W9-BMH-523

PEARSON

ALWAYS LEARNING

Skills with Microsoft® for Excel® 2013

Custom Edition for Ryerson University

Taken from:
Skills for Success with Microsoft® Office 2013
by Kris Townsend, Catherine Hain, and Stephanie Murre Wolf

Go! With Microsoft® Excel® 2013 Comprehensive
by Shelley Gaskin, Alicia Vargas, and Debra Geoghan

Cover Art: Courtesy of Photodisc/Getty Images.

Taken/Excerpts taken from:

Skills for Success with Microsoft® Office 2013
by Kris Townsend, Catherine Hain, and Stephanie Murre Wolf
Copyright © 2014 by Pearson Education, Inc.
Upper Saddle River, New Jersey 07458

Go! With Microsoft® Excel® 2013 Comprehensive
by Shelley Gaskin, Alicia Vargas, and Debra Geoghan
Copyright © 2014 by Pearson Education, Inc.

All rights reserved. No part of this book may be reproduced, in any form or by any means, without permission in writing from the publisher.

This special edition published in cooperation with Pearson Learning Solutions.

All trademarks, service marks, registered trademarks, and registered service marks are the property of their respective owners and are used herein for identification purposes only.

Pearson Learning Solutions, 501 Boylston Street, Suite 900, Boston, MA 02116
A Pearson Education Company
www.pearsoned.com

Printed in Canada

1 2 3 4 5 6 7 8 9 10 V0YA 18 17 16 15 14 13

000200010271805076

LF

ISBN 10: 1-269-55969-9
ISBN 13: 978-1-269-55969-0

Contents in Brief

Taken from *Skills for Success with Microsoft® Office 2013,* by Kris Townsend, Catherine Hain, and Stephanie Murre Wolf

Table of Contents

Microsoft Excel

Contributors

We'd like to thank the following people for their work on Skills for Success:

Focus Group Participants

Rose Volynskiy	Howard Community College	Lex Mulder	College of Western Idaho
Fernando Paniagua	The Community College of Baltimore County	Kristy McAuliffe	San Jacinto College South
Jeff Roth	Heald College	Jan Hime	University of Nebraska, Lincoln
William Bodine	Mesa Community College	Deb Fells	Mesa Community College

Reviewers

Barbara Anderson	Lake Washington Institute of Technology	Deb Fells	Mesa Community College
Janet Anderson	Lake Washington Institute of Technology	Tushnelda C Fernandez	Miami Dade College
Ralph Argiento	Guilford Technical Community College	Jean Finley	Asheville-Buncombe Technical Community College
Tanisha Arnett	Pima County Community College		
Greg Ballinger	Miami Dade College	Jim Flannery	Central Carolina Community College
Autumn Becker	Allegany College of Maryland	Alyssa Foskey	Wiregrass Georgia Technical College
Bob Benavides	Collin College	David Freer	Miami Dade College
Howard Blauser	North GA Technical College	Marvin Ganote	University of Dayton
William Bodine	Mesa Community College	David Grant	Paradise Valley Community College
Nancy Bogage	The Community College of Baltimore County	Clara Groeper	Illinois Central College
Maria Bright	San Jacinto College	Carol Heeter	Ivy Tech Community College
Adell Brooks	Hinds Community College	Jan Hime	University of Nebraska
Judy Brown	Western Illinois University	Marilyn Holden	Gateway Technical College
Maria Brownlow	Chaminade	Ralph Hunsberger	Bucks County Community College
Jennifer Buchholz	UW Washington County	Juan Iglesias	University of Texas at Brownsville
Kathea Buck	Gateway Technical College	Carl Eric Johnson	Great Bay Community College
LeAnn Cady	Minnesota State College—Southeast Technical	Joan Johnson	Lake Sumter Community College
John Cameron	Rio Hondo College	Mech Johnson	UW Washington County
Tammy Campbell	Eastern Arizona College	Deborah Jones	Southwest Georgia Technical College
Patricia Christian	Southwest Georgia Technical College	Hazel Kates	Miami-Dade College, Kendall Campus
Tina Cipriano	Gateway Technical College	Jane Klotzle	Lake Sumter Community College
Paulette Comet	The Community College of Baltimore County	Kurt Kominek	Northeast State Community College
Jean Condon	Mid-Plains Community College	Vivian Krenzke	Gateway Technical College
Joy DePover	Minneapolis. Com. & Tech College	Renuka Kumar	Community College of Baltimore County
Gina Donovan	County College of Morris	Lisa LaCaria	Central Piedmont Community College
Alina Dragne	Flagler College	Sue Lannen	Brazosport College
Russ Dulaney	Rasmussen College	Freda Leonard	Delgado Community College
Mimi Duncan	University of Missouri St. Louis	Susan Mahon	Collin College
Paula Jo Elson	Sierra College	Nicki Maines	Mesa Community College
Bernice Eng	Brookdale Community College	Pam Manning	Gateway Technical College
Jill Fall	Gateway Technical College	Juan Marquez	Mesa Community College

Alysia Martinez — *Gateway Technical College*
Kristy McAuliffe — *San Jacinto College*
Robert McCloud — *Sacred Heart University*
Susan Miner — *Lehigh Carbon Community College*
Namdar Mogharreban — *Southern Illinois University*
Daniel Moix — *College of the Ouachitas*
Lindsey Moore — *Wiregrass Georgia Technical College*
Lex Mulder — *College of Western Idaho*
Patricia Newman — *Cuyamaca College*
Melinda Norris — *Coker College*
Karen Nunan — *Northeast State Community College*
Fernando Paniagua — *The Community College of Baltimore County*
Christine Parrish — *Southwest Georgia Technical College*
Linda Pennachio — *Mount Saint Mary College*
Amy Pezzimenti — *Ocean County College*
Leah Ramalingam — *Riversity City College*
Mary Rasley — *Lehigh Carbon Community College*
Cheryl Reuss — *Estrella Mountain Community College*
Wendy Revolinski — *Gateway Technical College*
Kenneth Rogers — *Cecil College*

Jeff Roth — *Heald College*
Diane Ruscito — *Brazosport College*
June Scott — *County College of Morris*
Vicky Seehusen — *MSU Denver*
Emily Shepard — *Central Carolina Community College*
Pamela Silvers — *A-B Tech*
Martha Soderholm — *York College*
Yaacov Sragovich — *Queensborough Community College*
Jody Sterr — *Blackhawk Technical College*
Julia Sweitzer — *Lake-Sumter Community College*
Laree Thomas — *Okefenokee Technical College*
Joyce Thompson — *Lehigh Carbon Community College*
Barbara Tietsort — *University of Cincinnati, Blue Ash College*
Rose Volynskiy — *Howard Community College*
Sandra Weber — *Gateway Technical College*
Steven Weitz — *Lehigh Carbon Community College*
Berthenia Williams — *Savannah Technical College*
David Wilson — *Parkland College*
Allan Wood — *Great Bay Community College*
Roger Yaeger — *Estrella Mountain Community College*

What's New For Office 2013

With Office 2013, Microsoft is taking the office to the cloud. The Skills for Success series shows students how to get the most out of Office 2013 no matter what device they are using—a traditional desktop or tablet.

Whether you are tapping and sliding with your finger or clicking and dragging with the mouse, Skills for Success shows you the way with the hallmark visual, two-page, easy-to-follow design. It covers the essential skills students need to know to get up and running with Office quickly, and it addresses Web Apps, touch screens, and the collaborative approach of Office 365. Once students complete the Instructional Skills, they put their knowledge to work with a progression of review, problem-solving, and challenging, end-of-chapter projects.

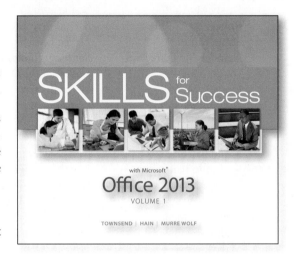

What's New for Office 2013

3 new chapters—Intro to Computer Concepts, Windows 8, and Internet Explorer 10 give you all the content you need to teach your course!

Coverage of new features of Office 2013 in an approach that is easy and effective for teaching students the skills they need to get started with Microsoft Office.

Skills Summary—new summary chart of all the Skills and Procedures covered in the chapter makes remembering what was covered easier!

Application Introductions—provide a brief overview of each application and put the chapters in context for students.

Student Training Videos—new, author-created training videos for each Skill in the chapters!

Application Capstone Projects—each application will conclude with a capstone project to help students and instructors ensure that students are ready to move onto the next application. These will also be grader projects in MyITLab.

Integrated Projects—integrated projects follow each application so that as students learn a new application, they also learn how to use it with other applications.

Web Apps Projects (formerly Collaboration Project)—use a variety of the web apps available at the end of each application. Also includes an "On Your Own" project to let students try an additional project.

Additional Grader Projects—two new grader projects based on the Skills Review provide a broader variety of homework and assessment options; written by the book authors.

New Training and Assessment Simulations—written by the book authors to provide enhanced one-to-one content match in MyITLab.

SkyDrive Coverage included in the Common Features chapter.

Office 365 Coverage included in the Concepts chapter.

MOS mapping—located on the Instructor Resource Site provides a guide to where the MOS Core exam objectives are covered in the book, on the Companion website, and in MyITLab to help students prepare to ace the exam!

Skills for Success

with Microsoft® Office 2013 *Volume 1*

- **10 × 8.5 Format**— Easy for students to read and type at the same time by simply propping the book up on the desk in front of their monitor

- **Clearly Outlined Skills**— Each skill is presented in a single two-page spread so that students can easily follow along

- **Numbered Steps and Bulleted Text**— Students don't read long paragraphs of text, instead they get a step-by-step, concise presentation

- **Broad Coverage of Skills**— Gives students the knowledge needed to get up and running quickly

NEW Application Introductions provide students with a concise overview of each application to put the chapters in context

Two Page Chapter Introduction— Briefs students on what is important and sets the stage for the project they will create

File Summary— A quick summary of the files the students need to open and the names of the files they will turn in

Outcome— Shows students up front what their completed project will look like

Clock— Tells how much time students need to complete the chapter

Student Training Videos for each Skill in the chapter provide a personal, instructor-led walk through

Sequential Pagination— Saves you and your students time in locating topics and assignments

Skills List— A visual snapshot of what skills they will complete in the chapter

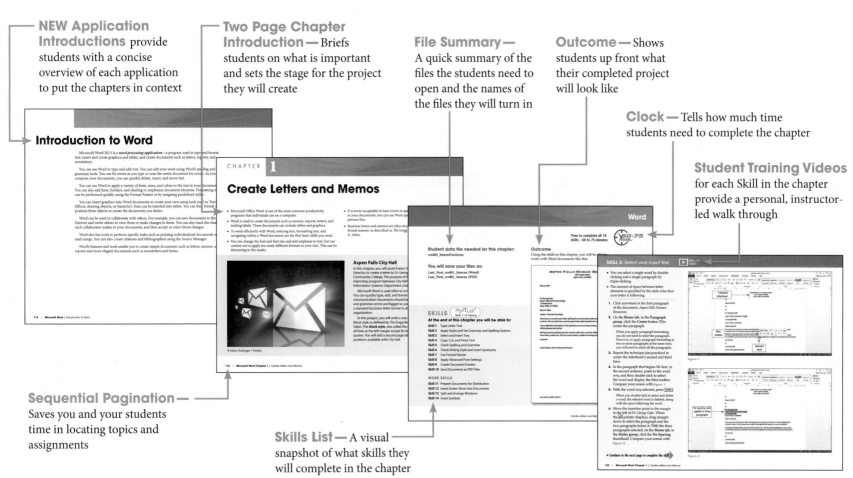

Skills for Success

Written for Today's Students — Skills are taught with numbered steps and bulleted text so students are less likely to skip valuable information

Two-Page Spreads — Each skill is presented in a concise, two-page spread to give students the visual illustration right with the steps—no flipping pages

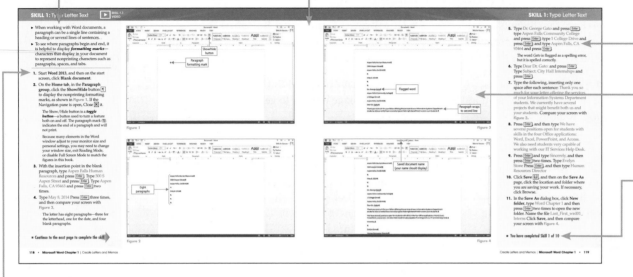

Colored Text — Clearly shows what a student types

Larger Screen Images — Provide a view of the full ribbon and include concise callouts for easy reference

Done! — Students always know when they've completed a skill

Hands-On — Students start working on their skills from Step 1

New BizSkills Videos — Covering the important business skills students need to succeed: *Communication, Dress for Success, Interview Prep,* and more

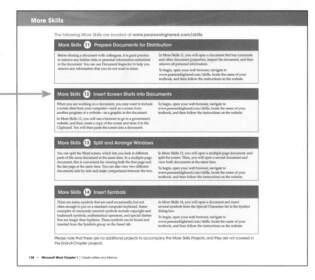

More Skills — Additional skills included online

Skills for Success

End-of-Chapter Material — Several levels of review and assessment so you can assign the material that best fits your students' needs

NEW Skills and Procedures Summary Chart — Provides a quick review of the skills and tasks covered in each chapter

A stronger progression from point and click to practice, and to critical thinking.

From Point and Click to Critical Thinking

Skills 1–10 Guided learning	Annotated linear steps that tell 'where to click' and *why*.
Skills Review Guided practice	Linear steps that tell them 'where to click' one more time.
2 Skills Assessments Independent practice	Linear steps that tell them 'what to click' but not necessarily where.
Visual Skills Assessment Non-linear problem-solving	Students determine their own steps to create the document shown in the figure and described in the directions.
My Skills Transfer of skills	Students transfer their skills to a different scenario—a personal document, instead of business document.
Skills Challenge 1 Apply skills to fix problems	Typically a document that needs 'fixed' by apply the skills in the chapter. The problems are described in a way that the *challenge* is deciding how to fix the problems, not figuring out what the directions mean or how it will be graded.
Skills Challenge 2 Conduct research to solve a problem	Typically a project that requires some research to determine the content of the document. Directions are written in a way that the *challenge* is deciding what to say and how best to format the document, not figuring out what the directions mean or how it will be graded.

NEW MyITLab grader project covering all 10 skills (homework and assessment versions)

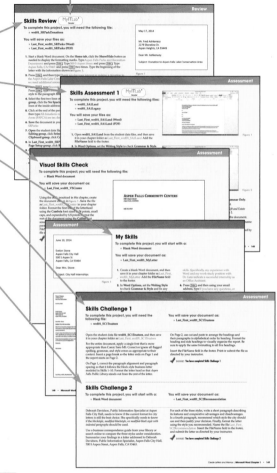

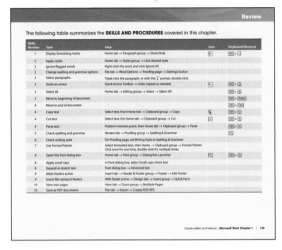

Integrated Projects — Follow each application so they are easier to manage and provide practice immediately after students work with each new application.

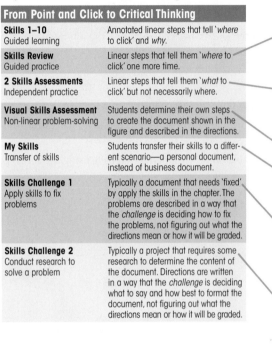

NEW Application Capstone —

For each application we provide a comprehensive project covering all of the Skills. Also available as a Grader project in MyITLab.

Web App Projects — Students use Cloud computing to save files; create, edit, and share Office documents using Office Web Apps; and create Windows Live groups.

MyITLab

Skills for Success combined with MyITLab gives you a completely integrated solution: Instruction, Training, & Assessment

- eText
- Training & Assessment Simulations
- Grader Projects

Student Videos!

Student Training Videos — Each skill within a chapter comes with an instructor-led video that walks students through each skill.

BizSkills Video Cover the important business skills students need to be successful—*Interviewing, Communication, Dressing for Success,* and more.

Student Data — Files are all available on the Companion Website using the access code included with your book. pearsonhighered.com/skills

About the Authors

Kris Townsend is an Information Systems instructor at Spokane Falls Community College in Spokane, Washington. Kris earned a bachelor's degree in both Education and Business, and a master's degree in Education. He has also worked as a public school teacher and as a systems analyst. Kris enjoys working with wood, geocaching, and photography. He commutes to work by bike and also is a Lewis and Clark historical reenactor.

Catherine Hain is an instructor at Central New Mexico Community College in Albuquerque, New Mexico. She teaches computer applications classes in the Business and Information Technology School, both in the classroom and through the distance learning office. Catherine holds a bachelor's degree in Management and Marketing and a master's degree in Business Administration.

Stephanie Murre Wolf is a Technology and Computer Applications instructor at Moraine Park Technical College in Wisconsin. She is a graduate of Alverno College and enjoys teaching, writing curriculum, and authoring textbooks. In addition to classroom instruction, Stephanie actively performs corporate training in technology. She is married and has two sons; together, the family enjoys the outdoors.

A Special Thank You

Pearson Prentice Hall gratefully acknowledges the contribution made by Shelley Gaskin to the first edition publication of this series—*Skills for Success with Office 2007*. The series has truly benefited from her dedication toward developing a textbook that aims to help students and instructors. We thank her for her continued support of this series.

Introduction to Excel

Microsoft Excel 2013 is a ***spreadsheet application***—a program used to store information and to perform numerical analysis of data that is arranged in a grid of cells. This grid is organized in rows identified by numbers and columns identified by letters.

A business spreadsheet can be used for many purposes including tracking budgets and summarizing results. You can create formulas using mathematical operations such as addition, subtraction, multiplication, and division. Formulas can refer to the value stored in a cell and when you change the value of the cell, the formula will recalculate the results. Because the results are immediately displayed, Excel is frequently used by businesses to help make decisions.

Once you have entered your data and formulas into Excel, you can format the text and values, or wrap text in a cell and merge cells to improve the look of the spreadsheet. You can change the row height and the column width, and insert or delete rows and columns.

You can sort and filter data, or apply conditional formatting to data to help you find the information you are looking for more quickly. You can also use cell styles, borders, or font colors and shading to highlight important data.

You can present your Excel data in a wide variety of charts, including pie charts, line charts, or bar charts. Charts show trends and make comparisons. Your charts and data can be displayed in an Excel workbook or copied to a Word document or a PowerPoint presentation. Excel can be used to collaborate with others. For example, you can save workbooks to the Internet and then invite others to view or make changes to your workbooks.

Cell styles applied

Merged cells

Formatted values

Column chart

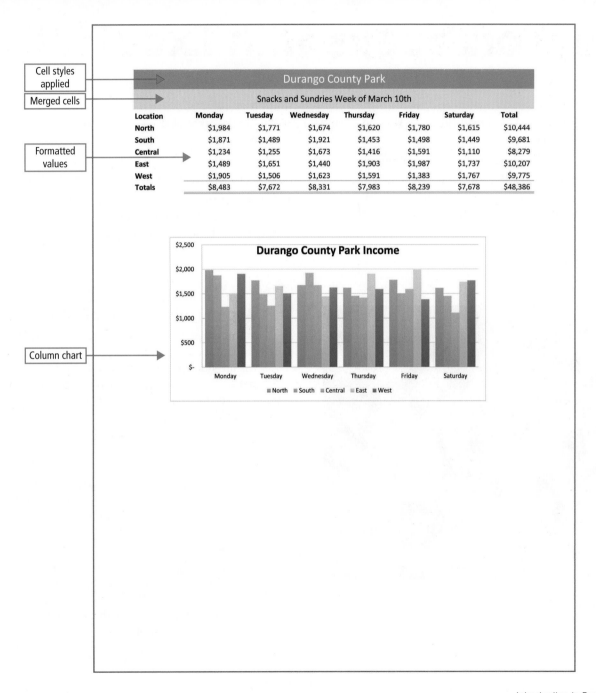

Location	Monday	Tuesday	Wednesday	Thursday	Friday	Saturday	Total
North	$1,984	$1,771	$1,674	$1,620	$1,780	$1,615	$10,444
South	$1,871	$1,489	$1,921	$1,453	$1,498	$1,449	$9,681
Central	$1,234	$1,255	$1,673	$1,416	$1,591	$1,110	$8,279
East	$1,489	$1,651	$1,440	$1,903	$1,987	$1,737	$10,207
West	$1,905	$1,506	$1,623	$1,591	$1,383	$1,767	$9,775
Totals	$8,483	$7,672	$8,331	$7,983	$8,239	$7,678	$48,386

CHAPTER 1

Create Workbooks with Excel 2013

- ▶ Microsoft Office Excel 2013 is used worldwide to create workbooks and to analyze data that is organized into columns and rows.

- ▶ After data is entered into Excel, you can perform calculations on the numerical data and analyze the data to make informed decisions.

- ▶ When you make changes to one or more number values, you can immediately see the effect of those changes in totals and charts that rely on those values.

- ▶ An Excel workbook can contain a large amount of data—up to 16,384 columns and 1,048,576 rows.

- ▶ The basic skills you need to work efficiently with Excel include entering and formatting data and navigating within Excel.

- ▶ When planning your worksheet, think about what information will form the rows and what information will form the columns. Generally, rows are used to list the items and columns to group or describe the items in the list.

© Elenathewise / Fotolia

Aspen Falls Outdoor Recreation

In this chapter, you will create a workbook for Amado Pettinelli, the Outdoor Recreation Supervisor. Mr. Pettinelli wants to know the attendance at each city attraction and the revenue each venue generates for the city. He plans to recommend to the Aspen Falls City Council that the busiest attractions receive more city funding in the next fiscal year.

A business spreadsheet can be used for many purposes including tracking budgets, manufacture measurements, or employees. The spreadsheet data can be manipulated using arithmetic and mathematical formulas commonly used in the modern-day business world. If you are asked to create a spreadsheet, you need to know if the results of the data manipulation will be presented in numerical or in graphical format.

In this project, you will create a new Excel workbook and enter data which displays the total number of visitors at the various city attractions in Aspen Falls. You will format the data, construct formulas, and insert functions. You will calculate the percent of weekday visitors at each of the locations and insert a footer. Finally, you will check the spelling in the workbook.

Time to complete all 10 skills – 60 to 90 minutes

Student data file needed for this chapter:

Blank Excel workbook

You will save your workbook as:

Last_First_exl01_Visitors

Outcome

Using the skills in this chapter, you will be able to work with Excel worksheets like this:

Aspen Falls Outdoor Recreation						
Visitors to City Attractions						
Location	Weekends	Weekdays	All Visitors	Difference	Entrance Fee	Total Fees
Zoo	3,169	1,739	4,908	1,430	$ 10	$ 49,080
Pool	5,338	3,352	8,690	1,986	$ 10	$ 86,900
Aquarium	9,027	3,868	12,895	5,159	$ 12	$ 154,740
Garden	4,738	2,788	7,526	1,950	$ 4	$ 30,104
Museum	3,876	913	4,789	2,963	$ 11	$ 52,679
Total	26,148	12,660	38,808			$ 373,503
Percent of Weekday Visitors						
Zoo	35.4%					
Pool	38.6%					
Aquarium	30.0%					
Garden	37.0%					
Museum	19.1%					

SKILLS  MyITLab®
Skills 1-10 Training

At the end of this chapter you will be able to:

Skill 1 Create and Save Workbooks

Skill 2 Enter Data and Merge and Center Titles

Skill 3 Construct Addition and Subtraction Formulas

Skill 4 Construct Multiplication and Division Formulas

Skill 5 Adjust Column Widths and Apply Cell Styles

Skill 6 Insert the SUM Function

Skill 7 AutoFill Formulas and Data

Skill 8 Format, Edit, and Check Spelling

Skill 9 Insert Footers and Adjust Page Settings

Skill 10 Display Formulas and Print Worksheets

MORE SKILLS

Skill 11 Create Workbooks from Templates

Skill 12 Insert Names into Formulas

Skill 13 Create Templates

Skill 14 Manage Document Properties

▶ An Excel **workbook** is a file that you can use to organize various kinds of related information. A workbook contains **worksheets**, also called **spreadsheets**—the primary documents that you use in Excel to store and work with data.

▶ The worksheet forms a grid of vertical columns and horizontal rows. The small box where one column and one row meet is a cell.

1. Start **Excel 2013**, and then click **Blank workbook**. In the lower right, notice the zoom—magnification level.

    Your zoom level should be 100%, but most figures in this chapter are zoomed to 120%.

2. Verify the cell in the upper left corner is the **active cell**—the cell outlined in green in which data is entered when you begin typing—as shown in Figure 1.

    In a worksheet, columns have alphabetical headings across the top, and rows have numerical headings down the left side. When a cell is active, the headings for the column and row in which the cell is located are shaded. The column letter and row number that identify a cell is the **cell address**, also called the **cell reference**.

3. In cell **A1**, type Aspen Falls Outdoor Recreation and then press [Enter] to accept the entry.

4. In cell **A2**, type Visitors and then press [Enter] two times. Compare your screen with Figure 2.

5. In cell **A4**, type Location and press [Tab] to make the cell to the right—**B4**—active.

■ Continue to the next page to complete the skill

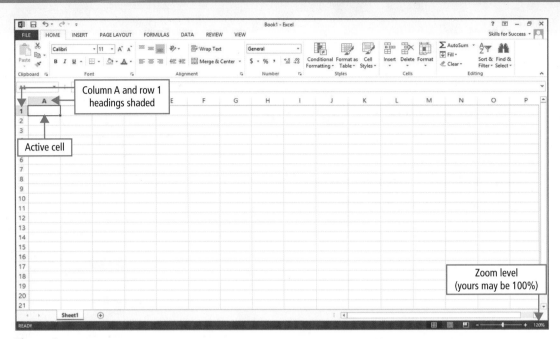

Figure 1

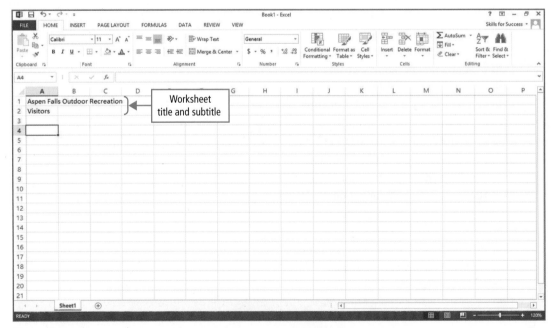

Figure 2

.

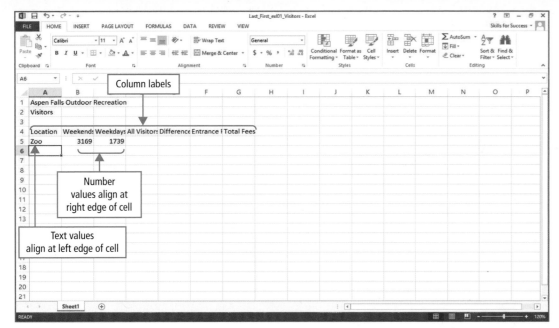

Figure 3

6. With cell **B4** the active cell, type the following labels, pressing Tab between each label:

Weekends
Weekdays
All Visitors
Difference
Entrance Fee
Total Fees

Labels at the beginning of columns or rows help readers understand the data.

To correct typing errors, click a cell and retype the data. The new typing will replace the existing data.

7. Click cell **A5**, type Zoo and then press Tab. Type 3169 and press Tab. Type 1739 and then press Enter. Compare your screen with **Figure 3**.

Data in a cell is called a *value*. You can have a *text value*—character data in a cell that labels number values, or a *number value*—numeric data in a cell. A text value is also referred to as a *label*. Text values align at the left cell edge, and number values align at the right cell edge.

8. Click **Save** 🖫. On the **Save As** page, click **Computer**, and then click the **Browse** button. In the **Save As** dialog box, navigate to the location where you are saving your files. Click **New folder**, type Excel Chapter 1 and then press Enter two times. In the **File name** box, name the workbook Last_First_exl01_Visitors and then press Enter.

9. Take a few moments to familiarize yourself with common methods to move between cells as summarized in the table in **Figure 4**.

■ **You have completed Skill 1 of 10**

Common Ways to Move or Scroll Through a Worksheet

Key	Description
Enter	Move down one row.
Tab	Move one column to the right.
Shift + Tab	Move one column to the left.
↓ ↑ → ←	Move one cell in the direction of the arrow.
Ctrl + Home	Move to cell A1.
Ctrl + End	Move to the lowest row and the column farthest to the right that contains data.

Figure 4

▶ To create an effective worksheet, you enter titles and subtitles and add labels for each row and column of data. It is a good idea to have the worksheet title and subtitle span across all the columns containing data.

1. In cell **A6**, type Aquarium and press [Tab].

2. In cell **B6**, type 9027 and press [Tab]. In cell **C6**, type 3868 and press [Enter].

3. In row **7** and row **8**, type the following data:

   Garden   5738   2877

   Museum   3876   913

4. In cell **A9**, type Total and press [Enter]. Compare your screen with **Figure 1**.

5. Click cell **B1**, type Worksheet and press [Enter]. Click cell **A1**, and then compare your screen with **Figure 2**.

   When text is too long to fit in a cell and the cell to the right of it contains data, the text will be *truncated*—cut off. Here, the text in cell A1 is truncated.

   The *formula bar*—a bar below the Ribbon that displays the value contained in the active cell and is used to enter or edit values or formulas.

   Data displayed in a cell is the *displayed value*. Data displayed in the formula bar is the *underlying value*. Displayed values often do not match their underlying values.

6. On the Quick Access Toolbar, click the **Undo** button ↺ to remove the text in cell **B1**.

   Long text in cells overlaps into other columns only when those cells are empty. Here, A1 text now overlaps B1 because that cell is empty.

■ **Continue to the next page to complete the skill** ▶

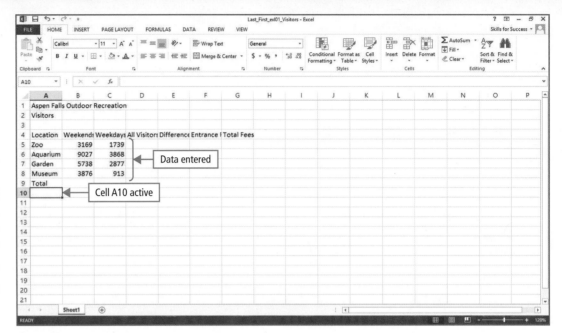

Figure 1

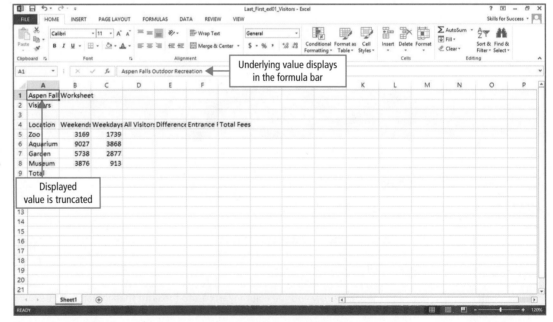

Figure 2

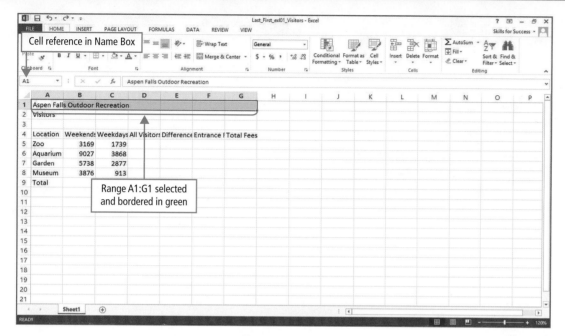

Figure 3

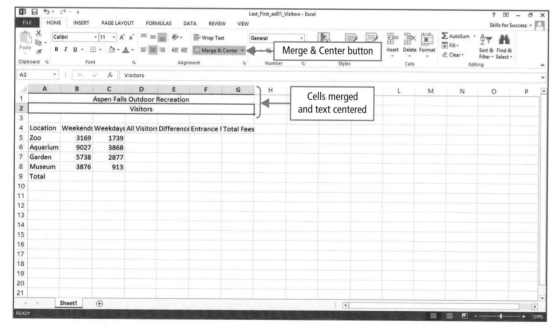

Figure 4

7. Point to the middle of cell **A1** to display the ⊕ pointer. Hold down the left mouse button, and then drag to the right to select cells **A1** through **G1**. Compare your screen with Figure 3. To select a range on a touch screen, tap the cell, and then drag the selection handle.

The selected range is referred to as *A1:G1* (A1 through G1) A *range* is two or more cells in a worksheet that are adjacent (next to each other). A colon (:) between two cell references indicates that the range includes the two cell references and all the cells between them.

When you select a range, a thick green line surrounds the range, and all but the first cell in the range are shaded. The first cell reference will be displayed in the *Name Box*—an area by the formula bar that displays the active cell reference.

8. On the **Home tab**, in the **Alignment group**, click the **Merge & Center** button.

The selected range, A1:G1, merges into one larger cell, and the data is centered in the new cell. The cells in B1 through G1 can no longer be selected individually because they are merged into cell A1.

9. Using the technique just practiced, merge and center the range **A2:G2**.

10. **Save** 🖫 the workbook, and then compare your screen with Figure 4.

■ **You have completed Skill 2 of 10**

▶ A cell's underlying value can be a text value, a number value, or a *formula*—an equation that performs mathematical calculations on number values in the worksheet.

▶ Formulas begin with an equal sign and often include an *arithmetic operator*—a symbol that specifies a mathematical operation such as addition or subtraction.

Symbols Used in Excel for Arithmetic Operators	
+ (plus sign)	Addition
- (minus sign)	Subtraction (also negation)
* (asterisk)	Multiplication
/ (forward slash)	Division
% (percent sign)	Percent
^ (caret)	Exponentiation

Figure 1

1. Study the symbols that Excel uses to perform mathematical operations, as summarized in the table in **Figure 1**.

2. In cell **D5**, type =B5+C5 and then press Enter.

   When you include cell references in formulas, the values in those cells are inserted. Here, the total number of visitors for the Zoo location equals the sum of the values in cells B5 and C5 (3169+ 1739 = 4908).

   When you type a formula, you might see a brief display of function names that match the first letter you type. This Excel feature, called *Formula AutoComplete*, suggests values as you type a function.

3. In cell **D6**, type the formula to add cells **B6** and **C6**, =B6+C6 and then press Enter.

4. In cell **D7**, type = and then click cell **B7** to automatically insert *B7* into the formula. Compare your screen with **Figure 2**.

   Cell **B7** is surrounded by a moving border indicating that it is part of an active formula.

5. Type + Click cell **C7**, and then press Enter to display the result *8615*.

   You can either type formulas or construct them by pointing and clicking in this manner.

■ **Continue to the next page to complete the skill** ▶

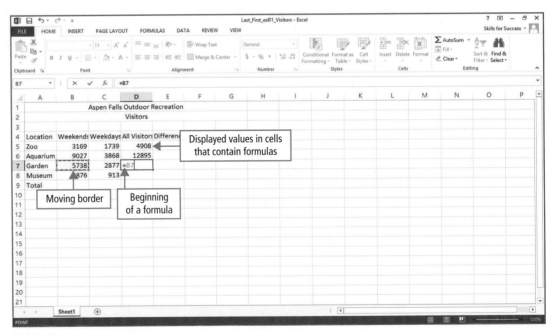

Displayed values in cells that contain formulas

Moving border

Beginning of a formula

Figure 2

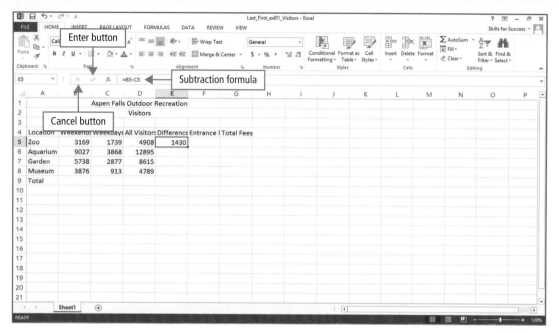

Figure 3

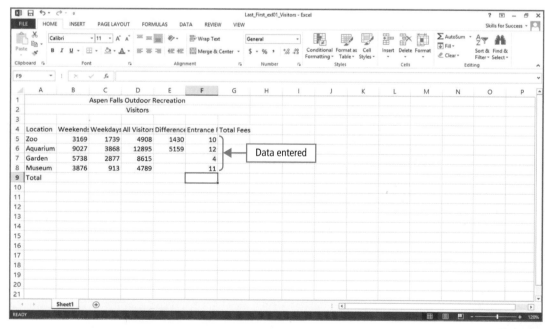

Figure 4

6. In cell **D8**, use point and click to construct a formula that adds cells **B8** and **C8**.

7. In cell **E5**, type =B5-C5 On the formula bar, click the **Enter** button ☑ to confirm the entry while keeping cell *E5* the active cell, and then compare your screen with **Figure 3**.

   Here, the underlying value for cell E5 displays as a formula in the formula bar and the displayed value, *1430*, displays in the cell as a result of the formula.

   If you make an error entering a formula, you can click the Cancel button and then start over. Alternately, you can press the ⌊Esc⌋ key.

8. In cell **E6**, use point and click to enter the formula =B6-C6 to display the difference for the Aquarium weekend and weekday visitors. (You will complete the column E formulas in Skill 7.)

9. Type the following data using the ⌊↓⌋ to move to the next row, and then compare your screen with **Figure 4**.

Cell	Value
F5	10
F6	12
F7	4
F8	11

10. Save 🖫 the workbook.

- **You have completed Skill 3 of 10**

▶ The four most common operators for addition (+), subtraction (-), multiplication (*), and division (/) can be found on the number keypad at the right side of a standard keyboard, or on the number keys at the top of a keyboard.

1. In cell **G5**, type =D5*F5—the formula that multiplies the total Zoo visitors by its entrance fee. On the formula bar, click the **Enter** button ☑, and then compare your screen with **Figure 1**.

    The *underlying formula*—the formula as displayed in the formula bar—multiplies the value in cell D5 (*4908*)—by the value in cell F5 (*10*) and displays the result in cell G5 (*49080*).

2. In the range **G6:G8**, enter the following formulas:

Cell	Formula
G6	=D6*F6
G7	=D7*F7
G8	=D8*F8

3. In cell **A11**, type Percent of Weekday Visitors and then press Enter. Compare your screen with **Figure 2**.

■ Continue to the next page to complete the skill ▶

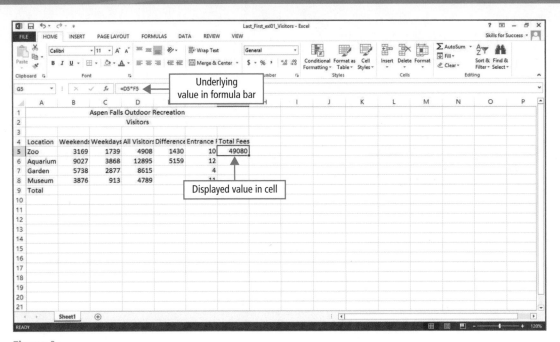

Figure 1

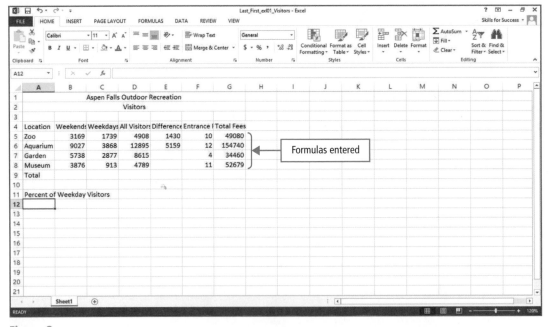

Figure 2

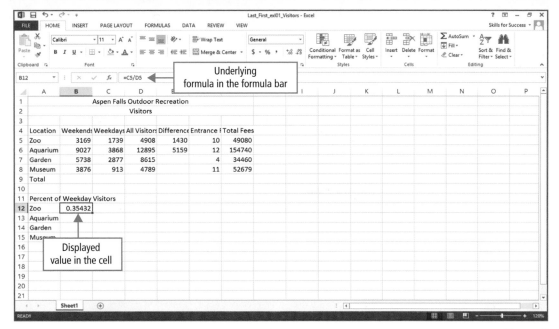

Figure 3

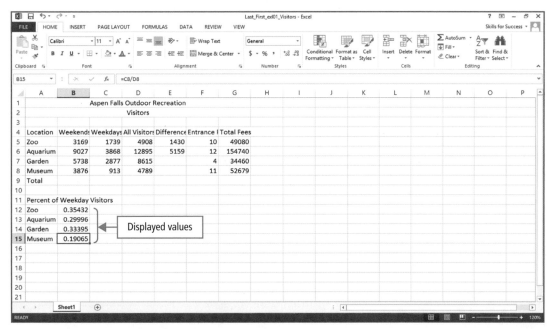

Figure 4

4. Select the range **A5:A8**, and then on the **Home tab**, in the **Clipboard group**, click the **Copy** button 📋. Click cell **A12**, and then in the **Clipboard group**, click the **Paste** button.

   The four location labels are copied to the range A12:A15.

5. Press [Esc] to remove the moving border around the copied cells.

6. In cell **B12**, construct the formula to divide the number of Weekday Zoo visitors by the Total Zoo visitors, =C5/D5 and then click the **Enter** button ✓. Compare your screen with Figure 3.

   Percentages are calculated by taking the amount divided by the total and will be displayed in decimal format. Here, the underlying formula in B12 (=C5/D5) divides the weekday Zoo visitors (1739) by the total Zoo visitors (4908).

7. Construct the formulas to calculate the percent of weekday visitors for each location, and then compare your screen with Figure 4.

Cell	Formula
B13	=C6/D6
B14	=C7/D7
B15	=C8/D8

8. **Save** 💾 the workbook.

■ **You have completed Skill 4 of 10**

▶ The letter that displays at the top of a column is the **column heading**. The number that displays at the left of a row is the **row heading**.

▶ **Formatting** is the process of specifying the appearance of cells or the overall layout of a worksheet.

1. Click cell **A4**. On the **Home tab**, in the **Cells group**, click the **Format** button, and then click **Column Width**. In the **Column Width** dialog box, type 13

2. Compare your screen with **Figure 1**, and then click **OK**.

> The default column width will display 8.43 characters when formatted in the standard font. Here, the width is increased to display more characters.

3. Select the range **B4:G4**.In the **Cells group**, click the **Format** button, and then click **Column Width**. In the **Column Width** dialog box, type 12 and then click **OK**.

4. Select cells **A11:B11**. On the **Home tab**, in the **Alignment group**, click the **Merge & Center arrow**, and then on the displayed list, click **Merge Across**. Compare your screen with **Figure 2**.

> Merge Across merges the selected cells without centering them.

5. Click cell **A1** to select the merged and centered range A1:G1. In the **Cells group**, click the **Format** button, and then click **Row Height**. In the **Row Height** dialog box, type 22.5 and then click **OK**.

■ **Continue to the next page to complete the skill**

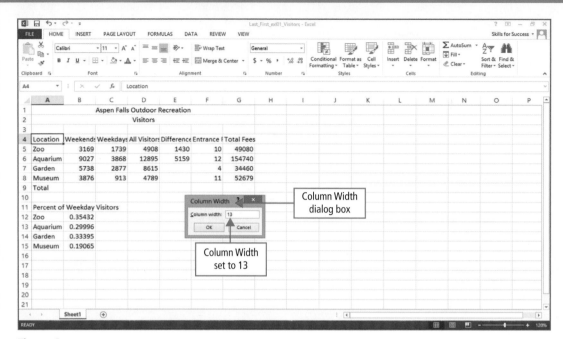

Figure 1

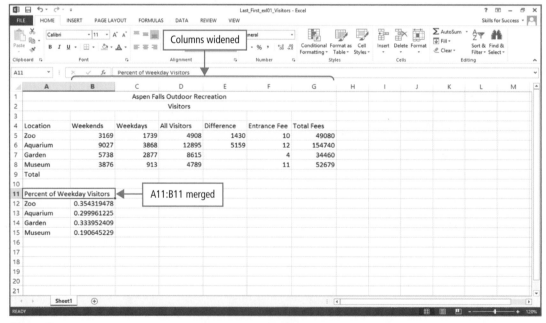

Figure 2

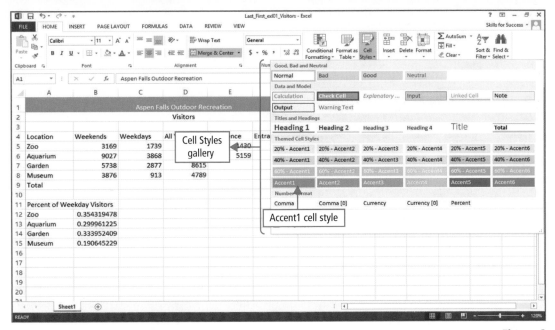

Figure 3

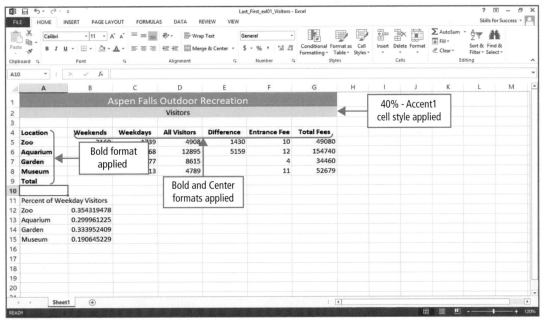

Figure 4

6. With **A1:G1** still selected, in the **Styles group**, click the **Cell Styles** button. In the **Cell Styles** gallery, under **Titles and Headings**, use Live Preview to view the title as you point to **Heading 1** and then **Heading 2**.

    A *cell style* is a prebuilt set of formatting characteristics, such as font, font size, font color, cell borders, and cell shading.

7. Under **Themed Cell Styles**, point to the **Accent1** style. Compare your screen with **Figure 3**, and then click **Accent1**.

8. In the **Font group**, click the **Font Size arrow** ⌷ and then click **16**.

9. Click cell **A2**, and then using the technique you just practiced, apply the **40% - Accent1** cell style. In the **Font group**, click the **Increase Font Size** button ⌷ one time to change the font size to **12**.

10. Select the range **B4:G4**. Right-click the selected range to display a shortcut menu and the Mini toolbar. On the Mini toolbar, click the **Bold** button ⌷ and then click the **Center** button ⌷ to apply bold and to center the text within each of the selected cells.

11. Select the range **A4:A9**. Display the Mini toolbar, and then apply **Bold** to the selected range. Click cell **A10**, and then compare your screen with **Figure 4**.

12. Save ⌷ the workbook.

■ **You have completed Skill 5 of 10**

▶ You can create your own formulas, or you can use a *function*—a prewritten Excel formula that takes a value or values, performs an operation, and returns a value or values.

▶ The AutoSum button is used to insert common summary functions into a worksheet.

▶ When cell references are used in a formula or function, the results are automatically recalculated whenever those cells are edited.

1. Click cell **B9.** On the **Home tab,** in the **Editing group,** click the **AutoSum** button, and then compare your screen with **Figure 1.**

    SUM is an Excel function that adds all the numbers in a range of cells. The range in parentheses, *(B5:B8),* indicates the range of cells on which the SUM function will be performed.

    When the AutoSum button is used, Excel first looks *above* the selected cell for a suitable range of cells to sum. When no suitable data is detected, Excel then looks to the *left* and proposes a range of cells to sum. Here, the range B5:B8 is surrounded by a moving border, and *=SUM(B5:B8)* displays in cell B9.

2. Press [Enter] to display the function result—*21810.*

3. Select the range **C9:D9.** In the **Editing group,** click the **AutoSum** button, and then compare your screen with **Figure 2.**

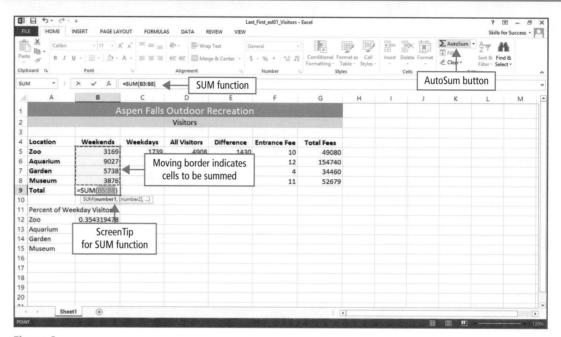

Figure 1

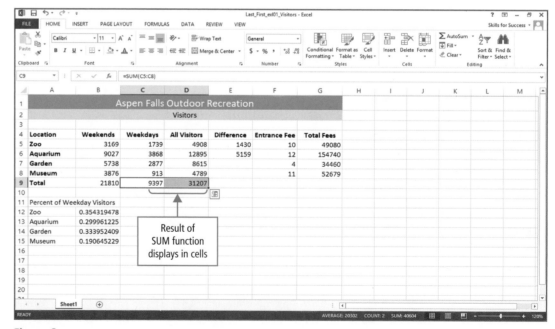

Figure 2

■ **Continue to the next page to complete the skill**

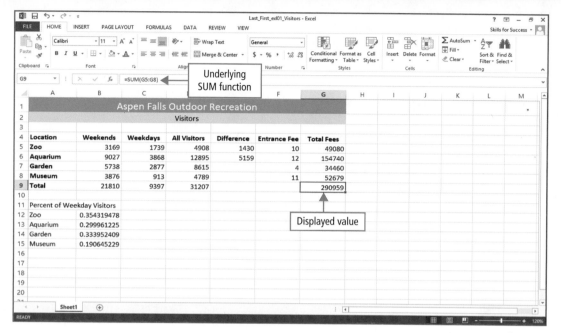

Figure 3

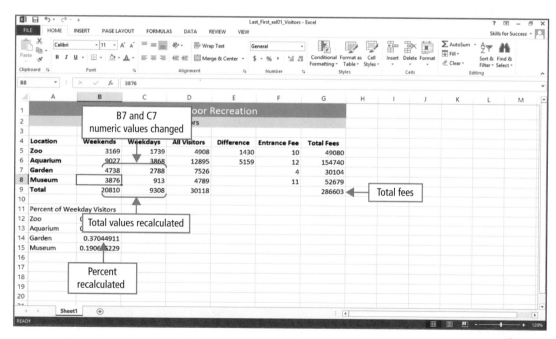

Figure 4

4. Click cell **C9**, and then in the formula bar, verify that the SUM function adds the values in the range *C5:C8*.

5. Click cell **D9**, and verify that the SUM function adds the values in the range *D5:D8*.

6. Using the technique just practiced, in cell **G9**, insert the SUM function to add the values in the range **G5:G8**. Verify cell **G9** is the active cell, and then compare your screen with Figure 3.

7. In cell **B7**, type 4738 Watch the total in cell **B9** update as you press Tab.

   In cell B9, the displayed value changed to 20810, but the underlying formula remained the same.

8. In cell **C7**, type 2788 and then press Enter to update the values in cells that contain formulas referring to cell C7. Compare your screen with Figure 4.

9. **Save** ▢ the workbook.

■ **You have completed Skill 6 of 10**

▶ Text, numbers, formulas, and functions can be copied down rows and also across columns to insert formulas and functions quickly.

▶ When a formula is copied to another cell, Excel adjusts the cell references relative to the new location of the formula.

1. Click cell **E6**. With cell **E6** selected, point to the **fill handle**—the small green square in the lower right corner of the selection—until the ✚ pointer displays as shown in **Figure 1**.

   To use the fill handle, first select the cell that contains the content you want to copy—here the formula =*B6-C6*.

2. Drag the ✚ pointer down to cell **E8**, and then release the mouse button.

3. Click cell **E7**, and verify on the formula bar that the formula copied from E6 changed to=*B7-C7*. Click cell **E8**, and then compare your screen with **Figure 2**.

   In each row, the cell references in the formula adjusted *relative to* the row number—B6 changed to B7 and then to B8. This adjustment is called a ***relative cell reference*** because it refers to cells based on their position *in relation to* (relative to) the cell that contains the formula.

■ **Continue to the next page to complete the skill**

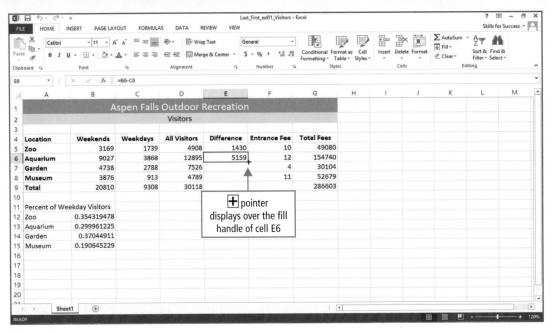

Figure 1

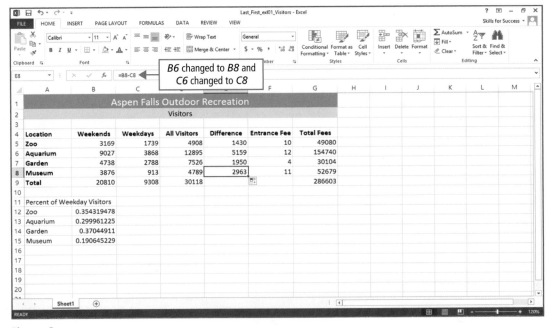

Figure 2

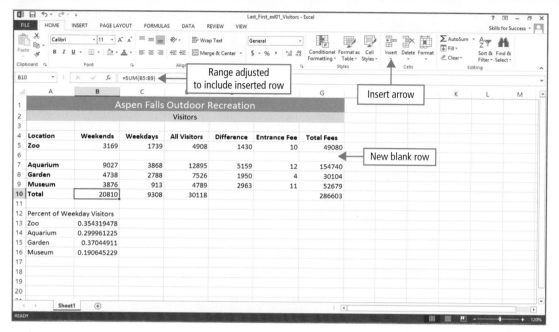

Figure 3

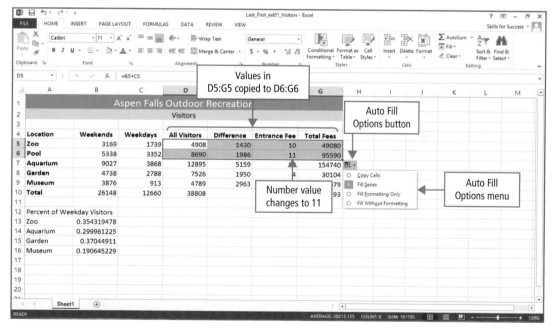

Figure 4

4. Click cell **A6**. In the **Cells group**, click the **Insert arrow**, and then click **Insert Sheet Rows**. Click cell **B10**, and then compare your screen with **Figure 3**.

   When you insert a new row or column, the cell references and the ranges in formulas or in functions adjust to include the new row or column. Here, in cell B10, the range in the function automatically updated to include the new row in the range.

5. In cell **A6**, type Pool and then press [Tab].

   By default, formatting (bold) from the row above is applied to an inserted row.

6. In cell **B6**, type 5338 and then press [Tab] to enter the value and update the column total in cell *B10* to *26148*.

7. In cell **C6**, type 3352 and press [Tab].

8. Select cells **D5:G5**. Point to the fill handle so that the ⊞ pointer displays, and then drag the ⊞ pointer down one row. Release the mouse button, and then click the **Auto Fill Options** button ⊞. Compare your screen with **Figure 4**.

   When you copy number values using the fill handle, the numbers automatically increment for each row or column. Here, the number value in cell F5 increased by one when it was copied to cell F6.

9. In the **Auto Fill Options** menu, click **Copy Cells**.

   With the Copy Cells option, number values are literally copied and do not increment. Here, the number value in cell F6 changes to *10*.

10. **Save** 🖫 the workbook.

■ **You have completed Skill 7 of 10**

▶ Always check spelling after you have finished formatting and editing your worksheet data.

1. Click cell **A14**, and repeat the technique used previously to insert a new row. In cell **A14**, type Pool and then press ⌷Enter⌷.

2. Click cell **B13**, and then use the fill handle to copy the formula down to cell **B14**.

3. Double-click cell **A2** to edit the cell contents. Use the arrow keys to move to the right of the word *Visitors*. Add a space, type to City Attractions and then press ⌷Enter⌷.

   Alternately, double-tap cell A2 to edit the cell.

4. Select the range **F5:G10**. In the **Styles group**, click the **Cell Styles** button, and then under **Number Format**, click **Currency [0]**. Take a few moments to familiarize yourself with the Number Formats as summarized in the table in **Figure 1**.

5. Select the range **B5:E10**. Click the **Cell Styles** button, and then under **Number Format**, click **Comma [0]**.

6. Select the range **B13:B17**. In the **Number group**, click the **Percent Style** button 🔲, and then click the **Increase Decimal** button 🔲 one time. Compare your screen with **Figure 2**.

   The Increase Decimal and Decrease Decimal buttons do not actually add or remove decimals, but they change how the underlying decimal values display in the cells.

■ **Continue to the next page to complete the skill**

Number Formats	
Format	**Description**
Comma	Adds commas where appropriate and displays two decimals.
Comma [0]	Adds commas where appropriate and displays no decimals.
Currency	Adds the dollar sign, commas where appropriate, and displays two decimals.
Currency [0]	Adds the dollar sign, commas where appropriate, and displays no decimals.
Percent	Adds the percent sign and multiplies the number by 100.

Figure 1

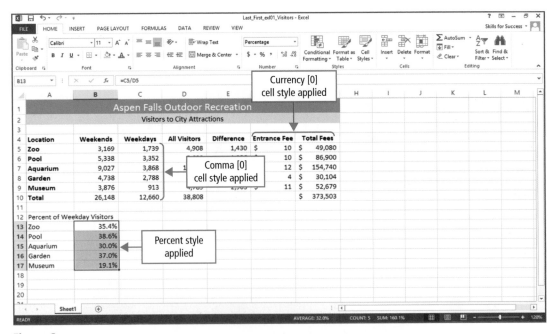

Figure 2

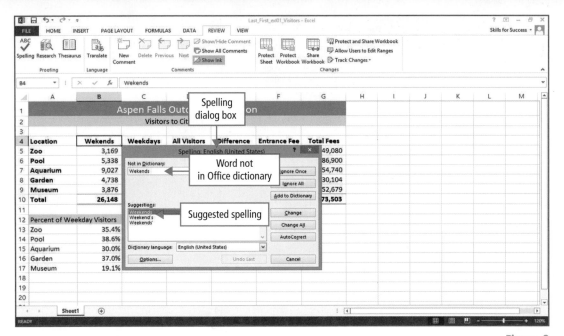

Figure 3

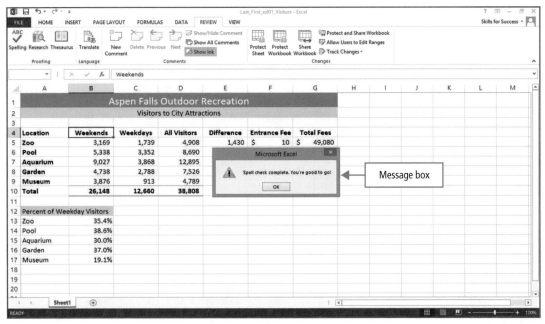

Figure 4

7. Select the range **B10:D10**. Hold down Ctrl, and then click cell **G10**. Click the **Cell Styles** button. Under **Titles and Headings**, click the **Total** style.

8. Select cell **A12**, and then click the **Cell Styles** button. Under **Themed Cell Styles**, click **40% - Accent1**.

9. Press Ctrl + Home to make cell **A1** active. On the **Review tab**, in the **Proofing group**, click the **Spelling** button.

   The spelling checker starts with the active cell and moves to the right and down, so making cell A1 the active cell before beginning is useful.

10. In the **Spelling** dialog box, under **Not in Dictionary**, a misspelled word displays as shown in Figure 3.

   This word is not in the Office dictionary; however, words not in the dictionary are not necessarily misspelled. Many proper nouns or less commonly used words are not in the Office dictionary.

   To correct a misspelled word and to move to the next word not in the Office dictionary, under Suggestions, verify that the correct spelling is selected, and then click the Change button.

11. Continue to use the spelling checker to correct any remaining errors you may have made. When the message **Spell check complete. You're good to go!** displays, as shown in Figure 4, click **OK**.

   When words you use often are not in the Office dictionary, you can click *Add to Dictionary* to add them.

12. **Save** 🖫 the workbook.

■ **You have completed Skill 8 of 10**

▶ In Excel, **Page Layout view** is used to adjust how a worksheet will look when it is printed.

1. Click the **Insert tab**, and then in the **Text group**, click the **Header & Footer** button to switch to **Page Layout view** and to display the **Header & Footer Tools Design** contextual tab.

2. On the **Design tab**, in the **Navigation group**, click the **Go to Footer** button to move to the Footer area. Click just above the word **Footer** to place the insertion point in the left section of the Footer area.

3. In the **Header & Footer Elements group**, click the **File Name** button. Compare your screen with **Figure 1**.

> Predefined headers and footers insert placeholders with instructions for printing. Here, the *& [File]* placeholder instructs Excel to insert the file name when the worksheet is printed.

4. In the **Header & Footer Elements group**, click in the middle section of the Footer area, and then click the **Current Date** button. Click the right section of the Footer area, and type City Attractions Click in a cell just above the footer to exit the Footer area.

5. Click the **Page Layout tab**. In the **Sheet Options group**, under **Gridlines**, select the **Print** check box.

6. In the **Page Setup group**, click the **Margins** button. Below the **Margins** gallery, click **Custom Margins**. In the **Page Setup** dialog box, under **Center on page**, select the **Horizontally** check box, and then compare your screen with **Figure 2**.

■ **Continue to the next page to complete the skill**

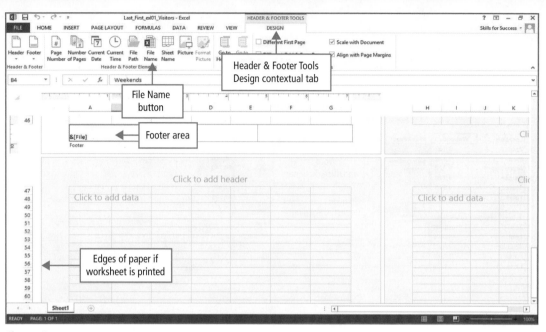

Figure 1

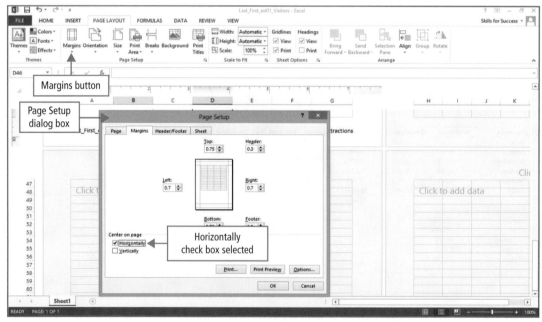

Figure 2

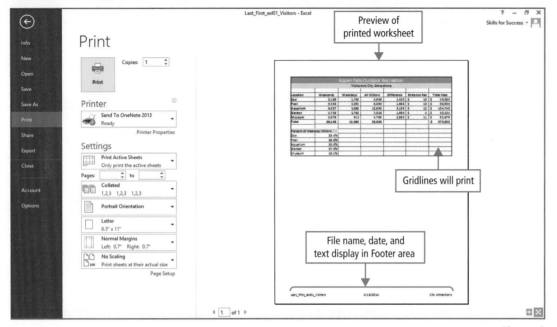

Figure 3

7. In the **Page Setup** dialog box, click **Print Preview**, and then compare your screen with **Figure 3**.

8. Click the **Back** button ⓒ. On the lower right side of the status bar, click the **Normal** button ▦ to return to Normal view, and then press `Ctrl` + `Home` to make cell **A1** active.

   Normal view maximizes the number of cells visible on the screen. The page break—the dotted line between columns G and H—indicates where one page ends and a new page begins.

9. At the bottom of your worksheet, right-click the **Sheet1** worksheet tab, and then from the shortcut menu, click **Rename**. Type Attraction Visitors and then press `Enter` to change the worksheet tab name. Compare your screen with **Figure 4**.

10. **Save** ▤ the workbook.

■ **You have completed Skill 9 of 10**

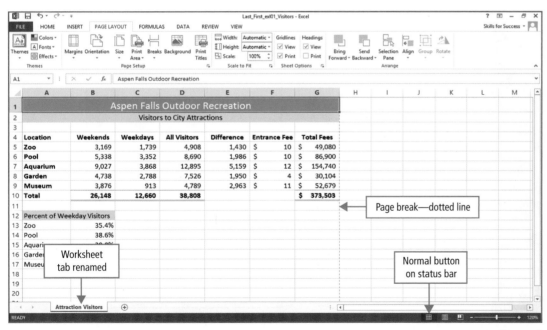

Figure 4

▶ Underlying formulas and functions can be displayed and printed.

▶ When formulas are displayed in cells, the orientation and worksheet scale may need to be changed so that the worksheet prints on a single page.

1. Click the **Formulas tab**. In the **Formula Auditing group**, click the **Show Formulas** button to display the underlying formulas in the cells. Compare your screen with **Figure 1**.

   Columns often become wider when formulas are displayed. Here, the printed worksheet extends to a second page.

2. Click the **File tab**, and then click **Print**.

   Below the preview of the printed page, *1 of 3* indicates that the worksheet will print on three pages.

3. In **Backstage** view, on the bottom of the **Print** page, click the **Next Page** button ▶ two times to view the second and the third pages, and then compare your screen with **Figure 2**.

4. Click the **Back** button ⟵. On the **Page Layout tab**, in the **Page Setup group**, click the **Orientation** button, and then click **Landscape** so that the page orientation will be wider than it is tall.

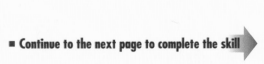
■ **Continue to the next page to complete the skill**

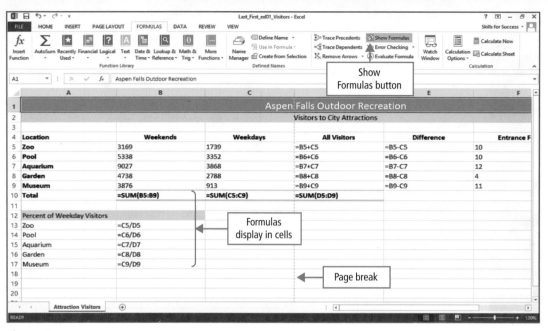

Figure 1

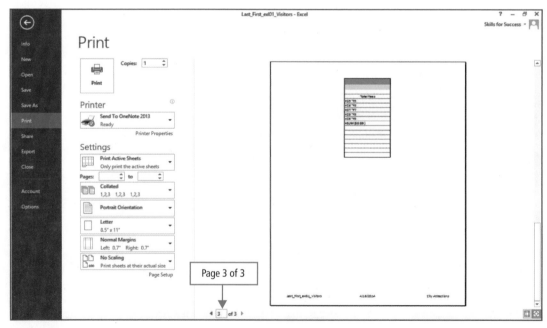

Figure 2

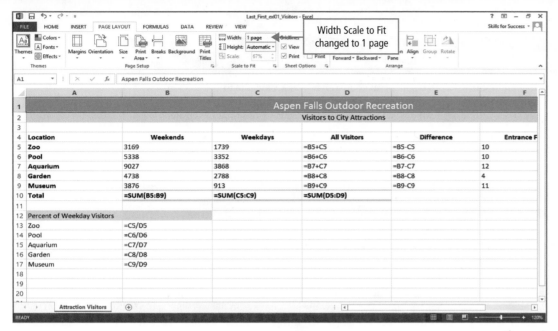

Figure 3

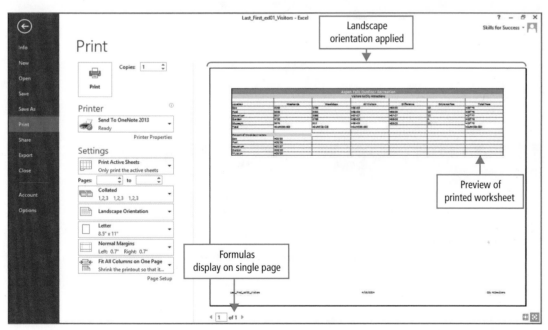

Figure 4

5. In the **Scale to Fit group**, click the **Width arrow**, and then click **1 page**. Compare your screen with Figure 3.

    Scaling adjusts the size of the printed worksheet to fit on the number of pages that you specify.

6. Click the **File tab**, and then click **Print**. Compare your screen with Figure 4.

    1 of 1 displays at the bottom of the Print page to notify you that the worksheet will now print on one page.

7. If you are directed by your instructor to submit a printout with your formulas displayed, click the Print button.

8. Click the **Back** button 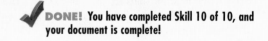. On the **Formulas tab** in the **Formula Auditing group**, click the **Show Formulas** button to hide the formulas.

9. If you are printing your work, print the worksheet with the values displayed and formulas hidden.

10. Save 🖫 the workbook, and then **Close** 🗙 Excel. Submit the workbook file or printouts as directed by your instructor.

✔ **DONE!** You have completed Skill 10 of 10, and your document is complete!

The following More Skills are located at **www.pearsonhighered.com/skills**

More Skills Create Workbooks from Templates

Templates are used to build workbooks without having to start from scratch. You can save time by using one of many predefined templates from Microsoft Office Online.

In More Skills 11, you will use a Calendar template downloaded from Microsoft Office Online to create a schedule.

To begin, open your web browser, navigate to www.pearsonhighered.com/skills, locate the name of your textbook, and then follow the instructions on the website.

More Skills Insert Names into Formulas

Instead of using cell references in formulas and functions, you can assign names that refer to the same cell or range. Names can be easier to remember than cell references, and they can add meaning to formulas, making them easier for you and others to understand.

In More Skills 12, you will open a workbook and practice various ways to name cell ranges. You will then use the names in formulas.

To begin, open your web browser, navigate to www.pearsonhighered.com/skills, locate the name of your textbook, and then follow the instructions on the website.

More Skills Create Templates

You can save one of your own workbooks as a template to use again, or you can download a template from Microsoft Office Online and then customize the template.

In More Skills 13, you will modify a Time Card template downloaded from Microsoft Office Online and then use the template to create a new weekly time card.

To begin, open your web browser, navigate to www.pearsonhighered.com/skills, locate the name of your textbook, and then follow the instructions on the website.

More Skills Manage Document Properties

Document properties are the detailed information about your workbook that can help you identify or organize your files, including the name of the author, the title, and keywords. Some workbook properties are added to the workbook when you create it. You can add others as necessary.

In More Skills 14, you will open a workbook, open the Document Information Panel, and add document properties.

To begin, open your web browser, navigate to www.pearsonhighered.com/skills, locate the name of your textbook, and then follow the instructions on the website.

Please note that there are no additional projects to accompany the More Skills Projects, and they are not covered in the End-of-Chapter projects.

The following table summarizes the **SKILLS AND PROCEDURES** covered in this chapter.

Skill Number	Task	Step	Icon	Keyboard Shortcut
2	Merge cells	Home tab → Alignment group → Merge & Center	Merge & Center	
3	Accept a cell entry	Formula bar → Enter	✓	Enter
5	Adjust Column Width	Home tab → Cells group → Format → Column Width		
5	Adjust Row Height	Home tab → Cells group → Format → Row Height		
5	Apply Cell Styles	Home tab → Styles group → Cell Styles		
6	Insert SUM function	Home tab → Editing group → AutoSum	Σ AutoSum	
7	Insert a row	Home tab → Cells group → Insert → Insert Sheet Rows		
8	Check spelling	Review tab → Proofing group → Spelling		F7
8	Edit inside cells	Double-click		F2
8	Increase Decimals	Home tab → Number group → Increase Decimal		
8	Decrease Decimals	Home tab → Number group → Decrease Decimal		
9	Display workbook in Normal View	Status bar → Normal		
9	Move to cell A1			Ctrl + Home
9	Insert text and fields into footers	Insert tab → Text group → Header & Footer		
9	Rename a worksheet tab	Right-click worksheet tab → Rename		
10	Display formulas	Formulas tab → Formula Auditing group → Show Formulas		Ctrl + [']
10	Scale to Print on one page	Page Layout tab → Scale to Fit group → Width		
10	Change Page Orientation	Page Layout tab → Page Setup group → Orientation		

Key Terms

Online Help Skills

1. Start **Excel 2013**, and then in the upper right corner of the start page, click the **Help** button.

2. In the **Excel Help** window **Search help** box, type Broken formula and then press Enter.

3. In the search result list, click **Why is my formula broken**, and then compare your screen with **Figure 1**.

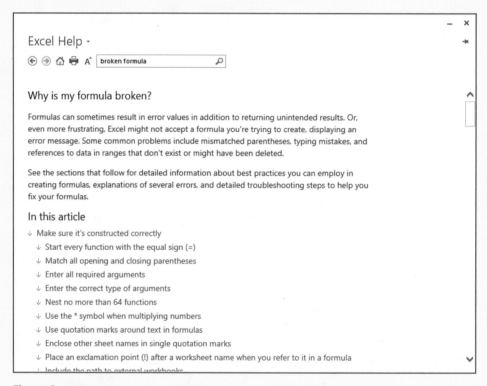

Figure 1

4. Read the article to answer the following questions: What results in a #DIV/0 error? What function can you nest with your division operation to avoid this error?

Matching MyITLab®

Match each term in the second column with its correct definition in the first column by writing the letter of the term on the blank line in front of the correct definition.

___ **1.** An Excel file that contains one or more worksheets.

___ **2.** The primary document that you use in Excel to store and work with data.

___ **3.** The cell, surrounded by a green border, ready to receive data or be affected by the next Excel command.

___ **4.** The identification of a specific cell by its intersecting column letter and row number.

___ **5.** Data in a cell—text or numbers.

___ **6.** Data in a cell made up of text only.

___ **7.** Data in a cell made up of numbers only.

___ **8.** Two or more cells on a worksheet.

___ **9.** The Excel window area that displays the address of a selected cell.

___ **10.** An Excel feature that suggests values as you type a function.

A Active cell

B Cell reference

C Formula AutoComplete

D Name Box

E Number value

F Range

G Text value

H Value

I Workbook

J Worksheet

BizSkills
Video

1. What are the best ways to network online?

2. What are some of the biggest pitfalls in using social media to communicate a personal brand?

Multiple Choice

Choose the correct answer.

1. An Excel window area that displays the value contained in the active cell.
   - A. Formula bar
   - B. Workbook
   - C. Name Box

2. The column letter and row number that identify a cell.
   - A. Cell window
   - B. Cell address
   - C. Cell file name

3. The data displayed in a cell.
   - A. Viewed value
   - B. Inspected value
   - C. Displayed value

4. An equation that performs mathematical calculations on number values.
   - A. Method
   - B. Formula
   - C. System

5. Page headers and footers can be changed in this view.
   - A. Print preview
   - B. Page Layout view
   - C. Normal view

6. Symbols that specify mathematical operations such as addition or subtraction.
   - A. Hyperlinks
   - B. Bookmarks
   - C. Arithmetic operators

7. The number that displays at the left of a row.
   - A. Row heading
   - B. Row name
   - C. Row border

8. A prewritten Excel formula.
   - A. Method
   - B. Function
   - C. Exponent

9. The small green square in the lowerright corner of the active cell.
   - A. Border
   - B. Fill handle
   - C. Edge

10. A view that maximizes the number of cells visible on the screen.
    - A. Page Layout view
    - B. Standard view
    - C. Normal view

Topics for Discussion

1. What is the advantage of using cell references instead of actual number values in formulas and functions?

2. What are some things you can do to make your worksheet easier for others to read and understand?

3. According to the Introduction to this chapter, how do you decide which information to put in columns and which to put in rows?

Skills Review

To complete this project, you will need the following file:

- Blank Excel document

You will save your file as:

- Last_First_exl01_SRFitness

1. Start **Excel 2013**. In cell **A1**, type Aspen Falls Fitness Events and then in cell **A2**, type Number of Participants In cell **A4**, type Department and then pressing `Tab` after each label, type Spring, Fall, Total Participants and Difference

2. In rows **5** through **9**, enter the following data starting in cell **A5**:

City Hall	185	140	Engineering	169	147
Finance	147	136	City Council	195	152
IT Services	130	117			

3. In cell **D5**, type =B5+C5 and then in cell **E5**, type =B5-C5 Select the range **D5:E5**. Point to the fill handle, and then drag down through row **9**. Compare your screen with **Figure 1**.

4. **Save** the workbook in your chapter folder with the name Last_First_exl01_SRFitness

5. On the **Insert tab**, in the **Text group**, click the **Header & Footer** button. In the **Navigation group**, click the **Go to Footer** button, and then click in the left footer. In the **Header & Footer Elements group**, click the **File Name** button. Click in a cell just above the footer. On the lower right side of the status bar, click the **Normal** button, and then press `Ctrl`+`Home`.

6. In cell **A10**, type Total and then select the range **B10:D10**. On the **Home tab**, in the **Editing group**, click the **AutoSum** button.

7. Click cell **A7**. In the **Cells group**, click the **Insert arrow**, and then click **Insert Sheet Rows**. In the new row **7**, type the following data: Public Works and 95 and 87

8. Select the range **D6:E6**, and then use the fill handle to copy the formulas down one row.

9. In cell **A13**, type Fall Participants as a Percent of Total

10. Select the range **A5:A10**, and then on the **Home tab**, in the **Clipboard group**, click the **Copy** button. Click cell **A14**, and then in the **Clipboard group**, click the **Paste** button. Press `Esc` and then compare your screen with **Figure 2**.

■ Continue to the next page to complete this Skills Review

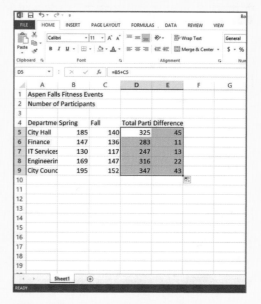

Figure 1

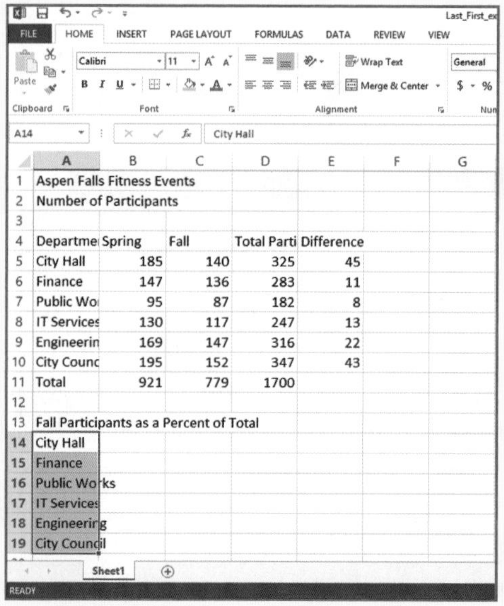

Figure 2

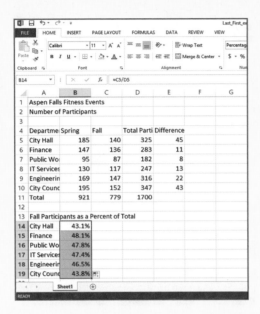

Figure 3

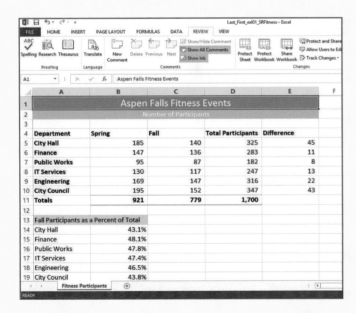

Figure 4

11. In cell **B14**, type =C5/D5 and then on the formula bar, click the **Enter** button. In the **Number group**, click the **Percent Style** button, and then click the **Increase Decimal** button one time. With cell **B14** still the active cell, use the fill handle to copy the formula down through row **19**. Compare your screen with **Figure 3**.

12. Select the range **A1:E1**, and then on the **Home tab**, in the **Alignment group**, click the **Merge & Center** button. In the **Styles group**, click the **Cell Styles** button, and then click **Accent 6**. In the **Font group**, click the **Font Size arrow**, and then click **16**. Select the range **A2:E2**, and then click the **Merge & Center** button. Click the **Cell Styles** button, and then click **60% - Accent 6**.

13. Select the range **A4:E4**. On the **Home tab**, in the **Cells group**, click the **Format** button, and then click **Column Width**. In the **Column Width** dialog box, type 16 and the click **OK**.

14. With the range **A4:E4** still selected, hold down [Ctrl], and then select the range **A5:A11**. In the **Font group**, click the **Bold** button.

15. Select range **B5:E11**. In the **Styles group**, click the **Cell Styles** button, and then click **Comma [0]**. Select the range **B11:D11**. Click the **Cell Styles** button, and then click the **Total** style.

16. Select the range **A13:B13**. In the **Alignment group**, click the **Merge & Center arrow**, and then click **Merge Across**. Click the **Cell Styles** button, and then click **40% - Accent6**.

17. Press [Ctrl] + [Home]. On the **Review tab**, in the **Proofing group**, click the **Spelling** button, and then correct any spelling errors.

18. Right-click the **Sheet1** worksheet tab, and from the shortcut menu, click **Rename**. Type Fitness Participants and then press [Enter]. **Save**, and then compare your screen with **Figure 4**. If directed by your instructor, display and format the worksheet formulas as described in Skill 10, and then print the worksheet.

19. Submit the printouts or workbook as directed by your instructor.

DONE! You have completed this Skills Review

Skills Assessment 1

MyITLab®
Grader

To complete this project, you will need the following file:

- exl01_SA1Path

You will save your workbook as:

- Last_First_exl01_SA1Path

Aspen Falls				
Bike Path Construction Costs				
Location	Brush Clearing	Paving	Landscaping	Total Cost
Cornish Forest	$ 5,883	$ 15,580	$ 3,271	$ 24,734
Haack Center	6,234	18,916	1,697	26,847
Aspen Lakes	4,763	18,846	1,498	25,107
Hamilton Hills Park	4,981	17,169	1,805	23,955
Hansen Hills	4,209	14,062	2,437	20,708
Plasek Park	3,247	12,691	3,971	19,909
Price Lakes	3,648	19,387	2,927	25,962
Rodman Creek	4,515	13,120	1,934	19,569
Schroder Brook	3,862	19,166	2,036	25,064
Terry Park	2,569	17,506	1,756	21,831
Total	$ 43,911	$ 166,443	$ 23,332	$ 233,686

Location	Increase	Cost Increase		
Cornish Forest	3%	$ 742.02		
Haack Center	3%	$ 805.41		
Aspen Lakes	5%	$ 1,255.35		
Hamilton Hills Park	5%	$ 1,197.75		
Hansen Hills	6%	$ 1,242.48		
Plasek Park	6%	$ 1,194.54		
Price Lakes	6%	$ 1,557.72		
Rodman Creek	6%	$ 1,174.14		
Schroder Brook	6%	$ 1,503.84		
Terry Park	6%	$ 1,309.86		

Figure 1

1. Start **Excel 2013**. From your student data files, open **exl01_SA1Path**. Save the workbook in your chapter folder as Last_First_exl01_SA1Path Add the file name to the worksheet's left footer, add the current date to the center footer, and then type Bike Path Costs in the right footer. Return to **Normal** view.

2. For the range **A1:E1**, merge and center and apply the **Accent5** cell style. Increase the font size to **18** points. For the range **A2:E2**, merge and center and apply the **40% - Accent 5** cell style. Widen column **A** to *20*. For all column and row labels, apply **Bold**.

3. For the range **E5:E13**, insert the **SUM** function to add the three costs for each row. In the range **B14:E14**, insert the **SUM** function to provide totals for each column.

4. Select the nonadjacent ranges **B5:E5** and **B14:E14**. Apply the **Currency [0]** cell style.

5. Select the range **B6:E13**, and then apply the **Comma [0]** cell style. Select the range **B14:E14**, and then apply the **Total** cell style.

6. Insert a new row above row **7**. In cell **A7**, type Aspen Lakes and as the costs for the new location, type 4763 and 18846 and 1498 Use the fill handle to copy the formula in cell **E6** to cell **E7**.

7. **Copy** the location names from the range **A5:A14** to the range **A20:A29**.

8. Making sure to type the decimals, in cells **B20** and **B21**, type .03 In cells **B22** and **B23**, type .05 and in cell **B24**, type .06 Use the fill handle to copy the value in cell **B24** down through cell **B29**. Select the range **B20:B29**, and then apply the **Percent Style** number format.

9. In cell **C20**, enter a formula that calculates the cost by multiplying cell **E5** by cell **B20**. AutoFill the formula in cell **C20** down through cell **C29**.

10. Rename the **Sheet 1** worksheet tab as Path Costs

11. Use **Page Setup** to center the worksheet **Horizontally**. Set the **Gridlines** to print.

12. Check and correct any spelling errors, ignoring the proper names.

13. **Save** the workbook. Submit the workbook as directed by your instructor. If you are instructed to do so, display the worksheet formulas, scale the worksheet to print on one page.

14. Compare your completed worksheet with **Figure 1**.

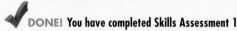
DONE! You have completed Skills Assessment 1

Skills Assessment 2

To complete this project, you will need the following file:

- exl01_SA2Guests

You will save your workbook as:

- Last_First_exl01_SA2Guests

---

1. Start **Excel 2013**. From the student data files, open **exl01_SA2Guests**. Save the workbook in your chapter folder as Last_First_exl01_SA2Guests Add the file name to the worksheet's left footer, and then add the Current Date to the right footer. Return to **Normal** view.

2. In cell **D5**, construct a formula to add the *1st Qtr.* and *2nd Qtr.* guests who are *Over 70*. In cell **E5**, construct a formula to calculate the increase of guests of the *2nd Qtr.* over the *1st Qtr.* guests who are *Over 70*.

3. In cell **F5** for the *Over 70* row, construct a formula to divide *2nd Qtr.* guests by the *1st Half Total Guests*.

4. AutoFill the formulas in the range **D5:F5** down through row **17**.

5. In cell **A18**, type Total and then in row **18**, insert the functions to total columns **B:D**.

6. Insert a new row above row **15**, and then in the new cell, **A15**, type 20 to 25 In cell **B15**, type 17196 and in cell **C15** type 19133

7. For the range **B5:E19** apply the **Comma [0]** cell style, and for the range **F5:F18** apply the **Percent** number style and display one decimal.

8. Merge and center the range **A1:F1**, and then apply the **Accent6** cell style. Increase the font size to **18**. Merge and center the range **A2:F2**, and then apply the **40% - Accent 6** cell style. Increase the font size to **14**.

9. Widen columns **A:C** to **11.00**, and then widen columns **D:F** to **14.00**.

10. For the column and row labels, apply **Bold**. In the range **B19:D19**, apply the **Total** cell style.

11. For the range **A22:C22**, apply the **Merge Across** alignment and the **40% - Accent 6** cell style.

12. In cell **C24**, construct a formula to multiply *1st Half Total Guests* in the *Over 70* row by the *Projected Percent Increase* in cell **B24**. Apply the **Comma [0]** cell style. AutoFill the formula down through row **37**.

13. Rename the worksheet tab Aspen Lakes Guests

14. Check and correct any spelling errors.

15. Use Page Setup to center the page **Horizontally**. Set the **Gridlines** to print, and then **Save** the workbook.

16. If you are instructed to do so, display the worksheet formulas, scale the worksheet to print on one page, and then print with the formulas displayed.

17. Switch to **Normal** view, and then compare your completed worksheet with **Figure 1**. **Close** Excel, and then submit the workbook as directed by your instructor.

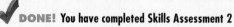 **DONE!** You have completed Skills Assessment 2

Aspen Lakes Recreation Area					
Number of Guests					
Ages	1st Qtr.	2nd Qtr.	1st Half Total Guests	2nd Qtr. Increase Over 1st Qtr.	2nd Qtr. as Percent of Total
Over 70	14,102	15,216	29,318	1,114	51.9%
65 to 70	15,125	17,854	32,979	2,729	54.1%
60 to 65	11,175	18,273	29,448	7,098	62.1%
55 to 60	15,110	16,572	31,682	1,462	52.3%
50 to 55	19,114	19,841	38,955	727	50.9%
45 to 50	18,475	21,418	39,893	2,943	53.7%
40 to 45	12,064	13,242	25,306	1,178	52.3%
35 to 40	14,628	16,232	30,860	1,604	52.6%
30 to 35	14,543	19,975	34,518	5,432	57.9%
25 to 30	17,933	19,724	37,657	1,791	52.4%
20 to 25	17,196	19,133	36,329	1,937	52.7%
15 to 20	30,516	32,597	63,113	2,081	51.6%
10 to 15	13,469	17,439	30,908	3,970	56.4%
Under 10	17,876	19,599	37,475	1,723	52.3%
Total	231,326	267,115	498,441		

Projected 2nd Half Guests			
Ages	Projected Percentage Increase	Projected Increase in Guests	
Over 70	2%	586	
65 to 70	8%	2,638	
60 to 65	4%	1,178	
55 to 60	1%	317	
50 to 55	5%	1,948	
45 to 50	6%	2,394	
40 to 45	9%	2,278	
35 to 40	3%	926	
30 to 35	6%	2,071	
25 to 30	15%	5,649	
20 to 25	14%	5,086	
15 to 20	18%	11,360	
10 to 15	21%	6,491	
Under 10	23%	8,619	

Figure 1

Visual Skills Check

To complete this project, you will need the following file:

- Blank Excel workbook

You will save your workbook as:

- Last_First_exl01_VSWorkers

Start **Excel 2013**. Open a new blank workbook, and then **Save** the workbook in your chapter folder as Last_First_exl01_VSWorkers Create the worksheet shown in **Figure 1**. The width of column **A** is 20 and the width of columns **B:F** is 13. Construct formulas that display the results shown in columns **D** and **F**, row **13**, and the range **B18:B25**. The title uses the **Accent4** cell style, and the font size is **20**. The subtitle uses the **40% - Accent 4** cell style, and the font size is **16**. The title and subtitle should be merged and centered. Using **Figure 1** as your guide, apply the **Currency [0]** cell style, the **Comma [0]** cell style, the **Total** cell style, the **Percent** number style, and the **Bold** format. On the range **A17:B17**, use Merge Across and apply the **40%-Accent2** cell style. Rename the *Sheet1* sheet tab as Park Workers Check and correct any spelling errors. Add the file name to the left footer. **Save** the workbook, and then submit the workbook as directed by your instructor.

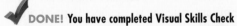 DONE! You have completed Visual Skills Check

Aspen Falls
Park Workers

	Price Park	Silkwood Park	Total Workers	Wage		Total Wages
Ticket Sellers	75	52	127	$ 15	$	1,905
Security	92	79	171	25		4,275
Landscapers	19	11	30	20		600
Life Guards	23	23	46	15		690
Cashiers	73	58	131	15		1,965
Parking Attendants	15	11	26	15		390
Maintenance	21	28	49	20		980
Cleaning	29	17	46	18		828
Total	347	279	626		$	11,633

Price Park as Percent of Total Workers	
Ticket Sellers	59.1%
Security	53.8%
Landscapers	63.3%
Life Guards	50.0%
Cashiers	55.7%
Parking Attendants	57.7%
Maintenance	42.9%
Cleaning	63.0%

Figure 1

My College Enrollment				
Course Name	Fall	Spring	Summer	Course Total
Algebra	1,173	938	415	2,526
Intro to Computers	1,043	857	497	2,397
Biology	578	311	253	1,142
World History	688	549	372	1,609
American History	824	598	397	1,819
Management	367	228	103	698
English	1,292	1,125	573	2,990
Semester Total	5,965	4,606	2,610	13,181

Summer as a Percent of Total	
Algebra	16.4%
Intro to Computers	20.7%
Biology	22.2%
World History	23.1%
American History	21.8%
Management	14.8%
English	19.2%

Figure 1

My Skills

To complete this project, you will need the following file:

- exl01_MYCollege

You will save your workbook as:

- Last_First_exl01_MYCollege

1. Start **Excel 2013**. From the student data files, open **exl01_MYCollege**. Save the workbook in your chapter folder as Last_First_ exl01_MYCollege Add the file name to the worksheet's left footer, and then return to **Normal** view.

2. For the range **A1:E1**, merge and center and apply the **Accent3** cell style.

3. Widen column **A** to 20, and then widen columns **B:E** to 12

4. For the range **B3:E3**, center the labels. For all column and row labels, apply **Bold**.

5. In cell **E4**, insert the **SUM** function to provide the total for the row. AutoFill the formula in cell **E4** down through cell **E9**.

6. For the range **B10:E10**, insert the **SUM** function to provide totals for each column. With the range **B10:E10** still selected, apply the **Total** cell style.

7. For the range **B4:E10**, apply the **Comma [0]** cell style.

8. Insert a new row above row 7. In cell **A7**, type World History and as the enrollment for the new course, type 688 and 549 and 372 AutoFill the formula in cell **E6** to cell **E7**.

9. **Copy** the course names from the range **A4:A10** to the range **A15:A21**.

10. In cell **B15**, create a formula that calculates the summer semester as a percent of the total course enrollment by dividing cell **D4** by cell **E4**. Apply the **Percent Style** number format, and display one decimal. AutoFill the formula in cell **B15** down through cell **B21**.

11. For the range **A14:B14**, merge across and apply the **40% - Accent3** cell style.

12. Rename the **Sheet 1** worksheet tab as Enrollment

13. Use **Page Setup** to center the worksheet **Horizontally**.

14. Check and correct any spelling errors.

15. **Save** the workbook. Submit the workbook as directed by your instructor. If you are instructed to do so, display the worksheet formulas, scale the worksheet to print on one page.

16. Compare your completed worksheet with Figure 1.

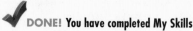 **DONE!** You have completed My Skills

Skills Challenge 1

To complete this project, you will need the following file:

- exl01_SC1Employees

You will save your workbook as:

- Last_First_exl01_SC1Employees

Start **Excel 2013**, and then open the workbook **exl01_SC1Employees**. Save the workbook in your chapter folder as Last_First_exl01_SC1Employees Duncan Chueng, the Park Operations Manager for Aspen Falls, wants to total and compare the number of employees at the city recreation areas. Using the skills you practiced in this chapter, correct the SUM function for each row and column. Format the worksheet using cell styles and number formats as practiced in this chapter. Merge and center the title across the correct columns.

Correct the number formats. No decimals should display in rows 5:11. Adjust column widths as necessary to display all data. Set the gridlines to print, and center the data horizontally on the page. Add the file name in the worksheet's left footer, and check for spelling errors. Save the workbook, and then submit the workbook as directed by your instructor.

✔ **DONE! You have completed Skills Challenge 1**

Skills Challenge 2

To complete this project, you will need the following file:

- exl01_SC2Painting

You will save your workbook as:

- Last_First_exl01_SC2Painting

Start **Excel 2013**, and then open the workbook **exl01_SC2Painting**. Save the workbook in your chapter folder as Last_First_exl01_SC2Painting The Art Center wants to total and compare the number of students enrolled in the painting classes in the different neighborhoods. Using the skills you practiced in this chapter, insert appropriate formulas and functions. Adjust column widths and row heights as necessary

to display all data. Format the worksheet as appropriate. Add the file name in the worksheet's left footer, and check for spelling errors. Save the workbook, and then submit the workbook as directed by your instructor.

✔ **DONE! You have completed Skills Challenge 2**

CHAPTER 2

Insert Summary Functions and Create Charts

- Functions are prewritten formulas that have two parts—the name of the function and the arguments that specify the values or cells to be used by the function.

- Functions analyze data to answer financial, statistical, or logical questions. Summary functions are used to recap information.

- Excel provides various types of charts that can make your data easier to understand.

- Column charts show data changes over a period of time or illustrate comparisons among items.

- Pie charts illustrate how each part relates to the whole. Pie charts display the relative sizes of items in a single data series.

- Charts can be enhanced with effects such as 3-D and soft shadows to create compelling graphical summaries.

Fotolia: Zwei Frauen im Büro © Jeanette Dietl

Aspen Falls City Hall

In this chapter, you will finish a workbook for Thelma Perkins, a Risk Management Specialist in the Finance Department. The workbook displays the department expenditures for Aspen Falls. The City Council requires that the Finance Department present departmental information annually for review and approval.

Companies use formulas and statistical functions to manipulate and summarize data to make better decisions. Summary results can include the data totals or averages. Results can be displayed graphically as charts, providing a visual representation of data. Commonly used chart types include line charts to illustrate trends over time or bar charts to illustrate comparisons among individual items. Based on the type of data selected, the Quick Analysis tools provide chart type options.

In this project, you will open an existing workbook, construct formulas containing absolute cell references, and AutoFill the formulas to other cells. You will insert the statistical functions AVERAGE, MAX, and MIN. You will create and format column charts and pie charts, and insert WordArt. Finally, you will prepare the chart sheet and the worksheet to meet printing requirements.

Time to complete all 10 skills – 60 to 90 minutes

Student data file needed for this chapter:

exl02_Expenditures

You will save your workbook as:

Last_First_exl02_Expenditures

Outcome

Using the skills in this chapter, you will be able to work with Excel worksheets like this:

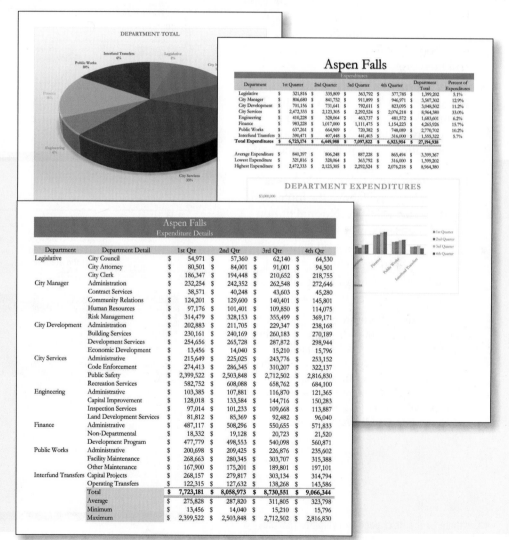

SKILLS

Skills 1-10 Training

At the end of this chapter you will be able to:

Skill 1 Align and Wrap Text

Skill 2 Apply Absolute Cell References

Skill 3 Format Numbers

Skill 4 Insert the AVERAGE Function

Skill 5 Insert the MIN and MAX Functions

Skill 6 Create Column Charts

Skill 7 Format Column Charts

Skill 8 Create and Format Pie Charts

Skill 9 Update Charts and Insert WordArt

Skill 10 Preview and Print Multiple Worksheets

MORE SKILLS

Skill 11 Insert, Edit, and Delete Comments

Skill 12 Change Chart Types

Skill 13 Copy Excel Data to Word Documents

Skill 14 Fill Data with Flash Fill

▶ The ***Text wrap*** format displays text on multiple lines within a cell.

1. Start **Excel 2013**, open the student data file **exl02_Expenditures**, and then compare your screen with **Figure 1**.

2. On the **File tab**, click **Save As**. On the **Save As** page, click the **Browse** button. Navigate to the location where you are saving your files. Click **New folder**, type Excel Chapter 2 and then press [Enter] two times. In the **File name** box, name the workbook Last_First_exl02_Expenditures and then press [Enter].

3. Verify *Expenditures* is the active worksheet. On the **Insert tab**, in the **Text group**, click the **Header & Footer** button. In the **Navigation group**, click the **Go to Footer** button. Click just above the word **Footer**, and then in the **Header & Footer Elements group**, click the **File Name** button. Click a cell above the footer. On the status bar, click the **Normal** button, and then press [Ctrl] + [Home].

4. Click cell **B2**. Point at the fill handle to display the [+] pointer, and drag right through cell **E2** to AutoFill the labels. Compare your screen with **Figure 2**.

> Excel's AutoFill feature can generate a series of values into adjacent cells. A ***series*** is a group of numbers, text, dates, or time periods that come one after another in succession. For example, the months *January, February, March* are a series. Likewise, *1st Quarter, 2nd Quarter, 3rd Quarter,* and *4th Quarter* form a series.

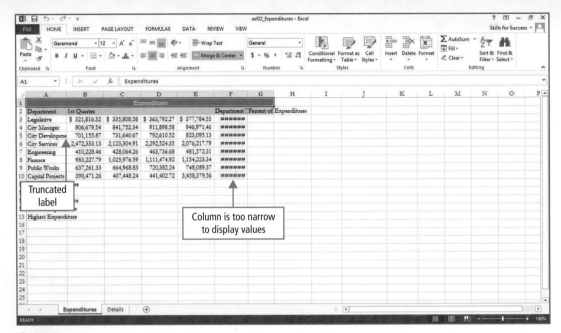

Figure 1

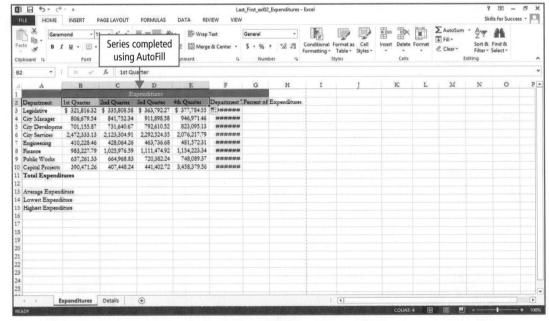

Figure 2

■ **Continue to the next page to complete the skill**

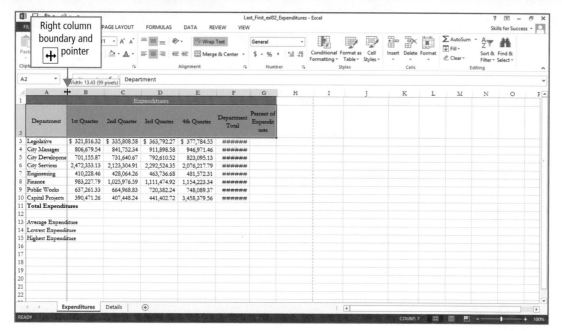

Figure 3

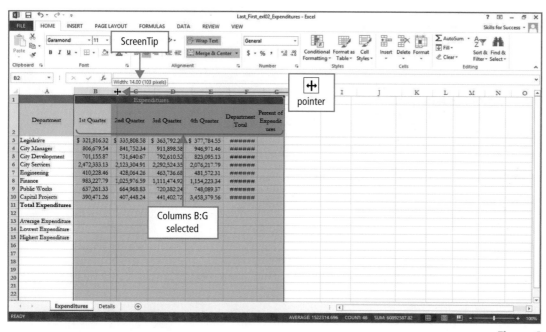

Figure 4

5. Select the range **A2:G2**. On the **Home tab**, in the **Alignment group**, click the **Wrap Text** button, the **Middle Align** button ☰, and the **Center** button ☰.

6. In the column heading area, point to the right boundary of column **A** to display the ⊞ pointer, as shown in **Figure 3**.

7. With the ⊞ pointer displayed, double-click to *AutoFit* the column—automatically change the column width to accommodate the longest entry.

8. In the column heading area, click the column **B** heading, and then drag right through column **G** to select columns **B:G**. Click the right boundary of column **B** to display the ⊞ pointer, and then drag to the right until the ScreenTip indicates *Width: 14:00 (103 pixels)* as shown in **Figure 4**. Release the mouse button.

9. Select the range **A3:A10**, and then in the **Alignment group**, click the **Increase Indent** button ☰.

10. **Save** 🖫 the workbook.

■ **You have completed Skill 1 of 10**

▶ The Quick Analysis Lens button is used to apply conditional formatting or to insert charts and totals.

▶ Excel uses rules to check for formula errors. When a formula breaks a rule, the cell displays an **error indicator**—a green triangle that indicates a possible error in a formula.

▶ An **absolute cell reference** is a cell reference that remains the same when it is copied or filled to other cells. To make a cell reference absolute, insert a dollar sign ($) before the row and column references.

1. Select **B3:F10**, click the **Quick Analysis Lens** button, and then compare your screen with **Figure 1**.

2. In the **Quick Analysis** gallery, click **Totals**, and then click the first option—**SUM**—to insert column totals.

3. Click **G3**, and then type =F3/F11 On the **formula bar**, click the **Enter** button ✓. Double-click **G3** to display the range finder, and then compare your screen with **Figure 2**.

   The **range finder** outlines all of the cells referenced in a formula. It is useful for verifying which cells are used in a formula and for editing formulas.

4. Press Esc to close the range finder. Point to the **G3** fill handle, and then AutoFill the formula down through **G10** to display **error values**—messages that display whenever a formula cannot perform the calculations in a formula. The #DIV/0! error value displays in a cell whenever the underlying formula attempts to divide by zero.

■ **Continue to the next page to complete the skill**

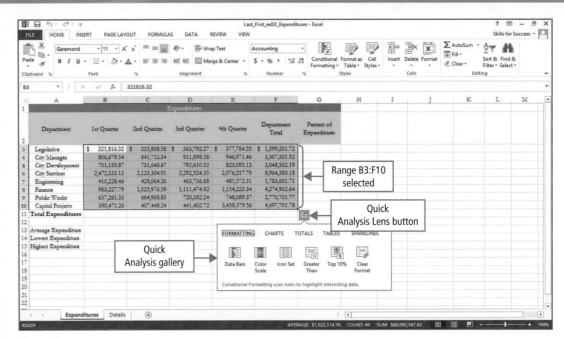

Figure 1

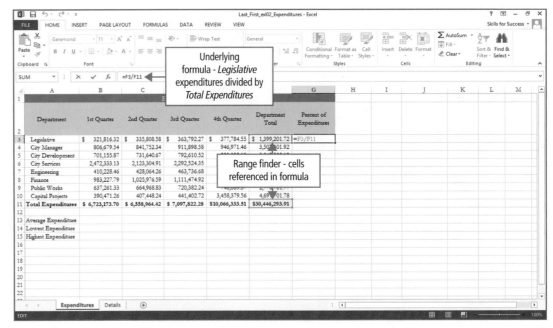

Figure 2

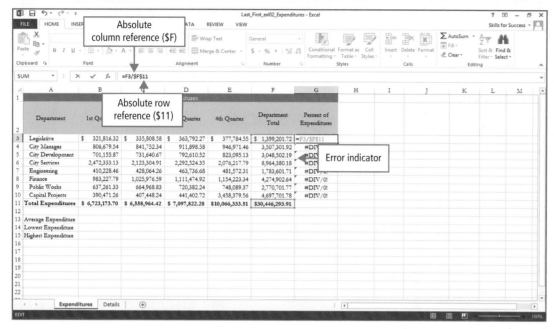

Figure 3

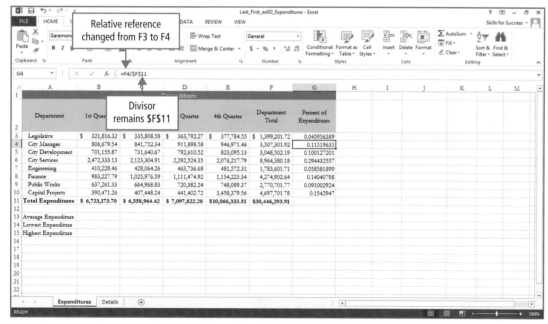

Figure 4

5. Click cell **G4**. To the left of the cell, point to the **Error Message** button ▾ to display the ScreenTip—*The formula or function used is dividing by zero or empty cells.*

6. Double-click cell **G4** to display the range finder.

> The formula was copied with a relative cell reference. In the copied formula, the cell reference to cell F4 is correct, but the formula is dividing by the value in cell F12, an empty cell. In this calculation, the divisor must be cell F11.

7. Press Esc and then double-click cell **G3**. In the formula, click the reference to cell **F11**, and then press F4 to insert a dollar sign ($) before the column reference *F* and the row reference *11* as shown in **Figure 3**.

> The dollar signs are used to indicate an absolute cell reference.

8. On the **formula bar**, click the **Enter** button ✓ and then AutoFill the formula in cell **G3** down through cell **G10**.

9. Click cell **G4**, and verify that the divisor refers to cell *$F$11*, as shown in **Figure 4**.

> The cell reference for the row *City Manager Department Total* changed relative to its row; however, the value used as the divisor— *Total Expenditures* in cell F11—remains absolute.

10. Press the ↓ two times and verify that the divisor remains constant—$F$11—while the dividend changes relative to the row.

11. **Save** 🖫 the workbook.

■ **You have completed Skill 2 of 10**

▶ A ***number format*** is a specific way that Excel displays numbers. For example, the number of decimals, or whether commas and special symbols such as dollar signs display.

▶ By default, Excel displays the ***General format***—a number format that does not display commas or trailing zeros to the right of a decimal point.

1. Click cell **B2**, and then on the **Home tab**, in the **Number group**, notice that *General* displays. Compare your screen with Figure 1.

2. Select the range **B3:F11**. In the **Number group**, click the **Decrease Decimal** button [.00→] two times to round the number and hide the decimals. Click cell **B6**, and then compare your screen with Figure 2.

    The Decrease Decimal button hides the displayed value decimals. The underlying value shows the decimals.

3. Select the range **G3:G10**. In the **Number group**, click the **Percent Style** button [%] and then click the **Increase Decimal** button [←.0] one time to add one decimal to the applied Percent Style. In the **Alignment group**, click the **Center** button [≡].

■ **Continue to the next page to complete the skill**

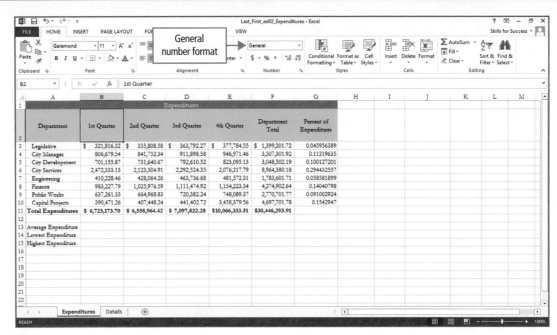

Figure 1

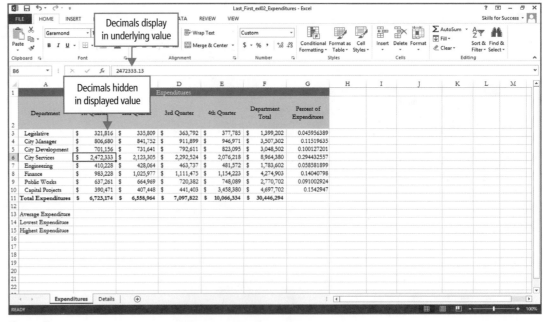

Figure 2

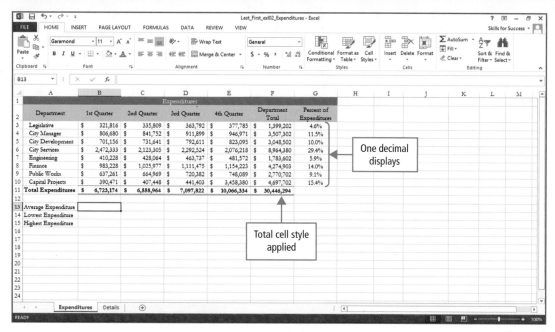

Figure 3

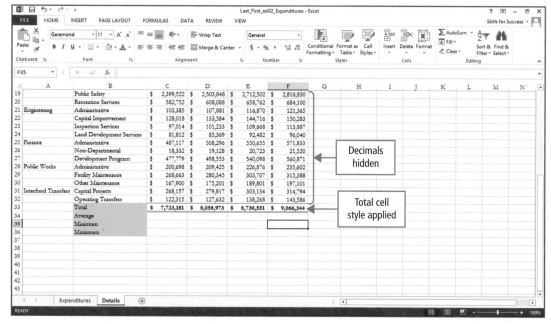

Figure 4

4. Select the range **B11:F11**. In the **Styles group**, click the **Cell Styles** button, and then under **Titles and Headings**, click **Total**. Click cell **B13**, and then compare your screen with **Figure 3**.

5. Along the bottom of the Excel window, notice the **worksheet tabs**, the labels along the lower border of the workbook window that identify each worksheet. Click the **Details** worksheet tab to make it the active worksheet.

6. Click cell **C5**. Hold down the Ctrl + Shift keys. With both keys held down, press the ↓ one time and the → one time to select the range **C5:F32**.

7. With the range **C5:F32** selected, click the **Quick Analysis Lens** button. In the **Quick Analysis** gallery, click **Totals**, and then click the first option—**SUM**.

8. With the range **C5:F32** still selected, hold down the Shift key and press the ↓ one time to include row 33—the range *C5:F33* is selected. In the **Number group**, click the **Decrease Decimal** button two times.

9. Select the range **C33:F33**, and then apply the **Total** cell style. Click cell **F35**, and then compare your screen with **Figure 4**.

10. **Save** the workbook.

■ **You have completed Skill 3 of 10**

▶ **Statistical functions** are predefined formulas that describe a collection of data—for example, averages, maximums, and minimums.

▶ The **AVERAGE function** adds a group of values and then divides the result by the number of values in the group.

1. Click the **Expenditures** worksheet tab, and then click cell **B13**. On the **Home tab**, in the **Editing group**, click the **AutoSum arrow**, and then in the list of functions, click **Average**. Look in the formula bar and in cell B13 to verify that the range B3:B12 is the suggested range of cells that will be averaged as shown in **Figure 1**.

The range in parentheses is the function **argument**—the values that a function uses to perform operations or calculations. The arguments each function uses are specific to that function. Common arguments include numbers, text, cell references, and range names.

When data is above or to the left of a selected cell, the function argument will automatically be entered. Often, you will need to edit the argument range.

2. With the insertion point in the function argument, click cell **B3**. On the range finder, click a sizing handle, and then drag down to select the argument range **B3:B10**, to exclude the *Total Expenditures* value in cell B11. On the formula bar, click the **Enter** button ✔ to display the result *$840,397*. Compare your screen with **Figure 2**.

■ Continue to the next page to complete the skill ▶

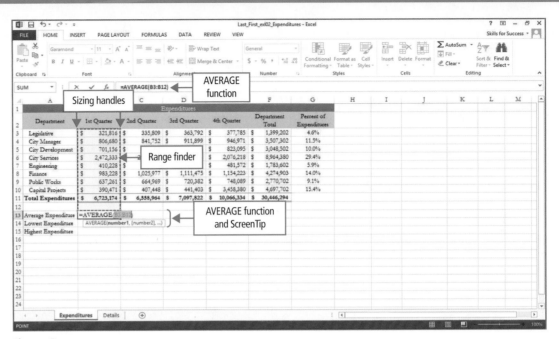

Figure 1

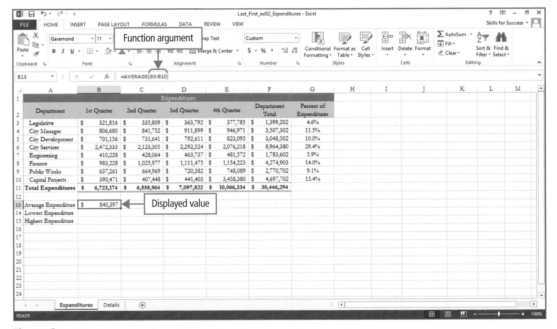

Figure 2

3. Click cell **C13**. In the **Editing group**, click the **AutoSum arrow**, and then in the list of functions, click **Average**. In the formula bar and in the cell, notice that Excel proposes to average the value in cell *B13*, not the values in column C.

4. With cell reference B13 highlighted in the function argument, click cell **C3**, and then use the range finder sizing handle to select the range **C3:C10**. On the formula bar, click the **Enter** button ✔ to display the result *$819,871*.

5. Click cell **D13**. Using the techniques just practiced, enter the **AVERAGE** function using the argument range **D3:D10**, and then on the formula bar, click the **Enter** button ✔.

6. Verify that cell **D13** is the active cell, and then AutoFill the function to the right through cell **F13**. Compare your sheet to Figure 3.

7. Click the **Details** worksheet tab, and then click cell **C34**. Enter the **AVERAGE** function using the argument range **C5:C32**. Do not include the *Total* value in cell *C33* in the function argument. Compare your sheet to Figure 4.

8. Display the worksheet footers, click in the left footer, and then click the **File Name** button. Click in the right footer, and then click the **Sheet Name** button. Return to Normal view.

9. **Save** 💾 the workbook.

■ **You have completed Skill 4 of 10**

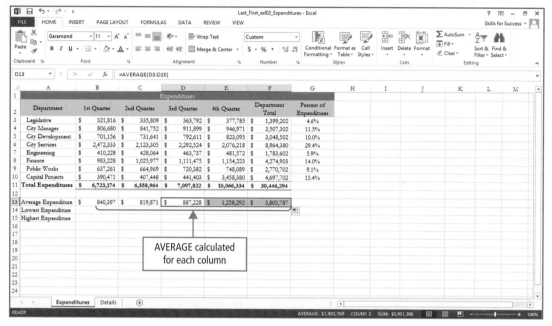

Figure 3

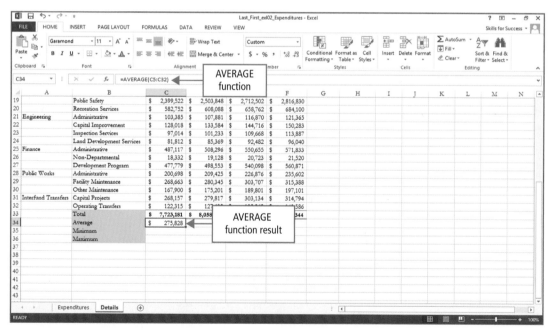

Figure 4

▶ The *MIN function* returns the smallest value in a range of cells.

▶ The *MAX function* returns the largest value in a range of cells.

1. Click cell **C35**. Type =Mi and then in the Formula AutoComplete list, double-click **MIN**. With the insertion point blinking in the function argument, click cell **C32**, and then use the range finder sizing handles to drag up and select the range **C5:C32**. Press ⌈Enter⌉ to display the result *$13,456*.

   The MIN function evaluates the range provided in the function argument—C5:C32—and then returns the lowest value—*$13,456*. Here, the *Total* and *Average* values in cells *C33* and *C34* should not be included in the argument range.

2. Verify that **C36** is the active cell. Type =Ma and then in the Formula AutoComplete list, double-click **MAX**. Using the technique just practiced, select the range **C5:C32**, and then on the formula bar, click the **Enter** button ✓ to display the result *$2,399,522*. Compare your screen with **Figure 1**.

   The MAX function evaluates all of the values in the range C5:C32 and then returns the highest value found in the range.

3. Select the range **C34:C36**. AutoFill the formulas to the right through column **F**, and then compare your screen with **Figure 2**.

   In this manner, you can AutoFill several different functions or formulas at the same time. Here, the different functions at the beginning of each row are filled across the columns.

■ **Continue to the next page to complete the skill**

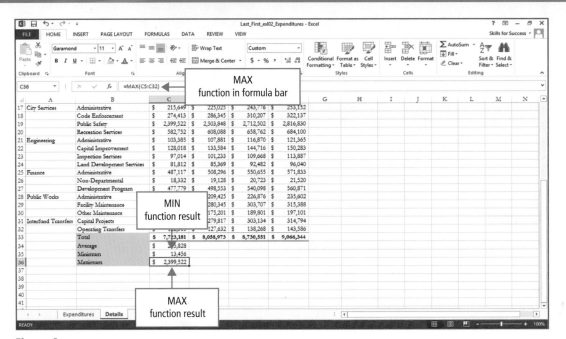

Figure 1

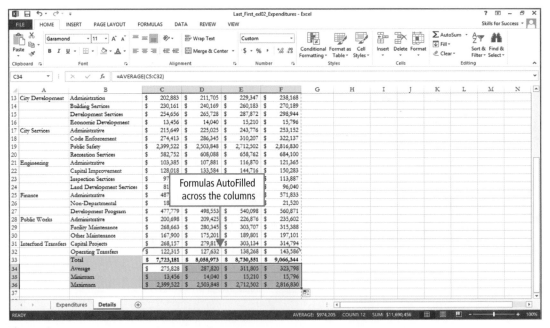

Figure 2

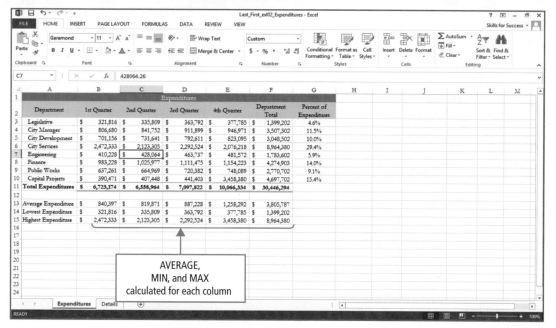

AVERAGE, MIN, and MAX calculated for each column

Figure 3

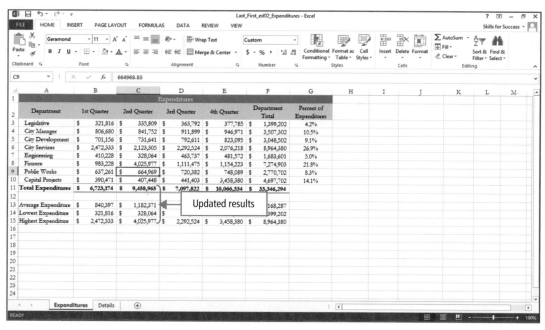

Updated results

Figure 4

4. Click the **Expenditures** worksheet tab. In cell **B14**, repeat the technique just practiced to insert the **MIN** function, using the range **B3:B10** as the function argument in the parentheses. Verify that the result is *$321,816*.

5. In cell **B15**, insert the **MAX** function using the range **B3:B10** as the function argument. Verify that the result is *$2,472,333*. Take care that the argument range does not include the cells with the total expenditures or average expenditures.

6. AutoFill the formulas in **B14:B15** to the right through column **F**. Review the functions, and verify that the lowest and highest values in each column were selected from each of the ranges for the MIN and MAX functions. Click cell **C7**, and then compare your screen with **Figure 3**.

7. With cell **C7** as the active cell, type 328,064 and then press Enter. In cell **C8**, type 4,025,977 and then press Enter. Verify that the MIN and MAX values in cells **C14** and **C15**, and the SUM and AVERAGE functions were automatically updated. Compare your screen with **Figure 4**.

8. Save 💾 the workbook.

■ **You have completed Skill 5 of 10**

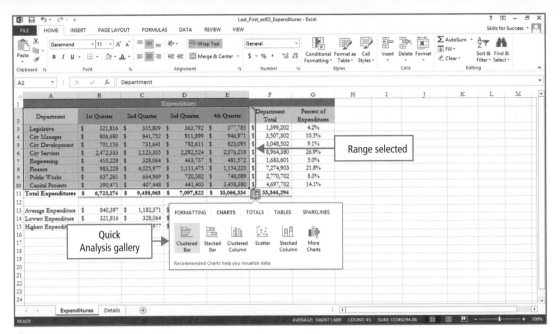

▶ A ***chart*** is a graphical representation of data used to show comparisons, patterns, and trends.

▶ A ***column chart*** is useful for illustrating comparisons among related numbers.

1. Verify *Expenditures* is the active worksheet. Select the range **A2:E10**—do *not* include the *Department Total* column or the *Total Expenditures* row in your selection. Click the **Quick Analysis Lens** button, and then in the **Quick Analysis** gallery, click **Charts**. Compare your screen with **Figure 1**.

2. In the **Quick Analysis** gallery, click the third chart—**Clustered Column**—to insert the chart and display the *Chart Tools* contextual tabs. Compare your screen with **Figure 2**.

When you insert a chart in this manner, an ***embedded chart***—a chart that is placed on the worksheet containing the data—is created. Embedded charts are beneficial when you want to view or print a chart with its source data.

An ***axis*** is a line bordering the chart plot area that is used as a frame of reference for measurement. The ***category axis*** is the axis that displays the category labels. A ***category label*** is nonnumeric text that identifies the categories of data. Here, the worksheet's row labels—the department names in A2:A10—are used for the category labels.

The ***value axis*** is the axis that displays the worksheet's numeric data.

The ***y-axis*** is the vertical axis of a chart, and the ***x-axis*** is the horizontal axis of a chart.

■ **Continue to the next page to complete the skill** ▷

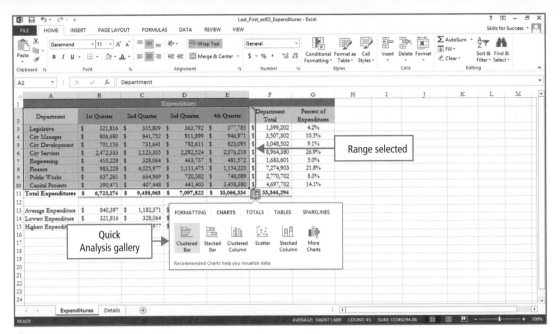

Figure 1

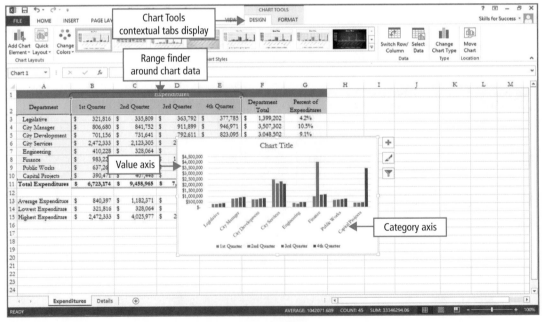

Figure 2

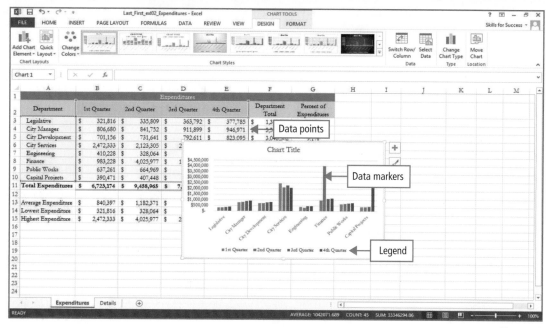

Figure 3

3. On the left side of the chart, locate the numerical scale, and then on the bottom, locate the quarters displayed in the legend. Compare your screen with Figure 3.

In the worksheet, each cell in the blue range finder is referred to as a **data point**—a chart value that originates in a worksheet cell. Each data point is represented in a chart by a **data marker**—a column, a bar, an area, a dot, a pie slice, or another symbol that represents a single data point.

Data points that are related to one another form a **data series**, and each data series has a unique color or pattern represented in the chart **legend**—a box that identifies the patterns or colors that are assigned to the data series or categories in the chart. Here, each quarter is a different data series, and the legend shows the color assigned to each quarter.

4. Point to the upper border of the chart to display the ⬚ pointer, and then move the chart to position its upper left corner in the middle of cell **A17**. If you are working with a touch screen, you can touch the chart and slide it to the correct position.

5. Scroll down to display row **36**. Point to the lower right corner of the chart to display the ⬚ pointer, and then drag to resize the chart to display the lower right chart corner in the middle of cell **G36**. Click cell **G15** and then compare your screen with Figure 4.

6. **Save** 🖫 the workbook.

■ **You have completed Skill 6 of 10**

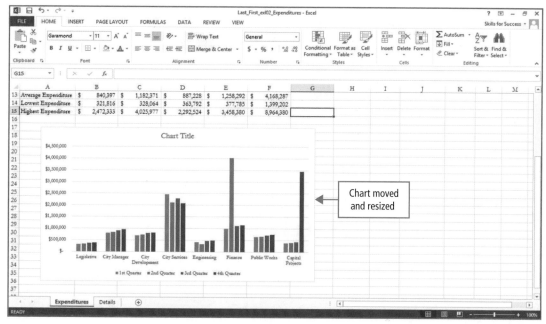

Figure 4

▶ You can modify the overall look of a chart by applying a ***chart layout***—a pre-built set of chart elements that can include a title, a legend, or labels.

▶ You can modify the overall look of a chart by applying a ***chart style***—a pre-built chart format that applies an overall visual look to a chart by modifying its graphic effects, colors, and backgrounds.

1. Click the border of the chart to select the chart and display the chart buttons.

2. To the right of the chart, click the **Chart Styles** button 🖌, and then click **Style 3**. At the top of the **Chart Styles** gallery, click the **Color tab**, and then under **Colorful**, click **Color 3**. Compare your screen with **Figure 1**.

3. Click the **Chart Styles** button 🖌 to close the gallery.

4. On the **Design tab**, in the **Chart Layouts group**, click the **Quick Layout** button. Point at the different layouts to preview the layouts on the chart. Point at **Layout 9**, and then compare your screen with **Figure 2**.

5. In the **Quick Layout** gallery, click **Layout 9** to add the axes titles and to move the legend to the right side of the chart.

■ **Continue to the next page to complete the skill**

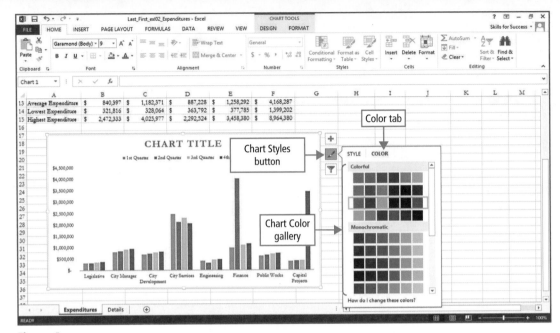

Figure 1

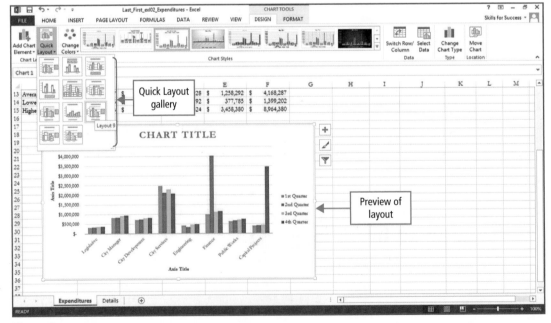

Figure 2

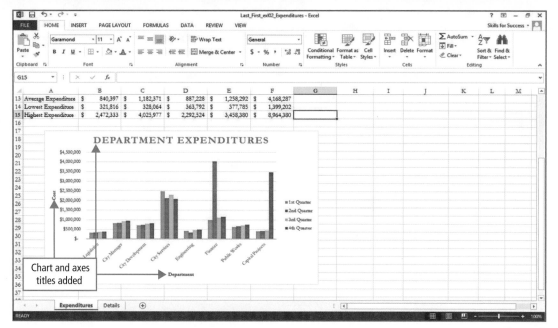

Figure 3

6. At the top of the chart, click the text *Chart Title*, and then type Department Expenditures to insert the text into the formula bar. Press [Enter] to accept the text. Verify that your text replaced any text in the chart title.

7. Below the horizontal axis, click the text *Axis Title*, type Department and then press [Enter].

8. To the left of the vertical axis, click the text *Axis Title*, type Cost and then press [Enter].

9. Click cell **G15** to deselect the chart. **Save** the workbook, and then compare your screen with **Figure 3**.

10. Take a moment to examine the various types of charts available in Excel, as summarized in **Figure 4**.

■ **You have completed Skill 7 of 10**

Chart Types Commonly Used in Excel	
Chart type	**Used to**
Column	Illustrate data changes over a period of time or illustrate comparisons among items.
Line	Illustrate trends over time, with time displayed along the horizontal axis and the data point values connected by a line.
Pie	Illustrate the relationship of parts to a whole.
Bar	Illustrate comparisons among individual items.
Area	Emphasize the magnitude of change over time.

Figure 4

▶ A **pie chart** displays the relationship of parts to a whole.

▶ A **chart sheet** is a workbook sheet that contains only a chart and is useful when you want to view a chart separately from the worksheet data.

1. Verify *Expenditures* is the active sheet. Select the range **A2:A10**. Hold down Ctrl, and then select the nonadjacent range **F2:F10**.

2. On the **Insert tab**, in the **Charts group**, click the **Recommended Charts** button, and then compare your screen with **Figure 1**.

3. In the **Insert Chart** dialog box, click the **Pie** thumbnail, and then click **OK**.

   Here, the row labels identify the slices of the pie chart, and the department totals are the data series that determine the size of each pie slice.

4. On the **Design tab**, in the **Location group**, click the **Move Chart** button. In the **Move Chart** dialog box, select the **New sheet** option button. In the **New sheet** box, replace the highlighted text *Chart1* with Expenditure Chart as shown in **Figure 2**.

5. In the **Move Chart** dialog box, click **OK** to move the pie chart to a chart sheet.

6. On the **Design tab**, in the **Type group**, click the **Change Chart Type** button. In the **Change Chart Type** dialog box, click the **3-D Pie** thumbnail and then click **OK**.

   The chart is changed from a two-dimensional chart to a three-dimensional chart. **3-D**, which is short for **three-dimensional**, refers to an image that appears to have all three spatial dimensions—length, width, and depth.

■ **Continue to the next page to complete the skill**

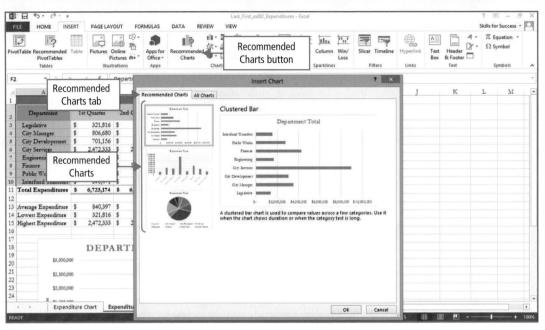

Figure 1

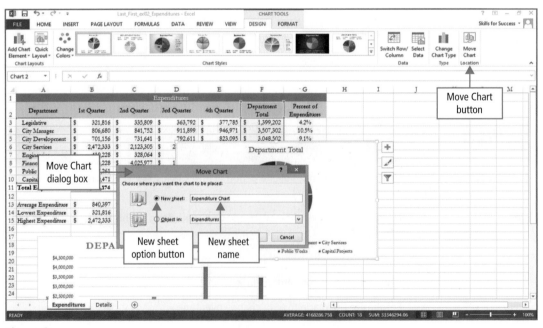

Figure 2

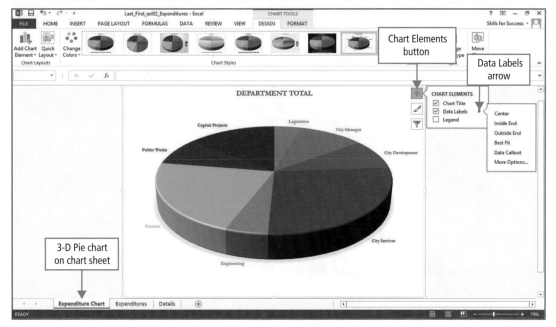

Figure 3

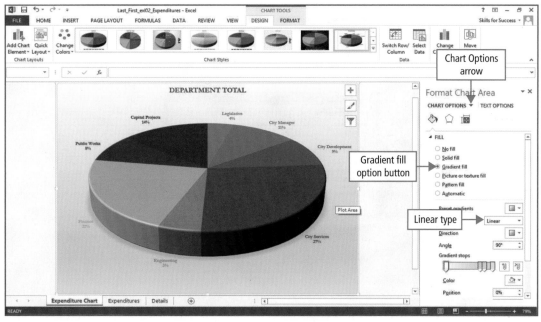

Figure 4

7. To the right of the chart, click the **Chart Styles** button. In the **Chart Styles** gallery, scroll down, and then click **Style 8**.

8. To the right of the chart, click the **Chart Elements** button. Under **Chart Elements**, point at **Data Labels**, and then click the **Data Labels arrow**. Compare your screen with Figure 3.

9. In the **Data Labels** list, click **More Options** to open the Format Data Labels pane.

10. In the **Format Data Labels** pane, under **Label Contains**, select the **Percentage** check box. Verify that the **Category Name** check box is selected, and then clear any other check boxes.

11. At the top of the pane, click the **Label Options arrow** and then click **Chart Area**, to open the Format Chart Area pane. In the **Format Chart Area** pane, click the **Fill & Line** button, and then click **Fill**. Click the **Gradient fill** option button, and verify that the Type is *Linear*. Compare your screen with Figure 4.

12. **Close** the **Format Chart Area** pane.

13. On the **Insert tab**, in the **Text group**, click the **Header & Footer** button. In the **Page Setup** dialog box, click the **Custom Footer** button. Verify that the insertion point is in the **Left section** box, and then click the **Insert File Name** button. Click in the **Right section** box, and then click the **Insert Sheet Name** button. Click **OK** two times.

14. **Save** the workbook.

■ **You have completed Skill 8 of 10**

▶ A chart's data series and labels are linked to the source data in the worksheet. When worksheet values are changed, the chart is automatically updated.

1. Click the **Expenditures** worksheet tab to display the worksheet. Scroll as necessary to display row **8** at the top of the window and the chart at the bottom of the window. In the column chart, note the height of the *Finance* data marker for the 2nd Quarter and the *Capital Projects* data marker for the 4th Quarter.

2. Click cell **C8**. Type 1,017,000 and then press [Enter] to accept the new value. Notice the animation in the chart when changes are made to its source data. Compare your screen with **Figure 1**.

3. Click cell **E10**, type 316,000 and then press [Enter].

   In cell G10, the *Capital Projects* expenditure now represents 5.7% of the projected total.

4. Click the **Expenditure Chart** worksheet tab to display the pie chart. Verify that in the pie chart, the slice for *Capital Projects* displays 6%.

   When underlying data is changed, the pie chart percentages and pie slices are automatically recalculated and resized. On the chart, 5.7% is rounded up to 6%.

5. Right-click the **Capital Projects** data label to select all of the data labels, and in the shortcut menu click **Font**. In the **Size** box, type 11 Compare your screen with **Figure 2**, and then click **OK**.

■ **Continue to the next page to complete the skill** ➤

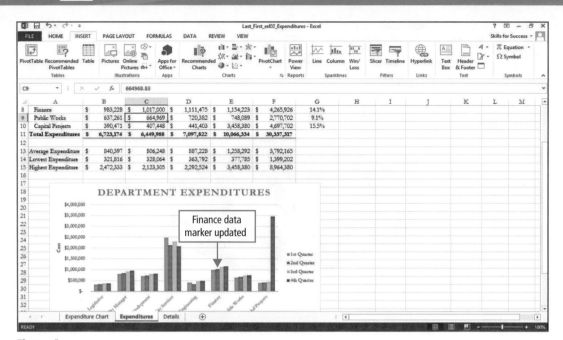

Figure 1

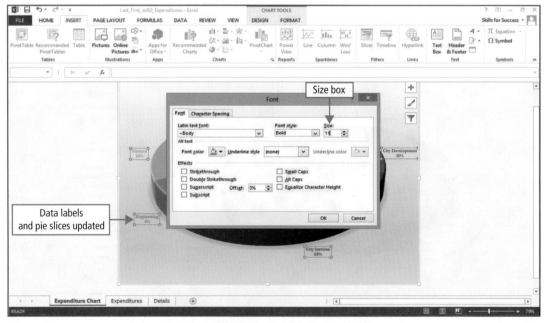

Figure 2

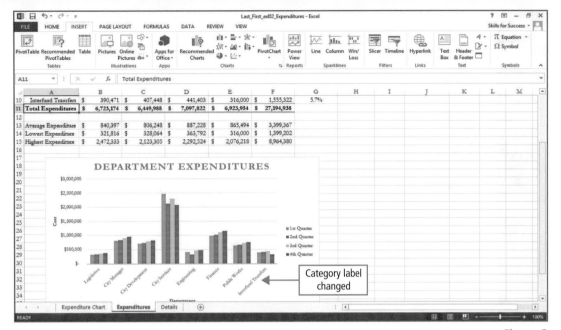

Figure 3

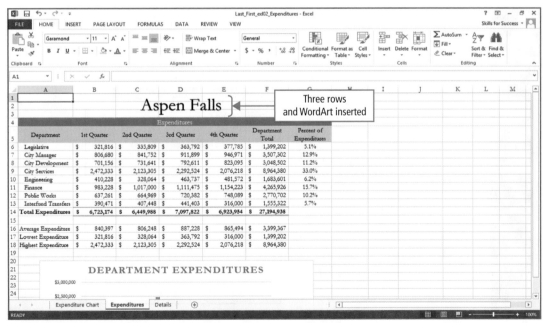

Figure 4

6. Click the **Expenditures** worksheet tab, and then in cell **A10**, change *Capital Projects* to Interfund Transfers Press Enter and then scroll down to verify that the column chart category label changed. Compare your screen with Figure 3.

7. Click the **Expenditure Chart** worksheet tab, and verify that the data label on the pie chart displays as *Interfund Transfers*.

8. Click the **Expenditures** worksheet tab. Scroll up, and then select the range **A1:G3**. On the **Home tab**, in the **Cells group**, click the **Insert arrow**, and then click **Insert Sheet Rows** to insert three blank rows.

9. On the **Insert tab**, in the **Text group**, click the **Insert WordArt** button. In the **WordArt** gallery, click the first style in the first row—**Fill - Black**, **Text 1**, **Shadow**. Immediately type Aspen Falls

10. Select the WordArt text. In the mini toolbar, click the **Font Size** button and then click **32**.

11. Point to the bottom border of the WordArt box, and then with the pointer, drag to position the WordArt object to approximately the range **C1:E3**. Click cell **A1** to deselect the WordArt, and then compare your screen with Figure 4.

12. **Save** the workbook.

▪ **You have completed Skill 9 of 10**

▶ Before you print an Excel worksheet, you can use Page Layout view to preview and adjust the printed document.

1. Verify *Expenditures* is the active worksheet. Scroll down, and then click the column chart to select the chart. Click the **File tab**, and then click **Print**. Compare your screen with **Figure 1**.

   When an embedded chart is selected, only the chart will print.

2. Click the **Back** button ⊙. Click cell **A19** to deselect the chart.

3. On the **View tab**, in the **Workbook Views group**, click the **Page Layout** button. On the left side of the status bar, notice that *Page: 1 of 2* displays, informing you that the data and the column chart would print on two pages.

4. On the **Page Layout tab**, in the **Scale to Fit group**, click the **Width arrow**, and then click **1 page**. Click the **File tab**, and then click **Print**. Compare your screen with **Figure 2**.

   1 of 1 displays at the bottom of the screen, indicating that the WordArt, the data, and the column chart will all print on one page.

5. Click the **Back** button ⊙. On the status bar, click the **Normal** button ▦ and then press ⌨Ctrl + ⌨Home to make cell **A1** the active cell.

■ **Continue to the next page to complete the skill** ▶

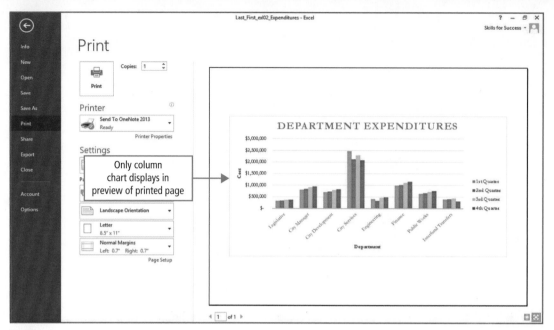

Figure 1

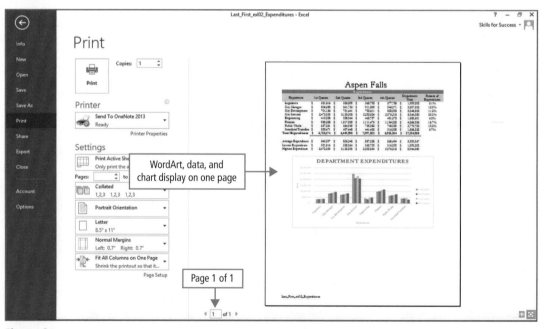

Figure 2

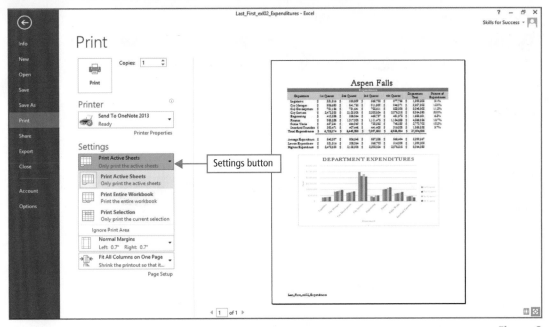

Settings button

Figure 3

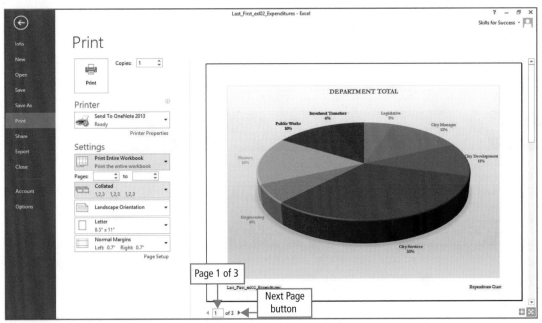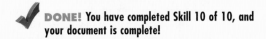

Page 1 of 3

Next Page button

Figure 4

6. On the **Review tab**, in the **Proofing group**, click the **Spelling** button, and then check the spelling of the worksheet. When the message *Spell check complete. You're good to go!* displays, click **OK**.

7. **Save** 🖫 the workbook.

8. Click the **File tab**, and then click **Print**. Under **Settings**, click the first button. Compare your screen with Figure 3.

9. On the displayed list, click **Print Entire Workbook**. Notice at the bottom of the screen, *1 of 3* displays, and the chart sheet with the pie chart is the first page. Compare your screen with Figure 4.

10. At the bottom of the screen, click the **Next Page** button ▶ to preview the worksheet containing your WordArt, the data, and the column chart. Save 🖫 the workbook. Submit the workbook as directed by your instructor. If you are printing your work for this project, print the workbook. Otherwise, click the **Back** button ←.

11. If your instructor asked you to print formulas, display the worksheet formulas, AutoFit the column widths, and then print the formulas.

12. **Close** ✖ Excel. Submit the file or printouts as directed by your instructor.

✔ **DONE!** You have completed Skill 10 of 10, and your document is complete!

More Skills

The following More Skills are located at **www.pearsonhighered.com/skills**

More Skills Insert, Edit, and Delete Comments

You can add comments to cells in a worksheet to provide reminders, to display clarifying information about data within the cells, or to document your work. When you point to a cell that contains a comment, the comment and the name of the person who created the comment display.

In More Skills 11, you will insert, edit, and delete comments.

To begin, open your web browser, navigate to www.pearsonhighered.com/skills, locate the name of your textbook, and then follow the instructions on the website.

More Skills 12 Change Chart Types

After you create a chart, you may determine that a different chart type might be easier for the readers of your chart to understand. For example, you can change a bar chart to a column chart. The column chart and a bar chart are good choices to illustrate comparisons among items.

In More Skills 12, you will create a bar chart and then change the chart type to a column chart.

To begin, open your web browser, navigate to www.pearsonhighered.com/skills, locate the name of your textbook, and then follow the instructions on the website.

More Skills 13 Copy Excel Data to Word Documents

You can copy the data and objects created in one application to another application, saving time and ensuring accuracy because data is entered only one time.

In More Skills 13, you will create a chart in Excel and then copy the chart and paste it into a Word document.

To begin, open your web browser, navigate to www.pearsonhighered.com/skills, locate the name of your textbook, and then follow the instructions on the website.

More Skills Fill Data with Flash Fill

Instead of entering data manually, you can use Flash Fill to recognize a pattern in your data and automatically enter the rest of your data. You can use the fill handle or the fill command to AutoFill data that follow a pattern or series—for example, hours, days of the week, or numeric sequences such as even numbers.

In More Skills 14, you will use Flash Fill to enter data in cells.

To begin, open your web browser, navigate to www.pearsonhighered.com/skills, locate the name of your textbook, and then follow the instructions on the website.

Please note that there are no additional projects to accompany the More Skills Projects, and they are not covered in the End-of-Chapter projects.

The following table summarizes the **SKILLS AND PROCEDURES** covered in this chapter.

Skill Number	Task	Step	Icon	Keyboard Shortcut
1	Wrap text	Home tab → Alignment group → Wrap Text		
1	Middle align text	Home tab → Alignment group → Middle Align	▤	
1	Center text	Home tab → Alignment group → Center	▤	
1	Increase indent	Home tab → Alignment group → Increase Indent	▤	
2	Insert the SUM function	Quick Analysis Lens button → Totals → SUM	▣	
2	Create an absolute cell reference	Select cell reference → Type $		F4
3	Apply the Percent style	Home tab → Number group → Percent Style	%	
3	Increase the number of display decimals	Home tab → Number group → Increase Decimal	▣	
4	Calculate an average	Home tab → Editing group → Sum arrow → Average		
5	Calculate a minimum	Home tab → Editing group → Sum arrow → Min		
5	Calculate a maximum	Home tab → Editing group → Sum arrow → Max		
6	Insert a chart using the Quick Analysis Lens	Quick Analysis Lens button → Charts → select desired chart	▣	
7	Apply a chart style	Chart Style → Style		
7	Apply a chart layout	Design tab → Chart Layouts group → Quick Layout → Layout		
8	Insert a recommended chart	Insert tab → Charts group → Recommended Charts → select desired chart		
8	Move a chart to its own worksheet	Design tab → Locations group → Move Chart → New sheet		
8	Change the chart type	Design tab → Type group → Change Chart Type → Type		
8	Change chart data labels	Chart Elements → Data labels arrow → More Options → Format Data labels pane		
9	Insert WordArt	Insert tab → Text group → WordArt	𝐴 ▾	
10	Adjust scale	Page Layout tab → Scale to Fit group → Width arrow → Page		
10	Print an entire workbook	File tab → Print → Settings → Print Entire Workbook		

Key Terms

Online Help Skills

1. Start **Excel 2013**, and then in the upper right corner of the start page, click the **Help** button ⟦ ? ⟧.

2. In the **Excel Help** window **Search help** box, type Keyboard shortcuts and then press ⟦ Enter ⟧.

3. In the search result list, click **Keyboard shortcuts in Excel**, and then compare your screen with Figure 1.

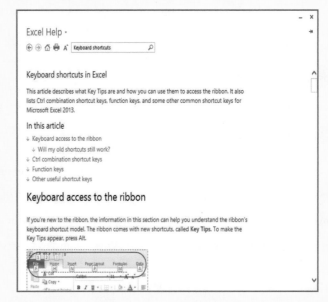

Figure 1

4. Read the article to answer the following question: How can you use Key Tips to access the ribbon?

Matching

Match each term in the second column with its correct definition in the first column by writing the letter of the term on the blank line in front of the correct definition.

___ **1.** A command with which you can display text on multiple lines within a cell.

___ **2.** A cell reference that refers to a cell by its fixed position in a worksheet and does not change when the formula is copied.

___ **3.** Rules that specify the way numbers should display.

___ **4.** The default format applied to numbers.

___ **5.** The value(s) that determine how a function should be used.

___ **6.** A graphical representation of data in a worksheet that shows comparisons, patterns, and trends.

___ **7.** A chart line that contains words as labels.

___ **8.** A chart line that contains numeric data.

___ **9.** The function that adds a group of values and then divides the result by the number of values in the group.

___ **10.** The Excel feature that outlines all of the cells referenced in a formula.

A Absolute cell reference

B Argument

C AVERAGE

D Category axis

E Chart

F General format

G Number format

H Range finder

I Text wrap

J Value axis

BizSkills Video

1. Why should you practice for an interview?

2. How should you answer a question about a missing reference?

Multiple Choice MyITLab®

Choose the correct answer.

1. Automatically changing the column width to accommodate the longest column entry.
   - A. Drag and drop
   - B. AutoFit
   - C. Auto adjust

2. A green triangle that indicates a possible error in a formula.
   - A. Error indicator
   - B. Message
   - C. Dialog Box Launcher

3. A chart type useful for illustrating comparisons among related numbers.
   - A. Pie chart
   - B. Area chart
   - C. Column chart

4. A chart placed on a worksheet with the source data.
   - A. Chart sheet
   - B. Column chart
   - C. Embedded chart

5. The related data points in a chart.
   - A. Column
   - B. Data series
   - C. Chart point

6. The box that identifies the patterns or colors assigned to the data series.
   - A. Legend
   - B. Dialog box
   - C. Message box

7. A predesigned combination of chart elements.
   - A. 3-D chart
   - B. Chart layout
   - C. Chart

8. A pre-built chart format that applies an overall visual look to a chart.
   - A. Data marker
   - B. Chart finder
   - C. Chart style

9. The chart type that best displays the relationship of parts to a whole.
   - A. Pie chart
   - B. Area chart
   - C. Column chart

10. A worksheet that contains only a chart.
    - A. Worksheet
    - B. Chart area
    - C. Chart sheet

Topics for Discussion

1. Search current newspapers and magazines for examples of charts. Which charts catch your eye and why? Do the charts appeal to you because of their color or format? Is something intriguing revealed to you in the chart that you have never considered before? What are some formatting changes that you think make a chart interesting and valuable to a reader?

2. Do you think 3-D pie charts distort the data in a way that is misleading? Why or why not?

Skills Review

To complete this project, you will need the following file:

- exl02_SRRevenue

You will save your file as:

- Last_First_exl02_SRRevenue

1. Start **Excel 2013**, and open the file **exl02_SRRevenue**. **Save** the file in your chapter folder as Last_First_exl02_SRRevenue Add the file name in the worksheet's left footer, and the sheet name in the right footer. Return to Normal view.

2. In the column heading area, point to the right boundary of column **A** and double-click to AutoFit the column width. Click the column **B** heading, and then drag right to select columns **B:F**. Click the right boundary of column **B**, and then drag to the right until the ScreenTip indicates *Width:13:00 (109 pixels)*.

3. Select the range **A1:F1**. On the **Home tab**, in the **Alignment group**, click the **Wrap Text**, **Middle Align**, and **Center** buttons.

4. Select the range **B2:E13**. Click the **Quick Analysis** button, click **Totals**, and then click the first option—**SUM**.

5. Select the range **B2:E14**. In the **Number group**, click the **Decrease Decimal** button two times. Select the range **B14:E14**. In the **Styles group**, click the **Cell Styles** button, and then click **Total**.

6. In cell **F2**, type =E2/$E$14 and then on the formula bar, click the **Enter** button. With cell F2 the active cell, in the **Number group**, click the **Percent Style** button, and the **Increase Decimal** button. In the **Alignment group**, click the **Center** button. AutoFill the formula in cell **F2** down through cell **F13**. Click cell **A15**, and then compare your screen with **Figure 1**.

7. Click cell **B16**. Type =Av and then in the formula AutoComplete list, double-click **AVERAGE**. For the function argument, select the range **B2:B13**, and then press Enter . Using the same function argument range, in cell **B17**, enter the **MAX** function. Select the range **B16:B17**, and then AutoFill the formulas to the right through column **D**. Compare your screen with **Figure 2**.

- Continue to the next page to complete this Skills Review

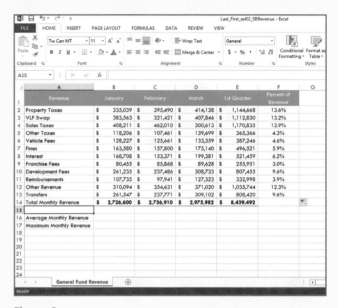

Figure 1

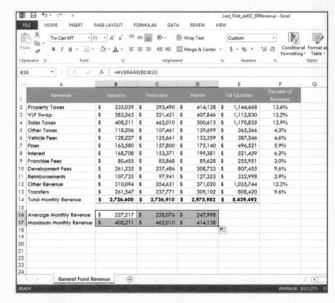

Figure 2

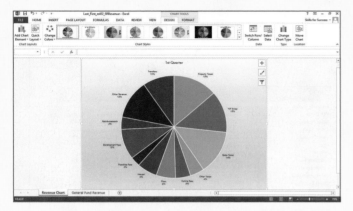

Figure 3

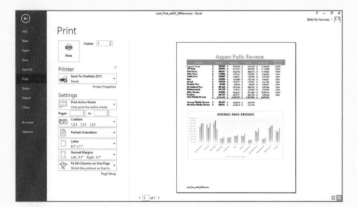

Figure 4

8. Select the range **A1:D13**. Click the **Quick Analysis Lens** button, click **Charts**, and then click the **Clustered Column** thumbnail. Move and resize the chart to display in approximately the range **A20:F40**. At the top right corner of the chart, click the **Chart Styles** button, and then click the **Style 9** thumbnail. Click the **Chart Title**, type General Fund Revenue and then press [Enter].

9. Select the nonadjacent ranges **A1:A13** and **E1:E13**. On the **Insert tab**, in the **Charts group**, click the **Recommended Charts** button. On the **All Charts tab**, click **Pie**, and then click **OK**.

10. On the **Design tab**, in the **Location group**, click the **Move Chart** button. In the **Move Chart** dialog box, select the **New sheet** option button, type the sheet name Revenue Chart and then click **OK**.

11. On the **Design tab**, in the **Chart Layouts group**, click the **Quick Layout** button, and then click **Layout 1**.

12. Click the **Chart Elements** button, click the **Data Labels arrow**, and then click **More Options**. In the **Format Data Labels** pane, under **Label Position**, click **Outside End**.

13. Click the **Label Options arrow**, and then click **Chart Area**. In the **Format Chart Area** pane, click the **Fill & Line** button, and then click **Fill**. Select the **Gradient fill** option button, and then **Close** the Format Chart Area pane. Compare your screen with Figure 3.

14. On the **Insert tab**, in the **Text group**, click the **Header & Footer** button. In the **Page Setup** dialog box, click the **Custom Footer** button. Insert the **File Name** in the left section, and insert the **Sheet Name** in the right section.

15. Click the **General Fund Revenue** worksheet tab. Select the range **A1:A3**. On the **Home tab**, in the **Cells group**, click the **Insert arrow**, and then click **Insert Sheet Rows**. On the **Insert tab**, in the **Text group**, click the **Insert WordArt** button, and then in the first row, click the second thumbnail—**Fill - Turquoise, Accent 1 Shadow**. Immediately type Aspen Falls Revenue Select the text in the WordArt. On the mini toolbar, change the **Font Size** to **36**. Point to the bottom border of the WordArt, and then move the WordArt to approximately the range **B1:E3**.

16. Click cell **A1**. Click the **Page Layout tab**. In the **Scale to Fit group**, click the **Width** arrow, and then click **1 page** button.

17. Click the **File tab**, and then click **Print**. Compare your screen with Figure 4.

18. **Save** the workbook, and then submit the workbook as directed by your instructor.

 **DONE! You have completed the Skills Review**

Skills Assessment 1  MyITLab® Grader

To complete this project, you will need the following file:

- exl02_SA1Debt

You will save your workbook as:

- Last_First_exl02_SA1Debt

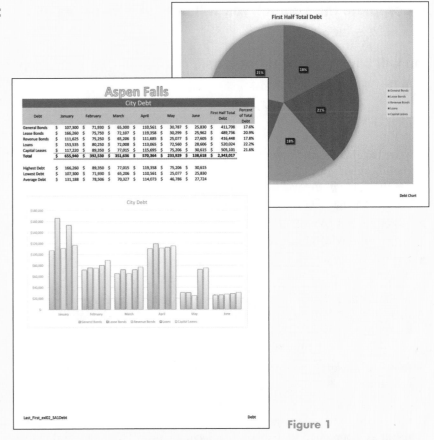

Figure 1

1. Start **Excel 2013**, and open the file **exl02_SA1Debt**. **Save** the workbook in your chapter folder as Last_First_exl02_SA1Debt Add the file name in the worksheet's left footer and the sheet name in the right footer. Return to Normal view.

2. Select the range **A2:I2**, and then apply the alignment **Wrap Text** and **Middle Align**.

3. Select the column headings **B:I**, and then AutoFit the column widths.

4. In the range **B8:H8**, insert the column totals, and apply the **Total** cell style.

5. Select the range **B3:H8**, and then display no decimals.

6. In cell **I3**, calculate the *Percent of Total Debt*. In the formula, use an absolute cell reference when referring to cell **H8**. AutoFill the formula down through cell **I7**, and then format the results as percentages with one decimal place.

7. In the range **B10:G10**, insert a function to calculate the highest monthly debt. In the range **B11:G11**, insert a function to calculate the lowest monthly debt. In the range **B12:G12**, insert a function to calculate the average monthly debt.

8. Insert a **Pie** chart based on the nonadjacent ranges **A2:A7** and **H2:H7**. Move the pie chart to a chart sheet with the sheet name Debt Chart

9. For the pie chart, apply **Layout 6**, and then apply the **Chart Style 3**. Change the data label **Font Size** to **12**. Add the file name in the chart sheet's left footer and the sheet name in the right footer.

10. On the **Debt** worksheet, insert a **Clustered Column** chart based on the range **A2:G7**. Move the chart below the data, and then resize the chart to approximately the range **A15:I38**. Apply the chart **Style 5**. Change the chart title to City Debt

11. Insert three sheet rows at the top of the worksheet. Insert **WordArt**, using the style **Gradient Fill – Purple**, **Accent 4**, **Outline - Accent 4**. Change the WordArt text to Aspen Falls and then change the **Font Size** to **36**. Move the WordArt to the top of the worksheet, centering it above the data.

12. Adjust the **Scale to Fit** to fit the WordArt, data, and column chart on one page.

13. **Save** the workbook, and then compare your completed workbook with **Figure 1**.

14. **Close** Excel, and then submit the workbook as directed by your instructor.

 **DONE! You have completed Skills Assessment 1**

Skills Assessment 2

To complete this project, you will need the following file:

- exl02_SA2Cost

You will save your workbook as:

- Last_First_exl02_SA2Cost

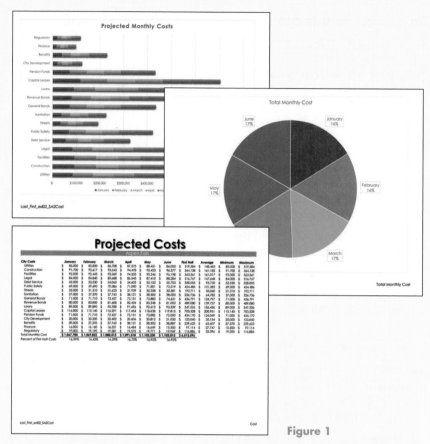

1. Start **Excel 2013**, and open the file **exl02_SA2Cost**. **Save** the workbook in your chapter folder as Last_First_exl02_SA2Cost Add the file name in the worksheet's left footer, and the sheet name in the right footer. Return to Normal view.

2. For column **A**, AutoFit the column width. For columns **B:K**, change the column width to **11.00 (93 pixels)**.

3. In the range **B3:K3**, apply the **Center** alignment. In the range **A4:A20**, apply the **Increase Indent** alignment.

4. In the range **I4:I20**, insert a function to calculate the average monthly cost. In the range **J4:J20**, insert a function to calculate the minimum monthly cost. In the range **K4:K20**, insert a function to calculate the maximum monthly cost.

5. In row **21**, insert totals for columns **B:H**, and then apply the **Total** cell style.

6. In cell **B22**, calculate the *Percent of First Half Costs*. In the formula, use an absolute cell reference when referring to cell **H21**. Format the result as a percent and display two decimals. AutoFill the formula to the right through column **G**.

7. Insert a **Stacked Bar** chart based on the range **A3:G20**. Move the stacked bar chart to a chart sheet named Projected Costs Chart Apply the chart **Style 11**. Change the Chart Title to Projected Monthly Costs Add the file name in the chart sheet's left footer and the sheet name in the right footer.

8. Click the **Cost** worksheet tab. Insert a **Pie** chart based on the nonadjacent ranges **A3:G3** and **A21:G21**. Move the pie chart to a chart sheet named Total Monthly Cost Apply the chart **Layout 1**. Change the data label position to **Data Callout**, and change the data label **Font Size** to **12**. Add the file name in the chart sheet's left footer and the sheet name in the right footer.

Figure 1

9. On the **Cost** worksheet, insert four blank lines at the top of the worksheet. Insert a WordArt with the **Fill - Black**, **Text 1**, **Outline - Background 1**, **Hard Shadow - Background 1** style. In the WordArt, type the text Projected Costs and then change the **Font Size** to **44**. Move the WordArt to the top of the worksheet, centering it above the data.

10. Scale the **Cost** worksheet to print on **1 page**.

11. **Save** the workbook, and then compare your completed workbook with **Figure 1**.

12. **Close** Excel, and then submit the workbook as directed by your instructor.

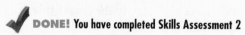

DONE! You have completed Skills Assessment 2

Visual Skills Check

To complete this project, you will need the following file:

- exl02_VSNetAssets

You will save your workbook as:

- Last_First_exl02_VSNetAssets

Start **Excel 2013**, and open the file **exl02_VSNetAssets**. **Save** the workbook in your chapter folder as Last_First_exl02_VSNetAssets Create the worksheet as shown in **Figure 1**. Calculate the *Percent of Total Net Assets* using an absolute cell reference. In rows **13:15**, insert the statistical functions that correspond with the row labels. Format the values and text as shown. Create the pie chart, and then move and resize the chart as shown in the figure. The chart uses the **Layout 4** chart layout, data label font size **11**, and in the chart area the **Linear Down** gradient fill. Insert the file name in the worksheet's left footer. **Save** the workbook, and then submit the workbook as directed by your instructor.

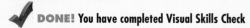 **DONE! You have completed Visual Skills Check**

Aspen Falls					
Net Assets					
Business-type Activities					

Asset	July	August	September	Total	Percent of Total Net Assets
Transportation	$ 268,755	$ 275,082	$ 282,086	$ 825,923	25.9%
Port	$ 242,886	$ 245,688	$ 247,253	$ 735,827	23.1%
Water	$ 175,885	$ 180,256	$ 193,008	$ 549,149	17.2%
Power	$ 117,006	$ 108,832	$ 115,038	$ 340,876	10.7%
Hospital	$ 213,468	$ 250,865	$ 275,066	$ 739,399	23.2%
Total Net Assets	$ 1,018,000	$ 1,060,723	$ 1,112,451	$ 3,191,174	
Minimum Asset	$ 117,006	$ 108,832	$ 115,038		
Maximum Asset	$ 268,755	$ 275,082	$ 282,086		
Average Asset	$ 203,600	$ 212,145	$ 222,490		

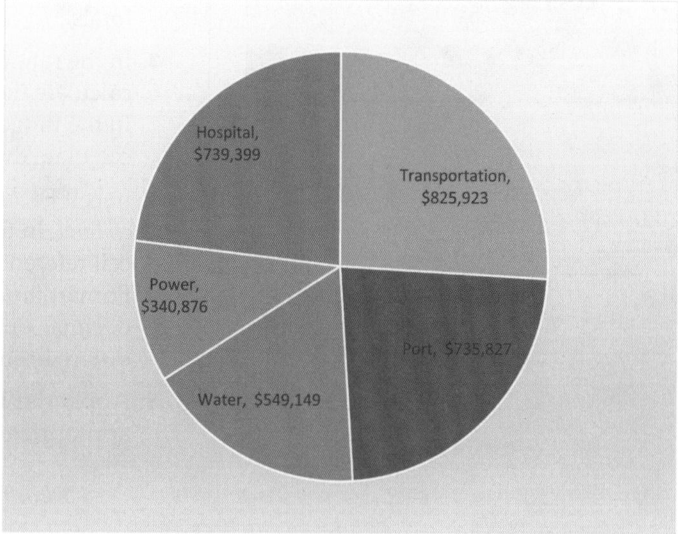

Hospital, $739,399

Transportation, $825,923

Power, $340,876

Port, $735,827

Water, $549,149

Last_First_exl02_VSNetAssets

Figure 1

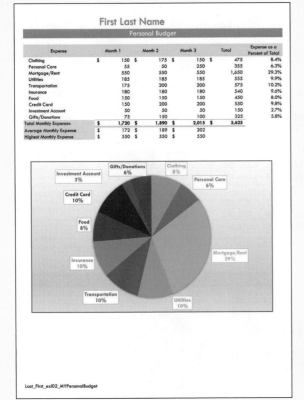

First Last Name

Personal Budget

Expense		Month 1		Month 2		Month 3		Total	Expense as a Percent of Total
Clothing	$	150	$	175	$	150	$	475	8.4%
Personal Care		55		50		250		355	6.3%
Mortgage/Rent		550		550		550		1,650	29.3%
Utilities		185		185		185		555	9.9%
Transportation		175		200		200		575	10.2%
Insurance		180		180		180		540	9.6%
Food		150		150		150		450	8.0%
Credit Card		150		200		200		550	9.8%
Investment Account		50		50		50		150	2.7%
Gifts/Donations		75		150		100		325	5.8%
Total Monthly Expenses	$	1,720	$	1,890	$	2,015	$	5,625	
Average Monthly Expense	$	172	$	189	$	202			
Highest Monthly Expense	$	550	$	550	$	550			

Last_First_exl02_MYPersonalBudget

Figure 1

My Skills

To complete this project, you will need the following file:

- exl02_MYPersonalBudget

You will save your workbook as:

- Last_First_exl02_MYPersonalBudget

1. Start **Excel 2013**, and open the file **exl02_MYPersonalBudget**. **Save** the workbook in your chapter folder as Last_First_exl02_MYPersonalBudget Add the file name in the worksheet's left footer, and then return to Normal view.

2. Change the alignments of the row **3** labels, and indent the column **A** expense labels. In the range **B14:E14**, insert the column totals.

3. In the range **B15:D15**, insert a function to calculate the average monthly expense. In the range **B16:D16**, insert a function to calculate the maximum monthly expense.

4. In cell **F4**, calculate the *Expense as a Percent of Total*. In the formula, use an absolute cell reference when referring to the total. Format the results as percentages with one decimal, and then AutoFill the formula down through cell **F13**.

5. Apply the **Total** cell style where appropriate.

6. Insert a **Pie** chart based on the nonadjacent ranges **A3:A13** and **E3:E13**.

7. Move the pie chart to an appropriate location below your data, and then resize the chart.

8. Format the pie chart with any of the chart options of your choice including layout, style, or color.

9. At the top of the worksheet, insert three blank rows. Insert a WordArt using your first and last names as the WordArt text. Move the WordArt above the data and resize to fit in the blank rows.

10. Adjust the scaling to fit the data and the pie chart on one page when printed.

11. **Save** the workbook, and then submit the workbook as directed by your instructor. Compare your completed workbook with Figure 1.

 **DONE! You have completed My Skills**

Skills Challenge 1

To complete this project, you will need the following file:

- exl02_SC1Budget

You will save your workbook as:

- Last_First_exl02_SC1Budget

Start **Excel 2013.** Open the file **exl02_SC1Budget**, and then save the workbook in your chapter folder as Last_First_exl02_SC1Budget During the fourth quarter of this year, the Accounting Department developed a summary of the proposed Aspen Falls budget. Correct the errors in the statistical functions—you may want to display the formulas. Use an absolute cell reference when correcting the percent. Correct the number formats, and format the labels

appropriately. Modify the WordArt and the column chart. Verify that the WordArt, data, and column chart will print on one page. Add the file name in the worksheet's left footer. Save the workbook, and then submit the workbook as directed by your instructor.

 DONE! You have completed Skills Challenge 1

Skills Challenge 2

To complete this project, you will need the following file:

- exl02_SC2Classes

You will save your workbook as:

- Last_First_exl02_SC2Classes

Start **Excel 2013**, and then open the workbook **exl02_SC2Classes**. Save the workbook in your chapter folder as Last_First_exl02_SC2Classes Carter Horikoshi, the Art Center Supervisor, created a workbook to track how many students attended Community Center classes last summer. He wants to determine if he should offer more classes this summer based on the number of students from last summer. He wants to know the total enrollment and the average enrollment for each

month and for each class. He would like to view a chart that summarized the enrollment data. Using the skills you learned in this chapter, provide Mr. Horikoshi a workbook to assist him in his decision. Add the file name in the worksheet's left footer. Save the workbook, and then submit the workbook as directed by your instructor.

 DONE! You have completed Skills Challenge 2

CHAPTER 3

Manage Multiple Worksheets

- Organizations typically create workbooks that contain multiple worksheets. In such a workbook, the first worksheet often summarizes the detailed information in the other worksheets.

- In an Excel workbook, you can insert and move worksheets to create the detailed worksheets and summary worksheet that you need.

- By grouping worksheets, you can edit and format the data in multiple worksheets at the same time. The changes you make on the active sheet are reflected in all of the sheets included in the group.

- You can create multiple worksheets quickly by copying and pasting information from one worksheet to other worksheets.

- You can color code each worksheet tab so that detailed information can be quickly located.

- When you use multiple math operators in a single formula, you must take care to ensure the operations are carried out in the intended order.

- When building a summary worksheet, you will typically use formulas that refer to cells in the other worksheets.

© Jas

Aspen Falls City Hall

In this chapter, you will work with a spreadsheet for Diane Payne, the Public Works Director in Aspen Falls. She wants to know the revenue generated from parking meters and parking tickets in different locations throughout the city. Understanding how much revenue is generated from the meters and tickets and the costs associated with park maintenance and upgrades will help Diane decide if more meters should be added and if more personnel should be hired to enforce parking regulations.

A workbook, composed of multiple worksheets, allows Diane to collect data from different worksheets but analyze those worksheets grouped together as a whole. When you have a large amount of data to organize in a workbook, dividing the data into logical elements, such as locations or time periods, and then placing each element in a separate worksheet often makes sense. In other words, it is often better to design a system of worksheets instead of trying to fit all of the information on a single worksheet. You can then collect and input the data on an individual basis and see the summarized results with minimal effort.

In this project, you will work with grouped worksheets to enter formulas and apply formatting on all selected worksheets at the same time. You will create formulas that use multiple math operators, construct formulas that refer to cells in other worksheets, and create and format a clustered bar chart.

Time to complete all 10 skills – 60 to 90 minutes

Student data file needed for this chapter:

exl03_Parking

You will save your workbook as:

Last_First_exl03_Parking

Outcome

Using the skills in this chapter, you will be able to work with Excel worksheets like this:

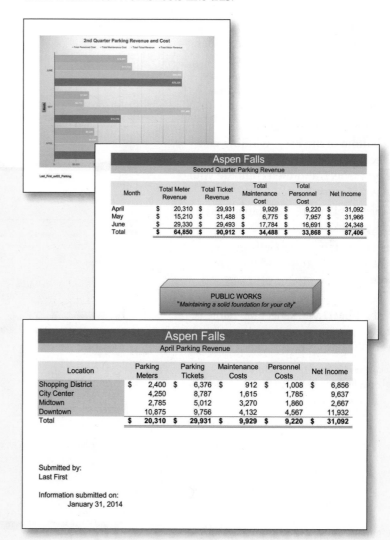

SKILLS  Skills 1-10 Training

At the end of this chapter you will be able to:

Skill 1 Organize Worksheet Tabs

Skill 2 Enter and Format Dates

Skill 3 Clear Cell Contents and Formats

Skill 4 Move Cell Contents and Use Paste Options

Skill 5 Enter Data in Grouped Worksheets

Skill 6 Insert Multiple Math Operators in Formulas

Skill 7 Format Grouped Worksheets

Skill 8 Insert, Hide, Delete, and Move Worksheets

Skill 9 Create Summary Worksheets

Skill 10 Create Clustered Bar Charts

MORE SKILLS

Skill 11 Create Organization Charts

Skill 12 Create Line Charts

Skill 13 Set and Clear Print Areas

Skill 14 Create, Edit, and Delete Hyperlinks

SKILL 1.1 VIDEO

▶ When a workbook contains more than one worksheet, you can move among worksheets by clicking the worksheet tabs.

▶ **Tab scrolling buttons** are buttons to the left of worksheet tabs used to display worksheet tabs that are not in view.

1. Start **Excel 2013**, and then open the student data file **exl03_Parking**. Click the **File tab**, and then click **Save As**. Click the **Browse** button, and then navigate to the location where you are saving your files. Click **New folder**, type Excel Chapter 3 and then press [Enter] two times. In the **File name** box, using your own name, name the workbook Last_First_exl03_ Parking and then press [Enter].

2. At the bottom of the Excel window, click the **Sheet2** worksheet tab to make it the active worksheet, and then compare your screen with **Figure 1**.

3. Click the **Sheet1** worksheet tab to make it the active worksheet.

4. On the **Home tab**, in the **Cells group**, click the **Format** button, and then click **Rename Sheet**. Compare your screen with **Figure 2**.

5. Verify the **Sheet1** worksheet tab name is selected, type April and then press [Enter] to accept the name change.

> You can use up to 31 characters in a worksheet tab name.

Figure 1

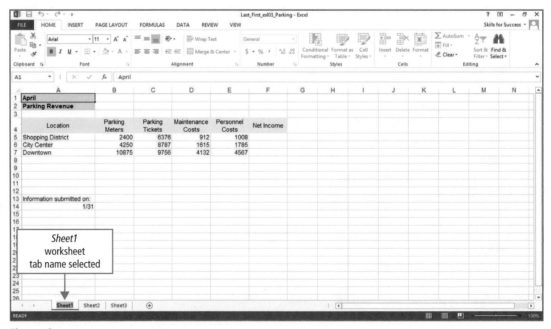

Figure 2

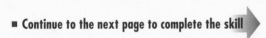
■ Continue to the next page to complete the skill ▶

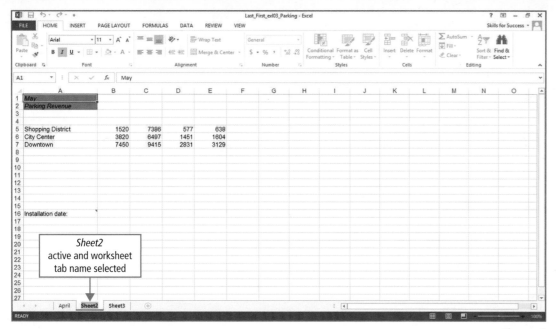

Figure 3

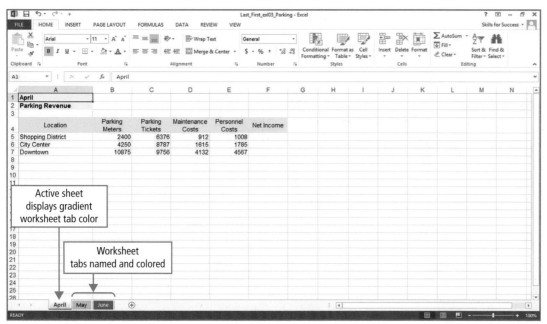

Figure 4

6. Double-click the **Sheet2** worksheet tab to make it the active sheet and to select the sheet name. Compare your screen with **Figure 3**.

7. With the **Sheet2** worksheet tab name selected, type May and then press [Enter].

8. Using either of the two methods just practiced, rename the **Sheet3** worksheet tab as June and then press [Enter].

9. Verify that the **June** sheet is the active worksheet. On the **Page Layout tab**, in the **Themes group**, click the **Colors** button. Scroll down, and then click **Slipstream** to change the theme colors for this workbook.

10. On the **Home tab**, in the **Cells group**, click the **Format** button, and then point to **Tab Color** to display the colors associated with the *Slipstream* theme colors. Click the fifth color in the first row—**Blue, Accent 1**. Alternately, right-click the worksheet tab, and then click Tab Color.

   A gradient color on a worksheet tab indicates that the worksheet is active. When a worksheet is not active, the entire worksheet tab is filled with the selected color.

11. Use the technique just practiced to change the worksheet tab color of the **May** worksheet tab to the sixth color in the first row—**Turquoise, Accent 2**.

12. Change the worksheet tab color of the **April** worksheet tab to the seventh color in the first row—**Green, Accent 3**. Compare your screen with **Figure 4**.

13. **Save** 🖫 the workbook.

■ **You have completed Skill 1 of 10**

► When you enter a date, it is assigned a *serial number*—a sequential number.

► Dates are stored as sequential serial numbers so they can be used in calculations. By default, January 1, 1900, is serial number 1. January 1, 2014, is serial number 41640 because it is 41,640 days after January 1, 1900. Serial numbers make it possible to perform calculations on dates, for example, to find the number of days between two dates by subtracting the older date from the more recent date.

► When you type any of the following values into cells, Excel interprets them as dates: *7/4/10, 4-Jul, 4-Jul-10, Jul-10*. When typing in these date formats, the [-] (hyphen) key and the [/] (forward slash) key function identically.

► You can enter months using the entire name or first three characters. Years can be entered as two or four digits. When the year is left off, the current year will be inserted.

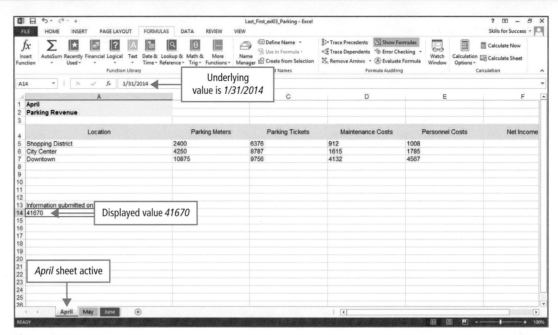

Figure 1

1. On the **April** sheet, click cell **A14** to display the underlying value *1/31/2014* in the formula bar. On the **Formulas tab**, in the **Formula Auditing group**, click the **Show Formulas** button. Compare your screen with **Figure 1**.

   The date, *January 31, 2014*, displays as 41670—the number of days since the reference date of January 1, 1900.

2. On the **Formulas tab**, in the **Formula Auditing group**, click the **Show Formulas** button to display the date.

3. On the **Home tab**, in the **Number group**, click the **Number Format arrow** (**Figure 2**).

   In the Number Format list, you can select common date, time, and number formats, or click *More Number Formats* to display additional built-in number formats.

■ **Continue to the next page to complete the skill** ▶

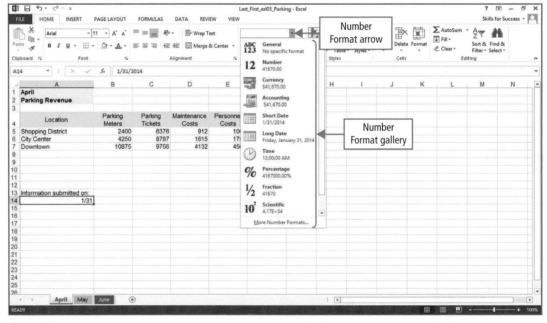

Figure 2

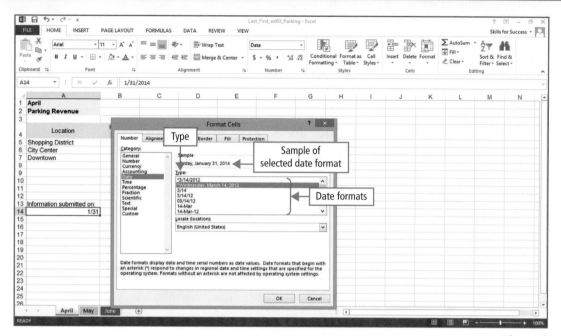

Figure 3

Date Format AutoComplete	
Date Typed As	**Completed by Excel As**
7/4/14	7/4/2014
7-4-98	7/4/1998
7/4 or 7-4	4-Jul (current year assumed)
July 4 or Jul 4	4-Jul (current year assumed)
Jul/4 or Jul-4	4-Jul (current year assumed)
July 4, 1998	4-Jul-98
July 2014	Jul-14
July 1998	Jul-98

Figure 4

4. At the bottom of the **Number Format** list, click **More Number Formats**. On the **Number tab** of the **Format Cells** dialog box, notice Date is selected at the left. Under **Type**, click ***Wednesday, March 14, 2012**, to show a sample of the selected date format. Compare your screen with **Figure 3**.

> The date *Wednesday, March 14, 2012*, will not display in your worksheet. This is a sample of a format that can be applied to your current date.

5. Under **Type**, scroll down, click **March 14, 2012**, and then click **OK** to display the date in cell A14 as *January 31, 2014*.

6. Click the **May** worksheet tab to make it the active worksheet, and then click cell **A17**. Type 8/11/98 and then on the **formula bar**, click the **Enter** button ☑ to accept the entry and change the year from *98* to *1998*.

> When a two-digit year between 30 and 99 is entered, a twentieth-century date is applied to the date format—*8/11/1998*.

7. Click the **June** worksheet tab, and then click cell **A17**. Hold down Ctrl and press ;—the semicolon key. Press Enter to confirm the entry and to enter the current date.

> The Ctrl + ; shortcut enters the current date, obtained from your computer, into the selected cell using the default date format. The table in **Figure 4** summarizes how Excel interprets various date formats.

8. **Save** 🖫 the workbook.

■ **You have completed Skill 2 of 10**

▸ Cells can contain formatting, comments, hyperlinks, and *content*—underlying formulas and data.

▸ You can clear the formatting, comments, hyperlinks, or the contents of a cell.

1. Click the **April** worksheet tab, and then click cell **A1**. On the **Home tab**, in the **Editing group**, click the **Clear** button, and then compare your screen with **Figure 1**.

2. On the menu, click **Clear Contents**. Look at cell **A1**, and verify that the text has been cleared but that the fill color applied to the cell still displays.

   Alternately, to delete the contents of a cell, you can press Delete , or you can tap a cell and then on the Mini toolbar, click Clear.

3. In cell **A1**, type Parking Revenue and then on the **formula bar**, click the **Enter** button ✓.

4. With cell **A1** still selected, in the **Editing group**, click the **Clear** button, and then click **Clear Formats** to clear the formatting from the cell. Compare your screen with **Figure 2**.

5. Select cell **A2**. On the **Home tab**, in the **Editing group**, click the **Clear** button, and then click **Clear All** to clear both the cell contents and the cell formatting.

■ **Continue to the next page to complete the skill**

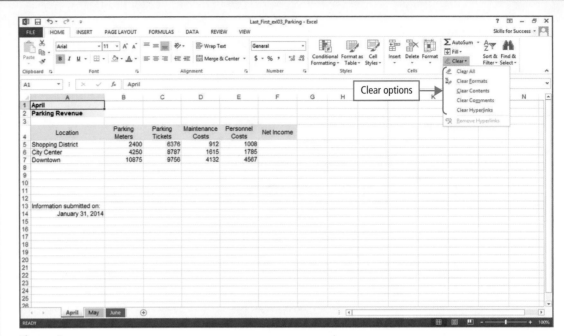

Figure 1

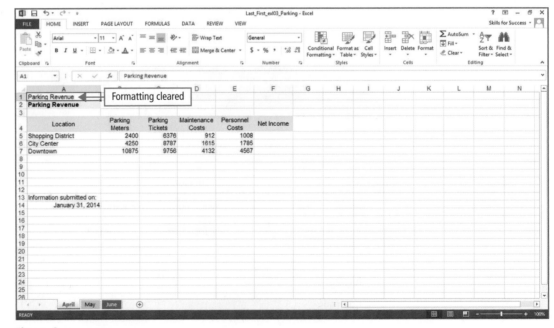

Figure 2

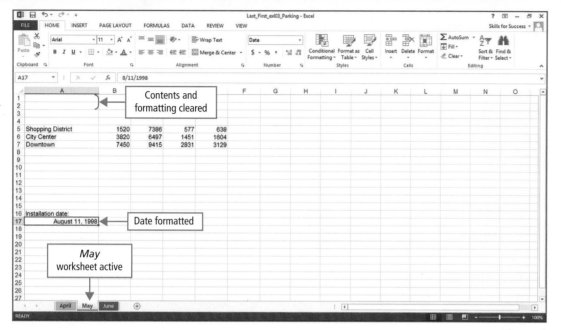

Contents and formatting cleared

Date formatted

May worksheet active

Figure 3

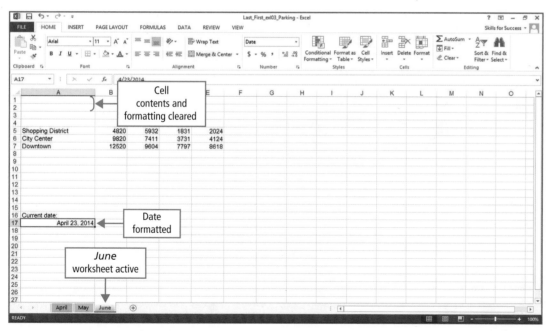

Cell contents and formatting cleared

Date formatted

June worksheet active

Figure 4

6. Display the **May** worksheet, and then select the range **A1:A2**. In the **Editing group**, click the **Clear** button, and then click **Clear All**.

7. Click cell **A16** to display the comment. On the **Home tab**, in the **Editing group**, click the **Clear** button, and then click **Clear Comments** to clear the comment from the cell.

8. Click cell **A17**. On the **Home tab**, in the **Number group**, click the **Number Format arrow**. At the bottom of the **Number Format** list, click **More Number Formats**. In the **Format Cells** dialog box, under **Type**, scroll down, click **March 14, 2012**, and then click **OK** to display the date in cell **A17** as *August 11, 1998*. Compare your screen with Figure 3.

9. Display the **June** worksheet. Select the range **A1:A2**, and then use the technique just practiced to clear the contents and formatting from the selected range.

10. Click cell **A17**, and then use the technique just practiced to apply the date format *March 14, 2012*, to the current date. Compare your screen with Figure 4.

11. Make **April** the active sheet, and then **Save** 🖫 the workbook.

■ **You have completed Skill 3 of 10**

▶ Data from cells and ranges can be copied and then pasted to other cells in the same worksheet, to other worksheets, or to worksheets in another workbook.

▶ The **Clipboard** is a temporary storage area for text and graphics. When you use either the Copy command or the Cut command, the selected data is placed in the Clipboard, from which the data is available to paste.

1. On the **April** sheet, select the range **A13:A14**. Point to the lower edge of the green border surrounding the selected range until the [ ] pointer displays. Drag downward until the ScreenTip displays *A16:A17*, as shown in Figure 1, and then release the left mouse button to complete the move.

   Drag and drop is a method of moving objects in which you point to the selection and then drag it to a new location.

2. Select the range **A4:F4**. In the **Clipboard group**, click the **Copy** button [ ].

   A moving border surrounds the selected range, and a message on the status bar indicates *Select destination and press ENTER or choose Paste,* confirming that your selected range has been copied to the Clipboard.

3. Display the **May** sheet, and then click cell **A4**. In the **Clipboard group**, click the **Paste arrow** to display the **Paste Options** gallery. Point at the second option in the second row—**Keep Source Column Widths** [ ], and then compare your screen with Figure 2.

■ Continue to the next page to complete the skill ▶

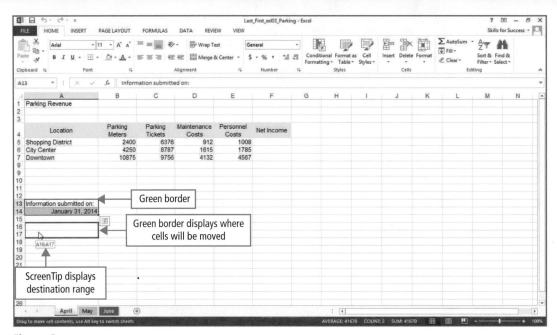

Figure 1

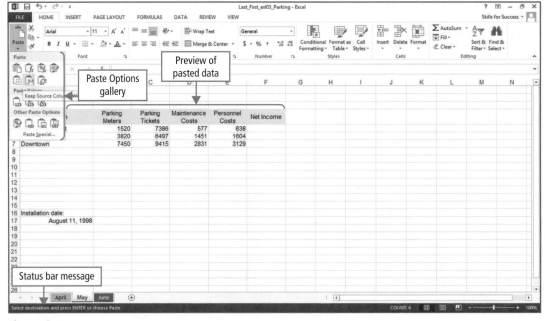

Figure 2

Paste Options		
Option	**Icon**	**Content and format pasted**
Paste		Both the contents and cell formatting
Formulas		Only the formula
Formulas & Number Formatting		Both the formula and the number formatting
Keep Source Formatting		All content and cell formatting from original cells
No Borders		All content and cell formatting except borders
Keep Source Column Widths		All content and formatting including the column width format
Transpose		Orientation of pasted entries change—data in rows are pasted as columns
Formatting		Only the formatting

Figure 3

4. In the **Paste Options** gallery, click the option **Keep Source Column Widths** to paste the column labels and to retain the column widths from the source worksheet. The table in Figure 3 summarizes the Paste Options.

   When pasting a range of cells, you need to select only the cell in the upper left corner of the *paste area*—the target destination for data that has been cut or copied. When an item is pasted, it is not removed from the Clipboard, as indicated by the status bar message.

5. Display the **June** sheet, and then click cell **A4**. Using the technique just practiced, paste the column labels using the Paste Option **Keep Source Column Widths**.

6. Click cell **A17**, and then point to the upper green border surrounding the cell to display the pointer. Drag up to move the cell contents to cell **A16**. In the message box *There's already data here. Do you want to replace it?* click **OK** to replace the contents. Compare your screen with Figure 4.

7. Click the **April** worksheet tab. **Save** workbook.

■ **You have completed Skill 4 of 10**

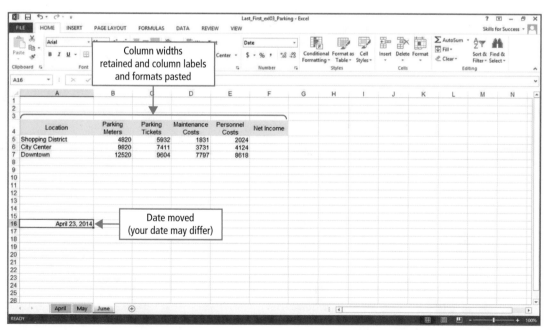

Figure 4

▶ You can group any number of worksheets in a workbook. After the worksheets are grouped, you can edit data or format cells in all of the grouped worksheets at the same time.

▶ Grouping worksheets is useful when you are creating or modifying a set of worksheets that are similar in purpose and structure.

1. Right-click the **April** worksheet tab, and then from the shortcut menu, click **Select All Sheets**.

2. At the top of the screen, on the title bar, verify that *[Group]* displays as shown in **Figure 1**.

   Here, all three worksheet tabs are shaded with a gradient color and *[Group]* displays on the title bar to indicate that the three worksheets are active as a group.

3. Select the range **A5:A7**, and then apply the **40% - Accent1** cell style.

4. Display the **May** worksheet to ungroup the sheets and to verify that the cell style you selected in the previous step displays as shown in **Figure 2**.

   In the worksheet tab area, both the *April* worksheet tab and the *June* worksheet tab display a solid color, indicating that they are no longer active in the group. At the top of your screen, *[Group]* no longer displays on the title bar.

   Selecting a single worksheet cancels a grouping. Because the worksheets were grouped, formatting was applied to all of the selected worksheets. In this manner, you can make the same changes to all selected worksheets at the same time.

■ **Continue to the next page to complete the skill**

Figure 1

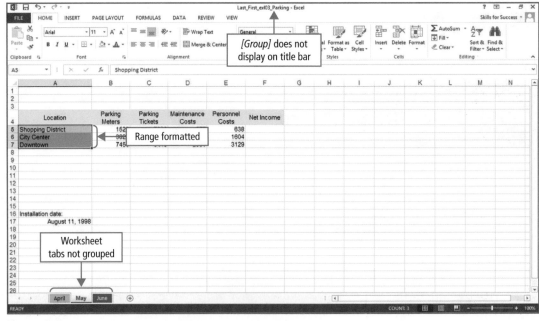

Figure 2

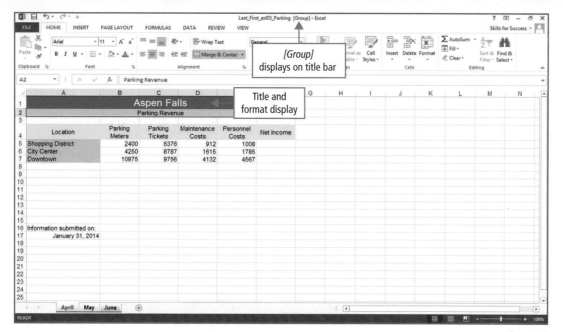

Figure 3

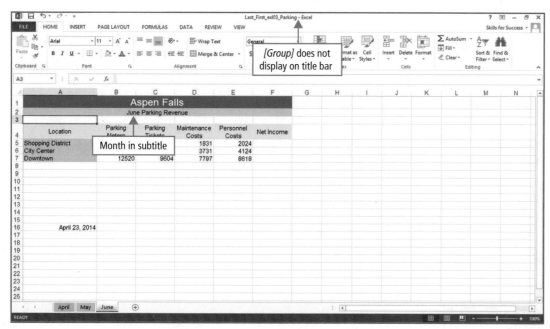

Figure 4

5. Right-click the **April** worksheet tab, and then from the shortcut menu, click **Select All Sheets**.

6. In cell **A1**, press [Delete], type Aspen Falls and then press [Enter]. Select the range **A1:F1**, and then in the **Alignment group**, click the **Merge & Center** button. Apply the **Accent1** cell style. Click the **Font Size** button [11 ▾], and then click **18**.

7. In cell **A2**, type Parking Revenue and then press [Enter]. Select the range **A2:F2**, and then click the **Merge & Center** button. Apply the **40% - Accent1** cell style, and then compare your screen with **Figure 3**.

8. Right-click the **April** worksheet tab, and then from the shortcut menu, click **Ungroup Sheets**. Verify that *[Group]* no longer displays on the title bar.

9. Double-click cell **A2** to edit the cell contents. Use the arrow keys to move to the left of the word *Parking*. Type April and add a space, and then press [Enter]. Display the **May** worksheet. Using the same technique, edit cell **A2** to May Parking Revenue Display the **June** worksheet, and then edit cell **A2** to June Parking Revenue Compare your screen with **Figure 4**.

10. Save 🖫 the workbook.

■ **You have completed Skill 5 of 10**

▶ When you combine several math operators in a single formula, ***operator precedence***—a set of mathematical rules for performing calculations within a formula—are followed. Expressions within parentheses are calculated first. Then, multiplication and division are performed before addition and subtraction.

▶ When a formula contains operators with the same precedence level, Excel evaluates the operators from left to right. Multiplication and division are considered to be on the same level of precedence. Addition and subtraction are considered to be on the same level of precedence.

1. Right-click the **June** worksheet tab, and then click **Select All Sheets**. Verify that *[Group]* displays on the title bar.

2. Click cell **F5**, enter the formula =(B5+C5)-(D5+E5) and then compare your screen with **Figure 1**.

   The formula *Net Income = Total Revenue – Total Cost* is represented by (*Parking Meters + Parking Tickets*) – (*Maintenance Cost + Personnel Cost*). By placing parentheses in the formula, the revenue is first added together, the costs are added together, and then the total costs are subtracted from the total revenues. Without the parentheses, the formula would give an incorrect result.

3. On the **formula bar**, click the **Enter** button ✔. AutoFill the formula down through cell **F7**. Compare your screen with **Figure 2**.

■ Continue to the next page to complete the skill

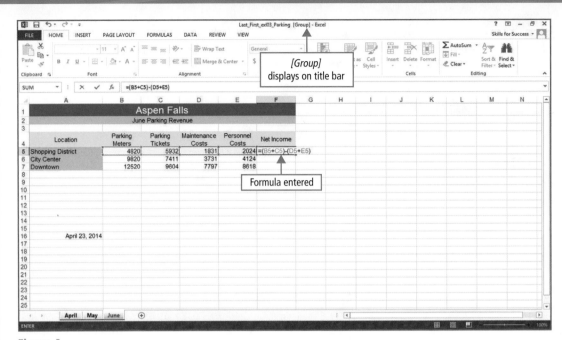

Figure 1

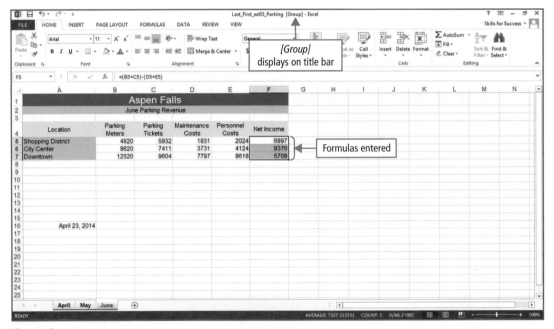

Figure 2

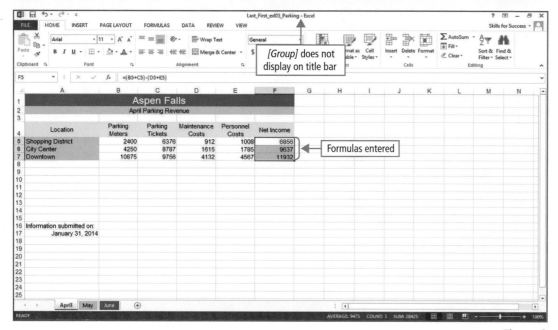

Figure 3

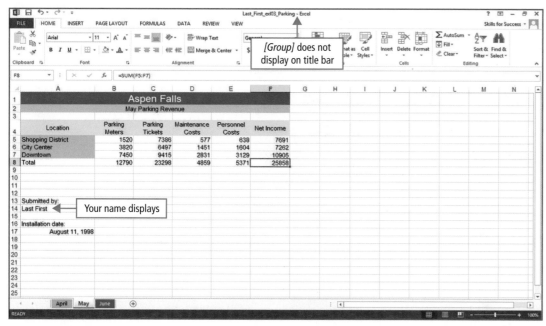

Figure 4

4. Display the **April** worksheet to ungroup the sheets and to verify that the formula results display in the worksheet. Compare your screen with **Figure 3**.

    Because the worksheets were grouped, the formulas have been entered on all selected worksheets.

5. Right-click the **April** worksheet tab, and then click **Select All Sheets**. Verify that *[Group]* displays on the title bar.

6. In cell **A8**, type Total and then press [Enter]. Select the range **B8:F8**, and then on the **Home tab**, in the **Editing group**, click the **AutoSum** button to insert the column totals.

7. Click cell **A13**, type Submitted by: and then press [Enter]. In cell **A14**, using your name, type Last First and then press [Enter].

8. Click the **May** worksheet tab. Click cell **F8**, and then compare your screen with **Figure 4**.

    On the *May* worksheet, the formula in cell F8 displays as the value *25858*.

9. **Save** ⊟ the workbook.

■ **You have completed Skill 6 of 10**

▶ When worksheets are grouped, any changes made to a single worksheet are made to each worksheet in the group. For example, if you change the width of a column or add a row, all the worksheets in the group are changed in the same manner.

1. Right-click the **May** worksheet tab, and then click **Select All Sheets**.

2. In the row heading area, point to row **7** to display the ➡ pointer. Right-click, and then compare your screen with **Figure 1**.

3. From the shortcut menu, click **Insert** to insert a new blank row above the *Downtown* row in all of the grouped worksheets. In cell **A7**, type Midtown and press [Tab].

4. Click the **April** worksheet tab to make it the active worksheet and to ungroup the worksheets. Beginning in cell **B7**, enter the following *Midtown* data for April:

| 2785 | 5012 | 3270 | 1860 |

5. Click the **May** worksheet tab, and then beginning in cell **B7**, enter the following *Midtown* data for May:

| 2420 | 8190 | 1916 | 2586 |

6. Click the **June** worksheet tab, and then beginning in cell **B7**, enter the following *Midtown* data for June:

| 2170 | 6546 | 4425 | 1925 |

7. Click each of the worksheet tabs, and then verify that you entered the values correctly. Click the **June** worksheet tab, and then compare your screen with **Figure 2**.

■ **Continue to the next page to complete the skill**

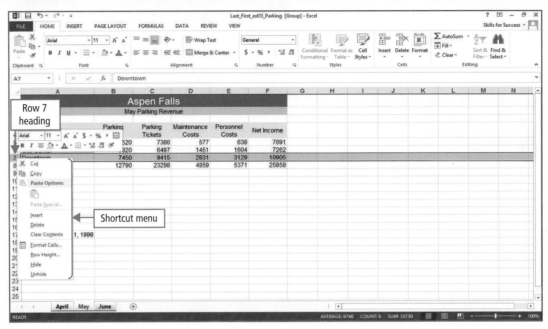

Figure 1

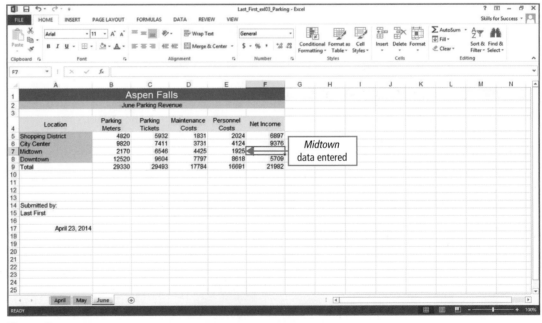

Figure 2

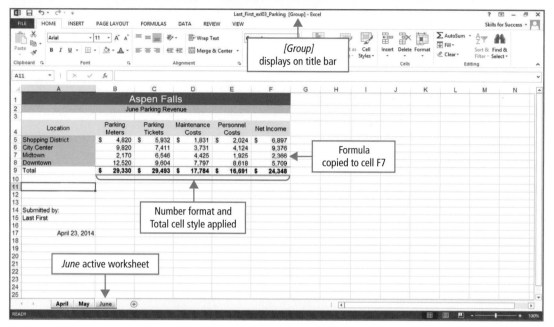

Figure 3

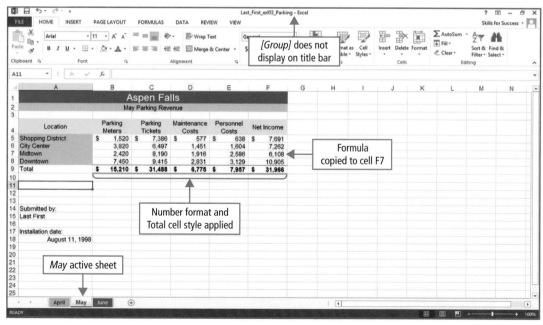

Figure 4

8. Right-click the **June** worksheet tab, and then click **Select All Sheets**. Click cell **F6**, and then AutoFill the formula down to cell **F7**.

   On the *June* worksheet, the formula in cell *F9* displays as the value *$24,348*.

9. Select the range **B5:F5**, hold down Ctrl, and then select the range **B9:F9**. With the nonadjacent ranges selected, in the **Styles group**, click the **Cell Styles** button, and then click **Currency [0]**.

10. Select the range **B6:F8**, and then apply the **Comma [0]** cell style.

11. Select the range **B9:F9**, and then apply the **Total** cell style. Click cell **A11**, and then compare your screen with **Figure 3**.

12. Display the **April** sheet, and then verify that the same formatting was applied.

13. Click the **May** worksheet tab to make it the active worksheet, and verify that the formulas and formatting changes were made. Compare your screen with **Figure 4**.

    On the *May* sheet, the formula in cell *F9* displays as the value *$31,966*.

14. Save the workbook.

■ **You have completed Skill 7 of 10**

▶ To organize a workbook, you can position worksheet tabs in any order you desire.

▶ You can add new worksheets to accommodate new information.

1. Right-click the **April** worksheet tab, and then from the shortcut menu, click **Unhide**. Compare your screen with Figure 1.

2. In the **Unhide** dialog box, verify *1st Qtr* is selected and then click **OK**. Use the same technique to **Unhide** the **2010** and the **2011** worksheets.

3. Right-click the **2010** worksheet tab, and then click **Delete**. Read the message that displays, and then click **Delete**. Use the same technique to **Delete** the **2011** worksheet.

> Because you can't undo a worksheet deletion, it is a good idea to verify that you selected the correct worksheet before you click Delete.

4. To the right of the **June** worksheet tab, click the **New Sheet** button ⊕ to create a new worksheet. Rename the new worksheet tab as Summary

5. In cell **A2**, type Second Quarter Parking Revenue and press Enter . In cell **A4**, type Month and then press Tab . Type the following labels in row **4**, pressing Tab after each label: Total Meter Revenue, Total Ticket Revenue, Total Maintenance Cost, Total Personnel Cost, Net Income

6. In cell **A5**, type April and then AutoFill the months down through cell **A7**.

7. Change the **Column Width** of columns **A:F** to 12 Click cell **A9**, and then compare your screen with Figure 2.

■ **Continue to the next page to complete the skill**

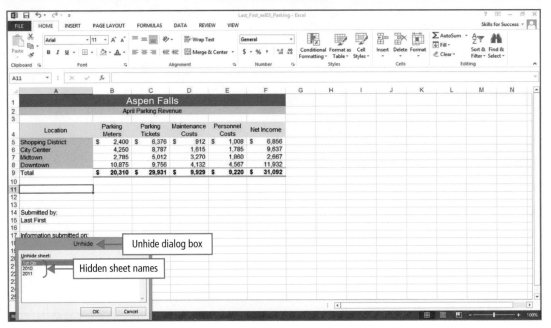

Figure 1

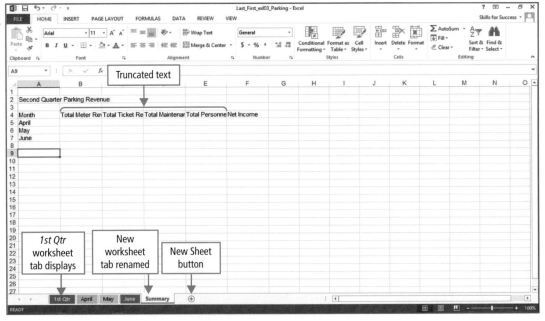

Figure 2

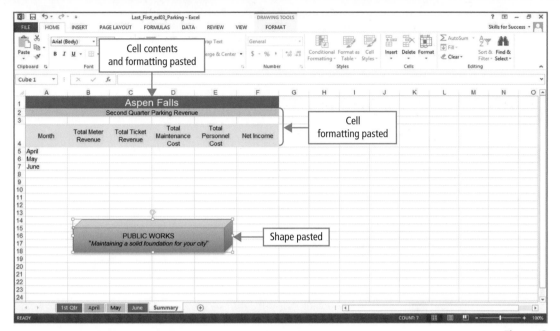

Figure 3

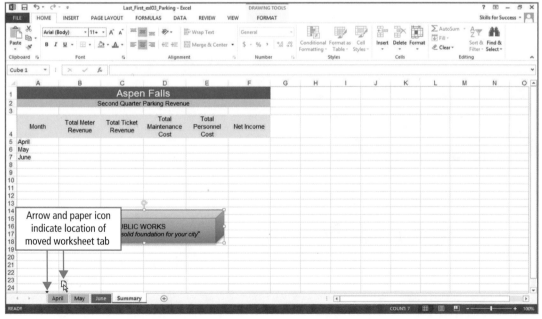

Figure 4

8. Display the **June** sheet. Click cell **A1**, and then in the **Clipboard group**, click the **Copy** button. Display the **Summary** sheet. Click cell **A1**, and then click the **Paste** button to paste the cell content and format.

9. Display the **June** sheet, and then press **Esc** to remove the moving border. Select the range **A2:F4**, and then click the **Copy** button. Display the **Summary** sheet, and then click cell **A2**. In the **Clipboard group**, click the **Paste arrow**. In the **Paste Options** gallery, under **Other Paste Options**, click the first option—**Formatting** to paste only the format.

10. Display the **1st Qtr** sheet. Click the shape, and then click the **Copy** button. Display the **Summary** sheet. In the **Clipboard group**, click the **Paste** button. Move the shape to approximately the range **B14:E18**. Compare your screen with **Figure 3**.

11. Right-click the **1st Qtr** worksheet tab, and then click **Hide**.

12. Click the **Summary** worksheet tab. Hold down the left mouse button and drag to the left to display an arrow and the pointer. Drag to the left until the arrow is to the left of the **April** worksheet tab, as shown in **Figure 4**.

13. Release the left mouse button to complete the worksheet move. **Save** the workbook.

■ **You have completed Skill 8 of 10**

▶ A **summary sheet** is a worksheet that displays and summarizes totals from other worksheets. A **detail sheet** is a worksheet with cells referred to by summary sheet formulas.

▶ Changes made to the detail sheets that affect totals will automatically recalculate and display on the summary sheet.

1. On the **Summary** sheet, click cell **B5**. Type = and then click the **April** worksheet tab. On the **April** sheet, click cell **B9**, and then press Enter to display the April sheet *B9* value in the Summary sheet *B5* cell.

2. In the **Summary** sheet, click cell **B5**. In the formula bar, notice that the cell reference in the underlying formula includes both a worksheet reference and a cell reference as shown in **Figure 1**.

   By using a formula that refers to another worksheet, changes made to the Total in cell *B9* of the *April* sheet will be automatically updated in this *Summary* sheet.

3. Click cell **B6**, type = and then click the **May** worksheet tab. On the **May** sheet, click cell **B9**, and then press Enter.

4. On the **Summary** sheet, repeat the technique just practiced to display the **June** sheet **B9** value in the **Summary** sheet **B7** cell.

5. On the **Summary** sheet, select the range **B5:B7**, and then AutoFill to the right through column **F**. Click cell **F7**, and then compare your screen with **Figure 2**.

■ **Continue to the next page to complete the skill**

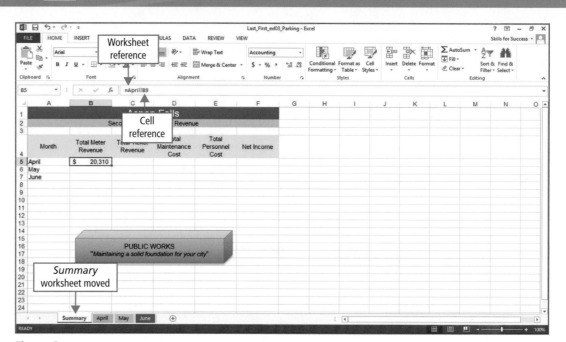

Figure 1

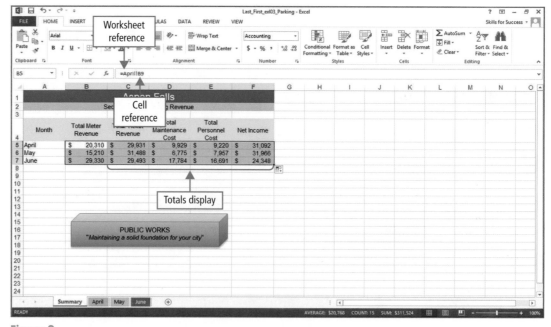

Figure 2

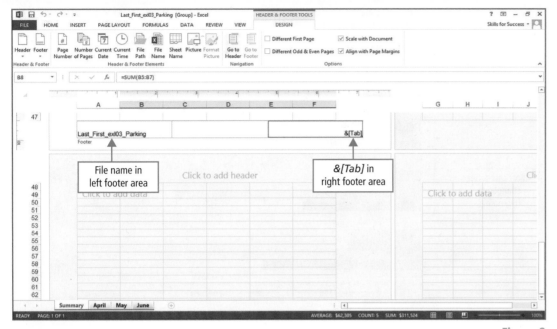

File name in
left footer area

&[Tab] in
right footer area

Figure 3

6. On the **Summary** sheet, click cell **A8**, type Total and then select the range **B8:F8**. In the **Editing group**, click the **AutoSum** button, and then apply the **Total** cell style.

7. Right-click the **Summary** worksheet tab, and then click **Select All Sheets**.

8. Insert the file name in the worksheet's left footer. Click the right section of the footer, and then in the **Header & Footer Elements group**, click the **Sheet Name** button, and then compare your screen with **Figure 3**.

   By grouping worksheets, you can insert headers and footers into each worksheet quickly and consistently.

9. Click in a cell just above the footer to exit the **Footer area**. On the lower right side of the status bar, click the **Normal** button ▦. Hold down Ctrl, and press Home to make cell **A1** the active cell on all selected worksheets.

10. With the sheets still grouped, click the **File tab**, and then click **Print**. At the bottom of the screen, click the **Next Page** button ▶ three times to view each of the four worksheets, and then compare your screen with **Figure 4**.

    Because the worksheets are grouped, all four worksheets are included in the preview.

11. **Save** 🖫 the workbook.

▪ **You have completed Skill 9 of 10**

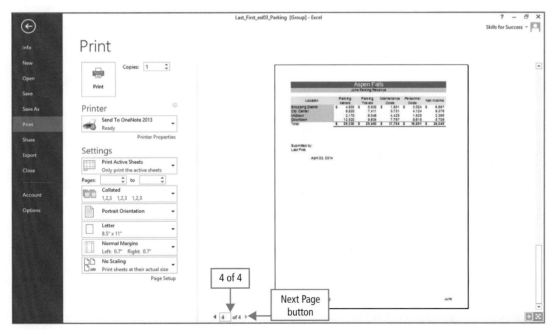

4 of 4

Next Page
button

Figure 4

▶ SKILL 1.10
VIDEO

▶ A ***clustered bar chart*** is useful when you want to compare values across categories; bar charts organize categories along the vertical axis and values along the horizontal axis.

1. Click the **Back** button ⊙. Right-click the **Summary** worksheet tab, and then click **Ungroup Sheets**. On the **Summary** sheet, select the range **A4:E7**. On the **Insert tab**, in the **Charts group**, click the **Recommended Charts** button. In the **Insert Chart** dialog box, verify the first choice is selected—**Clustered Bar**, and then click **OK**.

2. On the **Design tab**, in the **Location group**, click the **Move Chart** button. In the **Move Chart** dialog box, select the **New sheet** option button, type 2nd Qtr Chart and then click **OK**.

3. On the **Design tab**, in the **Data group**, click the **Switch Row/Column** button to display the months on the vertical axis. Compare your screen with **Figure 1**.

    Because you want to look at revenue and costs by month, displaying the months on the vertical axis is useful.

4. In the **Chart Layouts group**, click the **Quick Layout** button, and then click **Layout 3**.

5. To the right of the chart, click the **Chart Styles** button ✎, and then click **Style 3**.

6. Edit the **Chart Title** to 2nd Quarter Parking Revenue and Cost and then compare your screen with **Figure 2**.

■ **Continue to the next page to complete the skill** ➤

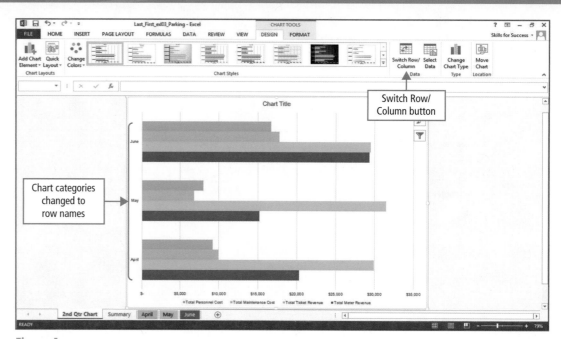

Figure 1

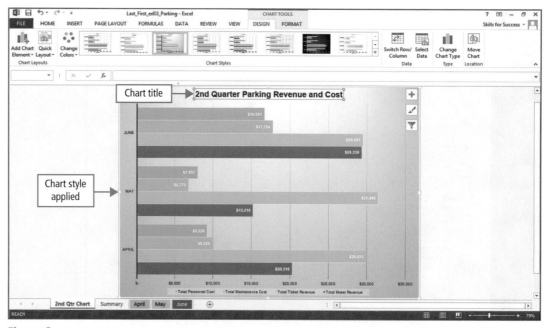

Figure 2

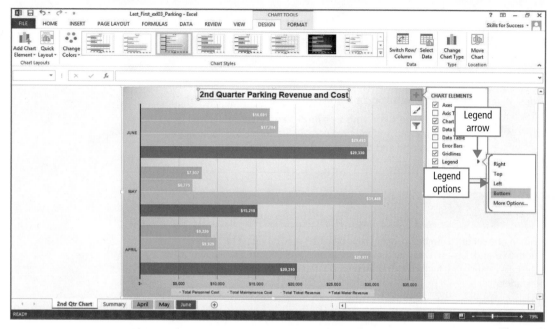

Figure 3

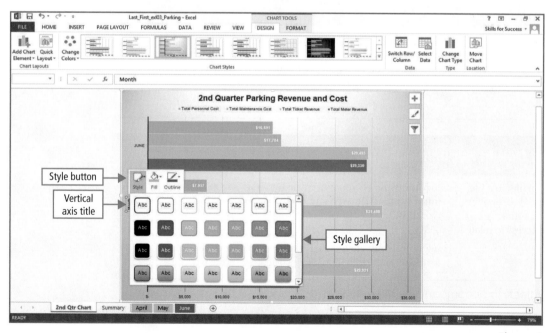

Figure 4

7. At the top right corner of the chart, click the **Chart Elements** button ➕. Point to **Legend**, and then click the **Legend arrow**. Compare your screen with Figure 3.

8. In the list, click **Top** to move the legend to the top of the chart sheet.

9. In the **Chart Elements** gallery, point to **Axis Titles**, and then click the **Axis Titles arrow**. Select the **Primary Vertical** check box to add the vertical axis title. Click the **Chart Elements** button ➕ to close the gallery.

10. On the left side of the chart, change the vertical **Axis Title** text to Month Right-click the *Month* title, and then on the Mini toolbar, click the **Style** button and compare your screen with Figure 4.

11. In the **Style** gallery, click the second thumbnail in the fourth row—**Subtle Effect - Blue**, **Accent 1**.

12. On the **Insert tab**, in the **Text group**, click the **Header & Footer** button. In the **Page Setup** dialog box, click the **Custom Footer** button. In the **Footer** dialog box, verify the insertion point is in the **Left section** and then click the **Insert File Name** button. Click the **Right section** of the footer, and then click the **Insert Sheet Name** button. Click **OK** two times.

13. Save the workbook, and then **Close** Excel. Submit the project as directed by your instructor.

 DONE! You have completed Skill 10 of 10, and your document is complete!

More Skills

The following More Skills are located at **www.pearsonhighered.com/skills**

More Skills 11 Create Organization Charts

You can add SmartArt graphics to a worksheet to create timelines, illustrate processes, or show relationships. When you click the SmartArt button on the Ribbon, you can select from among a broad array of graphics, including an organization chart. An organization chart graphically represents the relationships between individuals and groups in an organization.

In More Skills 11, you will insert and modify a SmartArt graphic to create an organization chart.

To begin, open your web browser, navigate to www.pearsonhighered.com/skills, locate the name of your textbook, and then follow the instructions on the website.

More Skills 12 Create Line Charts

Use a line chart when you want to compare more than one set of values over time. Time is displayed along the bottom axis and the data point values are connected with a line. The curves and directions of the lines make trends obvious to the reader.

In More Skills 12, you will create a line chart comparing three sets of values.

To begin, open your web browser, navigate to www.pearsonhighered.com/skills, locate the name of your textbook, and then follow the instructions on the website.

More Skills 13 Set and Clear Print Areas

If you are likely to print the same portion of a particular worksheet over and over again, you can save time by setting a print area.

In More Skills 13, you will set and then clear print areas in a worksheet.

To begin, open your web browser, navigate to www.pearsonhighered.com/skills, locate the name of your textbook, and then follow the instructions on the website.

More Skills 14 Create, Edit, and Delete Hyperlinks

You can insert a hyperlink in a worksheet that can link to a file, a location in a file, a web page on the World Wide Web, or a web page on an organization's intranet. Creating a hyperlink in a workbook is a convenient way to provide quick access to related information. You can edit or delete hyperlinks.

In More Skills 14, you will create hyperlinks to related information on the web and to other worksheets in the workbook.

To begin, open your web browser, navigate to www.pearsonhighered.com/skills, locate the name of your textbook, and then follow the instructions on the website.

Please note that there are no additional projects to accompany the More Skills Projects, and they are not covered in the End-of-Chapter projects.

The following table summarizes the **SKILLS AND PROCEDURES** covered in this chapter.

Skills Number	Task	Step	Keyboard Shortcut
1	Rename worksheet tabs	Right-click worksheet tab → Rename → Type new name → Enter	
1	Rename worksheet tabs	Double-click worksheet tab → Type new name → Enter	
1	Format worksheet tabs	Home tab → Cells group → Format → Tab Color	
1	Format worksheet tabs	Right-click worksheet tab → Tab Color	
2	Format dates	Home tab → Number group → Number Format arrow → More Number Formats	
2	Enter the current date		Ctrl + ;
3	Clear cell contents	Home tab → Editing group → Clear → Clear Contents	Delete
3	Clear cell formatting	Home tab → Editing group → Clear → Clear Formats	
3	Clear cell contents and formatting	Home tab → Editing group → Clear → Clear All	
4	Paste with options	Home tab → Clipboard group → Paste Arrow → Select desired option	
5	Group worksheets	Right-click worksheet tab → Select All Sheets	
5	Ungroup worksheets	Right-click worksheet tab → Ungroup Sheets or click a single worksheet tab	
8	Insert worksheets	Home tab → Cells group → Insert arrow → Insert Sheet	
8	Delete worksheet	Home tab → Cells group → Delete arrow → Delete Sheet	
8	Hide worksheet	Right-click worksheet tab → Hide	
8	Unhide worksheet	Right-click worksheet tab → Unhide → Worksheet name	
8	Move worksheet tab	Drag worksheet tab to new location	

Key Terms

Online Help Skills

1. Start **Excel 2013**, and then in the upper right corner of the start page, click the **Help** button ⟨ ? ⟩.

2. In the **Excel Help** window **Search help** box, type numbers to dates and then press ⟨Enter⟩.

3. In the search result list, click **Stop automatically changing numbers to dates**, and then compare your screen with **Figure 1**.

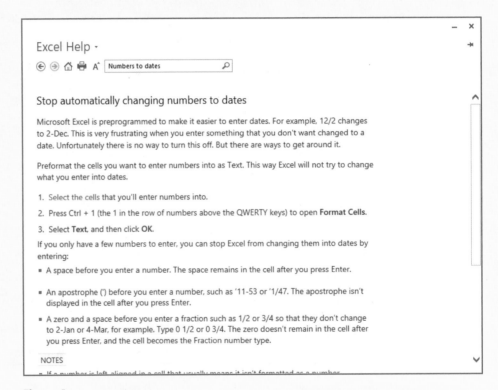

Figure 1

4. Read the article to answer the following question: What cell format can be applied to stop changing numbers into dates?

Matching

Match each term in the second column with its correct definition in the first column by writing the letter of the term on the blank line in front of the correct definition.

___ **1.** The labels along the lower edge of the workbook window that identify each worksheet.

___ **2.** Controls to the left of the worksheet tabs used to display worksheet tabs that are not in view.

___ **3.** A sequential number assigned to a date.

___ **4.** A temporary storage area for text and graphics.

___ **5.** A method of moving or copying the content of selected cells in which you point to the selection and then drag it to a new location.

___ **6.** The target destination for data that has been cut or copied using the Clipboard.

___ **7.** The mathematical rules that specify the order in which calculations are performed.

___ **8.** A worksheet that displays and recaps totals from other worksheets.

___ **9.** A worksheet that contains the detailed information in a workbook.

___ **10.** A chart type that is useful when you want to compare values across categories.

A Clipboard

B Clustered bar chart

C Detail sheet

D Drag and drop

E Operator precedence

F Paste area

G Serial number

H Summary sheet

I Tab scrolling buttons

J Worksheet tabs

BizSkills
Video

1. Why should you arrive early for an interview?

2. What should you do at the end of an interview?

Multiple Choice

Choose the correct answer.

1. An active worksheet tab will display in this way.
   A. With a solid tab color
   B. With a gradient tab color
   C. Always as the first worksheet

2. Worksheets can be grouped in this way.
   A. Right-clicking a worksheet tab and then clicking Select All Sheets
   B. Double-clicking a worksheet tab
   C. Clicking the New Sheet button

3. Clearing the contents of a cell deletes this.
   A. Only the contents
   B. Only the formatting
   C. Both contents and formatting

4. When pasting a range of cells, this cell needs to be selected in the paste area.
   A. Bottom right cell
   B. Center cell
   C. Top left cell

5. Worksheets can be hidden in this way.
   A. Move the worksheet as the last sheet
   B. Right-click a worksheet tab and then click Hide
   C. Double-click a worksheet tab

6. If a workbook contains grouped worksheets, this word will display on the title bar.
   A. [Collection]
   B. [Set]
   C. [Group]

7. When a formula contains operators with the same precedence level, the operators are evaluated in this order.
   A. Left to right
   B. Right to left
   C. From the center out

8. Addition and this mathematical operator are considered to be on the same precedence level.
   A. Multiplication
   B. Division
   C. Subtraction

9. Changes made in a detail worksheet will automatically recalculate and display on this sheet.
   A. Summary
   B. Final
   C. Outline

10. The paste option Keep Source Column Widths will paste this.
    A. The cell formatting
    B. Only the column width formatting
    C. All content and cell formatting including the column width format

Topics for Discussion

1. Some people in an organization will only view the summary worksheet without examining the detail worksheets. When might this practice be acceptable and when might it cause mistakes?

2. Illustrate some examples of how a formula's results will be incorrect if parentheses are not used to group calculations in the order they should be performed. Think of a class where you have three exam grades and a final exam grade. If the three tests together count as 50 percent of your course grade, and the final exam counts as 50 percent of your course grade, how would you write the formula to get a correct result?

Skills Review

MyITLab®
Grader

To complete this project, you will need the following file:

- exl03_SRPayroll

You will save your file as:

- **Last_First_exl03_SRPayroll**

1. Start **Excel 2013**. From your student data files, open **exl03_SRPayroll**. Save the workbook in your chapter folder as Last_First_exl03_SRPayroll

2. Right-click the worksheet tab, and then click **Select All Sheets**. Click cell **A19**. On the **Home tab**, in the **Editing group**, click the **Clear** button, and then click **Clear All**. Select the range **A4:F4**, and then apply the **40% - Accent3** cell style. In the **Alignment group**, click the **Wrap Text** and the **Center** buttons.

3. In cell **F5**, type =B5-(C5+D5+E5) and then press [Enter] to construct the formula to compute the Net Pay as *Total Gross Pay – (Income Tax + Social Security (FICA) Tax + Health Insurance)*. AutoFill the formula in cell **F5** down through cell **F12**. Compare your screen with Figure 1.

4. Verify that the worksheets are still grouped. Select the range **B6:F12**, and then apply the **Comma [0]** cell style. Select the range **B13:F13**, and then apply the **Total** cell style. Click the **Courthouse** worksheet tab.

5. To the right of the **Courthouse** worksheet tab, click the **New Sheet** button. Rename the new worksheet tab Summary and then change the **Tab Color** to **Orange**, **Accent 6**. Click the **Summary** worksheet tab, and drag it to the left of the *Community Center* worksheet tab. Compare your screen with Figure 2.

6. Right-click the worksheet tab, and then click **Select All Sheets**. Add the file name in the worksheet's left footer. Click the right footer section, and then in the **Header & Footer Elements group**, click the **Sheet Name** button. Return to Normal view, and then press [Ctrl] + [Home].

Figure 1

Figure 2

■ Continue to the next page to complete this Skills Review

Figure 3

Figure 4

7. Display the **Community Center** sheet, select the range **A1:F4**, and then click **Copy**. Display the **Summary** sheet and then click cell **A1**. Click the **Paste arrow** and then click **Keep Source Column Widths**. In cell **A2**, replace the text with City Payroll in cell **A4**, replace the text with Location and then press [Enter]. Type the following labels in column **A**, pressing [Enter] after each label: Community Center, City Center, Courthouse, and Total

8. On the **Summary** sheet, click **B5**, type = and then click the **Community Center** worksheet tab. On the **Community Center** sheet, click cell **B13**, and then press [Enter]. Use the same technique in cells **B6** and **B7** to place the *Total Gross Pay* amounts from the *City Center* and the *Courthouse* sheets on the *Summary* sheet.

9. On the **Summary** sheet, select the range **B5:B7**. Click the **Quick Analysis Lens** button, click **Totals**, and then click the first option **Sum**. Select the range **B5:B8**, and then AutoFill the formulas to the right through column **F**. Select the range **B8:F8**, and then apply the **Total** cell style. Click cell **A10**, and then compare your screen with Figure 3.

10. On the **Summary** sheet, select the nonadjacent ranges **A4:A7** and **C4:E7**. On the **Insert tab**, in the **Charts group**, click the **Recommended Charts** button. In the **Insert Chart** dialog box, click **Clustered Bar**, and then click **OK**. On the **Design tab**, in the **Location group**, click the **Move Chart** button. In the **Move Chart** dialog box, select the **New sheet** option button, type Payroll Adjustments and then click **OK**.

11. On the **Design tab**, in the **Data group**, click the **Switch Row/Column** button. Click the **Chart Styles** button, and then click **Style 2**. Change the **Chart Title** to Payroll Adjustments by Location

12. On the **Summary** sheet, click cell **A12**, type Date Created and then click [Enter]. In cell **A13**, press [Ctrl] + ; (the semicolon), and then press [Enter].

13. Right-click the **Summary** worksheet tab, and then click **Unhide**. In the **Unhide** dialog box, click **OK**. Right-click the **Art Center** worksheet tab, and then click **Delete**. In the message box, click **Delete**.

14. **Group** the worksheets, and then check the spelling.

15. Click the **File tab**, and then click **Print**. Compare your workbook with Figure 4.

16. **Save** the workbook, and then submit the workbook as directed by your instructor.

DONE! You have completed this Skills Review

Skills Assessment 1

To complete this workbook, you will need the following file:

- exl03_SA1Center

You will save your workbook as:

- Last_First_exl03_SA1Center

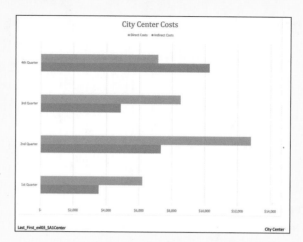

1. Start **Excel 2013**, and open the file **exl03_SA1Center**. **Save** the workbook in your chapter folder as Last_First_exl03_SA1Center

2. Group the worksheets. In cell **E5**, construct a formula to compute *Net Income = Income – (Indirect Costs + Direct Costs)*. AutoFill the formula down through cell **E7**.

3. In the nonadjacent ranges **B5:E5** and **B8:E8**, apply the **Currency [0]** cell style.

4. Insert a new worksheet. Rename the new worksheet tab Summary and apply the worksheet tab color **Brown, Accent 5**. Move the new worksheet tab to make it the first worksheet in the workbook.

5. Copy the range **A1:E4** from any of the detail worksheets, and then on the **Summary** sheet, click cell **A1**. Paste the range using the **Keep Source Column Widths** paste option. Change the subtitle of cell **A2** to City Center Annual Revenue and then change the label in cell **A4** to Quarter

6. In cell **A5**, type 1st Quarter and then AutoFill the labels in the range **A6:A8**. In cell **A9**, type Total

7. In the *Summary* worksheet, enter a formula in cell **B5** setting the cell to equal cell **B8** in the *1st Quarter* worksheet. Enter the *Income* total from the *2nd Quarter,* the *3rd Quarter,* and the *4th Quarter* worksheets in the range **B6:B8**.

8. Select the range **B5:B8**, and then use the **Quick Analysis Lens** button to insert the column total.

9. AutoFill the range **B5:B9** to the right through **column E**. In **row 9**, apply the **Total** cell style.

10. Insert a **Clustered Bar** chart using the nonadjacent ranges **A4:A8** and **C4:D8** as the source data. Move the chart to a chart sheet with the sheet name City Center

Aspen Falls
City Center Annual Revenue

Quarter	Income	Indirect Costs	Direct Costs	Net Income
1st Quarter	$ 17,700	$ 3,540	$ 6,195	$ 7,965
2nd Quarter	$ 36,590	$ 7,318	$ 12,806	16,466
3rd Quarter	$ 24,320	$ 4,864	$ 8,511	10,945
4th Quarter	$ 25,604	$ 10,270	$ 7,126	8,208
Total	$ 104,214	$ 25,992	$ 34,638	$ 43,584

Aspen Falls
City Center Rental Revenue: 1st Quarter

Rental Item	Income	Indirect Costs	Direct Costs	Net Income
City Center Rental	$ 9,200	$ 1,840	$ 3,220	$ 4,140
AV Equipment	4,800	960	1,680	2,160
Display Equipment	3,700	740	1,295	1,665
Total	$ 17,700	$ 3,540	$ 6,195	$ 7,965

Figure 1

11. Apply the **Style 10** chart style. Change the **Chart Title** to City Center Costs

12. Group the worksheets. Add the file name in the left footer and the sheet name in the right footer. Return to Normal view, and then press [Ctrl] + [Home].

13. Check the spelling of the workbook, and then ungroup the sheets.

14. **Save** the workbook. Compare your completed workbook with Figure 1. Submit the workbook as directed by your instructor.

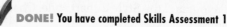

DONE! You have completed Skills Assessment 1

Skills Assessment 2

To complete this workbook, you will need the following file:

- exl03_SA2Taxes

You will save your workbook as:

- Last_First_exl03_SA2Taxes

1. Start **Excel 2013**, and open the file **exl03_SA2Taxes**. **Save** the workbook in your chapter folder as Last_First_exl03_SA2Taxes

2. Group the sheets. In cell **F5**, construct a formula to compute *Net Revenue = (Taxes Paid + Late Fees) – (Office Costs + Personnel Costs)*. AutoFill the formula down through **row 10**.

3. Select the nonadjacent ranges **B5:F5** and **B11:F11**, and then apply the **Currency [0]** cell style.

4. Ungroup the worksheets, and then hide the **April** worksheet. Compare the *January* worksheet with **Figure 1**.

5. Insert a new sheet, rename the worksheet tab 1st Qtr Summary and then change the worksheet tab color to **Brown, Text 2**. Move the worksheet to the first position in the workbook. Copy the range **A1:F4** from another sheet, and then paste the range at the top of the *1st Qtr Summary* sheet using the **Keep Source Column Widths** paste option.

6. On the **1st Qtr Summary** sheet, change the subtitle in cell **A2** to 1st Quarter Tax Revenue and then change the label in cell **A4** to Month In the range **A5:A7**, enter the months January, February, and March and in cell **A8**, type Total

7. In cell **B5**, enter a formula setting the cell to equal the total *Taxes Paid* in the *January* worksheet. In cells **B6** and **B7** of the **1st Qtr Summary** sheet, enter the total *Taxes Paid* from the *February* and the *March* worksheets.

8. Total column **B** and then AutoFill the range **B5:B8** to the right through column **F**. In the range **B8:F8**, apply the **Total** cell style.

9. Select the range **A4:C7**, and then insert a **Stacked Bar** chart. Move the chart to approximately the range **A10:F26**.

10. Apply the **Layout 9** chart layout and the **Style 2** chart style. Change the chart title to 1st Quarter

11. Group the worksheets and then check the spelling of the workbook. Add the file name in the left footer and the sheet name in the right footer. Return to Normal view, and then press [Ctrl] + [Home].

12. **Save** the workbook. Compare your *1st Qtr Summary* sheet with **Figure 1**. Submit the workbook as directed by your instructor.

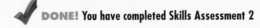 **DONE!** You have completed Skills Assessment 2

Aspen Falls
1st Quarter Tax Revenue

Month	Taxes Paid	Late Fees	Office Costs	Personnel Costs	Net Revenue
January	$ 630,090	$ 274,527	$ 23,357	$ 284,629	$ 596,631
February	$ 654,466	$ 338,305	$ 22,029	$ 263,466	$ 707,276
March	$ 771,693	$ 407,095	$ 22,915	$ 320,350	$ 835,523
Total	$ 2,056,249	$ 1,019,927	$ 68,301	$ 868,445	$ 2,139,430

1ST QUARTER

■January ■February ■March

LATE FEES $274,527 / $338,305 / $407,095

TAXES PAID $630,090 / $654,466 / $771,693

Aspen Falls
January Tax Revenue

Tax	Taxes Paid	Late Fees	Office Costs	Personnel Costs	Net Revenue
Motor Vehicle	$ 82,831	$ 58,255	$ 2,879	$ 49,255	$ 88,952
Sales	154,520	47,280	3,796	51,529	146,475
Franchise	72,956	46,998	4,915	60,061	54,978
Utilities	98,750	35,107	5,688	38,378	89,791
Property	120,000	40,762	3,200	24,320	133,242
Other	101,033	46,125	2,879	61,086	83,193
Totals	$ 630,090	$ 274,527	$ 23,357	$ 284,629	$ 596,631

Figure 1

Visual Skills Check

To complete this workbook, you will need the following file:

- exl03_VSWater

You will save your workbook as:

- Last_First_exl03_VSWater

Start **Excel 2013**, and open the file **exl03_VSWater**. Save the workbook in your chapter folder as Last_First_exl03_VSWater Complete the **Summary** sheet as shown in Figure 1. Create a summary sheet for the 4th Quarter with the totals from each month and the titles as shown in the figure. Name the worksheet tab 4th Qtr Summary and apply the worksheet tab color **Orange, Accent 1**. Move the **Summary** sheet to be the first worksheet. Insert a **Clustered Bar** chart based on the range **A4:D7**, and then move the chart below the data. Apply the **Style 12** chart style. On all sheets, add a footer with the file name in the left section and the sheet name in the right section. **Save** the workbook, and then submit the workbook as directed by your instructor.

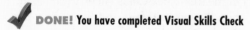 **DONE! You have completed Visual Skills Check**

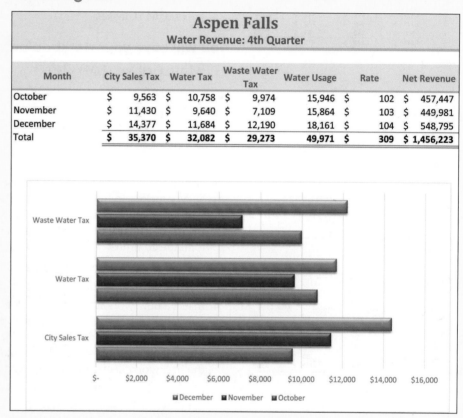

Aspen Falls
Water Revenue: 4th Quarter

Month	City Sales Tax	Water Tax	Waste Water Tax	Water Usage	Rate	Net Revenue
October	$ 9,563	$ 10,758	$ 9,974	15,946	$ 102	$ 457,447
November	$ 11,430	$ 9,640	$ 7,109	15,864	$ 103	$ 449,981
December	$ 14,377	$ 11,684	$ 12,190	18,161	$ 104	$ 548,795
Total	$ 35,370	$ 32,082	$ 29,273	49,971	$ 309	$ 1,456,223

Aspen Falls
Water Revenue: October

Building Type	City Sales Tax	Water Tax	Waste Water Tax	Water Usage	Rate	Net Revenue
Residential	$ 1,575	$ 1,890	$ 1,507	3,181	$ 19	$ 65,411
Commercial	4,233	5,762	5,671	5,440	27	162,546
Industrial	3,170	2,404	2,191	6,118	31	197,423
Apartments	585	702	605	1,207	25	32,067
Total	$ 9,563	$ 10,758	$ 9,974	15,946	$ 102	$ 457,447

Figure 1

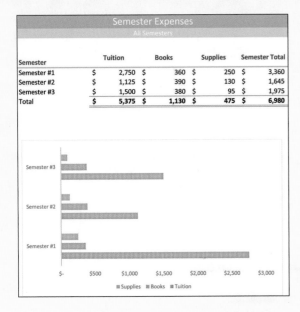

Figure 1

My Skills

To complete this workbook, you will need the following file:

- exl03_MYClasses

You will save your workbook as:

- Last_First_exl03_MYClasses

1. Start **Excel 2013**, and open the file **exl03_MyClasses**. **Save** the workbook in your chapter folder as Last_First_exl03_MYClasses

2. Group the worksheets. In cell **E5**, use the SUM function to total the row and then AutoFill the formula down through cell **E9**. In **row 10**, use the SUM function to total the columns.

3. Select cell **A2**, and then apply the **60% - Accent3** cell style.

4. Insert a new worksheet. Rename the new worksheet tab Semester Costs and apply the worksheet tab color **Blue**, **Accent 5**. Move the new worksheet tab to make it the first worksheet in the workbook.

5. Copy the range **A1:E4** from any of the detail worksheets, and then on the **Semester Costs** worksheet, click cell **A1**. Paste the range using the **Keep Source Column Widths** paste option. Change the subtitle of cell **A2** to All Semesters then change the label in cell **A4** to Semester and then change the label in cell **E4** to Semester Total

6. In cell **A5**, type Semester #1 and then AutoFill the label down through **A7**. In cell **A8**, type Total

7. In cell **B5** insert a formula to equal the value in cell **B10** in the *Semester #[?]1* worksheet. In the cells **B6** and **B7**, insert

formulas that equal the *Tuition* total from the *Semester #2* and *Semester #3* worksheets.

8. Use the **Quick Analysis Lens** button to insert the **column B** total, and then AutoFill the formulas in **column B** to the right through **column E**. Select the range **B8:E8**, and then apply the **Total** cell style.

9. Insert a **Clustered Bar** chart using the range **A4:D7** as the source data. Move and resize the chart to display below the data in approximately the range **A12:E28**.

10. Apply the **Style 2** chart style, and then delete the **Chart Title**. Move the legend to the bottom of the chart.

11. On the **Semester Costs** sheet, in cell **A36**, enter the current date, and then apply the **March 14, 2012**, date format.

12. Group the worksheets. Add the file name in the left footer and the sheet name in the right footer. Return to Normal view, and then press [Ctrl] + [Home].

13. Check the spelling of the workbook, and then ungroup the sheets.

14. **Save** the workbook. Compare your completed workbook with **Figure 1**. Submit the workbook as directed by your instructor.

 DONE! You have completed My Skills

Skills Challenge 1

To complete this workbook, you will need the following file:

- exl03_SC1Visitors

You will save your workbook as:

- Last_First_exl03_SC1Visitors

During each quarter, Carter Horikoshi, the Art Center Supervisor, tracked the revenue and costs at the Art Center. Open the file **exl03_SC1Visitors**, and then save the workbook in your chapter folder as Last_First_exl03_SC1Visitors Hide the Convention Center worksheet, and then move the remaining worksheets into the correct order. Assign a tab color to each worksheet tab. Group the worksheets, and then adjust the column widths to display all values. Format the labels in rows 1 through 4 consistently across all the worksheets. In cell F5, insert parentheses so that the sum of *Marketing Costs* and *Operating Costs* is subtracted from the sum of *Entrance Fees* and *Food Revenue*. Copy the corrected formula down. Format

the numbers appropriately. Unhide the Annual Summary worksheet, and move it as the first worksheet. Move and resize the bar chart to display below the data. On the Annual Summary sheet, format the values and the chart appropriately. Verify the formulas on the Summary sheet are correct. On all sheets, insert the file name in the left footer and the sheet name in the right footer. Check the spelling of the workbook and then verify that each sheet will print on one page. Save the workbook, and then submit the workbook as directed by your instructor.

 DONE! You have completed Skills Challenge 1

Skills Challenge 2

To complete this workbook, you will need the following file:

- exl03_SC2Durango

You will save your workbook as:

- Last_First_exl03_SC2Durango

During each month of the summer season, Duncan Chueng, the Park Operations Manager, tracked the revenue and cost at the various locations in the Durango County Recreation Area. Open the file **exl03_SC2Durango**, and then save the workbook in your chapter folder as Last_First_exl03_SC2Durango Using the skills you learned in the chapter, create a new summary worksheet with an appropriate sheet name. On the summary sheet, insert a clustered bar chart that displays the revenue for

each month. Format the chart appropriately. Move the summary sheet to the first position in the workbook. On all sheets, insert the file name in the left footer and the sheet name in the right footer. Adjust the page settings to print each worksheet on one page. Save the workbook, and then submit the workbook as directed by your instructor.

 DONE! You have completed Skills Challenge 2

CHAPTER 4

More Functions and Excel Tables

▶ The Excel Function Library contains hundreds of special functions that perform complex calculations quickly.

▶ Function Library categories include statistical, financial, logical, date and time, and math and trigonometry.

▶ Conditional formatting helps you see important trends and exceptions in your data by applying various formats such as colored gradients, data bars, or icons.

▶ You can convert data that is organized in rows and columns into an Excel table that adds formatting, filtering, and AutoComplete features.

▶ An Excel table helps you manage information by providing ways to sort and filter the data and to analyze the data using summary rows and calculated columns.

© alisonhancock

Aspen Falls City Hall

In this chapter, you will revise a spreadsheet for Jack Ruiz, the Aspen Falls Community Services Director. He has received permission from the City Council to create community gardens in open space areas in Aspen Falls. In order to promote the gardens, the city will provide materials to community members. He has a workbook with a list of materials and wants to know if any items need to be reordered and if new suppliers should be contacted for quotes when replacing the items. He is also tracking the donations received from local retail stores.

Using workbooks to track information is a primary function of a spreadsheet application. Because spreadsheets can be set up to globally update when underlying data is changed, managers often use Excel to help them make decisions in real time. An effective workbook uses functions, conditional formatting, summary statistics, and charts in ways that describe past trends and help decision makers accurately forecast future needs.

In this project, you will use the functions TODAY, NOW, COUNT, and IF to generate useful information for the director. You will apply conditional formatting to highlight outlying data and create sparklines to display trends. To update the underlying data, you will use the Find and Replace tool. Finally, you will create and format Excel tables, and then search the tables for data.

Time to complete all 10 skills – 60 to 90 minutes

Student data file needed for this chapter:

exl04_Garden

You will save your workbook as:

Last_First_exl04_Garden

Outcome

Using the skills in this chapter, you will be able to work with Excel worksheets like this:

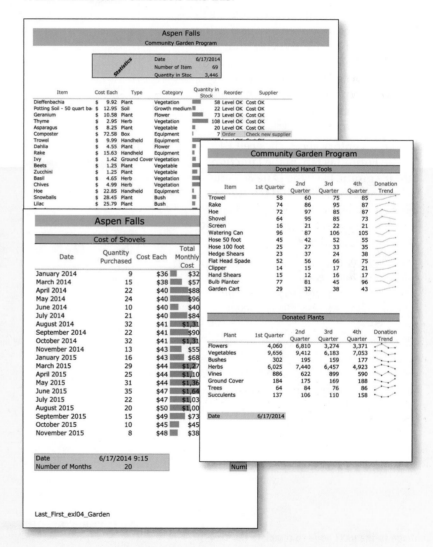

SKILLS

MyITLab®
Skills 1-10 Training

At the end of this chapter you will be able to:

Skill 1 Insert the TODAY, NOW, and COUNT Functions

Skill 2 Insert the IF Function

Skill 3 Move Functions, Add Borders, and Rotate Text

Skill 4 Apply Conditional Formatting

Skill 5 Insert Sparklines

Skill 6 Use Find and Replace

Skill 7 Freeze and Unfreeze Panes

Skill 8 Create, Sort, and Filter Excel Tables

Skill 9 Filter Data

Skill 10 Convert Tables to Ranges, Hide Rows and Columns, and Format Large Worksheets

MORE SKILLS

Skill 11 Apply Conditional Color Scales with Top and Bottom Rules and Clear Rules

Skill 12 Insert the Payment (PMT) Function

Skill 13 Create PivotTable Reports

Skill 14 Use Goal Seek

▶ The **TODAY** *function* returns the serial number of the current date.

▶ The **NOW** *function* returns the serial number of the current date and time.

▶ The **COUNT** *function* counts the number of cells that contain numbers.

1. Start **Excel 2013**, and then open the student data file **exl04_Garden**. Click the **File tab**, and then click **Save As**. Click the **Browse** button, and then navigate to the location where you are saving your files. Click **New folder**, type Excel Chapter 4 and then press [Enter] two times. In the **File name** box, using your own name, name the workbook Last_First_exl04_ Garden and then press [Enter].

2. On the **Inventory** sheet, click cell **E4**. On the **Formulas tab**, in the **Function Library group**, click the **Date & Time** button, and then click **TODAY**. Read the message that displays, compare your screen with **Figure 1**, and then click **OK** to enter the function.

> The TODAY function takes no arguments, and the result is *volatile*—the date will not remain as entered but rather will be updated each time this workbook is opened.

3. Click the **Donations** worksheet tab, scroll down, and then click cell **B36**. Use the technique just practiced to enter the TODAY function. Compare your screen with **Figure 2**.

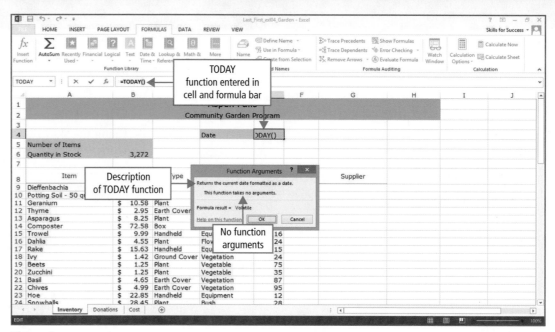

Figure 1

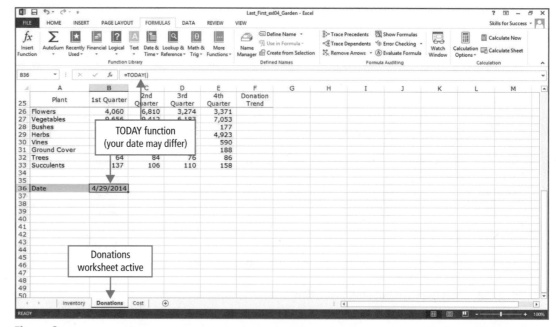

Figure 2

■ **Continue to the next page to complete the skill** ➤

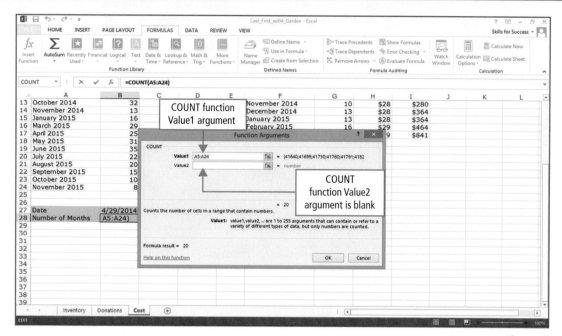

Figure 3

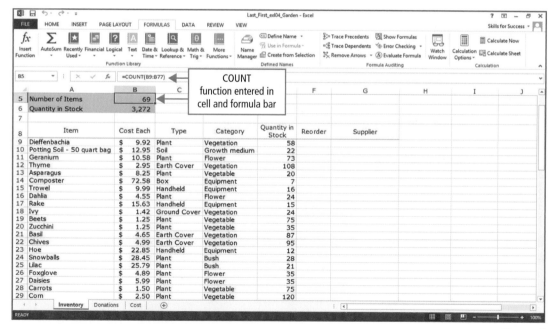

Figure 4

4. Click the **Cost** worksheet tab, scroll down and then click the merged cell **B27**. In the **Function Library group**, click the **Date & Time** button, and then click **NOW**. Read the message that displays, and then click **OK** to insert the function.

5. Click cell **B28**. In the **Function Library group**, click the **More Functions** button. Point to **Statistical**, and then click **COUNT**.

6. In the **Function Arguments** dialog box, in the **Value1** box, type A5:A24 and then compare your screen with **Figure 3**.

7. In the **Function Arguments** dialog box, click **OK**.

   The number of cells in the range A5:A24 that contain values is *20*.

8. Click cell **G28**. Use the technique just practiced to enter a **COUNT** function with the range F5:F17 as the **Value1** argument. The result should be *13*.

9. Click the **Inventory** worksheet tab, and then click cell **B5**. In the **Function Library group**, click the **More Functions** button, point to **Statistical**, and then click **COUNT**. If necessary, move the Function Arguments dialog box to the right to view column **B**. In the **Function Arguments** dialog box, with the insertion point in the **Value1** box, click cell **B9**. Press [Ctrl] + [Shift] + [↓] to select the range **B9:B77**. Click **OK** to display the result *69*. Compare your screen with **Figure 4**.

10. **Save** 🖫 the workbook.

■ **You have completed Skill 1 of 10**

▶ A *logical function* applies a logical test to determine whether a specific condition is met.

▶ A *logical test* is any value or expression that can be evaluated as TRUE or FALSE and *Criteria* are the conditions specified in the logical test.

▶ The *IF function* is a logical function that checks whether criteria are met and then returns one value when the condition is TRUE and another value when the condition is FALSE.

1. On the **Inventory** worksheet, click cell **F9**. In the **Function Library group**, click the **Logical** button, and then on the list, point to **IF**. Read the ScreenTip, and then click **IF**.

2. In the **Function Arguments** dialog box, with the insertion point in the **Logical_test** box, type E9<10

    A *comparison operator* compares two values and returns either TRUE or FALSE. Here, the logical test *E9<10* uses the less than comparison operator, and will return TRUE only when the value in E9 is less than 10. The table in **Figure 1** lists commonly used comparison operators.

3. Press [Tab] to move the insertion point to the **Value_if_true** box, and then type Order

4. Press [Tab] to move the insertion point to the **Value_if_false** box, type Level OK and then compare your screen with **Figure 2**.

    In function arguments, text values are surrounded by quotation marks. Here, quotation marks display around *Order* and will automatically be inserted around *Level OK* after you click OK.

■ **Continue to the next page to complete the skill** ▶

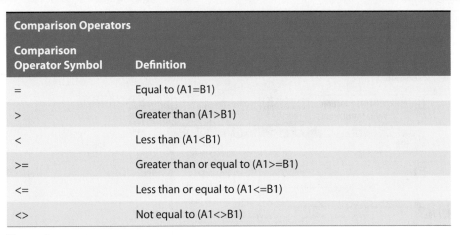

Comparison Operators	
Comparison Operator Symbol	Definition
=	Equal to (A1=B1)
>	Greater than (A1>B1)
<	Less than (A1<B1)
>=	Greater than or equal to (A1>=B1)
<=	Less than or equal to (A1<=B1)
<>	Not equal to (A1<>B1)

Figure 1

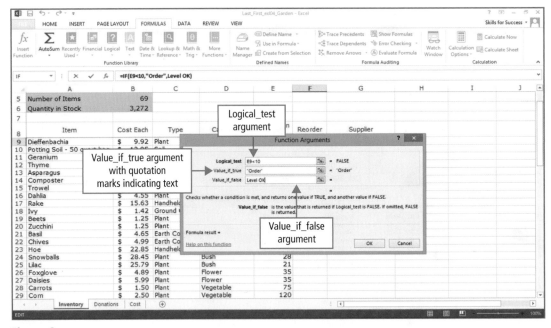

Figure 2

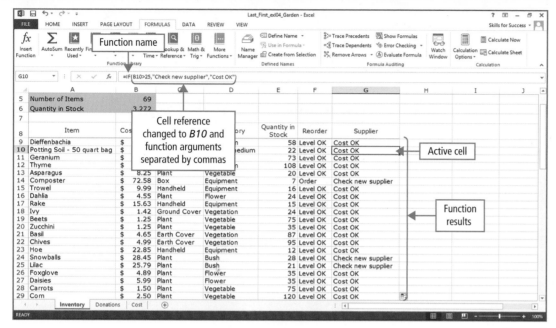

Figure 3

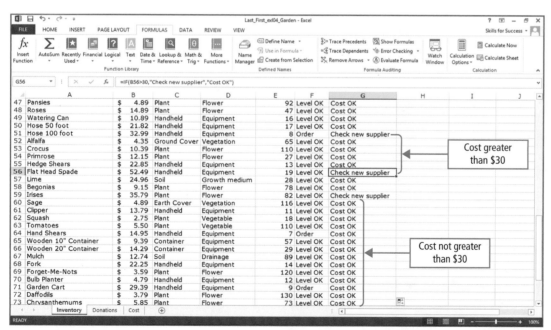

Figure 4

5. Click **OK** to display the result *Level OK*.

The IF function tests whether E9 is less than 10. When this condition is TRUE, *Order* will display. Because E9 contains the value *58*, the condition is FALSE, and *Level OK* displays.

6. Click cell **G9**. In the **Function Library group**, click the **Logical** button, and then click **IF**. In the **Logical_test** box, type B9>25 and then in the **Value_if_true** box, type Check new supplier In the **Value_if_false** box, type Cost OK and then click the **OK** button to display *Cost OK*.

7. Select the range **F9:G9**. Point to the fill handle to display the ⊞ pointer, and then double-click to AutoFill the functions down through row **77**. Click **G10**, and then compare your screen with **Figure 3**.

In each row of column G, the function evaluates the value in column B. When the value in column B is greater than $25, the text *Check new supplier* displays. Otherwise, the text *Cost OK* displays.

When a function has multiple arguments, each argument is separated by a comma.

When the function was copied down to G10, the cell reference changed from B9 to B10.

8. Scroll down and verify that nine items meet the condition and display the text *Check new supplier*. Click cell **G9**. In the formula bar, change the number *25* to *30* and then, click the **Enter** button ✓. AutoFill the function down through cell **G77**. Scroll down to verify that five items meet the changed condition. Click cell **G56**, and then compare your screen with **Figure 4**.

9. Save 🖫 the workbook.

■ **You have completed Skill 2 of 10**

▶ When you move cells containing formulas or functions by dragging them, the cell references in the formulas or functions do not change.

▶ Borders and shading emphasize a cell or a range of cells, and rotated or angled text draws attention to text on a worksheet.

1. On the **Inventory** worksheet, press Ctrl + Home. Select the range **A5:B6**. Point to the top edge of the selected range to display the ⬚ pointer. Drag the selected range to the right until the ScreenTip displays the range **D5:E6**, as shown in Figure 1, and then release the mouse button to complete the move.

2. Click cell **E5**. Notice that the cell references in the function did not change.

3. Click the **Donations** worksheet tab. Select the merged cell **A3**. On the **Home tab**, in the **Font group**, click the **Border arrow** ⬚ ▾, and then click **Top and Bottom Border**.

4. Click the merged cell **A23**. In the **Font group**, click the **Border** button ⬚ ▾ to apply a top and bottom border. Click cell **A5**, and then compare your screen with Figure 2.

5. Click the **Cost** worksheet tab. Click the merged cell **A3**. Hold down Ctrl and then click the merged cell **F3**. Use the technique just practiced to apply a top and bottom border.

■ **Continue to the next page to complete the skill**

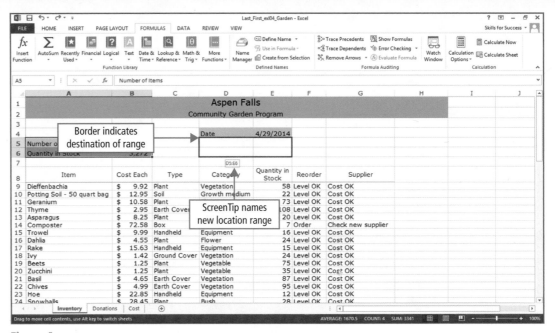

Figure 1

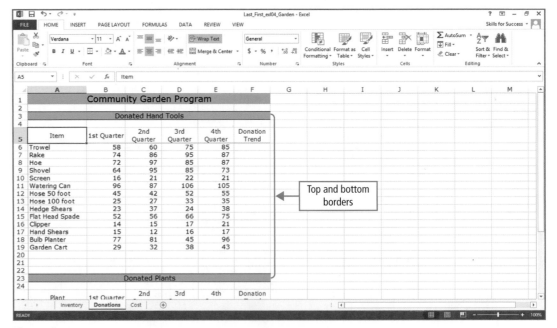

Figure 2

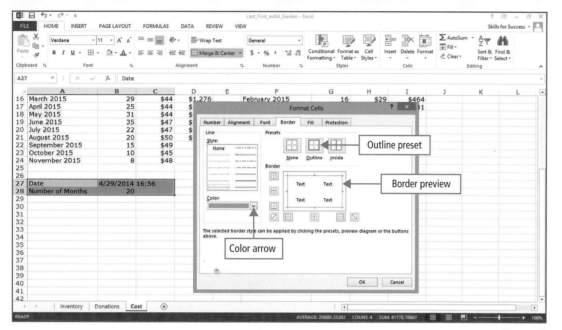

Figure 3

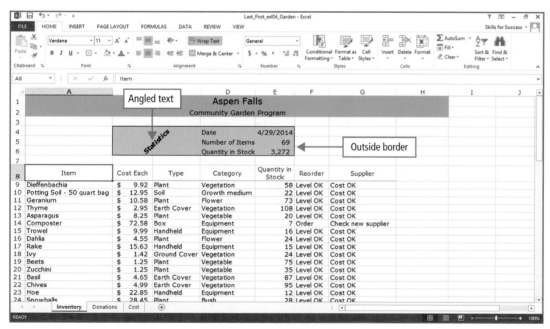

Figure 4

6. Scroll down, and then select the range **A27:C28**. In the **Font group**, click the **Border arrow**. At the bottom of the **Border** gallery, click **More Borders**.

7. In the **Format Cells** dialog box, click the **Color arrow**, and then click the fifth color in the first row—**Orange, Accent 1**. Under **Presets**, click **Outline**. Compare your screen with **Figure 3**, and then click **OK**.

8. Select the range **F28:G28**. Press F4 to repeat the last command, and then click cell **F30**.

   Pressing F4 will repeat the last command. In this instance it will apply an orange border to the selected range.

9. Click the **Inventory** worksheet tab. Click cell **B4**, type Statistics and then press Enter.

10. Select the range **B4:C6**. On the **Home tab**, in the **Alignment group**, click the **Merge & Center** button. Apply the **40% - Accent 4** cell style, and then click **Middle Align**, **Bold** B, and **Italic** I.

11. With the merged cell still selected, in the **Alignment group**, click the **Orientation** button, and then click **Angle Counterclockwise**.

12. Select the range **B4:E6**. In the **Font group**, click the **Border arrow**, and then click **Outside Borders**. Click cell **A8**, and then compare your screen with **Figure 4**.

13. **Save** the workbook.

■ **You have completed Skill 3 of 10**

▶ **Conditional formatting** is a format, such as cell shading or font color, that is applied to cells when a specified condition is true.

▶ Conditional formatting makes analyzing data easier by emphasizing differences in cell values.

1. On the **Inventory** worksheet, click cell **F9**. Press [Ctrl] + [Shift] + [↓] to select the range **F9:F77**.

2. Click the **Quick Analysis Lens** button, and then click **Text Contains**. In the **Text That Contains** dialog box, delete the text in the first box, and then type Order Compare your screen with **Figure 1**, and then click **OK**.

   Within the range F9:F77, cells that contain the text *Order* display with light red fill and dark red text formatting.

3. Using the technique just practiced, select the range **G9:G77**, and then open the **Text That Contains** dialog box. In the first box, type Check new supplier To the right of the format box, click the **arrow**, and then compare your screen with **Figure 2**.

   You can use the Text That Contains dialog box to specify the formatting that should be applied when a condition is true. If the formatting choice you need is not listed, you can open the Format Cells dialog box by clicking the Custom Format command.

■ **Continue to the next page to complete the skill**

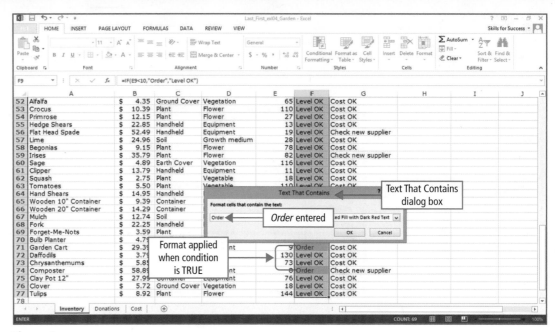

Figure 1

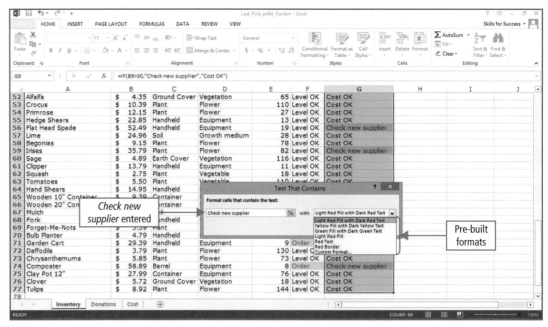

Figure 2

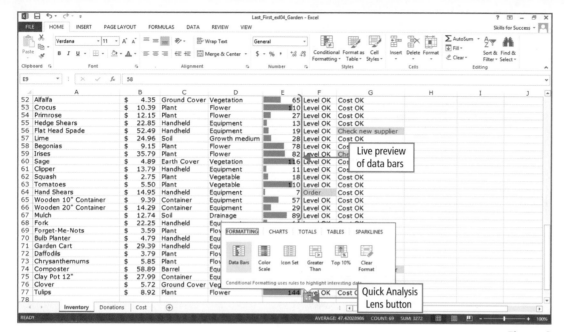

Figure 3

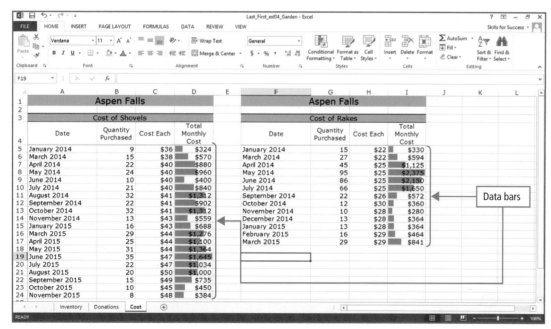

Figure 4

4. In the list of conditional formats, click **Green Fill with Dark Green Text**, and then click **OK**.

5. Select the range **E9:E77**. Click the **Quick Analysis Lens** button 📋, and then point to **Data Bars**. Compare your screen with **Figure 3**.

A *data bar* is a format that provides a visual cue about the value of a cell relative to other cells in a range. Data bars are useful to quickly identify higher and lower numbers within a large group of data, such as very high or very low levels of inventory.

6. In the **Quick Analysis** gallery, click **Data Bars** to apply the conditional formatting.

7. Scroll up, and then click cell **E15**. Type 190 and then press Enter to adjust all data bars to the new value.

Data bars are sized relative to the maximum value within a range. Here, when a new maximum value of 190 was entered, all the data bars adjusted.

8. Click the **Cost** worksheet tab. Select the range **D5:D24**, and then use the technique just practiced to apply the default data bar conditional format.

9. Select the range **I5:I17**, and then apply the default data bar conditional format. Click cell **F19**, and then compare your screen with **Figure 4**.

10. Save 💾 the workbook.

■ **You have completed Skill 4 of 10**

▶ A ***sparkline*** is a chart contained in a single cell that is used to show data trends.

1. Click the **Donations** worksheet tab to make it the active sheet, and then select the range **B6:E19**.

2. Click the **Quick Analysis Lens** button, and then click **Sparklines**. In the **Sparklines** gallery, point to **Line** to display sparklines in **column F**. Compare your screen with **Figure 1**, and then click **Line**.

3. With the range **F6:F19** selected, on the **Design tab**, in the **Show group**, select the **High Point** check box to mark the highest point of data on each sparkline.

4. In the **Style group**, click the **Sparkline Color** button, and then click the fifth color in the first row—**Orange, Accent 1**. Click cell **E20**, and then compare your screen with **Figure 2**.

> The sparklines in column F show that the donation levels of hand tools are generally increasing over time.

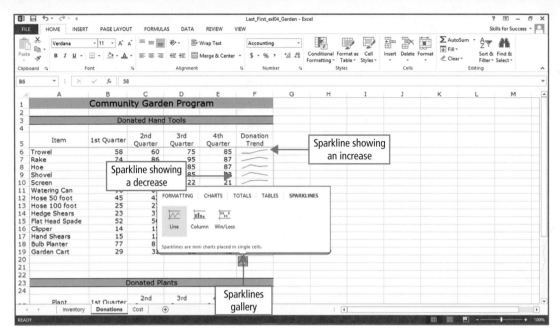

Figure 1

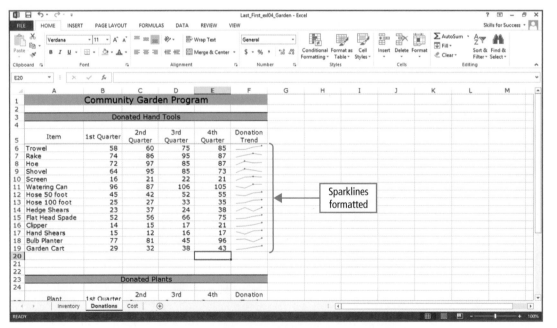

Figure 2

■ **Continue to the next page to complete the skill** ➤

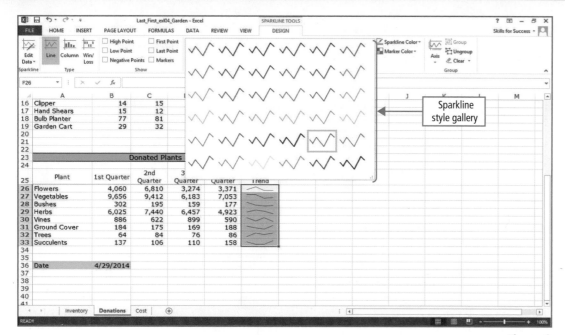

Figure 3

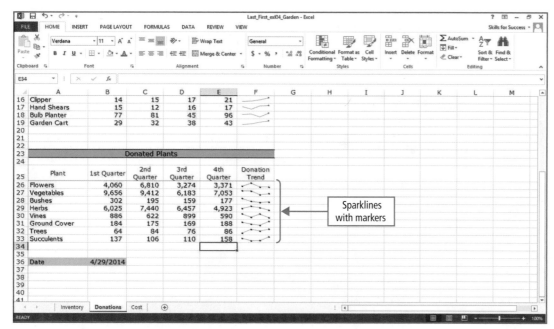

Figure 4

5. Scroll down and then select the range **B26:E33**. Use the techniques just practiced to insert the default **Line** sparklines.

6. With the range **F26:F33** selected, on the **Design tab**, in the **Style group**, click the **More** button ⏷, and then compare your screen with Figure 3.

7. In the **Style** gallery, click the first color in the third row—**Sparkline Style Accent 1**, **(no dark or light)**.

8. In the **Style group**, click the **Marker Color** button. In the displayed list, point to **Markers**, and then click the second color in the first row—**Black, Text 1** to mark each data point on the sparklines. Click cell **E34**, and then compare your screen with Figure 4.

9. Right-click the **Donations** worksheet tab, and then click **Select All Sheets**. Add the file name to the worksheet's left footer and the sheet name to the right footer. Return to **Normal** view and then press Ctrl + Home to make cell **A1** the active cell on each of the grouped worksheets.

10. Right-click the **Donations** worksheet tab, and then click **Ungroup Sheets**. Save 🖫 the workbook.

■ **You have completed Skill 5 of 10**

▶ The ***Replace*** feature finds and then replaces a character or string of characters in a worksheet or in a selected range.

1. Click the **Inventory** worksheet tab, and then verify that cell **A1** is the active cell. On the **Home tab**, in the **Editing group**, click the **Find & Select** button, and then click **Replace**.

2. In the **Find and Replace** dialog box, in the **Find what** box, type Earth Cover and then press Tab. In the **Replace with** box, type Herb and then compare your screen with **Figure 1**.

3. Click the **Find Next** button, and then verify that cell **C12** is the active cell. In the **Find and Replace** dialog box, click the **Replace** button to replace the value in cell **C12** with *Herb* and to select the next occurrence of *Earth Cover* in cell *C21*.

4. In the **Find and Replace** dialog box, click the **Replace All** button. Read the message that displays. Compare your screen with **Figure 2**, and then click **OK**.

   The Replace All option replaces all matches of an occurrence of a character or string of characters with the replacement value. Here, six values were replaced. Only use the Replace All option when the search string is unique.

■ **Continue to the next page to complete the skill** ➤

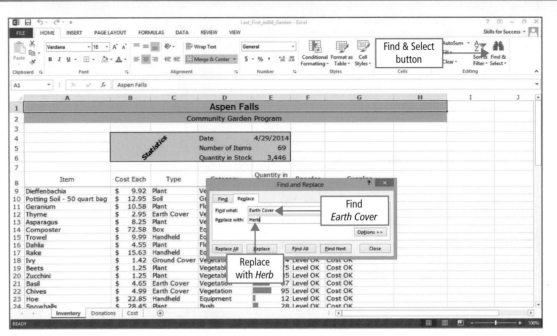

Figure 1

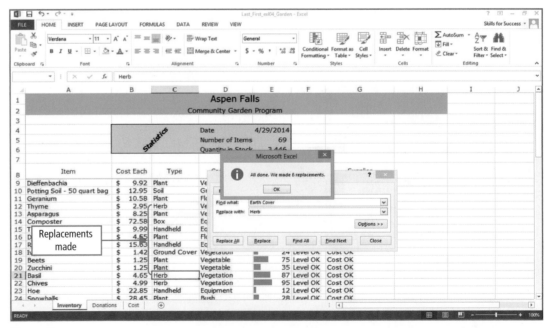

Figure 2

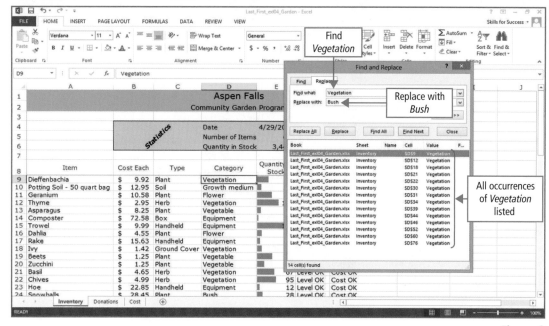

Figure 3

5. In the **Find and Replace** dialog box, in the **Find what** box, replace the text *Earth Cover* with Vegetation and then press ⌈Tab⌋. In the **Replace with** box, replace the text *Herb* with Bush and then click the **Find All** button.

6. In the **Find and Replace** dialog box, point to the bottom border, and then with the ⇕ pointer, drag down to resize the dialog box until each listed occurrence displays as shown in **Figure 3**. If necessary, move the dialog box to display all occurrences.

    The Find All option finds all occurrences of the search criteria.

7. In the lower portion of the **Find and Replace** dialog box, in the **Cell** column, click **$D$31** to make cell **D31** the active cell, and then click the **Replace** button. Compare your screen with **Figure 4**.

    In this manner you can find all occurrences of cell text and use the list to replace only the occurrences you desire.

8. Use the technique just practiced to replace the two occurrences of the word Clay with the word Terracotta and then close all message and dialog boxes.

9. **Save** 🖫 the workbook.

■ **You have completed Skill 6 of 10**

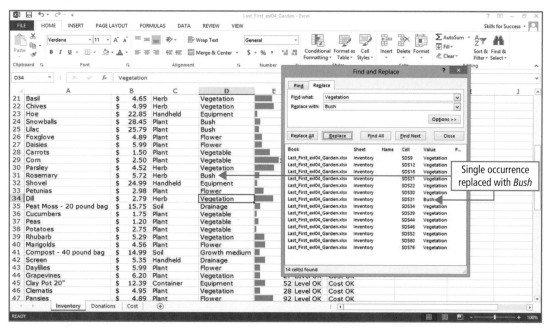

Figure 4

▶ SKILL 1.7
VIDEO

▶ The *Freeze Panes* command keeps rows or columns visible when you are scrolling in a worksheet. The frozen rows and columns become separate panes so that you can always identify rows and columns when working with large worksheets.

1. On the **Inventory** sheet, scroll until **row 50** displays at the bottom of your window and the column labels are out of view. Compare your screen with **Figure 1**.

    When you scroll in large worksheets, the column and row labels may not be visible, which can make identifying the purpose of each row or column difficult.

2. Press [Ctrl] + [Home], and then click cell **C15**. On the **View tab**, in the **Window group**, click the **Freeze Panes** button, and then click **Freeze Panes** to freeze the rows above and the columns to the left of C15—the active cell.

    A line displays along the upper border of row 15 and on the left border of column C to show where the panes are frozen.

3. Click the **Scroll Down** [∨] and **Scroll Right** [>] arrows to display cell **M80**, and then notice that the top and left panes remain frozen. Compare your screen with **Figure 2**.

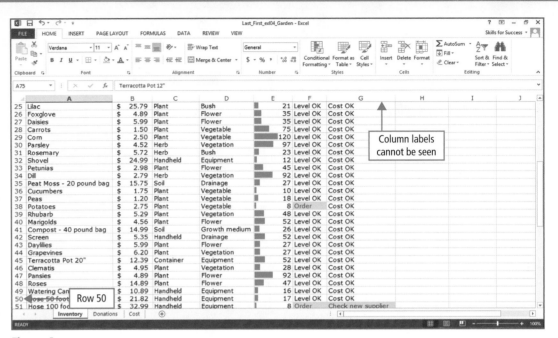

Figure 1

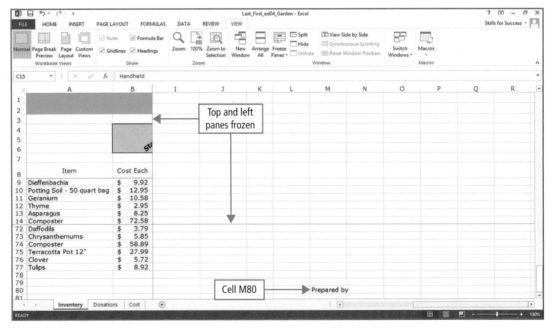

Figure 2

■ Continue to the next page to complete the skill ▶

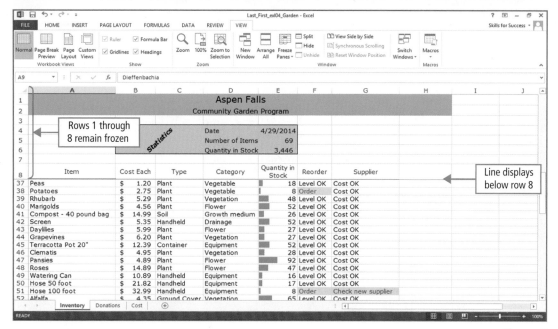

Rows 1 through 8 remain frozen

Line displays below row 8

Figure 3

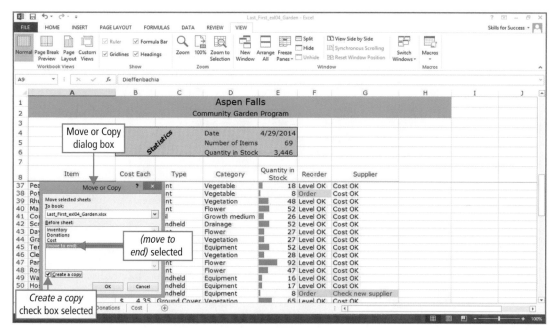

Move or Copy dialog box

(move to end) selected

Create a copy check box selected

Figure 4

4. Click cell **M80** and then press ⟨Delete⟩.

5. In the **Window group**, click the **Freeze Panes** button, and then click **Unfreeze Panes**.

   The rows and columns are no longer frozen, and the border no longer displays on row 15 and on column C.

6. Click cell **A9**. In the **Window group**, click the **Freeze Panes** button, and then click **Freeze Panes** to freeze the rows above **row 9**.

7. Watch the row numbers below **row 8** as you scroll down to **row 50**. Compare your screen with Figure 3.

   The labels in row 1 through row 8 stay frozen while the remaining rows of data continue to scroll.

8. Right-click the **Inventory** worksheet tab, and then from the list, click **Move or Copy**. In the **Move or Copy** dialog box, click **(move to end)**, and then select the **Create a copy** check box. Compare your screen with Figure 4.

9. In the **Move or Copy** dialog box, click **OK** to create a copy of the worksheet named *Inventory (2)*.

   A *(2)* displays in the name since two sheets in a workbook cannot have the same name.

10. Right-click the **Inventory (2)** worksheet tab, click **Rename**, type Sort by Cost and then press ⟨Enter⟩.

11. In the **Window group**, click the **Freeze Panes** button, and then click **Unfreeze Panes** to unfreeze the panes.

12. Click the **Inventory** worksheet tab, and verify that on this worksheet, the panes are still frozen.

13. **Save** 🖫 the workbook.

■ **You have completed Skill 7 of 10**

▶ To analyze a group of related data, you can convert a range into an ***Excel table***—a series of rows and columns that contain related data that has been formatted as a table. Data in an Excel table are managed independently from the data in other rows and columns in the worksheet.

▶ Data in Excel tables can be sorted in a variety of ways—for example, in ascending order or by color.

1. Click the **Sort by Cost** worksheet tab, and then click cell **A11**. On the **Home tab**, in the **Styles group**, click the **Format as Table** button. In the gallery, under **Light**, click the fifth choice—**Table Style Light 5**.

2. In the **Format as Table** dialog box, under **Where is the data for your table?** verify that the range **=$A$8:$G$77** displays. Verify that the **My table has headers** check box is selected. Compare your screen with **Figure 1**, and then click **OK** to convert the range to an Excel table.

    When creating an Excel table, you only need to click in the data. The layout of column and row headings determines the default range provided in the Format As Table dialog box.

3. Click cell **H8**, type Total Cost and then press [Enter] to automatically add the formatted column to the Excel table.

4. In cell **H9**, type =B9*E9 and then press [Enter] to create a ***calculated column***—a column in an Excel table that uses a single formula which adjusts for each row. Compare your screen with **Figure 2**.

■ **Continue to the next page to complete the skill** ▶

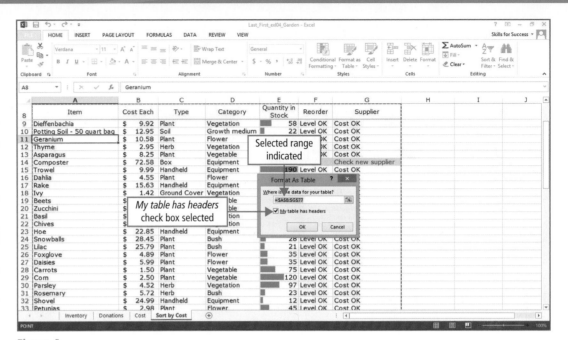

Figure 1

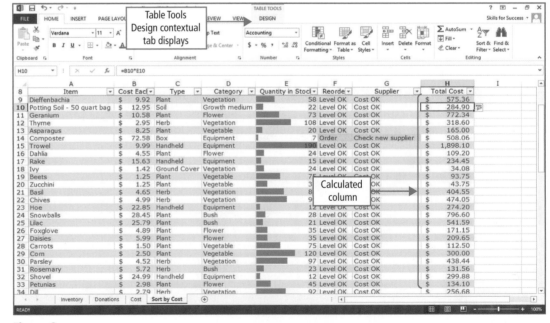

Figure 2

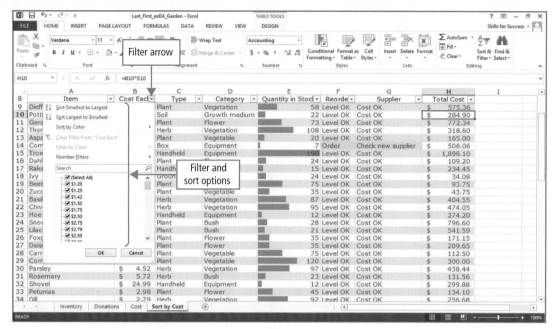

Figure 3

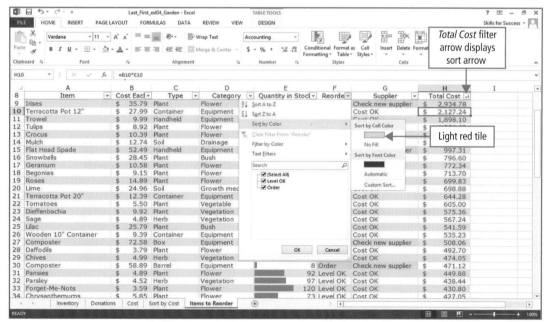

Figure 4

5. In the header row of the Excel table, click the **Cost Each filter arrow**, and then compare your screen with Figure 3.

6. In the **Filter** gallery, click **Sort Smallest to Largest**.

   The rows in the table are sorted by the *Cost Each* values, from the lowest to the highest, as indicated by the up arrow on the column's filter button.

7. In the header row, click the **Total Cost filter arrow**, and then click **Sort Largest to Smallest**.

   The rows in the table are now sorted from the highest to lowest *Total Cost* value, and the small arrow in the Total Cost filter arrow points down, indicating a descending sort. The previous sort on the *Cost Each* column no longer displays.

8. Right-click the **Sort by Cost** worksheet tab, and then click **Move or Copy**. In the **Move or Copy** dialog box, click **(move to end)**, select the **Create a copy** check box, and then click **OK**.

9. Rename the **Sort by Cost (2)** worksheet tab, as Items to Reorder.

10. In the **Items to Reorder** worksheet, click the **Reorder filter arrow**, and then point to **Sort by Color**. Notice that the color formats in **column F** display in the list. Compare your screen with Figure 4.

    If you have applied manual or conditional formatting to a range of cells, you can sort by these colors.

11. In the list, under **Sort by Cell Color**, click the **light red tile** to place the six items that need to be ordered at the top of the Excel table.

12. Save 🖫 the workbook.

■ **You have completed Skill 8 of 10**

▶ You can *filter* data to display only the rows of a table that meet specified criteria. Filtering temporarily hides rows that do not meet the criteria.

1. On the **Items to Reorder** worksheet, click the **Category filter arrow**. From the menu, clear the **(Select All)** check box to clear all the check boxes. Select the **Equipment** check box, as shown in **Figure 1**, and then click **OK** to display only the rows containing *Equipment*.

   The rows not meeting this criteria are hidden from view.

2. On the **Design tab**, in the **Table Style Options group**, select the **Total Row** check box to display the column total in cell **H78**.

   The *Total row* provides summary functions in drop-down lists for each column. Here, *Total* displays in cell A78. In cell H78, the number *$10,400.26* indicates the SUM of the Total Cost column for the filtered *Equipment* rows.

3. In the **Total** row, click cell **D78**, and then click the **arrow** that displays to the right of the selected cell. Compare your screen with **Figure 2**.

4. In the list of summary functions, click **Count** to count only the visible rows in **column D**—*20*.

5. In the header row, click the **Type filter arrow**. From the menu, clear the **Handheld** check box, and then click **OK**.

   Filters can be applied to more than one column. Here, both the Type and Category columns are filtered.

■ **Continue to the next page to complete the skill**

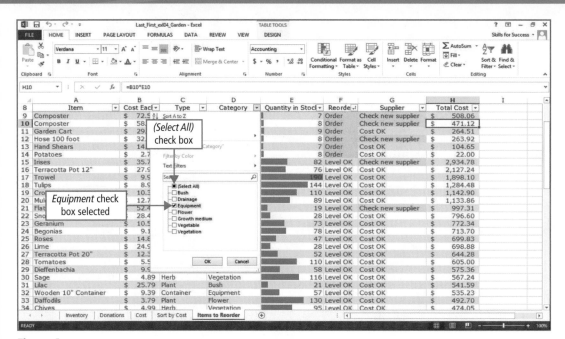

Figure 1

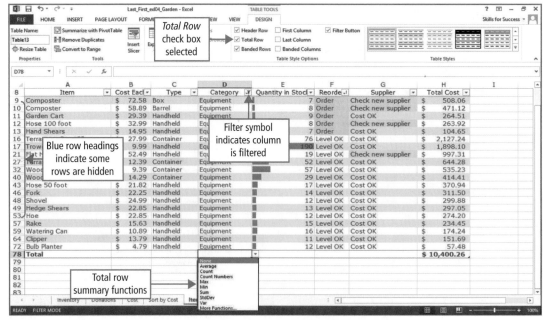

Figure 2

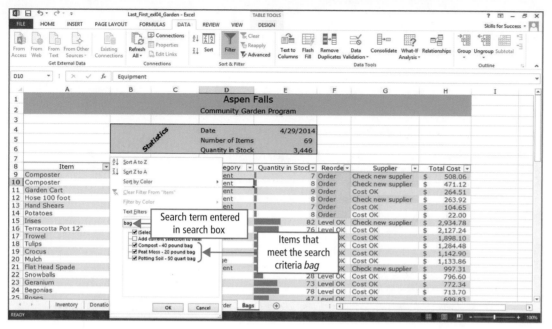

Figure 3

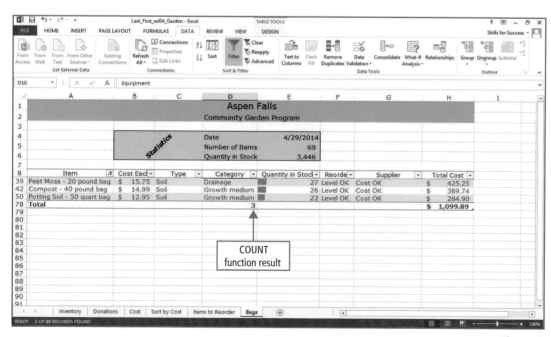

Figure 4

6. Right-click the **Items to Reorder** worksheet tab, and then using the techniques you just practiced, create a copy of the worksheet and move the sheet to the end. Rename the **Items to Reorder (2)** worksheet tab as Bags

7. With the **Bags** worksheet active, click any cell in the Excel table to make the Excel table active. On the **Data tab**, in the **Sort & Filter group**, click the **Clear** button to clear all the filters and to display all the rows in the Excel table.

8. In the header row, click the **Item filter arrow**. In the **Filter** list, click in the **Search** box, type bag and then compare your screen with **Figure 3**.

9. Click **OK** to display the three rows containing the text bag in the **Item** column. Compare your screen with **Figure 4**.

In the Total row, the Category count in cell D78 and the Total Cost in cell H78 display the results of the filtered rows.

10. Save 🖫 the workbook.

■ **You have completed Skill 9 of 10**

▶ An Excel table can be converted into a range retaining the table format.

▶ When a large worksheet is too wide or too long to print on a single page, row and column headings can be printed on each page.

1. Right-click the **Bags** worksheet tab, create a copy of the sheet, and move it to the end of the workbook. Rename the **Bags (2)** worksheet tab as All Items

2. In the **All Items** sheet, click cell **A8**. On the **Design tab**, in the **Tools group**, click the **Convert to Range** button. Read the message box, as shown in **Figure 1**, and then click **Yes**.

   > When converting an Excel table into a range, all filters are removed and the heading row no longer displays filter buttons. Any existing sorts and formatting remain.

3. Click the **File tab**, and then click **Print**. Click the **Next Page** button ▶ three times to view the four pages.

4. Click the **Back** button ⬅. On the **Page Layout tab**, in the **Scale to Fit group**, click the **Width arrow**, and then click **1 page**. Click the **Height arrow**, and then click **1 page**.

5. Click the **Inventory** worksheet tab. In the **Scale to Fit group**, click the **Width** arrow, and then click **1 page**.

6. In the **Page Setup group**, click the **Print Titles** button, and then in the **Page Setup** dialog box, under **Print titles**, click in the **Rows to repeat at top** box. In the worksheet, click **row 8**, and then compare your screen with **Figure 2**.

■ Continue to the next page to complete the skill ▶

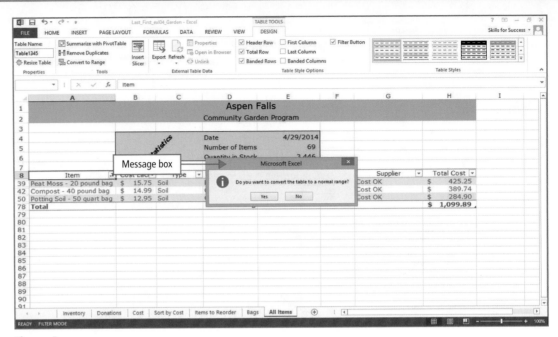

Figure 1

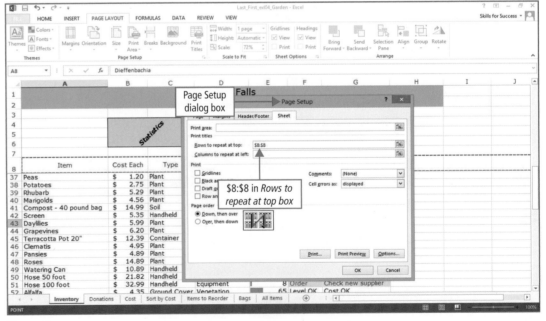

Figure 2

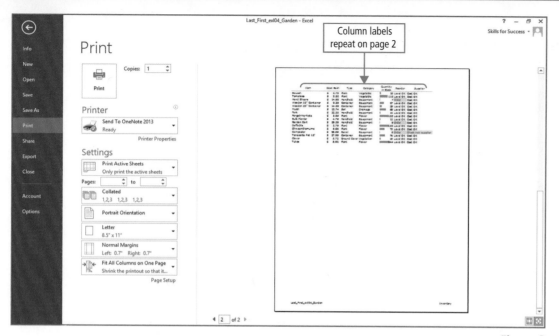

Figure 3

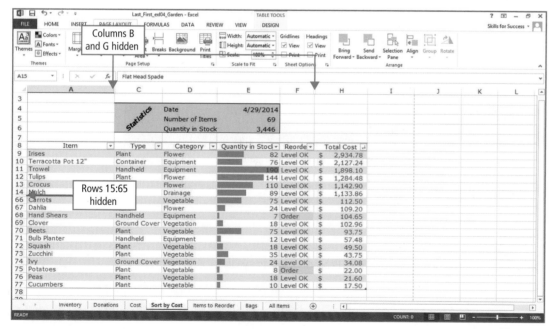

Figure 4

7. In the **Page Setup** dialog box, click the **Print Preview** button. Click the **Next Page** button ▶ to verify that the column labels from **row 8** display at the top of page 2. Compare your screen with **Figure 3**.

8. Click the **Back** button ⬅.

9. Click the **Cost** worksheet tab. Hold down `Ctrl`, and then click the **Items to Reorder** and the **Bags** worksheet tabs to group the three worksheets. In the **Page Setup group**, click the **Orientation** button, and then click **Landscape**. In the **Scale to Fit group**, click the **Width** arrow, and then click **1 page**.

   With the worksheets grouped, the orientation and scaling are applied to all three worksheets.

10. Click the **Sort by Cost** worksheet tab to select the worksheet and ungroup the three worksheets. Click cell **B13**. On the **Home tab**, in the **Cells group**, click the **Format** button, point to **Hide & Unhide**, and then click **Hide Columns**. Use the same technique to hide **column G**.

11. Select **rows 15:65**. In the **Cells group**, click the **Format** button, point to **Hide & Unhide**, and then click **Hide Rows**.

12. On the **Page Layout tab**, in the **Page Setup group**, click the **Orientation** button, and then click **Landscape**. Compare your screen with **Figure 4**.

13. **Save** 🖫 the workbook, and then **Close** ✖ Excel. Submit the workbook as directed by your instructor.

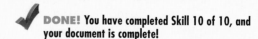

DONE! You have completed Skill 10 of 10, and your document is complete!

The following More Skills are located at **www.pearsonhighered.com/skills**

More Skills Apply Conditional Color Scales with Top and Bottom Rules and Clear Rules

You can apply color scales, which apply different colors to the cells, and top/bottom rules, which format the highest or lowest values. Conditional formatting rules can be cleared when no longer needed.

In More Skills 11, you will apply these additional types of conditional formats.

To begin, open your web browser, navigate to www.pearsonhighered.com/skills, locate the name of your textbook, and then follow the instructions on the website.

More Skills Insert the Payment (PMT) Function

The PMT function calculates the periodic payment for loans based on the loan amount, interest rate, and length of the loan. When you borrow money from a bank, the amount charged for your use of the borrowed money is called interest, and the interest amount is included in the PMT function.

In More Skills 12, you will use the PMT function to calculate various loan payments.

To begin, open your web browser, navigate to www.pearsonhighered.com/skills, locate the name of your textbook, and then follow the instructions on the website.

More Skills Create PivotTable Reports

A PivotTable report is an interactive way to summarize large amounts of data quickly, to analyze numerical data in depth, and to answer unanticipated questions about your data.

In More Skills 13, you will create a PivotTable report, pivot the data, and then filter the data.

To begin, open your web browser, navigate to www.pearsonhighered.com/skills, locate the name of your textbook, and then follow the instructions on the website.

More Skills Use Goal Seek

Goal Seek is a method to find a specific value for a cell by adjusting the value of another cell. With Goal Seek, you work backward from the desired outcome to find the necessary input to achieve your goal.

In More Skills 14, you will use Goal Seek to determine how much money can be borrowed to achieve a specific monthly payment.

To begin, open your web browser, navigate to www.pearsonhighered.com/skills, locate the name of your textbook, and then follow the instructions on the website.

Please note that there are no additional projects to accompany the More Skills Projects, and they are not covered in the End-of-Chapter projects.

The following table summarizes the **SKILLS AND PROCEDURES** covered in this chapter.

Skills Number	Task	Step	Icon	Keyboard Shortcut
1	Insert TODAY functions	Formula tab → Function Library group → Date & Time → TODAY		
1	Insert NOW functions	Formula tab → Function Library group → Date & Time → NOW		
1	Insert COUNT functions	Formula tab → Function Library group → More Functions → Statistical → COUNT		
2	Insert IF functions	Formula tab → Function Library group → Logical → IF		
3	Add borders	Home tab → Font group → Border arrow → Border		
3	Angle text	Home tab → Alignment group → Orientation		
4	Apply conditional formatting to text	Quick Analysis Lens button → Text Contains		
4	Apply conditional formatting to data bars	Quick Analysis Lens button → Data Bars		
5	Insert sparklines	Quick Analysis Lens button → Sparklines		
5	Add sparkline high points	Design tab → Show group → High Point		
6	Use Find and Replace	Home tab → Editing group → Find & Select → Replace		Ctrl + H
7	Freeze panes	View tab → Window group → Freeze Panes		
7	Unfreeze panes	View tab → Window group → Unfreeze Panes		
8	Create Excel tables	Home tab → Styles group → Format as Table		
8	Filter Excel tables	Click the column filter arrow		
8	Sort Excel tables	Column filter arrow		
9	Search Excel tables	Column filter arrow → Search criteria		
9	Insert Total rows	Design tab → Table Style Options group → Total Row		
10	Convert Excel tables to ranges	Design tab → Tools group → Convert to Range		
10	Repeat rows at the top of each printed page	Page Layout tab → Page Setup group → Print Titles		
10	Hide columns	Home tab → Cells group → Format → Hide & Unhide → Hide Columns		
10	Hide rows	Home tab → Cells group → Format → Hide & Unhide → Hide Rows		

Key Terms

Online Help Skills

1. Start **Excel 2013**, and then in the upper right corner of the start page, click the **Help** button ? .

2. In the **Excel Help** window **Search help** box, type use formulas in Excel tables and then press Enter .

3. In the search result list, click **Using formulas in Excel tables**, and then compare your screen with **Figure 1**.

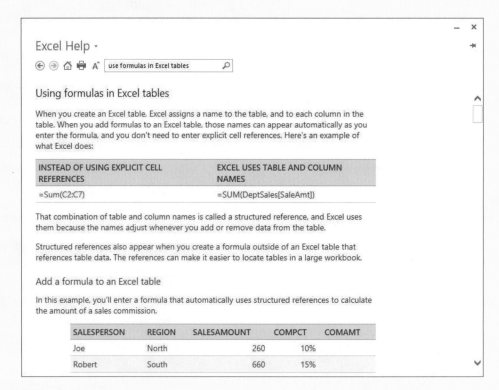

Figure 1

4. Read the article to answer the following questions: What are structured references and why would you use them?

Matching

Match each term in the second column with its correct definition in the first column by writing the letter of the term on the blank line in front of the correct definition.

___ **1.** An Excel function that returns the serial number of the current date.

___ **2.** The result of a function that will be updated each time the workbook is opened.

___ **3.** The type of function that tests for specific conditions and typically uses conditional tests to determine whether specified conditions are TRUE or FALSE.

___ **4.** Conditions that determine how conditional formatting is applied or what values are returned in logical functions.

___ **5.** A cell shading or font color that is applied to cells when a specified circumstance is met.

___ **6.** A chart inside a single cell used to show data trends.

___ **7.** A series of rows and columns that are formatted together.

___ **8.** A column in an Excel table that uses a single formula that adjusts for each row.

___ **9.** A command to display only the rows of a table that meet specified criteria.

___ **10.** A row in an Excel table that provides summary functions.

A Calculated column

B Conditional formatting

C Criteria

D Excel table

E Filter

F Logical function

G Sparkline

H TODAY function

I Total row

J Volatile

BizSkills Video

1. What are some of the positive behaviors of the second applicant?

2. If you were the interviewer, which applicant would you hire and why would you hire that person?

Multiple Choice

Choose the correct answer.

1. This function checks whether criteria are met and returns one value if TRUE and another value if FALSE.
   A. IF
   B. UNKNOWN
   C. NEW

2. These symbols are inserted into logical functions to determine whether a condition is true or false—(<) and (=), for example.
   A. Comparison operators
   B. Mathematical operators
   C. Logical symbols

3. Applying this format to text draws attention to the text on a worksheet.
   A. Angle
   B. Slope
   C. Slant

4. This word describes a format, such as cell shading, that is applied to cells when a specified condition is true.
   A. Filtered
   B. Conditional
   C. Calculated

5. This format provides a visual cue about the value of a cell relative to other cells.
   A. Cell style
   B. Quick style
   C. Data bar

6. This command ensures that header rows and columns remain visible when a worksheet is scrolled.
   A. Total Panes
   B. Excel Panes
   C. Freeze Panes

7. Data in an Excel table can be sorted in this way.
   A. Large to largest
   B. Smallest to largest
   C. Small to smallest

8. This command displays only the rows of a table that meet specified criteria.
   A. Filter
   B. Standard
   C. Chart

9. This row displays as the last row in an Excel table and provides summary statistics.
   A. Total
   B. Sorted
   C. Changeable

10. This word describes the result of a function that is updated each time a workbook is opened.
    A. Volatile
    B. Changeable
    C. Unstable

Topics for Discussion

1. Think about current news stories, including sports stories, and identify statistical data that is presented by the media. What are the advantages of using conditional formatting with this type of data?

2. Sorting and filtering are two of the most valuable ways to analyze data. If you were presented with an

Excel table containing names and addresses, what are some of the ways you might sort or filter the data? If you were presented with an Excel table of a day's cash transactions at your college's cafeteria, what are some ways you could sort, filter, and total?

Skills Review

To complete this project, you will need the following file:

- exl04_SRAuction

You will save your file as:

- Last_First_exl04_SRAuction

1. Start **Excel 2013**, and then open the file **exl04_SRAuction**. Save the workbook in your chapter folder as Last_First_exl04_SRAuction

2. On the **Materials List** sheet, click cell **B4**. On the **Formulas tab**, in the **Function Library group**, click the **Date & Time** button, and then click **TODAY**. In the message box, click **OK**. Click cell **B5**. In the **Function Library group**, click the **More Functions** button. Point to **Statistical**, and then click **COUNT**. In the **Value1** box, enter the range B9:B48, and then press Enter. Compare your screen with **Figure 1**.

3. Select the range **A4:B6**. Point to the right border of the selected range, and then move the data to the range **D4:E6**.

4. In cell **B4**, type Surplus and then merge and center the title in the range **B4:C6**. On the **Home tab**, in the **Alignment group**, click the **Middle Align** button. Click the **Orientation** button, and then click **Angle Counterclockwise**. Select the range **B4:E6**. In the **Font group**, click the **Border arrow**, and then click **Outside Borders**.

5. Click cell **A1**. In the **Editing group**, click the **Find & Select** button, and then click **Replace**. In the **Find what** box, type Sedan In the **Replace with** box, type Car and then click **Replace All**. Click **OK**, and then **Close** the dialog box.

6. Click cell **G9**. On the **Formulas tab**, in the **Function Library group**, click **Logical**, and then click **IF**. In the **Logical_test** box, type E9="Yes" In the **Value_if_true** box, type B9*F9 In the **Value_if_false** box, type 0 and then click **OK**. AutoFill the function down through **G48**, and then compare your screen with **Figure 2**.

7. Click cell **A9**. On the **View tab**, in the **Window group**, click the **Freeze Panes** button, and then click **Freeze Panes**.

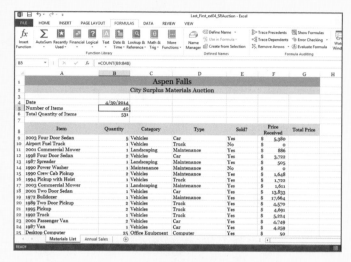

Figure 1

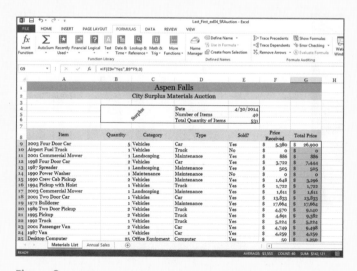

Figure 2

- Continue to the next page to complete this Skills Review

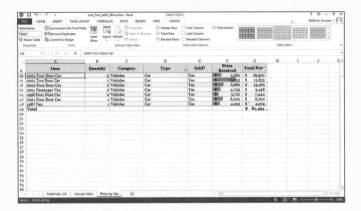

Figure 3

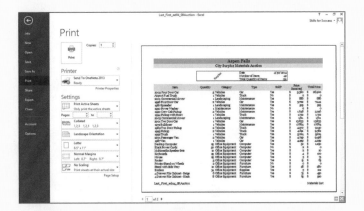

Figure 4

8. Right-click the **Materials List** worksheet tab, and then click **Move or Copy**. In the **Move or Copy** dialog box, click **(move to end)**, select the **Create a copy** check box, and then click **OK**. Rename the new worksheet tab as Price by Car

9. On the **Price by Car** sheet, in the **Window group**, click the **Freeze Panes** button, and then click **Unfreeze Panes**. On the **Home tab**, in the **Styles group**, click the **Format as Table** button, and then click **Table Style Light 17**. In the **Format As Table** dialog box, verify that the **My table has headers** check box is selected, and then click **OK**.

10. Click the **Type filter arrow**, and then clear the **(Select All)** check box. Select the **Car** check box, and then click **OK**. Click the **Total Price filter arrow**, and then click **Sort Largest to Smallest**. On the **Design tab**, in the **Table Style Options group**, select the **Total Row** check box.

11. Select the range **F9:F48**. Click the **Quick Analysis Lens** button, and then click **Data Bars**. Click cell **A9**, and then compare your screen with **Figure 3**.

12. Create a copy of the **Price by Car** sheet, move to the end, and then rename the new worksheet tab Pickups On the **Data tab**, in the **Sort & Filter group**, click the **Clear** button. Click the **Item filter arrow**. In the **Search** box, type Pickup and then click **OK**.

13. On the **Annual Sales** worksheet, select the range **B4:F9**. Click the **Quick Analysis Lens** button, click **Sparklines**, and then click the **Column** button.

14. Right-click the worksheet tab, and then click **Select All Sheets**. On the **Page Layout tab**, in the **Page Setup group**, click the **Orientation** button, and then click **Landscape**. In the **Scale to Fit group**, change the **Width** to **1 page**. Click the **Insert tab**, and add the file name in the left footer and the sheet name in the right footer. Return to **Normal** view, and then ungroup the worksheets.

15. Click the **Materials List** worksheet tab. On the **Page Layout tab**, in the **Page Setup group**, click the **Print Titles** button. In the **Page Setup** dialog box, click in the **Rows to repeat at top** box, click row **8**, and then click **OK**.

16. **Save** the workbook. Click the **File tab**, and then click the **Print tab**. Compare your workbook with **Figure 4**. Submit the workbook as directed by your instructor.

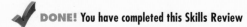

DONE! You have completed this Skills Review

Skills Assessment 1  MyITLab® Grader

To complete this project, you will need the following file:

- exl04_SA1Recycling

You will save your workbook as:

- Last_First_exl04_SA1Recycling

---

1. Start **Excel 2013**, and open the file **exl04_SA1Recycling**. Save the file in your chapter folder as Last_First_exl04_SA1Recycling

2. In **E3**, insert the **NOW** function. Select **A5:G5**, and apply a **Bottom Border**.

3. In **F6:F27**, insert **Line Sparklines** using the data in **columns B:E**. Show the **Low Point**.

4. In **G6**, insert the **IF** function. For the logical test, check whether the **FY 2014** result is greater than the **FY 2013** value in the same row. If the logical test is TRUE, Yes should display, and if it is FALSE, Needs Work should display. **Center** the results, and then AutoFill **G6** down through **G27**.

5. Select **G6:G27**. Apply a **Text Contains** conditional format that will display any cells that contain *Needs Work* formatted with **Light Red Fill**.

6. Create a copy of the sheet, and move the copy to the end of the workbook. Rename the new worksheet tab Improvements

7. On the **Improvements** sheet, format **A5:G27** as an Excel table, using the **Table Style Light 16**. Filter **column G** to display only the rows that improved from the previous year.

8. Display the **Total** row, and then display the four FY sums. In **G28**, select **None**.

9. Sort the **FY 2014** column from the smallest to the largest value.

10. Hide **column B**.

11. Group the worksheets. Change the page orientation to **Landscape**. Add the file name in the left footer and the sheet name in the right footer. Return to **Normal** view, and ungroup the sheets.

12. On the **Recycling** sheet, change the Page Setup to repeat the titles in **row 5**. On the **Improvements** sheet, change the **Height** scale to fit on one page.

13. **Save** the file. Click the **File tab**, click **Print**, and then compare your workbook with **Figure 1**. Submit the file as directed by your instructor.

 DONE! You have completed Skills Assessment 1

Recycling Volumes
Aspen Falls (in tons)

11/25/2012 16:32

Type	FY 2011	FY 2012	FY 2013	FY 2014	Trend	Improved from previous year?
Glass	$ 10,820	$ 8,857	$ 10,928	$ 11,036		Yes
Tin Cans	$ 825	$ 650	$ 833	$ 842		Yes
White goods	$ 11,010	$ 12,250	$ 11,120	$ 11,230		Yes
Other ferrous	$ 61,150	$ 63,000	$ 61,762	$ 62,373		Yes
Aluminum cans	$ 1,150	$ 1,320	$ 1,262	$ 1,173		Needs Work
Non-ferrous	$ 13,160	$ 13,270	$ 13,292	$ 13,423		Yes
High Grade Paper	$ 1,830	$ 2,490	$ 1,848	$ 1,867		Yes
Newsprint	$ 14,790	$ 13,370	$ 14,938	$ 15,086		Yes
Cardboard	$ 19,640	$ 16,350	$ 21,836	$ 20,033		Needs Work
Other paper	$ 4,340	$ 5,900	$ 4,383	$ 4,427		Yes
PETE	$ 703	$ 960	$ 710	$ 717		Yes
HDPE	$ 417	$ 710	$ 421	$ 425		Yes
Other plastics	$ 588	$ 920	$ 594	$ 600		Yes
Yard waste	$ 57,200	$ 55,829	$ 59,772	$ 58,344		Needs Work
Wood waste	$ 10,630	$ 11,825	$ 11,736	$ 10,843		Needs Work
Batteries	$ 2,900	$ 3,030	$ 2,929	$ 2,958		Yes
Oil	$ 8,840	$ 6,360	$ 8,928	$ 9,017		Yes

Recycling Volumes
Aspen Falls (in tons)

11/25/2012 16:32

Type	FY 2012	FY 2013	FY 2014	Trend	Improved from previous year?
Gypsum	$ 180	$ 227	$ 230		Yes
HDPE	$ 710	$ 421	$ 425		Yes
Other plastics	$ 920	$ 594	$ 600		Yes
PETE	$ 960	$ 710	$ 717		Yes
Tin Cans	$ 650	$ 833	$ 842		Yes
Tires	$ 806	$ 1,020	$ 1,030		Yes
High Grade Paper	$ 2,490	$ 1,848	$ 1,867		Yes
Electronics	$ 1,050	$ 1,869	$ 1,887		Yes
Other	$ 2,500	$ 2,010	$ 2,030		Yes
Batteries	$ 3,030	$ 2,929	$ 2,958		Yes
Other paper	$ 5,900	$ 4,383	$ 4,427		Yes
Textiles	$ 6,208	$ 6,474	$ 6,538		Yes
Oil	$ 6,360	$ 8,928	$ 9,017		Yes
Glass	$ 8,857	$ 10,928	$ 11,036		Yes
White goods	$ 12,250	$ 11,120	$ 11,230		Yes
Non-ferrous	$ 13,270	$ 13,292	$ 13,423		Yes
Newsprint	$ 13,370	$ 14,938	$ 15,086		Yes
Other ferrous	$ 63,000	$ 61,762	$ 62,373		Yes
Total	142,511	144,287	145,715		

Figure 1

Skills Assessment 2

To complete this project, you will need the following file:

- exl04_SA2Equipment

You will save your workbook as:

- Last_First_exl04_SA2Equipment

Quantity in Stock	Item	Cost Each	Type	Category	Stock Level	Total Cost
11	Radio Chest Harness	$35	Safety	Safety Equipment	Level OK	$ 385
87	Rope Gloves	$32	Gloves	Outerwear	Level OK	$ 2,784
28	Safety Harness	$199	Safety	Safety Equipment	Level OK	$ 5,572
29	Chest Harness	$99	Safety	Safety Equipment	Level OK	$ 2,871
35	EMS Jacket	$399	Coat	Outerwear	Level OK	$ 13,965
47	EMS Pants	$289	Pants	Outerwear	Level OK	$ 13,583
89	Breakaway Vest	$29	Vest	Outerwear	Level OK	$ 2,581
15	Mesh Vest	$17	Vest	Outerwear	Level OK	$ 255
25	Mesh Traffic Vest	$29	Vest	Outerwear	Level OK	$ 725
89	Reflective Nylon Vest	$11	Vest	Outerwear	Level OK	$ 979
16	Handheld Remote Siren	$289	Siren	Traffic	Level OK	$ 4,624
19	Siren	$189	Siren	Traffic	Level OK	$ 3,591
27	Traffic Baton	$19	Baton	Traffic	Level OK	$ 513
37	Flare Beacon Kit	$305	Light	Traffic	Level OK	$ 11,285
90	Flares with Stands	$99	Light	Traffic	Level OK	$ 8,910
26	Traffic Flashlight	$18	Light	Traffic	Level OK	$ 468
56	Night Barrier Tape	$15	Tape	Traffic	Level OK	$ 840
17	Water Rescue Kit	$119	Safety	Water Rescue	Level OK	$ 2,023
38	Water Rescue Vest	$99	Safety	Water Rescue	Level OK	$ 3,762
4	Water Tether System	$59	Safety	Water Rescue	Order	$ 236
18	Wildfire Helmet	$59	Helmet	Outerwear	Level OK	$ 1,062
17	Full-Brim Helmet	$59	Helmet	Outerwear	Level OK	$ 1,003
58	Firefighting Goggles	$49	Helmet	Safety Equipment	Level OK	$ 2,842
31	Water Throw Bag	$59	Safety	Water Rescue	Level OK	$ 1,829
32	Dry Bag	$18	Safety	Water Rescue	Level OK	$ 576

1. Start **Excel 2013**, and open the file **exl04_SA2Equipment**. Save the workbook in your chapter folder as Last_First_exl04_SA2Equipment Insert the file name in the worksheet's left footer and the sheet name in the right footer. Return to **Normal** view.

2. In cell **A2**, insert the **TODAY** function.

3. Select the range **A4:G4**, and then apply **Outside Borders**.

4. In cell **F5**, insert the **IF** function. For the logical test, check whether the **Quantity in Stock** is less than **10**. If the logical test is TRUE, Order should display. If the logical test is FALSE, Level OK should display.

5. AutoFill the function in cell **F5** down through cell **F63**.

6. Select the range **F5:F63**, apply a **Text Contains** conditional format that will display any cells that indicate *Order* formatted with **Red Text**.

7. Find all occurrences of Removal and replace with Extrication

8. Format the range **A4:G63** as an Excel table, using the **Table Style Medium 10** table style.

9. Change the page orientation to **Landscape**, and then set the titles in **row 4** to repeat on each printed page.

10. Create a copy of the worksheet, and move the copied sheet to the end of the workbook. Rename the new worksheet tab Safety On the **Safety** worksheet, **Sort** the table in alphabetical order by **Category**. **Filter** the Excel table to display the **Safety** type.

11. Display the **Total** row, and then in cell **B64**, display the count for column B.

				Aspen Falls		
				11/24/2012		
Quantity in Stock	Item		Type	Category	Stock Level	Total Cost
9	Gas Mask		Safety	Safety Equipment	Order	$ 2,331
9	Gas Mask Pouch		Safety	Safety Equipment	Order	$ 315
13	Respirator		Safety	Safety Equipment	Level OK	$ 4,797
45	Disaster Safe Bag		Safety	Safety Equipment	Level OK	$ 585
57	Disaster Kit		Safety	Safety Equipment	Level OK	$ 5,643
11	Radio Chest Harness		Safety	Safety Equipment	Level OK	$ 385
28	Safety Harness		Safety	Safety Equipment	Level OK	$ 5,572
29	Chest Harness		Safety	Safety Equipment	Level OK	$ 2,871
17	Water Rescue Kit		Safety	Water Rescue	Level OK	$ 2,023
38	Water Rescue Vest		Safety	Water Rescue	Level OK	$ 3,762
4	Water Tether System		Safety	Water Rescue	Order	$ 236
31	Water Throw Bag		Safety	Water Rescue	Level OK	$ 1,829
32	Dry Bag		Safety	Water Rescue	Level OK	$ 576
Total		13				$ 30,925

Figure 1

12. Hide **column D**.

13. **Save** your workbook, and then compare your workbook with Figure 1. Submit the workbook as directed by your instructor.

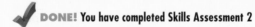 **DONE!** You have completed Skills Assessment 2

Visual Skills Check

To complete this project, you will need the following file:

- exl04_VSArt

You will save your workbook as:

- Last_First_exl04_VSArt

Start **Excel 2013**, and then open the file **exl04_ VSArt**. Save the workbook in your chapter folder as Last_First_exl04_VSArt Add the file name in the worksheet's left footer. Insert the current date using a date function. Your date may be different than shown. In **column F**, use a logical function indicating *Insure* for art with a value greater than $50,000. The conditional formatting in the **Insurance** column is **Light Red Fill with Dark Red Text**. Display Data Bars in **column C**. The Excel table is formatted using the **Table Style Light 14** table style. Filter and sort the Excel table, and display the functions on the **Total** row as shown in **Figure 1**. **Save** the workbook, and then submit the workbook as directed by your instructor.

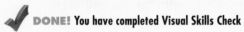 **DONE! You have completed Visual Skills Check**

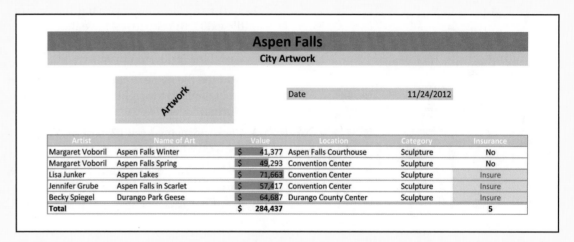

Figure 1

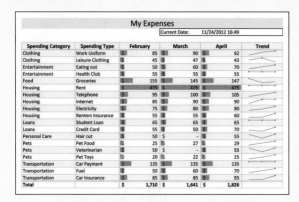

Figure 1

My Skills

To complete this project, you will need the following file:

- exl04_MYExpenses

You will save your workbook as:

- Last_First_exl04_MYExpenses

1. Start **Excel 2013**, and open the file **exl04_MYExpenses**. Save the workbook in your chapter folder as Last_First_exl04_MYExpenses

2. Add the file name in the left footer and the sheet name in the right footer. Return to **Normal** view.

3. Click the merged cell **E2**, and then insert the **NOW** function.

4. Select the range **D2:F2**, and then apply the **Outside Borders**.

5. Select the range **C5:E23**, and then insert **Data Bars**.

6. In the range **F5:F23**, insert **Line Sparklines** using the data in the **columns C:E**. On the sparklines, show the **High Point**.

7. Format the range **A4:F23** as an Excel table, using **Table Style Light 19**. Sort the

Spending Category column to display in alphabetical order.

8. Display the **Total** row, display the sums for **C24:E24**, and in the **Trend** column, select **None**.

9. Change the **Width** scale to fit on one page.

10. Create a copy of the worksheet, and move the copied sheet to the end of the workbook. Rename the new worksheet tab High Expenses

11. On the **High Expenses** worksheet, sort the **April** column from largest to smallest. Hide **rows 19:23**.

12. **Save** your workbook. Click the **File tab**, click **Print**, and then compare your workbook with **Figure 1**. Submit the workbook as directed by your instructor.

 DONE! You have completed My Skills

Skills Challenge 1

To complete this project, you will need the following file:

- exl04_SC1Classes

You will save your workbook as:

- Last_First_exl04_SC1Classes

Start **Excel 2013**, and then open the file **exl04_SC1Classes**. Save the workbook in your chapter folder as Last_First_exl04_SC1Classes Carter Horikoshi, the Art Center Supervisor, has started a workbook to track the art classes offered at different locations. He is concerned about large class sizes and wonders if he should hire an assistant for the instructors. Using the skills you practiced in this chapter, on the Classes worksheet, correct the date function. The panes no longer need to be frozen. In the Excel table, display all rows. In column D, the Data Bars should be applied to all cells. In column E, the logical function should calculate whether a class needs a Class Assistant—a class needs a Class Assistant if the class size is greater than 30. The Excel table should be filtered to show the Computer Basics, Drawing, Painting, and Woodworking classes, and sorted from the largest to smallest class size. The titles in row 6 should repeat on each page. On the Enrollment sheet, the sparklines should be formatted to emphasize the high and low values in each row. The Enrollment sheet should print on one page. On both worksheets, add the file name in the left footer and the sheet name in the right footer. Save your workbook, and then submit the workbook as directed by your instructor.

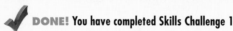 **DONE! You have completed Skills Challenge 1**

Skills Challenge 2

To complete this project, you will need the following file:

- exl04_SC2Water

You will save your workbook as:

- Last_First_exl04_SC2Water

Start **Excel 2013**, and then open the file **exl04_SC2Water**, and save the workbook in your chapter folder as Last_First_exl04_SC2Water Diane Payne, the Public Works Director, is responsible for testing the city water supply. She has started a workbook to track the water test results. Using the skills you practiced in this chapter, insert functions in the Water worksheet that provide the current date and count the number of samples. Insert a logical function to determine if the High Test amount is greater than the Farm Water Limit for each quarter. Display Yes if TRUE and No if FALSE. Format the data as an Excel table using the table style of your choice, and then filter the Excel table to display violations. On the Test Results worksheet, insert sparklines to display trends. On both worksheets, add the file name in the left footer and the sheet name in the right footer. Each worksheet should print on one page. Save your workbook, and then submit the workbook as directed by your instructor.

 **DONE! You have completed Skills Challenge 2**

CAPSTONE PROJECT

To complete this workbook, you will need the following file:
exl_CAPBudget

You will save your workbook as:
Last_First_exl_CAPBudget

1. Start **Excel 2013**, and open the student data file **exl_CAPBudget**. **Save** the workbook in your chapter folder as Last_First_exl_CAPBudget

2. Group the worksheets. Widen **columns B:E** to *13.00*. Change the height of **row 4** to *15.00*. In cell **E5**, insert a function to total the row, and then AutoFill **E5** down through **E14**. In the range **E6:E14**, apply the **Comma [0]** cell style. In the range **B15:E15**, insert a function to total the columns, and then apply the **Total** cell style.

3. With the worksheets still grouped, in cell **B16**, insert a function to calculate the average *North* budget item. In cell **B17**, insert a function to calculate the highest *North* budget item.

4. In cell **B18**, insert a function to calculate the lowest *North* budget item.

5. AutoFill the range **B16:B18** to the right through **column D**, and then compare your screen with **Figure 1**.

6. Ungroup the worksheets. Insert a new worksheet. Rename the new worksheet tab Summary and apply the worksheet tab color **Orange**, **Accent 2**. Move the new worksheet tab to make it the first worksheet in the workbook.

7. Copy the range **A1:E4** from any of the quarter worksheets, and then on the **Summary** worksheet, paste the range into **A1:E4** using the **Keep Source Column Widths** paste option.

8. On the **Summary** worksheet, change the subtitle of cell **A2** to Annual Budget and then change the label in cell **A4** to Quarter

9. On the **Summary** worksheet, in cell **A5** type 1st Quarter and then AutoFill **A5** down through cell **A8**. In cell **A9**, type Annual Total

10. On the **Summary** worksheet, enter a formula in cell **B5** setting the cell equal to cell **B15** in the **First Quarter** worksheet. **Save** the workbook, and then compare your screen with **Figure 2**.

■ Continue to the next page to complete the skill

Figure 1

Figure 2

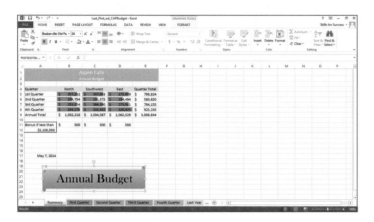

Figure 3

11. On the **Summary** worksheet, enter a formula for the *North* total from the **Second Quarter**, the **Third Quarter**, and the **Fourth Quarter** worksheets in the range **B6:B8**. AutoFill the range **B5:B8** to the right through **column E**.

12. On the **Summary** worksheet, in the range **B9:E9**, insert a function to calculate the column totals.

13. In cell **A11**, type Bonus if less than and then in cell **A12** type $1,100,000 Select the range **A11:A12**, and then apply the **Outside Borders**.

14. In cell **B11**, insert the **IF** function. For the logical test, check whether the *North* total is less than the value in cell **A12**. If the logical test is true, 500 should display, and if the logical test is false, 50 should display. In the function, use an absolute cell reference when referring to cell **A12**.

15. In cell **B11**, apply the **Currency [0]** cell style, and then AutoFill cell **B11** to the right through cell **D11**.

16. Select the range **B5:D8**, insert the default **Data Bars** conditional format.

17. In cell **A17**, insert the **TODAY** function. Format the date with the **March 14, 2012**, date format.

18. Unhide the **Last Year** worksheet. **Copy** the *Annual Budget* shape and then paste the shape in the **Summary** worksheet. Move the shape to approximately the range **A19:E24**, and then compare your screen with Figure 3.

19. **Hide** the **Last Year** worksheet.

20. Group the worksheets, and then press [Ctrl] + [Home]. Find and replace the four occurrences of Qtr with Quarter

21. With the worksheets still grouped, check and correct any spelling errors. Add the file name to the left footer and the sheet name to the right footer. Return to **Normal view**, and then make cell **A1** the active cell. Ungroup the worksheets.

22. Make the **Summary** worksheet the active worksheet. Insert a **3-D Pie** chart based on the nonadjacent ranges **A4:A8** and **E4:E8**. Move the pie chart to a chart sheet with the sheet name Budget Chart

23. For the pie chart, apply **Layout 1**, and then apply the **Chart Style 8**. Change the chart title to Aspen Falls Annual Budget and then for the data labels, change the font size to **12**. Add the file name in the chart sheet's left footer and the sheet name in the right footer. Compare your screen with Figure 4.

24. **Save**, and then **Close** the workbook. Submit the project as directed by your instructor.

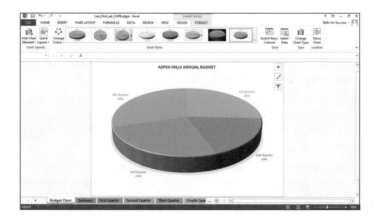

Figure 4

 DONE! You have completed the Excel Capstone Project

Copy Word Tables into Excel Worksheets

▶ Each Microsoft Office application has different strengths. For example, you can use Word to convert text into tables, and Excel to insert functions and formulas into table cells.

▶ Exporting data from one application to another enables you to use the strengths of each application without having to retype the data.

▶ To move data from Word to Excel, you must organize the information into rows and columns. One way to format data is to create a table in Word.

© Vitaly Krivosheev

Aspen Falls City Hall

In this Integrated Project, you will create documents for the Aspen Falls Community Services Office, which has been working on various sustainability programs for the citizens of Aspen Falls, California. As part of their sustainability program, Aspen Falls is working with the local community college to increase the number of students riding city buses instead of driving their cars to campus. Students will be given a sticker to affix to their student ID, and then by showing this ID to a bus driver, the students can ride a city bus for free. You will assist Jack Ruiz, Community Services Director, to complete a letter to the college president stating more students will be permitted to participate in the free bus ride program.

In Word, you can use tabs to organize text into rows and columns. The tabbed text can be converted into a table that can be formatted with table styles. A Word table can be copied and pasted into other applications such as Excel.

You will convert tabbed Word text into a table, add data to the table, and then format the table. You will then copy the table from the Word document and paste it into an Excel worksheet.

Time to complete this project – 30 to 60 minutes

30-60 min.

Student data files needed for this project:

exl_IP03Riders (Word)
exl_IP03Pass (Excel)

You will save your files as:

Last_First_exl_IP03Riders
(Word)

Last_First_exl_IP03Pass
(Excel)

Outcome

Using the skills in this project, you will be able to work with Office documents like this:

SKILLS (MyITLab®)

At the end of this project you will be able to:

▶ Convert text to a table
▶ Copy a Word table into an Excel workbook
▶ Match destination formatting when pasting

ASPEN FALLS COMMUNITY SERVICES

275 Elm Street, Room 122C
Aspen Falls, CA 93463

June 17, 2014

Dr. Dan Cheek
President
Aspen Falls Community College
817 Wisteria Lane
Aspen Falls, CA 93468

Dear Dr. Cheek:

We have been pleased with the involvement of the Aspen Falls Commun
sustainability programs. As you know, the city has been promoting "Ride
provides each student a sticker to affix to a student ID. By showing the st
student can ride a city bus for free. Student participation in this program

We still have funds available for this program and are pleased to inform
who signed up after the deadline may now pick up a free city bus ride sti

First Name	Last Name
Carmelina	Goforth
Florine	Dupont
Valentina	Blunt
Erik	Zook
Scotty	Whittle
Kareen	Whitehurst
First	Last

Thank you again for encouraging your students to take part in this sustai

Sincerely,

Jake Ruiz
Community Services Director

Last_First_exl_IP03Riders

Aspen Falls
Student Bus Passes

First Name	Last Name	Bus Pass Issued
Dane	Borders	Yes
Junko	Bachman	Yes
Donovan	Tisdale	Yes
Hugh	Tavares	Yes
Brandi	Schmid	Yes
Viviana	Pickard	Yes
Willy	Jasper	Yes
Denita	Gulley	Yes
Riley	Fonseca	Yes
Genevie	Condon	Yes
Sulema	Clancy	Yes
Errol	Batista	Yes
Dodie	Wicks	Yes
Delmer	New	Yes
Zoe	Martell	Yes
Misha	Lo	Yes
Yuki	Littleton	Yes
Cedrick	Ison	Yes
Lady	Haag	Yes
Joy	Folsom	Yes
China	Brumfield	Yes
Terence	Broyles	Yes
Gregg	Brito	Yes
Lane	Mireles	Yes
Glen	McDonnell	Yes
Valeria	LeClair	Yes
Lupe	Hamblin	Yes
Jonelle	Gough	Yes
Abel	Fanning	Yes
Freddie	Binder	Yes
Rueben	Winfield	Yes
Kathrine	Whitworth	Yes
Carmelina	Goforth	No
Florine	Dupont	No
Valentina	Blunt	No
Erik	Zook	No
Scotty	Whittle	No
Kareen	Whitehurst	No
First	Last	No

1. Start **Excel 2013**, and then open the student data file **exl_IP03Pass**. Save 💾 the workbook in your chapter folder as Last_First_exl_IP03Pass

2. Add the file name in the worksheet's left footer, and then return to **Normal view**. Minimize ⎯ the Excel window.

3. Start **Word 2013**, and then open the student data file **exl_IP03Riders**. Save 💾 the file in your chapter folder as Last_First_exl_IP03Riders Add the file name to the footer, and then close the footer.

4. At the bottom of the Word document, beginning with the text *First Name,* select the seven lines of tabbed text. Do not select the blank line above or below the tabbed text.

5. On the **Insert tab**, in the **Tables group**, click the **Table** button, and then click **Convert Text to Table**. Compare your screen with Figure 1.

6. In the **Convert Text to Table** dialog box, click **OK**.

7. On the **Design tab**, in the **Table Styles group**, click the **More** button ⎽. In the **Table Style gallery**, scroll down and then under **List Tables**, point at the fourth style—**List Table 1 Light - Accent** 3. Compare your screen with Figure 2, and then click the fourth style.

8. In the **Table Style Options group**, clear the **First Column** check box.

9. On the **Layout tab**, in the **Cell Size group**, click the **AutoFit** button, and then click **AutoFit Contents**.

■ **Continue to the next page to complete the skill**

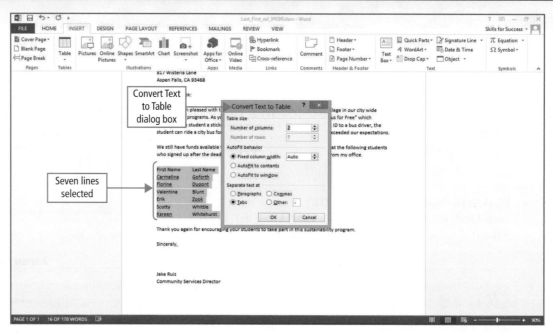

Figure 1

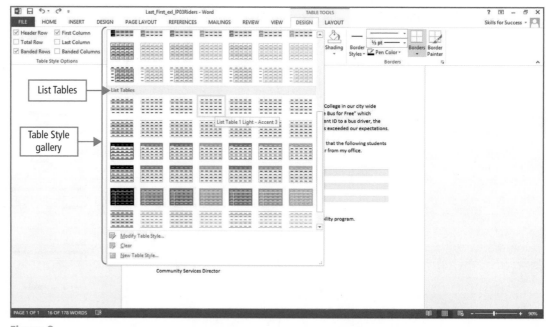

Figure 2

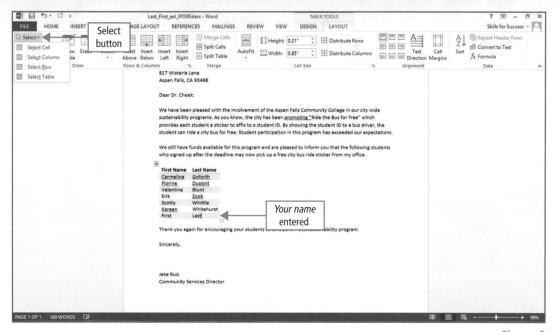

Figure 3

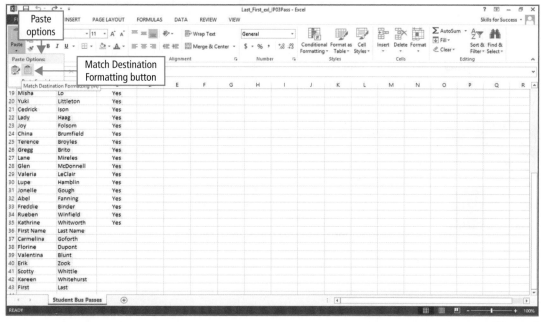
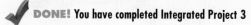

Figure 4

10. In the last table row, click in the cell with the text *Whitehurst*, and then press `Tab` to insert a new row. Type your first name, press `Tab`, and then type your last name. **Save** 🖫 the Word document.

11. On the **Layout tab**, in the **Table group**, click the **Select** button, and then compare your screen with Figure 3.

12. In the list, click **Select Table**. On the **Home tab**, in the **Clipboard group**, click the **Copy** button 📋.

13. On the taskbar, click the **Excel** button 📊 to make the Excel window active.

14. Scroll down, and then click cell **A36**. On the **Home tab**, in the **Clipboard group**, click the **Paste arrow**. Under **Paste Options**, point to the second button 📋—**Match Destination Formatting**. Compare your screen with Figure 4.

15. Click the **Match Destination Formatting** button 📋.

16. Click cell **A36**. In the **Cells group**, click the **Delete arrow**, and then click **Delete Sheet Rows** to delete the header row from the copied table.

17. Click cell **C36**, type No and then on the formula bar, click **Enter** ✓. AutoFill cell **C36** down through **C42**.

18. **Save** 🖫 the Excel workbook, and then **Close** ✖ the workbook. **Save** 🖫 the Word document, and then **Close** ✖ the document. Submit the project as directed by your instructor.

✔ **DONE! You have completed Integrated Project 3**

Link Data from Excel

▶ You can copy a chart from an Excel workbook and paste it into a Word document.

▶ When you copy data from Excel, you can paste it into a Word document as a table, or you can create a link between Excel and Word so that any changes made in an Excel document will also be reflected in a linked Word table.

▶ When you update data in an Excel file that has been linked to a Word document, the information will be updated in the Word document.

▶ Excel charts or data that have been pasted into a Word document can be formatted in the Word document.

© Africa Studio

Aspen Falls City Hall

In this Integrated Project, you will complete a memo for the Library Director, Douglas Hopkins. Mr. Hopkins has been working with the Friends of the Aspen Falls Public Library. The group operates a bookstore and donates the revenue to the public library. The group tracks their bookstore revenue in an Excel workbook and Mr. Hopkins plans to present the revenue information to the Board of Trustees. You will complete a memo to the Board of Trustees and include a chart and linked data from the Excel workbook in your memo.

Each Microsoft Office application has different strengths; for example, you can use Excel to create charts based on values in an Excel workbook. An Excel chart can be copied and then pasted into a Word document such as a memo or a report. You can link data from one file to another file, and when you update the data in the original file, the linked data will also be updated.

You will open an Excel workbook and a Word document, and you will paste a chart from the Excel worksheet into the Word document. You will also link data from the Excel worksheet to the Word document, and then update the link.

Introduction

Time to complete this
project – 30 to 45 minutes

Student data files needed for this project:

exl_IP04Report (Word)
exl_IP04BookSales (Excel)

You will save your files as:

Last_First_exl_IP04Report
(Word)

Last_First_exl_IP04BookSales
(Excel)

Outcome

Using the skills in this project, you will be able to
create documents that look like this:

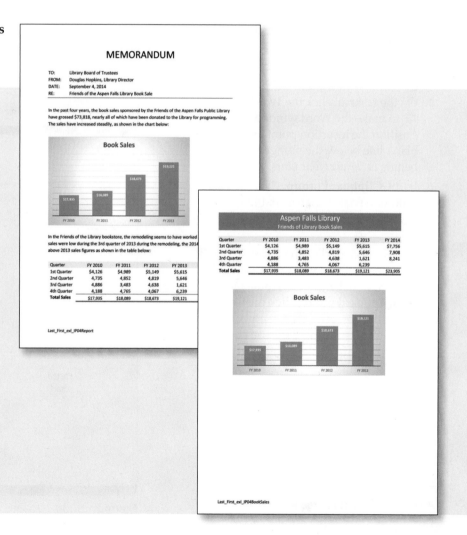

SKILLS MyITLab®

At the end of this project you will be able to:

► Copy Excel charts and paste them into Word documents
► Link Excel data to Word documents
► Link and keep the source formatting
► Update linked data

1. Start **Word 2013**, and then open the student data file **exl_IP04Report**. **Save** 🖫 the file in your chapter folder as Last_First_exl_IP04Report Add the file name to the footer, and then close the footer.

2. Start **Excel 2013**, and then open the student data file **exl_IP04BookSales**. **Save** 🖫 the workbook in your chapter folder as Last_First_exl_IP04BookSales Add the file name in the worksheet's left footer, and then return to **Normal view**.

3. In Excel, click the chart border to select the chart. Compare your screen with **Figure 1**.

4. On the **Home tab**, in the **Clipboard group**, click the **Copy** button 📋.

5. On the taskbar, click the **Word** button 📃 to make the Word window active. Position the insertion point in the first blank line below the paragraph that begins *In the past four years.*

6. In the **Clipboard group**, click the **Paste** button to paste the chart in the Word document. Compare your screen with **Figure 2**.

7. On the taskbar, click the **Excel** button 📊 to make the Excel window active. Select the range **A4:F9**. On the **Home tab**, in the **Clipboard group**, click the **Copy** button 📋.

▪ **Continue to the next page to complete the skill**

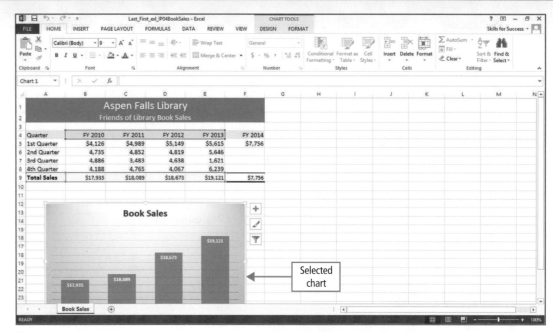

Figure 1

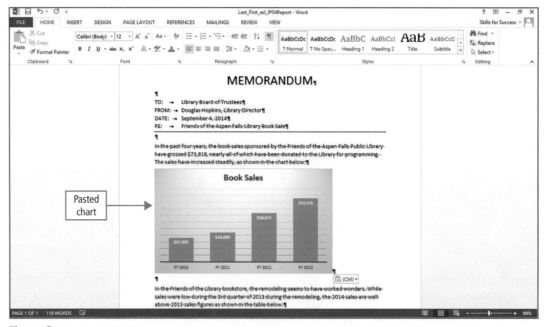

Figure 2

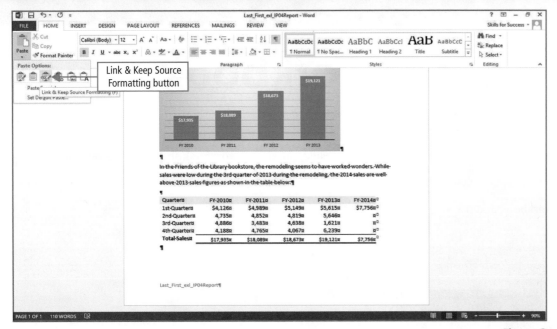

Figure 3

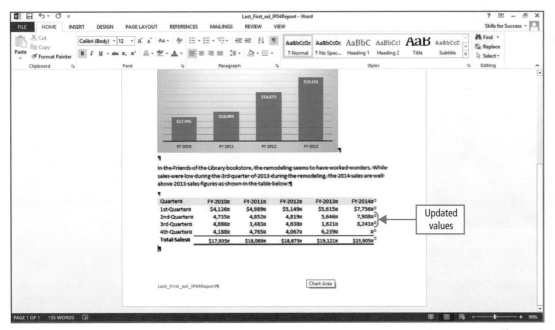

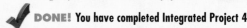

Figure 4

8. On the taskbar, click the **Word** button.

9. Position the insertion point in the blank line at the end of the document. On the **Home tab**, in the **Clipboard group**, click the **Paste arrow**, and then under **Paste Options**, point to the third button —**Link & Keep Source Formatting**. Compare your screen with **Figure 3**.

    A preview of the data displays at the insertion point.

10. Click the **Link & Keep Source Formatting** button.

11. On the taskbar, click the **Excel** button. Press [Esc] to remove the moving border.

12. In cell **F6** type 7908 and then press [Enter]. In cell **F7** type 8241 and then press [Enter].

13. **Save** the Excel file.

14. On the taskbar, click the **Word** button.

15. In the Word document, right-click the Excel table that you pasted previously, and then click **Update Link** to check for any changes in the linked Excel data. Compare your screen with **Figure 4**.

    In the Word document, the updated 2nd Quarter and 3rd Quarter values display, and the 2014 total is updated.

16. **Save** the Word document, and then **Close** [x] the document. **Close** the Excel workbook. Submit the project as directed by your instructor.

DONE! You have completed Integrated Project 4

Refer to Cells in Other Workbooks

▶ An ***external reference***—a reference to a cell in another workbook—is useful when keeping worksheets together in the same workbook is not practical.

▶ An external reference must include the name of the workbook and the name of the worksheet.

▶ After a link is created, the source workbook should not be renamed or moved to a different location.

© Gunnar3000

Aspen Falls City Hall

In this Integrated Project, you will assist Kim Leah, Parks and Recreation Director, to complete a list of contacts for the city parks and golf courses. The Course Managers at the Aspen Lakes Golf Course and at the Hamilton Golf Course each maintain an Excel workbook that contains information about the employees working at their golf courses. You will link the contact information from these two workbooks into a third workbook that contains the parks contact information.

If employees are in different locations, sometimes it isn't practical to keep data in the same workbook. Data can be linked from one workbook to another workbook using external references.

You will link data from two Excel workbooks to a third workbook. You will update the data in the original workbooks and verify that the data is updated in the linked workbook, and then you will apply conditional formatting.

Time to complete this
project – 30 to 60 minutes

Student data files needed for this project:

exl_IP05Golf1   exl_IP05Contacts
exl_IP05Golf2

You will save your files as:

Last_First_exl_IP05Golf1   Last_First_exl_IP05Contacts
Last_First_exl_IP05Golf2

Outcome

Using the skills in this project, you will be able to work with an Excel workbook like this:

SKILLS   MyITLab®

At the end of this project you will be able to:

▶ Link data from one Excel workbook to another
▶ Update linked data
▶ Insert conditional formatting

Aspen Falls Parks and Recreation				
Employee Contact Information				
First Name	**Last Name**	**Position**	**Phone**	**Location**
First	Last	Parks and Recreation Manager	(805) 555-1479	City Hall, Room 416
Amado	Pettinelli	Outdoor Recreation Supervisor	(805) 555-1417	City Hall, Room 440
Leah	Kim	Parks and Recreation Director	(805) 555-1410	City Hall, Room 412
Lorrine	Deely	Community Center Supervisor	(805) 555-1153	City Hall, Room 434
Booker	Berhe	Aquatics Supervisor	(805) 555-1350	City Hall, Room 432
Irving	Siravo	Capital Improvement Supervisor	(805) 555-1310	City Hall, Room 426
Keith	Hansen	Park Operations Manager	(805) 555-1112	City Hall, Room 414
Jacquetta	Ronald	Planning and Design Supervisor	(805) 555-1031	City Hall, Room 430
Neely	Ramsburg	Design and Development Manager	(805) 555-1403	City Hall, Room 420
Vic	Fowler	Aspen Lakes Course Manager	(805) 555-1010	Aspen Lakes Golf Course
Lee	Garrett	Golf Instructor	(805) 555-1787	Aspen Lakes Golf Course
Kyle	Burress	Golf Instructor	(805) 555-5851	Aspen Lakes Golf Course
Diego	Alvarez	Mechanic	(805) 555-7985	Aspen Lakes Golf Course
Ariana	Korpela	Landscaper	(805) 555-2775	Aspen Lakes Golf Course
Brooke	Whitlow	Bookkeeper	(805) 555-5595	Aspen Lakes Golf Course
Timothy	Dominik	Clubhouse Associate	(805) 555-2523	Aspen Lakes Golf Course
Jesse	Periera	Clubhouse Associate	(805) 555-6944	Aspen Lakes Golf Course
Chloe	Tauer	Maintenance Associate	(805) 555-3989	Aspen Lakes Golf Course
Rosaria	Cabiness	Food and Beverage	(805) 555-6814	Aspen Lakes Golf Course
Tracy	Lecroy	Hamilton Course Manager	(805) 555-1010	Hamilton Golf Course
Mandee	Covey	Golf Instructor	(805) 555-8675	Hamilton Golf Course
Ollie	Wizen	Golf Instructor	(805) 555-3593	Hamilton Golf Course
Dylan	Lee	Mechanic	(805) 555-9124	Hamilton Golf Course
Marissa	Madeiros	Landscaper	(805) 555-7781	Hamilton Golf Course
Sabrina	Mak	Bookkeeper	(805) 555-5221	Hamilton Golf Course
Chester	Schillinger	Clubhouse Associate	(805) 555-7279	Hamilton Golf Course
Byron	Hoese	Maintenance Manager	(805) 555-9737	Hamilton Golf Course

Last_First_exl_IP05Contacts

1. Start **Excel 2013**, and then open the student data file **exl_IP05Contacts**. **Save** 🖫 the workbook in your chapter folder as Last_First_exl_IP05Contacts

2. Click cell **A5**, type your first name, and then press ⌷Tab⌷. In cell **B5** type your last name, and then press ⌷Enter⌷. **Save** 🖫 the workbook, and then compare your screen with Figure 1.

3. **Open** the student data file **exl_IP05Golf1**. **Save** 🖫 the workbook in your chapter folder as Last_First_exl_IP05Golf1

4. Right-click the **Golf Lessons** worksheet tab, and then click **Select All Sheets**. Add the file name in the worksheet's left footer, and then return to **Normal view**. Right-click the worksheet tab, and then click **Ungroup Sheets**.

5. Click the **Aspen Lakes Contacts** worksheet tab, and then select the range **A4:E13**. On the **Home tab**, in the **Clipboard group**, click the **Copy** button 📋.

6. Make **Last_First_exl_IP05Contacts** the active workbook, and then click cell **A14**. On the **Home tab**, in the **Clipboard group**, click the **Paste arrow**. Under **Other Paste Options**, click the second button 📋—**Paste Link**. Click cell **A14**, and then compare your screen with Figure 2.

   The reference to the source workbook, worksheet, and cell displays in the formula bar.

7. Make **Last_First_exl_IP05Golf1** the active workbook. **Save** 🖫 the workbook and then **Close** ⌷ ✕ ⌷ the workbook.

■ **Continue to the next page to complete the skill**

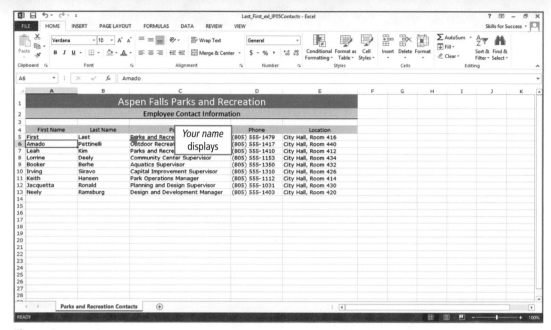

Figure 1

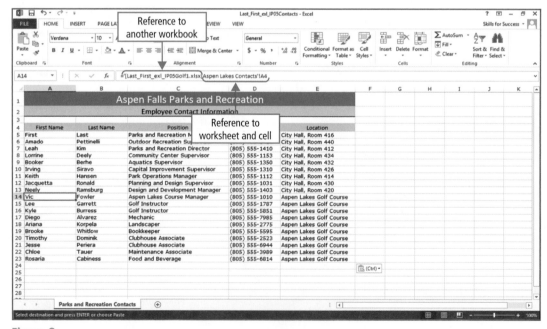

Figure 2

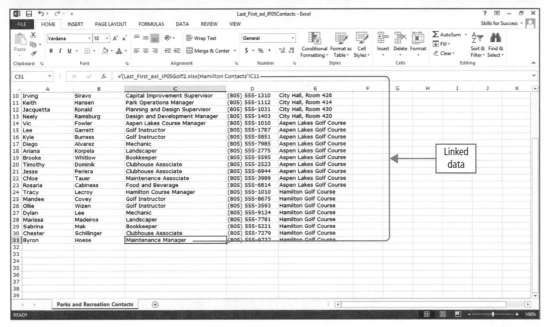

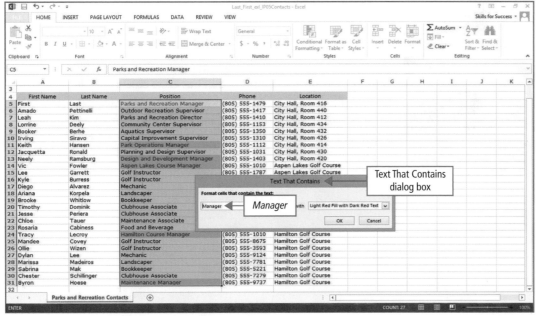

Figure 3

Figure 4

8. **Open** the student data file **exl_IP05Golf2**. **Save** 🖫 the workbook in your chapter folder as Last_First_exl_IP05Golf2

9. Using the techniques just practiced **Select All Sheets**, add the file name in the worksheet's left footer, return to **Normal view**, and then **Ungroup Sheets**.

10. Click the **Hamilton Contacts** worksheet tab, and then select the range **A4:E11**. On the **Home tab**, in the **Clipboard group**, click the **Copy** button 🖹.

11. Make **Last_First_exl_IP05Contacts** the active workbook, and then click cell **A24**. In the **Clipboard group**, click the **Paste arrow**. Under **Other Paste Options**, click the **Paste Link** button 🖹.

12. Make **Last_First_exl_IP05Golf2** the active workbook, and then click cell **C11**. Type Maintenance Manager and then press Enter. **Save** 🖫 the workbook.

13. Make **Last_First_exl_IP05Contacts** the active workbook. Click cell **C31**, and then compare your screen with **Figure 3**.

14. Select the range **C5:C31**. Click the **Quick Analysis Lens** button 🖳, and then click the **Text Contains** button. In the **Text That Contains** dialog box, in the first box replace the text with Manager Compare your screen with **Figure 4**, and then click **OK**.

16. **Save** 🖫 the Excel workbooks, and then **Close** ☒ the workbooks. Submit the project as directed by your instructor.

✔ **DONE! You have completed Integrated Project 5**

Create Workbooks Using Excel Web App

▶ **Excel Web App** is a cloud-based application used to complete basic spreadsheet formulas using a web browser.

▶ Excel Web App can be used to create or edit workbooks using a web browser instead of the Excel program—Excel 2013 does not need to be installed on your computer.

▶ When you create a document using Excel Web App, it is saved on your SkyDrive so that you can work with it from any computer connected to the Internet.

▶ You can use Excel Web App to insert a chart and perform basic chart formatting tasks.

▶ If you need a feature not available in Excel Web App, you can edit the workbook in Microsoft Excel and save it on your SkyDrive.

© Maxim_Kazmin

Aspen Falls City Hall

In this project, you will assist Taylor and Robert Price, energy consultants for the city of Aspen Falls. They have asked you to use Excel Web App to create a spreadsheet that shows the energy consumption of a city building.

Excel Web App is used to create or open Excel workbooks from any computer or device connected to the Internet. When needed, you can edit text, enter formulas, or insert charts. You can save these workbooks on your SkyDrive, and continue working with them later when you are at a computer that has Excel 2013 available.

In this project, you will use Excel Web App to create a new workbook. You will enter data and then apply formats and number styles. You will insert formulas, functions, and a chart. Finally, you will open the workbook in Excel 2013 to format the chart and check the spelling in the worksheet.

Time to complete this
project – 30 to 60 minutes

Student data file needed for this project:

New blank Excel Web App workbook

You will save your file as:

Last_First_exl_WAEnergy

SKILLS MyITLab®

At the end of this project you will be able to:

▶ Create new Excel workbooks from SkyDrive
▶ Enter data in Editing View
▶ Apply number styles
▶ Enter summary functions
▶ Enter formulas using absolute cell references
▶ Insert and format bar charts
▶ Edit workbooks created in Excel Web App in Excel 2013

Outcome

Using the skills in this project, you will be able to create and edit an Excel Web App workbook like this:

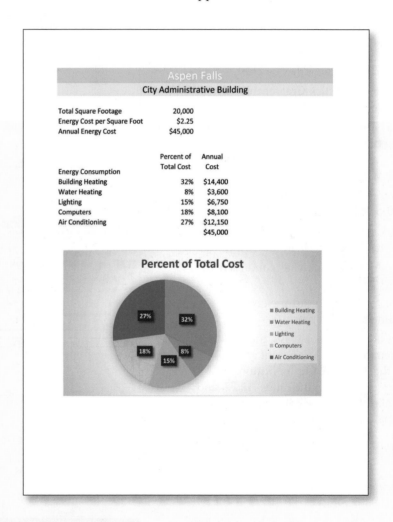

1. Start **Internet Explorer**, navigate to live.com and log on to your Microsoft account. If you do not have an account, follow the links and directions on the page to create one.

2. After logging in, navigate as needed to display the **SkyDrive** page.

   SkyDrive and Web App technologies are accessed through web pages that may change and the formatting and layout of some pages may often be different from the figures in this book. When this happens, you may need to adapt the steps to complete the actions they describe.

3. On the toolbar, click **Create**, and then click **Excel workbook**.

4. In the **New Microsoft Excel workbook** dialog box, name the file Last_First_exl_WAEnergy and then compare your screen with **Figure 1**.

5. Click the **Create** button to save the workbook and start Excel Web App.

   The Excel Web App displays four tabs in Editing View: File, Home, Insert, and View.

6. In cell **A1** type Aspen Falls and then press Enter.

7. In cell **A2** type City Administrative Building and then press Enter.

8. Select the range **A1:F1**, and then on the **Home tab**, in the **Alignment group**, click the **Merge & Center** button. Select the range **A2:F2**, and then click the **Merge & Center** button. Compare your screen with **Figure 2**.

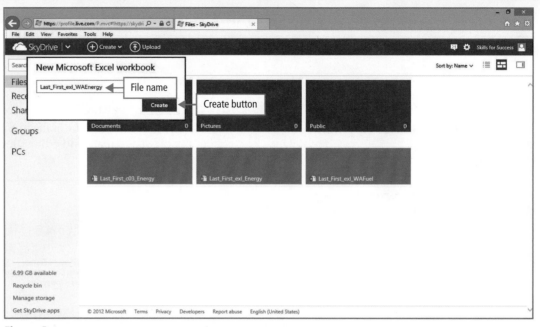

Figure 1

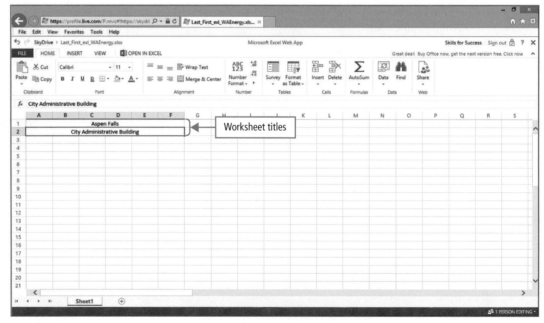

Figure 2

 **Continue to the next page to complete the skill**

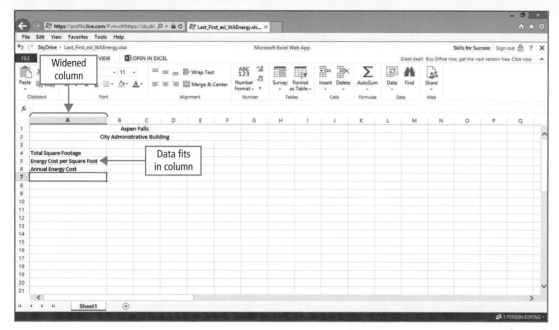

Figure 3

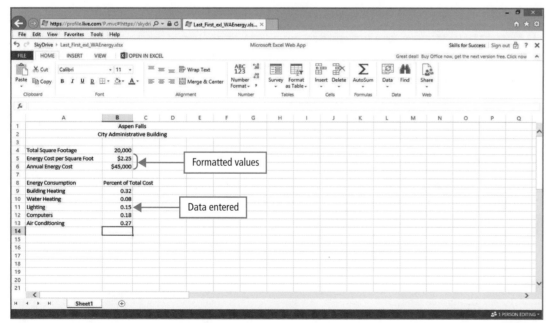

Figure 4

9. In cell **A4** type Total Square Footage and then press Enter.

10. In cell **A5** type Energy Cost per Square Foot and then press Enter.

11. In cell **A6** type Annual Energy Cost and then press Enter.

12. In the column heading area, point to the right boundary of **column A** to display the ➕ pointer. Double-click between **columns A** and **B** to display all of the contents of cell **A5** in the column. Compare your screen with **Figure 3**.

13. Make cell **B4** the active cell. Type 20,000 and then press Enter.

14. In cell **B5** type 2.25 and then press Enter.

15. In cell **B6** type =B4*B5 and then press Enter.

16. Click cell **B5**. On the **Home tab**, in the **Number group**, click the **Number Format** button, and then click **Currency**.

17. Click cell **B6**, and then apply the **Currency** number format. Click the **Decrease Decimal** button ⌗ two times.

18. Click cell **A8**, type Energy Consumption and then press Enter.

19. In the range **A9:A13**, pressing Enter after each entry, type Building Heating, Water Heating, Lighting, Computers and then Air Conditioning.

20. Click cell **B8**, type Percent of Total Cost and then press Enter.

21. In **B9:B13**, making sure you type the decimal in front of each number, type the following values: .32, .08, .15, .18 and then .27 Compare your screen with **Figure 4**.

■ **Continue to the next page to complete the skill**

22. Select the range **B9:B13**. In the **Number group**, click the **Number Format** button, and then click **Percentage**. Click the **Decrease Decimal** button ⯆ two times.

23. Click **C8**, type Annual Cost and then press Enter.

24. Select the range **B8:C8**. In the **Alignment group**, click the **Wrap Text** button, click the **Middle Align** button ☰, and then click the **Center** button ☰.

25. Click **C9**, type =B9*$B$6 and then press Enter.

26. Click **C9**, point at the fill handle, and then compare your screen with **Figure 5**.

27. While still pointing at the fill handle, drag the fill handle to copy the formula down through cell **C13**.

> The absolute cell reference to $B$6 is copied to each of the other formulas.

28. Click **C14**. In the **Formulas group**, click the **AutoSum** button, and then press Enter.

29. Select the range **A8:B13**. On the **Insert tab**, in the **Charts group**, click the **Pie** button, and then point at the first chart—**2-D Pie**. Compare your screen with **Figure 6**, and then click the first chart.

> A contextual tab—the Chart Tools tab—displays on the Ribbon.

30. Move the chart to approximately the range **A16:F30**.

31. To the right of the tabs, click the **Open in Excel** button. If prompted, enter your ID and password.

32. If prompted, at the top of the screen, on the **Protected View** bar, click **Enable Editing**.

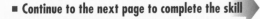
■ Continue to the next page to complete the skill

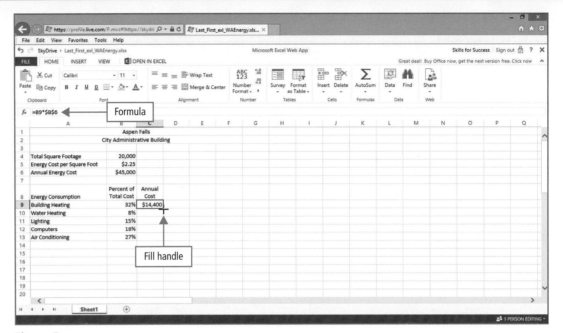

Figure 5

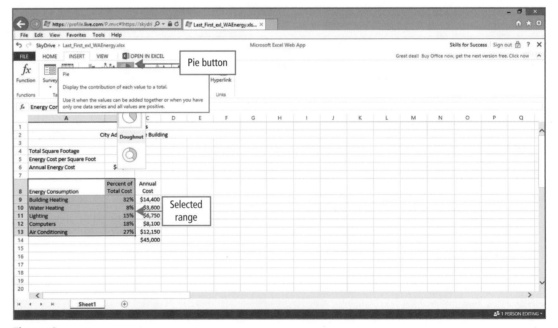

Figure 6

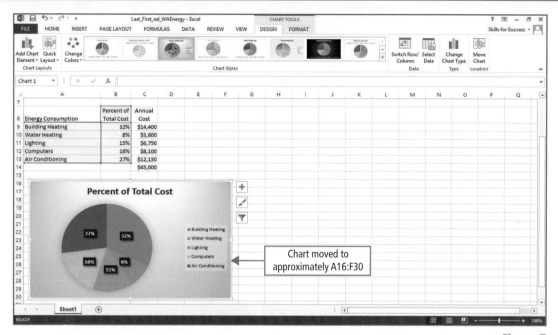

Figure 7

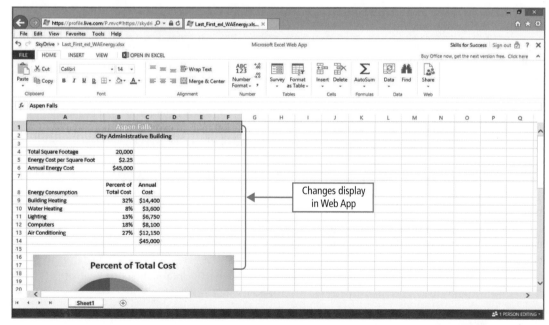

Figure 8

33. Click cell **A1**. On the **Home tab**, in the **Styles group**, click the **Cell Styles** button, and then click **Accent 4**. In the **Font group**, click the **Font Size** button [11 ▾], and then click **14**. In the **Cells group**, click the **Format** button, and then click **Row Height**. In the **Row Height** dialog box, type 20 and then click **OK**.

34. Click cell **A2**. In the **Styles group**, click the **Cell Styles** button, and then click **40% - Accent 4**. In the **Font group**, click the **Font Size** button [11 ▾], and then click **12**.

35. Click the chart to select the chart, and then on the **Design tab**, in the **Chart Styles group**, click the third style—**Style 3**. Compare your screen with **Figure 7**.

36. On the **Review tab**, in the **Proofing group**, click the **Spelling** button to check and correct any spelling errors. **Save** 🖫 your workbook and then **Close** [x] Excel 2013.

37. On the **SkyDrive** page, open the workbook in the Excel Web App. Compare your screen with **Figure 8**.

> The cell styles and the chart style 3 have been applied. Features not supported by Excel Web App, such as styles, cannot be changed in the Web App but they can be viewed.

38. Click the **View tab**, and then click **Reading View**. **Print** or **Share** the document as directed by your instructor.

39. In the top-left corner of the Internet Explorer window, click the **sign out** link, and then **Close** ⊠ the browser window.

 **DONE! You have completed Excel Web App Project!**

Glossary

.docx extension The file extension typically assigned to Word documents.

.pdf extension The file extension assigned to PDF documents.

3-D Short for three-dimensional.

Absolute cell reference The exact address of a cell, regardless of the position of the cell that contains the formula, that remains the same when the formula is copied. An absolute cell reference takes the form $A$1.

Accelerator A feature that searches the web for information related to the text that you select.

Action argument An additional instruction that determines how the macro action should run.

Active cell The cell outlined in green in which data is entered when you begin typing.

Active content A program downloaded with a web page that provides additional functionality.

ActiveX script A small program that allows websites to provide content such as learning management systems.

Add-on A small program added to a web browser to add functionality.

After Previous Begins the animation sequence immediately after the completion of the previous animation.

Alias A descriptive label used to identify a field in expressions, datasheets, or forms and reports.

Alignment Guide A line that displays when an object is aligned with a document object such as a margin or heading.

Anchor A symbol that displays to the left of a paragraph to indicate which paragraph an object is associated with.

And logical operator A logical comparison of two criteria that is true only when both criteria outcomes are true.

Animation Special visual effect added to an image, chart, or text on a slide.

Animation Painter Tool used to copy animation settings from one object to another.

Annotate Using the Pen tool to write on the slide while the slide show is running.

App A program use to perform a similar set of tasks. For example, Calendar is used to make appointments, and Bing Weather is used to track weather.

App Short for application, often a program purchased through the computer or device application store.

App command A button and command in an application that remains hidden until you need it.

Append row The last row of a datasheet into which a new record is entered.

Application Another word for app or program.

Application software Software used to accomplish specific tasks such as word processing and surfing the Internet.

Area chart A chart type that emphasizes the magnitude of change over time.

Argument The values that a function uses to perform operations or calculations.

Arithmetic operator A symbol that specifies a mathematical operation such as addition or subtraction.

Aspect ratio The width-to-height ratio of a screen.

Asterisk (*) wildcard A wildcard character that matches any combination of characters.

Attachment data type A data type used to store files such as Word documents or digital photo files.

Author-date citation A short citation format that contains the author's last name, the publication year, and the page number if one is available.

AutoComplete A menu of commands that match the characters you type.

AutoCorrect A feature that corrects common spelling errors as you type.

AutoFit A command that automatically changes the column width to accommodate the longest entry.

AutoNumber A field that automatically enters a unique, numeric value when a record is created.

AVERAGE function A function that adds a group of values, and then divides the result by the number of values in the group.

Avg An operator that calculates the average of the values in each group.

Axis A line bordering the chart plot area used as a frame of reference for measurement.

Backstage view A collection of pages on the File tab used to open, save, print, and perform other file management tasks.

Bar chart A chart type that illustrates comparisons among individual items.

Between ... And operator A comparison operator that finds all numbers or dates between and including two values.

Bibliography A compilation of sources referenced in a report and listed on a separate page.

Bing Internet Explorer's default search provider.

Black slide A slide that appears at the end of a presentation in Slide Show view, indicating that the slide show is over.

Block style A business letter format that begins all lines at the left margin except for letterheads, tables, and block quotes. Also known as full-block style.

Bluetooth A wireless technology that connects devices using radio waves over short distances.

Body font Font applied to all text on slide, except for the title.

Browser Software used to view and navigate the Web.

Browsing history The information that Internet Explorer stores as you browse the web.

Bullet Point An individual line of bulleted text on a slide.

Bulleted list A list of items with each item introduced by a symbol—such as a small circle or check mark—in which the list items can be presented in any order.

C drive The internal drive that stores the operating system. It is commonly assigned the letter 'C.'

Calculated column A column in an Excel table that uses a single formula that adjusts for each row.

Calculated field A field in a table or query that derives its values from other fields in the table or query.

Caption A field property that determines what displays in datasheet, form, and report labels.

Card reader A collection of ports designed to accept flash-based memory cards.

Cascading delete A referential integrity option in which you can delete a record on the one side of the relationship and all the related records on the many side will also be deleted.

Cascading update A referential integrity option in which you can edit the primary key values in a table and all the related records in the other table will update accordingly.

Category axis The axis that displays the category labels.

Category label Label that identifies the categories of data in a chart.

Category label Nonnumeric text that identifies the categories of data.

Cell A box formed by the intersection of a row and column into which text, objects, and data can be inserted.

Cell address The column letter and row number that identify a cell; also called the cell reference.

Cell reference The column letter and row number that identify a cell; also called a cell address.

Cell style A prebuilt set of formatting characteristics, such as font, font size, font color, cell borders, and cell shading.

Central Processing Unit The hardware responsible for controlling the computer commands and operations.

Charm A button accessed from the right edge of the screen that can be used to quickly perform common tasks.

Chart A graphical representation of data used to show comparisons, patterns, and trends.

Chart layout A prebuilt set of chart elements that can include a title, legend, or labels.

Chart sheet A workbook sheet that contains only a chart and is useful when you want to view a chart separately from the worksheet data.

Chart style A prebuilt chart format that applies an overall visual look to a chart by modifying its graphic effects, colors, and backgrounds.

Chrome The area of a web browser devoted to toolbars, address boxes, tabs, and menus.

Citation A note in the document that refers the reader to a source in the bibliography.

Click To click the left mouse button.

Clip Art An image, drawing, or photograph accessed from Microsoft Office Online and other online providers.

Clipboard A temporary memory location maintained by the operating system used to copy or move text, objects, files, or folders.

Cloud backup A service that copies your files to a server so that you if you need to, you can recover them.

Cloud computing Services such as file storage, file sharing, and applications provided via the Internet.

Cloud-based service A Cloud-computing resource such as SkyDrive, Facebook, and Flickr.

Clustered bar chart A chart type that is useful when you want to compare values across categories; bar charts organize categories along the vertical axis and the values along the horizontal axis.

Color scales A conditional format that uses color to help the user visualize data distribution and variation.

Column break A nonprinting character that forces the text following the break to flow into the next column.

Column chart A chart type useful for illustrating comparisons among related numbers.

Column chart Used to show comparison among related categories.

Column heading The letter that displays at the top of a column.

Columnar layout A layout that places labels in the first column and data in the second column.

Command An action used to complete a task.

Comment A note that is attached to a cell, separate from other cell content.

Compact and Repair A process that rebuilds database files so that data and database objects are stored more efficiently.

Comparison operator An operator that compares two values, such as > (greater than) or < (less than).

Comparison operator Compares two values and returns either TRUE or FALSE.

Compatibility mode A mode that limits formatting and features to ones that are supported in earlier versions of Office.

Compressed folder A file or group of files compressed into a single file.

Computer A programmable electronic device that can input, process, output, and store data.

Computer window A File Explorer folder window used to access the drives available on your computer.

Conditional formatting A format such as cell shading or font color, which is applied to cells when a specified condition is true.

Content Underlying formulas and data in a cell.

Contextual tab A tab that displays on the Ribbon only when a related object such as a graphic or chart is selected. This tab contains tools used on the object.

Contrast The difference in brightness between two elements on a slide, such as the background and the text or the background and a graphic.

Control An object on a form or in a report such as a label or a text box.

Cookie A small text file written by some websites as you visit them. It is used to add functionality to the page or to analyze the way that you use the website.

Copy A command that places a copy of the selected text or object on the Office Clipboard.

Copyright-free image An image that is not protected by copyright.

Count An operator that calculates the number of records in each group.

COUNT function A function that counts the number of cells that contain numbers.

CPU Central Processing Unit.

CPU cache A storage area dedicated to the processor.

CPU speed A computer specification measured in calculations per second.

Criteria (Access) Conditions in a query used to select the records that answer the query's question.

Criteria (Excel) The condition that is specified in the logical test.

Crosstab query A select query that calculates a sum, an average, or a similar statistic, and then groups the results by two sets of values.

Currency data type A data type that stores numbers formatted as monetary values.

Custom Range A user-determined selection of slides; includes only a selection of the slides in the presentation.

Cut A command that deletes the selected text or object and places a copy in the Office clipboard.

Data bar A format that provides a visual cue to the reader about the value of a cell relative to other cells. The length of the data bar represents the value in the cell.

Data label Text that identifies a data marker in a chart.

Data marker A column, bar, area, dot, pie slice, or other symbol that represents a single data point.

Data point A chart value that originates in an Excel worksheet cell, a Word table cell, or an Access field. Individual data plotted in a chart.

Data series In a chart, data points that are related to one another.

Data series Related data points on a chart; assigned a unique color or pattern represented in the chart legend.

Data source The file that contains the information—such as names and addresses—that changes with each letter or label in the main mail merge document.

Data Type A field property that specifies the type of information that the field will hold; for example, text, number, date, or currency.

Database A collection of structured tables designed to store data.

Database software Software used to store large amounts of data and retrieve that data in useful and meaningful ways.

Database system A program used to both store and manage large amounts data.

Datasheet The presentation of a database table.

Datasheet view An Access view that features the data but also has contextual tabs on the Ribbon so that you can also change the table's design.

Date/Time data type A data type that stores serial numbers that are converted into and formatted as dates or times.

Default home page The page that first displays when you open a web browser.

Default printer The printer that is automatically selected when you do not choose a different printer.

Delay Animation starts after a predetermined amount of time.

Desktop A GUI element that simulates a real desktop in which files are placed. A screen that you use to organize and work with your files and applications.

Desktop app An application that runs from the desktop.

Desktop computer A computer designed to be placed permanently on a desk or at a workstation.

Desktop icon A shortcut to a program, file, or location on your computer.

Desktop publishing software Software designed to produce professional publications such as newsletters, letterheads, business cards, and brochures.

Detail control The area of a report that repeats for each record in the table or query.

Detail sheet A worksheet with cells referred to by summary sheet formulas.

Device A common term for smartphone or tablet.

Displayed value Data displayed in a cell.

Document Information Panel A panel that displays above the worksheet window in which properties or property information is added, viewed, or updated.

Document properties Details about a file that describe or identify the file, such as the title, author name, and keywords.

Document properties Information about a document that can help you identify or organize your files, such as the name of the document author, the file name, and key words.

Domain name A unique name assigned to a website on the World Wide Web.

Dot leader A series of evenly spaced dots that precede a tab stop.

Double-click To click the left mouse button two times quickly without moving the mouse.

Double-spacing The equivalent of a blank line of text displays between each line of text.

Double-tap To tap the screen in the same place two times quickly.

Drag To press and hold the left mouse button while moving the mouse.

Drag and drop A method of moving objects, in which you point to a selection and drag it to a new location.

Drop cap The first letter (or letters) of a paragraph, enlarged and either embedded in the text or placed in the left margin.

DVD A storage device that uses optical laser technology to read and write data.

E-mail attachment A file that is sent with an e-mail message so that the recipient can open and view the file.

E-mail software Software used to receive and send e-mail. Many e-mail programs also include tools for managing appointments, contacts, and tasks.

Edit To insert, delete, or replace text in an Office document, workbook, or presentation.

Edit mode A mode that selects the text inside a control, not the control itself.

Em dash A long dash based on the width of the capital letter M in the current font and font size.

It marks a break in thought, similar to a comma but stronger.

Embedded chart A chart that is placed on the worksheet containing the data.

Embedded computer A small, specialized computer built into a larger component such as an automobile or appliance.

Emphasis effect Animation that emphasizes an object or text that is already displayed.

Endnote A note or comment placed at the end of a section or a document.

Ensure Fit (Slide Size) A setting that scales information down so that it all appears on the slide.

Entrance effect Animation that appears as an object or text is moved onto the screen.

Error indicator A green triangle that indicates a possible error in a formula.

Error value A message that displays whenever a formula or function cannot perform its calculations.

Excel table A series of rows and columns that contains related data that have been formatted as a table.

Exit effect Animation that appears as an object or text is moved off the screen.

Explode To drag a section of a pie chart out to add emphasis.

Expression A combination of fields, mathematical operators, and prebuilt functions that calculates values in tables, forms, queries, and reports.

External drive A solid-state disk drive that attaches to the computer via a USB port.

Eyedropper Tool used to select color from any object or image on a slide and apply the color to another area of the slide; often used to create a cohesive color scheme.

Fair use A rule that allows limited reproduction of images for educational purposes.

Favorite A stored web address that can be clicked to navigate to that page quickly.

Fax service provider A company that receives faxes sent to them from the Internet and then relays the fax to the recipient using phone lines.

Fax service providers typically charge fees for their service.

Field (Access) A common characteristic of the data that the table will describe, such as city, state, or postal code.

Field (Excel) In a PivotTable, a cell that summarizes multiple rows of information from the source data.

Field (Word) A category of data—such as a file name, a page number, or the current date—that can be inserted into a document.

Field size A field property that limits the number of characters that can be typed into a text or number field.

File A collection of data that is saved, opened, and changed by applications.

File Explorer An application that is used to view, find, and organize your files and folders.

File system An organized method to save and retrieve files.

Fill handle The small black square in the lower right corner of the selection.

Filter A command to display only the rows of a table that meet specified criteria. Filtering temporarily hides rows that do not meet the criteria.

Fingerprint scanner An input device that reads fingerprints to authorize computer users.

First line indent The location of the beginning of the first line of a paragraph in relation to the left edge of the remainder of the paragraph.

Flagged error A wavy line indicating a possible spelling, grammar, or style error.

Floating object An object that you can move independently of the surrounding text.

Folder A container in which you store your files.

Folder window A File Explorer window that displays files and folders.

Font A set of characters with the same design and shape; measured in points.

Footer A reserved area for text, graphics, and fields that displays at the bottom of each page in a document.

Footer The text that displays at the bottom of every slide or that prints at the bottom of a sheet of slide handouts.

Footnote A note or comment placed at the bottom of the page.

Foreign key A field that is used to relate records in a second related table. The foreign key field is often the second table's primary key.

Form A database object that is used to find, update, and add table records.

Form data Information that you have typed into forms, such as your sign-in name, e-mail address, and street address.

Format To change the appearance of the text—for example, changing the text color to red.

Format Painter A tool that copies *formatting* from one selection of text to another.

Formatting The process of specifying the appearance of cells or the overall layout of a worksheet.

Formatting mark A character that displays in your document to represent a nonprinting character such as a paragraph, space, or tab.

Formula An equation that performs mathematical calculations on number values in the worksheet.

Formula AutoComplete A feature that suggests values as you type a function.

Formula bar A bar below the Ribbon that displays the value contained in the active cell and is used to enter or edit values or formulas.

Freeze Panes A command used to keep rows or columns visible when scrolling in a large worksheet. The frozen rows and columns become separate panes.

Full Page Slide A printout in which the slide is fit to letter-size paper (8.5 by 11 inches).

Full-block style A business letter format that begins all lines at the left margin except for letterheads, tables, and block quotes. Also known as block style.

Function A prewritten Excel formula that takes a value or values, performs an operation, and returns a value or values.

Future value (Fv) In a loan, the value at the end of the time periods, or the cash balance you want to attain after the last loan payment is made. The future value for a loan is usually zero.

Gallery A visual display of selections from which you can choose.

Gateway A network device that enables communication between networks.

GB The abbreviation for gigabyte.

General format The default number format. It does not display commas or trailing zeros to the right of a decimal point.

Gesture A motion that is performed on a touch display that is interpreted as a command.

Gigabyte A unit of measure for storage devices. One gigabyte can store about one thousand digital photos.

Goal Seek A what-if analysis tool used to find a specific value for a cell by adjusting the value of another cell.

GPU A graphic processing unit.

Gradient fill Gradual progression of colors and shades, usually from one color to another, or from one shade to another shade of the same color, used to add a fill to a shape or placeholder. Gradients come in light and dark variations.

Graphic processing unit A card attached to the computer's main board to improve computer performance.

Graphical user interface A visual system used to interact with the computer.

Group A collection of objects treated as one unit that can be copied, moved, or formatted.

Group By An operator that designates which query column contains the group of values to summarize as a single record, one for each group.

GUI Graphical user interface.

Guide A line that displays on the ruler to give you a visual indication of where the pointer is positioned.

Handout A printout that features multiple slides on a single page; can contain between two and nine slides per page.

Hanging indent An indent where the first line extends to the left of the rest of the paragraph.

Hard disk drive A common storage device in desktop computers that stores data using magnetic charges.

HDD Hard disk drive.

Header A reserved area for text, graphics, and fields that displays at the top of each page in a document.

Header The text that prints at the top of each page of slide handouts.

Headings font Font applied to slide titles.

Home page The starting point for the remainder of the pages at a website.

Homegroup A Windows networking tool that makes it easy to share pictures, videos, music, documents, and devices such as printers.

Hosted e-mail A service used to provide e-mail addresses and related resources.

HTML document A text file with instructions for displaying its content in a web browser. *See also* Hypertext Markup Language document.

Hyperlink (PowerPoint) A connection from one slide to another slide in the same presentation or to a slide in another presentation, an email address, a web page, or a file.

Hyperlink Text or a graphic that you click to go to a file, a location in a file, a web page on the World Wide Web, or a web page on an organization's intranet.

Hyperlink data type A data type that stores links to websites or files located on your computer.

Hypertext Markup Language document A text file that includes instructions for displaying its content in a web browser.

Icon A small button used to represent a file, folder, or command.

IF function A logical function that checks whether criteria is met, and then returns one value when the condition is TRUE, and another value when the condition is FALSE.

Indent The position of paragraph lines in relation to the page margins.

Indeterminate relationship A relationship that does not enforce referential integrity.

Information processing cycle The four basic computer functions that work together in a cycle: input, processing, output, and storage.

InPrivate Browsing An Internet Explorer window that limits the browsing history that is written.

Input The process of gathering information from the user through input devices.

Input device Computer hardware such as keyboards, mice, touch displays, and microphones.

Input mask A set of special characters that control what can and cannot be entered in a field.

Insertion point A flashing vertical line that indicates where text will be inserted when you start typing.

Integrated graphics card A graphics card built into the computer's main board.

IntelliSense A feature that displays Quick Info, ToolTips, and AutoComplete boxes as you type.

Interest The charge for borrowing money; generally a percentage of the amount borrowed.

Internet A global collection of networks that facilitate electronic communication such as e-mail, file sharing, and the World Wide Web.

Internet Explorer A program used to browse the World Wide Web.

Internet service provider An organization that provides Internet connections, typically for a fee.

Internet zone The default security zone applied to all websites.

Intranet A web site that is accessed by only individuals within the organization.

IP address A unique set of numbers assigned to each computer on the Internet.

Is Not Null An operator that tests if a field contains a value (is not empty).

Is Null An operator that tests if a field is empty.

ISP Internet service provider.

Justified text A paragraph alignment that aligns the text with both the left and right margins.

Keep Source Formatting One of the Paste Options, applies the original formatting of the pasted text.

Keep Text Only One of the Paste Options, removes all formatting from the selection.

Keyboard An input device used to type characters and perform common commands.

Keyboard shortcut A combination of CTRL, ALT, WINDOWS, and character keys that perform a command when pressed.

Keyboard shortcut A combination of keys that performs a command.

Label Text data in a cell that identifies a number value.

Label A control on a form or in a report that describes other objects in the report or on the form.

Label report A report formatted so that the data can be printed on a sheet of labels.

Landscape An orientation that is wider than it is tall.

Layout A format that determines how data and labels are arranged in a form or report.

Layout (PowerPoint) The arrangement of the text and graphic elements or placeholders on a slide.

Layout gallery A visual *representation* of several content layouts that you can apply to a slide.

Layout view An Access view used to format a form or report while you are viewing a sample of the data.

Leader A series of characters that form a solid, dashed, or dotted line to fill the space preceding a tab stop.

Leader character The symbol used to fill the space in a leader.

Legend A box that identifies the patterns or colors that are assigned to the data series or categories in the chart.

Legend Identifies the patterns or colors that are assigned to the data in the chart.

Library A collection of folders and files assembled from various locations.

Line chart A chart type that illustrates trends over time, with time displayed along the x-axis and the data point values connected by a line.

Line spacing The vertical distance between lines of text in a paragraph; can be adjusted for each paragraph.

Linked table A table that exists in a file different from the one you are working on; created by an application such as Access or Excel but that can be opened as a table in Access.

List Level A hierarchy of bullets and sub-bullets; each level has its own formatting.

Live Preview A feature that displays what the results of a formatting change will be if you select it.

Local account An account where you can only access one computer and you must create separate accounts for each computer that you use.

Local intranet zone A security zone designed for web content stored on internal networks that is accessed only by those within the organization.

Lock screen A screen that displays shortly after you turn on a computer or device running Windows 8. It also displays when you are not signed in to prevent unauthorized individuals from logging on to your computer.

Logical function A function that applies a logical test to determine if a specific condition is met.

Logical test Any value or expression that can be evaluated as being TRUE or FALSE.

Long Text data type A data type that can store up to 65,535 characters in each record.

Macro A set of saved actions that you can use to automate tasks.

Macro action A prebuilt set of instructions that performs tasks when the macro is run.

Macro Builder An object tab with pre-built commands that you can select and modify to build a macro.

Mail merge A Word feature used to customize letters or labels by combining a main document with a data source.

Main document The mail merge document that contains the text that remains constant.

Malware A type of program designed to harm your computer, control your computer, or discover private information.

Manual page break A document feature that forces a page to end at a location you specify.

Margins The spaces between the text and the top, bottom, left, and right edges of the paper.

Masked character Text that is hidden by displaying characters such as bullets.

MAX function A function that returns the largest value in a range of cells.

Maximize (PowerPoint) A setting that keeps slide content as large as possible and allows some areas to be cropped if needed.

Maximize To size a window to fill the entire screen.

Merge Selected cells are combined into a single cell.

Merge field A field that merges and displays data from a specific column in the data source.

Metadata Information and personal data that is stored with your document.

MHTML file Another name for a web archive.

Microsoft account A single logon used to log on to Windows Cloud-based services such as Hotmail and SkyDrive.

Microsoft Office A suite of productivity programs.

MIN function A function that returns the smallest value in a range of cells.

Mini toolbar A toolbar with common formatting commands that displays near selected text.

Minimize To close a window but leave the application open and its button displayed on the taskbar.

Modal form A form with its Modal property set to Yes so that when the form opens, the Navigation Pane is collapsed, and when the form is closed, the Navigation Pane displays again.

Modem A device that translates signals between a router and an ISP.

Mouse An input device used to point to and click on screen elements.

Name A word that represents a cell or range of cells that can be used as a cell or range reference.

Name Box An area that displays the active cell reference.

Navigation bar A vertical or horizontal bar with hyperlinks to the main pages of a website.

Navigation form A form that contains a Navigation Control with tabs that you can use to quickly open forms and reports.

Navigation toolbar Displays in the lower left corner of the slide in Slide Show view; can be used to move to any slide while the slide show is running.

Network drive A hard drive that is accessed through a network.

Network interface card A card that connects a computer to a network.

NIC Network interface card.

Normal view (Excel) A view that maximizes the number of cells visible on the screen.

Normal View (PowerPoint) A view in which PowerPoint window is divided into two areas—the Slide pane and the left pane, which contains thumbnails of each slide.

Notebook The name given to a OneNote document. It is a loose structure of digital pages.

Notes page Printouts that contain the slide image in the top half of the page and speaker notes in the lower half of the page.

Notes pane The area of the Normal View window used to type notes that can be printed below an image of each slide.

NOW function A function that returns the serial number of the current date and time.

Nudge To move an object in small increments by pressing one of the arrow keys.

Number data type A data type that stores numeric values.

Number format A specific way that Excel displays numbers.

Number value Numeric data in a cell.

Numbered list A list of items with each item introduced by a consecutive number or letter to indicate definite steps, a sequence of actions, or chronological order.

Office 2013 RT A version of Office optimized for working on portable devices with touch screens such as Windows phones and tablets.

Office 365 A Cloud service built around the Office suite of programs.

Office on Demand A streaming version of Office that enables you to work from a computer that does not have Office installed.

Office RT An app version of Office designed to work on tablets with an ARM processor.

Office.com Clip Art A collection of online pictures, provided through Office.com, including pictures, drawings, and graphics.

On Click Animation begins the animation sequence when the mouse button is clicked or the spacebar is pressed.

One-to-many form A two-part form in which the main form displays in Single Form view and the related records display in a subform in Datasheet view.

One-to-many relationship A relationship in which a record in the first table can have many associated records in the second table.

OneNote A program used to collect notes, drawings, and media from multiple participants.

Online pictures A collection of images stored online and made available for use in presentations.

Onscreen keyboard A virtual keyboard that displays on a touch screen.

Open source software Software that can be sold or given away as long as the source code is provided for free.

OpenDocument Presentation A presentation that can be opened by PowerPoint and other presentation software, including Impress and Google Docs.

Operating system software Software that controls the way the computer works while it is running.

Operator precedence The mathematical rules for performing calculations within a formula.

Or logical operator A logical comparison of two criteria that is true if either of the criteria outcomes is true.

Organization chart A chart that graphically represents the reporting relationships between individuals and groups in an organization.

Orphan The first line of a paragraph that displays as the last line of a page.

Outline A printout that displays the slide text only.

Output The computer process of displaying information through output devices.

Output device Hardware that provides information to the user such as monitors, speakers, and printers.

Page Layout view A view used to adjust how a worksheet will look when it is printed.

Paint A drawing program that is installed with most versions of Windows.

Paragraph spacing The vertical distance above and below each paragraph; can be adjusted for each paragraph.

Password protect To require a password to open a shared file.

Paste A command that inserts a copy of the text or object from the Office Clipboard.

Paste area The target destination for data that has been cut or copied.

PDF document An image of a document that can be viewed using a PDF reader such as Adobe Acrobat Reader instead of the application that created the original document.

.pdf extension The file extension assigned to PDF documents.

PDF file *See* Portable Document Format file.

Peer-to-peer network A small network that connects computers and devices without the need for a server.

Permission level The privilege to read, rename, delete, or change a file.

Phishing website A dishonest website posing as a legitimate site to gain personal information, such as your logon and bank account number.

Photo album A presentation composed primarily of pictures.

Picture An image created with a scanner or digital camera and saved with a graphic file extension such as .jpg, .png, .tif, or .bmp.

Picture One of the Paste Options, pastes the text as a picture.

Picture effect A picture style that includes shadows, reflections, glows, soft edges, bevels, and 3-D rotations.

Picture Style Prebuilt set of formatting borders, effects, and layouts applied to a picture.

Pie chart A chart type that illustrates the relationship of parts to a whole.

Pie chart Used to illustrate percentages or proportions and includes only one data series.

Pinch Slide two fingers closer together to shrink or zoom out.

PivotTable report An interactive, cross-tabulated Excel report used to summarize and analyze data.

Placeholder A box with dotted borders; holds text or objects such as pictures, charts, and tables.

Placeholder A reserved, formatted space into which you enter your own text, pictures, charts, or tables. If nothing is entered, the placeholder text will not print.

Placeholder character A symbol in an input mask that is replaced as you type data into the field.

PMT function A function that calculates the payment for a loan based on constant payments and a constant interest rate.

Point A unit of measure with 72 points per inch typically used for font sizes and character spacing.

Pop-up A small window that displays in addition to the web page you are viewing.

Port The connectors on the outside of the computer to which you connect external devices.

Portable Document Format file A file format that preserves document layout and formatting so that files can be viewed in Word, Windows 8 Reader, or Adobe Acrobat Reader.

Portrait An orientation that is taller than it is wide.

PowerPoint 97-2003 Presentation A presentation which is saved in an older, .ppt format.

PowerPoint Picture Presentation A presentation in which each slide is saved as a picture, rather than a slide with individual components.

PowerPoint Presentation A presentation that can be opened using Microsoft PowerPoint.

PowerPoint Show A PowerPoint presentation which opens automatically as a slide show without the use of presentation software.

Present value (Pv) The total amount that a series of future payments is worth today, often the initial amount of a loan.

Presentation software Software used to arrange information in slides that can be projected on a large screen in front of an audience.

Presenter view A view available in which slides are projected in Slide Show view. Shows notes and slide on computer screen while only the slide is projected to the audience; requires only one monitor.

Primary key A field that uniquely identifies each record in a table.

Principal The initial amount of the loan; the total amount that a series of future payments is worth today. Also called the present value (Pv) of a loan.

Print A command that opens the Print dialog box so that you can select a different printer or different print options.

Print Preview A command that opens a preview of the table with Ribbon commands that enable you

to make adjustments to the object you are printing.

Privacy policy A document that explains what types of information are collected and how the information will be used.

Processing The computer process of transforming, managing, and making decisions about the data and information.

Productivity software Software used to accomplish tasks such as reading and composing e-mail, writing documents, and managing tasks.

Program Another word for application or software.

Protected Mode A feature that makes it more difficult for malware to be installed on your computer.

Protected View A view applied to documents downloaded from the Internet that allows you to decide if the content is safe before working with the document.

Public A shared file that does not require a password.

Public computer A computer that is available to others when you are not using it.

Public web site A web site designed for public access.

QAT An acronym for Quick Access Toolbar.

Query A database object that displays a subset of data in response to a question; a database object used to ask questions about—query—the data stored in database tables.

Query design grid The lower half of the Query Design view window that contains the fields the query will display and the query settings that should be applied to each field.

Query design workspace The upper half of the Query Design view window that displays the tables that the query will search.

Question mark (?) wildcard A wildcard character that matches any single character.

Quick Access Toolbar A small toolbar that contains buttons for commonly used commands such as Save and Undo.

Quick Info An IntelliSense box with a message that explains the purpose of the selected AutoComplete command.

Quick Print A command that prints the object directly. You cannot make any adjustments to the

object, choose a different printer, or change the printer settings.

Quick Start field A set of fields that can be added with a single click. For example, the Name Quick Start data type inserts the LastName and FirstName fields and assigns the Text data type to each.

Quick Style A style that can be accessed from a Ribbon gallery of thumbnails.

RAM Random access memory; a computer's temporary electronic memory.

Random access memory An electronic chip that provides temporary storage.

Range Two or more cells in a worksheet that are adjacent or nonadjacent.

Range finder An Excel feature that outlines all of the cells referenced in a formula. It is useful for verifying which cells are used in a formula and it can be used to edit formulas.

Rate The percentage that is paid for the use of borrowed money.

Read Mode A view that is used when you need to read, but not edit, electronic documents.

Read privilege A permission level that allows you to open the document, but not change it.

Reader A tablet-like computer designed to bring entertainment features such as books and movies.

Recently Used Fonts Listing of fonts you have selected and applied in the existing presentation.

Record A collection of related data, such as the contact information for a person.

Recycle Bin An area on your drive that stores files you no longer need.

Referential integrity A rule that keeps related values synchronized. For example, the foreign key value must be present in the related table.

Relative cell reference Refers to cells based on their position in relation to (relative to) the cell that contains the formula.

Replace A feature that finds and then replaces a character or string of characters, or in a selected range.

Report A database object that presents tables or query results in a way that is optimized for onscreen viewing or printing.

Report Layout view A view that can be used to format a report while viewing the report's data.

Report view A view optimized for onscreen viewing of reports.

Restricted sites zone A security zone in which you place sites that you explicitly do not trust.

Ribbon An application area that contains commands placed in groups that are organized by tabs.

Rich Text Format file A document file format designed to work with many different types of programs.

Right-click To click one time with the right mouse button.

Router A network device that enables communication between different networks.

Row heading The number that displays at the left of a row.

Royalty-free image An image that can be used in a publication after paying a one-time fee, rather than paying a fee each time the image is printed.

RTF file *See* Rich Text Format file.

Sans serif font A font where the letters do not have serifs.

Scanner An input device that can convert paper images into a digital image.

Screen saver An animation that displays on your screen after a set period of computer inactivity.

Screenshot A snapshot of any window that is open on your desktop.

Script Code downloaded from a web page that provides additional functionality.

SDD Solid-state Disk Drive.

Search provider A website that provides a way for you to search for information on the web.

Search suggestion A word or phrase that displays as you type in a search box.

Section A portion of a document that can be formatted differently from the rest of the document.

Section break A nonprinting character that marks the end of one section and the beginning of another section.

Select query A type of query that selects and displays the records that answer a question without changing the data in the table.

Separator character A character such as a tab or comma designated as the character to separate columns of unformatted text.

Serial number A sequential number.

Series A group of things that come one after another in succession; for example, the months January, February, March.

Serif An extra detail or hook at the end of a character stroke.

Serif font A font where the letters have serifs or extra details or hooks at the end of each stroke.

Server A computer dedicated to providing services to other computers on a network.

Setting A saved preference that changes the way Windows or a program behaves or appears.

SharePoint A web application server designed for organizations to develop an intranet.

Shift-click To click a file while holding down the [Shift] key. Shift-clicking is often used to select a continuous range of files.

Short Text data type A data type that stores up to 255 characters of text.

Sign in The process of connecting to a computer.

Sign-in screen The screen you use to type your logon information.

Single Form view A view that displays one record at a time with field names in the first column and field values in the second column.

Site index A page of hyperlinks that outline a website.

Site map Another name for site index.

Sizing handle A small square or circle on an object's border that is used to resize the object by dragging.

SkyDrive A Cloud-based service that is used to store and share files.

Slide (PowerPoint) An individual page in a presentation that can contain text, pictures, or other objects.

Slide (touch screen) Touch an object and then move the finger across the screen.

Slide handout A printed image of slides on a sheet of paper.

Slide master The highest level slide in a hierarchy of slides, stores theme and slide layout information.

Slide show A series of pictures that change at a set interval.

Slide Sorter view The view that displays all of the slides in your presentation as thumbnails.

Slide transition A motion effect that occurs in a slide show as you move from one slide to another.

Small caps A font effect that displays all characters in uppercase while making any character originally typed as an uppercase letter taller than the ones typed as lowercase letters.

Smart Guide A dashed line that appears on the slide when objects are spaced nearly evenly; indicates when objects are evenly spaced.

Smart phone A cellular phone with an operating system.

SmartArt graphic A visual representation of information that you can use to communicate your message or ideas effectively.

SmartScreen Filter A feature that helps protect you from online threats.

Snap To quickly position a window to either half of the screen by dragging the title bar and the pointer to the screen's edge.

Snip A screenshot created with the Snipping Tool.

Snipping Tool An application used to create screenshots called snips.

Social media A Cloud service where content is shared through the interactions of people connected through social networks.

Software A set of instructions stored on your computer.

Solid-state disk drive A drive that that stores data using electricity and retains the data when the power is turned off.

Source The reference used to find information or data.

Source data The data that is used to create a PivotTable.

Sparkline A chart contained in a single cell that is used to show data trends.

Speech recognition An input technology that performs commands or types text based on words spoken into a microphone.

Split bar A bar that splits a document into two windows.

Spreadsheet The primary document that you use in Excel to store and work with data; also called a worksheet.

Spreadsheet software Software used to organize information in a tabular structure with numeric data, labels, formulas, and charts.

SQL select query A command that selects data from a data source based on the criteria you specify.

Start screen The initial screen that displays when starting PowerPoint 2013, Word 2013, or Excel 2013.

Start screen app An application that runs from the Start screen.

Statistical function A predefined function that describes a collection of data; for example, totals, counts, and averages.

Storage The location where data resides on a computer.

Storage device Computer hardware that stores information after a computer is powered off.

Streaming media A Cloud-based service that provides video and music as you watch or listen to it.

Stretch Slide two fingers apart to enlarge or zoom in.

Student data file A file that you need to complete a project in a textbook.

Style A prebuilt collection of formatting settings that can be assigned to text.

Stylus A pen-like pointing device used with touch screens.

Subdatasheet A datasheet that displays related records from another table by matching the values in the field that relates the two tables. In a datasheet, the subdatasheet displays below each record.

SUM An Excel function that adds all the numbers in a range of cells.

Sum An operator that calculates the total of the values in each group.

Summary sheet A worksheet that displays and summarizes totals from other worksheets.

Summary statistic A calculation for each group of data such as a total, an average, or a count.

Superscript Text that is positioned higher and smaller than the other text.

Swipe Slide in from a screen edge to display app commands, charms, or other temporary areas.

Synonym Words with the same meaning.

Tab scrolling buttons The buttons to the left of the worksheet tabs used to display Excel worksheet tabs that are not in view.

Tab stop A specific location on a line of text marked on the Word ruler to which you can move the insertion point by pressing the Tab key.

Tabbed browsing A feature that you use to open multiple web pages in the same browser window.

Table (Access) A database object that stores the database data so that records are in rows and fields are in columns.

Table The object that stores the data by organizing it into rows and columns. Each column is a field, and each row is a record.

Table Design view An Access view that features table fields and their properties.

Table style Borders and fill colors applied to the entire table in a manner consistent with the presentation theme.

Tablet A portable computer built around a single touch screen.

Tabular layout A layout in which the controls are positioned as table cells in rows and columns.

Tap To touch once with the finger.

Taskbar An area that displays buttons along the bottom of the desktop that represent applications and windows.

TB The abbreviation for terabyte.

Template A pre-built document into which you insert text using the layout and formatting provided in that document.

Template (Excel) A pre-built workbook used as a pattern for creating new workbooks; used to build workbooks without having to start from a blank workbook.

Temporary Internet file A copy of a web page and its images stored in your personal folder. This is used to improve the time that it takes for a frequently visited page to display.

Terabyte A unit of measure for storage devices. One terabyte is approximately a thousand gigabytes.

Text Alignment The placement of text within a placeholder.

Text box (Access) A control on a form or in a report that displays the data from a field in a table or query.

Text box (PowerPoint) An object used to position text anywhere on a slide.

Text box (Word) A movable, resizable container for text or graphics.

Text effect A prebuilt set of decorative formats, such as outlines, shadows, text glow, and colors, that make text stand out in a document.

Text value Character data in a cell that labels number values.

Text wrap A format that displays text on multiple lines within a cell.

The Cloud The collection of services provided by Cloud computing.

Theme A group of pre-built settings, including desktop background, window border color, screen saver, and system sounds.

Theme (PowerPoint) Set of unified, pre-built design elements—colors, fonts, and effects—that provides a unique look for your presentation.

Theme variant Variations of the current theme, with different accent colors.

Thesaurus A reference that lists words that have the same or similar meaning to the word you are looking up.

Three-color scale A conditional format that compares a range of cells and applies a gradation of three colors; the shades represent higher, middle, or lower values.

Three-dimensional Refers to an image that appears to have all three spatial dimensions: length, width, and depth.

Thumb drive Another name for a USB flash drive.

Thumbnail A small graphic representing a larger picture or photo.

Tile A small window that runs an application that presents live, updated information.

TODAY function A function that returns the serial number of the current date.

Toggle button A button used to turn a feature both on and off.

Top-level domain Letters after a domain name that specify the type of organization sponsoring a website—*.gov*, for example.

Top/Bottom Rules A conditional format used to apply formatting to the highest and lowest values in a range of cells.

Total row A row that displays as the last row in an Excel table and provides summary functions in drop-down lists for each column.

Touch display A screen that interprets commands when you touch it with your finger.

Touchpad A flat area on which you can move the finger to position the pointer.

TPL An acronym for Tracking Protection List.

Tracking cookie Gathers information about your web browsing behaviors across multiple websites. They are used to provide ads and services based on your interests.

Tracking Protection List An Internet Explorer add-on that helps prevent websites from collecting information about your visit.

Truncated Cut off.

Trusted sites zone A security zone in which you place sites that you trust not to harm your computer.

Two-color scale A conditional format that compares a range of cells and applies a gradation of two colors; the shade of the color represents higher or lower values.

Underlying formula The formula as displayed in the formula bar.

Underlying value Data displayed in the formula bar.

Unicode (UTF-8) A system for representing a large variety of text characters and symbols. It is used often in HTML documents.

Uniform Resource Locator The unique address of a page on the Internet.

Unsecured network A network that does not require a password to connect to it.

Unzip To decompress a compressed (zipped) folder.

URL Uniform Resource Locator, or web address.

USB flash drive A small, portable solid-state drive about the size of the human thumb.

Use Destination Theme One of the Paste Options, applies the formatting of the slide to which the text is pasted.

Utility program A small program designed to perform a routine task or computer housekeeping task.

Validation rule A field property that requires that specific values be entered into a field.

Value Data in a cell.

Value axis The axis that displays the worksheet's numeric data.

Vertical alignment The space above and below a text or object in relation to the top and bottom of a table cell or top and bottom margins.

Volatile The result of a function that does not remain as entered, but is updated each time the workbook is opened.

Web Another name for World Wide Web.

Web album A Cloud-based service that you use to store, organize, and share photos and video.

Web app An application that runs in a web browser.

Web archive A file that saves web page text and pictures in a single file. These files are typically assigned the *.mht* file extension.

Web browser A program used to navigate the World Wide Web.

Website A collection of connected pages located at a single domain name.

Widow The last line of a paragraph that displays as the first line of a page.

Wildcard A special character, such as an asterisk, used in query criteria to allow matches for any combination of letters or characters.

Windows 8 Store app Software that is downloaded and installed from the Windows 8 Store and run in the Start screen.

Wired network A network that transmits signals through wires.

Wireless network A network that transmits signals via radio waves.

With Previous Animation begins the animation sequence at the same time as any animation preceding it or, if it is the first animation, with the slide transition.

Word processing software Software used to create, edit, format, and print documents containing primarily text and graphics.

Word wrap Words at the right margin automatically move to the next line if they do not fit.

WordArt (PowerPoint) A pre-built set of fills, outlines, and effects used to create decorative effects in your presentation.

WordArt (Word) A set of graphic text styles that can be used to make text look like a graphic.

Workbook A file that you can use to organize various kinds of related information.

Worksheet The primary document that you use in Excel to store and work with data; also called a spreadsheet.

Worksheet tab The labels along the lower border of the workbook window that identify each worksheet or chart sheet.

World Wide Web A collection of linked pages designed to be viewed from any computer connected to the Internet.

WWW An acronym for World Wide Web.

X-axis Another name for the horizontal axis.

XML Paper Specification A file format that preserves formatting and embeds its fonts in such a way that it can be shared on many different devices and programs.

XPS An acronym for XML Paper Specification.

Y-axis Another name for the vertical axis.

Yes/No data type A data type that stores variables that can have one of two possible values—for example, yes or no, or true or false.

Zipped folder Another name for a compressed folder.

GO!
with Microsoft®
Excel® 2013
Comprehensive

Brief Contents

Taken from *Go! With Microsoft® Excel® 2013 Comprehensive*, by Shelley Gaskin, Alicia Vargas, and Debra Geoghan

Table of Contents

Chapter 7 Creating PivotTable and PivotChart Reports and Using BI Tools in Excel

About the Authors

Shelley Gaskin, Series Editor, is a professor in the Business and Computer Technology Division at Pasadena City College in Pasadena, California. She holds a bachelor's degree in Business Administration from Robert Morris College (Pennsylvania), a master's degree in Business from Northern Illinois University, and a doctorate in Adult and Community Education from Ball State University (Indiana). Before joining Pasadena City College, she spent 12 years in the computer industry, where she was a systems analyst, sales representative, and director of Customer Education with Unisys Corporation. She also worked for Ernst & Young on the development of large systems applications for their clients. She has written and developed training materials for custom systems applications in both the public and private sector, and has also written and edited numerous computer application textbooks.

This book is dedicated to my students, who inspire me every day.

Alicia Vargas is a faculty member in Business Information Technology at Pasadena City College. She holds a master's and a bachelor's degree in business education from California State University, Los Angeles, and has authored several textbooks and training manuals on Microsoft Word, Microsoft Excel, and Microsoft PowerPoint.

This book is dedicated with all my love to my husband Vic, who makes everything possible; and to my children Victor, Phil, and Emmy, who are an unending source of inspiration and who make everything worthwhile.

Debra Geoghan is a professor in the Science, Technology, Engineering, and Mathematics (STEM) Department at Bucks County Community College in Pennsylvania where she is coordinator of the Computer Science area. Deb teaches computer classes ranging from basic computer literacy to cybercrime, computer forensics, and networking. She holds a B.S. in Secondary Science Education from Temple University and an M.A. in Computer Science Education from Arcadia University, and has earned certifications from Microsoft, CompTIA, and Apple. Deb has taught at the college level since 1996 and also spent 11 years in the high school classroom.

Throughout her teaching career Deb has worked with educators to integrate technology across the curriculum. At Bucks she serves on many technology committees, presents technology workshops for faculty, and runs a summer workshop for local K–12 teachers interested in using technology in their classrooms. Deb is an avid user of technology, which has earned her the nickname "gadget lady."

This book is dedicated to my husband Joe, and my sons Joe and Mike, whose love and support have made this project possible.

GO! with Excel 2013

GO! with Excel 2013 is the right solution for you and your students in today's fast-moving, mobile environment. The GO! Series content focuses on the real-world job skills students need to succeed in the workforce. They learn Office by working step-by-step through practical job-related projects that put the core functionality of Office in context. And as has always been true of the GO! Series, students learn the important concepts when they need them, and they never get lost in instruction, because the GO! Series uses Microsoft procedural syntax. Students learn how and learn why—at the teachable moment.

After completing the instructional projects, students are ready to apply the skills in a wide variety of progressively challenging projects that require them to solve problems, think critically, and create projects on their own. And, for those who want to go beyond the classroom and become certified, GO! provides clear MOS preparation guidelines so students know what is needed to ace the Core exam!

What's New

New Design reflects the look of Windows 8 and Office 2013 and enhances readability.

Enhanced Chapter Opener now includes a deeper introduction to the A and B instructional projects and more highly defined chapter Objectives and Learning Outcomes.

New Application Introductions provide a brief overview of the application and put the chapters in context for students.

Coverage of New Features of Office 2013 ensures that students are learning the skills they need to work in today's job market.

New Application Capstone Projects ensure that students are ready to move on to the next set of chapters. Each Application Capstone Project can be found on the Instructor Resource Center and is also a Grader project in MyITLab.

More Grader Projects based on the E, F, and G mastering-level projects, both homework and assessment versions! These projects are written by our GO! authors, who are all instructors in colleges like yours!

New Training and Assessment Simulations are now written by the authors to match the book one-to-one!

New MOS Map on the Instructor Resource Site and in the Annotated Instructor's Edition indicates clearly where each required MOS Objective is covered.

Three Types of Videos help students understand and succeed in the real world:

- *Student Training Videos* are broken down by Objective and created by the author—a real instructor teaching the same types of courses that you do. Real personal instruction.
- *GO! to Work* videos are short interviews with workers showing how they use Office in their jobs.
- *GO! for Job Success* videos relate to the projects in the chapter and cover important career topics such as *Dressing for Success, Time Management,* and *Making Ethical Choices.* **Available for Chapters 1–3 only.**

New GO! Learn It Online section at the end of the chapter indicates where various student learning activities can be found, including multiple choice and matching activities.

New Styles for In-Text Boxed Content: Another Way, Notes, More Knowledge, Alerts, and **new** *By Touch* **instructions** are included in line with the instruction and not in the margins so that the student is more likely to read this information.

Clearly Indicated Build from Scratch Projects: GO! has always had many projects that begin "from scratch," and now we have an icon to really call them out!

New Visual Summary focuses on the four key concepts to remember from each chapter.

New Review and Assessment Guide summarizes the end-of-chapter assessments for a quick overview of the different types and levels of assignments and assessments for each chapter.

New Skills and Procedures Summary Chart (online at the Instructor Resource Center) summarizes all of the shortcuts and commands covered in the chapter.

New End-of-Chapter Key Term Glossary with Definitions for each chapter, plus a comprehensive end-of-book glossary.

New Flipboards and Crossword Puzzles enable students to review the concepts and key terms learned in each chapter by completing online challenges.

Teach the Course You Want in Less Time

A Microsoft® Office textbook designed for student success!

- **Project-Based** – Students learn by creating projects that they will use in the real world.

- **Microsoft Procedural Syntax** – Steps are written to put students in the right place at the right time.

- **Teachable Moment** – Expository text is woven into the steps—at the moment students need to know it—not chunked together in a block of text that will go unread.

- **Sequential Pagination** – Students have actual page numbers instead of confusing letters and abbreviations.

New Design – Provides a more visually appealing and concise display of important content.

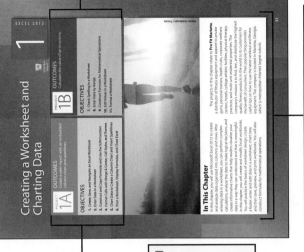

Student Outcomes and Learning Objectives – Objectives are clustered around projects that result in student outcomes.

Scenario – Each chapter opens with a job-related scenario that sets the stage for the projects the student will create.

Project Files – Clearly shows students which files are needed for the project and the names they will use to save their documents.

Project Results – Shows students what successful completion looks like.

New Feature

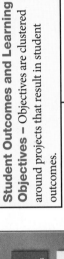

Simulation Training and Assessment – Give your students the most realistic Office 2013 experience with open, realistic, high-fidelity simulations.

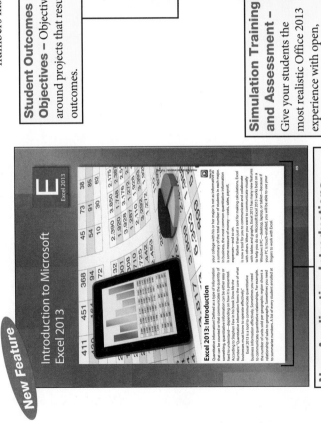

New Application Introductions – Provide an overview of the application to prepare students for the upcoming chapters.

Project Activities – A project summary stated clearly and quickly.

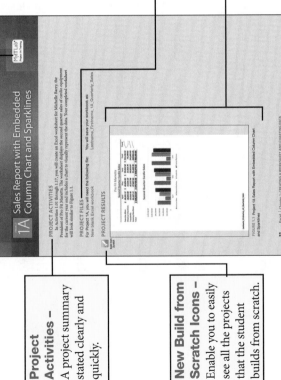

New Build from Scratch Icons – Enable you to easily see all the projects that the student builds from scratch.

In-Text Features
Another Way, Notes, More Knowledge, Alerts, and By Touch Instructions

Microsoft Procedural Syntax – Steps are written to put the student at the right place at the right time.

Color Coding – Each chapter has two instructional projects, which is less overwhelming for students than one large chapter project. The two projects are differentiated by different colored numbering and headings.

Teachable Moment – Expository text is woven into the steps—at the moment students need to know it—not chunked together in a block of text that will go unread.

Objective List – Every end-of-chapter project includes a listing of covered objectives from Projects A and B.

Sequential Pagination – Students are given actual page numbers to navigate through the textbook instead of confusing letters and abbreviations.

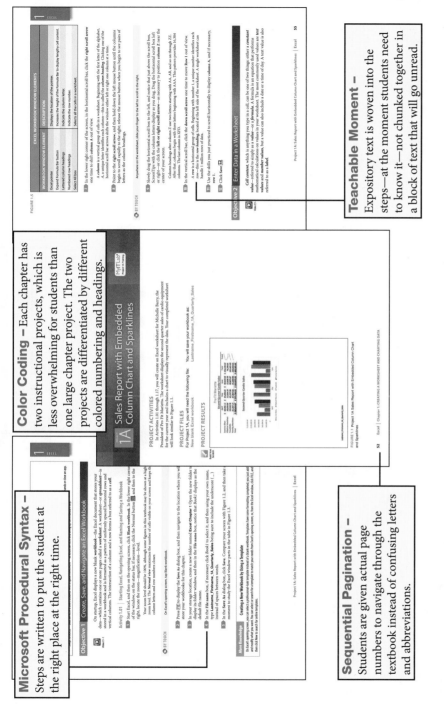

End-of-Chapter
Content-Based Assessments – Assessments with defined solutions.

Review and Assessment Chart – Displays a comprehensive list of each chapter assessment with a description and location to make planning easier.

End-of-Chapter Glossary – Gives students an easy way to review key terms.

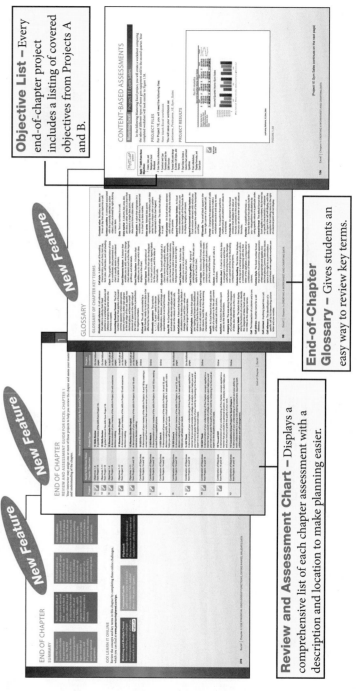

End-of-Chapter

Content-Based Assessments – Assessments with defined solutions. (continued)

Grader Projects – Each chapter has six MyITLab Grader projects—three homework and three assessment—clearly indicated by the MyITLab logo.

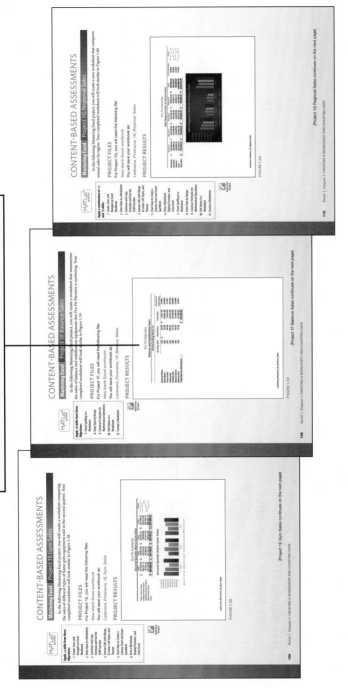

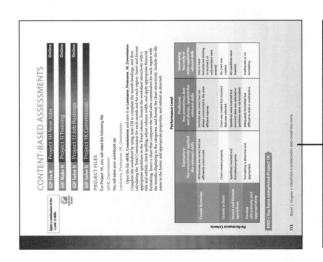

Task-Specific Rubric – A matrix specific to the GO! Solve It projects that states the criteria and standards for grading these defined-solution projects.

End-of-Chapter

Outcomes-Based Assessments – Assessments with open-ended solutions.

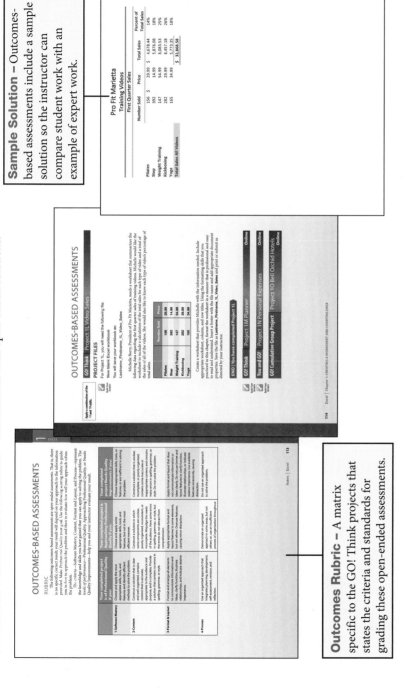

Sample Solution – Outcomes-based assessments include a sample solution so the instructor can compare student work with an example of expert work.

Outcomes Rubric – A matrix specific to the GO! Think projects that states the criteria and standards for grading these open-ended assessments.

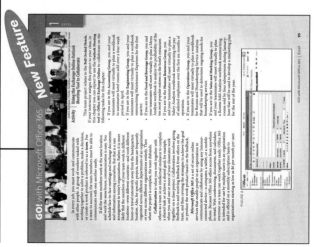

GO! with Microsoft Office 365 — **New Feature** — A collaboration project for each chapter teaches students how to use the cloud-based tools of Office 365 to communicate and collaborate from any device, anywhere. **Available for Chapters 1–3 only.**

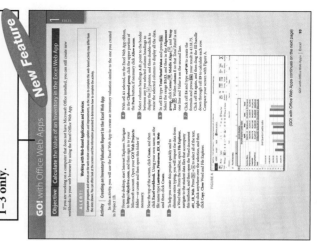

Office Web Apps – For each instructional project, students can create the same or similar result in the corresponding Office Web Apps - 24 projects in all! **Available for Chapters 1–3 only.**

GO! with MyITLab

Gives you a completely integrated solution

Instruction ■ Training ■ Assessment

All of the content in the book and MyITLab is written by the authors, who are instructors, so the instruction works seamlessly with the simulation trainings and grader projects — true 1:1. eText, Training and Assessment Simulations, and Grader Projects

Student Materials

Student Data Files – All student data files are available to all on the companion website: www.pearsonhighered.com/go.

3 Types of Videos help students understand and succeed in the real world:

- **Student Training Videos** are by Objective and created by the author—a real instructor teaching the same types of courses that you teach.

- *GO! to Work* videos are short interviews with workers showing how they use Office in their job.

- *GO! for Job Success* videos related to the projects in the chapter cover important career topics such as *Dressing for Success*, *Time Management*, and *Making Ethical Choices*. **Available for Chapters 1–3 only.**

Flipboards and crossword puzzles provide a variety of review options for content in each chapter.
Available on the companion website using the access code included with your book.
pearsonhighered.com/go

Reviewers

GO! Focus Group Participants

Kenneth Mayer — Heald College
Carolyn Borne — Louisiana State University
Toribio Matamoros — Miami Dade College
Lynn Keane — University of South Carolina
Terri Hayes — Broward College
Michelle Carter — Paradise Valley Community College

Diane Santurri — Johnson & Wales University
Roland Sparks — Johnson & Wales University
Ram Raghuraman — Joliet Junior College
Eduardo Suniga — Lansing Community College
Kenneth A. Hyatt — Lone Star College - Kingwood
Glenn Gray — Lone Star College - North Harris
Gene Carbonaro — Long Beach City College
Betty Pearman — Los Medanos College
Diane Kosharek — Madison College
Peter Meggison — Massasoit Community College
George Gabb — Miami Dade College
Lennie Alice Cooper — Miami Dade College
Richard Mabjish — Miami Dade College
Victor Giol — Miami Dade College
John Meir — Midlands Technical College
Greg Pauley — Moberly Area Community College
Catherine Glod — Mohawk Valley Community College
Robert Huyck — Mohawk Valley Community College
Kevin Engellant — Montana Western
Philip Lee — Nashville State Community College
Ruth Neal — Navarro College
Sharron Jordan — Navarro College
Richard Dale — New Mexico State University
Lori Townsend — Niagara County Community College
Judson Curry — North Park University
Mary Zegarski — Northampton Community College
Neal Stenlund — Northern Virginia Community College
Michael Goeken — Northwest Vista College
Mary Beth Tarver — Northwestern State University
Amy Rutledge — Oakland University
Marcia Braddock — Okefenokee Technical College
Richard Stocke — Oklahoma State University - OKC
Jane Stam — Onondaga Community College
Mike Michaelson — Palomar College
Kungwen (Dave) Chu — Purdue University Calumet
Wendy Ford — City University of New York - Queensborough Community College

Lewis Hall — Riverside City College
Karen Acree — San Juan College
Tim Ellis — Schoolcraft College
Dan Combellick — Scottsdale Community College
Pat Serrano — Scottsdale Community College
Rose Hendrickson — Sheridan College
Kit Carson — South Georgia College
Rebecca Futch — South Georgia State College
Brad Hagy — Southern Illinois University Carbondale
Mimi Spain — Southern Maine Community College
David Parker — Southern Oregon University
Madeline Baugher — Southwestern Oklahoma State University
Brian Holbert — St. Johns River State College
Bunny Howard — St. Johns River State College
Stephanie Cook — State College of Florida
Sharon Wavle — Tompkins Cortland Community College
George Fiori — Tri-County Technical College
Steve St. John — Tulsa Community College
Karen Thessing — University of Central Arkansas
Richard McMahon — University of Houston-Downtown
Shohreh Hashemi — University of Houston-Downtown
Donna Petty — Wallace Community College
Julia Bell — Walters State Community College
Ruby Kowaney — West Los Angeles College
Casey Thompson — Wiregrass Georgia Technical College
DeAnnia Clements — Wiregrass Georgia Technical College

GO! Reviewers

Abul Sheikh — Abraham Baldwin Agricultural College
John Percy — Atlantic Cape Community College
Janette Hicks — Binghamton University
Shannon Ogden — Black River Technical College
Karen May — Blinn College
Susan Fry — Boise State University
Chigurupati Rani — Borough of Manhattan Community College / CUNY
Ellen Glazer — Broward College
Kate LeGrand — Broward College
Mike Puopolo — Bunker Hill Community College
Nicole Lytle-Kosola — California State University, San Bernardino
Nisheeth Agrawal — Calhoun Community College
Pedro Diaz-Gomez — Cameron
Linda Friedel — Central Arizona College
Gregg Smith — Central Community College
Norm Cregger — Central Michigan University
Lisa LaCaria — Central Piedmont Community College
Steve Siedschlag — Chaffey College
Terri Helfand — Chaffey College
Susan Mills — Chambersburg
Mandy Reininger — Chemeketa Community College
Connie Crossley — Cincinnati State Technical and Community College
Marjorie Deutsch — City University of New York - Queensborough Community College
Mary Ann Zlotow — College of DuPage
Christine Bohnsak — College of Lake County
Gertrude Brier — College of Staten Island
Sharon Brown — College of The Albemarle
Terry Rigsby — Columbia College
Vicki Brooks — Columbia College
Donald Hames — Delgado Community College
Kristen King — Eastern Kentucky University
Kathie Richer — Edmonds Community College
Gary Smith — Elmhurst College
Wendi Kappersw — Embry-Riddle Aeronautical University
Nancy Woolridge — Fullerton College
Abigail Miller — Gateway Community & Technical College
Deep Ramanayake — Gateway Community & Technical College
Gwen White — Gateway Community & Technical College
Debbie Glinert — Gloria K School
Dana Smith — Golf Academy of America
Mary Locke — Greenville Technical College
Diane Marie Roselli — Harrisburg Area Community College
Linda Arnold — Harrisburg Area Community College - Lebanon
Daniel Schoedel — Harrisburg Area Community College - York Campus
Ken Mayer — Heald College
Xiaodong Qiao — Heald College
Donna Lamprecht — Hopkinsville Community College
Kristen Lancaster — Hopkinsville Community College
Johnny Hurley — Iowa Lakes Community College
Linda Halverson — Iowa Lakes Community College
Sarah Kilgo — Isothermal Community College
Chris DeGeare — Jefferson College
David McNair — Jefferson College

4

Use Financial and Lookup Functions, Define Names, Validate Data, and Audit Worksheets

PROJECT

4A

OUTCOMES

Calculate loan options and create a loan amortization schedule.

OBJECTIVES

1. Use Financial Functions
2. Use Goal Seek
3. Create a Data Table
4. Use Defined Names in a Formula

PROJECT

4B

OUTCOMES

Automate workbooks to look up information automatically and to validate data. Audit workbook formulas to locate and correct errors.

OBJECTIVES

5. Use Lookup Functions
6. Validate Data
7. Audit Worksheet Formulas
8. Use the Watch Window to Monitor Cell Values

GO! to Work
Video E4

Yuri Arcurs/Fotolia

In This Chapter

In this chapter, you will use Financial functions and What-If Analysis tools to make your worksheets more valuable for analyzing data and making financial decisions. In addition, you will define names and use them in a formula. You will use the Lookup functions to locate information that is needed in a form and create a validation list to ensure that only accurate data is entered. In this chapter, you will also use Excel's auditing features to help you understand the construction of formulas in a worksheet, and locate and correct any errors. For example, by tracing relationships you will be able to test your formulas for accuracy.

The projects in this chapter relate to **Jesse Jewelers**, a Toronto-based retailer of jewelry and accessories for men and women. Jesse sells unique and beautiful items at a great price. Products include necklaces, bracelets, key chains, business cases, jewelry boxes, handmade bags, and personalized items. Founded in 2005 by two college friends, this growing company has several retail locations and an online store. It distributes its products to department and specialty stores throughout the United States and Canada. Jesse Jewelers provides exceptional customer service from a well-trained staff of product experts.

PROJECT 4A

Amortization Schedule and Merchandise Costs

PROJECT ACTIVITIES

In Activities 4.01 through 4.09, you will create a worksheet for Alaina Dubois, International Sales Director for Jesse Jewelers, that details the loan information to purchase furniture and fixtures for a new store in Houston. You will also define names for ranges of cells in a workbook containing quarterly and annual merchandise costs for the new store. Your completed worksheets will look similar to Figure 4.1.

PROJECT FILES

For Project 4A, you will need the following files:

e04A_Merchandise_Costs
e04A_Store_Loan

You will save your workbooks as:

Lastname_Firstname_4A_Merchandise_Costs
Lastname_Firstname_4A_Store_Loan

PROJECT RESULTS

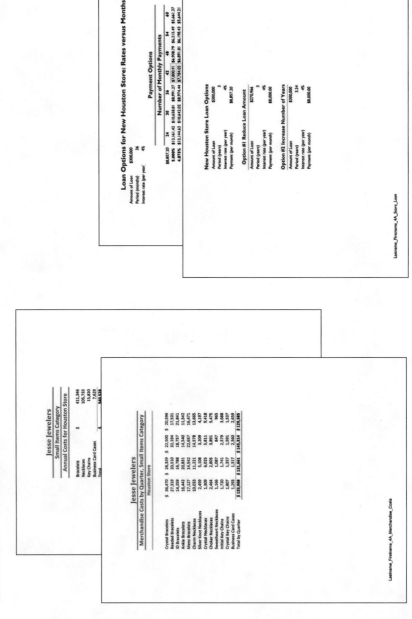

FIGURE 4.1 Project 4A Amortization Schedule and Merchandise Costs

NOTE

If You Are Using a Touchscreen

- Tap an item to click it.
- Press and hold for a few seconds to right-click; release when the information or commands display.
- Touch the screen with two or more fingers and then pinch together to zoom in or stretch your fingers apart to zoom out.
- Slide your finger on the screen to scroll—slide left to scroll right and slide right to scroll left.
- Slide to rearrange—similar to dragging with a mouse.
- Swipe from edge: from right to display charms; from left to expose open apps, snap apps, or close apps; from top or bottom to show commands or close an app.
- Swipe to select—slide an item a short distance with a quick movement—to select an item and bring up commands, if any.

Objective 1 | Use Financial Functions

Video E4-1

Financial functions are prebuilt formulas that make common business calculations such as calculating a loan payment on a vehicle or calculating how much to save each month to buy something. Financial functions commonly involve a period of time such as months or years.

When you borrow money from a bank or other lender, the amount charged to you for your use of the borrowed money is called *interest*. Loans are typically made for a period of years, and the interest that must be paid is a percentage of the loan amount that is still owed. In Excel, this interest percentage is called the *rate*.

The initial amount of the loan is called the *Present value (Pv)*, which is the total amount that a series of future payments is worth now, and is also known as the *principal*. When you borrow money, the loan amount is the present value to the lender. The number of time periods—number of payments—is abbreviated *Nper*. The value at the end of the time periods is the *Future value (Fv)*—the cash balance you want to attain after the last payment is made. The future value is usually zero for loans, because you will have paid off the full amount at the end of the term.

Activity 4.01 | Inserting the PMT Financial Function

In this activity, you will calculate the monthly payments that Jesse Jewelers must make to finance the purchase of the furniture and fixtures for a new store in Houston, the total cost of which is $300,000. You will calculate the monthly payments, including interest, for a three-year loan at an annual interest rate of 4.0%. To stay within Alaina's budget, the monthly payment must be approximately $8,000.

1 Start Excel. From your student files, open e04A_Store_Loan. Display the **Save As** dialog box, navigate to the location where you will store your workbooks for this chapter, and then create a new folder named **Excel Chapter 4** Open the folder, and then **Save** the workbook as **Lastname_Firstname_4A_Store_Loan**

2 In the range **A2:B5**, enter the following row titles and data. Recall that you can format the numbers as you type by typing them with their symbols as shown. Compare your screen with Figure 4.2.

Amount of Loan	$300,000
Period (years)	3
Interest Rate (per year)	4%
Payment (per month)	

FIGURE 4.2

3 ▶ Click cell **B5**. On the **FORMULAS tab**, in the **Function Library group**, click **Financial**. In the list, scroll down as necessary, and then click **PMT**.

The Function Arguments dialog box displays. Recall that *arguments* are the values that an Excel function uses to perform calculations or operations.

4 ▶ If necessary, drag the Function Arguments dialog box to the right side of your screen so you can view columns A:B.

The *PMT function* calculates the payment for a loan based on constant payments and at a constant interest rate.

5 ▶ With your insertion point positioned in the **Rate** box, type **b4/12** and then compare your screen with Figure 4.3.

Excel will divide the annual interest rate of 4%, which is 0.04 in decimal notation, located in cell B4 by 12 (months), which will result in a *monthly* interest rate.

When borrowing money, the interest rate and number of periods are quoted in years. The payments on a loan, however, are usually made monthly. Therefore, the number of periods, which is stated in years, and the *annual* interest rate, must be changed to a monthly equivalent in order to calculate the monthly payment amount. You can see that calculations like these can be made as part of the argument in a function.

FIGURE 4.3

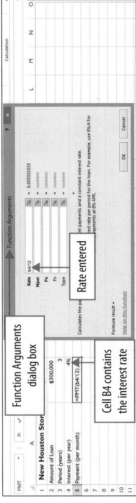

6 ▶ Press [Tab] to move the insertion point to the **Nper** box. In the lower portion of the dialog box, notice Excel points out that *Nper is the total number of payments for the loan* (number of periods).

7 ▶ Type **b3*12** to have Excel convert the number of years in the loan in cell **B3** (3 years) to the total number of months.

Recall that the PMT function calculates a *monthly* payment. Therefore, all values in the function must be expressed in months. To complete the PMT function, you must determine the total number of loan payment periods (months), which is 3 years × 12 months, or 36 months.

8 ▶ Press [Tab] to move to the **Pv** box, and then type **b2** to indicate the cell that contains the amount of the loan.

Pv represents the present value—the amount of the loan before any payments are made. In this instance, the Pv is $300,000.

9 In cell **B5** and on the **Formula Bar**, notice that the arguments that comprise the PMT function are separated by commas. Notice also, in the **Function Arguments** dialog box, that the value of each argument displays to the right of the argument box. Compare your screen with Figure 4.4.

N O T E   Optional Arguments

The PMT function has two arguments not indicated by bold; these are optional. The Future value (Fv) argument assumes that the unpaid portion of the loan should be zero at the end of the last period. The *Type argument* indicates when the loan payment is due. If not specified, the Type argument assumes that the payment will be made at the end of each period. These default values are typical of most loans and may be left blank.

FIGURE 4.4

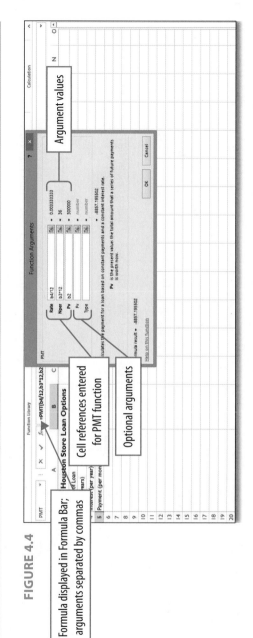

Formula displayed in Formula Bar; arguments separated by commas

Cell references entered for PMT function

Optional arguments

Argument values

10 In the lower right corner of the **Function Arguments** dialog box, click **OK**.

The monthly payment amount—($8,857.20)—displays in cell B5. The amount displays in red and in parentheses to show that it is a negative number, a number that will be paid out. This monthly payment of $8,857.20 is over the $8,000 per month that Alaina has budgeted for her payments.

11 Click in the **Formula Bar**, and then using the arrow keys on the keyboard, position the insertion point between the equal sign and PMT. Type – (minus sign) to insert a minus sign into the formula, and then press [Enter].

By placing a minus sign in the formula, the monthly payment amount, $8,857.20, displays in cell B5 as a *positive* number, which is more familiar and simpler to work with.

12 Save 🖫 your workbook.

Objective 2   Use Goal Seek

Video E4-2

What-If Analysis is a process of changing the values in cells to determine how those changes affect the outcome of formulas on the worksheet; for example, you might vary the interest rate to determine the amount of loan payments.

Goal Seek is part of a suite of data tools used for a What-If Analysis. It is a method to find a specific value for a cell by adjusting the value of one other cell. With Goal Seek, you can work backward from the desired outcome to find the number necessary to achieve your goal. If you have a result in mind, you can try different numbers in one of the cells used as an argument in the function until you get close to the result you want.

Activity 4.02 | Using Goal Seek to Produce a Desired Result

Alaina knows that her budget cannot exceed $8,000 per month for the new store loan. The amount of $300,000 is necessary to purchase the furniture and fixtures to open the new store. Now she has two options: borrow less money and reduce the amount or quality of the furniture and fixtures in the store or extend the time to repay the loan. To find out how much she can borrow for three years to stay within the budget or how much to increase the repayment period, you will use the Goal Seek tool.

1 Click cell **B5**. On the **DATA tab**, in the **Data Tools group**, click **What-If Analysis**, and then in the list, click **Goal Seek**. In the **Goal Seek** dialog box, in the **Set cell** box, confirm that *B5* displays.

The cell address in this box is the cell that will display the desired result.

2 Press Tab. In the **To value** box, type the payment goal of **8000** and press Tab. In the **By changing cell** box, type **b2** which is the amount of the loan, and then compare your dialog box with Figure 4.5.

FIGURE 4.5

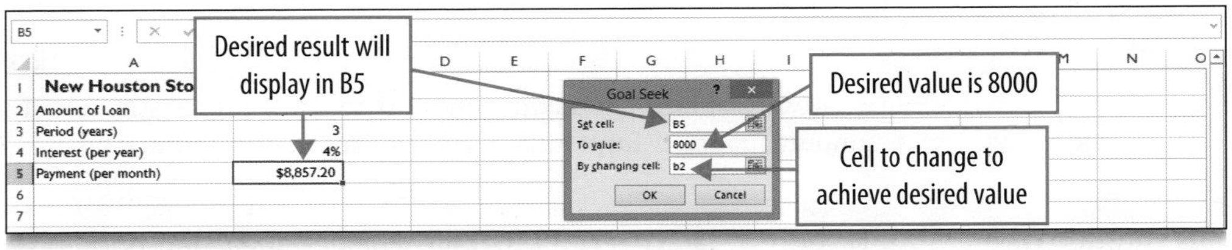

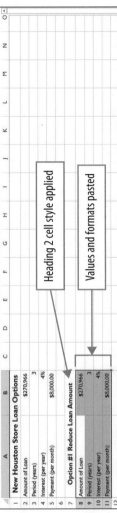

Desired result will display in B5

Desired value is 8000

Cell to change to achieve desired value

3 Click **OK**, and then in the **Goal Seek Status** dialog box, click **OK**.

Excel's calculations indicate that to achieve a monthly payment of $8,000.00 using a three-year loan, Alaina can borrow only *$270,966*—not $300,000.

4 Click cell A7. Type **Option #1 Reduce Loan Amount** and then on the **Formula Bar**, click **Enter** to keep the cell active. **Merge and Center** this heading across the range **A7:B7**, on the **HOME tab**, display the **Cell Styles** gallery, and then under **Titles and Headings**, click the **Heading 2** cell style.

5 Select the range **A2:B5**, right-click, and then click **Copy**. Point to cell **A8**, right-click, point to **Paste Special**, and then under **Paste Values**, click the **second button—Values & Number Formatting (A)**. Press Esc to cancel the moving border.

ANOTHER WAY   Click cell A8, right-click, and then click Paste Special. In the Paste Special dialog box, under Paste, click the Values and number formats option button, and then click OK.

6 **Save** your workbook, and then compare your worksheet with Figure 4.6.

Recall that by using the Paste Special command, you can copy the *value* in a cell, rather than the formula, and the cell formats are retained—cell B5 contains the PMT function formula, and here you need only the value that *results* from that formula.

FIGURE 4.6

Heading 2 cell style applied

Values and formats pasted

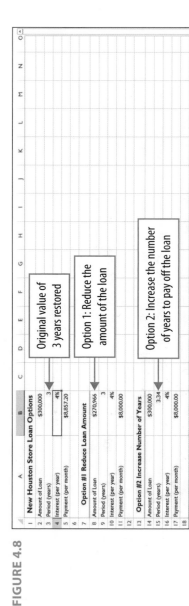

Activity 4.03 | Using Goal Seek to Find an Increased Period

For Alaina's purchase of furniture and fixtures for the new store in Houston, an alternative to borrowing less money—which would mean buying fewer items or items of lesser quality—would be to increase the number of years of payments.

1 In cell **B2**, replace the existing value by typing **300000** and then press Enter to restore the original loan amount. Click cell **B5**. On the **DATA tab**, in the **Data Tools group**, click **What-If Analysis**, and then click **Goal Seek**.

2 In the **Set cell** box, confirm that *B5* displays. Press Tab. In the **To value** box, type **8000** and then press Tab. In the **By changing cell** box, type **b3** which is the number of years for the loan. Compare your screen with Figure 4.7.

FIGURE 4.7

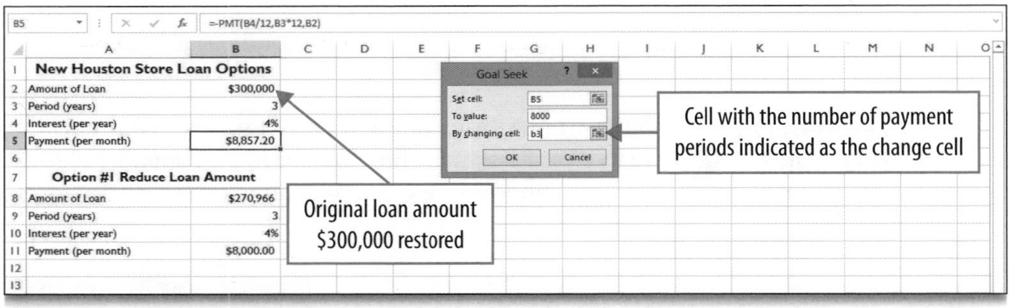

3 Click **OK** two times.

Excel's calculations indicate that by making payments for 3.3 years—3.343845511—the monthly payment is the desired amount of $8,000.00.

4 Click cell **A13**. Type **Option #2 Increase Number of Years** and then press Enter. Right-click over cell **A7**, on the mini toolbar, click **Format Painter**, and then click cell **A13** to copy the format.

5 Select the range **A2:B5**, right-click, and then click **Copy**. Point to cell **A14**, right-click, point to **Paste Special**, and then under **Paste Values**, click the **second button—Values & Number Formatting (A)**. Press Esc to cancel the moving border.

BY TOUCH Press and hold an item to display a shaded square and then release to right-click it.

6 Click cell **B15**, right-click to display the mini toolbar, and then click **Decrease Decimal** until the number of decimal places displayed is two. Click cell **B3**. Type **3** and then press Enter to restore the original value. **Save** your workbook, and then compare your screen with Figure 4.8.

FIGURE 4.8

Project 4A: Amortization Schedule and Merchandise Costs | Excel **237**

Video E4-3

A *data table* is a range of cells that shows how changing certain values in your formulas affects the results of those formulas. Data tables make it easy to calculate multiple versions in one operation, and then to view and compare the results of all the different variations.

For example, banks may offer loans at different rates for different periods of time, which require different payments. By using a data table, you can calculate the possible values for each argument.

A *one-variable data table* changes the value in only one cell. For example, use a one-variable data table if you want to see how different interest rates affect a monthly payment. A *two-variable data table* changes the values in two cells—for example, if you want to see how different interest rates and different payment periods will affect a monthly payment.

Activity 4.04 | Designing a Two-Variable Data Table

Recall that the PMT function has three required arguments: Present value (Pv), Rate, and Number of periods (Nper). Because Alaina would still like to borrow $300,000 and purchase the fixtures and furniture that she has selected for the new store in Houston, in this data table, the present value will *not* change. The two values that will change are the Rate and Number of periods. Possible periods will range from 24 months (2 years) to 60 months (5 years) and the rate will vary from 5% to 3%.

1 At the lower edge of the worksheet, click the **New sheet button** ⊕. Double-click the **Sheet1 tab**, type **Payment Table** and then press Enter.

2 In cell **A1**, type **Loan Options for New Houston Store: Rates versus Months** and then press Enter. **Merge and Center** 🔲▾ this title across the range **A1:J1**, and then apply the **Title** cell style.

3 In the range **A2:B4**, enter the following row titles and data:

Amount of Loan	$300,000
Period (months)	36
Interest rate (per year)	4%

4 Point to the border between **columns A** and **B** and double-click to AutoFit **column A**. In cell **C5**, type **Payment Options** and press Enter, and then **Merge and Center** 🔲▾ this title across the range **C5:I5**. From the **Cell Styles** gallery, under **Titles and Headings**, click the **Heading 1** cell style.

5 In cell **C6**, type **Number of Monthly Payments** and press Enter, and then use the **Format Painter** ⭐ to apply the format of cell **C5** to cell **C6**.

6 In cell **C7**, type **24** and then press Tab. Type **30** and then press Tab. Select the range **C7:D7**, point to the fill handle, and then drag to the right through cell **I7** to fill in a pattern of months from 24 to 60 in increments of six months.

Recall that the Auto Fill feature will duplicate a pattern of values that you set in the beginning cells.

7 In cell **B8**, type **5.000%** and then press Enter. In cell **B9**, type **4.875%** and then press Enter.

Excel rounds both values to two decimal places.

8 Select the range **B8:B9**. Point to the fill handle, and then drag down through cell **B24** to fill a pattern of interest rates in decrements of .125 from 5.00% down to 3.00%.

9 Right-click anywhere over the selected range, and then on the mini toolbar, click **Increase Decimal**. **Save** your workbook. Compare your screen with Figure 4.9.

Row 7 represents the number of monthly payments, and column B represents a range of possible annual interest rates. These two arguments will be used to calculate varying payment arrangements for a loan of $300,000.

FIGURE 4.9

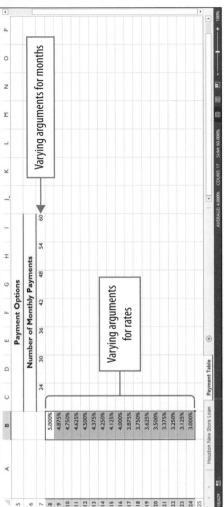

10 In cell **A8**, type **Rates** and then press **Enter**. Select the range **A8:A24**. On the **HOME tab**, in the **Alignment group**, click **Merge and Center**, click **Align Right**, and then click **Middle Align**. Display the **Cell Styles** gallery, and then under **Data and Model**, click the **Explanatory Text** style. Compare your screen with Figure 4.10.

FIGURE 4.10

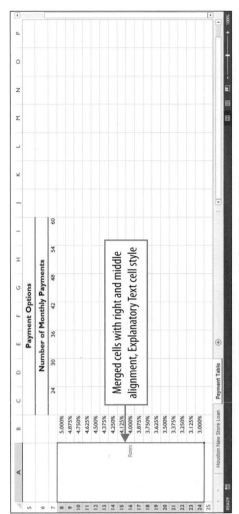

Activity 4.05 | Using a Data Table to Calculate Options

Recall that a data table is a range of cells that shows how changing certain values in your formulas affects the results of those formulas.

In this activity, you will create a table of payments for every combination of payment periods, which are represented by the column titles under *Number of Monthly Payments*, and interest rates, which are represented by the row titles to the right of *Rates*. From the resulting table, Alaina can find a combination of payment periods and interest rates that will enable her to go forward with her plan to borrow $300,000 to purchase the necessary furniture and fixtures for the new store in Houston.

1 Press Ctrl + Home to view the top of your worksheet. Then, in cell **B7**, type **=** Notice that in the upper left corner of your screen, in the **Name Box**, *PMT* displays indicating the most recently used function. Click in the **Name Box** to open the **Function Arguments** dialog box and select the **PMT** function.

When creating a data table, you enter the PMT function in the upper left corner of your range of data, so that when the data table is completed, the months in row 7 and the rates in column B will be substituted into each cell's formula and will fill the table with the range of months and interest rate options.

2 In the **Rate** box, type **b4/12** to divide the interest rate per year shown in cell **B4** by 12 and convert it to a monthly interest rate.

3 Press Tab to move the insertion point to the **Nper** box. Type **b3** which is the cell that contains the number of months, and then press Tab.

The periods in cell B3 are already stated in months and do not need to be changed.

4 In the **Pv** box, type **-b2** to enter the amount of the loan as a negative number. Compare your dialog box with Figure 4.11.

FIGURE 4.11

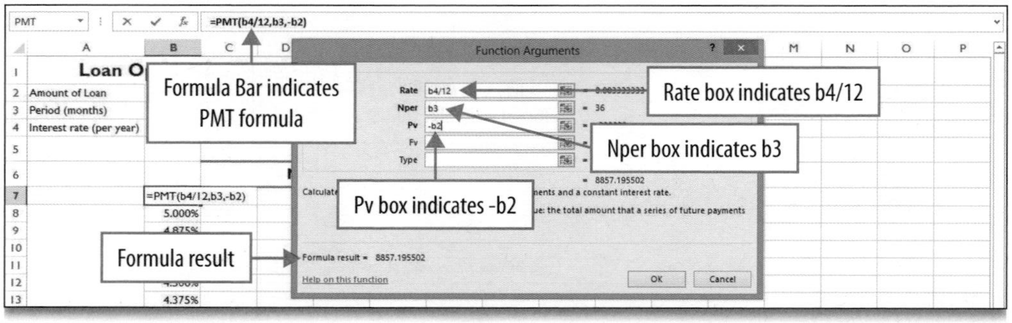

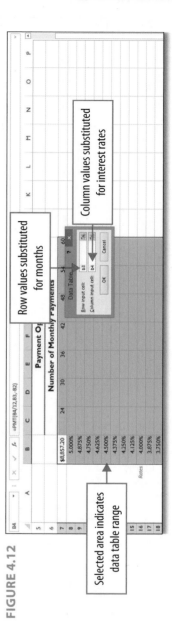

Formula Bar indicates
PMT formula

Rate box indicates b4/12

Nper box indicates b3

Pv box indicates -b2

Formula result

5 Click **OK** to close the **Function Arguments** dialog box and display the result in cell **B7**.

The payment—$8,857.20—is calculated by using the values in cells B2, B3, and B4. This is the same payment that you calculated on the first worksheet. Now it displays as a positive number because you entered the loan amount in cell B2 as a negative number.

6 Select the range **B7:I24**, which encompasses all of the months and all of the rates. With the range **B7:I24** selected, on the **DATA tab**, in the **Data Tools group**, click **What-If Analysis**, and then click **Data Table**.

7 In the **Data Table** dialog box, in the **Row input cell** box, type **b3** and then press Tab. In the **Column input cell** box, type **b4** and then compare your screen with Figure 4.12.

The row of months will be substituted for the value in cell B3, and the column of interest rates will be substituted for the value in cell B4.

FIGURE 4.12

Selected area indicates
data table range

Row values substituted
for months

Column values substituted
for interest rates

8 Click **OK**. Click cell **F8**, and then examine the formula in the **Formula Bar**. Compare your screen with Figure 4.13.

The table is filled with payment options that use the month and interest rate corresponding to the position in the table. So, if Alaina chooses a combination of 42 months at an interest rate of 5.0%, the monthly payment will be $7,800.91, which is slightly under the monthly payment she wanted. The data table is one of a group of Excel's What-If Analysis tools.

FIGURE 4.13

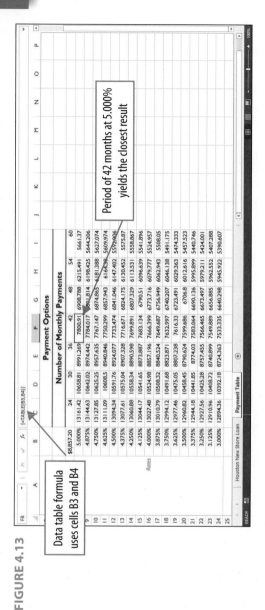

F8   {=TABLE(B3,B4)}

Data table formula uses cells B3 and B4

Period of 42 months at 5.000% yields the closest result

Payment Options

Number of Monthly Payments

$8,857.20	24	30	36	42	48	54	60
5.000%	13161.42	10658.81	8991.269	7800.91	6908.788	6215.491	5661.137
4.875%	13144.63	10642.02	8974.442	7784.017	6891.814	6198.425	5644.206
4.750%	13127.85	10625.25	8957.635	7767.147	6874.865	6181.388	5627.074
4.625%	13111.09	10608.5	8940.846	7750.299	6857.943	6164.39	5609.974
4.500%	13094.34	10591.76	8924.077	7733.474	6841.046	6147.402	5592.906
4.375%	13077.61	10575.04	8907.328	7716.671	6824.175	6130.452	5575.87
4.250%	13060.88	10558.34	8890.598	7699.891	6807.329	6113.531	5558.867
4.125%	13044.17	10541.65	8873.887	7683.134	6790.51	6096.639	5541.896
4.000%	13027.48	10524.98	8857.196	7666.399	6773.716	6079.777	5524.957
3.875%	13010.79	10508.32	8840.524	7649.687	6756.949	6062.943	5508.05
3.750%	12994.12	10491.68	8823.871	7632.997	6740.207	6046.138	5491.175
3.625%	12977.46	10475.05	8807.238	7616.33	6723.491	6029.363	5474.333
3.500%	12960.82	10458.45	8790.624	7599.686	6706.8	6012.616	5457.523
3.375%	12944.18	10441.85	8774.03	7583.064	6690.136	5995.899	5440.746
3.250%	12927.56	10425.28	8757.455	7566.465	6673.497	5979.211	5424.001
3.125%	12910.96	10408.72	8740.899	7549.889	6656.885	5962.552	5407.288
3.000%	12894.36	10392.18	8724.363	7533.335	6640.298	5945.922	5390.607

Rates

Houston New Store Loan   Payment Table

9 Point to cell **B7**, right-click, and then on the mini toolbar, click **Format Painter**. With the pointer, select the range **C8:I24** to apply the same format. AutoFit columns **C:I** to display all values.

10 Select the range **F8:F19**. From the **HOME tab**, display the **Cell Styles** gallery, and then under **Data and Model**, click the **Note** cell style to highlight the desired payment options.

11 Select the range **B8:B24**, hold down [Ctrl], and then select the range **C7:I7**. Right-click over the selection, and then on the mini toolbar, click **Bold B** and then click **Center**. Click anywhere to deselect the range, and then compare your worksheet with Figure 4.14.

🔁 **BY TOUCH**   Swipe to select the range B8:B24, hold it, and then select the range C7:I7.

By using a data table of payment options, you can see that Alaina must get a loan for a 42-month period (3.5 years) for any of the interest rates between 5.000% and 3.000% in order to purchase the furniture and fixtures she wants and still keep the monthly payment under $8,000.

FIGURE 4.14

For a 42-month period, loan options in this range will be within the budget

Payment Options

Number of Monthly Payments

$8,857.20	24	30	36	42	48	54	60
5.000%	$13,161.42	$10,658.81	$8,991.27	$7,800.91	$6,908.79	$6,215.49	$5,661.37
4.875%	$13,144.63	$10,642.02	$8,974.44	$7,784.02	$6,891.81	$6,198.43	$5,644.21
4.750%	$13,127.85	$10,625.25	$8,957.63	$7,767.15	$6,874.87	$6,181.39	$5,627.07
4.625%	$13,111.09	$10,608.50	$8,940.85	$7,750.30	$6,857.94	$6,164.38	$5,609.97
4.500%	$13,094.34	$10,591.76	$8,924.08	$7,733.47	$6,841.05	$6,147.40	$5,592.91
4.375%	$13,077.61	$10,575.04	$8,907.33	$7,716.67	$6,824.17	$6,130.45	$5,575.87
4.250%	$13,060.88	$10,558.34	$8,890.60	$7,699.89	$6,807.33	$6,113.53	$5,558.87
4.125%	$13,044.17	$10,541.65	$8,873.89	$7,683.13	$6,790.51	$6,096.64	$5,541.90
4.000%	$13,027.48	$10,524.98	$8,857.20	$7,666.40	$6,773.72	$6,079.78	$5,524.96
3.875%	$13,010.79	$10,508.32	$8,840.52	$7,649.69	$6,756.95	$6,062.94	$5,508.05
3.750%	$12,994.12	$10,491.68	$8,823.87	$7,633.00	$6,740.21	$6,046.14	$5,491.18
3.625%	$12,977.46	$10,475.05	$8,807.24	$7,616.33	$6,723.49	$6,029.36	$5,474.33
3.500%	$12,960.82	$10,458.45	$8,790.62	$7,599.69	$6,706.80	$6,012.62	$5,457.52
3.375%	$12,944.18	$10,441.85	$8,774.03	$7,583.06	$6,690.14	$5,995.90	$5,440.75
3.250%	$12,927.56	$10,425.28	$8,757.45	$7,566.47	$6,673.50	$5,979.21	$5,424.00
3.125%	$12,910.96	$10,408.72	$8,740.90	$7,549.89	$6,656.88	$5,962.55	$5,407.29
3.000%	$12,894.36	$10,392.18	$8,724.36	$7,533.34	$6,640.30	$5,945.92	$5,390.61

Rates

12 Right-click the **Payment Table sheet tab** and click **Select All Sheets**. With the two sheets grouped, insert a footer in the **left section** that includes the **file name**. Click outside the footer area. On the status bar, click **Normal** . Press [Ctrl] + [Home] to move to the top of the worksheet. Click the **PAGE LAYOUT tab**, in the **Page Setup group**, set the **Orientation** to **Landscape**. Click **Margins**, and then click **Custom Margins**. In the **Page Setup** dialog box, under **Center on page**, select **Horizontally**, and then click **OK**.

13 Click the **FILE tab** to display **Backstage view**. On the right, at the bottom of the **Properties** list, click **Show All Properties**. On the list of **Properties**, in the **Tags** box, type **amortization schedule, payment table** In the **Subject** box, type your course name and section #. Under **Related People**, be sure that your name displays as the author. If necessary, right-click the author name, click Edit Property, type your name, click outside of the Edit person dialog box, and then click OK.

14 Click **Print**, examine the **Print Preview**, make any necessary adjustments, and then **Save**  and Close your workbook.

15 Hold this workbook until the end of this project, and then print or submit the two worksheets in this workbook electronically as directed by your instructor. If required, print or create an electronic version of your worksheets with formulas displayed using the instructions in Project 1A.

Objective 4 Use Defined Names in a Formula

Video E4-4

A *name*, also referred to as a *defined name*, is a word or string of characters in Excel that represents a cell, a range of cells, a formula, or a constant value. A defined name that is distinctive and easy to remember typically defines the *purpose* of the selected cells. When creating a formula, the defined name may be used instead of the cell reference.

All names have a *scope*, which is the location within which the name is recognized without qualification. The scope of a name is usually either to a specific worksheet or to an entire workbook.

Activity 4.06 | Defining a Name

In this activity, you will use three ways to define a name for a cell or group of cells. After defining a name, you can use the name in a formula to refer to the cell or cells. Names make it easier for you and others to understand the meaning of formulas in a worksheet.

1 From your student files, open the file e04A_Merchandise_Costs, and then **Save** the file in your **Excel Chapter 4** folder as **Lastname_Firstname_4A_Merchandise_Costs**

2 Select the range **B6:E17**. In the lower right corner of the selection, click **Quick Analysis**. Click **TOTALS**, compare your screen to Figure 4.15, and then click the first **Sum** button to total the columns. Click anywhere to cancel the selection.

Use this technique to sum a group of columns or rows simultaneously.

ANOTHER WAY   Select the range B6:E18, which includes the adjacent empty cells in row 18, and then click AutoSum.

FIGURE 4.15

Range selected

SUM columns

Quick analysis

---

3 Select the range **B6:E6**, hold down [Ctrl], and select the range **B18:E18**. From the **Cell Styles** gallery, under **Number Format**, click the **Currency [0]** cell style. Select the range **B7:E17**, display the **Cell Styles** gallery, and then, under **Number Format**, click **Comma [0]**.

You can use these number formats in the Cell Styles gallery in a manner similar to the Accounting Number Format button and the Comma Style button on the ribbon. The advantage to using these styles from the Cell Styles gallery is that you can select the option that formats automatically with zero [0] decimal places.

4 Select the range **B18:E18**, and then from the **Cell Styles** gallery, under **Titles and Headings**, click the **Total** cell style. Press [Ctrl] + [Home] to move to the top of the worksheet, and then compare your screen with Figure 4.16.

FIGURE 4.16

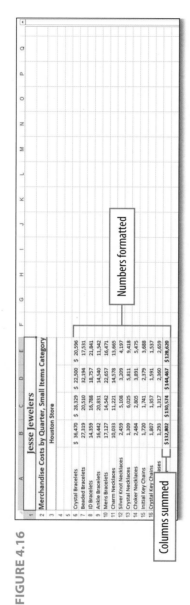

Numbers formatted

Columns summed

---

5 Select the range **B6:E9**. On the **FORMULAS tab**, in the **Defined Names group**, click **Define Name**. Compare your screen with Figure 4.17.

The New Name dialog box displays. In the Name box, Excel suggests *Crystal_Bracelets* as the name for this range of cells, which is the text in the first cell adjacent to the selected range. Excel will attempt to suggest a logical name for the selected cells. Notice that Excel replaces the blank space with an underscore, as defined names cannot contain spaces.

FIGURE 4.17

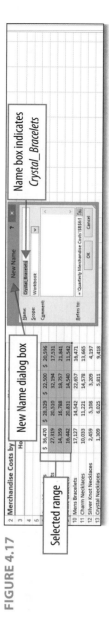

Selected range

New Name dialog box

Name box indicates
Crystal_Bracelets

---

6 With *Crystal_Bracelets* selected, type **Bracelet_Costs** as the name.

Naming cells has no effect on the displayed or underlying values; it simply creates an easy-to-remember name that you can use when creating formulas that refer to this range of cells.

7 At the bottom of the dialog box, at the right edge of the **Refers to** box, point to and click **Collapse Dialog Box** ⬚. Compare your screen with Figure 4.18.

The dialog box collapses (shrinks) so that only the *Refers to* box is visible, and the selected range is surrounded by a moving border. When you define a name, the stored definition is an absolute cell reference and includes the worksheet name.

FIGURE 4.18

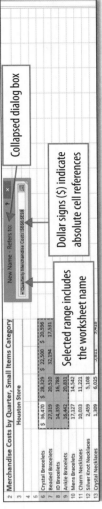

Collapsed dialog box

Dollar signs ($) indicate absolute cell references

Selected range includes the worksheet name

8 If necessary, drag the collapsed dialog box by its title bar to the right of your screen so that it is not blocking the selection. Then, change the range selection by selecting the range **B6:E10**.

A moving border surrounds the new range. The range, formatted with absolute cell references, displays in the *Refers to* box of the collapsed dialog box. In this manner, it is easy to change the range of cells referred to by the name.

9 Click **Expand Dialog Box** ⬚ to redisplay the entire **New Name** dialog box, and then click **OK**.

10 Select the range **B11:E14**. In the upper left corner of the Excel window, to the left of the **Formula Bar**, click in the **Name Box**, and notice that the cell reference *B11* moves to the left edge of the box and is highlighted in blue. Type **Necklace_Costs** as shown in Figure 4.19.

FIGURE 4.19

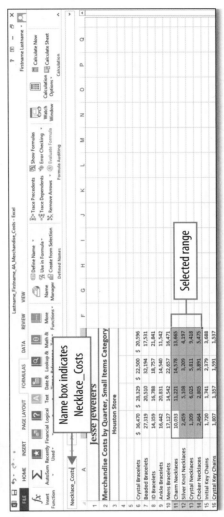

Name box indicates Necklace_Costs

Selected range

11 Press [Enter], and then take a moment to study the rules for defining names, as described in the table in Figure 4.20.

RULES FOR DEFINING NAMES

The first character of the defined name must be a letter, an underscore (_), or a backslash (\).

After the first character, the remaining characters in the defined name can be letters, numbers, periods, and underscore characters.

Spaces are not valid in a defined name; use a period or the underscore character as a word separator, for example, 1st.Quarter or 1st_Qtr.

The single letter C or R in either uppercase or lowercase cannot be defined as a name, because these letters are used by Excel for selecting a row or column when you enter them in a Name or a Go To text box.

A defined name can be no longer than 255 characters; short, meaningful names are the most useful.

Defined names cannot be the same as a cell reference, for example M$10.

Defined names can contain uppercase and lowercase letters; however, Excel does not distinguish between them. So, for example, if you create the name Sales and then create another name SALES in the same workbook, Excel considers the names to be the same and prompts you for a unique name.

FIGURE 4.20

12 Click any cell to cancel the selection. Then, click the **Name Box arrow** and compare your screen with Figure 4.21. If necessary, resize the Name Box by dragging the three vertical dots to the right, to display the full names.

Your two defined names display in alphabetical order.

FIGURE 4.21

List of defined names

13 From the list, click **Bracelet_Costs** and notice that Excel selects the range of values that comprise the cost of various Bracelet styles.

14 Click the **Name Box arrow** again, and then click **Necklace_Costs** to select the range of values that comprise the Necklace costs.

15 Select the range **B15:E16**. On the **FORMULAS tab**, in the **Defined Names group**, click **Name Manager**, and notice that the two names that you have defined display in a list.

16 In the upper left corner of the **Name Manager** dialog box, click **New**. With *Initial_Key_Chains* selected, type **Key_Chain_Costs** and then click **OK**. Compare your screen with Figure 4.22. **Close** the **Name Manager** dialog box and **Save** 🖫 your workbook.

This is another method to define a name—by creating a new name in the Name Manager dialog box. The Name Manager dialog box displays the three range names that you have created, in alphabetical order.

FIGURE 4.22

Name Manager dialog box

New button

List of named ranges

Activity 4.07 | Inserting New Data into a Named Range

You can insert new data into the range of cells that a name represents. In this activity, you will modify the range named *Necklace_Costs* to include new data.

1 On the left side of your window, click the **row 15** heading to select the entire row. Right-click over the selected row, and then click **Insert** to insert a new blank row above.

A new row 15 is inserted, and the remaining rows move down one row. Recall that when new rows are inserted in this manner, Excel adjusts formulas accordingly.

2 Click the **Name Box arrow**, and then click **Key_Chain_Costs**. Notice that Excel highlights the correct range of cells, adjusting for the newly inserted row.

If you insert rows, the defined name adjusts to the new cell addresses to represent the cells that were originally defined. Likewise, if you move the cells, the defined name goes with them to the new location.

3 In cell **A15**, type **Sweetheart Necklaces** and then press Tab. In cell **B15**, type **1166** and press Tab. In cell **C15**, type **1087** and press Tab. In cell **D15**, type **847** and press Tab. In cell **E15**, type **965** and press Enter.

The cells in the newly inserted row adopt the Currency [0] format from the cells above.

4 On the **FORMULAS tab**, from the **Defined Names group**, click **Name Manager.**

5 In the **Name Manager** dialog box, in the **Name** column, click **Necklace_Costs**. At the bottom of the dialog box, click in the **Refers to** box and edit the reference, changing **$E$14** to **$E$15** as shown in Figure 4.23.

This action will include the Sweetheart Necklace values in the named range.

FIGURE 4.23

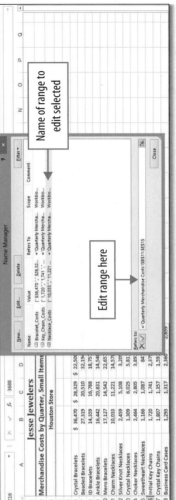

6 In the **Name Manager** dialog box, click **Close**, and click **Yes** to save the changes you made to the name reference. In the upper left corner of the window, click the **Name Box arrow** and then click the range name **Necklace_Costs**. Notice that the selected range now includes the new row 15. **Save** your workbook.

NOTE   **Changing a Defined Name**

If you create a defined name and then decide to change it, you can use the Name Manger to edit the name. Display the Name Manager dialog box, select the defined name, and then at the top of the dialog box, click Edit. If the defined name is used in a formula, the new name is automatically changed in any affected formulas.

Activity 4.08 | Creating a Defined Name by Using Row and Column Titles

You can use the Create from Selection command to use existing row or column titles as the name for a range of cells.

1 Select the range **A18:E18**. On the **FORMULAS tab**, in the **Defined Names group**, click **Create from Selection**. Compare your screen with Figure 4.24.

The Create Names from Selection dialog box displays. A check mark displays in the *Left column* check box, which indicates that Excel will use the value of the cell in the leftmost column of the selection as the range name, unless you specify otherwise.

FIGURE 4.24

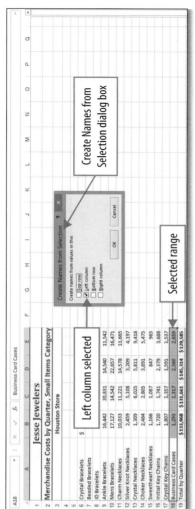

2 In the **Create Names from Selection** dialog box, click **OK**, and then click anywhere to cancel the selection.

3 Click the **Name Box arrow**, and then click the name **Business_Card_Cases**, and notice that in the new range name, Excel inserts the underscore necessary to fill a blank space in the range name. Also notice that the actual range consists of only the numeric values, as shown in Figure 4.25. **Save** your workbook.

This method is convenient for naming a range of cells without having to actually type a name— Excel uses the text of the first cell to the left of the selected range as the range name and then formats the name properly.

FIGURE 4.25

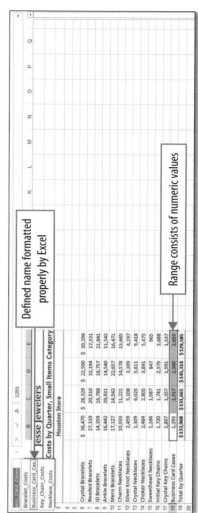

N O T E   **Deleting a Defined Name**

If you create a defined name and then decide that you no longer need it, you can delete the name and its accompanying range reference. Display the Name Manager dialog box, select the defined name, and then at the top of the dialog box, click Delete. Deleting a defined name does not modify the cell contents or formatting of the cells. Deleting a defined name does not delete any cells or any values. It deletes only the name that you have applied to a group of cells. However, any formula that contains the range name will display the #NAME? error message, and will have to be adjusted manually.

Activity 4.09 | Using Defined Names in a Formula

The advantage to naming a range of cells is that you can use the name in a formula in other parts of your workbook. The defined name provides a logical reference to data. For example, referring to data as Bracelet_Costs is easier to understand than referring to data as B6:E10.

When you use a defined name in a formula, the result is the same as if you typed the cell references.

1 Display the **Annual Merchandise Costs** worksheet.

2 In cell **B5**, type **=sum(B** and then scroll to the bottom of the AutoComplete list; compare your screen with Figure 4.26.

The Formula AutoComplete list displays containing all of Excel's built-in functions that begin with the letter B and any defined names in this workbook that begin with the letter B. To the left of your defined name *Bracelet_Costs*, a defined name icon [icon] displays.

FIGURE 4.26

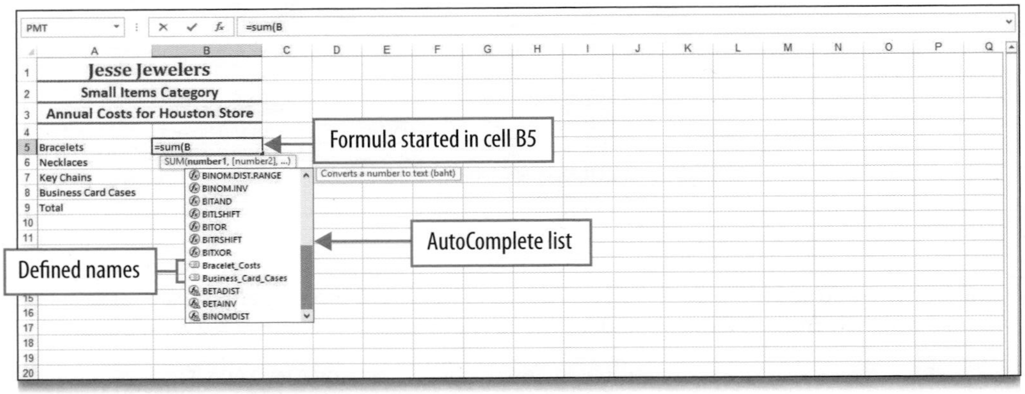

3 Double-click **Bracelet_Costs** and then press [Enter].

Your result is *411346*. Recall that SUM is a function—a formula already built by Excel—that adds all the cells in a selected range. Therefore, Excel sums all the cells in the range you defined as Bracelet_Costs on the first worksheet in the workbook, and then places the result in cell B5 of this worksheet.

ANOTHER WAY You can simply type the defined name in the formula.

4 In cell **B6**, type **=sum(N** and then on the **Formula AutoComplete** list, double-click **Necklace_Costs** to insert the formula. Press [Enter] to display the result *105,733*.

5 In cell **B7**, type **=sum(** and then on the **FORMULAS tab**, in the **Defined Names group**, click **Use in Formula**. In the list, click **Key_Chain_Costs**, and then press [Enter] to display the total *15,820*.

6 In cell **B8**, use any of the techniques you just practiced to sum the cells containing the costs for **Business Card Cases** and to display a result of *7,629*. In cell **B9**, in the **Function Library group**, click **AutoSum** ∑ AutoSum ▾ to sum **column B** and display a result of *540,528*.

7 Select the nonadjacent cells **B5** and **B9**, and then on the **HOME tab**, display the **Cell Styles** gallery. Under **Number Format**, click the **Currency [0]** cell style. Select the range **B6:B8**, display the **Cell Styles** gallery, and then under **Number Format**, click **Comma [0]**.

8 Click cell **B9** and under **Titles and Headings**, click the **Total** cell style. Click cell **B5** and then compare your screen with Figure 4.27.

FIGURE 4.27

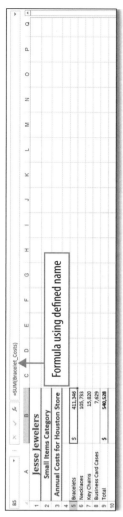

	A	B	C	D	E	F	G	H
B5				=SUM(Bracelet_Costs)				
1		Jesse Jewelers						
2		Small Items Category						
3		Annual Costs for Houston Store						
4								
5	Bracelets	$ 411,346						
6	Necklaces	105,733						
7	Key Chains	15,820						
8	Business Card Cases	7,629						
9	Total	$ 540,528						
10								

Formula using defined name

9 Select both worksheets so that *[Group]* displays in the title bar. With the two worksheets grouped, insert a footer in the **left section** that includes the file name. Return to **Normal view** and make cell **A1** active. **Center** the worksheets **Horizontally** on the page.

10 Click the **FILE tab** to display **Backstage** view. On the right, at the bottom of the **Properties** list, click **Show All Properties**. Under **Related People**, be sure that your name displays as the author. If necessary, right-click the author name, click Edit Property, and then type your name. In the **Subject** box, type your course name and section #, and in the **Tags** box, type **small items category, merchandise costs** Display the grouped worksheets in **Print Preview, Close** the **Print Preview,** and then make any necessary corrections or adjustments. Right-click any of the grouped sheet tabs, and then click **Ungroup Sheets.**

11 **Save** ▣ your workbook. Print or submit the two worksheets in this workbook electronically as directed by your instructor. If required, print or create an electronic version of your worksheets with formulas displayed. **Close** Excel.

END | You have completed Project 4A

8 Click cell **C9**, type **12** as the quantity ordered and press Tab. In cell **D9**, type **Silver** and press Tab.

9 With cell **E9** as the active cell, on the **FORMULAS tab**, in the **Function Library group**, click **Lookup & Reference**, and then click **VLOOKUP**.

10 With the insertion point in the **Lookup_value** box, click cell **A9** to look up information for Item G-ID. Click in the **Table_array** box, display the **Product Information** sheet, and then select the range **A4:C11**. Press F4 to make the values in the range absolute.

11 In the **Col_index_num** box, type **3** to look up the price in the third column of the range, and then click **OK**.

The Unit Price for the ID Bracelet—$17.00—displays in cell E9.

12 Click cell **F9**, and notice that a formula to calculate the total for the item, Quantity times Unit Price, has already been entered in the worksheet.

This formula has also been copied to the range F10:F18.

13 Click cell **E9**, and then copy the VLOOKUP formula down through cell **E18**. Compare your screen with Figure 4.33.

The #N/A error notation displays in the cells where you copied the formula, and also in cells F10:F18, because the formulas there have no values yet with which to perform a calculation—values have not yet been entered in column A in those rows.

FIGURE 4.33

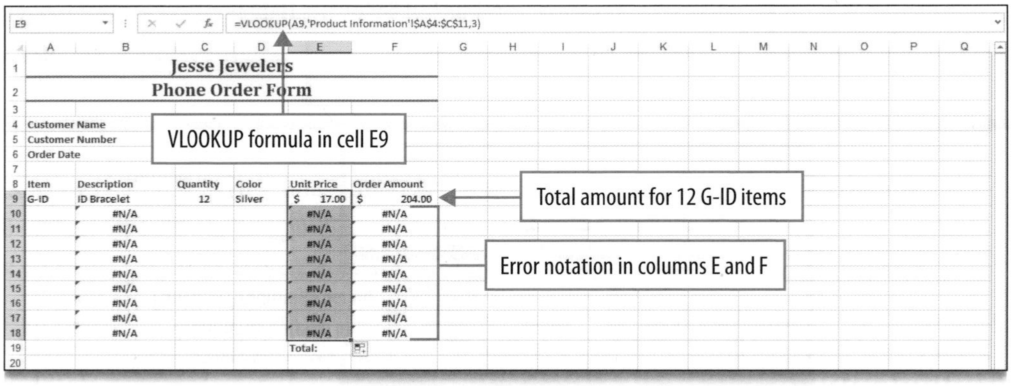

14 Click cell **A10**, type **N-CB** and press Tab two times.

Excel looks up the product description and the product price in the vertical table array on the Product Information sheet, and then displays the results in cells B10 and E10.

15 In cell **C10**, type **24** and press Tab. Notice that Excel calculates the total for this item in cell F10—*432.00.*

16 In cell **D10**, type **White** and then press Enter. Notice that after data is entered in the row, the error notations no longer display. **Save** your workbook. Compare your screen with Figure 4.34.

FIGURE 4.34

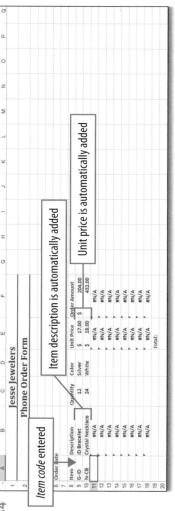

Item code entered

Item description is automatically added

Unit price is automatically added

Objective 6 Validate Data

Video E4-6

Another technique to improve accuracy when completing a worksheet is *data validation*—a technique in which you control the type of data or the values that are entered into a cell. This technique improves accuracy because it limits and controls the type of data an individual, such as an order taker, can enter into the form.

One way to control the type of data entered is to create a *validation list*—a list of values that are acceptable for a group of cells. Only values in the list are valid; any value *not* in the list is considered invalid. For example, in the Phone Order sheet, it would be useful if in the Item column, only valid Style Codes could be entered.

Activity 4.12 | Creating a Validation List

A list of valid values must either be on the same worksheet as the destination cell, or if the list is in another worksheet, the cell range must be named. In this activity, you will create a defined name for the Style Codes, and then create a validation list for column A of the Phone Order worksheet.

1 Display the **Product Information** worksheet. Select the range **A4:A11**. On the **FORMULAS tab**, in the **Defined Names group**, click **Create from Selection**.

Recall that by using the Create from Selection command, you can automatically generate a name from the selected cells that uses the text in the top row or the leftmost column of a selection.

2 In the **Create Names from Selection** dialog box, be sure the **Top row** check box is selected, and then click **OK** to use *Style Code* as the range name.

3 In the **Defined Names group**, click **Name Manager**, and then notice that the new defined name is listed with the name *Style_Code*.

Style_Code displays as the defined name for the selected cells. Recall that Excel replaces spaces with an underscore when it creates a range name.

4 **Close** the **Name Manager** dialog box. Display the **Phone Order** sheet, and then select the range **A9:A18**.

Before you set the validation requirement, you must first select the cells that you want to restrict to only valid entries from the list.

5 On the **DATA tab**, in the **Data Tools group**, click **Data Validation**. In the **Data Validation** dialog box, be sure the **Settings tab** is selected.

6 Under **Validation criteria**, click the **Allow arrow**, and then click **List**.

A Source box displays as the third box in the Data Validation dialog box. Here you select or type the source data.

7 Click to position the insertion point in the **Source** box, type **=Style_Code** and then compare your screen with Figure 4.35.

FIGURE 4.35

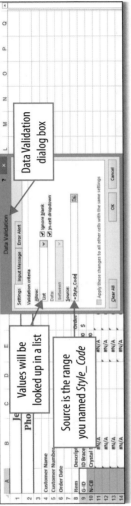

Data Validation dialog box

Values will be looked up in a list

Source is the range you named *Style_Code*

8 Click **OK**. Click cell **A11**, and notice that a list arrow displays at the right edge of the cell.

9 In cell **A11**, click the **list arrow** to display the list, and then compare your screen with Figure 4.36.

FIGURE 4.36

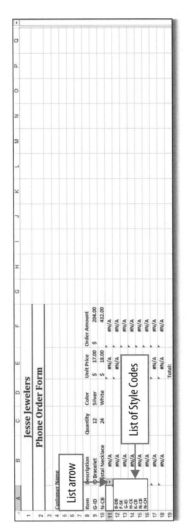

Jesse Jewelers
Phone Order Form

List arrow

List of Style Codes

10 From the list, click **B-DB**.

The Style Code is selected from the list and the Item, Description, and Unit Price cells are filled in for row 11.

11 Press [Tab] two times, type **24** and press [Tab], type **Multi** and then press [Enter] to return to the beginning of the next row. Compare your screen with Figure 4.37.

You can see that when taking orders by phone, it will speed the process if all of the necessary information can be filled in automatically. Furthermore, accuracy will be improved if item codes are restricted to only valid data.

FIGURE 4.37

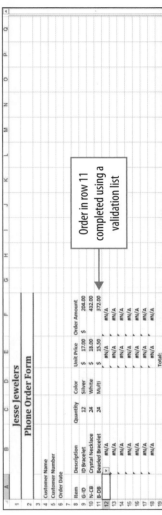

Jesse Jewelers
Phone Order Form

Order in row 11 completed using a validation list

12 With cell **A12** active, click the **list arrow**, and then click **F-SK**. As the **Quantity**, type **18** and as the **Color**, type **Antique** and then press Enter.

13 In cell **A13**, type **G-W** and press Tab.

An error message displays indicating that you entered a value that is not valid; that is, it is not on the validation list you created. If the order taker mistakenly types an invalid value into the cell, this message will display.

Restricting the values that an order taker can enter will greatly improve the accuracy of orders. Also, encouraging order takers to select from the list, rather than typing, will reduce the time it takes to fill in the order form.

14 In the error message, click **Cancel**. Click the **list arrow** again, click **H-CK**, and press Tab two times. As the **Quantity**, type **18** and as the **Color**, type **Ivory** and then press Enter.

15 Select the unused rows **14:18**, right-click over the selection, and then click **Delete**.

16 In cell **F14**, sum the **Order Amount** column, and apply the **Total** cell style.

17 Select both worksheets so that *[Group]* displays in the title bar. With the two worksheets grouped, insert a footer in the **left section** that includes the file name. **Center** the worksheets **Horizontally** on the page. Return to **Normal** view and make cell **A1** active.

18 Click the **FILE tab** to display **Backstage** view. On the right, at the bottom of the **Properties** list, click **Show All Properties**. On the list of **Properties**, in the **Tags** box, type **phone order form** In the **Subject** box, type your course name and section #. Under **Related People**, be sure that your name displays as the author. If necessary, right-click the author name, click Edit Property, type your name, click outside of the Edit person dialog box, and then click OK. Display the grouped worksheets in **Print Preview**, **Close** the **Print Preview**, and then make any necessary corrections or adjustments.

19 Ungroup the worksheets and then **Save** your workbook. Hold this workbook until the end of this project, and then print or submit the two worksheets in this workbook electronically as directed by your instructor. If required, print or create an electronic version of your worksheets with formulas displayed. **Close** this workbook.

More Knowledge | **Creating Validation Messages**

In the Data Validation dialog box, you can use the Input Message tab to create a ScreenTip that will display when the cell is selected. The message can be an instruction that tells the user what to do. You can also use the Error Alert tab to create a warning message that displays if invalid data is entered in the cell.

Objective 7 | Audit Worksheet Formulas

Video E4-7

Auditing is the process of examining a worksheet for errors in *formulas*. Formulas are equations that perform calculations on values in your worksheet. A formula consists of a sequence of values, cell references, names, functions, or operators in a cell, which together produce a new value. Recall that a formula always begins with an equal sign.

Excel includes a group of *Formula Auditing* features, which consists of tools and commands accessible from the FORMULAS tab that help you to check your worksheet for errors. In complex worksheets, use these Formula Auditing features to show relationships between cells and formulas, to ensure that formulas are logical and correct, and to resolve error messages. Although sometimes it is appropriate to hide the error message, at other times error notations can indicate a problem that should be corrected.

Activity 4.13 | Tracing Precedents

Precedent cells are cells that are referred to by a formula in another cell. The *Trace Precedents command* displays arrows that indicate what cells affect the values of the cell that is selected. By using the Trace Precedents command, you can see the relationships between formulas and cells. As an auditing tool, the process of tracing a formula is a way to ensure that you constructed the formula correctly.

1 From your student files, open the file **e04B_Miami_Revenue**, and then **Save** the file in your **Excel Chapter 4** folder as **Lastname_Firstname_4B_Miami_Revenue** Compare your screen with Figure 4.38.

The worksheet details the revenue and expenses related to the Miami store over a six-month period. Several error notations are present (#VALUE!, #REF!, #DIV/0!), green triangles display in the top left corners of several cells indicating a potential error, and two columns are too narrow to fit the data which Excel indicates by displaying pound signs—#####.

FIGURE 4.38

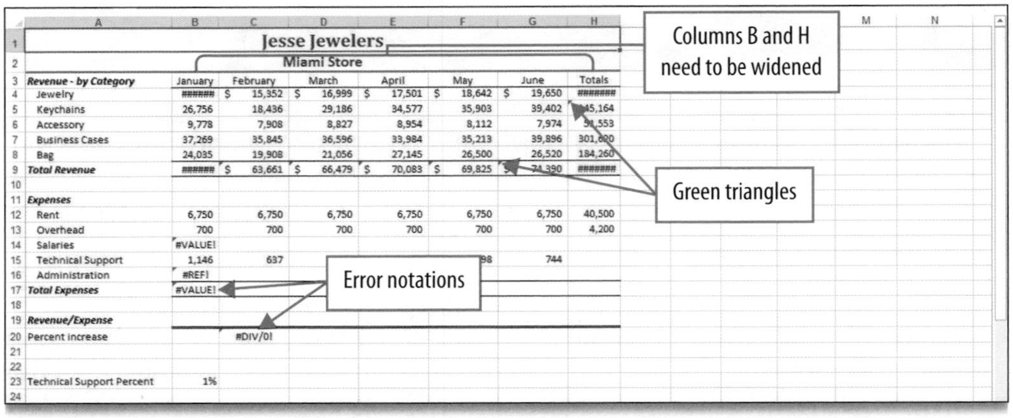

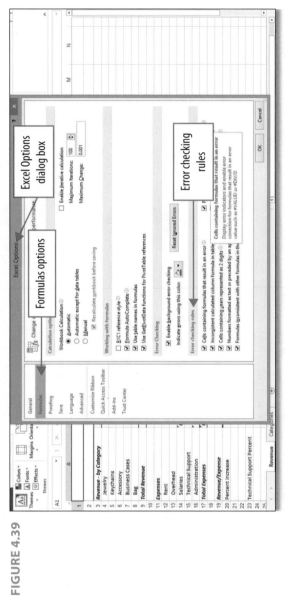

Columns B and H need to be widened

Green triangles

Error notations

2 Click the **FILE tab**, and then on the left, click **Options**. In the **Excel Options** dialog box, click **Formulas**. Under **Error checking rules**, point to the small information icon after the first Error checking rule to display the ScreenTip. Compare your screen with Figure 4.39.

Here you can control which error checking rules you want to activate, and you can get information about each of the rules by clicking the small blue information icon at the end of each rule. By default, all but the next to last rule are selected, and it is recommended that you maintain these default settings. This textbook assumes the default settings.

FIGURE 4.39

Excel Options dialog box

Formulas options

Error checking rules

3 In the lower right corner of the dialog box, click **Cancel** to close the dialog box.

4 Take a moment to study the table in Figure 4.40, which details some common error values that might display on your worksheet.

An *error value* is the result of a formula that Excel cannot evaluate correctly.

FIGURE 4.40

MICROSOFT EXCEL ERROR VALUES		
ERROR VALUE	**MEANING**	**POSSIBLE CAUSE**
#####	Cannot see data.	The column is not wide enough to display the entire value.
#DIV/0!	Cannot divide by zero.	The divisor in a formula refers to a blank cell or a cell that contains zero.
#NAME?	Does not recognize a name you used in a formula.	A function or a named range may be misspelled or does not exist.
#VALUE!	Cannot use a text field in a formula.	A formula refers to a cell that contains a text value rather than a numeric value or a formula.
#REF!	Cannot locate the reference.	A cell that is referenced in a formula may have been deleted or moved.
#N/A	No value is available.	No information is available for the calculation you want to perform.
#NUM!	Invalid argument in a worksheet function.	An unacceptable argument may have been used in a function. Or, a formula result could be too large or too small.
#NULL!	No common cells.	A space was entered between two ranges in a formula to indicate an intersection, but the ranges have no common cells.

5 On your worksheet, in the **column heading area**, select **column B**, hold down [Ctrl], and then select **column H**. Point to the right edge of either of the selected column headings to display the ✛ pointer, and then double-click to apply AutoFit.

AutoFit widens the columns to accommodate the longest values in each column; the ##### errors no longer display.

⟳ BY TOUCH Tap the column B heading and hold it, then tap column H. With both columns selected double-tap the border to the right edge of either of the selected column headings to apply AutoFit.

6 Click cell **C9**, and then notice the **green triangle** in the top left corner of the cell.

A green triangle in the upper left corner of a cell indicates that the formula in the cell is suspect for some reason. Typically, this is because the formula does not match the formula in the cells next to it, or because it does not include all of the adjacent cells.

7 In cell **C9**, to the left of the cell, point to **Error Checking** ◈ ▾, and then read the **ScreenTip** that displays. Compare your screen with Figure 4.41.

The ScreenTip indicates that adjacent cells containing numbers are not included in the formula. It is possible that the formula purposely consists of a group of cells that excludes some of the cells adjacent to it. However, because that is not as common as including *all* of the cells that are adjacent to one another, Excel flags this as a potential error.

FIGURE 4.41

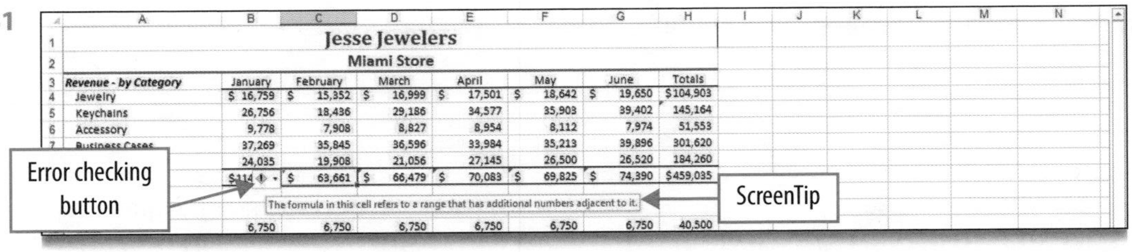

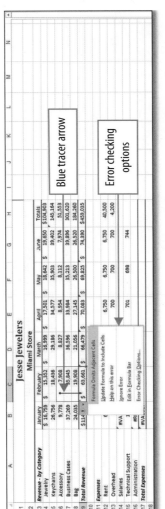

8 ▶ On the **FORMULAS tab**, in the **Formula Auditing group**, click **Trace Precedents**. Notice that the range **C6:C8** is bordered in blue and a blue arrow points to cell **C9**.

Recall that precedent cells are cells that are referred to by a formula in another cell. Here, the precedent cells are bordered in blue. A blue arrow, called a *tracer arrow*, displays from C6:C8, pointing to the selected cell C9. A tracer arrow shows the relationship between the active cell and its related cells. Tracer arrows are blue when pointing from a cell that provides data to another cell.

Because this total should include *all* of the revenue categories for February, this is an error in the formula—the formula should include the range C4:C8. By tracing the precedents, you can see that two cells were mistakenly left out of the formula.

9 ▶ To the left of cell **C9**, click **Error Checking** ◈ ▾ to display a list of error checking options. Compare your screen with Figure 4.42.

FIGURE 4.42

10 ▶ In the list, notice that Excel indicates the potential error highlighted in blue—*Formula Omits Adjacent Cells*. Notice also that you can update the formula, seek help with the error, ignore the error, edit the formula in the **Formula Bar**, or display the **Error Checking Options** in the **Excel Options** dialog box. Click **Update Formula to Include Cells**, and then look at the formula in the **Formula Bar**.

As shown in the Formula Bar, the formula is updated to include the range C4:C8; the green triangle no longer displays in the cell.

11 ▶ Click cell **D9**, which also displays a green triangle, and then point to **Error Checking** ◈ ▾ to display the **ScreenTip**.

The same error exists in cell D9—not all adjacent cells in the column were included in the formula. This error also exists in the range E9:G9. You can click in each cell and use the Error Checking button's options list to correct each formula, or, you can use the fill handle to copy the corrected formula in cell C9 to the remaining cells.

12 ▶ Click cell **C9**, drag the fill handle to copy the corrected formula to the range **D9:G9** and then notice that all the green triangles are removed from the range.

13 ▶ Click cell **H5**, point to **Error Checking** ◈ ▾, and read the **ScreenTip**.

The formula in this cell is not the same as the formula in the other cells in this area of the worksheet.

14 On the **FORMULAS tab**, in the **Formula Auditing group**, click **Trace Precedents**. Compare your screen with Figure 4.43.

A blue border surrounds the range B8:G8, and a blue tracer arrow displays from the cell B8 to cell H5. This indicates that the formula in cell H5 is summing the values in row 8 rather than the values in row 5.

FIGURE 4.43

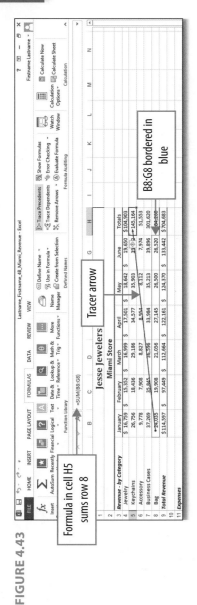

15 To the left of cell **H5**, click **Error Checking** to display the list of error checking options, notice the explanation *Inconsistent Formula*, examine the formula in the **Formula Bar**, and then click **Copy Formula from Above**. If necessary, AutoFit column H to display the values correctly.

16 Look at the **Formula Bar** to verify that the formula is summing the numbers in **row 5**—the range **B5:G5**. With cell H5 still selected, from the **HOME tab**, display the **Cell Styles gallery**, and then, under **Number Format**, click the **Comma [0] number format**.

The blue tracer arrow no longer displays, the formula sums row 5, and the proper number format is applied.

17 Click cell **H4**. On the **FORMULAS tab**, in the **Formula Auditing group**, click **Trace Precedents**. Notice the tracer arrow indicates that the appropriate cells are included in the formula, as shown in Figure 4.44.

FIGURE 4.44

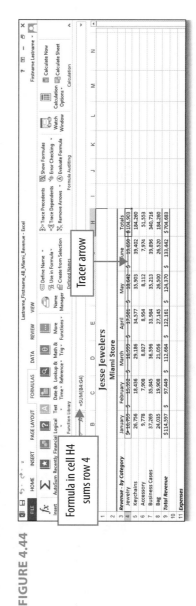

18 Click cell **H5**, click **Trace Precedents**, notice the **tracer arrow**, and then click cell **H6**. Click **Trace Precedents**, notice the tracer arrow, and verify that the correct cells are included in the formula.

19 Click cell **H7**, click **Trace Precedents**, and then click cell **H8**. Click **Trace Precedents**. Compare your screen with Figure 4.45.

Cells H7 and H8 display blue tracer arrows that are inconsistent with the other formulas in this column. However, green triangle indicators do not display in either of these cells. When auditing a worksheet, you cannot rely on the error notations and triangle indicators alone. To ensure the accuracy of a worksheet, you should use the tracer arrows to verify that all of the formulas are logical and correct.

FIGURE 4.45

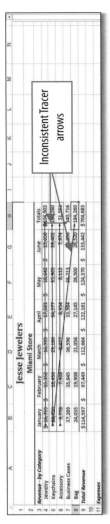

20 In the **Formula Auditing group**, click **Remove Arrows**. Click cell **H6** and then use the fill handle to copy the correct formula down to cells **H7:H8**.

21 **Save** your workbook.

Activity 4.14 | Tracing Dependents

Dependent cells are cells that contain formulas that refer to other cells—they depend on the values of other cells to display a result. The *Trace Dependents command* displays arrows that indicate what cells are affected by the value of the currently selected cell.

1 Click cell **B14**, which displays the error *#VALUE!*. To the left of the cell, point to **Error Checking** and read the ScreenTip.

This formula contains a reference to a cell that is the wrong data type—a cell that does not contain a number.

2 In the **Formula Auditing group**, click **Trace Precedents**.

A blue tracer arrow indicates that cell B3 is included in the formula. Because cell B3 contains text—*January*—and not a number, no mathematical calculation is possible. The salaries should be calculated as 5% of *Total Revenue*, plus the constant amount of $36,000.

3 In the **Formula Auditing group**, click **Trace Dependents**. Compare your screen with Figure 4.46.

A red tracer arrow displays showing that the formula in cell B17 depends on the result of the formula in cell B14. Tracer arrows are red if a cell contains an error value, such as #VALUE!.

FIGURE 4.46

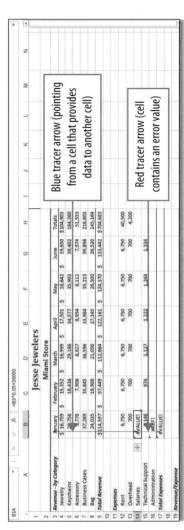

4 Click **Error Checking** ◈ ▾ and then click **Show Calculation Steps.**

The Evaluate Formula dialog box opens and indicates the formula as =*"January"*0.05+36000. January is not a number, nor is it a range name that refers to a group of numbers; so, it cannot be used in a mathematical formula. At the bottom of the dialog box, Excel indicates that the next evaluation will result in an error.

5 At the bottom of the dialog box, click **Evaluate.**

The formula in the Evaluation box indicates *#Value!+36000.* You can use this box to evaluate each step of the formula. With complex formulas, this can be helpful in examining each piece of a formula to see where the error has occurred.

6 **Close** the **Evaluate Formula** dialog box. With cell **B14** still the active cell, click in the **Formula Bar** and edit the formula to change cell **B3** to **B9,** and then press Enter. If necessary, AutoFit column B.

The error is removed and the result—41,730—displays in cell B14.

7 Click cell **B14.** Drag the fill handle to copy the corrected formula in cell **B14** across the row to cells **C14:G14.**

8 Click cell **B9.** In the **Formula Auditing group,** click **Trace Dependents.** Compare your screen with Figure 4.47.

Each cell where an arrowhead displays indicates a dependent relationship.

FIGURE 4.47

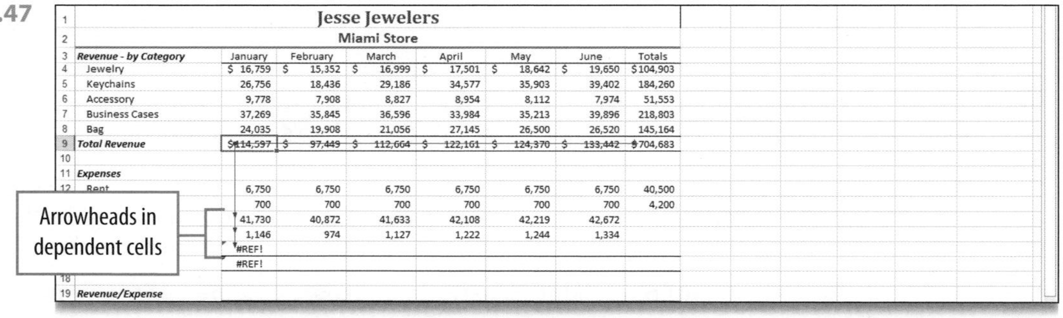

9 In the **Formula Auditing group,** click **Remove Arrows. Save** 🖫 your workbook.

Activity 4.15 | Tracing Formula Errors

Another tool you can use to help locate and resolve an error is the *Trace Error command.* Use this command to trace a selected error value such as #VALUE!, #REF!, #NAME?, or #DIV/0!.

1 Click cell **B16,** point to **Error Checking** ◈ ▾ and read the **ScreenTip.**

The error message indicates that a cell that was referenced in the formula has been moved or deleted, or the function is causing an invalid reference error. In other words, Excel does not know where to look to get the value that should be used in the formula.

2 In the **Formula Auditing group,** click the **Error Checking arrow** to display a list, and then compare your screen with Figure 4.48.

FIGURE 4.48

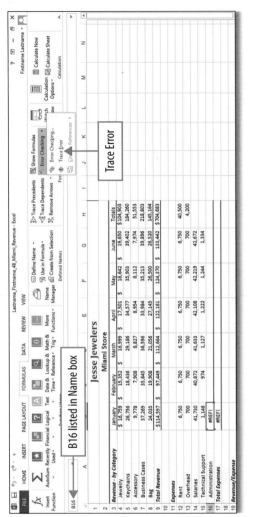

FIGURE 4.48

> **3** In the list, click **Trace Error**.
>
> A precedent arrow is drawn from cell B9 to B16.

> **4** In the **Formula Auditing group**, click the **Error Checking arrow** again, and then click **Trace Error** again.
>
> An arrow is drawn between cells B9 and B4 and the range B4:B8 is bordered in blue. The blue border indicates that this range is used in the formula in cell B9, which sums the values.

> **5** Click in cell A24. Type **Admin Percent** and press [Tab], type **2** and then press [Enter].
>
> The percent used to calculate administrative expenses was moved or deleted from the worksheet causing the #REF! error. You must re-enter the value so that it can be referenced in the formula in cell B16.

> **6** Click **B16**. Click **Error Checking ◇ ▾** to display the list of error checking options, and then click **Edit in Formula Bar**. The insertion point displays in the **Formula Bar** so that you can edit the formula.

> **7** Delete **#REF!**. Type **b24** and press [F4] to make the cell reference absolute, and then press [Enter].
>
> The error notation in cell B16 is replaced with 2,292. The corrected formula needs to be copied across row 16, and it needs to use an absolute reference. That way, the 2% Admin Percent will be applied for each month.

> **8** Click cell **B16** and then drag the fill handle to copy the formula to the right into cells **C16:G16**.

> **9** **Save 🖫** your workbook, press [Ctrl] + [Home], and then compare your screen with Figure 4.49.

FIGURE 4.49

Activity 4.16 | Using Error Checking

The **Error Checking command** checks for common errors that occur in formulas. The behavior is similar to checking for spelling; that is, the command uses a set of rules to check for errors in formulas. The command opens the Error Checking dialog box, which provides an explanation about the error and enables you to move from one error to the next. Therefore, you can review all of the errors on a worksheet.

1 Be sure that cell **A1** is the active cell. In the **Formula Auditing group**, click the **Error Checking arrow**, and then click **Error Checking.**

The Error Checking dialog box displays, and indicates the first error—in cell C20. Here the error notation *#DIV/0!* displays. The Error Checking dialog provides an explanation of this error—a formula or function is trying to divide by zero or by an empty cell.

2 In the **Error Checking** dialog box, click **Show Calculation Steps.**

The Evaluate Formula dialog box displays, and in the Evaluation box, *0/0* displays.

3 In the **Evaluate Formula** dialog box, click **Evaluate.**

The Evaluation box displays the error *#DIV/0!* And the Evaluate button changes to Restart.

4 Click **Restart.**

The formula *(C19-B19)/C19* displays; the first reference to C19 is underlined. The underline indicates that this is the part of the formula that is being evaluated. Each time you click the Evaluate button, it moves to the next cell reference or value in the formula.

5 In the **Evaluate Formula** dialog box, click **Step In**. Compare your screen with Figure 4.50.

A second box displays, which normally displays the value in the referenced cell. In this instance, the cell that is referenced is empty, as indicated in the message in the lower part of the dialog box. In a complex formula, this dialog box can help you examine and understand each part of the formula and identify exactly where the error is located.

FIGURE 4.50

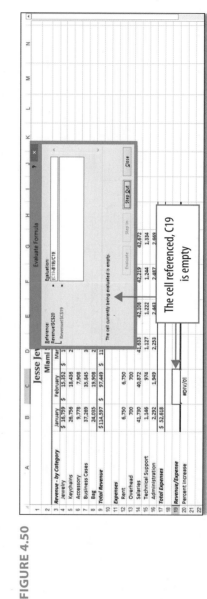

The cell referenced, C19 is empty

6 Click **Step Out.**

The cell evaluation box closes and the underline moves to the next cell in the formula—B19—which you can visually verify is empty by looking at the worksheet. To remove this error, you must complete the remainder of the worksheet.

7 Close the **Evaluate Formula** dialog box. In the **Error Checking** dialog box, click **Next.**

A message box displays stating that the error checking is complete for the entire sheet.

8 Click **OK.**

Both the message box and the Error Checking dialog box close.

9 Click cell **H13** and then use the fill handle to copy this formula down to cells **H14:H16**. Click cell **B17** and use the fill handle to copy this formula to the right into cells **C17:H17**. AutoFit any columns, if necessary, to display all of the data.

The formulas in the rows and columns are completed.

10 Click cell **B19** and type **=b9-b17** Press [Enter], and then copy the formula to the right into cells **C19:H19**.

The revenue/expense for each month is calculated. Notice that the *#DIV/0!* error in cell C20 is removed, but the formatting of the cell needs to be changed from dollars to percent.

11 Click cell **C20**, and on the **HOME tab**, in the **Number group**, click **Percent Style** %. Copy the formula to the right into cells **D20:G20**.

This formula calculates the percent change in revenue versus expenses, month to month.

12 Press [Ctrl] + [Home], **Save** 💾 your workbook. Compare your screen with Figure 4.51.

FIGURE 4.51

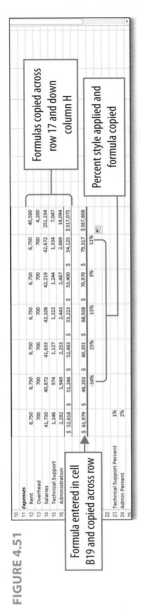

10								
11	**Expenses**							
12	Rent	6,750	6,750	6,750	6,750	6,750	6,750	40,500
13	Overhead	700	700	700	700	700	700	4,200
14	Salaries	41,730	40,872	41,633	42,108	42,219	42,672	251,234
15	Technical Support	1,146	974	1,127	1,222	1,244	1,334	7,047
16	Administration	2,292	1,949	2,253	2,443	2,487	2,669	14,094
		$ 52,618	$ 51,246	$ 53,400	$ 54,125	$317,075		
		$ 61,979	$ 46,203	$ 60,201	$ 53,223	$ 68,938	$ 70,970	$ 79,317	$ 387,608
		-34%	23%	13%	3%	11%		
22								
23	Technical Support Percent	1%						
24	Admin Percent	2%						

Formula entered in cell B19 and copied across row

Formulas copied across row 17 and down column H

Percent style applied and formula copied

More Knowledge

One common error in Excel worksheets is a ***circular reference***, in which a formula directly or indirectly refers to itself. The result is an ***iterative calculation***, where Excel recalculates the formula over and over. To prevent this, Excel flags the formula as an error and does not perform the calculation. If you need to, you can enable iterative calculations and specify the maximum number of iterations Excel performs in the Excel Options dialog box.

Activity 4.17 | Circling Invalid Data

If you use validation lists in a worksheet, you can apply data validation and instruct Excel to circle invalid data. In this manner you can verify that valid values—values from the list—have been entered on the worksheet.

1 Click the **Categories sheet tab**.

This worksheet lists the merchandise types included in each category; only merchandise types from these categories are valid.

2 Click the **Name Box arrow**, and then click **Items**, which is the only range name that displays in the list box. Compare your screen with Figure 4.52.

The named range in row 2 is highlighted.

FIGURE 4.52

	A	B	C	D	E	F	G	H	I	J	K	L	M
1		Revenue categories include the following items:											
2	Jewelry	Keychains	Accessories	Business Cases	Bags								
3	Bracelets	Keychains	Belts	Leather	Handbags								
4	Necklaces		Scarves	Engraved	Laptop Cases								
5	Earrings				E-reader Covers								
6	Rings												
7													

Named range

3 Display the **Revenue** worksheet. On the **DATA tab**, in the **Data Tools group**, click the **Data Validation arrow**, and then click **Circle Invalid Data.** Compare your screen with Figure 4.53.

Red circles display around Accessory and Bag.

FIGURE 4.53

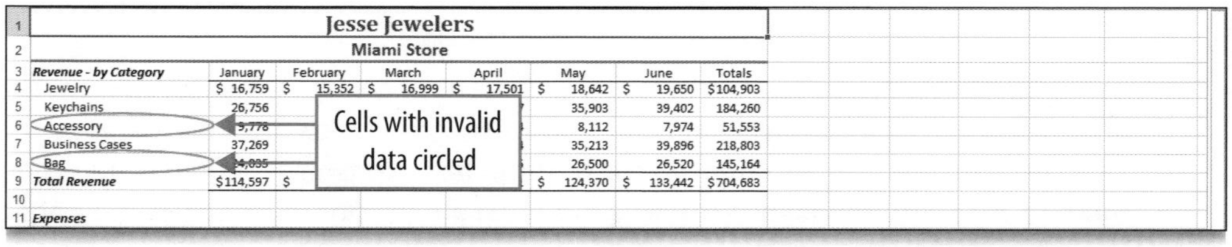

Jesse Jewelers

Miami Store

Revenue - by Category	January	February	March	April	May	June	Totals
Jewelry	$ 16,759	$ 15,352	$ 16,999	$ 17,501	$ 18,642	$ 19,650	$104,903
Keychains	26,756		35,903		8,112	35,402	184,260
Accessory	37,778				8,112	7,974	51,553
Business Cases	37,269				35,213	39,896	218,803
Bag	36,035				26,500	26,520	145,164
Total Revenue	$114,597	$			124,370	$ 133,442	$704,683
Expenses							

Cells with invalid data circled

4 Click cell **A6** and click the arrow that displays at the right side of the cell.

The validation list displays.

5 In the list, click **Accessories.**

The item is corrected but the red circle is not removed.

6 Click cell **A8**, click the arrow, and then click **Bags.**

7 In the **Data Tools group**, click the **Data Validation arrow**, and then click **Clear Validation Circles** to remove the circles.

8 In the **Data Tools group**, click the **Data Validation arrow**, and then click **Circle Invalid Data.**

No circles are applied, which confirms that the data is now valid against the validation list.

9 **Save** your workbook.

10 Select both worksheets so that *[Group]* displays in the title bar. With the two worksheets grouped, insert a footer in the **left section** that includes the file name. **Center** the worksheets **Horizontally** on the page and set the **Orientation** to **Landscape.** On the status bar, click **Normal**. Press Ctrl + Home.

11 Click the **FILE tab** to display **Backstage** view. On the right, at the bottom of the **Properties** list, click **Show All Properties.** On the list of **Properties**, in the **Tags** box, type **Miami revenue** In the **Subject** box, type your course name and section #. Under **Related People**, be sure that your name displays as the author. If necessary, right-click the author name, click Edit Property, type your name, click outside of the Edit person dialog box, and then click OK. Display the grouped worksheets in **Print Preview, Close** the print preview, and then make any necessary corrections or adjustments.

12 Ungroup the worksheets, **Save** and **Close** your workbook.

13 Hold this workbook until the end of this project, and then print or submit the two worksheets in this workbook electronically as directed by your instructor. If required, print or create an electronic version of your worksheets with formulas displayed using the instructions in Project 1A.

Objective 8 Use the Watch Window to Monitor Cell Values

Video E4-8

You can monitor cells in one part of a workbook while working on another part of the workbook using the *Watch Window*—a window that displays the results of specified cells. You can monitor cells on other worksheets and see the results as soon as formulas are calculated or changes are made that affect the outcome of the watched cells. This feature is also useful on large worksheets for which the total rows and columns are not visible on the screen with the details.

Activity 4.18 | Using the Watch Window to Monitor Changes

Mike Connor's assistant is preparing the 1st Quarter sales worksheets using the Watch Window for sales totals for the four largest retail stores.

1 From your student files, open the file e04B_First_Quarter_Sales and then **Save** the file in your **Excel Chapter 4** folder as **Lastname_Firstname_4B_First_Quarter_Sales**

2 On the **Toronto** worksheet, click cell **E8**. On the **FORMULAS tab**, in the **Formula Auditing group**, click **Watch Window.**

The Watch Window displays on your screen. As you create totals for the columns and rows on each worksheet in this activity, you will be able to use the Watch Window to view the results for all the worksheets at once.

3 In the upper left corner of the **Watch Window**, click **Add Watch**. Drag the window below your data, and then compare your screen with Figure 4.54.

The Add Watch dialog box displays the address for the selected cell—Toronto!$E$8

FIGURE 4.54

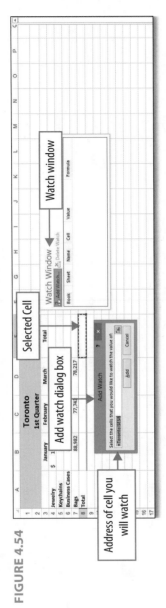

4 In the **Add Watch** dialog box, click **Add.**

Because there is no value or formula in the cell at this time, the Name, Value, and Formula columns are empty.

5 Display the **Houston** worksheet and then click cell **E8**. In the **Watch Window**, click **Add Watch,** and then in the **Add Watch** dialog box, click **Add.** Compare your screen with Figure 4.55.

A second cell is added to the Watch Window.

FIGURE 4.55

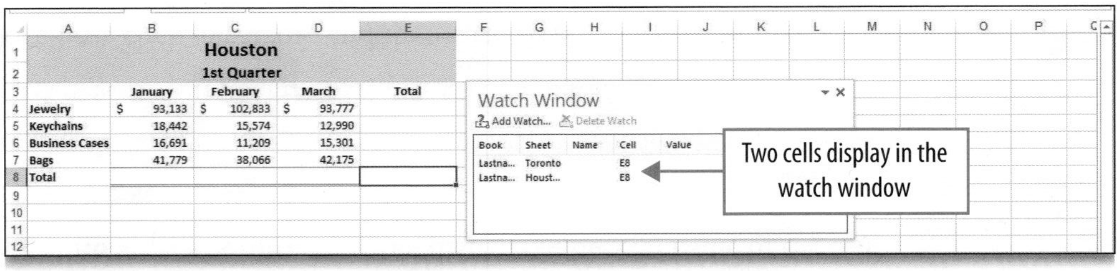

6 Following the same procedure, add cell **E8** from the **New York** sheet and from the **Miami** sheet to the **Watch Window.** Adjust the size of the **Watch Window** columns as necessary to view all four sheets. Compare your screen with Figure 4.56, and verify cell **E8** is listed for each of the four worksheets.

FIGURE 4.56

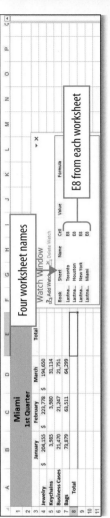

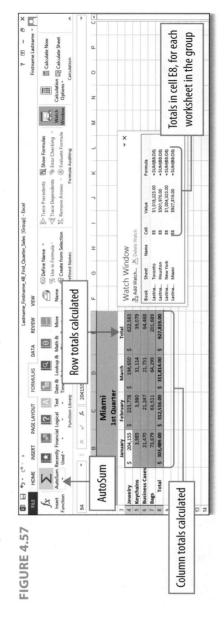

Four worksheet names

E8 from each worksheet

---

7 With the **Miami** worksheet active, hold down Shift, and then click the **Toronto sheet tab.**

The four store worksheets are selected and *[Group]* displays in the title bar.

8 In the **Miami** worksheet, select the range **B4:E8.**

This includes the data and the empty row and column immediately adjacent to the data. Because the sheets are grouped, this action is taking place on all four worksheets.

9 On the **FORMULAS tab,** in the **Function Library group,** click **AutoSum.** Compare your screen with Figure 4.57.

The totals for the rows and columns in this worksheet, as well as in the other three worksheets, are calculated. The results display immediately in the Watch Window, indicating that calculations took place on all four sheets simultaneously.

FIGURE 4.57

AutoSum

Row totals calculated

Column totals calculated

Totals in cell E8, for each worksheet in the group

---

10 Close ☒ the **Watch Window.**

11 With the four worksheets grouped, insert a footer in the **left section** that includes the file name. **Center** the sheets **Horizontally.** On the status bar, click **Normal** 🎬. Press Ctrl + Home to move to the top of the worksheet.

12 Click the **FILE tab** to display **Backstage** view. On the right, at the bottom of the **Properties** list, click **Show All Properties.** On the list of **Properties,** in the **Tags** box, type **first quarter sales** In the **Subject** box, type your course name and section #. Under **Related People,** be sure that your name displays as the author. If necessary, right-click the author name, click Edit Property, type your name, click outside of the Edit person dialog box, and then click OK. Display the grouped worksheets in **Print Preview,** and then view your worksheets. **Close** the print preview, and then make any necessary corrections or adjustments.

13 Right-click any sheet tab and click **Ungroup Sheets. Save** 🖫 and **Close** your workbook and **Exit** Excel. Print or submit the four worksheets in this workbook electronically as directed by your instructor. If required, print your worksheets with formulas displayed.

END | You have completed Project 4B

END OF CHAPTER

SUMMARY

The PMT function is used to calculate the payment for a loan. The PMT function has three required arguments: Rate (interest), Nper (number of payments), and Pv (present value), and two optional arguments.

Two of Excel's What-If Analysis tools are Goal Seek—used to find a specific value for a cell by adjusting the value of another cell; and Data Tables—which display the results of different inputs into a formula.

A defined name can represent a cell, range of cells, formula, or constant value and can be used in a formula. A Lookup function looks up data located in another part of a workbook to find a corresponding value.

Data validation is used to control the type of data or the values that are entered into a cell. Formula auditing improves the accuracy of data entry and checks a worksheet for various types of errors.

GO! LEARN IT ONLINE

Review the concepts and key terms in this chapter by completing these online challenges, which you can find at **www.pearsonhighered.com/go.**

Matching and Multiple Choice:
Answer matching and multiple choice questions to test what you learned in this chapter. MyITLab®

Crossword Puzzle:
Spell out the words that match the numbered clues, and put them in the puzzle squares.

Flipboard:
Flip through the definitions of the key terms in this chapter and match them with the correct term.

END OF CHAPTER

REVIEW AND ASSESSMENT GUIDE FOR EXCEL CHAPTER 4

Your instructor may assign one or more of these projects to help you review the chapter and assess your mastery and understanding of the chapter.

Review and Assessment Guide for Excel Chapter 4

Project	Apply Skills from These Chapter Objectives	Project Type	Project Location
4C	Objectives 1–4 from Project 4A	**4C Skills Review** A guided review of the skills from Project 4A.	On the following pages
4D	Objectives 5–8 from Project 4B	**4D Skills Review** A guided review of the skills from Project 4B.	On the following pages
4E	Objectives 1–4 from Project 4A	**4E Mastery (Grader Project)** A demonstration of your mastery of the skills in Project 4A with extensive decision making.	In MyITLab and on the following pages
4F	Objectives 5–8 from Project 4B	**4F Mastery (Grader Project)** A demonstration of your mastery of the skills in Project 4B with extensive decision making.	In MyITLab and on the following pages
4G	Combination of Objectives from Projects 4A and 4B	**4G Mastery (Grader Project)** A demonstration of your mastery of the skills in Projects 4A and 4B with extensive decision making.	In MyITLab and on the following pages
4H	Combination of Objectives from Projects 4A and 4B	**4H GO! Fix It** A demonstration of your mastery of the skills in Projects 4A and 4B by creating a correct result from a document that contains errors you must find.	Online
4I	Combination of Objectives from Projects 4A and 4B	**4I GO! Make It** A demonstration of your mastery of the skills in Projects 4A and 4B by creating a result from a supplied picture.	Online
4J	Combination of Objectives from Projects 4A and 4B	**4J GO! Solve It** A demonstration of your mastery of the skills in Projects 4A and 4B, your decision making skills, and your critical thinking skills. A task-specific rubric helps you self-assess your result.	Online
4K	Combination of Objectives from Projects 4A and 4B	**4K GO! Solve It** A demonstration of your mastery of the skills in Projects 4A and 4B, your decision making skills, and your critical thinking skills. A task-specific rubric helps you self-assess your result.	On the following pages
4L	Combination of Objectives from Projects 4A and 4B	**4L GO! Think** A demonstration of your understanding of the Chapter concepts applied in a manner that you would use outside of college. An analytic rubric helps you and your instructor grade the quality of your work by comparing it to the work an expert in the discipline would create.	On the following pages
4M	Combination of Objectives from Projects 4A and 4B	**4M GO! Think** A demonstration of your understanding of the Chapter concepts applied in a manner that you would use outside of college. An analytic rubric helps you and your instructor grade the quality of your work by comparing it to the work an expert in the discipline would create.	Online
4N	Combination of Objectives from Projects 4A and 4B	**4N You and GO!** A demonstration of your understanding of the Chapter concepts applied in a personal situation. An analytic rubric helps you and your instructor grade the quality of your work.	Online

GLOSSARY

GLOSSARY OF CHAPTER KEY TERMS

Arguments The values that an Excel function uses to perform calculations or operations.

Auditing The process of examining a worksheet for errors in formulas.

Circular reference An Excel error that occurs when a formula directly or indirectly refers to itself.

Data table A range of cells that shows how changing certain values in your formulas affect the results of those formulas and that makes it easy to calculate multiple versions in one operation.

Data validation A technique by which you can control the type of data or the values that are entered into a cell by limiting the acceptable values to a defined list.

Defined name A word or string of characters in Excel that represents a cell, a range of cells, a formula, or a constant value; also referred to as simply a *name*.

Dependent cells Cells that contain formulas that refer to other cells.

Error Checking command A command that checks for common errors that occur in formulas.

Error value The result of a formula that Excel cannot evaluate correctly.

Financial functions Pre-built formulas that perform common business calculations such as calculating a loan payment on a vehicle or calculating how much to save each month to buy something; financial functions commonly involve a period of time such as months or years.

Formula An equation that performs mathematical calculations on values in a worksheet.

Formula Auditing Tools and commands accessible from the FORMULAS tab that help you check your worksheet for errors.

Future value (Fv) The value at the end of the time periods in an Excel function; the cash balance you want to attain after the last payment is made—usually zero for loans.

Goal Seek One of Excel's What-If Analysis tools that provides a method to find a specific value for a cell by adjusting the value of one other cell—find the right input when you know the result you want.

HLOOKUP An Excel function that looks up values that are displayed horizontally in a row.

Interest The amount charged for the use of borrowed money.

Iterative calculation When Excel recalculates a formula over and over because of a circular reference.

LOOKUP An Excel function that looks up values in either a one-row or one-column range.

Lookup functions A group of Excel functions that look up a value in a defined range of cells located in another part of the workbook to find a corresponding value.

Name A word or string of characters in Excel that represents a cell, a range of cells, a formula, or a constant value; also referred to as *a defined name.*

Nper The abbreviation for *number of time periods* in various Excel functions.

One-variable data table A data table that changes the value in only one cell.

PMT function An Excel function that calculates the payment for a loan based on constant payments and a constant interest rate.

Precedent cells Cells that are referred to by a formula in another cell.

Present value (Pv) The total amount that a series of future payments is worth now; also known as the *principal.*

Principal The total amount that a series of future payments is worth now; also known as the *Present value (Pv).*

Rate In the Excel PMT function, the term used to indicate the interest rate for a loan.

Scope The location within which a defined name is recognized without qualification—usually either to a specific worksheet or to the entire workbook.

Table array A defined range of cells, arranged in a column or a row, used in a VLOOKUP or HLOOKUP function.

Trace Dependents command A command that displays arrows that indicate what cells are affected by the value of the currently selected cell.

Trace Error command A tool that helps locate and resolve an error by tracing the selected error value.

Trace Precedents command A command that displays arrows to indicate what cells affect the value of the cell that is selected.

Tracer arrow An indicator that shows the relationship between the active cell and its related cell.

Two-variable data table A data table that changes the values in two cells.

Type argument An optional argument in the PMT function that assumes that the payment will be made at the end of each time period.

Validation list A list of values that are acceptable for a group of cells; only values in the list are valid and any value *not* in the list is considered invalid.

VLOOOKUP An Excel function that looks up values that are displayed vertically in a column.

Watch Window A window that displays the results of specified cells.

What-If Analysis The process of changing the values in cells to see how those changes affect the outcome of formulas in a worksheet.

CHAPTER REVIEW

Skills Review | Project 4C Auto Loan

Apply 4A skills from these Objectives:

1 Use Financial Functions
2 Use Goal Seek
3 Create a Data Table
4 Use Defined Names in a Formula

In the following Skills Review, you will create a worksheet for Patricia Murphy, U.S. Sales Director, which details loan information for purchasing seven automobiles for Jesse Jewelers sales representatives. The monthly payment for the seven automobiles cannot exceed $3,500. You will also help Ms. Murphy calculate quarterly Store Supply costs using Defined Names. Your completed two worksheets will look similar to Figure 4.58.

PROJECT FILES

For Project 4C, you will need the following files:

e04C_Auto_Loan
e04C_Store_Supplies

You will save your workbooks as:

Lastname_Firstname_4C_Auto_Loan
Lastname_Firstname_4C_Store_Supplies

PROJECT RESULTS

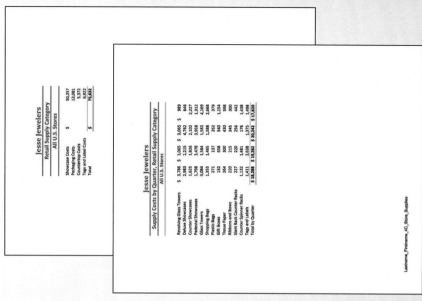

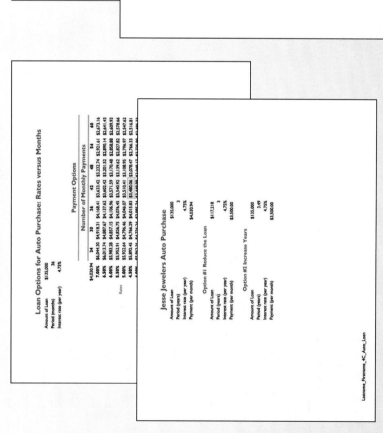

FIGURE 4.58

(Project 4C Auto Loan continues on the next page)

CHAPTER REVIEW

Skills Review   Project 4C Auto Loan (continued)

1 Start Excel. From your student files, open the file e04C_Auto_Loan, and then **Save** the file in your **Excel Chapter 4** folder as **Lastname_Firstname_4C_Auto_Loan**

a. In the range **A2:B5**, enter the following row titles and data.

Amount of Loan	$135,000
Period (years)	3
Interest Rate (per year)	4.75%
Payment (per month)	

b. Click cell **B5**. On the **FORMULAS tab**, in the **Function Library group**, click **Financial**, and then scroll down and click **PMT**. Drag the **Function Arguments** dialog box to the right side of your screen so you can view **columns A:B**.

c. In the **Rate** box, type **b4/12** to convert the annual interest rate to a monthly interest rate. Press [Tab], and then in the **Nper** box, type **b3*12** to have Excel convert the number of years in the loan (3) to the total number of months. Press [Tab], and then in the **Pv** box, type **b2** to enter the present value of the loan. Click **OK** to create the function. In the **Formula Bar**, between the equal sign and PMT, type **–** (minus sign) to insert a minus sign into the formula, and then press [Enter] to display the loan payment as a positive number.

2 Click cell **B5**. On the **DATA tab**, in the **Data Tools group**, click **What-If Analysis**, and then in the list, click **Goal Seek**. In the **Goal Seek** dialog box, in the **Set cell** box, confirm that **B5** displays.

a. Press [Tab]. In the **To value** box, type the payment goal of **3500** and then press [Tab]. In the **By changing cell** box, type **b2** which is the amount of the loan. Click **OK** two times. For three years at 4.75%, Lauren can borrow only $117,218 if she maintains a monthly payment of $3,500.

b. Click cell **A7**. Type **Option #1 Reduce the Loan** and then on the **Formula Bar**, press **Enter**. **Merge and Center** the title across the range **A7:B7**, display the **Cell Styles** gallery, and then apply the **Heading 2** cell style.

c. Select the range **A2:B5**, right-click, and then click **Copy**. Point to cell **A8**, right-click, point to **Paste**

Special, and then under **Paste Values**, click the second button—**Values & Number Formatting (A)**. Press [Esc] to cancel the moving border.

d. In cell **B2**, type **135000** and then press [Enter] to restore the original loan amount. Click cell **B5**. On the **DATA tab**, in the **Data Tools group**, click **What-If Analysis**, and then click **Goal Seek**.

e. In the **Set cell** box, confirm that **B5** displays. Press [Tab]. In the **To value** box, type **3500** and then press [Tab]. In the **By changing cell** box, type **b3** which is the number of years for the loan. Click **OK** two times.

f. Click **A13**. Type **Option #2 Increase Years** and then press [Enter]. Use the **Format Painter** to copy the format from cell **A7** to cell **A13**. Select the range **A2:B5**, right-click, and then click **Copy**. Point to cell **A14**, right-click, point to **Paste Special**, and then under **Paste Values**, click the second button—**Values & Number Formatting (A)**. Press [Esc] to cancel the moving border.

g. Point to cell **B15**, right-click to display the mini toolbar, and then click **Decrease Decimal** until the number of decimal places is two. Click cell **B3**. Type **3** and then press [Enter] to restore the original value. Press [Ctrl] + [Home] to move to the top of the worksheet. **Save** your workbook.

3 To determine how variable interest rates and a varying number of payments affect the payment amount, Lauren will set up a two-variable data table. Click the **New sheet** button to create a new worksheet. Double-click the **Sheet1 tab**, rename it **Payment Table** and then press [Enter]. In cell **A1**, type **Loan Options for Auto Purchase: Rates versus Months** and then press [Enter]. **Merge and Center** this title across the range **A1:I1**, and then apply the **Title** cell style.

a. In the range **A2:B4**, enter the following row titles and data.

Amount of Loan	$135,000
Period (months)	36
Interest Rate (per year)	4.75%

b. Change the width of **column A** to **20.** Click cell **C8.** Type **24** and then press [Tab]. Type **30** and then press [Tab]. Select the range **C8:D8**. Drag the fill handle to

(Project 4C Auto Loan continues on the next page)

CHAPTER REVIEW

Skills Review   Project 4C Auto Loan (continued)

the right through cell I8 to fill a pattern of months from 24 to 60 in increments of six months.

c. In cell B9, type 7.0% and press [Enter]. Type 6.5% and press [Enter]. Select the range B9:B10, and then drag the fill handle down through cell B16 to fill a pattern of interest rates in increments of .5% from 7.00% down to 3.50%. If necessary, adjust to display two decimal places.

d. Click cell C6. Type Payment Options and then press [Enter]. Merge and Center this title across the range C6:I6. Apply the Heading 1 cell style. Click cell C7. Type Number of Monthly Payments and then use the Format Painter to apply the format of cell C6 to cell C7.

e. Click cell A9, type Rates and then press [Enter]. Select the range A9:A16. On the HOME tab, in the Alignment group, click Merge and Center, click Align Right, and then click Middle Align. Apply the Explanatory Text cell style.

f. Click cell B8. On the FORMULAS tab, in the Function Library group, click Financial, and then click PMT. In the Rate box, type b4/12 to divide the interest rate per year by 12 to convert it to a monthly interest rate. Press [Tab], and then in the Nper box, type b3 and press [Tab]. In the Pv box, type -b2 and then click OK.

g. Select the range B8:I16. On the DATA tab, in the Data Tools group, click What-If Analysis, and then in the list, click Data Table. In the Data Table dialog box, in the Row input cell box, type b3 and then press [Tab]. In the Column input cell box, type b4 In the Data Table dialog box, click OK to create the data table. Click in any cell outside of the table to deselect.

h. Use the Format Painter to copy the format from cell B8 to the range C9:I16.

i. Select the range F14:F16 and apply the Note cell style to highlight the desired payment option. Select the nonadjacent ranges C8:I8 and B9:B16, apply Bold and Center. On the PAGE LAYOUT tab, set the Orientation for this worksheet to Landscape.

j. Group both worksheets. Click the INSERT tab, insert a footer, and then in the left section, click File Name. Click in a cell just above the footer to exit the Footer area and view your file name. From the PAGE LAYOUT tab, display the Page Setup dialog

box, and on the Margins tab, select the Horizontally check box. Click OK, and then on the status bar, click Normal. AutoFit columns C:I. Press [Ctrl] + [Home] to move to the top of the worksheet.

k. Click the FILE tab to display Backstage view. On the right, at the bottom of the Properties list, click Show All Properties. On the list of Properties, in the Tags box, type amortization schedule, payment table In the Subject box, type your course name and section #. Under Related People, be sure that your name displays as the author. If necessary, right-click the author name, click Edit Property, type your name, click outside of the Edit person dialog box, and then click OK. Return to Normal view and make cell A1 active. Display each worksheet in Print Preview, and then make any necessary corrections or adjustments. Close the Print Preview.

l. Ungroup the worksheets, Save and Close your workbook but leave Excel open. Print or submit the two worksheets in this workbook electronically as directed by your instructor. If required, print or create an electronic version of your worksheets with formulas displayed using the instructions in Project 1A.

4 Open the file e04C_Store_Supplies, and then Save the file in your Excel Chapter 4 folder as Lastname_Firstname_4C_Store_Supplies

a. Select the range B6:E18, which includes the empty cells in row 18, and then click AutoSum. Click anywhere to cancel the selection. Select the range B6:E6, hold down [Ctrl] and select the range B18:E18, and then from the Cell Styles gallery, under Number Format, apply the Currency [0] cell style. Select the range B7:E17, display the Cell Styles gallery, and then under Number Format, click Comma [0]. Select the range B18:E18, and then apply the Total cell style.

b. Select the range B6:E9. On the FORMULAS tab, in the Defined Names group, click Define Name. With Revolving_Glass_Towers selected, type Showcase_Costs as the name. At the bottom of the dialog box, at the right edge of the Refers to box, point to and click Collapse Dialog Box. Change the range by selecting the range B6:E10.

c. Click Expand Dialog Box to redisplay the New Name dialog box, and then click OK. Select the

(Project 4C Auto Loan continues on the next page)

CHAPTER REVIEW

range B11:E14. In the upper left corner of the Excel window, to the left of the Formula Bar, click in the Name Box. Type **Wrapping_Costs** and press Enter.

d. Select the range B15:E16. On the **FORMULAS tab**, in the **Defined Names group**, click **Name Manager**. In the upper left corner of the Name Manager dialog box, click **New**. With *Slant_Back_Counter_Racks* selected, type **Countertop_Costs** and then click **OK. Close** the Name Manager dialog box and **Save** your workbook.

e. On the left side of your window, in the **row heading area**, point to the **row 15** heading and right-click to select the entire row and display a shortcut menu. Click **Insert** to insert a new blank row above. Click cell A15, type **Ribbons and Bows** and then press Tab. In cell B15, type **220** and press Tab. In cell C15, type **215** and press Tab. In cell D15, type **345** and press Enter. In cell E15, type **300** and press Enter.

f. On the **FORMULAS tab**, from the **Defined Names group**, display the **Name Manager** dialog box. In the Name Manager dialog box, in the **Name** column, click **Wrapping_Costs**. At the bottom of the dialog box, click in the **Refers to** box and edit the reference, changing **$E$14** to **$E$15** to include the new row in the range. **Close** the Name Manager dialog box, and click **Yes** to save the changes you made to the name reference.

g. On the **FORMULAS tab**, from the **Defined Names group**, display the **Name Manager** dialog box. Click **Wrapping_Costs**, and then click **Edit**. In the **Edit Name** dialog box, with *Wrapping_Costs* selected, type **Packaging_Costs** Click **OK**, and then **Close** the Name Manager dialog box. In the upper left corner of the window, click the **Name Box arrow** and notice the modified range name, Packaging_ Costs. Click any cell to close the list, and then **Save** your workbook.

h. Select the range A18:E18. On the **FORMULAS tab**, in the **Defined Names group**, click **Create from Selection**. In the Create Names from Selection dialog box, click **OK**, and then click anywhere to cancel the selection. Click the **Name Box arrow**, and then click the name **Tags_and_Labels**. Notice that in the new range name, Excel inserted the underscore necessary to fill a blank space in the range name.

5 Display the **Annual Supply Costs** worksheet.

a. In cell B5, type **=sum(S** Continue typing **Showcase_ Costs** and then press Enter. Your result is 50257. In cell B6, type **=sum(P** and then on the **Formula AutoComplete list**, double-click **Packaging_Costs** to insert the formula. Press Enter to display the result 13081.

b. In cell B7, type **=sum(** and then on the **FORMULAS tab**, in the **Defined Names group**, click **Use in Formula**. In the list, click **Countertop_ Costs** and then press Enter to display the total 5372.

c. In cell B8, use any of the techniques you just practiced to sum the cells containing the costs for **Tags and Labels Costs** and to display a result of 6922. Click cell B9, hold down Alt and press = to insert the SUM function, and then press Enter to display a total of 75632.

d. Select the nonadjacent cells **B5** and **B9**, and then from the **HOME tab**, display the **Cell Styles** gallery. Under **Number Format**, click the **Currency [0]** cell style. To the range B6:B8, apply the **Comma [0]** cell style. Click cell **B9** and apply the **Total** cell style.

e. Select both worksheets so that *[Group]* displays in the title bar. With the two worksheets grouped, insert a footer in the left section that includes the file name. **Center** the worksheets **Horizontally** on the page.

f. Click the **FILE tab** to display Backstage view. On the right, at the bottom of the Properties list, click **Show All Properties**. On the list of **Properties**, in the **Tags** box, type **retail supply category, supply costs** In the **Subject** box, type your course name and section #. Under **Related People**, be sure that your name displays as the author. If necessary, right-click the author name, click Edit Property, type your name, click outside of the Edit person dialog box, and then click OK. Return to **Normal** view and make cell **A1** active, display the grouped worksheets in **Print Preview, Close the Print Preview**, and then make any necessary corrections or adjustments. Right-click any of the grouped sheet tabs, and then click **Ungroup Sheets**.

g. **Save** your workbook. Print or submit the two worksheets in both workbooks electronically as directed by your instructor. If required, print or create an electronic version of your worksheets with formulas displayed. **Close** Excel.

END | You have completed Project 4C

CHAPTER REVIEW

Skills Review | Project 4D Quarterly Cost Report and Lookup Form

Apply 4B skills from these Objectives:

5 Use Lookup Functions

6 Validate Data

7 Audit Worksheet Formulas

8 Use the Watch Window to Monitor Cell Values

In the following Skills Review, you will assist Mike Connor, the Vice President of Marketing at Jesse Jewelers by adding lookup functions to a Packing Slip form so that an order taker can complete the form quickly. You will use the Formula Auditing tools to review a revenue worksheet for the Houston store and you will use the Watch Window to edit the store's utility cost worksheets. Your completed workbooks will look similar to Figure 4.59.

PROJECT FILES

For Project 4D, you will need the following files:

e04D_Houston Revenue

e04D_Packing_Slip

e04D_Utilities

You will save your workbooks as:

Lastname_Firstname_4D_Houston Revenue

Lastname_Firstname_4D_Packing_Slip

Lastname_Firstname_4D_Utilities

PROJECT RESULTS

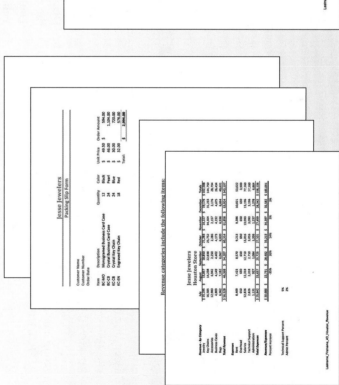

FIGURE 4.59

(Project 4D Quarterly Cost Report and Lookup Form continues on the next page)

CHAPTER REVIEW

1 From your student files, open the file e04D_Packing_Slip, and then **Save** the file in your **Excel Chapter 4** folder as **Lastname_Firstname_4D_Packing_Slip**.

a. Display the **Product Information** worksheet. Select the range **A4:C11**. On the **DATA tab**, in the **Sort & Filter group**, click **Sort**. If necessary, drag the Sort dialog box to the right side of your screen so you can view columns A:C.

b. In the **Sort** dialog box, under **Column**, click the **Sort by arrow**. Notice that the selected range is now **A5:C11** and that the column titles in the range **A4:C4** display in the **Sort by** list. In the **Sort by** list, click **Style Code**. Under **Sort On**, verify that **Values** displays, and under **Order**, verify that **A to Z** displays. Click **OK** to sort the data by Style Code in ascending order. **Save** your workbook.

c. Display the **Packing Slip** worksheet. In cell **A9**, type **BC-MO** and press **Tab**. With cell **B9** as the active cell, on the **FORMULAS tab**, in the **Function Library group**, click **Lookup & Reference**, and then click **VLOOKUP**.

d. With the insertion point in the **Lookup_value** box, click cell **A9** to look up the description of Item BC-MO. Click in the **Table_array** box, and then at the bottom of the workbook, click the **Product Information sheet tab**. On the **Product Information** sheet, select the range **A4:C11**, and then press **F4**. Click in the **Col_index_num** box, type **2** and then click **OK**.

e. With cell **B9** as the active cell and containing the VLOOKUP formula, point to the fill handle in the lower right corner of the cell, and then drag to fill the VLOOKUP formula down through cell **B18**.

f. Click cell **C9**, type **12** as the quantity ordered, and then press **Tab**. In cell **D9**, type **Black** and press **Tab**. With cell **E9** as the active cell, on the **FORMULAS tab**, in the **Function Library group**, click **Lookup & Reference**, and then click **VLOOKUP**.

g. With the insertion point in the **Lookup_value** box, click cell **A9** to look up information for Item BC-MO. Click in the **Table_array** box, display the **Product Information** sheet, and then select the range **A4:C11**. Press **F4** to make the values in the range absolute.

h. In the **Col_index_num** box, type **3** to look up the price in the third column of the range, and then

click **OK**. The Unit Price for the Monogrammed Business Card Case displays in cell **E9**. Click cell **F9**, and notice that a formula to calculate the total for the item, Quantity times Unit Price, has already been entered in the worksheet.

i. Click cell **E9**, and then copy the VLOOKUP formula down through cell **E18**.

j. Click cell **A10**, type **BC-CB** and press **Tab** two times. In cell **C10**, type **24** and press **Tab**. Notice that Excel calculates the total for this item in cell **F10**—1,104.00. In cell **D10**, type **Pearl** and then press **Enter**. **Save** your workbook.

2 Display the **Product Information** sheet. Select the range **A4:A11**. On the **FORMULAS** tab, in the **Defined Names** group, click **Create from Selection**.

a. In the **Create Names from Selection** dialog box, be sure only the **Top row** check box is selected, and then click **OK**.

b. Display the **Packing Slip** worksheet, and then select the range **A9:A18**. On the **DATA tab**, in the **Data Tools group**, click **Data Validation**. In the **Data Validation** dialog box, be sure the **Settings tab** is selected.

c. Under **Validation criteria**, click the **Allow arrow**, and then click **List**. Click to position the insertion point in the **Source box**, type **=Style_Code** and then click **OK**.

d. Click cell **A11**, and notice that a list arrow displays at the right edge of the cell. In cell **A11**, click the list arrow to display the list. In the list, click **KC-CB**. Press **Tab** two times, type **24** and press **Tab**, type **Blue** and then press **Enter** to return to the beginning of the next row.

e. With cell **A12** active, click the **list arrow**, and then click **KC-EN**. As the **Quantity**, type **18** and as the **Color**, type **Red** and press **Enter**. In cell **A13**, type **B-W** and press **Tab**. An error message displays indicating that you entered a value that is not valid; that is, it is not on the validation list you created. In the error message, click **Cancel** and then **Save** your workbook.

f. Select the unused **rows 13:18**, right-click over the selected rows, and then click **Delete**. In cell **F13**, **Sum** the order amounts and then apply the **Total** cell style.

3 Select both worksheets so that [Group] displays in the title bar. With the two worksheets grouped, insert

(Project 4D Quarterly Cost Report and Lookup Form continues on the next page)

CHAPTER REVIEW

a footer in the left section that includes the file name. Center the worksheets **Horizontally** on the page.

a. Click the **FILE tab** to display **Backstage** view. On the right, at the bottom of the **Properties** list, click **Show All Properties**. On the list of **Properties**, in the **Tags** box, type **luggage, bag, order form** In the **Subject** box, type your course name and section #. Under **Related People**, be sure that your name displays as the author. If necessary, right-click the author name, click Edit Property, type your name, click outside of the Edit person dialog box, and then click OK.

b. Return to **Normal** view and make cell **A1** active, display the grouped worksheets in **Print Preview, Close** the **Print Preview**, and then make any necessary corrections or adjustments. Ungroup the worksheets, **Save** and **Close** your workbook.

c. Print or submit the two worksheets in this workbook electronically as directed by your instructor. If required, print or create an electronic version of your worksheets with formulas displayed.

4 From your student files, open the file **e04D_Houston Revenue**. In your Excel Chapter 4 folder, **Save** the file as **Lastname_Firstname_4D_Houston Revenue**

a. In the **column heading area**, select **column B**, hold down Ctrl, and then select **column H**. Point to the *right* edge of either of the selected column headings to display the pointer, and then double-click to AutoFit the columns.

b. Click cell **C9**. On the **FORMULAS tab**, click **Trace Precedents**. To the left of the cell, click **Error Checking**, and then click **Update Formula to Include Cells**. Drag the fill handle to copy the corrected formula in cell **C9** to the range **D9:G9**.

c. Click cell **H5**, and then point to the **Error Checking** button to read the ScreenTip. On the **FORMULAS tab**, in the **Formula Auditing group**, click **Trace Precedents**. To the left of cell **H5**, click **Error Checking** to display the list of error checking options, click **Copy Formula from Above**, and then look at the **Formula Bar** to verify that the formula is summing the numbers in **row 5**. With cell **H5** still selected, from the **HOME tab**, display the **Cell Styles** gallery, and then click the **Comma [0]** number format.

d. Click cell **H6**, on the **FORMULAS tab**, click **Trace Precedents**, and then verify that the row is correctly summed. Click cell **H7**, click **Trace Precedents.** Notice that the formula is not correct. Click cell **H8**, click **Trace Precedents**; notice that the formula is not correct. In the **Formula Auditing group**, click **Remove Arrows**. Click cell **H6**, and then use the fill handle to copy the correct formula down to cells **H7:H8**.

5 Click cell **B14**, which displays the error *#VALUE!*. To the left of the cell, point to **Error Checking** and read the ScreenTip. In the **Formula Auditing group**, click **Trace Precedents**.

a. Click **Error Checking**, and then, click **Show Calculation Steps.** Notice that the formula is multiplying by a text value.

b. **Close** the **Evaluate Formula** dialog box. With cell **B14** still the active cell, click in the **Formula Bar**, and then edit the formula to change the reference to cell **B3** to **B9** and press Enter. Click cell **B14**, and then drag the fill handle to copy the corrected formula across the row to cells **C14:G14**.

6 Click cell **B16**, point to **Error Checking**, and read the ScreenTip. In the **Formula Auditing group**, click the **Error Checking arrow** to display a list. Click **Trace Error.** In the **Formula Auditing group**, click the **Error Checking arrow**, and then click **Trace Error** again to view the precedent cells. Click in cell **A24**. Type **Admin Percent** and press Tab, and then type **2** to fill in the missing data.

a. Click cell **B16**. Remove the arrows. Click **Error Checking** to display the list of error checking options, and then click **Edit in Formula Bar**. Delete *#REF!*. Type **b24** and press F4 to make the cell reference absolute. Press Enter. Click cell **B16**, and then use the fill handle to copy the formula to the right into cells **C16:G16**.

7 Click cell **A1**. In the Formula Auditing group, click the **Error Checking arrow**, and then click **Error Checking**—cell **C20** is selected. In the **Error Checking** dialog box, click **Show Calculation Steps;** notice that the divisor is an empty cell. In the Evaluate Formula dialog box, click **Evaluate.** Click **Restart.**

a. In the **Evaluate Formula** dialog box, click **Step In** to examine the formula. Click **Step Out**. Close the **Evaluate Formula** dialog box.

(Project 4D Quarterly Cost Report and Lookup Form continues on the next page)

CHAPTER REVIEW

b. In the **Error Checking** dialog box, click **Next**. Click **OK**. Click cell **H13**, and then use the fill handle to copy this formula down to cells **H14:H16**. Click cell **B17** and drag the fill handle to copy this formula to the right into cells **C17:H17**.

c. Click cell **B19** and type **=b9-b17** Press Enter, and then copy the formula to the right into cells **C19:H19**. Click cell **C20**, and then on the **HOME tab**, in the **Number group**, click **Percent Style**. Copy the formula to the right into cells **D20:G20**.

8 Display the **Categories** worksheet. To the left of the **Formula Bar**, click the **Name Box arrow**, and then click **Bags**. In the **Data Tools group**, click the **Data Validation arrow**, and then click **Clear Validation Circles**.

a. Redisplay the **Revenue** worksheet. On the **DATA tab**, in the **Data Tools group**, click the **Data Validation arrow**, and then click **Circle Invalid Data**.

b. Click cell **A8**, and then click the arrow at the right side of the cell. From the list, click **Bags**. In the **Data Tools group**, click the **Data Validation arrow**, and then click **Clear Validation Circles**.

c. Select both worksheets so that *[Group]* displays in the title bar. With the two worksheets grouped, insert a footer in the **left section** that includes the file name. **Center** the worksheets **Horizontally**. Set the **Orientation** to **Landscape**. On the status bar, click **Normal**. Press Ctrl + Home.

d. Click the **FILE tab** to display **Backstage** view. On the right, at the bottom of the **Properties** list, click **Show All Properties**. On the list of **Properties**, in the **Tags** box, type **Houston revenue** In the **Subject** box, type your course name and section #. Under **Related People**, be sure that your name displays as the author. If necessary, right-click the author name, click Edit Property, type your name, click outside of the Edit person dialog box, and then click OK.

e. Display the grouped worksheets in **Print Preview**, close the print preview, and then make any necessary corrections or adjustments. Ungroup the worksheets, **Save** and **Close** your workbook. Print or submit the two worksheets in this workbook electronically as directed by your instructor. If required, print or create an electronic version of your worksheets with formulas displayed.

9 From your student files, open the file **e04D_Utilities**, and then **Save** the file in your **Excel Chapter 4** folder as **Lastname_Firstname_4D_Utilities** Display the **Toronto** worksheet, and then click cell **E8**. On the **FORMULAS tab**, in the **Formula Auditing group**, click **Watch Window**. In the upper left corner of the **Watch Window**, click **Add Watch**. In the **Add Watch** dialog box, click **Add**.

a. Display the **Houston** worksheet, and using the same technique, add cell **E8** from the **Houston** worksheet. Repeat this for the **New York** worksheet and for the **Miami** worksheet. Adjust the size of the **Watch Window** and columns as necessary to view all four sheets, and verify that cell **E8** is listed for each of the four worksheets.

b. With the **Miami** worksheet active, hold down Shift and click the **Toronto sheet tab** to select all four worksheets. In the **Miami** worksheet, select the range **B4:E8**. On the **FORMULAS tab**, in the **Function Library group**, click **AutoSum**. **Close the Watch Window**. Select the range **E5:E7**, and then apply **Comma Style** with zero decimal places.

c. With the four worksheets grouped, insert a footer in the **left section** that includes the file name. **Center** the sheets **Horizontally**. On the status bar, click **Normal**. Press Ctrl + Home to move to the top of the worksheet.

d. Click the **FILE tab** to display **Backstage** view. On the right, at the bottom of the **Properties** list, click **Show All Properties**. On the list of **Properties**, in the **Tags** box, type **Utilities** In the **Subject** box, type your course name and section #. Under **Related People**, be sure that your name displays as the author. If necessary, right-click the author name, click Edit Property, type your name, click outside of the Edit person dialog box, and then click OK.

e. Display the grouped worksheets in **Print Preview**. Redisplay the worksheets. Make any necessary corrections or adjustments. Right-click any of the grouped sheet tabs, and then click **Ungroup Sheets**. **Save** your workbook. Print or submit the four worksheets in this workbook electronically as directed by your instructor. If required, print or create an electronic version of your worksheets with formulas displayed. **Close** Excel.

END | You have completed Project 4D

CONTENT-BASED ASSESSMENTS

EXCEL

Mastering Excel | Project 4E Condo Loan and Quarterly Cost Report

MyITLab®
grader

Apply 4A skills from these Objectives:

1 Use Financial Functions
2 Use Goal Seek
3 Create a Data Table
4 Use Defined Names in a Formula

In the following Mastering Excel project, you will create a worksheet for Jacques Celestine, President of Jesse Jewelers, which analyzes loan options for a condo in Toronto that the company is considering purchasing. Jacques wants to provide a lodging facility for company visitors, but would like to keep the monthly loan payment below $6,250. You will also define names for ranges of cells in a workbook containing quarterly Advertising costs. The worksheets of your workbooks will look similar to Figure 4.60.

PROJECT FILES

For Project 4E, you will need the following files:

e04E_Advertising_Costs
e04E_Condo_Loan

You will save your workbooks as:

Lastname_Firstname_4E_Advertising_Costs
Lastname_Firstname_4E_Condo_Loan

PROJECT RESULTS

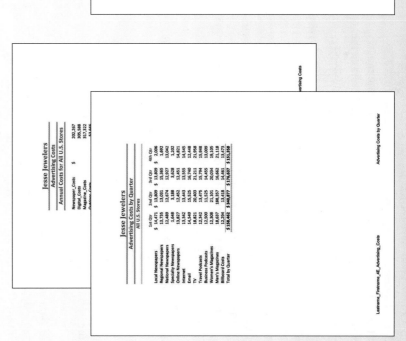

FIGURE 4.60

(Project 4E Condo Loan and Quarterly Cost Report continues on the next page)

Project 4E: Condo Loan and Quarterly Cost Report | Excel **281**

CONTENT-BASED ASSESSMENTS

Mastering Excel   Project 4E Condo Loan and Quarterly Cost Report (continued)

1 Start Excel. From your student files, locate and open e04E_Condo_Loan. **Save** the file in your **Excel Chapter 4** folder as **Lastname_Firstname_4E_Condo_Loan** In cell **B5**, insert the **PMT** function using the data from the range **B2:B5**—be sure to divide the interest rate by 12, multiply the years by 12, and display the payment as a positive number. The result, $6,598.44, is larger than the payment of $6,250.

2 Use **Goal Seek** to change the amount of the loan so that the payment is under $6,250. Then, in **A7**, type **Option #1 Reduce the Loan** and then **Copy** the format from cell **A1** to cell **A7**. **Copy** the range **A2:B5**, and then **Paste the Values & Number Formatting (A)** to cell **A8**. In cell **B2**, type **615000** to restore the original loan amount.

3 Use **Goal Seek** to change the period of the loan so that the payment does not exceed $6,250. In **A13**, type **Option #2 Increase Years** Format the cell the same as cell **A7**. **Copy** the range **A2:B5**, and then **Paste the Values & Number Formatting (A)** to cell **A14**. Display the value in **B15** with two decimal places, and then in cell **B3**, type **10** to restore the original value. Insert a footer with the **File Name** in the left section, and then **Center** the worksheet **Horizontally** on the page.

4 **Save** and return to **Normal** view. Set up a two-variable data table. Rename the **Sheet2 tab** to **Condo Payment Table** In the range **A2:B4**, enter the following row titles and data.

Amount of Loan	$615,000
Period (months)	120
Interest Rate (per year)	5.25%

5 In cell **C8**, type **60**—the number of months in a five-year loan. In **D8**, type **120**—the number of months in a 10-year loan. Fill the series through cell **H8**; apply **Bold and Center.**

6 Beginning in cell **B9**, enter varying interest rates in decrements of .5% beginning with **7.5%** and ending with **4.0%** Format all the interest rates with two decimal places, and then **Bold** and **Center** the range **B8:B16**. In cell **B8**, enter a PMT function using the information in cells **B2:B4**. Be sure that you convert the interest rate to a monthly rate and that the result displays as a positive number.

7 Create a **Data Table** in the range **B8:H16** using the information in cells **B2:B4** in which the **Row input cell**

is the **Period** and the **Column input cell** is the **Interest rate.** Copy the format from **B8** to the results in the data table. Format cell **D16** with the **Note** cell style as payment option that is close to but less than $6,250 per month. Change the **Orientation** to **Landscape.** Insert a footer with the **File Name** in the left section, and **Center** the worksheet **Horizontally** on the page. Return to **Normal** view and move to cell **A1.**

8 Click the **FILE tab** to display **Backstage** view. On the right, at the bottom of the **Properties** list, click **Show All Properties.** On the list of **Properties**, in the **Tags** box, type **condo, payment table** In the **Subject** box, type your course name and section # Under **Related People,** be sure that your name displays as the author. If necessary, right-click the author name, click Edit Property, type your name, click outside of the Edit person dialog box, and then click OK. **Print Preview,** make any necessary corrections or adjustments, ungroup the worksheets, and **Save and Close** your workbook. Print or submit electronically as directed.

9 From your student files, open **e04E_Advertising_Costs. Save** it in your **Excel Chapter 4** folder as **Lastname_Firstname_4E_Advertising_Costs** Display the **Advertising Costs by Quarter** worksheet, and then apply appropriate **Currency [0], Comma [0],** and **Total** cell styles.

10 Name the following ranges: **B6:E10 Newspaper_Costs; B10:E14 Digital_Costs; B15:E16 Magazine_Costs; B17:E17 Billboard_Costs** Insert a new row 15. In cell **A15,** type **Business Podcasts** In cell **B15,** type **12500** In cell **C15,** type **11525** In cell **D15,** type **14455** In cell **E15,** type **13009.**

11 Display **Name Manager,** click **Digital_Costs,** and then change cell **E14** to **E15.** Select the **Billboard_Costs,** and **Edit** the name to **Outdoor_Costs.** Display the **Annual Advertising Costs** sheet. In cell **B5,** type **=sum(N** and sum Newspaper costs using its defined name in the formula. Do this for the other named ranges. Sum all the costs. Apply **Currency [0], Comma [0],** and **Total** cell styles to the appropriate cells. Group the worksheets, insert a footer that includes the file name. **Center** the worksheets **Horizontally** on the page. Document properties should include the tags **advertising costs** Ungroup the worksheets, **Save** your file and then print or submit your worksheet electronically as directed by your instructor. **Close** Excel.

END | You have completed Project 4E

CONTENT-BASED ASSESSMENTS

Mastering Excel | **Project 4F Lookup Form and Sales Revenue**

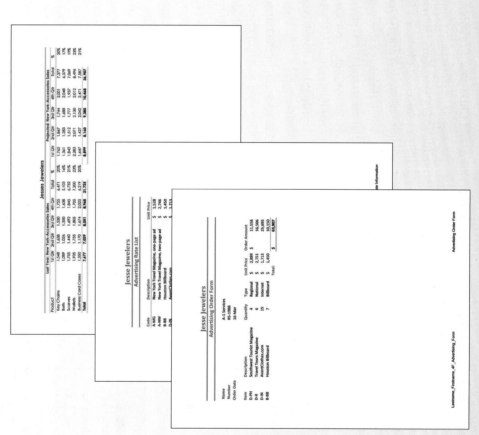

MyITLab® grader

Apply 4B skills from these Objectives:

5 Use Lookup Functions

6 Validate Data

7 Audit Worksheet Formulas

8 Use the Watch Window to Monitor

In the following Mastering Excel project, you will assist Mike Connor, the Vice President of Marketing at Jesse Jewelers, by adding lookup functions to an Advertising Order form so that an order taker can complete the form quickly. You will also use the Formula Auditing features and visual inspection to find and correct several types of errors. Your completed workbooks will look similar to Figure 4.61.

PROJECT FILES

For Project 4F, you will need the following files:

e04F_Advertising_Form
e04F_New_York_Revenue

You will save your workbooks as:

Lastname_Firstname_4F_Advertising_Form
Lastname_Firstname_4F_New_York_Revenue

PROJECT RESULTS

FIGURE 4.61

(Project 4F Lookup Form and Sales Revenue continues on the next page)

Project 4F: Lookup Form and Sales Revenue | Excel **283**

CONTENT-BASED ASSESSMENTS

Mastering Excel   Project 4F Lookup Form and Sales Revenue (continued)

1 Open e04F_Advertising_Form. Save the file in your Excel Chapter 4 folder as **Lastname_Firstname_4F_Advertising_Form** Display the Advertising Rate Information sheet, select the range A4:C11, and **Sort by Code.** Name the range A4:A11 using **Create from Selection.** Display the **Advertising Order Form** sheet; in the range **A9:A18** create a **data validation list** using the defined name *Code.*

2 Click cell **A9**, click the **list arrow**, click **D-PH.** With cell **B9** as the active cell, insert a **VLOOKUP** function that will look up the **Description** from the **Advertising Rate Information** sheet using the **Item** number.

3 With cell **B9** as the active cell, fill the VLOOKUP formula through cell **B18.** In cell **C9**, type **4** and in cell **D9**, type **Regional** With cell **E9** as the active cell, insert a **VLOOKUP** function to look up Unit Price. **Copy** the VLOOKUP formula through cell **E18.** Add the following orders:

Item	Quantity	Type
D-R	6	**National**
D-IN	15	**Internet**
B-BB	7	**Billboard**

4 Delete unused rows, sum the **Order Amount**, and apply **Total** cell style. Group the worksheets, insert a footer that includes the file name. **Center** the worksheets **Horizontally** on the page. Document properties should include the tags **advertising costs** and **form** Ungroup the

worksheets, **Save** and **Close** your workbook but leave Excel open.

5 Open the file e04F_New_York_Revenue, and then **Save** the file in your Excel Chapter 4 folder as **Lastname_Firstname_4F_New_York_Revenue**

6 Click cell **I5**, which displays a green triangle indicating a potential error, and then on the **FORMULAS tab**, click **Trace Precedents.** Click **Error Checking,** and then click **Edit in Formula Bar.** Change *$B$14* to *$B$15* so that the formula is using the Growth Assumption for *Belts,* not for Key Chains.

7 On the **FORMULAS tab**, in the **Formula Auditing group**, click **Error Checking** to begin checking for errors from this point in the worksheet. In cell **M6**, the flagged error, notice the formula is trying to divide by cell **L10**, which is empty. Click **Edit in Formula Bar,** change **10** to **9** and then in the **Error Checking** dialog box, click **Resume.**

8 In cell **F7**, examine the error information, and then click **Copy Formula from Above.** Examine the error in cell **J8**, and then click **Copy Formula from Left.** Use **Format Painter** to copy the format in cell **M5** to cell **M6.**

9 Insert a footer with the file name in the **left section,** center the worksheet **Horizontally.** Display the **Document Properties,** add your name as the **Author,** type your course name and section # in the **Subject** box, and as the **Tags,** type **New York revenue** Save your workbook. Display and examine the **Print Preview,** make any necessary corrections, ungroup the worksheets, **Save,** and then print or submit electronically as directed by your instructor. If you are directed to do so, print the formulas. **Close** Excel.

END | You have completed Project 4F

CONTENT-BASED ASSESSMENTS

MyITLab® grader

Apply 4A and 4B skills from these Objectives:

1 Use Financial Functions
2 Use Goal Seek
3 Create a Data Table
4 Use Defined Names in a Formula
5 Use Lookup Functions
6 Validate Data
7 Audit Worksheet Formulas
8 Use the Watch Window to Monitor Cell Values

Mastering Excel | Project 4G Warehouse Loan and Staff Lookup Form

In the following Mastering Excel project, you will create a worksheet for Jacques Celestine, President of Jesse Jewelers, which analyzes loan options for a warehouse that the company is considering purchasing. Jacques wants to establish an additional storage facility in the United States, but would like to keep the monthly loan payment below $10,000. You will also assist Mike Connor, the Vice President of Marketing at Jesse Jewelers, by adding lookup functions to a Staff Planning Form so that a manager can complete the form quickly. You will also use Formula Auditing to check a workbook for errors. Your completed workbooks will look similar to Figure 4.62.

PROJECT FILES

For Project 4G, you will need the following files:

e04G_Online_Bracelet_Revenue
e04G_Staff_Form
e04G_Warehouse_Loan

You will save your workbooks as:

Lastname_Firstname_4G_Online_Bracelet_Revenue
Lastname_Firstname_4G_Staff_Form
Lastname_Firstname_4G_Warehouse_Loan

PROJECT RESULTS

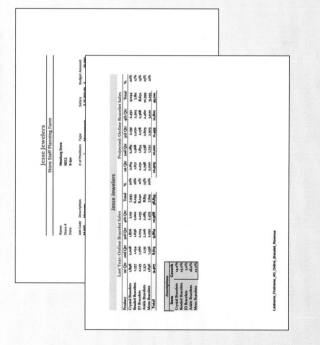

FIGURE 4.62

(Project 4G Warehouse Loan and Staff Lookup Form continues on the next page)

CONTENT-BASED ASSESSMENTS

Mastering Excel   Project 4G Warehouse Loan and Staff Lookup Form (continued)

1 In your student files, locate and **open** the file **e04G_Warehouse_Loan**, and **Save** it in your Excel Chapter 4 folder as **Lastname_Firstname_4G_Warehouse_Loan** Display the **Warehouse Payment Table** sheet. In cell **B9**, enter rates in decrements of .5% beginning with **7.5%** and ending with **4%** in cell **B16**. Format rates with two decimal places.

2 In cell **B8**, enter a **PMT** function using the information in cells **B2:B4**. Create a **Data Table** in the range **B8:H16** using the information in cells **B2:B4** in which the **Row input cell** is the **Period** and the **Column input cell** is the **Interest rate**. Apply the format from **B8** to the results in the data table. Select the payment option closest to $10,000 per month and format the option with the **Note** cell style.

3 Insert a footer that includes the file name, and document properties that include your firstname and lastname as the **Author**, your course name and section # as the **Subject**, and the tags **warehouse loan** Change the **Orientation** to **Landscape**, **center Horizontally**, and return to **Normal** view. **Print Preview**, **Save**, and then print or submit electronically as directed. **Close** this workbook.

4 Open the file **e04G_Staff_Form**, and **Save** it in your Excel Chapter 4 folder as **Lastname_Firstname_4G_Staff_Form** On the **Job Information** sheet, select the range **A4:C11**, and then **Sort** the selection by **Job Code**. Name the range **A4:A11** by the name in the top row. Display the **Staffing Plan** sheet, and select the range **A9:A18**. Display the **Data Validation** dialog box, and validate from a **List** using the **Source =Job_Code**

5 Click cell **A9**, and then click **M-MG**. Click cell **B9**, and insert a **VLOOKUP** function that looks up the **Description** from the **Job Information** worksheet using the **Job Code**.

6 With cell **B9** as the active cell, fill the **VLOOKUP** formula through cell **B18**. In cell **C9**, type **1** as the **# of Positions** and in cell **D9**, type **Management** as the **Type**. In cell **E9**, insert the **VLOOKUP** function that looks up the **Salary** from the **Job Information** worksheet using the **Job Code** Copy the **VLOOKUP** formula down into cell **E18**.

7 Beginning in cell **A10**, add these staff positions:

8 Delete any unused rows between the last item and the Total row. Sum the **Budget Amount** column and apply the **Total** cell style. Group the worksheets, insert a footer in the left section with the file name, **center** the worksheets **Horizontally**, and change the **Orientation** to **Landscape**. Update the document properties with your name and course name and section #, and add the **Tags planning, staff Print Preview**, ungroup the worksheets, **Save**, and then submit it as directed. **Close** this workbook.

9 From your student files, open **e04G_Online_Bracelet_Revenue**, and then **Save** the file in your Excel Chapter 4 folder as **Lastname_Firstname_4G_Online_Bracelet_Revenue**

10 Click cell **I5**, and then on the **FORMULAS tab**, click **Trace Precedents**. Click **Error Checking**, and then click **Edit in Formula Bar**. Change *$B$14* to **$B$15** so that the formula is using the Growth Assumption for *Beaded Bracelets*, not for *Crystal Bracelets*.

11 On the **FORMULAS tab**, in the Formula Auditing **group**, click **Error Checking**. In cell **M6**, notice the formula is trying to divide by cell **L10**, which is empty. Click **Edit in Formula Bar**, change **10** to **9** and then in the **Error Checking** dialog box, click **Resume**.

12 In cell **F7**, examine the error information, and then click **Copy Formula from Above**. Examine the error in cell **J8**, and then click **Copy Formula from Left**. Click **OK**. Use **Format Painter** to copy the format in cell **M5** to cell **M6**.

13 Insert a footer with the file name in the **left section** and **center** the worksheet **Horizontally**. To the **Document Properties**, add your firstname and lastname as the **Author**, add your course name and section # as the **Subject**, and add **online bracelet revenue** as the **Tags**. Display and examine the **Print Preview**, make any necessary corrections, ungroup the worksheets, **Save**, and then print or submit electronically as directed by your instructor. If required, print or create an electronic version of your worksheets with formulas displayed. **Close** Excel.

Item	# of Positions	Type
C-CASH	3	Cashier
C-CSA	1	Customer Service
M-AMG	3	Management

END | You have completed Project 4G

CONTENT-BASED ASSESSMENTS

Apply a combination of the 4A and 4B skills.

GO! Fix It	Project 4H Bag Costs by Quarter	**Online**
GO! Make It	Project 4I Arizona Store Loan	**Online**
GO! Solve It	Project 4J Store Furnishings	**Online**
GO! Solve It	Project 4K Order Form	

PROJECT FILES

For Project 4K, you will need the following file:

e04K_Order_Form

You will save your workbook as:

Lastname_Firstname_4K_Order_Form

Open the file **e04K_Order_Form** and save it as **Lastname_Firstname_4K_Order_Form** Prepare the Product Information worksheet for a VLOOKUP function by sorting the items by Style Code, and then create a named range for the Style Code information. On the Order Form worksheet, using the named range, set data validation for the Item column. Insert the VLOOKUP function in column B and column E, referencing the appropriate data in the Product Information worksheet. Then enter the data below.

Item	Description	Quantity	Color
C-S		12	White
C-T		15	Natural
M-MC		25	Assorted
M-CF		50	Green

Delete the unused row. Construct formulas to total the order, and then apply appropriate financial formatting. On both sheets, include your file name in the footer, add appropriate properties, and then submit them as directed.

Project 4K: Order Form | Excel   287

CONTENT-BASED ASSESSMENTS

GO! Solve It   Project 4K Order Form (continued)

Performance Level

Performance Criteria	Exemplary	Proficient	Developing
Use Lookup Functions	The VLOOKUP function correctly looks up data on the Validation List.	The VLOOKUP function looks up some but not all data on the Validation List.	The VLOOKUP function does not look up any of the correct information.
Validate Data	The Validation List is sorted correctly and used on the order form.	The Validation List was sorted, but not used on the order form.	The Validation List is not sorted and not used on the order form.
Calculate and Format the Order Amount	The Order Amount and financial information is properly calculated and formatted.	Some, but not all, of the Order Amount and financial information is properly calculated and formatted.	Incorrect formulas and/or incorrect financial formatting were applied in most of the cells.

END | You have completed Project 4K

OUTCOMES-BASED ASSESSMENTS

RUBRIC

The following outcomes-based assessments are open-ended assessments. That is, there is no specific correct result; your result will depend on your approach to the information provided. Make Professional Quality your goal. Use the following scoring rubric to guide you in how to approach the problem and then to evaluate how well your approach solves the problem.

The criteria—Software Mastery, Content, Format and Layout, and Process—represent the knowledge and skills you have gained that you can apply to solving the problem. The levels of performance—Professional Quality, Approaching Professional Quality, or Needs Quality Improvements—help you and your instructor evaluate your result.

	Your completed project is of Professional Quality if you:	Your completed project is Approaching Professional Quality if you:	Your completed project Needs Quality Improvements if you:
1-Software Mastery	Choose and apply the most appropriate skills, tools, and features and identify efficient methods to solve the problem.	Choose and apply some appropriate skills, tools, and features, but not in the most efficient manner.	Choose inappropriate skills, tools, or features, or are inefficient in solving the problem.
2-Content	Construct a solution that is clear and well organized, contains content that is accurate, appropriate to the audience and purpose, and is complete. Provide a solution that contains no errors in spelling, grammar, or style.	Construct a solution in which some components are unclear, poorly organized, inconsistent, or incomplete. Misjudge the needs of the audience. Have some errors in spelling, grammar, or style, but the errors do not detract from comprehension.	Construct a solution that is unclear, incomplete, or poorly organized; contains some inaccurate or inappropriate content; and contains many errors in spelling, grammar, or style. Do not solve the problem.
3-Format & Layout	Format and arrange all elements to communicate information and ideas, clarify function, illustrate relationships, and indicate relative importance.	Apply appropriate format and layout features to some elements, but not others. Overuse features, causing minor distraction.	Apply format and layout that does not communicate information or ideas clearly. Do not use format and layout features to clarify function, illustrate relationships, or indicate relative importance. Use available features excessively, causing distraction.
4-Process	Use an organized approach that integrates planning, development, self-assessment, revision, and reflection.	Demonstrate an organized approach in some areas, but not others; or, use an insufficient process of organization throughout.	Do not use an organized approach to solve the problem.

OUTCOMES-BASED ASSESSMENTS

Apply a combination of the 4A and 4B skills.

GO! Think   Project 4L Key Chains

PROJECT FILES

For Project 4L, you will need the following file:

e04L_Key_Chains

You will save your workbook as:

Lastname_Firstname_4L_Key_Chains

From your student files, open the file **e04L_Key_Chains**, and then save it in your chapter folder as **Lastname_Firstname_4L_Key_Chains** So that order takers do not have to type the Style Code, Description, and Unit Price in the Order Form worksheet, use the information on the Product Information sheet to create a validation list for the Item and then insert a VLOOKUP function in the Description and Unit Price columns. Then create an order for two of the Plush Animal Key Chains (K–S) and two of the Classic Key Chains (M–TF). Delete unused rows, create appropriate totals, apply financial formatting, and then save and submit it as directed.

END | You have completed Project 4L

GO! Think   Project 4M Delivery Van Purchase   Online

Build from
Scratch

You and GO!   Project 4N Vehicle Loan   Online

Build from
Scratch

Build from
Scratch

7

Creating PivotTable and PivotChart Reports and Using BI Tools in Excel

GO! to Work
Video E7

quasarphotos/Fotolia

PROJECT 7A

OUTCOMES

Query large amounts of data, subtotal and aggregate numeric data, and filter and group data to analyze for relationships and trends.

OBJECTIVES

1. Create a PivotTable Report
2. Use Slicers and Search Filters
3. Modify a PivotTable Report
4. Create a PivotChart Report

PROJECT 7B

OUTCOMES

Use the Excel Business Analysis Tools: Data Model, PowerPivot, and Power View, to analyze data from multiple sources.

OBJECTIVES

5. Create a Data Model Using PowerPivot
6. Create a PivotTable Using PowerPivot
7. Create a Dashboard Using Power View

In This Chapter

In this chapter, you will use Excel's Business Intelligence (BI) tools to create a PivotTable and a PivotChart report, and use Power View to organize and display data. Organizations gather large amounts of data, but the data is not useful until it is organized in a manner that reveals patterns or trends. You will subtotal, aggregate, and summarize data. You will extract information from data by organizing the data into groups from which trends, comparisons, patterns, and relationships can be determined, and you will create different views of the data so that more than one pattern or trend can be observed.

The projects in this chapter relate to **Golden Grove**, a growing city located between Los Angeles and San Diego. Just 10 years ago the population was under 100,000; today it has grown to almost 300,000. Community leaders have always focused on quality and economic development in decisions on housing, open space, education, and infrastructure, and encourage best environmental practices, making the city a model for other communities its size around the United States. The city provides many recreational and cultural opportunities with a large park system, thriving arts, and a friendly business atmosphere.

PROJECT 7A

PivotTable and PivotChart

MyITLab®
Project 7A Training

PROJECT ACTIVITIES

In Activities 7.01 through 7.13, you will create a PivotTable report and a PivotChart report that summarize calls handled at Fire Department stations and Police Department precincts during the first quarter of the year for the City of Golden Grove. Your completed worksheets will look similar to Figure 7.1.

PROJECT FILES

For Project 7A, you will need the following file:

e07A_Fire_Police

You will save your workbook as:

Lastname_Firstname_7A_Fire_Police

PROJECT RESULTS

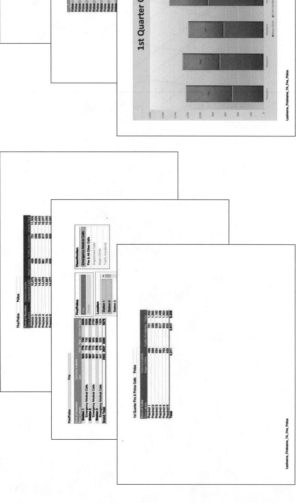

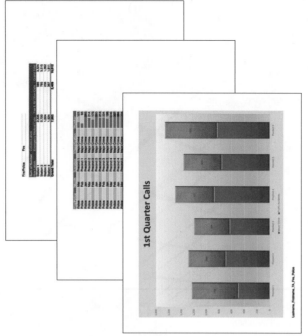

FIGURE 7.1 Project 7A PivotTable and PivotChart

NOTE   If You Are Using a Touchscreen

- Tap an item to click it.
- Press and hold for a few seconds to right-click; release when the information or commands display.
- Touch the screen with two or more fingers and then pinch together to zoom in or stretch your fingers apart to zoom out.
- Slide your finger on the screen to scroll—slide left to scroll right and slide right to scroll left.
- Slide to rearrange—similar to dragging with a mouse.
- Swipe from edge: from right to display charms; from left to expose open apps, snap apps, or close apps; from top or bottom to show commands or close an app.
- Swipe to select—slide an item a short distance with a quick movement—to select an item and bring up commands, if any.

Objective 1   Create a PivotTable Report

Video E7-1

A long list of numerical data is not useful until it is organized in a way that is meaningful to the reader. To combine and compare large amounts of data, use Excel's PivotTable report—also called simply a *PivotTable*—which is an interactive Excel report that summarizes and analyzes large amounts of data.

Using a PivotTable report, you can show the same data in a table in more than one arrangement. For example, you can manipulate the rows and columns of the table to view or summarize the data from different perspectives. In this manner, you pivot—turn—the information around to get varying views of the data. A PivotTable report is especially useful when you want to analyze related totals, such as when you have a long list of numbers to sum and you want to compare several facts about each total. The *source data* for a PivotTable must be formatted in columns and rows, and can be located in an Excel worksheet or an external source.

Activity 7.01   Creating a PivotTable Report

The data you use to create your PivotTable report should be in the format of a list—a series of rows that contains related data—with column titles in the first row. Subsequent rows should contain data appropriate to its column title, and there should be no blank rows. Excel will use your column titles as the *field names*—the categories of data. The data in each column should be of the same type.

Michael Thomas, Director of Public Safety, prepares quarterly reports about Fire Department and Police Department calls. He tracks the total number of calls at each location grouped by the classifications used by the Fire Department and the Police Department.

To prepare for each City Council meeting, Mr. Thomas needs to know the average number of calls handled by each location during the quarter. He also needs a separate report regarding the number of major crimes reported by each Police Department precinct. Finally, he needs to know which Fire Department station had the lowest number of emergency medical calls during the quarter, in the event the City Council votes to close or combine facilities.

1 Start Excel. From your student files, open the file **e07A_Fire_Police**. Display the **Save As** dialog box, navigate to the location where you will store your workbooks for this chapter, and then create a new folder named **Excel Chapter 7** Open your new folder, and then **Save** the workbook as **Lastname_Firstname_7A_Fire_Police**

2 Take a moment to scroll through the worksheet and examine the data.

Recall that a PivotTable report combines and compares large amounts of data. This worksheet displays three months of calls. There are two classifications for Fire Department calls and three classifications for Police Department calls.

To place the information in proper locations on the PivotTable report, think about the questions Mr. Thomas wants to answer. For his internal tracking report, he needs to know the total number of calls handled at each Fire Department station or Police Department precinct during the first quarter—grouped according to the classifications used by the Fire Department and the Police Department.

3 Click cell **A2**. On the **INSERT tab**, in the **Tables group**, click **Recommended PivotTables**. Compare your screen with Figure 7.2.

The Recommended PivotTables dialog box displays and a moving border surrounds the range of data—this is referred to as the source data. A cell in your data must be active before you create a PivotTable; in this manner you identify the source of your data.

FIGURE 7.2

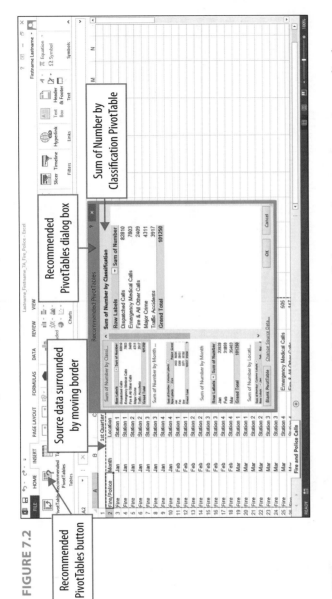

4 In the **Recommended PivotTables** dialog box, scroll down, point to each preview to display a ScreenTip, and then click the fifth PivotTable—**Sum of Number by Location** (+). Compare your screen with Figure 7.3.

Excel suggests PivotTables based upon the organization of your data.

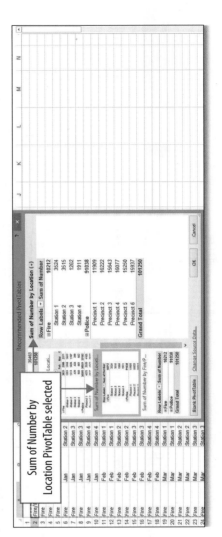

BY TOUCH Select the range A2:E80 and tap Quick Analysis. Tap the TABLES tab and point to each PivotTable example to view a preview of the selection, then tap the table you wish to create.

FIGURE 7.3

5 Click **OK**.

Excel adds a new sheet—Sheet1—to the workbook. On the left side of the new worksheet, Excel generates a PivotTable report.

On the right side of the window, Excel displays the PivotTable Fields pane. The upper portion, referred to as the field section, lists the field names—the column titles from your source data. Use the field section to add fields to and remove fields from the PivotTable. The lower portion, referred to as the layout section, displays four areas where you can build the PivotTable by rearranging and repositioning fields. On the ribbon, the PIVOTTABLE TOOLS adds two tabs—ANALYZE and DESIGN.

More Knowledge

If your source data is already formatted as an Excel table, you can create a PivotTable easily. Select a single cell within the source data, and then on the DESIGN tab, in the Tools group, click Summarize with PivotTable

6 Save your workbook, and then take a moment to study Figure 7.4 and the table in Figure 7.5.

FIGURE 7.4

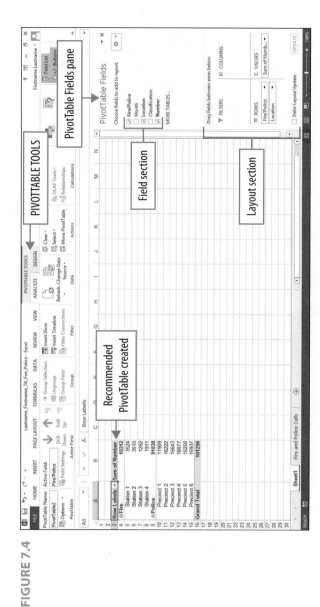

A L E R T !
If the PivotTable Fields Pane Does Not Display

If the PivotTable Fields pane is not visible, click any cell in the PivotTable report to display it. If you accidently close the PivotTable Fields pane, you can redisplay it by clicking any cell in the PivotTable report to display the PivotTable Tools tabs on the ribbon. On the ANALYZE tab, in the Show group, click Field List.

FIGURE 7.5

PIVOTTABLE SCREEN ELEMENTS	
SCREEN ELEMENT	**DESCRIPTION**
PivotTable Fields pane	A window that lists, at the top, all of the fields—column titles—from the source data for use in the PivotTable report and at the bottom, an area in which you can arrange the fields in the PivotTable.
FILTERS area	An area to position fields by which you want to filter the PivotTable report, enabling you to display a subset of data in the PivotTable report.
COLUMNS area	An area to position fields that you want to display as columns in the PivotTable report. Field names placed here become column titles, and the data is grouped in columns by these titles.
ROWS area	An area to position fields that you want to display as rows in the PivotTable report. Field names placed here become row titles, and the data is grouped by these row titles.
VALUES area	An area to position fields that contain data that is summarized in a PivotTable report or PivotChart report. The data placed here is usually numeric or financial in nature and the data is summarized—summed. You can also perform other basic calculations such as finding the average, the minimum, or the maximum.
Layout section	The lower portion of the PivotTable Fields pane containing the four areas for layout; use this area to rearrange and reposition fields in the PivotTable.
Field section	The upper portion of the PivotTable Fields pane containing the fields—column titles—from your source data; use this area to add fields to and remove fields from the PivotTable.

Activity 7.02 | Adding Fields to a PivotTable Report

Recall that a PivotTable report can combine and compare large amounts of data for the purpose of analyzing related totals. By viewing the combined information in different ways, you can answer questions. Mr. Thomas, for example, wants to know how many calls of every classification were handled by each Fire Department station and Police Department precinct during the first quarter.

There are several ways to place the data from your list into the PivotTable report. From the PivotTable Fields pane, you can drag field names from the field section at the top and then drop them into one of the four areas in the layout section at the bottom. Or, you can select a field name in the field section at the top, and Excel will place the field in a default location based on the field's data type. If you want an arrangement other than the one you get by default, you can move fields from one location to another by simply dragging them between the various areas in the layout section.

1 On the right side of the worksheet, in the **PivotTable Fields** pane, in the **field section**, notice that **Fire/Police** check box is selected, and Excel has placed the field in the **ROWS area** of the **layout section**.

By default, non-numeric fields are added to the ROWS area and numeric fields are added to the VALUES area, but you can move fields as desired.

2 In the **layout section**, in the **ROWS area**, point to **Fire/Police**, hold down the left mouse button, and then drag the field name upward into the **FILTERS area**.

Mr. Thomas wants to use the PivotTable report to analyze the call data by Department—either Fire Department calls or Police Department calls. To do so, filter the report based on the Fire/Police field by moving this field to the FILTERS area. The Report Filter filters the entire report based on this field.

As you drag, a small blue icon attaches to the mouse pointer to indicate you are moving a field. *Fire/Police* displays in the FILTERS area. On the left, the Fire/Police field is added at the top of the PivotTable report.

🔄 **ANOTHER WAY**   In the ROWS area, click the Fire/Police arrow, and then click Move to Report Filter.

3 In the **PivotTable Fields** pane, in the **field section,** verify the **Location** field check box is selected.

In the layout section, the Location field displays in the ROWS area. The Location names—Precincts and Stations—display as rows in the PivotTable report. There are six Police Department precincts and four Fire Department stations. Recall that by default, non-numeric fields are added to the ROWS area.

4 In the **PivotTable Fields** pane, in the **field section,** select the **Classification** field check box. Right-click cell **A4,** point to **Expand/Collapse,** and then click **Expand Entire Field.** Compare your screen with Figure 7.6.

In the layout section, the Classification field displays as the second field in the ROWS area. The Classification names are added as indented row headings under each Police Department precinct location and under each Fire Department station location. In this manner, a row that is lower in position in the ROWS area is nested within the row immediately above it. Notice that, under each precinct location, only the call classifications related to the Police Department display. Likewise, as you scroll down, under station locations, only the call classifications related to the Fire Department display.

FIGURE 7.6

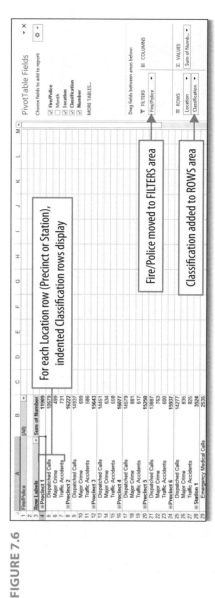

For each Location row (Precinct or Station), indented Classification rows display

Fire/Police moved to FILTERS area

Classification added to ROWS area

5 In the **PivotTable Fields** pane, from the **field section,** drag the **Month** field down to the **COLUMNS area.** Verify that **Sum of Number** displays in the **VALUES area.** Compare your screen with Figure 7.7.

Use any of these techniques to place fields in the layout section. The arrangement of fields in the layout section reflects the arrangement of the data in the PivotTable report.

The PivotTable report is complete; the result is a group of related totals. The long list of figures from the Fire and Police Calls worksheet is summarized, and you can make comparisons among the data. *Sum of Number* displays in cell A3, which refers to the field name *Number*—the number of calls for each call classification has been summed.

FIGURE 7.7

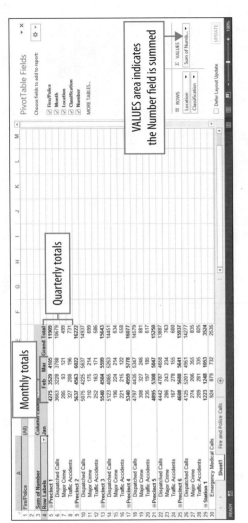

Monthly totals

Quarterly totals

VALUES area indicates
the Number field is summed

6 Click cell **B5**, point to the selected cell, and then notice the ScreenTip that displays.

Now that the data is organized and the number of calls calculated, you can view and compare various facts about the data. For example, you can see that in January, in Precinct 1, there were a total of 4275 calls, compared with 3529 calls in February. This summary information was not available in the original worksheet. By summarizing and pivoting (turning) data in various ways, you can see different information. Additionally, ScreenTips describe the cell contents.

7 On the **DESIGN tab**, in the **PivotTable Styles group**, click **More**, and then under **Medium**, in the second row, click the fourth style—**Pivot Style Medium 11**. Compare your screen with Figure 7.8.

FIGURE 7.8

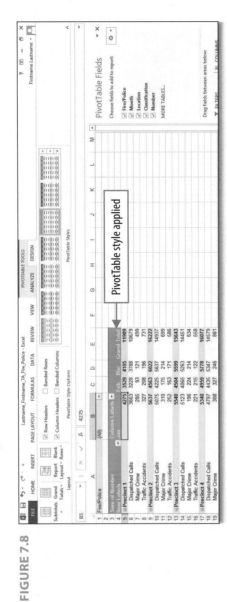

PivotTable style applied

8 **Close** the **PivotTable Fields** pane, and then **Save** your workbook.

Video E7-2

You can *filter*—limit the display of data to only specific information—a PivotTable by using a search filter or by using slicers. *Slicers* are easy-to-use filtering controls with buttons that enable you drill down through large amounts of data. Slicers display as movable floating objects on your worksheet in the same manner as charts and shapes and make it easy to see what filters are currently applied.

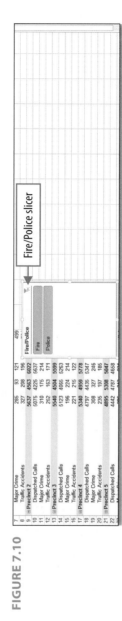

Activity 7.03 | Using Slicer to Filter a PivotTable

Limiting the data displayed enables you to focus on parts of the data without the distraction of the data you do not need to see. Mr. Thomas wants to limit the data to only the Fire Department information and then determine which Fire Department station had the lowest number of emergency medical calls. Then he wants to hide that station and look at the numbers for the remaining stations.

1 On the **ANALYZE tab**, in the **Filter group**, click **Insert Slicer**. Compare your screen with Figure 7.9.

The Insert Slicers dialog box displays all the field names from your PivotTable report.

FIGURE 7.9

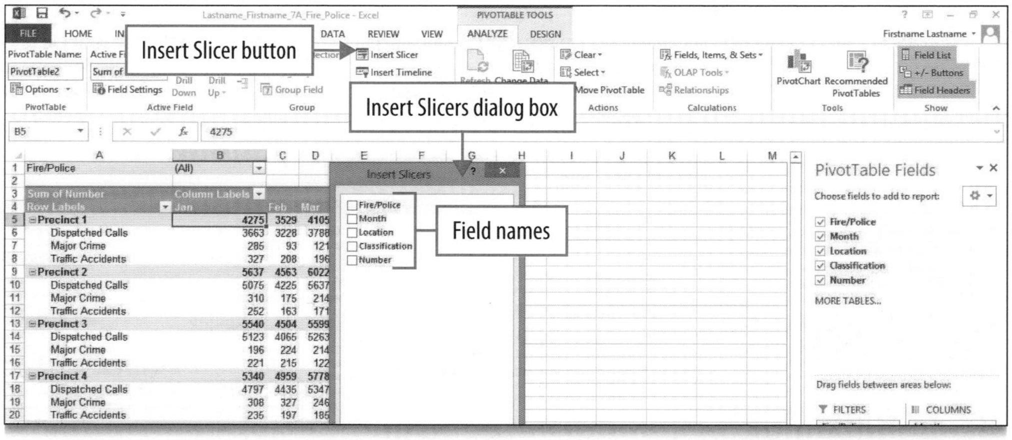

2 Select the **Fire/Police** check box, and then click **OK**. Compare your screen with Figure 7.10.

The Fire/Police slicer displays.

FIGURE 7.10

3 Point to the upper border of the **Fire/Police** slicer to display the pointer, and then drag the slicer up to align with the top of the PivotTable and to the right so that it is not blocking your view of the PivotTable.

4 Point to the lower sizing handle on the **Fire/Police** slicer list until the pointer displays, and then drag upward to shorten the length of the slicer to just below **Police**. Compare your screen with Figure 7.11.

A slicer includes a *slicer header* that indicates the category of the slicer items, *filtering buttons* to select the item by which to filter, and a Clear Filter button. When a filtering button is selected, the item is included in the filter. *Clear Filter* removes a filter. You can move a slicer to another location on the worksheet, and resize it as needed.

FIGURE 7.11

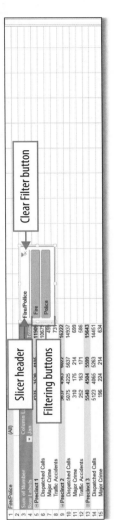

5 On the **OPTIONS tab**, in the **Slicer Styles group**, click **More** ▾, and then under **Dark**, click the second slicer style—**Slicer Style Dark 2**. Compare your screen with Figure 7.12.

You can apply various styles to slicers to make them easier to differentiate or to match the PivotTable report.

FIGURE 7.12

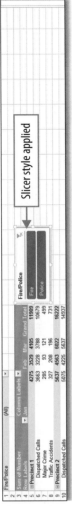

6 In the PivotTable report, notice that the Police Department precincts display first. Then, on the **Fire/Police slicer**, click the **Fire** filtering button, move your pointer out of the slicer, and then compare your screen with Figure 7.13.

The records for the Police Department precincts are hidden and only the Fire Department station items display. Recall that filtering displays only the data that you want to see. A filtering button that is not selected—displays in gray—indicates that the item is *not* included in the filtered list. By looking at this slicer, you can see that only Fire items are included. Because slicers indicate the current filtering state, it is easy to see exactly what is shown in the PivotTable report—and also to see what is *not* shown.

FIGURE 7.13

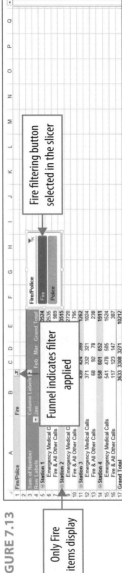

7 Click any cell in the PivotTable. On the **ANALYZE tab**, in the **Filter group**, click **Insert Slicer**. In the **Insert Slicers** dialog box, select the **Classification** check box, and then click **OK**.

8 Drag the **Classification** slicer to the right of the **Fire/Police** slicer, and then resize the field list to remove the blank area below **Traffic Accidents**. Notice that call classifications associated with the Police Department—Dispatched Calls, Major Crime, and Traffic Accidents—are dimmed.

Because the PivotTable is currently filtered by Fire, no filters related to Police are available.

9 Display the **Slicer Styles** gallery, and then apply **Slicer Style Light 4**. If necessary, widen the slicer to view the entire name of each filtering button, click cell **A1** to select the PivotTable, and then compare your screen with Figure 7.14.

FIGURE 7.14

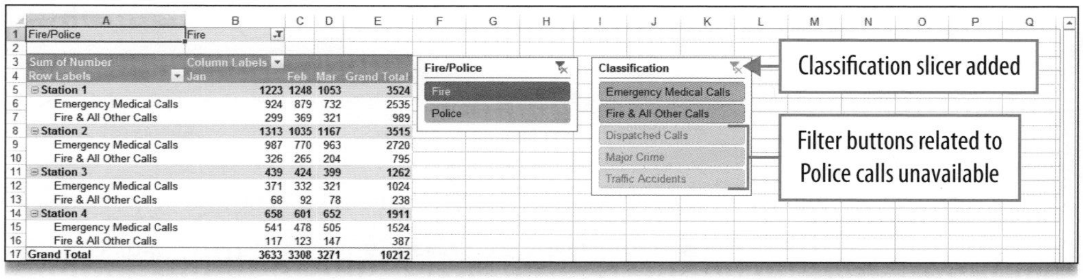

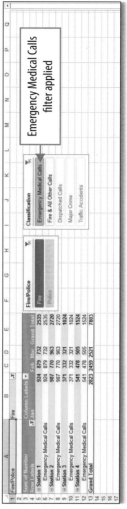

Classification slicer added

Filter buttons related to Police calls unavailable

10 On the **Classification slicer**, click the **Emergency Medical Calls** filtering button, and then compare your screen with Figure 7.15.

The data is further filtered by the call classification *Emergency Medical Calls*; that is, only Fire Department station items with *Emergency Medical Calls* as the call classification displays in the PivotTable report. Now, at a glance, Mr. Thomas can see which Fire Department station had the lowest number of emergency medical calls. Mr. Thomas may want to investigate this further to find the reason for the low number and to determine if the number is up or down from previous quarters.

FIGURE 7.15

Emergency Medical Calls filter applied

11 With cell **A1** active, on the **ANALYZE tab**, in the **Filter group**, click **Insert Slicer**. In the **Insert Slicers** dialog box, select the **Location** check box, and then click **OK**.

12 Drag the **Location slicer** below the **Fire/Police slicer**, and notice that the **Precinct** filtering buttons are dimmed.

Because the PivotTable is already filtered by Fire Department stations, and no Police Department precincts display in the PivotTable, the Precinct filtering buttons are dimmed—unavailable—for filtering in the current arrangement.

13 Shorten the **Location slicer** to display only the Stations, and then from the **Slicer Styles** gallery, apply **Slicer Style Light 6**. Click cell **A1**, and then compare your screen with Figure 7.16.

For each field of data in the PivotTable, you can display a slicer to enable ways to slice—display a thin piece of—the data in meaningful ways.

FIGURE 7.16

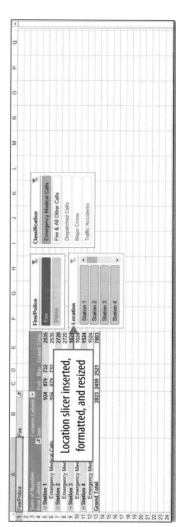

Location slicer inserted, formatted, and resized

14 To display all the stations *except* Station 3, hold down [Ctrl], and then in the **Location slicer**, click the **Station 3** filtering button. Release [Ctrl], move the pointer away from the PivotTable, and then compare your screen with Figure 7.17.

Use the [Ctrl] key in this manner to select all the filtering buttons *except* the one that you click. In the Location slicer, Stations 1, 2, and 4 are selected and Station 3 is not. In the PivotTable report, the Station 3 data is hidden, and only the data for Stations 1, 2, and 4 displays.

The number of Emergency Medical Calls for the remaining Fire Department stations range from a low of 478 in February at Station 4 to a high of 987 in January at Station 2. The Grand Total recalculates to reflect only the three stations currently displayed.

FIGURE 7.17

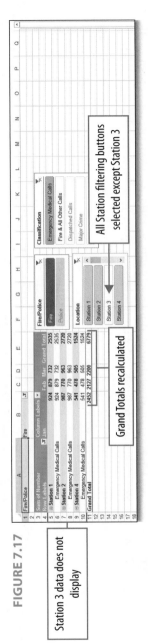

Station 3 data does not display

Grand Totals recalculated

All Station filtering buttons selected except Station 3

15 In the sheet tab area at the lower left of your screen, point to the **Sheet1 sheet tab**, right-click, and then, click **Move or Copy**. In the **Move or Copy** dialog box, at the lower left, select the **Create a copy** check box. Compare your screen with Figure 7.18.

FIGURE 7.18

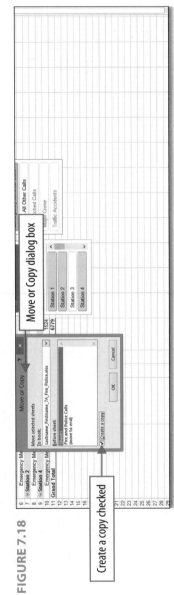

Create a copy checked

Move or Copy dialog box

16 Click **OK**. Right-click the **Sheet 1 (2) sheet tab**, click **Rename**, and then type **Slicers** Press [Enter].

The sheet is copied and renamed. In this worksheet, your instructor will be able to verify that you have filtered the worksheet using slicers and the slicers are formatted.

17 **Save** 🖫 your workbook.

Activity 7.04 | Clearing Filters and Filtering by Using the Search Box

Using the search filter is another way to filter data in a PivotTable report and find relevant information easily.

1 At the bottom of the Excel window, click the **Sheet1 sheet tab** to display this worksheet.

2 In the **Sheet1** worksheet, in the **Location slicer**, click **Clear Filter** 🗙.

This action clears all the filters within a slicer; therefore, the data for all four Fire Department stations displays.

3 In the **Classification slicer**, click the **Fire & All Other Calls** filtering button, and then compare your screen with Figure 7.19.

Clicking a filtering button cancels the selection of another filtering button, unless you hold down the Ctrl key to include multiple filters. By examining this data, Mr. Thomas can see that Station 3 also has the lowest number of *Fire & All Other Calls*. Mr. Thomas will need to investigate further to determine why Station 3 has the lowest number of calls in both classifications and whether this represents a trend.

FIGURE 7.19

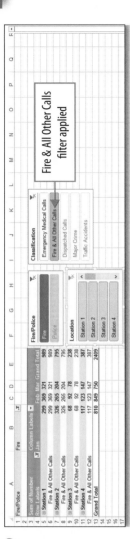

Fire & All Other Calls filter applied

4 In the **Classification slicer**, click **Clear Filter**. In the **Fire/Police** slicer, click **Clear Filter**.

No filters are applied and data from both the Police Department and the Fire Department displays.

5 Point to the **Fire/Police slicer header** and right-click. Click **Remove "Fire/Police"**. By using the same technique, remove the **Location slicer** and the **Classification slicer**.

6 Click cell **A1** to select the PivotTable, and then on the **ANALYZE tab**, in the **Show group**, click **Field List** to display the **PivotTable Fields** pane. In the **field section**, point to **Location**, and then on the right, click the **Location arrow**. Click in the **Search** box, type **Station 3** and then click **OK**. Compare your screen with Figure 7.20.

The filter is applied and only Station 3 data displays.

FIGURE 7.20

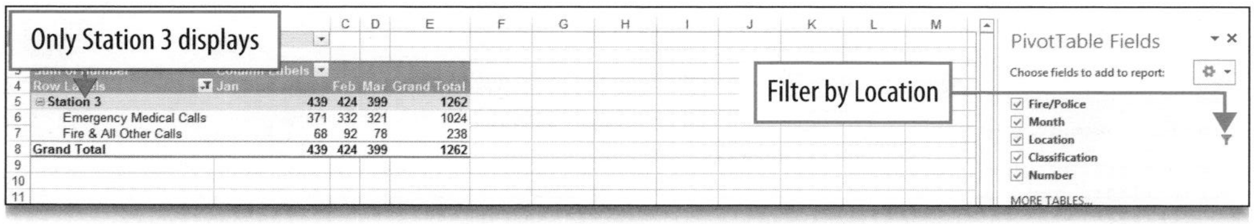

Only Station 3 displays

7 With cell **A1** still active, on the **ANALYZE tab**, in the **Actions group**, click **Clear**, and then click **Clear Filters**.

You can also clear filters by using this command.

8 Save your workbook.

Objective 3 Modify a PivotTable Report

Video E7-3

You have seen how, after you have added fields to the PivotTable report, you can pivot (turn) the information in various ways; for example, by removing or rearranging the fields. With different views of your data, you can answer different questions. You can display a field as a column rather than a row. You can display parts of the data on separate pages; for example, by creating separate pages for the Fire Department calls and Police Department calls. After data is displayed in a useful way, you can format it using any methods you have practiced.

Activity 7.05 | Rearranging a PivotTable Report

In the Fire/Police PivotTable report, a large amount of detail information displays. Although totals display for both the rows and the columns for each location and for each classification, it is still difficult for a reader to make comparisons across precincts and stations. Mr. Thomas needs to be able to respond to questions from City Council members representing different sections of the city. He must know the average number of service calls by department, by classification, and by precinct or station. For the City Council meeting, he does not need to see the monthly detail. In this activity, you will remove and rearrange fields to produce arrangements of this data that will be useful for answering questions at the City Council meeting.

1 In the **layout section** of the **PivotTable Fields** pane, from the **COLUMNS area**, drag the **Month** field name upward into the white **field section**—a black X attaches to the pointer as you drag—and then release the mouse button. Compare your screen with Figure 7.21.

The X indicates that the field is being removed from the PivotTable report. When you release the mouse button, the details for each month no longer display in the PivotTable report; only the quarterly totals for the various call classifications at each location display. In PivotTable Fields pane, *Month* is no longer selected or bold.

ANOTHER WAY   Click the Month arrow, and then click Remove Field.

FIGURE 7.21

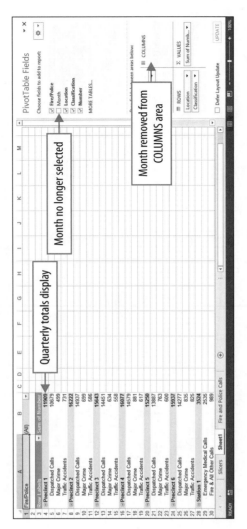

2 In the **layout section** of the **PivotTable Fields** pane, from the **ROWS area**, drag the **Classification** field into the **COLUMNS area.** Compare your screen with Figure 7.22.

By moving *Classification* from the ROWS area to the COLUMNS area, the various classifications become column titles instead of row titles. The classifications are arranged alphabetically across columns B:F. Now the police-related calls—Dispatched Calls, Major Crime, and Traffic Accidents—display as separate classifications.

FIGURE 7.22

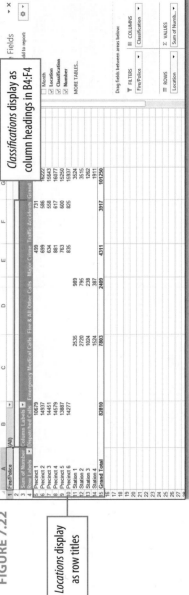

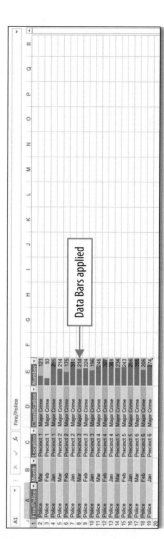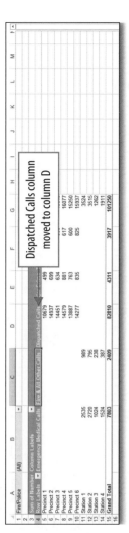

3 **Close** ✕ the **PivotTable Fields** pane. Click cell **B4**—the column title *Dispatched Calls*. Right-click, point to Move, and then click **Move "Dispatched Calls" Down**.

The Dispatched Calls column moves one column to the right.

4 Click cell **C4**, and then use the same technique to move the **Dispatched Calls** column to the right one column again. **Save** 🖫 your workbook, and then compare your screen with Figure 7.23.

By placing the three police-related call classifications adjacent to one another, you have a clearer view of the activity by location.

FIGURE 7.23

Activity 7.06 | Displaying PivotTable Report Details in a New Worksheet

From the PivotTable report, you can display details for a particular category of information in a separate worksheet. Mr. Thomas needs a separate report showing major crimes reported each month by precinct.

1 Click cell **E15**—the total for the *Major Crime* classification—and then point to the selected cell to view the ScreenTip.

To display the Major Crime field as a separate report, first select the total. Recall that the ScreenTips provide details about the cell's contents.

2 Right-click cell **E15**, and then click **Show Details**.

A new sheet—*Sheet3*—is added to your workbook, and the records for the Major Crime calls display in a table, along with the other fields from the Excel source data. Notice that the *Month* field is included, even though that field is not used in the PivotTable report.

ANOTHER WAY   Double-click a total to display the data on a new worksheet.

3 On **Sheet3**, with the table selected, in the lower right corner, click **Quick Analysis** 📊, and then click **Data Bars**.

Conditional formatting is applied to the data in column E.

4 Rename the **Sheet3** tab **Major Crimes** Click cell **A1** to deselect the data, and then **Save** 🖫 your workbook. Compare your screen with Figure 7.24.

FIGURE 7.24

Activity 7.07 | Displaying PivotTable Data on Separate Pages

Recall that Mr. Thomas wanted to analyze the call data by Department—Police Department and Fire Department. To do so, you moved the Fire/Police field to the FILTERS area and filtered the entire report on this field.

Adding a field to the FILTERS area is optional; however, if the report is filtered in this manner, you can display multiple pages for your PivotTable data. For example, you can display the Fire Department calls on one page and the Police Department calls on another page. Doing so will make it easier to answer questions about the calls handled by each Department.

1 Click the **Sheet1 tab**, and then rename it **Combined Calls PivotTable**

2 Click cell **A1** to select the PivotTable report. On the ANALYZE tab, in the **PivotTable group**, click the **Options arrow**. Click **Show Report Filter Pages**. Click **OK**.

Because the Fire/Police field was placed in the FILTERS area, this action adds two new sheets to the workbook, one labeled *Fire* and another labeled *Police*.

3 Click the **Police sheet tab**.

The data for the Police Department calls displays on a separate sheet. The data remains in the form of a PivotTable—you can move fields from a row position to a column position and vice versa.

4 Click the **Fire sheet tab. Save** 🖫 your workbook, and then compare your screen with Figure 7.25.

The data for the Fire calls displays on a separate sheet.

FIGURE 7.25

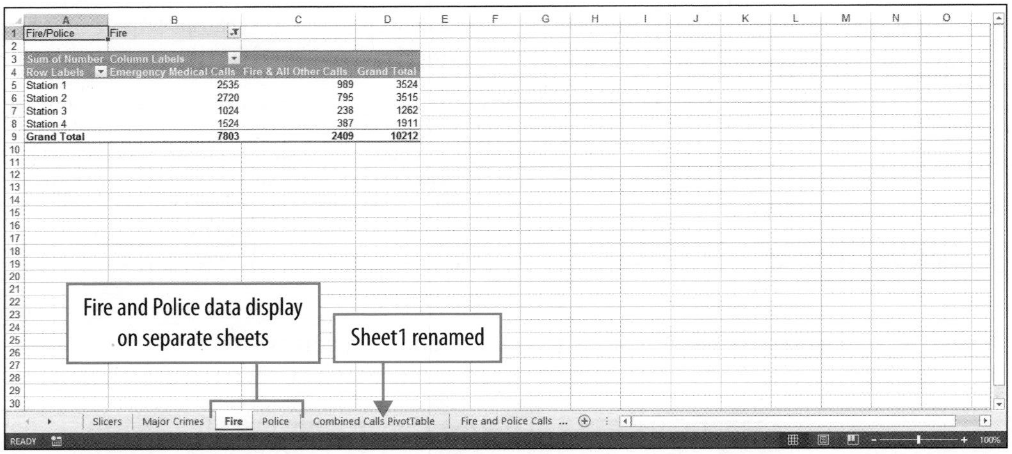

Fire and Police data display on separate sheets

Sheet1 renamed

Activity 7.08 | Changing Calculations in a PivotTable Report

A PivotTable report combines and compares large amounts of data so that you can analyze related totals. The default calculation in a PivotTable report is to *sum* the numeric data. You can modify the calculation to display an average, minimum, maximum, or some other calculation. Here, Mr. Thomas needs to report the *average* number of calls for the first quarter.

1 Display the **Combined Calls PivotTable** worksheet. Point to any cell containing numerical data, right-click, and then click **Value Field Settings**.

The Value Field Settings dialog box displays. In the Custom Name box, *Sum of Number* displays; in the Summarize value field by list, *Sum* is selected.

ANOTHER WAY   On the ANALYZE tab, in the Active Field group, click Field Settings.

420   **Excel | Chapter 7: CREATING PIVOTTABLE AND PIVOTCHART REPORTS AND USING BI TOOLS IN EXCEL**

2 Under **Summarize value field by**, click **Average**. Compare your screen with Figure 7.26.

The Custom Name box displays *Average of Number*.

FIGURE 7.26

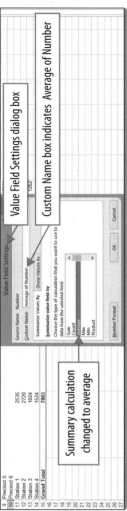

3 Click **OK**.

An average for the three months is calculated and displays with six decimal places in the data cells. Cell A3 indicates *Average of Number*.

4 Right-click any numeric value, and then on the shortcut menu, click **Value Field Settings**. In the lower left corner of the dialog box, click **Number Format**.

The Format Cells dialog box displays, with only the Number tab included.

5 Under **Category**, click **Number**. Change the **Decimal places** box to **0**. Select the **Use 1000 Separator (,)** check box. Click **OK** two times to close both dialog boxes. Click cell **A1**, and then compare your screen with Figure 7.27.

The average figures display as whole numbers with the 1000 separator comma appropriately applied.

FIGURE 7.27

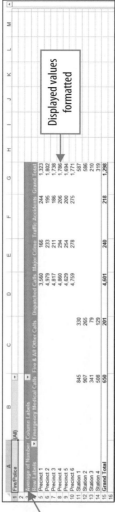

6 **Save** your workbook.

Activity 7.09 | **Formatting a PivotTable Report**

You can apply a PivotTable Style to the entire PivotTable report and change field names to make them easier to understand. For example, the field name *Average of Number* would be easier to understand as *Average Number of Calls*.

1 In cell **A1**, type **1st Quarter Fire & Police Calls** and then press Enter.

2 Click cell **A3**, type **Average Number of Calls** and then press Enter. AutoFit **column A**.

3 On the **DESIGN tab**, in the **PivotTable Styles group**, click **More** .

4 Under **Medium**, in the first row, click the sixth style—**Pivot Style Medium 6**. Click cell **G4** and type **Average** and press Enter. Notice that cell **A15** changes to *Average*. Compare your screen with Figure 7.28.

FIGURE 7.28

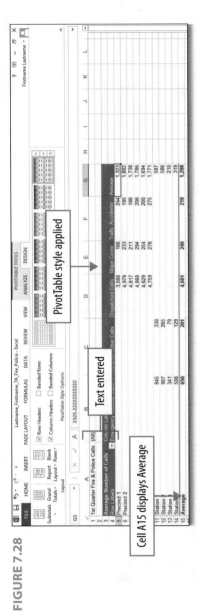

5 Display the **Police** worksheet. On the **DESIGN tab**, in the **PivotTable Styles group**, display the **PivotTable Styles** gallery, and then under **Medium**, in the first row apply the second style—**Pivot Style Medium 2**.

6 Point to any numerical value, right-click, and then click **Value Field Settings**. In the lower left corner, click **Number Format**. Under **Category**, click **Number**. Change the **Decimal places** box to **0**, and then select the **Use 1000 Separator (,)** check box. Click **OK** two times to close both dialog boxes. Click cell **A1**, and then compare your screen with Figure 7.29.

FIGURE 7.29

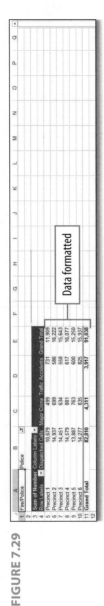

7 Display the **Fire** worksheet. Using the techniques you just practiced, apply the **Pivot Style Medium 3** style to this PivotTable and format the numbers to display using the 1000 comma separator with no decimal places.

8 Save your workbook.

Activity 7.10 | Updating PivotTable Report Data

In the previous activities, you created a combined PivotTable report to display the *average* number of calls by classification type for the Police Department precincts and the Fire Department stations. You created a separate PivotTable report for Fire and for Police to show the *total* number of calls for the quarter by Location and Classification. You also created a separate list of the major crimes by precinct. Finally, Station 3 was identified as the fire station with the lowest call numbers; Mr. Thomas plans to gather supporting information to determine if this is a change from previous quarters.

In this activity, you will update some of the data. If you change the underlying data on which the PivotTable report is based, you must also *refresh*—update—the PivotTable to reflect the new data.

1 On the **Fire** worksheet, in cell **B5**, notice that the total **Emergency Medical Calls for Station 1** is *2,535*.

2 Display the **Combined Calls PivotTable** worksheet, and then click cell **B11**. Notice that the *average* number of **Emergency Medical Calls for Station 1** is *845*.

3 Display the **Fire and Police Calls** worksheet—your original source data. Click cell **E3** and change the number from 924 to **824** Press Enter, and then click cell **E11** and change the number from 879 to **779** and press Enter.

The calls for January and February were both mistakenly overstated by 100 calls and are reduced from 924 and 879 to 824 and 779, respectively.

4 Display the **Combined Calls PivotTable** worksheet. Although you adjusted the underlying data, notice that in cell **B11**, the average number of Emergency Medical Calls for Station 1 has not changed—it still indicates 845.

5 On the **ANALYZE tab**, in the **Data group**, click the **Refresh arrow**, and then click **Refresh.** Compare your screen with Figure 7.30.

The average number of Emergency Medical Calls for Station 1 updates to 778, and the average for this type of call from all stations changes to 634.

FIGURE 7.30

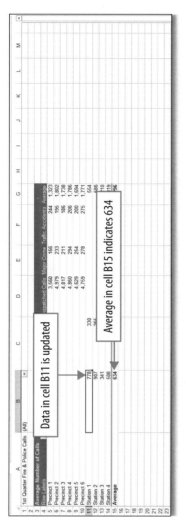

Data in cell B11 is updated

Average in cell B15 indicates 634

6 Display the **Fire** worksheet, and then click cell **B5**. Notice that the total number of Emergency Medical Calls for Station 1 has been updated to 2,335. **Save** your workbook.

Objective 4   Create a PivotChart Report

Video E7-4

A **PivotChart report** is a graphical representation of the data in a PivotTable—referred to as the **associated PivotTable report.** A PivotChart report usually has an associated PivotTable and the two are interactive; that is, if you change the field layout or data in the associated PivotTable report, the changes are immediately reflected in the PivotChart report. A PivotChart report and its associated PivotTable report must be in the same workbook.

Most of the operations you have practiced in standard charts work the same way in a PivotChart. A PivotChart report displays data series, categories, data markers, and axes in the same manner as a standard chart. There are some differences. For example, whereas standard charts are linked directly to a range of worksheet cells, PivotChart reports are based on the data source of the associated PivotTable report.

Activity 7.11 | Creating a PivotChart Report from a PivotTable Report

Mr. Thomas wants to analyze Police calls—specifically the calls related to Major Crime and Traffic Accidents—and he thinks that a chart would be useful to City Council members to convey this information.

1 Display the **Combined Calls PivotTable** worksheet, and then press Ctrl + Home to make cell **A1** the active cell and to select the PivotTable.

2 On the **ANALYZE tab**, in the **Tools group**, click **PivotChart**. In the **Insert Chart** dialog box, on the left side, if necessary, click **Column**, and then click **OK** to accept the default chart— **Clustered Column.** Compare your screen with Figure 7.31.

The PivotChart displays *field buttons*. You can click on any button with an arrow to choose a filter and so change the data that is displayed in the chart. Filters you apply will be reflected in the PivotTable report and vice versa. After your chart is complete, you can hide the field buttons from view. Here, the Classification field items form the legend, and the Location field items form the category axis.

FIGURE 7.31

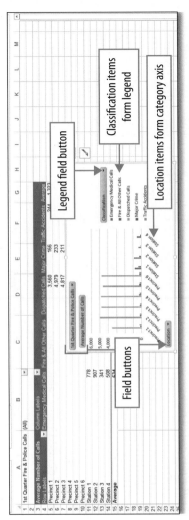

3 On the **DESIGN tab**, in the **Location group**, click **Move Chart**. In the **Move Chart** dialog box, click the **New sheet** option, replace the highlighted text *Chart1* by typing **1st Quarter Chart** and then click **OK.**

4 In the **1st Quarter Chart** sheet, on the **DESIGN tab**, in the **Chart Layouts group**, click **Quick Layout**, and then click the third chart layout—**Layout 3**—which places the legend at the bottom of the chart. In the **Chart Styles group**, click **More**, and then apply **Style 14.**

5 Click the **Chart Title** and watch the **Formula Bar** as you type **1st Quarter Calls** and press **Enter** to display the title text in the chart. Compare your screen with Figure 7.32.

FIGURE 7.32

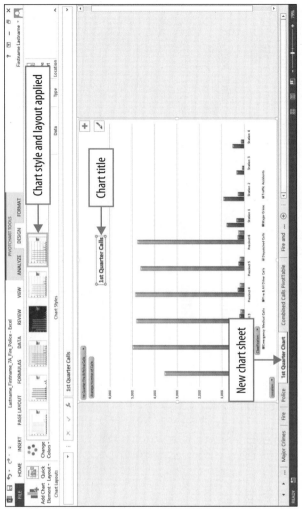

6 On the **INSERT tab**, in the **Text group**, click **Header & Footer**. In the **Page Setup** dialog box, click **Custom Footer**. With the insertion point in the **left section**, from the small toolbar in the dialog box, click **Insert File Name**. Click **OK** two times. **Save** your workbook.

Activity 7.12 | Modifying a PivotChart Report

You can filter and change the values of the data in the PivotChart report by using the gray field buttons that display on the chart. Recall that you can click on any button with an arrow to choose a filter, and that filters you apply will be reflected in the PivotTable report.

For example, most of the calls number in the hundreds, but the Dispatched Calls number in the thousands, resulting in a larger vertical scale. This disparity prevents Mr. Thomas from being able to easily compare the other two call classifications—Major Crime and Traffic Accidents. In this activity, you will filter the data to show only Police calls in the Major Crime and Traffic Accidents classifications. You will also change the summary data back to *total* number of calls rather than the average.

1 In the upper left corner of the chart, click the **Report Filter** field button, which indicates *1st Quarter Fire & Police Calls.* In the lower left corner of the list, select the **Select Multiple Items** check box. Click to clear the (**All**) check box, and select the **Police** check box. Click **OK**, and then compare your screen with Figure 7.33.

Only the Police precinct calls display.

FIGURE 7.33

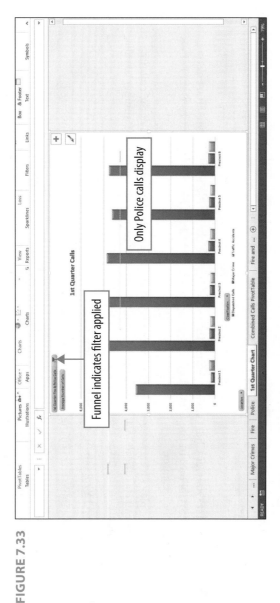

2 At the bottom of the PivotChart, click the **Classification** button above the chart legend. Click to *clear* the check box for **Dispatched Calls**, and then click **OK.**

This action removes the Dispatched Calls classification; only the two remaining call classifications for Police precincts display. The Legend field button displays a funnel icon to indicate that a filter is applied. Because the number of dispatched calls is in the thousands, compared to hundreds for the other call types, removing this classification allows for a clearer comparison of the other call classifications.

3 On the **DESIGN tab,** in the **Type group,** click **Change Chart Type.** In the **Change Chart Type** dialog box, with **Column** selected, click the second chart type—**Stacked Column**—and then click **OK.** Compare your screen with Figure 7.34.

Stacked columns display the two call classifications by location. Within each location, the stacked column shows the amount of activity as part of a whole.

FIGURE 7.34

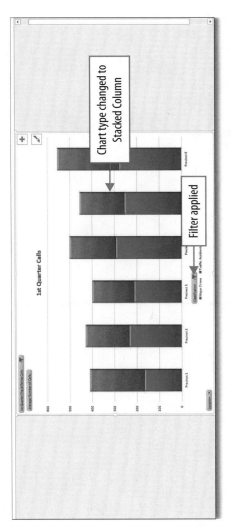

4 Display the **Combined Calls PivotTable** worksheet, and then compare your screen with Figure 7.35.

The data is rearranged and only the precinct calls display. The fire station calls do not currently display on the Combined PivotTable sheet. Each time you changed the PivotChart, the underlying PivotTable changed to reflect the new display of the data.

FIGURE 7.35

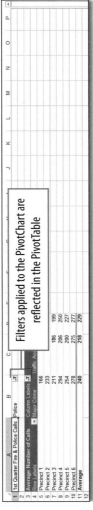

5 Click the **1st Quarter Chart sheet tab** and then click in the chart title to make the chart active. On the **DESIGN tab**, in the **Chart Layouts group**, click **Add Chart Element**, point to **Data Labels**, and then click **Center**.

Labels display on each segment of the columns showing the value for that portion of the column. For the call classification at a particular station, the number represents the *average* number of calls per month in the three months that comprise the first quarter.

6 On the **ANALYZE tab**, in the **Show/Hide group**, click **Field List.**

The PivotTable Fields pane displays. Here you can change the way the data is summarized.

7 In the **PivotChart Fields** pane, in the **VALUES area**, click **Average Number of Calls**, and then click **Value Field Settings.** In the dialog box, click **Sum**, and then click **OK**. On the **chart**, click **Chart Elements** ⊞, point to **Data Labels**, click the arrow, and then click **Center**. Click **Chart Elements** ⊞ to close the **CHART ELEMENTS** list, and then, compare your screen with Figure 7.36.

The chart changes to display the *total* number of calls rather than the average number of calls.

FIGURE 7.36

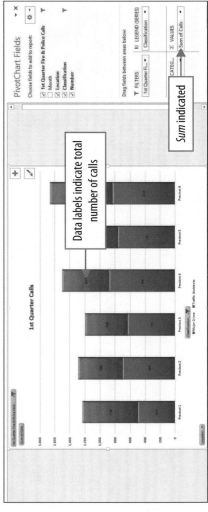

8 Display the **Combined Calls PivotTable** worksheet. **Close**  the **PivotTable Fields** pane. In cells **D4** and **A11**, notice that *Average* is still indicated. Click cell **A11** and type **Total** Press Enter.

Total displays in both cells D4 and A11.

9 Redisplay the **1st Quarter** sheet. On the **FORMAT tab**, in the **Current Selection group**, click the **Chart Elements arrow**, click **Chart Area**, and then click **Format Selection**. In the **Format Chart Area** pane, click **FILL**. Click **Solid fill**, click the **Fill Color arrow**, and then in the fifth column, click the second color—**Blue Accent 1, Lighter 80%**.

10 In the **Format Chart Area** pane, click the arrow next to **CHART OPTIONS** to display the **Chart Elements** list, and then click **Plot Area**. Click **Gradient fill**, click the **Preset gradients arrow**, and then in the second column, click the first color—**Light Gradient – Accent 2**. **Close**  the **Format Plot Area** pane. Right-click the **Chart Title**, click **Font**, and then change the font size to **32** and change the font color to the first color in the fourth column—**Dark Blue, Text 2**. Click **OK**.

11 On the **ANALYZE tab**, in the **Show/Hide group**, click **Field Buttons arrow**, and then click **Hide All**. Click an outer edge of the chart to select the entire chart, and then compare your screen with Figure 7.37.

FIGURE 7.37

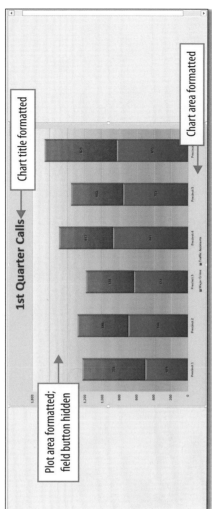

Chart title formatted

1st Quarter Calls

Plot area formatted; field button hidden

Chart area formatted

Activity 7.13 | Arranging and Hiding Worksheets in a Multi-sheet Workbook

1 At the bottom of the Excel window, to the left of the sheet tabs, click the **left arrow** twice and make the **Slicers** worksheet active. To the right of the sheet tabs, locate the horizontal scroll bar. At the left end of the scroll bar, point to the three vertical dots to display the pointer, and then drag to the right to decrease the width of the scroll bar to display all seven worksheets in this workbook as shown in Figure 7.38.

FIGURE 7.38

Seven worksheet tabs display

Horizontal scroll bar

2 Drag the **Combined Calls PivotTable sheet tab** to the left until it is the first worksheet. In the same manner, rearrange the remaining sheet tabs so they are in the following order: Combined Calls PivotTable, Slicers, Major Crimes, Fire, Police, 1st Quarter Chart, Fire and Police Calls. Click the **Fire and Police Calls sheet tab** and then compare your screen with Figure 7.39.

FIGURE 7.39

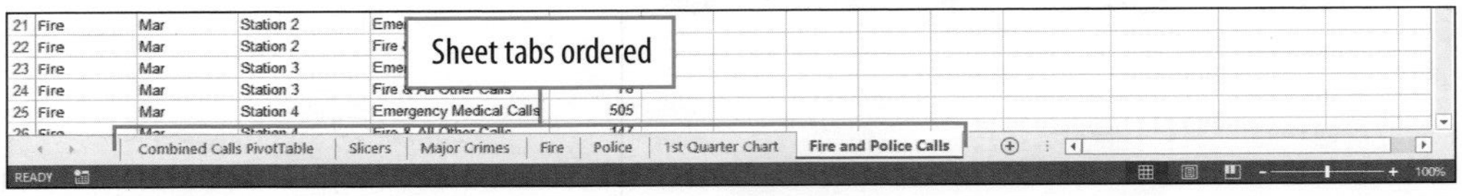

Sheet tabs ordered

3 Right-click the **Fire and Police Calls sheet tab** and then click **Hide**.

In this manner you can hide a worksheet to prevent a user from altering the data.

4 Point to the **Combined Calls PivotTable sheet tab**, right-click, and then click **Select All Sheets**. Insert a footer in the **left section** that includes the file name. From the **PAGE LAYOUT tab**, center the worksheets horizontally on the page, change the Orientation to **Landscape**, and then in the **Scale to Fit group**, set the **Width** to **1 page**. On the status bar, click **Normal** ▦. Press [Ctrl] + [Home] to move to the top of the worksheet.

5 Display the **document properties** and under **Related People**, be sure that your name displays as the author. If necessary, right-click the author name, click **Edit Property**, and then type your name. In the **Subject** box, type your course name and section #, and in the **Tags** box, type **fire, police, call activity**

6 With the sheets still grouped, display the **Print Preview**, and then examine the six visible pages of your workbook. Return to the worksheet and make any necessary corrections or adjustments. Ungroup the worksheets.

7 **Save** ▤ your workbook.

8 Print or submit the workbook electronically as directed by your instructor.

END | You have completed Project 7A

MyITLab®
Project 7B Training

PROJECT
7B

PowerPivot and Power View

PROJECT ACTIVITIES

In Activities 7.14 through 7.21, you will use two of Excel's Business Intelligence tools, PowerPivot and Power View, to create a report and dashboard for the district recreation center. Your completed worksheets will look similar to Figure 7.40.

PROJECT FILES

For Project 7B, you will need the following files:

New blank Excel workbook
e07B_Medical_Supplies

You will save your workbook as:

Lastname_Firstname_7B_First_Aid

PROJECT RESULTS

Build from
Scratch

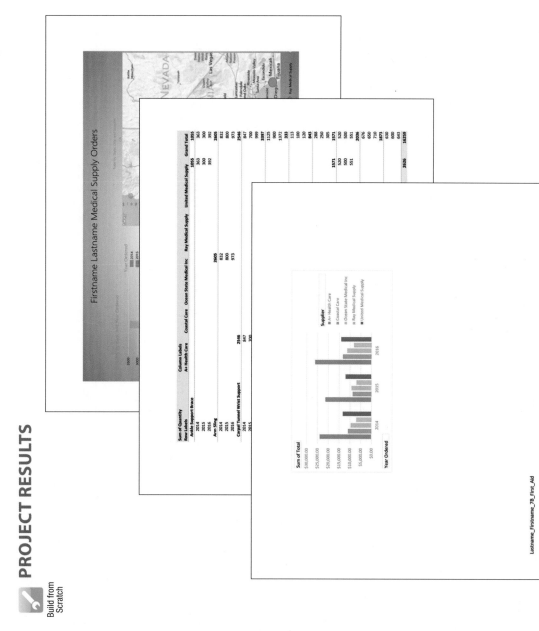

FIGURE 7.40 Project 7B PowerPivot and Power View

Objective 5   Create a Data Model Using PowerPivot

Video E7-5

Excel includes several **Business Intelligence tools** that can be used to perform analysis and create sophisticated charts and reports. The **Data Model** is a method of incorporating data from multiple, related tables into an Excel worksheet. The data can be in an Excel workbook, imported from an Access database, or imported from an external source such as a corporate database, a public data feed, or an analysis service. The related tables can be used to create PivotTables, Pivot Charts, and Power View reports.

Traditional PivotTables use data from a single table. With **PowerPivot**, you can analyze data from multiple sources, work with multiple data tables, and create relationships between tables. A **relationship** is an association between tables that share a common field.

Power View allows you to create and interact with multiple charts, slicers, and other data visualizations in a single sheet.

Activity 7.14 │ Enabling the PowerPivot and Power View Add-ins

The PowerPivot and Power View Add-ins are disabled by default. You must enable PowerPivot and Power View from the Excel Options dialog box. In this activity, you will enable PowerPivot and Power View and add the PowerPivot tab to the ribbon.

1 Start Excel and open a new blank workbook. Click the **FILE tab** to display **Backstage** view, and then click **Options.**

2 In the **Excel Options** dialog box, on the left, click **Add-Ins.** At the bottom of the **Excel Options** dialog box, click the **Manage arrow** and click **COM Add-Ins.** Click **Go.** Select the **Microsoft Office PowerPivot for Excel 2013** and **Power View** check boxes. Compare your dialog box with Figure 7.41

Add-ins are optional commands and features that are not immediately available; you must first install and/or activate an add-in to use it.

FIGURE 7.41

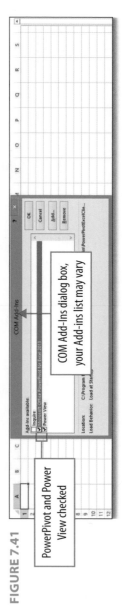

PowerPivot and Power View checked

COM Add-Ins dialog box, your Add-ins list may vary

3 Click **OK.** If the **POWERPIVOT tab** is not displayed on the ribbon, right-click the **VIEW tab** and click **Customize the Ribbon.** On the right, under **Customize Ribbon,** verify **Main Tabs** is selected, select the **Power View** and **PowerPivot** check boxes, and then click **OK.**

The PowerPivot tab is displayed on the ribbon.

Activity 7.15 │ Importing Data into the Excel Data Model

In this activity, you will import multiple tables from an Access database into the Data Model using PowerPivot.

1 Click the **POWERPIVOT tab,** and then, in the **Data Model group,** click **Manage.**

The PowerPivot for Excel window opens.

2 Maximize the **PowerPivot** window. In the **Get External Data group**, click **From Database**, and then click **From Access**. Compare your screen with Figure 7.42

FIGURE 7.42

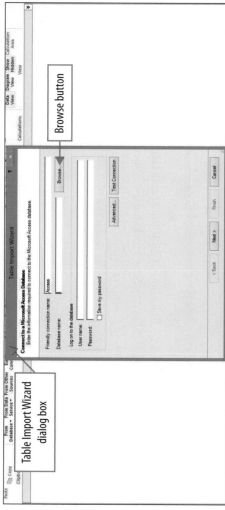

Table Import Wizard dialog box

Browse button

3 In the **Table Import Wizard**, click **Browse**. Navigate to your student files, click **e07B_Medical_Supplies**, and then click **OK**. Click **Next**.

4 Verify *Select from a list of tables and views to choose the data to import* is selected and then click **Next**. Compare your screen with Figure 7.43

FIGURE 7.43

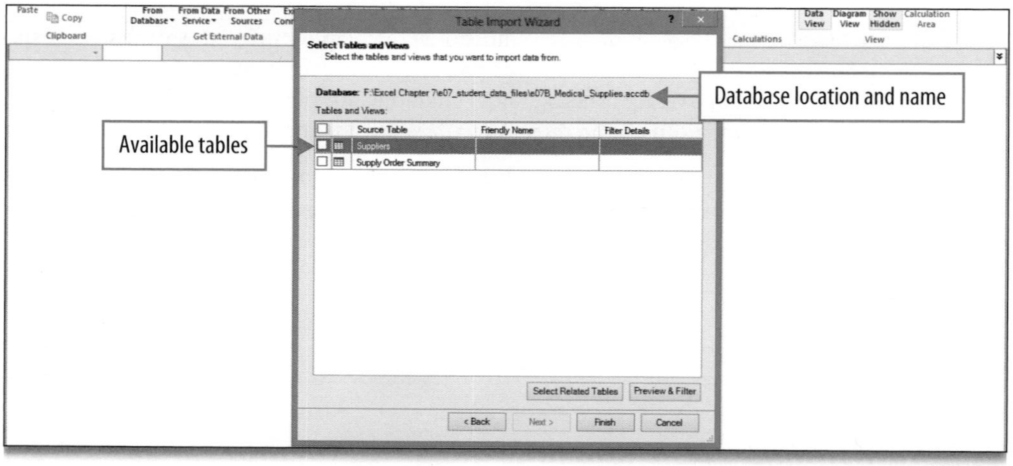

Available tables

Database location and name

5 Select both tables and then click **Finish** to import the tables into the Excel Data Model. Compare your screen with Figure 7.44.

FIGURE 7.44

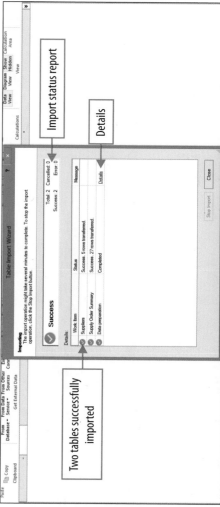

Two tables successfully imported

Import status report

Details

6 Click **Details** to verify a relationship was created between the imported tables. Click **OK**. Click **Close**. Compare your screen with Figure 7.45.

The two tables are imported into the Data Model and display in the PowerPivot window. The data does not display in the Excel workbook. To work with multiple tables in Excel, a relationship must be created between the tables.

FIGURE 7.45

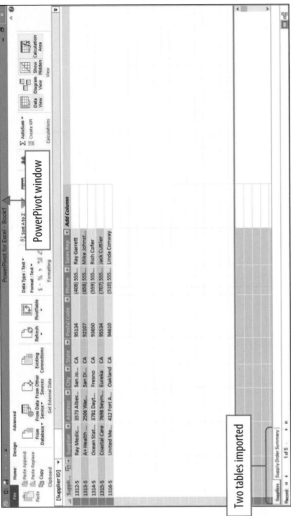

PowerPivot window

Two tables imported

7 In the **PowerPivot** window, with the **Suppliers** table active, click the **Design tab**. In the **Relationships group**, click **Manage Relationships**. Compare your screen with Figure 7.46.

The Manage Relationships dialog box indicates a relationship between the Supplier ID field in the Supply Order Summary table and the Suppliers table. Because the two tables were imported together, the relationship between them was detected and created in the Excel Data Model. You can also manually create, edit, or delete relationships between tables.

FIGURE 7.46

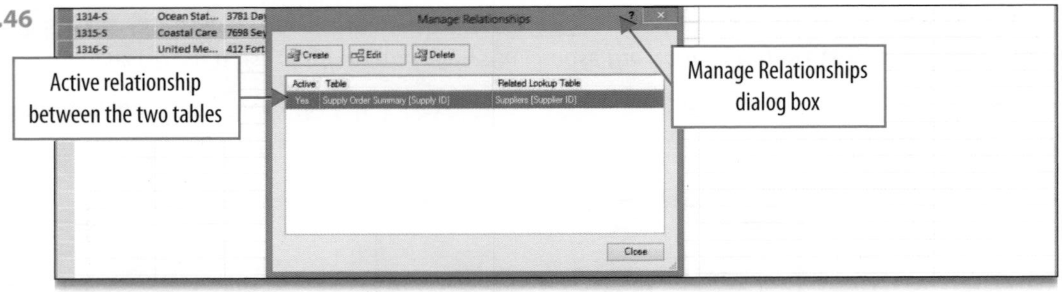

Manage Relationships dialog box

Active relationship between the two tables

8 In the **Manage Relationships** dialog box, click **Close**. Click the **Home tab**, and then click **PivotTable**. In the **Insert Pivot** dialog box, verify **New Worksheet** is selected and then click **OK**. Compare your screen with Figure 7.47.

Notice the PivotTable is created in the Excel workbook, not in the PowerPivot window.

FIGURE 7.47

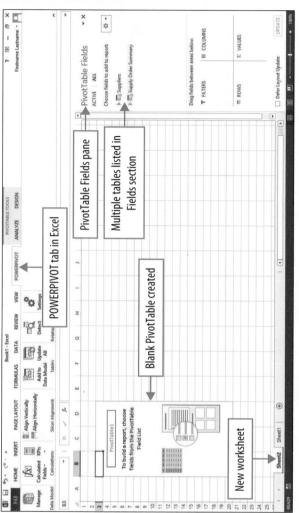

9 Save your file in your Excel Chapter 7 folder as **Lastname_Firstname_7B_First_Aid**

Objective 6   Create a PivotTable Using PowerPivot

Activity 7.16 | Creating a PivotTable Using Multiple Tables

 Video E7-6

The Data Model allows you to use PowerPivot to create PivotTables using the data from multiple, related tables.

1 In the **PivotTable Fields** pane, notice there are two tabs: **ACTIVE** and **ALL**. With the **ALL tab** active, expand the **Suppliers** table, and then drag the **Supplier** field to the **COLUMNS area**. Collapse the **Suppliers** table, expand the **Supply Order Summary** table, and then drag the **Item** and **Year Ordered** fields to the **ROWS area**. Drag the **Quantity** field to the **VALUES area**. Compare your screen with Figure 7.48.

You have created a PivotTable using data from two related tables.

FIGURE 7.48

2 Click cell **B5**. In the lower right corner of the cell, click **Quick Explore** [icon]. Expand **Supply Order Summary** and compare your screen with Figure 7.49.

Quick Explore allows you to drill down through PivotTable data with a single click.

FIGURE 7.49

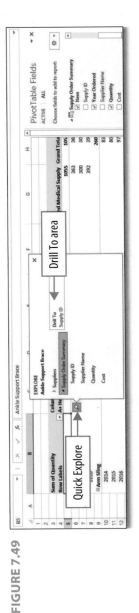

3 Click **Drill to Supply ID**. With cell **B5** selected, click **Quick Explore** [icon] and then click **Drill to Item**. Compare your screen with Figure 7.50.

In this manner you can drill through the data in a PivotTable.

FIGURE 7.50

4 Click **Undo** [icon] two times. **Save** [icon] your workbook.

Activity 7.17 | Adding a Calculated Field and Creating a PivotChart Using PowerPivot

The imported data does not include a total column, so you will add one in PowerPivot.

1 On the **Windows taskbar**, click the **PowerPivot** button to switch to the **PowerPivot** window. Click the **Supply Order Summary sheet tab**. Click the **Add Column** header and in the **Formula Bar**, type =[and then, double-click [**Quantity**]. Type *[and then double-click [**Cost**]. Press [Enter]. Compare your screen with Figure 7.51.

The tables in the PowerPivot window do not contain row and column headings like an Excel worksheet, but rather field names like a database. This formula uses the field names *Quantity* and *Cost*. A new calculated column is created in the Data Model that can be used in the PivotTables and other reports.

FIGURE 7.51

2 Right-click the **CalculatedColumn1** and click **Rename Column**. Type **Total** and then press [Enter].

3 On the **Home tab**, click the **PivotTable arrow** and then click **PivotChart**. In the **Insert Pivot** dialog box, verify that **New Worksheet** is selected, and then click **OK**.

4 In the **PivotChart Fields** pane, expand the **Suppliers** table, and then drag the **Supplier** field to the **LEGEND (SERIES) area.** Collapse the **Suppliers** table, expand the **Supply Order Summary** table, and then drag the **Total** field to the **VALUES area.** Drag the **Year Ordered** field to the **AXIS (CATEGORY) area.** Compare your screen with Figure 7.52. **Save** your workbook.

Using PowerPivot, a PivotChart does not have to be associated with a PivotTable.

FIGURE 7.52

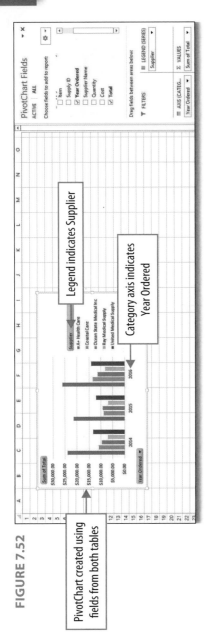

PivotChart created using fields from both tables

Legend indicates Supplier

Category axis indicates Year Ordered

Objective 7 | Create a Dashboard Using Power View

Video E7-7

Power View is a data visualization tool that can be used to create interactive dashboards and reports. Power View can be used with data in worksheet tables or with data in the Data Model. The charts and other objects created on a Power View worksheet are related, and can be cross-filtered. Filtering one object will also filter the other objects on the worksheet. You can create multiple Power View sheets in a workbook.

Activity 7.18 | Create a Power View Worksheet and Column Chart Visualization

In this activity, you will create a Power View worksheet and a Column chart.

1 Click the **Sheet1 sheet tab.** Click the **INSERT tab.** In the **Reports group**, click **Power View.** Compare your screen with Figure 7.53.

A new Power View worksheet is created. The Power View canvas displays on the left and the Power View Fields pane displays on the right. The *canvas* is the area of a Power View worksheet that contains data visualizations.

NOTE

The Power View Add-in is installed by default, but must be enabled the first time it is used. You must also have Silverlight installed. If you do not have Silverlight installed, Excel will prompt you to install it at this point.

FIGURE 7.53

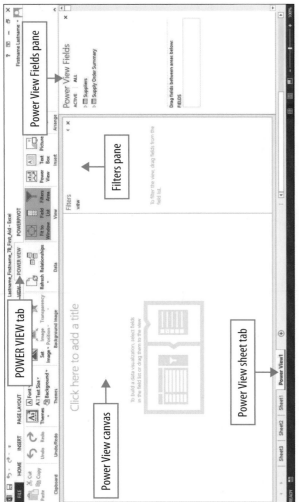

2 At the top of the **Power View** worksheet, click *Click here to add a title*, and then type **Firstname Lastname Medical Supply Orders**

3 Notice both tables are visible in the **Power View Fields** pane. Expand the **Supply Order Summary** table. Drag the **Item**, **Quantity**, and **Year Ordered** fields to the **FIELDS area**. Compare your screen with Figure 7.54.

A table is created in the upper left quadrant of the Power View canvas.

 BY TOUCH   Tap the check box next to a field to select it.

FIGURE 7.54

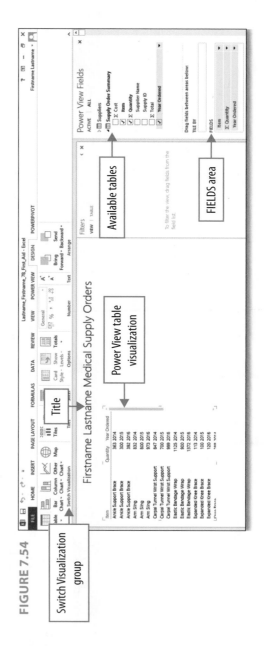

4 On the **DESIGN tab**, in the **Switch Visualization group**, click the **Column Chart arrow** and then click **Stacked Column**. Compare your screen with Figure 7.55. **Save** your workbook.

The table is changed to a stacked column chart.

FIGURE 7.55

Activity 7.19 | Create a Power View Pie Chart Visualization

In this activity, you will add a pie chart to the Power View worksheet.

1 Click a blank area of the **Power View** canvas to deselect the column chart. In the **Power View Fields** pane, expand the **Suppliers** table and drag the **Supplier** field to the **FIELDS area**. From the **Supply Order Summary** table drag the **Total** field to the **FIELDS area**. Compare your screen with Figure 7.56.

Recall that the Total field is a calculated field that you created in the Data Model.

FIGURE 7.56

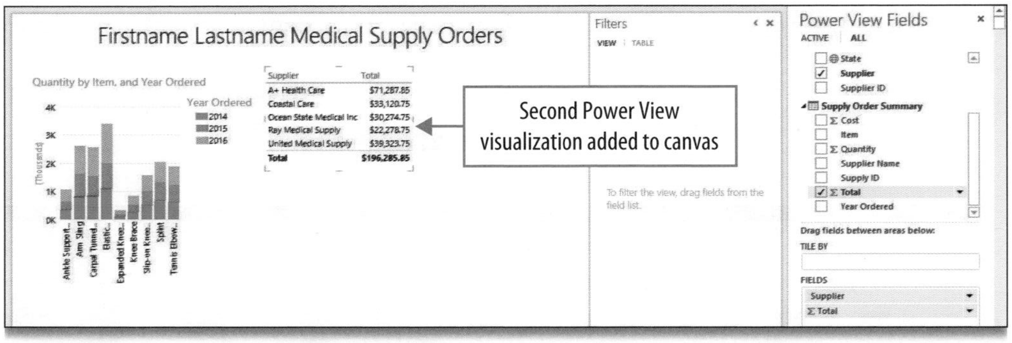

2 On the **DESIGN tab**, in the **Switch Visualization group**, click **Other Chart** and then click **Pie**. Point to the lower right edge of the pie chart to display the pointer, and then drag the pie chart below the column chart. Point to the lower right corner of the pie chart area to display the pointer and drag to resize the pie chart until it is the same width as the column chart and touches the bottom edge of the canvas. Compare your screen with Figure 7.57. **Save** your workbook.

FIGURE 7.57

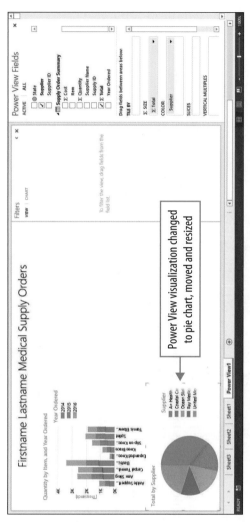

Activity 7.20 | Create a Power View Map

Power View can use the Bing map service to generate a map if your data contains location information. In this activity, you will create a map of local suppliers.

1 Click a blank area of the **Power View** canvas to deselect the pie chart. In the **Power View Fields** pane, from the **Suppliers** table, drag the **City**, **State**, and **Supplier** fields to the **FIELDS area.** From the **Supply Order Summary** table drag the **Total** field to the **FIELDS area.**

2 On the **DESIGN tab**, in the **Switch Visualization group**, click **Map**. If necessary, in the **PRIVACY WARNING** bar, click **Enable Content**. Drag the lower right corner of the map to resize it to fill the right side of the canvas. Compare your screen with Figure 7.58. **Save** 🖫 your workbook.

FIGURE 7.58

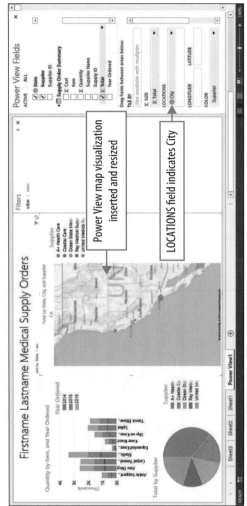

Power View map visualization inserted and resized

LOCATIONS field indicates City

Activity 7.21 | Formatting the Power View Worksheet

A Power View report can be formatted to make it more attractive.

1 Click the canvas to deselect the map. **Close** ⊠ the **Filters** pane. On the **POWER VIEW tab**, in the **Themes group**, click **Text Size**, and then click **75%**.

This makes the text smaller so more of the text is visible on the sheet.

2 In the **Themes group**, click **Background**, and then click the first color in the third row—**Light 1 Center Gradient**.

3 Click the map to select it. Click the **LAYOUT tab**, in the **Labels group**, click **Legend**, and then click **Show Legend at Bottom**.

4 **Close** ⊠ the **Power View Fields** pane, **Save** 🖫 your workbook, and then compare your screen with Figure 7.59.

FIGURE 7.59

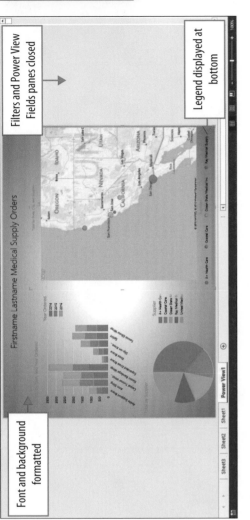

Font and background formatted

Filters and Power View Fields panes closed

Legend displayed at bottom

5 On the pie chart, click the blue slice that represents *A+ Health Care*. Notice that the other slices on the pie chart are dimmed. Also notice the effect on the column chart and map. Compare your screen with Figure 7.60.

The objects on the Power View sheet are related, so highlighting or filtering one object also affects the other objects.

FIGURE 7.60

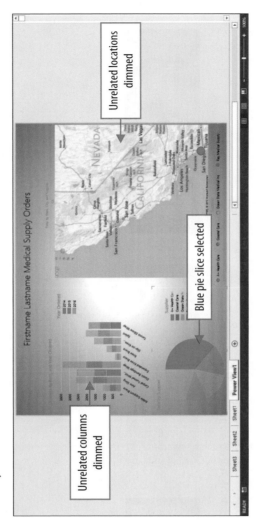

Unrelated columns dimmed

Unrelated locations dimmed

Blue pie slice selected

6 Rename **Sheet3 PivotChart** Rename **Sheet2 PivotTable** Delete Sheet1. Group the **PivotChart** and **PivotTable** worksheets and insert a footer with the file name in the **left section**. Return to **Normal** view, center horizontally, change the **Orientation** to **Landscape**, and scale the **Width** and **Height** to **1 page**. Press Ctrl + Home to return to cell A1.

7 Display the **document properties** and under **Related People**, be sure that your name displays as the author. If necessary, right-click the author name, click **Edit Property**, and then type your name. In the **Subject** box, type your course name and section #, and in the **Tags** box, type **first aid, BI** Return to your worksheet, ungroup the worksheets, and **Save** your workbook.

8 Print or submit the workbook electronically as directed by your instructor. **Close** your workbook and **Close** Excel.

NOTE

A Power View worksheet must be printed separately from the other worksheets.

END | You have completed Project 7B

END OF CHAPTER

SUMMARY

PivotTables and PivotCharts are used to organize and display data. PivotTables are useful for summarizing and analyzing large amounts of data. PivotCharts graphically represent the data in PivotTables.

By manipulating data in PivotTable and PivotChart reports you can present and organize information into groups from which trends, comparisons, patterns, and relationships can be determined.

Business Intelligence tools in Excel, including PowerPivot and Power View, can be used to perform data analysis and create sophisticated charts and reports using data from multiple sources and tables.

Excel uses the Data Model to incorporate data from multiple sources into related tables in Excel. The data can come from an Excel worksheet or external sources such as databases and data feeds.

GO! LEARN IT ONLINE

Review the concepts and key terms in this chapter by completing these online challenges, which you can find at **www.pearsonhighered.com/go.**

Matching and Multiple Choice:
Answer matching and multiple choice questions to test what you learned in this chapter. MyITLab®

Crossword Puzzle:
Spell out the words that match the numbered clues, and put them in the puzzle squares.

Flipboard:
Flip through the definitions of the key terms in this chapter and match them with the correct term.

END OF CHAPTER

REVIEW AND ASSESSMENT GUIDE FOR EXCEL CHAPTER 7

Your instructor may assign one or more of these projects to help you review the chapter and assess your mastery and understanding of the chapter.

	Review and Assessment Guide for Excel Chapter 7		
Project	**Apply Skills from These Chapter Objectives**	**Project Type**	**Project Location**
7C	Objectives 1–4 from Project 7A	**7C Skills Review** A guided review of the skills from Project 7A.	On the following pages
7D	Objectives 5–7 from Project 7B	**7D Skills Review** A guided review of the skills from Project 7B.	On the following pages
7E	Objectives 1–4 from Project 7A	**7E Mastery (Grader Project)** A demonstration of your mastery of the skills in Project 7A with extensive decision making.	In MyITLab and on the following pages
7F	Objectives 5–7 from Project 7B	**7F Mastery (Grader Project)** A demonstration of your mastery of the skills in Project 7B with extensive decision making.	In MyITLab and on the following pages
7G	Objectives 1–7 from Projects 7A and 7B	**7G Mastery (Grader Project)** A demonstration of your mastery of the skills in Projects 7A and 7B with extensive decision making.	In MyITLab and on the following pages
7H	Combination of Objectives from Projects 7A and 7B	**7H GO! Fix It** A demonstration of your mastery of the skills in Projects 7A and 7B by creating a correct result from a document that contains errors you must find.	Online
7I	Combination of Objectives from Projects 7A and 7B	**7I GO! Make It** A demonstration of your mastery of the skills in Projects 7A and 7B by creating a result from a supplied picture.	Online
7J	Combination of Objectives from Projects 7A and 7B	**7J GO! Solve It** A demonstration of your mastery of the skills in Projects 7A and 7B, your decision-making skills, and your critical thinking skills. A task-specific rubric helps you self-assess your result.	Online
7K	Combination of Objectives from Projects 7A and 7B	**7K GO! Solve It** A demonstration of your mastery of the skills in Projects 7A and 7B, your decision-making skills, and your critical thinking skills. A task-specific rubric helps you self-assess your result.	On the following pages
7L	Combination of Objectives from Projects 7A and 7B	**7L GO! Think** A demonstration of your understanding of the chapter concepts applied in a manner that you would outside of college. An analytic rubric helps you and your instructor grade the quality of your work by comparing it to the work an expert in the discipline would create.	On the following pages
7M	Combination of Objectives from Projects 7A and 7B	**7M GO! Think** A demonstration of your understanding of the chapter concepts applied in a manner that you would outside of college. An analytic rubric helps you and your instructor grade the quality of your work by comparing it to the work an expert in the discipline would create.	Online
7N	Combination of Objectives from Projects 7A and 7B	**7N You and GO!** A demonstration of your understanding of the chapter concepts applied in a manner that you would in a personal situation. An analytic rubric helps you and your instructor grade the quality of your work.	Online

GLOSSARY

GLOSSARY OF CHAPTER KEY TERMS

Add-in An optional command or feature that is not immediately available; you must first install and/or activate an add-in to use it.

Associated PivotTable report The PivotTable report in a workbook that is graphically represented in a PivotChart.

Business Intelligence tools Tools that can be used to perform data analysis and create sophisticated charts and reports.

Canvas The area of a Power View worksheet that contains data visualizations.

Clear Filter A button that removes a filter.

COLUMNS area An area to position fields that you want to display as columns in the PivotTable report. Field names placed here become column titles, and the data is grouped in columns by these titles.

Data Model A method of incorporating data from multiple, related tables into an Excel worksheet.

Field button A button on a PivotChart with an arrow to choose a filter, and thus change the data that is displayed in the chart.

Field names The column titles from source data that form the categories of data for a PivotTable.

Field section The upper portion of the PivotTable Fields pane containing the fields—column titles—from your source

data; use this area to add fields to and remove fields from the PivotTable.

Filter To limit the display of data to only specific information.

FILTER area An area in the lower portion of the PivotTable Fields pane to position fields by which you want to filter the PivotTable report, enabling you to display a subset of data in the PivotTable report.

Filtering button A button on a slicer which you use to select the item by which to filter.

Layout section The lower portion of the PivotTable Fields pane containing the four areas for layout; use this area to rearrange and reposition fields in the PivotTable.

PivotChart report A graphical representation of the data in a PivotTable report.

PivotTable An interactive Excel report that summarizes and analyzes large amounts of data.

PivotTable Fields pane A window that lists, at the top, all of the fields—column titles—from the source data for use in the PivotTable report and at the bottom, an area in which you can arrange the fields in the PivotTable.

Power View An Excel BI tool that allows you to create and interact with multiple charts, slicers, and other data visualizations in a single sheet.

PowerPivot An Excel BI tool that allows you to analyze data from multiple sources, work with multiple data tables, and create relationships between tables.

Quick Explore A tool that allows you to drill down through PivotTable data with a single click.

Refresh The command to update a worksheet to reflect the new data.

Relationship An association between tables that share a common field.

ROWS area An area to position fields that you want to display as rows in the PivotTable report. Field names placed here become row titles, and the data is grouped by these row titles.

Slicer Easy-to-use filtering control with buttons that enable you to drill down through large amounts of data.

Slicer header The top of a slicer that indicates the category of the slicer items.

Source data The data for a PivotTable, formatted in columns and rows, which can be located in an Excel worksheet or an external source.

VALUES area An area to position fields that contain data that is summarized in a PivotTable report or PivotChart report. The data placed here is usually numeric or financial in nature and the data is summarized—summed. You can also perform other basic calculations such as finding the average, the minimum, or the maximum.

CHAPTER REVIEW

Skills Review   Project 7C Parks and Pools Calls

Apply 7A skills from these Objectives:

1 Create a PivotTable Report
2 Use Slicers and Search Filters
3 Modify a PivotTable Report
4 Create a PivotChart Report

In the following Skills Review, you will assist Lindsay Johnson, Director of Parks and Recreation, in preparing a comparative report for phone calls received by the various park and pool facilities in the city. You will create and modify a PivotTable report and PivotChart report. The first six worksheets in your workbook will look similar to Figure 7.61.

PROJECT FILES

For Project 7C, you will need the following file:

e07C_Parks_Pools

You will save your workbook as:

Lastname_Firstname_7C_Parks_Pools

PROJECT RESULTS

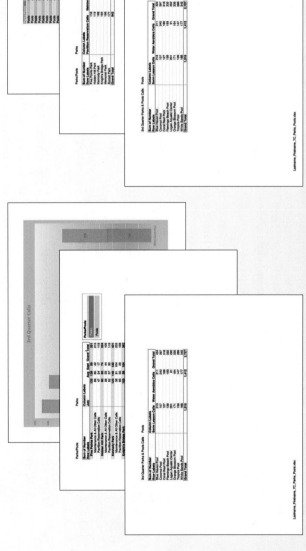

FIGURE 7.61

(Project 7C Parks and Pools Calls continues on the next page)

CHAPTER REVIEW

1 Start Excel. From your student files, open e07C_Parks_Pools. Save the file in your Excel Chapter 7 folder as **Lastname_Firstname_7C_Parks_Pools** Click cell A2. On the **INSERT tab**, in the **Tables group**, click **Recommended PivotTables**, and then, in the **Recommended PivotTables** dialog box, click **Sum of Number by Location (+) PivotTable**. Click **OK**.

a. In the **PivotTable Fields** pane, in the **layout section**, verify **Parks/Pools** and **Location** are listed in the **ROWS area**, and **Sum of Number** is listed in the **VALUES area**.

b. Drag the **Parks/Pools** field from the **ROWS area** up to the **FILTERS area**.

c. In the **field section**, select the **Classification** field check box. Right-click cell **A4**, point to **Expand/Collapse**, and then click **Expand Entire Field**.

d. In the **PivotTable Fields** pane, from the **field section**, drag the **Month** field down to the **COLUMNS area**.

e. On the **DESIGN tab**, in the **PivotTable Styles group**, click **More**, and then under **Light**, click **Pivot Style Light 8**.

2 On the **ANALYZE tab**, in the **Filter group**, click **Insert Slicer**. Select the **Parks/Pools** check box, and then click **OK**. Drag the **Parks/Pools** slicer to the right of the PivotTable. Shorten the slicer to just below **Pools**.

a. On the **OPTIONS tab**, in the **Slicer Styles group**, click **More**, and then under **Dark**, click **Slicer Style Dark 6**. Click cell **A1**. On the **Parks/Pools slicer**, click the **Parks** filtering button. Point to the **Sheet1 sheet tab**, right-click, and then click **Move or Copy**. In the **Move or Copy** dialog box, select the **Create a copy** check box. Click **OK**. Right-click the **Sheet 1 (2) sheet tab**, click **Rename**, and then type **Filtered by Parks**

b. Display the **Sheet1** worksheet. In the **Parks/Pools slicer**, click **Clear Filter**. Point to the **Parks/Pools slicer header**, right-click, and then click **Remove "Parks/Pools"**.

3 In the layout section of the **PivotTable Fields** pane, from the **COLUMNS area**, drag the **Month** field name upward into the white field section and then release the mouse button. In the **layout section**, from the **ROWS area**, drag the **Classification** field into the **COLUMNS area**. **Close** the **PivotTable Fields** pane.

a. Click cell **B4**. Right-click, point to **Move**, and then click **Move "Maintenance & All Other Calls" Down**. Point to cell **E19** and right-click; click **Show Details**. In in the lower right corner, click **Quick Analysis**, and then click **Data Bars**. Rename the **Sheet3 tab Swim Lesson Calls** Click cell A1.

b. Click the **Sheet1 tab**, and then rename it **Combined Calls PivotTable** Click cell A1. On the **ANALYZE tab**, in the **PivotTable group**, click the **Options arrow**, and then click **Show Report Filter Pages**. In the dialog box, click **OK** to create worksheets for Parks and for Pools.

c. Display the **Combined Calls PivotTable** worksheet. Point to any cell with numerical data, right-click, and then click **Value Field Settings**. Click **Number Format**, click **Number**, and then set the **Decimal places** to **0** and select the **Use 1000 Separator** check box. Click **OK** two times.

d. Click cell A1. Type **3rd Quarter Parks & Pools Calls** press [Enter], and then apply AutoFit to column A. Display the **Parks and Pools Calls** worksheet, which is your source data. Change the value in cell E3 from 95 to **85** and then press [Enter]. Display the **Combined Calls PivotTable** worksheet. Click cell A1. On the **ANALYZE tab**, in the **Data group**, click the **Refresh arrow**, and then click **Refresh**.

4 On the **ANALYZE tab**, in the **Tools group**, click **PivotChart**. In the **Insert Chart** dialog box, on the left verify **Column** is selected, on the right, verify the first chart—**Clustered Column** is selected, and then click **OK**. On the **DESIGN tab**, in the **Location group**, click **Move Chart**. In the **Move Chart** dialog box, click the **New sheet** option, replace the highlighted text *Chart1* by typing **3rd Quarter Chart** and then click **OK**. In the new chart sheet, on the **DESIGN tab**, in the **Chart Layouts group**, click **Quick Layout**, and then click **Layout 3**. In the **Chart Styles group**, click **More**, and then apply **Style 13**.

a. Click the **Chart Title** and watch the **Formula Bar** as you type **3rd Quarter Calls** and press [Enter]. On the **INSERT tab**, in the **Text group**, click **Header & Footer**. In the **Page Setup** dialog box, click **Custom Footer**. With the insertion point in the **left section**, from the small toolbar in the dialog box, click **Insert File Name**, and then click **OK** two times.

(Project 7C Parks and Pools Calls continues on the next page)

CHAPTER REVIEW

b. In the upper left corner of the chart, click **Report Filter**, which indicates *3rd Quarter Parks & Pools Calls*. In the lower left corner of the list, select (place a check mark in) the **Select Multiple Items** check box. Click to clear the **(All)** check box, select the **Pools** check box, and then click **OK**. At the bottom of the PivotChart, click **Legend**, which indicates *Classification*. Click to *clear* the check box for **Pool Party Calls**, and then click **OK**.

c. On the **DESIGN tab**, in the **Type group**, click **Change Chart Type**. In the **Change Chart Type** dialog box, click **Stacked Column**, and then click **OK**. On the **DESIGN tab**, in the **Chart Layouts group**, click **Add Chart Element**, point to **Data Labels**, and then click **Center**.

d. On the **FORMAT tab**, in the **Current Selection group**, click the **Chart Elements arrow**, click **Chart Area**, and then click **Format Selection**. In the **Format Chart Area** pane, click **FILL**. Click **Solid fill**, click the **Fill Color arrow**, and then in the fifth column, click the third color—**Green, Accent 1, Lighter 60%**. Format the **Plot area** with **Gradient fill**. Click the **Preset gradients arrow**, and then in the second column, click the first color—**Light Gradient – Accent 2**. **Close** the **Format Plot Area** pane.

e. On the **ANALYZE tab**, in the **Show/Hide group**, click the **Field Buttons arrow**, and then click **Hide All**.

f. Drag the **Combined Calls PivotTable sheet tab** to the left until it is the first worksheet. Arrange the remaining sheet tabs so they are in the following order: Combined Calls PivotTable, Filtered by Parks, 3rd Quarter Chart, Swim Lesson Calls, Parks, Pools, Parks and Pool Calls. Hide the **Parks and Pool Calls** worksheet.

g. Point to the **Combined Calls PivotTable sheet tab**, right-click, and then click **Select All Sheets**. Insert a footer in the **left section** that includes the file name. From the **PAGE LAYOUT tab**, center the worksheets horizontally on the page, change the **Orientation** to **Landscape**, and then in the **Scale to Fit group**, set the **Width** to **1 page**. On the status bar, click **Normal**. Press Ctrl + Home to move to the top of the worksheet. Display the **document properties** and under **Related People**, be sure that your name displays as the author. If necessary, right-click the author name, click **Edit Property**, and then type your name. In the **Subject** box, type your course name and section #, and in the **Tags** box, type **parks, pools, call activity** With the sheets still grouped, display the **Print Preview**, and then examine the six visible pages of your workbook. If necessary, make any necessary corrections or adjustments and ungroup the worksheets. Submit the workbook electronically as directed by your instructor.

END | You have completed Project 7C

CHAPTER REVIEW

Skills Review   Project 7D Office Supplies

Apply 7B skills from these Objectives:

5 Create a Data Model Using PowerPivot

6 Create a PivotTable Using PowerPivot

7 Create a Dashboard Using Power View

In the following Skills Review, you will assist City Council Office Manager Jake Curley create a Data Model, PivotTable, and PivotChart using PowerPivot. You will also create a Power View worksheet. Your results will look similar to those in Figure 7.62.

PROJECT FILES

For Project 7D, you will need the following files:

New blank workbook
e07D_Office_Supplies

You will save your workbook as:

Lastname_Firstname_7D_Council_Office

PROJECT RESULTS

Build from Scratch

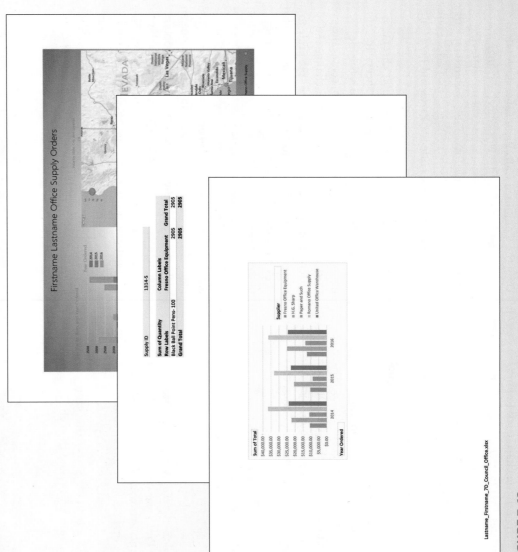

Lastname_Firstname_7D_Council_Office.xlsx

FIGURE 7.62

(Project 7D Office Supplies continues on the next page)

CHAPTER REVIEW

Skills Review Project 7D Office Supplies (continued)

1 Start Excel and display a new blank workbook. If the **POWERPIVOT** tab is not visible, follow the directions in Activity 7.14 to enable it. Click the **POWERPIVOT tab**, and then, in the **Data Model group**, click **Manage.**

a. Maximize the **PowerPivot** window. In the **Get External Data group**, click **From Database**, and then click **From Access.** In the **Table Import Wizard**, click **Browse.** Navigate to your student files and open the file **e07D_Office_Supplies.** Click **Next.** Verify *Select from a list of tables and views to choose the data to import* is selected and then click **Next.** Select both tables and then click **Finish.** Click **Close.**

b. In the **PowerPivot** window, with the **Suppliers** table active, click the **Design tab.** In the **Relationships group**, click **Manage Relationships.** Verify the relationship was created between the two imported tables and then **Close the Manage Relationships** dialog box.

c. Click the **Home tab**, and then click **PivotTable.** In the **Insert Pivot** dialog box, verify **New Worksheet** is selected and then click **OK. Save** your file in your **Excel Chapter 7** folder as **Lastname_Firstname_7D_Council_Office**

2 In the **PivotTable Fields** pane, with the **ALL tab** active, expand the **Suppliers** table, and then drag the **Supplier** field to the **COLUMNS area.** Expand the **Supply Order Summary** table and drag the **Item** and **Year Ordered** fields to the **ROWS area.** Drag the **Quantity** field to the **VALUES area.**

a. Click cell **B5.** In the lower right corner of the cell, click the **Quick Explore** icon. Expand **Supply Order Summary.** Click **Drill to Supply ID.** With cell **B5** selected, click **Quick Explore** and then click **Drill to Item.**

3 Use the buttons on the **Windows taskbar** to return to the **PowerPivot** window. Click the **Supply Order Summary sheet tab.** Click the **Add Column** header and in the **Formula Bar**, type **=[** Double-click **[Quantity]**, type ***[** Double-click **[Cost]**, and then press [Enter].

a. Right-click the **CalculatedColumn1** and click **Rename Column.** Type **Total** and then press [Enter].

b. Click the **PivotTable arrow** and then click **PivotChart.** Verify that **New Worksheet** is selected in the **Insert Pivot** dialog box and then click **OK.**

c. In the **PivotChart Fields** pane, expand the **Suppliers** table, and then drag the **Supplier** field to the **LEGEND (SERIES) area.** Expand the **Supply Order Summary** table and drag the **Total** field to the **VALUES area.** Drag the **Year Ordered** field to the **AXIS (CATEGORY) area.**

4 Click the **Sheet1 sheet tab.** On the **INSERT tab**, in the **Reports group**, click **Power View.** At the top of the **Power View** worksheet, click *Click here to add a title*, and then type **Firstname Lastname Office Supply Orders**

a. In the **Power View Fields** pane, expand the **Supply Order Summary** table. Drag the **Item, Quantity,** and **Year Ordered** fields to the **FIELDS area.**

b. On the **DESIGN tab**, in the **Switch Visualization group**, click the **Column Chart arrow** and then click **Stacked Column.**

5 Click a blank area of the **Power View** canvas to deselect the column chart. In the **Power View Fields** pane, expand the **Suppliers** table and drag the **Supplier** field to the **FIELDS area.** From the **Supply Order Summary** table drag the **Total** field to the **FIELDS area.**

a. In the **Switch Visualization group**, click **Other Chart** and then click **Pie.** Point to the lower right edge of the pie chart to display the selection pointer, and then drag the pie chart below the column chart. Point to the lower right corner of the pie chart area to display the diagonal resize pointer and drag to resize the pie chart until it is the same width as the column chart and touches the bottom edge of the canvas.

b. Click a blank area of the **Power View** canvas to deselect the pie chart. In the **Power View Fields** pane, from the **Suppliers** table drag the **City, State,** and **Supplier** fields to the **FIELDS area.** From the **Supply Order Summary** table drag the **Total** field to the **FIELDS area.**

c. In the **Switch Visualization group**, click **Map.** If necessary, click **Enable Content.** Drag the lower right corner of the map to resize it to fill the right side of the canvas.

(Project 7D Office Supplies continues on the next page)

CHAPTER REVIEW

Project 7D Office Supplies (continued)

6 Click the canvas to deselect the map. **Close** the **Filters** pane. On the **POWER VIEW tab**, in the **Themes group**, click **Text Size**, and then click **75%**.

a. Click **Background**, and then click the first color in the third row—**Light 1 Center Gradient**.

b. Click the map to select it. Click the **LAYOUT tab**, in the **Labels group**, click **Legend**, and then click **Show Legend at Bottom**. **Close** the **Power View Fields** pane and close the **Filters** pane.

7 Rename **Sheet3 PivotChart** Rename **Sheet2 PivotTable** Delete **Sheet1**. Group the **PivotChart** and **PivotTable** worksheets and insert a footer with the file name in the **left section**. Return to **Normal** view, center horizontally, change the **Orientation** to **Landscape**, and scale the **Width and Height to 1 page.** Press Ctrl + Home to return to cell **A1**.

8 Display the **document properties** and under **Related People**, be sure that your name displays as the author. If necessary, right-click the author name, click **Edit Property**, and then type your name. In the **Subject** box, type your course name and section #, and in the **Tags** box, type **office supplies**, **BI Save** your workbook. Print or submit the workbook electronically as directed by your instructor.

END | You have completed Project 7D

CONTENT-BASED ASSESSMENTS

Mastering Excel   Project 7E Concessions

MyITLab® grader

Apply 7A skills from these Objectives:

1 Create a PivotTable Report

2 Use Slicers and Search Filters

3 Modify a PivotTable Report

4 Create a PivotChart Report

In the following Mastering Excel project, you will help Lindsay Johnson, the Director of Parks and Recreation, create and modify a PivotTable report and PivotChart report to analyze revenue from park concessions such as food, boat rentals, and golf fees. Your completed workbooks will look similar to Figure 7.63.

PROJECT FILES

For Project 7E, you will need the following file:

e07E_Concessions_Revenue

You will save your workbook as:

Lastname_Firstname_7E_Concessions_Revenue

PROJECT RESULTS

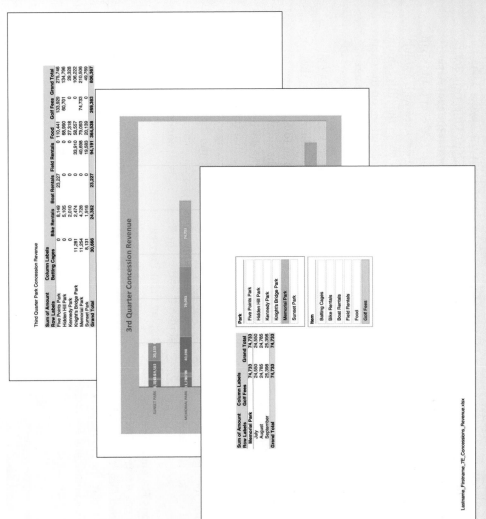

Lastname_Firstname_7E_Concessions_Revenue.xlsx

FIGURE 7.63

(Project 7E Concessions continues on the next page)

CONTENT-BASED ASSESSMENTS

Mastering Excel | Project 7E Concessions (continued)

1 Start Excel. From your student files, open **e07E_Concessions_Revenue** and **Save** the file in your Excel Chapter 7 folder as **Lastname_Firstname_7E_Concessions_Revenue**

2 Click cell **A2**. Insert the Recommended PivotTable *Sum of Amount by Park*. Add the **Month** field to the **ROWS** area. Place the **Item** field in the **COLUMNS area. Close** the **PivotTable Fields** pane.

3 Insert a slicer for the **Park** field and a slicer for the **Item** field. Resize and move the slicers so that they are to the right of the PivotTable, with the Park slicer above the Item slicer. Apply **Slicer Style Light 4** and **Slicer Style Light 6** to the slicers, respectively.

4 Filter first by **Memorial Park**, and then by **Golf Fees.** Right-click any value in the PivotTable report, display the **Value Field Settings** dialog box, and then format the **Number** category to display zero decimal places and the **1000 Separator.** Move the two slicers to the immediate right of the filtered PivotTable, and then make a copy of this worksheet. Name the copied worksheet **Memorial-3Q Golf Fees**

5 Rename **Sheet1 Concessions Revenue** Clear the filters and remove the slicers. In cell A1, type **Third Quarter Park Concession Revenue** Display the **Field List,** and then *remove* the **Month** field from the **ROWS area** to display only the grand totals for each park and for each item. **Close** the **PivotTable Fields** pane.

6 Insert a **PivotChart** using the **Stacked Bar** chart type. Move the chart to a new worksheet named **3rd Quarter Concessions Chart** Apply the **Layout 3** chart layout and **Chart Style 4**. As the **Chart Title,** type **3rd Quarter Concession Revenue** Format the **Plot Area** with the **Gradient fill Light Gradient-Accent 6,** the sixth column, first color. Format the **Chart Area** with a solid fill using **Blue, Accent 1, Lighter 60%** in the fifth column, the third color. Hide all of the field buttons on the chart. Insert a custom footer with the file name in the **left section.**

7 Hide the **Park Concessions** worksheet. Select all worksheets. Insert a footer with the file name in the **left section.** Change the **Orientation** to **Landscape,** set the **Width** to **1 page,** and center the sheets horizontally. Return to **Normal** view. Display the **document properties** and under **Related People,** be sure that your name displays as the author. If necessary, right-click the author name, click **Edit Property,** and then type your name. In the **Subject** box, type your course name and section #, and in the **Tags** box, type **concession revenue** Display **Print Preview,** make corrections or adjustments and ungroup the worksheets. **Save** and **Close** the workbook. Print or submit electronically as directed.

> **END** | You have completed Project 7E

CONTENT-BASED ASSESSMENTS

MyITLab® grader

Apply 7B skills from these Objectives:

5 Create a Data Model Using PowerPivot
6 Create a PivotTable Using PowerPivot
7 Create a Dashboard Using Power View

Mastering Excel   **Project 7F Vehicle Maintenance**

In the following Skills Review, you will assist Caryn Black, the Vehicle Fleet Manager, create a Data Model, PivotTable, and PivotChart using PowerPivot. You will also create a Power View worksheet. Your results will look similar to those in Figure 7.64.

PROJECT FILES

For Project 7F, you will need the following files:

New blank workbook
e07F_Vehicle_Parts

You will save your workbook as:

Lastname_Firstname_7F_Fleet_Maintenance

PROJECT RESULTS

Build from Scratch

Lastname_Firstname_7F_Fleet_Maintenance.xlsx

FIGURE 7.64

(Project 7F Vehicle Maintenance continues on the next page)

CONTENT-BASED ASSESSMENTS

Mastering Excel | Project 7F Vehicle Maintenance (continued)

1 Start Excel and display a new blank workbook. If the **POWERPIVOT tab** is not visible, follow the directions in Activity 7.14 to enable it. Use **POWERPIVOT tab**, to import the Access database **e07F_Vehicle_Parts** into the **Data Model**. Verify the relationship was created between the two imported tables. Insert a **PivotTable** in a new worksheet. **Save** your file in your Excel Chapter 7 folder as **Lastname_Firstname_7F_Fleet_Maintenance**

2 Place the **Supplier** field from the **Suppliers** table in the **COLUMNS area**. From the **Supply Order Summary** table, place the **Item** and **Year Ordered** fields in the **ROWS area**, and the **Quantity** field in the **VALUES area**. In cell **B5**, use **Quick Explore** to drill to **Supply ID**, and then drill to **Item**.

3 Return to the **PowerPivot** window. On the **Supply Order Summary** worksheet, add a calculated column that multiplies **[Quantity] * [Cost]**. Rename the column **Total**

4 Insert a **PivotChart** in a new worksheet. Place the **Supplier** field from the **Suppliers** table in the **LEGEND (SERIES) area**. From the **Supply Order Summary** table, place the **Total** field to the **VALUES area**, and place the **Year Ordered** field to the **AXIS (CATEGORY) area**.

5 Click the **Sheet1 sheet tab**. Insert a **Power View** report. Add the title **Firstname Lastname Vehicle Maintenance Orders** From the **Supply Order Summary** table, place the **Item**, **Quantity**, and **Year Ordered** fields in the **FIELDS area**. Change the visualization to a **Stacked Column** chart. Drag to widen the chart until all nine columns are visible.

6 Create a pie chart by placing the **Suppliers** table **Supplier** field, and the **Supply Order Summary** table **Total** field, in the **FIELDS area**. Move and resize the pie chart to fit below the column chart.

7 Insert a Map visualization using the **City**, **State**, and **Supplier** fields from **Suppliers** and the **Total** field from the **Supply Order Summary**. Resize the map to fill the right side of the canvas. Set the legend to display at the bottom.

8 Change the **Power View** worksheet **Text Size** to **75%**. Set the background, to the first color in the third row—**Light 1 Center Gradient**. Close the **Power View Fields** pane and Close the **Filters** pane.

9 Rename **Sheet3 PivotChart** Rename **Sheet2 PivotTable** Delete **Sheet1**. Group the **PivotChart** and **PivotTable** worksheets and insert a footer with the file name in the **left section**. Return to **Normal** view, center horizontally, change the **Orientation** to **Landscape**, and scale the **Width** and **Height** to **1 page**. Press [Ctrl] + [Home] to return to cell **A1**. Display the document properties and under **Related People**, be sure that your name displays as the author. If necessary, right-click the author name, click **Edit Property**, and then type your name. In the **Subject** box, type your course name and section #, and in the **Tags** box, type **vehicle maintenance, BI** **Save** your workbook. Print or submit the workbook electronically as directed by your instructor.

END | You have completed Project 7F

CONTENT-BASED ASSESSMENTS

Mastering Excel | Project 7G Aquatics Revenue

MyITLab® grader

Apply 7A and 7B skills from these Objectives:

1 Create a PivotTable Report
2 Use Slicers and Search Filters
3 Modify a PivotTable Report
4 Create a PivotChart Report
5 Create a Data Model Using PowerPivot
6 Create a PivotTable Using PowerPivot
7 Create a Dashboard Using Power View

In the following Mastering Excel project, you will assist Lindsay Johnson, the Director of Pools and Recreation, in creating and modifying a PivotTable report and a PivotChart report to analyze revenue from the Aquatics Program. Your completed workbooks will look similar to Figure 7.65.

PROJECT FILES

For Project 7G, you will need the following files:

e07G_Aquatics_Revenue
e07G_Pool_Supplies

You will save your workbooks as:

Lastname_Firstname_7G_Aquatics_Revenue
Lastname_Firstname_7G_Pool_Orders

PROJECT RESULTS

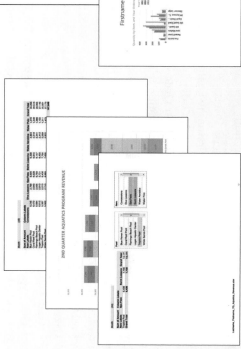

FIGURE 7.65

(Project 7G Aquatics Revenue continues on the next page)

CONTENT-BASED ASSESSMENTS

Mastering Excel | Project 7G Aquatics Revenue (continued)

1 From your student files, open the file e07G_Aquatics_Revenue. Save the file as **Lastname_Firstname_7G_Aquatics_Revenue** in your Excel Chapter 7 folder.

2 Click cell **A2**, and then insert a **PivotTable**. Use the **Month** field as the **Report Filter**. Use the **Pool** field as the row labels and the **Item** field as the column labels. Place the **Amount** field in the **VALUES area. Close the PivotTable Fields** pane.

3 Right-click any value in the PivotTable report, display the **Value Field Settings** dialog box, and then format the **Number** category to display zero decimal places and the **1000 Separator.**

4 Insert a slicer for the **Pool** field and for the **Item** field. Apply **Slicer Style Light 4** and **Slicer Style Light 5** to the slicers, respectively.

5 By using the two slicers, filter the data to show, for the **Tropics Pool**, the total revenue for **Spa Fees and Swim Lessons.** Resize and move the two slicers to the right of the filtered PivotTable, and then make a copy of this worksheet. Name the copied worksheet **Tropics Pool - 2Q**

6 Rename **Sheet1 2Q Revenue** In each slicer, click the **Clear Filter** button, and then remove the slicers from the worksheet. Insert a **PivotChart** using the **Stacked Column** chart type. Move the chart to a new worksheet named **2Q Revenue Chart** Apply the **Layout 3** chart layout and **Chart Style 9.** As the **Chart Title,** type **2nd Quarter Aquatics Program Revenue** Add centered data labels, and then hide all of the field buttons on the chart. Insert a custom footer with the file name in the **left section.**

7 Hide the worksheet that contains your source data. Display the **2Q Revenue** worksheet, select all the worksheets, and then insert a footer with the file name in the **left section.** Change the **Orientation to Landscape,** set the **Width to 1 page,** and center the sheets horizontally. Display the **document properties** and under **Related People,** be sure that your name displays as the author. If necessary, right-click the author name, click **Edit Property,** and then type your name. In the **Subject** box, type your course name and section #, and in the **Tags** box, type **aquatics program, revenue** Display **Print Preview,** make any corrections or adjustments, ungroup the worksheets, and then **Save** the workbook. Print or submit electronically as directed by your instructor. **Close** this workbook, but leave Excel open.

8 Open a new blank workbook. Use PowerPivot to import the Access database **e07G_Pool_Supplies** into the **Data Model.** Verify the relationship was created between the two imported tables. On the **Supply Order Summary** worksheet, add a calculated column that multiplies **[Quantity] * [Cost].** Rename the column **Total**

9 Insert a **PivotTable** in a new worksheet. Rename the new sheet **PivotTable** Place the **Supplier** field from the new sheet **Suppliers** table in the **COLUMNS area.** From the **Supply Order Summary** table, place the **Item** field in the **ROWS area,** and the **Quantity** field in the **VALUES area.** In cell **B5,** use **Quick Explore** to drill to **Supply ID,** and then drill to **Item.** Insert a footer with the file name in the **left** section.

10 Insert a **Power View** report. Add the title **Firstname Lastname Pool Supplies Orders** From the **Supply Order Summary** table, place the **Item, Quantity, and Year Ordered** fields in the **FIELDS area.** Change the visualization to a **Clustered Column** chart.

11 Insert a Map visualization using the **City, State,** and **Supplier** fields from **Suppliers** and the **Total** field from the **Supply Order Summary.** Resize the map to fill the right side of the canvas. Set the legend to display at the bottom. Close the **Power View Fields** and **Filters** panes.

12 **Save** your file in your Excel Chapter 7 folder as **Lastname_Firstname_7G_Pool_Orders** Delete **Sheet1.** Display the **document properties** and under **Related People,** be sure that your name displays as the author. If necessary, right-click the author name, click **Edit Property,** and then type your name. In the **Subject** box, type your course name and section #, and in the **Tags** box, type **pool supplies, BI Save** your workbook. Print or submit both workbooks electronically as directed by your instructor.

END | You have completed Project 7G

CONTENT-BASED ASSESSMENTS

GO! Fix It	Project 7H Park Revenue	Online
GO! Make It	Project 7I City Services Revenue	Online
GO! Solve It	Project 7J Fixed Assets	Online
GO! Solve It	Project 7K Park Expenses	

Apply a combination of the 7A and 7B skills.

PROJECT FILES

For Project 7K, you will need the following file:

e07K_Park_Expenses

You will save your workbook as:

Lastname_Firstname_7K_Park_Expenses

Open the file e07K_Park_Expenses and save it as **Lastname_Firstname_7K_Park_Expenses** From the source data, create a PivotTable. Use the Month and Park fields as row labels. Use the Expense Item field as a column label. Place the Amount field in the VALUES area. Format the numbers to display zero decimal places and the 1000 separator. Format the PivotTable with an attractive style. Create a PivotChart on a separate sheet using the column chart style, and then use the report filters on the chart to show only the data for June, only the data for Knight's Bridge, Five Points, and Sunset Parks, and only the expenses for Equipment, Grounds & Maintenance, and Utilities. Format the chart attractively. Hide the Park Expenses worksheet. On all sheets, insert the file name in the footer in the left section. Set the orientation to landscape and center horizontally. Add appropriate information to the document properties including the tag **park grounds expenses** and submit as directed by your instructor.

(Project 7K Park Expenses continues on the next page)

CONTENT-BASED ASSESSMENTS

GO! Solve It   Project 7K Park Expenses (continued)

Performance Level

Performance Criteria	Exemplary	Proficient	Developing
Create a PivotTable Report	The PivotTable Report displays Month and Park as row labels, Expense Item in COLUMNS area, and amount field in the VALUES area.	The PivotTable Report displays some of the items from the field list, but not all according to the directions.	The PivotTable was not created.
Format a PivotTable Report	The PivotTable is formatted with the numbers displaying zero decimal places, the 1000 separator, and an attractive style.	The PivotTable is formatted with some but not all of the formatting, numbers displaying zero decimal places, the 1000 separator, and some attractive formatting.	The PivotTable was not formatted.
Create and Format a PivotChart	A PivotChart displays on a separate sheet using the column chart style. The chart is filtered showing the data for June, only for Knight's Bridge, Five Points, and Sunset Parks, and only the expenses for Equipment, Grounds & Maintenance, and Utilities. The chart is formatted attractively.	A PivotChart displays on a separate sheet using the column chart style. The chart is filtered showing some but not all of the data for June, only for Knight's Bridge, Five Points, and Sunset Parks, and only the expenses for Equipment, Grounds & Maintenance, and Utilities. Some of the chart is formatted attractively.	The PivotChart was not created.

END | You have completed Project 7K

OUTCOMES-BASED ASSESSMENTS

RUBRIC

The following outcomes-based assessments are open-ended assessments. That is, there is no specific correct result; your result will depend on your approach to the information provided. Make Professional Quality your goal. Use the following scoring rubric to guide you in how to approach the problem and then to evaluate how well your approach solves the problem.

The *criteria*—Software Mastery, Content, Format and Layout, and Process—represent the knowledge and skills you have gained that you can apply to solving the problem. The *levels of performance*—Professional Quality, Approaching Professional Quality, or Needs Quality Improvements—help you and your instructor evaluate your result.

	Your completed project is of Professional Quality if you:	Your completed project is Approaching Professional Quality if you:	Your completed project Needs Quality Improvements if you:
1–Software Mastery	Choose and apply the most appropriate skills, tools, and features and identify efficient methods to solve the problem.	Choose and apply some appropriate skills, tools, and features, but not in the most efficient manner.	Choose inappropriate skills, tools, or features, or are inefficient in solving the problem.
2–Content	Construct a solution that is clear and well organized, contains content that is accurate, appropriate to the audience and purpose, and is complete. Provide a solution that contains no errors in spelling, grammar, or style.	Construct a solution in which some components are unclear, poorly organized, inconsistent, or incomplete. Misjudge the needs of the audience. Have some errors in spelling, grammar, or style, but the errors do not detract from comprehension.	Construct a solution that is unclear, incomplete, or poorly organized; contains some inaccurate or inappropriate content; and contains many errors in spelling, grammar, or style. Do not solve the problem.
3–Format & Layout	Format and arrange all elements to communicate information and ideas, clarify function, illustrate relationships, and indicate relative importance.	Apply appropriate format and layout features to some elements, but not others. Overuse features, causing minor distraction.	Apply format and layout that does not communicate information or ideas clearly. Do not use format and layout features to clarify function, illustrate relationships, or indicate relative importance. Use available features excessively, causing distraction.
4–Process	Use an organized approach that integrates planning, development, self-assessment, revision, and reflection.	Demonstrate an organized approach in some areas, but not others; or, use an insufficient process of organization throughout.	Do not use an organized approach to solve the problem.

OUTCOMES-BASED ASSESSMENTS

Apply a combination of the 7A and 7B skills.

GO! Think   Project 7L Golf Course Revenue

PROJECT FILES

For Project 7L, you will need the following file:

e07L_Golf_Courses

You will save your workbook as:

Lastname_Firstname_7L_Golf_Courses

Open the file e07L_Golf_Courses, and then save it in your Excel Chapter 7 folder as **Lastname_Firstname_7L_Golf_Courses** From the source data, create a PivotTable and filter the report on Month. Use Course as row label and Item as column label. Sum the amounts. Create an attractive PivotChart report for the 3rd Quarter Revenue. Exclude Logo Shirts and Golf Balls from the PivotChart. Hide the source data worksheet. Insert the file name in the left section of the footer on each page, center horizontally, set the orientation to landscape, add appropriate information to the document properties, including the tags **golf courses revenue** and submit as directed by your instructor.

END | You have completed Project 7L

GO! Think   Project 7M Pool Expenses   Online

You and GO!   Project 7N Inventory   Online

Build from Scratch

EXCEL 2013

8

Using the Data Analysis, Solver, and Scenario Features, and Building Complex Formulas

GO! to Work
Video E8

PROJECT
8A

OUTCOMES
Analyze sales data to evaluate business solutions and compare data with a line chart.

OBJECTIVES
1. Calculate a Moving Average
2. Project Income and Expenses
3. Determine a Break-Even Point

PROJECT
8B

OUTCOMES
Use Solver and Scenario Tools, and create complex formulas.

OBJECTIVES
4. Use Solver
5. Create Scenarios
6. Use Logical Functions
7. Create Complex Formulas

Lasse Kristensen/Fotolia

In This Chapter

Organizations forecast future results based on current trends. You will use Excel tools to analyze data, project values, determine the moving average of sales, project sales based on an expected growth rate, and determine a break-even point.

You will use the Solver and Scenario tools to search for solutions to problems. Solver can analyze financial planning problems that involve a quantity that changes over time. By using a scenario, you can look at a set of values and project forward to focus on possible results. Finally, you will create complex formulas to determine which employees meet specific performance criteria.

The projects in this chapter relate to **Brina's Bistro,** which is a chain of 25 casual, full-service restaurants based in Ft. Lauderdale, Florida. The Brina's Bistro owners plan an aggressive expansion program. To expand by 15 additional restaurants in Tennessee, Florida, Georgia, North Carolina, and South Carolina by 2021, the company must attract new investors, develop new menus, and recruit new employees, all while adhering to the company's quality guidelines and maintaining its reputation for excellent service. To succeed, the company plans to build on its past success and maintain its quality elements.

MyITLab®
Project 8A Training

PROJECT 8A

Sales Analysis

PROJECT ACTIVITIES

In Activities 8.01 through 8.06, you will use Excel's data analysis tools to determine the moving average of sales for the first six weeks at the new Brina's Bistro restaurant in Charlotte, North Carolina. Then you will project sales based on an expected growth rate and determine the break-even point for the restaurant. Your completed worksheets will look similar to Figure 8.1.

PROJECT FILES

For Project 8A, you will need the following file:

e08A_Charlotte_Sales

You will save your workbook as:

Lastname_Firstname_8A_Charlotte_Sales

PROJECT RESULTS

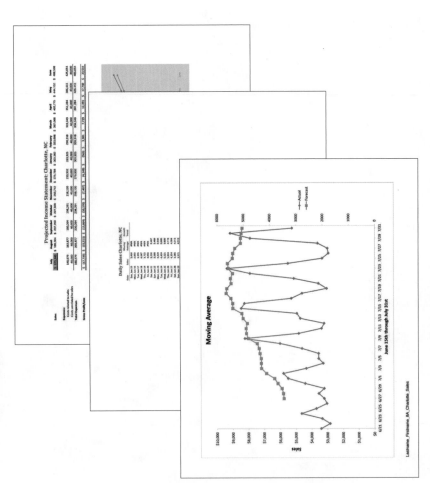

Lastname_Firstname_8A_Charlotte_Sales

FIGURE 8.1 Project 8A Sales Analysis

NOTE   If You Are Using a Touchscreen

- Tap an item to click it.
- Press and hold for a few seconds to right-click; release when the information or commands display.
- Touch the screen with two or more fingers and then pinch together to zoom in or stretch your fingers apart to zoom out.
- Slide your finger on the screen to scroll—slide left to scroll right and slide right to scroll left.
- Slide to rearrange—similar to dragging with a mouse.
- Swipe from edge: from right to display charms; from left to expose open apps, snap apps, or close apps; from top or bottom to show commands or close an app.
- Swipe to select—slide an item a short distance with a quick movement—to select an item and bring up commands, if any.

Objective 1   Calculate a Moving Average

Video E8-1

Start-up businesses usually operate at a loss while the business grows, with an expectation that at some future point, the business will become profitable. Owners and investors want to know if the business is on track to become profitable and when the point of profitability is likely to occur.

Excel offers Data Analysis tools, which range from basic to very sophisticated, to help you project future results based on past performance. One of the basic tools is a moving average. A *moving average* is a sequence of averages computed from parts of a data series. In a chart, a moving average smoothes the fluctuations in data, showing a pattern or trend more clearly. When you use a moving average, you choose how many preceding intervals to include in the average. A series of averages is calculated by moving—or changing—the range of cells used to calculate each average.

Activity 8.01   Creating a Custom Number Format

Kelsey Tanner, the Chief Financial Officer of Brina's Bistro, wants to see how sales have grown in the first six weeks at the new restaurant in Charlotte, North Carolina. Because there is a wide variation in sales at restaurants between weekday and weekend sales, Ms. Tanner first needs to add the day of the week to the Charlotte sales report. To accomplish this, you will customize the format applied to the date. You can customize numbers or dates when the available options do not match your needs.

1 Start Excel. From your student files, open the file **e08A_Charlotte_Sales**. Display the **Save As** dialog box, navigate to the location where you will store your workbooks for this chapter, and then create a new folder named **Excel Chapter 8** In your new folder, **Save** the workbook as **Lastname_Firstname_8A_Charlotte_Sales**

2 Select the range **A3:AV4**. Right-click anywhere over the selection and click **Copy**. Click cell **A5**. Right-click and under **Paste Options**, click **Transpose (T)** Compare your screen with Figure 8.2.

If the data in a worksheet is arranged in rows but you want to work with columns instead, you can use this method to *transpose*, or switch, the rows and columns.

FIGURE 8.2

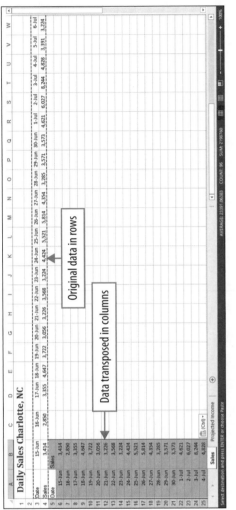

Original data in rows

Data transposed in columns

More Knowledge | **The Transpose Function**

You can use the TRANSPOSE function to swap rows and columns. TRANSPOSE is an array function. The advantage to using the TRANSPOSE function is that a link is maintained between the original and transposed data.

3 Delete **rows 2:4**. In cell **C2**, type **Moving Average** In cell **D2**, type **Growth Trend** Select the range **A2:D2** and apply the **Heading 3** cell style. In the **Alignment group**, click **Wrap Text**.

4 Click cell **A3**. On the **HOME tab**, in the **Number group**, click the **Dialog Box Launcher** ⟱. In the **Format Cells** dialog box, be sure the **Number tab** is selected. Under **Category**, click **Custom**. Examine the table in Figure 8.3 to familiarize yourself with the codes used to create a custom date format.

Custom codes display under Type, and the code for the selected date in cell A3 displays in the Type box. You can use this format as a starting point and then modify it or you can type a new code in the Type box.

FIGURE 8.3

DATE CODES	
TO DISPLAY	**USE THIS CODE**
Months as 1–12	m
Months as 01–12	mm
Months as Jan–Dec	mmm
Months as January–December	mmmm
Months as the first letter of the month	mmmmm
Days as 1–31	d
Days as 01–31	dd
Days as Sun–Sat	ddd
Days as Sunday–Saturday	dddd
Years as 00–99	yy
Years as 1900–9999	yyyy

5 Select the code in the **Type** box and type **ddd, mmm dd** to replace it. Compare your screen with Figure 8.4.

As you type, you can see the date displayed in the new format in the Sample box. This code creates a date that displays as *Sun, Jun 15*. The comma displays as a comma.

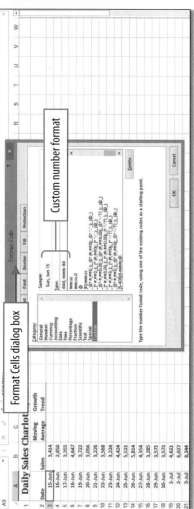

FIGURE 8.4

Format Cells dialog box

Custom number format

---

6 Click **OK**, if necessary, AutoFit column A, and notice the new date format in cell **A3**. Drag the fill handle to copy the new format down through cell **A49**. Click cell **A50** and type **Total** Click cell **B50** and in the **Editing group**, click **AutoSum**. Verify that the range to be summed is **B3:B49** and then press **Enter**. Apply the **Currency [0]** cell style to cell **B50**. Your total equals *$232,844*. Apply the **Total** cell style to the range **A50:B50**. Press **Ctrl** + **Home**, AutoFit **column A**, click **Save** ⊞, and then compare your screen with Figure 8.5.

FIGURE 8.5

Custom date format applied

Activity 8.02 | Calculating a Moving Average

Recall that a moving average calculates an average for a group of numbers over a specified interval. The number range that is averaged is constantly changing, dropping off the first number in the range and adding on the most recent number. In this manner, you can see a trend for widely fluctuating numbers. The sales activity for the new Charlotte restaurant has been strong on the weekends and slower during the week. You need to determine if, overall, the sales activity is trending upward or downward. The moving average tool is one of several Data Analysis tools.

1 Click the **FILE tab** and then click **Options**. In the **Excel Options** dialog box, on the left, click **Add-Ins**. At the bottom of the dialog box, verify that the **Manage** box displays *Excel Add-ins*, and then click **Go**. In the **Add-Ins** dialog box, if necessary, select the **Analysis ToolPak** check box. Compare your screen with Figure 8.6.

Recall that *Add-ins* are optional commands and features that are not immediately available; you must first install and/or activate an add-in to use it.

FIGURE 8.6

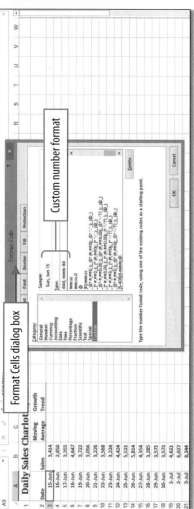

2 Click **OK**, and then click cell **A2** to make it the active cell. On the **DATA tab**, in the **Analysis group**, click **Data Analysis**. Scroll the list as necessary, and then click **Moving Average**. Click **OK**.

The Moving Average dialog box displays. Here you define the input range, the *interval*—the number of cells to include in the average—and the output range.

3 With the insertion point blinking in the **Input Range** box, type **b2:b49** and then click the **Labels in First Row** check box.

The input range consists of the sales figures for the first six weeks, from Jun 15 through Jul 31. The first cell in the range, B2, contains the label *Sales*.

NOTE Moving Average Using Data in Rows

When using data that is listed in rows, rather than columns, do not check the Labels in First Row box.

4 Click in the **Interval** box, and then type **7**

The moving average will be a weekly (7-day) average of sales. The first average will be from Sun, Jun 15 through Sat, Jun 21. The next average will be from Mon, Jun 16 through Sun, Jun 22. This pattern—dropping the oldest date and adding in the next date—will continue for the entire range.

5 Click in the **Output Range** box, type **c3** and then click the **Chart Output** check box. Compare your **Moving Average** dialog box with Figure 8.7.

FIGURE 8.7

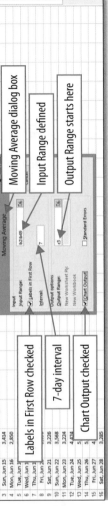

- Labels in First Row checked
- 7-day interval
- Chart Output checked
- Moving Average dialog box
- Input Range defined
- Output Range starts here

6 Click **OK**. Save your workbook, and then compare your screen with Figure 8.8.

The moving averages display in column C and a chart is added to the worksheet. The first six cells in column C display the error code *#N/A* because there were not seven numbers available to use in the average. Green triangles display because the formulas in these cells refer to a range that has additional numbers adjacent. The first average—for Sun, Jun 15 through Sat, Jun 21—is 3,467.

FIGURE 8.8

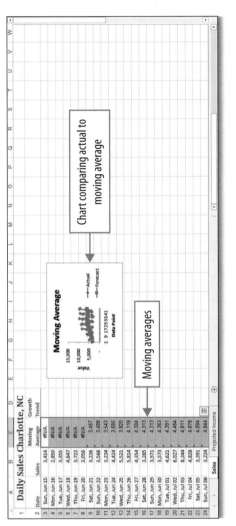

- Chart comparing actual to moving average
- Moving averages

Activity 8.03 | Modifying the Moving Average Chart

To gain a clearer image of a trend, you can modify the moving average chart. In the moving average chart, the moving average is labeled Forecast. A *forecast* is a prediction of the future, often based on past performances.

1 Click the outer edge of the chart to select it, and then on the **DESIGN tab**, in the **Location group**, click **Move Chart.**

2 Click **New sheet**, type **Sales Trend Chart** and then click **OK.**

By displaying this chart on a separate chart sheet, you can more easily see the actual data points—in dark blue—versus the moving average—in red—which is labeled *Forecast*. The horizontal category axis—the X-axis—is titled *Data Point*. This represents the dates for each sales figure. You can see by the red line that, overall, the sales activity for the first six weeks is trending slightly upward.

3 At the bottom of the chart, point to any of the data points to display the ScreenTip *Horizontal (Category) Axis*, and then click to select the axis. On the **DESIGN tab**, in the **Data group**, click **Select Data.**

In the Select Data Source dialog box, you can change the category axis labels to display the range of dates that correspond to the sales figures. You can also use this method to add or edit the data series used in a chart.

ANOTHER WAY   Right-click the axis, and then click Select Data.

4 In the **Select Data Source** dialog box, under **Horizontal (Category) Axis Labels,** click **Edit.** Click the **Sales sheet tab** to display the *Sales* worksheet, and then select the range **A9:A49.** Compare your screen with Figure 8.9.

The selected range displays in the dialog box. You can select the range of cells to use as labels for the category axis. Start with cell A9 because that is the first row for which there is a moving average calculation.

FIGURE 8.9

Label range defined

Axis Labels dialog box

5 In the **Axis Labels** dialog box, click **OK.** In the **Select Data Source** dialog box, click **OK.**

Dates display along the category axis at the bottom of the chart.

6 Right-click the **Horizontal (Category) Axis,** and then click **Format Axis.** In the **Format Axis** pane, with **Axis Options** ▶ selected, scroll down and click **Number,** scroll down and click the **Category arrow,** and then click **Date.** Click the **Type arrow,** click the **3/14 format,** and then **Close** ✖ the **Format Axis pane.**

This action shortens the date format displayed on the axis.

7 Click the **Horizontal (Category) Axis Title**—*Data Point*—to select it. On the **Formula Bar,** type **June 15th through July 31st** and then press Enter. Click the **Horizontal Axis Title,** triple-click to select the text, and then on the mini toolbar, change the font size to **12.** Click the **Vertical (Value) Axis Title**—*Value*—to select it. On the **Formula Bar** type **Sales** and then press Enter. Point to the **Vertical Axis Title,** double-click, and then on the mini toolbar, change the font size to **12.**

The Horizontal Axis and Vertical Axis titles are changed and formatted.

8 Right-click any value on the **Vertical (Value) Axis,** and then click **Format Axis.** In the **Format Axis** pane, click **Number,** scroll down and click the **Category arrow,** and then click **Currency.** If necessary, set **Decimal places** to **0,** and then **Close** ✖ the **Format Axis** pane.

This action changes the values to Currency with 0 decimal places.

9 On the **FORMAT tab**, in the **Current Selection group**, click the **Chart Elements arrow**, and then click **Series "Forecast"**. In the same group, click **Format Selection**. In the **Format Data Series** pane, if necessary, click the **Series Options icon** ◢. Under **Plot Series on**, click **Secondary Axis**. **Close** the **Format Data Series pane**. **Save** 🔲 your workbook, and then compare your chart with Figure 8.10.

Plotting the Forecast series on the secondary axis makes the trend easier to visualize because the scale is adjusted to reflect the smaller differences in the Forecast series values. A *dual-axis chart* is useful when comparing data series that use different scales or different types of measurements.

FIGURE 8.10

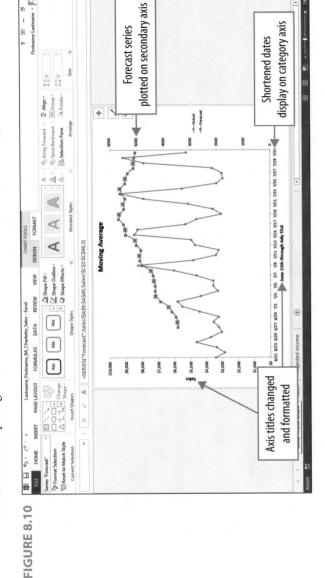

Forecast series plotted on secondary axis

Shortened dates display on category axis

Axis titles changed and formatted

More Knowledge

Using a Moving Average to Forecast Trends

It is common to see moving averages used to calculate stock or mutual fund performance, where fluctuations in value may be frequent, but the overall trend is what is important. Moving averages can also be used as a tool to help predict how much inventory will be needed to meet demand. Although this is a forecasting tool, it is important to recognize its limitations. A moving average is based on historical data, and it is not necessarily a good prediction of what will occur in the future. Changes in the economy, competition, or other factors can affect sales dramatically, causing the moving average trend to change.

Activity 8.04 | **Calculating Growth Based on a Moving Average**

You can also use a moving average to calculate the growth rate at different intervals.

1 Display the **Sales** worksheet. Scroll to position **row 21** near the top of your screen. Click cell **D21, type =(c21-c14)/c14 and click Enter** ✓.

This formula calculates a weekly sales growth percentage from one Saturday to the next, based on the moving average.

2 Point to cell **D21**, right-click, and then on the mini toolbar, click **Percent Style** %. Click **Increase Decimal** one time to display one decimal place—your result is *16.8%*.

3 With cell **D21** still selected, point to the cell and right-click, and then click **Copy**. Point to cell **D28**, right-click, and then under **Paste Options**, click **Paste (P)** 🗐.

The formula is copied to the next date that is a Thursday.

4 Point to cell **D35**, right-click, and then click **Paste (P)** 🗐. Continue in the same manner to paste the formula in cells **D42** and **D49** for the next two Thursday dates. Click **Save** 🔲, and then compare your screen with Figure 8.11.

The formula results show that the trend has moved up and down over five weeks of business.

FIGURE 8.11

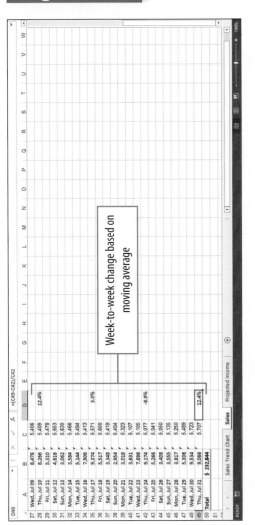

Week-to-week change based on moving average

Objective 2   Project Income and Expenses

Video E8-2

Income generally consists of sales for products and services. In a restaurant, this includes the sale of food and beverages. Expenses can be classified into two broad categories: fixed expenses and variable expenses. *Fixed expenses* remain the same each month regardless of the amount of activity. They include items such as rent, utilities, insurance, and general overhead. *Variable expenses* vary depending on the amount of sales. In a restaurant, the cost of the food—otherwise known as cost of goods sold—and wages are the two most common variable expenses. In this activity, you will work with a worksheet that uses these two broad categories of expenses.

Activity 8.05 | Projecting Income and Expenses

1 Click cell **A51**, type **July Sales** Click cell **B51**, type **=SUM(B19:B49)** and then press [Enter]. Display the **Projected Income** worksheet. Click cell **B3**. Type **=** click the **Sales sheet tab**, click cell **B51**, the July sales total, click **Enter** ✓, and then compare your screen with Figure 8.12.

This sheet contains the first portion of an income statement for the Charlotte restaurant. You have referenced the July total from the Sales worksheet. You will use that value to project sales and expenses through June of next year.

FIGURE 8.12

Cell B3 refers to cell B51 in the Sales worksheet

2 Click cell **B2**, and then use the fill handle to fill the months for a year—from July to June—across to **column M**. With the range **B2:M2** selected, apply **Center** ▤.

3 Click cell **C3**, type **=b3*(1+b12)** and then click **Enter** ✓. Apply the **Currency [0]** cell style.

This formula takes the previous month's sales in cell B3 and multiplies it by 110% to determine a growth rate of 10 percent over the previous month—*$188,364*. Cell B12 indicates the Required Sales Growth rate of 10%, and the absolute cell reference is used so this formula can be copied across the row.

4 With cell **C3** as the active cell, use the fill handle to copy the formula and the formatting across to **column M**. Compare your screen with Figure 8.13.

Based on this projection, by June of next year, the Charlotte restaurant should have $488.568 in monthly sales.

FIGURE 8.13

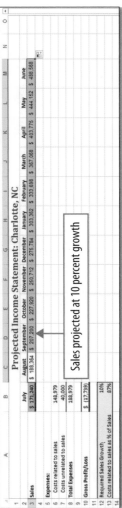

Sales projected at 10 percent growth

5 Click cell **B6** and examine the formula.

This formula multiplies the sales for July by the value in cell B13—87%. It is estimated that variable expenses for the first year will be 87 percent of sales. An absolute reference is used so this formula can be copied across the worksheet.

6 Use the fill handle to copy the formula from cell **B6** across the row to **column M**.

The variable expenses, which are based on sales, are projected for the next year. Variable expenses for June are calculated to be *425,054*.

7 Click cell **B7**. Use the fill handle to copy the value from cell **B7** across the row to **column M**.

These are fixed costs—costs such as rent and insurance that are not directly tied to sales—which total *40,000*.

8 Select the range **C8:M8**, and then on the **HOME tab**, in the **Editing group**, click **AutoSum** Σ AutoSum ▾ .

For each month, the total expenses are calculated.

9 Click cell **B10**.

This formula calculates the gross profit or loss for a month—sales minus expenses.

10 Use the fill handle to copy the formula from cell **B10** across to **column M**. **Save** 🖫 your workbook, and then compare your screen with Figure 8.14.

FIGURE 8.14

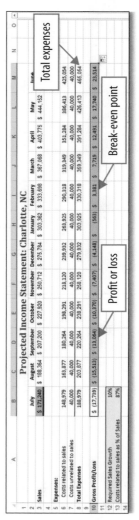

Profit or loss

Break-even point

Total expenses

Objective 3   Determine a Break-Even Point

Video E8-3

The goal of a business is to make a profit. However, a new business often operates at a loss for a period of time before becoming profitable. The point at which a company starts to make a profit is known as the ***break-even point***. A break-even point can be calculated for a product, a branch office, a division, or an entire company. The Brina's Bistro restaurants use a model for new restaurants that projects 10 percent growth, month-to-month, in the first year, with the expectation that sometime during the first year the restaurant will start to make a profit. Ms. Tanner wants to estimate when the new Charlotte restaurant will become profitable, based on sales for its first full month of business.

Activity 8.06 | Charting the Break-Even Point with a Line Chart

You can chart the results of the estimated income statement to create a visual image of the income and expenses and the projected break-even point.

Recall that a line chart displays trends over time. Time is displayed along the bottom axis and the data point values are connected with a line. If you want to compare more than one set of values, each group is connected by a different line. The curves and directions of the lines make trends noticeable to the reader.

1 Be sure that **columns A:M** display on your screen. If necessary, in the lower right corner of your screen, set the Zoom to 80%. Select the range **A2:M3**.

By including the months in row 2 and the labels in column A in the selection, the chart will be properly labeled.

2 On the **INSERT tab**, in the **Charts group**, click **Recommended Charts**. In the **Insert Chart** dialog box, with the **Line chart** selected, click **OK**.

3 On the **DESIGN tab**, in the **Data group**, click **Select Data**. In the **Select Data Source** dialog box, under **Legend Entries (Series)**, click **Add**. With the insertion point in the **Series name** box, click cell **A8**. Press [Tab], select the range **B8:M8** and then click **OK**. Verify that the **Chart data range** is *$A2:$M3* and *$A8:$M8*. Compare your screen with Figure 8.15.

By selecting the income totals and the expense totals, you will be able to see where they cross each other on a graph when you chart the break-even point. The Chart data range box displays the selected range—including the sheet name—using absolute references.

FIGURE 8.15

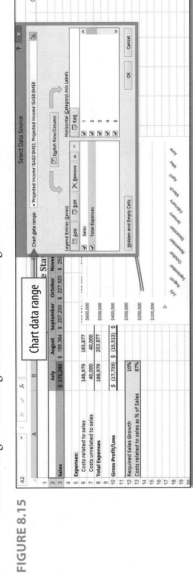

Chart data range

4 Click **OK**. On the **DESIGN tab**, in the **Chart Layouts group**, click **Quick Layout**, and then click **Layout 3**. Click **Chart Title**, and then watch the **Formula Bar** as you type **Expected Break-Even Point** Press [Enter].

5 By using the pointer, drag to position the upper left corner of the chart inside the upper left corner of cell **B15**.

6 Scroll to position **row 13** at the top of your screen. Drag the lower right sizing handle of the chart inside the lower right corner of cell **M36**. Compare your chart with the one shown in Figure 8.16.

FIGURE 8.16

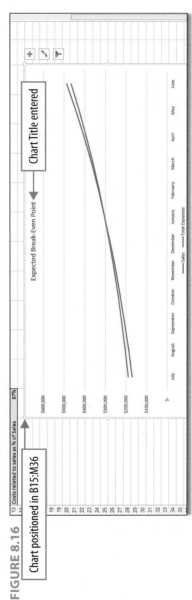

Chart positioned in B15:M36

Chart Title entered

Expected Break-Even Point

7 On the **DESIGN tab**, apply **Chart Style 12**.

8 On the left side of the chart, right-click the **Vertical (Value) Axis**, and then click **Format Axis**. In the **Format Axis** pane, verify that **Axis Options** 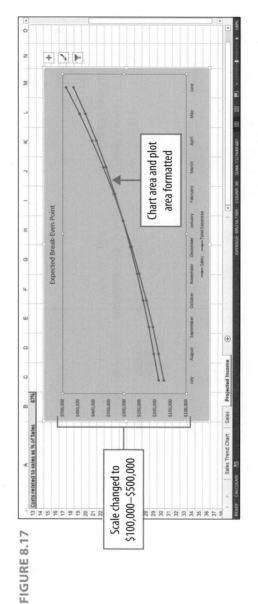 is selected. Under **AXIS OPTIONS**, in the **Minimum** box, type **100000** Press Enter. In the same manner, change the **Maximum** value to **500000**

Because there are no figures less than $100,000, changing the scale in this manner provides more vertical space on the chart and results in a more dramatic slope on the line.

9 Click the **AXIS OPTIONS arrow** and then click **Chart Area**. Click **Fill & Line**. Click **Solid Fill**, and then click the **Fill Color arrow**. Click the second color in the third column, **Tan, Background 2, Darker 10%**. Click the **CHART OPTIONS arrow** and click **Plot Area**. Format the **Plot Area** with the same fill. **Close** the **Format Plot Area** pane. Compare your screen with Figure 8.17.

FIGURE 8.17

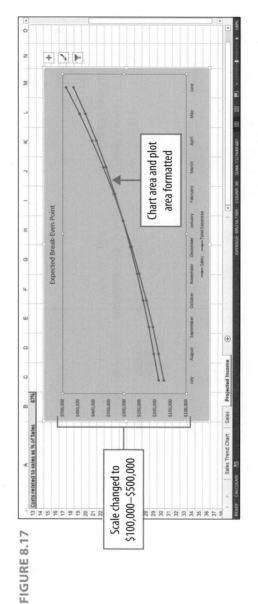

10 Display the **Sales Trend Chart** worksheet, and then insert a custom footer with the file name in the **left section**. Display the **Projected Income** worksheet, click anywhere outside the chart, and then, if necessary, set the **Zoom** back to **100%**. Right-click the **sheet tab**, and then click **Select All Sheets** so that *[Group]* displays in the title bar. Insert a footer in the **left section** that includes the file name. Click the cell above the footer to deselect it.

11 On the **PAGE LAYOUT tab**, set the **Orientation** to **Landscape**, and then in set the **Width** to **1 page** and the **Height** to **1 page**. Center the worksheets horizontally on the page. On the status bar, click **Normal**. Press Ctrl + Home to move to the top of the worksheet.

12 Display the **document properties** and under **Related People**, be sure that your name displays as the author. If necessary, right-click the author name, click **Edit Property**, and then type your name. In the **Subject** box, type your course name and section #, and in the **Tags** box, type **moving average**, **break-even point** Display the grouped worksheets in **Print Preview**. Make any necessary corrections or adjustments.

13 **Save** your workbook, and then **Print** the three worksheets or submit your workbook electronically as directed. If required, print or create an electronic version of your worksheets with formulas displayed. **Close** Excel.

END | You have completed Project 8A

Staffing Analysis

PROJECT ACTIVITIES

In Activities 8.07 through 8.17, you will assist Jillian Zachary, manager of the Ft. Lauderdale restaurant, in determining the most efficient work schedule for the server staff. You will also evaluate sales to determine which servers are eligible for Employee of the Week status. Your completed worksheets will look similar to Figure 8.18.

PROJECT FILES

For Project 8B, you will need the following file:

e08B_Staffing_Analysis

You will save your workbook as:

Lastname_Firstname_8B_Staffing_Analysis

PROJECT RESULTS

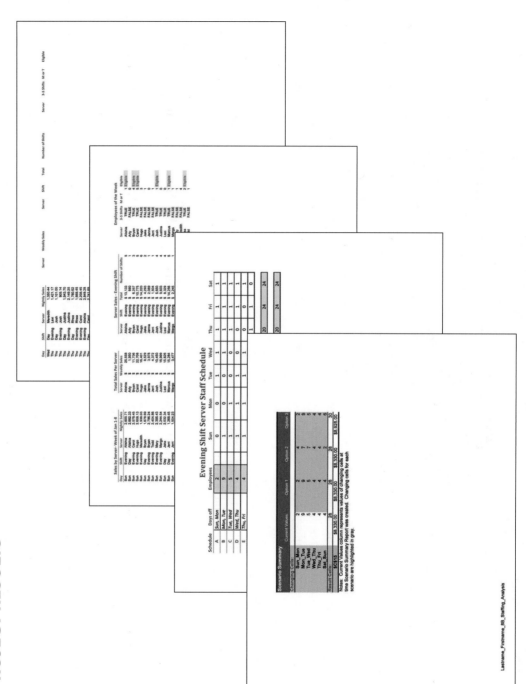

Lastname_Firstname_8B_Staffing_Analysis

FIGURE 8.18 Project 8B Staffing Analysis

Objective 4 | Use Solver

Video E8-4

Solver is an Excel's what-if analysis tool with which you can find an optimal (maximum or minimum) value for a formula in one cell—referred to as the objective cell—subject to constraints, or limits, on the values of other formula cells on a worksheet.

Use Solver when you need to make a decision that involves more than one variable. For example, the manager of the Ft. Lauderdale restaurant needs to determine the number of servers to assign to each evening shift so there are enough servers to handle customer demand, but not too many servers for the work required. Additionally, the schedule must allow each server to have two consecutive days off. Solver can help determine values like these—values that result in minimums, maximums, or specific results.

When you use Solver, the focus is on the *objective cell*—the cell that contains a formula for the results you are trying to determine, such as minimum weekly payroll expense. Your worksheet will have *decision variables*—also referred to as *variable cells*—that are cells in which the values will change to achieve the desired results. Your worksheet will also have *constraint cells*—cells that contain values that limit or restrict the outcome. As an example of a constraint, in determining a work schedule, you cannot schedule more than the total number of employees on the payroll.

Activity 8.07 | Installing Solver

Recall that add-ins are optional commands and features that are not immediately available; you must first install and/or activate an add-in to use it. Solver is an add-in.

1 ▶ Start Excel and display a new blank workbook. Click the **DATA tab**, and then at the right end of the **DATA tab**, check to see whether the **Analysis group** and **Solver** display. Compare your screen with Figure 8.19.

FIGURE 8.19

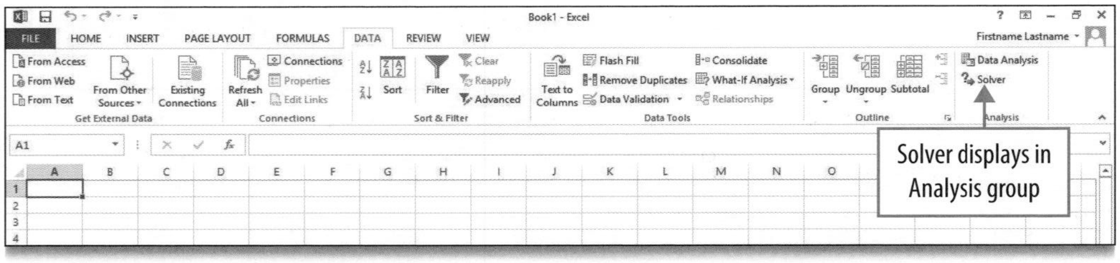

Solver displays in Analysis group

2 ▶ If **Solver** displays, Solver has been installed on your computer and you can move to Activity 8.08. If Solver does *not* display, complete the remaining steps in this activity to install it.

3 ▶ On the **FILE tab**, click **Options**. In the Excel **Options dialog** box, on the left, click **Add-Ins**, and then at the bottom of the screen, in the **Manage** box, if necessary, select **Excel Add-ins**. Compare your screen with Figure 8.20.

FIGURE 8.20

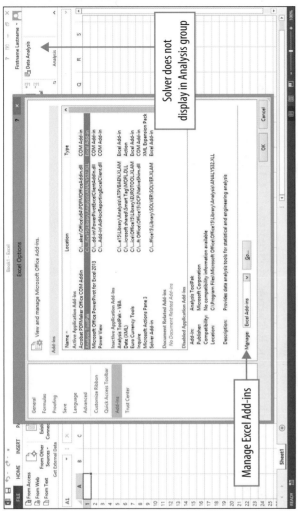

Solver does not display in Analysis group

Manage Excel Add-ins

4 Click **Go**.

The Add-Ins dialog box displays.

5 In the **Add-Ins** dialog box, select the **Solver Add-in** check box, and then click **OK**.

The Solver Add-in is installed. On the DATA tab, in the Analysis group, Solver displays.

Activity 8.08 | Understanding a Solver Worksheet

The manager of the Ft. Lauderdale restaurant wants to minimize the weekly payroll expense by scheduling only enough servers to handle established customer activity. She has reviewed customer activity for the past three months and determined how many servers are needed for the evening schedule on each day of the week. For example, more servers are needed on Friday and Saturday evenings than on Tuesday and Wednesday evenings. You will use Solver to determine the number of servers to schedule for each evening shift to meet the demand while minimizing the payroll expense. Before you can solve the problem of minimizing payroll expenses, familiarize yourself with the components of the worksheet.

1 From your student files, open the file **e08B_Staffing_Analysis**. Display the **Save As** dialog box, navigate to your **Excel Chapter 8** folder, and then **Save** the workbook as **Lastname_Firstname_8B_Staffing_Analysis**

2 Examine the range **A2:K8**, and then compare your screen with Figure 8.21.

Six possible schedules are labeled—A through F. Column B lists the two consecutive days off for each schedule. For example, servers who work Schedule B have Monday and Tuesday off. Servers who work Schedule C have Tuesday and Wednesday off.

For each schedule, the cells in columns E through K indicate a 0 for days off and a 1 for days worked. For example, Schedule B indicates 0 under Mon and Tue—the days off—and 1 under Sun, Wed, Thu, Fri, and Sat—the days worked.

FIGURE 8.21

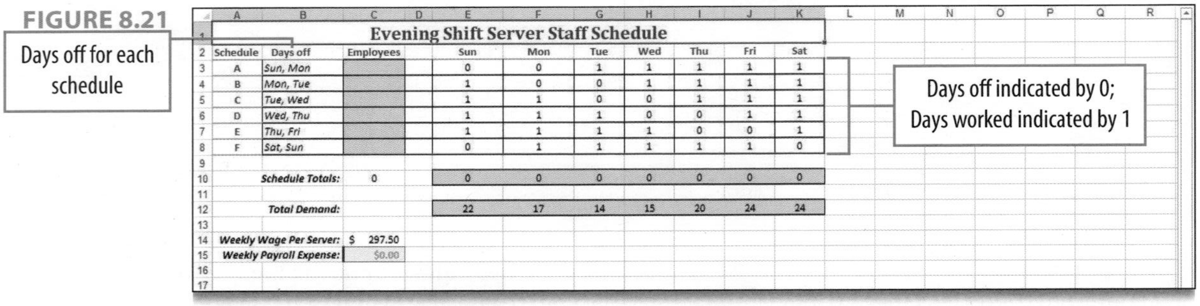

Days off for each schedule

	A	B	C	D	E	F	G	H	I	J	K	L	M	N	O	P	Q	R
1			Evening Shift Server Staff Schedule															
2	Schedule	Days off	Employees	Sun	Mon	Tue	Wed	Thu	Fri	Sat								
3	A	Sun, Mon		0	0	1	1	1	1	1								
4	B	Mon, Tue		1	0	0	1	1	1	1								
5	C	Tue, Wed		1	1	0	0	1	1	1								
6	D	Wed, Thu		1	1	1	0	0	1	1								
7	E	Thu, Fri		1	1	1	1	0	0	1								
8	F	Sat, Sun		1	1	1	1	1	0	0								
9																		
10		Schedule Totals:	0	0	0	0	0	0	0	0								
11																		
12		Total Demand:		22	17	14	15	20	24	24								
13																		
14		Weekly Wage Per Server:	$	297.50														
15		Weekly Payroll Expense:		$0.00														
16																		
17																		

Days off indicated by 0;
Days worked indicated by 1

3 ▶ Click cell **C10**, and then look at the **Formula Bar.**

Cell C10 sums the range C3:C8. It represents the number of servers who are assigned to each schedule. It is currently zero because no servers have been assigned to a schedule. The range C3:C8 is shaded in orange. These are the decision variables—the values that will change to achieve the desired results. Here, the desired result is to have only enough staff assigned to meet customer demand and hence minimize payroll expense.

4 ▶ Click cell **C14** and examine the formula.

This formula calculates the weekly wage, based on $8.50 per hour, multiplied by seven hours worked each day, multiplied by five days worked per week. The proposed schedule shows all servers working five days each week.

5 ▶ Click cell **C15**, which is formatted using the **Calculation cell** style, and examine the formula.

This cell calculates the total weekly payroll expense by multiplying the number of servers scheduled to work—cell C10—by the Weekly Wage Per Server—cell C14. Cell C15 is the objective cell. Recall that the objective cell contains the result that you are trying to achieve. In this instance, you are trying to achieve the minimum payroll expense that must be paid while maintaining enough servers on duty to meet established customer demand.

6 ▶ Select the range **E12:K12.**

These cells represent the minimum number of servers required to serve the number of customers expected each day of the week. The cells in this row will be one of the constraints used to determine the minimum weekly payroll expense. Recall that *constraints* are conditions or restrictions that must be met. In this case, the number of servers scheduled must be equal to or greater than the number required for each day.

7 ▶ Click cell **E10.**

The formulas in this row multiply the number of people assigned to work each schedule, arriving at a total number available each day of the week.

8 ▶ Click cell **C3**, and then click the **Name Box arrow.** Notice that cell C3 has been named *Sun_Mon.* Compare your screen with Figure 8.22 and take a moment to review each of the cells you will work with in this project.

The cells in the range C3:C8, the decision variables, have been named with their corresponding days off.

FIGURE 8.22

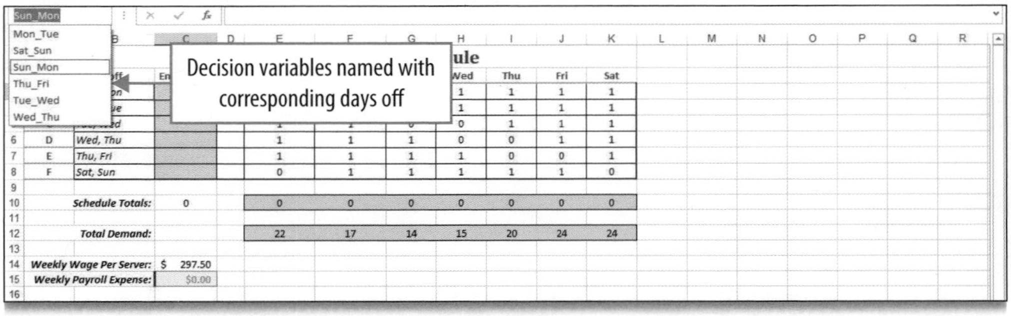

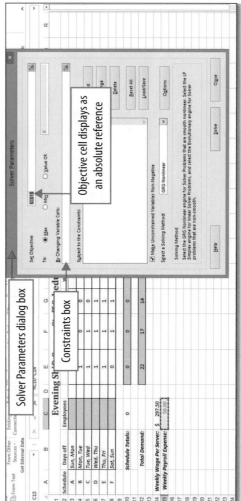

Decision variables named with corresponding days off

Activity 8.09 | Using Solver

In this activity, you will use Solver to determine the minimum payroll expense; that is, the minimum number of servers who can be on duty and still meet expected customer demand. This process involves identifying the objective cell, the decision variable cells, and the constraint cells.

1 Click cell **C15**—the objective cell. On the **DATA tab**, in the **Analysis group**, click **Solver**. If necessary, drag the **Solver Parameters** dialog box to the right side of your worksheet. Compare your screen with Figure 8.23.

The Solver Parameters dialog box displays and cell C15 displays as an absolute reference in the Set Objective box.

FIGURE 8.23

Solver Parameters dialog box

Constraints box

Objective cell displays as an absolute reference

2 To the right of **To**, click **Min**.

The three option buttons here enable you to use the Solver tool to maximize, minimize, or solve for a specific value.

3 Click in the **By Changing Variable Cells** box, and then select the range **C3:C8**.

The range displays as an absolute reference. In this cell range, Solver will place the optimum number of servers who must be assigned to each schedule to minimize payroll and meet the constraints that are set.

4 To the right of the **Subject to the Constraints** area, click **Add**.

In the Add Constraint dialog box, you enter constraints—limitations caused by various circumstances.

5 With the insertion point blinking in the **Cell Reference** box, select the range C3:C8.

6 In the middle box, click the **arrow**, and then click **int**. Compare your screen with Figure 8.24.

This constraint requires that only an *integer*—a whole number—can be used, because you cannot assign part of a person as a server. In the Add Constraint dialog box, in the Constraint box, *integer* displays.

FIGURE 8.24

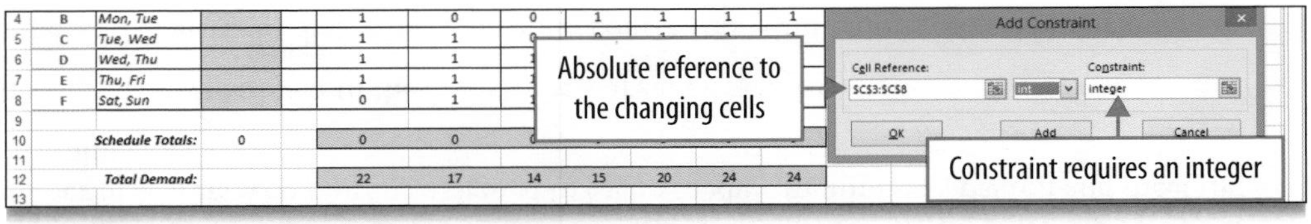

Absolute reference to the changing cells

Constraint requires an integer

7 Click **OK**.

The Add Constraint dialog box closes and the first constraint is added to the Solver Parameters dialog box.

8 Click **Add**. With the insertion point in the **Cell Reference** box, select the range **C3:C8**. In the middle box, click the **arrow**, and then click **>=**. In the **Constraint** box, type **0** Compare your dialog box with Figure 8.25.

This constraint (limitation) requires that the number of servers assigned to each schedule be a positive number—a negative number of servers cannot be assigned.

FIGURE 8.25

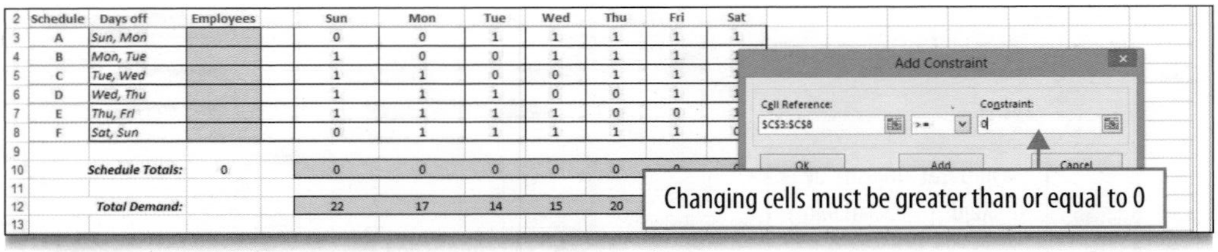

Changing cells must be greater than or equal to 0

9 Click **OK**.

The second constraint is added to the Solver Parameters dialog box.

10 Click **Add**. In the **Cell Reference** box, select the range **E10:K10**. In the middle box, click the **arrow**, and then click **>=**. In the **Constraint** box, select the range **E12:K12**.

This constraint requires that the number of servers assigned to each shift be greater than or equal to the number of servers required each day to meet the projected demand. For example, on Saturday, the number of servers assigned must be at least 24.

11 Click **OK**. Compare your dialog box with Figure 8.26.

Three constraints display in the Solver Parameters dialog box. First, the number of servers assigned to any given schedule—C3:C8—must be a whole number. Second, the number of servers—C3:C8—assigned to any given schedule must be a positive number equal to or greater than zero. Third, the number of servers—E10:K10—assigned to each day's shift must be equal to or greater than the number of servers needed to meet the established demand in cells E12:K12. With the constraints established, you can solve for (calculate) the minimum payroll expense.

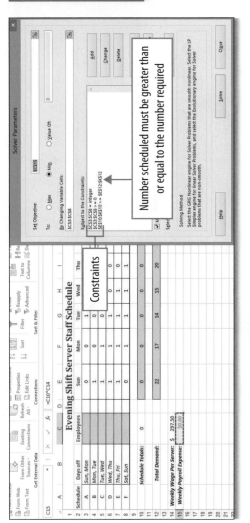

FIGURE 8.26

Constraints

Number scheduled must be greater than or equal to the number required

---

12 At the bottom of the **Solver Parameters** dialog box, click **Solve**. In the **Solver Results** dialog box, with **Keep Solver Solution** selected, click **OK**. **Save** 🖫 your workbook, and then compare your screen with Figure 8.27.

The Solver Results dialog box displays. The decision variables—the cell range C3:C8—displays the number of servers who should be assigned to each schedule to meet the demand while minimizing payroll. Cell C15—the objective cell—shows the Weekly Payroll Expense as *$8,330.00*, and the number of servers who will work each schedule displays in cells E10:K10. Thus, to adequately staff the evening shifts and to give servers two consecutive days off requires a total of 28 servers each working 5 days a week and 7 hours each day—cell C10. The minimum payroll expense for 28 servers is $8,330.00—28 servers times $297.50.

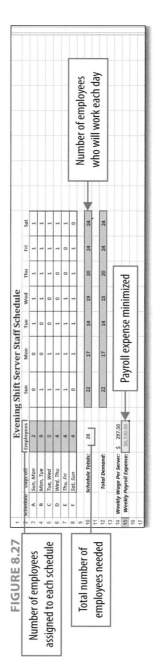

FIGURE 8.27

Number of employees assigned to each schedule

Total number of employees needed

Number of employees who will work each day

Payroll expense minimized

---

13 This is one possible solution. Later, you will consider alternatives with a different distribution of staff over the week.

More Knowledge

Solver Reports

The Solver Results dialog box offers three reports—Answer, Sensitivity, and Limits—that can be created to help you understand the results. The Answer Report displays the original and final values for the objective cell and the decision variables. It also shows the impact of the constraints on determining values for the decision variables and whether the result for each cell is binding or nonbinding. It helps you understand where there may be some flexibility in the results if you want to do further analysis or consider other alternatives. The Sensitivity and Limits reports are not meaningful in the current example because of the integer constraints that have been applied.

Video E8-5

The current solution indicates nine servers assigned to *Schedule B, Mon and Tue off,* and only two servers assigned to *Schedule A, Sun and Mon off.* Ms. Zachary wants to see what would happen if she assigned more servers to Schedule A. You can create several possible solutions to a problem and then use Excel's *Scenario Manager* what-if analysis tool to compare the alternatives. A *scenario* is a set of values that Excel saves and can substitute automatically in your worksheet.

Activity 8.10 │ Creating a Scenario Using the Scenario Manager

You can create a scenario from the Solver dialog box, or you can open the Scenario Manager dialog box and create a scenario. Here, you will use the Scenario Manager dialog box to save the existing solution for minimizing the weekly server staff payroll.

1 Select the range **C3:C8.**

These are the decision variable cells defined in Solver that are used to calculate the minimum payroll expense while matching the staffing requirements that are shown in row 12.

2 On the **DATA tab,** in the **Data Tools group,** click **What-If Analysis,** and then click **Scenario Manager.** Compare your screen with Figure 8.28.

The Scenario Manager dialog box displays. It shows that no scenarios have been defined.

FIGURE 8.28

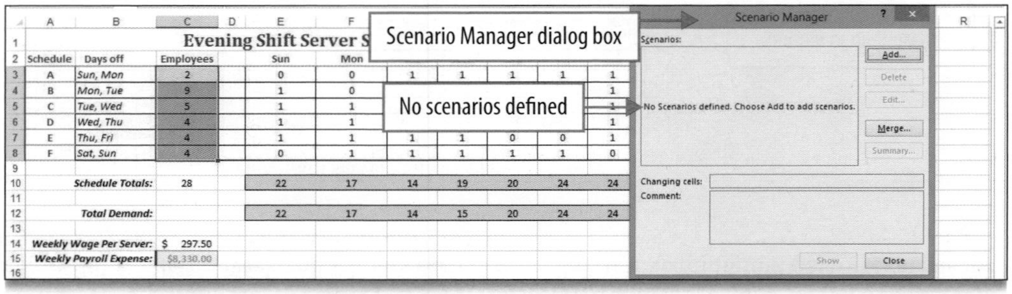

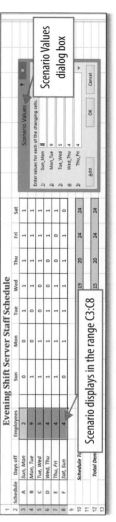

3 In the **Scenario Manager** dialog box, click **Add.**

The Add Scenario dialog box displays. Here you name the scenario and identify the decision variable cells.

4 In the **Scenario Name** box, type **Option 1** Verify that the **Changing cells** box displays C3:C8. You will save the existing solution as your first scenario.

5 Click **OK.** Compare your screen with Figure 8.29.

The Scenario Values dialog box displays and the current value in each of the decision variable cells is listed. You will accept the values that are displayed.

FIGURE 8.29

6 In the **Scenario Values** dialog box, click **OK**.

The Scenario Manager dialog box redisplays, and the first scenario is listed in the Scenarios box as *Option 1*.

7 In the **Scenario Manager** dialog box, click **Close**. **Save** 🔲 your workbook.

Activity 8.11 | Creating a Scenario Using Solver

You can also create a scenario using the Solver Parameters dialog box. Ms. Zachary wants to add another schedule option that would assign more servers to Schedule A so more people could be off on Sunday, a more traditional day off, and to help balance the numbers of shifts among employees.

1 Click cell **C15**—the objective cell. On the **DATA tab**, in the **Analysis group**, click **Solver**. In the **Solver Parameters** dialog box, verify that the **Set Objective** box displays *$C$15* and the **By Changing Variable Cells** box displays *$C$3:$C$8*.

The values from the first solution display in the Solver Parameters dialog box.

2 To the right of **Subject to the Constraints** box, click **Add**.

3 In the **Add Constraint** dialog box, click the **Cell Reference** box, and then click cell **C3**. In the middle box, click the **arrow**, and then click **=**. In the **Constraint** box, type **4**

This constraint will assign four servers to *Schedule A—Sun and Mon off.*

4 Click **OK**.

A fourth constraint is added to the Solver Parameters dialog box. Recall that because each of the cells in the range C3:C8 were named, the constraint displays as Sun_Mon =4. The range name displays when you summarize the alternatives you are creating.

5 In the lower right corner of the dialog box, click **Solve**. Drag the **Solver Results** dialog box to the right side of the screen and compare your screen with Figure 8.30.

A new solution is found and the Solver Results dialog box displays. The Weekly Payroll Expense remains at $8,330.00, but the servers are more evenly distributed across the schedules, with more servers scheduled on Friday and Saturday when the restaurant is the busiest. This provides a better distribution of staff on the busiest weekend days, while giving more people Sunday off. This shows that there may be more than one acceptable solution to the problem of minimizing the payroll.

FIGURE 8.30

The number of employees assigned to each schedule is changed

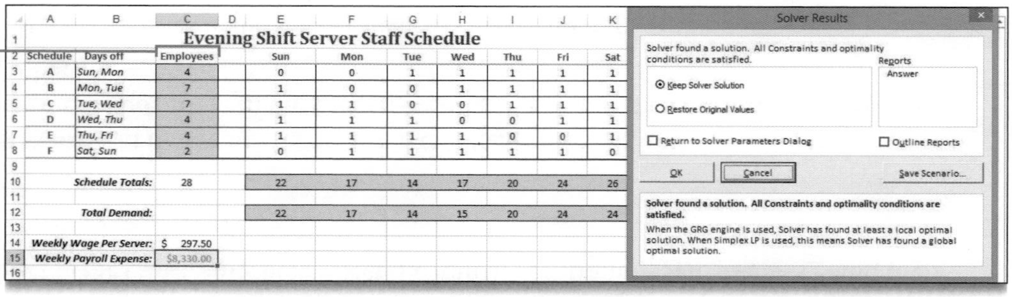

6 Click **Save Scenario** to display the **Save Scenario** dialog box.

7 In the **Scenario Name box**, type **Option 2** and then click **OK**.

A second scenario is saved and the Solver Results dialog box displays.

8 In the **Solver Results** dialog box, click **Restore Original Values**, and then click **OK**. **Save** 🔲 your workbook.

The dialog box closes and the previous solution is redisplayed on the worksheet.

Activity 8.12 | Creating a Scenario Summary

Ms. Zachary wants to see what would happen if she schedules six servers to have Saturday off. Schedule F includes both Saturday and Sunday off, which would give more employees a traditional weekend off. After the third scenario is created, you will view a summary of the results of all three alternatives.

1 Verify that cell **C15** is still the active cell. On the **DATA tab**, in the **Analysis group**, click **Solver**.

In the Solver Parameters dialog box, all four constraints (from Option 2) display, even though the currently displayed solution—Option 1—does not use the constraint that requires four servers be assigned to schedule A—*Sun_Mon = 4*.

2 In the **Subject to the Constraints** box, select the fourth constraint—**Sun_Mon = 4**—and then click **Delete**.

3 Click **Add**.

4 In the **Add Constraint** dialog box, click in the **Cell Reference** box, and then click cell **C8**. Change the middle box to =. In the **Constraint** box, type **6** and then click **OK**. Compare your screen with Figure 8.31.

Four constraints are listed in the Solver Parameters dialog box.

FIGURE 8.31

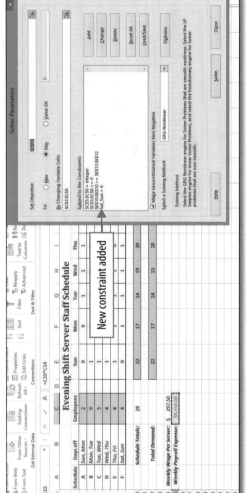

5 Click **Solve**.

A new solution is found; however, the Weekly Payroll Expense in cell C16 increases to $8,925.00, and the number of servers required to meet this scenario in cell C10 increases to 30.

6 Click **Save Scenario**. In the **Save Scenario** dialog box, type **Option 3** and then click **OK**.

The third scenario is saved and the Solver Results dialog box displays.

7 Click **Restore Original Values**, and then click **OK**.

The previous solution is restored to the worksheet.

8 On the **DATA tab**, in the **Data Tools group**, click **What-If Analysis**, and then click **Scenario Manager**. Compare your screen with Figure 8.32.

The Scenario Manager dialog box displays the three scenario names that you have created.

FIGURE 8.32

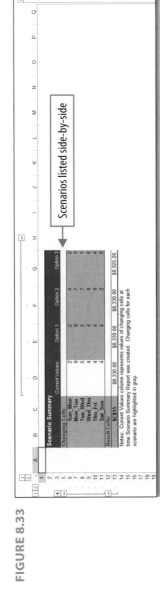

9 In the **Scenario Manager** dialog box, click **Summary**.

The Scenario Summary dialog box displays. Here you can choose between a Scenario Summary, which displays the data in a table, or a Scenario PivotTable report.

10 Be sure **Scenario Summary** is selected, and then click **OK**. Compare your screen with Figure 8.33.

Excel inserts a new worksheet in your workbook—the *Scenario Summary* sheet, which compares the three options side-by-side. The results for Option 1 and Option 2 indicate the same amount in the results cell—$8,330.00—and Option 3 indicates $8,925.00 in payroll expenses. The outline pane displays along the top and left side of the worksheet.

FIGURE 8.33

11 Select the range **D12:G12** and then, on the **HOME tab**, in the **Editing group**, click **AutoSum** . **Save** your workbook.

The total number of servers required for each scenario is added to the Scenario Summary sheet. Options 1 and 2 require 28 servers to fill the schedule and Option 3 requires 30 servers.

Objective 6 | Use Logical Functions

Video E8-6

There are a number of *logical functions* that are used to test for specific conditions. The results of a logical test are either TRUE or FALSE. Recall that the SUM function adds values in a specified range of cells. The *SUMIF function* contains a logic test—it will add values in a specified range that meet a certain condition or criteria. The *SUMIFS function* is similar to the SUMIF function, but allows you to specify multiple ranges and multiple criteria to test. The *COUNTIF function* and *COUNTIFS function* work in the same way, counting cells that meet specific criteria in specified ranges. The *syntax*, or arrangement of the arguments in a function, displays in a ScreenTip as you begin to build the function.

Activity 8.13 | Using the SUMIF Function

Ms. Zachary wants to see the total each server has sold over the past week. SUMIF can be used to add values in a range that meet a specific condition or criteria. In this activity you will use SUMIF to calculate the total weekly sales for each server.

1 Display the **Weekly Sales** worksheet.

This worksheet lists the sales for each server that has worked the day or evening shift the week of January 1–8.

2 Click cell **G3**, and then type **=sumif(** Compare your screen with Figure 8.34.

The syntax displays for the SUMIF function. It has two required arguments: *range* and *criteria*, and one optional argument: *sum_range*.

FIGURE 8.34

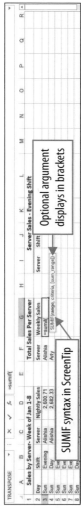

3 Notice *range* is bold in the ScreenTip that displays. Select the range **C3:C102** and press F4 to make the value absolute. Type , (a comma) and notice *criteria* is now bold in the ScreenTip.

4 Click cell **F3**, and then type , (a comma).

5 Notice *[sum_range]* is now bold. Select the range **D3:D102** and press F4. Type **)** and then, on the **Formula Bar**, click **Enter** ✓.

The brackets around *sum_range* indicate it is an optional argument. If you do not include it, Excel will attempt to determine what range to use for the calculation.

6 Drag the fill handle to copy the formula down through cell **G19**. Format the range **G3:G19** using cell style **Currency [0]**. **Save** 🖫 your workbook and compare your screen with Figure 8.35.

FIGURE 8.35

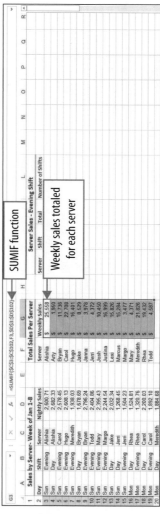

Activity 8.14 | Using the SUMIFS Function

Because each server may work multiple shifts, you can use the SUMIFS function to include a second criteria—Shift—to SUM. In this activity, you will use SUMIFS to calculate sales for each server for the evening shift.

1 Select the range **F3:F19**, which contains the server names. Right-click over the selection and click **Copy**. Right-click cell **I3** and click **Paste (P)** 🗎. Click cell **J3**, and then type **Evening** and then copy the cell down through **I19**.

2 Click cell **K3** and type **=sumifs(** Compare your screen with Figure 8.36.

In the SUMIFS function, the *sum_range* argument is specified first, followed by the first *criteria_range1* and *criteria1*. Additional *criteria_range* and *criteria* arguments can follow, up to a maximum of 127.

FIGURE 8.36

3 Select the range **D3:D102** and press F4 to make the value absolute. Type , (a comma), select the range **C3:C102**, and press F4 . Type , (a comma). Click cell **I3**, and then type , (a comma).

The optional arguments [criteria_range2, criteria2] display in brackets in the ScreenTip.

4 Select the range **B3:B102** and then press F4 . Type , (a comma) and then click cell **J3**. Type **)** and then click **Enter** ✓ .

5 Drag the fill-handle to copy the formula down through cell **K19**. Format the range **K3:K19** using cell style **Currency [0]**. **Save** 🖫 your workbook and compare your screen with Figure 8.37.

In this SUMIFS function, you used the Nightly Sales as the sum_range, the Server as the first criteria, and the Shift as the second criteria.

FIGURE 8.37

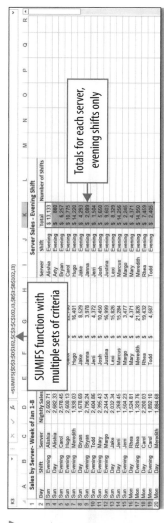

Activity 8.15 | Using the COUNTIFS Function

Ms. Zachary wants to see the number of evening shifts each server has worked over the past week. The COUNTIFS function can be used to count items that meet multiple conditions—in this case, the server and the shift worked.

1 Click cell **L3** and type **=countifs(** Compare your screen with Figure 8.38.

The COUNTIFS function has two required arguments: *criteria_range1* and *criteria1*. Additional *criteria_range* and *criteria* arguments can follow.

FIGURE 8.38

2 Select the range **C3:C102** and press **F4** to make the value absolute. Type , (a comma), click cell **I3**, and then type , (a comma).

The optional arguments [criteria_range2, criteria2] display in brackets in the ScreenTip.

3 Select the range **B3:B102** and then press **F4**. Type , (a comma) and then click cell **J3**. Type **)** and then click **Enter** ✓.

4 Drag the fill handle to copy the formula down through cell **L19**. **Save** 🖫 your workbook and compare your screen with Figure 8.39.

Using the COUNTIFS function, Ms. Zachary is able to see how many evening shifts each server worked this week.

FIGURE 8.39

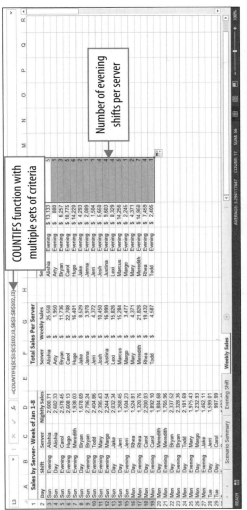

COUNTIFS function with multiple sets of criteria

Number of evening shifts per server

Objective 7 | Create Complex Formulas

Video E8-7

The logical functions AND and OR can be used to develop compound logical tests using up to 255 arguments. The *AND function* returns a result of TRUE if *ALL* of the conditions are met. The *OR function* returns a value of TRUE if *ANY* of the conditions are met. The *NOT function* takes only one argument and is used to test one condition. If the condition is true, NOT returns the logical opposite false. If the condition is false, then true is returned.

Activity 8.16 | Building Compound Conditional Tests Using AND

To determine the Employee of the Week, Ms. Zachary needs to determine the server with the best sales that worked at least three shifts but no more than five evening shifts during the week, and worked a least one shift during the slower days Monday and Tuesday. To do this, she needs to use a compound conditional test.

1 Click cell **N1** and type **Employees of the Week** and press **Enter**. **Merge & Center** the text over the range **N1:Q1** and apply the **Heading 2** cell style. In cell **N2**, type **Server** In cell **O2**, type **3-5 Shifts** In cell **P2**, type **M or T** Copy the server names from **I3:I19** to **N3:N19**.

2 Select the range **A3:A102**, in the **Name Box**, type **DAY** and then press **Enter**. Select the range **B3:B102**, in the **Name Box**, type **SHIFT** and then press **Enter**. Select the range **C3:C102**, in the **Name Box**, type **SERVER** and then press **Enter**.

By naming the ranges, you have made it easier to construct and understand complex formulas.

3 In cell **O2**, type **=and(** and compare your screen with Figure 8.40.

The AND function takes the argument *logical1*, followed by optional additional logical tests.

FIGURE 8.40

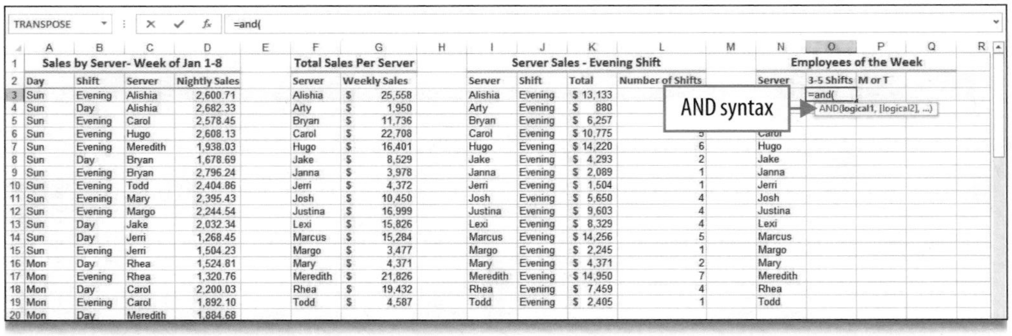

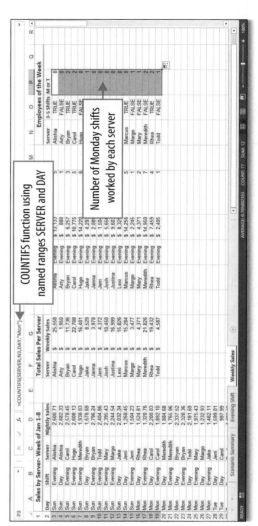

4 Click cell **L3**, type **>=3,** (include the comma) Click cell **L3**, and type **<=5)** Click **Enter** ✓ and copy the formula down through cell **O19.** Compare your screen with Figure 8.41.

The AND function performs two logical tests *L3>=3* and *L3<=5*. Both of the tests must be true for the function to return TRUE. If either or both tests fail, the function returns the result FALSE.

FIGURE 8.41

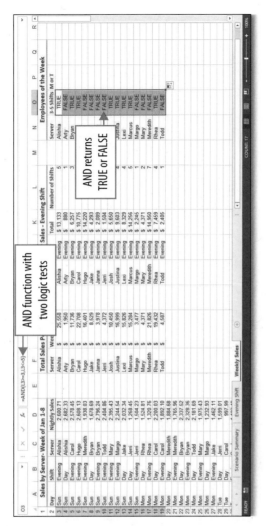

5 Click cell **P3,** and then type the formula **=countifs(server,n3,day,"Mon")** Click **Enter** ✓ and copy the formula down through cell **P19.** Compare your screen with Figure 8.42.

This formula uses the named ranges SERVER and DAY as the criteria ranges to determine the number of Monday shifts each server has worked.

FIGURE 8.42

6 Click cell **P3** and in the **Formula Bar**, position the insertion point at the end of the formula. Type **+countifs(server,n3,day, "Tue")** Click **Enter** ☑ and copy the formula down through cell **P19**. **Save** 🔲 your worksheet and compare your screen with Figure 8.43.

The mathematical operators plus sign (+), minus sign (−), division sign (/), and multiplication sign (*) can be used to build complex formulas. In this case, by adding the results of two functions.

FIGURE 8.43

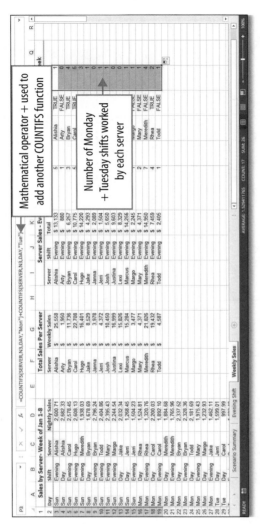

Activity 8.17 | Using Nested Functions

Complex formulas can be built by nesting functions. A *nested function* is contained inside another function. The inner, nested function is evaluated first and the result becomes the argument for the outer function. Recall that the IF function uses a single logic test and returns one value if true and another value if false. In this activity you will use an IF function with a nested AND function to determine which servers are eligible for Employee of the Week status.

1 Click cell **Q2**, type **Eligible** and then press [Enter].

2 In cell **Q3**, type **=if(and(o3, p3>=1), "Eligible", "")** Click **Enter** ☑ and copy the formula down through cell **Q19**. **Save** 🔲 your worksheet and compare your screen with Figure 8.44.

There are six servers that meet both criteria—O3 is true and P3 is greater than or equal to 1—and are listed as *Eligible*. The double quotes make the cell blank rather than displaying the word FALSE if the result is false.

FIGURE 8.44

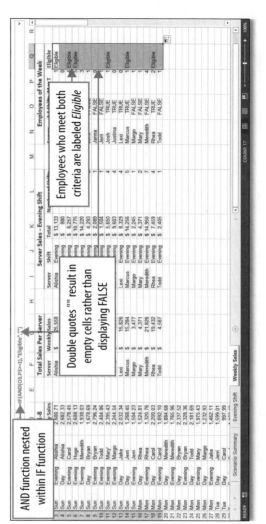

3 Press **Ctrl** + **Q** to open **Quick Analysis** at the bottom of the selection, and then click **Text Contains**. In the **Text That Contains** dialog box, verify **Format cells that contain the text** displays *Eligible*. Click the **with arrow**, and then click **Green Fill with Dark Green Text**. Compare your screen with Figure 8.45.

This applies conditional formatting to the cells in the selected range that contain text, which makes it easy for Ms. Zachary to see which employees are eligible.

FIGURE 8.45

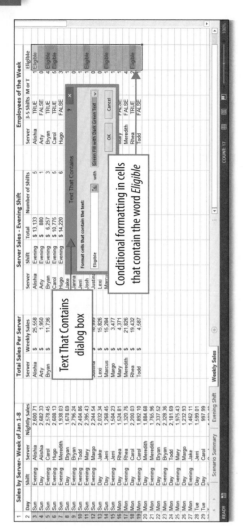

Text That Contains dialog box

Conditional formatting in cells that contain the word *Eligible*

4 Click **OK**. On the **PAGE LAYOUT tab**, click **Print Titles**. Under **Print Titles**, click in the **Rows to repeat at top** box, and then from the **row heading area**, select **row 2**. Click **OK**.

This worksheet will print on two pages so adding column titles will make it easier to understand the information on the second page.

5 Select all three worksheets so that *[Group]* displays in the title bar. With the worksheets grouped, set the **Orientation** to **Landscape**. Center the worksheets horizontally on the page and set the **Width** to **1 page**. Insert a footer in the **left section** that includes the file name. On the status bar, click **Normal** and make cell **A1** active.

6 Display the **document properties** and if necessary, right-click the author name, click **Edit Property**, and then type your name. In the **Subject box**, type your course name and section #, and in the **Tags box**, type **staff schedule** Display the grouped worksheets in **Print Preview**. If necessary, return to the workbook and make any necessary corrections or adjustments. Ungroup the worksheets and **Save** your workbook.

7 **Print** or submit the three worksheets in this workbook electronically as directed by your instructor. If required, print or create an electronic version of your worksheets with formulas. **Close** Excel.

END | You have completed Project 8B

END OF CHAPTER

SUMMARY

A moving average is a sequence of averages computed from parts of a data series. It smoothes the data, showing a pattern or trend. The break-even point is the point at which a company starts to make a profit.

Solver is a what-if analysis tool used to find an optimal value for a formula in one cell—referred to as the objective cell—subject to constraints, on the values of other formula cells in a worksheet.

You can create several possible solutions to a problem and use Scenario Manager to compare the alternatives. A scenario is a set of values that Excel saves and can substitute automatically in your worksheet.

Complex formulas can be built by nesting functions. A nested function is contained inside another function. The inner function is evaluated first and the result becomes the argument for the outer function.

GO! LEARN IT ONLINE

Review the concepts and key terms in this chapter by completing these online challenges, which you can find at **www.pearsonhighered.com/go.**

Matching and Multiple Choice:
Answer matching and multiple choice questions to test what you learned in this chapter. MyITLab®

Crossword Puzzle:
Spell out the words that match the numbered clues, and put them in the puzzle squares.

Flipboard:
Flip through the definitions of the key terms in this chapter and match them with the correct term.

END OF CHAPTER

REVIEW AND ASSESSMENT GUIDE FOR EXCEL CHAPTER 8

Your instructor may assign one or more of these projects to help you review the chapter and assess your mastery and understanding of the chapter.

Review and Assessment Guide for Excel Chapter 8

Project	Apply Skills from These Chapter Objectives	Project Type	Project Location
8C	Objectives 1–3 from Project 8A	**8C Skills Review** A guided review of the skills from Project 8A.	On the following pages
8D	Objectives 4–7 from Project 8B	**8D Skills Review** A guided review of the skills from Project 8B.	On the following pages
8E	Objectives 1–3 from Project 8A	**8E Mastery (Grader Project)** A demonstration of your mastery of the skills in Project 8A with extensive decision making.	In MyITLab and on the following pages
8F	Objectives 4–7 from Project 8B	**8F Mastery (Grader Project)** A demonstration of your mastery of the skills in Project 8B with extensive decision making.	In MyITLab and on the following pages
8G	Objectives 1–7 from Projects 8A and 8B	**8G Mastery (Grader Project)** A demonstration of your mastery of the skills in Projects 8A and 8B with extensive decision making.	In MyITLab and on the following pages
8H	Combination of Objectives from Projects 8A and 8B	**8H GO! Fix It** A demonstration of your mastery of the skills in Projects 8A and 8B by creating a correct result from a document that contains errors you must find.	Online
8I	Combination of Objectives from Projects 8A and 8B	**8I GO! Make It** A demonstration of your mastery of the skills in Projects 8A and 8B by creating a result from a supplied picture.	Online
8J	Combination of Objectives from Projects 8A and 8B	**8J GO! Solve It** A demonstration of your mastery of the skills in Projects 8A and 8B, your decision-making skills, and your critical thinking skills. A task-specific rubric helps you self-assess your result.	Online
8K	Combination of Objectives from Projects 8A and 8B	**8K GO! Solve It** A demonstration of your mastery of the skills in Projects 8A and 8B, your decision-making skills, and your critical thinking skills. A task-specific rubric helps you self-assess your result.	On the following pages
8L	Combination of Objectives from Projects 8A and 8B	**8L GO! Think** A demonstration of your understanding of the chapter concepts applied in a manner that you would use outside of college. An analytic rubric helps you and your instructor grade the quality of your work by comparing it to the work an expert in the discipline would create.	On the following pages
8M	Combination of Objectives from Projects 8A and 8B	**8M GO! Think** A demonstration of your understanding of the chapter concepts applied in a manner that you would use outside of college. An analytic rubric helps you and your instructor grade the quality of your work by comparing it to the work an expert in the discipline would create.	Online
8N	Combination of Objectives from Projects 8A and 8B	**8N You and GO!** A demonstration of your understanding of the chapter concepts applied in a manner that you would in a personal situation. An analytic rubric helps you and your instructor grade the quality of your work.	Online

GLOSSARY

GLOSSARY OF CHAPTER KEY TERMS

Add-in Optional command or feature that is not immediately available; you must first install and/or activate it to use it.

AND function A logical function that can be used to develop compound logical tests using up to 255 arguments. The function returns a result of TRUE if ALL of the conditions are met.

Break-even point The point at which a company starts to make a profit.

Constraint In Solver, a condition or restriction that must be met.

Constraint cell In Solver, a cell that contains a value that limits or restricts the outcome.

COUNTIF function A logical function that counts the cells that meet specific criteria in a specified range.

COUNTIFS function A logical function that counts the cells that meet specific criteria in multiple ranges.

Decision variable In Solver, a cell in which the value will change to achieve the desired results.

Dual-axis chart A chart that has one series plotted on a secondary axis. Useful when comparing data series that use different scales or different types of measurements.

Fixed expense Expense that remains the same each month regardless of the amount of activity.

Forecast A prediction of the future, often based on past performances.

Integer A whole number.

Interval The number of cells to include in the average.

Logical function A function that tests for specific conditions.

Moving average A sequence of averages computed from parts of a data series.

Nested function A function that is contained inside another function. The inner function is evaluated first and the result becomes the argument for the outer function.

NOT function A logical function that takes only one argument and is used to test one condition. If the condition is true, the function returns the logical opposite false. If the condition is false, true is returned.

Objective cell In Solver, a cell that contains a formula for the results you are trying to determine.

OR function A logical function that can be used to develop compound logical tests using up to 255 arguments. The function returns a value of TRUE if ANY of the conditions are met.

Scenario A set of values that Excel saves and can substitute automatically in your worksheet.

Scenario Manager A what-if analysis tool that compares alternatives.

Solver A what-if analysis tool with which you can find an optimal (maximum or minimum) value for a formula in one cell—referred to as the objective cell—subject to constraints, or limits, on the values of other formula cells on a worksheet.

SUMIF function A logical function that contains one logic test—it will add values in a specified range that meet certain conditions or criteria.

SUMIFS function A logical function that will add values in multiple ranges that meet multiple criteria.

Syntax The arrangement of the arguments in a function.

Transpose To switch the data in rows and columns.

Variable cell In Solver, a cell in which the value will change to achieve the desired results.

Variable expense Expense that varies depending on the amount of sales.

CHAPTER REVIEW

Skills Review   Project 8C Orlando Sales

Apply 8A skills from these Objectives:

1 Calculate a Moving Average
2 Project Income and Expenses
3 Determine a Break-Even Point

In the following Skills Review, you will create a worksheet for Kelsey Tanner, the Chief Financial Officer of Brina's Bistro, who wants to see how sales have grown in the first six weeks at the new restaurant in Orlando, Florida. Your completed worksheets will look similar to Figure 8.46.

PROJECT FILES

For Project 8C, you will need the following file:

e08C_Orlando_Sales

You will save your workbook as:

Lastname_Firstname_8C_Orlando_Sales

PROJECT RESULTS

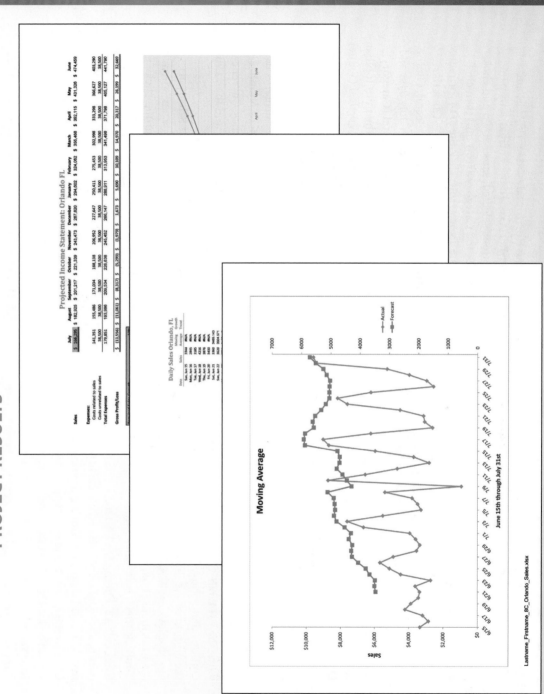

Lastname_Firstname_8C_Orlando_Sales.xlsx

FIGURE 8.46

(Project 8C Orlando Sales continues on the next page)

CHAPTER REVIEW

1 Start Excel. From your student files, open the file e08C_Orlando_Sales, and then in your Excel Chapter 8 folder, **Save** the file as **Lastname_Firstname_8C_Orlando_Sales**

a. Select the range **A3:AV4**. Right-click anywhere over the selection and click **Copy**. Click cell **A5**. Right-click and under **Paste Options**, click **Transpose (T)**. Delete rows **2:4**. In cell **C2** type **Moving Average** In cell **D2** type **Growth Trend** Select the range **A2:D2** and apply the **Heading 3** cell style and, in the **Alignment group**, click **Wrap Text**. Click cell **A3**. On the **HOME tab**, in the **Number group**, click the **Dialog Box Launcher**. In the **Format Cells** dialog box, be sure the **Number tab** is selected. Under **Category**, click **Custom**. Select the code in the **Type** box and type **ddd, mmm dd** to replace it. Click **OK**, and then drag the fill handle to copy the new format down through cell **A49**. Press Ctrl + Home.

b. Click the **FILE tab**, click **Options**. In the **Excel Options** dialog box, on the left, click **Add-Ins**. At the bottom of the dialog box, verify that the **Manage** box displays *Excel Add-ins*, and then click **Go**. In the **Add-Ins** dialog box, if necessary, select the **Analysis ToolPak** check box. Click **OK**.

c. Click cell **A2**. On the **DATA tab**, in the **Analysis group**, click **Data Analysis**. Scroll the list as necessary, and then click **Moving Average**. Click **OK**. Click in the **Input Range box**, type **b2:b49** and then select the **Labels in First Row** check box. Click in the **Interval box**, and then type **7** Click in the **Output Range box**, type **c3** and then select the **Chart Output** check box. Click **OK**.

d. Click the outer edge of the chart to select it and then, on the **DESIGN tab**, in the **Location group**, click **Move Chart**. Click **New sheet**, type **Sales Trend Chart** and then click **OK**. At the bottom of the chart, point to any of the data points to display the ScreenTip *Horizontal (Category) Axis*, and then click to select the axis. On the **DESIGN tab**, in the **Data group**, click **Select Data**. In the **Select Data Source** dialog box, click **Edit**. Display the **Sales** worksheet, and then select the range **A3:A49**. In the **Axis Labels** dialog box, click **OK**. In the **Select Data Source** dialog box, click **OK**.

e. Right-click the **Horizontal (Category)Axis**, and then click **Format Axis**. In the **Format Axis** pane, with **Axis Options** selected, scroll down and click **Number**, click the **Category arrow** and then click **Date**. Click the **Type arrow**, click the **3/14** format, and then **Close** the **Format Axis** pane. Click the **Horizontal (Category)Axis Title** to select it. On the **Formula Bar** type **June 15th through July 31st** and then press Enter. Point to the **Horizontal (Category) Axis Title**, triple-click, and then on the mini toolbar, change the font size to **12**. Click the **Vertical (Value) Axis Title** to select it. On the **Formula Bar** type **Sales** and then press Enter. Point to the **Vertical (Value) Axis Title**, double-click, and then on the mini toolbar, change the font size to **12**. Right-click the **Vertical (Value) Axis**, and then click **Format Axis**. In the **Format Axis** pane, scroll down to **Number**, click the **Category arrow**, and then click **Currency**. If necessary, set **Decimal places to 0**, and then **Close** the **Format Axis** pane.

f. On the **FORMAT tab**, in the **Current Selection group**, click the **Chart Elements arrow**, and then click **Series "Forecast"**. In the same group click **Format Selection**. In the **Format Data Series** pane, if necessary, click the **Series Options** icon. Under **Plot Series on**, click **Secondary Axis. Close** the **Format Data Series** pane.

g. Display the **Sales** worksheet. Click cell **D21**, and then type **=(c21-c14)/c14** Press Enter. Scroll to position **row 21** near the top of your screen. Point to cell **D21**, right-click, and then on the mini toolbar, click **Percent Style**. Click **Increase Decimal** one time to display one decimal. With cell **D21** still selected, point to the cell and right-click, and then click **Copy**. Point to cell **D28**, right-click, and then click **Paste**. In the same manner, paste it in cells **D35**, **D42**, and **D49**.

2 Click cell **A51**, type **July Sales** Click cell **B51**, type **=sum(b19:b49)** and then press Enter. Display the **Projected Income** worksheet. Click cell **B3**. Type **=** click the **Sales sheet tab**, click cell **B51**, the July sales total, click **Enter**. On the **Projected Income** worksheet, click cell **B2**, and then use the fill handle to fill the months for a year—from July to June—across to **column M**. With the range **B2:M2** selected, apply **Center**.

(Project 8C Orlando Sales continues on the next page)

CHAPTER REVIEW

Skills Review   Project 8C Orlando Sales (continued)

a. Click cell **B3**; in the **Formula Bar**, notice the cell reference. Click cell C3, type **=b3*(1+b12)** and then click Enter. Apply the **Currency [0]** cell style. Use the fill handle to copy the formula in cell C3 across the row to cell **M3**.

b. Click cell **B6** and examine the formula. Use the fill handle to copy the formula from cell **B6** across the row to cell **M6**. **Copy** the value in cell **B7** across the row to cell **M7**. Select the range **C8:M8**, and then on the **HOME tab**, in the **Editing group**, click **AutoSum. Copy** the formula in cell **B10** across the row to cell **M10**.

3 In the lower right corner of your screen, if necessary, set the **Zoom** to **80%** so that **columns A:M** display on your screen. Select the range **A2:M3**. On the **INSERT tab**, in the **Charts group**, click **Recommended Charts**. In the **Insert Chart** dialog box, with the **Line chart** selected, click **OK**.

a. On the **DESIGN tab**, in the **Data group**, click **Select Data**. In the **Select Data Source** dialog box, under **Legend Entries (Series)**, click **Add**. With the insertion point in the **Series name** box, click cell **A8**. Press [Tab], select the range **B8:M8** and then click **OK**. Verify that the **Chart data range** is *$A2:$M3* and *$A8:$M8*. Click **OK**. Click **Chart Title**, and then type **Expected Break-Even Point** Press [Enter].

b. Drag to position the upper left corner of the chart inside the upper left corner of cell **B15**. Scroll to position **row 13** near the top of your screen. Drag the lower right corner of the chart inside the lower right corner of cell **M36**.

c. On the **DESIGN tab**, apply **Chart Style 12**. On the left side of the chart, right-click the **Value (Value) Axis**, and then click **Format Axis**. In the **Format Axis** pane verify that **Axis Options** is selected. Under **AXIS OPTIONS**, in the **Minimum** box, type

150000 Press [Enter]. In the same manner, change the **Maximum** value to **500000**

d. Format both the **Plot Area** and the **Chart Area** with a **Solid fill** using the color **Light Yellow, Background 2. Close** the **Format Chart Area** pane.

e. Display the **Sales Trend Chart** worksheet. On this chart sheet, insert a custom footer with the file name in the **left section**.

4 Display the **Projected Income** worksheet, click anywhere outside the chart, and then, if necessary, set the **Zoom** back to **100%**. Right-click the **sheet tab**, and then click **Select All Sheets** so that *[Group]* displays in the title bar. With the worksheets grouped, insert a footer in the **left section** that includes the file name. Click the cell above the footer to deselect it.

a. On the **PAGE LAYOUT tab**, set the **Orientation** to **Landscape**, and then, set the **Width** to **1 page**, and the **Height** to **1 page**. Center the worksheets horizontally on the page. On the status bar, click **Normal**. Press [Ctrl] + [Home] to move to the top of the worksheet.

b. Display the **document properties** and under **Related People**, be sure that your name displays as the author. If necessary, right-click the author name, click **Edit Property**, and then type your name. In the **Subject** box, type your course name and section #, and in the **Tags** box, type **Orlando, break-even** Display the grouped worksheets in **Print Preview**; if necessary, return to the workbook and make any necessary corrections or adjustments. Ungroup the worksheets.

c. **Save** your workbook, and then **Print** the three worksheets or submit your workbook electronically as directed. If required, print or create an electronic version of your worksheets with formulas displayed. **Close** Excel.

END | You have completed Project 8C

CHAPTER REVIEW

Skills Review | Project 8D Charlotte Staffing

Apply 8B skills from these Objectives:

4 Use Solver
5 Create Scenarios
6 Use Logical Functions
7 Create Complex Formulas

In the following Skills Review, you will assist Stephanie Wheaton, manager of the Charlotte restaurant, in determining the most efficient work schedule for the evening server staff. Your completed worksheets will look similar to Figure 8.47.

PROJECT FILES

For Project 8D, you will need the following file:

e08D_Charlotte_Staffing

You will save your workbook as:

Lastname_Firstname_8D_Charlotte_Staffing

Build from Scratch

PROJECT RESULTS

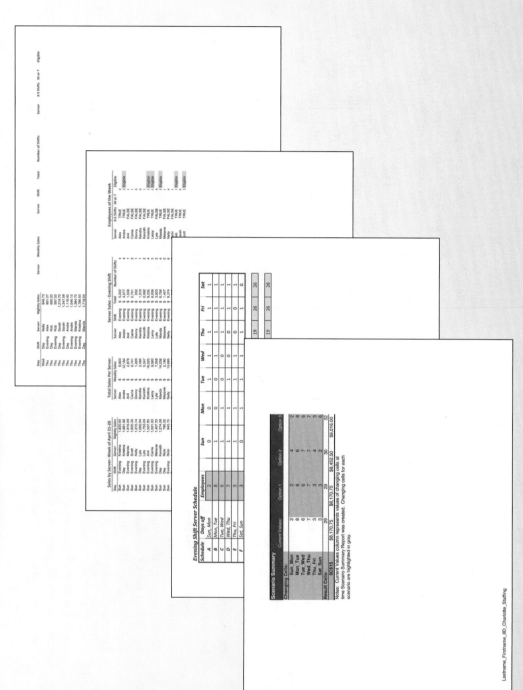

Lastname_Firstname_8D_Charlotte_Staffing

FIGURE 8.47

(Project 8D Charlotte Staffing continues on the next page)

CHAPTER REVIEW

Skills Review   Project 8D Charlotte Staffing (continued)

1 Start Excel. Click the **DATA tab**, and then at the right end of the **DATA tab**, check to see if the **Analysis group** and **Solver** display. If **Solver** displays, Solver is installed; move to Step a. If Solver does *not* display, on the **DATA FILE tab**, click **Options**. On the left, click **Add-Ins**, and then at the bottom of the screen, in the **Manage** box, if necessary, select **Excel Add-ins**. Click **Go**. Select the **Solver Add-in** check box, and then click **OK**.

a. From your student files, open the file **e08D_ Charlotte_Staffing**. Display the **Save As** dialog box, navigate to your Excel Chapter 8 folder, and then **Save** the workbook as **Lastname_Firstname_8D_Charlotte_Staffing**

b. Examine the formulas in cells C10, C14, and C15. Click cell C3, and then click the **Name Box arrow**; notice that cell C3 is named *Sun_Mon* and the other schedules also have been named.

c. Click cell **C15**—the objective cell. On the **DATA tab**, in the **Analysis group**, click **Solver**.

d. To the right of **To**, click **Min**. Click in the **By Changing Variable Cells** box, and then select the range **C3:C8**. To the right of the **Subject to the Constraints** area, click **Add** to add the first constraint. With the insertion point blinking in the **Cell Reference** box, select the range **C3:C8**. In the middle box, click the **arrow**, and then click **int**. Click **OK**—the result must be a whole number.

e. Click **Add** to add the second constraint. With the insertion point in the **Cell Reference** box, select the range **C3:C8**. In the middle box, click the **arrow**, and then click **>=**. In the **Constraint** box, type **0** Click **OK**.

f. Click **Add** to add the third constraint. In the **Cell Reference** box, select the range **E10:K10**. In the middle box, click the **arrow**, and then click **>=**. In the **Constraint** box, select the range **E12:K12**. Click **OK**; the result must be equal to or greater than the demand for each day. At the bottom of the **Solver Parameters** dialog box, click **Solve**. With **Keep Solver Solution** selected, click **OK**. Cell C15 indicates *$8,170.75*.

2 Select the range **C3:C8**. On the **DATA tab**, in the **Data Tools group**, click **What-If Analysis**, and then click **Scenario Manager**. In the **Scenario Manager** dialog box, click **Add**. In the **Scenario Name** box, type **Option 1** Verify

that the **Changing cells** box displays C3:C8. Click **OK**. In the **Scenario Values** dialog box, click **OK**. In the **Scenario Manager** dialog box, click **Close**.

a. Click cell C15—the objective cell. On the **DATA tab**, in the **Analysis group**, click **Solver**. In the **Solver Parameters** dialog box, verify that the **Set Objective** box displays *$C$15* and the **By Changing Variable Cells** box displays *$C$3:$C$8*.

b. To the right of **Subject to the Constraints** box, click **Add** to add an additional constraint. In the **Add Constraint** dialog box, click the **Cell Reference** box, and then click cell C3. In the middle box, click the **arrow**, and then click **=**. In the **Constraint** box, type **4** Click **OK**; this constraint will raise the number of employees who have Sunday and Monday off to 4.

c. In the lower right corner of the dialog box, click **Solve**. Click **Save Scenario** to display the **Save Scenario** dialog box. In the **Scenario Name** box, type **Option 2** and then click **OK**. In the **Solver Results** dialog box, click **Restore Original Values**, and then click **OK**.

d. Verify that cell C15 is still the active cell. On the **DATA tab**, in the **Analysis group**, click **Solver**. In the **Subject to the Constraints** box, select the fourth constraint—*Sun_Mon = 4*—and then click **Delete** to delete this constraint.

e. Click **Add**. In the **Add Constraint** dialog box, click in the **Cell Reference** box, and then select cell C8. Change the middle box to **=**. In the **Constraint** box, type **6** and then click **OK**; this constraint will raise the number of employees who have Saturday and Sunday off to 6.

f. Click **Solve**. Click **Save Scenario**. In the **Save Scenario** dialog box, type **Option 3** and then click **OK**. Click **Restore Original Values**, and then click **OK**.

g. On the **DATA tab**, in the **Data Tools group**, click **What-If Analysis**, and then click **Scenario Manager**. In the **Scenario Manager** dialog box, click **Summary**. Be sure **Scenario Summary** is selected, and then click **OK** to summarize the three options on a new worksheet. Select the range **D12:G12** and then, on the **HOME tab**, in the **Editing group**, click **AutoSum**.

3 Display the **Weekly Sales** worksheet. Click cell G3, and then type **=sumif(** Select the range C3:C102 and

(Project 8D Charlotte Staffing continues on the next page)

CHAPTER REVIEW

press [F4] to make the value absolute. Type , (a comma). Click cell F3, and then type , (a comma). Select the range D3:D102 and press [F4]. Type) and then, on the Formula Bar, click Enter.

a. Drag the fill handle to copy the formula down through cell G19. Format the range G3:G19 using cell style Currency [0].

b. Select the range F3:F19. Right-click over the selection and click Copy. Right-click cell I3 and click Paste (P). Click cell J3, and then type Evening and then copy the cell down through I19.

c. Click cell K3 and type =sumifs(Select the range D3:D102 and press [F4] to make the value absolute. Type , (a comma), select the range C3:C102, and press [F4]. Type , (a comma). Click cell I3, and then type , (a comma). Select the range B3:B102 and then press [F4]. Type , (a comma) and then click cell J3. Type) and then click Enter. Drag the fill handle to copy the formula down through cell K19. Format the range K3:K19 using cell style Currency [0].

d. Click cell L3 and type =countifs(Select the range C3:C102 and press [F4] to make the value absolute. Type , (a comma), click cell I3, and then type , (a comma). Select the range B3:B102, and then press [F4]. Type , (a comma) and then click cell J3. Type) and then click Enter. Drag the fill handle to copy the formula down through cell L19.

4 Click cell N1 and type Employees of the Week and press [Enter]. Merge & Center the text over cells N1:Q1 and apply the Heading 2 cell style. In cell N2 type Server In cell O2 type 3-5 Shifts In cell P3 type M or T Copy the server names from I3:I19 to N3:N19.

a. Select the range A3:A102, in the Name Box, type DAY and then press [Enter]. Select the range B3:B102, in the Name Box, type SHIFT and then press [Enter]. Select the range C3:C102, in the Name Box, type SERVER and then press [Enter].

b. In cell O3, type =and(Click cell L3, type >=3, (include the comma). Click cell L3 and type <=5) Click Enter and copy the formula down through cell O19.

c. Click cell P3, and then type the formula =countifs(server,n3,day,"Mon") Click Enter and copy the formula down through cell P19. Click cell P3 and in the Formula Bar, position the insertion point at the end of the formula. Type +countifs(server,n3,day,"Tue") Click Enter and copy the formula down through cell P19.

d. Click cell Q2, type Eligible and then press [Enter]. In cell Q3, type =if(and(o3, p3>=1),"Eligible", "") Click Enter and copy the formula down through cell Q19.

e. Press [Ctrl] + [Q] to open Quick Analysis at the bottom of the selection, and then click Text Contains. In the Text That Contains dialog box, in the Format cells that contain the text box type Eligible Click the with arrow, and then click Green Fill with Dark Green Text. Click OK. On the PAGE LAYOUT tab, click Print Titles. Under Print Titles, click in the Rows to repeat at top box, and then from the row heading area, select row 2. Click OK.

5 Select all worksheets so that [Group] displays in the title bar. With the worksheets grouped, insert a footer in the left section that includes the file name. On the status bar, click Normal. Press [Ctrl] + [Home].

a. Set the Orientation to Landscape. Center the worksheets horizontally on the page and set the Width to 1 page. Display the document properties and under Related People, be sure that your name displays as the author. If necessary, right-click the author name, click Edit Property, and then type your name. In the Subject box, type your course name and section #, and in the Tags box, Charlotte, server schedule

b. Display the grouped worksheets in Print Preview. If necessary, return to the workbook and make any necessary corrections or adjustments. Save your workbook. Print or submit the two worksheets in this workbook electronically as directed by your instructor. If required, print or create an electronic version of your worksheets with formulas displayed. Close Excel.

END | You have completed Project 8D

CONTENT-BASED ASSESSMENTS

MyITLab® grader

Apply 8A skills from these Objectives:

1 Calculate a Moving Average

2 Project Income and Expenses

3 Determine a Break-Even Point

Mastering Excel | Project 8E Seafood Inventory

In this Mastering Excel project, you will create a worksheet for Joe Flores, manager of the Dallas region, who wants to analyze the fluctuation in the quantity of shrimp that is used at the four Dallas restaurants. In this project, you will use the moving average tool to help identify the variation in shrimp usage in recipes over a four-week period. Your completed worksheets will look similar to Figure 8.48.

PROJECT FILES

For Project 8E, you will need the following file:

e08E_Seafood_Inventory

You will save your workbook as:

Lastname_Firstname_8E_Seafood_Inventory

PROJECT RESULTS

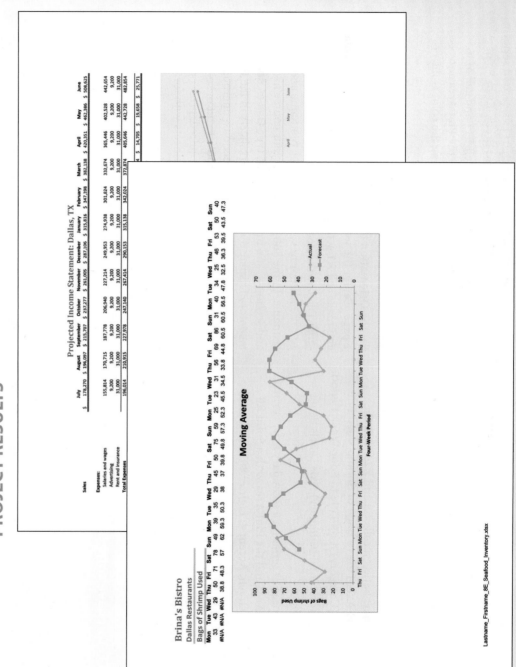

Lastname_Firstname_8E_Seafood_Inventory.xlsx

FIGURE 8.48

(Project 8E Seafood Inventory continues on the next page)

CONTENT-BASED ASSESSMENTS

Mastering Excel Project 8E Seafood Inventory (continued)

1 Start Excel. From your student files, open the file **e08E_Seafood Inventory**, and then **Save** it in your **Excel Chapter 8** folder as **Lastname_Firstname_8E_Seafood_Inventory** Be sure that the Analysis ToolPak is enabled.

2 On the **Moving Average** worksheet, insert a **Moving Average a5:ab5** as the **Input Range**, **4** as the **Interval**, and **a6** as the **Output Range**. Select the **Chart Output** check boxes. Do not select the **Labels in First Row** check box. Position the chart between cells **C8** and **Z29**. Edit the **Vertical (value) Axis Title** to **Bags of Shrimp Used** Edit the **Horizontal (Category) Axis Title** to **Four-Week Period**.

3 Edit the **Horizontal (Category) Axis Labels** using the range **A4:AB4**.

4 Plot the **Forecast series on a secondary axis**. Format both the **Chart Area** and the **Plot Area** with a **Solid fill** using the color **Green, Accent 4, Lighter 80%**. Format the range **D6:AB6** with **0** decimal places.

5 Display the **Projected Income** worksheet. Click cell **C3**, type **=b3*(1+b13)** and **Copy** the formula across to cell **M3**. **Copy** the formula in cell **B9** across to cell **M9**. Select the range **A2:M3**, and then insert a **Line chart**.

Add the range **A9:M9** to the Line chart as a second series. Change the **Chart Title** to **Expected Break-Even Point**

6 Position the chart between cell **B15** and cell **M36**. Apply **Chart Style 12**. Format both the **Plot Area** and the **Chart Area** with a **Solid fill** using the color **Gold, Accent 1, Lighter 80%**.

7 Deselect the chart. Select all the sheets and insert a footer in the **left section** that includes the file name. Set the **Orientation** to **Landscape**, and set the **Width to 1 page**. Center the worksheets horizontally. Click **Normal** and make cell **A1** active.

8 Display the **document properties** and, if necessary, edit the **Author** box, to display your firstname and your lastname. In the **Subject** box, type your course name and section #, and in the **Tags** box, type **Dallas, seafood inventory** Display the grouped worksheets in the **Print Preview**, make any necessary corrections, ungroup the worksheets, and **Save** your workbook. **Print** or submit your workbook electronically. If required, print or create an electronic version of your worksheets with formulas displayed.

END | You have completed Project 8E

CONTENT-BASED ASSESSMENTS

MyITLab®
grader

Apply 8B skills from these Objectives:

4 Use Solver
5 Create Scenarios
6 Use Logical Functions
7 Create Complex Formulas

Mastering Excel   Project 8F Seafood Chowder

In this Mastering Excel project, you will assist Jillian Zachary, manager of the Ft. Lauderdale East restaurant, by using Solver to create several scenarios for how much of each of the three seafood ingredients—scallops, shrimp, and fish—to include in the chowder at the new seasonal prices to maintain a profit margin of 35 percent on a serving of chowder at the current wholesale seafood costs. Your completed worksheet will look similar to Figure 8.49.

PROJECT FILES

For Project 8F, you will need the following file:

e08F_Seafood_Chowder

You will save your workbook as:

Lastname_Firstname_8F_Seafood_Chowder

Build from Scratch

PROJECT RESULTS

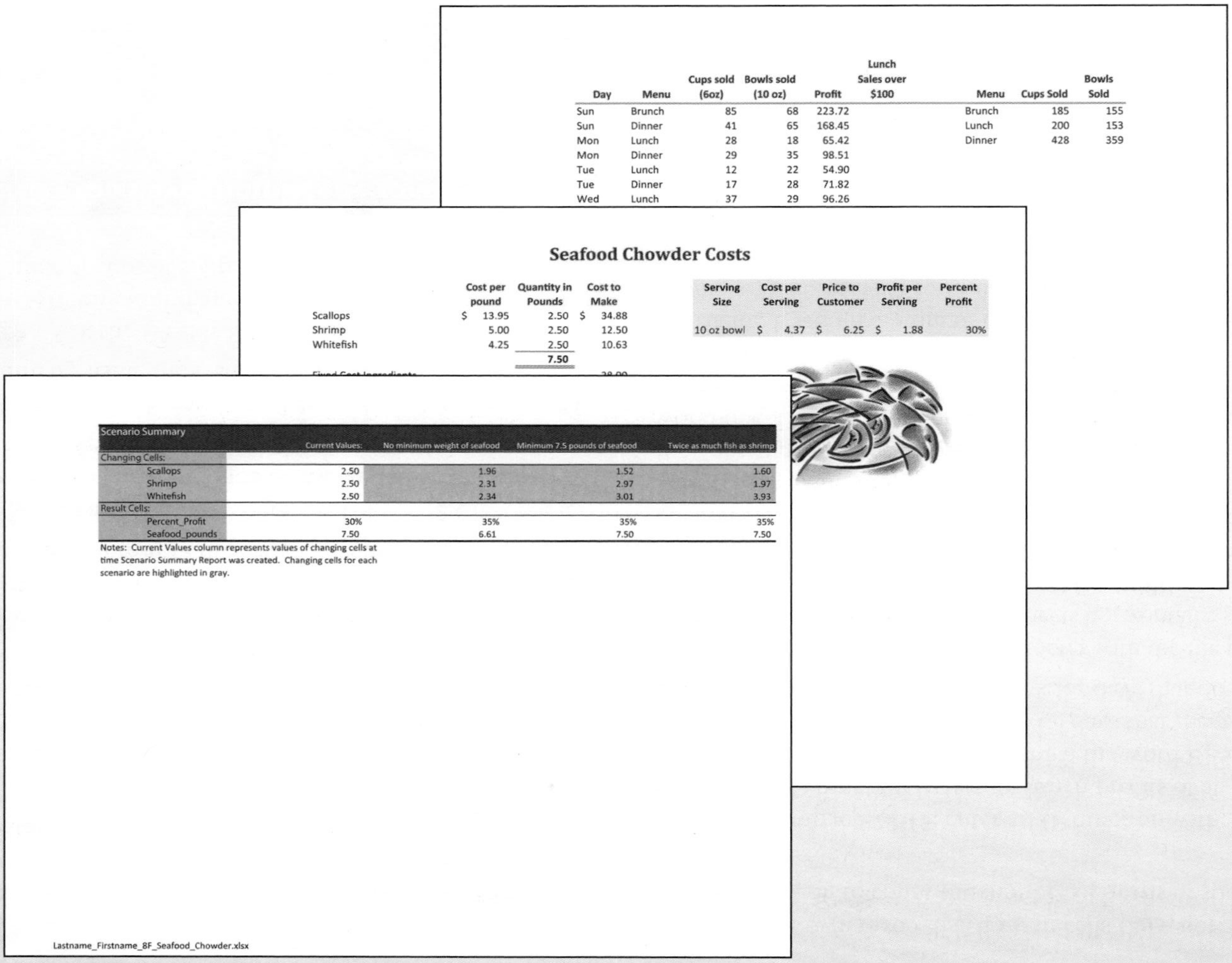

Day	Menu	Cups sold (6oz)	Bowls sold (10 oz)	Profit	Lunch Sales over $100
Sun	Brunch	85	68	223.72	
Sun	Dinner	41	65	168.45	
Mon	Lunch	28	18	65.42	
Mon	Dinner	29	35	98.51	
Tue	Lunch	12	22	54.90	
Tue	Dinner	17	28	71.82	
Wed	Lunch	37	29	96.26	

Menu	Cups Sold	Bowls Sold
Brunch	185	155
Lunch	200	153
Dinner	428	359

Seafood Chowder Costs

	Cost per pound	Quantity in Pounds	Cost to Make
Scallops	$ 13.95	2.50	$ 34.88
Shrimp	5.00	2.50	12.50
Whitefish	4.25	2.50	10.63
		7.50	

Serving Size	Cost per Serving	Price to Customer	Profit per Serving	Percent Profit
10 oz bowl	$ 4.37	$ 6.25	$ 1.88	30%

Scenario Summary				
	Current Values:	No minimum weight of seafood	Minimum 7.5 pounds of seafood	Twice as much fish as shrimp
Changing Cells:				
Scallops	2.50	1.96	1.52	1.60
Shrimp	2.50	2.31	2.97	1.97
Whitefish	2.50	2.34	3.01	3.93
Result Cells:				
Percent_Profit	30%	35%	35%	35%
Seafood_pounds	7.50	6.61	7.50	7.50

Notes: Current Values column represents values of changing cells at time Scenario Summary Report was created. Changing cells for each scenario are highlighted in gray.

Lastname_Firstname_8F_Seafood_Chowder.xlsx

FIGURE 8.49

(Project 8F Seafood Chowder continues on the next page)

CONTENT-BASED ASSESSMENTS

Mastering Excel | Project 8F Seafood Chowder (continued)

1 Start Excel. From your student files, open the file **e08F_Seafood_Chowder**, and then **Save** the file in your Excel Chapter 8 folder as **Lastname_Firstname_8F_Seafood_Chowder** Be sure that **Solver** is installed.

2 With the **Seafood Chowder Costs** worksheet active, open **Solver.** Set the objective cell **$J$5** to the value of **35%** and set the variable cells to the range **C4:C6.** **Save** the scenario as **No minimum weight of seafood** and then restore the original values.

3 Open **Solver.** Add a constraint where cell **C7 >= 7.5** Click **Solve. Save** the scenario as **Minimum 7.5 pounds of seafood** and restore the original values.

4 Add a constraint where cell **C6 = c5*2** Click **Solve. Save** the scenario as **Twice as much fish as shrimp Save** Restore the original values.

5 Open the **Scenario Manager** and create a Scenario Summary using the result cells **J5** and **C7.**

6 Click the **Weekly Sales** worksheet. In cell **I2,** enter a SUMIF function that uses Named Ranges to count the number of cups of soup sold for each menu and copy

the formula down through cell **I4.** In cells **J2:J4,** enter a **SUMIF** function to count the number of bowls of soup sold for each shift.

7 In the range **F2:F15,** enter an **IF** function with a nested **AND** function to test for lunch profits of at least $100. The function should return the word **BEST,** formatted with a red border for those days that meet both conditions, and leave the cells blank for days that do not.

8 Select **All Sheets** and insert a footer with the file name in the **left section,** center the worksheets horizontally, set the **Orientation** to **Landscape,** and then set the **Width** to **1 page.** Return to **Normal** view and make cell **A1** active. Display the **document properties,** add your name as the author; type your course name and section # in the **Subject** box, and as the **Tags,** type **seafood chowder, recipe costs Save** your workbook. Display and examine the **Print Preview,** make any necessary corrections, ungroup the worksheets, **Save,** and then **Print** or submit electronically as directed by your instructor. If required, print or create an electronic version of your worksheets with formulas displayed.

END | You have completed Project 8F

CONTENT-BASED ASSESSMENTS

Mastering Excel   Project 8G Income Model

MyITLab®
grader

Apply 8A and 8B skills from these Objectives:

1 Calculate a Moving Average
2 Project Income and Expenses
3 Determine a Break-Even Point
4 Use Solver
5 Create Scenarios
6 Use Logical Functions
7 Create Complex Formulas

In this Mastering Excel project, you will assist Kelsey Tanner, CFO of Brina's Bistro, and use a worksheet model and use Solver to create several scenarios that would result in breaking even six months after opening. In this model for projecting the income, a new restaurant is expected to break even eight months after opening. Management wants to examine the assumptions and see what changes are needed to shorten the time it takes to break even. Month 0 is the first month of operation and it assumes that a new restaurant will gross $156,250 in sales in the opening month. The costs related to sales are assumed to be 87 percent; fixed costs are $40,000; and the anticipated growth rate in the first year, month-to-month, is 10 percent. The worksheet extends these assumptions out to month 11, which is the end of the first year of operation. Your completed worksheets will look similar to Figure 8.50.

PROJECT FILES

For Project 8G, you will need the following file:

e08G_Income_Model

You will save your workbook as:

Lastname_Firstname_8G_Income_Model

PROJECT RESULTS

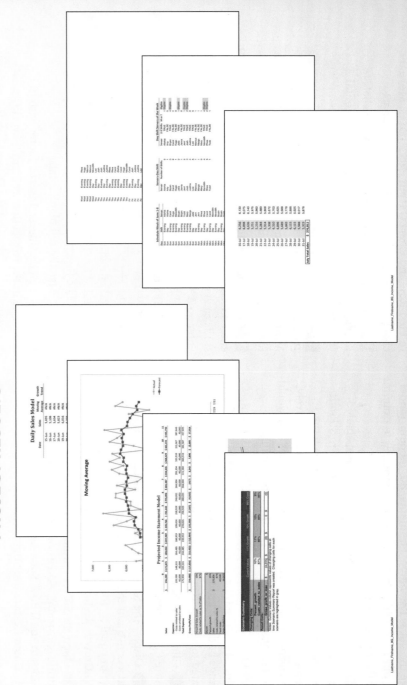

FIGURE 8.50

(Project 8G Income Model continues on the next page)

Project 8G: Income Model | Excel   **501**

CONTENT-BASED ASSESSMENTS

Mastering Excel   Project 8G Income Model (continued)

1 From your student files, open e08G_Income_Model. Save the file as **Lastname_Firstname_8G_Income_Model** in your **Excel Chapter 8** folder. Take a moment to examine the **Projected Income** worksheet.

2 Change cell **B15** to **6** Notice in the green shaded area that *Sales* changes to *$276,806* and the *Gross Profit/Loss* changes to (*$4,015*). Note that these match the figures under Month 6 in cells **H3** and **H10**, respectively. Management wants to create several scenarios that would result in breaking even six months after opening.

3 Open **Solver**. Set the **objective cell** to *$B$20* to a **Value of 0** and set the **Variable Cells** to *$B$16,$B$18* to change both the growth rate (in cell **B16**) and the costs related to sales percent (in cell **B18**).

4 Click **Solve**. **Save** this scenario as **11% Growth** and restore the original values.

5 Display the **Solver Parameters** dialog box again. Add a constraint that requires **Percent growth** to be less than or equal to **10% Solve** and then **Save** this scenario as **10% Growth** Restore the original values.

6 Open the **Solver Parameters** dialog box. Delete the existing constraint. Add a constraint for the **Costs related to sales** to equal **85% Solve** and then **Save** the scenario as **85% Costs** Restore the original values.

7 Open the **Scenario Manager**. Create a **Scenario Summary** worksheet with a summary of the scenarios.

8 Display the **Projected Income** worksheet. Select the range **A2:M3**, insert a **Line chart**, and then, add the range **A8:M8** to the chart as a second series. Change the **Chart Title** to **Expected Break-Even Point** Position the chart between cell **B22** and cell **L40**. Format both the **Plot Area** and the **Chart Area** with a **Solid fill** using the color **Olive Green, Accent 4, Lighter 80%**. Add a **Horizontal (Category) Axis Title** with the text **Month Number**

9 Display the **Sales** worksheet. Create a **Moving Average**. As the **Input Range**, type **b2:b49** as the **Interval**

type **7** and as the **Output Range** type **c3** Select the **Labels in First Row** and **Chart Output** check boxes. Move the chart to a new sheet named **Sales Trend Chart**

10 Edit the **Horizontal (Category) Axis Labels** to display the range **A9:A49**. Format the **Horizontal (Category) Axis** using the 3/14 **Date** format.

11 On the **Horizontal (Category) Axis**, change *Data Point* to **Date** On the **Vertical (Value) Axis**, set the *Minimum* to **3500** On this chart sheet, insert a custom footer with the file name in the **left section**.

12 Click the **Schedules sheet tab**. In the range **F3:F19**, enter a **COUNTIFS** function to count the number of day shifts each server is scheduled to work. In the range **I3:I19**, enter an **AND** function to determine which servers are scheduled for 2–5 day shifts. In the range **J3:J19**, enter a **COUNTIFS** function to calculate the number of Monday and Tuesday shifts each server is scheduled to work.

13 In the range **K3:K19**, enter an **IF** function with a nested **AND** function to determine which employees are scheduled for 2–5 day shifts, including a Monday or Tuesday. The function should return the word **Eligible** if true, and leave the cell blank if false.

14 Select all the sheets. Insert a footer with the file name in the **left section**, center the worksheets horizontally, and then set the **Orientation to Landscape** and the **Width** to **1 page** and **Height** to **2 pages**. Return to **Normal** view and make cell **A1** active. To the **document properties**, add your firstname and lastname as the **Author**, add your course name and section # as the **Subject**, and add **income, sales model** as the **Tags**. **Save** your workbook. Display and examine the **Print Preview**, make any necessary corrections, ungroup the worksheets, **Save**, and then **Print** or submit electronically as directed by your instructor. If required, print or create an electronic version of your worksheets with formulas displayed.

END | You have completed Project 8G

CONTENT-BASED ASSESSMENTS

GO! Fix It	Project 8H Maintenance Expenses	Online
GO! Make It	Project 8I Oyster Usage	Online
GO! Solve It	Project 8J Tampa Income	Online
GO! Solve It	Project 8K Oceana Salad	Online

PROJECT FILES

For Project 8K, you will need the following file:

e08K_Ahi_Salad

You will save your workbook as:

Lastname_Firstname_8K_Ahi_Salad

Open the file e08K_Ahi_Salad and save it as **Lastname_Firstname_8K_Ahi_Salad** Be sure that Solver is installed. Create three scenarios and a summary. Set the objective cell to J5, value of 60%. Solve for **No minimum weight of vegetables** by changing variable cells to the range C4:C6. Solve for **Minimum 5 pounds of vegetables** by using the constraints cell C5, >=, and 5. Solve for **Twice as many vegetables as greens** by using the constraints cell C5, =, C6*2. Create a Scenario Summary. On all sheets, insert the file name in the footer in the left section. Set the Orientation to Landscape, Width to 1 page, and center horizontally. Add appropriate information to the document properties including the tag **Ahi salad** and submit as directed by your instructor.

(Project 8K Oceana Salad continues on the next page)

CONTENT-BASED ASSESSMENTS

GO! Solve It   Project 8K Oceana Salad (continued)

Performance Level

Performance Criteria	Exemplary	Proficient	Developing
Use Solver to Create Scenarios	Three scenarios were created using Solver based on the instructions.	Two scenarios were created using Solver based on the instructions.	None or one scenario was created using Solver based on the instructions.
Create a Scenario Summary	A Scenario Summary listing three scenarios was created.	A Scenario Summary listing two scenarios was created.	A Scenario Summary was not created.

END | You have completed Project 8K

OUTCOMES-BASED ASSESSMENTS

RUBRIC

The following outcomes-based assessments are open-ended assessments. That is, there is no specific correct result; your result will depend on your approach to the information provided. Make Professional Quality your goal. Use the following scoring rubric to guide you in how to approach the problem and then to evaluate how well your approach solves the problem.

The *criteria*—Software Mastery, Content, Format and Layout, and Process—represent the knowledge and skills you have gained that you can apply to solving the problem. The *levels of performance*—Professional Quality, Approaching Professional Quality, or Needs Quality Improvements—help you and your instructor evaluate your result.

	Your completed project is of Professional Quality if you:	Your completed project is Approaching Professional Quality if you:	Your completed project Needs Quality Improvements if you:
1-Software Mastery	Choose and apply the most appropriate skills, tools, and features and identify efficient methods to solve the problem.	Choose and apply some appropriate skills, tools, and features, but not in the most efficient manner.	Choose inappropriate skills, tools, or features, or are inefficient in solving the problem.
2-Content	Construct a solution that is clear and well organized, contains content that is accurate, appropriate to the audience and purpose, and is complete. Provide a solution that contains no errors in spelling, grammar, or style.	Construct a solution in which some components are unclear, poorly organized, inconsistent, or incomplete. Misjudge the needs of the audience. Have some errors in spelling, grammar, or style, but the errors do not detract from comprehension.	Construct a solution that is unclear, incomplete, or poorly organized; contains some inaccurate or inappropriate content; and contains many errors in spelling, grammar, or style. Do not solve the problem.
3-Format & Layout	Format and arrange all elements to communicate information and ideas, clarify function, illustrate relationships, and indicate relative importance.	Apply appropriate format and layout features to some elements, but not others. Overuse features, causing minor distraction.	Apply format and layout that does not communicate information or ideas clearly. Do not use format and layout features to clarify function, illustrate relationships, or indicate relative importance. Use available features excessively, causing distraction.
4-Process	Use an organized approach that integrates planning, development, self-assessment, revision, and reflection.	Demonstrate an organized approach in some areas, but not others; or, use an insufficient process of organization throughout.	Do not use an organized approach to solve the problem.

OUTCOMES-BASED ASSESSMENTS

Apply a combination of the 8A and 8B skills

GO! Think | Project 8L Seasonings Inventory

PROJECT FILES

For Project 8L, you will need the following file:

e08L_Seasonings_Inventory

You will save your workbook as:

Lastname_Firstname_8L_Seasonings_Inventory

Open the file e08L_Seasonings_Inventory, and then save it in your chapter folder as **Lastname_Firstname_8L_Seasonings_Inventory** From the source data, create a Moving Average chart to help identify the variation in seafood seasoning used over a four-week period using a seven-day interval. Begin the output range in cell A6. Move the chart to a new sheet. Format the chart attractively. Insert the file name in the left section of the footer on each page, center horizontally, set the Orientation to Landscape, add appropriate information to the document properties, including the tag **seasonings inventory** and submit as directed by your instructor.

END | You have completed Project 8L

GO! Think | Project 8M PT Staff | Online

You and GO! | Project 8N Entertainment | Online

Build from Scratch

Glossary

3-D The shortened term for *three-dimensional*, which refers to an image that appears to have all three spatial dimensions—length, width, and depth.

Absolute cell reference A cell reference that refers to cells by their fixed position in a worksheet; an absolute cell reference remains the same when the formula is copied.

Accessibility Checker An Excel tool that finds any potential accessibility issues and creates a report so that you can resolve the issues to make your file easier for those with disabilities to use.

Accounting Number Format The Excel number format that applies a thousand comma separator where appropriate, inserts a fixed U.S. dollar sign aligned at the left edge of the cell, applies two decimal places, and leaves a small amount of space at the right edge of the cell to accommodate a parenthesis for negative numbers.

Active cell The cell, surrounded by a black border, ready to receive data or be affected by the next Excel command.

ActiveX control Graphic object, such as a check box or button, that you place on a form to display or enter data, perform an action, or make the form easier to read. When the person filling in the form clicks the ActiveX control, VBA code runs that automates a task or offers options.

Add-in An optional command or feature that is not immediately available; you must first install and/or activate an add-in to use it.

Additive The term that describes the behavior of a filter when each additional filter that you apply is based on the current filter, and that further reduces the number of records displayed.

Address bar (Internet Explorer) The area at the top of the Internet Explorer window that displays and where you can type a URL—Uniform Resource Locator—which is an address that uniquely identifies a location on the Internet.

Address bar (Windows) The bar at the top of a folder window with which you can navigate to a different folder or library, or go back to a previous one.

Advanced Filter A filter that can specify three or more criteria for a particular column, apply complex criteria to two or more columns, or specify computed criteria.

Alignment The placement of text or objects relative to the left and right margins.

Alignment guides Green lines that display when you move an object to assist in alignment.

Alt text Text used in documents and webpages to provide a text description of an image.

And comparison operator The comparison operator that requires each and every one of the comparison criteria to be true.

AND function A logical function that can be used to develop compound logical tests using up to 255 arguments. The function returns a result of TRUE if ALL of the conditions are met.

App The term that commonly refers to computer programs that run from the device software on a smartphone or a tablet computer—for example, iOS, Android, or Windows Phone—or computer programs that run from the browser software on a desktop PC or laptop PC—for example, Internet Explorer, Safari, Firefox, or Chrome.

App for Office A webpage that works within one of the Office applications, such as Excel, and that you download from the Office Store.

Apps for Office 2013 and SharePoint 2013 A collection of downloadable apps that enable you to create and view information within your familiar Office programs.

Arguments The values that an Excel function uses to perform calculations or operations.

Arithmetic operators The symbols +, -, *, /, %, and ^ used to denote addition, subtraction (or negation), multiplication, division, percentage, and exponentiation in an Excel formula.

Arrange All The command that tiles all open program windows on the screen.

Ascending The term that refers to the arrangement of text that is sorted alphabetically from A to Z, numbers sorted from lowest to highest, or dates and times sorted from earliest to latest.

Associated PivotTable report The PivotTable report in a workbook that is graphically represented in a PivotChart.

Auditing The process of examining a worksheet for errors in formulas.

Auto Fill An Excel feature that generates and extends values into adjacent cells based on the values of selected cells.

AutoCalculate A feature that displays three calculations in the status bar by default—Average, Count, and Sum—when you select a range of numerical data.

AutoComplete A feature that speeds your typing and lessens the likelihood of errors; if the first few characters you type in a cell match an existing entry in the column, Excel fills in the remaining characters for you.

AutoFilter menu A drop-down menu from which you can filter a column by a list of values, by a format, or by criteria.

AutoFit An Excel feature that adjusts the width of a column to fit the cell content of the widest cell in the column.

AutoSum A button that provides quick access to the SUM function.

AVERAGE function An Excel function that adds a group of values, and then divides the result by the number of values in the group.

Axis A line that serves as a frame of reference for measurement and that borders the chart plot area.

Background image An image inserted in a worksheet that is behind, not in the worksheet cells.

Backstage tabs The area along the left side of Backstage view with tabs to display screens with related groups of commands.

Backstage view A centralized space for file management tasks; for example, opening, saving, printing, publishing, or sharing a file. A navigation pane displays along the left side with tabs that group file-related tasks together.

Base The starting point when you divide the amount of increase by it to calculate the rate of increase.

Bevel A shape effect that uses shading and shadows to make the edges of a shape appear to be curved or angled.

Break-even point The point at which a company starts to make a profit.

Business Intelligence tools Tools that can be used to perform data analysis and create sophisticated charts and reports.

Canvas The area of a Power View worksheet that contains data visualizations.

Category axis The area along the bottom of a chart that identifies the categories of data; also referred to as the x-axis.

Category labels The labels that display along the bottom of a chart to identify the categories of data; Excel uses the row titles as the category names.

Cell The intersection of a column and a row.

Cell address Another name for a cell reference.

Cell content Anything typed into a cell.

Cell reference The identification of a specific cell by its intersecting column letter and row number.

Cell style A defined set of formatting characteristics, such as font, font size, font color, cell borders, and cell shading.

Center alignment The alignment of text or objects that is centered horizontally between the left and right margins.

Certificate authority A commercial organization that issues digital certificates, keeps track of who is assigned to a certificate, signs certificates to verify their validity, and tracks which certificates are revoked or expired.

Change history Information that is maintained about changes made in past editing sessions.

Chart The graphic representation of data in a worksheet; data presented as a chart is usually easier to understand than a table of numbers.

Chart area The entire chart and all of its elements.

Chart elements Objects that make up a chart.

Chart Elements button A button that enables you to add, remove, or change chart elements such as the title, legend, gridlines, and data labels.

Chart Filters button A button that enables you to change which data displays in the chart.

Chart layout The combination of chart elements that can be displayed in a chart such as a title, legend, labels for the columns, and the table of charted cells.

Chart sheet A workbook sheet that contains only a chart.

Chart style The overall visual look of a chart in terms of its graphic effects, colors, and backgrounds; for example, you can have flat or beveled columns, colors that are solid or transparent, and backgrounds that are dark or light.

Chart Styles button A button that enables you to set a style and color scheme for your chart.

Chart Styles gallery A group of predesigned chart styles that you can apply to an Excel chart.

Chart types Various chart formats used in a way that is meaningful to the reader; common examples are column charts, pie charts, and line charts.

Check box A type of ActiveX control that the person filling in the form can select to indicate a choice.

Circular reference An Excel error that occurs when a formula directly or indirectly refers to itself.

Clear Filter A button that removes a filter.

Click The action of pressing and releasing the left button on a mouse pointing device one time.

Clip art Downloadable predefined graphics available online from Office.com and other sites.

Clipboard A temporary storage area that holds text or graphics that you select and then cut or copy.

Cloud computing Refers to applications and services that are accessed over the Internet, rather than to applications that are installed on your local computer.

Cloud storage Online storage of data so that you can access your data from different places and devices.

Collaborate To work with others as a team in an intellectual endeavor to complete a shared task or to achieve a shared goal.

Collaboration In Excel, the process of working jointly with others to review, comment on, and make necessary changes to a shared workbook.

Column A vertical group of cells in a worksheet.

Column chart A chart in which the data is arranged in columns and that is useful for showing data changes over a period of time or for illustrating comparisons among items.

Column heading The letter that displays at the top of a vertical group of cells in a worksheet; beginning with the first letter of the alphabet, a unique letter or combination of letters identifies each column.

COLUMNS area An area to position fields that you want to display as columns in the PivotTable report. Field names placed here become column titles, and the data is grouped in columns by these titles.

Comma delimited file A file type that saves the contents of the cells by placing commas between them and an end-of-paragraph mark at the end of each row; also referred to as a CSV (comma separated values) file.

Comma Style The Excel number format that inserts thousand comma separators where appropriate and applies two decimal places; Comma Style also leaves space at the right to accommodate a parenthesis when negative numbers are present.

Commands An instruction to a computer program that causes an action to be carried out.

Common dialog boxes The set of dialog boxes that includes Open, Save, and Save As, which are provided by the Windows programming interface, and which display and operate in all of the Office programs in the same manner.

Comparison operators Symbols that evaluate each value to determine if it is the same (=), greater than (>), less than (<), or in between a range of values as specified by the criteria.

Compatibility Checker An Excel tool that finds any potential compatibility issues that might cause a significant loss of functionality or a minor loss of fidelity in an earlier version of Excel, and creates a report so that you can resolve the issues.

Compatibility Mode Using a workbook in Excel 97-2003 file format (.xls) instead of the newer XML-based file format (.xlsx).

Compound criteria The use of two or more criteria on the same row—all conditions must be met for the records to be included in the results.

Compound filter A filter that uses more than one condition—and one that uses comparison operators.

Compressed file A file that has been reduced in size and thus takes up less storage space and can be transferred to other computers quickly.

Compressed folder A folder that has been reduced in size and thus takes up less storage space and can be transferred to other computers quickly; also called a *zipped* folder.

CONCATENATE A text function used to join up to 255 strings of characters.

Conditional format A format that changes the appearance of a cell—for example, by adding cell shading or font color—based on a condition; if the condition is true, the cell is formatted based on that condition, and if the condition is false, the cell is *not* formatted.

Constant value Numbers, text, dates, or times of day that you type into a cell.

Constraint In Solver, a condition or restriction that must be met.

Constraint cell In Solver, a cell that contains a value that limits or restricts the outcome.

Context menus Menus that display commands and options relevant to the selected text or object; also called *shortcut menus*.

Context sensitive A command associated with the currently selected or active object; often activated by right-clicking a screen item.

Context-sensitive commands Commands that display on a shortcut menu that relate to the object or text that you right-clicked.

Contextual tabs Tabs that are added to the ribbon automatically when a specific object, such as a picture, is selected, and that contain commands relevant to the selected object.

Copy A command that duplicates a selection and places it on the Clipboard.

COUNT A statistical function that counts the number of cells in a range that contain numbers.

COUNTIF function A statistical function that counts the number of cells within a range that meet the given condition and that has two arguments—the range of cells to check and the criteria.

COUNTIFS function A logical function that counts the cells that meet specific criteria in multiple ranges.

Criteria Conditions that you specify in a logical function or filter.

Criteria range An area on your worksheet where you define the criteria for the filter, and that indicates how the displayed records are filtered.

CSV (comma separated values) file A file type in which the cells in each row are separated by commas and an end-of-paragraph mark at the end of each row; also referred to as a comma delimited file.

Custom filter A filter with which you can apply complex criteria to a single column.

Custom list A sort order that you can define.

Cut A command that removes a selection and places it on the Clipboard.

Cycle A category of SmartArt graphics that illustrates a continual process.

Data Facts about people, events, things, or ideas. Data is represented by text or numbers in a cell.

Data bar A cell format consisting of a shaded bar that provides a visual cue to the reader about the value of a cell relative to other cells; the length of the bar represents the value in the cell—a longer bar represents a higher value and a shorter bar represents s lower value.

Data connection A link to external data that automatically updates an Excel workbook from the original data whenever the original data source gets new information.

Data labels Labels that display the value, percentage, and/or category of each particular data point and can contain one or more of the choices listed—Series name, Category name, Value, or Percentage.

Data marker A column, bar, area, dot, pie slice, or other symbol in a chart that represents a single data point; related data points form a data series.

Data Model A method of incorporating data from multiple, related tables into an Excel worksheet.

Data point A value that originates in a worksheet cell and that is represented in a chart by a data marker.

Data series Related data points represented by data markers; each data series has a unique color or pattern represented in the chart legend.

Data table A range of cells that shows how changing certain values in your formulas affect the results of those formulas and that makes it easy to calculate multiple versions in one operation.

Data validation A technique by which you can control the type of data or the values that are entered into a cell by limiting the acceptable values to a defined list.

Database An organized collection of facts related to a specific topic or purpose.

DAVERAGE function A function that determines an average in a database that is limited by criteria set for one or more cells.

DCOUNT function A function that counts the number of occurrences of a specified condition in a database.

Decision variable In Solver, a cell in which the value will change to achieve the desired results.

Default The term that refers to the current selection or setting that is automatically used by a computer program unless you specify otherwise.

Defined name A word or string of characters in Excel that represents a cell, a range of cells, a formula, or a constant value; also referred to as simply a *name*.

Delimited A text file in which the text is separated by commas or tabs.

Dependent cells Cells that contain formulas that refer to other cells.

Descending The term that refers to the arrangement of text that is sorted alphabetically from Z to A, numbers sorted from highest to lowest, or dates and times sorted from latest to earliest.

Deselect The action of canceling the selection of an object or block of text by clicking outside of the selection.

Design mode An Excel mode or view in which you can work with ActiveX controls.

Desktop In Windows, the screen that simulates your work area.

Desktop app The term that commonly refers to a computer program that is installed on your computer and requires a computer operating system like Microsoft Windows or Apple OS to run.

Detail data The subtotaled rows that are totaled and summarized; typically adjacent to and either above or to the left of the summary data.

Detail sheets The worksheets that contain the details of the information summarized on a summary sheet.

Dialog box A small window that contains options for completing a task.

Dialog Box Launcher A small icon that displays to the right of some group names on the ribbon, and which opens a related dialog box or pane providing additional options and commands related to that group.

Digital certificate An electronic means of proving identity issued by a certificate authority.

Digital signature An electronic, encrypted, stamp of authentication. A means of proving identity and authenticity that ensures that a file originated from the signer and has not been changed.

Displayed value The data that displays in a cell.

Document Inspector An Excel feature that can find and remove hidden properties and personal information in a workbook.

Document properties Details about a file that describe or identify it, including the title, author name, subject, and keywords that identify the document's topic or contents; also known as *metadata*.

Drag The action of holding down the left mouse button while moving your mouse.

Drag and drop The action of moving a selection by dragging it to a new location.

DSUM function A function that sums a column of values in a database that is limited by criteria set for one or more cells.

Dual-axis chart A chart that has one series plotted on a secondary axis. Useful when comparing data series that use different scales or different types of measurements.

Edit The process of making changes to text or graphics in an Office file.

Ellipsis A set of three dots indicating incompleteness; an ellipsis following a command name indicates that a dialog box will display if you click the command.

Embed The action of inserting something created in one program into another program.

Embedded chart A chart that is inserted into the same worksheet that contains the data used to create the chart.

Encryption The process by which a file is encoded so that it cannot be opened without the proper password.

Enhanced ScreenTip A ScreenTip that displays more descriptive text than a normal ScreenTip.

Enterprise fund A municipal government fund that reports income and expenditures related to municipal services for which a fee is charged in exchange for goods or services.

Error Checking command A command that checks for common errors that occur in formulas.

Error value The result of a formula that Excel cannot evaluate correctly.

Event The action that causes a program or macro to run, such as clicking a button or a command or pressing a combination of keys.

Excel pointer An Excel window element with which you can display the location of the pointer.

Excel table A series of rows and columns that contains related data that is managed independently from the data in other rows and columns in the worksheet.

Expand Formula Bar button An Excel window element with which you can increase the height of the Formula Bar to display lengthy cell content.

Expand horizontal scroll bar button An Excel window element with which you can increase the width of the horizontal scroll bar.

Explode The action of pulling out one or more pie slices from a pie chart for emphasis.

Extensible Markup Language (XML) A language that structures data in text files so that it can be read by other systems, regardless of the hardware platform or operating system.

Extract The process of pulling out multiple sets of data for comparison purposes. Or, to decompress, or pull out, files from a compressed form.

Extract area The location to which you copy records when extracting filtered rows.

Field A specific type of data such as name, employee number, or social security number that is stored in columns.

Field button A button on a PivotChart with an arrow to choose a filter, and thus change the data that is displayed in the chart.

Field names The column titles from source data that form the categories of data for a PivotTable.

Field section The upper portion of the PivotTable Fields pane containing the fields—column titles—from your source data; use this area to add fields to and remove fields from the PivotTable.

File A collection of information stored on a computer under a single name, for example, a Word document or a PowerPoint presentation.

File Explorer The program that displays the files and folders on your computer, and which is at work anytime you are viewing the contents of files and folders in a window.

Fill The inside color of an object.

Fill handle The small black square in the lower right corner of a selected cell.

Filter The process of displaying only a portion of the data based on matching a specific value to show only the data that meets the criteria that you specify.

FILTER area An area in the lower portion of the PivotTable Fields pane to position fields by which you want to filter the PivotTable report, enabling you to display a subset of data in the PivotTable report.

Filtering A process in which only the rows that meet the criteria display; rows that do not meet the criteria are hidden.

Filtering button A button on a slicer which you use to select the item by which to filter.

Financial functions Pre-built formulas that perform common business calculations such as calculating a loan payment on a vehicle or calculating how much to save each month to buy something; financial functions commonly involve a period of time such as months or years.

Find A command that finds and selects specific text or formatting.

Find and replace A command that searches the cells in a worksheet—or in a selected range—for matches and then replaces each match with a replacement value of your choice.

Fixed expense Expense that remains the same each month regardless of the amount of activity.

Flash Fill An Excel feature that predicts how to alter data based upon the pattern you enter into the cell at the beginning of the column. The data must be in the adjacent column to use Flash Fill. Use it to split data from two or more cells or to combine data from two cells.

Folder A container in which you store files.

Folder window In Windows, a window that displays the contents of the current folder, library, or device, and contains helpful parts so that you can navigate the Windows file structure.

Font A set of characters with the same design and shape.

Font styles Formatting emphasis such as bold, italic, and underline.

Footer A reserved area for text or graphics that displays at the bottom of each page in a document.

Forecast A prediction of the future, often based on past performances.

Form An Excel worksheet or object that contains fields and controls that enable a user to easily enter or edit data.

Form control A graphic object that does not require VBA code. A Form control is compatible with versions of Excel that do not support ActiveX.

Format Changing the appearance of cells and worksheet elements to make a worksheet attractive and easy to read.

Formatting The process of establishing the overall appearance of text, graphics, and pages in an Office file—for example, in a Word document.

Formatting marks Characters that display on the screen, but do not print, indicating where the Enter key, the Spacebar, and the Tab key were pressed; also called *nonprinting characters*.

Formula An equation that performs mathematical calculations on values in a worksheet.

Formula Auditing Tools and commands accessible from the Formulas tab that help you check your worksheet for errors.

Formula AutoComplete An Excel feature that, after typing an = (equal sign) and the beginning letter or letters of a function name, displays a list of function names that match the typed letter(s), and from which you can insert the function by pointing to its name and pressing the Tab key or double-clicking.

Formula Bar An element in the Excel window that displays the value or formula contained in the active cell; here you can also enter or edit values or formulas.

Freeze Panes A command that enables you to select one or more rows or columns and freeze (lock) them into place so that they remain on the screen while you scroll; the locked rows and columns become separate panes.

Function A predefined formula—a formula that Excel has already built for you—that performs calculations by using specific values in a particular order or structure.

Fund A sum of money set aside for a specific purpose.

Future value (Fv) The value at the end of the time periods in an Excel function; the cash balance you want to attain after the last payment is made—usually zero for loans.

Gallery An Office feature that displays a list of potential results instead of just the command name.

General format The default format that Excel applies to numbers; this format has no specific characteristics—whatever you type in the cell will display, with the exception that trailing zeros to the right of a decimal point will not display.

General fund The term used to describe money set aside for the normal operating activities of a government entity such as a city.

Get External Data A group of commands that enables you to bring data from an Access database, from the web, from a text file, or from an XML file into Excel without repeatedly copying the data.

Go To A command that moves to a specific cell or range of cells that you specify.

Go To Special A command that moves to cells that have special characteristics, for example, to cells that are blank or to cells that contain constants, as opposed to formulas.

Goal Seek One of Excel's What-If Analysis tools that provides a method to find a specific value for a cell by adjusting the value of one other cell—find the right input when you know the result you want.

Google Docs Google's free web-based word processor, spreadsheet, slide show, and form service, that along with free data storage, is known as Google Drive.

Google Drive Google's free web-based word processor, spreadsheet, slide show, and form service, that includes free data storage.

Gradient fill A fill effect in which one color fades into another.

Gridlines Lines in the plot area that aid the eye in determining the plotted values.

Groups On the Office ribbon, the sets of related commands that you might need for a specific type of task.

Header A reserved area for text or graphics that displays at the top of each page in a document.

Hierarchy A category of SmartArt graphics used to create an organization chart or show a decision tree.

HLOOKUP An Excel function that looks up values that are displayed horizontally in a row.

Horizontal Category axis (x-axis) The area along the bottom of a chart that identifies the categories of data; also referred to as the x-axis.

HTML (Hypertext Markup Language) A language web browsers can interpret.

Hyperlink Text or graphics that, when clicked, take you to another location in the worksheet, to another file, or to a webpage on the Internet or on your organization's intranet.

Icon set A set of three, four, or five small graphic images that make your data visually easier to interpret.

IF function A function that uses a logical test to check whether a condition is met, and then returns one value if true, and another value if false.

Info tab The tab in Backstage view that displays information about the current file.

Information Data that has been organized in a useful manner.

Insertion point A blinking vertical line that indicates where text or graphics will be inserted.

Integer A whole number.

Interest The amount charged for the use of borrowed money.

Interval The number of cells to include in the average.

Intranet A network within an organization that uses Internet technologies.

Iterative calculation When Excel recalculates a formula over and over because of a circular reference.

Keyboard shortcut A combination of two or more keyboard keys, used to perform a task that would otherwise require a mouse.

KeyTip The letter that displays on a command in the ribbon and that indicates the key you can press to activate the command when keyboard control of the ribbon is activated.

Keywords Custom file properties in the form of words that you associate with a document to give an indication of the document's content; used to help find and organize files. Also called *tags*.

Label Another name for a text value, and which usually provides information about number values. Or, column and row headings that describe the values and help the reader understand the Chart.

Landscape orientation A page orientation in which the paper is wider than it is tall.

Layout Options A button that displays when an object is selected and that has commands to choose how the object interacts with surrounding text.

Layout section The lower portion of the PivotTable Fields pane containing the four areas for layout; use this area to rearrange and reposition fields in the PivotTable.

LEFT A text function that returns the specified number of characters from the beginning (left) of a string of characters.

Left alignment The cell format in which characters align at the left edge of the cell; this is the default for text entries and is an example of formatting information stored in a cell.

Legend A chart element that identifies the patterns or colors that are assigned to the categories in the chart.

Lettered column headings The area along the top edge of a worksheet that identifies each column with a unique letter or combination of letters.

Line charts A chart type that is useful to display trends over time; time displays along the bottom axis and the data point values are connected with a line.

List A category of SmartArt graphics used to show non-sequential information. Or, a series of rows that contains related data that you can group by adding subtotals.

Live Preview A technology that shows the result of applying an editing or formatting change as you point to possible results—*before* you actually apply it.

Location Any disk drive, folder, or other place in which you can store files and folders.

Locked [cells] In a protected worksheet, data cannot be inserted, modified, deleted, or formatted in these cells.

Logical function A function that tests for specific conditions.

Logical functions A group of functions that test for specific conditions and that typically use conditional tests to determine whether specified conditions are true or false.

Logical test Any value or expression that can be evaluated as being true or false.

LOOKUP An Excel function that looks up values in either a one-row or one-column range.

Lookup functions A group of Excel functions that look up a value in a defined range of cells located in another part of the workbook to find a corresponding value.

LOWER A text function that changes the case of the characters in a string, making all characters lowercase.

Macro An action or a set of actions with which you can automate tasks by grouping a series of commands into a single command.

Macro virus Unauthorized programming code in a macro that erases or damages files.

Major sort A term sometimes used to refer to the first sort level in the Sort dialog box.

Major unit The value in a chart's value axis that determines the spacing between tick marks and between the gridlines in the plot area.

Major unit value A number that determines the spacing between tick marks and between the gridlines in the plot area.

Mark as Final command Prevents additional changes to the document and disables typing, editing comments, and proofing marks.

Matrix A category of SmartArt graphics used to show how parts relate to a whole.

MAX function An Excel function that determines the largest value in a selected range of values.

MEDIAN function An Excel function that finds the middle value that has as many values above it in the group as are below it; it differs from AVERAGE in that the result is not affected as much by a single value that is greatly different from the others.

Merge & Center A command that joins selected cells in an Excel worksheet into one larger cell and centers the contents in the merged cell.

Metadata Details about a file that describe or identify it, including the title, author name, subject, and keywords that identify the document's topic or contents; also known as *document properties*.

Microsoft Access A database program used to manage database files.

MID A text function that extracts a series of characters from a text string given the location of the beginning character.

MIN function An Excel function that determines the smallest value in a selected range of values.

Mini toolbar A small toolbar containing frequently used formatting commands that displays as a result of selecting text or objects.

Module The programming code written in VBA when you record a new macro; the place where the VBA code is stored.

Moving average A sequence of averages computed from parts of a data series.

MRU Acronym for *most recently used*, which refers to the state of some commands that retain the characteristic most recently applied; for example, the Font Color button retains the most recently used color until a new color is chosen.

Name A word or string of characters in Excel that represents a cell, a range of cells, a formula, or a constant value; also referred to as *a defined name*.

Name Box An element of the Excel window that displays the name of the selected cell, table, chart, or object.

Navigate The process of exploring within the organizing structure of Windows. Or, the process of moving within a worksheet or workbook.

Navigation pane In a folder window, the area on the left in which you can navigate to, open, and display favorites, libraries, folders, saved searches, and an expandable list of drives.

Nested function A function that is contained inside another function. The inner function is evaluated first and the result becomes the argument for the outer function.

Nonprinting characters Characters that display on the screen, but do not print, indicating where the Enter key, the Spacebar, and the Tab key were pressed; also called *formatting marks*.

Normal view A screen view that maximizes the number of cells visible on your screen and keeps the column letters and row numbers close to the columns and rows.

NOT function A logical function that takes only one argument and is used to test one condition. If the condition is true, the function returns the logical opposite false. If the condition is false, true is returned.

Notification bar An area at the bottom of an Internet Explorer window that displays information about pending downloads, security issues, add-ons, and other issues related to the operation of your computer.

NOW function An Excel function that retrieves the date and time from your computer's calendar and clock and inserts the information into the selected cell.

Nper The abbreviation for *number of time periods* in various Excel functions.

Number format A specific way in which Excel displays numbers in a cell.

Number values Constant values consisting of only numbers.

Numbered row headings The area along the left edge of a worksheet that identifies each row with a unique number.

Object A text box, picture, table, or shape that you can select and then move and resize.

Objective cell In Solver, a cell that contains a formula for the results you are trying to determine.

Office Web Apps The free online companions to Microsoft Word, Excel, PowerPoint, Access, and OneNote.

One-variable data table A data table that changes the value in only one cell.

Open dialog box A dialog box from which you can navigate to, and then open on your screen, an existing file that was created in that same program.

Option button In a dialog box, a round button that enables you to make one choice among two or more options.

Options dialog box A dialog box within each Office application where you can select program settings and other options and preferences.

Or comparison operator The comparison operator that requires only one of the two comparison criteria that you specify to be true.

OR function A logical function that can be used to develop compound logical tests using up to 255 arguments. The function returns a value of TRUE if ANY of the conditions are met.

Order of operations The mathematical rules for performing multiple calculations within a formula.

Organization chart A type of graphic that is useful to depict reporting relationships within an organization.

Page Layout view A screen view in which you can use the rulers to measure the width and height of data, set margins for printing, hide or display the numbered row headings and the lettered column headings, and change the page orientation; this view is useful for preparing your worksheet for printing.

Pane A portion of a worksheet window bounded by and separated from other portions by vertical and horizontal bars.

Paragraph symbol The symbol ¶ that represents the end of a paragraph.

Password An optional element of a template added to prevent someone from disabling a worksheet's protection.

Paste The action of placing cell contents that have been copied or moved to the Clipboard into another location.

Paste area The target destination for data that has been cut or copied using the Office Clipboard.

Paste Options gallery A gallery of buttons that provides a Live Preview of all the Paste options available in the current context.

Path A sequence of folders that leads to a specific file or folder.

PDF The acronym for Portable Document Format, which is a file format that creates an image that preserves the look of your file; this is a popular format for sending documents electronically because the document will display on most computers.

PDF (Portable Document Format) A file format developed by Adobe Systems that creates a representation of electronic paper that displays your data on the screen as it would look when printed, but that cannot be easily changed.

Percent for new value = base percent + percent of increase The formula for calculating a percentage by which a value increases by adding the base percentage—usually 100%—to the percent increase.

Percentage rate of increase The percent by which one number increases over another number.

Picture A category of SmartArt graphics that is used to display pictures in a diagram.

Picture element A point of light measured in dots per square inch on a screen; 64 pixels equals 8.43 characters, which is the average number of characters that will fit in a cell in an Excel worksheet using the default font.

Pie chart A chart that shows the relationship of each part to a whole.

PivotChart report A graphical representation of the data in a PivotTable report.

PivotTable An interactive Excel report that summarizes and analyzes large amounts of data.

PivotTable Fields pane A window that lists, at the top, all of the fields—column titles—from the source data for use in the PivotTable report and at the bottom, an area in which you can arrange the fields in the PivotTable.

Pixel The abbreviated name for a picture element.

Plot area The area bounded by the axes of a chart, including all the data series.

PMT function An Excel function that calculates the payment for a loan based on constant payments and a constant interest rate.

Point The action of moving your mouse pointer over something on your screen.

Point and click method The technique of constructing a formula by pointing to and then clicking cells; this method is convenient when the referenced cells are not adjacent to one another.

Pointer Any symbol that displays on your screen in response to moving your mouse.

Points A measurement of the size of a font; there are 72 points in an inch.

Portable Document Format A file format that creates an image that preserves the look of your file, but that cannot be easily changed; a popular format for sending documents electronically, because the document will display on most computers.

Portrait orientation A page orientation in which the paper is taller than it is wide.

Power View An Excel BI tool that allows you to create and interact with multiple charts, slicers, and other data visualizations in a single sheet.

PowerPivot An Excel BI tool that allows you to analyze data from multiple sources, work with multiple data tables, and create relationships between tables.

Precedent cells Cells that are referred to by a formula in another cell.

Present value (Pv) The total amount that a series of future payments is worth now; also known as the *principal*.

Principal The total amount that a series of future payments is worth now; also known as the *Present value (Pv)*.

Print Preview A view of a document as it will appear when you print it.

Print Titles An Excel command that enables you to specify rows and columns to repeat on each printed page.

Procedure A named sequence of statements in a computer program that performs an action.

Process A category of SmartArt graphics that is used to show steps in a process or timeline.

Progress bar In a dialog box or taskbar button, a bar that indicates visually the progress of a task such as a download or file transfer.

PROPER A text function that capitalizes the first letter of each word.

Properties The details about a file that describe or identify the file, including the title, author name, subject, and tags that identify the file's topic or contents. Also known as *metadata*.

Protected View A security feature in Office 2013 that protects your computer from malicious files by opening them in a restricted environment until you enable them; you might encounter this feature if you open a file from an email or download files from the Internet.

Protection This prevents anyone from altering the formulas or changing other template components.

pt The abbreviation for *point*; for example, when referring to a font size.

Pyramid A category of SmartArt graphics that uses a series of pictures to show relationships.

Query A process of restricting records through the use of criteria conditions that will display records that will answer a question about the data.

Quick Access Toolbar In an Office program window, the small row of buttons in the upper left corner of the screen from which you can perform frequently used commands.

Quick Analysis tool A tool that displays in the lower right corner of a selected range with which you can analyze your data by using Excel tools such as charts, color-coding, and formulas.

Quick Explore A tool that allows you to drill down through PivotTable data with a single click.

Range Two or more selected cells on a worksheet that are adjacent or nonadjacent; because the range is treated as a single unit, you can make the same changes or combination of changes to more than one cell at a time.

Range finder An Excel feature that outlines cells in color to indicate which cells are used in a formula; useful for verifying which cells are referenced in a formula.

Rate In the Excel PMT function, the term used to indicate the interest rate for a loan.

Rate = amount of increase/base The mathematical formula to calculate a rate of increase.

Read-Only A property assigned to a file that prevents the file from being modified or deleted; it indicates that you cannot save any changes to the displayed document unless you first save it with a new name.

Recommended Charts An Excel feature that displays a customized set of charts that, according to Excel's calculations, will best fit your data based on the range of data that you select.

Record All the categories of data pertaining to one database item such as a person, place, thing, event, or idea, stored in a horizontal row in a database.

Record Macro A command that records your actions in Visual Basic for Applications (VBA).

Refresh The command to update a worksheet to reflect new data.

Relationship A category of SmartArt graphics that is used to illustrate connections.

Relationship An association between tables that share a common field.

Relative cell reference In a formula, the address of a cell based on the relative positions of the cell that contains the formula and the cell referred to in the formula.

Ribbon A user interface in both Office 2013 and File Explorer that groups the commands for performing related tasks on tabs across the upper portion of the program window.

RIGHT A text function that returns the specified number of characters from the end (right) of a string of characters.

Right-click The action of clicking the right mouse button one time.

Rotation handle A circle that displays on the top side of a selected object used to rotate the object up to 360 degrees.

Rounding A procedure in which you determine which digit at the right of the number will be the last digit displayed and then increase it by one if the next digit to its right is 5, 6, 7, 8, or 9.

Row A horizontal group of cells in a worksheet.

Row heading The numbers along the left side of an Excel worksheet that designate the row numbers.

ROWS area An area to position fields that you want to display as rows in the PivotTable report. Field names placed here become row titles, and the data is grouped by these row titles.

Sans serif font A font design with no lines or extensions on the ends of characters.

Scale The range of numbers in the data series that controls the minimum, maximum, and incremental values on the value axis.

Scale to Fit Excel commands that enable you to stretch or shrink the width, height, or both, of printed output to fit a maximum number of pages.

Scaling The group of commands by which you can reduce the horizontal and vertical size of the printed data by a percentage or by the number of pages that you specify.

Scenario A set of values that Excel saves and can substitute automatically in your worksheet.

Scenario Manager A what-if analysis tool that compares alternatives.

Schema An XML file that contains the rules for what can and cannot reside in an XML data file.

Scope The location within which a defined name is recognized without qualification—usually either to a specific worksheet or to the entire workbook.

Screenshot An image of an active window on your computer that you can insert into a worksheet.

ScreenTip A small box that displays useful information when you perform various mouse actions such as pointing to screen elements or dragging.

Scroll bar A vertical or horizontal bar in a window or a pane to assist in bringing an area into view, and which contains a scroll box and scroll arrows.

Scroll box The box in the vertical and horizontal scroll bars that can be dragged to reposition the contents of a window or pane on the screen.

Select All box A box in the upper left corner of the worksheet grid that, when clicked, selects all the cells in a worksheet.

Selecting Highlighting, by dragging with your mouse, areas of text or data or graphics, so that the selection can be edited, formatted, copied, or moved.

Self-signed A project signed with a certificate that you create yourself.

Series A group of things that come one after another in succession; for example, January, February, March, and so on.

Serif font A font design that includes small line extensions on the ends of the letters to guide the eye in reading from left to right.

Shared workbook A workbook set up to allow multiple users on a network to view and make changes to the workbook at the same time.

SharePoint Collaboration software with which people in an organization can set up team sites to share information, manage documents, and publish reports for others to see.

Sheet tab scrolling buttons Buttons to the left of the sheet tabs used to display Excel sheet tabs that are not in view; used when there are more sheet tabs than will display in the space provided.

Sheet tabs The labels along the lower border of the Excel window that identify each worksheet.

Shortcut menu A menu that displays commands and options relevant to the selected text or object; also called a *context menu*.

Show Formulas A command that displays the formula in each cell instead of the resulting value.

Signature line Specifies the individual who must sign the document.

Sizing handles Small squares that indicate a picture or object is selected.

SkyDrive Microsoft's free cloud storage for anyone with a free Microsoft account.

Slicer Easy-to-use filtering control with buttons that enable you to drill down through large amounts of data.

Slicer header The top of a slicer that indicates the category of the slicer items.

SmartArt graphic A visual representation of information and ideas.

Solver A what-if analysis tool with which you can find an optimal (maximum or minimum) value for a formula in one cell—referred to as the objective cell—subject to constraints, or limits, on the values of other formula cells on a worksheet.

Sort The process of arranging data in a specific order based on the value in each field.

Sort dialog box A dialog box in which you can sort data based on several criteria at once, and that enables a sort by more than one column or row.

Source data The data for a PivotTable, formatted in columns and rows, which can be located in an Excel worksheet or an external source.

Sparkline A tiny chart in the background of a cell that gives a visual trend summary alongside your data; makes a pattern more obvious.

Split The command that enables you to view separate parts of the same worksheet on your screen; splits the window into multiple resizable panes to view distant parts of the worksheet at one time.

Split button A button divided into two parts and in which clicking the main part of the button performs a command and clicking the arrow opens a menu with choices.

Spreadsheet Another name for a worksheet.

Standardization All forms created within the organization will have a uniform appearance; the data will always be organized in the same manner.

Start search The search feature in Windows 8 in which, from the Start screen, you can begin to type and by default, Windows 8 searches for apps; you can adjust the search to search for files or settings.

Statistical functions Excel functions, including the AVERAGE, MEDIAN, MIN, and MAX functions, which are useful to analyze a group of measurements.

Status bar The area along the lower edge of the Excel window that displays, on the left side, the current cell mode, page number, and worksheet information; on the right side, when numerical data is selected, common calculations such as Sum and Average display.

Style A group of formatting commands, such as font, font size, font color, paragraph alignment, and line spacing that can be applied to a paragraph with one command.

Sub Short for a sub procedure.

Sub procedure A unit of computer code that performs an action.

Subfolder A folder within a folder.

Subtotal command The command that totals several rows of related data together by automatically inserting subtotals and totals for the selected cells.

SUM function A predefined formula that adds all the numbers in a selected range of cells.

SUMIF function A logical function that contains one logic test—it will add values in a specified range that meet certain conditions or criteria.

SUMIFS function A logical function that will add values in multiple ranges that meet multiple criteria.

Summary sheet A worksheet where totals from other worksheets are displayed and summarized.

Switch Row/Column A charting command to swap the data over the axis—data being charted on the vertical axis will move to the horizontal axis and vice versa.

Synchronization The process of updating computer files that are in two or more locations according to specific rules—also called syncing.

Syncing The process of updating computer files that are in two or more locations according to specific rules—also called synchronization.

Syntax The arrangement of the arguments in a function.

Tab delimited text file A file type in which cells are separated by tabs; this type of file can be readily exchanged with various database programs.

Table Data stored in a format of rows and columns.

Table array A defined range of cells, arranged in a column or a row, used in a VLOOKUP or HLOOKUP function.

Tabs (ribbon) On the Office ribbon, the name of each activity area.

Tags Custom file properties in the form of words that you associate with a document to give an indication of the document's content; used to help find and organize files. Also called *keywords*.

Taskbar The area along the lower edge of the desktop that displays buttons representing programs.

Template A special workbook that may include formatting, formulas, and other elements, and that is used as a pattern for creating other workbooks.

Text function A function that can be used to combine or separate data, change case, and apply formatting to a string of characters.

Text pane The pane that displays to the left of the graphic, is populated with placeholder text, and is used to build a graphic by entering and editing text.

Text values Constant values consisting of only text, and which usually provide information about number values; also referred to as labels.

Theme A predesigned set of colors, fonts, lines, and fill effects that look good together and that can be applied to your entire document or to specific items.

Tick mark labels Identifying information for a tick mark generated from the cells on the worksheet used to create the chart.

Tick marks The short lines that display on an axis at regular intervals.

Title bar The bar at the top edge of the program window that indicates the name of the current file and the program name.

Toggle button A button that can be turned on by clicking it once, and then turned off by clicking it again.

Toolbar In a folder window, a row of buttons with which you can perform common tasks, such as changing the view of your files and folders or burning files to a CD.

Trace Dependents command A command that displays arrows that indicate what cells are affected by the value of the currently selected cell.

Trace Error command A tool that helps locate and resolve an error by tracing the selected error value.

Trace Precedents command A command that displays arrows to indicate what cells affect the value of the cell that is selected.

Tracer arrow An indicator that shows the relationship between the active cell and its related cell.

Track Changes An Excel feature that logs details about workbook changes including insertions and deletions.

Transpose To switch the data in rows and columns.

Trendline A graphic representation of trends in a data series, such as a line sloping upward to represent increased sales over a period of months.

TRIM A text function that removes extra blank spaces from a string of characters.

Triple-click The action of clicking the left mouse button three times in rapid succession.

Trusted Documents A security feature in Office that remembers which files you have already enabled; you might encounter this feature if you open a file from an email or download files from the Internet.

Two-variable data table A data table that changes the values in two cells.

Type argument An optional argument in the PMT function that assumes that the payment will be made at the end of each time period.

Underlying formula The formula entered in a cell and visible only on the Formula Bar.

Underlying value The data that displays in the Formula Bar.

Uniform Resource Locator An address that uniquely identifies a location on the Internet.

Unlocked [cells] Cells in a protected worksheet that may be filled in.

UPPER A text function that changes the case of the characters in a string, making all characters uppercase.

URL The acronym for Uniform Resource Locator, which is an address that uniquely identifies a location on the Internet.

USB flash drive A small data storage device that plugs into a computer USB port.

Validation list A list of values that are acceptable for a group of cells; only values in the list are valid and any value *not* in the list is considered invalid.

Value Another name for a constant value.

Value after increase = base x percent for new value The formula for calculating the value after an increase by multiplying the original value—the base—by the percent for new value (see the *Percent for new value* formula).

Value axis A numerical scale on the left side of a chart that shows the range of numbers for the data points; also referred to as the Y-axis.

VALUES area An area to position fields that contain data that is summarized in a PivotTable report or PivotChart report. The data placed here is usually numeric or financial in nature and the data is summarized—summed. You can also perform other basic calculations such as finding the average, the minimum, or the maximum.

Variable cell In Solver, a cell in which the value will change to achieve the desired results.

Variable expense Expense that varies depending on the amount of sales.

VBA The abbreviation for the Visual Basic for Applications programming language.

VBA construct An instruction that enables a macro to perform multiple operations on a single object.

Vertical Value axis (y-axis) A numerical scale on the left side of a chart that shows the range of numbers for the data points; also referred to as the y-axis.

Visual Basic Editor The window in which you can view and edit Visual Basic code.

Visual Basic for Applications The programming language used to write computer programs in the Microsoft Windows environment.

VLOOKUP An Excel function that looks up values that are displayed vertically in a column.

Volatile A term used to describe an Excel function that is subject to change each time the workbook is reopened; for example the NOW function updates itself to the current date and time each time the workbook is opened.

Walls and floor The areas surrounding a 3-D chart that give dimension and boundaries to the chart.

Watch Window A window that displays the results of specified cells.

Watermark A faded image or text used as a background of a document.

What-If Analysis The process of changing the values in cells to see how those changes affect the outcome of formulas in a worksheet.

Wildcard A character, for example the asterisk or question mark, used to search a field when you are uncertain of the exact value or when you want to widen the search to include more records.

Window A rectangular area on a computer screen in which programs and content appear, and which can be moved, resized, minimized, or closed.

Wizard A feature in Microsoft Office programs that walks you step by step through a process.

WordArt A feature with which you can insert decorative text in your document.

Workbook An Excel file that contains one or more worksheets.

Workbook-level buttons Buttons at the far right of the ribbon tabs that minimize or restore a displayed workbook.

Worksheet The primary document that you use in Excel to work with and store data, and which is formatted as a pattern of uniformly spaced horizontal and vertical lines.

Worksheet grid area A part of the Excel window that displays the columns and rows that intersect to form the worksheet's cells.

X-axis Another name for the horizontal (category) axis.

.xlsx file name extension The default file format used by Excel 2013 to save an Excel workbook.

XML Paper Specification A Microsoft file format that creates an image of your document and that opens in the XPS viewer.

XPS The acronym for XML Paper Specification—a Microsoft file format that creates an image of your document and that opens in the XPS viewer.

XPS (XML Paper Specification) A file type, developed by Microsoft, which creates a representation of electronic paper that displays your data on the screen as it would look when printed.

Y-axis Another name for the vertical (value) axis.

Zipped folder A folder that has been reduced in size and thus takes up less storage space and can be transferred to other computers quickly; also called a *compressed* folder.

Zoom The action of increasing or decreasing the size of the viewing area on the screen.

Index

Taken from *Skills for Success with Microsoft® Office 2013*, by Kris Townsend, Catherine Hain, and Stephanie Murre Wolf

 The internet icon represents Index entries found within More Skills on the Companion Website: www.pearsonhighered.com/skills

Skills for Success Office 2013 | Index **I-1**

Insert Chart dialog box, 322, 360, 368, (CW) Excel, ch 2, More Skills 12, (CW) Excel, ch 3, More Skills 12

legends, 319

line, 306, 321, 362, (CW) Excel, ch 3, More Skills 12

Move Chart dialog box, 322, 329, 334, 360, 368, (CW) Excel, ch 3, More Skills 12

organization charts, 362, (CW) Excel, ch 3, More Skills 11

pie charts
  creating, 322–323
  defined, 306, 321, 322
  formatting, 322–323
  3-D, 322–323

Recommended Charts button, 322, 329, 334, 360, 368, (CW) Excel, ch 2, More Skills 12, (CW) Excel, ch 3, More Skills 12

sparklines, 384–385, 397, 402–403, 406–407

types, 321

update, 324–325

WordArt in, 324–325

chart layout, 320–321

chart sheets, 322–323, 327, 335–336, 361, 369

chart styles, Excel charts, 320–321, 323, 329, 334–336

check spelling and grammar. *See* spelling and grammar options

clear cell contents and formats, 346–347, 363

clearing print areas, 362, (CW) Excel, ch 3, More Skills 13

clipboard, 348

cloud-based applications. *See* web apps

clustered bar charts, 360–361, 368–369, 371–373, (CW) Excel, ch 2, More Skills 12

colors
  worksheet tabs, 343

color scales, top/bottom rules and, 396, (CW) Excel, ch 4, More Skills 11

columns. *See also* tables; worksheets
  calculated, 390
  Freeze Panes command, 388–389, 397, 402
  heading, 282
  hide, 394–395
  Keep Source Column Widths option, 348–349, 368–370, 372
  Unfreeze Panes command, 388–389, 397, 402
  widths
    adjust, 282–283
    AutoFit, 309, 327, 333, 335–336

column charts
  bar charts to column charts, 328, (CW) Excel, ch 2, More Skills 12
  create, 318–319
  defined, 306, 321
  formatting, 320–321

comments, in cells, 328, (CW) Excel, ch 2, More Skills 11

comparison operators, 378–379. *See also* queries

conditional formatting
  cells, 374, 382–383, 397, 403–405, (CW) Excel, ch 4, More Skills 11

content, 346. *See also* cells

Convert Text to Table dialog box, 412, (CW) Word, ch 3, More Skills 13

converting
  Excel tables to ranges, 394–395, 397
  Word tables to worksheets, 410–413, (CW) Excel, IP03

COUNT function, 376–377, 393, 397, 401

creating. *See specific entries*

criteria. *See also* queries
  logical test and, 378–379, 401, 403–404

currency, number format, 288

Cut command, 348

data. *See also* files; *specific data*

data bars, 383, 397, 402, 405–407

data labels, chart, 323–324, 329

data markers, 319, (CW) Excel, ch 2, More Skills 12

data points, 319, (CW) Excel, ch 2, More Skills 12

data series, 319, 324, (CW) Excel, ch 2, More Skills 12

databases. *See also* forms; queries; tables

datasheets. *See also* tables

dates
  NOW function, 376–377, 397, 403, 406
  TODAY function, 376–377, 397, 401, 404
  volatile, 376
  in worksheets, 344–345, 363–364

decimals
  Decrease Decimal button, 288, 295, 312–313, 333, 425–426
  Increase Decimal button, 288, 295, 300, 312, 329, 333, (CW) Excel, ch 4, More Skills 14

Decrease Decimal button, 288, 295, 312–313, 333, 425–426

deleting
  comments, from cells, (CW) Excel, ch 2, More Skills 11
  worksheets, 356–357, 363

design, of presentation. *See* presentations

design grid. *See* query design grid

design workspace. *See* query design workspace

detail sheets, 358, 366, 369, 372. *See also* worksheets

dialog boxes
  Convert Text to Table, 412, (CW) Word, ch 3, More Skills 13
  Export - Excel Spreadsheet, (CW) Access, ch 2, More Skills 11
  Export - HTML Document, (CW) Access, ch 2, More Skills 12
  Find and Replace, 386–387
  Format Cells, 345, 347, 381–382, (CW) Excel, ch 4, More Skills 13
  Function Arguments, 377–378, (CW) Excel, ch 4, More Skills 12

Insert Chart, 322, 360, 368, (CW) Excel ch 2 More Skills 12, (CW) Excel, ch 3, More Skills 12

Insert Hyperlink, (CW) Excel, ch 3, More Skills 14

Move Chart, 322, 329, 334, 360, 368, (CW) Excel, ch 3, More Skills 12

Move or Copy, 389, 391, 402

Name Manager, (CW) Excel, ch 1, More Skills 12

Page Setup, 290–291, 334, 361, 394–395, 402, (CW) Excel, ch 2, More Skills 11, (CW) Excel, ch 4, More Skills 11

Select Table, 413

Text That Contains, 382, 421

dictionaries. *See also* spelling and grammar options; synonyms
  words not in Office dictionary, 289

digital images. *See* clip art; graphics; photos; pictures

digital photos. *See* photos

discussion topics. *See* topics for discussion

display formulas, 292–293

displayed value, cells, 276

#DIV/0 *error, cell*, 296, 310

division (/), 278

division formulas, 280–281

documents, Word. *See also* flyers; spelling and grammar options; tables; text
  Excel charts copied to, 328, (CW) Excel, ch 2, More Skills 13
  linked with Excel workbook, 414–417, (CW) Excel, IP04

Document Information Panel, 294, (CW) Excel, ch 1, More Skills 14, (CW) Word, ch 4, More Skills 13

document properties
  workbooks, 294, (CW) Excel, ch 1, More Skills 14

drag and drop, 348

editing
  comments, in cells, (CW) Excel, ch 2, More Skills 11
  worksheets, 288–289

Editing view, web apps, 424

electronic mail. *See* e-mail

embedded charts, 318

equal to (=), 378

errors. *See also* spelling and grammar options
  #DIV/0 error, 296, 310

error indicator, 310–311

error values, formulas, 310

Excel 2013. *See also* common features; workbooks; worksheets
  bar charts
    changed to column chart, 328, (CW) Excel, ch 2, More Skills 12
    clustered, 360–361, 368–369, 371–373, (CW) Excel, ch 2, More Skills 12
    defined, 331

BizSkills, 297, 331, 365, 399

Capstone Project, 408–409

grouped worksheets, 359
placeholders, 290
Help
    online
        Excel 2013, 296, 330, 364, 398
hide rows and columns, worksheets, 394–395
hide worksheets, 356–357, 363
hyperlinks. *See also* linking
    Insert Hyperlink, Ⓒ Excel, ch 3, More Skills 14,
    in worksheets and cells, 362, Ⓒ Excel, ch 3, More Skills 14

IF function, 378–379, 397, 401, 403–404
images. *See* clip art; graphics; photos; pictures
Increase Decimal button, 288, 295, 300, 312, 329, 333,
        Ⓒ Excel, ch 4, More Skills 14
Increase Indent button, 309, 329, 336
Insert Chart dialog box, 322, 360, 368, Ⓒ Excel, ch 2, More
        Skills 12, Ⓒ Excel, ch 3, More Skills 12
insert footnotes. *See* footnotes
Insert Hyperlink dialog box, Ⓒ Excel, ch 3, More Skills 14,
        Ⓒ PowerPoint, ch 4, More Skills 12, Ⓒ Word, ch 4,
        More Skills 14
inserting
    comments, in cells, Ⓒ Excel, ch 2, More Skills 11
    worksheets, 356–357, 363
Integrated Projects
    cells linked to other workbooks, 418–421, Ⓒ Excel, IP05
    Word tables converted to Excel worksheets, 410–413,
        Ⓒ Excel, IP03
interest, Ⓒ Excel, ch 4, More Skills 12
ISPs. *See* Internet service providers

Keep Source Column Widths, 348–349, 368–370, 372
Keep Source Formatting option, 349, 417, Ⓒ Excel, IP04
key terms
    Excel 2013, 296, 330, 364, 398
keyboard shortcuts. *See also* skills and procedures
    Excel, 330

labels. *See also* cells; mail merge
    category labels, 318
    data labels, charts, 323–324, 329
    text value as, 275
landscape orientation
    worksheets, 292–293, 402–404
large worksheets, formatting, 394–395
layouts
    chart, 320–321
    Page Layout view, 290, 326
legend, 319
less than (<), 378
less than or equal to (<=), 378
line charts, 306, 321, 362, Ⓒ Excel, ch 3, More Skills 12

Link & Keep Source Formatting button, 417, Ⓒ Excel, IP04
linking. *See also* hyperlinks; Integrated Projects
    cells between workbooks, 418–421, Ⓒ Excel, IP05
    Excel workbook and Word document, 414–417, Ⓒ Excel,
        IP04
logical functions, 378, 405, 407
logical test, 378–379, 401, 403–404

matching
    Excel 2013, 297, 331, 365, 399
    math operators, in formulas, 352–353
MAX function, 316–317
Merge & Center button, 277, 282, 295, 300, 351, 381, 424,
        Ⓒ Excel Web App
merge and center worksheet titles, 276–277
Microsoft Office 2013. *See* Office 2013
middle align text, in cell, 309, 329, 333, 335, 381
MIN function, 316–317
misspelled words. *See* spelling and grammar options
Modern Language Association. *See* MLA
Move Chart dialog box, 322, 329, 334, 360, 368, Ⓒ Excel, ch 3,
        More Skills 12
Move or Copy dialog box, 389, 391, 402
move through worksheets, 275
moving
    cell contents, 348–349
    functions, 380–381
    worksheet tabs, 363
    worksheets, 356–357
multiple choice
    Excel 2013, 298, 332, 366, 400
multiple worksheets. *See also* grouped worksheets;
        worksheets
    managing, 340–373
    printing, 326–327
multiplication (*), 278
multiplication formulas, 280–281
My Skills
    Excel 2013, 304, 338, 372, 406

Name Box, 277
Name Manager dialog box, Ⓒ Excel, ch 1, More
        Skills 12
names, in formulas, 294, Ⓒ Excel, ch 1, More Skills 12
no borders, worksheet Paste Option, 349
not equal to (<>), 378
NOW function, 376–377, 397, 403, 406
Nper argument box, Ⓒ Excel, ch 4, More Skills 12
number formats, 288, 312
number value, cells, 275

Office 2013. *See also* Access 2013; common features;
        Excel 2013; PowerPoint 2013; Word 2013

Office Clipboard, 348
Office dictionary. *See* dictionaries
Office.com
    workbook templates, Ⓒ Excel ch 1 More Skills 11,
        Ⓒ Excel ch 1 More Skills 13
operators. *See also specific operators*
    arithmetic, 278
    comparison, 378–379
    math, in formulas, 352–353
    percent (%), 278
operator precedence, 352
organization charts, 362, Ⓒ Excel, ch 3, More Skills 11
organize
    worksheet tabs, 342–343
orientation
    change, 295
    landscape
        worksheets, 292–293

Page Layout view, 290, 326
page orientation. *See* orientation
page settings, worksheets, 290–291
Page Setup dialog box, 290–291, 334, 361, 394–395, 402,
        Ⓒ Excel, ch 2, More Skills 11, Ⓒ Excel, ch 4,
        More Skills 11
paste area, 349
Paste Options
    worksheets, 348–349, 363
Payment function. *See* PMT function
percent, number format, 288
percent (%) operator, 278
Percent Style button, 288, 300, 312, 329, 333
pie charts
    creating, 322–323
    defined, 306, 321, 322
    formatting, 322–323
    3-D, 322–323
PivotTable reports, 396, Ⓒ Excel, ch 4, More Skills 13
PMT (Payment) function, 396, Ⓒ Excel, ch 4, More Skills 12
precedence, operator, 352
present value, Ⓒ Excel, ch 4, More Skills 12
principal, Ⓒ Excel, ch 4, More Skills 12
print areas, setting and clearing, 362, Ⓒ Excel, ch 3,
        More Skills 13
print preview
    worksheets, 326–327
printing
    comments, in cells, Ⓒ Excel, ch 2, More Skills 11
    multiple worksheets, 326–327
    workbooks, 329
    worksheets, 292–293
procedures. *See* skills and procedures
Professional Business Skills. *See* BizSkills

Index

Taken from *Go! With Microsoft® Excel® 2013 Comprehensive*, by Shelley Gaskin, Alicia Vargas, and Debra Geoghan

P9-DNN-886

Microsoft Office 2003: Essentials Course

Microsoft Office 2003: Essentials Course

BRIAN FAVRO
Labyrinth Publications

RUSSEL STOLINS
Santa Fe Community College

SANDRA CALDWELL
Community College of Allegheny County

JUDY MARDAR
Community College Workforce Alliance

MICHELLE MAROTTI
DeKalb Technical College

JILL MURPHY
ExecuTrain of San Francisco

LABYRINTH
PUBLICATIONS®

Microsoft Office 2003: Essentials Course
by Brian Favro, Russel Stolins, Sandra Caldwell,
Judy Mardar, Michelle Marotti, Jill Murphy

Copyright © 2003 by Labyrinth Publications

LABYRINTH
PUBLICATIONS®

Labyrinth Publications
P.O. Box 20820
El Sobrante, California 94803
800.522.9746
On the Web at labpub.com

President and Publisher:
Brian Favro

Interior Design:
Seventeenth Street Studios

Illustrations: Tom Brooks

Series Editor: Russel Stolins

Managing Editor:
Laura A. Lionello

Production Management,
Composition: Rad Proctor

Indexing: Joanne Sprott

Cover Design:
Seventeenth Street Studios

Printer: Courier, Kendallville

All rights reserved. Printed in the United States of America. No part of this material protected by this copyright notice may be reproduced or utilized in any form or by any means, electronic or mechanical, including photocopying, recording, scanning, or by information storage and retrieval systems without written permission from the copyright owner.

No part of this publication may be reproduced or transmitted in any form or by any means without the prior written permission from the publisher.

Labyrinth Publications® and the Labyrinth Publications logo are registered trademarks of Labyrinth Publications. Microsoft®, Outlook®, PowerPoint®, and Windows® are registered trademarks of Microsoft Corporation. Other product and company names mentioned herein may be the trademarks of their respective owners.

The example companies, organizations, products, people, and events depicted herein are fictitious. No association with any real company, organization, product, person, or event is intended or should be inferred.

Screen shots reprinted with permission from Microsoft Corporation.

ISBN-10: 1-59136-027-7
ISBN-13: 978-1-59136-027-8

Manufactured in the United States of America.

10 9 8

Microsoft
Office 2003:
Essentials
Course

Contents in Brief

Contents

UNIT 1

COMPUTER CONCEPTS
AND WINDOWS

LESSON 1 COMPUTER CONCEPTS 4

LESSON 2 WORKING WITH
WINDOWS PROGRAMS 42

LESSON 3 FILE MANAGEMENT
AND ONLINE HELP 84

UNIT 2

INTERNET EXPLORER

LESSON 4 BROWSING THE WEB   120

UNIT 3

OUTLOOK 2003

LESSON 5 INTRODUCING OUTLOOK 2003   154

LESSON 6 SENDING AND RECEIVING EMAIL   176

UNIT 8

COMPREHENSIVE INTEGRATION

LESSON 25 INTEGRATION PROJECT: MULTITASKING WITH OFFICE 2003   734

UNIT 9

APPENDICES

Keyboard Shortcut Summary

KEYSTROKES FOR ALL APPLICATIONS

Bold	`Ctrl`+`B`
Help	`F1`
Italics	`Ctrl`+`I`
Underline	`Ctrl`+`U`
Cut	`Ctrl`+`X`
Copy	`Ctrl`+`C`
Open	`Ctrl`+`O`
Paste	`Ctrl`+`V`
Undo	`Ctrl`+`Z`
Redo/repeat	`Ctrl`+`Y`
Save	`Ctrl`+`S`
Print	`Ctrl`+`P`

UNIT 1: COMPUTER CONCEPTS AND WINDOWS

Close active program window	`Alt`+`F4`

UNIT 2: INTERNET EXPLORER

Move back one page	`Alt`+`←`
Move forward one page	`Ctrl`+`→`
Move to bottom of page	`End`
Move to top of page	`Home`
Open a new browser window	`Ctrl`+`N`

UNIT 3: OUTLOOK 2003

Create a new email message	`Ctrl`+`Shift`+`M`
Create a new folder	`Ctrl`+`Shift`+`E`

UNIT 4: WORD 2003

1.5 spacing	`Ctrl`+`5`
Align center	`Ctrl`+`E`
Align left	`Ctrl`+`L`
Align right	`Ctrl`+`R`
Decrease font size one point	`Ctrl`+`[`
Delete from insertion point to beginning of word	`Ctrl`+`Backspace`
Delete from insertion point to end of word	`Ctrl`+`Delete`
Demote	`Tab`
Double-spacing	`Ctrl`+`2`
Find	`Ctrl`+`F`
Go To dialog box	`Ctrl`+`G`
Hanging indent	`Ctrl`+`T`
Hanging indent, remove	`Ctrl`+`Shift`+`T`
Increase font size one point	`Ctrl`+`]`
Insert date	`Alt`+`Shift`+`D`
Insert page break	`Ctrl`+`Enter`
Insert time	`Alt`+`Shift`+`T`
Justify	`Ctrl`+`J`
Left indent	`Ctrl`+`M`
Left indent, remove	`Ctrl`+`Shift`+`M`
Open dialog box	`Ctrl`+`O`
Promote	`Shift`+`Tab`

Keyboard Shortcut Summary (continued)

Replace	Ctrl + H
Show/hide characters	Ctrl + Shift + 8
Single spacing	Ctrl + 1
Start Spelling and Grammar checker	F7
Thesaurus dialog box	Shift + F7

UNIT 5: EXCEL 2003

AutoSum	Alt + =
Comma style	Ctrl + Shift + !
Currency style	Ctrl + Shift + $
Delete to end of line	Ctrl + Delete
Display formulas	Ctrl + ~
Format Cells dialog box	Ctrl + 1
General style	Ctrl + Shift + ~
Percent style	Ctrl + Shift + %

UNIT 6: ACCESS 2003

Delete selected object	Delete
Open selected object	Enter
Open selected object in Design view	Ctrl + Enter

Quick Reference Table Summary

Quick Reference Table Summary (continued)

Preface

Microsoft® Office 2003: Essentials Course is a complete survey of the Office 2003 system. The text begins with basic computer concepts, introduces Windows®, and surveys Office 2003 applications. Students are introduced to Internet Explorer, Outlook®, Word, Excel, Access, and PowerPoint®. The text also includes integration lessons and ends with a comprehensive integration project that brings the Office applications together.

Over the last 10 years of writing and publishing Microsoft Office courses, Labyrinth has developed a unique instructional design that makes learning faster and easier for students at all skill levels. Teachers have found that the Labyrinth model helps them focus on the most complex topics and allows them more time to devote to students having difficulty with the material. The instructions are carefully written and the compelling case studies demonstrate the relevance of topics in practical situations. We've crafted 235 Hands-On and Critical Thinking exercises to reinforce the subject matter and ensure mastery of the material.

Microsoft Office 2003: Essentials Course has a companion online course that includes integrated multimedia content and is available for the Blackboard Learning System™. The same strengths of instructional design and carefully crafted, hands-on exercises that work so well in the classroom also enable students to study effectively at home or the office with minimal need to contact an instructor for assistance.

The course is also supported on the Labyrinth Web site with a comprehensive instructor support package that includes detailed lesson plans, PowerPoint presentations, a course syllabus, extensive test banks, and more.

We are grateful to the many teachers who have used Labyrinth titles and suggested improvements to us during the 10 years we have been writing and publishing Office books. *Microsoft Office 2003: Essentials Course* has benefited from the reviewing and suggestions of Jaclyn Winskie M. ED at Southeastern Technical College.

About the Authors

Sandra Caldwell (BA, Liberal Arts) has provided corporate training, technical writing, workshop leadership, and consulting to corporate and small businesses in Boston, Chicago, Philadelphia, and Pittsburgh for more than a decade. She is presently a corporate trainer with the Institute for Corporate and Professional Development at the Community College of Allegheny County as well a Microsoft technologies instructor for the Lifetime Learning division of the college. Sandra is also a computer instructor with Washington & Jefferson College.

Brian Favro (BSc, Computer Engineering) began teaching adult education classes in Richmond, CA in 1991. He found that few books on computer applications met the needs of students and began writing materials to meet those needs. From this experience, he launched Labyrinth Publications and developed the "ease of understanding" format that evolved, with the help of Russel Stolins, into the instructional model that makes Labyrinth books so unique. Other instructors liked what he was doing and soon Brian was selling his books to them, and Labyrinth Publications was born.

Judy Mardar has been an independent computer trainer, technical writer, and consultant for many years. She teaches, writes, and consults at the Community College Workforce Alliance, as well as with private training companies, the state government, and small businesses. She is a certified Microsoft Office Expert and has trained thousands of people to use computers and business software over the last 10 years.

Michelle Marotti (BS, Computer Science; MS, Education) earned her degrees from Southern Oregon University. While at Southern Oregon, she began teaching seminars for Word, Excel, and Access, helping the staff migrate to these new applications. After receiving her teaching certificate, she went on to teach high school computer classes. Since June of 2000, she has taught at DeKalb Technical College outside of Atlanta, Georgia as a computer instructor.

Jill Murphy (BS, Education) has 20 years of experience with the IBM Corporation in technical support, curriculum development, training trainers, and training management. In her many years of training in the corporate environment, Jill has developed a deep understanding of adult learning principles and accelerated learning techniques. This experience has given her the background for writing effective training materials. Currently, she focuses on instructional design and curriculum development. Jill is a coauthor on the Labyrinth Silver Series title *Welcome to Computer Concepts and Microsoft Works.*

Russel Stolins (MA, Educational Technology) teaches at Santa Fe Community College. He has been teaching adults about technology since 1982, including courses on desktop publishing, computer concepts, Microsoft Office applications, multimedia design, and the Internet. He is recognized nationwide as an expert in classroom teaching techniques and instructional technology, often being invited to present at education conferences throughout the U.S. In the fall of 2000, Russel developed his first Web-based course using the Blackboard Learning System in Georgia. The course has since been rolled out nationwide and new courses for the Blackboard Learning System and WebCT are currently under development. Russel's latest books, *Laying a Foundation with Windows XP* and *Welcome to the Internet,* were published by Labyrinth Publications in 2003.

Introduction

Welcome to Labyrinth Publications, where you'll find your course to success. Our real world, project-based approach to education helps students grasp concepts, not just read about them, and prepares them for success in the workplace. Our straightforward, easy-to-follow language is ideal for both instructor-led classes and self-paced labs. At Labyrinth, we're dedicated to one purpose: delivering quality courseware that is comprehensive yet concise, effective, and affordable. It's no wonder that Labyrinth is a recognized leader in Microsoft Office and operative system courseware.

More than a million users have learned Office our way. At Labyrinth, we believe that successful teaching begins with exceptional courseware. That's why we've made it our goal to develop innovative texts that empower both teachers and students. We give educators the necessary resources to deliver clear, relevant instruction and students the power to take their new skills far beyond the classroom.

Labyrinth Series Give You More Choices

Labyrinth offers seven exceptionally priced series to meet your needs:

- Microsoft® Office 2003 Series—These full-length, full-featured texts explore applications in the new Office 2003 series. All application specific books in this series are Microsoft Office Specialist approved for the Core certification exam and the Word and Excel books are approved for the Expert level certification exam.

- Silver™ Series—Designed especially for adult learners, seniors, and non-native speakers, this series includes larger fonts and screens, our unmistakable straightforward design, and fun hands-on projects.

- ProStart Foundations™ Series—These full-length, full-featured texts for operating systems and applications include the new Microsoft Windows titles and are designed to lay a solid foundation for students.

- ProStart™ Series for Office XP—These full-length, full-featured texts walk students through the basic and advanced skills of the primary Office XP applications. Most are Microsoft Office Specialist approved. The Office XP Essentials and Comprehensive courses offer surveys of all the primary Office XP applications.

- Briefcase™ Series for Office XP—The popular and inexpensive choice for short classes, self-paced courses, and accelerated workshops (or mix and match for longer classes), these concise texts provide quick access to key concepts. Most are Microsoft Office Specialist approved.

- Off to Work™ Series for Office 2000—Full-length, full-featured texts set the standard for clarity and ease of use in this series. All books in this series are Microsoft Office Specialist approved.

- Briefcase Series for Office 2000—Designed for short classes, self-paced courses, and accelerated workshops, each lesson in this series is broken down into subtopics that provide quick access to key concepts. All books in this series are Microsoft Office Specialist approved.

Microsoft Office 2003 Series Teaching Resources

Instructor Support Material

To back your success, Labyrinth provides a complete instructor support package that includes the following:

- Comprehensive classroom setup instructions
- Sample syllabi
- Detailed lesson plans, including a topic sequence and suggested classroom demonstrations
- PowerPoint presentations for use in lecturing (also available online to students)
- Student exercise files
- Printer-friendly exercise solution guides
- Answer keys for Concepts Review questions at the end of each lesson
- Teacher-customizable, project-based assessment exercises
- Teacher-customizable test banks for each lesson
- TestComposer test generator for editing test banks with Microsoft Word (or create new question banks and online tests)

These resources are available on our Web site at *http://labpub.com* and on our instructor support CD, which you can obtain my calling our customer service staff at 1-800-522-9746.

Web Site

The Web site *http://labpub.com/learn/oe3* features content designed to support the lessons and provide additional learning resources for this book. This main page contains links to individual lesson pages. Some of the items you will find at this site are described below.

PowerPoint Presentations The same presentations available to instructors are accessible online. This makes an excellent tool for review, particularly for students who miss a class session.

 Web-Based Simulations Some exercises contain topics that have Web-based simulations. These simulations can be accessed through the lesson pages.

Downloads Required course files can be downloaded on the lesson pages.

Student Exercise Diskette Files Files included on the exercises diskette that comes with the book are also available for download. These are starting point files used in the Hands-On, Skill Builder, Assessment, and Critical Thinking exercises.

Labyrinth's Successful Instruction Design

In conjunction with the straightforward writing style, Labyrinth books feature a proven instructional design. The following pages point out the carefully crafted design elements that build student confidence and ensure success.

Lesson introductions present clear learning objectives.

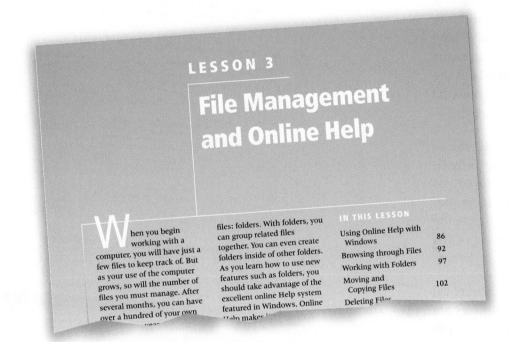

Case studies introduce a practical application that integrates topics presented in each lesson.

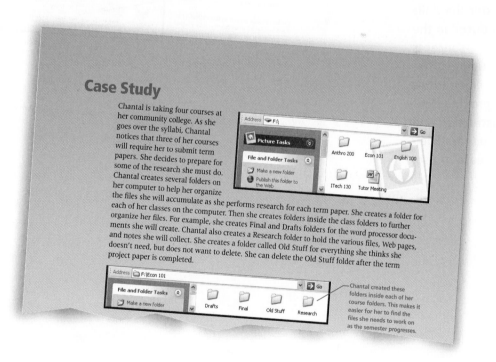

Concepts discussions are kept concise and use illustrations for added clarity and to help students understand the material introduced.

Quick Reference tables provide generic procedures for key tasks that work outside the context of the lesson.

Hands-On exercises are detailed tutorials that help students master the skills introduced in the concepts discussions. The illustrations provide clear instruction and allow unparalleled ease of use.

Browsing through Files

As you work with Windows programs such as WordPad and Paint, you will want to locate and open files you have created previously. Although you can open files from within an application program, sometimes it is more convenient to search directly through all of the files you have saved to a hard drive or floppy disk. This is the sort of task for which the My Computer window is perfectly suited.

QR **QUICK REFERENCE: MOUSE MOTIONS**

Motion	How to Do It	This motion is used...
Click	Gently tap and immediately to release the left mouse button.	to "press" a button or select a menu option or object on the screen.
Double-click	Click twice in rapid succession.	as a shortcut for many types of common commands.
Drag	Press and hold down the left mouse button while sliding the mouse. Release the mouse button when you reach your destination.	to move an object, select several objects, draw lines, and select text.
Right-click	Gently tap and immediately release the right mouse button.	to display a context-sensitive menu for the object at which you are pointing.
Point	Slide the mouse without pressing a button until the pointer is in the desired location.	to position the pointer before using one of the four motions above, to select an object on the screen, or to get a menu to appear.

Hands-On 2.7 Move and Size the WordPad Window

In this exercise, you will move the WordPad window to a different location on the Desktop, then change the size of the window.

1. Follow these steps to move the WordPad window:

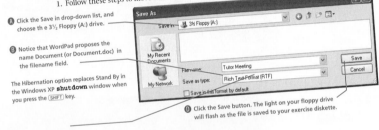

Ⓐ Click the Save in drop-down list, and choose the 3½ Floppy (A:) drive.

Ⓑ Notice that WordPad proposes the name Document (or Document.doc) in the filename field.

The Hibernation option replaces Stand By in the Windows XP **shutdown** window when you press the (SHIFT) key.

Ⓓ Click the Save button. The light on your floppy drive will flash as the file is saved to your exercise diskette.

The Concepts Review section at the end of each lesson includes both true/false and multiple choice questions.

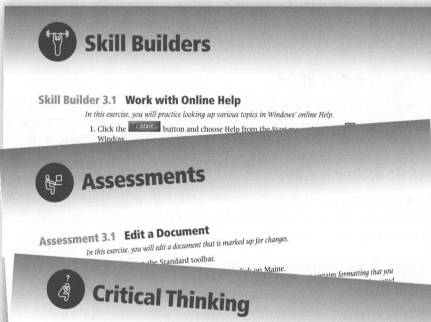

Concepts Review

True/False Questions

1. A Contents (or Home in Windows XP) search of online Help lets you locate Help topics by typing keywords. TRUE FALSE
2. A My Computer window lets you view the files and folders on the computer. TRUE FALSE
3. Windows organizes drives and folders in a hierarchy. TRUE FALSE
4. You can use the CTRL key to randomly select a group of files. TRUE FALSE
5. Folders can have subfolders within them. TRUE FALSE
6. You can use the Cut and Paste commands to move files. TRUE FALSE
7. Files are sent to the Recycle Bin when they are deleted from floppy disks. TRUE FALSE
8. The Properties command displays how much space is left on a floppy disk. TRUE FALSE
9. An Exploring window gives you a two-panel view of files and folder. TRUE FALSE
10. A quick way to open a file is to double-click on it in a My Computer windows. TRUE FALSE

Multiple Choice Questions

1. Which of the following methods would you use to view files and folders on the computer:
   a. Open a My Computer Window

3. Which command is used to create a new folder?
   a. File→Folder→Create
   b. File→New→Folder

Skill Builders, Assessments, and Critical Thinking exercises provide fun, hands-on projects with reduced levels of detailed instruction so students can test their mastery of the material.

Skill Builders

Skill Builder 3.1 Work with Online Help

In this exercise, you will practice looking up various topics in Windows' online Help.

1. Click the ⧉ start button and choose Help from the Start menu
   Window

Assessments

Assessment 3.1 Edit a Document

In this exercise, you will edit a document that is marked up for changes.

the Standard toolbar.

click on Maine.

contains formatting that you

Critical Thinking

Critical Thinking 3.1 On Your Own

Compose a new letter to Donna Wilson using the AutoCorrect shortcut you just created. Request that Donna send you information on Citizen Bank's new Small Business Credit Line program. Let Donna know that because you are starting a new business venture (you choose the venture), you are interested in obtaining financing from the bank. Save the letter as **Wilson Letter 2** then close it.

How This Book Is Organized

This book is organized according to the primary applications taught. This organization is designed to familiarize you with each application program and offers sufficient reinforcement so routine commands become second nature.

Unit 1: Computer Concepts and Windows

These lessons introduce the basics of running a computer with Windows. We begin with an overview of computer hardware and software. We then move on to running application programs, moving and sizing program windows, and saving work. Finally, we discuss Window's online Help and how to move and copy files on a floppy disk.

Unit 2: Internet Explorer

This lesson covers the basics of browsing the World Wide Web. We learn how to navigate to Web site with Web addresses (URLs) and hyperlinks. We also learn how to use Internet search engines and to print Web pages we find particularly interesting and informative.

Unit 3: Outlook 2003

This lesson discusses the essential features of Outlook 2003. We learn how to compose email messages, check for incoming messages, and how to reply to messages that we receive. We also explore Outlook's Help feature and learn how to create folders to organize our messages.

Unit 4: Word 2003

These lessons introduce word processing with Word 2003. We begin with the basic techniques for keying and editing documents, and pay particular attention to business letters. We round out our discussion with the advanced topics of desktop publishing and emailing Word documents.

Unit 5: Excel 2003

These lessons cover worksheet skills with Excel 2003. We begin with how to construct and edit worksheets, and then move on to formatting. We conclude with a discussion of the advanced topics of charting and publishing workbooks to the World Wide Web.

Unit 6: Access 2003

These lessons cover database concepts and skills with Access 2003. We begin with an introductory discussion of database setup and the use of tables, queries, and reports. We conclude by learning how to output data from Access to Excel.

Unit 7: PowerPoint 2003

These lessons introduce presentation techniques with PowerPoint 2003. We learn the skills necessary to develop effective presentations, including working with templates, graphics, and animation. We also give specific tips and notes on how to deliver dynamic electronic presentations.

Unit 8: Comprehensive Integration

This lesson is a sophisticated project that joins the major Office 2003 applications. You will create, email, and post documents to the Web. This integrated project is designed to test your knowledge of the material presented in this book.

Unit 9: Appendices

Three appendices cover procedures that may not apply to all students:

- Appendix A: Using File Storage Media
- Appendix B: Using Outlook with Hotmail and Other Email Services
- Appendix C: Using Web-Based Email Simulations

Visual Conventions

This book uses many visual and typographic cues to guide you through the lessons. This page provides examples and describes the function of each cue.

Type this text   Anything you should type at the keyboard is printed in this typeface.

Tips, Notes, and Warnings are used throughout the text to draw attention to certain topics.

Command→Command   This convention indicates multiple selections to be made from a menu bar. For example, File→Save means to select File, and then select Save.

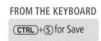 These margin notes indicate shortcut keys for executing a task described in the text.

 Quick Reference tables provide generic instructions for key tasks. Only perform these tasks if you are instructed to in an exercise.

 This icon indicates the availability of a Web-based simulation for an exercise. You may need to use a WebSim if your computer lab is not set up to support particular exercises.

 Hands-On exercises are introduced immediately after concept discussions. They provide detailed, step-by-step tutorials so you can master the skills presented.

 The Concepts Review section includes both true/false and multiple choice questions designed to gauge your understanding of concepts.

 Skill Builder exercises provide additional hands-on practice with moderate assistance.

 Assessment exercises test your skills by describing the correct results without providing specific instructions on how to achieve them.

 Critical Thinking exercises are the most challenging. They provide general instructions, allowing you to use your skills and creativity to achieve the result you envision.

Microsoft Office 2003: Essentials Course

UNIT 1

Computer Concepts and Windows

These lessons introduce the basics of how computers work and how to run Windows programs. You begin by learning basic hardware and software concepts that can help transform a computer from a mysterious box to a familiar tool. You will get a view of the major components of a computer system and how they interact to help you work and play. Next, you learn how to launch programs, arrange program windows on the screen, and save your work in files. Then you'll move on to working with the powerful online help built into Windows and most Windows programs. Finally, you learn how to browse for files and how to move and copy them from one location to another.

LESSON 1

Computer Concepts

When most people look inside a typical desktop computer, they see a bewildering array of cables, circuit boards, wires, and computer chips. However, the primary components of a computer system are easier to understand than you might expect. In this lesson, you will learn about the physical components of computer systems (hardware) and the logical components (software). You will learn how a computer system's hardware and software work together to help you work, play games, and access the Internet. By the end of this lesson, you should be able to identify the primary components of a typical computer system and make sense of the computer specifications featured in advertisements.

Additional learning resources are available at labpub.com/learn/oe3/

Case Study

Karen wants to purchase a computer system that will effectively meet her needs. Depending on the types of work she expects to perform on the computer, some features and capabilities will be more valuable than others. Here are some examples.

If she uses the system primarily for . . .	She will want these types of features . . .
Browsing the Internet	A basic system with a fast modem and an ink-jet printer
Desktop publishing	A fast system with a large monitor and a laser printer
Computer games	The latest video hardware for 3-D graphics
Video editing	A Firewire port that connects the computer to her digital video camera and a very large hard drive on which to edit videos

!TIP!

Spend your money on features and performance that make a tangible difference in your productivity and enjoyment.

Getting the Most for Your Money

The fastest, most feature-packed system is not necessarily Karen's best choice. She needs a balanced system, with all of its parts able to perform efficiently. For example, if she spends less money on the microprocessor (the computer's "brain"), she will have more money to spend on a better printer, a larger monitor (screen), and other features that could make the computer more useful for its primary tasks. The latest and fastest hardware almost always costs more than the previous generation, even though the previous generation may be just slightly slower.

Obsolescence

As Karen considers the purchase of a new computer system, she worries that it could soon become outdated. She even feels tempted to wait a few months for the next generation of technology to become available. Here are two factors she should keep in mind:

- Every computer eventually becomes obsolete—that is, unable to run the software you must use to get work done. But most new computers can keep up with developments for at least three to four years. That is enough time to benefit from your investment.

- If Karen waits several months for the next generation of computers, that is time she could have spent learning how to use the computer and becoming more productive. This time could be worth hundreds or even thousands of dollars to her. For example, it could lead to a better job or a promotion.

Learning the Basics

Before she makes her purchase decision, Karen decides to learn more about what's inside the computer itself. This has always been a mystery to her, but a friend explained that it's not really all that complicated to understand the basic components of the computer and the functions they perform.

Computer Systems

A computer system is a complex machine built with various mechanical parts, electronic circuits and program codes. All of these components must work together precisely. Later topics will explain many of these components in detail. This topic describes the most basic classifications of computer systems.

Basic Components

All the components of a computer system can be grouped into two types:

- **Hardware**—Hardware is the physical part of the computer system. Examples of hardware are the keyboard, the monitor, and any other physical component of the computer.

- **Software**—Software is the logical part of the computer system. Software consists of the programming instructions that let the computer interact with you to accomplish tasks. Software is typically stored on hard drives, CD-ROM disks, and floppy disks. Examples of software are Windows XP™ and Microsoft Word™.

Types of Computers

The first electronic computers were constructed in the 1940s. They were very large machines that filled a room with vacuum tubes and wiring. As computers have evolved, they have become smaller and faster. Two basic types of computers are:

- **Mainframe**—Mainframe computers can fit in a typical living room. They are designed to support large, corporate-level data processing. Hundreds of users can work simultaneously on a mainframe computer.

- **Personal Computers**—Personal computers (PCs), are small enough to fit on a desktop or inside a briefcase. A personal computer gets its computing power from a silicon chip called a microprocessor and is designed for operation by a single user.

Types of Personal Computers

There are three basic types of personal computer systems:

- **Desktop**—A desktop computer is designed to sit on top of your desk, or as a tower unit that sits alongside or under your desk. Desktop computers are easy to upgrade with new capabilities and devices.

- **Notebook**—Notebook computers are designed to be light enough to carry with you. They contain batteries, so they can operate without being plugged into a power outlet. This portability comes at a price. A notebook computer usually costs at least twice as much as a desktop computer with similar capabilities.

- **Handheld**—Handheld computers have become very popular among business users. They are very small and light and can easily fit into a purse or pocket. Also called a Personal Digital Assistant (PDA), this type of computer is designed to hook up to the user's primary computer to exchange schedules, phone numbers, and other information.

Network Servers

A network server usually looks similar to a desktop computer system, but runs special operating system software that provides network services to many other computers. Network servers let computer users share files and printers, send and receive email messages, and may also provide Internet and security services. Most personal computers used in business are connected to a network.

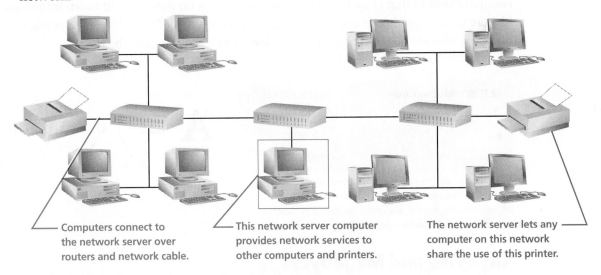

Computers connect to the network server over routers and network cable.

This network server computer provides network services to other computers and printers.

The network server lets any computer on this network share the use of this printer.

Desktop Computer Components

Desktop computer hardware is divided into the following components:

- **System Unit**—This is the box that holds the most fundamental components of the computer, such as the microprocessor, random access memory, and disk drives.

The system unit

- **Peripherals**—These are the hardware components outside the system unit. Examples of peripherals are the keyboard, mouse, monitor, and printer.

Units of Measure

The computer industry has its own terminology to describe and measure the performance and features of computer systems. These terms are explained in various sections of this lesson:

Term	What it Measures	See page ...
Bits	The most basic element of computer data	8
Bytes	The size of software files, the capacity of disk drives, and random access memory (RAM)	8
Gigahertz (GHz) Megahertz (MHz)	The speed of the computer's microprocessor	10
Resolution	The sharpness of output from a printer or the dots displayed on the computer screen	17

Bits and Bytes

The most basic unit of information on the computer is the bit. A bit is a single circuit in the computer system that is switched on or off. By itself, a bit doesn't hold much information. But if 8 bits are strung together in a specific order, they form a byte. This is like interpreting the dots and dashes of Morse Code. In the examples below, notice how varying the position of a single bit changes the meaning of each byte.

Letter	Morse Code	Byte (ASCII)*
A	. -	10000001
B	- - - .	10000010
C	- . - .	10000011

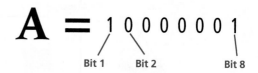

*ASCII (pronounced "ask-ee") is an internationally accepted code for representing characters in the computer. It defines byte codes for 128 different alphabetic, numeric, and symbol characters. (The name is an acronym for American Standard Code for Information Interchange.)

Kilobytes and Megabytes

The table below lists the most common terms used to describe the size of software files and the capacity of random access memory, hard drives, and other storage devices explained later in this lesson.

Term	Description	Examples
Bit	A single on-off switch in a computer circuit	0 or 1
Byte	A single character of data	A, B, C, $, @, {, \
Kilobyte (KB)	Approximately one thousand bytes of data	About one single-spaced typed page of text
Megabyte (MB)	Approximately one million bytes of data	About 3 average-length novels
Gigabyte (GB)	Approximately one billion bytes of data	3,000 novels' worth of text, or about 1,500 large color pictures

> **!NOTE!** *The exact size of a kilobyte is actually 1,024 bytes. However, most people just round off those extra 24 bytes. Similarly, most people round off the extra bytes when referring to a megabyte or gigabyte.*

Inside the System Unit, Part 1

Most of a computer's processing power is determined by the components inside the system unit. Nearly all system units have an open-architecture design with modular parts that can be snapped in and out of the system. Open architecture permits the upgrading of a computer with new features and capabilities long after it is originally built. Part 1 describes the basic processing components of the system unit:

- System board
- Microprocessor
- Random access memory (RAM)
- Disk drives

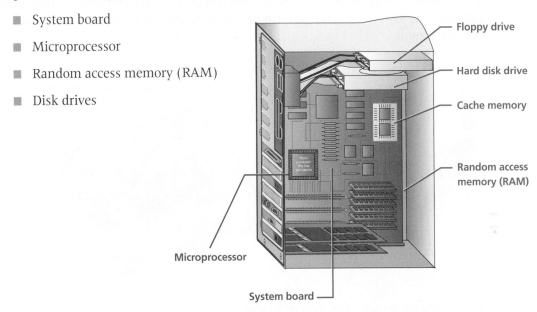

The System Board

The system board (also called the "motherboard") contains sockets and connectors that hold the essential circuitry of the computer. System boards on newer computers may also contain additional features such as built-in sound hardware and connectors to plug in disk drives.

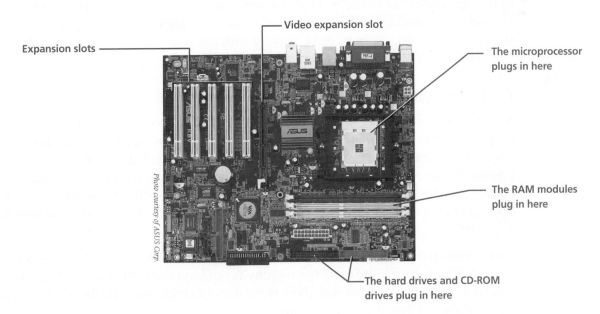

!NOTE!

*See the Lesson 1
Web page for
links to more
information on
microprocessors.*

The Microprocessor

A microprocessor is a single silicon chip containing the complete circuitry of a computer. The microprocessor serves as the "brain" of a microcomputer. Because it determines the basic processing power of the computer, most advertisements start by telling you the make and model of the microprocessor. Intel's Celeron™ and Pentium 4™ series are popular microprocessors for personal computers. Advanced Micro Devices (AMD) sells a speedy competitor to Intel's Pentium 4 microprocessor called Athlon. Many used computers have Pentium II microprocessors, which run more slowly but can still perform useful work such as word processing, Web browsing, and electronic mail.

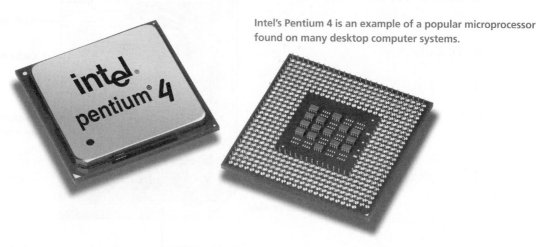

Intel's Pentium 4 is an example of a popular microprocessor found on many desktop computer systems.

Microprocessor Performance

Several design elements combine to set the performance of a microprocessor. The internal architecture of the microprocessor, its physical dimensions (die size), the efficiency of its most basic commands (instruction set), and features such as Hyper-Threading, are examples of these design elements. The quality of other components in the computer are also critical to the performance of its microprocessor. For example, a fast microprocessor in a computer equipped with very little random access memory (or RAM, described in the next major topic) may run programs more slowly than a slower microprocessor working with plenty of RAM. The most tangible factor in a microprocessor's performance is its clock speed.

Clock Speed

A microprocessor contains an internal clock that is set to a specific speed. One cycle (or one "tick" of the internal clock) is a single pulse of electrical current flowing through the microprocessor. The microprocessor carries out one action for each cycle—even if it's just registering something typed at the keyboard. The speed of the newest microprocessors is expressed in gigahertz (GHz), billions of cycles per second. Most ads for microcomputers indicate the microprocessor model and clock speed. For example: Intel Celeron/2.2 GHz, AMD Athlon 3200/2.2 GHz, and Intel Pentium 4/3.2 GHz.

Today's most powerful microprocessors can run at speeds of 2.4 GHz or faster. This top speed rating continues to increase every few months as vendors compete to put the fastest microprocessor on the market. However, sheer speed doesn't always translate literally into performance. That's where benchmarks can be helpful.

!NOTE!

e the Lesson 1
Web page for
links to more
formation on
icroprocessors.

Benchmarks

How can you compare one microprocessor with another? The best method is to research their ratings on a benchmark. Benchmarks are programs that measure the performance of a computer system. You can get a good idea of the relative performance of three microprocessors when you compare their benchmark test results on similarly configured systems.

Microsoft Office Performance Benchmark

Pentium 4 3.6 GHz	300
AMD FX-51 2.2 GHz	247
Pentium 4 2.4 GHz	208

Benchmark tests allow you to compare the performance of microprocessors.

Cost

If you want the fastest microprocessor available, you will pay a high premium for it. The very fastest model of a microprocessor can cost up to 50% more than the models just one or two levels below it. Thus, you could pay several hundred dollars more for a microprocessor that might give you just 10% more processing speed—a speed difference you might not even be able to notice as you work with your programs. If you are purchasing your first computer and expect to run basic programs, such as a word processor or a Web browser, you are probably better off buying a microprocessor that is a few notches below the top of the line but still meets your needs. The money you save (perhaps $400 or more) could be spent on other parts of the computer, such as a larger monitor or a better printer.

Random Access Memory

Random access memory (RAM) is a special type of chip that temporarily stores data as it is processed. While the microprocessor is the single most important component inside the system unit box, RAM plays a critical role in the computer's operation. Everything you see on the computer screen is actually temporarily stored in your computer's RAM. Think of RAM as the workbench of your computer.

How RAM Works

The microprocessor never accesses software directly from the computer's disk drives. Instead, the operating system software loads software from the disk drives into RAM. Then the microprocessor reads the software from RAM for processing and places the results of processing back into RAM. The process of transferring data in and out of the microprocessor to RAM is repeated millions of times each second. The diagram below displays the sequence that one operating system, Windows, follows to run programs and process data as you work.

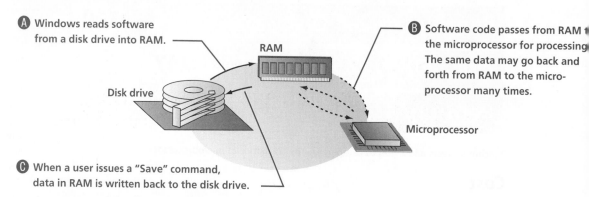

A Windows reads software from a disk drive into RAM.

RAM

B Software code passes from RAM to the microprocessor for processing. The same data may go back and forth from RAM to the microprocessor many times.

Disk drive

Microprocessor

C When a user issues a "Save" command, data in RAM is written back to the disk drive.

RAM is Volatile Memory

The moment you switch off power to your computer, all of the data residing in RAM is erased. Because it can change so instantly, RAM is sometimes referred to as volatile memory. In order to safely store your work for future work sessions, you must save it to a disk drive. Since RAM temporarily stores correspondence and other work you perform on the computer, it is very important to remember to save your work before you switch off your computer.

Locations of RAM

A computer system actually has various types of RAM in several locations inside the system unit. However, when you see an advertisement describing the amount of RAM within a computer, the designation always refers to the main system RAM. Other types of RAM include cache RAM (see page 13) and video RAM (described on page 18).

Types of RAM Modules

RAM chips are on small modules that plug into special slots in the system board. The capacity of these modules is rated in megabytes (MB). Popular sizes are 128, 256, and 512 MB. There are two basic types of RAM modules found in most new computers:

- **DDRAM**—double data rate (DDR) RAM has the potential to operate twice as fast as the older SDRAM modules. They do this by reading and writing data simultaneously (thus doubling the speed). However, to harness this potential performance boost, the design of key components of the computer system, particularly the system board and microprocessor, must be compatible with this new technology.

- **SDRAM**—Until recently, SDRAM modules were the most common form of RAM on new computers. These snap-in modules are reliable and easy to upgrade and replace.

An SDRAM (DIMM) module

Cache RAM

Most computers also come with another form of RAM called a cache (pronounced "cash"). This is expensive, high-speed RAM that stores the most recently used program code and data. Any time the microprocessor needs fresh data to process, it checks to see if any of the data it needs is already in the cache. The microprocessor can work with data in the cache much more quickly than if it must go to normal RAM or the hard drive to process the data. Modern microprocessors have internal (also called Level 1) cache memory built right into them, and external (Level 2) cache memory installed on the system board.

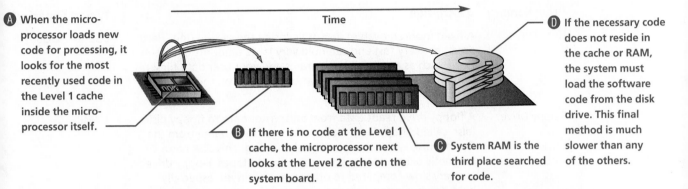

Ⓐ When the microprocessor loads new code for processing, it looks for the most recently used code in the Level 1 cache inside the microprocessor itself.

Time

Ⓑ If there is no code at the Level 1 cache, the microprocessor next looks at the Level 2 cache on the system board.

Ⓒ System RAM is the third place searched for code.

Ⓓ If the necessary code does not reside in the cache or RAM, the system must load the software code from the disk drive. This final method is much slower than any of the others.

How Much RAM Do You Need?

The system RAM in your computer is measured in megabytes. Most new computers are equipped with 256 to 512 megabytes of RAM. This is enough to run most popular programs. It is relatively easy to install additional RAM into a computer. The following points can help you determine the amount of system RAM you need for your computer:

■ The more RAM your computer has, the more programs you can run simultaneously.

■ Sophisticated application programs for computer graphics and databases require plenty of RAM to run efficiently. See the table on page 34 for a comparison of the RAM requirements of different types of application programs.

■ When you purchase application software, the amount of system RAM necessary to run the software is indicated on the package.

Disk Drives

When software is installed on a computer, it is stored on various disk drives in the system unit. Some types of disks are fixed inside the computer, while others are removable. The various disk drives are often referred to as the computer's mass-storage devices.

Listed below are the most popular types of disk drives for personal computers. Each type has capabilities that make it ideal for particular tasks.

Drive Name	Description	Typical Capacity*
Hard Drive	A fixed (nonremovable) disk drive inside the system unit. Hard drives are very fast and can hold very large amounts of software, such as application programs and your user data files. When you install a new application program on the computer, it is stored on the hard drive.	6GB to 100GB
Floppy Drive	A floppy drive reads data from and writes data to floppy disks (also called "floppies"). Floppy disks get their name from the flexible disk within the plastic disk housing. This disk has a magnetic oxide coating similar to cassette tapes. Floppy drives are very slow compared to other types of drives, especially hard drives. Floppy disks are most convenient for carrying work to another computer.	1.4MB
USB Flash Drive	A USB flash drive stores your data on a flash memory chip. You simply plug it into a USB port on any computer and Windows immediately recognizes it as an additional disk drive. The first USB drives supported the slower USB 1.1 standard (see page 23). Newer USB drives transfer data up to 40 times faster when plugged into a USB 2.0 port.	32–512MB
CD-ROM Drive	A CD-ROM (compact disk-read only memory) drive can hold large amounts of data. CD-ROM disks look similar to music CDs but store information differently—though most CD-ROM drives can play music CDs. CD-ROM drives are rated according to transfer speed. A 40x CD-ROM drive transfers data 40 times faster than the first CD-ROM drives that appeared in the late 1980s.	650MB
CD-RW Drive	CD-RW (compact disk-read write) drives allow you to write data to blank CDs and can read data from standard CD-ROM discs. Recordable CD-ROM discs are excellent media for long-term storage of important computer files. For example, you would want to store an electronic family photo album on a recordable CD-ROM disc.	650MB
DVD Drive	A DVD (digital video disk) drive can read both DVD and CD-ROM discs. This makes it a popular compliment to a CD-RW drive on many new computers. Bundled software allows you to view DVD movies on your computer monitor.	Up to 17GB
Removable Disk Drive	A removable-disk drive stores data on disk cartridges. By adding more disk drives, you can create virtually unlimited data storage space. The Iomega Zip™ is one popular example of a removable disk drive. You can store the equivalent of about 180 floppy disks on a single Zip disk.	100MB to 250MB

*The abbreviations for capacity are KB for kilobyte, MB for megabyte, and GB for gigabyte. For a description of these, see the glossary.

How Disk Drives Work

Most hard drives use disks covered with a magnetic oxide material similar to that used for cassette tapes. A read/write head hovers over the disks as they spin at high speed (4800 to 9600 rpm). The read/write head applies positive and negative charges to the surface of the disk to record data. Each positive or negative charge represents one bit of data.

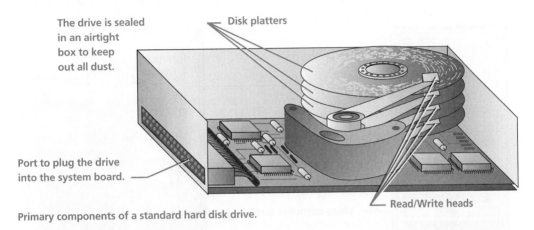

The drive is sealed in an airtight box to keep out all dust.

Disk platters

Port to plug the drive into the system board.

Read/Write heads

Primary components of a standard hard disk drive.

TIP!

Never move a computer while it is running. When the read/write heads are not in the "parked" position, there is a higher risk that they could touch the hard drive platters if the computer is moved.

Hard drives are extremely reliable, but they can be damaged. Hard drives are sealed in an air-tight box to keep out dust particles. If one of the read/write heads touches a disk, it can damage the hard drive and result in the loss of data—perhaps all of the data on the hard drive. When you switch off the computer, the read/write heads are automatically moved to a safe, "park" position, which keeps them away from the data on the hard drive.

RAM Compared to Disk Drives

Although RAM and the capacity of disk drives are both measured in megabytes, the two are very different. Many people who are new to computers confuse RAM with storage space on the disk drives. You can avoid this confusion if you think of RAM as the computer's temporary workbench memory and disk drives as the computer's permanent mass-storage devices.*

There are two important distinctions between RAM and mass storage:

- When you switch off the power to your computer, any data in RAM is erased, whereas data stored on disk drives is saved for future work sessions.

- Hard drives have far more capacity than RAM. A new computer usually has 40 or more times more hard drive storage space than the size of its RAM.

*The word permanent should not be taken literally. Like any electromechanical device, a disk drive might someday fail. It is also possible to inadvertently give a command to erase some or all of the data on the disk drive.

Inside the System Unit, Part 2

Although the microprocessor, RAM, and disk drives are critical to the performance of a computer, they require the support of many other components. Part 2 describes the video system that creates the image on the computer display and the expansion cards that give the computer additional capabilities.

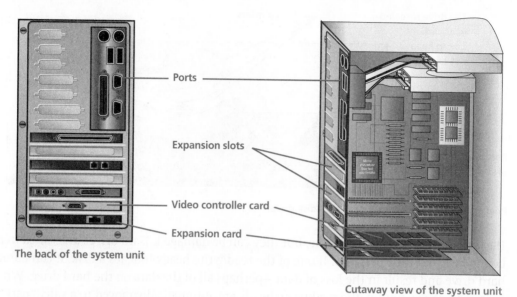

Ports

Expansion slots

Video controller card

Expansion card

The back of the system unit

Cutaway view of the system unit

Computer Video

A computer screen display is made up of hundreds of thousands of individual dots of light called pixels. Each pixel receives commands 60 to 80 times per second that control exactly which color it should display. These commands generate patterns of pixels to create the text, windows, controls, and other images you see on the screen.

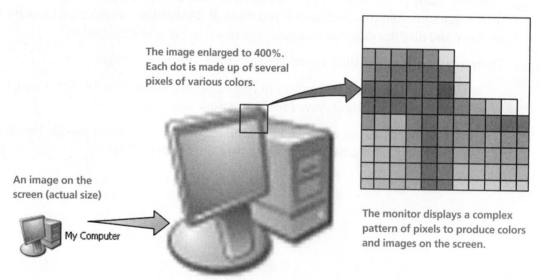

The image enlarged to 400%. Each dot is made up of several pixels of various colors.

An image on the screen (actual size)

My Computer

The monitor displays a complex pattern of pixels to produce colors and images on the screen.

Key Components

Three key hardware and software components make up the video subsystem of a computer:

- **Video monitor**—Most monitors appear similar to television sets, but contain more sophisticated and precise circuitry. Video monitors come in two primary types: traditional cathode ray tube (CRT) monitors and liquid crystal display (LCD) panels.

- **Video controller**—This is an expansion card inside the computer's system unit that sends video signals to the monitor. It controls the display of all the images you see on the monitor. Many computers have a video controller built right into the system board.

- **Video driver**—This is software that tells Windows how to work effectively with the video controller card and monitor.

Video Performance

There are three important ways to measure the performance of a video controller and monitor:

- *Resolution* is the number of pixels that the monitor can display. Displaying more pixels on your monitor will make the images on your computer screen appear sharper and smaller. The most basic resolution setting is 800 pixels across by 600 pixels down (written 800 × 600). Many computers are capable of almost double this resolution at 1024 × 768.

800 × 600   1024 × 768   1280 × 1024   1600 × 1200

- The *color depth* indicates how many different colors the screen can potentially display. A higher color-depth setting gives the most accurate display of graphics. If you want to display photo-realistic color images, make sure the video controller is capable of 24-bit color, which allows the monitor to display up to 16.7 million colors.

- The *refresh rate* is important when you purchase a CRT monitor (see page 19). A monitor that supports a refresh rate of 75 Hz or greater will reduce annoying and fatiguing flicker on the screen. LCD monitors do not suffer from a flicker problem and most operate with a refresh rate of 60 Hz.

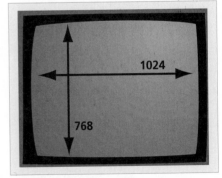

The screen resolution is measured horizontally and vertically in pixels.

Video RAM

The video controller has its own RAM that is separate from the RAM on the system board. This RAM is devoted to video display. Most computers sold today have plenty of video RAM to display millions of colors at all of the resolutions your video controller and monitor can display.

Choosing a Monitor

In June 2003, monthly sales of flat panel monitors surpassed sales of traditional CRT (cathode ray tube) monitors for the first time. Both types of monitors have advantages and disadvantages. Your choice of a monitor may be affected by the budget for your purchase, space available to set up a monitor, and the resolution setting your computing activities require.

Purchasing a Flat Panel Monitor

Flat panel monitors are becoming an increasingly popular replacement for standard CRT monitors. Most flat panel monitors use a technique called thin film transfer (TFT) to produce a bright image that can change rapidly to display movies and animation with the necessary speed and fluidity. Compared to traditional CRT monitors, flat panel monitors are much smaller and lighter, more expensive, and may not display some colors quite as accurately.

Key LCD Specifications

While many specifications and features define the quality of an LCD panel, the most important specifications are the panel's contrast ratio, viewing angle, and brightness. Other specifications indicate panel performance as well. In the final analysis, it is best to purchase an LCD monitor after you've had a chance to view it and compare it to similar monitors.

Specification	Description
Contrast ratio	This specification measures the difference between the brightest and darkest pixels (points of light) the screen can generate to form an image. The higher the contrast ratio, the greater the range of colors a panel can display.
Viewing angle	This specification measures the angle up to which you can see a clear, bright image on the screen. Images viewed on an LCD panel from outside its viewing angle will appear faded and washed out.
Resolution	This specification refers to the number of pixels the monitor can display. A 15-inch monitor usually displays 1024 pixels across by 768 pixels down (1024 × 768). A 17-inch monitor usually displays at 1280 × 1024. The more pixels the monitor displays, the sharper the image. LCD panels display at lower resolutions but the picture will either be significantly smaller or not as clear.
DVI or Analog input	A DVI (Digital Visual Interface) connection sends digital signals to the monitor. An analog connection must be converted from an analog (wave) signal to digital information when it reaches the monitor. Less expensive flat panel monitors usually only offer an analog input. Most high-end flat panel monitors feature both a DVI and an analog input. In terms of performance, a DVI connection usually results in a sharper image than an analog connection. NOTE: To use a DVI connection, your computer's video hardware must support this feature.

Purchasing a CRT Monitor

You should consider several features when purchasing a monitor. Remember that the screen resolution and refresh rate settings your monitor is capable of should also be compatible with the capabilities of your computer's video controller.

Feature	Description	
Screen size	Like television screens, the size of a computer screen is measured diagonally. Monitors also have a viewable area rating that measures the largest screen area you can display. For example, many 17" monitors have a viewable area of 15.9".	
Maximum resolution	A high-quality monitor can display a maximum resolution of 1024 × 768 pixels or greater.	
Dot pitch	Dot pitch refers to the size of the individual points of light (pixels) on the screen. A larger dot pitch causes images on the screen to appear fuzzier and coarser.	
Vertical frequency	A vertical frequency setting of 70 hertz or better results in a very steady image with no noticeable flicker.	

3-D Video Controllers

Some video controllers are specially optimized for computer games. Many of the latest computer games have some dazzling 3-D special effects. However, these special effects can appear jagged and jerky on older hardware. The latest generation of 3-D video controllers plug into system boards equipped with an Accelerated Graphics Port (AGP) and can display textured 3-D images with great speed and detail.

Expansion Cards

Expansion cards are modular circuit boards that plug into the computer to add new features and capabilities, some of which might not even have existed when the computer was manufactured. For example, you could add an expansion card to connect a scanner or video camera to the computer.

Examples of Expansion Cards

There are numerous expansion cards you can purchase and plug into your computer. Any time you buy an expansion card, it also comes with the software necessary to use its features.

Card type	Description
Modem	A modem lets you dial over a standard phone line to connect to other computers. An internal modem is installed on an expansion card. An external modem is a peripheral. (See page 24 for details on modems).
Sound	A sound card can generate high-quality sound and music on the computer. This is useful for games and programs such as online encyclopedias. Some sound cards connect to a musical keyboard so you can create your own compositions.
Video capture	The video capture card has a connector for a video camera and software that helps you capture (record) video onto your computer's hard drive. You can edit captured video to add special effects and titles. After editing, you can record the video from the hard drive back to videotape.
Network or LAN	The network card lets you connect your computer to a local area network (LAN). If you have network cards on two or more computers in your home, you can set up a small version of a LAN called a peer-to-peer network.
TV	A TV card can display a television picture in a window on your monitor. It can connect to an antenna or cable TV service. The card comes with software to tune in channels.

Expansion Slots

Expansion cards plug into expansion slots on the system board. Most computers sold today come with two or three PCI (Peripheral Component Interconnect) expansion slots. However, with the popularity of devices that plug into USB ports (see page 23), the need for expansion slots and expansion cards has diminished. Before you purchase an expansion card, you should always check to see that you have an open slot for it. The open slot and the expansion card must be of the same type.

Slot Type	Description
PCI	This is a very fast connection to your computer's microprocessor. Many new types of expansion cards are designed for this type of slot. For example, video capture and network cards are now typically designed to fit into a PCI slot. PCI is short for Peripheral Component Interconnect.
ISA	This is an older type of slot. It is not as fast as PCI, but there are still many types of expansion cards for which this slot is fast enough for good performance. ISA is short for Industry Standard Architecture.

The Bus

Expansion slots connect to the microprocessor by a data path called the bus. This path allows the RAM ports and expansion slots on the computer to communicate with the microprocessor. A faster bus means that the computer's devices can share data more rapidly, contributing to overall system performance.

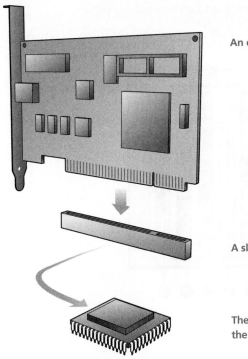

An expansion card

A slot on the system board

The bus acts as a highway from the slot to the microprocessor

Ports

A port is a place to plug a cable or peripheral device into your computer's system unit. The keyboard, mouse, and monitor plug into ports. Many expansion cards provide additional ports for specific devices. For example, a scanner may connect to the computer through a port on an expansion card. All computer systems come with several different ports built into the back of the system unit. Various cables are designed to work with the ports. For example, you would use a parallel cable to connect a printer to the parallel port.

The table below lists the most common types of ports, and they are shown in the figure at the bottom of this page. A computer system may have some or all of these ports.

	This port type . . .	is commonly used to connect . . .
❶	PS/2	a mouse and keyboard.
❷	USB port	a growing variety of peripheral devices, including scanners, keyboards, cameras, and monitors.
❸	Serial (Com1, Com2)	an external modem.
❹	Parallel (LPT1)	a printer.
❺	SCSI	a scanner or external disk drive.
❻	FireWire (IEEE 1394)	a digital video camera or external hard drive.
❼	Video	the monitor.
❽	Miniplugs	speakers, microphone, and sound sources.
❾	Joystick	a joystick for games.
❿	Phone jack	a telephone line to an internal modem.
⓫	RS-14	a network cable.

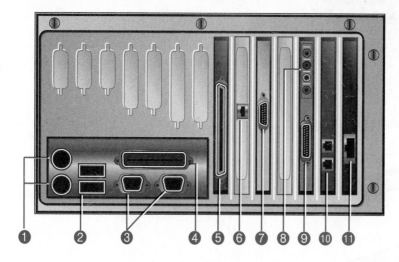

Selecting Peripherals

A peripheral is hardware outside the computer's system unit box. Peripherals are usually associated with entering data into the computer (input) or outputing data in the form of screen displays, printouts, and sound. The monitor is one example of a peripheral covered earlier in this lesson.

Plug and Play

Plug and Play devices are designed for Windows to recognize automatically. When Windows detects a new Plug and Play device, it searches for and loads the necessary software to work with the device or prompts you to perform an installation from a CD that came with the device.

USB Ports

USB (Universal Serial Bus) ports allow you to connect many different types of devices to the computer. This connection has become very popular for connecting scanners, printers, digital cameras, keyboards, mice, and other peripherals. USB ports allow you to chain several different devices to a single port on your computer. You can also plug and unplug a USB device while the computer is running. This capability is called "hot swapping." Many new computers now have two USB ports at the back of the computer (see figure on the previous page) as well as two USB ports at the front.

USB 1.0 and 2.0

The first version of USB ports available were versions 1.0 and 1.1. These supported data transfer speeds of up to 12 Mbps (megabits per second). USB 2.0 devices can support data transfer speeds 40 times faster than USB 1.0 devices (up to 480 Mbps). USB 1.1 devices will work in USB 2.0 ports but at a reduced speed.

Keyboard

The keyboard is the main data entry device for a microcomputer. There are numerous makes of keyboards, and they can differ considerably in quality. You may want to consider an ergonomic keyboard. These spread out the keys or even split the keyboard in half to give your hands a more natural typing angle. The style and placement of the computer keyboard is an important factor in healthy computing habits. See page 35 for tips on setting up your computer with the keyboard at the proper height.

Microsoft's Natural Multimedia Keyboard features an
ergonomic shape for more comfortable typing.
Photo courtesy of Microsoft Corporation.

The Mouse

The mouse is a pointing device to give commands to the computer by pointing and clicking at specific places on the screen. An ergonomically designed mouse fits very comfortably in your hand; some also have a third button or scroll wheel you can program to issue special commands. A typical mouse uses a small rolling ball at the bottom of the device to sense movement. An optical mouse uses a light sensor to track movement.

This cordless mouse features a scroll wheel to make browsing in data windows easier.

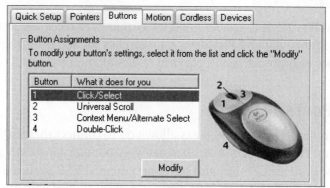

You can program certain mouse buttons and the scroll wheel to perform custom functions

Trackballs

A popular alternative to the mouse is called a trackball. It uses a rotating ball that you roll with your thumb or fingers. Some users prefer a trackball because it saves desktop space. Others find rolling the trackball more comfortable than moving a mouse. A combined trackball and mouse is also available.

A trackball mouse can save space on your desk

Dial-Up Modems

A modem (MOdulator/DEModulator) is a device that translates the digital data of computer communication into analog sound waves that can be transmitted over a voice telephone line. At the other end of the line, another modem converts the sound back into digital data. With a modem you can:

- dial up and exchange information with other computers.

- connect to an Internet service provider (ISP) for Web browsing and email.

- use your computer to send and receive faxes.

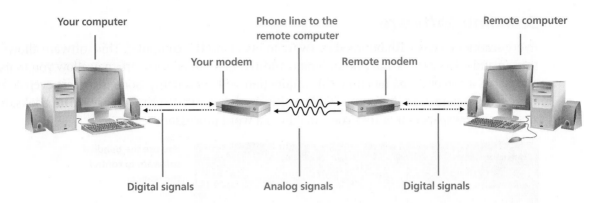

Your computer

Phone line to the
remote computer

Remote computer

Your modem

Remote modem

Digital signals

Analog signals

Digital signals

Types of Dial-Up Modems

Modems come in both external and internal models. Internal modems are expansion cards you can plug into an expansion slot inside the system unit. An external modem is a peripheral that sits on your desk and plugs into the back of your computer with a serial cable. Most new computers come with an internal modem as standard equipment. Some modems even offer voice mail capabilities (for example: "To leave a message for Bob, dial 1; to leave a message for Sue, dial 2," and so on).

Photo courtesy of 3Com Corporation.

Modem Speed

A faster modem is useful if you frequently browse the Web. You measure a modem's speed as the bits per second of digital data it can transmit over a telephone line under ideal conditions. For example, under ideal conditions a 56K modem can send and receive data at nearly 56,000 bits per second (or about 7,000 bytes per second). However, telephone line quality, the facilities of Internet service providers, and other factors may reduce a modem's actual speed to less than its rated speed.

Other Types of Modems

Most modems in use today work on standard telephone lines. However, a new generation of telecommunications technology is beginning to replace phone modems. These technologies are becoming widely available in major metropolitan areas.

■ A *cable modem* allows you to access the Internet at speeds up to 35 times faster than standard phone modems. Cable modems connect to the same cables that carry cable television signals.

■ *DSL* (Digital Subscriber Line) modems offer data speeds up to 50 times faster than a telephone modem. DSL modems connect to a standard telephone line.

Scanners

A scanner turns pictures and photographs into computer files that you can place into documents or attach to email messages. Flatbed scanners work similarly to copy machines. You place the original face down the scanner's glass plate, then run software to select and scan the part of an image you wish to save as a computer file.

Photo courtesy of Hewlett-Packard Corp.

Scanning Software

Every scanner comes with bundled software to install on the computer. This software allows you to scan and edit pictures and photographs. Additional bundled software may allow you to use the scanner as a copier or fax machine (in conjunction with a modem). Some scanners even come with optical character recognition (OCR) software that converts printed pages from books, magazines, and newspapers into text you can edit in a word processor.

You use the bundled software to control the scanner.

Printers

A printer is a very useful peripheral for many types of work. A printer can help you create professional looking documents, custom business cards, large signs, and other types of printouts. Modern printers produce very sharp output inexpensively and quickly. Two types of printers work best for home and office use:

- **Laser**—Laser printers use a laser to trace a pattern on a drum that picks up toner and fuses it to the paper to print text and graphics. Laser printers are very fast and they print sharp images; however, most laser printers print only in black and white. Color laser printers cost more than black-and-white models. A good color laser printer costs about twice as much as an equivalent black and white model.

- **Ink-jet**—These printers spray microscopic drops of ink on the page. Compared to laser printers, ink-jets are slower and cannot print as sharply. But most ink-jet printers are capable of color printing. When used with special paper, and set to a low speed, some ink-jet printers can create photo-realistic color pictures.

There are two important measures of printer performance:

- The resolution of printing is measured in dots per inch (DPI). The higher the resolution of a printout, the sharper the appearance of graphics and text on the page. Early laser printers and most ink-jet printers can print up to 600 DPI. Most new laser printers now print at 1200 DPI.

- The speed of a printer is typically measured as the number of pages per minute (PPM) it is able to print.

The table below is a generalized comparison of laser and ink-jet printers.

Printer Type	Speed	Prints color	Printer resolution printing in . . .	
			Color	Black and White
Laser	6–24 PPM	No	N/A	600–1200 DPI
Color Laser	6 PPM color 18 PPM b/w	Yes	600 DPI	1200 DPI
Ink-Jet	2–5 PPM color 5–9 PPM b/w	Yes	300 DPI	600 DPI

Digital Camera

Digital cameras have become a popular way of taking photographs that are easy to transfer over the Internet and copy to a CD-ROM disc. The number of pixels it can capture in a single shot measures the capability of most cameras. For example, a 1-mega pixel camera can take a picture composed of approximately 1 million pixels. A 3.35-mega pixel camera can take photographs that result in a clear 8" x 10" printed image. Most digital cameras rely on a removable memory cartridge to store photos. Some digital cameras can also take small movies with sound.

The Nikon CoolPix 4500 is an example of a digital camera.

Attribution: Photo courtesy of Nikon USA.

Digital Video Camera

Digital video cameras are similar to traditional video cameras, except that they capture and store video as a series of digital images instead of as analog images on videotape. Digital video cameras can store images on various media, including memory cards, digital videotape, and CDs. One advantage of digital video cameras is that it is easy to transfer the video to a computer via a USB or FireWire (IEEE 1394) connection. Since the video is already digitized, you can use software to edit it and apply special effects.

Surge Protector

A computer has very sensitive circuitry. A power surge can burn out the most important and expensive components of your computer. To prevent this, your computer and its peripherals should always be connected to a surge protector. Most computer hardware also requires a grounded (three-prong) power outlet. Some surge protectors come with several on-off switches for the outlets. This is very convenient, since it makes switching off individual components of the computer system when they are not in use easy to do.

Photo courtesy of Kensington Technology Group.

Uninterruptible Power Source

If your electrical utility is subject to frequent blackouts and brownouts, you should consider the purchase of an uninterruptible power source (UPS). This device contains a power sensor that instantly switches to a high-capacity battery any time the power to your computer is cut off. The UPS will also sound an audible tone that warns you the computer is running off the battery. The amount of time a UPS can keep the computer running depends on the size of the UPS battery and the computer's power requirements. Typically, the UPS should be able to power the computer for at least five minutes. This provides enough time to save your work and shut down the computer normally.

An example of a UPS for home or office computer.

Photo courtesy American Power Conversion Corporation.

Computer Software

Computer software is the invisible, logical component of the computer. Most software exists in the form of program instructions that control how the computer functions and performs tasks for you. Software also stores the results of the work you perform on the computer. Without software, a computer is useless.

COMPUTER SOFTWARE		
Program Files		**User Files**
Operating Systems	**Applications**	
Windows XP	Word	Letter
Windows 2000	Excel	Digital Photo
Macintosh System X	Internet Explorer	Name & address list
Linux 3.3	Quicken	Web page
DOS 6.0	Outlook Express	Digital Video clip

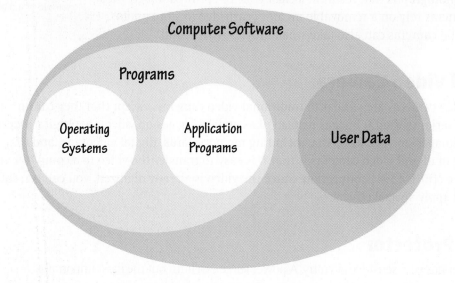

Files

The basic unit of software is the file. A file is a collection of computer data that has some common purpose. Examples of files are application programs, digital images, or a letter you have typed. Depending on the programs you install and use, the computer may have thousands of files stored on its disk drive.

Programs

A program is software code designed to run the computer and help you get work done. A simple program can be a single software file. Complex programs like Word and Excel are made up of dozens of files, each of which helps you use some feature of the program. There are two basic types of programs in a computer system: the operating system and application programs.

Operating System

The operating system (OS) is the basic software your computer needs in order to run. The operating system software takes control of the computer soon after it is turned on and controls all of the basic functions of your computer. The operating system also helps you browse through and organize your user files (see the next page). This makes finding and opening documents and other types of work you have created previously easier.

Every computer requires an operating system in order to function. Windows XP is an operating system. Other popular operating systems include System X for the Macintosh, Windows 98, Linux, and Unix.

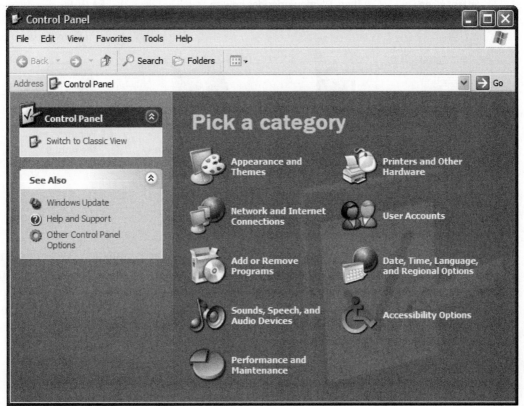

Most of the settings in the Windows XP Control Panel are controlled by the operating system.

Examples of the Operating System at Work

Here are two examples of how the operating system plays a vital role in every task you perform on the computer:

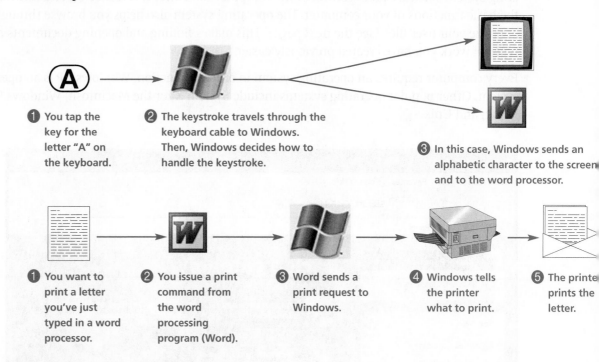

① You tap the key for the letter "A" on the keyboard.

② The keystroke travels through the keyboard cable to Windows. Then, Windows decides how to handle the keystroke.

③ In this case, Windows sends an alphabetic character to the screen and to the word processor.

① You want to print a letter you've just typed in a word processor.

② You issue a print command from the word processing program (Word).

③ Word sends a print request to Windows.

④ Windows tells the printer what to print.

⑤ The printer prints the letter.

Application Programs

Application programs (or simply "applications") help you accomplish tasks. For example, you use a word processing program to type letters and create other documents. You can use financial management programs to balance checkbooks and investment accounts. You use graphics programs to create drawings and other graphic art. Even games for entertainment are a form of application program. Here are some examples of popular application programs:

This application . . .	helps you to . . .
Word	write letters, memos, reports, and other text documents.
Excel	work with numbers on a spreadsheet.
Outlook	keep a schedule, and send and receive electronic mail messages.
Access	keep track of large amounts of data.
PowerPoint	create on-screen presentations.
Internet Explorer	browse sites on the World Wide Web.
Photoshop	edit and add special effects to photographs.
PageMaker	create newsletters, flyers, and books.
Quicken	write checks and keep track of your personal finances.
TurboTax	fill out tax forms and print a tax return, or file the return electronically.
FrontPage	create your own Web sites.
Windows Movie Maker	create and combine your own digital videos by adding titles and special effects.

User Files

User files (or simply "files") contain information and work that users have created in application programs. When you finish a piece of work, you will usually save it as a file on a hard drive or floppy disk. Examples of work you might store in user files are a:

- letter you typed and saved with a word processor
- drawing or digital photograph
- database of names and addresses
- record of your checking account transactions
- game you have saved to play later

Computer Viruses

A computer virus is a software program designed to cause trouble on a computer system. Viruses can invisibly transmit themselves to "infect" a computer without your knowledge. For example, if you copy a virus-infected program to a floppy disk, then run that program on another computer, the virus may infect other programs on the new "host" computer. There are many types of computer viruses, and new ones are discovered almost every day. Most viruses are harmless, but a very few have been known to do great damage, such as erase your hard drive!

Antivirus Software

A special type of application software designed to detect and erase viruses is called an antivirus program. It is a good idea to purchase and install antivirus software on a new computer. An antivirus program watches all software activities on the computer, and halts the processing of any program it considers to be performing a "suspicious" activity. Antivirus programs can detect the unseen activities of most viruses when they try to invade your system and can usually "clean" (erase) a virus in an infected file.

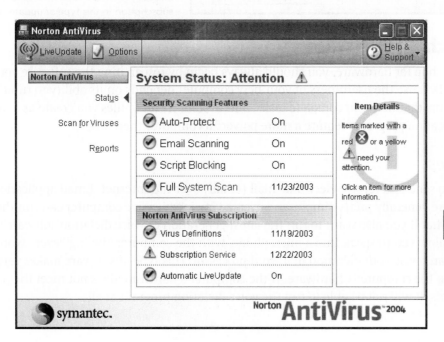

This antivirus program loads itself automatically when the computer is powered up. It watches for suspicious activity that could indicate a virus attempting to infect the system.

Macro Viruses

A macro virus is a small program embedded within a word processor, spreadsheet, or other type of user data file. These macro viruses are the first viruses not contained inside program files. (A macro is a saved series of keystrokes and commands that you can "replay" to perform repetitive tasks.) Most modern antivirus software can detect and clean macro viruses.

Virus Definition Updates

New strains (types) of computer virus are discovered almost daily. Since many viruses use similar techniques to invisibly "infect" a computer system, many antivirus programs can detect new strains of virus without having detailed information about them. If the computer has a connection to the Internet or is equipped with a modem, many antivirus programs can utilize a special updating feature. This feature dials out and copies (downloads) the most up-to-date virus definitions onto your hard drive. These updates can ensure that your antivirus program has the latest information on new types of viruses.

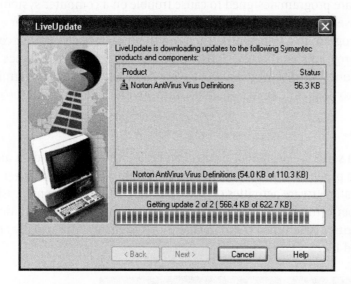

This screen walks a user through contacting the vendor for the latest virus definitions. Most antivirus software vendors offer a free one-year subscription to this type of update service.

Researching Software

Before you shop for hardware, you should always begin by researching the software you expect to run. Why? Because the usefulness of your new computer depends on its ability to run the application programs that help you complete tasks, and to store the data files you create as you work. Some application programs require a more powerful computer than others.

Examples

You want to send and receive electronic mail (email) over the Internet. Email application programs are generally pretty simple, and even a very inexpensive computer can run them. However, what if you also want to run the latest generation of voice dictation software? These programs allow you to speak into a microphone, with the computer "typing" every word you say. Then you can revise your dictation in a word processor. This type of software makes very high demands on the computer's hardware. If the computer's hardware does not meet the program's requirements, it will not be able to run the voice dictation program at all.

Reading Software Requirements

When you purchase software in a store, the package will indicate the type of hardware and operating system required to run the software. Before you purchase a computer, you should examine the packaging of programs you intend to run. Pay close attention to all of the requirements specified for each program. This research will help you determine exactly which features and equipment are necessary and most valuable. For example, you may discover that the fastest microprocessor on the market will not be as useful to you as more RAM.

Making Your Purchase Decision

Once you have completed your software research, you are ready to make your purchase decision. The table below summarizes the basic specifications to keep in mind when you shop for your computer.

Requirement	Notes	Examples
Microprocessor	This specification tells you the model and speed of the microprocessor required to run the software. A slower or older model microprocessor may not be able to handle the demands of a sophisticated application program. On the other hand, many basic programs will run fine with the slower microprocessor you might find in a used computer.	Pentium 4, 3.2 GHz Celeron, 1.8 GHz Pentium II, 266 MHz
Operating system	Application programs are designed to run with specific versions of Windows or some other operating system. Most programs designed for earlier versions of Windows will also (but not always) work smoothly with a later version of Windows.	Windows 2000 Windows XP Macintosh System X
RAM	More sophisticated programs typically require more RAM to run efficiently. If you intend to run several programs at once, you probably want to have at least twice as much RAM as is required by the most demanding program you will run.	512 MB of RAM with Windows XP
Hard drive storage space	Some programs require a large amount of space on your hard drive to run efficiently. There may be a minimal installation option that takes less hard drive space, and a full installation option that installs all the optional features of the program.	160 GB of hard drive space
CD-ROM or DVD drive	You will install most programs from a CD-ROM disc. Computer DVD drives can also read CD-ROM discs. Some very large programs (such as encyclopedias) may be available on DVD disc.	CD-RW drive DVD-RW drive
Extras	Some software applications may recommend additional hardware to provide more value from the program.	56K modem Firewire (IEEE 1394) port

Software System Requirements

All software application programs have specific requirements for the computer hardware and operating system on which they run. For example, some newer application programs will not run on older versions of Windows and certain programs require more RAM than others to run efficiently. Software vendors print system requirements on the retail boxes and on their Web pages.

 TIP! *Before you purchase new hardware make sure it meets or exceeds the system requirements of all software you intend to run on the computer.*

System Requirements Example

The following table compares the software requirements of two similar application program suites.

SYSTEM REQUIREMENTS	MICROSOFT OFFICE 2003 STANDARD EDITION	WORDPERFECT OFFICE 11 STANDARD EDITION
Microprocessor	Pentium 233 MHz or higher	Pentium 166 or higher
System RAM	128 MB	64 MB (128 recommended)
Hard Drive Space	260 MB	370 MB
Operating System	Windows 2000 with SP3[1] Windows XP or later	Windows 98 Second Edition Windows NT 4.0 with SP6a Windows ME Windows 2000 with SP3 Windows XP
Other Required or Recommended Items	▪ Pentium II 400 MHz and a close-talk microphone required to use the speech recognition feature ▪ Some features require an Internet connection	

[1]This means "Service Pack 3." A service pack is essentially a package of software updates (sometimes called "bug fixes.")

Setting Up a Computer

When you set up a computer, you can take specific measures to make your work and play more productive and comfortable. This section offers advice on setting up a computer and developing healthy work habits that can reduce the risk of discomfort or injury.

Ergonomics

Ergonomics is the science of designing the equipment we work with to maximize productivity and reduce fatigue. When you set up a computer system at your home or office, it is important to consider how you can sit and work at the computer as comfortably as possible. A few rules of thumb can help you arrange your computer workstation ergonomically.

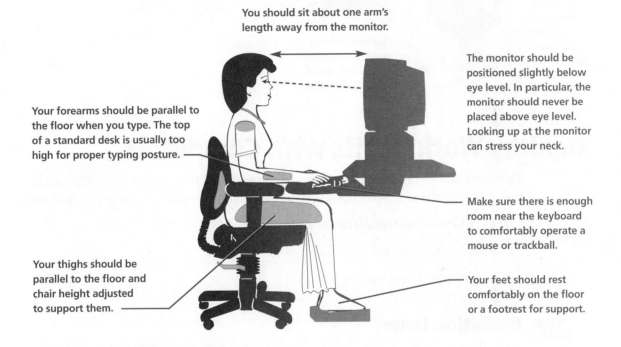

You should sit about one arm's length away from the monitor.

Your forearms should be parallel to the floor when you type. The top of a standard desk is usually too high for proper typing posture.

The monitor should be positioned slightly below eye level. In particular, the monitor should never be placed above eye level. Looking up at the monitor can stress your neck.

Make sure there is enough room near the keyboard to comfortably operate a mouse or trackball.

Your thighs should be parallel to the floor and chair height adjusted to support them.

Your feet should rest comfortably on the floor or a footrest for support.

Computer Furniture

Many stores carry furniture designed especially for computers. For example, certain desks equipped with keyboard drawers that place the keyboard at the optimal level for typing. If you expect to spend a great deal of time at the computer, good furniture is a sound investment in your health and comfort.

Photo courtesy of Computer Furniture Direct.

Your Chair

A high-quality chair is another key to working comfortably at the computer. It should have adjustments for the seat back and height. The chair should also give good support to your lower back. If the chair is equipped with arms, they should be adjustable.

An affordable alternative to an expensive computer chair is to purchase an ergonomic backrest instead. Backrests can save you 80% or more over the purchase of a chair.

See the Lesson 1 Web page for links to Web sites about computer-related ergonomics.

This backrest may give good support at 20% the cost of an equivalent chair.

Photos courtesy of Obusforme.

Healthy Work Habits with Computers

Operating any piece of equipment over a long period of time carries risks. The specific health risks posed by frequent computer operation are still being identified. Some of the risks under study are:

- radiation from computer monitors
- eye strain from full-time use
- repetitive stress injuries

Radiation Issues

Sit at least an arm's length away from the monitor.

All computer monitors emit radiation while in use. CRT (but not flat panel) monitors and television sets both use the same cathode ray tube (CRT) technology. However, CRT monitors are built with much better shielding to reduce radiation. The amount of radiation emitted by CRT monitors is not directly related to the size of the screen. In other words, a small, older monitor may emit more radiation than a new, larger one. Also, CRT monitors put out more radiation from the sides and rear than from the front.

Eye Strain

Periodically focus your eyes across the room or out a window (a different distance from the monitor).

Some computer users have reported blurred vision after long work sessions in front of a monitor. This can be caused by staring at a fixed distance for long periods of time. Our eyes are used to focusing at various distances every few minutes.

!TIP!

If you think you are experiencing a repetitive stress injury, seek medical advice as early as possible.

Repetitive Stress Injuries

Repetitive stress injuries (RSIs) can occur when the same motion is repeated over and over again for prolonged periods. If you are typing at a computer keyboard all day long, the muscles in your hands and wrists can become stressed. Some intense projects, such as graphic design, may require hundreds of motions each hour to maneuver the mouse and give commands from the keyboard.

Awareness is Key!

Awareness may be the best medicine to prevent the painful and debilitating effects of repetitive stress injuries. One symptom can be numbness and tingling sensations in the wrist, palm, or forearm. In a severe case, every motion of the affected area can become quite painful.

In recent years, there has been an increase in computer-related repetitive stress injuries, including tendonitis and carpal tunnel syndrome. This is a result of the widespread use of computers and the long hours people are working on them. These injuries are difficult to treat, so be careful and take preventive measures.

!TIP!

See the Lesson 1 Web page for links to Web sites about computer-related health issues.

Preventive Measures

With good work habits, your risk of injury is greatly reduced. The following tips can help you avoid a repetitive stress injury, even if you work at a computer many hours each day.

- Take frequent rest breaks.

- Do hand-strengthening exercises (keep a squeeze ball near the computer).

- Maintain proper hand positioning at the keyboard; a wrist rest may help you.

- Invest in ergonomic computer furniture and hardware, including a comfortable chair, keyboard, and mouse.

- Apply an ice pack to your hand and wrist to help reduce inflammation, but see a doctor if any type of discomfort continues.

Concepts Review

True/False Questions

1. The primary chip on a personal computer system board is called a microprocessor. TRUE FALSE

2. A megabyte is larger than a gigabyte. TRUE FALSE

3. Software designed to help you get work done is called user data files. TRUE FALSE

4. A computer's RAM works just like the storage space on the hard drive. TRUE FALSE

5. The sharpness of a printer's output is measured by its resolution. TRUE FALSE

6. The latest, fastest microprocessor is always the best choice for a new computer. TRUE FALSE

7. The image you see on the computer's monitor (screen) is made up of pixels. TRUE FALSE

8. Floppy disks can hold just as much data as hard drives. TRUE FALSE

9. Software that controls the computer's basic functions is called an operating system. TRUE FALSE

10. Because they are much smaller, notebook computers generally cost less than desktop computers. TRUE FALSE

Multiple Choice Questions

1. Which statement best describes how you should shop for a new computer?
   a. Get the fastest computer available.
   b. Get a computer that meets the requirements of the application program you plan to use.
   c. Get the least expensive computer available.
   d. None of the above

2. Hardware components that are outside the system unit case are called:
   a. Accessories
   b. Printers and modems
   c. Pointing devices
   d. Peripherals

3. Among the health risks of working with computers are the following:
   a. Radiation
   b. Gamer's elbow
   c. Repetitive stress injury
   d. Eyestrain
   e. a, c, and d
   f. a, b, c, and d

4. The three primary types of software are:
   a. Anti-virus, user data, applications
   b. Applications, user data, operating system
   c. Operating system, word processor, spreadsheet
   d. Applications, utilities, operating system

Concept Matrix

Place a check mark in the correct column for each term:

Item	Hardware	Software
Modem	_____	_____
Windows XP	_____	_____
Printer	_____	_____
Floppy disk	_____	_____
Word processing application	_____	_____
Floppy drive	_____	_____
Letter document file	_____	_____
Computer system	_____	_____
Peripherals	_____	_____
Application program	_____	_____

Skill Builders

Skill Builder 1.1 Research Software Requirements

- Visit a store that sells computer software.

- Examine at least four software application programs you would like to run on your own computer. They should be programs that help you get useful work done in your job or as a hobby.

- Make notes on the system requirements of each software application program.

- Use these notes to create a basic requirements list for the computer system you will research in the next exercise.

Skill Builder 1.2 Research Your Own Computer System

Look up computer system advertisements in a local periodical or visit a local computer store. Determine the following information for at least two different systems:

- The model of microprocessor and its clock speed

- The system RAM

- The video RAM

- The capacity of the hard drive

- The size and type (CRT or LCD) of the video monitor, its dot pitch, and its resolution

Skill Builder 1.3 Make a Purchase Recommendation

Using the information presented in this lesson, write a specification for a system you would like to purchase for your use at home or work.

- Include any additional peripherals (such as a scanner or video capture card).

LESSON 2

Working with Windows Programs

As you learned in Lesson 1, the operating system is software that controls the basic functions of your computer. When you work with application programs such as those in the Office 2003 Suite, the Windows operating system controls your interactions with the programs and peripherals, such as the printer. This lesson introduces many basic techniques for working with programs in Windows XP and Windows 2000.

These techniques work with virtually any Windows program, not just the Office 2003 Suite. You will learn how to start programs, adjust the size of program windows, and how to run more than one program at once (multitasking). You will also learn the basics of saving your work and giving commands with menu bars and dialog boxes. By the end of this lesson, you should be able to work with the basic commands of almost any Windows application program.

Additional learning resources are available at labpub.com/learn/oe3/

Case Study

Michael has just purchased his first computer, a discount model that didn't set him back much but has all the features he needs. It isn't the fastest computer on the market, but Michael made sure it was powerful enough to run the basic types of programs he will use for the next couple of years. The only software that came with the computer was the operating system, Windows 98. But Michael discovers that Windows features several basic application programs called applets. When a friend asks Michael to help him put together a meeting announcement, he is eager to demonstrate what his computer and printer can do.

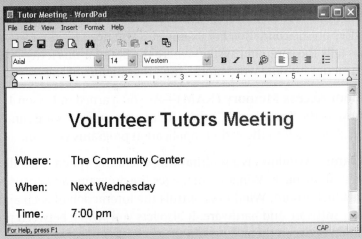

WordPad is a basic word processing application that you can use to type simple documents, like a one-page letter, with ease.

Michael's friend also wants to print a map with directions to the meeting, so he starts the Paint program and has soon drawn a map showing the location of the meeting.

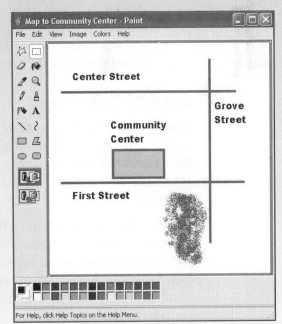

The Paint applet is a simple drawing program. It features tools you use for drawing lines, boxes, circles, and text. It even has a spray paint tool.

Introducing Windows

Windows is an operating system. As you may recall from Lesson 1, there are three primary categories of software: the operating system, application programs, and user data files. As the operating system, Windows controls all the basic functions of the computer. Windows serves as the interface between you and the hardware and software that make up the computer system.

Roles of an Operating System

Windows plays several critical roles, such as those described below.

- **Managing file storage**—Windows controls the hard disk drives, floppy drive, and any other storage devices on the computer. For example, if you need to edit a letter you typed recently, Windows tells the computer system where the data for this letter is located and how to retrieve the letter into the word processing program for editing.

- **Managing Random Access Memory (RAM)**—As you learned in Lesson 1, your computer uses RAM as the "workbench" where all of your programs are run. Windows controls RAM and allocates it to the various application programs you run.

- **Managing Programs**—Windows is a multitasking operating system that allows several programs to run simultaneously. Windows manages the programs and ensures they have adequate RAM in which to run. Windows controls the interaction of each application program with other software and hardware. It also lets you switch between programs and copy information between them.

- **Managing Hardware and Peripherals**—Windows controls the hardware inside the system unit. For example, when you click with the mouse or tap a key on the keyboard, Windows receives your command and either executes it or passes the command on the application program you are running. Windows also controls the display of everything you see on the computer monitor. When you print a document, Windows sends the commands and data that tell the printer what to print.

Ease of Learning

Imagine if every make of car had its gas and brake pedals in a different location from other makes. Or if you had a turn signal control on the steering wheel in one make of car and on the left side of the dashboard in another. That's the way software was in the early days of personal computers (PCs). Learning one program did not necessarily help you learn the next one. Fortunately, this is no longer the case.

As you make your way through these lessons, you will learn basic commands and techniques that apply to virtually any Windows program you may encounter. This consistency is an important feature of Windows and of software that uses a Graphic User Interface (GUI). It makes learning how to use computers and various computer programs much easier than it was in the past. Computers were once the realm of programmers and specialists. Now, anyone can learn to use a computer effectively.

Switching On the Computer

The On-Off Switch

Most computers have an on-off switch located on the front of the system unit (the box that holds the basic components).

The on-off switch
(usually on the front
of the system unit)

The monitor

The mouse

Before You Switch On the System Unit

Most computers have peripheral devices attached to the system unit. You should switch on these peripherals before switching on the system unit. This ensures that the system unit will recognize the peripherals as it "wakes up." Examples of peripheral devices are:

- A printer

- A graphic scanner

- An external CD-ROM drive

 ## Hands-On 2.1 Switch On the Computer

In this exercise, you will switch on your computer. In many computer labs, the computers remain running as long as the lab is open.

1. Remove any floppy disks from the floppy drive.

   The computer may not start properly if a floppy disk is in the drive. A small button on the floppy drive on the front of the computer allows you to eject any floppy disk in the drive.

2. Follow these steps to switch on the computer:

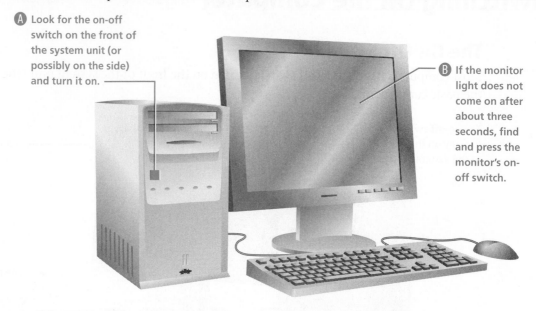

Ⓐ Look for the on-off switch on the front of the system unit (or possibly on the side) and turn it on.

Ⓑ If the monitor light does not come on after about three seconds, find and press the monitor's on-off switch.

Starting Windows

Depending on the speed of your computer, Windows requires about one minute to start after you switch on the computer. During this time, the computer performs an internal self-check to ensure the hardware is functioning properly. When Windows has completed its start-up, one of the following features usually appears:

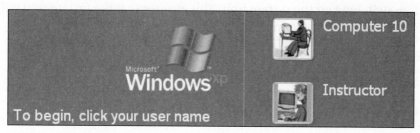

■ A logon screen (Windows XP)

■ An *Enter Password* dialog box (Windows 2000)

Depending on your computer's configuration, it is also possible that Windows XP will have an Enter Password dialog box similar to the one for Windows 2000. It is also possible to configure Windows 2000 to log on with a particular user name automatically.

Windows XP Editions

Windows XP comes in two primary editions:

- **Home Edition**—This version is optimized for home use. It comes installed on most consumer-oriented desktop and notebook computers. The features left off the Home edition are rarely of interest to home users.

- **Professional Edition**—This version contains additional features for use in business environments and on networks. For example, it contains remote access features, so you can access the computer from another location while travelling. It also contains encryption (code) software to help protect files and additional system backup features.

Both editions of Windows XP are based on the same foundation of software code. If you know how to run one edition, you know the basics of the other edition. Microsoft is planning to release additional editions of Windows. For example, a *Media Center* edition was released near the end of 2002. This edition allows you to run home media equipment from your computer and with a single remote control.

 NOTE! *See the Lesson 2 Web page for a link to a comparison of Windows XP Home and Professional editions and more information on the Windows XP Media Center edition.*

Logging On to Windows

Most Windows systems are configured for users to log on before they can work with programs. Logging on can make a difference in the menus and programs that are available. If you are connected to a network, you cannot access resources such as printers and disk drives without a proper login.

Logging On to Windows XP

Windows XP normally displays a log on screen when you first power up the computer. This screen displays the available user names. If a user name requires a password, Windows also displays a space to enter the password. You can even see a password hint in case you forget the password.

Click the Question Mark button to display a password hint.

Logging On to Windows 2000

2000 only

Windows allows you to either set the computer to log on as a specific user automatically or to enter a user name and password. If Windows is set up to require a user name and password, a dialog box similar to the one displayed in the next exercise appears. A dialog box is one way to issue commands to Windows. Many home systems are set up to perform an automatic log on, but in most classrooms you will need to follow a log on procedure.

User Names

User names serve an important function in Windows. Each user has a customizable Start menu, My Documents folder, and Desktop. The user name also controls access to devices such as printers and network drives on a *local area network* (LAN). Your instructor will tell you which user name to use in the Hands-On exercise below.

Hands-On 2.2 Log On to Windows

In this exercise, you will log on to Windows with a user name to display the Windows Desktop. Depending on the Windows configuration you are using, you will use either a home-style login or network login.

Before You Begin: You can skip this exercise if the Windows Desktop is already visible.

Follow the instructions below for your version of Windows:

Windows XP Home Login

1. If you do not see a login screen similar to the one shown in step 2, skip the Windows XP section and go to step 1 of the *Windows 2000 and Windows XP Network Login* section below.

2. Follow these steps to log on to Windows XP:

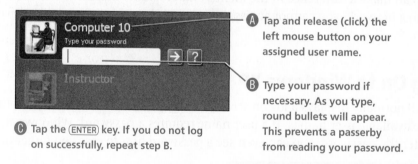

Ⓐ Tap and release (click) the left mouse button on your assigned user name.

Ⓑ Type your password if necessary. As you type, round bullets will appear. This prevents a passerby from reading your password.

Ⓒ Tap the (ENTER) key. If you do not log on successfully, repeat step B.

The Windows Desktop appears and you are logged on.

Windows 2000 and Windows XP Network Login

1. If you do not see a Log On dialog box, hold down the (CTRL) and (ALT) keys on the keyboard, then tap the (DELETE) key.

    If it was not there before, a Log On dialog box appears.

2. If you need a username and password to log on to Windows take a moment now to write them in the spaces below:

    User Name: _____ Password:_____ ❑ No password required

3. Follow these steps if you were given a password, otherwise skip to step 4:

    ■ If necessary, tap the (TAB) key on the left side of the keyboard until you see the insertion point blinking in the password box.

    You are now ready to type a password in this box.

    ■ Type your password in the password box.

    As you type the password, an asterisk will appear for each letter. This prevents others from seeing the password as you type. The use of a password is optional. You might want to use a password to keep other users from viewing and changing your personal Desktop setup in Windows. If your computer is hooked up to a network, a password might give you access to additional storage space and printers on the network.

4. Tap the (ENTER) key on the keyboard.

    You should be logged on and the Desktop should appear. If you did not log on successfully, repeat step 2, taking care to type the password exactly as it was given to you.

The Desktop

After you log on, Windows will display the Desktop. Depending on how the computer is set up, Windows may also automatically run one or more programs. For example, you may see an anti-virus program start after the Desktop appears (see "Antivirus software" on page 31 Lesson 1). The Desktop is the workspace where you run programs in Windows. Your Desktop will look similar to the following illustration but may differ in a few details.

⚠ NOTE! *Depending on programs installed and other setup options, your Desktop will likely differ from the illustration.*

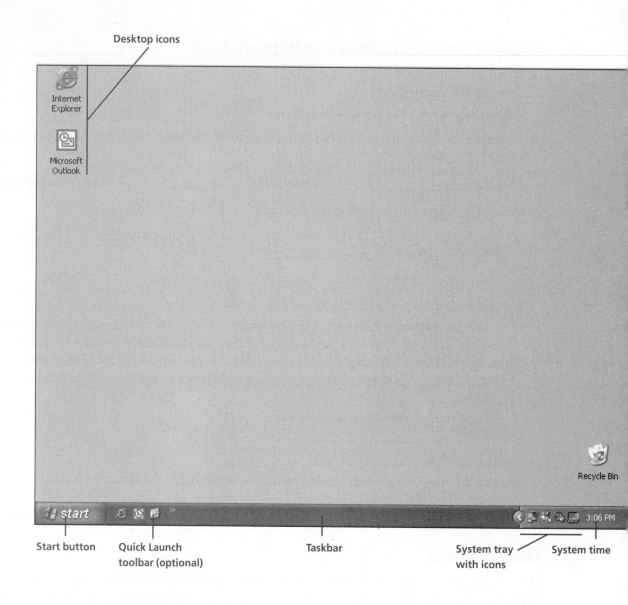

Desktop icons

Internet Explorer

Microsoft Outlook

Recycle Bin

start

Start button   Quick Launch   Taskbar   System tray   System time
                toolbar (optional)   with icons

Icons and Buttons

An *icon* is a small picture that represents a device, command, or software. A *button* is an object that you "press" (by clicking with the mouse) to execute a command. Windows uses a variety of icons and buttons. Here are several examples taken from the Desktop and other parts of Windows:

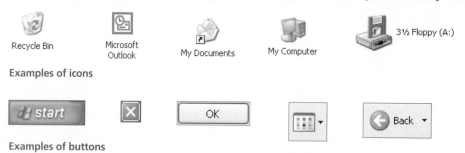

Recycle Bin   Microsoft Outlook   My Documents   My Computer   3½ Floppy (A:)

Examples of icons

start   OK   Back

Examples of buttons

Using a Mouse

You will give most of your commands to Windows with a mouse. A mouse is a pointing device; it lets you point to various screen locations and issue commands. Douglas Englebart, a Stanford professor, introduced the mouse in 1968. It probably got its name from the tail-like cable that connects it to the computer. If you have never used a mouse before, this lesson and the ones to follow will give you plenty of practice.

Mouse Buttons

A typical mouse has two buttons for issuing commands. Some mice have three buttons, and the middle button has various functions depending on the program with which it is used. The two main mouse buttons are shown below.

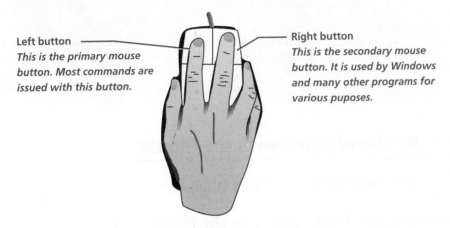

Left button
This is the primary mouse button. Most commands are issued with this button.

Right button
This is the secondary mouse button. It is used by Windows and many other programs for various pupeses.

You can perform five basic motions with a mouse. Each motion has specific uses in Windows and other programs.

Are You Left-Handed?

If you are left-handed, Windows has an option that lets you reverse the role of the two mouse buttons. You should also feel free to position the mouse to the left of your keyboard. (Most users keep the mouse on the right side of the keyboard.)

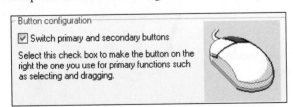

Button configuration
☑ Switch primary and secondary buttons
Select this check box to make the button on the right the one you use for primary functions such as selecting and dragging.

The Windows control panel includes options to switch the primary and secondary mouse buttons. You can use Windows' online Help (covered in Lesson 3) to learn more about this feature.

Motion		How to Do It	This motion is used...
Click		Gently tap and immediately to release the left mouse button.	to "press" a button or select a menu option or object on the screen.
Double-click		Click twice in rapid succession.	as a shortcut for many types of common commands.
Drag		Press and hold down the left mouse button while sliding the mouse. Release the mouse button when you reach your destination.	to move an object, select several objects, draw lines, and select text.
Right-click		Gently tap and immediately release the right mouse button.	to display a context-sensitive menu for the object at which you are pointing.
Point		Slide the mouse without pressing a button until the pointer is in the desired location.	to position the pointer before using one of the four motions above, to select an object on the screen, or to get a menu to appear.

 ## Hands-On 2.3 Hold and Point with the Mouse

In this exercise, you will practice holding and pointing with the mouse.

Hold the Mouse and Reposition It on the Mouse Pad

1. Take a few moments to study the following illustrations before you take hold of the mouse.

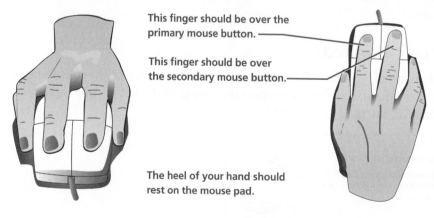

This finger should be over the primary mouse button.

This finger should be over the secondary mouse button.

The heel of your hand should rest on the mouse pad.

2. Gently hold the mouse as shown above, but don't press the buttons.

3. Grasp the sides of the mouse with your thumb and ring finger (use your thumb and little finger if you have a three-button mouse).

4. Lift the mouse off the pad slightly, then reposition it near the center of the pad.

   Use this technique to reposition the mouse whenever you run out of room on the mouse pad.

5. Lift the mouse off the pad and reposition it at various locations on the mouse pad.

Practice Moving the Pointer

6. Rest your wrist on the edge of the mouse pad and slide the mouse from side to side, as shown below.

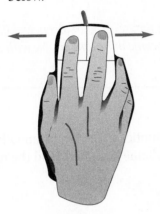

The mouse pointer ⇖ will move from side to side on the screen. Most side-to-side motions can be made without moving your forearm.

7. Slide your wrist and forearm forward and backward to shift the mouse pointer up and down on the screen.

8. Slide the mouse pointer all the way to the top-left corner of the screen.

   It's OK to move your hand on the mouse pad as you do this.

9. Locate the Recycle Bin icon on the Desktop and position the mouse pointer ⇗ on it.

Recycle Bin   Recycle Bin

Some text appears, indicating the function of the icon (a Screen Tip).

10. Point at the Start button and then at the System Time at the bottom-right corner of the screen.

!NOTE! *Don't worry if you have trouble pointing with the mouse. As with any new skill, using a mouse may require some practice. Be patient. You will become more comfortable with a mouse by the time you finish this book.*

The Clicking Motion

After pointing, clicking is one of the most basic mouse motions. The key to smooth clicking is to tap and release the left mouse button in one quick motion. Some beginners hold the mouse button down too long during a click.

The Right-Click Motion

You use a right-click to issue special commands in Windows and many application programs. When you right-click, you tap and release the secondary (right) mouse button, rather than the primary (left) mouse button. Right-clicks often cause a context-sensitive pop-up menu to appear on the screen.

Hands-On 2.4 Practice Clicking with the Mouse

In this exercise, you will practice pointing and clicking. You will see the difference between a normal click and a right-click on the Start button.

Follow the instructions below for your version of Windows. The Windows 2000 exercise begins on the next page.

Windows XP

1. Follow these steps to practice clicking:

Ⓐ Point at the center of the Start button at the bottom-left corner of the Desktop, then tap and release the left mouse button in one smooth motion (click).

Ⓑ Slowly slide your mouse pointer straight up to point at the All Programs menu. The All Programs menu lists the programs that are available on your computer.

Ⓒ Point on a clear area on the Desktop, then click to make the menus disappear.

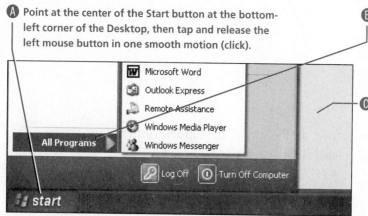

2. Follow these steps to practice right-clicking:

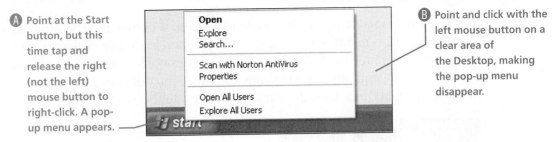

Ⓐ Point at the Start button, but this time tap and release the right (not the left) mouse button to right-click. A pop-up menu appears.

Ⓑ Point and click with the left mouse button on a clear area of the Desktop, making the pop-up menu disappear.

Windows 2000

1. Follow these steps to practice clicking:

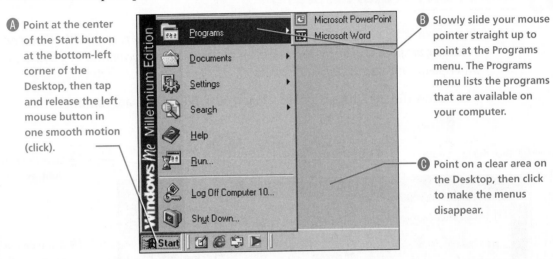

Ⓐ Point at the center of the Start button at the bottom-left corner of the Desktop, then tap and release the left mouse button in one smooth motion (click).

Ⓑ Slowly slide your mouse pointer straight up to point at the Programs menu. The Programs menu lists the programs that are available on your computer.

Ⓒ Point on a clear area on the Desktop, then click to make the menus disappear.

2. Follow these steps to practice right-clicking:

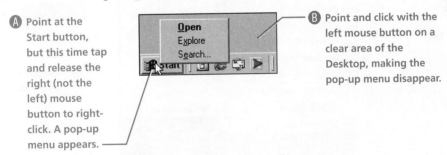

Ⓐ Point at the Start button, but this time tap and release the right (not the left) mouse button to right-click. A pop-up menu appears.

Ⓑ Point and click with the left mouse button on a clear area of the Desktop, making the pop-up menu disappear.

Starting Programs

You can start a program by clicking the Start  button and choosing the desired program from the Programs menu. You can also start a program by double-clicking a Desktop icon for the program (if a Desktop icon exists). For example, the Internet Explorer Web browser program typically has a Desktop icon. Also, you can launch some programs from the optional Quick Launch toolbar that is next to the Start button.

Internet Explorer

The Quick Launch toolbar lets you start programs with a single click.

Hands-On 2.5 Start WordPad

In this exercise, you will use the Start menu to launch the WordPad program. WordPad is an entry-level word processing program you can use to create letters and other simple documents. In a later exercise, you will use WordPad to compose a meeting announcement.

1. Follow the steps below for the version of Windows you are running:

Windows 2000

Ⓐ Click the Start button. — Ⓑ Slide the mouse up to Programs. — Ⓒ Slide the mouse pointer to the right, and point at Accessories.

Ⓓ If you do not see the WordPad program, click the expand menu command to make it appear.

Ⓔ Slide the mouse pointer to the right, and click WordPad.

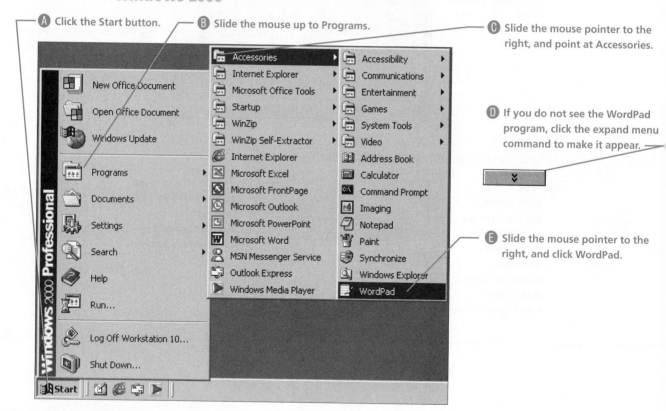

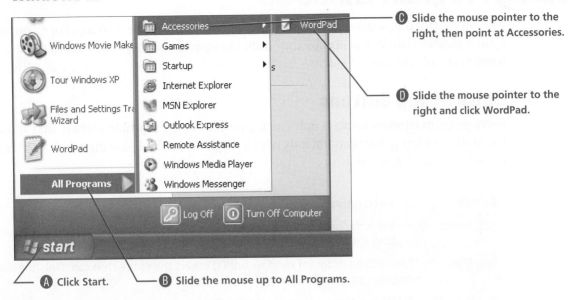

Ⓒ Slide the mouse pointer to the right, then point at Accessories.

Ⓓ Slide the mouse pointer to the right and click WordPad.

Ⓐ Click Start.

Ⓑ Slide the mouse up to All Programs.

The WordPad program window appears on the Desktop.

Elements of a Program Window

Every program runs in its own program window. The WordPad window you have open now is a good example of a typical Windows program. Since the controls in most program windows work similarly, once you have mastered a program such as WordPad, you are well on your way to mastering Windows programs in general. Take a few moments to look over the common features shown in the following illustration.

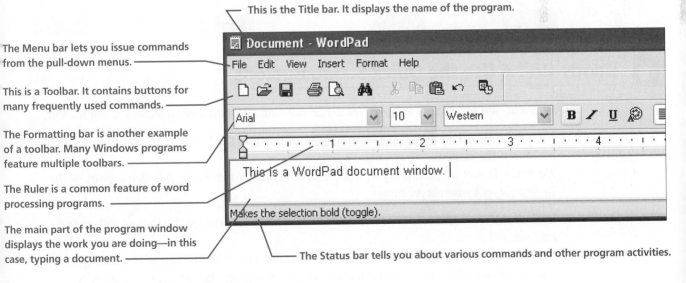

This is the Title bar. It displays the name of the program.

The Menu bar lets you issue commands from the pull-down menus.

This is a Toolbar. It contains buttons for many frequently used commands.

The Formatting bar is another example of a toolbar. Many Windows programs feature multiple toolbars.

The Ruler is a common feature of word processing programs.

The main part of the program window displays the work you are doing—in this case, typing a document.

The Status bar tells you about various commands and other program activities.

Sizing Program Windows

You can control the position and size of program windows on the Desktop. For example, you may want a program window to occupy the entire Desktop or you may want two or more program windows displayed side-by-side.

Quick Sizing Buttons

Every program window displays quick sizing buttons at the top-right corners that allow you to give the most common window commands with a single click. The following table describes the function of each quick sizing button.

Button	Description
Minimize	Removes the program window from the Desktop but keeps the program running. Clicking the program button on the Taskbar restores the program window.
Maximize	Expands the program window until it covers the entire Desktop. Only the maximized program and the Taskbar are visible.
Restore	Restores a program window to the size it was set to before it was maximized. A restored window usually covers only a portion of the Desktop.
Close	Closes a document window or exits a program.

The Switching Restore and Maximize Buttons

The Maximize and Restore buttons never appear together. Instead, when either button is clicked, the window changes and displays the other button, as shown in the example below:

When you click the maximize button here . . .

. . . the middle button displays the restore button . . .

. . . and if you click the restore button . . .

. . . it changes back to the maximize button.

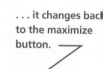

Hands-On 2.6 Use the Quick Sizing Buttons

In this exercise, you will practice using the Minimize, Maximize, Restore, and Close quick sizing Buttons.

1. Notice the WordPad  button near the Start button on the Taskbar at the bottom of the screen.
   The button is recessed (pushed in) because WordPad is the active program. A button appears on the Taskbar for each running program.

2. Look at the top-right corner of the WordPad window and notice the three quick sizing buttons.
   If the window is already maximized, then the Restore button will be displayed in the center of the trio. If the last WordPad user sized the window to cover just part of the Desktop, then the Maximize button will be displayed.

3. If the middle quick sizing button is the Maximize button, then click it.
   At this point, the WordPad window will be maximized. Only the WordPad window, the Taskbar, and the Start button should be visible.

4. Click the Minimize button on the WordPad window.
   The window vanishes, but the WordPad button is still visible on the Taskbar.

5. Click the WordPad ▤ Document - WordPad button on the Taskbar and the window will reappear.
   You can always restore a minimized window by clicking that program's button on the Taskbar.

6. Click the Restore ▣ button, and the window will occupy only part of the Desktop.
   Leave the WordPad window open.

Moving Program Windows

You can move a window on the Desktop to various screen locations by dragging on its title bar. The only time you cannot move a window is if it is maximized. You can tell when a window is maximized because it will have a Restore quick sizing button.

Changing the Size of a Program Window

You can adjust the size and shape of an open window by dragging the window's borders. When you point to the border of a window that is restored (i.e., not maximized), you will see a double-arrow appear. The arrows will point in the directions you can resize the window.

⚠️**TIP!** *You cannot change the size of a maximized window.*

Hands-On 2.7 Move and Size the WordPad Window

In this exercise, you will move the WordPad window to a different location on the Desktop, then change the size of the window.

1. Follow these steps to move the WordPad window:

⚠️**NOTE!** *It's OK if your WordPad window has different dimensions than shown below.*

Windows XP users will probably not see My Computer and Network Neighborhood icons on the Desktop. These are now found in the Start menu.

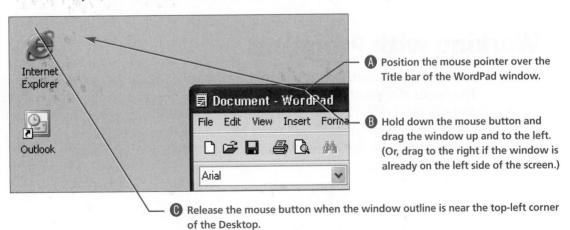

Ⓐ Position the mouse pointer over the Title bar of the WordPad window.

Ⓑ Hold down the mouse button and drag the window up and to the left. (Or, drag to the right if the window is already on the left side of the screen.)

Ⓒ Release the mouse button when the window outline is near the top-left corner of the Desktop.

2. Drag on the title bar of the WordPad window again, but this time drag down toward the bottom-right of the Desktop.

3. Drag the title bar once more to place the WordPad window at the top-center of the Desktop.

Change the Size of the Window

4. Follow these steps to change the size of the WordPad window:

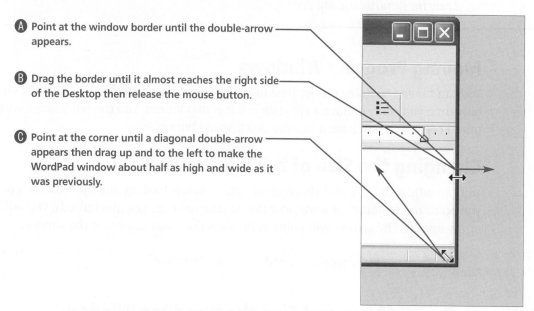

Ⓐ Point at the window border until the double-arrow appears.

Ⓑ Drag the border until it almost reaches the right side of the Desktop then release the mouse button.

Ⓒ Point at the corner until a diagonal double-arrow appears then drag up and to the left to make the WordPad window about half as high and wide as it was previously.

5. Change only the height of the window by dragging the bottom border up or down.

6. Practice some more until you can place and size the WordPad window at any desired location on the Desktop.
   This skill will become very useful when you run more than one program at once and need to arrange them on the Desktop so you can see the contents of one window as you work in a different window.

7. When you are finished, maximize ▣ the WordPad window.
   It is often easier to work in a maximized window, because it covers any distracting elements that may be on the Desktop.

Working with Programs

Application programs such as WordPad are designed to help you get work done on the computer. Thousands of application programs are available to help you accomplish a wide variety of tasks. Many of the techniques you use to work with the WordPad program in these exercises will apply to other Windows programs as well. Most programs let you give commands with pull-down menus, toolbars, and keyboard shortcuts. You will use all three types of commands in the Hands-On exercises in this lesson.

Using Toolbars

WordPad's toolbars include buttons for the most frequently used commands. Most of these buttons are either toggles that you switch on and off, or have drop-down lists from which you make a selection.

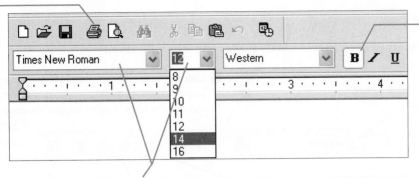

his toolbar utton issues he Print ommand.

A click on this button activates the Bold command. Notice how the button appears to be "pressed" when compared to the button next to it.

These toolbar boxes have drop-down lists from which you make a selection. You can also type directly into the boxes.

Hands-On 2.8 Type a Meeting Announcement

In this exercise, you will use some of WordPad's toolbar commands as you type a simple meeting announcement. The commands you will use let you change the look of the text in the document.

Format and Type a Heading

1. Tap the **(ENTER)** key six times to add space to the top margin of the announcement.
   Each time you tap the (ENTER) key in a word processing document, you add a new line to the document. Each new line is usually about one-sixth of an inch high.

2. Follow these steps to set the format for the announcement heading:

Ⓐ Point (don't click) on the Font Size drop-down list on the toolbar. Notice the description of the command on the status bar at the bottom-left corner of the WordPad window.

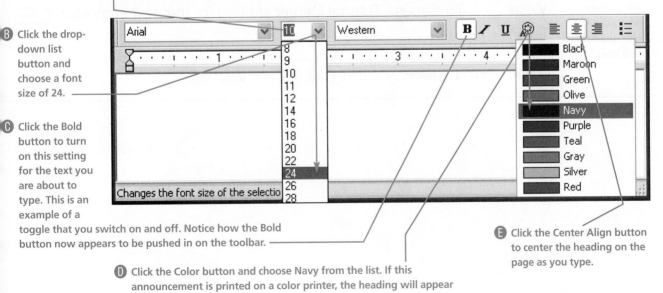

Ⓑ Click the drop-down list button and choose a font size of 24.

Ⓒ Click the Bold button to turn on this setting for the text you are about to type. This is an example of a toggle that you switch on and off. Notice how the Bold button now appears to be pushed in on the toolbar.

Ⓓ Click the Color button and choose Navy from the list. If this announcement is printed on a color printer, the heading will appear dark blue.

Ⓔ Click the Center Align button to center the heading on the page as you type.

3. Type the heading for the announcement: **Volunteer Tutors Meeting**
   The size and color of the letters will match the settings you made in the previous step.

4. Tap the (ENTER) key on the keyboard twice to add space between the heading and the body of the announcement that you are about to type.

Format and Type the Body of the Announcement

5. Follow these steps to format the body text of the announcement:

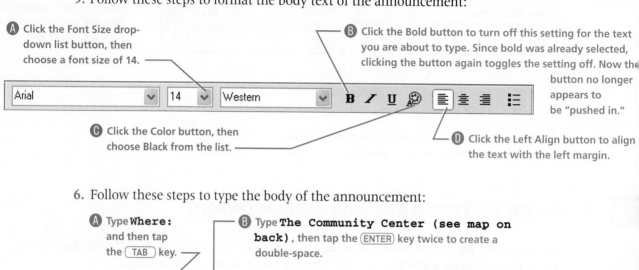

A Click the Font Size drop-down list button, then choose a font size of 14.

B Click the Bold button to turn off this setting for the text you are about to type. Since bold was already selected, clicking the button again toggles the setting off. Now the button no longer appears to be "pushed in."

C Click the Color button, then choose Black from the list.

D Click the Left Align button to align the text with the left margin.

6. Follow these steps to type the body of the announcement:

A Type **Where:** and then tap the (TAB) key.

B Type **The Community Center (see map on back)**, then tap the (ENTER) key twice to create a double-space.

C Continue typing the rest of the announcement. You may need to tap the (TAB) key twice after Time and What to make these lines even with the first two lines.

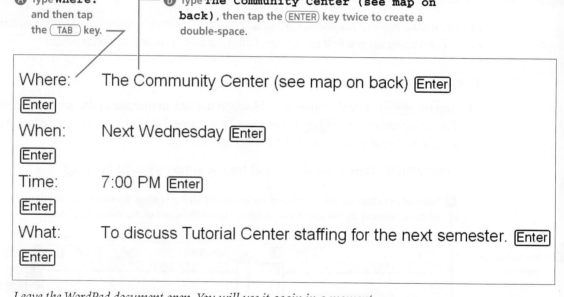

Leave the WordPad document open. You will use it again in a moment.

Using Pull-Down Menus

You use pull-down menus frequently in Windows programs to initiate commands. Almost all Windows programs use pull-down menus. Several symbols that appear on pull-down menus. You should be familiar with. The following illustration displays significant features in WordPad's File menu.

When you click a command with three dots after it, a dialog box with additional choices will be displayed. The three dots are called an ellipsis.

This command has a keyboard shortcut you can use to issue the command by holding down the first key and then tapping the second key.

WordPad stores a list of the most recently saved documents here. This makes it easier to open a document you just worked on.

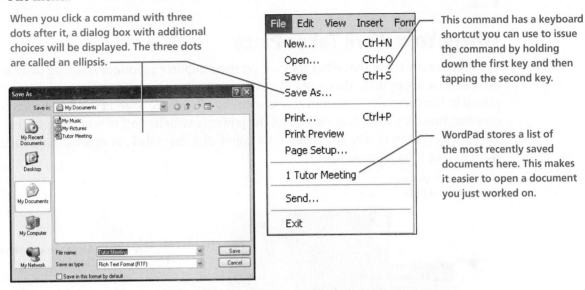

Hands-On 2.9 Issue a Command from the Menu Bar

In this exercise, you will work with menu bar to access the Print Preview feature of WordPad.

1. Follow these steps to issue a command from the menu bar:

A Click the File command on the menu bar.

B Click the Print Preview command in the drop-down menu.

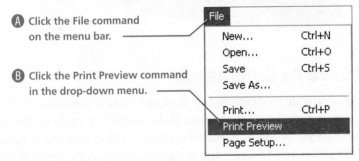

In the rest of this book, a command like this will be written File→Print Preview.

A preview of the printed page will appear in the WordPad window. This displays exactly how your document will appear when it is printed. The dashed lines indicate the margins of the document and will not appear in print.

2. Click the ⬜ Close button on the top-right side of the WordPad window.
This closes the Print Preview window. Now you are back in normal document view.

Saving Files

You create documents by using application programs like WordPad. The word file refers to any document that has been saved onto a storage device. A typical hard disk drive has thousands of files stored on it. With most Windows programs, you use the Save command to save your work in a file.

Where Your Work Takes Place

Many beginners think that what they see on the computer's monitor is taking place in the hard drive or on a floppy disk. This is not the case. As you use an application program, your work is placed in the computer's random access memory (RAM; see page 11) and is displayed on the monitor. However, RAM is erased when the power is switched off or when the system is restarted. This is why you must save your work on a floppy disk, hard disk, or other storage media if you want to save it for later use.

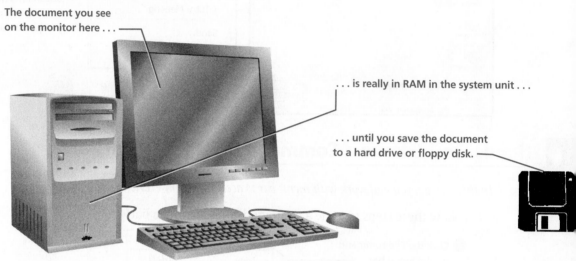

The document you see on the monitor here . . .

. . . is really in RAM in the system unit . . .

. . . until you save the document to a hard drive or floppy disk.

The Save and Save As Commands

FROM THE KEYBOARD

CTRL+S to Save the current file.

Most Windows programs provide two commands that let you save documents. The File→Save command saves the current document onto a disk. If the document had previously been saved, then the old version is replaced by the new edited version. If the document is new, then a *Save As* dialog box appears. This allows you to name the document and specify the disk drive and folder to which you wish to save the document. You can also use the File→Save As command to make a copy of an existing document by saving the document with a new name.

Naming Files

When you save a file for the first time, you must give it a name. Windows has specific rules for naming files. The following Quick Reference table lists the rules for naming files.

QUICK REFERENCE: RULES FOR FILE NAMES

Rule	Description
Filename length	A filename can contain up to 255 characters.
Characters that are allowed in filenames	A filename may contain numbers, spaces, periods, commas, semicolons, dashes, and parentheses.
Characters that are not allowed in filenames	A filename cannot contain the following characters: \ / : * ? " < > l.

Storing Your Exercise Files

This book contains a single floppy disk located on the inside back cover with various files used in many exercises. You will also create entirely new files for some lessons and save them to a storage location. The exercises in this book assume that you will store and open files on a floppy disk. However, you can also save files to another storage location such as the My Documents folder or a USB flash drive. Appendix A at the back of this book contains detailed instructions on the use of these alternative file storage locations.

NOTE! *Take a moment to review Appendix A now if you do not intend to store your work for this lesson on the floppy disk.*

 ## Hands-On 2.10 **Save the Announcement**

In this exercise, you will save the WordPad document that is currently in RAM to your floppy disk.

1. Insert your exercise diskette into the floppy drive. The disk should be placed with the label side facing up and the metal plate facing in as shown in the following figure.

2. Follow these steps to issue the Save command:

Ⓐ Click File on the WordPad menu bar and the File menu will drop-down, as shown here. ─────

Ⓑ Slide the mouse down, and click Save on the drop-down menu. ─────

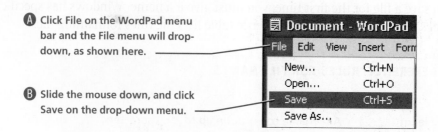

3. Follow these steps to finish saving the document to your floppy disk:

Ⓐ Click the Save in drop-down list, and choose the 3½ Floppy (A:) drive. ─────

Ⓑ Notice that WordPad initially proposes the name Document (or Document.doc) in the filename field. ─────

Ⓒ Click in the Filename box to the right of the name Document. Use the (BACKSPACE) key on the keyboard to delete the name Document, and then type the name **Tutor Meeting**, as shown here. ─────

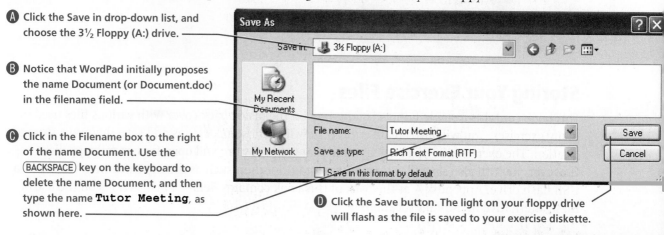

Ⓓ Click the Save button. The light on your floppy drive will flash as the file is saved to your exercise diskette.

Notice that the new name of your document is now displayed on the title bar at the top-left corner of the WordPad window.

Closing Program Windows

FROM THE KEYBOARD
(ALT)+(F4) to close the active program window.

When you are finished working with a program, you will usually want to close the program window. This not only removes clutter from the Desktop, it also conserves RAM so you can run other programs more efficiently. Virtually all Windows programs have a File→Exit command you can use to close the program window. You can also close a program window with the Close quick sizing button at the top-right corner of the window.

Hands-On 2.11 **Close WordPad**

In this exercise, you will close WordPad using commands on the menu bar.

1. Choose File→Exit from the menu bar. Click No if you are asked if you wish to save your document.
   The program window will close. If you type something in the document after issuing a Save command, WordPad asks if you wish to save the changes. In this case, there is no need to save the change.

Editing Files

After you have typed a document, it is easy to make changes. For example, let's say that another volunteer tutors meeting is to take place next month. Rather than typing the document again from scratch, you can simply change some of the information, then save the document again.

Working on a Previously Saved File

If you want to work on a previously saved file, you must open it in the application program. After you have changed the file, you have two ways to save your changes:

- **Save**—This command overwrites the old version of the file with the new version you have just edited.

- **Save As**—This command allows you to create a new file with the changes you have made, leaving the old version intact with the old filename.

Hands-On 2.12 Open and Edit a File

In this exercise, you will open the meeting announcement you created earlier, edit it, then save the announcement with a new name.

Open the Meeting Announcement File

1. Click the Start button, then slide the mouse pointer up to the All Programs menu (or Programs if you are running Windows 2000).

2. Slide the mouse pointer to the right, then up to Accessories, and then click the WordPad program at the bottom of the menu.

3. If the WordPad window is not already maximized, click the Maximize 🔲 quick sizing button to make the WordPad window cover the Desktop.

4. Click the Open 📂 button on the WordPad toolbar.

5. Follow these steps to open the announcement file you saved to your floppy disk:

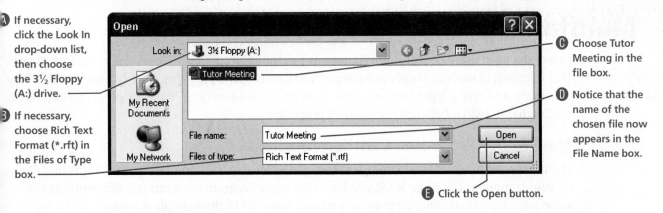

You will see the floppy drive light flash as the file is loaded from the floppy drive into the computer's RAM. After it is loaded into RAM, the announcement document will be displayed in the WordPad window.

6. Follow these steps to change the date for the meeting:

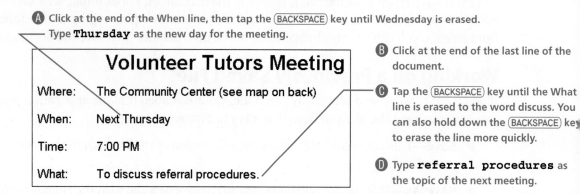

A Click at the end of the When line, then tap the (BACKSPACE) key until Wednesday is erased. Type **Thursday** as the new day for the meeting.

B Click at the end of the last line of the document.

C Tap the (BACKSPACE) key until the What line is erased to the word discuss. You can also hold down the (BACKSPACE) key to erase the line more quickly.

D Type **referral procedures** as the topic of the next meeting.

Volunteer Tutors Meeting

Where:	The Community Center (see map on back)
When:	Next Thursday
Time:	7:00 PM
What:	To discuss referral procedures.

7. Choose File→Save As from the menu bar.

8. Follow these steps to save the file with a new name:

A Click at the end of the filename. If you see .doc at the end of the filename, tap the (BACKSPACE) key until the .doc portion of the filename deleted. (WordPad will add the .doc back to the end of the filename when you save the document.)

B Tap the spacebar, then type **(September)** at the end of the filename with parentheses, as shown here. Windows lets you use several types of punctuation characters in filenames.

File name:	Tutor Meeting

File name:	Tutor Meeting (September)		Save
Save as type:	Rich Text Format (RTF)		Cancel

C Click the Save button to execute the command.

Now two versions of the announcement are saved to your floppy disk. The first version has not been changed.

9. Click the Restore 🗗 button at the top-right corner of the WordPad window. *Now WordPad occupies just a portion of the Desktop.*

Multitasking

One of the most useful features of Windows is the ability to run multiple programs simultaneously. This is known as multitasking. For example, you can download files from the Internet, print a long document, and type a letter in a word processor all at the same time. You click program buttons on the Taskbar to switch between multitasked programs.

How Many Programs Can You Multitask?

The number of programs you can run at the same time depends on how much RAM is installed on your computer. The more RAM you have, the more programs you can run efficiently at the same time. Large and complex programs require more RAM than simple programs. If you try to run more than one large program on a computer with a small amount of RAM, Windows will run much more slowly.

Hands-On 2.13 Start Paint

In this exercise, you will start a second program to run simultaneously with WordPad. Paint is a simple drawing program that comes with Windows.

1. Click the Start button, then point at the Programs (or All Programs) menu.

2. Slide the mouse pointer over to choose the Accessories menu, then click the Paint program. If you are using Windows 2000 and you do not see the Paint program in the Accessories menu, click the Expand Menu [⏦] command to make the entire menu appear.
   The Paint program window opens.

3. If Paint is not already maximized, click the maximize ⬜ button.
   Paint's program window now covers the entire Desktop. However, you can see from the two buttons on the Taskbar that WordPad is still running. Since you just started Paint, it is now the active program. Notice how Paint's button on the Taskbar appears "pushed in" compared to the WordPad button.

Switching between Windows

When you run multiple programs, only one program window at a time can be active. The other program windows are inactive. You use the Taskbar to switch between the programs you are running. As you did in a previous exercise, you also use the Taskbar to restore a minimized program window.

Hands-On 2.14 Switch between Paint and WordPad

In this exercise, you will practice making WordPad and Paint the active program.

1. Click the [📄 Tutor Meeting - Word...] button on the Taskbar to activate the WordPad program.
   Now WordPad's Taskbar button appears "pushed in." Notice also that WordPad's title bar has a different color than the title bar for the Paint window.

2. Click the [🎨 untitled - Paint] button on the Taskbar.
   That's all there is to switching from one program to another. The Paint window now appears on top of the WordPad window.

3. Click the Restore ⬜ button on the Paint window.
   Now Paint's window occupies just a portion of the Desktop.

4. If the WordPad window is not visible, point at the title bar on the Paint window, then drag the Paint window to a new position on the Desktop so that both windows are partially visible. For example, drag the title bar down and to the right.

The Paint window title bar ⎯⎯

5. Click anywhere in the WordPad window to activate it.
   Whenever you click in a program window, it becomes the active program.

6. Click the Close button on the WordPad window to exit the program. Click Yes if WordPad asks you to save changes to the document.

7. Click the Maximize ▢ button on the Paint window.
   Leave the Paint window open, since you will begin drawing in a moment.

Using Dialog Boxes

Dialog boxes allow you to set options and controls for a command. You will encounter a variety of controls in dialog boxes. You used a dialog box earlier in this lesson to adjust the speed of double-clicks with the mouse. The following illustrations describe several common types of dialog box controls.

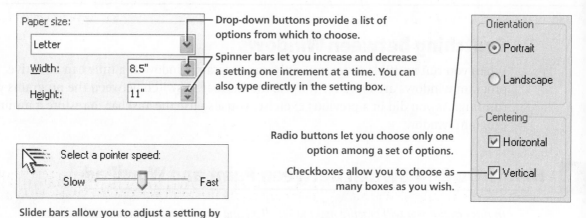

Slider bars allow you to adjust a setting by dragging the slider control.

Hands-On 2.15 Specify the Drawing Size

In this exercise, you will use a dialog box to specify the size of your drawing. The options you set will reduce the size of the Paint file that you will save to your exercise diskette. This is necessary because the Paint program produces graphic files. Graphic files occupy a large amount of disk space when compared to text files. One Paint file can occupy your entire diskette if you do not make the settings defined in this exercise.

1. Choose Image on the Paint menu bar.
   Notice that the Attributes command has three dots (ellipses) after its name. This indicates that this command uses a dialog box.

2. Choose the Attributes command.
   You will use this dialog box to specify the drawing size. The drawing size also affects the size of the file when you save this drawing.

3. Follow these steps to set the drawing size (be sure to complete the steps in order: A, B, C, etc.):

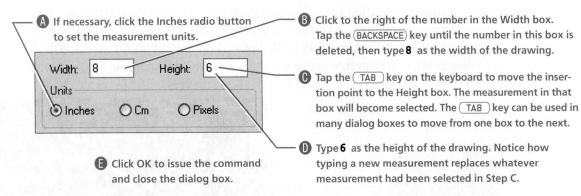

Ⓐ If necessary, click the Inches radio button to set the measurement units.

Ⓑ Click to the right of the number in the Width box. Tap the (BACKSPACE) key until the number in this box is deleted, then type **8** as the width of the drawing.

Ⓒ Tap the (TAB) key on the keyboard to move the insertion point to the Height box. The measurement in that box will become selected. The (TAB) key can be used in many dialog boxes to move from one box to the next.

Ⓓ Type **6** as the height of the drawing. Notice how typing a new measurement replaces whatever measurement had been selected in Step C.

Ⓔ Click OK to issue the command and close the dialog box.

The image size is set to 8" by 6". In the next few steps, you will save the empty drawing to your exercise diskette. You will use a drop-down button on the Save As dialog box to set the Save As Type. Most programs have a Save As Type option that lets you specify the type of file you wish to create. In the Paint program, you use the Save As Type option to determine the amount of color information that is stored in the file. You will reduce the amount of color information to conserve space on your diskette.

4. Choose File→Save from the menu bar.

5. Follow these steps to set the image file type for your drawing:

Ⓐ Click the Save in drop-down list, and choose the 3½ Floppy [A:] drive.

Ⓑ Type **Map to Community Center** in the File Name box.

Ⓒ Click the Save as Type drop-down list, then choose JPEG as the drawing type.

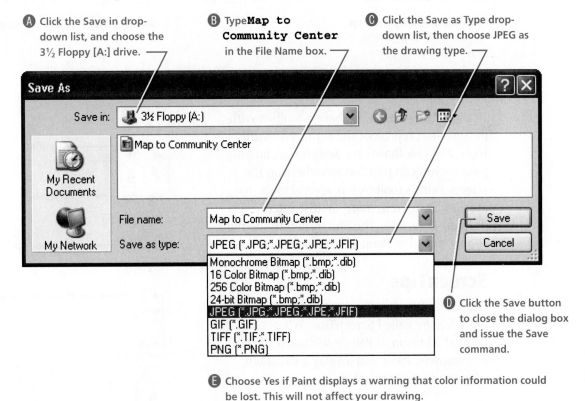

Ⓓ Click the Save button to close the dialog box and issue the Save command.

Ⓔ Choose Yes if Paint displays a warning that color information could be lost. This will not affect your drawing.

Working with the Paint Program

Paint is a small application (called an applet) that is bundled with Windows. Paint lets you use a mouse to create drawings and graphic images. Paint is known as a "bit map" program because images are formed by turning dots (called pixels) on and off on the screen. The dots are too tiny to see when printed. However, you can see them if you zoom in on the Paint screen.

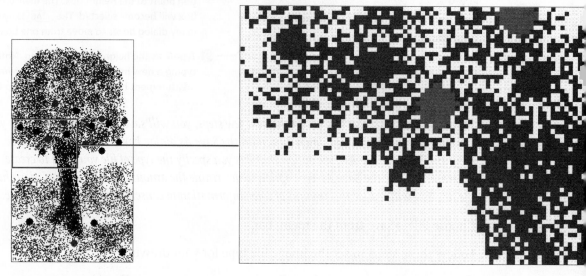

This tree is actually made up of numerous dots (pixels).

A close-up view of the tree drawing.

Using Tools from a Toolbox

Drawing programs often have a toolbox with buttons that represent the various drawing tools. Most toolboxes are designed as floating palettes you can position anywhere on the screen. Paint's toolbox has several tools that are also featured in more sophisticated drawing programs. The illustration to the right shows several of Paint's basic tools.

ScreenTips

Like many Windows programs, Paint's toolbox has a feature called ScreenTips. When you point at a button in Paint's toolbox for about two seconds, Paint will display a small box with the name of the tool.

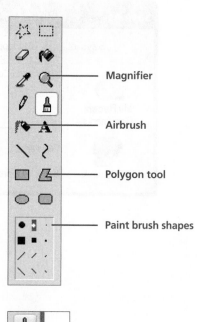

Magnifier

Airbrush

Polygon tool

Paint brush shapes

Hands-On 2.16 Draw a Map

In this exercise, you will use several of Paint's tools to draw a simple map. When you are finished, you will save the drawing. Before you begin, take a look at the map on page 75 to see what the final version of the map will look like.

1. Follow these steps to draw lines for the streets on the map:

!TIP! *The (SHIFT) key helps you to draw perfectly straight lines.*

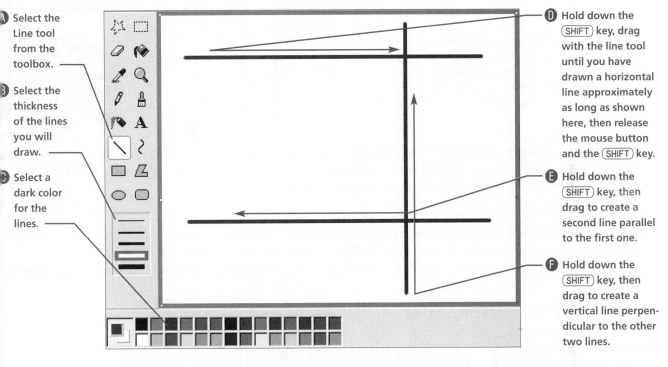

Ⓐ Select the Line tool from the toolbox.

Ⓑ Select the thickness of the lines you will draw.

Ⓒ Select a dark color for the lines.

Ⓓ Hold down the (SHIFT) key, drag with the line tool until you have drawn a horizontal line approximately as long as shown here, then release the mouse button and the (SHIFT) key.

Ⓔ Hold down the (SHIFT) key, then drag to create a second line parallel to the first one.

Ⓕ Hold down the (SHIFT) key, then drag to create a vertical line perpendicular to the other two lines.

2. Follow these steps to draw a rectangle for the community center and fill it with color:

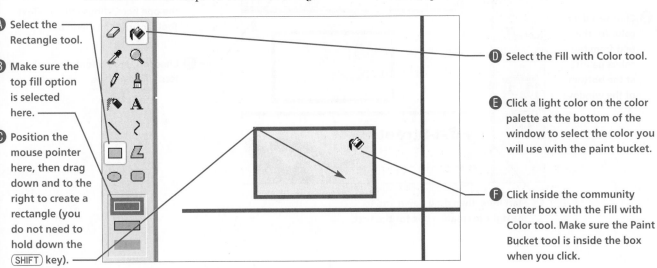

Ⓐ Select the Rectangle tool.

Ⓑ Make sure the top fill option is selected here.

Ⓒ Position the mouse pointer here, then drag down and to the right to create a rectangle (you do not need to hold down the (SHIFT) key).

Ⓓ Select the Fill with Color tool.

Ⓔ Click a light color on the color palette at the bottom of the window to select the color you will use with the paint bucket.

Ⓕ Click inside the community center box with the Fill with Color tool. Make sure the Paint Bucket tool is inside the box when you click.

3. Follow these steps to add a park to the drawing:

!TIP!

If you do not like the results of a command, choose Edit→Undo from the menu bar.

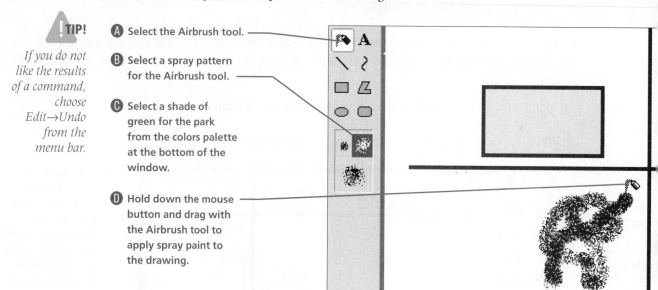

A Select the Airbrush tool.

B Select a spray pattern for the Airbrush tool.

C Select a shade of green for the park from the colors palette at the bottom of the window.

D Hold down the mouse button and drag with the Airbrush tool to apply spray paint to the drawing.

Anytime you have completed a substantial amount of work on a project, it is a good idea to save your work. That way if the computer crashes (stops running) or some other problem occurs, you can still open the most recently saved version of the drawing.

4. Choose File→Save from the menu bar to save your drawing.
You will see the floppy drive light go on as the file is saved. Since you have saved this drawing once already (when you set the drawing type), the Save As dialog box does not appear. The blank version of the drawing is replaced by what is on your screen. The drawing is saved with the same settings you made originally.

5. Follow these steps to add a street name to the drawing:

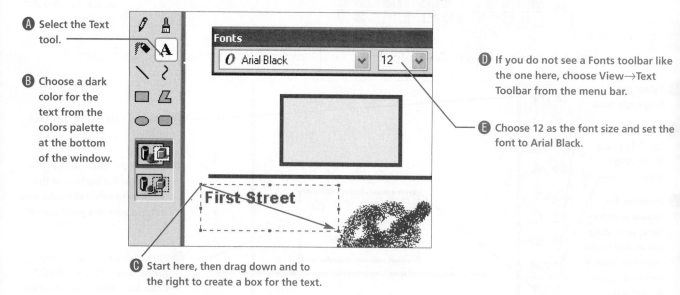

A Select the Text tool.

B Choose a dark color for the text from the colors palette at the bottom of the window.

Fonts

O Arial Black   12

D If you do not see a Fonts toolbar like the one here, choose View→Text Toolbar from the menu bar.

E Choose 12 as the font size and set the font to Arial Black.

First Street

C Start here, then drag down and to the right to create a box for the text.

6. Add additional street names and the community center name to the drawing as shown below. Don't worry if these are not placed perfectly.

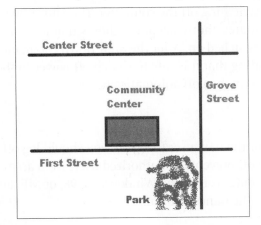

TIP!

If you need to move the Fonts toolbar out of the way, drag on the title bar (where the word Fonts appears on the toolbar).

Paint has many more features than can be covered in this brief tutorial. Most Windows drawing programs use toolboxes and drawing tools that are similar to the Paint tools you have used in this exercise.

Printing Files

Almost all Windows programs have a File→Print command or a Print button on a toolbar that you can use to print your documents. The File→Print command usually displays a dialog box that lets you choose the printer, as well as other options. A document with color (such as a Paint drawing) will only print in color if you have a color printer (such as an ink-jet printer). Otherwise, the colors will print as shades of gray.

 Hands-On 2.17 Print the Map

In this exercise, you will print the drawing you completed in the last exercise..

1. Choose File→Save to save your drawing.

TIP!

It is always a good idea to save your work before you print.

2. Choose File→Print to view the Print dialog box.
   Look over the Print dialog box options for a moment. There is no need to change any of the options.

3. Click OK to print the drawing; retrieve the drawing from the printer.

4. Feel free to enhance your drawing and experiment with some of the other Paint tools.

5. When you are finished with the drawing, choose File→Save from the menu bar to save the finished version of your drawing.

6. Click the Close [X] button to exit the Paint program. Choose Yes if you are asked if you wish to save your drawing.
   If any changes were made since you last gave the Save command, Paint will ask if you wish to save those changes. If you want to discard the most recent changes, you can click No, and the changes will not be saved. Usually, however, you will want to save any changes to a file when you exit a program.

Shutting Down Windows

You must shut down Windows before switching off the computer. The Shut Down command closes all running programs. It also initiates "housekeeping" chores that let Windows start properly the next time the computer is switched on. After the Shut Down command is completed, Windows will display a message indicating that it is safe to switch off power to the computer. On many new computers, the power is switched off automatically.

Logging Off

If you want to leave the computer on for the next user to log on, you should log off Windows rather than shut down the computer. Logging off prevents unauthorized users from accessing network resources. However, if the computer is running Windows 95, 98, or ME, anyone can get to the Windows Desktop by clicking the Cancel button.

Hibernation

Windows 2000 and XP support a feature called Hibernation. Normally, when you shut down the computer all program windows are closed. Hibernation allows you to suspend the computer with program windows open and ready to work again. Windows prepares the computer for hibernation by writing all of the data in RAM onto the hard drive. When you restart the computer, this data is restored to RAM and all program windows and open files appear just as they were when you sent the computer into hibernation. This makes it easy to resume your work.

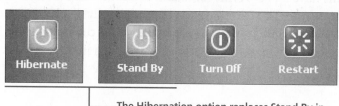

The Hibernation option replaces Stand By in the Windows XP shutdown window when you press the (SHIFT) key.

QUICK REFERENCE: SHUTTING DOWN WINDOWS

Task	Procedure
Log off Windows 2000 Professional	■ Click Start on the Windows Taskbar, then choose Shut down. ■ Choose Log Off [Your User Name] from drop-down list and click OK.
Log Off Windows XP	■ Click Start→Log Off. ■ Click Log Off to confirm logging off.
Shut down Windows 2000	■ Click Start on the Windows Taskbar, then choose Shut Down. ■ Choose the Shut down option and click Yes or OK.
Shut down Windows XP	■ Click Start. ■ Click Turn Off Computer. ■ Choose the desired shut down method.

Hands-On 2.18 Log Off Windows

In this exercise, you will log off and leave the computer running for the next user.

1. Click Start, then examine the lower-left side of the Start menu to see which version of Windows you are using.

2. Follow the log-off procedure for the version of windows you are running:

   ■ **Windows 2000**—Click Shut Down, then choose the Log Off [Your Log on Name] option from the drop-down list and click OK.

   ■ **Windows XP**—Click ![Log Off] at the bottom of the Start menu, then click the Log Off button in the Log Off Windows box.

You should now be logged off, and a sign-on screen should appear.

Concepts Review

True/False Questions

1. Windows is responsible for file, memory, and program management.   TRUE   FALSE

2. You double-click by pressing the secondary (right) mouse button twice in rapid succession.   TRUE   FALSE

3. You can start a program by clicking the Start button and choosing the desired program from the Programs menu.   TRUE   FALSE

4. You use the File→Open command to save a document to a floppy disk.   TRUE   FALSE

5. Filenames can have up to 255 characters in Windows.   TRUE   FALSE

6. Windows is a multitasking operating system.   TRUE   FALSE

7. You can choose as many radio buttons as desired when setting options in a dialog box.   TRUE   FALSE

8. You should always shut down Windows prior to switching off the computer system.   TRUE   FALSE

9. The Windows Taskbar lets you switch between program windows.   TRUE   FALSE

10. You can change the size of a maximized program window by dragging on the window borders.   TRUE   FALSE

Multiple Choice Questions

1. Which of the following buttons restores a window?
   a. ▭
   b. ▢
   c. ▤
   d. ✕

2. Which of the following buttons minimizes a window?
   a. ▭
   b. ▢
   c. ▤
   d. ✕

3. Which of the following techniques is used to move a program window?
   a. Maximize the window and drag the Title bar.
   b. Restore the window and drag the Title bar.
   c. Minimize the window and drag the Title bar.
   d. Drag a corner-sizing handle.

4. Which of the following commands can be used to print in most programs?
   a. File→Save
   b. File→Open
   c. View→Print
   d. None of the above

Skill Builders

Skill Builder 2.1 **Type a To Do List**

1. Log on to Windows.

2. Choose Start→Programs→Accessories→WordPad to start the WordPad program. Or use Start→All Programs→Accessories→WordPad if you are running Windows XP.

3. Maximize 🔲 the WordPad window.

4. Type **To Do List** as a heading for the document, then tap the (ENTER) key three times to add lines beneath the heading.

5. Type a list of things you need to do this week. Tap (ENTER) twice after each line to double-space the list.

6. Save your list to your exercise diskette using a descriptive name. Make sure that the 3½ Floppy (A:) drive is displayed in the Save in box. Keep in mind that you can use up to 255 characters in the filename including spaces.

7. Use File→Print to print your To Do list.

8. Close ❌ WordPad and save any changes (if WordPad gives you that option).

Skill Builder 2.2 **Paint a House**

1. Start the Paint program with Start→Program→Accessories→Paint. Or use Start→All Programs→Accessories→Paint if you are running Windows XP.

2. Choose File→Save from the menu bar.

3. Set the Save As Type (at the bottom of the dialog box) to 16 Color Bitmap.
   This setting reduces the number of colors you can use in the drawing, but will significantly reduce the size of the file when you save it.

4. Save the empty drawing to your exercise diskette as **A House**. Make sure that the 3½ Floppy (A:) drive is displayed in the Save in box before you click the Save button.

5. Use your investigative skills, creativity, and some trial and error to draw a house. Try to include objects such as doors, windows, a roof, and perhaps landscaping.

   !TIP! *If you make a mistake, immediately select Edit→Undo from the menu bar to undo your most recent command. If you are running Windows 98 or later, Paint will let you undo the three most recent commands.*

6. Feel free to print your drawing.

7. Close Paint, and save any changes (if Paint gives you that option).

Skill Builder 2.3 Use the Calculator

This Skill Builder will show you how to use the Windows Calculator applet.

1. Click the Start [start] button and slide the mouse up to All Programs (or Programs if you are running Windows 2000).

2. Slide the mouse to Accessories and choose Calculator. If you are running Windows 2000, ME, or XP and you do not see the Calculator in the Accessories menu, click the Menu Extension [⁀] command in the list to display the entire Accessories menu.

3. Follow these steps to add two numbers:

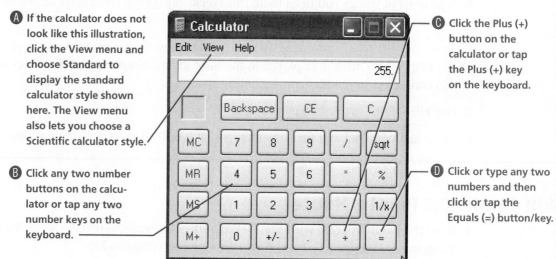

Ⓐ If the calculator does not look like this illustration, click the View menu and choose Standard to display the standard calculator style shown here. The View menu also lets you choose a Scientific calculator style.

Ⓑ Click any two number buttons on the calculator or tap any two number keys on the keyboard.

Ⓒ Click the Plus (+) button on the calculator or tap the Plus (+) key on the keyboard.

Ⓓ Click or type any two numbers and then click or tap the Equals (=) button/key.

4. Feel free to experiment with the calculator.

5. Click the Minimize [_] button to minimize the calculator.

6. Click the Calculator [Calculator] button on the Taskbar to restore the calculator. *Notice that you can hide the calculator when you are not using it and display it when you need it. This technique is often used when working with multiple programs.*

7. Close [X] the calculator window when you have finished experimenting, then continue with the Assessment exercises.

Assessments

Assessment 2.1 Create and Save a WordPad Document

1. Start the WordPad program.

2. Type the document displayed below.

   Your document does not have to match this document exactly, but it should contain the same information.

   ### Parts of a Personal Computer System

   #### Hardware
   System Unit
   Monitor
   Mouse
   Keyboard
   Printer

   #### Software
   Operating System
   Application Programs
   User Files

   [Your Name]

   ---

3. Save the document to your exercise diskette as **Assessment Exercise for Lesson 2**.

4. Close ☒ WordPad.

Assessment 2.2 Open and Print a WordPad Document

1. Start the WordPad Program.

2. Open the Assessment Exercise For Lesson 2 document you created in the previous assessment exercise.

3. Change the title of the document to **Personal Computer Components**.

4. Save the change to the document, then print the document. Retrieve the printout from the printer.

5. Close WordPad.

6. Turn in the printed page for grading.

Assessment 2.3 Configure Two Program Windows

1. Start the WordPad Program.

2. If WordPad is maximized, click the Restore ▣ button to restore the window.

3. Drag on WordPad's program window borders so that the WordPad window covers the left half of the Desktop.

4. Start the Paint Program. Make sure the Paint window is not maximized.

5. Drag on Paint's program window borders so that the Paint window covers the right half of the Desktop.

6. Close the program windows.

LESSON 3

File Management and Online Help

When you begin working with a computer, you will have just a few files to keep track of. But as your use of the computer grows, so will the number of files you must manage. After several months, you can have over a hundred of your own files. After a year, you can have hundreds more. Fortunately, Windows gives you a very effective tool for managing files: folders. With folders, you can group related files together. You can even create folders inside of other folders. As you learn how to use new features such as folders, you should take advantage of the excellent online Help system featured in Windows. Online Help makes it easy to find the answer to many types of questions with three ways to search for the information you need.

IN THIS LESSON

Additional learning resources are available at labpub.com/learn/oe3/

Case Study

Chantal is taking four courses at her community college. As she goes over the syllabi, Chantal notices that three of her courses will require her to submit term papers. She decides to prepare for some of the research she must do. Chantal creates several folders on her computer to help her organize

the files she will accumulate as she performs research for each term paper. She creates a folder for each of her classes on the computer. Then she creates folders inside the class folders to further organize her files. For example, she creates Final and Drafts folders for the word processor documents she will create. Chantal also creates a Research folder to hold the various files, Web pages, and notes she will collect. She creates a folder called Old Stuff for everything she thinks she doesn't need, but does not want to delete. She can delete the Old Stuff folder after the term project paper is completed.

Chantal created these folders inside each of her course folders. This makes it easier for her to find the files she needs to work on as the semester progresses.

As Chantal learns new ways to organize her work, she also learns how to look up the answers to her questions with online Help. For example, when she could not recall how to create a new folder on her computer, she looked it up in online Help. Chantal likes to be as self-reliant as possible where computers are concerned, and online Help is one of the ways she can do this.

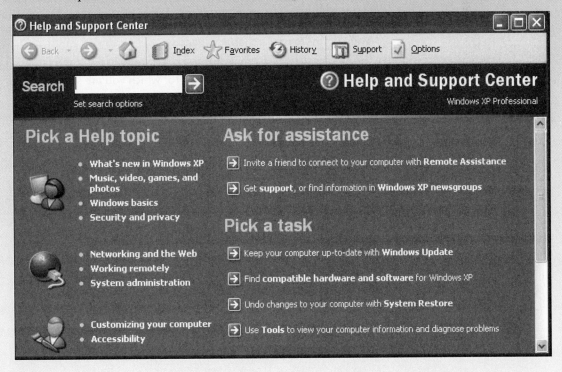

Using Online Help with Windows

Windows provides an online Help system that can answer questions about running application programs or completing tasks with Windows itself. Online Help has proven so effective that many vendors no longer publish the sort of lengthy manuals that used to come with most programs. For example, the Microsoft Office XP Suite provides just a thin "Discovering" manual with an overview of what's new and how to use basic features of the software.

Finding the Information You Need

Your goal when using online Help is to locate a Help topic. The Help feature provides several methods that you can use to locate topics. All Help topics have keywords that identify them. For example, a Help topic that discusses copying files can probably be located by using the keywords *copying files*. Regardless of which method you use, the goal is to locate a topic. Once you locate the desired topic, you can display it and follow its instructions.

Search Methods

Depending on the version of Windows you are using, the following methods are available for searching online Help:

Search Method	Description
Contents	The Contents method is useful if you are trying to locate a topic but you aren't really sure how to describe it. The Contents method lets you navigate through a series of categories until the desired topic is located.
Index	The Index method lets you locate a topic by typing keywords. An alphabetically indexed list of topics is displayed from which you can choose the desired topic. This method is most useful if you know the name of the topic or feature with which you need assistance.
Search	The Search method searches inside of the Help topics for the keywords you enter. This provides an in-depth search and lets you locate topics that may not be found using the other search methods. However, sometimes this method will find more topics than you need.
Web Help (Windows 2000 only)	This Help option takes you directly to Microsoft's Web site. Web Help can locate the latest information on the topic for which you are searching.

QUICK REFERENCE: STARTING ONLINE HELP

Task	Procedure
Start Windows online Help.	■ Choose Start→Help from the Start menu. ■ Choose the desired search method.
Start online Help in an application program.	■ Choose Help from the menu bar or tap the (F1) function key, then select the type of Help you require.

Hands-On 3.1 Search Online Help

In this exercise, you will determine which version of Windows you are running. This will determine whether you perform section a or b of the exercise.

Before You Begin: Choose the correct version of the exercise according to your version of Windows:

- **Windows 2000**—*Complete Hands-On Exercise 3.1a starting below.*
- **Windows XP**—*Complete Hands-on Exercise 3.1b starting on page 88.*

 Hands-On 3.1a Search Online Help in Windows 2000

1. Click the Start button, and choose ![Help] from the menu.
   The Windows Help window will appear. In the next few steps, you will look up a Help topic on copying files or folders.

2. Follow these steps to conduct a search using the Contents method:

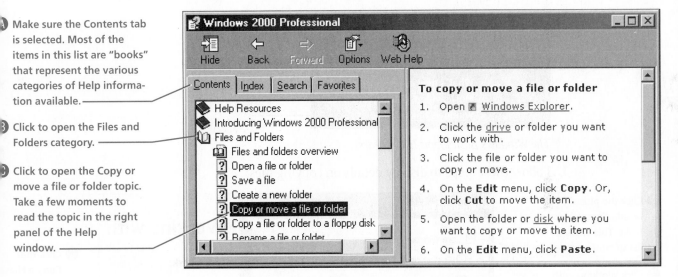

Ⓐ Make sure the Contents tab is selected. Most of the items in this list are "books" that represent the various categories of Help information available.

Ⓑ Click to open the Files and Folders category.

Ⓒ Click to open the Copy or move a file or folder topic. Take a few moments to read the topic in the right panel of the Help window.

3. Follow these steps to adjust the size of the panels in the Help window:

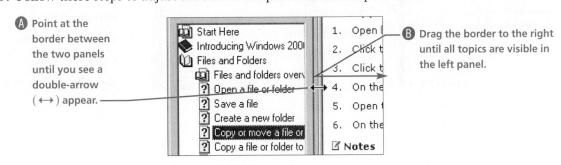

Ⓐ Point at the border between the two panels until you see a double-arrow (↔) appear.

Ⓑ Drag the border to the right until all topics are visible in the left panel.

4. Click the Hide button on the left side of the Help window toolbar.
This command conserves screen space by hiding the category list. Now only the Help topic you displayed earlier is visible.

5. Click the Show button on the left side of the Help window toolbar.
Now the category list is visible again; thus, this control works as a toggle to switch the display of the category list on and off.

Leave the Help window open, and continue with the Index Search topic on page 89.

 ## Hands-On 3.1b Search Online Help in Windows XP

Windows XP continues the refinements in the Windows Help system introduced in Windows ME. It contains a table of contents navigation scheme that is easier to use.

1. Click the Start button and choose Help and Support 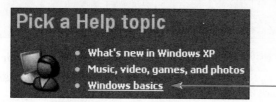 from the menu.
The Windows Help window will appear. In the next few steps, you will look up a Help topic on copying files or folders.

2. Click the Windows Basics link.

Pick a Help topic
- What's new in Windows XP
- Music, video, games, and photos
- <u>Windows basics</u>

The Windows Basics topic list appears.

3. Follow these steps to display details on copying files:

Ⓐ Click the plus sign beside Core Windows tasks. This expands a list of subtopics.

Ⓑ Click Working with Files and Folders. A further list of topics appears in the right panel of the Help window.

Ⓒ Click the Copy a File or Folder topic. This displays detailed information on the topic in the right panel.

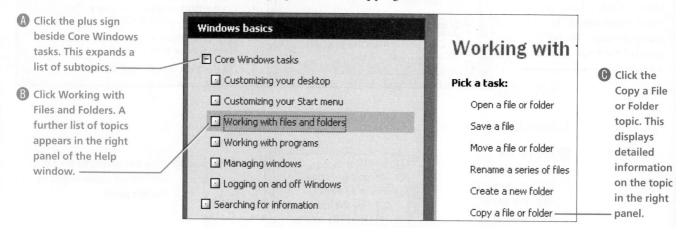

4. Follow these steps to adjust the size of the panels in the Help window:

<table>
<tr><td>Windows basics</td></tr>
<tr><td>☐ Core Windows tasks
☐ Customizing your desktop
☐ Customizing your Start menu</td></tr>
</table>

To copy a file or folder
1. Open 🗎 My Documents.
If the file or folder you w
its subfolders, use Searc
then click **Search**.

A Point at the border between the two Help window panels until a double-pointed arrow appears.

B Drag the border to the right until it is about one-half as wide as the Help window.

Depending on the screen size of your monitor, you may sometimes wish to change the area displaying Help instructions.

5. Point at the border between the Help panels and drag the border to the left until the left panel is a good size to display the Windows Basics topics.
Leave the Help window open and continue with the Index Search topic below.

Index Search

The Index search lets you find Help topics by searching for a keyword in the topic titles. Every topic that includes the keyword in its title is displayed in a search results window.

Hands-On 3.2 **Search with the Index Method**

In this exercise, you will use the Index search method to find the same topic on copying files and folders.

1. Follow the steps for your version of Windows to perform an Index search. (Windows XP users will find their steps on the following page.)

A Click the Index tab near the top of the Help window.

B Type the keyword **copying** in the keyword box.

C Look over the search results in this list, then use the instructions in the next step to open the appropriate topic.

D Go on to Step 2.

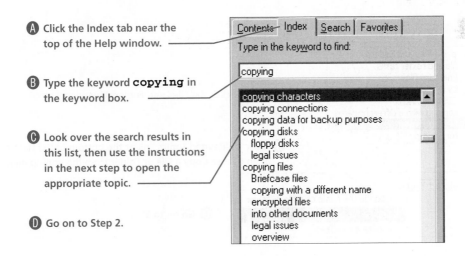

Contents | Index | Search | Favorites
Type in the keyword to find:

copying

copying characters
copying connections
copying data for backup purposes
copying disks
  floppy disks
  legal issues
copying files
  Briefcase files
  copying with a different name
  encrypted files
  into other documents
  legal issues
  overview

Windows 2000

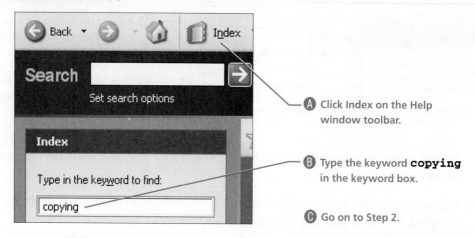

Ⓐ Click Index on the Help window toolbar.

Ⓑ Type the keyword **copying** in the keyword box.

Ⓒ Go on to Step 2.

Windows XP

2. Follow the instructions for the version of Windows you are using:

Ⓐ Double-click the overview topic under copying files.

> Click a topic, then click Display.
>
> | Title |
> |---|
> | Copy or move a file or folder |
> | Using Windows Explorer |

Ⓑ Choose Copy or move a file or folder from the Topics Found window, then click the Display button at the lower-right corner of the window. The topic will be displayed in the right panel of the Help window.

> copying files
>   Briefcase files
>   copying to floppy disks
>   legality of
>   overview
>   viewing copied files using
> copying floppy disks

Ⓒ Go to Step 3.

Windows 2000

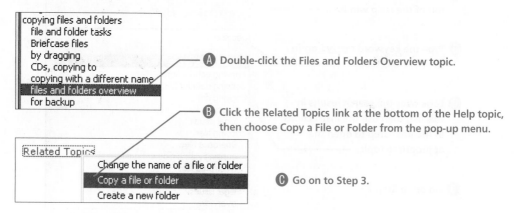

> copying files and folders
>   file and folder tasks
>   Briefcase files
>   by dragging
>   CDs, copying to
>   copying with a different name
>   files and folders overview
>   for backup

Ⓐ Double-click the Files and Folders Overview topic.

Ⓑ Click the Related Topics link at the bottom of the Help topic, then choose Copy a File or Folder from the pop-up menu.

> Related Topics
> | Change the name of a file or folder |
> |---|
> | Copy a file or folder |
> | Create a new folder |

Ⓒ Go on to Step 3.

3. Follow the steps for your version of Windows to return to the Contents search method:

   ▧ **Windows 2000**—Click the Contents tab.

   ▧ **Windows XP**—Click the Home 🏠 button on the Toolbar.

4. Use the Contents search method to browse for new features in your version of Windows. Look for topics such as Introducing Windows, or Using Windows, What's New….

5. Use the Index search method to search for help on the following topics.

   ▧ Cascading Windows

   ▧ Undeleting Files

6. When you are finished with the additional searches in Step 5, close ✕ any open Help windows before moving on to the next topic.

Accessing Help in an Application Program

FROM THE KEYBOARD

F1 to display the Help system.

Most Windows programs have online Help built into them. You access a program's online Help system with the Help command from the program's menu bar. Many Windows application programs use an online Help window that works just like Windows Help. The Microsoft Office 2003 Suite features a question box that allows you to search for Help topics by typing a question in plain English.

Hands-On 3.3 Look Up Help for an Application Program

In this exercise, you will start the WordPad program and look up a Help topic in WordPad's online Help.

1. Choose Start→Programs→Accessories→WordPad to start the WordPad program.

2. Choose Help→Help Topics from WordPad's menu bar.
   WordPad displays its Help window. This window will look similar to the Help window you used in the previous exercises.

3. Choose the Index tab, then type **undo** as the search keyword.
   A list of Help topics beginning with the same letters as this keyword will appear.

4. Double-click to open the topic in the results list that begins with the word undo or undoing.
   WordPad's Help displays a method to undo your most recent action. This can be useful if you accidentally delete some text or make some other mistake as you work.

5. Click the Help Window's Close ✕ button.

6. Tap the F1 function key in the top row of keys on the keyboard.
   Most Windows programs treat F1 as the Help key.

7. Close ✕ the Help window again.

8. Close ✕ the WordPad window.

Browsing through Files

In Lesson 2, you stored documents and an image as files on your exercise diskette. In this lesson, you will learn how to organize the growing number of files that can accumulate as you work with a computer. Besides your own files, there are hundreds or even thousands of files on the hard drive that run Windows and the application programs you use. Learning how all these files are organized will help you save and find your own files more easily.

How Files are Organized

Windows uses a flexible hierarchy that is common to most personal computers. The three levels in the hierarchy are listed below:

Level	Definition	Examples
Drive	This is a physical place in which you store files.	▪ A floppy disk ▪ A hard drive
Folder	This is an electronic location in which you store groups of related files. It is also possible to place folders inside of other folders.	▪ A folder to store all the files for an application program ▪ A folder to store all the letters you type for a project
File	This is a collection of computer data that has some common purpose.	▪ A letter you've typed ▪ A picture you've drawn

Browsing with the My Computer Window

As you work with Windows programs such as WordPad and Paint, you will want to locate and open files you have created previously. Although you can open files from within an application program, sometimes it is more convenient to search directly through all of the files you have saved to a hard drive or floppy disk. This is the sort of task for which the My Computer window is perfectly suited.

The following illustrations describe the major features of the My Computer window. Take a moment to review these features before beginning the next Hands-On exercise.

Windows 2000

The toolbar in Windows 2000 differs slightly from earlier versions of Windows. —

This button displays the drives and folders on the system in a new panel. —

These buttons let you move, copy, and delete files. —

These links display other useful locations in which files and folders may be stored. —

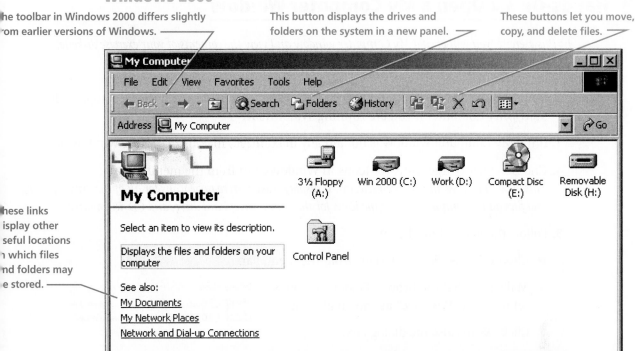

Windows XP

The address bar displays the location you are currently browsing. —

These panels contain links to display system task commands and other places you may wish to browse. —

This panel displays details on whichever item you select in the right panel. —

You can double-click any items in this panel to view their contents. —

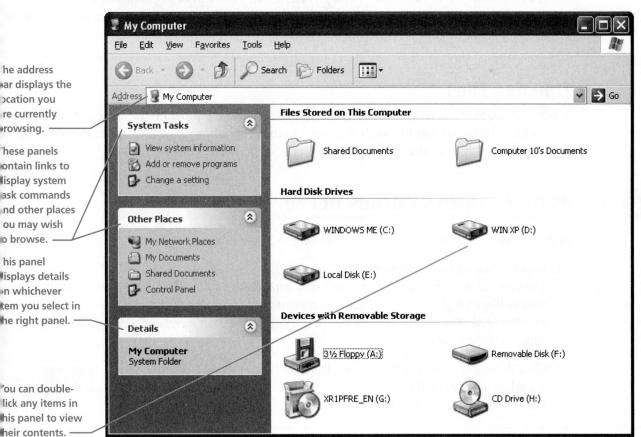

Hands-On 3.4 **Open a My Computer Window**

In this exercise, you will open a My Computer window and view the contents of your exercise diskette.

1. Close any open windows on the Desktop.

2. Double-click the My Computer 🖳 icon near the top-left corner of the Desktop, or click Start→My Computer if you are running Windows XP.

3. If the My Computer window is not already maximized, maximize ▣ the window now.

4. Choose View→Large Icons (or Icons in Windows XP) from the menu bar.
   This view may have already been selected. It displays easy-to-recognize icons for all of the drives, folders, and files on the computer. Notice the icons for the floppy drive, hard drive, and CD-ROM drive.

5. Follow the instructions below:

   ▨ Choose Tools→Folder Options from the menu bar.

   ▨ Make sure that the Browse Folders option is set to "Same Window," as shown at right.

   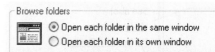

   ▨ Click OK to close the dialog box.

6. Place your exercise diskette in the floppy drive, with the label side up and the metal side in.

7. Double-click the 3½ Floppy (A:) 💾 or 🖴 icon to view the exercise diskette.
   You stored some files on this diskette in the previous lesson. But WordPad's Open and Save As dialog boxes only display document files that the program can open. In the My Computer window you can see all of the files on the diskette. Leave the My Computer window open and continue with the next topic.

Opening Files

When you double-click on a file in a My Computer window, the program used to create or edit that type of file is launched and the file is displayed in the program window. This is a convenient way to start working with a file after you find it.

 ## Hands-On 3.5 **Open a Document File**

In this exercise, you will open the WordPad document you created in a previous lesson.

1. Double-click on the Tutor Meeting document file.
   Windows will start the program that is associated with document files. This will probably be Microsoft Word or WordPad. If Word is installed on the computer, it is programmed to open files that were created with WordPad. However, you can also start WordPad from the Start menu and use WordPad's Open command to open the file.

2. Click the upper Close ⊠ button, as shown at right. Click No if you are asked to save the file.
   Now only the My Computer window should be open.

Changing the View

There are several ways to view drives and folders in a My Computer window. You have been using the Large Icons view thus far. This view represents each file and folder with a larger icon than the other views. You can change the view from the My Computer View menu or with the Views toolbar button. Depending on the version of Windows you are using, the Views button will match one of the examples below:

Windows 2000

Windows XP

 ## Hands-On 3.6 Try out Different Views

In this exercise, you will experiment with different formats for viewing files.

1. Choose View→List from the menu bar.
   Use this view when you want to display as many folder and file names as possible.

2. Choose View→Details from the menu bar.
   This view gives you additional information about the files, such as the date each file was created or modified. Depending on how this view was last used, you may or may not be able to see the entire filename in the leftmost column.

3. Follow these steps to adjust the width of a column in Details view:

Ⓐ Point here until you see the double-arrow, then double-click. The column width is adjusted to the length of the longest item in the column. ⟶

Ⓑ Point here until you see the double-arrow, then press the mouse button and drag to the left to make the column narrower ⟶

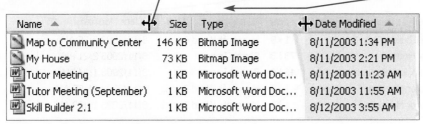

Ⓒ Double-click to make the column you just narrowed as wide as its longest item.

4. Choose View→Thumbnails from the menu bar. After you have seen the Thumbnails view, return to the Details view.
   The Thumbnails view displays a miniature view of each image file. Notice that the map you created in Lesson 2 is now displayed as a small thumbnail image.

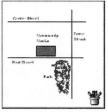

Map to Community Center

Sorting Files

The My Computer window may contain many files and folders. You can sort the files and folders in a variety of ways. This can be useful if you are trying to find a specific file. The files and folders can be sorted by name, size, type, or date. These four parameters are known as Sort Keys. You can also sort files in ascending order (A to Z) or descending order (Z to A). The four sort keys are described in the following table.

Sort Key	How it Sorts the Files and Folders
Name	Alphabetically by filename
Size	By the size of the files
Type	By the function of the file, such as word processing document, spreadsheet, or database
Date	By the date that the file was created or most recently modified

Hands-On 3.7 Sort the Files

In this exercise, you will view the files on your exercise diskette in various sort orders.

1. Make sure that the Details view is displayed, then follow these steps to sort the files in various ways:

    A Click the Modified or Date Modified column heading to sort the files by date. The most recently modified file is listed first. ⟶

    B Click the Modified or Date Modified column heading again. Now files with the most recent date are at the bottom of the list. When you click the same column a second time, the list is sorted in descending rather than ascending order. ⟶

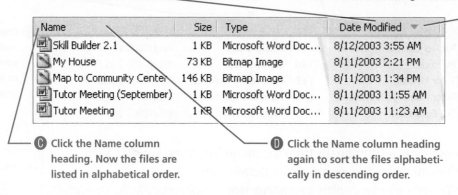

    C Click the Name column heading. Now the files are listed in alphabetical order.

    D Click the Name column heading again to sort the files alphabetically in descending order.

2. Try sorting the files by clicking on the other columns.
    Sorting the files can often help you locate a particular file. For example, sorting the files by date can help you find a file you created or modified recently.

3. Set the view to Large Icons (or Icons).
    You can also sort files when you are in one of the other view modes, as you will do in the next step.

4. Choose View→Arrange Icons→By Size from the menu bar.
   Your Map to Community Center file should be last in the list. Image files like the map are usually much larger than word processing documents. The Tutor Meeting file appears toward the top of the list, because it is a very small document.

5. Close ☒ the My Computer window.

Working with Folders

Folders are important tools for organizing files. You may have just a few files when you begin using a computer, but after a year or two you may have hundreds of files. What if you could only view your files in a single, long list? This would be similar to finding a book in a library that had only one long bookshelf. You could find the book eventually, but you would need to scan through many titles first.

Folders Hierarchy

Folders are organized into a hierarchy on each drive of a Windows system. Windows creates many folders when it is installed on the computer. You can create your own folders as well. The following illustration displays a common folders hierarchy on a Windows system. This is an example of the *Exploring* window. You will learn how to open an Exploring window later in this lesson.

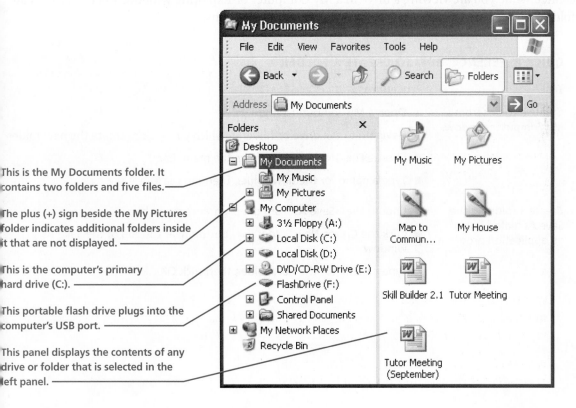

This is the My Documents folder. It contains two folders and five files.

The plus (+) sign beside the My Pictures folder indicates additional folders inside it that are not displayed.

This is the computer's primary hard drive (C:).

This portable flash drive plugs into the computer's USB port.

This panel displays the contents of any drive or folder that is selected in the left panel.

The My Documents Folder

Windows features a special folder called My Documents. This folder stores files on the computer's hard drive. The My Documents folder is associated with your log-on name. This means that each user with his or her own log on name has a unique My Documents folder. If you are running a program in the Office 2003 Suite, you can access the My Documents folder with a single click.

This button in the Word 2003 Save As dialog box navigates you to the My Documents folder with a single click.

Creating Folders

You can create folders on a floppy disk or the hard drive whenever you need them. Folders can be created while you are viewing a drive in a My Computer or Exploring window. You can also create folders from the Save As dialog box of most Windows programs.

QUICK REFERENCE: HOW TO CREATE A FOLDER

Task	Procedure
Create a folder from a My Computer window.	■ Open a My Computer Window.
	■ Navigate to the drive or folder in which you wish to create the new folder.
	■ Choose File→New→Folder from the menu bar.
	■ Type a name for the new folder, then tap the (ENTER) key.
Create a folder in the Save As dialog box of an application program.	■ Choose File→Save As from the program's menu bar.
	■ Click the Create New Folder [icon] button near the top of the Save As window.
	■ Type a name for the new folder, then click OK.

Hands-On 3.8 Create Folders on Your Floppy Disk

In this exercise, you will create two folders on your exercise diskette. Later in this lesson you will move and copy files into these folders.

1. Follow the step for your version of Windows:

   ■ **Windows 2000**—Double-click the My Computer icon on the Desktop.

   ■ **Windows XP**—Choose Start→My Computer.

2. If necessary, maximize 🔲 the window.

3. Make sure your exercise diskette is properly inserted, then double-click the 3½ Floppy (A:) drive.

4. Choose View→Icons (or View→Large Icons in Windows 2000).

5. Follow these steps to create a new folder:

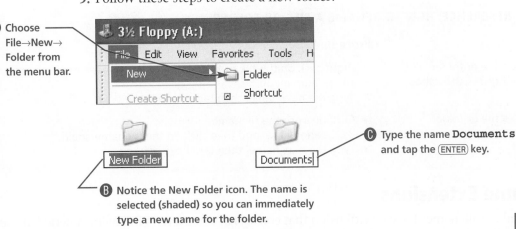

Ⓐ Choose File→New→ Folder from the menu bar.

Ⓒ Type the name **Documents** and tap the (ENTER) key.

Ⓑ Notice the New Folder icon. The name is selected (shaded) so you can immediately type a new name for the folder.

6. Double-click the Documents folder icon to navigate to your new folder.
   Notice that the name of your folder is displayed in the Address bar near the top of the My Computer window as well as in the Title bar. This folder is empty now, but you will place files in it later.

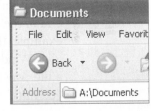

7. Follow these steps to navigate to the 3½ Floppy (A:) drive using the Address Bar:

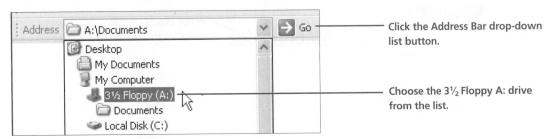

Click the Address Bar drop-down list button.

Choose the 3½ Floppy A: drive from the list.

Now the drive or My Documents folder is displayed in the Address bar. Looking at the Address bar as you navigate in the system helps you keep track of where you are.

8. Choose File→New→Folder from the menu bar. Type **Graphics** as the name for the new folder and tap the (ENTER) key.

9. Double-click on the Graphics folder.
   Notice that the name of the folder is displayed in the Address bar.

10. Click the Up  or button on the toolbar to return to the 3½ Floppy (A:) drive level.
   The Up button jumps you one level up in the drive/folder hierarchy. This button is often easier to use than the drop-down list you used in Step 7.

Renaming Files and Folders

In Lesson 2, you learned how to save a file with a new name to create a copy of the file. It is also easy to rename a file without making a copy. To rename a file that is displayed in a My Computer window, right-click on the file and choose Rename from the pop-up menu.

 QUICK REFERENCE: HOW TO RENAME A FILE OR FOLDER

Task	Procedure
Rename a file or folder with the right-click method.	■ Right-click on the file or folder icon, then choose Rename from the pop-up menu. ■ Type the new name, then tap the (ENTER) key.
Rename a file or folder with the click-pause method.	■ Click on once the filename. ■ Pause about 1 second then click on the filename again. ■ Type the new name, then tap the (ENTER) key.

Filename Extensions

Most Windows filenames have an extension that consists of three letters following a period at the end of the filename. Filename extensions identify the type of file you are working with. For example, the Tutor Meeting file is a word processing document, so it has a filename extension of .doc. Windows application programs add this extension to any filename you type when you save a file. Most Windows systems hide the filename extension. But if your system is set to display it, you must type out the extension whenever you rename a file.

The filename ——— Tutor Meeting.doc ——— The extension. Most Windows systems are set to hide the extension.

Hands-On 3.9 Rename a File

In this exercise, you will use both methods to rename one of the files you created in Lesson 2.

1. Follow these steps to issue the Rename command with the right-click method:

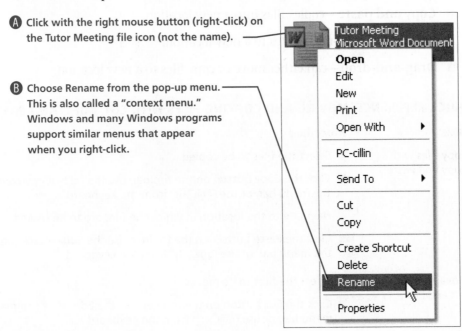

A Click with the right mouse button (right-click) on the Tutor Meeting file icon (not the name).

B Choose Rename from the pop-up menu. This is also called a "context menu." Windows and many Windows programs support similar menus that appear when you right-click.

Windows highlights the filename for renaming. It may or may not display a three-letter extension of .doc.

2. Examine the filename, then follow the instructions that match the filename:

   - If the filename reads Tutor Meeting, type **April Meeting** and tap (ENTER).

   - If the filename reads Tutor Meeting.doc, type **April Meeting.doc** and tap (ENTER).

   The old name is deleted and replaced by the new name.

3. Click on a clear area of the My Computer window to deselect the April Meeting file.

4. Click on the filename (not the icon) for the April Meeting file. Pause about two seconds, and then click again on the filename.
   The name will be highlighted for editing. You need to pause so that Windows does not mistake your command for a double-click (which is done much faster).

5. Tap the left arrow ← key until the insertion point is blinking just to the right of the *l* in April, then tap the (BACKSPACE) key until the word April is deleted.
   The arrow key allows you to move the insertion point back without deleting the word Meeting.

6. Type **Tutor** as the first word in the filename, then tap the (ENTER) key to complete the rename command.
   Leave the My Computer window open.

Moving and Copying Files

Windows lets you move and copy files from one drive to another, and from one folder to another. There are several techniques you can use to move and copy files. This lesson will teach you three methods:

- **Copy and paste**—copies files into a new location.

- **Cut and paste**—moves files to a new location.

- **Drag-and-drop**—can either move or copy files to a new location.

QUICK REFERENCE: MOVING AND COPYING FILES WITH CUT, COPY, AND PASTE

Task	Procedure
Copy files with Copy and Paste.	■ Select the files to be copied.
	■ Click the Copy button on the toolbar, use the Edit→Copy command on the menu bar, or use CTRL+C from the keyboard.
	■ Navigate to the location in which the files are to be copied.
	■ Click the Paste button on the toolbar, use the Edit→Paste command on the menu bar, or use CTRL+V from the keyboard.
Move Files with Cut and Paste.	■ Select the files to be moved.
	■ Click the Cut button on the toolbar, use the Edit→Cut command on the menu bar, or use CTRL+X from the keyboard.
	■ Navigate to the location in which the files are to be moved.
	■ Click the Paste button on the toolbar, use the Edit→Paste command on the menu bar, or use CTRL+V from the keyboard.

Selecting Multiple Files for Move and Copy Commands

You can move and copy a single file or dozens of files with the same command. Before you give the Cut or Copy command, select the file(s) you wish to be affected by the command. To select a single file, you simply click on it. The two easiest methods of selecting multiple files are described in the Quick Reference table that follows. You can combine these two techniques as your needs dictate.

QUICK REFERENCE: HOW TO SELECT MULTIPLE FILES FOR COMMANDS

Technique	Procedure
CTRL+Click technique to select several files.	■ Click the first file you wish to select.
	■ Press and hold CTRL while you click on any other files you wish to select.
	■ Release the CTRL key when you have made all of your selections.
SHIFT+Click technique to select several files in a row.	■ Click the first file you wish to select.
	■ Press and hold SHIFT while you click last file in the group that you wish to select, then release SHIFT.
Deselect a selected file.	■ Press and hold CTRL while you click on the file you wish to deselect.

Hands-On 3.10 **Move and Copy Files**

Move a File with Cut and Paste

In this part of the exercise, you will use the Cut and Paste technique to move a single file into one of your new folders.

1. Make sure the My Computer window is displaying the correct drive (floppy, USB flash drive, or My Documents folder). Look at the top-left corner of the My Computer window's title bar to confirm that you are at the right location.

2. Click to select the Map to Community Center file in the My Computer window.

3. Choose Edit→Cut from the menu bar.
   Notice that the icon for the file you selected is "dimmed." This indicates that the file has been cut and will be moved when you give the Paste command.

4. Double-click to open the Graphics folder.
   This navigates you to the empty Graphics folder.

5. Choose Edit→Paste from the menu bar.
   After the file has been moved, it will be displayed in the window.

6. Click the Up or ⬆ button to return to the floppy drive or other file storage location.
   Notice that the Map to Community Center file is no longer listed with the other files; it was moved to a different folder.

⚠️ **!NOTE!**

The first level of a drive is also called the root.

Copy Multiple Files

In this part of the exercise, you will select more than one file for the Copy and Paste commands.

7. Hold down the (CTRL) key as you click on the two Tutor Meeting document files, then release the (CTRL) key.
   Both files should now be selected.

8. Choose Edit→Copy from the menu bar.

9. Double-click to open the Documents folder.

10. Choose Edit→Paste from the menu bar.
    The files will appear in the window as they are copied.

11. Click the Up ⬆ or ⬆ button to return to the floppy drive or other file storage location.
    Notice that the document files are still displayed in the window; they were copied rather than moved.

Moving and Copying Files with Drag-and-Drop

The Drag-and-Drop technique is an easy way to move or copy files or folders by dragging them to the desired location. The easiest way to use the Drag-and-Drop technique is to hold down the right (not the left) mouse button as you drag. This will give you a pop-up menu from which you select the Move or Copy command.

QUICK REFERENCE: MOVING AND COPYING FILES WITH DRAG AND DROP

Task	Procedure
Drag-and-Drop with the right-drag technique.	■ Select the files or folders to be moved or copied.
	■ Point at one selected file or folder, press and hold the right mouse button, and drag the files or folders to the desired location.
	■ Release the mouse button at the destination, then select Move Here, Copy Here, or Cancel from the pop-up menu.
Move files on the same disk drive with Drag-and-Drop.	■ Select the files or folders to be moved.
	■ Point at one selected file or folder and drag with the left mouse button to a new location on the same disk drive.
Copy files to a different disk drive with Drag-and-Drop.	■ Select the files or folders to be copied.
	■ Point at one selected file or folder and drag with the left mouse button to the new location on a different disk drive.

Hands-On 3.11 Move Files with Drag and Drop

In this exercise, you will select two files with the (CTRL)+Click technique.

1. Click to select the Tutor Meeting file. Press (CTRL), click on the Tutor Meeting (September) document file, and release (CTRL).

2. Follow these steps to move the files with the Drag-and-Drop technique:
   The two files will disappear from the My Computer window as they are moved.

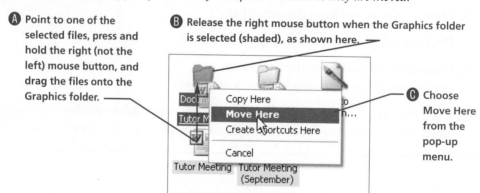

Ⓐ Point to one of the selected files, press and hold the right (not the left) mouse button, and drag the files onto the Graphics folder.

Ⓑ Release the right mouse button when the Graphics folder is selected (shaded), as shown here.

Ⓒ Choose Move Here from the pop-up menu.

3. Double-click to open the Graphics folder.
   The two files you dragged and dropped should now be in the folder.

4. Click the Up ⤴ or 📁 button on the toolbar to return to the 3½ Floppy (A:) drive level.

Deleting Files and Folders

You can delete files and folders by selecting them and tapping the (DELETE) key. When you delete a folder, any files inside that folder are deleted as well.

What Happens to Deleted Files?

Windows does not physically erase a deleted file from the hard drive. Instead, the file is placed in the Recycle Bin. The Recycle Bin holds the deleted files until you give a command to empty it, or it runs out of the space allotted to store deleted files. If you delete files from the hard drive, you can recover them by opening the Recycle Bin, selecting the files you wish to recover, then choosing File→Restore from the menu bar.

 !WARNING! *Files and folders deleted from floppy disks are not sent to the Recycle Bin! They are permanently deleted when you issue the delete command.*

 Hands-On 3.12 Delete Files and a Folder

In this exercise, you will delete one of the files in the Documents folder. Then you will delete the Documents folder itself (erasing the other document file).

1. Double-click to open the Documents folder on your floppy disk.
   You still have a copy of these files in the Graphics folder, so it is safe to delete the ones in this folder.

2. Select one of the document files in the folder, then tap the (DELETE) key on the keyboard.
   Depending on how Windows is configured, you may see a prompt asking if you really want to delete the file you selected. This is a safeguard to help prevent the accidental deletion of files. This confirmation feature can be switched on and off.

3. Choose Yes if Windows asks you to confirm deleting the file.
   Windows will briefly display an animation of the files being deleted.

 !TIP!

Always make sure you know what's inside a folder before you delete it.

4. Click the Up 🔼 or 🔼 button to return to the floppy drive.

5. Follow the step for your version of Windows:

   ■ **Windows 2000**—Select the Documents folder then click the Delete ⊠ button on the Toolbar. Choose Yes if you are asked to confirm the deletion.

   ■ **Windows XP**—Select the Select the Documents folder then click Delete this Folder on the task panel on the left side of the Window. Choose Yes if you are asked to confirm the deletion.

Checking Space on a Drive

As you create and save files to your floppy disk, the disk may eventually run out of space. Thus, you may want to check the space available on the floppy disk from time to time. You can use the Properties command to display a pie chart of the available space on a drive. Windows 2000 can also display a pie chart as part of a My Computer or Exploring window, as can all other versions of Windows if they are configured to do so.

QUICK REFERENCE: CHECKING THE AVAILABLE SPACE ON A DISK DRIVE

Task	Procedure
View a pie chart of how much space is available on a disk drive.	■ Open a My Computer or Exploring window.
	■ Right-click on the desired drive, then choose Properties from the pop-up menu.

Hands-On 3.13 Check the Properties of Your Disk

In this exercise, you will find out how much space is available on your floppy disk using the Properties option.

1. Click the Up ⬆ or 📁 button on the toolbar to return to the My Computer level in the computer system.

2. Follow these steps to view the properties of the floppy disk:

Ⓐ Right-click the 3½ Floppy (A:) drive.

Ⓑ Choose Properties from the context menu.

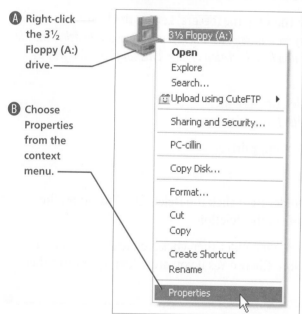

A Properties window for the floppy drive will appear. The pie chart and numbers indicate how much space is available on the floppy disk.

3. Close ⊠ the Properties window.

4. Click (don't double-click) on the 3½ Floppy (A:) drive.
   Depending on how your version of Windows is configured, you may see a similar pie chart on the left side of the My Computer window.

5. Close ⊠ the My Computer window.

The Exploring View

Windows gives you two ways of searching through files on the computer: the My Computer window and the Exploring Window. The My Computer window displays these items in a single panel. The Exploring window splits the display into two panels. Below is an example of an Exploring window.

This panel displays the structure of the computer's drives and folders.

This Folders button switches the Folders panel on and off.

This panel displays the contents of any drive or folder that you select for viewing. What you see in this panel is exactly the same as what you would see in a My Computer window.

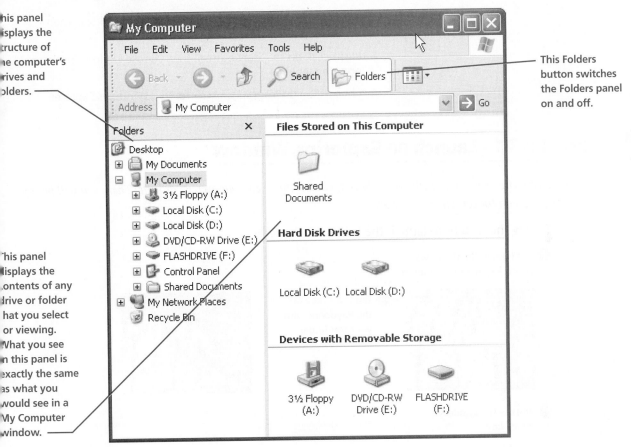

Why Two Views?

Microsoft researched the way people interact with computers. They found that most beginners are more comfortable with the single-panel view of the My Computer window. It is a simpler, more intuitive view of the computer system. Experienced users tend to prefer the flexibility of the Exploring window. They find it easier to navigate quickly in the computer with the Exploring view. Thus, providing both views satisfies the needs of beginners and experienced users.

You have used the My Computer window for most of the exercises in this lesson. Now you will have an opportunity to try the Exploring window. After you have tried both methods, you can decide which view works best for your file management activities. You may find that you prefer the My Computer view for the first year or two that you work with Windows. That's fine. You can perform the same tasks in either view.

QUICK REFERENCE: OPENING AN EXPLORING WINDOW

Task	Procedure
Open an Exploring Window.	You can use any of the following methods:

■ Hold down the Windows key on the keyboard and tap the Ⓔ key.

■ Right-click on the My Computer icon on the Desktop, then choose Explore from the pop-up menu.

■ Right-click on the Start button, then choose Explore from the pop-up menu.

■ Choose Start→Programs→Accessories→Windows Explorer.

Hands-On 3.14 Launch an Exploring Window

In this exercise, you will launch an Exploring window and view your exercise diskette. Then, you will briefly view folders on the computer's hard drive.

1. Follow these steps to launch the Windows Explorer:

Ⓐ Hold down the Windows (Start) key with your thumb.

Ⓑ Tap the Ⓔ key on the keyboard with your forefinger.

Ⓒ Release the Windows (Start) key.

2. Maximize 🔲 the Exploring window if necessary then choose View→Large Icons (or Icons in Windows XP) from the menu bar.

3. Follow these steps to view files on your floppy disk:

Ⓐ Click the 3½ Floppy (A:) icon in the left panel to display its contents in the right panel of the Exploring window.

Ⓑ If necessary, click the (+) sign to expand the display of the folder on this drive.

Ⓒ Click the Graphics folder in the left panel.

Ⓓ The files inside the Graphics folder appear in the right panel.

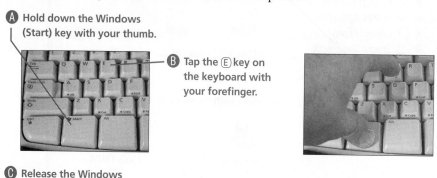

Move Files with Drag-and-Drop

4. Choose View→List from the menu bar.

5. Click on the first file in the list, and press (SHIFT), then click on the last file in the list.
   The (SHIFT)+Click selection technique selects all of the files between your first and last click.

6. Click on one of the files (do not hold down the (SHIFT) key).
   Now only the file you clicked is selected. To select more than one file, you must always hold down the (SHIFT) or (CTRL) key as you click additional files.

7. Choose Edit→Select All from the menu bar.
   This command selects all of the files displayed in the right panel. This command is faster than the (CTRL)+Click or (SHIFT)+Click methods when you want to select all of the files in a folder.

8. Choose View→Large Icons (or Icons) from the menu bar.

9. Follow these steps to move the files back to the top (root) level of the drive or My Documents folder with the drag and drop technique:

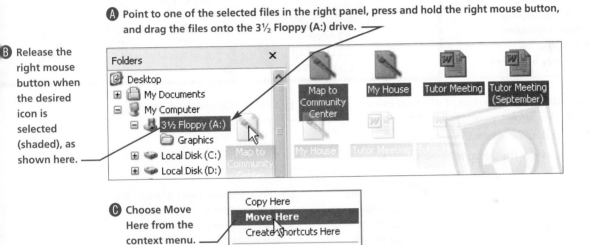

Ⓐ Point to one of the selected files in the right panel, press and hold the right mouse button, and drag the files onto the 3½ Floppy (A:) drive.

Ⓑ Release the right mouse button when the desired icon is selected (shaded), as shown here.

Ⓒ Choose Move Here from the context menu.

When the Move command is completed, the Graphics folder will be empty.

10. Follow these steps to delete the empty Graphics folder:

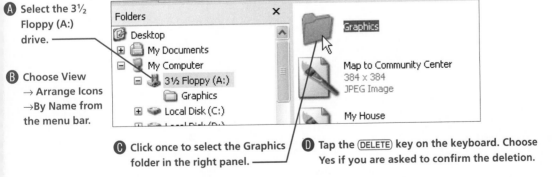

Ⓐ Select the 3½ Floppy (A:) drive.

Ⓑ Choose View → Arrange Icons →By Name from the menu bar.

Ⓒ Click once to select the Graphics folder in the right panel.

Ⓓ Tap the (DELETE) key on the keyboard. Choose Yes if you are asked to confirm the deletion.

Explore the Hard Drive

Compared to your floppy disk, a typical hard drive stores many thousands more files in a much more complex folder structure. Now you will browse a few of the folders on a hard drive.

11. Follow these steps to browse folders on the hard drive:

A Click the plus (+) sign next to the hard drive (C:) to expand the view of folders on this drive. The C: drive may not be named the same as the illustration.

B **Windows XP Only**—Click Show the Contents of this Folder in the right panel if the contents of the C: drive is hidden.

C Click the plus (+) sign beside the Program Files folder to expand the view of other folders inside this folder. This folder holds most application programs installed on the computer. There may be dozens of folders here.

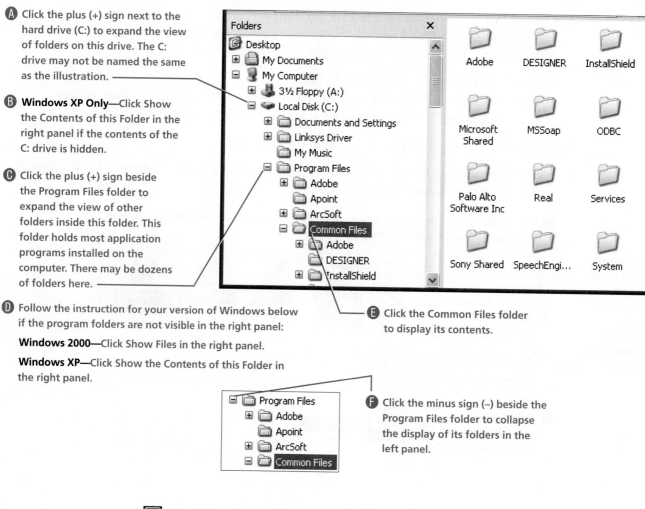

D Follow the instruction for your version of Windows below if the program folders are not visible in the right panel:

Windows 2000—Click Show Files in the right panel.

Windows XP—Click Show the Contents of this Folder in the right panel.

E Click the Common Files folder to display its contents.

F Click the minus sign (–) beside the Program Files folder to collapse the display of its folders in the left panel.

12. Close ☒ the Exploring window.

Concepts Review

True/False Questions

1. A Contents (or Home in Windows XP) search of online Help lets you locate Help topics by typing keywords.   TRUE   FALSE

2. A My Computer window lets you view the files and folders on the computer.   TRUE   FALSE

3. Windows organizes drives and folders in a hierarchy.   TRUE   FALSE

4. You can use the (CTRL) key to randomly select a group of files.   TRUE   FALSE

5. Folders can have subfolders within them.   TRUE   FALSE

6. You can use the Cut and Paste commands to move files.   TRUE   FALSE

7. Files are sent to the Recycle Bin when they are deleted from floppy disks.   TRUE   FALSE

8. The Properties command displays how much space is left on a floppy disk.   TRUE   FALSE

9. An Exploring window gives you a two-panel view of files and folder.   TRUE   FALSE

10. A quick way to open a file is to double-click on it in a My Computer windows.   TRUE   FALSE

Multiple Choice Questions

1. Which of the following methods would you use to view files and folders on the computer:
   a. Open a My Computer Window
   b. Open an Exploring Window
   c. Both A and B
   d. None of the Above

2. Which of the following views displays columns with the filename, size, type, and modified date?
   a. Large Icons
   b. Small Icons
   c. List
   d. Details
   e. Thumbnails

3. Which command is used to create a new folder?
   a. File→Folder→Create
   b. File→New→Folder
   c. Click the ⬆ or ⬆ button
   d. All of the above

4. If one filename is already selected in a My Computer or Exploring window, which key could be used to select several more files by clicking just once?
   a. (SHIFT)
   b. (ALT)
   c. (CTRL)
   d. None of the above

Skill Builders

Skill Builder 3.1 **Work with Online Help**

In this exercise, you will practice looking up various topics in Windows' online Help.

1. Click the ⊞ start button and choose Help from the Start menu. Maximize ☐ the Help Window.

2. Choose the Index search method in the Help window.

3. Start typing the search keywords **recycle bin**. You will notice that the phrase Recycle Bin appears after you type the letters recy.
   You usually only need to type the first few characters of the desired search phrase.

4. Double-click to open the topic according to the operating system you are running:
   - **Windows 2000:** emptying
   - **Windows XP:** emptying

5. Read the topic.

6. Use the Index search method to get Help on the following topics.

Windows Version	Search Keyword(s)	Help Topics to Open
Windows 2000	My Computer	opening files or folders
	Windows Explorer	copying files or folders
	copying files	overview→copy or move a file or folder
	dragging files	overview→move files by dragging
Windows XP	my computer	overview
	windows explorer	copy files and folders by dragging
	copying files	files and folders overview
	selecting	selecting multiple files and folders...

These Help topics will give you tips and alternatives to the methods you have already learned.

Use the Contents Search Method

7. Click the Contents tab (or Home if you are running Windows ME or XP).

8. Choose a topic according to the operating system you are running:
   - **Windows 2000:** Files and folders
   - **Windows XP**: Windows basics: Core Windows tasks: working with files and folders

9. Locate five different Help Sub-topics for the topic listed above for your operating system. Take the time to open the Help topics and read them.

10. Experiment with Help until you are confident that you can find topics when the need arises, using the most efficient search method.

11. Close ☒ the Help window.

Skill Builder 3.2 **Create a Folder**

In this exercise, you will create a new folder.

1. Open a My Computer window, and double-click the $3\frac{1}{2}$ Floppy (A:) drive to display your exercise files. If necessary, maximize the window.

2. Double-click the Map to Community Center file.
   The Paint program, or another program assigned to open Paint files will launch, and your map will be displayed in the program window.

   ■ **Windows XP Only**: This version of Windows may open the map in a viewer. Click the Edit File button as shown at the right to open the Paint file in the Paint program.

3. Close ☒ the Paint (or other program) window. Click No if you are asked to save the file.

4. Choose View→Details from the menu bar, then click on the Modified heading to sort the files by date.

5. Use File→New→Folder to create a folder named **Backup**. If the folder name is not selected when you create it, right-click on the folder icon, then use the Rename command to change the name.

Skill Builder 3.3 **Copy Files**

In this exercise, you will copy files to the new Backup folder, then delete them.

Windows 2000 and XP feature Move To and Copy To commands on their menu bars, toolbar buttons (2000), and task panel (XP). These commands help you navigate to the destination for a move or copy command. In this exercise, you will try this method.

⚠️**TIP!**

Use the CTRL *or* SHIFT *key to select multiple files.*

1. A My Computer window should be open, using the Details view to display the contents of the $3\frac{1}{2}$ floppy (A:) drive.

2. Click the Size column heading to sort the list of files by size, then select the two smallest files in the list.

3. **Windows 2000:** Click the Copy To 📋 button on the toolbar.

   Windows XP: Click the Copy the Selected Items task in the File and Folder Tasks section of

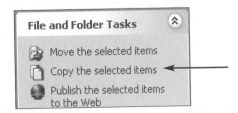

the window, as shown below.

4. Follow these steps to select the destination of the Copy command:

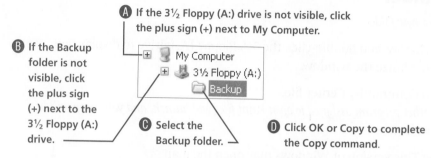

A If the 3½ Floppy (A:) drive is not visible, click the plus sign (+) next to My Computer.

B If the Backup folder is not visible, click the plus sign (+) next to the 3½ Floppy (A:) drive.

C Select the Backup folder.

D Click OK or Copy to complete the Copy command.

5. Double-click to open the Backup folder and verify that the files were copied. *The two files you selected should appear in the folder.*

6. Click the Up 🔼 or 📁 button on the My Computer toolbar.

7. Select the Backup folder, then delete the folder.

Skill Builder 3.4 Check the Hard Drive Properties

In this exercise, you will determine the amount of space left on your hard drive and floppy disk.

1. In a My Computer window, right-click on the (C:) drive icon, then choose Properties from the context menu.

2. Write down how much free space there is left on the hard drive: _____.
Many megabytes, or even gigabytes, of space will probably be available on the hard drive.

3. Click Cancel to close the Properties window.

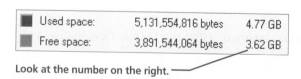

Look at the number on the right. ———

4. Make sure your exercise diskette is inserted properly.

5. Right-click the 3½ Floppy (A:) drive icon and choose Properties from the context menu.

6. Write down the storage spaced currently used in your storage location: _____.
It's easy to see how much storage space you are using and how much space remains on a device such as a floppy disk, hard drive, or USB flash drive.

7. Click Cancel to close the Properties window.

8. Close ☒ the My Computer window.

Assessments

Assessment 3.1 Search Online Help

1. Start the WordPad program.

2. Type your name at the top of the WordPad document, tap (ENTER) twice, type **Shutting Down the Computer**, then tap (ENTER).

3. Start Windows online Help and look up the following topic for your version of Windows:

   - **Windows 2000:** Search for "Shutting down the computer"

   - **Windows XP:** Search for "Turning Off the computer"

   NOTE! Do not try to look up the topic in WordPad's online help.

4. Arrange the Help and WordPad windows one above the other or side-by-side so that the Help window is visible as you type in WordPad. Remember that you cannot change the size of a maximized window.

5. In WordPad, type the first line of instructions for the Help topic, then tap the (ENTER) key twice.

6. Type **Creating a Folder**, then tap (ENTER).

7. Look up the following topic in Windows online Help: creating a folder or creating new folders.

8. In WordPad, type the first three steps of the instructions for the Help topic, then tap the (ENTER) key twice.

9. Save the WordPad document to your exercise diskette as **Online Help**.

10. Print the document and turn it in to your instructor for grading.

11. Close ⊠ the WordPad and Help windows.

Assessment 3.2 Create a Folder and Copy Files

1. Open a My Computer or Exploring window and display the $3\frac{1}{2}$ Floppy (A:) drive.

2. Create a new folder on your storage location named **Lesson 3**.

3. Copy the Tutor Meeting and the Tutor Meeting (September) files to the new folder.

4. Close ⊠ the My Computer or Exploring window.

Assessment 3.3 Navigate in an Exploring Window

1. Open an Exploring (not a My Computer) window.

2. Choose the 3½ Floppy (A:) drive in the left panel of the Exploring window.

3. Display the contents of the Lesson 3 folder in the right panel of the Exploring window.

UNIT 2

Internet Explorer

This unit introduces basic World Wide Web browsing skills. You learn the skills necessary to navigate your way through Web sites with hyperlinks and how to use an Internet search engine to find useful information on the over three billion Web pages currently online.

LESSON 4

Browsing the Web

The World Wide Web (or "the Web") is the most dynamic and exciting service on the Internet. The Web organizes information onto pages connected by objects on those pages called *hyperlinks,* which you can click to jump to other pages of information. Thousands of new pages are added to the Internet every day. In order to view pages on the Web, you use an application program called a *Web browser.* Microsoft's *Internet Explorer* is one of the most popular Web browsers. In this lesson, you will learn the basics of browsing the Web with Internet Explorer. You will also learn how to use an Internet search engine to find Web pages on almost any topic among the billions of Web pages now online.

IN THIS LESSON

Additional learning resources are available at labpub.com/learn/oe3

Case Study

Jasmine is planning to drive to the airport tomorrow morning. She lives about a two-hour drive away from the airport in good weather. Since it's early spring, she could still encounter snow or sleet during her drive. Jasmine decides to check the latest weather report. Many Web sites offer weather information. Jasmine uses one called AccuWeather.com. Using links on the Web browser and other browsing controls, Jasmine looks up an hour-by-hour weather forecast so she can plan when to depart for the airport.

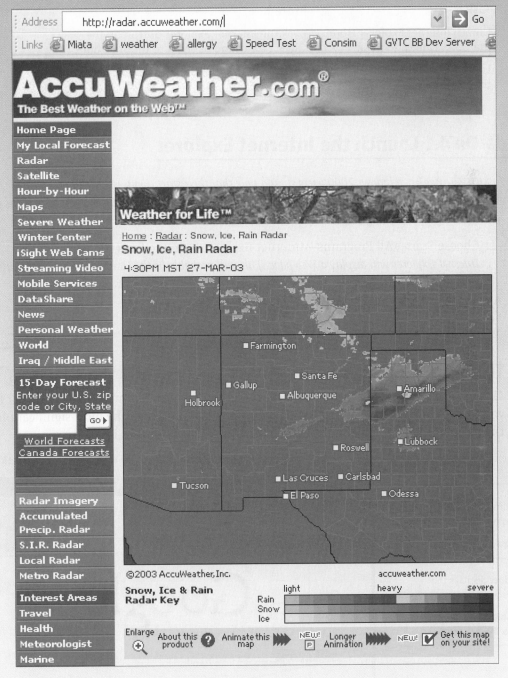

AccuWeather.com allows you to look up the latest weather by zip code or city name.

Launching Internet Explorer

Internet Explorer is an application program similar to a word processor or spreadsheet. It is designed to help you browse Web pages on the Internet. There are several ways to launch Internet Explorer. When you start the browser, it will either begin searching for a page on the Internet, or it may look for a page that is on your hard drive.

QUICK REFERENCE: LAUNCHING INTERNET EXPLORER

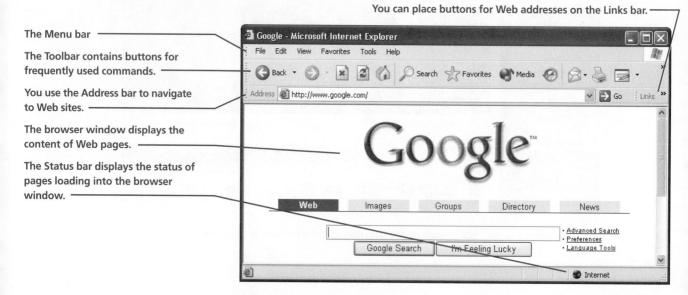

Task	Procedure
Launch Internet Explorer from the Quick Launch toolbar.	Click the Internet Explorer button on the Quick Launch toolbar next to the Start button.
Launch Internet Explorer from the Start menu.	Click Start→Programs→Internet Explorer

Hands-On 4.1 Launch the Internet Explorer

Before You Begin: Windows 2000 users should note that their start menu uses Programs (rather than All Programs) to launch most programs. Please interpret Start→All Programs in the instructions for this lesson to mean Start→Programs.

1. Choose Start→All Programs→Internet Explorer from the Start menu.
    Internet Explorer will display a Web page. This will probably be the Home page of the institution where you are taking this class.

2. If necessary, Maximize ☐ the Internet Explorer window.

The Internet Explorer Window

Like many other application programs, the Internet Explorer has menus and a toolbar that allow you to give commands. The illustration below points out some of the most significant features of the Internet Explorer window. You will use many of these features in this lesson.

You can place buttons for Web addresses on the Links bar.

The Menu bar

The Toolbar contains buttons for frequently used commands.

You use the Address bar to navigate to Web sites.

The browser window displays the content of Web pages.

The Status bar displays the status of pages loading into the browser window.

The Home Page

When you launch Internet Explorer, the first page you see displayed is called the home page. This page is important, since it is the easiest page to navigate to. Internet Explorer allows you to set any page on the Web as your home page. The home page you are viewing now may be the MSN (Microsoft Network) Web site, or it may be set to a page for the school at which you are studying.

Customizable Home Pages

The Lesson 4 Web page contains links to several popular Web portal sites.

There are many Web sites that are designed to serve as your initial point of entry to the Web when you launch Internet Explorer. These sites are often called portals. You can even customize the portal's home page to display topics that interest you. For example, you can customize the home page to display breaking news, weather, sports scores, and other information.

Home Page
Make this your home page
Personalize this page

This option on the MSN.com page is typical of many home page sites.

About HTML

Web pages are designed with a programming language called HTML (HyperText Markup Language). Most Web page files end with a filename extension of .htm or .html. These extensions help the computer know what type of data the file contains and thus which program it should use to open the file. The diagram below displays a small example of the HTML code typically behind the Web pages you view.

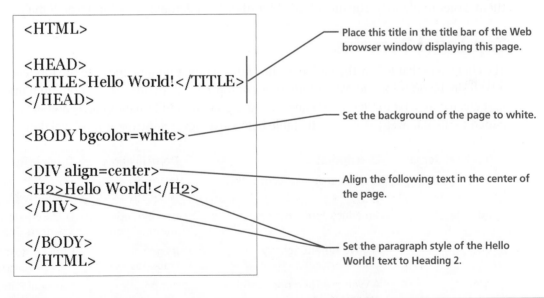

```
<HTML>

<HEAD>
<TITLE>Hello World!</TITLE>
</HEAD>

<BODY bgcolor=white>

<DIV align=center>
<H2>Hello World!</H2>
</DIV>

</BODY>
</HTML>
```

Place this title in the title bar of the Web browser window displaying this page.

Set the background of the page to white.

Align the following text in the center of the page.

Set the paragraph style of the Hello World! text to Heading 2.

Here is an example of HTML code and what it displays on a Web page.

Hello World!

Navigating the Web

In order to navigate through the Web, you need to tell your browser which sites you wish to view. Every page on the Web has a unique identifying address, called a URL (Uniform Resource Locator). When you enter a URL in the Internet Explorer's address bar, the browser loads the Web page contained at that address.

URLs

A URL (pronounced "you are el") is essentially a mailing address for a Web page. Similar to residential addresses, URLs contain several parts that help your browser find the exact page you are looking for. Every URL contains a domain name. A URL may also contain file and folder names that point to a specific Web page. If page names and folder names are part of a URL, each is separated by a normal slash (/)—not the DOS backslash (\).

The components of a URL are shown below:

When you type a domain name, you can leave out the http:// protocol portion of the URL.

Domains

A domain is a particular computer network that is connected to the Internet. A domain can consist of a single computer or hundreds of computers networked together. Every computer connected to the Internet is part of a domain. Most domains have a domain name to make them easier to identify. The most basic identifier for a domain is its top-level domain.

Top-Level Domains

The characters that follow the period at the end of a domain name indicate the top-level domain a Web site belongs to. There are many types of top-level domains. When domain names were first created, several top-level domains were designated. Additional top-level domains have been added to the list over the years. The table below lists several different top-level domains.

Top-level domain	Description	Domain name	Organization
.com	A commercial, for-profit Web site	microsoft.com sears.com	Microsoft, Inc. Sears, Roebuck & Co.
.edu	An educational institution	berkeley.edu stanford.edu	U.C. Berkeley Stanford University
.gov	A government agency	irs.gov state.gov	Internal Revenue Service US Secretary of State
.org	A Web site for a nonprofit organization	npr.org amnesty.org	National Public Radio Amnesty International
.mil	A military organization	navy.mil	The US Navy
.net	An organization dedicated to providing network resources	earthlink.net technet.net	The Earthlink ISP New Mexico Technet
.jp	An organization based in Japan	japantimes.co.jp yahoo.co.jp	Japan Times Publications Yahoo! Japan
.ca	An organization based in Canada	canada.gc.ca aircanada.ca	Government of Canada Air Canada (airline)

Example

Jasmine's teacher has handed out two Web addresses to Web pages in the assignment. Jasmine must navigate to those pages in order to view the information. Jasmine can learn a bit about where the pages are and what they are about just by interpreting the domain names of the URLs. For example, if its URL contains .edu in the domain name, Jasmine knows that the Web page is located at an educational institution.

Navigating with the Address Bar

The most basic control for navigating the Web with Internet Explorer is the Address bar. This bar allows you to type the URL of the Web page you wish to visit. It also lists the most recent Web sites that have been visited. This can be a handy shortcut when you wish to return to a Web site a day or two later. The Address bar is just one of several shortcuts that help you navigate quickly to favorite sites or sites you have viewed recently.

You can navigate to any site on the Web by typing its URL in the Address bar.

Navigating to Pages

!TIP!

Some Web sites require that you type www. in front of the domain name, others do not.

Like a computer's hard drive, the content of sophisticated Web sites is organized into folders. If you know the folder a page is located in and the name of the page, you can navigate directly to that particular page with the Address bar.

Examples: www.nmipa.org/main/meetings.shtml
            labpub.com/learn/oe3

AutoComplete

As you type a URL in the Address bar, you may see it display some Web addresses in a drop-down list. This is the AutoComplete feature at work. AutoComplete keeps track of all the Web sites you have visited recently. If you start to type the address of one of these sites, AutoComplete displays other URLs similar to what you are entering. If you want to accept a URL in the AutoComplete box, simply click on it with the mouse.

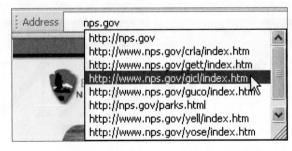

You simply point and click to navigate to a URL displayed in the AutoComplete list.

QUICK REFERENCE: NAVIGATING WITH THE ADDRESS BAR

Task	Procedure
Navigate by typing a URL.	■ Click in the Address bar to highlight the current URL.
	■ Type the new URL, and tap the (ENTER) key.
Navigate with AutoComplete.	■ Click in the Address bar to highlight the current URL.
	■ Start to type the new URL until you see the AutoComplete list appear with the domain you are navigating to.
	■ Tap the Down arrow ⊕ key to select the URL you want; then tap the (ENTER) key, or click on the desired URL with the mouse.

 Hands-On 4.2 Navigate to Sites Via the Address Bar

In this exercise, you will practice navigating from one Web site to another by entering URLs into the Address Bar.

1. Follow these steps to navigate to a Web site:

Ⓐ Click in the Address bar to highlight the Web address (URL). This is the home (default) address that the Internet Explorer is set to display whenever you launch it. The address you see on your display will probably be different from the one shown here. ────

Ⓑ Type the following URL exactly as it appears here: **labpub.com**, and tap the (ENTER) key. You do not need to type http://; this will be filled in for you automatically. If you see a list of AutoComplete suggestions drop down, ignore it for now. ────

Ⓒ Click in the Address bar again to highlight the URL. ────

Ⓓ Type the URL **nps.gov**, and tap the (ENTER) key. The National Park Service Web site appears. Most Web sites tend to change frequently, so the ParkNet site may not exactly match the one you see illustrated here. ─

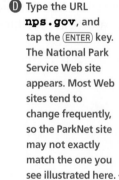

Try AutoComplete

2. Follow these steps to navigate to a recently visited Web site with AutoComplete:

A Click in the Address bar to highlight the current URL, and start to type **labp**. AutoComplete will usually display a list of Web addresses that match the first few letters you type. ————

B Click on **http://labpub.com/home.asp** ————

3. Click in the Address bar, and tap the (END) key on the keyboard.
   This removes the selection from the URL. Now you can type at the end of the current URL without the URL being deleted. In the next step, you will navigate to a specific page on the Web site.

4. Tap the (BACKSPACE) key on the keyboard to delete the words: Home.asp, then type **modems.htm** at the end of the URL as shown at right and tap (ENTER).
   This navigates you to a Web page about modems.

5. Click in the Address bar to highlight the current URL; begin to type **nps**, and then pause. Watch for AutoComplete to display a list of URLs, then tap the Down arrow (↓) key on the keyboard to select http://nps.gov. Now navigate to that URL by tapping (ENTER).
   You should now be back at the National Park Service Web site. This technique lets you keep your hands on the keyboard as you select the AutoComplete URL suggestion.

6. Click in the Address bar to highlight the current URL, and type **labpub.com**. Tap the Forward Slash (/) key; then tap the **M** key.
   AutoComplete displays the pages that start with the letter M. This makes the AutoComplete list much shorter.

7. Tap the Down arrow (↓) key to choose the labpub.com/modems.htm page. Then tap (ENTER).
   You are back at the About Modems page. Leave the Internet Explorer window open. You will continue using it in a moment.

Adjusting the Display of Web Pages

You can adjust the size of text displayed in Web pages at any time. For example, you can make the text display larger if it is difficult to read at the normal (medium) setting. It is also possible to make the Internet Explorer window fill the entire monitor, which allows more room to display the content of the Web pages you are browsing.

QUICK REFERENCE: ADJUSTING THE VIEW OF WEB PAGES

Task	Procedure
Adjust the size of text.	■ Choose View→Text Size from the menu bar.
	■ Select the desired size of text from the options menu.
Set Internet Explorer in Full Screen mode.	■ Choose View→Full Screen from the menu bar, or tap the (F11) function key on the keyboard.
	■ Click the Restore ⟳ button in the top-right corner of the screen to exit full screen mode, or tap the (F11) function key again.

Hands-On 4.3 Adjust the Display of Text

1. Follow these steps to adjust the display of text in the Internet Explorer window:

Ⓐ Choose View→Text Size→Largest from the menu bar.

Ⓑ If you do not see the illustration, tap the (PGDN) key. Notice that the text in the diagram did not change size. This is because this "text" is a picture of the letters rather than text that can change size.

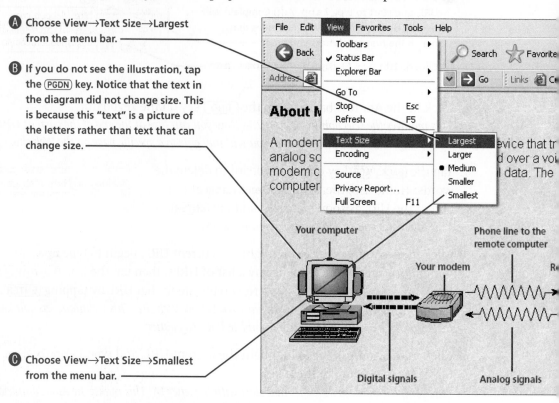

Ⓒ Choose View→Text Size→Smallest from the menu bar.

2. Choose View→Text Size→Medium from the menu bar.
   This is the default size for text in Internet Explorer and should work well under most conditions. However, as you browse the Web in this and other lessons, you can change the text size if it makes it easier for you to read the text on Web pages.

3. Choose View→Full Screen from the menu bar.
   The Internet Explorer window will immediately cover the entire screen. Notice that the Internet Explorer window covers even the Windows Taskbar, which is usually at the bottom of the screen. The navigation buttons at the top-left corner are also smaller. These adjustments provide the maximum amount of space for browsing the content of the Web pages.

4. Click the restore button in the top-right corner of the screen to restore the Internet Explorer window to the size it had before you gave the Full Screen command.

5. Tap the (F11) function key at the top of the keyboard.
   This function key is a handy shortcut to switch to full-screen mode.

6. Tap the (F11) function key again to restore the Internet Explorer window.
   This type of command is called a toggle *because tapping the same key toggles you between the full screen and restore commands. Leave the Internet Explorer window open.*

Navigating with Hyperlinks

After URLs, a hyperlink is the most basic navigation tool you can use to navigate on the Web. A hyperlink is essentially an object on a Web page that points to some other location on the same page, a different page, or even a different Web site altogether. Web pages with hyperlinks are an example of hypertext. Ted Nelson coined this term in 1963, while a sociology student at Harvard. He envisioned a book with hypertext connections to all human knowledge. Hyperlinks usually navigate you to a Web page or a specific location on a Web page. Some hyperlinks may perform other functions, such as generating an email message that is addressed automatically to a particular recipient.

Once Jasmine has navigated to one of the Web sites assigned to her, she also needs to navigate inside the Web site. If Jasmine had to type out the URL for each page she wanted to view, she'd be in for a lot of typing! Fortunately, hyperlinks make it easy to navigate Web pages by simply pointing and clicking.

If you think an element on a Web page may be a hyperlink, point at it. If the mouse pointer changes to a hand, you know you have found a hyperlink.

Examples of Hyperlinks

A hyperlink can take on several forms. It may be some text on a Web page. A hyperlink can also be an image or part of an image. There is one feature that will be consistent for all forms of hyperlinks. Whenever you place the mouse pointer over a hyperlink, the mouse pointer will change its shape to a hand. Some examples of hyperlinks are displayed below. You will work with several types of hyperlinks in the following Hands-On exercise.

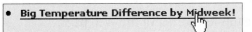

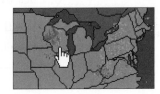

Anything on a Web page that causes the pointer to change to a hand functions as a link. If you think a piece of text, a button, or some other item on a Web page is a link, just point to it to find out.

Hands-On 4.4 Navigate with Links

In this exercise, you will use links to navigate various views in a simulation of a weather report Web page.
Before You Begin: The Lesson 4 Web page should be displayed on your screen.

1. Click on the address bar, type the URL **labpub.com/learn/oe3/lesson4.html**, then tap the (ENTER) key.
   Internet Explorer displays the Lesson 4 Web page.

2. Point (don't click) over the <u>Hands-On Exercise 4.4</u> link on the Lesson 4 Web page.
   Notice that the pointer arrow turns into a hand. This indicates that the text to which you are pointing is a link. Notice also that the link text is highlighted when you point over it. Many (but not all) links display a visual effect like this.

3. Click the <u>Hands-On Exercise 4.4</u> link.
   This command jumps you to the first page of the exercise. This weather Web site is a simulation, so it will not display the correct date or weather. Later, you can check out the live Web site. Most links jump you directly to another Web page or to a specific section of the current Web page.

4. Enter the zip code **87505** in the 15-Day Forecast box on the left side of the Web page then tap the (ENTER) key.
   A local weather forecast page appears.

underscored text links

Notice the various underscored text items on this page. These are links. The buttons along the left side of the Web page also serve as links.

5. Click <u>Today</u> in the 15-Day Weather Forecast column as shown at right.
   This link jumps you to a more detailed forecast.

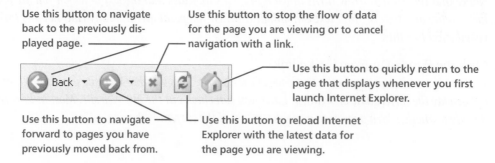

6. Click the <u>Go Hourly For Even More Detail</u> link at the bottom of the Day column, then scroll down the page until the entire forecast is visible.

7. Point (don't click) over the [NEXT 8 HOURS ▶] button on the right side of the forecast.
   Notice how the pointer turns into a hand. This button functions as a link.

8. Click the [NEXT 8 HOURS ▶] button on the right side of the forecast.

9. Click the AccuWeather.com logo on the top-left corner of the Web page.
   Most corporate logos in this location navigate you back to the Web site's Home page.

Navigating with Browsing Controls

FROM THE KEYBOARD

(ALT)+(←) to navigate back one page

(ALT)+(→) to navigate forward one page

(HOME) to navigate to the top of the page

(END) to navigate to the bottom of the page

Web pages may or may not have extensive navigation controls built into them. Fortunately, your Web browser has basic navigation controls that are always available. These basic navigation controls allow you to navigate reliably in any type of Web site. They also have some features that ordinary links lack.

Basic Navigation Buttons

The most basic navigation controls on Internet Explorer are the Forward and Back buttons. There are a few other buttons that you can use to browse Web sites. The diagram below lists and describes the navigation buttons.

Use this button to navigate back to the previously displayed page.

Use this button to stop the flow of data for the page you are viewing or to cancel navigation with a link.

Use this button to quickly return to the page that displays whenever you first launch Internet Explorer.

⊙ Back ▾ ⊙ ▾ ✕ ⟳ ⌂

Use this button to navigate forward to pages you have previously moved back from.

Use this button to reload Internet Explorer with the latest data for the page you are viewing.

Making Multi-Page Jumps

The Back and Forward navigation buttons feature a drop-down list button with which you can jump several pages at once. This can be much faster than clicking the button repeatedly. For example, you can jump from deep within a Web site back to its Home page with a single jump.

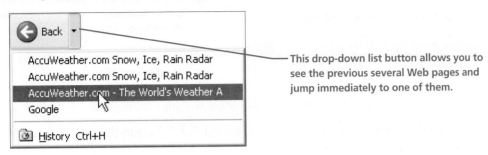

This drop-down list button allows you to see the previous several Web pages and jump immediately to one of them.

 ## Hands-On 4.5 Use Navigation Buttons

 In this exercise, you will use the browser's navigation buttons to view various pages on the Web site.
Before You Begin: The Accuweather.com Home page should be displayed.

Navigate with the Back and Forward Buttons

1. Point (don't click) anywhere over the eastern half of the United States.
   The pointer turns into a hand, indicating that this map is also a link.

2. Click on the New Mexico area of the map as shown by the yellow highlight.
   You zoom in to a closer view of the area over which you clicked.

3. Click again on New Mexico on the map as shown by the yellow highlight.

4. Click Santa Fe on the map.
   This link zooms you to the closest level. Notice that your pointer tool no longer displays a hand but instead is now an arrow. This means that the map no longer functions as a link. You have zoomed in as far as you can.

5. Click the main portion of the browser's Back ⊙ Back button on the toolbar.
   This navigates you back to the previously viewed page.

6. Click the Back ⊙ Back button two more times to return to the Web site's Home page.

7. Click the main portion of the browser's Forward ⊙ button.
   This navigates you forward to the page you just moved back from.

8. Click the Forward ⊙ button two more times until you return to the detail-level map.
   Notice that the Forward button is now dimmed. You can only move forward to pages from which you previously moved back.

9. Follow these steps to navigate with the Back button's drop-down list

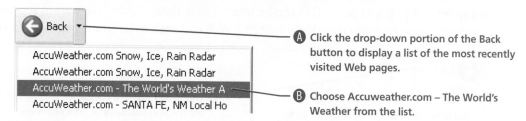

A Click the drop-down portion of the Back button to display a list of the most recently visited Web pages.

B Choose Accuweather.com – The World's Weather from the list.

Internet Explorer immediately jumps you back to the Web site's Home page.

10. Click the drop-down list portion of the Forward button then choose AccuWeather.com Local Radar at the bottom of the list.
Internet Explorer immediately jumps you back to this local weather map.

Navigate with the Home Button

11. Click the Home button.
Internet Explorer jumps back to the browser's Home page.

12. Click the Refresh button.
Internet Explorer reloads the currently displayed page. The refresh button is useful when a Web page does not appear to load properly on the first try. The refresh button also updates data on time-sensitive Web pages. For example, on the "live" AccuWeather.com Web site the refresh button would reload the latest weather report information.

Printing Web Pages

You may often wish to print information from Web pages. For example, if you order a product or travel tickets online and wish to keep a permanent record of the transaction, it is a good idea to print the page when you make a purchase. In general, printing a Web page is like printing a document with a word processor.

Print Preview

The Print Preview command works similarly to the Print Preview command featured in WordPad and many other Windows programs. Print Preview displays how your page will print with the current print option settings. You can also change some of the print options from the Print Preview window.

Print Options

The Internet Explorer offers several useful print options. Depending on what is on the page you are printing, one or more of these options will be useful.

Option	Description
Print Frames.	If the Web page you are printing uses frames, you have the option to print either the entire page or just the currently selected frame on the page. This option is always grayed out if the page you are about to print does not use frames.
Print linked documents.	This option will print pages for all the hyperlinks on the page you are about to print. *Tip: Use this option with care! If the page has numerous hyperlinks, you may end up with more pages than you want.*
Print a table of links.	This option prints an additional page after the contents of the page itself. A table of hyperlinks is useful if you want to do additional research on the hyperlinks.

QUICK REFERENCE: PRINTING A WEB PAGE

Task	Procedure
Preview a printed Web page.	■ Choose File→Print Preview from the menu bar.
Print a Web page with the current print options.	■ Click the Print button on the Internet Explorer toolbar, or choose File→Print from the menu bar.
Print the current Web page and change the print options.	■ Choose File→Print from the menu bar. ■ Select the options you desire for the print job.

Hands-On 4.6 **Print a Web Page**

In this exercise, you will preview then print the Home page.

1. Choose File→Print Preview from the menu bar.
   Internet Explorer displays a preview of how the page will appear in print. Depending on the length of the page you are viewing, the printed version may stretch across two or even three printed pages.

2. Click the Print button at the top-left corner of the Window.
   The Print dialog box appears. This allows you to customize the print settings if you wish.

3. Choose Current Page in the Page Range section of the dialog box, as shown below.

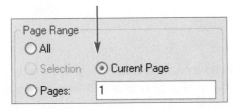

4. Click the Print button. Retrieve the page from the printer.

Searching the Web

An Internet search engine is a Web site designed to help you locate and navigate to Web pages that contain the information for which you are looking. Search engines typically display a list of links (called hits), which you use to navigate to sites that meet your search criteria. As you will see, there are many types of search engines from which to choose, and the search engine you select can make a difference in the success or failure of your searches. This topic will introduce basic techniques for locating Web pages.

!NOTE! *The exercises in this lesson use the Google.com search engine because it is an excellent general search engine that is also easy to use. The techniques you use to work with Google.com will also work well with other search engines. It will be easier to master your first lesson with search engines by focusing on just one.*

Search Methods

Most search engines offer three different types of search methods to use their Web site database. Most of the time, the standard search method will work best. The advanced search and search directory methods are beyond the scope of this lesson.

Method	Description
Standard search	With this method, you simply enter one or more words or a phrase to conduct a search.
Advanced search	An advanced search allows you to limit the search in specific ways. For example, you could specify that pages that do not have a particular word on them should be included in the list of "hits."
Search Directory	Many search engines also offer a hierarchical directory of the indexed Web pages. Examples of search directory categories include travel, news, education, people, and real estate.

Performing a Standard Search

A standard search asks the search engine to find Web pages with a specific word or several words. Standard searches are quick and easy to execute, and will often yield the information you are seeking. The results of a search are typically reported as a results list of Web pages, with a short summary of each page. Each Web page in the search results list is called a "hit." Sometimes, a search may yield no hits at all. Other times, you may get millions of hits—more than you would have time to browse through.

Selecting Search Words

!TIP!

Start most of your searches with two to three words.

A standard search can consist of a singe search word, or several. The more words you include in a search, the more likely it is that the search results will be relevant to your needs. However, you don't want to start out with so many search words that you miss Web sites that did not include some of the search words, but would still be of interest. When you perform a standard search with more than one word, most search engines will show you the pages that contain all the words first, then pages that contain only a few of the words. The illustration on the next page displays the features of a typical search results page.

The statistics of your search.

The search terms you used.

The web directory categories relevant to your search terms.

The first Web site that Google considered most relevant to your search.

The next most relevant Web page located by your search.

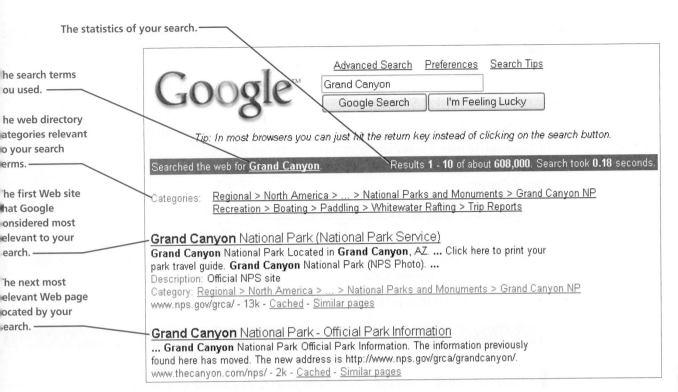

Every Internet search engine has its own rules and conventions (called syntax) for searching. However, the two rules show in the following Quick Reference table will work with most Internet search engines.

QUICK REFERENCE: TYPING SEARCH WORDS

Rule	Examples
Use capital letters only when typing proper nouns. If you type more than one name in a search, separate each name with a comma.	Robin Williams, Grand Canyon
If you wish to search for an exact phrase, enclose the phrase in quotation marks.	"global warming trends"

Hands-On 4.7 Perform a Standard Search

In this exercise, you will perform a simulated standard search. You will run the simulation from the Labyrinth Publications Web site.

Launch Internet Explorer and Navigate to the Simulation

1. Click in the Address bar and begin typing `labpub.com/learn/oe3/lesson4.html`.

2. Choose the Lesson 4 Web page from the AutoComplete list as shown at right.

3. Click the Standard Search link.

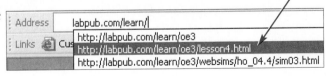

4. Read the instructions on the Standard Search page; then click Continue at the bottom of the page.
   You will see a simulation of the Google.com home page.

Perform a Standard Search

5. Enter the search words **Grand Canyon** in the search box; then tap the (ENTER) key.
   AutoComplete may display the search words as you type.

   After a pause, the first page of search results will appear. It contains the first ten search results, as well as other search options you can select.

6. Look over the search results in the blue bar near the top of the page.

> Searched the web for **Grand Canyon**.   Results **1 - 10** of about **608,000**. Search took **0.18** seconds.

   Notice that your search located over 600,000 Web pages related to your search words. Of course this is more than you would have time to review. However, Google.com tries to list the search results in the order it thinks is most relevant to your search. Let's see how close it came.

7. Scroll the page up and down to briefly glance over the first 10 hits from your search.
   Notice that this first page of search results is quite relevant to finding general information about the Grand Canyon. Now let's examine the search results in detail.

Interpreting Search Results

Most search engines offer several types of information about each hit scored by a search. This helps you select the hits most likely to have the content you are seeking. This is one area where search engines can differ quite a bit. The illustration below displays the search result list of the Google.com search engine.

> **!NOTE!** *This is just one example of a particular search engine. Other search engines have their own ways of displaying search results.*

this page is listed in Google's search directory, the categories it is listed under are shown here. A search directory is a table of contents-style search that is indexed by humans rather than a computer.

The title of the Web page. This first search result is the one Google thought would most likely contain the information you are looking for.

The URL of the page. This may give you clues about its origin and content. For example, notice that the top-level domain for this page is .gov. This means it is on a government agency Web site—in this case, the National Park Service.

When more than one page at a site is considered relevant, an additional page is indented after the primary page. The More Results link allows you to see the rest of the relevant pages on this Web site.

This link displays the version of the page that Google saved (cached) when it indexed the page. If you can't display the page directly, this saved version will let you see what the page contained.

The overall statistics of your search.

Searched the web for **Grand Canyon**.   Results **1 - 10** of about **662,000**. Search took **0.60** seconds.

Categories: Regional > North America > ... > National Parks and Monuments > Grand Canyon NP
Recreation > Boating > Paddling > Whitewater Rafting > Trip Reports

Grand Canyon National Park (National Park Service)
Grand Canyon National Park Located in **Grand Canyon**, AZ. ... Click here to print your park travel guide. **Grand Canyon** National Park (NPS Photo) ...
Description: Official NPS site
Category: Regional > North America > ... > National Parks and Monuments > Grand Canyon NP
www.nps.gov/grca/ - 13k - Cached - Similar pages

Grand Canyon National Park - Official Park Information
... **Grand Canyon** National Park Official Park Information. The information previously found here has moved. The new address is http://www.nps.gov/grca/grandcanyon/.
www.thecanyon.com/nps/ - 2k - Cached - Similar pages

Grand Canyon, **Grand Canyon** National Park, **Grand Canyon** ...
... **Grand Canyon** Coaches Located at the **Grand Canyon** National Park Airport, **Grand Canyon** Coaches is your local expert in tours, taxi, shuttles, Colorado River ...
Description: Visitor resources--tourism and a whole lot more. This site has a wealth of **Canyon** information, including...
Category: Regional > North America > ... > National Parks and Monuments > Grand Canyon NP
www.thecanyon.com/ - 15k - Cached - Similar pages
[More results from www.thecanyon.com]

This link immediately conducts a new search for pages similar to this one.

Relevance Ratings

When you search with one or more words, search engines look for pages that contain all of the words, and pages that contain any of the words. Pages containing more of your search words are scored higher for relevance than pages containing just one or a few of the words. Google.com orders the search results by relevance rating. Some search engines also list a percentage rating (e.g. 95%) of how likely the page is to contain information relevant to your search.

Opening Additional Browser Windows

Sometimes as you browse, you may wish to leave a Web page open on the desktop and browse additional pages. For example, you might want to compare two sites side by side, or browse a hyperlink from one page without losing your place on that page. This is easily done at any time. You can use two methods to open multiple browser windows.

QUICK REFERENCE: OPENING ADDITIONAL WINDOWS

Task	Procedure
Open an additional browsing window.	■ Choose File→New Window from the Internet Explorer menu bar, or press the (CTRL) key; then tap the (N) key.
Open an additional browsing window from a hyperlink.	■ Right-click on a hyperlink; then choose Open Link In New Window from the pop-up menu.

FROM THE KEYBOARD
(CTRL)+(N) to open a new browser window

Hands-On 4.8 Browse Search Results

Examine the First Search Result

1. Scroll the page so that the first three or four search results are visible.

2. Follow these steps to examine the first search result:

A Point (don't click) at the title link for the first search result.

B Notice the URL for this link on the status bar.

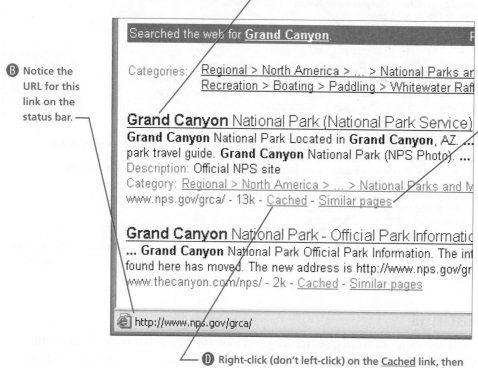

C Point (don't click) on the Similar Pages link, then look at the URL listed for this link in the status bar. In this case, the link initiates a new search. At the end of this URL are the words related=www.nps.gov/grca/, which is how Google relates the new search to this web page.

D Right-click (don't left-click) on the Cached link, then choose Open In New Window from the pop-up menu. A new page will appear with a copy of this Web page that Google stored when it last indexed (crawled) this Web page.

3. Look over the cached page. Notice that the search words are highlighted in color.

4. Close ☒ the page when you are done reviewing it, or click the Back ⬅ Back button if it is active (not dimmed).
   It may be useful to review the cached (saved) version of a Web page if the original page is no longer accessible on the Web.

5. Right-click on the Grand Canyon National Park (National Park Service) link for the first search result, then choose Open in New Window from the pop-up menu.

The page appears in a new Internet Explorer window. This technique is quite useful to quickly open search results, without needing to backtrack to the search result page. Unlike the cached version you viewed earlier, the search words are not highlighted.

6. When you are done reviewing the Web page, examine the Back button on your browser toolbar, then follow the appropriate instruction below.

   ▪ Close ⊠ the page if the Back button is dimmed like this example:

   ▪ Click the Back button if the button is not dimmed as in this example: Back

Examine Another Search Result

The first search result had a top-level domain of .gov. This means that it is maintained by a US government agency. The top-level domain name of a link can offer significant clues to the Web site's origins and content.

7. Follow these steps to navigate to the 3½ Floppy (A:) drive using the Address Bar:

Ⓐ Notice that the top-level domain for this Web site is .com. This means that it is most likely a commercial Web site, not run by a government agency.

Ⓑ Right-click on the title link, then choose Open in New Window from the context menu.

8. Review the contents of this commercial Web page.
   Notice that this page is geared to selling. For example, there is a banner ad at the very top of the page. Please also note that this page is a simulation—not the actual Web page—so most of its information will be out of date.

9. Close ⊠ the page when you are done reviewing it, or click the Back Back button on the toolbar if you did not open this page in a new window.

10. Tap the (END) key on the keyboard, then click the Next link as shown below.

The next page of search results will appear.

11. Briefly review search results 11 to 20, but do not click any of the links to these pages.
    With over 660,000 search results, you could potentially search over 66,000 of these search pages. Life is too short for such an inefficient search! Fortunately, you can narrow your search to reduce the sheer number of search results.

    Leave the browser window open.

Narrowing a Search

When a search yields tens of thousands of hits, it will be very time-consuming to browse through even a fraction of the pages to find the information you are searching for. Fortunately, it is possible to conduct another search only on the hits that were listed for a previous search. This means that you can conduct a broad search, then add more terms to the search to reduce the number of hits. This is called "narrowing" your search, since a narrower cross-section of Web sites will match your multiple search criteria.

Most search engines allow you to add words to a search and search only within the results from the previous search.

Example

Jasmine likes getting lots of hits on her searches, but soon discovers that there are some disadvantages to a large number of hits. She finds herself looking through screen after screen of hit lists. Since she and her friends decided to take a rafting trip through the Grand Canyon, Jasmine decides to narrow her search to pages that contain references to rafting trips.

Methods

There are two methods you can use to narrow a search. The method that works best depends on the popularity of the topic you are searching and your search engine.

Method	Example	Notes
Gradual Perform a search for each word, telling the search engine to search only within the previous results.	Perform three searches: ■ Grand Canyon Search within results for: ■ Rafting ■ Whitewater	This method takes more time, but is more likely to end up with relevant sites in your hit list.
Quick Create one search that uses several words you think are relevant to what you are searching for.	Perform one search: ■ Grand Canyon rafting whitewater	This method is faster, but you may be more likely to miss a site that does not happen to contain all of the words you entered. There will probably be more irrelevant sites in your search as well.

!TIP! *If you are searching on an obscure topic with most Internet search engines, the gradual method is recommended. If you are searching with Google, however, both methods produce the same result and thus the Quick method is recommended.*

Hands-On 4.9 Narrow a Search

Now you will narrow your search to find only Web sites related to the Grand Canyon which mention white-water rafting.

1. Tap the (END) key to jump to the bottom of the page.

2. Click the <u>Search Within Results</u> link.

Advanced Search	Preferences	Search Tips	
Grand Canyon		Google Search	Search within results ←

Google displays a special Search within results page. Notice the 608,000 results for Grand Canyon near the top of the page. Let's see how much we can reduce this number.

3. Type the word **rafting** in the search box, then click the Search within Results button.
   Google displays a new search result page. Notice that the number of search results has been reduced dramatically—down to 28,000.

4. Take a moment to review the first ten search results, but don't click on any of the links.
   Notice that most of these search results are for .com domains. Some of these links describe rafting in general. You can narrow the search even more if you look for pages specifically about whitewater rafting.

Narrow the Search Again

5. Tap the (END) key to jump to the bottom of the page, then click the <u>Search Within Results</u> link.
   Another Search within results page appears.

6. Type the word **whitewater** in the search box, then click the Search within Results button.
   Google displays a new search result page. Now the number of search results is down to 10,400.

Try the I'm Feeling Lucky Button

Google has a special search button that jumps you directly to the first search result in a search.

7. Notice that the first search result on this page is Arizona River Runners.

8. Click the I'm Feeling Lucky button near the top of the search results page.
   Google immediately opens the first search result. This same page would have opened if you simply typed Grand Canyon rafting whitewater in the search box and then clicked I'm Feeling Lucky. This button is a convenient shortcut if you think Google is likely to find the page you are looking for in its first result.

9. Click the Back button, then take a moment to look over the first ten search results. If yo wish, you can click on one or two of the results to see how relevant the pages are to your search topic. Use the Back button to return to the search results page if you look at other pages.

NOTE! *The links on this page are "live." That is, they are active pages on the Internet. Some of these pages may have changed or gone offline since this chapter was written. If you come upon a dead (inactive) link, just click the Back button and try another link.*

Notice how all of your search terms are listed on these pages. Google prioritizes pages in search results that include all of your search terms. In general, pages that mention these terms most often will appear at the top of your search.

Leave the browser window open when you are done and continue reading the next topic.

Search Directories

Some Internet search engines feature a search directory. Unlike standard search engine results, most Web directories are created by humans. That is, the directory is assembled by people who actually look at the Web pages, decide how to categorize them, and may even assign a quality rating to the Web site. Web directories place all of their search results into categories. You search for information by moving down into increasingly specific categories related to your topic or question.

TIP!

Search directories are an excellent way to search for information on topics you know little about.

One Advantage of Search Directories

You can learn a great deal about a topic just by looking over how it's organized in a search directory. In addition to listings of Web pages on very specific topics, search directories also feature pages devoted to more general information about a broad topic. For example, a search directory page about Geography may include links to pages about mapmaking, census bureaus and general geography, along with links to maps of specific geographic regions and countries.

Hands-On 4.10 Use a Search Directory

In this exercise, you will use a search directory to locate Web pages related to Mark Twain.

1. Click in the Address Bar, then enter the following URL:
   labpub.com/learn/oe3/lesson4.html
   then tap the (ENTER) key. You can also click this URL if it appears in the autocomplete list. *This immediately navigates you back to the Lesson 4 Web page.*

2. Click the Directory Search link.
   This exercise starts at a simulation of the Google.com Home page.

3. Click the More link, then click the Directory link on the Google Services page.
   This command opens the Web Directory page. Since Mark Twain was an author, let's start with the Arts category.

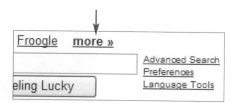

4. Click the <u>Arts</u> link on the Web Directory page.
   This page displays all of the categories under which Arts-related pages have been indexed. At the bottom of the page are some links to related categories that are not within Arts.

5. Click the <u>Literature</u> link.
   This page displays sub-categories under Literature.

6. Scroll down the page until the Web Pages section becomes visible.
   The Web Pages section contains a listing of pages devoted to literature in general. Some sub-categories will have numerous pages in this section; others may have just one or two.

   Notice the green bars beside the Web pages. A longer bar indicates that human indexers have judged this page as being more valuable. Many Web directories rate the quality of each page according to the indexer's subjective judgment.

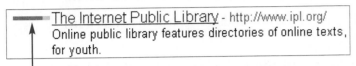

7. Tap the (HOME) key, then click the <u>Authors</u> link.
   This page is devoted to links and pages about authors in general.

8. Take a moment to scroll down the page and review the links about authors.
   Since we are still searching for links about Mark Twain, we will continue deeper into this Web directory.

9. Tap the (HOME) key, then click the <u>T</u> link under Authors Categorized by Letter.
   This page lists all authors whose last name begins with T which have been indexed. Notice the numbers in parenthesis beside each name. This indicates how many individual Web pages are indexed for that author.

10. Scroll down the list, then click the <u>Twain, Mark</u> link.
    There are quite a few pages devoted to Mark Twain in general and also to specific works that he wrote. You could learn a great deal about Mark Twain just by looking over these links. This is one of the strengths of search directories. It may take longer to find the related links, but you can learn more about the topic just by reviewing the links it's related to.

11. Take some time to look over some of the links and categories under Mark Twain.

12. When you are finished, close ⊠ the Internet Explorer window.

Concepts Review

True/False Questions

1. A URL is essentially the address of a Web page. TRUE FALSE

2. You can only use the Back [Back] button to navigate backwards a single page at a time. TRUE FALSE

3. You can always use the Forward button to navigate forward through a Web site. TRUE FALSE

4. The Refresh button reloads text and images into the page you are currently viewing. TRUE FALSE

5. Whenever you print a Web page, it always prints just as you see it on the screen. TRUE FALSE

6. You can have several Internet Explorer browser windows open at the same time, each viewing a different Web page. TRUE FALSE

7. A Web site designed to help you locate Web pages is called an Internet search engine. TRUE FALSE

8. The domain name of a Web site gives you some clues about the type of organization that is posting that site. TRUE FALSE

9. You can change the size of text displayed on Web pages. TRUE FALSE

10. It is possible to search within results you obtained in a previous search. TRUE FALSE

Multiple Choice Questions

1. A URL is very similar to _____.

   a. a highway sign.
   b. a computer terminal.
   c. a mailing address.
   d. All of the above

2. Which of these is not a part of a URL?

   a. Domain name
   b. Top-level domain
   c. Page name
   d. Hyperlink name

3. Internet Explorer's AutoComplete feature _____.

   a. lists the names of recently visited Web pages similar to the name you are typing.
   b. allows you to choose URLs from a list.
   c. appears below the address bar.
   d. All of the above

4. Adding additional search words to reduce the number of hits in a search is called

   a. expanding the search.
   b. a reduced search.
   c. narrowing the search.
   d. All of the above

Skill Builders

Skill Builder 4.1 Browse Another Computer Museum

Compared to the first computer museum you browsed in this lesson, the Obsolete Computer Museum has a much more primitive interface. There is no navbar at the top of the pages. In fact, some pages don't have any hyperlinks at all. However, since you are now familiar with the navigation buttons on the Internet Explorer toolbar, you should find it easy to navigate in this Web site.

Start Internet Explorer and Navigate to the Web Pages

1. Start Internet Explorer.

2. Click in the Address bar, then enter the URL **labpub.com/learn/oe3**, and tap the (ENTER) key.

3. Click the Lesson 4 - Browsing the Web hyperlink on the right side of the page, under the WebSims and Other Links heading.

4. Click the Obsolete Computer Museum hyperlink near the bottom of the Web page.

5. Read over the introduction to this simulation; then click the Continue hyperlink at the bottom of the page.
   The home page of the Obsolete Computer Museum will appear. On the home page is a long list of the computer systems exhibited in the museum. Most of the hyperlinks on this page are disabled. For space reasons, it was not possible to put the entire museum online here. You can view the full museum later in this exercise.

Browse the Commodore 64 Exhibit

6. Scroll the museum's computer list down to the Commodore section, and click the C64 hyperlink.
   The Commodore 64 page will appear. This was a popular home microcomputer in the early 1980s. The computer's electronics were all contained within the keyboard unit.

7. Scroll down the page until you see the C64 Screen Shot hyperlink, and click the hyperlink.
   Notice that there is no text on this page. There aren't any hyperlinks either. The only way to navigate out of this page is to use the Back button on the toolbar.

   Looks like this computer is booted up. Are you ready to compute?

8. Click the Back [Back] button to navigate back to the Commodore 64 page.

9. Tap the (END) key to jump to the bottom of the page.

Check the Destination of a Hyperlink

10. Look at the first part of the current address on the Address bar at the top of the Internet Explorer window.
    Notice the first part of the URL. The current domain you are browsing is labpub.com.

11. Follow these steps to analyze one of the hyperlinks:

Ⓐ Point (don't click) at
the C64 Home Page
hyperlink.

• C64 Home Page
• Other Commodore Sites

Ⓑ Look at the hyperlink's destination in the lower-left corner of the status bar.
Notice that the URL for this hyperlink is in a different domain. This means that
the hyperlink will take you to a different Web site.

http://www.hut.fi/~msmakela/cbm/

12. Click the C64 Home Page hyperlink.
*Depending on the present status of this site, you will navigate to the page or receive an indication that the
page is not available because the site has been taken down.*

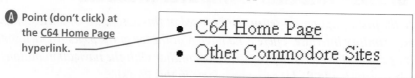

Navigate Back to Your Starting Point

13. Click the drop-down arrow on the Back button; then select
Obsolete Computer Museum.
*Now you are back at the Obsolete Computer museum page in a
single jump.*

14. Click the Back button again.
This takes you back to the page which introduced this exercise.

15. If you wish, click the Obsolete Computer Museum link to visit the current version of the
Web site.

Skill Builder 4.2 Browse with the Address Bar

In this exercise, you will navigate to Web pages with the Address bar.

1. Navigate to the home page of at least two Web sites from the following selection of sites. If you see an error message, check for a typo in the Address bar, and try again.
   Sometimes a Web site may not be available due to some technical problem on the network. You may need to try the site again in an hour or two, or the next day.

2. If you find a Web site that interests you, feel free to navigate in the site for a few minutes. Look for hyperlinks on the page in the form of navbars, images, and underscored text.

!TIP! *Remember, many pictures are also hyperlinks. When you point at a picture, watch for the pointer to change into a hand. Look at the lower-left corner of the status bar to see where the hyperlink is pointing.*

http://edspace.nasa.gov/

Site Name	URL
National Geographic Magazine	www.nationalgeographic.com
National Archives	www.nara.gov
Yosemite National Park	www.nps.gov/yose
Hertz Rent A Car	www.hertz.com
Amazon	www.amazon.com
Smithsonian Institution	www.si.edu
Library of Congress	lcweb.loc.gov*
eBay Auction site	www.ebay.com
Project Gutenberg	promo.net/pg*
National Aeronautics and Space Administration	www.nasa.gov
Southwest Airlines	www.iflyswa.com

*Note: Not all URLs begin with www. These links are examples.

!NOTE! *These are live Web links. It is possible for a link to have changed locations or to have shut down since this book was printed. Or, a link may be down temporarily due to technical problems. If you try a link and it does not work, try another link.*

Skill Builder 4.3 Narrow a Search

In this exercise, you will search for Web pages about used notebook computers. You will narrow your search to focus on pages offering used notebook computers for a specific brand for sale.

!NOTE! *Please note that you are now searching on live search engine pages. Due to the changing nature of most Web sites, the Google.com site may not work exactly as outlined in this exercise. When the live page does not match the instructions, use common sense to interpret how to accomplish each instruction on the live pages.*

1. Launch Internet Explorer, then enter the following URL into the address bar: **google.com**
   Notice that it was not necessary to enter www. in front of the URL. This is the case with many Web sites.

2. Enter the search words **computer notebook used** in the search box, then tap the (ENTER) key.
   Even with three search words, this search turned up several hundred thousand pages in the search results.

3. Look over the first ten search results, then tap the (END) key and click Next to view the next ten search results. Make a mental note of the number of pages your search turned up.

Use a Search Modifier and Narrow the Search

Some of your search results may include pages indicating that someone wants to buy a used notebook computer. Since these pages are not relevant to your search, you will use a special command to exclude pages containing the word wanted. You can do this by placing a minus sign (-) in front of the word to exclude.

!TIP! *Most search engines allow you to use modifiers such as the minus sign in a search. Check Search Tips or links pages in your favorite search engine to learn more about the modifiers it supports.*

4. Tap the (HOME) key, enter the search words **computer notebook used-wanted** in the search box, then tap the (ENTER) key.
   Notice that the number of search results is less than your previous search turned up. In this case, less is more.

   Now let's narrow your search within these results. You will search for all of the pages that include the Toshiba brand name.

5. Tap the (END) key, then click the Search Within Results link.
   Google.com displays its special search within results page.

6. Type **Toshiba** in the search box, then tap the (ENTER) key.
   Notice how the number of search results has been significantly reduced—probably down to around 10% of the previous results.

7. Click some of the links in your first two pages of search results and see how relevant they are to the objective of purchasing a used Toshiba notebook computer.

 !TIP! *You may want to right-click on the links, then choose Open In New Window from the pop-up menu. This makes it easy to return to your original search results page.*

Skill Builder 4.4 **Use a Search Directory**

In this exercise, you will use Google.com's Web Directory to search for Live Links!

 !NOTE! *Please note that you are now searching on live search engine pages. Due to the changing nature of most Web sites, the Google.com site may not work exactly as outlined in this exercise. When the live page does not match the instructions, use common sense to interpret how to accomplish each instruction on the live pages.*

1. Launch Internet Explorer, then enter the following URL into the address bar: **google.com**

2. Click the More link, then click the Directory link on the Google Services page.
   The directory page appears. This subdivides the entire direc-tory into many primary categories. Now you will start navi-gating through the directory to find Web sites devoted to weather in your State.

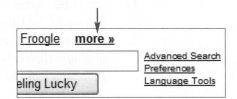

3. Click the <u>News</u> category link, then click the <u>Weather</u> category link.
   Notice the various subdivisions of this category, such as Air Quality and UV Index. You can learn more about your selected topic just by viewing information such as this.

4. Click the <u>By Region</u> category link, then click <u>North America</u>, and <u>United States</u>.

5. Click the <u>By State</u> link, then choose your State.

 !TIP! *In the next step, right-click each link, then choose Open in New Window. By opening each link in a new window, your search page will always be available for you to try another link.*

6. Open a few links and look for differences among the various services. In particular, take note of the services rated highly compared to those rated less highly (as shown by the length of their green bars at the left of each link). Do you see much difference in quality?

Try Another Directory Search

7. Close any other open Internet Explorer windows so that only your directory search page remains open.

8. Tap the (HOME) key on the keyboard, then click the <u>Go to Directory Home</u> link near the top-right side of the page.

9. Decide on a topic to search for, then start making your way through the various search directory categories toward that topic. Feel free to explore new ideas that occur to you as you browse the directories.

10. When you are done, return to the Search Directory Home page.

Search within the Directory

Notice that there is a search box at the top of the search directory page. This allows you to conduct a normal search, or to search within the directory. This can help you jump quickly through many layers of the directory. (You can also perform a normal Google search from this box.)

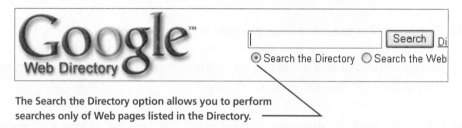

The Search the Directory option allows you to perform searches only of Web pages listed in the Directory.

11. Type **[the name of your State] weather** in the search directory box. Make sure that the Search The Directory option is chosen immediately below the search box, then tap (ENTER). *Google jumps you immediately to the Weather directory you browsed to earlier in this exercise. This type of search only displays Web pages listed in the directory. This usually results in a much shorter search results list, and you have the quality ratings for each page in the list.*

12. Return to the search directory home page, then try searching for another topic within the search directory.

Assessments

Assessment 4.1 Navigate to Web Pages and Print Them

1. Launch the Internet Explorer.

2. Navigate to the Web sites listed below. At each Web site, print the home page.

URL	Description
www.yahoo.com	A popular Internet search engine and portal
www.microsoft.com/ie	Home page for Internet Explorer online support

Assessment 4.2 Navigate with Hyperlinks

1. Navigate to the following Web page: **labpub.com/learn/oe3/test4.html**
   There are no hyperlinks to this page. You must use the Address bar.

2. Navigate with the hyperlinks on this and other pages until you reach the page titled Stop, you made it!
   Not all of the hyperlinks will be obvious. You will have to search for them on the pages. Some hyperlinks will be text hyperlinks; others will be images.

3. Print the *Stop, you made it!* page.

Assessment 4.3 Search for Web Pages

1. Start Internet Explorer and navigate to **google.com**

2. Perform a standard search on *one* of the topics in the list below. Your search should contain at least three hits that appear to be relevant.

   - A major league sports franchise in or near your city

   - Works by a selected author

   - State government information

   - Travel to your state

   - Travel to a region of your choice

3. After you complete the search, print the first search results page.

4. Write your name and the name of your topic at the top of the page.

5. Circle three hits that are relevant to your topic.

UNIT 3

Outlook 2003

This unit covers the skills you need to correspond with others using electronic mail (email). You begin with an introduction to Outlook 2003, a powerful personal information manager. You learn how to navigate to Outlook's various features such as the Calendar and Task view. Next, you learn the basics of sending and receiving email messages with Outlook. You learn how email accounts are set up, how to send messages, and how to reply to the messages you receive.

Introducing Outlook 2003

Outlook 2003 is a program that allows you to organize all of your personal information in a single place. Outlook can help you manage your calendar, contacts list, email, and tasks. Outlook also interacts with other Office 2003 programs to share this information. In this lesson, you will learn about Outlook's basic functions and how to store your personal information. You will learn how Outlook uses folders and how you can create your own folders. You will also learn how Outlook uses your Internet connection to help you send and receive email messages. By the end of the lesson, you will have a basic understanding of how to get around in the program, and of many of the features it offers to help you organize your personal information.

Additional learning resources are available at labpub.com/learn/oe3/

Case Study

Erin is just starting a new job. Her cubicle is equipped with a new personal computer and Windows. Her company has installed Office 2003 on all computers and has designated Outlook 2003 as its standard email and scheduling program. Having spent the morning at a new employee orientation, Erin now sits down at her desk and boots up her computer.

Although she is skilled in Microsoft Word and Excel, Erin is new to Outlook and email. She's used Hotmail for a couple of years for her personal email, but now she can expect to receive a dozen or more email messages each day. So, her first task is to learn about how Outlook works and how it can help her to manage her personal information. The moment she starts the program, Erin sees that the Navigation pane makes navigating among the various views of her data simple.

Erin knows that excellent online help is a feature of Office 2003 applications. As she learns the program, Erin enters questions in plain English in a question box on the program window. Outlook displays lists of Help topics related to her question. She can also right-click on many dialog box options to view a quick summary of an option or feature.

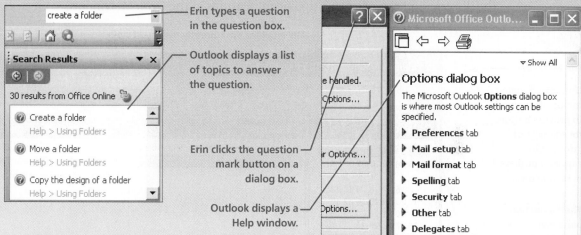

Erin types a question in the question box.

Outlook displays a list of topics to answer the question.

Erin clicks the question mark button on a dialog box.

Outlook displays a Help window.

Erin is also interested in the way Outlook stores and organizes her information. Everything she sees in the Outlook view is stored in folders. Soon, Erin learns how to create her own folders.

What is Outlook?

Outlook is a program for managing your email, calendar, names and addresses of contacts, and task lists. The Outlook program features a flexible interface that allows you to shift among these various functions. A list of Outlook's basic functions appears below.

- **Electronic Mail (email)**—Outlook lets you send and receive email messages. You can organize messages into folders and create settings that help you manage your email. For example, you can create a new folder to hold all of your email messages from a specific correspondent.

- **Calendar**—Outlook lets you create appointments and display them in daily, weekly, and monthly views. You can set reminders for especially important appointments.

- **Contacts**—Outlook can maintain the names and addresses of all your correspondents. The Contacts list also stores email addresses, web page addresses (URLs), telephone numbers, and many other types of information.

- **Tasks**—Outlook lets you create task (to-do) lists and set reminders when various tasks are due. You can also attach documents to a task.

- **Notes**—Outlook lets you create the electronic equivalent of Post It™ notes. You can even display notes directly on the Windows Desktop.

The illustration below displays significant features of the Outlook window.

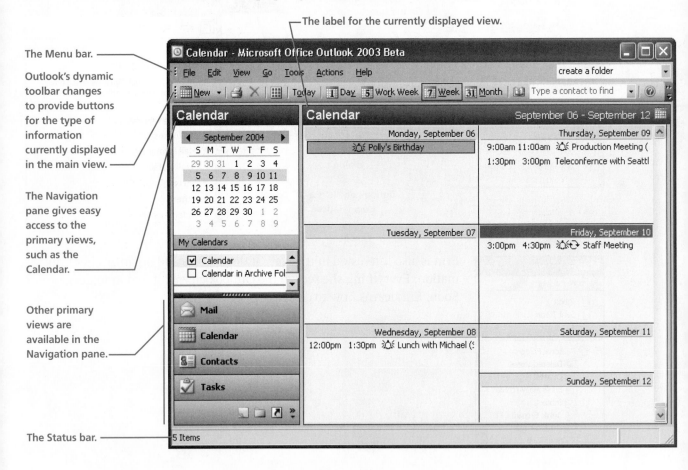

Starting Outlook

You can start Outlook from the Start button menu with Start→Programs→Microsoft Outlook. When Office 2003 is installed with the default settings, an Outlook icon is also placed on your Desktop. You can also place an Outlook shortcut in the Quick Launch toolbar with Windows 2000 and XP.

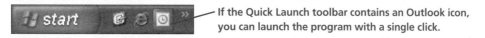

If the Quick Launch toolbar contains an Outlook icon, you can launch the program with a single click.

The Navigation Pane

Outlook's Navigation pane contains buttons and controls to help you navigate among the various program views. You can customize the Navigation pane with popular options for specific views, frequently used email folders, and other features. The appearance of the top portion of the Navigation pane changes with the currently displayed view.

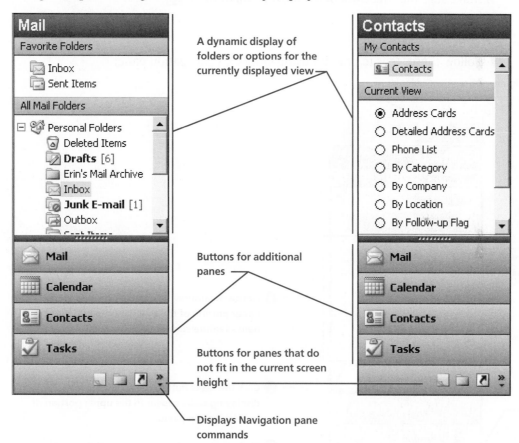

Hands-On 5.1 Start Outlook and Navigate to Various Views

In this exercise, you will start the Outlook program and browse views of some program features.

Before You Begin: Windows 2000 users should note that their start menu uses Programs (rather than All Programs) to launch most programs. Please interpret Start→All Programs in the instructions for this lesson to mean Start→Programs.

1. Choose Start→All Programs→Microsoft Office→Microsoft Office Outlook 2003 from the Start menu.
   The Outlook program window appears.

2. Choose Yes if you are asked to make Outlook your default email client.
   You may be prompted to answer this question if another email program, such as Outlook Express, is also installed on your computer.

3. Make sure that the Outlook window is Maximized ▣.

Outlook Views

4. Follow these steps to practice using Outlook's Navigation pane:

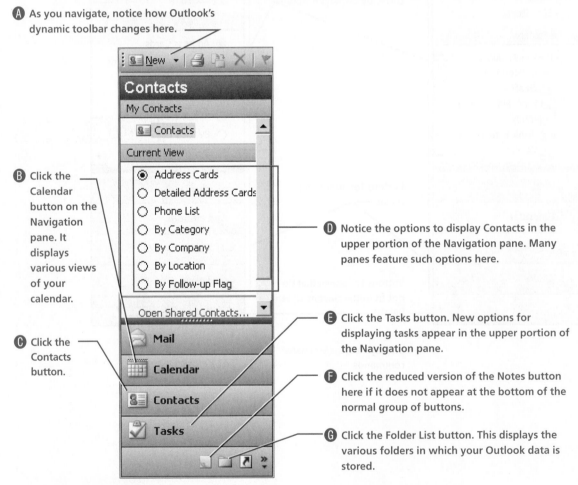

Ⓐ As you navigate, notice how Outlook's dynamic toolbar changes here.

Ⓑ Click the Calendar button on the Navigation pane. It displays various views of your calendar.

Ⓒ Click the Contacts button.

Ⓓ Notice the options to display Contacts in the upper portion of the Navigation pane. Many panes feature such options here.

Ⓔ Click the Tasks button. New options for displaying tasks appear in the upper portion of the Navigation pane.

Ⓕ Click the reduced version of the Notes button here if it does not appear at the bottom of the normal group of buttons.

Ⓖ Click the Folder List button. This displays the various folders in which your Outlook data is stored.

5. Follow these steps to continue your navigation practice:

Ⓐ Choose Personal Folders in the Folder list to display the Outlook Today pane. This pane displays a summary of information from several other panes. ─────────

Ⓑ Choose the Contacts folder to display your Contacts list. You can navigate to any Outlook data via the folder list. However, notice that the display choices you saw in the previous step are not displayed in the Folders list. ─────────

Ⓒ Click the Mail button in the Navigation pane. ─────

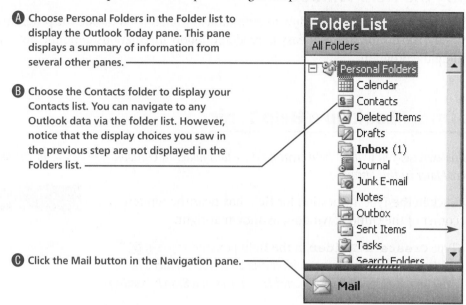

Many Outlook users prefer to use this pane as their default view. It allows them to see incoming email messages whenever they switch to Outlook from other programs.

Getting Help

All Office 2003 applications include excellent online help features. In fact, Outlook and the other Office 2003 applications no longer come with the traditional, printed manual that used to be enclosed with most application programs. Any information you may need is usually available directly from Outlook's online help.

The Help Box

A Help box near the top-right corner of the Outlook window is another handy way to get online help. The Help box uses powerful, natural language processing to interpret your question and display several items that are likely to contain the answer. Simply type your question in the box, then tap the (ENTER) key. Outlook will display a list of choices it thinks will answer your question.

After you type a question and tap (ENTER) the Help box displays topics it thinks will provide the answer.

Tiling the Help Window

You can tell the Help window to automatically align itself beside the program window. This AutoTile button makes it easy to read and follow instructions in online help while you are running the program.

Hands-On 5.2 **Look up a Help Topic**

In this exercise, you will get help creating a custom folder in Outlook. The details of Outlook folders are covered later in this lesson.

1. Click in the Type a Question for Help box near the top-left corner of the Outlook window, as shown at right.

2. Type **Create a Folder** in the Help box and tap (ENTER).
   Outlook Help searches sources online and on your computer's hard drive and displays a list of suggested Help topics in a Search Results pane.

3. Click the Create a Folder topic near the top of the Search Results pane.
   After a pause, which varies with the speed of your Internet connection, Help opens a new window to display a basic procedure to create a folder in Outlook.

4. Click the Tile Windows ⊞ button on the top-left corner of the Help window.
   The Outlook program window and Help window move side by side so that it's easy to read and follow the procedure steps.

Help Sources

All of the Office 2003 application programs feature several sources of help. Each source has specific uses. The two sources you will probably use most often are listed below.

■ **Microsoft Office Online**—This help source compiles the latest help information and makes it available over the Internet. You must have an Internet connection to access this help source.

■ **Offline Help**—This help source relies on files stored on your computer's hard drive. This information is always available, whether you are online or offline.

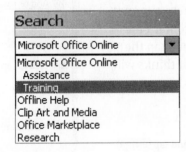

The Search box in the Help pane offers the choice of several sources of online help.

New Help Resources

Microsoft Office Online Help features some new resources to help you learn and use its application programs. These resources are only available over an Internet connection.

- **Assistance**—This resource consists of brief articles, tips, and other information about specific topics.

- **Training**—This resource consists of brief, self-paced courses that cover specific topics. They are online courseware that is self-paced, often contains animated demonstrations and audio content, and includes instructions for hands-on practice.

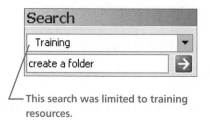

This search was limited to training resources.

The first two search results display courses about creating folders in Outlook.

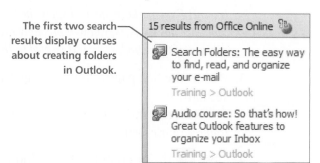

Printing Help Topics

 You can print any help topic. Simply display the topic and click the Print button on the Help window. A print dialog box allows you to select a printer and give the print command.

Hands-On 5.3 Search for Training Articles

In this exercise, you will search for training articles related to creating Outlook folders.

Before You Begin: Make sure your computer has a working Internet connection. If you do not have an Internet connection, skip this exercise and continue reading the next topic.

Search for Training

1. Follow these steps to set Help to search for training topics:

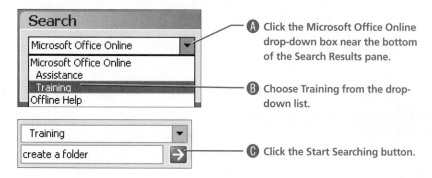

Ⓐ Click the Microsoft Office Online drop-down box near the bottom of the Search Results pane.

Ⓑ Choose Training from the drop-down list.

Ⓒ Click the Start Searching button.

A new search results list appears. This displays only training articles from the Microsoft Office Online resource.

2. Choose the So That's How! topic near the top of the search results list. If this topic does not appear in the list, choose any other topic.

Outlook Help searches sources online and on your computer's hard drive and displays a list of suggested Help topics in a Search Results pane.

!NOTE! *Because these training topics are located online and subject to change, this topic may no longer be available or its title may have changed.*

Internet Explorer launches to display the first Web page containing the brief training course. If your computer has speakers, you will probably hear a narrator talking about the course. He or she is reading the contents of the introductory text located in the right column of the Web page.

3. Review the first page of the training course, particularly the Goals and About this Course sections.

Do not start the training course at this time. This lesson will teach you some of the techniques that the training course covers.

4. Close [X] the Internet Explorer window when you are finished.

Search for a Procedure in Offline Help

5. Click the Search type box and choose Offline Help as shown at right.
   This sets Help to search only for topics on your computer's hard drive.

6. Click the Start Searching [→] button.
   The search results topics do not include training courses now since these are only available online.

7. Click the Create a Folder link near the top of the Search Results list.

8. Click the Print [🖨] button on the Help window then click the Print button to print the topic on the default printer. Retrieve the printout from the printer.

9. Close the Help topic window.

10. Close [x] the Search Results task pane.

Outlook Folders

Outlook organizes all of your information into folders. Folders in Outlook function just like folders in the My Computer or Exploring windows: they allow you to assemble groups of related types of information. For example, there is a folder in which Outlook stores all of your contacts. Other folders store incoming and outgoing email messages. You can also create your own folders. For example, Erin may want to create a folder to store all of the email messages she receives from a particular client. In this topic, you will learn how to view Outlook folders and to add new folders.

The Folders Hierarchy

Outlook folders are organized in a hierarchy similar to the one illustrated below. Personal Folders serves as the primary folder for your information—all of the other folders are located within this folder. Outlook comes with many basic folders already created. You can also add custom folders to Outlook to further organize your personal information.

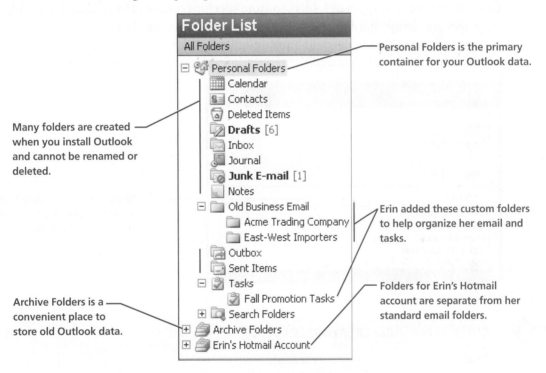

Personal Folders is the primary container for your Outlook data.

Many folders are created when you install Outlook and cannot be renamed or deleted.

Erin added these custom folders to help organize her email and tasks.

Folders for Erin's Hotmail account are separate from her standard email folders.

Archive Folders is a convenient place to store old Outlook data.

Viewing Folders

Outlook normally hides folders from view, which saves space in the program window. Most users like to navigate to various folder views with the Navigation Pane. However, if you want to see all of your folders, simply display the Folder List. You can display the Folder list anytime by clicking the Folder List button near or at the bottom of the Navigation pane.

TIP! *When you select a view with the Navigation pane, you are actually viewing the contents of an Outlook folder.*

Creating Folders

FROM THE KEYBOARD

(CTRL)+(SHIFT)+(E)
to create a new folder.

Outlook lets you create new folders at any time, and create as many as you need. Folder names can be up to 255 characters long, including symbols such as the forward slash (/) and hyphen (-). When you create a folder, you can place it beneath the Outlook Today folder or inside another folder. You create new folders with the File→Folder→New Folder command from the menu bar.

Example

As Erin uses email at work, the number of messages she sends and receives continues to grow. At first, it is not too difficult to scan through a list of twenty or thirty messages in the Inbox. However, after the list grows to over fifty messages, Erin finds that she is scrolling up and down more than sh likes. It also becomes difficult to find messages sent by a particular person and to keep track of corre spondence. Erin creates folders to organize her email.

Folder Types

Outlook uses various types of folders to store specific types of information. For example, email messages are always stored in email folders, and contacts are always stored in contact folders. Whenever you create a folder, you must designate which type of folder you wish to create. Outlook uses a different icon to represent the type of information contained in each folder.

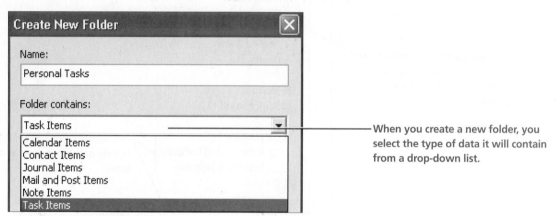

When you create a new folder, you select the type of data it will contain from a drop-down list.

QUICK REFERENCE: CREATING FOLDERS

Task	Procedure
Create a new folder.	■ Choose File→Folder→New Folder from the menu bar, or use (CTRL)+(SHIFT)+(E) from the keyboard.
	■ Type the folder name.
	■ Make sure that the folder type is correct.
	■ Click the folder under which the new folder should be created.
	■ Click OK to complete the command.

Adaptive Menus

Office 2003 programs feature an adaptive menu system that hides menu bar commands that are seldom used. This reduces the number of menu commands on the menu bar. Thus, you have two types of menus on the menu bar, as described below.

- **Short menu**—This menu contains only the most frequently used commands. Outlook displays the short menu when you first click on a menu bar command.

- **Expanded menu**—This menu contains all of the available commands. When you choose a command from the expanded menu, the command is moved to the short menu.

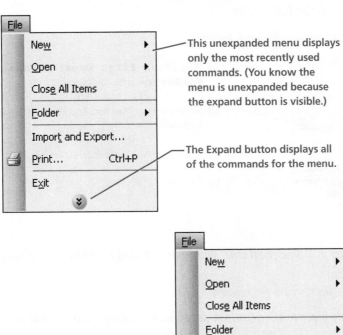

This unexpanded menu displays only the most recently used commands. (You know the menu is unexpanded because the expand button is visible.)

The Expand button displays all of the commands for the menu.

Seldom used (normally hidden) commands have dark bars beside them.

Hands-On 5.4 Create a New Folder

In this exercise, you will create a new folder for email. You will learn how to move and copy email messages to this folder in Lesson 6.

Create a Mail Folder

1. Make sure the Mail button is chosen in the Navigation pane.

2. Choose File→Folder→New Folder from the menu bar.
   The Create New Folder dialog box appears.

3. Follow these steps to create the new folder:

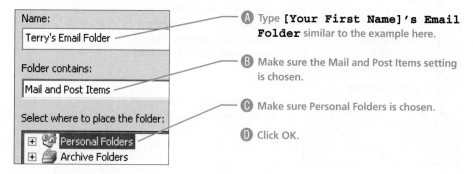

A Type **[Your First Name]'s Email Folder** similar to the example here.

B Make sure the Mail and Post Items setting is chosen.

C Make sure Personal Folders is chosen.

D Click OK.

The new folder appears in alphabetical order within the All Mail Folders section of the Navigation pane.

Create a Folder in Archive Folders

Archive Folders is a handy place to store Outlook data that is no longer current but may be useful to reference in the future.

4. Choose File→Folder→New Folder from the menu bar.

5. Follow these steps to create the new folder:

A Type **[Your First Name]'s Old Calendar** similar to the example here.

B Choose Calendar Items from the Folder Contains list.

C If necessary, click the plus (+) sign beside Archive Folders to expand this folder list.

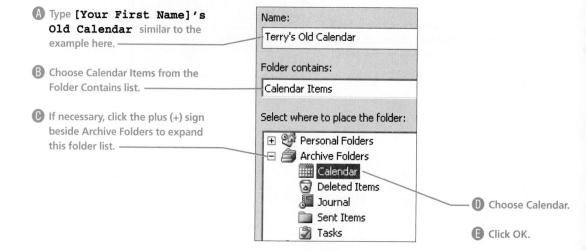

D Choose Calendar.

E Click OK.

Outlook creates the new folder, though it is not visible in the Navigation pane. This is because the new folder is not a Mail folder. To view this folder you must display the Calendar or Folder List pane.

6. Click the Calendar button in the Navigation pane.
   The calendar folder you created should be visible in the My Calendars list.

7. Place a checkmark in the box beside [Your Name's] Old Calendar, as shown below.

Outlook displays this calendar on the right side of the Calendar pane.

8. Uncheck the [Your Name's] Old Calendar box.
   The calendar disappears from the Calendar pane.

9. Click the Folder List button on the Navigation pane in either of the two locations shown below.

10. If necessary, scroll down until the Archive Folders becomes visible. Click the plus (+) signs next to the folder names to make the [Your Name]'s Old Calendar folder visible similar to the figure at right.

11. Click the minus sign beside Archive Folders in the navigation bar if it is visible.
    This collapses the display of these folders.

12. Click the Mail button on the Navigation pane.
    Because it is an email folder, the [Your Name]'s Email Folder is visible in the Navigation pane.

Outlook and the Internet

Outlook contains several features that allow you to communicate over the Internet. The most important of these features is electronic mail (email). The Internet is the world's largest computer network. It is an interconnected system of computers that resides on every continent. These computers talk to each other with a common set of rules (called protocols). Every computer on the Internet can send information to any other computer that is also connected to the Internet.

Services on the Internet

The Internet supports many services for global communications. The two most commonly used services on the Internet are the World Wide Web (Web) and email. It is important to remember that the Internet is a communication network, not a single service such as the Web. Use of the Web is becoming so common that many beginners think that the Web is the Internet. This is not true. The Web is a service, and it needs the Internet in order to function.

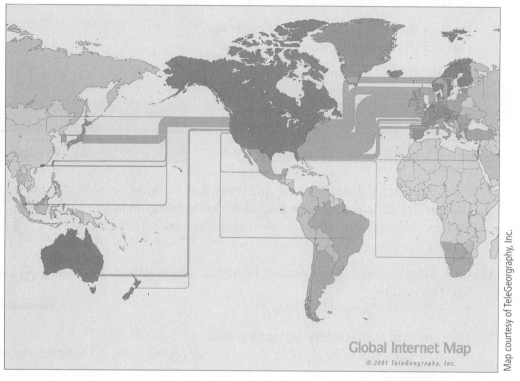

Global Internet Map
© 2001 TeleGeography, Inc.

Map courtesy of TeleGeorgraphy, Inc.

This is an example of an Internet map. It displays the relative capacities of Internet data lines between the US and other regions of the world.

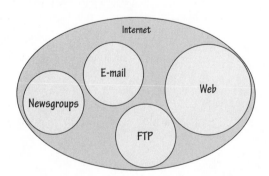

The Web and email are two services that run over the Internet and that you can access with Outlook 2003.

How the Internet Works

The Internet functions according to rules of operation called protocols. Just as the interactions between nations are guided by accepted protocols, all of the computers on the Internet function according to protocols. The two most critical protocols on the Internet are the Transmission Control Protocol (TCP) and Internet Protocol (IP). These are usually abbreviated as TCP/IP.

Packet-Switched Networking

Data that is sent out over the Internet is broken down into small chunks called packets. In ideally democratic fashion, every single packet on the Internet receives the same treatment—whether it is part of a small message, or a large message. IP controls how packets are addressed to arrive at their intended destination. Once the packets arrive, they must be sorted into the proper order to re-create the original form of the data; TCP takes care of this task. The figure below illustrates how a Web page travels through the Internet from a Web server computer to display in a user's Web browser window.

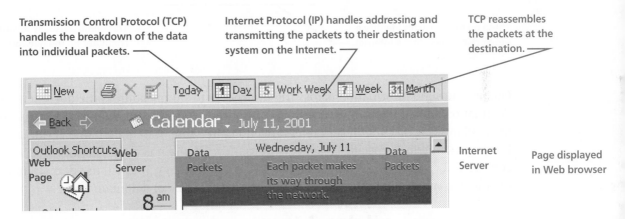

Transmission Control Protocol (TCP) handles the breakdown of the data into individual packets.

Internet Protocol (IP) handles addressing and transmitting the packets to their destination system on the Internet.

TCP reassembles the packets at the destination.

Internet Server

Page displayed in Web browser

All of the information transmitted over the internet is sent in small packets.

An Analogy

To better understand how information travels over the internet, consider this example. Let's say that rather than sending a Web page, you need to ship a dinosaur skeleton to a museum across the country. (This is a rather large-scale example, but it will do.)

First, you wouldn't send the entire skeleton in one box! Rather, you would break it down. So, you would set your museum staff to taking the skeleton apart and packaging each piece for shipment. Each package would have a label with the address of the receiving museum.

Next, you would take all of the packages to Federal Express for shipment. FedEx knows where the shipment will go because each package is properly addressed. FedEx is not going to devote an entire plane to the shipment; instead, it will fit what it can among the rest of the package traffic going in the same general direction as your packages. Some of the packages will ship right away, and others will ship later, as space is available.

FedEx delivers the packages as they arrive in the destination city. At the hosting museum, the packages are sorted into the proper order, according to a catalog that lists every package in the shipment. Then, the skeleton is reassembled for the exhibit.

In miniature fashion, TCP/IP performs the analogous tasks in transmitting data over the Internet that FedEx and the museum staff performed to ship the dinosaur skeleton. The museum staffs at both ends of the shipment perform a task similar to that of TCP, disassembling and assembling all of the packets that compose the data being sent over the Internet. FedEx performs a role analogous to IP, deciding how to route the packets and ensuring that they reach their destination.

IP Addresses and Domains

Every computer connected to the Internet has a unique, 12-digit identifying number called an IP Address. For example, the computer this lesson is being written on has a temporary IP address of 205.184.198.66. The first three sets of numbers usually identify the network with which the Internet server is part. The fourth set of numbers usually identifies a specific computer on that network. This system allows the unique identification of approximately four billion computers on the Internet.

An example of a typical IP address.

These numbers usually identify a network attached to the Internet. ———

——— This number usually identifies a computer on the network.

One way to send information across the Internet is to simply address the document or file to the destination's IP address. However, since 12-digit numbers are not easy for humans to memorize, most addressing on the Internet refers to a domain name. A domain name is simply a plain-language name for a specific IP address. A top-level domain is a category of Internet site such as commercial (.com), education (.edu), or government (.gov). You will use domain names in the next lesson when you address email. Below is an example of a domain name.

The domain name ——— The top-level domain name

NOTE! *You will learn about addressing email messages in Lesson 6.*

Concepts Review

True/False Questions

1.	Outlook can help you manage a wide variety of personal information.	TRUE	FALSE
2.	All of the information in Outlook is stored in folders.	TRUE	FALSE
3.	Outlook's online help is only organized as a table of contents.	TRUE	FALSE
4.	Outlook's online help does not access information directly from the Internet.	TRUE	FALSE
5.	Outlook's online help includes training courses.	TRUE	FALSE
6.	You can place folders within other folders.	TRUE	FALSE
7.	Outlook contains features that help you schedule your appointments.	TRUE	FALSE
8.	When you create a folder, you must indicate the type of data it will store.	TRUE	FALSE
9.	You cannot create new folders in Outlook's Archive folder.	TRUE	FALSE
10.	You can mix different types of Outlook data in the same folder.	TRUE	FALSE

Multiple Choice Questions

1. Which of the following activities is not supported by a feature in Outlook?
   a. Calendar scheduling
   b. Word processing
   c. Notes
   d. Electronic mail
   e. Task list

2. Which method is probably the easiest way to search for online help?
   a. Use the Index search feature to display the longest list of possible help items.
   b. Type a question in plain English in the Question box.
   c. Search the Table of Contents under the type of task with which you need help.
   d. None of the above

3. Where can you create a new folder?
   a. In Personal Folders.
   b. In Archive Folders.
   c. Only in the Email Inbox.
   d. Both A and B

4. When data is sent out over the Internet,
   a. it travels as a single entity until it reaches its destination.
   b. it is split up into small packets that travel together.
   c. it is split up into small packets that travel independently.
   d. None of the above

Skill Builder 5.1 **Look up a Help Topic**

In this exercise, you will look up how to delete a folder, then you will print the topic.

1. Start Outlook, then type **Delete a Folder** in the question box near the top-right corner of the window and tap the (ENTER) key.

2. Click the Delete a folder item in the Search Results pane. Read over the steps in the topic.

3. Click the Print 🖨 button on the help window toolbar to print the topic, then click Print to complete the command.

4. Close ⊠ the Help window.

Skill Builder 5.2 **Create a Folder**

In this exercise, you will create a new folder, then delete it.

1. Click the Mail button on the Navigation pane.

2. Choose File→Folder→New Folder from the menu bar.

3. Follow these steps to create the folder:

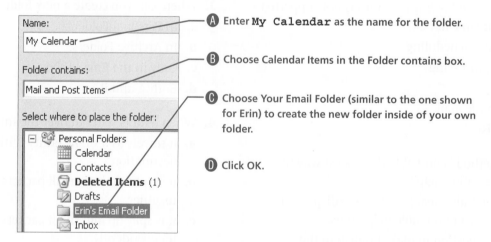

Ⓐ Enter **My Calendar** as the name for the folder.

Ⓑ Choose Calendar Items in the Folder contains box.

Ⓒ Choose Your Email Folder (similar to the one shown for Erin) to create the new folder inside of your own folder.

Ⓓ Click OK.

Notice that the new folder does not appear in All Mail Folders on the Navigation pane. This is because the Mail pane does not display other types of folders.

4. Click the Calendar button on the Navigation pane.

My Calendar should now appear at the bottom of the My Calendars section of the Calendar pane.

Delete the Calendar Folder

5. Display the Folders List by clicking whichever version of this button is visible.

6. Follow these steps to delete the folder:

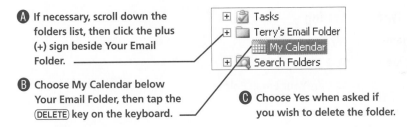

Ⓐ If necessary, scroll down the folders list, then click the plus (+) sign beside Your Email Folder.

Ⓑ Choose My Calendar below Your Email Folder, then tap the ⟨DELETE⟩ key on the keyboard.

Ⓒ Choose Yes when asked if you wish to delete the folder.

Outlook places the folder in the Deleted Items folder.

7. Follow these steps to empty the Deleted Items folder:

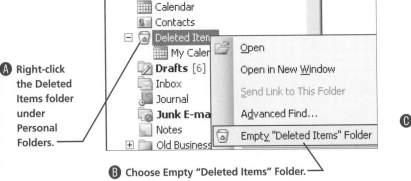

Ⓐ Right-click the Deleted Items folder under Personal Folders.

Ⓑ Choose Empty "Deleted Items" Folder.

Ⓒ Choose Yes to confirm emptying Deleted Items.

Assessments

Assessment 5.1 Print an Online Help Topic

In this assessment test, you will look up two Help topics using any method of your choice. You will then print the topics.

1. Look up a procedure to copy a folder in online help.
2. Print the topic.
3. Look up how to change email account settings.
4. Print the topic.

Assessment 5.2 Create a Folder

In this assessment test, you will create a new folder, add a shortcut to the folder on the Outlook bar, then delete the folder and remove the shortcut.

Part A: Create the Folder

1. Create a new folder according to the specifications below:

Setting Type	Setting
Folder Name	My Tasks
Folder Type	Task Items
Location	Within Your Email Folder

Part B: Delete the Folder

2. Delete the My Tasks folder from the Folder List.
3. Empty the Deleted Items Folder.

LESSON 6

Sending and Receiving Email

Electronic mail (email) is one of the most popular services on the Internet. With an email account, you can exchange messages, documents, images, and virtually any other type of information with other email users—anywhere in the world. The use of Internet email is growing at such a pace that it will become as common as the telephone within a few more years. It is not even necessary to have a computer in order to access email. Small, inexpensive devices are being sold that can put email in the palm of your hand. In this lesson, you will learn the basics of sending, receiving, and replying to email messages. You will learn various methods to delete, restore, and move messages into different folders. You will also learn how to flag messages for future attention.

Additional learning resources are available at labpub.com/learn/oe3/

Case Study

Daniel has just started a new job at the Acme Trading Company. Acme is an import/export business that works with other vendors in many countries. Daniel will be responsible for tracking Acme's shipments of dishware and glassware. Daniel uses a company email account to correspond with his contacts at other vendor companies. Daniel has never used email before, but he finds it easy to send and receive his first messages. Soon, Daniel comes to prefer email to sending letters by postal mail. The vendors with whom he exchanges email prefer it, too.

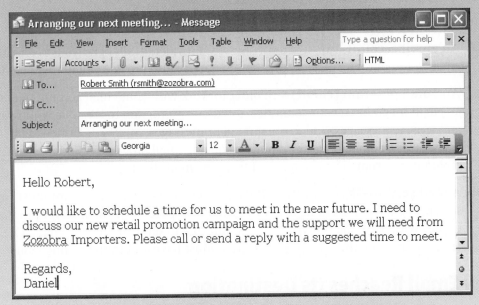

A typical Outlook email message looks like this. You will also reply to email messages you receive and forward messages to other email users.

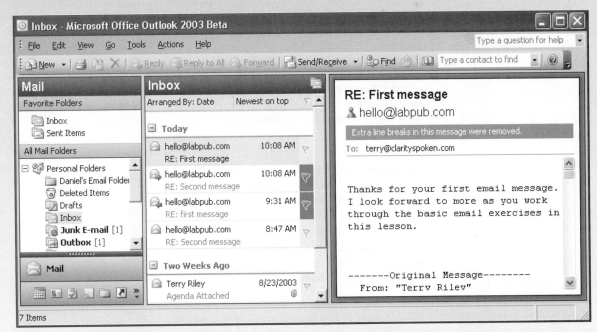

Outlook features several views that let you review, respond to, and print email messages. The Inbox view lists new email messages as they are delivered.

About Electronic Mail

Along with the Web, electronic mail (email) is the most popular of all Internet services. Email is simply the capability to send a message to a specific individual's email address anywhere in the world. An email message can also have one or more computer files (attachments) sent with it. With email you can send and receive messages, send a message to more than one recipient, and exchange documents and images.

Components of Email Service

You need the following services in order to work with email on the Internet:

- **An email account**—Most Internet Service Providers (ISPs) give you an email account when you sign up for service. Your company may also provide you with an email account.

- **An email program (client)**—In order to work with your email account, you must install an email program on your computer. You use this program to create new messages, receive and reply to messages, and to organize your messages. Microsoft Outlook 2002 is one example of an email program. Another popular email program is Eudora Light. An email program may sometimes be referred to as an email client.

- **A mail server**—The company or ISP that provides your email account must run a mail server program on one of its network system computers. The mail server program communicates with other mail servers over the Internet to send and receive email. Of course, in order to function, the mail server program must have an Internet connection.

How Email Reaches its Destination

When you send an email message, the following process takes place to move your message to its destination:

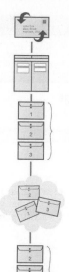

You use Outlook to create and compose the message, then give the send command.

The message is transmitted via your modem or local area network to the outgoing mail server at the office of your ISP or corporate information systems department. The mail server figures out how to find the addressee's mail server at the destination.

The message is broken up into packets and sent through the Internet to the addressee's incoming mail server destination.

The message packets arrive at the incoming mail server and are reassembled into the message.

The addressee gives a send/receive mail command from his or her email program. The message is transmitted from the incoming mail server to the addressee's email program and is copied to the addressee's hard drive. The addressee can then open, view, and reply to the message.

Email Settings in Outlook

In order to help you use email, Outlook must have information about your email account. Your email account is probably set up already. A summary of the email settings Outlook needs is listed in the following table.

Setting	Description	Example
Server type	Outlook allows you to access several different types of email. For example, a POP3 server type controls sending and receiving standard Internet email. An HTTP server allows you to access Web email services such as Hotmail.	POP3 HTTP Exchange
Your name	Your name as it will appear on email that you send to others. This name can be changed as needed, without affecting your email address.	Bob Smith Betsy Jones
Email address	The address others will use to send you email. Many companies follow a standard convention when they assign email names of first initial and last name. Some people prefer to use a pseudonym for their email name.	mjones@college.edu clevername@hotmail.com anon@santa-fe.cc.nm.us
Incoming mail (POP) server	This is a program on the mail server computer in the network. It controls all *incoming* email.	Pop3.sfsu.edu
Outgoing mail (SMTP) server	This is another program on the mail server computer on the network. It controls all *outgoing* email. *Note: Sometimes the names of the Pop server and SMTP server will be identical.*	smtp.sfsu.edu
User name	This is the name the email system uses to identify you when Outlook logs on to send or receive mail. In most cases, your account name will be identical to your email address, but without the domain name.	mjones clevername
Password	A secret password that allows you to send and receive mail to the mail servers. Some computer facilities have special rules for acceptable passwords. For example, a password may be required to have a certain length or to contain both alphabetic characters and numerals.	Student12 4access What6Ever

Setting Up Multiple Email Accounts

Outlook allows you to set up more than one email account to use with the program. For example, you could set up an email account that you use on the job and a personal email account from your ISP. Outlook can check all of your email accounts with a single command, or you can check accounts individually with the Tools→Send/Receive command.

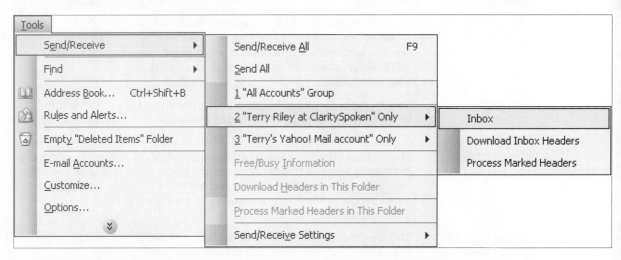

The Tools→Send/Receive command allows you to check for messages on individual accounts.

Outlook and Webmail

Webmail is an email account that you can access from any Web browser with an Internet connection. Compared to normal email, Webmail uses a different type of mail server (HTTP rather than POP). Outlook 2002 allows you to access email from many types of Webmail accounts, including Hotmail.

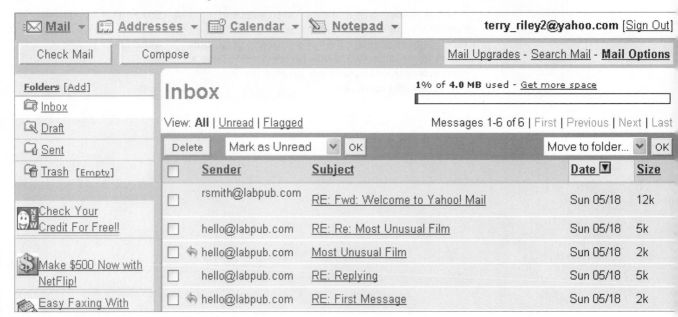

Hotmail is a popular example of a Webmail service.

Depending on your computer classroom is set up, an email account may already be set up in Outlook. However, some computer labs may require students to use a Webmail account such as Hotmail with Outlook.

Hands-On 6.1 View Your Email Settings

In this exercise, you will open a window to display information about your Internet email account. You will enter your own name as the name to display on outgoing email messages.

Before You Begin: If you must set up your computer to work with your Hotmail account, you should skip this exercise and see Appendix A for detailed account set up instructions. Please perform Hands-On Exercise A.1 in lieu of Exercise 6.1 below.

WebSim Users Only—If your computer cannot access an email account, read the instructions on the Web-Based Simulations in Appendix B. Be sure to run the two exercises listed below:

- *Perform the instructions in Hands-On Exercise B.2 to load some required files into Outlook.*
- *Follow the instructions in Hands-On Exercise B.1 to run a simulation of this exercise.*

1. Start Outlook. Choose Yes if you are asked to make Outlook your default email client. Choose Cancel if Outlook asks for the passwords to any email accounts.

2. Choose Tools→Email Accounts from the menu bar.

!**TIP!** *Click the Expand* 🔽 *button to expand the menu if the command is not visible.*

3. Make sure that the View Or Change Existing Email Accounts option is chosen, then click Next.
The Email Accounts dialog box appears. This lists all of the email accounts set up for Outlook. Outlook allows you to send and receive email for more than one email account.

4. If more than one email account is visible, select your email account, then click the Change button.
The primary settings for your email account are displayed. Notice the Server Information settings at the top-right corner.

5. Change the name in (only) the User Information section to your own name.

!**NOTE!** *Do not change the email address setting.*

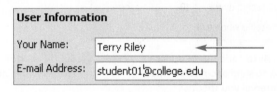

6. If a Test Account Settings button is visible, click the button, then click Close after the account settings test is complete. Otherwise, skip to Step 7.
Outlook can test your settings on standard Internet email accounts. A test is not required for Hotmail/HTTP email accounts.

7. Click Next, then click Finish to close the E-mail Accounts dialog box.
Depending on how Outlook is configured, the test message sent in Step 7 may arrive at the inbox.

Setting Outlook Options

Outlook has many options you can set for its email functions. For example, you can set Outlook to check for new email messages automatically. The settings that are made when Outlook is first installed serve the needs of most users. These initial settings are called defaults. However, there may be times when you want to change a default setting. You can do this with the Tools→Options command.

Hands-On 6.2 Change Mail Setup Options

In this exercise, you will set Outlook to hold outgoing email messages until you give the Send/Receive command. You will also set Outlook to automatically check for new email messages every 10 minutes.

1. Choose Tools→Options from the menu bar. Click the Expand ⏬ button to expand the menu if the Options command is not displayed.

2. Follow these steps to set the Mail Delivery options:

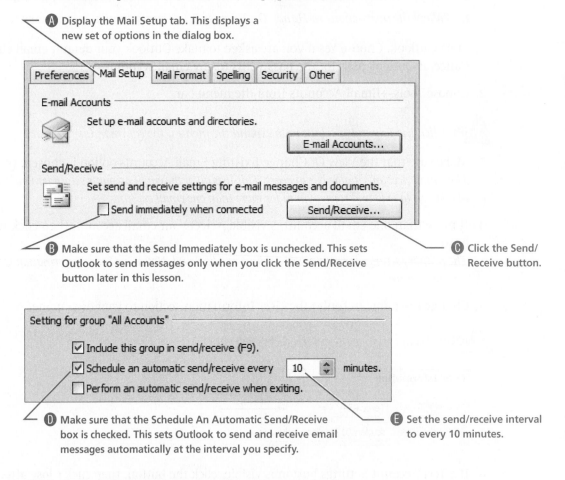

Ⓐ Display the Mail Setup tab. This displays a new set of options in the dialog box.

Ⓑ Make sure that the Send Immediately box is unchecked. This sets Outlook to send messages only when you click the Send/Receive button later in this lesson.

Ⓒ Click the Send/ Receive button.

Ⓓ Make sure that the Schedule An Automatic Send/Receive box is checked. This sets Outlook to send and receive email messages automatically at the interval you specify.

Ⓔ Set the send/receive interval to every 10 minutes.

3. Click Close, then click OK to close the Options dialog box.

Sending an Email Message

Sending an email message is easy. If you know how to use a word processor, you know more than enough to create and send an email message. This topic will take you through the steps of sending your first email message with Outlook. To start an email message, simply choose File→New→Mail Message, or click the New button on the toolbar and choose Mail Message.

FROM THE KEYBOARD

(CTRL)+(SHIFT)+(M) to create a new email message.

Email Addresses

When you receive an email account, you are also given an email address. This address uniquely identifies your email account and where your mail server can be located. An email address looks similar to, and functions much like, the URL for a Web page. The diagram below shows the parts of a typical email address.

rstolins@labpub.com

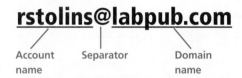

Account name   Separator   Domain name

QUICK REFERENCE: RULES FOR EMAIL ADDRESSES

■ Email addresses always contain the @ symbol to separate the account name from the domain name.

■ An email address cannot contain space characters.

■ An email address can contain certain punctuation characters, such as a dash and periods.

AutoFill

As you type an email address, Outlook's AutoFill feature automatically displays a list of similar email addresses you've used before. You can use the arrow keys or the mouse to select from the list, then Outlook automatically enters the rest of the email address. This can help prevent typos in your email addresses.

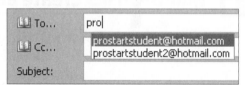

Outlook displays a list of contacts whose name begins with the letters typed in the To box.

Message Importance (Priority)

When you send a message, you can give it one of three different importance levels, as described below:

■ **Normal**—This is the default importance setting for messages. Most messages you send and receive will use this priority.

■ **High**—This importance level indicates that the message should be opened and responded to right away.

■ **Low**—This importance level is rarely used. If you know your recipient receives a lot of email every day, and your message is not very important, you can set it to low importance.

When someone receives a high or low importance email message, it will have an importance flag on its row in the Inbox.

TIP! *The importance that you set to a message has nothing to do with how fast it is actually transmitted. The Internet treats every email message the same, regardless of its importance setting.*

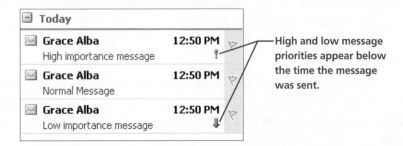

High and low message priorities appear below the time the message was sent.

QUICK REFERENCE: SEND AN EMAIL MESSAGE

Task	Procedure
Send an email message.	■ Choose New→Mail Message from the menu bar or click the New button on the Outlook toolbar and choose Mail Message.
	■ Address the message and enter a subject.
	■ Fill in the body of the message, then click the Send button.
Assign a priority to an email message.	■ Start the message.
	■ Click the appropriate priority button if the message is high or low priority.

Hands-On 6.3 Create and Send Email Messages

WebSim *In this exercise, you will create a new email message and send it to an email address at labpub.com. This email address will automatically send a message back to you.*

1. Make sure that the Inbox (or Hotmail Inbox) view is displayed.

2. Click the New Mail Message [New] button at the left side of the Outlook toolbar.
   A new email message window will appear on the screen. Outlook always gives you a separate window to compose email messages.

3. Follow these steps to begin composing your first email message:

!NOTE! *As you type the email address, Outlook may display an AutoFill option below the To box similar to the one shown at right. Just continue to type the address manually if you see this. You will use the AutoFill feature on your next message.*

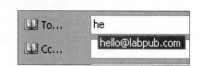

A Type **hello@labpub.com** as the address for the message. ⟶

B Tap the (TAB) key two or three times to jump the insertion point down to the Subject field. Type **First message** as the subject of your message. ⟶

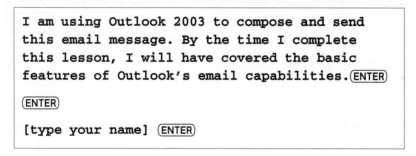

C Tap the (TAB) key once to jump down to the body of the message. You should see the insertion point blinking on the first line of the body portion of the message.

4. Read the comment below, then type the message that follows:
   Don't worry about the message lines wrapping around exactly as they appear below. When you type to the end of the message box, a new line will be started for you automatically. You only need to tap (ENTER) when you want to start a new line at the end of a paragraph, or insert a blank line in the message. If you tap (ENTER) at the end of each line, your message may be difficult for the addressee to read.

```
I am using Outlook 2003 to compose and send
this email message. By the time I complete
this lesson, I will have covered the basic
features of Outlook's email capabilities.(ENTER)

(ENTER)

[type your name] (ENTER)
```

Set the Message Importance

5. Click the High Importance ⚠ button on the message toolbar, then move your mouse pointer away from the button.
   The button now has a border around it. This indicates that High Importance is set for this message.

6. Click the High Importance ⚠ button again, then move the mouse pointer away from the button.
   Now the button no longer has a border. The High Importance setting has been switched off.

7. Click the High Importance ⚠ button one last time.

Send the Message

8. Look over the message and fix any typographical errors. If you see an error, click just to the right of the error, then tap the (BACKSPACE) key to delete it. You can then retype the word and it will be inserted into the message. After you've made any necessary corrections, go on to the next step.

   Many users make typos in their email messages. It's a good idea to scan your messages for typos before you send them. You should use the same level of care with business correspondence via email as you would use in a standard business letter.

9. Click the ⬛️Send button on the message toolbar to send your message.

   This command does not actually send the message to the mail server system just yet. This is because you configured Outlook in the previous exercise not to send messages immediately upon giving the Send command

10. Click the Outbox folder on the Navigation pane.

    Your message should be listed here. The Outbox is a folder that holds all outgoing email messages. When you give the Send/Receive command, messages in this folder are transmitted to the outgoing mail server on the system that provides your Internet connection.

11. Click the ⬛️Send/Receive ▾ button on the Outlook toolbar.

    Outlook may display a window that shows the progress of sending and receiving messages. Since your message is short, the window appears for only a few seconds. A portion of the window is displayed below.

If the progress window is not visible, you should see a display at the bottom-right corner of the Outlook window in the Status bar. The Status bar can display information about making a connection to the mail server and the delivery of email messages.

Click on the status message, then choose Details to view detailed information on the progress of the Send/Receive command.

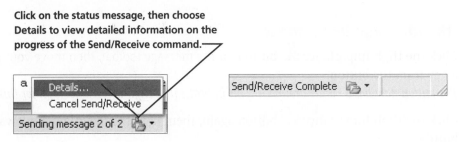

12. Choose the Sent Items folder in the Navigation pane.

Now your message should appear in this list. Note the time that the message was sent in the Sent column of the list. Outlook keeps a copy of every email message you send.

Congratulations! You've just sent your first email message with Outlook 2003.

Send a Second Message

13. Click the New Mail Message ⟨New⟩ button at the left side of the Outlook toolbar.
In the next step, you will use Outlook's AutoFill feature to enter the email address.

14. Follow these steps to enter the email address:

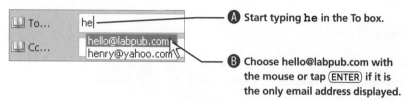

Ⓐ Start typing **he** in the To box.

Ⓑ Choose **hello@labpub.com** with the mouse or tap ⟨ENTER⟩ if it is the only email address displayed.

Outlook enters the email address for you. Notice that it has also underlined the address and added a semicolon after the address. This is because you separate multiple email addresses with semicolons.

15. Tap the ⟨TAB⟩ key until the insertion point is blinking in the Subject line, type **Second message**, then tap the ⟨TAB⟩ key to jump to the body of the message.

16. Type the body of the message as shown below:

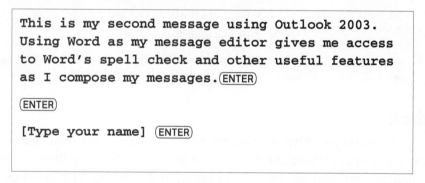

17. Click the ⟨Send⟩ button on the message toolbar to send your message.
The message has been sent to the Outbox, where it will be ready for delivery.

18. Click the ⟨Send/Receive ▾⟩ button on the Outlook toolbar.
Your message is delivered to the mail server system. It now begins its journey over the Internet to the addressee. Notice that the Second message is now listed at the top of the Sent Items view. You may also hear a sound play if a response to your first message arrives during this Send/Receive command.

Receiving Messages

When a new message arrives, it is stored in the mail server computer at your ISP or business network until you give the send/receive command to retrieve it. Outlook gives you two ways to retrieve messages:

- **Give the command manually**—You can click the Send/Receive button at any time to check for new messages and to send messages that are currently in your Outbox.

- **Give the command automatically**—You can set Outlook to check for new messages every few minutes or every few hours. You adjusted this setting in a previous Hands-On exercise.

> Setting for group "All Accounts"
>
> ☑ Include this group in send/receive (F9).
> ☑ Schedule an automatic send/receive every 10 ⌃⌄ minutes.
> ☐ Perform an automatic send/receive when exiting.

You make a setting in the Outlook options dialog box to check for new messages at a regular time interval.

QR **QUICK REFERENCE: SETTING AUTOMATIC CHECKS FOR NEW MESSAGES**

Task	Procedure
Set Outlook to check for new messages automatically.	■ Choose Tools→Options from the menu bar.
	■ Click the Mail Delivery tab.
	■ Make sure that the Check for new messages option is checked, then set the time interval for automatic checks.

The Inbox

 Inbox When messages arrive, they are placed in your Inbox. The Inbox normally holds all the messages sent to you until you place them into other folders, or delete them. Outlook uses several folders to manage your email account. For example, in the previous Hands-On exercise you viewed the Outgoing and Sent Items folders. You can also create your own email folders in Outlook, as you learned to do in Lesson 5.

The Send/Receive Command

Send/Receive The Send/Receive command in Outlook prompts the program to contact your mail-server to check for new messages. If you have incoming messages, they will be placed into your Inbox. At the same time, Outlook also sends any messages in your Outbox to the mail server system for delivery to their destinations.

Outlook has three ways to notify you that messages have arrived:

- A new message sound will play.

- A number will appear by the inbox label.

- A small envelope icon will appear in the bottom-right side of the Windows taskbar.

Reading Incoming Messages

You can preview messages in the Outlook window or you can double-click to open any message in a window of its own. The preview option is handy if you wish to review many messages quickly. When you come across a longer message, you may want to open it in a separate message window. Finally, you can also click the Previous and Next buttons in a message window to review messages in that window.

The Previous and Next buttons allow you to scroll through messages in a message window.

Sorting Messages in the Inbox

Messages in your Inbox may be sorted whenever the need arises. Simply click the Arranged By: column heading and choose the sort order you want. Most of the time you will probably sort your messages by the date received but you may also sort messages by sender, subject line, and other useful orders.

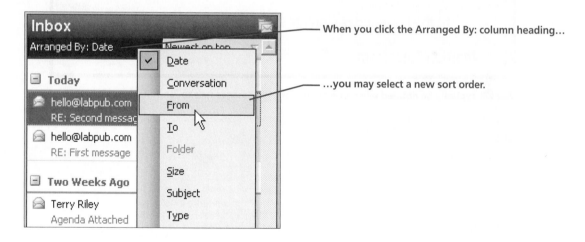

When Things Go Wrong

Sometimes you may receive a message that another message you tried to send did not go through. This may happen for a variety of reasons. For example, you may have typed the wrong address for the message or the recipient's mail server system may have been out of operation. The mail server for your account will make several attempts, if necessary, to deliver each message. When it fails to get the message through, you will receive an error message.

!TIP! *If you receive an error notification for a message, you can try sending it again. Select the message in the Sent Items view, double-click to open the message, then choose Actions→Resend this Message from the message window menu bar.*

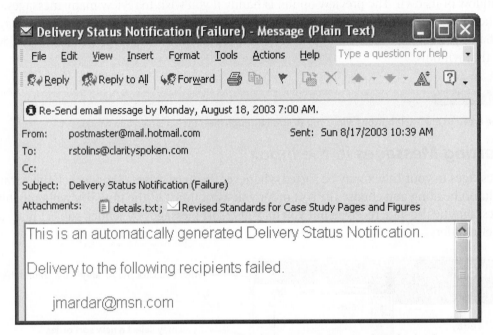

You will typically be notified when one of your email messages fails to reach its destination.

Hands-On 6.4 Check for New Messages

 In this exercise, you will check for new messages in your Inbox folder. You will also view these messages in Inbox view as well as a separate window, and sort the messages in your Inbox in several ways.

1. Choose the Inbox in the Favorite Folders section of the Navigation Pane.
   You used the Send/Receive command earlier to transmit your email message to the outgoing mail server. You will use the same command to check the incoming mail server for newly arrived email messages.

2. Click the ⬜ Send/Receive button on the Outlook toolbar.
   Depending on how Outlook is configured, you may see a dialog box that displays the progress of the Send/Receive command. The status bar will also display the progress of your send/receive command.

3. If a new message does not arrive, click the Send/Receive button every 30 seconds until you receive the second message.
   Depending on the level of traffic on the Internet, two or three minutes may pass before your first message is received and the reply reaches the mail server for your email account. Sometimes, the turn-around takes one minute or less.

Read the New Messages

4. Follow these steps to view the new email messages:

Ⓐ Choose RE: Second Message below Today in the Inbox.

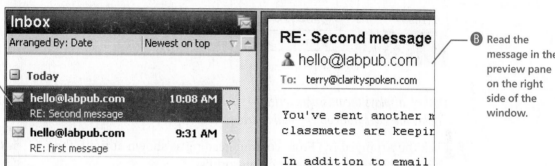

Ⓑ Read the message in the preview pane on the right side of the window.

5. Click the RE: First Message in the Inbox to view the response to your first message.
   The Up and Down arrow keys are a handy way to navigate through your email messages. Also, notice that the icon for your second message has changed from a closed envelope ✉ to an open ✉ one.

6. Click RE: Second Message in the Inbox to view this message again.

7. Follow these steps to change the width of the message preview pane:

Ⓐ Point at the border between the Inbox and Preview pane until the double-arrow appears, then drag to the right.

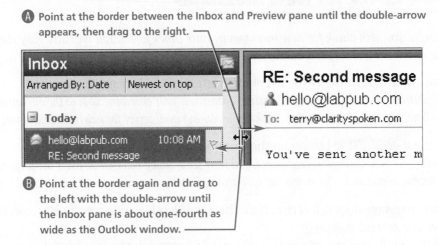

Ⓑ Point at the border again and drag to the left with the double-arrow until the Inbox pane is about one-fourth as wide as the Outlook window.

Sort the Inbox Messages

8. Follow these steps to sort messages in the Inbox:

Ⓐ Click the Arranged By: Date column heading.

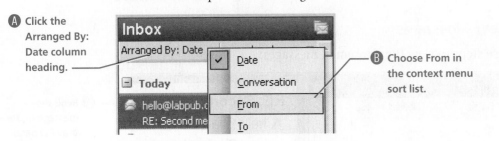

Ⓑ Choose From in the context menu sort list.

Outlook displays the messages sorted by sender. This may list only messages from Hello or it may also display messages from other email addresses.

9. Click the Arranged By: From column heading as shown at right, then choose Date from the context menu sort list.
Outlook reverts to the default sort by date display.

Read a Message in its Own Window

10. Double-click on the RE: Second message message at the top of the Inbox list.
The reply from hello@labpub.com opens in a message window.

11. Minimize ▬ the Outlook (not the message) window.

12. Point at the bottom border of the message window until you see the double-arrow ↕. Then, drag down on the bottom margin of the message window to make it larger on the screen and easier to read. You can also drag up on the window's title bar (see figure below) if it is already near the bottom of the Windows Desktop.

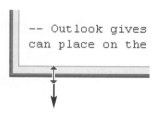

The title bar.

13. Click the Next Item ⬇ button on the message window toolbar to view the next message. This should be the response to your first message.
You can use the Next and Previous buttons to navigate through all of your messages in the Inbox.

14. Click the Next Item ⬇ button again.
The next message in the Inbox will appear, or the message window will close if there are no more messages to display.

15. Close ☒ the message window if it is still open.

16. Click the ⬛ Inbox - Microsoft Offi... button on the Windows Taskbar to restore the program window to the Desktop.

Flagging Messages

You can flag messages in the Inbox as a reminder to follow up on them. For example, you can flag a message and set a reminder to send a reply or place a phone call to the sender. Flags are especially useful when you need to follow up on specific messages but don't have the time to do so when you initially read the messages. You can flag the most important messages as you read, then later re-read the flagged messages.

You can type a custom message for the Flag. ⎯

You can set a reminder for the Flag. Outlook will display a reminder message at the selected date and time. ⎯

⚠TIP! *When you can't deal with an important message at the time you read it, be sure to flag it with a reminder setting.*

QUICK REFERENCE: FLAGGING MESSAGES

Task	Procedure
Flag a message.	■ Right-click on the message to be flagged, then choose a flag color or Add Reminder from the context menu.
	■ If you wish, you can change the label for the flag and set a reminder date.
Clear the flag from a message.	■ Right-click on the message with the flag, then choose Clear Flag or Flag Complete from the context menu.

 TIP! *To perform a right-click, you click the right (not the left) mouse button. This displays a special context menu in most Windows programs.*

Hands-On 6.5 **Flag a Message**

In this exercise, you will create a flag for the reply to the first message you sent, reminding you in one month to follow up on this correspondence.

 WebSim Users Only—Click the Internet Explorer button on the Windows Taskbar, then run the simulatio_ of this exercise.

Hotmail/HTTP Email Users Only—Skip this exercise if you are using Hotmail. Outlook does not permit the flagging of Hotmail messages. If you wish, navigate to the Lesson Web page and perform the Web-base_ simulation for this exercise.

1. Make sure that the Inbox view is displayed.

2. Follow these steps to flag two messages:

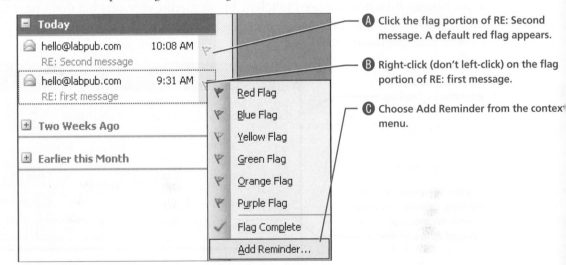

Ⓐ Click the flag portion of RE: Second message. A default red flag appears.

Ⓑ Right-click (don't left-click) on the flag portion of RE: first message.

Ⓒ Choose Add Reminder from the contex_ menu.

Outlook displays a Flag for Follow Up dialog box.

3. Follow these steps to set a follow up for the flag:

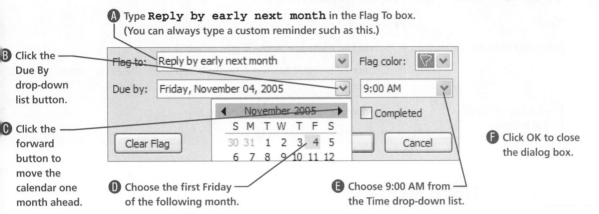

A Type **Reply by early next month** in the Flag To box.
(You can always type a custom reminder such as this.)

B Click the Due By drop-down list button.

C Click the forward button to move the calendar one month ahead.

D Choose the first Friday of the following month.

E Choose 9:00 AM from the Time drop-down list.

F Click OK to close the dialog box.

A flag appears beside the message. A reminder will appear on the date and time you've just set, giving you a convenient way to re-open and reply to this message.

4. Click the flag on RE: Second message to mark it completed.
   A checkmark replaces the flag. This helps you track messages that do not require further attention.

Printing Messages

You use the same commands to print email messages that you use with other Windows programs such as Word and Excel (File→Print). The toolbar of the Outlook window and each message window contains a Print button. Use the Print button whenever you wish to print an entire message. Outlook also offers a print preview option that displays how the message will print. Besides individual messages, you can also print a list of the email messages in the Inbox.

FROM THE KEYBOARD
CTRL+P to print.

Print Styles

Outlook offers two basic print styles:

- **Items**—When you print an item, Outlook prints whichever type of item is currently selected. For example, Outlook can print an individual email message or an event on the calendar. Items always print in the Memo print style.

- **Views**—Outlook can print the list, calendar, or other type of information displayed in a view. For example, if you are displaying the Inbox view, Outlook can print a list of the email messages displayed in the view.

!TIP! *When the print dialog box displays print styles other than Memo, these styles print views rather than items.*

QUICK REFERENCE: PRINTING EMAIL MESSAGES

Task	Procedure
Print an Email message.	■ Select the message in the Outlook window.
	■ Choose File→Print from the menu bar, or click the Print button on the toolbar.
Print a list of messages in the Inbox.	■ Choose File→Print from the menu bar.
	■ Choose the Table print style.

Hands-On 6.6 **Print a Message**

 In this exercise, you will experiment with the Print Preview feature, then print an Email message.

1. Select the RE: Second Message in the Inbox.

2. Choose File→Print from the menu bar to display the print dialog.

3. Click the Table Style option, then click the Preview button at the bottom-right corner of the Print dialog box.
   Outlook displays a preview of the message list as it will print. This is an example of printing a view rather than an item, such as an email message.

4. Click once near the top of the preview to zoom in for a closer look.

5. Close ⊠ the Print Preview window.

6. Click the Print 🖨 button on the toolbar. (This prints the currently selected message in Memo Style.) Retrieve the printout from the printer.
   The Memo style prints the full text of all selected messages. You may notice some additional code in this message. This is due to the autoresponder system. You should rarely see messages with so much "junk" code.

Responding to Messages

🔄 Reply   In a previous exercise, you received a message. On many occasions you will want to reply to a message immediately. The Reply commands make it easy to respond to a message without having to retype the email address. In addition, Outlook automatically adds an RE: prefix to the subject line so that your correspondent knows you are replying to a message.

Outlook places an RE: in front of the original subject line of every reply.

Reply Compared to Reply to All

 If you look at the toolbar, you will notice a second reply button, called Reply to All. The table below describes the difference between the two commands.

Command	What it Does
Reply	This command creates a message addressed only to the sender of the original message.
Reply to All	This command creates a message addressed to the sender of the original message and to everyone else who received the original message.

Including the Previous Message

Outlook will automatically place a copy of the message to which you are responding in your reply. This helps the person you are replying to know exactly what your reply is about. If you don't want to include the original message in a particular reply, you can always select and delete it, as you can in the body of a normal message.

Forwarding Messages

Forward Sometimes you may receive a message that should be handled by someone else. Or, you may want to share it with another correspondent. You can use Copy and Paste commands to copy the text of the message and paste it into a new message. But, it is much easier to use the Forward command instead. This command makes a copy of the message and lets you address it to a different addressee. The subject line of the message also reflects that the message is being forwarded (i.e., it originated from someone other than you).

Subject: FW: first message

Outlook automatically places a prefix of FW: in front of the original subject line when yu forward a message.

Emoticons (Smileys)

One disadvantage of email over making a telephone call is that all you have to communicate with is written words. Since English is an inflectional language, some meaning can be lost when something is expressed in writing alone. One way to overcome the lack of inflection is to use emoticons (also called smileys) from time to time in your messages. An emoticon can help convey the attitude or emotion behind a phrase. Below are a few examples of emoticons.

Emoticon	Meaning
:-)	Joking
:-0	Bored
;-)	Winking
:-(	Sad
:-<	Frowning

To create an emoticon, use some of the punctuation keys on the keyboard. For example, the joking emoticon is composed of a colon, followed by a dash, followed by a close parenthesis.

There are literally hundreds of emoticons available. The Web page for this lesson contains links to Web pages that list some of the most popular and creative emoticons. In the next exercise, you will use an emoticon.

WebSim Users Only—Click the Internet Explorer button on the Windows Taskbar, then run the simulation of this exercise.

In this exercise, you will send a reply to the message you received from Hello. You will also forward the message.

1. Follow these steps to create a reply to a message you just received:

Ⓐ Select **RE: first message** in the Inbox.

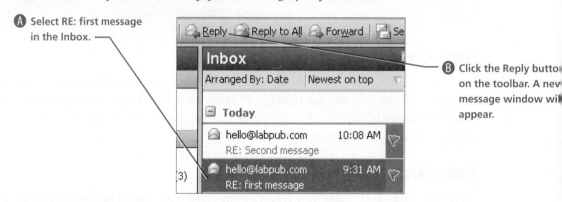

Ⓑ Click the **Reply** button on the toolbar. A new message window will appear.

Notice that the address of the sender (hello@labpub.com) is already typed in the To: field. The subject line has been filled in for you as well and a copy of the original message is already printed in the message body. The insertion point should be blinking in the first line of the message body, ready for you to type the text of your reply.

2. Follow these steps to change the subject line of your reply:
   You can change the subject line of a reply at any time.

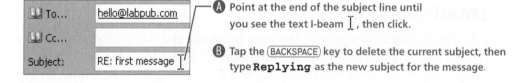

Ⓐ Point at the end of the subject line until you see the text I-beam Ⅰ, then click.

Ⓑ Tap the (BACKSPACE) key to delete the current subject, then type **Replying** as the new subject for the message.

3. Tap the (TAB) key to jump the cursor down to the body of the message, then type the following:

> **Thanks for your prompt reply. The way you turned around my message, it seems that you spend all your time watching for new email. Is this a hobby of yours?**

4. Now you will type a smiley emoticon that will look like this: **:-)** .

   ■ Tap the (SPACE BAR) to add a space after the question mark.

   ■ Hold down the (SHIFT) key and type a colon **:**.

   ■ Release the (SHIFT) key and type a hyphen **-**.

   ■ While holding down the (SHIFT) key, type a close parenthesis **)**.

5. Continue typing the rest of the message:

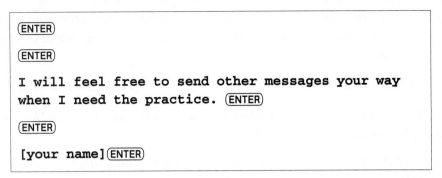

6. Review the message and correct any typos, then click the ⊟ Send button to send the message to the Outbox.
Notice that the icon for the message you replied to now displays a small arrow ▧. This indicates that you have replied to the message. The message will be held in the Outbox until you give the send/receive command later in this exercise.

Forward a Message

7. Double-click to open the RE: Second message email message in its own window.

8. Click the ▧ Forward button on the toolbar of the message window that just popped up.
A new message window appears with the body of the message you are forwarding already copied. An FW: prefix has been placed at the beginning of the subject line. The Reply and Forward buttons are always available from the main Outlook window and individual message windows.

9. In the To box, address the forwarded message to yourself (that is, type your own email address).

⚠ **TIP!** *If you do not recall your email address, you can see it in the body of the message. Notice the To line of the original message.*

10. Tap the (TAB) key until you see the insertion point blinking in the body of the message. Then type the following message:

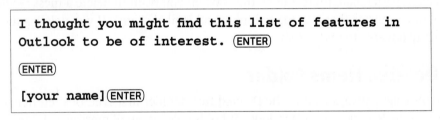

11. Click the ⊟ Send button to send the message.
You are back to viewing the message you forwarded. Notice the yellow bar across the top of the message, indicating when you forwarded it. Outlook always records this information when you reply to or forward a message.

12. Close ⊠ message window of the message you just forwarded.
Notice that the icon for the message you replied to now displays a small arrow. This indicates that you have forwarded the message. Notice also that this arrow points in the opposite direction of the replied to message arrow.

   📩 **You forwarded this message.**   📩 **You replied to this message.**

Hotmail Users Only—Outlook does not mark Hotmail messages with the special icons shown above. Your messages will retain their Read Message 📖 icons.

13. Click 📧 Send/Receive on the Outlook toolbar to send your outgoing messages and check for new messages.

Check for New Mail

14. Wait about one minute, then click 📧 Send/Receive to check for new messages. Keep clicking the Send/Receive button once a minute until you receive the new messages (a reply to Hello, and the message you forwarded to yourself).
   The message you sent to yourself will probably arrive first, since it does not need to travel over the Internet to reach your mail server system.

15. Read the new messages in the preview window.
   Leave the Outlook window open.

16. **WebSim Users Only**—Minimize the Internet Explorer window. You can perform the rest of the exercises directly in Outlook.
   Leave the Outlook window open.

⚠️ **NOTE!** *If you have not already done so, perform Hands-On exercise C.2 in Appendix C to import data into Outlook.*

Deleting and Marking Messages

As you work with email, there will be times when you want to delete a message that is no longer relevant or a message that is actually junk email (called spam). If you delete a message by mistake, it is usually possible to undelete it.

The Deleted Items Folder

Deleted messages always go into the Deleted Items folder first. The Deleted Items folder works similarly to the Recycle Bin in Windows. It holds deleted email messages, folders, and other types of Outlook items such as appointments and tasks. If you later decide that you wish to keep a message you had deleted previously, you can look for it in the Deleted Items folder and retrieve the message by moving it into a different folder.

When the Deleted Items folder is emptied, all the messages in it are permanently erased. To save disk space, you should empty the Deleted Items folder from time to time.

QUICK REFERENCE: DELETING AND RETRIEVING MESSAGES

Task	Procedure
Delete a message.	■ Select the message in a view. ■ Drag it to the Deleted Items folder, click the Delete button on the toolbar, or tap (DELETE) to delete the selected items.
Retrieve (undelete) a message.	■ Select the Deleted Items folder. ■ Drag the item to be undeleted to the Navigation pane folder where it should be restored—for example, to the Inbox.
Permanently delete messages.	■ Right-click the Deleted Items folder. ■ Select Empty "Deleted Items" Folder from the context menu.

Marking Messages

Outlook displays each new message with a closed envelope icon. After you read a message and choose another, Outlook automatically marks the message as having been "read" with an open envelope icon. Sometimes you may want to mark one or more messages as "unread" as a reminder to read them again. Or you may want to select a whole batch of messages and mark them as "read." You can change the marked icon for messages at any time.

Unread
message

Read
message

TIP! *You can use the* (CTRL) *and* (SHIFT) *keys to select multiple messages for Mark Messages and other commands.*

QUICK REFERENCE: MARKING AND SELECTING MESSAGES

Task	Procedure
Change the mark on messages.	■ Select the desired messages (see the methods below). ■ Right-click on one of the messages, then choose Mark as Read or Mark as Unread from the context menu.
Select multiple messages with the (CTRL) key.	■ Click the first message you wish to select, then hold down (CTRL) and click to select additional messages. You can release the (CTRL) key when you are finished making selections. ■ Hold down (CTRL) and click any currently selected message to deselect it.
Select a group of consecutive messages with the (SHIFT) key.	■ Click the first message in a consecutive group of messages, then hold down (SHIFT) and click the last message in the group. Release the (SHIFT) key. ■ You can still select additional messages by holding down the (CTRL) key. Or, you can deselect any currently selected message by clicking while you hold down the (CTRL) key.
Select all of the messages in a folder.	■ Display the desired folder, then choose Edit→Select All from the menu bar, or use (CTRL)+(A).

In this exercise, you will practice marking, deleting, and retrieving email messages. You will also permanently delete messages in your Deleted Items folder.

Mark Messages

1. Make sure that the Inbox is displayed in the Outlook window.

2. Right-click on the RE: Replying message that you just received from hello@labpub.com, then choose Mark As Unread from the context menu.
   Notice that the message now displays an unread ✉ icon. This is a simple way to remind yourself to reread the message without setting up a follow-up flag.

3. Right-click on the RE: Replying message you just marked as unread.
   Notice that now the context menu now displays Mark as Read.

4. Choose Mark As Read from the context menu.

5. Click the top message in the Inbox, then hold down the (CTRL) key and click the second message from the top.
   The two messages should now have a selection highlight.

6. Right-click on one of the messages, then choose Mark As Unread from the menu bar.
   Now both of the selected messages are marked as unread. You can use the (SHIFT) and (CTRL) keys to select several messages at a time for the Mark as Read or Mark as Unread commands.

Delete Messages

7. Follow these steps to delete some email messages:
   Notice that the two messages you dragged have disappeared from the Inbox. Now one of the messages remaining in the Inbox is selected.

   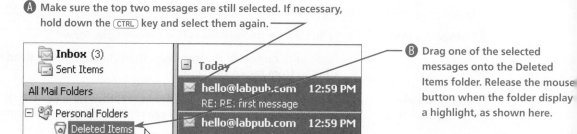

   Ⓐ Make sure the top two messages are still selected. If necessary, hold down the (CTRL) key and select them again.

   Ⓑ Drag one of the selected messages onto the Deleted Items folder. Release the mouse button when the folder display a highlight, as shown here.

8. Click the Delete ☒ button on the Outlook toolbar to delete the currently selected message.
   This message has also been sent to the Deleted Items folder.

9. Click the Deleted Items folder in the Navigation pane.
    You will see the messages you just deleted in Steps 7 and 8. The messages will stay in this folder until you "empty" the Deleted Items folder.

> **NOTE!** *Hotmail Users Only—Outlook will not display the message you sent to yourself in the Deleted Items folder. Instead, this message will be in your Hotmail Deleted Items folder. Skill Builder 6.3 will give you practice viewing this folder from within Outlook.*

10. Drag one of the messages in the Deleted Items view over the Inbox (or Hotmail Inbox) folder in the Navigation pane. Release the mouse button when you see a border around the Inbox folder, as shown to the right.
    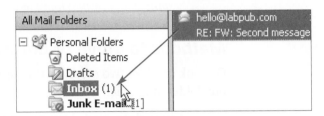
    You have just "undeleted" the message from the Deleted Items folder. Anytime you delete a message by mistake, you can retrieve it from the Deleted Items folder.

11. Drag-and-drop another message from Deleted Items into the Inbox.

12. Click the Inbox on the Navigation pane and confirm that both messages were undeleted.

Empty the Deleted Items Folder

13. Click the Deleted Items folder. Notice that one message you deleted earlier is still there.

> **NOTE!** *Hotmail Users Only—Your Outlook Deleted Items folder may be empty at this point; however, you can still perform the next step.*

14. Right-click the Deleted Items folder on the Navigation pane, then choose Empty "Deleted Items" Folder from the context menu.
    You will see a warning that you are about to permanently delete the contents of this folder. You cannot retrieve items after they have been emptied from the Deleted Items folder. However, when you permanently delete unneeded messages, they will no longer take up space on the computer's hard drive.

15. Choose Yes to confirm that the messages in the folder should be permanently deleted.
    The Deleted Items folder should now be empty.

Moving and Copying Messages

You learned how to create new folders in Lesson 5. Most of the time, you will create new folders in which to store specific Outlook items. For example, you can create a folder to store all of your email messages to and from a specific correspondent. Or, you can create a folder to store contacts from a specific organization, such as a club or a business. Once you have created an email folder, you can move and copy messages into it.

 TIP! *You can only move or copy email messages into a folder designated for this type of data. For example, you cannot move or copy email messages into the Contacts folder.*

Methods to Move or Copy Messages

Outlook provides two methods that are particularly useful for moving or copying messages from one folder to another:

- **Right-drag-and-drop method**—With this method, you select the items to be copied, display the folder to which you wish to copy the items, then use the right (not the left) mouse button to drag and drop the items into the destination folder on the Navigation pane. When you release the mouse button, Outlook displays a context menu from which you can choose the Move or Copy command.

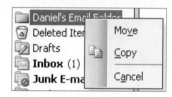

The right-drag-and-drop method displays a context menu to move or copy the selected items.

- **Menu method**—With this method, you select the items to be moved, then choose Edit→Move to Folder or Edit→Copy to Folder from the menu bar. Outlook displays the folder list and you choose the destination for the move or copy command.

 TIP! *These methods work for any type of Outlook item (such as appointments and tasks), not just email messages.*

QUICK REFERENCE: MOVING AND COPYING ITEMS TO A FOLDER

Task	Procedure
Move or copy items from one Outlook folder to another with the drag-and-drop commands.	■ Display the folder containing the items to be moved.
	■ Select the items to be moved. You can use the (CTRL) and (SHIFT) keys to select multiple items for the command.
(Right-drag method)	■ Point at one of the selected items to be moved, drag it with the right (not the left) mouse button to the destination folder, then release the mouse button.
	■ Choose Move or Copy from the context menu.
Move or copy items from one Outlook folder to another with the Move (or Copy) to Folder command.	■ Display the folder containing the items to be moved.
	■ Select the items to be moved. You can use the (CTRL) and (SHIFT) keys to select multiple items for the command.
(Menu method)	■ Choose Edit→Move to Folder or Edit→Copy to Folder from the (Menu method) menu bar.
	■ Select the destination folder from the folder list, then click OK.

Hands-On 6.9 Move Email Messages

In this exercise, you will move the email messages you received during this lesson into Your Email Folder.

Move Email Messages into a Folder

1. If necessary, choose the Inbox in the Navigation pane.

2. Click on the top message in the Inbox view, then hold down the (SHIFT) key and click on the first message you received during this lesson.

3. Choose Edit→Move to Folder from the menu bar.
   Outlook will display a folder list.

Hotmail/HTTP email Users Only—In the next step, remember that Your Email Folder is in Outlook Today [Personal Folders], not in your Hotmail/HTTP email folder.

4. Choose Your Email Folder in the dialog box, then click OK.
   The email messages will disappear from the Inbox as they are moved to your email folder.

5. Choose Your Email Folder in the Navigation pane.
   The email messages you moved should now appear in this folder.

6. Choose Edit→Select All from the menu bar.
    This selects all of the messages in Your Email Folder.

7. Follow these steps to execute the copy command with the drag-and-drop method:

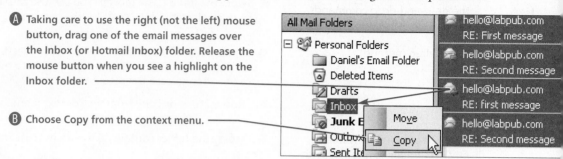

Ⓐ Taking care to use the right (not the left) mouse button, drag one of the email messages over the Inbox (or Hotmail Inbox) folder. Release the mouse button when you see a highlight on the Inbox folder. ————

Ⓑ Choose Copy from the context menu. ————

Notice that all of your messages remain in Your Email Folder, since this was a copy command rather than a move.

8. Choose the Inbox in the Navigation pane.
    The messages you copied in the previous step should be visible.

Delete Messages

Since you don't really need the extra copy of your messages in the Inbox, you will delete them.

9. Click the first message in the Inbox, then hold down the (SHIFT) key and click the last of your messages in the Today section.
    This will select all of the consecutive messages between the two clicks.

10. Tap the (DELETE) key on the keyboard.
    All of the selected messages are sent to the Deleted Items folder.

Exit Outlook

11. Choose File→Exit from the menu bar to close the Outlook program window.

Concepts Review

True/False Questions

1. Outlook's toolbar looks exactly the same, no matter which view you are using (such as the Inbox, Contacts, Calendar or Tasks). TRUE FALSE

2. You can set Outlook to automatically check for new mail. TRUE FALSE

3. When an email message arrives at the mail server at your company or ISP, it is immediately transmitted to your Inbox. TRUE FALSE

4. When you compose a message and click the Send button, the message is always immediately transmitted to the mail server that serves your email account. TRUE FALSE

5. To manually check for incoming email messages, click the Send/Receive button. TRUE FALSE

6. The Reply button automatically addresses a new message to the sender of the message to which you are replying. TRUE FALSE

7. You can use Outlook for email even if you do not have an ISP, online service, or business network system with which to connect. TRUE FALSE

8. Messages set as high priority are transmitted to their destination faster than messages set as low priority. TRUE FALSE

9. Once a message has been marked as read, you cannot change it back to unread. TRUE FALSE

10. When you flag a message for follow up, you can also prompt Outlook when to display a pop-up reminder about the message. TRUE FALSE

Multiple Choice Questions

1. What must you have in order to use email?
   a. An email program such as Outlook.
   b. An email account and an email program.
   c. An Internet connection, an email account, and an email program.
   d. An Internet connection.

2. Mail server programs usually run at which locations?
   a. Inside your computer.
   b. At the ISP that supports your account.
   c. At the company network (if you have a corporate email account).
   d. Both b and c

3. Which of the following is not a valid email address?
   a. bsmith@labpub.com
   b. smith@labpub.com
   c. bruce@labpub.com
   d. www.amazon.com
   e. Both b and d

4. What happens when you delete a message?
   a. The message is permanently deleted.
   b. The message is placed in the Deleted Items folder and may be retrieved.
   c. The message is archived and may be retrieved.
   d. None of the above

Skill Builders

Skill Builder 6.1 **Send a Message**

In this exercise, you will practice sending a message, then printing it.

 WebSim Users Only—If your computer does not have an email account, perform the following steps to start a WebSim for this and the next Skill Builder exercise:

- *Launch Internet Explorer.*
- *Click in the address bar, type* **labpub.com/learn/oe3**, *and then tap* (ENTER).
- *Click the Lesson 6 - Sending and Receiving Email hyperlink.*
- *Click the Skill Builder Exercise 6.1 hyperlink.*
- *Begin the exercise with Step 1.*

1. Start Outlook. You can use Start→E-Mail if you are running Windows XP. Enter your password if prompted to do so.

2. Make sure that the Inbox (or Hotmail Inbox) view is displayed.

3. Click the Send/Receive button on the Outlook toolbar. Read any new messages that may have been delivered.

Send a Message

4. Click the ⌐New button on the Outlook toolbar to start a new email message.

5. Address the message to **hello@labpub.com**.

6. Tap the (TAB) key two or three times until the insertion point is blinking in the Subject box, then type **The best film I've seen lately** in the subject line and tap the (TAB) key to jump to the body of the message.

7. Compose a brief message about the best film that you've seen recently, with perhaps a line or two about what you liked about it. Type your name at the bottom of the message.
   Note: don't give away the ending! ;-)

8. Click the ⌐Send button on the message toolbar to send your message to the Outbox.

9. Click the Send/Receive button on the Outlook toolbar.
   Your message is transmitted to the outgoing mail server system for delivery over the Internet to the addressee's incoming mail server system.

Print the Message You Just Sent

10. Display the Sent Items folder.

⚠️**NOTE!** *If you use Hotmail, be sure to choose the Sent Items folder in the Hotmail section of the email folders as shown at right.*

11. Make sure that The best film I've seen lately message is selected, then click Print 🖨 on the Outlook toolbar. Choose the Memo Print Style, then click OK. Retrieve the message from the printer.

12. Display the email Inbox.

Skill Builder 6.2 Check for Messages and Respond

WebSim *WebSim Users Only—There is a simulation for this exercise.*

In this exercise, you will check for a reply to the message you sent in the previous Skill Builder exercise.

1. Click the Send/Receive button on the Outlook toolbar. Continue to check for new messages until you receive a reply from Hello to your best film message.
Depending on the level of traffic on the Internet, the reply may take a few minutes to arrive.

2. Make sure the Inbox view is displayed. Select the new message and read it in the Preview Pane.

Change the Message Delivery Option

3. Choose Tools→Options from the Outlook toolbar, then click the Mail Setup tab.

4. Check the Send Immediately when Connected option. Click OK to close the Options window.

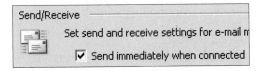

Now your messages will be transmitted to the outgoing mail server immediately when you click the Send *button on the message window.*

Forward the Message then Send a Reply

5. Forward the Most Unusual Film message to another student in the class or to yourself. In the body of the message, type **I'm forwarding this interesting comment on a film from someone named "Hello."** Enter your name as well. When you have finished typing in the body of the message, click Send.
   Outlook transmits the message immediately. It was unnecessary to type your name at the end of the message since it will appear on the From *line when the message is received.*

6. Make sure that the Most Unusual Film message is selected. Click ⟨Reply⟩ to start a reply to this message. Type a line or two about the most unusual film you've ever seen—do not change the subject line—then send the message.

7. After about one minute, click the Send/Receive button to check for newly arriving messages. If the response from hello@labpub.com does not arrive on your first try, repeat the Send/Receive command about every 30 seconds until you receive the response.

8. Read the response from Hello, then print it in Memo style.

Hotmail/HTTP Email Users Only—Unless you intend to perform the Assessment exercises at the end of this chapter during this class session, you should deactivate your Hotmail account. Perform Hands-On Exercise A.2 Deactivate Hotmail in Appendix A if you are finished working with email for this class session.

Skill Builder 6.3 Delete and Retrieve a Message

In this exercise, you will send an email message to the Deleted Item folder, then retrieve that message and put it back into your Inbox.

WebSim Users Only—You should repeat Hands-On Exercise B.2 in Appendix B before you perform Skill Builders 6.3 and 6.4. This will allow you to perform the exercises directly in Outlook.

1. Display the Inbox.

2. Select one of the messages you have received from hello@labpub.com.

3. Click the Delete ⓧ button on the Outlook toolbar.
   Although the message disappears from the Inbox, it has not yet been permanently deleted. Instead, the message has been placed into the Deleted Items *folder. As long as the message remains in Deleted Items, you can still retrieve it.*

⚠ **NOTE!** *Perform only the set of instructions that apply to your type of email account.*

POP Email Account (or No Email Account Installed)

4. Display the Deleted Items folder.

5. Using the right (not the left) mouse button, drag-and-drop the message you just deleted onto the Inbox folder in the Navigation pane to retrieve (undelete) the message. Choose Move from the context menu after you release the mouse button.
The message disappears from the Deleted Items folder.

6. Click the Inbox folder in the Navigation pane and confirm that the message was retrieved.
You are finished with this exercise. Continue with Skill Builder 6.4.

Hotmail or HTTP Email Account

4. Choose the Deleted Items folder under your Hotmail account folder list (not under Outlook Today).
Notice that the deleted message is in this list. This is the same list you would see if you viewed your account in a Web browser.

5. Using the right (not the left) mouse button, drag-and-drop the message you just deleted onto your Hotmail Inbox folder in the Navigation pane, then choose Move from the context menu.
Your message is undeleted and disappears from the Deleted Items folder.

6. Click the Hotmail Inbox folder in the Navigation pane and confirm that the message was undeleted.

Skill Builder 6.4 Move Messages to Your Email Folder

In this exercise, you will move all the messages you received during this lesson into Your Email folder. Then, using shortcut buttons, you will confirm that the messages were moved correctly.

1. Make sure that the Inbox is displayed.

2. Click the top message in the Inbox. While holding down the (SHIFT) key, click the last message in the Inbox that you have received during this work session.
The (SHIFT) key method is a very handy way to select several messages quickly.

3. Choose Edit→Move to Folder from the menu bar, then select Your Email Folder from the list and click OK.
The messages disappear from the Inbox. Now you will view Your Email Folder.

4. Choose Your Email Folder in the Navigation pane. Confirm that the messages were moved properly in the previous step.

5. Display the Inbox.
The Inbox or Calendar views are typically the best views to have visible while you work with Outlook.

Assessments

Assessment 6.1 Compose and Send a Message

1. Start Outlook.

2. Start a new email message, then follow these instructions to compose it:

To:	hello@labpub.com
Subject:	Email Facts
Message body	■ Compose a brief statement on the most important two facts about working with email that you have learned in this lesson.
	■ Be sure to type your name at the end of the message.

3. Send the message. Make sure that the message goes out to the outgoing mail server.

4. Check for a reply to your message.

Assessment 6.2 Reply to a Message

1. Reply to the RE: Email Facts message.

2. In the body of your reply, state one more fact about working with email that you learned in this lesson and type your name at the end of the message.

3. Send the message, then check for a response to the message.

4. You should now have received a total of two messages from hello@labpub.com.

Assessment 6.3 Print Messages from the Previous Assessment Exercises

1. Print both of the messages you received from hello@labpub.com in the previous two assessment exercises.

2. Print the message you sent in Assessment Exercise 6.1. (The message with the subject Email Facts. You can find it in the Sent Items view.)

3. After you have printed the three messages, turn in the printouts to your instructor for grading.

UNIT 4

Word 2003

The lessons in this unit give you practice using Word 2003 and many of its great features. You will learn how to create business letters, memoranda, reports, and flyers. You will also email Word documents. You will work with the Undo feature to reverse changes you make in a document. Whether you make a mistake or just change your mind, Word can fix it for you! You'll work with proofreading aids such as spell check and grammar check, and enrich your writing skills with the thesaurus. You will gain formatting skills to give your documents professional polish, and you'll work with Clip Art and other tools that add impact and pizzazz.

Use AutoComplete

1. Tap (ENTER) six times.
   Each time you tap (ENTER), the insertion point moves down one line. (ENTER) is used to insert blank lines in documents.

2. Notice the vertical position indicator on the status bar as shown below.

   The vertical position indicator shows the vertical position of the insertion point within the document.——

   | Page 1 | Sec 1 | 1/1 | At 2.1" | Ln 7 | Col 1 |

You can turn AutoComplete on and off via Insert→ AutoText→ AutoText then check or uncheck Show AutoComplete Suggestions.

3. Type the first few letters of the current month and tap (ENTER) to accept the month when the yellow date tip appears, as shown at the right.
   The example at the right uses February as the month. You should type the current month. AutoComplete only prompts for month names that are longer than four characters.

   February (Press ENTER to Inser

4. If AutoComplete displays the tip, continue typing until it suggests the rest of the date and tap (ENTER). Otherwise, complete today's date by typing it.
   You can always accept an item that AutoComplete proposes by tapping (ENTER).

Complete the Inside Address

5. Tap (ENTER) four times.
   Business letters require four returns after the date. Word will most likely underline the date with a purple dotted line. This indicates that a smart tag is associated with the date.

Turn Smart tags on and off by issuing the Tools→ AutoCorrect Options command then checking or unchecking the desired choices on the Smart Tags tab.

6. Position the mouse pointer over the date to display the Smart Tag button.

7. Click the Smart Tag ⑤ button to display the list of available actions.

8. Choose Remove This Smart Tag to remove the tag.
   This example showed you how to remove a smart tag. However, it isn't necessary to remove smart tags unless you find them distracting.

9. Now complete the inside address and salutation as shown to the right.
   Only tap (ENTER) in the locations indicated.

   February 10, 2004 [ENTER]
   [ENTER]
   [ENTER]
   [ENTER]
   Ms. Sandra Smith [ENTER]
   Vice President of Operations [ENTER]
   Integrated Office Solutions, Inc. [ENTER]
   2756 Industrial Lane, Suite 104 [ENTER]
   Los Angeles, CA 90024 [ENTER]
   [ENTER]
   Dear Ms. Smith: [ENTER]
   [ENTER]

10. Now complete the letter as shown below. Only tap (ENTER) in the indicated locations. Use (BACKSPACE) to correct any typing mistakes. Word automatically checks spelling and grammar as you type. Word underlines misspelled words with wavy red underlines and grammar errors with wavy green underlines. For now, ignore any red or green underlining that may appear.

Dear Ms. Smith:

It was a pleasure meeting with you yesterday. Both Richard Brown and I were quite impressed with your facilities and the quality of your team. You certainly have a group of hard-working people. [Enter]
[Enter]
Our meeting was designed to give you an overview of our copiers, laser printers, fax machines, and digital scanners. We would like to follow up our presentation with a live demonstration. You must see our products in action to truly appreciate their benefits. I will contact you early next week to arrange a demonstration. [Enter]
[Enter]
In the meantime, please feel free to contact me if I can be of further assistance. [Enter]
[Enter]
Sincerely, [Enter]
[Enter]
[Enter]
[Enter]
Susan Adams [Enter]
Sales Representative

Save Concepts

One important lesson to learn is to save your documents frequently! Power outages and careless accidents can result in lost data. The best protection is to save your documents every 10 or 15 minutes, or after making significant changes. Documents are saved to storage locations such as floppy disks, hard disks, or to Web sites on the Internet.

Save Command

The Save 🖫 button on the Standard toolbar and the File→Save command both initiate the Save command. If the document had previously been saved, then Word replaces the previous version with the new edited version. If the document had never been saved, then Word displays the Save As dialog box. The Save As dialog box lets you specify the name and storage location of the document. You can also use the Save As dialog box to make a copy of a document by saving it under a new name or to a different location. You can use filenames containing as many as 255 characters. The following illustration describes the Save As dialog box.

FROM THE KEYBOARD
(CTRL)+(S) for save

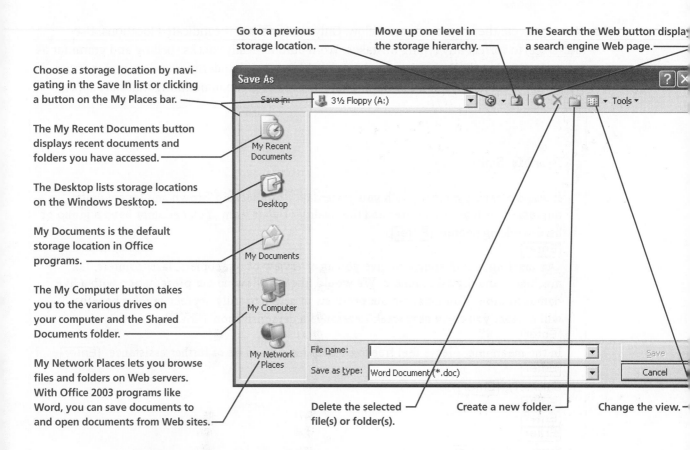

Go to a previous storage location.

Move up one level in the storage hierarchy.

The Search the Web button displays a search engine Web page.

Choose a storage location by navigating in the Save In list or clicking a button on the My Places bar.

The My Recent Documents button displays recent documents and folders you have accessed.

The Desktop lists storage locations on the Windows Desktop.

My Documents is the default storage location in Office programs.

The My Computer button takes you to the various drives on your computer and the Shared Documents folder.

My Network Places lets you browse files and folders on Web servers. With Office 2003 programs like Word, you can save documents to and open documents from Web sites.

Delete the selected file(s) or folder(s).

Create a new folder.

Change the view.

Storing Your Exercise Files

This book contains a single floppy disk located on the inside back cover with various files used in many exercises. You will also create entirely new files for some lessons and save them to a storage location. The exercises in this book assume that you will store and open files on a floppy disk. However, you can also save files to another storage location such as the My Documents folder or a USB flash drive. Appendix A at the back of this book contains detailed instructions on the use of these alternative file storage locations.

 NOTE! *Take a moment to review Appendix A now if you do not intend to store your exercise files for the book on a floppy disk.*

Hands-On 7.3 **Save the Letter**

⚠️ **IMPORTANT!** *The Standard and Formatting toolbars can appear in either one row (side by side) or in two rows (one on top of the other). If the toolbars are in one row, some of the buttons may be hidden. Click the Toolbar Options* 🔽 *button at the end of each toolbar to reveal any hidden buttons for that toolbar. You can also click this button to choose whether the toolbars appear on one or two rows.*

In this exercise, you will save the letter that was created in the previous exercise.

Before You Begin: Please see Appendix A if you intend to save your files to a storage location other than the floppy disk.

1. Click the Save 💾 button and the Save As dialog box will appear.

2. Follow these steps to save the letter:
   Keep in mind that your dialog box will contain more files than shown here.

Ⓐ Click here and choose the disk drive with your exercise diskette. ⎯⎯⎯

Ⓑ Notice that Word proposes the first part of the date as the name. Word always proposes the first line of text as the filename.

Ⓒ Type the name **Hands-On Lesson 7** and it will replace the proposed name. (If you switched disk drives, then you may need to click in the File Name box, delete the proposed name with the (DELETE) and/or (BACKSPACE) key, then type the new name.) ⎯⎯⎯

Ⓓ Click the Save button.

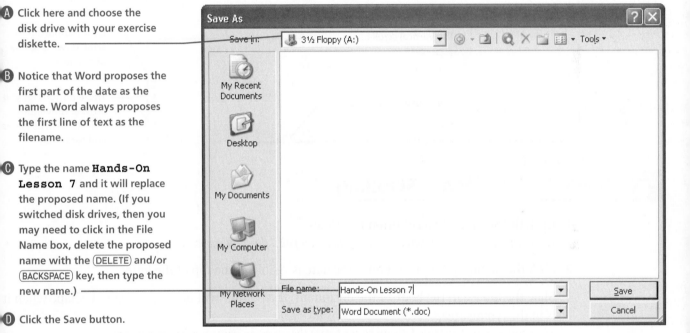

Notice that the letter was saved and remains on the screen. You will continue to use the letter throughout this lesson.

Scrolling Documents and Repositioning the Insertion Point

The vertical and horizontal scroll bars let you browse through documents. However, scrolling does not move the insertion point. You must click in the document to reposition the insertion point. The vertical scroll bar is on the right side of the document window and the horizontal scroll bar is at the bottom of the document window. Scroll bars also appear in many dialog boxes. The following illustration shows the scroll bars and their components.

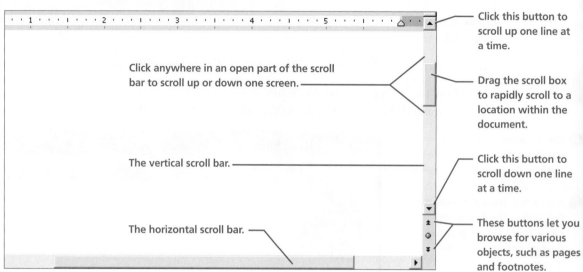

Click this button to scroll up one line at a time.

Click anywhere in an open part of the scroll bar to scroll up or down one screen.

Drag the scroll box to rapidly scroll to a location within the document.

The vertical scroll bar.

Click this button to scroll down one line at a time.

The horizontal scroll bar.

These buttons let you browse for various objects, such as pages and footnotes.

 ## Hands-On 7.4 Practice Scrolling

1. Click the Scroll Down ▾ button five times.
   Notice that the document scrolls, but the insertion point does not move.

2. Click the Scroll Up ▴ button until the date is visible at the top of the letter.

3. Slide the mouse in the body of the document; the pointer will have an I-Beam I shape when it is in the typing area.
   The pointer must have this I-Beam shape before the insertion point can be repositioned.

4. Click the I-Beam anywhere on the date, and the blinking insertion point will be positioned there.

5. Move the I-Beam into the left margin area, and it will become an arrow ⇖.
   This arrow should not be present if you are trying to reposition the insertion point.

6. Position the I-Beam on the first line of the inside address just in front of Ms., and click the left mouse button.
   The insertion point should be positioned just in front of Ms. If a black background appears behind the text, then you have accidentally selected it. Selecting is discussed later in this lesson. If you accidentally selected the text, then deselect it by clicking the mouse pointer outside of it.

7. Take a few minutes to practice scrolling and repositioning the insertion point.

Inserting and Overtyping Text

You will almost always work in Insert mode.

Insert mode is the default editing mode in Word. In insert mode, existing text moves to the right as new text is typed. The new text is thus inserted into the document. Thus far, you have been working in insert mode. In overtype mode, existing text is replaced as new text is typed. You switch between insert mode and overtype mode by double-clicking the OVR (overtype) indicator on the status bar as shown in the following illustration.

Double-clicking the OVR (overtype) indicator switches between insert mode and overtype mode. The mode is set to overtype when the OVR indicator is bold as shown here.

Page 1	Sec 1	1/1	At 1"	Ln 1	Col 1	REC	TRK	EXT	OVR	

 ## Hands-On 7.5 Inserting and Overtyping Text

Insert Text

1. Click just in front of the word *yesterday* in the first body paragraph as shown below.

2. Type the phrase **and the rest of your staff**, and tap the (SPACE BAR) once.

Click here

It was a pleasure meeting with you |yesterday.

3. Use the technique in Steps 1 and 2 to insert the phrase **and creative** in front of the word *people* at the end of the paragraph. The completed paragraph is shown below.

Overtype Text

It was a pleasure meeting with you and the rest of your staff yesterday. Both Richard Brown and I were quite impressed with your facilities and the quality of your team. You certainly have a group of hard-working and creative people.

4. Position the insertion point in the inside address in front of the *S* in *Smith*.

5. Double-click the OVR button on the status bar.
   The OVR button should now appear bold.

6. Type the word **Evans**, and *Smith* should be replaced by *Evans*.
   If insert mode had been active, the name Smith would have moved to the right, making room for Evans.

7. Now click in front of the name *Smith* in the salutation line, and type **Evans**.

8. Double-click the OVR button on the status bar when you have finished.
   The letters OVR will be dimmed on the status bar, indicating that insert mode is active.

9. Click the Save 🖫 button to save the changes to your exercise diskette.

Selecting Text

You must select text if you wish to perform some action on that text. Suppose you want to delete an entire paragraph. You would select the paragraph first and then tap the (DELETE) key. Selected text is usually displayed in white on a black background. The illustration to the right shows a selected paragraph in the inside address of your letter.

Ms. Sandra Evans
Vice President of Operations
Integrated Office Solutions, Inc.

Selection Techniques

Word provides many selection techniques using both the mouse and keyboard. The mouse techniques are usually more intuitive; however, beginners may find it difficult to control the mouse. The keyboard techniques tend to provide greater control. You can use the keyboard techniques if you have difficulty controlling the mouse. The following quick reference table illustrates the available selection techniques.

QUICK REFERENCE: SELECTION TECHNIQUES

Item to be Selected	Mouse Technique	Keyboard Technique
One word	Double-click the desired word.	Click at beginning of word, press and hold (SHIFT) and (CTRL) while tapping (→).
A phrase or continuous section of text	Drag the I-beam I in any direction over the desired text.	Click at beginning of phrase, press and hold (SHIFT) while tapping any arrow keys. You can also click at beginning of phrase, press and hold (SHIFT), and then click at end of phrase.
A line	Position the mouse pointer to the left of the line, and click when the pointer has an arrow shape.	Press (SHIFT)+(END) to select from insertion point to end of line. Press (SHIFT)+(HOME) to select from insertion point to beginning of line.
One paragraph	Triple-click anywhere on the paragraph. You can also position the mouse pointer to the left of the paragraph in the margin and double-click when the pointer has an arrow shape.	
Multiple paragraphs	Drag the I-beam I over the desired paragraphs. You can also position the mouse pointer to the left of the paragraphs and drag up or down when the pointer has an arrow shape.	
Entire document	Triple-click to the left of any paragraph, or press and hold (CTRL) and click to the left of any paragraph.	Press (CTRL)+(A) to execute Select All command, or press (CTRL) and click in left margin.
Noncontiguous Areas	Press and hold the (CTRL) key while dragging over the selected text.	

Hands-On 7.6 Practice Selecting Text

Select Using the Left Margin

1. Follow these steps to select text using the left margin:

A Place the mouse pointer to the left of this line and it will have this shape. Click the mouse button to select the entire line. ⟶

B Click here to select this line. Notice that the previously selected paragraph is no longer selected. ⟶

C Select this paragraph by double-clicking in front of it. ⟶

Ms. Sandra Evans
Vice President of Operations
Integrated Office Solutions, Inc.
2756 Industrial Lane, Suite 104
Los Angeles, CA 90024

Dear Ms. Evans:

It was a pleasure meeting with you and the rest of your staff yesterday. Both Richard Brown and I were quite impressed with your facilities and the quality of your team. You certainly have a group of hard-working and creative people.

2. Try dragging the mouse pointer 𝄞 down in the left margin.
   Be sure to press and hold the left mouse button as you drag, and multiple lines will be selected.

TIP!

Also, you can select the entire document by pressing (CTRL) and clicking in the left margin.

3. Try triple-clicking the mouse pointer 𝄞 anywhere in the left margin.
   The entire document will become selected. Triple clicking can be tricky, so you may need to try it several times.

4. Deselect the document by clicking anywhere in the text area.

Select Words

5. Double-click the I-beam I on any word.
   The word should become selected.

6. Double-click a different word, and notice that the previous word has been deselected.

7. Select five different words one after another by double-clicking them.

8. Deselect the last word you selected by clicking the I-Beam I anywhere outside of it.

Noncontiguous Selections

9. Select any word or paragraph.

10. Press and hold the (CTRL) key while you select another word or paragraph.
    Both your first and your second selections will be in effect. You can select as many noncontiguous areas of a document as desired using this technique. This can be quite useful when formatting documents.

Drag Select

11. Follow these steps to drag select a phrase:

A Position the I-beam here just in front of *It was a pleasure . . .*

B Press and hold the left mouse button, then drag to the right until the phrase *It was a pleasure meeting with you* is selected.

C Release the mouse button and the text will remain selected.

Dear Ms. Evans:

⎯⎯⎯⎯⎯⎯⎯⎯⎯⎯⎯⎯⎯⎯➤

It was a pleasure meeting with you and the rest of your staff Brown and I were quite impressed with your facilities and t certainly have a group of hard-working and creative people.

12. Practice drag selecting text in the second large paragraph. Try dragging the mouse in all directions.
    Notice how the selection block expands and contracts as you move the mouse.

!TIP!

Use Undo if you accidentally move text. Undo is discussed at the bottom of this page.

13. Deselect by clicking anywhere on the selected text.

14. Take two minutes to practice selecting text using the drag technique.

15. Take five minutes to practice selecting text using all of the techniques discussed in the table at the beginning of this topic. In particular, try using the keystroke techniques discussed in the table.

Editing Text

FROM THE KEYBOARD

(CTRL)+(BACKSPACE) to delete from insertion point to beginning of word.
(CTRL)+(DELETE) to delete from insertion point to end of word.

The (DELETE) and (BACKSPACE) keys are used to remove text from a document. (DELETE) removes the character to the right of the insertion point and (BACKSPACE) removes the character to the left of the insertion point. You can also remove an entire selection by tapping (DELETE) or (BACKSPACE). If you are removing just a few characters, it is usually more efficient to click in front of the characters and tap (DELETE) one or more times. If you are removing a word, phrase, or paragraph, it is more efficient to select the desired text and then tap (DELETE) to remove the selection.

You can replace text by selecting the desired text and then typing the replacement text. Selected text is removed as you begin typing replacement text. The replacement text is then inserted in the document as you continue to type.

Undo and Redo

Word's Undo button lets you reverse your last editing action(s). You can reverse simple actions such as accidental text deletions, or you can reverse more complex actions such as margin changes. Most actions can be undone. Actions that cannot be undone include commands such as printing documents and saving documents.

FROM THE KEYBOARD

(CTRL)+(Z) for undo
(CTRL)+(Y) for redo

The Redo button reverses Undo. Use Redo when you Undo an action but decide to go through with that action after all.

Undoing and Redoing Multiple Actions

The arrows ⏷ on the Undo and Redo buttons display lists of actions that can be undone or redone. You can undo or redo multiple actions by dragging the mouse over the desired actions. You can undo or redo an almost unlimited number of actions using this method. However, you must undo or redo actions in the order in which they appear on the drop-down list.

Repeat

The Edit→Repeat command lets you repeat your last action. For example, imagine you want to change the font size at several locations in a document. To accomplish this, you could change the font size at one location, reposition the insertion point, and then issue the Repeat command. The Repeat command would set the font size at the new location to the same size you set at the previous location. You can repeat an action as many times as desired. However, the Repeat command is only available when the Redo button is unavailable. The Edit→Repeat command changes to Edit→Redo as soon as you undo an action.

FROM THE KEYBOARD
CTRL + Y for repeat

Hands-On 7.7 Edit the Letter and Use Undo

Delete Several Words

1. Follow these steps to delete text from the inside address block:

Ⓐ Drag the mouse pointer over the phrase *of Operations* as shown here. ⎯

Ⓑ Tap DELETE to remove the phrase, then tap BACKSPACE to remove the space after the word President.

```
Ms. Sandra Evans
Vice President of Operations
Integrated Office Solutions, Inc.
2756 Industrial Lane, Suite 104
```

Ⓒ Select the word *Inc* by double-clicking it, then tap DELETE to delete the word.

Ⓓ Tap DELETE once to remove the period, then tap BACKSPACE once to remove the comma.

Ⓔ Click in front of this comma, then tap DELETE repeatedly to remove *, Suite 104*.

Select and Replace Words

2. Follow these steps to select and replace several words and to insert a phrase:

Ⓐ Double-click the last name *Brown* and type the replacement name **Jones**. ⎯

Ⓑ Double-click the word *meeting* and type the replacement word **presentation**.

Ⓒ Click in front of the word *copiers*, type the phrase **high-performance**, and tap SPACE BAR. The new phrase should be inserted in front of the word *copiers*.

It was a pleasure meeting with you and the rest of your staff yesterday. Brown and I were quite impressed with your facilities and the quality of certainly have a group of hard-working and creative people.

Our meeting was designed to give you an overview of our copiers, laser machines, and digital scanners. We would like to follow up our presenta demonstration. You must see our products in action to truly appreciate t will contact you early next week to arrange a demonstration.

In the meantime, please feel free to contact us if we can be of further as

Ⓓ Select the word *us* and type the replacement word **me**. ⎯

Ⓔ Replace *we* with **I**.

Use Undo to Override AutoCorrect

! TIP!

To turn off Auto
capitalization,
choose Tools→
AutoCorrect
Options and
uncheck the
Capitalize First
Letter Of
Sentences box.

AutoCorrect is a tool that automatically corrects many common spelling errors, and looks for other potential problems. One of these potential problems is the lack of capitalization at the start of a sentence. AutoCorrect will automatically capitalize the first letter of a sentence if you fail to capitalize it yourself. This is acceptable most of the time, but there are occasions when you may want to override AutoCorrect.

3. Scroll to the bottom of the document, and click to the right of the title Sales Representative in the signature block.

4. Tap (ENTER) twice.

5. Type your initials in lowercase, and then type a colon (**:**).
   AutoCorrect should spring into action, capitalizing your first initial. Unfortunately, typists initials should appear in lowercase in business correspondence.

6. Click Undo, 🔄 and the capital letter should return to lowercase.
   You can always use Undo to override AutoCorrect.

7. Tap (SPACE BAR), and type the document name **Hands-On Lesson 7**.
   The completed signature block should be xx: Hands-On Lesson 7, where xx are your initials.

8. Click Save 💾 to save the changes to your document.

! IMPORTANT! *It is important to save now because you will begin experimenting with Undo and Redo.*

Practice Using Undo and Redo

9. Delete any word in the letter.

10. Click Undo 🔄 and the word will be restored.

11. Select any paragraph, then tap (DELETE) to remove the paragraph.

12. Click Undo 🔄 to restore the paragraph.

13. Click Redo 🔄 and the paragraph will vanish again.
    Redo always reverses the most recent Undo.

14. Click Undo 🔄 again to restore the paragraph.

Undo and Redo Multiple Actions

15. Follow these steps to explore the Undo actions list, and to delete three items:

Ⓐ Click the drop-down button next to Undo, and a list of all preceding actions will be displayed. Don't worry if your list does not match the list in this illustration. ⎯⎯

Ⓑ Use the scroll bar to browse through the list of actions. Scroll to the top of the list when you are finished browsing and make a mental note of the first three or four actions on the list. ⎯⎯

Ⓒ Tap the ⌈ESC⌋ key to close the list.

Ⓓ Select the month, and delete it. ⎯⎯

Ⓔ Delete the word Vice from the title. ⎯⎯

Ⓕ Select the street number 2756, and type the replacement number **2989**. ⎯⎯

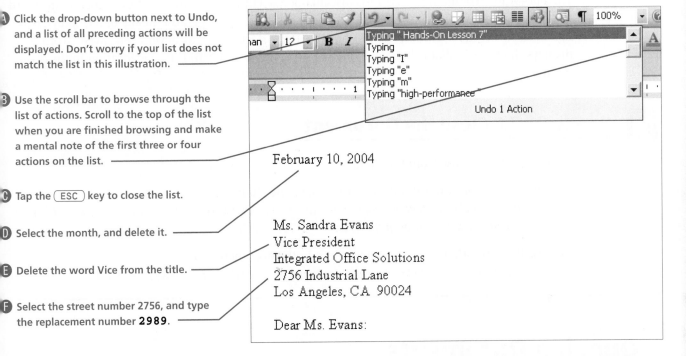

16. Follow these steps to undo the last few changes:

Ⓐ Click the Undo drop-down button, and notice that the last few changes are at the top of the list. Your most recent action was typing the number 2989, so it appears on top of the list. Each action is given a descriptive name to help identify it.⎯⎯

Ⓑ Position the mouse pointer on the first action, at the top of the list then slide the mouse down (there is no need to press the mouse button) highlighting up to Typing "Hands-On Lesson 7" as shown here.⎯⎯

Ⓒ Click when the actions are selected, and the recent changes will be undone. Your document should be exactly as it was prior to making the changes.

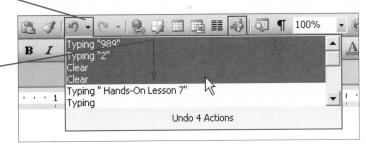

17. Feel free to experiment with Undo and Redo.

Closing Documents

The File→Close command is used to close an open document. When you close a document, Word prompts you to save the changes. If you choose Yes at the prompt, and the document previously had been saved, then Word saves the changes. If the document has never been saved, Word displays the Save As dialog box, allowing you to assign a name and storage location to the document.

 Hands-On 7.8 Close the Document

1. Choose File→Close from the menu bar.

2. Click the No button if Word asks you to save the changes.
   You can always close without saving to eliminate changes that have occurred since the last save. The next exercise will instruct you to open the letter.

3. Finally, notice that there is no document in the document window.
   The document window always has this appearance when all documents have been closed.

Opening Documents

FROM THE KEYBOARD

(CTRL)+(O) to display open dialog box.

The Open [icon] button on the Standard toolbar and the File→Open command display the Open dialog box. The Open dialog box lets you navigate to any storage location and open previously saved documents. Once a document is open, you can browse it, print it, or even make editing changes. The organization and layout of the Open dialog box is similar to the Save dialog box discussed earlier in this lesson.

Hands-On 7.9 **Open the Letter**

1. Click Open on the Standard toolbar.

2. Follow these steps to open the Hands-On Lesson 7 document:
   Keep in mind that your dialog box will display files not shown here.

A Choose the disk drive containing your exercise diskette. It is most likely in 3½ Floppy (A:).

B Choose the file named Hands-On Lesson 7.

C Click the Open button.

⚠️ **TIP!**

You can also double-click a document on the list.

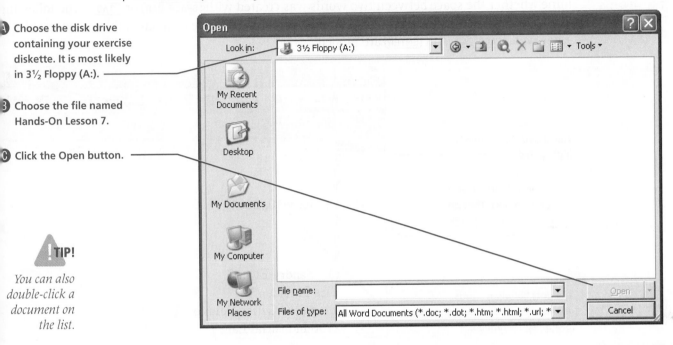

Showing Nonprinting Characters

The Show/Hide ¶ button on the Standard toolbar shows or hides all nonprinting characters in a document. Nonprinting characters include spaces, tab characters, and carriage returns that do not appear on the printed page. Showing these characters can be important, especially when editing a document. For example, you may need to display the nonprinting characters to determine whether the space between two words was created with (SPACE BAR) or (TAB). The following illustration shows the location of the Show/Hide button and the characters that are inserted whenever (SPACE BAR) and (ENTER) are tapped.

FROM THE KEYBOARD

(CTRL)+(SHIFT)+(8)
to show or hide
characters

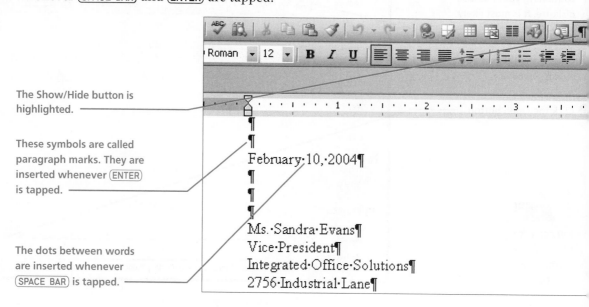

The Show/Hide button is highlighted.

These symbols are called paragraph marks. They are inserted whenever (ENTER) is tapped.

The dots between words are inserted whenever (SPACE BAR) is tapped.

Inserting and Deleting Paragraph Marks

Paragraph marks ¶ (or carriage returns) play an important role in Word documents. Every paragraph ends with a paragraph mark. A paragraph mark is inserted whenever (ENTER) is tapped. Paragraph marks affect the appearance and format of documents. You may need to delete paragraph marks as you edit and format documents. For example, suppose you want to combine two paragraphs into one large paragraph. To accomplish this, you would delete the paragraph mark separating the paragraphs. It is usually best to display the nonprinting characters with the Show/Hide button before deleting paragraph marks and other nonprinting characters. You can delete the paragraph mark to the right of the insertion point using (DELETE).

Hands-On 7.10 Insert and Delete Paragraph Marks

In this exercise, you will restructure several paragraphs in the letter. Remember to use Undo if you make a mistake.

Combine Two Paragraphs

1. Click Show/Hide ¶ to display the symbols.

2. Position the insertion point in front of the paragraph mark at the end of the second main paragraph as shown here.

> presentation·with·a·live·demonstration.·You·must·see·our·products·in·action·to·truly·
> appreciate·their·benefits.·I·will·contact·you·early·next·week·to·arrange·a·demonstration.¶
> ¶
> In·the·meantime,·please·feel·free·to·contact·me·if·I·can·be·of·further·assistance.¶

Position insertion point here.

3. Tap (DELETE) once.
   The paragraph mark to the right of the insertion point will be deleted. The mark below the paragraph will immediately move up to take its place. Notice that the gap between the paragraphs is no longer a double-space.

4. Tap (DELETE) again, and the paragraphs will be joined together.

5. Tap (SPACE BAR) once to create space between the two sentences in the combined paragraph.

Split the Combined Paragraph

6. Follow these steps to split the paragraph into two smaller paragraphs:

> Our·presentation·was·designed·to·give·you·an·overview·of·our·high-performance·copiers,·
> laser·printers,·fax·machines,·and·digital·scanners.·We·would·like·to·follow·up·our·
> presentation·with·a·live·demonstration.·You·must·see·our·products·in·action·to·truly·
> appreciate·their·benefits.·I·will·contact·you·early·next·week·to·arrange·a·demonstration.·In·
> the·meantime,·please·feel·free·to·contact·me·if·I·can·be·of·further·assistance.¶

A Click here just in front of the word I.

B Tap (ENTER) twice to push the last two sentences down and to form a new paragraph.

7. Click Show/Hide ¶ to hide the symbols.

Print Preview

The Print Preview button and the File→Print Preview command display the Print Preview window, which shows how a document will look when it is printed. Print Preview can save time, paper, and wear-and-tear on your printer. Print Preview is especially useful when printing long documents, or with documents containing intricate graphics and formatting. It is always wise to preview a long or complex document before sending it to the printer.

When you display the Print Preview window, the standard toolbars are replaced by the Print Preview toolbar. The following illustration describes the important buttons on the Print Preview toolbar.

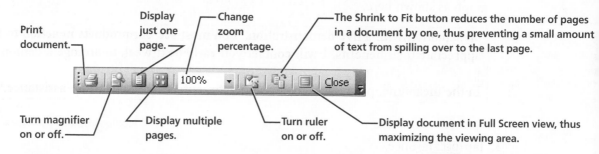

Hands-On 7.11 Use Print Preview

1. Click Print Preview on the Standard toolbar.

2. Make sure the Magnifier button is highlighted on the toolbar.

3. Position the mouse pointer over the document, and the pointer will look like a magnifying glass.

4. Zoom in by clicking anywhere on the document.

5. Zoom out by clicking anywhere on the document.
You can zoom in and out whenever the magnifier is on. When the magnifier is off, the mouse pointer functions normally, allowing you to edit the document in Print Preview mode.

6. Feel free to experiment with the other buttons on the Print Preview toolbar.

7. When you have finished, click the Close button on the Print Preview toolbar to exit from Print Preview.

Printing

The Print button on the Standard toolbar sends the entire document to the current printer. You must display the Print dialog box if you want to change printers, specify the number of copies to be printed, print selected pages, and to set other printing options. The Print dialog box is displayed with the File→Print command. When you print a document, a printer icon appears on the status bar. The Printer icon indicates that Word is processing the print job and is preparing to send the job to the printer. The following illustration explains the most important options available in the Print dialog box.

FROM THE KEYBOARD

(CTRL)+(P) to display Print dialog box

You choose printers from this drop-down list.

You can specify the number of copies here. The Collate option is useful when you are printing more than one copy of a multiple page document. If the Collate box is checked, the first copy is printed before the second copy begins printing, etc.

You can choose to print all pages, the current page, or a range of pages. You specify a range of pages by typing the desired range in the Pages box. The example text below the Pages box shows the entry required to print pages 1, 3, and 5 through 12.

You can choose to print odd or even pages only with the Print option.

The Pages Per Sheet option lets you print multiple copies of the document on a single page. For example, you may want to print several business cards on a single page. The Scale to Paper Size option lets you squeeze a document onto various predefined paper sizes.

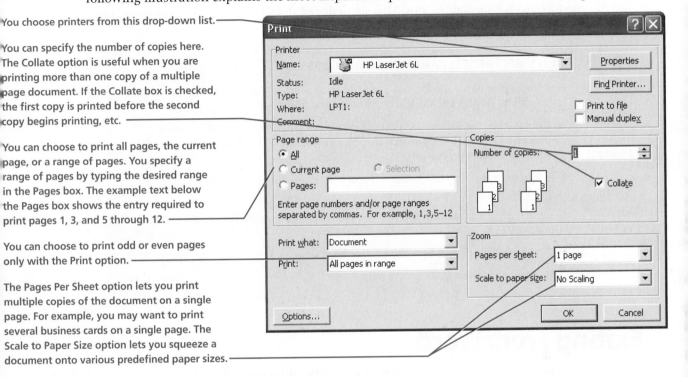

Hands-On 7.12 Print the Document

1. Choose File→Print to display the Print dialog box.

2. Take a few moments to check out the dialog box options.

3. When you are ready to print, make sure the options are set as shown in the preceding illustration, and click the OK button.
   Keep in mind that your printer will probably be different than the printer shown in the Name box in the illustration.

4. Retrieve your document from the printer.

Canceling Print Jobs

Sometimes you will want to cancel a print job after issuing the Print command. When you print a document, Word processes the print job and sends it to the printer. Most modern printers contain memory where the print job is stored while it is being printed. For this reason, it is not always possible to terminate a print job from Word or other Office programs. The difficult work of canceling the print job must often be done at the printer. This is especially true with newer computers. Newer computers are so fast that the print job is often sent to the printer before you have time to cancel it from within the application. The following quick reference steps can be used to effectively cancel print jobs. This sequence of steps is designed to save paper, prevent jamming of the printer, and effectively terminate the print job.

QUICK REFERENCE: CANCELING PRINT JOBS

- Remove the paper stack from the printer, or remove the paper tray. You should be able to do this even if the printer is in the middle of printing a page.

- Double-click the Printer icon on the status bar. This will terminate further processing of the job by Word. The Printer icon won't be visible if Word has finished processing the job.

- If a page was being printed when you pulled out the paper tray, make sure it has finished printing.

- Switch off the power on the printer. This will clear the job out of the printer's memory.

- Pause 30 seconds and turn the printer back on.

- Reinsert the paper stack or the paper tray.

Turning off the printer may disrupt other users in a networked computer lab or office environment.

Exiting From Word

The File→Exit command is used to close the Word program. You should close Word and other programs if you are certain you won't be using them for some time. This will free up memory for other programs. When you close Word, you will be prompted to save any documents that have unsaved edits.

Hands-On 7.13 Exit from Word

1. Choose File→Exit from the menu bar.

2. Choose Yes when Word asks if you would like to save the changes.
   Word will close, and the Windows desktop will appear. Continue with the questions and exercises on the following pages.

Concepts Review

True/False Questions

1. The insertion point is automatically repositioned when you scroll through a document. TRUE FALSE

2. (ENTER) can be used to end one paragraph and begin another. TRUE FALSE

3. The Show/Hide button is used to display nonprinting characters, such as paragraph marks. TRUE FALSE

4. The (ENTER) key should be tapped twice when creating space between the date and the inside address in a business letter. TRUE FALSE

5. A single word can be selected by clicking once on the word. TRUE FALSE

6. Paragraph marks cannot be deleted once they have been inserted in a document. TRUE FALSE

7. (BACKSPACE) deletes the character to the right of the insertion point. TRUE FALSE

8. The (SHIFT) key is used to select noncontiguous parts of a document. TRUE FALSE

9. You can change printers by clicking the drop-down arrow on the Print button and choosing a printer from the list. TRUE FALSE

10. If you type "7, 10, 15-18" in the Pages field of the Print dialog box, pages 7, 10, and 15 through 18 will print. TRUE FALSE

Multiple Choice Questions

1. Which shape does the mouse pointer have when it is in the text area?
   a. Right-pointing arrow
   b. I-beam
   c. Left-pointing arrow
   d. None of the above

2. Which of the following methods can be used to select a paragraph?
   a. Double-click anywhere in the paragraph.
   b. Triple-click anywhere in the paragraph.
   c. Triple-click anywhere in the left margin.
   d. None of the above

3. What is happening if your existing text is disappearing as you type new text?
   a. You are in overtype mode.
   b. You are in insert mode.
   c. You are tapping (DELETE) by accident.
   d. None of the above

4. Which of the following statements is true?
   a. Undo is only available if Redo has been used.
   b. Redo is only available if Undo has been used.
   c. Both a and b
   d. Neither a nor b

Skill Builders

Skill Builder 7.1 Create a Block Style Letter

1. Start Word, and a new document window will appear. If you did not exit Word at the end of the last exercise, then click the New Blank Document button on the Standard toolbar (first button on the toolbar). The New Blank Document button is used to open a new document.

2. Type the following letter, tapping (ENTER) only as indicated. Notice the six hard returns shown at the top of the document. These hard returns position the date at approximately the 2" position.

ENTER
ENTER
ENTER
ENTER
ENTER
ENTER
February 10, 2004 ENTER
ENTER
ENTER
ENTER
Ms. Melissa Thompson ENTER
Customer Service Representative ENTER
Urbana Software Services ENTER
810 Ivanhoe Way ENTER
Urbana, IL 61801 ENTER
ENTER
Dear Ms. Thompson: ENTER
ENTER
I would like to take this opportunity to thank you for your excellent customer service.
You were patient, courteous, and very helpful. The installation assistance you provided
was invaluable. ENTER
ENTER
I have already put your program to good use. As you know, application programs can
boost personal productivity. Your program has allowed me to manage my business much
more effectively. I have enclosed the $45 fee you requested. ENTER
ENTER
Please send me a receipt and a catalog. ENTER
ENTER
Sincerely, ENTER
ENTER
ENTER
ENTER
Denise Smith ENTER
Administrative Assistant ENTER

3. Use Show/Hide ¶ to display the hidden characters.

4. Position the insertion point just in front of the sentence *I have enclosed the $45 . . .* in the second paragraph, and tap (ENTER) twice to create a new paragraph.

5. Position the insertion point at the end of the new paragraph just in front of the paragraph mark.

6. Tap (DELETE) twice to remove the two paragraph marks separating the new paragraph from the following paragraph.

7. Tap (SPACE BAR) once to insert a space between the two sentences in the combined paragraph.

8. Position the insertion point just to the right of the sentence *The installation assistance . . .* at the end of the first paragraph. The insertion point should be just to the right of the period ending the sentence.

9. Tap (SPACE BAR), and then type the sentence **I also appreciate the overnight delivery.**

10. Type **The program is also a lot of fun.** at the end of the second paragraph.

11. Insert your initials, below the signature block.

12. Save the document to your exercise diskette with the name **Skill Builder 7.1**; then close the document.

Skill Builder 7.2 Edit a Document

1. Click Open 📂 on the Standard toolbar.

2. Navigate to your exercise diskette, and double-click the file named Skill Builder 7.2.
   You will edit this document during this exercise. Notice that this document contains formatting that you have not yet learned about. For example, the title is centered and bold, and the paragraphs are formatted with double line spacing. This document is formatted like this because it is a report.

3. Follow these guidelines to make the editing changes shown below.

- If only one or two characters require deletion, then position the insertion point in front of the character(s) and use (DELETE) to remove them.

- If one or more words require deletion, then select the text and use (DELETE) to remove the selected text.

- If a word or phrase needs to be replaced with another word or phrase, then select the desired text and type the replacement text.

- Use Undo [↺] if you make mistakes.

4. When you have finished, save the changes, and close the document.

MAINE – THE PINE TREE STATE

Maine is recognized as one of the most ~~healthy~~ *healthful* states in the nation with temperatures averaging 70°F and winter temperatures averaging 20°F. It has 3,~~7~~00 miles of coastline, is about 5 *summer*

320 miles long and 210 miles wide, with a total area of 33,215 square miles or about as big as all

of the other five New England States combined. It comprises 16 counties with 22 cities, 424

towns, 51 plantations, and 416 unorganized townships. Aroostook county is so large (6,453

square miles) that it covers an area greater than the combined size of Connecticut. *and* *Rhode Island*

Maine abounds in natural assets—542,629 acres of state and national parks, including the

92-mile Allagash Wilderness Waterway, Acadia National Park (second most visited national

park in the United States), and Baxter State Park (location of Mt. Katahdin and the northern end

of the Appalachian Trail). Maine has one mountain ~~which~~ *that* is approximately one mile high—Mt.

Katahdin (5,268 ft. above sea level) and also claims America's first chartered city: York, 1641.

Maine's blueberry crop is the largest ~~blueberry crop~~ in the nation—98% of the low-bush

blueberries. Potatoes rank third in acreage and third in production nationally. Maine is nationally *in the United States* *lobster*

famed for its shellfish; over 46 million pounds of ~~shellfish~~ were harvested in 1997. The total of

all shellfish and fin fish harvested was approximately 237 million pounds with a total value of *in 1997*

$273 million ~~during the 1997 fishing season.~~

Skill Builder 7.3 **Create a Modified Block Style Letter**

A modified block style letter has the same elements and similar formatting as a block style letter. However, the modified block style positions the date, complimentary close, and signature block near the center of the lines.

1. Click the New Blank Document ⬜ button to open a new document window.

2. Type the following modified block style letter. Start the letter approximately 2" down from the top of the page. Tap TAB seven times to begin the date, complimentary close, and signature block just past the center of the lines. Finally, use the correct number of hard returns between the various paragraphs so that you have a properly formatted business letter.

3. When you have finished, save the document with the name **Skill Builder 7.3**, and then close the document.

Today's Date

Ms. Jessica Simms
811 Fairview Drive
Kansas City, MO 64106

Dear Ms. Simms:

I am pleased to inform you that you had excellent scores on all of your placement tests. You scored 98% on the word processing test, 97% on the spreadsheet test, and 99% on the office procedures test. These scores were far above average and are a testament to the quality of the vocational training program you recently completed.

I am pleased to offer you employment with Wilkinson Legal Services. Sarah Adams is looking forward to working with you should you decide to accept our offer.

I know you have several other job offers, and I hope you will give Wilkinson serious consideration. Sarah has already expressed an interest in having you train our staff members due to your excellent knowledge in Word and Excel. You will certainly have a bright future at Wilkinson.

Ms. Simms, please contact me soon. We look forward to having you as part of the Wilkinson team.

Sincerely,

Cynthia Lentz
Director, Human Resources

xx

Skill Builder 7.4 Create a Personal Style Business Letter

Personal business letters are used when an individual representing himself or herself sends a letter to a recipient in a business. Personal business letters can be composed using either the block or modified block style. Notice below that the return address is included in the signature block.

1. Start a new document, space down 2", and type the letter shown below.

2. When you have finished, save the document with the name **Skill Builder 7.4**, and then close the document.

Today's Date

Mr. Richard Johnson
Customer Service Manager
Colonial Credit Corporation
1000 Sherwood Place
East Brunswick, NJ 08816

Dear Mr. Johnson:

I have been with Colonial Credit for three years, and I have always paid my bills promptly. My annual income has also increased 30% in the past three years. For these reasons, I would like my credit limit raised to $3,000. The increase is necessary because I am traveling on business quite often.

Please respond as soon as possible. I appreciate your assistance.

Sincerely,

Jill Simms
2010 Washington Way
Racine, WI 53403

Assessments

Assessment 7.1 Block Style Letter

1. Create the block style business letter shown below. Space down the proper distance from the top of the page, and use proper spacing between paragraphs.

2. Save the letter to your exercise diskette with the name **Assessment 7.1**.

3. Print the letter, and then close the document.

Today's Date

Mrs. Suzanne Lee
8445 South Princeton Street
Chicago, IL 60628

Dear Mrs. Lee:

Thank you for your interest in the Back Bay Users Group. We will be holding an orientation for new members on the first Thursday in April at our headquarters.

Please let us know if you can attend by calling the phone number on this letterhead. Or, if you prefer, you may respond in writing or via email.

Sincerely,

Jack Bell
Membership Chair

xx

Assessment 7.2 **Editing Skills**

1. Open 🗐 the document on your exercise diskette named Assessment 7.2.

2. Make the editing changes shown in the following document.

3. Use (ENTER) to push the entire document down so that the date is positioned at approximately the 2" position.

4. Click the insertion point at the beginning of the date line and use (TAB) to move the date to approximately the 3" position on the ruler.

5. Use the technique in Step 4 to move the complimentary close and signature block to approximately the 3" position on the ruler.
   Indenting the date, complimentary close, and signature block converts the letter from block style to modified block style.

6. When you have finished, save the changes, print the letter, and close the document.

Today's Date

~~Ms. Cynthia Wilson~~ Mr. Roosevelt Jackson
~~118 Upper Terrace~~ 8 Spring Street
~~Freehold, NJ 08845~~ Martinville, NJ 08836

Dear ~~Ms. Wilson~~: Mr. Jackson

Thank you for your recent letter concerning back injuries in your office. Yes, ^back^ injuries are a common problem for office workers today. It was estimated by the U. S. Bureau of Labor Statistics that in one year over ~~490~~,000 employees took time from work due to back injuries.
580

Encourage your office employees to make certain their work surface is at a ~~suitable~~ height. They should also be encouraged to take frequent breaks from their desks. *comfortable*

Please
~~Feel free to~~ contact my office if you would like more information.

Sincerely,

Elaine Boudreau
Ergonomics Specialist

Assessment 7.3 Personal Style Business Letter

1. Create the personal style business letter shown below.

2. Save the letter to your exercise diskette with the name **Assessment 7.3**.

3. Print the letter, and then close the document.

Today's Date

Mr. Jake Wilson
Rebate Manager
Sierra Snowboards
4200 University Avenue
Berkeley, CA 94702

Dear Mr. Wilson:

Thank you for your excellent advice on the snowboarding equipment I recently purchased. Sierra Snowboards certainly has the best equipment in the business.

I would like to know when I can expect the rebate on the board I purchased. I mailed in my rebate coupon last month and I have yet to hear from the company. Do rebates normally take this long? Please contact me as soon as possible at (510) 223-3344. Thank you for your assistance.

Sincerely,

Melissa Jackson
1223 Appian Way
El Sobrante, CA 94803

Critical Thinking

Critical Thinking 7.1 On Your Own

Cathy Jacobson is an Administrative Assistant in the Marketing Department of Big Time Video Distributors. Big Time distributes videos to small video stores throughout the local area. Cathy works for Donald Livingston, the Director of Marketing. Donald and his marketing team have decided to offer promotional discounts to customers depending upon their sales volume in the previous quarter. The discounts are designed to encourage customers to order all of their videos from Big Time and to entice larger accounts to begin ordering from Big Time. Donald has instructed Cathy to prepare a letter to be sent to all Big Time customers.

Follow these guidelines to prepare a formal business letter announcing the promotional offer:

- Use the following generic text for the inside address.
  Name
  Company
  Address
  City, State Zip

- Let the customers know that the promotion will begin on the first day of the coming month. Use today's date for the preparation date.

- The discount schedule is shown below. Describe the discount schedule in a paragraph rather than in the table format shown here.

Volume in Previous Quarter	Discount Percentage
$50,000	10%
$100,000	15%
$200,000	25%

- Inform the customers that in order to get the discount they must respond within 30 days by returning the enclosed card. Your letter should include an enclosure notation indicating that there is an enclosure.

Save your completed letter as **Critical Thinking 7.1**.

Critical Thinking 7.2 On Your Own

Compose a personal business letter to Donna Wilson, the Loan Manager of Citizen's Bank. The address of Citizen's Bank is 12300 West Washington Avenue, Los Angeles, CA 90024. The purpose of the letter is to thank Donna for approving your $15,000 automobile loan. Donna worked hard to secure the best interest rate and terms for your loan, so you should let her know just how much you appreciate her excellent service. Save your completed letter as **Critical Thinking 7.2**, and then close it.

Critical Thinking 7.3 **On Your Own**

Open the Critical Thinking 7.2 letter that you composed in the previous exercise. Insert a new paragraph requesting that Donna send you information on Citizen Bank's new Small Business Credit Line program. Let Donna know that you are starting a new business venture (you choose the venture), and you are interested in obtaining financing from the bank. Save the completed letter as `Critical Thinking 7.3`.

Critical Thinking 7.4 **Web Research**

George Wilson is a certified financial planner and the owner of PlanRight Retirement Services. George sends correspondence to his clientele quite often and he usually includes one or more helpful hints on ways they can save money. Use Internet Explorer and a search engine of your choice to locate the Web site Uniform Resource Locators (URLs) of American Airlines, United Airlines, and Southwest Airlines. Compose a letter from George to his clientele letting them know that their 2003 tax packages are ready and available for pickup or mailing. In addition, include a paragraph describing the savings that can be realized by booking airline reservations through the Web sites of United, American, and Southwest airlines. Include the Web site URLs so that George's customers can visit the sites. Use the same generic text for the inside address that you used in Critical Thinking 7.1. Save your completed letter as `Critical Thinking 7.4`.

Critical Thinking 7.5 **On Your Own**

You have started a new Web-based business named Health-e-Meals.com. Health-e-Meals.com delivers healthy, nutritious meals directly to homes, businesses, and school lunch programs. Compose a business letter to Donna Wilson at Citizen's Bank using the address information for Donna from Critical Thinking 7.2. Let Donna know that you are interested in establishing a $100,000 credit line with the bank and that you would like to schedule an appointment to meet with her. Write one short paragraph describing the clientele and the product/service you are offering, and another paragraph describing the current monthly sales, expenses, and growth rate of the company. Save your completed letter as `Critical Thinking 7.5`.

LESSON 8

Creating a Memorandum and Press Release

In this lesson, you will expand upon the basic skills you developed in the previous lesson. You will create a two-page document that uses a page break to separate the pages. Paragraph formatting is an important technique in Word. This lesson introduces paragraph formatting and paragraph alignment techniques. You will learn how to apply various text formats, and you will use Cut, Copy, and Paste to rearrange text and paragraphs. Finally, you will unleash the power of Word's Format Painter—a powerful tool that is used to rapidly format text and ensure formatting consistency throughout a document.

Case Study

Lashanda Robertson is the Public Affairs Representative for Flexico, Inc., a fabrics manufacturer specializing in materials for active wear. Image and public perception are important determinants of success in the high-profile world of fashion design. Flexico is a progressive company that understands the importance of image. As the Public Affairs Representative for Flexico, Lashanda's responsibilities include issuing press releases to inform clothing manufacturers and other potential customers of forthcoming fabrics and materials. Lashanda creates a memorandum to which she attaches her latest press release announcing the new FlexMax line of fabrics for active wear. Memorandums are used for internal communication within a company or organization, whereas business letters are used for external communication.

Lashanda uses several of Word's paragraph and text formatting features to create her press release. The formatting toolbar makes it quick and easy to format the heading lines: changing the font and point size, applying the bold attribute, and centering the lines.

The special characters available in the Symbol dialog box makes it easy for Lashanda to access the registered and trademark symbols that she needs to use frequently in her work.

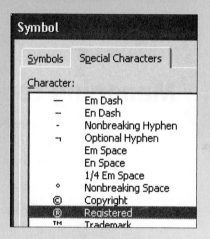

Flexico®, Inc.

Press Release

Flexico Announces FlexMax™ Fabric

Memorandum Styles

There are a variety of acceptable memorandum styles in use today. All memorandum styles contain the same elements but with varied formatting. Many new formats have emerged since the widespread use of computer and word processing technology. The style illustrated below is a traditional memorandum style with minimal formatting.

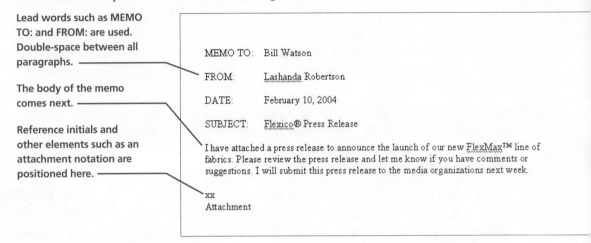

Lead words such as MEMO TO: and FROM: are used. Double-space between all paragraphs.

The body of the memo comes next.

Reference initials and other elements such as an attachment notation are positioned here.

MEMO TO: Bill Watson

FROM: Lashanda Robertson

DATE: February 10, 2004

SUBJECT: Flexico® Press Release

I have attached a press release to announce the launch of our new FlexMax™ line of fabrics. Please review the press release and let me know if you have comments or suggestions. I will submit this press release to the media organizations next week.

xx
Attachment

Managing Toolbars

Word 2003 includes more than 30 toolbars to assist you in creating and formatting documents. The Standard and Formatting toolbars contain the most frequently used buttons, so they are located at the top of the Word window just below the menu bar.

Displaying and Hiding Toolbars

You can display or hide toolbars by first displaying the Toolbars list and then choosing the desired toolbar(s) from the list. The Toolbars list is displayed using the View→Toolbars command or by right-clicking any displayed toolbar. A checkmark appears on the Toolbar list next to each toolbar that is currently displayed.

Moving Toolbars

You can move toolbars to any screen location. For example, many users like to position toolbars as floating pallets over the document area. You can move a toolbar by dragging the Move handle located on the left end of the toolbar.

The Move pointer appears when you point to a Move handle. You can move a toolbar to any screen location by dragging the Move handle.

Displaying the Standard and Formatting Toolbars on Separate Rows

In Word 2003, the Standard and Formatting toolbars are placed side-by-side on a single row, just below the menu bar. This arrangement was introduced in Word 2000. In earlier versions of Word, the Standard and Formatting toolbars were displayed on separate rows. The following illustration outlines the various toolbar options.

The Toolbar Options button appears on the right edge of all toolbars. Clicking this button displays a menu with several options. ————

If the Standard and Formatting toolbars are displayed on the same row, all of the included buttons will not fit on the toolbars. Buttons not visible on the toolbar are displayed on this list. You can choose a command by clicking a button on the list. ——→

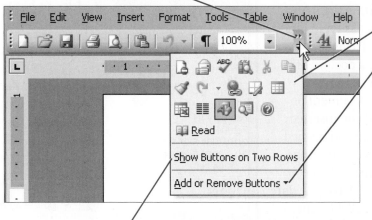

The Add or Remove Buttons option lets you add buttons to or remove buttons from a toolbar. You can also customize toolbars with this option.

The Show Buttons on Two Rows option positions the Standard and Formatting toolbars on separate rows. This option becomes Show Buttons on One Row if the toolbars are displayed on separate rows.

 ## Hands-On 8.1 Display the Formatting Toolbar on a Separate Row

1. Start Word, and follow these steps to display the Standard and Formatting toolbars on separate rows:

Ⓐ Click the Toolbar Options button on the right edge of the Standard toolbar. ————

Ⓑ If the Show Buttons on Two Rows option is available, choose it to display the Standard and Formatting toolbars on separate rows. If the Show Buttons on One Row option is available, note that your toolbars are already presented on separate rows. You can close the menu without choosing an option. ————

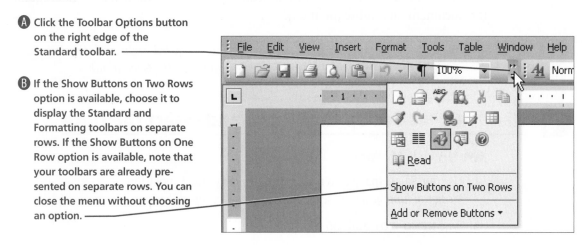

‼IMPORTANT! *From this point forward, the instructions in this text will assume that the Standard and Formatting toolbars are displayed on two rows. This will make it easier for you to locate buttons when instructed to do so.*

Inserting and Formatting the Date and Time

FROM THE KEYBOARD

(ALT)+(SHIFT)+(D) to insert date
(ALT)+(SHIFT)+(T) to insert time

Word lets you insert the current date and time using a variety of formats. For example, the date could be inserted as 2/10/04, February 10, 2004, or 10 February 2004. The Date and Time box is displayed with the Insert→Date and Time command. The desired date and/or time format can then be chosen and inserted.

The Update Automatically Option

You can insert the date and time as text or as a field. Inserting the date as text has the same effect as typing the date into a document. Fields, however, are updated whenever a document is opened or printed. For example, imagine you created a document on February 10, 2004, and you inserted the date as a field. If you had opened the document the next day, then the date would have automatically been updated to February 11, 2004. The date and time are inserted as fields whenever the Update Automatically box is checked, as shown to the right.

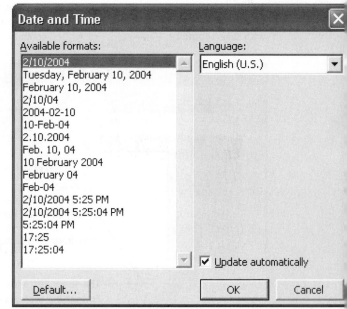

When to Use the Update Automatically Option

Maintaining the original date in a document may be important. For example, the date is important in documents such as business letters and legal agreements. If you insert the date in such documents using the Update Automatically option, then you will lose the original date if you open the document on a subsequent day.

!TIP! *To find the original date that a document was created, right-click the document in My Computer or Windows Explorer, choose Properties, and click the General tab.*

Hands-On 8.2 Set Up the Memo and Insert the Date

Set Up the Memo

1. Use (ENTER) to space down to approximately the 2" position.
   Memorandums generally begin 2" down from the top of the page.

2. Type **MEMO TO:** and tap the (TAB) key.

3. Type **Bill Watson**, and tap (ENTER) twice.

4. Type **FROM:** and tap the (TAB) key.

5. Type **Lashanda Robertson**, and tap (ENTER) twice.

6. Type **DATE:** and tap the (TAB) key twice.
   It was necessary to tap (TAB) twice to align the date with the names. The first tab aligned the insertion point with the ½" mark on the ruler (located just above the document). The second tab aligned the insertion point with the 1" position on the ruler.

Choose a Date Format and Insert the Date

TIP!

If the date and time are not accurate on your computer, double-click the time on the right end of the Taskbar, set the correct date and time, and click OK.

7. Choose Insert→Date and Time from the menu bar.

8. Make sure the Update Automatically box is checked at the bottom of the dialog box.
   This option instructs Word to insert the date as a field. Once again, be careful when using this option. It is being used in this memorandum for instructional purposes only. You may want to avoid using this feature in business correspondence.

9. Choose the third date format on the list, and click OK.

10. Click in the date.
    Notice that the date appears to be in a shaded box, which indicates that the date is inserted as a field.

11. Complete the remainder of the memorandum as shown in the following illustration.
    Make sure you double-space after the date line, the subject line, and after the main paragraph. Also, use (TAB) to line up the phrase Flexico Press Release after the SUBJECT: lead word.

MEMO TO: Bill Watson

FROM: Lashanda Robertson

DATE: February 10, 2004

SUBJECT: Flexico Press Release

I have attached a press release to announce the launch of our new FlexMax line of fabrics. Please review the press release and let me know if you have comments or suggestions. I will submit this press release to the media organizations next week.

xx
Attachment

---

12. Click the Save button, and save the memorandum as **Hands-On Lesson 8**.
    You will continue to enhance the memorandum throughout this lesson.

Inserting Symbols

Word lets you insert a variety of symbols, typographic characters, and international characters not found on the keyboard. Most symbols are inserted by using the Insert→Symbol command and choosing the desired symbols from the Symbol dialog box. You can also use keystrokes to insert common typographic symbols such as the Registered ® symbol and some international characters. The following illustration shows the organization of the Symbol dialog box.

The Special Characters tab contains commonly used characters such as the Registered ® symbol and various English language symbols. ——————

There are several symbol fonts from which you can choose. Each font displays different symbols in the dialog box. Some fonts, such as Wingdings, contain interesting symbols. ——————

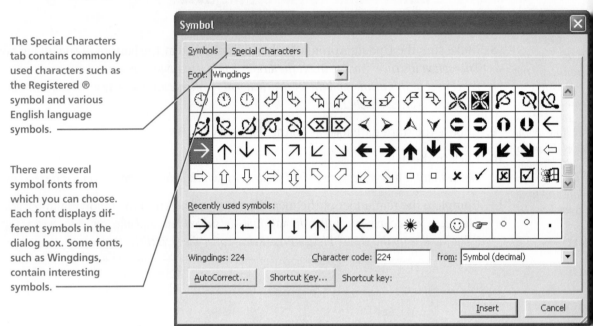

Hands-On 8.3 Insert Symbols

1. Position the insertion point to the right of the word Flexico on the SUBJECT: line.
   You will insert a Registered Trademark ® symbol in the next few steps. A registered trademark gives a company the exclusive right to use a trademark (Flexico in this case) nationwide.

2. Choose Insert→Symbol from the menu bar.

3. Click the Special Characters tab.

4. Choose the Registered ® symbol, and click the Insert button.
   The Registered ® symbol is inserted in the document, and the Symbol dialog box remains open. Word leaves the dialog box open in case you wish to insert additional symbols.

5. Click the insertion point to the right of the word FlexMax in the main paragraph (you may need to drag the dialog box out of the way in order to see the word).

6. Insert the Trademark ™ symbol.
   The Trademark symbol indicates that a company claims a phrase or icon as their trademark, but they have not received federal protection (indicated by the Registered ® symbol).

7. Click the Symbols tab on the Symbol dialog box.

8. Try choosing a different font from the Font list, and you will see a new set of symbols.

9. When you have finished experimenting, click the Close button to close the dialog box.

10. Click the Save button to save the changes.

Views

Word lets you view documents in several ways. Each view is optimized for specific types of work, thus allowing you to work efficiently. The views change the way documents appear onscreen but have no impact on the appearance of printed documents. You can choose the desired view from the View menu or from the View bar at the left end of the horizontal scroll bar as shown to the right. The following table outlines the views available in Word 2003.

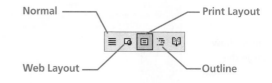

 QUICK REFERENCE: VIEWS

View	Description
Print Layout	Print Layout is the default view in Word 2003. In Print Layout, documents look almost exactly as they will when printed. Print Layout is the most versatile view, allowing you to see text, graphics, headers and footers, and other types of objects. You will probably use Print Layout view most of the time.
Normal	Normal view simplifies page layout by eliminating page numbers, page boundaries, and a few other elements from the view. Normal view can be useful if you want to concentrate on the text in your document. Normal view may also speed up scrolling and other tasks, especially if you have an older computer or large documents with many graphics.
Web Layout	Web Layout displays your document, as it would look on a Web page. Text, graphics, and background patterns are visible. The document is displayed on one long page without page breaks.
Outline	Outline view is useful for organizing documents.
Reading Layout	Reading layout is designed to make reading documents on the screen easier. Multiple page documents are displayed with two pages side by side, like an open book. You can change the size of the font to meet your reading needs without changing the font size in the document.

Hands-On 8.4 Experiment with Views

1. Locate the Views ≡ ⬛ 回 ⬛ 📖 bar on the left end of the horizontal scroll bar.

2. Position the mouse pointer over each button, and a descriptive ScreenTip will pop up.

3. Click each button to see how the appearance of the document changes.
   You may not notice much of a difference because your document lacks graphics and other more advanced elements.

4. Switch to Print Layout view when you have finished experimenting.

Zooming

The Zoom Control lets you "zoom in" to get a close-up view of a document or "zoom out" to see the "big picture." Zooming changes the size of onscreen text and graphics but has no affect on printed text and graphics. You can zoom from 10% to 500%.

You can type a zoom percentage in the Zoom box and tap Enter, or . . .

. . . you can click the drop-down button and choose an option from the list.

Notice how large the onscreen text appears; however, it will print in the normal size.

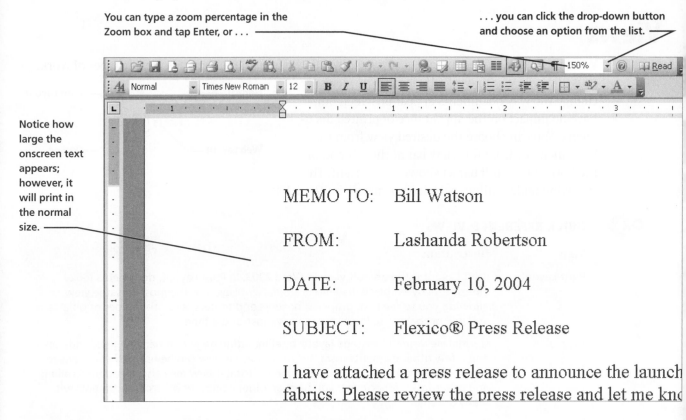

MEMO TO: Bill Watson

FROM: Lashanda Robertson

DATE: February 10, 2004

SUBJECT: Flexico® Press Release

I have attached a press release to announce the launch
fabrics. Please review the press release and let me kno

 ## Hands-On 8.5 **Use the Zoom Control**

1. Follow these steps to experiment with the zoom control:

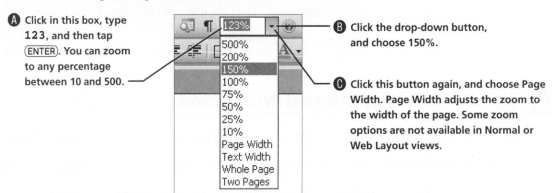

A Click in this box, type **123**, and then tap (ENTER). You can zoom to any percentage between 10 and 500.

B Click the drop-down button, and choose 150%.

C Click this button again, and choose Page Width. Page Width adjusts the zoom to the width of the page. Some zoom options are not available in Normal or Web Layout views.

2. Use the zoom control to select the following three zoom settings: Whole Page, 75%, and Page Width. Feel free to experiment with the zoom control.

Page Breaks

If you are typing text and the insertion point reaches the bottom of a page, Word automatically breaks the page and begins a new page. This is known as an automatic page break. The location of automatic page breaks may change as text is added to or deleted from a document. Automatic page breaks are convenient when working with long documents that have continuously flowing text. For example, imagine you were writing a novel, and you decided to insert a new paragraph in the middle of a chapter. With automatic page breaks, you could insert the paragraph, and Word would automatically repaginate the entire chapter.

You can force a page break to occur at any location in a document by inserting a manual page break. A manual page break remains in place unless you remove it. You insert manual page breaks whenever you want to control the starting point of a new page. You can insert a manual page break with the Insert→Break command.

FROM THE KEYBOARD
(CTRL)+(ENTER) to insert page break

Removing Manual Page Breaks

In Normal view, manual page breaks appear as a horizontal line with the phrase Page Break appearing on the line. The page break line also appears in Print Layout view if you click the Show/Hide button. You can remove a manual page break by positioning the insertion point on the page break line and tapping (DELETE), as shown in the following illustration.

You can remove a manual page break by showing the nonprinting characters, clicking on the Page Break line, and tapping (DELETE).

I have attached a press release to announce the launch of our new FlexMax™ line of fabrics. Please review the press release and let me know if you have comments or suggestions. I will submit this press release to the media organizations next week.

xx
Attachment
--Page Break--

Hands-On 8.6 Page Breaks

Insert a Page Break

1. Make sure you are in Print Layout view.

2. Position the insertion point to the right of the word Attachment on the attachment line.

3. Choose Insert→Break from the menu bar.
   Notice that several types of breaks are listed in the Break dialog box. This lesson only introduces page breaks.

4. Make sure Page Break is chosen, and click OK.
   You should be able to see the bottom portion of page 1 and the top of page 2.

5. Look at the Status bar at the bottom of the screen; it will show the insertion point is on Page 2.

Page 2   Sec 1   2/2

TIP!

You can remove a break without showing the nonprinting characters. However, this takes a little practice.

Remove the Page Break

6. Scroll up until the attachment line is visible.

7. Click the Show/Hide ¶ button, and a Page Break line will appear.

8. Click on the Page Break line, and tap (DELETE).

9. Try scrolling down to the second page, and you will see that it has been removed.

Reinsert the Break

10. Scroll up, and the insertion point should be just below the attachment line.

11. Press (CTRL)+(ENTER) to reinsert the page break.
This shortcut keystroke is useful to remember because page breaks are inserted often.

12. Click Show/Hide ¶ to hide the nonprinting characters.
The insertion point should be positioned at the top of the second page.

Formatting Paragraphs

The word paragraph has a special meaning in Word. A paragraph includes any text or objects followed by a paragraph mark. Word lets you format paragraphs in a variety of ways. For example, you can change paragraph alignment, add bullets and numbering to paragraphs, indent paragraphs, and apply paragraph styles.

A paragraph mark

You can click anywhere in a paragraph and apply the desired formats. When you tap (ENTER), the formats from the current paragraph are applied to the new paragraph. For example, if a heading is centered and you tap (ENTER), then the new paragraph will also be centered. You can format several paragraphs by first selecting the desired paragraphs and then applying the formats.

Aligning Text

The alignment buttons on the Formatting toolbar allow you to align paragraphs horizontally. Text can be left or right-aligned, centered, or justified. The alignment commands affect all text in a paragraph. To mix alignments within a line, you must use customized tab stops or tables.

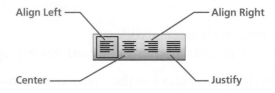

Hands-On 8.7 Set Up a Press Release

In this exercise, you will set up a press release. A press release is a type of announcement, so you will begin the first line 2" down from the top of the page.

Set Up the Title Lines

1. Make sure the insertion point is at the top of the new page, and tap (ENTER) several times to space down to approximately the 2" position.

2. Locate the alignment buttons on the Formatting toolbar, and notice that the Align Left ☰ button is highlighted.
   Left alignment is the default setting in Word.

3. Click the Center ☰ button.
   The insertion point moves to the center of the line.

4. Type the title **Flexico Announces FlexMax™ Fabric**, inserting the Trademark symbol as shown.

5. Tap (ENTER) twice, and notice that the center alignment is still in effect.
   Paragraph formats (including alignments) are copied to the next paragraph when (ENTER) is tapped.

6. Type **Press Release**, and tap (ENTER) twice.

7. Type **Flexico®, Inc.** inserting the Registered symbol as shown.

8. Tap (ENTER) twice; then click Align Left ☰ to restore left alignment.
   You are now ready to set up the body of the press release.

Set Up the Body

9. Type the heading **Announcement**, and tap (ENTER).

10. Type the phrase **San Francisco, Ca**.
    In the next step, you will insert an em dash. Em dashes are used as connectors within sentences and are available on the Symbols dialog box.

11. Display the Symbol dialog box, choose Em Dash from the Special Characters tab, and click Insert.

12. If necessary, move the Symbol dialog box out of the way, and click in the document to the right of the em dash.

13. Type the current date, and insert another em dash.

> **FROM THE KEYBOARD**
>
> Type two hyphens with no spaces before or after hyphens. Word will convert hyphens to an em dash when (SPACE BAR) is tapped after typing second connector word.

14. Close the Symbol dialog box, and complete the press release as shown below.

Flexico Announces FlexMax™ Fabric

Press Release

Flexico®, Inc.

Announcement
San Francisco, Ca.—February 12, 2004—Flexico, Inc. today announced the FlexMax fabric for active wear. FlexMax is ideally suited for active wear such as biking, hiking, and aerobics attire. This revolutionary fabric is designed by Flexico and allows for maximum range of motion while providing support, comfort, and moisture protection.

About Flexico
Founded in 1988, Flexico is a leading manufacturer of fabrics for active wear and outdoor activities. Flexico fabrics are used in fine active wear products worldwide.

FlexMax Styles
Initially, FlexMax fabrics will be available in two weights and a variety of colors. Contact Flexico or your distributor for information and samples.

Delivery and Availability
FlexMax products are designed to reach retailers by the third quarter of this year. Look for the distinctive Flexico log and the FlexMax trademark. FlexMax products will be available at most quality sporting goods stores.

---

15. Save ▣ the changes, and continue with the next topic.

Formatting Text

In Word and other Office programs, you can format text by changing the font, font size, and color. You can also apply various font formats including bold, italics, and underline. If no text is selected, the format settings take effect from that point forward or until you change them again. If you wish to format existing text, you must select the text and then apply the desired formats. Text can be formatted using options in the font box. The font box is displayed with the Format→Font command. In addition, you can format text with buttons on the Formatting toolbar, as shown in the following illustration.

FROM THE KEYBOARD

CTRL+B for Bold

CTRL+U for Underline

CTRL+I for Italics

CTRL+] to increase size one point

CTRL+[to decrease size one point

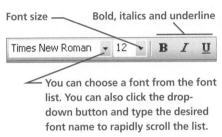

Font size — Bold, italics and underline

You can choose a font from the font list. You can also click the drop-down button and type the desired font name to rapidly scroll the list.

The Font Color button is on the right end of the Formatting toolbar. The color palette appears when you click the drop-down button. Once you choose a color, the color is displayed on the button. From that point forward, you can rapidly apply the color by clicking the button. —

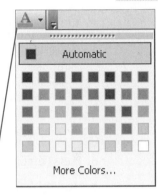

 ## Hands-On 8.8 **Format Text**

Format the Press Release Title Lines

1. Select the press release title lines by positioning the mouse pointer in the left margin and dragging down.

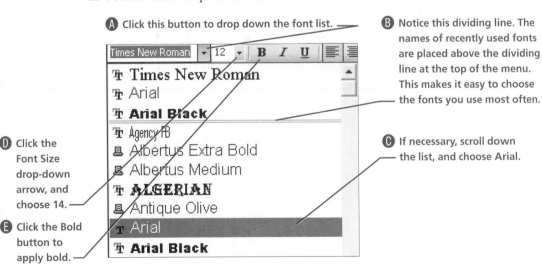

Flexico Announces FlexMax™ Fabric

Press Release

Flexico®, Inc.

2. Follow these steps to format the title lines:

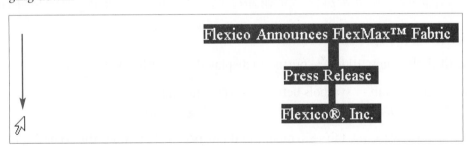

A Click this button to drop down the font list. —

B Notice this dividing line. The names of recently used fonts are placed above the dividing line at the top of the menu. This makes it easy to choose the fonts you use most often.

D Click the Font Size drop-down arrow, and choose 14. —

C If necessary, scroll down the list, and choose Arial.

E Click the Bold button to apply bold. —

3. Click the drop-down button on the Font Color 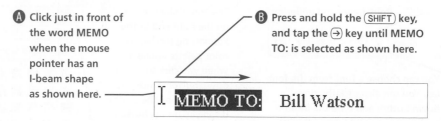 button (on the right end of the Formatting toolbar), and choose your favorite color.

Use Keystrokes to Select and Format

The following steps show you how to select using the keyboard. In some situations, keyboard selecting can give you greater precision and control.

4. Scroll up to the first page of the document to view the memorandum.

5. Follow these steps to select the phrase MEMO TO:

Ⓐ Click just in front of the word MEMO when the mouse pointer has an I-beam shape as shown here.

Ⓑ Press and hold the (SHIFT) key, and tap the ⊙ key until MEMO TO: is selected as shown here.

I **MEMO TO:**   Bill Watson

6. Press (CTRL)+(B) to apply bold to the words.

7. Use the techniques in the previous two steps to apply bold to the next lead word, FROM:.

8. Now apply bold to the lead word DATE:. You should see the date move one tab stop to the right, thus throwing off the alignment.
This occurred because the bold format increased the size of the lead word DATE:. The increased size pushed the lead word past the tab stop at the ½" position on the ruler. This in turn pushed the date past the tab stop at the 1" position. In the next few steps, you will solve this dilemma by removing a tab stop.

Remove a Tab Stop

9. Click the Show/Hide ¶ button to display the nonprinting characters.

10. Notice the tab → symbols between DATE: and the date.
The tab symbols show each location where the (TAB) key was tapped.

11. Click between the tab → symbols, and tap (DELETE) to remove the second symbol.
The date will move to the left, restoring proper alignment.

12. Click Show/Hide ¶ to hide the nonprinting characters.

13. Now apply bold to the SUBJECT: heading.

14. Save the changes, and continue with the next topic.

Cut, Copy, and Paste

Cut, Copy, and Paste are available in all Office 2003 applications. With Cut, Copy, and Paste you can move or copy text within a document, between documents, or between different Office applications. For example, you could use the Copy command to copy an important paragraph from one document, and the Paste command to paste the paragraph to another document. Cut, Copy, and Paste are most efficient for moving or copying text a long distance within a document or between documents. Cut, Copy, and Paste are easy to use if you remember the following concepts:

- You must select text before issuing a Cut or Copy command.

- You must position the insertion point at the desired location before issuing the Paste command. Otherwise, you will paste at the wrong location.

QUICK REFERENCE: USING CUT, COPY, AND PASTE

Command	Description	How to Issue the Command
Cut	The Cut command removes selected text from its original location and places it on the Office Clipboard.	Click the Cut button, or press CTRL+X.
Copy	The Copy command also places selected text on the Office Clipboard, but it leaves a copy of the text in the original location.	Click the Copy button, or press CTRL+C.
Paste	The Paste command pastes the most recently cut or copied text into the document at the insertion point location.	Click the Paste button, or press CTRL+V.

The Office Clipboard

The Office Clipboard lets you collect items from any Office document or program and paste them into any other Office document. For example, you can collect a paragraph from a Word document, data from an Excel worksheet, and a graphic from a PowerPoint slide and then paste them all into a Word document. The Office Clipboard can also be used within an application like Word to collect several items and then paste them as desired. The Office Clipboard can hold up to 24 items.

How it Works

You can place multiple items on the Office Clipboard using the standard Cut and Copy commands; however, the Office Clipboard must first be displayed in the Task Pane. The Office Clipboard is displayed with the Edit→Office Clipboard command. Once the Office Clipboard is displayed, you can choose an item and paste it into your document.

In this exercise, you will use Cut and Paste to rearrange the title lines in the press release.

1. Scroll down to the press release page.

2. Follow these steps to Cut and Paste a title line:

A Select this title line and the empty paragraph below it by dragging in the left margin.

B Click the Cut ✂ button on the Standard toolbar. The text will be cut from the document.

C Click the I-beam just in front of the first title line as shown here.

D Click the Paste 📋 button.

The Paste Options 📋 button will appear near the pasted text. The Paste Options button provides several options that allow you to control the formatting of the pasted text. For now, just ignore the presence of the Paste Options button.

The Press Release title and the paragraph mark below it should have pushed the Flexico Announces heading down, maintaining the double-spacing of the title lines. This occurred because of the way you selected the text prior to issuing the Cut command. By dragging in the margin to the left of the text, you selected both the text and the paragraph mark. The paragraph mark was pasted along with the text. The paragraph mark pushed the Flexico Announces paragraph down, maintaining the double-spacing. This was, by the way, the intended result.

3. Now select the third title line, Flexico®, Inc., and the empty paragraph below it by dragging in the left margin.

4. Click the Cut ✂ button.

5. Position the insertion point just in front of the first heading, Press Release.

6. Click the Paste 📋 button.
   Your headings should now have the arrangement shown to the right.

> **Flexico®, Inc.**
>
> **Press Release**
>
> **Flexico Announces FlexMax™ Fabric**

Use the Office Clipboard

7. Click the drop-down ▾ button on the Undo ↺▾ button.
   If you performed the preceding steps correctly, the first four items on the Undo list should be Paste, Cut, Paste, Cut.

8. Slide the mouse pointer over the first four items to select them, and click the mouse button.
   The press release headings should be in the same order they were in prior to cutting and pasting.

9. Choose Edit→Office Clipboard from the menu bar.

The Clipboard task pane will appear, displaying the Office Clipboard. Notice that the Office Clipboard displays a Paste All button that allows you to paste all items currently on the clipboard and a Clear All button that allows you to clear the clipboard. Individual items on the clipboard can be pasted by clicking them. Or, you can point at the desired item, which generates a drop-down button that you can click, and choose Paste from the list.

10. Click the Clear All button to clear the clipboard.

11. Select the Press Release heading and the empty paragraph below it.

12. Click the Cut ✂ button.

Notice that the item appears on the clipboard.

13. Select the Flexico®, Inc. heading and the empty paragraph below it.

14. Click the Cut ✂ button.

The clipboard should now display two items.

15. Position the insertion point just in front of the Flexico Announces title line.

16. Follow these steps to paste the Press Release item:

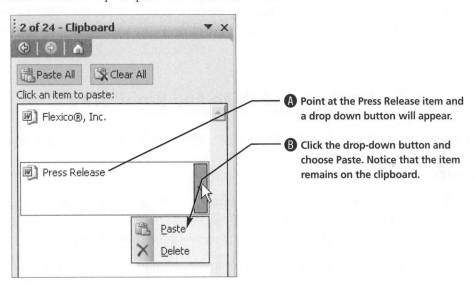

17. Position the insertion point just in front of the Press Release title line.

18. Now paste the Flexico®, Inc. item by simply clicking it on the clipboard.

As you can see, the Office Clipboard can be useful if you are collecting items from several places in a document. Keep in mind, however, that Cut, Copy, and Paste can be used without the Office Clipboard.

19. Click the Clear All button to clear the clipboard contents.

20. Close the Clipboard task pane by clicking its Close ⊠ button.

Drag and Drop

Drag and drop produces the same result as Cut, Copy, and Paste. However, Drag and Drop is usually more efficient if you are moving or copying text a short distance within the same document. If the original location and destination are both visible in the current window, then it is usually easier to use Drag and Drop. With Drag and Drop, you select the text you wish to move or copy and release the mouse button. Then you drag the text to the desired destination. If you press the (CTRL) key while releasing the mouse button, the text is copied to the destination.

Right Dragging

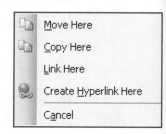

Right-Drag Pop-Up Menu

Right dragging is a variation of the drag-and-drop technique. Many beginners find Drag and Drop difficult to use because they have difficulty controlling the mouse. This difficulty is compounded if they are trying to copy text using Drag and Drop. This is because copying requires the (CTRL) key to be held while dragging the text. With the Right-Drag method, the right mouse button is used when dragging. When the right mouse button is released at the destination, a pop-up menu appears. The pop-up menu lets you choose Move, Copy, or Cancel. This provides more control because there is no need to use the (CTRL) key when copying, and you have the option of canceling the move or copy. The Right-Drag pop-up menu is shown in the illustration to the right.

Hands-On 8.10 Use Drag and Drop and Right Drag

In this exercise, you will use Drag and Drop and the Right-Drag method to rearrange paragraphs.

Use Drag and Drop

1. If necessary, scroll down until the paragraphs with the headings About Flexico, FlexMax Styles, and Delivery and Availability are all visible on the screen.
   Drag and Drop is most effective for moving or copying a short distance on the screen.

2. Follow these steps to move the Delivery and Availability paragraph and heading:

Ⓐ Select from the empty paragraph above the Delivery and Availability heading to the end of the paragraph as shown in the illustration.

Ⓑ Release the mouse button.

Ⓒ Position the mouse pointer on the selected text, and drag the text up until the move pointer is just above the About Flexico heading, as shown here.

Ⓓ Release the mouse button to drop the text above the About Flexico heading.

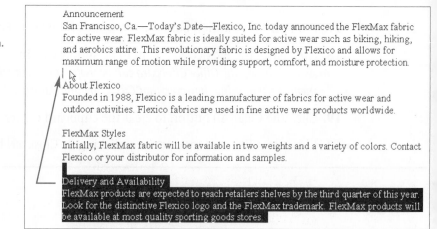

If you selected the empty paragraph above the text as shown and dropped the text in the empty space above the About Flexico heading, then your paragraphs should be properly spaced.

Use Right Drag

3. Follow these steps to move the FlexMax Styles paragraph and heading:

Ⓐ Select from the empty paragraph above the FlexMax Styles heading to the end of the paragraph as shown here; then release the mouse button.

Ⓑ Position the mouse pointer on the selected text, and press and hold the right mouse button.

Ⓒ Drag the mouse up while holding the right button until the move pointer is positioned just above the About Flexico heading, as shown here.

> Delivery and Availability
> FlexMax products are expected to reach retailers shelves by the third
> Look for the distinctive Flexico logo and the FlexMax trademark. Fle
> be available at most quality sporting goods stores.
>
> About Flexico
> Founded in 1988, Flexico is a leading manufacturer of fabrics for acti
> outdoor activities. Flexico fabrics are used in fine active wear produc
>
> FlexMax Styles
> Initially, FlexMax fabric will be available in two weights and a variet
> Flexico or your distributor for information and samples.

Ⓓ Release the mouse button, and choose Move Here from the pop-up menu that appears. Notice that the pop-up menu would have allowed you to cancel the move if desired.

Move a Sentence

4. Use any of the move techniques you have learned thus far to move the last sentence in the Announcement paragraph as shown in the following illustration. You can use Cut and Paste, Drag and Drop, or Right Drag.

Move the selected sentence to this location in front of the previous sentence. When the move is complete, you will need to insert a space after the moved sentence.

> Announcement
> San Francisco, Ca.—Today's Date—Flexico, Inc. today announced the FlexMax fabric
> for active wear. FlexMax fabric is ideally suited for active wear such as biking, hiking,
> and aerobics attire. This revolutionary fabric is designed by Flexico and allows for
> maximum range of motion while providing support, comfort, and moisture protection.

The Format Painter

The Format Painter lets you copy text formats from one location to another. This is convenient if you want the same format(s) applied to text in different locations. The Format Painter copies all text formats, including the font, font size, color, and character effects. The Format Painter saves time and helps create consistent formatting throughout a document. The Format Painter can also be used to copy paragraph formats, such as alignment settings.

QR

QUICK REFERENCE: COPYING TEXT FORMATS WITH THE FORMAT PAINTER

■ Click on the text with the format(s) you wish to copy.

■ Click the Format Painter once if you want to copy formats to one other location, or double-click if you want to copy to multiple locations.

■ Select the text at the new location(s) that you want to format. If you double-clicked in the previous step, the Format Painter will remain active, allowing you to select text at multiple locations. You can even scroll through the document to reach the desired location(s).

■ If you double-clicked in the first step, then click the Format Painter button when you have finished. This will turn off the Format Painter.

Hands-On 8.11 Use the Format Painter

Format Text

1. Select the Announcement heading (just above the first large paragraph of text).

2. Choose Format→Font to display the Font dialog box.

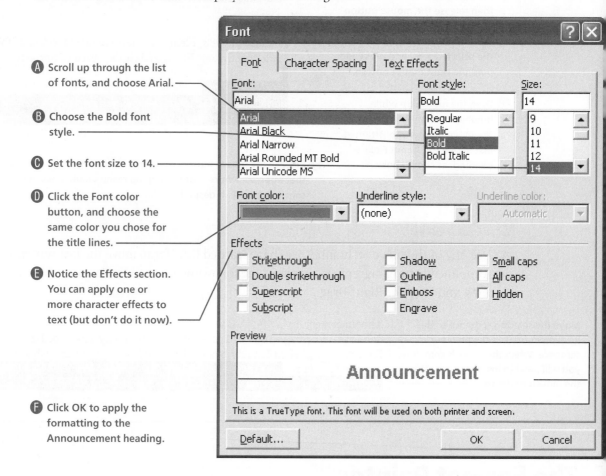

A Scroll up through the list of fonts, and choose Arial.

B Choose the Bold font style.

C Set the font size to 14.

D Click the Font color button, and choose the same color you chose for the title lines.

E Notice the Effects section. You can apply one or more character effects to text (but don't do it now).

F Click OK to apply the formatting to the Announcement heading.

Copy Formats to One Location

3. Make sure the insertion point is in the Announcement heading.

4. Click the Format Painter ![icon] button on the Standard toolbar.
   A paintbrush icon will be added to the I-beam pointer once it is positioned over the document.

5. Drag the mouse pointer across the Delivery and Availability heading and release the mouse button.
   The Arial, 14pt, bold, colored formats should be copied to the heading. The paintbrush icon also vanished because you clicked the Format Painter button just once in the previous step. If you want to copy formats to multiple locations, you must double-click the Format Painter. Actually, the 14pt heading is too large for these paragraphs. In the next few steps, you will change the size to 12pt for the Announcement heading and then copy the formats to the other headings in the press release.

Copy Formats to Several Locations

6. Select the Announcement heading.

7. Click the Font Size ![14] drop-down button on the Formatting toolbar, and choose 12.

8. Double-click the Format Painter ![icon].

9. Select the Delivery and Availability heading by either dragging the mouse over it or by clicking in front of it in the margin.

10. Select the FlexMax Styles heading to copy the formats to that heading.

11. If necessary, scroll down, and then select the About Flexico heading.

12. Click the Format Painter ![icon] to turn it off.

13. Scroll through your document, and take a moment to appreciate your work.

14. Feel free to experiment with any of the techniques you have learned in this lesson.

15. When you have finished, save the changes to your document then close the document.
    Continue with the end-of-lesson questions and exercises.

Concepts Review

True/False Questions

1. The zoom control changes the size of printed text. TRUE FALSE

2. The Formatting toolbar can be used to set all text formats and character effects. TRUE FALSE

3. Normal view is the default view in Word 2003. TRUE FALSE

4. The Format Painter is used to copy and paste text. TRUE FALSE

5. Manual page breaks remain in place until the user removes them. TRUE FALSE

6. The Right-Drag method displays a pop-up menu when the mouse button is released. TRUE FALSE

7. The Office Clipboard can hold up to 12 cut or copied items. TRUE FALSE

8. Items must be pasted from the Office Clipboard in the same order that they were placed on the Clipboard. TRUE FALSE

9. If you activate the Update Automatically checkbox in the Date and Time dialog box, the date will remain the same if you open the document on a subsequent day. TRUE FALSE

10. Toolbars can be positioned as floating pallets over the document area. TRUE FALSE

Multiple Choice Questions

1. In order to copy text formats to several locations in a document, you must
   a. click the Format Painter button and then select the desired text.
   b. double-click the Format Painter button and then select the desired text.
   c. use the Copy button.
   d. This cannot be done in Word.

2. Which of the following statements can be used to describe manual page breaks?
   a. Manual page breaks remain in place until they are deleted.
   b. Manual page breaks are inserted by the user.
   c. Manual page breaks can be inserted by pressing (CTRL)+(ENTER).
   d. All of the above

3. What is the percentage range of the zoom control?
   a. 25%–200%
   b. 10%–500%
   c. 25%–500%
   d. None of the above

4. Which key should you press if you want to copy while using drag-and-drop?
   a. (SHIFT)
   b. (CTRL)
   c. (ALT)
   d. (HOME)

Skill Builders

Skill Builder 8.1 Alignment and Formatting Practice

1. Click New Blank Document ⬜ button to start a new document.

2. Click the Center ▤ button.

3. Tap (ENTER) several times to space down to 2".

4. Set the font to Arial, the point size to 18, and turn on bold.

5. Click the drop-down button on the Font Color 🅰▾ button (on the right end of the Formatting toolbar), and choose your favorite color.

6. Type **The Wilson Family**, and tap (ENTER) *twice*.
   Notice you can apply text formats prior to typing text. The formats remain in effect until you change them or move the insertion point to a location with different formats.

7. Set the font size to 14.

8. Type **Is Having a**, and tap (ENTER) *twice*.

9. Set the font size to 18.

10. Type **Big Yard Sale**, tap (ENTER) *twice*, and set the alignment to left ▤.

11. Set the font to Times New Roman, the size to 14, turn off bold, and set the color to black.

12. Complete the document as shown below.

13. Save the document as **Skill Builder 8.1**, then close the document.

The Wilson Family

Is Having a

Big Yard Sale

Stop by our home at 22 Maple Street in Walnut Grove on July 21 for the yard sale of the summer! We'll have furniture, toys, electronics, antiques, and much more. We start at 8:00, so arrive early and be prepared to find bargains, one-of-a-kind items, and rare antiques!

Skill Builder 8.2 The Office Clipboard, Format Painter, and Drag and Drop

In this exercise, you will open a document on your exercise diskette. You will use the Office Clipboard to rearrange paragraphs, the Format Painter to paint formats, and Drag and Drop to move blocks of paragraphs.

Use the Office Clipboard

1. Open the document named Skill Builder 8.2 on your exercise diskette.
   Notice that the document contains a list of professional contacts. In the next few steps, you will use the Office Clipboard to reorganize the contacts by contact type. In other words, all of the attorneys will be grouped together, followed by the designers, then the bookkeepers.

2. Choose Edit→Office Clipboard from the menu bar.
   The Clipboard task pane appears, displaying the Office Clipboard. You must have the Office Clipboard displayed if you want to cut or copy multiple items to it.

3. If necessary, click the Clear All button to clear the clipboard.

4. Select the first attorney contact—David Roberts, Attorney—by clicking in front of the contact in the left margin.
   This will select the entire paragraph, including the paragraph mark.

5. Click the Cut ✄ button and the item will appear on the clipboard.

6. Select the next attorney—Lisa Wilson, Attorney—and Cut ✄ it to the clipboard.

7. Cut the remaining attorney contacts to the clipboard. Use Undo if you make a mistake. However, be careful because even if you use Undo, the item you cut will remain on the clipboard.

8. Now Cut ✄ the designer contacts to the clipboard.
   The bookkeeper contacts should now be grouped together in the document.

9. Tap (ENTER) to position the insertion point on a new line below the bookkeeper contacts.

10. Click the Paste All button on the Office Clipboard to paste the attorney and designer contacts.
    Notice that the contacts are pasted in the order they were cut, thus grouping the attorneys together and the designers together.

Create Headings

11. Click in front of the first bookkeeper contact, and tap (ENTER) to create a blank line.

12. Click on the blank line, and type **Bookkeepers**.

13. Use this technique to create an **Attorneys** heading above the first attorney contact, and a **Designers** heading above the first designer contact.

Use the Format Painter

14. Select the Professional Contacts heading at the top of the document.

15. Double-click the Format Painter 🖌.

16. Click the Bookkeepers heading to copy the formats to that heading.

17. Click the Attorneys and Designers headings.

18. Turn off the Format Painter 🖌.

19. Select the Professional Contacts heading, and increase the size to 14.

Use Drag and Drop

20. Select the Attorneys heading and the four attorney contacts by dragging in the left margin.

21. Release the mouse button.

22. Position the mouse pointer on the selection, and drag up until the pointer is just in front of the Bookkeepers heading.

23. Release the mouse button to move the Attorneys block above the Bookkeepers.

24. Now move the Designers heading and the designer contacts above the Bookkeepers.

Create Space and Center the Title

25. Position the insertion point just in front of the Attorneys heading, and tap (ENTER) to create a blank line between the Professional Contacts heading and the Attorneys heading.

26. Insert blank lines above the Designers and Bookkeepers headings.

27. Click on the Professional Contacts heading, and click the Center ▤ button.

28. Use (ENTER) to push the entire document down to approximately the 2" position.

29. Save the changes, close the Office Clipboard, and close the document.

Skill Builder 8.3 **Create a Memorandum**

1. Follow these guidelines to create the memorandum shown below:

   ■ Position the MEMO TO: line approximately 2" down from the top of the page.

   ■ Double-space between all paragraphs, and apply bold to the lead words MEMO TO:, FROM:, DATE:, and SUBJECT:.

   ■ Apply bold formatting as shown in the body paragraph.

   ■ Type your initials at the bottom of the memo.

2. Save the memo with the name **Skill Builder 8.3**, and then close the document.

MEMO TO: Jason Alexander

FROM: Tamika Jackson

DATE: Today's Date

SUBJECT: Monthly Sales Meeting

Our monthly sales meeting will be held in the conference room at **10:00 a.m.** on **Thursday, July 24**. Please bring your sales forecast for August and any important accounts that you wish to discuss. I will give you a presentation on our new products that are scheduled for release in September. I look forward to seeing you then.

xx

Skill Builder 8.4 Formatting Skills

1. Follow these guidelines to create the document shown below:

   ▓ Begin the document 2" down and enter all text. Center the titles as shown. Notice the dashes between the locations and days of the week in the Hands-On Workshops list and the other lists. These are em dashes inserted using the Special Characters tab of the Symbols dialog box. An easy way to insert these dashes is to insert the first one, select it, and copy it with the Copy command. Then, paste the dash at every other location where it is needed.

   ▓ Format the first title line with an Arial, bold, 16 pt font. Apply a color to the title.

   ▓ Use the Format Painter to copy the formats to the subtitle, then change the font size of the subtitle to 14 pt.

   ▓ Format the Hands-On Workshops heading with an Arial, bold, 12 pt font, and apply the same color you applied to the titles.

   ▓ Use the Format Painter to copy the formats from the Hands-On Workshops heading to the Seminar Series heading and the Internet Events heading.

2. Save the document with the name **Skill Builder 8.4**, and then close the document.

Southern California Computer Training

Summer Training Schedule

The following schedule is for hands-on workshops, seminars, and Internet events for July, August, and September. If you plan on attending an event, make your reservations early as we have limited seating. You should also pick up your training materials at least one week prior to your event.

Hands-On Workshops
Irvine—Tuesday, July 20
Los Angeles—Wednesday, July 21
San Diego—Wednesday, August 18
Riverside—Tuesday, September 21

Seminar Series
Irvine—Wednesday, July 21
Los Angeles—Thursday, August 19
Riverside—Wednesday, September 22

Internet Events
Los Angeles—Friday, August 20
Woodland Hills—Thursday, September 2

Assessments

Assessment 8.1 **Create a Memorandum**

1. Follow these guidelines to create the memorandum shown below:

   ▪ Begin the document 2" down from the top of the page.

   ▪ Boldface the lead words MEMO TO:, FROM:, DATE:, and SUBJECT: as shown.

   ▪ Use the em dash after the department names.

   ▪ Type your initials at the bottom of the memo.

2. Save the document to your exercise diskette with the name **Assessment 8.1**.

3. Print the document, and then close it.

MEMO TO: Mark Paxton

FROM: Tamara Niu

DATE: Today's Date

SUBJECT: Purchase Orders

The following departments have requested that purchase orders be issued for the specified products. Please conduct the necessary research and issue purchase orders as soon as possible.

Marketing—A cordless mouse that can be used at least six feet away from the base unit.

Systems—A flatbed scanner with high resolution. It should have software that allows enhancing of images even as scanning is taking place.

Research—A video camera that is supported by the Universal Serial Bus (USB) standard. The price should be lower than what we paid for the analog camera.

xx

Assessment 8.2

1. Open the document named Assessment 8.2 on your exercise diskette.

2. Follow these guidelines to modify the memorandum:

   - Apply bold formatting as shown below.

   - Insert the Do Not Try to Please Everyone line and the paragraphs following it as shown below, including the initials line and the attachment line.

MEMO TO: Office Staff

FROM: Ariel Ramirez

DATE: Today's Date

SUBJECT: Multiple Supervisors

Most executive assistants at our firm have multiple supervisors. Therefore, we are offering the following suggestions to make your work easier.

Prioritize—What is important may take preference over what is urgent. Which project can be delayed? Overall, which has the greatest importance to our firm? Evaluate and schedule your time accordingly.

Refuse Assignments—If you do not have the time, ask your supervisor if someone else can do the assignment. It's better to say no than to not meet the deadline.

Enjoy Multiple Projects—Learn to enjoy the challenge of switching from one project to another. You may not be able to finish them all, but realize the contribution you have made to each one.

Do Not Try to Please Everyone—There is no way you will please all of your supervisors all of the time. Set your own approval rating and go with it.

Listed on the attached sheet are some related workshops you may want to attend. Contact Human Resources for registration forms.

xx
Attachment

3. Tap (ENTER) once after the Attachment line; then insert a page break.

4. Follow these guidelines to create the following page:

   ■ Start the title line 2" down.

   ■ Center and bold the title as shown.

   ■ Apply the color of your choice to the title.

   ■ Double-space between all paragraphs.

RECOMMENDED WORKSHOPS

How to Mange Your Boss, April 23, Holiday Inn, Fremont, Phoenix Extension

The Perfect Support Person, April 30, Hyatt at the Airport, ProPeople Associates

Prioritizing Made Easy, May 5, Sheraton at the Wharf, CareerTech

Office Procedures for the Executive Assistant, May 7, SF Marriott, Phoenix Extension

---

5. Save the changes, print the document, and then close it.

Assessment 8.3

1. Open the document named Assessment 8.3.

2. Follow these guidelines to modify the document until it matches the following document:

   - Rearrange the paragraphs into groups as shown, using Cut and Paste, drag-and-drop, or the Office Clipboard. Use whichever method you prefer. The rearranged paragraphs should match the following example.

   - Insert a title, headings, and empty paragraphs as shown in the example.

   - Format the title and headings with an Arial bold font and a sea-green color. The title should have a font size of 16.

   - Use (ENTER) to push the entire completed document down to the 2" position.

3. Save the document, print the document, and then close it.

Bay Area Environmental Groups

Marin County
Marin Wetlands Conservation Corps, Marin County
Mt. Tamalpais Hiking Club, Marin County
John Muir Society, Marin County
Redwood Preservation Group, Marin County

East Bay
East Bay Conservation Corps, East Bay
El Cerrito Wetlands Restoration, East Bay
San Pablo Reservoir Water Reclamation, East Bay
Citizens for Environmental Restoration, East Bay

South Bay
South Bay Water Restoration, South Bay
San Jose Environmental Corps, South Bay
Gilroy Preservation Society, South Bay
Bay Wildlife Foundation, South Bay

Critical Thinking

Critical Thinking 8.1 On Your Own

Tanisha Johnson is the Director of Human Resources for Big Time Video Distributors. Tanisha works hard to provide Big Time employees with a variety of attractive fringe benefits. She realizes this is necessary in today's competitive job market. Recently, Tanisha set up the Big Time Discounts program with other local businesses. Through this program, Big Time employees are issued a Big Time discount card. The card gives Big Time employees a 10% discount on the products or services they purchase from participating businesses.

Set up a memorandum from Tanisha Johnson to the Big Time employees announcing the program. Let the employees know that the effective date will be the beginning of next month and that all employees are eligible to participate. Let them know that a 10% discount will be given to them on all purchases. Mention that the participating businesses list will be issued within a few days. Save your completed memorandum as **Critical Thinking 8.1**, then close it.

Critical Thinking 8.2 On Your Own

Tanisha Johnson has prepared the memorandum that was set up in Critical Thinking 8.1 but she changes her mind and decides not to send the memo until the participating businesses list is completed. Open the Critical Thinking 8.1 memorandum and save it as **Critical Thinking 8.2**. Add a second page to the memorandum that includes the following participating businesses list. You can use the (TAB) key to line up the list entries. Also, bold the headings as shown.

Discount Provider	Contact	Number
West Side Chiropractic	Dave Smith	223-1345
The Panda Restaurant	Sam Chin	223-0909
Spiffy Cleaners	Carol Caruso	222-9090
Southside Cinemas	Ken Turner	221-2121
Dave's Auto Repair	Dave Adams	221-4545

Include a centered title at the top of the second page. Edit the memorandum text on the first page to indicate that the participating businesses list is attached. Your memorandum should also have an attachment notation. Save the changes to the document, and then close it.

Critical Thinking 8.3 **Web Research**

Veronica Smith was recently promoted to Vice President of Operations for Veritime Systems. Veritime develops transaction processing systems and employs more than 1,500 people. One of Veronica's primary goals is to streamline the procurement process. She realizes that Veritime's procurement processes are outdated and too centralized. Veronica wants to push decision making down to the departmental level and use the Internet to streamline processes and ultimately save money.

The first directive that Veronica issues is to push purchasing decisions for office supplies down to the various department managers. Set up a memorandum from Veronica to all departmental managers. The memo should state that office supply purchases can now be made at the department level. Use Internet Explorer and a search engine of your choice to locate three office supply companies that allow purchases to be made from their Web sites. Add a second page to your memorandum listing the approved Web-based office supply stores. Include the URLs and 800 numbers of the stores. Save your completed memorandum as **Critical Thinking 8.3**.

Critical Thinking 8.4 **On Your Own**

Health-e-Meals.com (Critical Thinking 7.5 exercise) has been in business for over two years, and you have had tremendous success. The credit line that was secured through Citizen's Bank has allowed Health-e-Meals to surpass even your most optimistic projections. During this time, you have hired 16 employees to do everything from delivery to office management. To celebrate your success, you have decided to organize a company winter holidays party.

Set up a memorandum to all employees announcing the Winter Holiday party. Praise your employees for their hard work and the success of the company. Let them know how optimistic the future looks and how you look forward to the coming year. Insert a page break at the end of your memorandum. On page 2, outline the details of the party including date, time, location, and agenda. Save the completed memorandum as **Critical Thinking 8.4**.

LESSON 9

Professional Writing and Editing Tools

In this lesson, you will use online Help and professional writing and editing tools. Online Help allows you to get assistance at any time. Word 2003 provides spell checking, grammar checking, and a powerful thesaurus. Word 2003 even has automatic spell checking and grammar checking that check your work as you write. Another powerful tool in Word 2003 is Find and Replace, especially useful for finding and replacing text in large documents. Once you master the writing tools in Word 2003, you'll be able to write business documents, research papers, and reports with confidence.

IN THIS LESSON

Case Study

Sarah Thomas is a Health Science major at Upper State University. In order to fulfill the requirements of her Nutritional Studies class, Sarah has chosen to write a research paper on diabetes. She is interested in this topic since one of her family members was recently afflicted with diabetes. Sarah takes full advantage of the powerful writing and editing tools in Word 2003, using the spelling and grammar checkers to proof her paper prior to submission. She uses the thesaurus to find the best words to express her ideas, and finally, she uses the find and replace feature to make changes and ensure consistency throughout her paper.

Sarah uses spell check, shown to the right, as a proofreading aid to help ensure the accuracy of her report.

The grammar checker highlights questionable phrases and provides suggestions. This helps Sarah focus on content while creating a professional looking report.

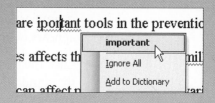

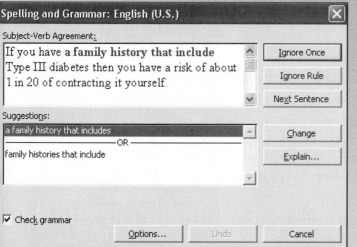

Choosing the right word to express her ideas is important to Sarah, and she relies on Word's thesaurus to provide a list of synonyms.

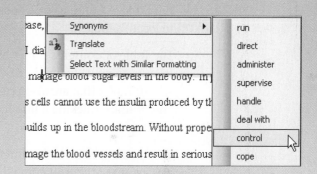

Online Help

Word's online Help puts a complete reference book at your fingertips. Help is available for just about any topic you can imagine. Online Help is important because Microsoft does not provide reference manuals with Office 2003. The reference manuals are now integrated into online Help.

Locating Help Topics

There are several methods you can use to locate Help topics:

- The Type a Question for Help `Type a question for help ▾ ✕` box appears at the right edge of the menu bar. Simply enter a question or search term in the box and a Search Results task pane appears with a list of topics you can choose from.

- Click the Help ⓦ button toward the right edge of the standard toolbar and the Word Help task pane appears. (You can also press F1 or choose Help→Microsoft Office Word Help from the menu bar to access the Word Help task pane.) In the task pane, you can enter a search term or click the Table of Contents link. The Table of Contents is similar to the Table of Contents in a book, which you can scan to locate a topic.

  The Table of Contents topics have book icons in front of them. When you click on the icon, you may see subtopics that are also preceded by book icons and/or links. Clicking a link takes you directly to that topic.

- When you have an active Internet connection, Help links you to Microsoft.com where you can find helpful information including tutorials, tips, frequently asked questions (FAQs), and more.

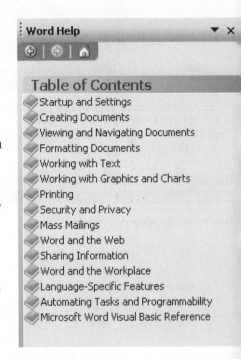

The Help Toolbars

The Word Help task pane has a toolbar at the top of the pane that allows you to navigate through Help panes.

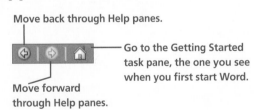

Move back through Help panes.

Go to the Getting Started task pane, the one you see when you first start Word.

Move forward through Help panes.

When you locate a topic you want to display, click the topic link and the Microsoft Office Word Help window appears. It contains the toolbar shown here.

The Auto Tile button causes the Help window to tile next to the Word window so you can read the Help information while working in the document. When the window is tiled, the button name changes to Untile. In Untile mode, the Help window minimizes to the task bar when you click in the Word document.

If you have looked at several Help topics the Back and Forward buttons allow you to navigate through those topics.

The Print button prints the topic currently in the Microsoft Office Word Help window.

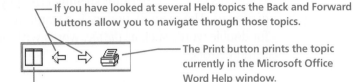

Hands-On 9.1 Use Online Help

1. Click the Help ⓘ button toward the right edge of the Standard toolbar.
   The Word Help task pane appears.

2. Type **spell check** in the Search For field toward the top of the task pane then click the green arrow ➡ button.
   The Search Results task pane appears.

3. Click the Check Spelling and Grammar link in the Search Results task pane.
   The Microsoft Office Word Help window appears, containing information on how to conduct a spell check. The window contains topic links that expand to reveal additional information when you click them.

4. Click the Close ☒ button in the upper-right corner of the Help window to close it.

5. Click the Close ☒ button in the upper-right corner of the Search Results task pane to close it.

6. Click the mouse in the Type a Question for Help box at the right edge of the menu bar and type **How do you print?**, then tap the (ENTER) key.
   The Search Results task pane appears again, this time containing topics that relate to printing.

7. Click the Help ⓘ button on the Standard toolbar to return to the Word Help task pane.

8. Click the Table of Contents link below the Search For field toward the top of the task pane to access the Table of Contents.

9. Click the book icon in front of the Formatting Documents topic to reveal the subtopics in that subject. Click the Margins and Page Setup link to display the relevant topics.
   Clicking one of the topic links would cause the Microsoft Office Word Help window to appear with detailed information about the topic. Clicking an open book icon closes the book and collapses the topic.

10. Close ☒ the Word Help task pane.

Spell Checking

Word checks a document for spelling errors by comparing each word to the contents of a main dictionary. The main dictionary is a standard, college-level dictionary. The spell checker also looks for double words such as *the the*, words with numbers such as *2004budget*, and a variety of capitalization errors.

Custom Dictionaries

Word actually compares your document with two (or more) dictionaries: the main dictionary and one or more custom dictionaries. Custom dictionaries contain words such as last names or company names that may not be in the main dictionary. You can add words to a custom dictionary during a spell check. For example, you may want to add last names or company names you frequently use in your work. The spell checker will ignore those words during future spell checks. Word also lets you use dictionaries for languages other than English. You can even purchase dictionaries with specific terminology, such as medical or legal terminology.

Automatic Spell Checking

Word can automatically check your spelling as you type. Word flags spelling errors by underlining them with wavy red lines. You can correct a flagged error by right-clicking the error and choosing a suggested replacement word or other option from the pop-up menu that appears.

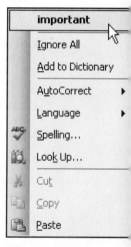

Spell Check Pop-Up Menu

 ## Hands-On 9.2 Use Automatic Spell Checking

Correct Spelling Errors

1. Open the document named Hands-On Lesson 9 on your exercise diskette.
   This document has plenty of spelling errors for you to correct.

2. Notice the word *iportant* in the first sentence has a wavy red underline.
   Misspelled words are identified by wavy red underlines.

3. *Right-click* the word *iportant,* and the following pop-up menu will appear.
   Take a few moments to study the following illustration.

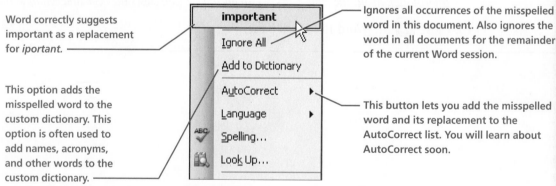

Word correctly suggests important as a replacement for *iportant.*

This option adds the misspelled word to the custom dictionary. This option is often used to add names, acronyms, and other words to the custom dictionary.

Ignores all occurrences of the misspelled word in this document. Also ignores the word in all documents for the remainder of the current Word session.

This button lets you add the misspelled word and its replacement to the AutoCorrect list. You will learn about AutoCorrect soon.

4. Choose important from the top of the list as shown in the preceding illustration. *Important will replace iportant.*

5. *Right-click* the word *millionAmericans* on the second line of the first paragraph, and choose *million Americans* from the pop-up menu.

Double Word and Capitalization Errors

6. Notice the double word *with with* in the third line. *Word reports these types of errors as well.*

7. *Right-click* the second occurrence of *with,* and choose Delete Repeated Word from the pop-up menu.

8. *Right-click* the word WIth at the start of the second paragraph.

9. Choose With from the pop-up menu. *As you can see, the spell checker looks for spelling, double words, and capitalization errors. You can always correct spelling as you type by right-clicking words with wavy red underlines and choosing an option from the pop-up menu.*

Grammar Checking

Word has a sophisticated grammar checker that can help improve your writing skills. Like the spell checker, the grammar checker can check grammar as you type. The grammar checker "flags" grammar errors by underlining them with wavy green lines. You can correct a flagged error by right-clicking the error and choosing a replacement phrase or other option from the pop up menu. Be careful when using the grammar checker, however, because it isn't perfect. There is no substitute for careful proofreading.

The Spelling and Grammar Dialog Box

The Spelling and Grammar dialog box is useful when you are spell checking and/or grammar checking a large document. It also provides access to customization options. For example, you use the Spelling and Grammar dialog box to choose a customized dictionary for the spell checker and to choose the writing style for the grammar checker. The Spelling and Grammar dialog box is displayed with the Tools→Spelling and Grammar command or by clicking the Spelling and Grammar button on the Standard toolbar.

FROM THE KEYBOARD
Press (F7) to start Spelling and Grammar checker

Use the Spell Checker

1. Click the Spelling and Grammar 🗹 button on the Standard toolbar.
   The spell check will begin, and the speller should stop on the misspelled word tretment *in the second paragraph.*

2. Take a few moments to study the following illustration.

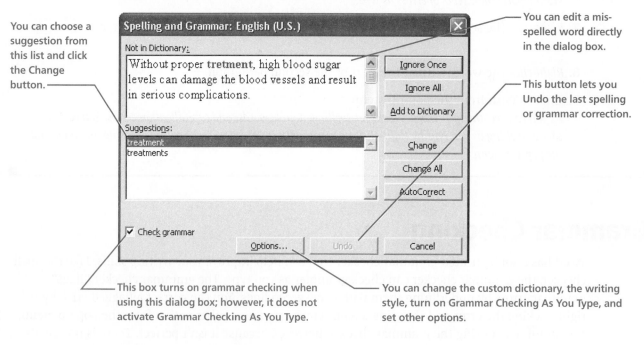

You can choose a suggestion from this list and click the Change button.

You can edit a mis-spelled word directly in the dialog box.

This button lets you Undo the last spelling or grammar correction.

This box turns on grammar checking when using this dialog box; however, it does not activate Grammar Checking As You Type.

You can change the custom dictionary, the writing style, turn on Grammar Checking As You Type, and set other options.

Use the Grammar Checker

3. Make sure that the Check Grammar box is checked.
   This will ensure that the grammar checking portion of this exercise works as it should.

4. Choose treatment from the Suggestions list, and click the Change button.
   Now the grammar checker should detect a grammatical error.

5. Follow these steps to explore the grammar checker options:

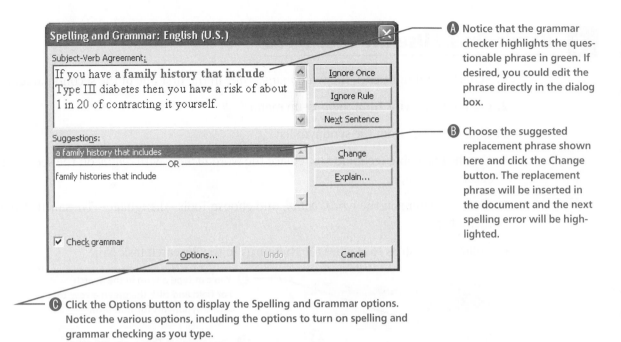

Ⓐ Notice that the grammar checker highlights the questionable phrase in green. If desired, you could edit the phrase directly in the dialog box.

Ⓑ Choose the suggested replacement phrase shown here and click the Change button. The replacement phrase will be inserted in the document and the next spelling error will be highlighted.

Ⓒ Click the Options button to display the Spelling and Grammar options. Notice the various options, including the options to turn on spelling and grammar checking as you type.

Ⓓ Close the Spelling and Grammar options box without changing any options.

6. Use the following guidelines to spell check and grammar check the remainder of this document:

  ▨ Use your best judgment to determine the correct spelling of all misspelled words.

  ▨ Use your best judgment to determine the correct grammar if Word reports grammar errors.

  ▨ From time-to-time, messages may pop up helping you with reported spelling and grammar errors. The messages will vanish as soon as you take any kind of action.

Thesaurus

The thesaurus can help improve your vocabulary and writing skills by providing synonyms (words with the same meaning) for words or phrases. The thesaurus can help you choose just the right words or phrases to accurately express your ideas. You can easily display a list of synonyms by right-clicking a selected word or phrase and choosing Synonyms from the pop up menu that appears. Thesaurus is also available via the Research task pane. You access the Research task pane with the thesaurus resource displayed by choosing Tools→Language→Thesaurus from the menu bar.

FROM THE KEYBOARD
(SHIFT)+(F7) to display the Thesaurus

1. Scroll up and right-click the word *manufacture* in the first line of the second paragraph.

2. Choose Synonyms from the pop-up menu.

3. Choose *produce* from the synonym list.

4. Use the preceding technique to replace the word *manage* with *control* on the second line of the second paragraph.

5. Click anywhere on the word *control*, and choose Tools→Language→Thesaurus from the menu bar.

6. Follow these steps to explore the thesaurus in the Research task pane:

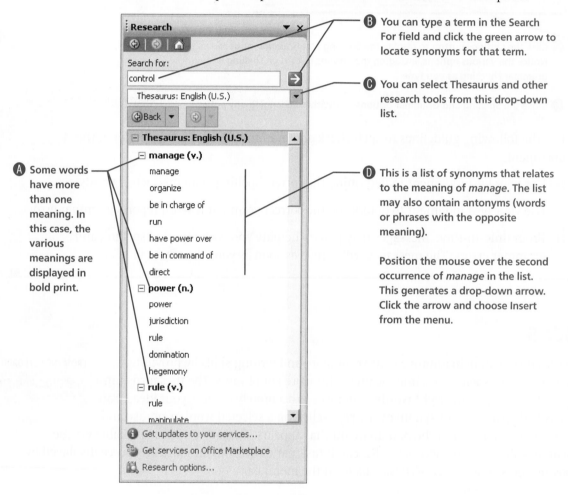

B You can type a term in the Search For field and click the green arrow to locate synonyms for that term.

C You can select Thesaurus and other research tools from this drop-down list.

A Some words have more than one meaning. In this case, the various meanings are displayed in bold print.

D This is a list of synonyms that relates to the meaning of *manage*. The list may also contain antonyms (words or phrases with the opposite meaning).

Position the mouse over the second occurrence of *manage* in the list. This generates a drop-down arrow. Click the arrow and choose Insert from the menu.

7. Right-click the word *manage*, and choose *control* from the Synonyms list on the pop-up menu.

8. Feel free to experiment with the thesaurus, then close the Research task pane.

9. Save 💾 your document and leave it open for the next exercise.

Find and Replace

Word's Find command lets you search a document for a particular word or phrase. You can also search for text formats, page breaks, and a variety of other items. Find is often the quickest way to locate a phrase, format, or item in a document. The Replace option lets you replace the found phrase, format, or item with a replacement phrase, format, or item. The Find and Replace dialog box is displayed with either the Edit→Find command or the Edit→Replace command.

FROM THE KEYBOARD

Press (CTRL)+(F) for Find
Press (CTRL)+(H) for Replace

Hands-On 9.5 Use Find

Find a Word

1. Position the insertion point at the top of the document, and make sure that no text is selected.

2. Choose Edit→Find from the menu bar.

3. Follow these steps to search for the word *pancreas:*

A Type **pancreas** in the Find What box. Notice the drop-down button at the right edge of the box. The drop-down button displays a list of previous words for which you have searched. ———

B Click this button if it is labeled More. The dialog box will expand and the Search and Find options will appear as shown here. ———

C Notice these check boxes. You will use these boxes later in this exercise. ———

D You can also choose to search either Up or Down from the insertion point. ———

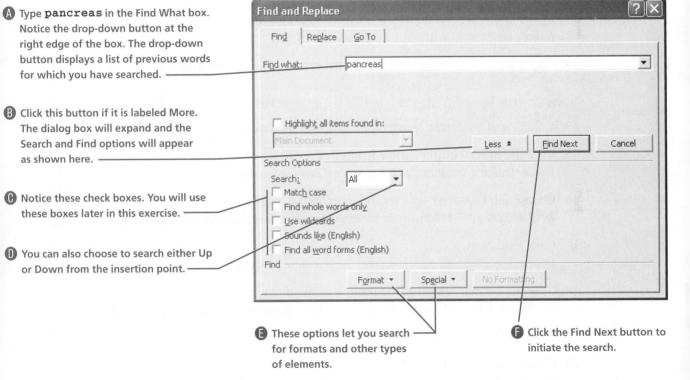

E These options let you search for formats and other types of elements.

F Click the Find Next button to initiate the search.

Find Another Word

4. Click in the Find What box, delete *pancreas* and type **With** (with a capital W) in its place.

5. Click the Find Next button, and *with* should be located in the second paragraph.

6. Click Find Next again, and the word *Without* should be located in the second paragraph.
   Notice that With was found even though it is part of the word Without. By default, Find is not case-sensitive, and it doesn't recognize the difference between a whole word or part of the word. You will change this, however, in the next few steps.

Use Match Case

7. Click the Match Case check box under the search options.
   This instructs Word to find only occurrences of the search string with the same matching case.

8. Click the Find Next button, and Word will locate the capitalized word *With* further down in the document.

9. Click Find Next again, and Word will indicate the entire document has been searched.
   Word skipped over several occurrences of with *in lowercase.*

10. Click OK on the message box, then uncheck the Match Case check box.

Search for a Whole Word

11. Scroll to the top of the document, and click the insertion point anywhere on the document title.
    Notice you can scroll while the Find and Replace box is open, although you may need to move the box out of your way.

12. Check the Find Whole Words Only check box.

13. Click Find Next several times until Word indicates that the entire document has been searched.
    Notice that the word without *was not located this time.*

14. Click OK on the message box, then uncheck the Find Whole Words Only check box.

Search for Text Formats and Tab Characters

Notice the Format and Special buttons at the bottom of the dialog box.

15. Click the Special button, and a list of items will appear.
    You can search a document for the presence of any item in this list.

16. Choose Tab Character (the second item on the list).
    Word will place a ^t character in the Find What box. This character tells Word to search for a tab.

17. Click Find Next.
    Word will select the space at the start of the first main paragraph. A tab created this space.

18. Click the Format button at the bottom of the dialog box.
    The Format button lets you search for specific fonts, paragraph formats, and other formats.

19. Choose Font from the list.

20. Choose Bold from the Font Style list, and click OK.
    The words Format: Font: Bold should appear below the Find What box.

21. Remove the ⁀t character from the Find What box; then click the Find Next button twice.
    Word should select the title because it is in bold.

22. Click the Cancel button to close the Find and Replace dialog box.

23. Click anywhere on the title to remove the selection.

Use Replace

24. Press (CTRL)+(H) to display the Find and Replace dialog box.
    Notice that the Replace tab is active in the dialog box. The shortcut keystroke you use determines which tab displays when the dialog box appears. Notice that there are tabs for Find, Replace, and Go To. Go To is covered later in this lesson.

25. Click the No Formatting button at the bottom of the dialog box.
    This turns off the bold setting that you searched for earlier in this exercise. In the next step, you will begin replacing the Roman numeral III with II.

26. Type the Roman numeral **III** (3 capital I's) in the Find What box and **II** in the Replace box.

27. Click the Find Next button.
    Word will locate and select the first occurrence of III.

28. Click the Replace button.
    Word replaces III with II and selects the next occurrence of III in the document.

29. Now click Replace All, and Word will replace all occurrences of III with II.
    Word should indicate that three replacements were made.

30. Click OK to dismiss the message box.

⚠WARNING! *Be careful with Replace All because you may make accidental replacements. For example, if you replace cat with dog, then words like* catapult *may become* dogapult. *You should use the Find Whole Words Only option if the word you are replacing might be part of a larger word (like* cat *and* catapult).

31. Move the insertion point to the top of the document and use Replace to replace the word *running* with *walking*. Make the replacements one at a time (rather than using Replace All). *Notice that Word maintains the appropriate capitalization for each replacement.*

32. Feel free to experiment with Find and Replace.

33. Close the Find and Replace dialog box when you have finished, but leave the document open.

Word Count

The word count feature counts the number of pages. words, characters, paragraphs, and lines in a document. Word count can be useful if you need to adjust your document to a specific length. For example, students who are creating reports or research papers often have length constraints. Word count is particularly useful to word processing professionals who bill clients by the word or page. You initiate word count with the Tools→Word Count command.

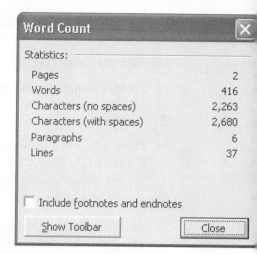

Word Count Statistics

 Hands-On 9.6 Use Word Count

1. Click anywhere in the document to make sure no words are selected.

2. Choose Tools→Word Count from the menu bar.
   Word will analyze the document and display the statistics.

3. Take a few moments to study the results, then click the Close button.
   Don't be concerned if your statistics do not match the illustration above. Your numbers depend on the changes you have made in the document so far.

4. Save the changes to the document, then close the document.

Recently Used File List

Word and other Office applications list up to nine of the most recently used files at the bottom of the File menu. You can open any of these documents by choosing them from the list. This is often the most efficient way to open a recently used document. The following Quick Reference steps explain how to adjust the number of files displayed on the Recently Used File List.

QUICK REFERENCE: MODIFYING THE RECENTLY USED FILE LIST

- Choose Tools→Options from the menu bar.
- Click the General tab.
- Adjust the number of entries in the Recently Used File List box.

Hands-On 9.7 Use the Recently Used Files List

1. Choose File from the menu bar.
   You will notice up to nine recently used documents are listed at the bottom of the menu. The Hands-On Lesson 9 document should be at the top of the list because you used it in the previous exercise.

2. Choose Hands-On Lesson 9 from the list, and the document will open.
   Leave the document open; you will continue to use it in the next exercise.

The Go To Command

The Go To command lets you rapidly locate a specific page in a document. Go To can also be used to locate objects (which you have not learned about) such as bookmarks, tables, footnotes, and endnotes. You choose the object you wish to go to in the Go To tab of the Find and Replace dialog box. You can display the Go To tab of the Find and Replace dialog box by choosing Edit→Go To from the menu bar. You can also display the Go To tab by double-clicking the page number section of the status bar.

FROM THE KEYBOARD
(CTRL)+(G) to display Go To dialog box

 Hands-On 9.8 Go To a Page

Use the Keyboard

1. Press (CTRL)+(G), and the Go To tab of the Find and Replace dialog box will appear.

2. Type **2** into the Enter Page Number box, and click the Go To button.
   The insertion point should move to the top of page 2.

3. Click the Close button in the dialog box.

Use the Status Bar

4. Double-click anywhere on the page number section of the status bar to display the Go To tab of the Find and Replace dialog box.

Page 2	Sec 1	2/2

   Notice that you can go to other locations, such as Sections, Lines, etc.

5. Type **1** into the Enter Page Number box, and then click the Go To button.

6. Close the Find and Replace dialog box.

Hyphenation

Word lets you hyphenate text automatically or manually. With automatic hyphenation, Word hyphenates words whenever it determines that hyphenation is necessary. With manual hyphenation, Word searches the document for words to hyphenate. When a word requiring hyphenation is located, Word prompts you to confirm the hyphen location within the word. Hyphenation is most useful in documents with short line lengths, such as documents containing newspaper style columns.

QUICK REFERENCE: HYPHENATING TEXT

To Hyphenate a Document Automatically:

- Choose Tools→Language→Hyphenation from the menu bar.
- Check the Automatically Hyphenate Document box, and click OK.

To Hyphenate a Document Manually:

- Choose Tools→Language→Hyphenation from the menu bar.
- Click the Manual button.
- If Word identifies a word to hyphenate and you want the hyphen positioned at the location Word proposes, click Yes. If you want the hyphen positioned at a different location in the word, then use the arrow keys on the keyboard to adjust the position, and then click Yes.

The Hyphenation Zone

The Hyphenation dialog box contains a Hyphenation Zone setting. The hyphenation zone lets you adjust the sensitivity of the hyphenation. You can widen the hyphenation zone by entering a larger number in the Hyphenation Zone box. This will reduce the number of words that are hyphenated. Likewise, you can increase the number of words that are hyphenated by entering a smaller number for the hyphenation zone.

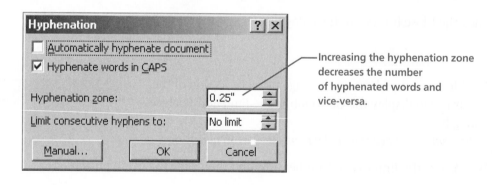

Increasing the hyphenation zone decreases the number of hyphenated words and vice-versa.

Nonbreaking Hyphens Nonbreaking Spaces

Some phrases (such as easy-to-use) require hyphens between the words in the phrase. You can use nonbreaking hyphens to ensure that all words in the phrase stay together on the same line. If you use nonbreaking hyphens and there is not enough space on a line for the entire phrase, then Word will move the entire phrase to the beginning of the next line. You insert nonbreaking hyphens with the (CTRL)+(SHIFT)+(-) keystroke combination. Likewise, you can insert nonbreaking spaces with the (CTRL)+(SHIFT)+(SPACE BAR) keystroke combination.

Hands-On 9.9 Use Hyphenation

1. Browse through the document and notice that there are no hyphenated words at the ends of the lines.
   This is because automatic hyphenation is turned off.

2. Scroll to the top of the document, and click on the title.

3. Choose Tools→Language→Hyphenation from the menu bar.

4. Make sure the hyphenation zone setting is set to .25", and click the Automatically Hyphenate Document check box.

5. Click OK, and browse through the document counting the number of end-of-line hyphens.
   You will increase the hyphenation zone setting in the next few steps and notice how this affects the number of hyphens.

6. Choose Tools→Language→Hyphenation from the menu bar.

7. Set the hyphenation zone to **.5"** and click OK.

8. Browse through the document, count the number of hyphens.
   The number of hyphens should have been reduced.

9. Choose Tools→Language→Hyphenation from the menu bar.

10. Uncheck the Automatically Hyphenate Document box, and click OK.

11. Browse through the document and notice that all automatic hyphens have been removed.

12. Save the document, close it, and continue with the end-of-lesson questions and exercises.

Concepts Review

True/False Questions

1. When you choose Tools→Language→Thesaurus from the menu bar, the Research task pane appears.   TRUE   FALSE

2. Word marks misspelled words with wavy red underlines.   TRUE   FALSE

3. You can correct a misspelled word by clicking it with the left mouse button and choosing a suggested replacement from the pop-up menu.   TRUE   FALSE

4. The Ignore All command on the Spelling and Grammar dialog box ignores a misspelled word for the current spell check only.   TRUE   FALSE

5. The spell checker can identify certain types of capitalization errors.   TRUE   FALSE

6. The Go To command can be initiated by pressing (ALT)+(G).   TRUE   FALSE

7. The thesaurus lets you find and replace misspelled words.   TRUE   FALSE

8. Increasing the hyphenation zone measurement increases the number of hyphenated words.   TRUE   FALSE

9. When you are using the Find dialog box, clicking the More button causes the dialog box to expand, revealing additional options.   TRUE   FALSE

10. The recently used file list is often the most efficient way to open a recently used document.   TRUE   FALSE

Multiple Choice Questions

1. Which of the following statements is true?
   a. The spell checker uses only a main dictionary.
   b. The only time a custom dictionary is used is with legal documents.
   c. The spell checker can use both a main and custom dictionary for all spell checks.
   d. None of the above

2. Which command initiates Word Count?
   a. Tools→Word Count
   b. Edit→Word Count
   c. Format→Word Count
   d. None of the above

3. Which of the following methods is used to access Help topics?
   a. Press the (F3) key.
   b. Enter a question or search term in the Type a Question for Help box.
   c. Choose Tools→Help from the menu bar.
   d. Click the Microsoft Office Word Help button on the standard toolbar.

4. On which menu is a list of the most recently used documents displayed?
   a. File
   b. Edit
   c. Insert
   d. Format

Skill Builders

Skill Builder 9.1 Use Online Help

1. Type the phrase **Office Clipboard** in the Type a Question for Help box and tap the (ENTER) key

2. Click the Display the Contents of the Office Clipboard topic that appears in the Search Results task pane.

3. Take a moment to read the topic, then close the Microsoft Office Word Help window.

4. Click the Help button on the standard toolbar to display the Word Help task pane.

5. Type **custom dictionaries** in the Search For field toward the top of the task pane and click the green arrow.

6. Click the Create and Use Custom Dictionaries link in the Search Result task pane.

7. Scan the topic, then close the Microsoft Office Word Help window.

8. Click the Back button toward the top of the Search Results task pane to return to the Word Help task pane.

9. Click the Table of Contents link below the Search For field.

10. Experiment with the Table of Contents by clicking book icons to view subtopics and links for various subjects.

11. If necessary, close the Microsoft Office Word Help window, then close the task pane.

Skill Builder 9.2 Spell Checking/Find and Replace

1. Start a new document, and type the business letter shown below. Use Word's automatic spell checking and grammar checking as you type the letter. Format the text with bold and italics as shown.

Today's date

Mr. Juan Lopez
Editor-in-Chief
Western Wildlife Publications
1450 Parker Lane
Ventura, CA 93003

Dear Mr. Lopez:

A short time ago, I subscribed to *Birds of Prey* magazine and I am enjoying it immensely. Your monthly tips have been especially useful. I have spotted more than twenty new species in my local area since I first subscribed to *Birds of Prey*. **Keep up the good work!**

One thing that I would like to see more of in *Birds of Prey* is recommendations on bird watching sites in the Western United States. I am especially interested in bald eagles and golden eagles. I would appreciate any suggestions you may have.

Sincerely,

Jason Torval
450 Lighthouse Lane
Manhattan Beach, CA 90266

---

2. Press (CTRL)+(H) to open the Find and Replace dialog box.

3. Replace all occurrences of Birds of Prey with Bird Watcher.
   Word should automatically italicize the phrase Bird Watcher because Birds of Prey was italicized.

4. Make sure there are no spelling errors in the document.

5. Save the document with the name **Skill Builder 9.2**, then close the document.

Skill Builder 9.3 **Using the Thesaurus**

In this exercise, you will modify the letter you created in the previous exercise.

1. Choose File from the menu bar, and then choose Skill Builder 9.2 from the list of recently used files.
   Suppose you want to use a word other than especially *in the second paragraph.*

2. Right-click anywhere on the word *especially* in the second paragraph.

3. Choose Synonyms from the pop-up menu, and then choose *particularly.*

4. Use the thesaurus to find replacements for the word *useful* in the first paragraph and *appreciate* in the second paragraph.

5. Select the phrase *A short time ago* at the beginning of the first paragraph.

6. Right-click the selected phrase.

7. Choose the replacement phrase *not long ago,* from the Synonym list.
   Notice that Word replaces the phrase but does not capitalize the first word of the sentence.

8. Click Undo ↻ to restore the original phrase.

9. Select *immensely* at the end of the first sentence in the first paragraph.

10. Choose Tools→Language→Thesaurus from the menu bar.

11. Choose *enormously* in the task pane to replace *immensely.*

12. Choose File→Save As from the menu bar.
    This command can be used to save a document under a new name.

13. Change the name Skill Builder 9.2 in the filename box to **Skill Builder 9.3**, and click the Save button.
    The Skill Builder 9.2 file remains unchanged, and Skill Builder 9.3 now also resides on your diskette.

14. Close the Research pane, close the document, and continue with the next exercise.

Skill Builder 9.4 **Editing a Business Letter**

1. Open the document on your exercise diskette named Skill Builder 9.4.

2. Use Find and Replace to replace all occurrences of the word *bill* with *account*.

3. Use Find and Replace to replace all occurrences of the word *payment* with *check*.

4. Use spell check and grammar check to review the entire document. Use your best judgment to make spelling and grammar choices.

5. Select the entire document, and change the font size to 12.

6. Use (ENTER) to start the date line at approximately the 2" position.

7. Replace the phrase Today's Date with the current date.

8. Move the address block from the bottom of the letter to the space between the last body paragraph and the complimentary close (Sincerely). If necessary, insert or remove hard returns until there is a double space between the address block and the last body paragraph, and between the address block and the complimentary close (sincerely).

9. Center the three address block lines horizontally on the page.

10. Insert your typist's initials and the document name below the signature block.

11. Save the changes; then close the document.

Assessments

Assessment 9.1

1. Open the document on your exercise diskette named Assessment 9.1.

2. Use spell checker and grammar checker to review the document. Use your best judgment to determine which replacements to use.

3. Use Find and Replace to make the following replacements. Also, write the number of replacements in the third column of the table.

Word	Replace With	Number of Replacements
breaks	fractures	_____
collarbone	clavicle	_____
movement	range-of-motion	_____

4. Print the document when you have finished.

5. Save the changes; then close the document.

Assessment 9.2

1. Open the document on your exercise diskette named Assessment 9.2.

2. Replace the phrase Today's Date with the current date, using the Date and Time feature. Insert the date as a field so that it updates automatically.

3. Use spell checker and grammar checker to review the document. Use your best judgment to determine which replacement words to use. Assume all proper names are spelled correctly.

4. Use Find and Replace to make the following replacements. Make sure the case (lowercase or uppercase) remains the same for all replacements. Also, write the number of replacements in the third column of the table.

Word or phrase	Replace With	Number of Replacements
Dan Do not replace Dan in the inside address	Mr. Heywood	_____
families	people	_____
special consideration	something special	_____

5. Print the document when you have finished.

6. Save the changes; then close the document.

Critical Thinking

Critical Thinking 9.1 **On Your Own**

Amanda Jackson is the owner of Amanda's Bookstore. Amanda's Bookstore is located in a small community and specializes in fiction and poetry books. For the past 15 years, Amanda has held weekly poetry readings by local and nationally recognized poets. Write a personal business letter to Amanda thanking her for the poetry readings. Let Amanda know that you enjoy the readings very much and that you would like her to hold monthly book signings. Try to sell her on the idea of holding book signings by convincing her that the events will complement the poetry readings by encouraging fiction enthusiasts to visit the store. The address of Amanda's Bookstore is:

Amanda Jackson
Amanda's Bookstore
3420 Colonial Lane
Atlanta, GA 30308

Use Word's spell checker and grammar checker to spell check and grammar check the letter. Use the thesaurus to find replacement words for at least five words in the letter. Save the completed letter as **Critical Thinking 9.1**.

Critical Thinking 9.2 **On Your Own**

Open the letter that you created in Critical Thinking 7.1. Use Word's spell checker and grammar checker to spell check and grammar check the letter. Use the thesaurus where necessary to replace words in the letter. Save the changes to the completed letter, and close it.

Spell check, grammar check, and use the thesaurus on Critical Thinking exercises 7.3, 7.4, 8.1, 8.2, and 8.3. Save the changes to each document, and then close it.

Critical Thinking 9.3 **On Your Own**

Bill Patterson is the Executive Director of the Southside Coalition for the Homeless. Bill wants to open a new housing center that will provide shelter, meals, counseling, and job training for needy single mothers and their children. Bill has found the perfect building for the new shelter, but he needs to raise $250,000 to renovate and furnish the building. In addition, he needs $185,000 per year for food, medical supplies, staff salaries, and other expenses. Bill has decided to solicit large corporations in the area for donations. He believes this could be a profitable venture for the corporations because they will receive the following benefits:

Tax deductions
Positive publicity in the community
A pool of trained job candidates

Write a letter for Bill requesting donations from the corporations. The letter should specify the total amount of money needed, how it will be spent, and the benefits realized by the corporations. In addition, ask for specific donation amounts. The recommended donation amounts for the building renovation are $10,000, $15,000, and $25,000. The recommended donation amounts for the annual expenditures are $2,500, $5,000, and $10,000.

Spell check and grammar check your letter, and use the thesaurus to choose the right words. In an important letter such as this, choosing the right words can be essential. Save your completed letter as `Critical Thinking 9.3`.

Critical Thinking 9.4 Web Research

Use Internet Explorer and a search engine of your choice to find information on dictionaries that can be used with Word 2003. There are many third-party dictionaries available with legal, medical, and scientific terminology. Try to locate Web sites of companies that offer such products. Create a Word document that documents your findings. Include the company names, Web site URLs, and any other relevant information that you find. Save your document as `Critical Thinking 9.4`.

Critical Thinking 9.5 On Your Own

Open the document you created in Critical Thinking 7.5. Spell check and grammar check the document. Use the thesaurus to choose replacement words for several words in the letter. Choose words that enhance the letter and make your sentences stronger. Try to choose the right word for each occasion. Save the changes to the letter when you have finished.

Open the memorandum you created in Critical Thinking 8.4. Spell check and grammar check the letter. Use the thesaurus to choose replacement words for several words. Save the changes to the memorandum when you have finished.

LESSON 10

Creating a Simple Report

In this lesson, you will create a simple report. Reports are important documents often used in business and education. You will format your report using various paragraph formatting techniques. Paragraphs are a fundamental part of any Word document. You will learn how to use Word 2003's Click and Type feature and change line spacing. In addition, you will master indenting techniques using the ruler and the indent buttons on the Formatting toolbar.

IN THIS LESSON

Case Study

Bill Nelson is a freshman at West Side Junior College. Bill has enrolled in an information systems course in which Office 2003 is an important component. Bill has been assigned the task of preparing a report on the importance of computer technology in the twenty-first century. Professor Williams has instructed Bill to use Word 2003. After conducting the necessary research, Bill uses the paragraph formatting techniques in Word 2003 to prepare a report that is properly formatted and has a professional appearance.

Bill knows that good use of white space makes reports easier to read. Word's Line Spacing button provides a quick way to lighten up the main body of the report by applying double spacing.

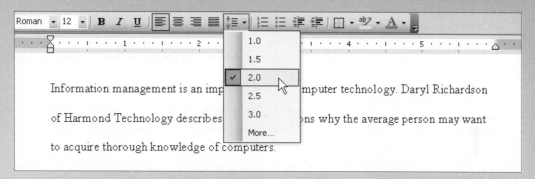

The indent markers on Word's ruler provide a simple method for emphasizing important facts in his report by offsetting the text from the margins.

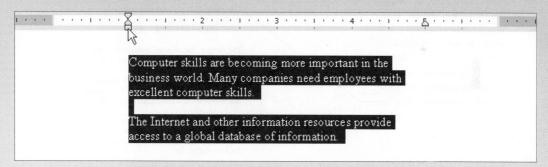

Report Formats

Overview

There are a variety of acceptable report formats. The example below shows a traditional business report in unbound format. Other report formats can be used for research papers and other types of documents.

Traditional Unbound Business Report Format

Double-spacing is typically set before beginning the report. Three double-spaced returns are used to space the title down to approximately the 2" position. ⎯⎯

The title is typed in upper-case, centered, and bold face. You can also apply a distinctive font to the title. ⎯⎯

The body of the report is double-spaced. The first line of each body paragraph is indented to 0.5". ⎯⎯

Quotations and other text you wish to emphasize are single-spaced and indented 0.5" to 1" on the left and right. You should double-space (by tapping ⎡ENTER⎤ twice) between quotes. ⎯⎯

COMPUTER TECHNOLOGY IN THE TWENTY-FIRST CENTURY

Our society has changed from a manufacturing-oriented society to an information society. Those with access to capital had power in the early 1900s. In the twenty-first century, however, power will come from access to information. The amount of worldwide information is growing at a rapid pace. Computer technology is responsible for much of this growth, but it can also help us manage the information.

Information management is an important use of computer technology. Daryl Richardson of Harmond Technology describes four other reasons why the average person may want to acquire thorough knowledge of computers.

> Computer skills are becoming more important in the business world. Many companies need employees with excellent computer skills.
>
> The Internet and other information resources provide access to a global database of information.
>
> Computer skills can often simplify ones personal life. Computers can be used to entertain, to manage finances, and to provide stimulating learning exercises for children.
>
> Using computers can provide a sense of accomplishment. Many people suffer from "computerphobia." Learning to use computers often creates a feeling of connection with the information age.

Click and Type

Click and Type lets you automatically apply formatting in blank areas of a document. Click and Type lets you set paragraph alignments (Align Left, Center, and Align Right), customize tab stops, insert tables, and apply other formats. To use Click and Type, position the mouse pointer in a blank area of a document and double-click. Click and Type inserts hard returns and adjusts the paragraph alignment as necessary to achieve the formatting you desire. Click and Type is only available in Print Layout, Web Layout, and Reading Layout views. The following illustrations demonstrate the use of Click and Type.

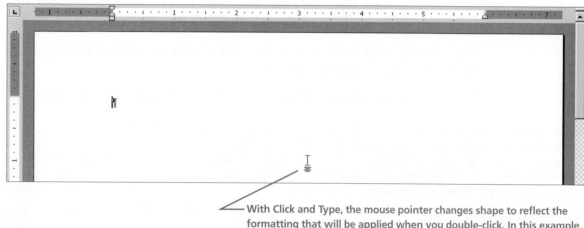

With Click and Type, the mouse pointer changes shape to reflect the formatting that will be applied when you double-click. In this example, the mouse pointer shows that center alignment will be applied.

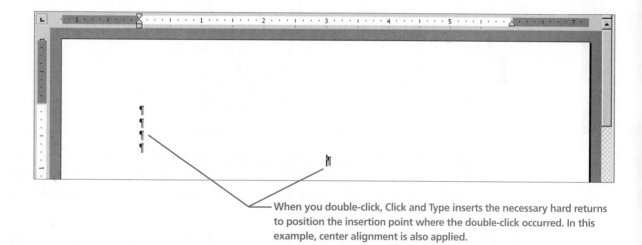

When you double-click, Click and Type inserts the necessary hard returns to position the insertion point where the double-click occurred. In this example, center alignment is also applied.

1. Start Word, and a blank document window will appear.

2. Make sure you are in Print Layout view. If necessary, use the View→Print Layout command to switch to Print Layout view.

3. Slide the mouse pointer to various locations in the blank document, and notice how the mouse pointer changes shape.
   The align left or align right shapes reflect the formatting that would be applied if you were to double-click.

4. Click the Show/Hide ¶ button to display the symbols.

5. Make sure the ruler is displayed at the top of the document window. If necessary, use the View→Ruler command to display the ruler.

6. Follow these steps to use Click and Type to format the title line of the report.

A Position the mouse pointer approximately 2" down and centered on the line. You can tell you are two inches down by looking at the vertical ruler. The 1" position on the white section of the vertical ruler means you are 2" down on the page. This is because the ruler's white section begins at the top margin, which is already 1" down from the top of the page.

B Double-click when the mouse pointer has the center alignment shape, as shown here.

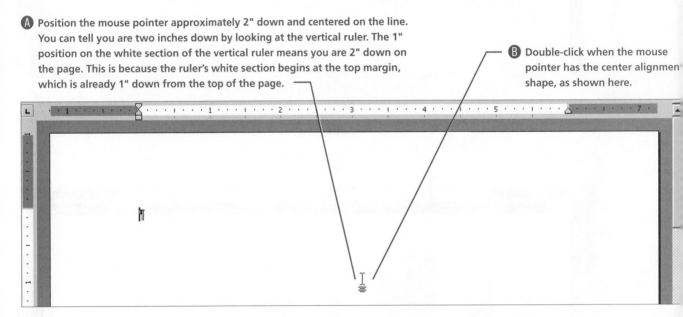

Word inserts paragraph marks as necessary and applies center alignment. Check the Status bar at the bottom of the window to ensure the insertion point is at approximately the 2" position. As you can see, Click and Type can be useful for rapidly applying formats. However, it does lack the precision that may be required for formatting some types of documents.

7. If the insertion point is not at the 2" position, use (ENTER) to insert hard returns as necessary to force it to the 2" position.

8. Turn on (CAPS LOCK), and click the Bold **B** button.

9. Type the report title **COMPUTER TECHNOLOGY IN THE TWENTY-FIRST CENTURY**.

10. Turn off bold, and tap (ENTER) twice.

11. Slide the mouse pointer to the left end of the current line.

12. Double-click when the mouse pointer has this shape $\overline{I}^{\overline{}}$.
    The alignment should change to left, and the insertion point should be positioned two lines below the title. Use Undo and try again if the alignment is not set to left.

13. Save the document to your exercise diskette with the name **Hands-On Lesson 10**.

Line Spacing

The Line Spacing button on the Formatting toolbar lets you set the line spacing for one or more paragraphs. Line spacing determines the amount of vertical space between lines in a paragraph. The default line spacing is single. Word makes a single-spaced line slightly higher than the largest character in the line. For example, if you are using a 12-point font, then single line spacing is slightly larger than 12 points. You apply line spacing by selecting the desired paragraph(s) and choosing the desired line spacing from the Line Spacing drop-down list. Line spacing can also be set using the Paragraph dialog box. The following table describes line spacing options available through the Paragraph dialog box.

FROM THE KEYBOARD
CTRL + 1 for single spacing
CTRL + 5 for 1.5 spacing
CTRL + 2 for double-spacing

Line Spacing	Description
Single	Default spacing in Word
1.5 Lines	1.5 times single-spacing
Double	Twice single-spacing
At Least	Specifies the minimum line spacing. The spacing may increase if the font size increases. However, the line spacing will never be smaller than the number of points specified in the At Least setting.
Exactly	Fixes the line spacing at the number of points specified. The line spacing remains fixed even if the font size of characters within the line changes.
Multiple	Lets you precisely control the line spacing by setting multiples such as 1.3 or 2.4.

Hands-On 10.2 Set Line Spacing

1. Make sure the insertion point is on the second blank line below the title.

2. Click the Line Spacing drop-down button, and choose 2.0.

3. Tap the (TAB) key once to create a 0.5" indent at the start of the paragraph.

4. Now type the following paragraph, but only tap (ENTER) after the last line in the paragraph.
   The lines will be double-spaced as you type them.

   Our society has changed from a manufacturing-oriented society to an information

   society. Those with access to capital had power in the early 1900s. In the twenty-first

   century, however, power will come from access to information. The amount of

   worldwide information is growing at a rapid pace. Computer technology is responsible

   for much of this growth, but it can also help us manage the information.

5. Make sure you tap (ENTER) after the last line. Then (TAB) once, and type the following paragraph.
   Notice the double-spacing has been carried to the new paragraph.

   Information management is an important use of computer technology. Daryl

   Richardson of Harmond Technology describes four other reasons why the average person

   may want to acquire thorough knowledge of computers.

6. Tap (ENTER) to complete the paragraph, then press (CTRL)+(1) to set single-spacing.
   The shortcut keystrokes can be quite useful for setting line spacing.

7. Now type the following paragraphs, tapping (ENTER) twice between paragraphs. There is no need to tab at the beginning of these paragraphs.

   Computer skills are becoming more important in the business world. Many companies
   need employees with excellent computer skills.

   The Internet and other information resources provide access to a global database of
   information.

   Computer skills can often simplify one's personal life. Computers can be used to
   entertain, to manage finances, and to provide stimulating learning exercises for children.

   Using computers can provide a sense of accomplishment. Many people suffer from
   "computerphobia." Learning to use computers often creates a feeling of connection with
   the information age.

8. Save 🖫 the changes, and continue with the next topic.

Indenting Text

Indenting offsets text from the margins. The left indent is the most widely used indent. The left indent sets off all lines in a paragraph from the left margin. Likewise, the right indent sets off all lines from the right margin. The first line indent sets off just the first line of paragraphs. This is similar to using ⟨TAB⟩ at the start of a paragraph. The hanging indent sets off all lines except the first.

The Increase Indent 🔲 button and Decrease Indent 🔲 button on the Formatting toolbar let you adjust the left indent. These buttons increase or decrease the left indent to the nearest tab stop. The default tab stops are set every 0.5", so the left indent changes 0.5" each time you click the buttons. You can also set indents using keystrokes, the Format→Paragraph dialog box, and by dragging indent markers on the horizontal ruler.

FROM THE KEYBOARD

⟨CTRL⟩+⟨M⟩ for left indent
⟨CTRL⟩+⟨SHIFT⟩+⟨M⟩ to remove left indent
⟨CTRL⟩+⟨T⟩ for hanging indent
⟨CTRL⟩+⟨SHIFT⟩+⟨T⟩ to remove hanging indent

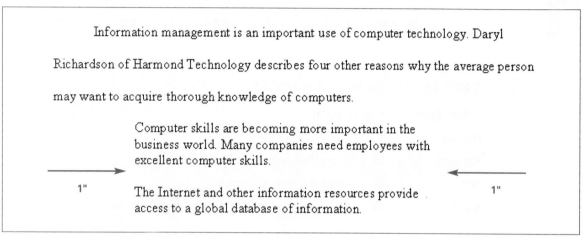

Information management is an important use of computer technology. Daryl Richardson of Harmond Technology describes four other reasons why the average person may want to acquire thorough knowledge of computers.

Computer skills are becoming more important in the business world. Many companies need employees with excellent computer skills.

1"

The Internet and other information resources provide access to a global database of information.

1"

These paragraphs are indented 1" from the left and right margins.

Hands-On 10.3 Experiment with Left Indents

Indent One Paragraph

1. Click in one of the single-spaced paragraphs you just typed.

2. Click the Increase Indent 🔲 button near the right end of the Formatting toolbar.
   The paragraph should be indented 0.5" on the left.

3. Click the Decrease Indent 🔲 button to remove the indent.

Indent Several Paragraphs

4. Use the mouse to select any part of two or more of the single-spaced paragraphs.
   You only need to select part of a paragraph when indenting or applying other paragraph formats.

5. Click Increase Indent 🔲 twice to create a 1" left indent on each of the selected paragraphs.

6. Now click Decrease Indent 🔲 twice to remove the indents.
   You will continue to work with indents in the next Hands-On exercise.

The Horizontal Ruler

You can set indents, margins, and tab stops by dragging markers on the horizontal ruler. When you use the ruler, you can see formatting changes as they are applied. The horizontal ruler is positioned just above the document in the document window. You can display or hide the ruler with the View→Ruler command. The following illustration shows the ruler, the margin boundaries, and the various indent markers.

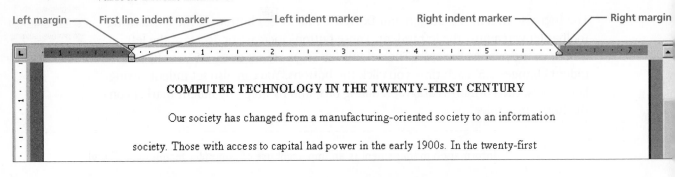

 QUICK REFERENCE: INDENT MARKERS

Indent Type		How to Set It
First line	▽	Drag this marker.
Hanging	⌂	Drag the top triangle.
Left	⌂	Drag the bottom square.
Right	△	Drag this marker on the right end of the ruler.

Hands-On 10.4 Use the Ruler to Indent Paragraphs

Set Left and Right Indents

1. If necessary, scroll down until the four single-spaced paragraphs at the bottom of your document are visible.

2. Select all four paragraphs by dragging the mouse pointer 𝔄 in the left margin.

3. Follow these steps to adjust the left and right indents:

Ⓐ Position the pointer on the Left Indent marker (the bottom box). A yellow Left Indent ScreenTip will appear, as shown here.

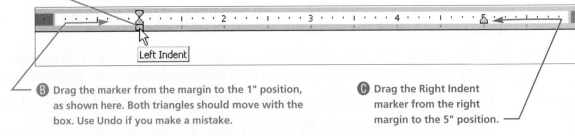

Ⓑ Drag the marker from the margin to the 1" position, as shown here. Both triangles should move with the box. Use Undo if you make a mistake.

Ⓒ Drag the Right Indent marker from the right margin to the 5" position.

4. Save the changes to your document, and then close the document.

Concepts Review

True/False Questions

1. The Increase Indent button changes the right indent. TRUE FALSE

2. The Decrease Indent button changes the right indent. TRUE FALSE

3. The ruler can be used to indent paragraphs. TRUE FALSE

4. The (CTRL)+(D) keystroke combination is used to set double-spacing. TRUE FALSE

5. The (CTRL)+(1) keystroke combination is used to set single-spacing. TRUE FALSE

6. With Click and Type, the mouse pointer changes shape to reflect the formatting that will be applied when you double-click in the document. TRUE FALSE

7. First Line indents only affect the first line of each selected paragraph. TRUE FALSE

8. The title begins 2" from the top of the page in a traditional business report. TRUE FALSE

9. When you choose At Least from the Line Spacing drop-down list on the Paragraph dialog box, the line spacing will never be smaller than the number of points specified. TRUE FALSE

10. When you use the Increase Indent button, the size of the indent is dependent on the position of the tab stops. TRUE FALSE

Multiple Choice Questions

1. In which of the following view modes is Click and Type available?
   a. Print Layout
   b. Web Layout
   c. Outline
   d. Reading Layout

2. If the font size of a paragraph is 12 point and the line spacing is set to single, then which of the following is true?
   a. The line spacing is slightly larger than 12 point.
   b. The line spacing is slightly smaller than 12 point.
   c. The line spacing is exactly 12 point.
   d. None of these

3. Which of the following actions should you take to adjust the right indent of three paragraphs?
   a. Drag the Right Indent marker.
   b. Select the paragraphs, and then drag the Right Indent marker.
   c. Select the paragraphs, and tap the (TAB) key.
   d. All of the above

4. Which command is used to display the horizontal ruler?
   a. View→Ruler
   b. Edit→Display Ruler
   c. Insert→Ruler
   d. File→Ruler

Skill Builders

Skill Builder 10.1 Indents and Line Spacing

1. Start a new document, and use the Line Spacing ⌄≣▾ button to set the line spacing to 2.0.

2. Click the Center ≣ button, and tap (ENTER) three times to approximately space down to the 2" position.

3. Set the font to Arial, bold, 12 pt, and type the title shown below.

4. Tap (ENTER), and set the alignment to left.

5. Turn off bold and set the font size to 11.

6. Type the first paragraph shown below, tapping (ENTER) once at the end of the paragraph.

7. Choose Format→Paragraph from the menu bar, and set the line spacing to single and the left and right indents to 1".
   The Paragraph dialog box is useful when setting several options, or when you want to precisely set line spacing, indents, or other options.

8. Click the Italic *I* button and type the quotations shown below. Use the Em Dash symbol from the Symbols dialog box between the end of paragraph periods and the author's names. Do not use italics on the author's names.

FAMOUS AMERICAN QUOTATIONS

Quotations have the power to inspire and define moments in our history. They are windows into the minds and lives of great people. Famous Americans certainly have contributed their share of famous quotations.

There was never yet an uninteresting life. Such a thing is an impossibility. Inside of the dullest exterior, there is a drama, a comedy, and a tragedy.—Mark Twain

We hold these truths to be sacred and undeniable; that all men are created equal and independent, that from that equal creation they derive rights inherent and inalienable, among which are the preservation of life, and liberty, and the pursuit of happiness.—Thomas Jefferson

I think, at a child's birth, if a mother could ask a fairy godmother to endow it with the most useful gift, that gift would be curiosity.—Eleanor Roosevelt

---

9. Save the document with the name **Skill Builder 10.1**.
   You will continue to use the document in the next exercise.

Skill Builder 10.2 Add Another Quotation

In this exercise, you will add a new quotation and a paragraph to the Skill Builder 10.1 document. The document should be open from the previous exercise.

1. Position the insertion point in front of the word *We* at the beginning of the second quote.

2. Tap (ENTER) twice to push the last two quotations down.

3. Tap (↑) twice to move the insertion point into the blank space between the paragraphs.

4. Now type the following quotation:

> *No one has been barred on account of his race from fighting or dying for America—There are no "white" or "colored" signs on the foxholes or graveyards of battle.—*
> John F. Kennedy

5. Now add the paragraph shown below to the bottom of the document. Make sure you double-space with (ENTER) between the last quote and the new paragraph. For the new paragraph, set the left and right indents to zero, the first line indent to 0.5", and the line spacing to 2.0. You will also need to turn off italics.

> Famous quotations help us express those hard-to-find words and feelings that
>
> are in all of our hearts. They become a part of our national conscience and memory.

6. Choose File→Save As from the menu bar.

7. Change the name of the document to **Skill Builder 10.2**, save it, and close it.

Skill Builder 10.3 **Format an Existing Document**

In this exercise, you will open a report on your exercise diskette. You will adjust the line spacing and indents and spell check the document.

Adjust the First Line Indent and Line Spacing

1. Open the document named Skill Builder 10.3.

2. Select the entire document by triple-clicking in the left margin, or choose Edit→Select All from the menu bar.

3. Drag the First Line Indent 🔽 marker to the 0.5" position on the ruler.
   This will indent the first line of all paragraphs by 0.5" (including the title).

4. Set the line spacing to double.

Format the Title and Credit Line

5. Use (ENTER) to push the title down to approximately the 2" position.

6. Center ▤ the title.
   Look at the ruler, and notice that the First Line Indent marker is at the 0.5" position. This will cause the title to be slightly off-center.

7. Set the First Line Indent 🔽 for the title paragraph to zero.

8. Format the title as Arial, bold, 14 pt.

9. Click on the credit line at the bottom of the report.

10. Set the First Line Indent 🔽 to zero, and right-align ▤ the paragraph.
    The paragraph should be flush with the right margin.

11. Format the title "Moss-Gathering" in the credit line with italics.

12. Spell check the entire document. Assume that the names of all people are correct.

13. Save the changes, and close the document.

Skill Builder 10.4 **Create an Announcement**

1. Follow these guidelines to create the announcement shown below:

   ■ Begin the announcement 2" down. Use 2.0 line spacing between all title lines and for the first body paragraph. Use (ENTER) to double-space between the cast member paragraphs. Use 1.0 line spacing within the cast member paragraphs.

   ■ Use an Arial font for the entire document. Use a font size of 12 for the body paragraphs. All title lines are centered, 14 pt, and bold.

   ■ Use Em Dash symbols after the names of the cast members. Indent the cast member paragraphs 0.5" on both the left and right.

2. Save the announcement with the name **Skill Builder 10.4**, and close the document.

The West Coast Playhouse

Presents

An Evening with Mabel

This fabulous play has been entertaining audiences since its opening night on

March 1, 1998. The cast is first-class, and the ambience is magical. You will find

this play delightfully humorous and deeply moving.

The Cast

> **Rebecca Thomas**—Rebecca is a graduate of the Smithton School of Dramatic Arts. Rebecca has played lead roles in 17 theatrical productions. She has also appeared on *Saturday Night Live* and other television productions.

> **Jim Oliver**—Jim is a recent graduate with a major in drama. Jim was voted the best overall actor in his graduating class, and he has won numerous other awards. We are confident that you will find Jim's performance truly memorable.

> **Clara Boyd**—Clara recently moved here from London, England, where she specialized in Shakespearean theatrical performances. Clara is also a world-class pianist.

Assessments

Assessment 10.1 Format an Existing Document

1. Open the document named Assessment 10.1 on your exercise diskette.

2. Apply 2.0 line spacing to the entire document.

3. Center the title, and apply bold formatting to the title.

4. Apply bold formatting to the two capitalized headings.

5. Apply a 0.5" First Line indent to all body paragraphs except for the headings.

6. Print the document, save the changes, and close the document.

Assessment 10.2 Create a Report Using Indents

1. Use the skills and report formatting knowledge you have acquired to create the report shown below. The single-spaced paragraphs are indented 1" on both the left and right.

2. Print the report, save it as **Assessment 10.2**, but leave it open, as you will continue to use it.

CLASSIFICATIONS OF EMPLOYMENT

CFEB Associates—Company Handbook

It is important that you understand how CFEB Associates classifies its employees.

We have established the following classifications for purposes of salary administration and eligibility for overtime payment and benefits.

Full-Time Regular Employees. These are staff members hired to work CFEB's normal, full-time workweek on a regular basis.

Part-Time Regular Employees. These are staff members hired to work at CFEB fewer than thirty-five hours per week on a regular basis.

Exempt Employees. These are staff members of CFEB Associates who are not required to be paid overtime, in accordance with applicable federal wage and hour laws, for work performed beyond forty hours in a workweek.

Nonexempt Employees. These are staff members of CFEB Associates who are required to be paid overtime at the rate of time and one-half their regular rate of pay for all hours worked beyond forty hours in a workweek.

Assessment 10.3 Add Paragraphs to a Document

1. Use the File→Save As command to save Assessment 10.2 with the name **Assessment 10.3**.

2. Add the following two paragraphs to the end of the Assessment 10.3 document. Notice that the first paragraph is indented and single-spaced, and the second paragraph is not indented and it is double-spaced.

3. If your report wraps to a second page after inserting the text, then remove hard returns from the top of the document until it fits on one page. If necessary, use a Whole Page zoom setting so that you can see the entire document. You should remove enough hard returns to center the document vertically on the page.

4. Print the report, save the changes, and close the document.

Temporary Employees. These are staff members of CFEB Associates who are engaged to work full-time or part-time on the firm's payroll with the understanding that their employment will be terminated no later than upon completion of a specific assignment.

You will be informed of your initial employment classification and of your

exempt or nonexempt status during your orientation session. Please direct any questions

regarding your employment classification or exemption status to the Director of Human

Resources.

Critical Thinking

Critical Thinking 10.1 On Your Own

Alexis Winston is a sophomore at Big State University majoring in computer science. Alexis has completed her freshman courses and is finally taking her first computer science course. Computer Science 101 provides an introduction to computing theory and requires each student to submit several reports. The topic of the first report assigned by Professor Carpenter is to research trends in computer science and technology. Each student must write a one-page report on the four most relevant computing trends of the twenty-first century. Alexis conducts the necessary research and decides upon the four trends that she considers to be the most relevant. She writes the following report text describing these trends.

The Internet—Use of the Internet has grown exponentially since 1995. The Internet has affected nearly every aspect of the computer world. Use of the Internet for business, education, communication, and other functions will continue to expand exponentially in the near future.

Open source—The move towards open source software (particularly operating systems) appears to be gathering momentum. The driving force behind the open source movement is the emergence of the Linux operating system. Linux has become the operating system of choice for many server systems and applications. Linux is also gaining recognition as a potential operating system for personal computers.

Internet appliances—Computing in the twenty-first century will no longer be restricted to personal computers and larger servers. The emergence of smart appliances and Internet-enabled consumer devices is a major trend. It is estimated that sales of Internet appliances in the United States will reach $15.3 billion by 2004.

Computers on a chip—The semiconductor industry has made remarkable advances in miniaturization and specialization. Soon, the functions of a motherboard will be condensed into a single chip. Single-chip computers will play a major role in a variety of devices from personal computers to cell phones, Internet appliances, and consumer electronics.

Write a one-page report on computing trends of the twenty-first century. Include a title, at least one main body paragraph, and the four trends discussed above. You can retype the trends exactly as they appear above. Format the report using the traditional unbound business report format shown in the Report Formats section at the beginning of this lesson. Indent the four trends 0.5" on both the left and right.

Spell check and grammar check your report. Use the thesaurus to find replacement words in the trends shown above. Save your completed report as `Critical Thinking 10.1`.

Critical Thinking 10.2 **Web Research**

Alexis Winston's CS 101 class incorporates a business component that addresses the impact of computing trends on business. Professor Carpenter has assigned a second report that requires each student to discuss the business implications of one of the trends mentioned in the previous report (the report written in Critical Thinking 10.1). Alexis decides to write her report on companies that will benefit from the emergence of Internet appliances.

Write a brief, one-page report on four companies that will benefit from the use of Internet appliances. Use Internet Explorer and a search engine of your choice to get information about the companies. You can choose any four companies. Some examples of companies that may benefit from this trend include Wind River Systems, Network Appliance, Cisco Systems, and Intel. Write a brief description of how each company may benefit from the use of Internet appliances. You can visit the Web sites of the companies or search for relevant articles on the Web. Position the information on the four companies below the main body paragraph, and indent them 1" on both the left and right. Use the unbound business report format with a title, at least one body paragraph, and the four indented paragraphs on the companies. If necessary, review the Report Formats section at the start of this lesson. Save your completed report as **Critical Thinking 10.2**.

LESSON 11

Margins and Lists

In this lesson, you will expand upon the formatting techniques you learned in the previous lesson and you will use margins, bulleted lists, and hanging indents to create a more sophisticated document. You will also learn how to customize bulleted and numbered lists, and you will work with outline-style numbered lists.

Additional learning resources are available at labpub.com/learn/oe3/

Case Study

Lisa Madison has found the summer job that most students dream about: she is a whitewater-rafting guide for Outdoor Adventures. Outdoor Adventures has been wooing thrill seekers for 25 years with rafting trips, helicopter skiing, wilderness trekking, and other high-octane adventures. Recently, Lisa realized that many guests have been forgetting to bring items, while others have been getting lost on the way to the starting points. Lisa decides to take charge of this situation using the power of Word 2003. She designs a pre-trip checklist that includes a list of recommendations, a bulleted list of items to bring, and directions to the starting points. With her take-charge attitude and her Office 2003 skills, Lisa should have no problem navigating the turbulent waters awaiting her in today's business world.

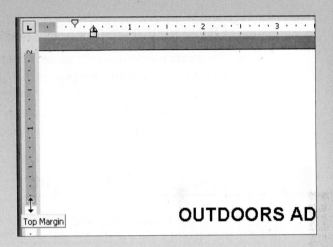

Lisa uses the mouse to drag the margin boundary on the ruler to quickly reset the top margin.

The Numbering button on the Formatting toolbar makes numbering lists as easy as 1-2-3.

Lisa creates bullets for her checklist by clicking the Bullets button.

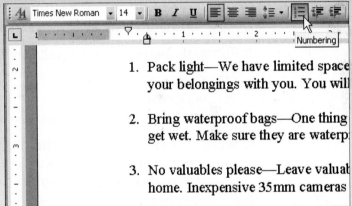

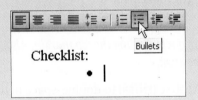

Margins

Margins determine the overall size of the text area on a page. In Word, the default top and bottom margins are 1", and the left and right margins are 1.25". You can set margins by dragging the margin boundaries on the rulers. You can also use the File→Page Setup command and set the margins in the Margins tab of the Page Setup dialog box. Margin settings are applied to the entire document or to an entire section (if the document has multiple sections). Sections are not discussed in this lesson.

Differences Between Margins and Indents

The margins determine the space between the text and the edge of the page. Indents are used to offset text from the margins. For example, imagine a document has a 1" left margin, and one of the paragraphs in that document has a 0.5" indent. The margin plus the indent will position the paragraph 1.5" from the edge of the page. If the margin were changed to 2", then the indented paragraph would be positioned 2.5" from the edge of the page (the 2" margin plus the 0.5" indent).

 ## Hands-On 11.1 Set Margins

1. Start Word, and choose File→Page Setup from the menu bar.
   The Page Setup dialog box lets you adjust a number of important settings that affect pages; for example, margins, paper size, page orientation, and headers and footers.

2. Make sure the Margins tab is selected, and notice the default settings for the margins.

3. Change the top margin to 1.5" and the left and right margins to 1".

4. Click OK to apply the changes.
   The top of the vertical ruler will have a 1.5" darkened area representing the top margin. Also, the Status bar will indicate that the insertion point is at the 1.5" position.

5. Set the font size to 14, and type the following text. Use (ENTER) to double-space between the title and subtitle and to triple-space between the subtitle and body paragraph. Also, use (ENTER) to double-space after the body paragraph.

   > OUTDOORS ADVENTURES
   >
   > Pre-Trip Checklist
   >
   >
   > **The following checklist and directions will help you prepare for your trip. Also, remember to keep three important things in mind:**

6. Format the title with an Arial 18 pt bold font, the subtitle with an Arial 16 pt bold font, and center both heading lines.

7. Save the document with the name **Hands-On Lesson 11**.
   You will continue to enhance this document throughout the lesson.

Setting Margins with the Rulers

You can set all four margins by dragging the margin boundaries on the rulers. The benefit of this technique is that you can see the effect immediately in the document. If you press the (ALT) key when dragging a margin boundary, Word displays the precise margin measurements on the rulers.

 ### Hands-On 11.2 **Change Margins with the Ruler**

1. Follow these steps to adjust the margins:

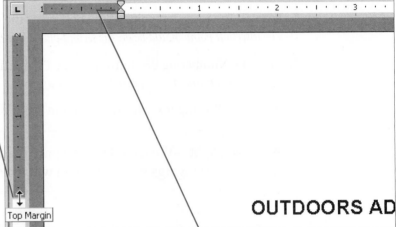

Ⓐ Position the mouse pointer here on the top margin boundary so that a double-headed arrow will appear.

Ⓑ Drag the margin boundary down until the numeral 2 appears at the top of the ruler. This indicates that the margin is set to 2".

Ⓒ Try adjusting the top margin again but press and hold the (ALT) key while dragging the margin boundary. Word will display the margin measurements on the ruler.

Ⓓ Set the top margin to 2".

Ⓔ Try changing the left margin by dragging this margin boundary. However, be patient because it requires delicate mouse moves to make the double-headed arrow appear between the top and bottom indent markers. When you have finished, make sure the left margin is set to 1".

Bulleted and Numbered Lists

You can create bulleted and numbered lists with the Bullets 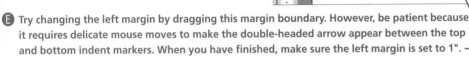 and Numbering buttons on the Formatting toolbar. In Word, a list is a series of two or more paragraphs. You can apply bullets and numbers to paragraphs by selecting the paragraphs and clicking the desired button. For a new list, you can turn on bullets or numbers when you begin typing the list. Word will format the first paragraph with a bullet or number. When you complete the paragraph and tap (ENTER), Word formats the next paragraph with a bullet or number. In a numbered list, Word numbers the paragraphs sequentially. Paragraphs in a numbered list are automatically renumbered if paragraphs are inserted or deleted.

AutoFormat as You Type

You can also start a bulleted list by typing an asterisk * followed by a space or a tab at the beginning of a new paragraph. When you complete the paragraph and tap (ENTER), Word converts the asterisk to a bullet character. Likewise, you can begin a numbered list by typing 1 followed by a space or tab and tapping (ENTER). This feature is known as AutoFormat as You Type.

Turning Bullets and Numbering Off

You can remove bullets or numbers from paragraphs by selecting the paragraphs(s) and clicking the Bullets button or the Numbering button. If you are typing a list, you should complete the list by tapping (ENTER) after the last paragraph in the list. You can then turn off bullets or numbering for the first paragraph following the list by clicking the Bullets button or the Numbering button.

Hands-On 11.3 Bullets and Numbers

Create a Numbered List

1. Position the insertion point at the bottom of the document.
   The insertion point should be on the second blank line below the body paragraph.

2. Click the Numbering ⊟ button on the Formatting toolbar.
   The indented numeral 1 appears followed by a period.

3. Type the following text, inserting the Em Dash symbol as shown:

> 1. **Pack light—We have limited space on our rafts, and you must carry all of your belongings with you. You will make more friends if you pack light.**

4. Tap (ENTER) once after typing the text.
   Notice that Word begins the next paragraph with the numeral 2. Paragraphs are numbered sequentially unless you tell Word otherwise. You will learn how to change the starting number later in this lesson.

5. Tap (ENTER) again, and numbering will be turned off for the new paragraph.
   Word assumes you want to turn off numbering when you tap (ENTER) without typing any text.

6. Click the Numbering ⊟ button again.
   Word will number the new blank paragraph with the numeral 2. Word continues the numbering from the previous list.

7. Type the following text:

> 2. **Bring waterproof bags—One thing you can count on is that your bag(s) will get wet. Make sure they are waterproof and they float.**

8. Tap (ENTER) and notice that Word creates a double-space and starts the numbering at 3.
   Word now understands that you want a double-space between each paragraph in the list.

9. Type the following text:

> 3. **No valuables please—Leave valuables such as camcorders and cameras at home. Inexpensive 35mm cameras are the safest bet.**

10. Tap (ENTER) and another double-space will be inserted.

11. Click the Numbering ⊟ button to turn off numbering for the new paragraph.

12. Type **Checklist:** and tap (ENTER) once.

13. Click the Bullets ⊞ button on the Formatting toolbar.
    Word will most likely insert a round • bullet (although another bullet style may appear). Also, the bullet may be indented further than the numbers in the numbered list.

14. Type **Sunglasses**, and tap (ENTER).
    Word formats the new paragraph with the bullet style.

15. Complete the following checklist:

    Checklist:
    - Sunglasses
    - Sunscreen
    - Insect repellant
    - Three sets of dry clothing
    - Tennis shoes
    - A warm, waterproof jacket

16. Tap (ENTER) twice after the last list item to turn off bullets.

The Bullets and Numbering Dialog Box

The Format→Bullets and Numbering command displays the Bullets and Numbering dialog box. The Bullets and Numbering dialog box lets you choose a style for your bulleted or numbered list, customize lists, and create outline numbered lists.

Built-in Bullet and Numbering Styles

Word provides seven built-in styles for bulleted and numbered lists. The styles are displayed in style galleries in the Bullets and Numbering dialog box. You can easily change the appearance of a bulleted or numbered list by choosing a style from the style galleries. The following illustration shows the built-in bullet and number styles available.

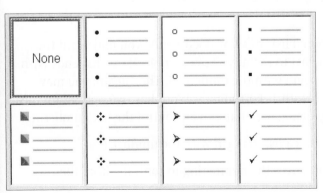

Bullet style gallery

Number style gallery

Hands-On 11.4 Change the Bullet Style

1. Select the bulleted list as shown below.

Checklist:
- Sunglasses
- Sunscreen
- Insect repellant
- Three sets of dry clothing
- Tennis shoes
- A warm, waterproof jacket

2. Choose Format→Bullets and Numbering from the menu bar.

3. Choose the Circle bullet style from the bullets gallery, and click OK.

Customizing Bullet and Number Styles

You can customize the built-in bullet and number styles in several ways. For example, you may want to use a bullet character other than the built-in bullet characters, or you may want to change the default indentation of a particular built-in bullet or number style. These and other customization options are available in the Customization dialog box. To display the Customization dialog box first display the Bullets and Numbering dialog box, and then choose a bullet or number style from the style galleries, and click the Customize button.

Resetting Customized Bullet and Number Styles

Once you customize a built-in bullet or number style, the new customized style replaces the built-in style in the style gallery from that point onward. Fortunately, the Bullets and Numbering dialog box contains a Reset button that restores a style in the gallery to its original built-in format. To reset a style, you choose the style from the style galleries and click the Reset button.

Modifying List Numbering

Many documents have more than one numbered list. In some documents, you may want the numbering to continue sequentially from one list to the next. For example, if one list ends with the numeral 4 you may want the next list to begin with the numeral 5. Then again, you may want the numbering in each new list to begin with 1. Fortunately, Word has two options on the Numbered tab of the Bullets and Numbering dialog box that let you control the list numbering:

- **Restart Numbering**—This option forces a list to begin with the number 1.

- **Continue Previous List**—This option forces the numbering to continue from the previous list.

Hands-On 11.5 Experiment with Customization

1. Scroll up, and click anywhere on the first numbered paragraph.

2. Choose Format→Bullets and Numbering from the menu bar.
   Notice the seven different number styles in the gallery. As with bullets, you can apply a style by choosing it from the gallery and clicking OK. When you use the Numbering button on the Formatting toolbar, it always applies the most recently used number style.

3. Notice the Restart Numbering and Continue Previous List options below the number styles.
   These options are used to adjust the starting number of a numbered list. These options will not be available for the paragraph numbered 1 because it is the first numbered paragraph in the document.

4. Click the Customize button.

5. Follow these steps to explore the Custom Numbered List dialog box:

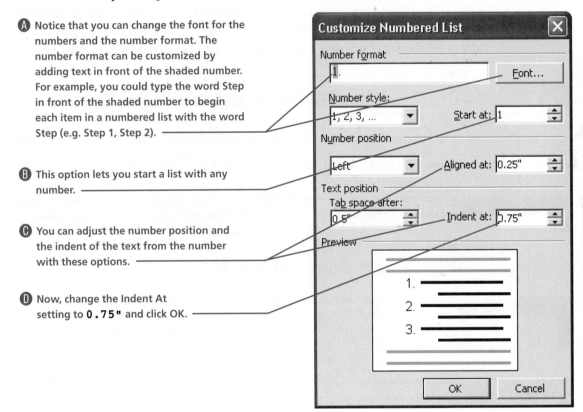

Ⓐ Notice that you can change the font for the numbers and the number format. The number format can be customized by adding text in front of the shaded number. For example, you could type the word Step in front of the shaded number to begin each item in a numbered list with the word Step (e.g. Step 1, Step 2).

Ⓑ This option lets you start a list with any number.

Ⓒ You can adjust the number position and the indent of the text from the number with these options.

Ⓓ Now, change the Indent At setting to **0.75"** and click OK.

The new number style should be applied to all numbered paragraphs. This will move the text following the number to the 0.75" position.

6. Make sure the insertion point is somewhere on the first paragraph in the numbered list.

7. Choose Format→Bullets and Numbering from the menu bar.
   The current number style should be highlighted in the gallery.

8. Locate the Reset button at the bottom of the dialog box.
   The Reset button will be available because the current number style has been customized.

9. Click the Reset button.

10. Click Yes on the message box that appears.

Word asks if you want to restore the gallery position to the default style. Each style has a position in the gallery. When you reset a style, you are resetting a particular gallery position to the default formats for that position. Notice that the Reset button is no longer available. The Reset button is only available if the highlighted gallery style has been customized.

11. Click OK, and the numbered paragraphs will be restored to their original format.

Keep in mind that you can customize bullet styles in a similar manner to number styles.

Adjusting Bullet and Number Alignment with the Ruler

You can easily adjust the indents of bulleted and numbered lists and the text following the bullets and numbers by dragging markers on the ruler. This technique is useful because it can be applied to specific paragraphs without changing the built-in styles in the style galleries. Drag the First Line Indent ▽ marker to adjust the bullet position and a Left Tab ⌐ marker to adjust the text position.

 Hands-On 11.6 Adjust Bullet Position and the Text Indent

1. Scroll to the bottom of the document, and select all of the bulleted paragraphs.

2. Follow this step to adjust the First Line Indent ▽ marker:

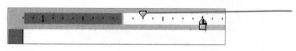

Ⓐ Drag the First Line Indent marker to the 0.25" position on the ruler as shown here. The bullets will move over to the 0.25" position. As you can see, the First Line Indent marker determines the bullet position.

3. Follow these steps to adjust the Left Tab ⌐ marker:

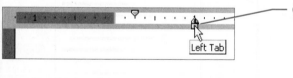

Ⓐ Position the mouse pointer on the Left Indent marker (the bottom square) and a Left Tab ScreenTip will appear. Notice a Left Tab marker is superimposed on the indent marker. The Left Tab marker appears whenever a paragraph has bullets or numbers.

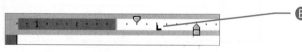

Ⓑ Drag the Left Tab marker until it is positioned at the 0.5" position as shown here. The bullet text should now be aligned at the 0.5" position.

4. Follow these steps to adjust the Hanging Indent marker:

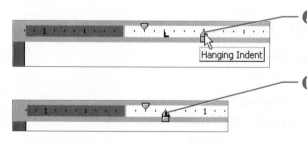

Ⓐ Position the mouse pointer on the Hanging Indent marker (the upward pointing triangle) and a Hanging Indent ScreenTip will appear.

Ⓑ Drag the Hanging Indent marker until it is positioned at the 0.5" position as shown here. You won't notice any change in the alignment at this point. You will learn about hanging indents in the next topic.

The bulleted checklist should have the appearance and alignment shown below.

> 3. No valuables please—Leave valuables such as camcorders and cameras at home. Inexpensive 35 mm cameras are the safest bet.
>
> Checklist:
> - ○ Sunglasses
> - ○ Sunscreen
> - ○ Insect repellant
> - ○ Three sets of dry clothing
> - ○ Tennis shoes
> - ○ A warm, waterproof jacket

5. Save the changes, and continue with the next topic.

Hanging Indents

The Hanging Indent ⬆ marker (upward-pointing triangle) offsets all lines of a paragraph except for the first line. Hanging indents are often used in bibliographic entries, glossary terms, and bulleted and numbered lists. You create hanging indents by dragging the Hanging Indent marker on the ruler or with the Paragraph dialog box.

> Middle Granite Canyon—Take Highway 240 to the Pine Meadows turnoff. Go right for two miles until you see a fork in the road. Go right for one mile to the starting point.

A paragraph with a hanging indent

 ## Hands-On 11.7 Create Hanging Indents

1. Position the insertion point on the second blank line below the checklist.

2. Type **Directions:** and tap (ENTER).

3. Type the following text. As you type, Word may underline various words or phrases with wavy green (grammar suggestion) or red (spelling suggestion) lines. You can remove the red or green underlines by right clicking them and choosing Ignore All from the pop-up menu. In addition, the street names (Forest Lake Drive and Creekside Lane) may be underlined with purple dotted lines. These Smart Tag indicators give you various options. You can remove a smart tag by pointing to the underlined street name, clicking the Smart Tag Options button that appears, and choosing Remove This Smart Tag.

> Upper Granite Canyon—Take Highway 240 to the Forest Lake exit. Take Forest Lake Drive to Creekside Lane and look for the starting point.

4. Click anywhere in the paragraph you just typed.

5. Follow these steps to create a hanging indent:

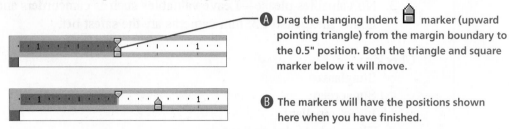

Ⓐ **Drag the Hanging Indent** ⬒ **marker (upward pointing triangle) from the margin boundary to the 0.5" position. Both the triangle and square marker below it will move.**

Ⓑ **The markers will have the positions shown here when you have finished.**

The formatted paragraph should match the following example. Notice how the second line is indented, but the first line remains at the margin.

> Upper Granite Canyon—Take Highway 240 to the Forest Lake exit. Take Forest
> Lake Drive to Creekside Lane and look for the starting point.

6. Now click the Increase Indent 🔲 button to increase both the First Line indent and the Hanging indent.

7. Position the insertion point at the end of the paragraph (to the right of the period).

8. Tap (ENTER) twice, then type the following text:

> Middle Granite Canyon—Take Highway 240 to the Pine Meadows turnoff.
> Go right for two miles until you see a fork in the road. Go right for
> one mile to the starting point.

9. Tap (ENTER) twice, and drag the First Line Indent marker and the Hanging Indent marker to the 0" position on the ruler.

10. Save the changes, and continue with the next topic.

Outline-Style Numbered Lists

An outline-style numbered list can have up to nine levels of numbers or bullet characters. Outline-style lists are often used in the legal profession where multiple numbering levels are required. You format paragraphs as an outline-style numbered list by displaying the Bullets and Numbering dialog box and choosing the desired style from the style gallery on the Outline Numbered tab.

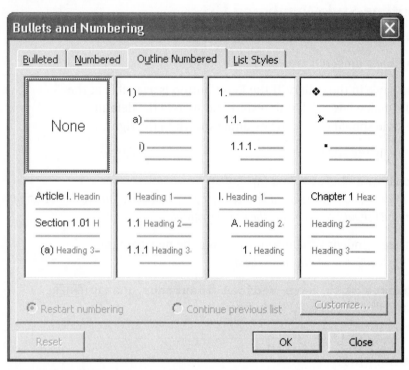

Outline numbered list styles

Promoting and Demoting List Items

The Increase Indent button and the Decrease Indent button are used to promote or demote paragraphs in an outline-style numbered list. The Increase Indent button indents selected paragraphs one level, thus demoting them one level. The Decrease Indent button reduces the indentation level and thus promotes the paragraph one level.

FROM THE KEYBOARD
(TAB) to demote
(SHIFT)+(TAB) to promote

 ## Hands-On 11.8 Create a Policies and Procedures Page

In this exercise, you will use outline-style numbered lists to create a policies and procedures page at the end of the document.

Set Up the New Page

1. Make sure the insertion point is at the end of the document and that the paragraph has no indents set.

2. Press (CTRL)+(ENTER) to insert a page break.
   Notice that the top margin is still set to 2".

3. Click the Center ![Center button] button.

4. Type **OUTDOOR ADVENTURES**, and tap (ENTER) twice.

5. Type **Policies and Procedures**, and tap (ENTER) three times.

6. Click the Align Left ![Align Left button] button.

Create an Outline-Style Numbered List

7. Choose Format→Bullets and Numbering from the menu.

8. Click the Outline Numbered tab.

9. Click the first style in the gallery. If the Reset button is available at the bottom of the dialog box, click it to restore the style to the default setting. The style should match the example shown to the right.

10. Click OK to apply the style.

11. Type **Medical and Injury**, and tap (ENTER).
    The heading Medical and Injury should be preceded by the number 1 followed by a closing parenthesis, and the number 2) should be applied to the new paragraph.

12. Click the Increase Indent ![Increase Indent button] button to demote the new paragraph.
    The number 2) should now become the letter a).

13. Type **All guests must have medical insurance**, and tap (ENTER).
    The new paragraph will be preceded by the letter b).

    ---
    1) Medical and Injury
       a) All guests must have medical insurance
       b) All guests must sign an injury waiver
       c) All guests agree to pay out-of-pocket medical expenses including:
       d)
    ---

14. Complete items b) and c) as shown below, tapping (ENTER) once after each paragraph. The insertion point should be on the new paragraph d) when you have finished.

15. Click the Increase Indent ![Increase Indent button] indent to demote the new paragraph.
    The new paragraph will be preceded by the letter i).

16. Type **Injuries resulting from on-trip accidents**, and tap (ENTER).

17. Complete the document as shown on the following page. You should double-space between the three list headings as shown. When you do this, the outline numbering will be turned off for the new heading paragraph. Turn the numbering on again using the Numbering button on the Formatting toolbar. Finally, format the title with an Arial 18 pt bold font and the subtitle with an Arial 16 pt bold font.

18. Save the changes, and close the document.

OUTDOOR ADVENTURES

Policies and Procedures

1) Medical and Injury
   a) All guests must have medical insurance
   b) All guests must sign an injury waiver
   c) All guests agree to pay out-of-pocket medical expenses including:
      i) Injuries resulting from on-trip accidents
      ii) Aero medical evacuation
      iii) Rehabilitation costs

2) Cancellations and Refunds
   a) A full refund will be given for cancellations with 60 days notice
   b) A 50% refund will be given for cancellations with 30 days notice
   c) No refund for cancellations with less than 30 days notice

3) Alternate Trip Destinations and Cancellations
   a) Your trip may be cancelled for any of the following reasons:
      i) Inclement weather
      ii) Poor water flow
      iii) Insufficient number of guests
      iv) Unavailability of a guide
   b) Your trip destination may be changed for any of the following reasons:
      i) Inclement weather
      ii) Poor water flow
      iii) Insufficient guest turnout requiring reorganization of trips

Concepts Review

True/False Questions

1. Margins can be set with the ruler.   TRUE   FALSE

2. The File→Page Setup command displays a dialog box that can be used to adjust margins.   TRUE   FALSE

3. Bullets can be offset from the margins.   TRUE   FALSE

4. Numbering always continues sequentially from one list to the next in documents with multiple lists.   TRUE   FALSE

5. Bullet formats are carried to the next paragraph when (ENTER) is tapped.   TRUE   FALSE

6. Bullet formats cannot be changed once (ENTER) is tapped.   TRUE   FALSE

7. Only the first line of a paragraph is indented when a hanging indent is applied.   TRUE   FALSE

8. Outline-style numbered lists can have up to seven numbering levels.   TRUE   FALSE

9. You can start a bulleted list by typing an asterisk * followed by a space or a tab at the beginning of a new paragraph.   TRUE   FALSE

10. If you are working with a numbered list in Outline Numbered style, you can use the Increase Indent button to demote a paragraph.   TRUE   FALSE

Multiple Choice Questions

1. Which of the following keys is used to display measurements on the ruler while the margin boundary is dragged?
   a. (ALT)
   b. (SHIFT)
   c. (CTRL)
   d. None of the above

2. Which command displays the Bullets and Numbering dialog box?
   a. Format→Bullets and Numbering
   b. Edit→Bullets and Numbering
   c. Format→Paragraph
   d. None of the above

3. Which technique indents the bullets in a bulleted list?
   a. Select the desired paragraphs, and drag the First Line Indent marker.
   b. Select the desired paragraphs, and drag the Left Tab symbol on the indent marker.
   c. Use the (TAB) key.
   d. None of the above

4. Which technique should you use to indent the text in a bulleted list?
   a. Select the desired paragraphs, and drag the First Line Indent marker.
   b. Select the desired paragraphs, and drag the Left Tab symbol on the indent marker.
   c. Use the (TAB) key.
   d. None of the above

Skill Builders

Skill Builder 11.1 Create a Personal Business Letter

In this exercise, you will create the document shown on the following page.

Set-Up the Letter

1. Start a new document, and Choose File→Page Setup from the menu bar.

2. Set the left and right margins to 1" and click OK.

3. Type the date, address, salutation, and first paragraph as shown on the following page.

Create the Numbered List

4. Tap (ENTER) twice after the first main paragraph, and then click the Numbering ⊞ button.
   It's OK if the number style and indentation are different than shown on the following page. You will adjust the style and indentation soon.

5. Type the three numbered paragraphs, tapping (ENTER) once after each paragraph.

6. Tap (ENTER) twice after the third numbered paragraph.
   This will turn off numbering.

7. Now complete the document as shown on the following page. Turn bullets on and off as necessary, and tap (ENTER) either once or twice between paragraphs as shown.
   Don't be concerned with text formats or bullet alignments at this point. You will be instructed to make those changes in the following steps.

Format the Lists and Headings

8. Select the three paragraphs in the numbered list.

9. Drag the First Line Indent ▽ marker to the 0" position on the ruler to align the numbers with the left margin.

10. Drag the Left Tab ∟ marker and the Hanging Indent ⌂ marker to the 0.25" position on the ruler. This will indent the text 0.25" from the numbers.

11. Now align the bulleted paragraphs the same way.

12. Format the headings with bold as shown on the following page.

13. If necessary, use the Format→Bullets and Numbering command to choose the numbering style and bullet style shown on the following page.

14. Save the document with the name **Skill Builder 11.1**, then close the document.

Today's Date

Mr. Dave Olson, President
Financial Freedom Network
300 South Meyers Fork Road
San Jose, CA 95136

Dear Mr. Olson:

I recently attended your quick start seminar on tax planning for retirement, and I was impressed with both the speaker and content of the presentation. I spoke with Mr. Barry after the presentation, and he asked me to provide you with three types of feedback:

1. Topics that I feel should be included in next year's presentation
2. Ways to improve the presentation
3. Comments on the facilities

I have organized my comments into the three lists that follow.

Topics to Include Next Year
✓ Information on 401K plans
✓ Method for calculating projected net worth
✓ Planning for children's college expenses

How to Improve the Presentation
✓ Make it longer (8 hours).
✓ Include more visuals.
✓ Have multiple speakers.

About the Facilities
✓ The food was excellent.
✓ The chairs were a little uncomfortable.
✓ The employees were very friendly and helpful.

Mr. Olson, I hope my feedback helps you plan for and improve next year's presentation. Please feel free to contact me if you need additional information.

Sincerely,

Richard Ellison, Seminar Participant
2400 Fairview Lane
Richmond, CA 94803

Skill Builder 11.2

1. Start a new document.

2. Set the top margin to 2" and the left and right margins to 1.5".

3. Follow these guidelines to create the document shown below:

   ■ Use a Times New Roman 16 pt font for all text except for the title and subtitle. Use an Arial bold 18 pt font for the title and an Arial bold 16 pt font for the subtitle.

   ■ Use (ENTER) to create the single-, double-, and triple-spacing shown below.

   ■ Use the bullet style shown below.

4. Save the document as **Skill Builder 11.2**, and close the document.

Baron's Model Train Supply

Going Out of Business Sale

Baron's Model Train Supply has provided the widest selection of model train accessories for over 43 years, but our lease has run out. We have decided to close up shop and liquidate our inventory. Please stop by before the end of June to take advantage of rock-bottom prices and a wide selection of accessories and collectibles. Here is just a sample of what you will find.

Accessories
   ❖ Scenery
   ❖ Tracks and switches
   ❖ Buildings

Collectibles
   ❖ Antique locomotives
   ❖ Antique cabooses
   ❖ Figures: Switchmen, engineers, animals, and more

Skill Builder 11.3

In this exercise, you will open a document on your exercise diskette. You will format the document until it matches the document on the following page.

1. Open the document named Skill Builder 11.3.

2. Look at the document on the following page, and notice the title shown at the top of the document. Insert the title, separating it from the first body paragraph with three hard returns. Format the title with an Arial 14 pt bold font and center align the title.

3. Select the first three body paragraphs, and apply double-spacing to them. Adjust the first line indent of the first three body paragraphs to 0.5".

4. Apply the bullet style shown on the following page to the next three paragraphs.

5. Use (ENTER) to double-space between the paragraphs. Remember that tapping (ENTER) will generate a new bullet on the blank line, so click the Bullets button to turn off the bullets on the blank lines.

6. Indent the last paragraph 1" on both the left and right as shown. You will also need to insert hard returns above and below the paragraph with the phrase "Lough adds a powerful statement."

7. Your completed document should match the document on the following page.

8. Save the changes to the document, and close it.

ELECTRIC CARS

Many people are not aware that electric cars have been used in the United States for nearly ninety years. In fact, before the introduction of the gasoline automobile, approximately 50,000 electric cars soared down American streets. Presently, electric cars are gaining attention as an effective means of improving our air quality, reducing pollution, and reducing the need to import oil into the United States.

Often referred to as "zero-emission vehicles," electric cars have the distinct advantage of releasing little or no pollution, reducing the amount of carbon monoxide in our air. Electric cars are also quieter than gasoline-fueled cars, and the batteries that power these cars have the potential to be recharged through renewable sources such as wind and solar power.

Steven Lough of Eco-Motion Electric Cars in Seattle, WA highlights a few of the many benefits of electric cars. A summary of his points follows:

- Electric cars are affordable. A used car in good condition sells for about $2,900 and new models start at $8,900.

- Electric cars are three times more efficient per dollar than gasoline-fueled cars. They improve air quality, limit pollution, and lessen U.S. dependence on imported coal and oil.

- Electric cars will improve over time. Already new batteries—including metal-nickel-hydride batteries and lithium batteries—are being researched. In the coming years these batteries will be available, doubling and tripling the per charge rate of these automobiles.

Lough adds a powerful statement, that:

> There are alternatives [to gasoline automobiles and the pollution and expense associated with them]…There is carpooling, public transportation, bicycles, telecommunications, and yes, electric cars.

Assessments

Assessment 11.1

1. Follow these guidelines to create the document shown below:

   ■ Set the top margin to 2".

   ■ Insert the date as a field using the Insert→Date and Time command.

   ■ Use the bullet style shown for the bulleted list.

2. Print the document, save it with the name **Assessment 11.1**, and close the document.

Current Date

Mr. John Upshaw
1204 Wilkins Drive
Sacramento, CA 90518

Dear Mr. Upshaw:

I am pleased to inform you that you have won the grand prize in our sweepstakes contest. Please contact me as soon as possible to verify receipt of this letter. You may contact me in any of the following ways.

   ➢ Stop by our office at 2400 Gerber Road.
   ➢ Call 1-916-682-9090 between the hours of 9:00 a.m. and 5:00 p.m.
   ➢ Write to me at the address listed on this letterhead.

I look forward to hearing from you soon. Please be prepared to present us with your verification number. Your verification number is JB101.

Sincerely,

Jerry Williams
Prize Notification Manager

Assessment 11.2

1. Follow these guidelines to create the document shown below:

   - Set the top margin to 2" and the left and right margins to 1".

   - Use an Arial bold 16 pt font for the title and a Times New Roman 14 pt font for all other text.

   - Center the title, and use three hard returns after the title.

   - Use single-spacing and double-spacing as necessary to format the document as shown.

   - Set the First Line Indent of the two body paragraphs to 0.5" as shown. Adjust the indents of the numbered paragraphs and the quotation as shown.

2. Print the document, save it with the name **Assessment 11.2**, and close the document.

SUCCESS

The quest for success is a driving force in the lives of many Americans.

This force drives the business world and often results in huge personal fortunes.

However, success can come in many forms, some of which are listed below.

1. Many people in America view success monetarily.

2. Our society also views public figures such as movie stars, athletes, and other celebrities as being successful.

3. Educational achievement such as earning an advanced degree is often perceived as successful.

It is easy to see that success means many things to many people. The poet

Ralph Waldo Emerson provides this elegant definition of success:

> To laugh often and much; to win the respect of intelligent people and the affection of children; to earn the appreciation of honest critics and endure the betrayal of false friends; to appreciate beauty, to find the best in others; to leave the world a bit better, whether by a healthy child, a garden patch or a redeemed social condition; to know even one life has breathed easier because you have lived. This is to have succeeded.

Assessment 11.3

1. Follow these guidelines to create the document shown below:

   ■ Set the top margin to 2".

   ■ Center the title, and use three hard returns after the title.

   ■ Use an Arial bold 16 pt font for the title and a Times New Roman 14 pt font for all other text. Apply bold to the list headings as shown.

   ■ Apply line spacing, indents, and bullets as shown.

2. Print the document, save it with the name **Assessment 11.3**, and close the document.

THE GOLDEN STATE

With more than thirty million people, California has become the most populous state in America. From the beaches of Southern California to the great redwood forests of Northern California, the Golden State is home to a diverse population and a vibrant economy.

A recent poll asked Californians to list the five things they liked best about life in California. The same poll also asked them to list the five biggest drawbacks to life in the Golden State. The poll results appear below.

Five Best Things
- Climate
- Cultural attractions
- Economic opportunities
- Educational opportunities
- Recreational activities

Five Biggest Drawbacks
- Air pollution
- Cost of living
- Crime
- Taxes
- Traffic and congestion

Critical Thinking

Critical Thinking 11.1 On Your Own

Jessica Owens is a student at Mid-Town High School. Jessica has always dreamed of working in the film industry. Jessica chose to attend Mid-Town High primarily because they offer college prep classes for film majors. Jessica just started her first film class, Film 101. Her instructor, Ms. Watkins, has asked students to prepare brief reports on their favorite films. Each report must include a report title and a brief paragraph describing the purpose of the report. In addition, Jessica must include brief paragraphs on her favorite comedy, drama, action, and love story films. The one- or two-sentence paragraphs should describe why she likes each film and why she believes the film is the best of its category. Use bullets for the category paragraphs. Save the completed report as **Critical Thinking 11.1**.

Critical Thinking 11.2 On Your Own

Jack Dennings loves to cook! He finds that the best way to relieve a little tension is to cook up a storm for friends and family. Recently, Jack started a monthly gourmet meal event at his home. Each month, he invites a group of friends and/or family to enjoy his feast. While preparing this month's menu, Jack was perusing his grandmother's recipes when he came across his childhood favorite—Glazed Garlic Prawns.

One of Jack's pet peeves is organization. He has computerized all of his menus by scanning or retyping them into Word documents. His grandmother's Glazed Garlic Prawns recipe was scribbled on a piece of paper as shown below:

Ingredients
1 pound of peeled prawns
1 tablespoon olive oil
1/4 cup coarse sea salt
3/4 cup chicken broth
2 tablespoons finely minced garlic
3 tablespoons fresh lemon juice
1/4 cup finely chopped parsley

Directions: 1. Rinse the prawns, pat dry, and brush with olive oil. 2. Spread the salt on a large plate and roll the prawns in the salt. Preheat the broiler. 3. Place the prawns directly on a rack and broil 4 inches from the heat 2 minutes per side. 4. Meanwhile, heat the chicken broth in a small saucepan over medium heat. Add the garlic, and cook for 2 minutes, stirring constantly. Add the lemon juice and parsley, and cook for 1 minute. Transfer the sauce to a serving bowl. Serve the prawns and dipping sauce immediately.

Enter the recipe above into a Word document. Use a descriptive title, put the ingredients in a bulleted list with the heading "Ingredients," and put the directions in a numbered list with the heading "Directions." If necessary, adjust the indents of the numbered list to allow the numbers to align with the bullets and the bullet text to align with the numbered text. Also, make sure you give Grandma credit for the recipe. Save the completed document as **Critical Thinking 11.2**.

Critical Thinking 11.3 Web Research

Bud Richardson works as an Administrative Assistant for Fremont Investment Group. Each month, Jerry Wilkins, Fremont's Chief Investment Advisor, sends a letter to his clients with his top stock picks of the month. Bud has been asked to prepare this month's letter and an attached stock pick page. Jerry's top technology recommendations for this month are 1. Oracle (ORCL), 2. Sun Microsystems (SUNW), 3. Cisco Systems (CSCO), 4. BMC Software (BMCS), and 5. Microsoft (MSFT). His top Dow Jones Industrial Average picks are 1. Citigroup (C), 2. Boeing Aircraft (BA), 3. Microsoft (MSFT), 4. Gillette (G), and 5. IBM (IBM).

Prepare a business letter to Fremont's clients from Jerry informing them that Jerry's top technology and Dow picks are attached. Use Internet Explorer to navigate to the Web site of a company that offers free stock quotations. Get the current stock price for each of the stocks listed above. Include an attachment page with a heading for each group of stocks, a brief paragraph describing some rationale for choosing the stocks, and a numbered list. The numbered lists should be numbered from 1 to 5 with each numbered item including the company name, stock symbol, and current price. Make sure the numbering starts over at 1 for the second list. Thus, each list will be numbered from 1 to 5. Save the completed document as **Critical Thinking 11.3**.

Critical Thinking 11.4 On Your Own

Health-e-Meals.com has been in business for over three years now and employs 42 people. You have done a remarkable job building the business. However, you realize that you cannot continue to grow at this rate without having a formal business plan and goals in place. You have decided to develop a business plan to help you with strategic planning and to help secure additional credit lines and financing. Part of the business plan is a list of the top five financial goals and the top five customer service goals for the next year.

Create a Word document that lists the top five financial goals and the top five customer service goals of Health-e-Meals.com in the current fiscal year. Use numbered lists to format the goals. Include a title and headings in the document. Save the completed document as **Critical Thinking 11.4**.

LESSON 12

Creating a Flyer

Word is a versatile program that gives you many options for designing documents. When you need to create a flyer, Word allows you to change the page orientation from tall (portrait) to wide (landscape). You can also add a border to a page. Like all of the Office XP programs, Word features an extensive library of clip art you can use to add visual interest to images. Much of this clip art is available online and does not take up space on your hard drive. The Clip Art task pane and the Clip Organizer make accessing the clip art collection easy. By the end of this lesson, you will be able to design custom flyers with Word that are visually attractive and effective.

IN THIS LESSON

Additional learning resources are available at labpub.com/learn/oe3/

Case Study

Nick manages an office equipment outlet in a medium-sized town. There's quite a bit of small business activity in the town. Most of these businesses depend on several computers. But when he visits offices, Nick notices that these computers are often set up very inefficiently. For example, he sees keyboards that are set too high for good typing posture and the mouse positioned so that the user must reach awkwardly to maneuver it. Ergonomics is the science of designing and setting up equipment and furniture in ways that workers find comfortable and efficient. One of Nick's sales associates has developed an hour-long presentation covering how to set up an ergonomically sound office space. He decides to mail a flyer to businesses in his area to promote this presentation, which will help generate interest in office furniture among new and established businesses. Nick uses Word to create the flyer. In the process, he learns more about Word's clip art and font features.

To advertise his "brown bag" presentation, Nick performs a keyword search of the clip art available for Microsoft Office programs. Over a dozen images matching his keyword appear. From here, Word pastes the selected artwork with a single click.

Nick uses the handles on the clip art images to change their size and shape right on the page.

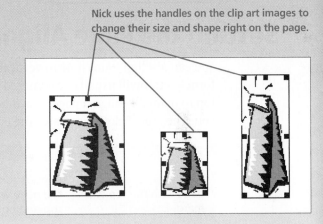

Page Orientation and Size

Setting the Page Orientation

When designing a specialized document such as a flyer, you may wish to make changes to the default page orientation and size. There are two types of page orientation:

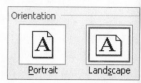

The Orientation setting in the Page Setup dialog box.

- **Portrait (tall)**—This is the default page orientation. Most documents use this orientation.

- **Landscape (wide)**—This orientation sets the page horizontally. It is especially useful for the display of long lines of information.

Setting the Paper Size

Most documents use the standard letter-size page. However, Word supports the use of many other standard paper sizes, and allows you to set a custom page size when necessary.

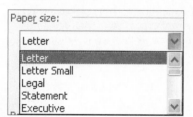

Word allows you to choose from a wide variety of paper sizes, and also supports setting a custom paper size.

Setting the Page Alignment

You can also tell Word how to vertically align the contents of an entire page. For example, a formal letter will usually be centered on the page. Although you could use extra paragraphs at the top to manually align a page, it is much easier to let Word make the alignment adjustment for you. The table below illustrates the effect of each page alignment setting.

Top	Center	Bottom	Justified
Aligns contents of the page with the top margin.	Centers contents of the page within the top and bottom margins.	Aligns contents of the page with the bottom margin.	Spreads contents of page evenly from top to bottom margin.

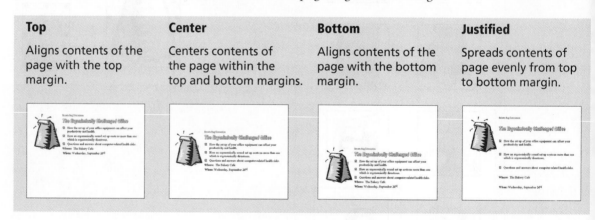

QUICK REFERENCE: SETTING PAGE ORIENTATION AND LAYOUT AND ALIGNMENT

Task	Procedure
Change the page orientation	▪ Choose File→Page Setup from the menu bar. ▪ Choose the Margins tab. ▪ Select the desired page orientation.
Change the paper size	▪ Choose File→Page Setup from the menu bar. ▪ Choose the Paper tab. ▪ Select the desired page size from the Paper drop-down list. ▪ If the necessary page size is not listed, scroll to the bottom of the list, choose Custom, and manually enter the custom page size.
Change the page alignment	▪ Choose File→Page Setup from the menu bar. ▪ Choose the Layout tab. ▪ Select the desired vertical alignment in the Page section of the dialog box.

Hands-On 12.1 **Adjust the Page Setup Settings**

In this exercise, you will change the page orientation and alignment.

1. Start Word, then choose View→Print Layout from the menu bar.

2. Choose Whole Page from the zoom box on the Word toolbar.
   The page is currently in the default portrait (tall) orientation. Viewing the whole page allows you to see this clearly.

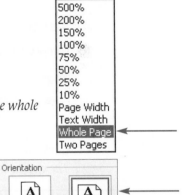

Adjust the Page Orientation and Margins

3. Choose File→Page Setup from the menu bar.

4. On the Margins tab set the page orientation to Landscape.

5. Change the page margins to 1 inch on top/bottom and 2 inches on left/right, as shown at right.

6. Click OK, and then choose Whole Page from the zoom box on the Word toolbar.

   Now the page is oriented in landscape (wide) configuration. By zooming the page again, you obtained a closer view. This is because the monitor is wider than tall, and thus fits portrait page orientation better.

View the Paper Size Options

7. Choose File→Page Setup from the menu bar.

8. Choose the Paper tab, then click the Paper Size drop-down list near the top of the dialog box.
This list contains all of the paper sizes pre-programmed for use with Word.

9. Tap the Ⓛ key on the keyboard.
The first page size matching the letter L appears.

10. Tap the Ⓛ key several more times to display other paper sizes that begin with this letter.
When you view a drop-down list, this keyboard shortcut scrolls to the first item that begins with the letter you tapped.

11. Tap the Ⓒ key on the keyboard until the Custom Size setting appears.
This is a quick shortcut to get to the Custom paper size setting. If the paper size you need is unavailable, you can always create a custom setting.

12. Tap the (HOME) key to jump up to the Letter size setting at the top of the list.

Adjust the Page Vertical Alignment

13. Choose the Layout tab, then choose Center as the Vertical Alignment setting.

14. Click OK.
The insertion point now blinks at the center of the page to reflect the centered vertical alignment setting.

Creating a Page Border

Word allows you to place a border around any page. You can adjust the color, line thickness, and other features of the border. You can even select various images to display around the border of a page. Word allows you to adjust the distance from the page margin that any border appears.

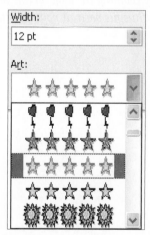

You can choose images to appear
around the border of a page.

The Borders and Shading Dialog Box

The Borders and Shading dialog box allows you to select and adjust any page border. You use the same dialog box to edit the borders of other objects such as images, tables, and around paragraphs. This dialog box displays a preview of how your page border will appear after you apply the command.

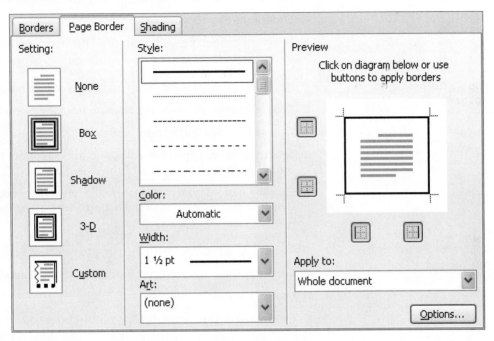

The Borders and Shading dialog box includes a tab for setting page borders.

A New Unit of Measure: The Point

⚠️ **TIP!**

72 points = 1 inch.
36 points = ½ inch.
24 points = ⅓ inch.

A point (pt) is $\frac{1}{72}$ of an inch. This is a common unit of measure in printing and is used by Word for many settings, such as page border margins, paragraph spacing, and other adjustments that benefit from this fine unit of measure.

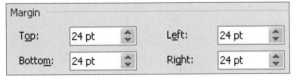

The page border option box is an example of a Word setting that uses points. In this case, each margin is set to 24 points (⅓ of an inch).

Adjusting the Page Border Margins

You can adjust the default margin settings for any page border. Normally, page border margins are set to one-third of an inch (24 points). Since most printers cannot print on the first quarter to-half-inch of the page, this setting works well with most printers. You adjust the page border margins from the options dialog box.

QUICK REFERENCE: APPLYING PAGE BORDERS

Task	Procedure
Apply a preset border to a page	■ Place the insertion point on the page to receive a border. ■ Choose Format→Borders and Shading from the menu bar. ■ Choose the Page Border tab. ■ Select the desired preset border from the items on the left side of the dialog box.
Apply a custom border to a page	■ Place the insertion point on the page to receive a border. ■ Choose Format→Borders and Shading from the menu bar. ■ Choose the Page Border tab. ■ Select the desired line style, color, and thickness from the drop-down lists in the center of the dialog box. ■ Click the desired borders to receive the line style or click a preset style icon on the left side of the dialog box to apply the custom line settings to all borders.
Apply artwork as the page border	■ Place the insertion point on the page to receive a border. ■ Choose Format→Borders and Shading from the menu bar. ■ Choose the Page Border tab. ■ Choose the desired artwork from the Art box and click OK.
Adjust the margins for a page border	■ Place the insertion point on the page on which you wish to adjust the page border margins. ■ Choose Format→Borders and Shading from the menu bar. ■ Choose the Page Border tab. ■ Click the Options button, make the desired margin adjustments, and click OK.

Hands-On 12.2 Apply a Page Border

In this exercise, you will apply a page border and change the margin from 24 points to 36 points (½ inch).

Add a Page Border

1. Choose Format→Borders and Shading from the menu bar.

2. Choose the Page Border tab.

3. Follow these steps to create a page border:

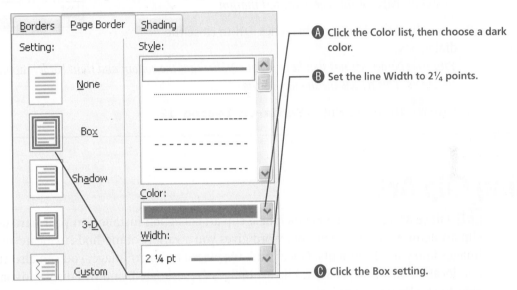

Ⓐ Click the Color list, then choose a dark color.

Ⓑ Set the line Width to 2¼ points.

Ⓒ Click the Box setting.

A border appears around the preview item according to your settings.

4. Click the None setting on the left side of the dialog box.
   The border disappears.

5. Follow these steps to place a border at the top and bottom of the page:

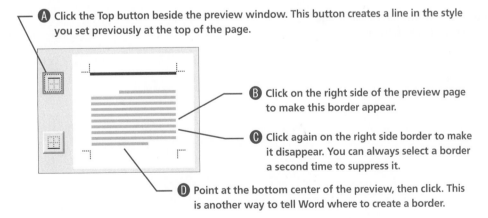

Ⓐ Click the Top button beside the preview window. This button creates a line in the style you set previously at the top of the page.

Ⓑ Click on the right side of the preview page to make this border appear.

Ⓒ Click again on the right side border to make it disappear. You can always select a border a second time to suppress it.

Ⓓ Point at the bottom center of the preview, then click. This is another way to tell Word where to create a border.

It's easy to set or customize the border settings with the preview box.

6. Click the Shadow setting box to create a shadowed border.
   This gives you a border around all four edges, with a shadow on the bottom and right sides of the border.

View the Border Margins

Now you will check the margins used for your page borders.

7. Click the Options button near the lower-right corner of the dialog box.

8. Click the Measure From drop-down list.
   Notice that you can measure the page border margin from either the edge of the paper or the edge of the text margin.

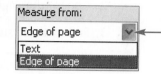

9. Click the Cancel button, then click OK to close the dialog box.
   Your page border settings should be visible. Notice that the bottom and right borders appear thicker than the others. This reflects the shadow setting.

10. Save 🖫 the document as **Hands-On Lesson 12**.

Using Clip Art

🖳 Office XP and Word 2002 include a clip art collection installed on your hard drive, even more clip art items are available online. Word gives you a variety of methods to locate and insert clip art images into your documents. Once you have placed a clip art image, you can also change its size and location on the page. Some clip art images are animated, and will display dynamically when viewed in a Web browser.

An icon indicates that this clip art image is animated.

An icon indicates that this clip art image came from the online collection.

Inserting Clip Art

Word offers two primary methods to locate and place clip art images into your documents.

- **The Clip Art Task Pane**—This method allows you to search for images by entering key words. When you search on a key word, the Task pane displays thumbnails of all images located by your search.

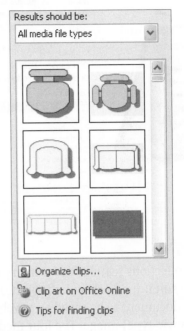

The Clip Art task pane makes searching for and reviewing clip art found with search keywords easy.

- **The Clip Organizer**—This method allows you to navigate among the major categories of clip art, viewing thumbnail images of the entire collection.

The Clip Organizer arranges clip art into folders.

Searching for Clip Art with Key Words

Each clip art image is associated with one or more key words to help you locate the images you need. Clip art images accessed from the Web may change from time-to-time.

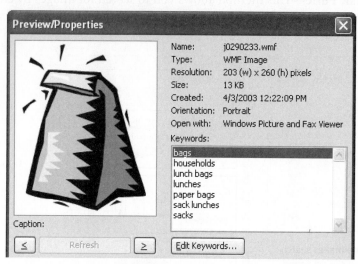

This clip art image has several key words associated with it.

Media Types

The clip art collections feature four primary media types. Each media type has specific characteristics that may suit it for a particular project. For example, a printed flyer will not benefit from a movie file. A document to be saved as a Web page, however, might benefit from the use of an animated (movie-type) image. The four media types are described below.

- **Clip Art**—These are images drawn by graphic artists.
- **Photographs**—These are photographs.
- **Movies**—These may be simple animated pictures or brief video clips.
- **Sounds**—These are sound effects, such as the noise made by a car horn or a modem establishing an online connection.

TIP!

Word is equipped to work with all of the file types represented by the clip art collections.

Items from each media type may reside in one of several file types. A file type is a specific method for saving computer data. Word files use the Word document file type. Picture files come in a variety of files types. For example, a photograph might be in a format optimized for print, such as tag image format file (TIFF), or in a format optimized for the Web, such as the JPEG file interchange format.

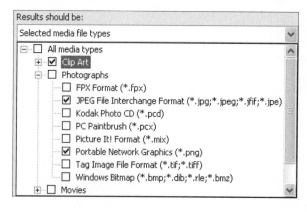

The Results Should Be box allows you to include or exclude specific media types and file types from your searches.

QUICK REFERENCE: INSERTING CLIP ART

Task	Procedure
Insert clip art with the task pane	■ Choose Insert→Picture→Clip Art from the menu bar.
	■ Enter one or more key words to search for images, then click Search.
	■ Click the thumbnail of the image to be inserted.
	■ To perform a new search, click the Modify button at the bottom of the task pane.
Insert clip art with the Clip Organizer	■ Choose Insert→Picture→Clip Art from the menu bar.
	■ Click the Organize Clips link near the bottom of the task pane.
	■ Navigate to locate the image you need among the folders in the Collections List, or use the Search button to perform a keyword search.
	■ Choose Insert→Picture→Clip Art from the menu bar. After you find the picture, click on the drop-down list button on the picture and choose copy from the pop-up menu.
	■ Click where you wish the picture to be placed in your document, then click the Paste button on the Word toolbar.

You can also drag-and-drop the image from the Clip Organizer window onto your document.

 Hands-On 12.3 Find and Insert Clip Art

In this exercise, you will search for a piece of clip art and place it on your document. Initially, you will just search clip art on the hard drive. Later, you will extend the search to include online images.

Insert Clip Art from the Task Pane

1. Choose Insert→Picture→Clip Art from the menu bar.
   The Clip Art task pane appears.

2. Follow these steps to limit your search to clip art on the hard drive:

Ⓐ Click the Search In: box. Depending on settings made by previous students, this box may read All Collections or Selected Collections. ⎯

Ⓑ Click the plus sign beside the Web Collections category. ⎯

Ⓒ Click the plus sign beside the Microsoft Office Online. This displays all of the subcategories you can search online. ⎯

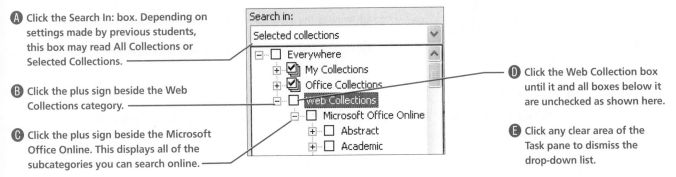

Ⓓ Click the Web Collection box until it and all boxes below it are unchecked as shown here.

Ⓔ Click any clear area of the Task pane to dismiss the drop-down list.

Now that you have deactivated searching the Web collection, let's search for clip art stored on your computer.

3. Follow these steps to search for clip art:

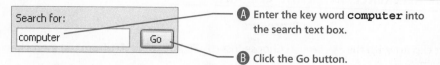

Ⓐ Enter the key word **computer** into the search text box.

Ⓑ Click the Go button.

The task pane displays all of the clip art files found by your search. This search is fast because it is searching only your hard drive.

4. Point (don't click) on any clip art picture in the task pane.
   A note pops up, describing details about the picture.

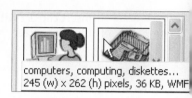

5. Click on any clip art picture in the task pane.
   After a brief pause, the picture is placed in your document at the insertion point. It's very easy to review clip art and insert selected items into your documents.

6. Click on the newly inserted clip art picture.
   Notice that the picture now has a set of small squares around its edges. These are called handles. Later in this lesson you will learn how to manipulate handles to scale an item.

7. Tap the (DELETE) key to delete the clip art picture.

Limit the Media Types in a Search

In addition to controlling the collection you search, you can limit your search to specific media.

8. Replace *computer* with the word **people** in the Search text box, and tap (ENTER).
   Several pictures will appear. As before, this search is limited to items stored on your hard drive, so the selection is relatively small. Now you will make it even smaller by limiting your search to photographs.

9. Follow these steps to limit the media types:

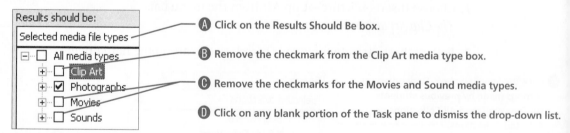

Ⓐ Click on the Results Should Be box.

Ⓑ Remove the checkmark from the Clip Art media type box.

Ⓒ Remove the checkmarks for the Movies and Sound media types.

Ⓓ Click on any blank portion of the Task pane to dismiss the drop-down list.

10. Click the Go button.
    Only a few items appear. Limiting the media file types on a search can be useful if you only want to consider specific types of images.

11. Follow these steps to resume searching all media types:

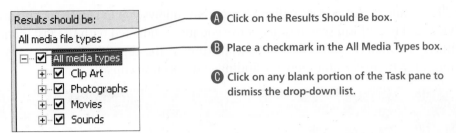

Ⓐ Click on the Results Should Be box.

Ⓑ Place a checkmark in the All Media Types box.

Ⓒ Click on any blank portion of the Task pane to dismiss the drop-down list.

Search the Web Collection

Now that you have searched the hard drive clip art, let's see the additional items you can locate online.

12. Replace *people* with the word **lunch bag** in the Search text box, then tap (ENTER).
    Few, if any, search results are displayed since the clip art search is limited to items on your hard drive.

13. Click Selected Collections in the Search in box, then click the checkbox for the Web Collections item to place a checkmark. Make sure that the checkbox has multiple squares below it as shown at right, not just one.

14. Click the Go button to repeat your search on the keywords *lunch bag*.
    There is a pause as the Web Collection is added to your search. When the results appear, notice that many items are displayed. The Web Collection of clip art is much more extensive than that on your hard drive. Notice the small globe icon at the lower-left corner of each image from the Web Collection.

15. Click in the scroll bar above the down scroll button to move to the next set of clip art, as shown at right.
    The next set of clip art pictures appears.

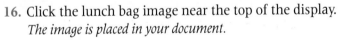

16. Click the lunch bag image near the top of the display.
    The image is placed in your document.

17. Close 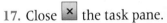 the task pane.

Using the Clip Organizer

The Clip Organizer featured on Office XP programs allows you to search for clip art in a Collection List view and to perform searches like those you just conducted with the task pane. The Clip Organizer also allows you to add your own pictures to the clip art collection. Thus, the Clip Organizer is a more versatile view for finding and selecting clip art.

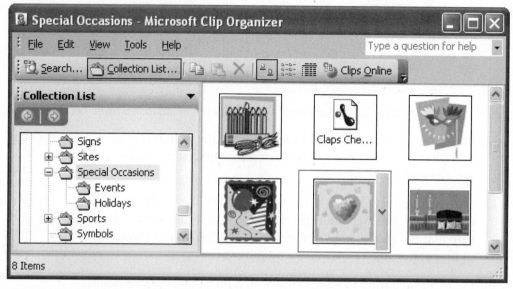

The Clip Organizer allows you to search the collection by category in the Collection List view. You can also add your own images to the collection.

The My Collections Folder

The Clip Organizer also allows you to save pictures to one or more folders within a My Collections folder. You can even save a picture found in the online Web Collections and place it on your hard drive for use when you are offline.

 ## Hands-On 12.4 **Work with the Clip Organizer**

Start the Clip Organizer

1. Choose Insert→Picture→Clip Art from the menu bar.

temp

⚠️ **TIP!**

If the Clip Organizer window appears small, you can resize or maximize the window as necessary.

2. Click the Organize Clips link near the bottom of the task pane.
   After a pause, the Clip Organizer window appears. An Add Clips to Organizer dialog box may also appear to ask if you wish to add media items on your hard drive to the Clip Organizer. In this case, you will indicate that you may wish to do so later.

3. Choose Later if the Add Clips to Organizer dialog box is visible.

x

x

Search for Clip Art in the Collection List View

4. Follow these steps to navigate in the Collection List view:

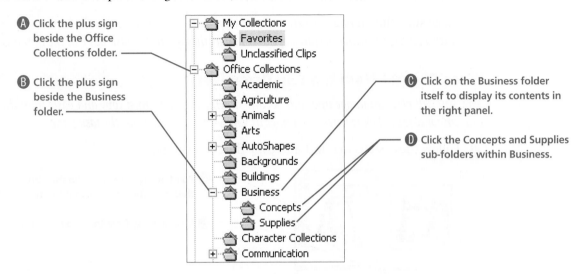

Ⓐ Click the plus sign beside the Office Collections folder.

Ⓑ Click the plus sign beside the Business folder.

Ⓒ Click on the Business folder itself to display its contents in the right panel.

Ⓓ Click the Concepts and Supplies sub-folders within Business.

The Clip Organizer stores images in a folder structure.

5. Follow these steps to continue to search the online Collection List:

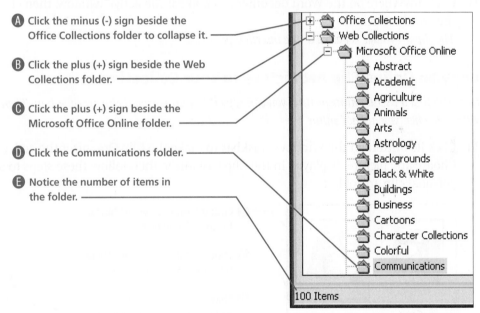

Ⓐ Click the minus (-) sign beside the Office Collections folder to collapse it.

Ⓑ Click the plus (+) sign beside the Web Collections folder.

Ⓒ Click the plus (+) sign beside the Microsoft Office Online folder.

Ⓓ Click the Communications folder.

Ⓔ Notice the number of items in the folder.

There will be a pause as thumbnail images for the online clip art downloads to the Clip Organizer. Depending on the speed of your Internet connection, several seconds or more may pass before all of the thumbnail images appear.

6. Scroll twice down the list of Communications thumbnail images. Each time you scroll there will be a pause as the Clip Organizer loads fresh thumbnails.
With about 100 clips to view, this could be a tedious way to search online clip art. Fortunately, the clip organizer gives you a method to search similar to the task pane.

7. Click the Search ![Search...] button on the Clip Organizer toolbar.
   Notice that your most recent search key word(s) appears in the Search text box.

8. Make sure "lunch bag" are the search keywords, then click the Go button.
   After a pause, the search results appear, much as they did in the task pane in the previous exercise.

Place Clip Art from the Clip Organizer

Now you will place an image into your document. However, you must copy and paste from the Clip Organizer; you cannot simply click to insert the image as you were able to do from the task pane.

9. Follow these steps to select and copy the clip art image:

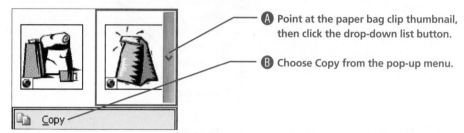

A Point at the paper bag clip thumbnail, then click the drop-down list button.

B Choose Copy from the pop-up menu.

The clip art image is now copied to the Windows clipboard.

10. Click anywhere on the Word document to make it the active window, then click Paste ![Paste] on the Word toolbar.
    The clip art image is pasted at the insertion point.

Copy an Online Clip Art Picture to Your Collection

Once you find a useful online picture, you can copy it to your personal clip art collection. Then it will be available even when you are not online.

11. Click its button on the Windows Taskbar to make the Clip Organizer the active window again. Choose any picture displayed in the Clip Organizer, then follow these steps to add it to your personal clip art folder:

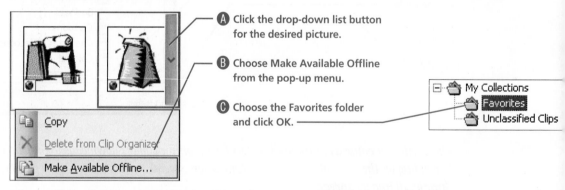

A Click the drop-down list button for the desired picture.

B Choose Make Available Offline from the pop-up menu.

C Choose the Favorites folder and click OK.

There will be a brief pause as the online clip art picture is copied to your hard drive.

12. Click the Collection List ![Collection List...] button on the Clip Organizer toolbar. Scroll to the top of the list, then click the Favorites folder.
    Your newly saved clip art picture should appear in the folder. Other images may be in this folder as well.

13. Close the Clip Organizer window. Click No if you are asked if you wish to keep pictures that are currently on the clipboard.
   Since you have already pasted the picture you need, there is no need to keep it on the clipboard.

14. Click on one of the paper bag pictures and tap the (DELETE) key.
   Now there should be just one paper bag picture on your document.

15. Save the document.

Scaling Pictures

Once you place a picture on a document, you can scale it to larger and smaller sizes. One especially easy way to scale a picture is to drag on its handles. Sizing a picture by its handles allows you to preview exactly how large it will be and adjust its size accordingly.

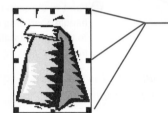

The small squares around the edge of an image are handles.

⚠ TIP! *Scaling and Proportions*

To scale an image proportionally, drag on its corner handles.

Most of the time, you will want to change the size of an image proportionally. That is, if you reduce the height, you will want the width to change by the same factor. If you don't scale an image proportionally, it will appear "scrunched" on the page.

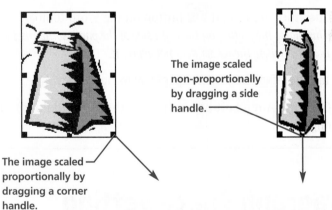

The original image.

The image scaled proportionally by dragging a corner handle.

The image scaled non-proportionally by dragging a side handle.

In this exercise, you will practice scaling a picture larger and smaller.

1. Click anywhere on the picture of the paper bag to display its handles.

2. Follow these steps to scale the picture larger and smaller:

Ⓐ Point to the handle on the lower-right corner of the picture, then drag down and to the right to scale it larger.

Ⓑ Point to the handle on the lower-right corner of the picture, then drag up and to the left to scale it smaller.

Ⓒ Point to the center-right handle, then drag directly to the right to scale the picture larger.

Notice how the picture is distorted by your last scale command. Since you dragged on a side-handle, the picture's proportions changed. Fortunately, it's easy to undo this if it was unintentional.

3. Click Undo 🔄 on Word's toolbar to undo your last scaling command.

4. Drag up and to the right on the upper-right handle until the picture is about one-third as tall as the size of the page.
There's no need to be exact about the picture size on this last step. If the picture turns out to be too large or too small, you can always scale it again later.

5. Click the Align Right ▤ button on the Word toolbar.
This places the picture on the right side of the page. Sometimes a picture is more effective when it appears in a spot where the reader does not expect it.

6. Tap the (END) key, then tap (ENTER) to start a new line.

7. Click the Align Left ▤ button on the Word toolbar to resume the normal horizontal alignment.

The Paragraph Space Setting

Thus far, when you have needed extra space between lines, you have simply tapped (ENTER) one or more times to create a double-space. While this technique is simple and effective, it often creates more space than you need. A more precise and elegant way to create extra space between paragraphs is the paragraph space setting. This allows you to pad the space between paragraphs with a precise amount of space (usually measured in points—see page 361.)

Paragraph Space Compared to Line Spacing

You create a new paragraph every time you tap the (ENTER) key. As your typing reaches the right margin, Word automatically creates a new line for you within the paragraph. The space between lines within a paragraph is set by the line space setting. The figures below illustrate the difference between the two settings.

These paragraph space settings add 6 points between this paragraph and other paragraphs.

This line space setting tells Word to double-space within this paragraph.

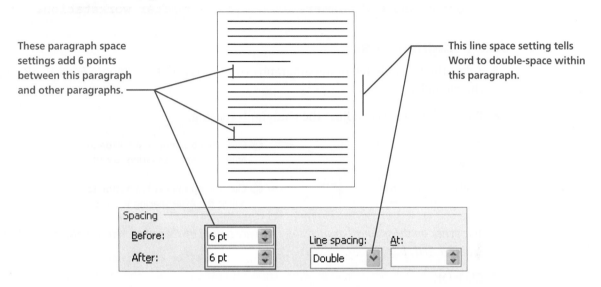

 QUICK REFERENCE: SETTING PARAGRAPH SPACE

Task	Procedure
Set paragraph space for text that has already been typed	■ Select the paragraph(s) to be formatted.
	■ Choose Format→Paragraph from the menu bar.
	■ Click the spinner bar buttons on the Before and After boxes in the Spacing section as desired (to adjust the spacing in 6 point increments), or manually type the desired space setting.

Hands-On 12.6 Set Paragraph Spacing

In this exercise, you will enter text for the flyer, then use paragraph spacing to adjust the space between many of the lines.

Enter Text for the Flyer

1. Set the font to Comic Sans MS.

2. Type **Brown bag discussion** on the line below the picture, then tap (ENTER).

3. Set the font size to 28 pt, type **The Ergonomically Challenged Office**, then tap (ENTER).

4. Set the font size to 18 pt, then click the Bullets 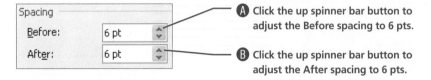 button on the toolbar and type the following bulleted text items:

- **How the setup of your office equipment can affect your productivity and health.**

- **Questions and answers about your computer workstation.**

Add Paragraph Space

5. Select the two bulleted item paragraphs you just typed, then choose Format→Paragraph from the menu bar.

6. Follow these steps to adjust the paragraph spacing:

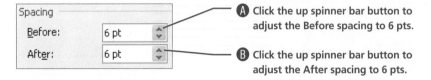

A Click the up spinner bar button to adjust the Before spacing to 6 pts.

B Click the up spinner bar button to adjust the After spacing to 6 pts.

Each click on the spinner bar increases the space setting by six points. You can also manually type a new setting directly into the box.

7. Click OK.
   There should now be additional space above and below each of the bulleted items. Next, you will add some additional space between the first bullet and the title.

8. Click anywhere on the title of the flyer, then choose Format→Paragraph from the menu bar.
   You do not have to select the entire paragraph when you make a paragraph-level format setting.

9. Select the current setting and manually enter **25 pt** as the spacing After the paragraph as shown at right, and click OK.
   Now there is a significant amount of space between the title and the first bullet. You could also have added to the Before space setting of the first bullet rather than adding to the space After setting of the title.

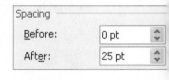

10. Click at the end of the last bulleted item and tap (ENTER) to start a new paragraph.

11. Click the Bullets 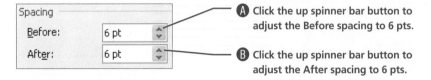 button on the toolbar to switch off the bulleted list.

Finish Typing the Flyer

12. Make a left tab setting at the 1.25 inch point on the ruler.

13. Type the remaining text for the flyer as shown below. Apply Bold font formatting to Where and When on the next two lines.

Where: The Bakery Cafe

When: Wednesday, September 27th at 12 Noon

A catered lunch will be provided.

14. Follow the steps below to scale the picture smaller if any of your text flows onto a new page. Otherwise, continue with the next step.

   ■ Scroll back up to page 1.

   ■ Click on the picture to make its handles appear.

   ■ Drag on a corner handle to scale the picture smaller, until all of your text appears on page 1 again.

15. Save ▣ the document.

Special Font Formatting

You already know about and use bold and italics for character-level font formatting. These are standard font formats offered by many other Windows programs. In addition to these standard font formats, Word features several special font formats you can apply to text. Each special font format has specific uses. Examples of special font formatting are shown in the bulleted list below:

   ■ Strikethrough   ~~This text should be eliminated from the final document.~~

   ■ Small Caps   THIS HELPS EMPHASIZE A TITLE

   ■ All caps   THIS LINE WAS TYPED IN LOWERCASE LETTERS

   ■ Shadow   Shadow should be used sparingly

   ■ Superscript   Text with a ^{superscript}

   ■ Subscript   Text with a $_{subscript}$

Animated Font Formatting

In addition to special font formatting, Word also allows you to apply several different animated font formats to your text. These formats are visible whenever the text is viewed in the Word program window.

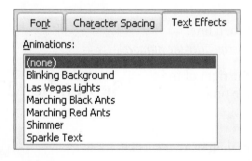

The Text Effects tab in the Font dialog box allows you to apply several types of animations to text characters.

QUICK REFERENCE: ADDING SPECIAL FONT FORMATTING

Task	Procedure
Apply a special font format to text.	■ Select the characters to be formatted.
	■ Choose Format→Font from the menu bar, then choose the Font tab.
	■ Click the checkbox(s) for the desired special font format(s) and click OK.
Apply an animation effect to text.	■ Select the characters to be formatted.
	■ Choose Format→Font from the menu bar, then choose the Text Effects tab.
	■ Choose the desired Animation effect from the list and click OK.

 Hands-On 12.7 Work with Special Font Formats

In this exercise, you will change the date for the discussion and use strikethrough to indicate that the original date was changed. You will also apply an animation effect to highlight the words catered lunch.

Apply Special Font Formatting

1. Select T*he Bakery Cafe* on the Where line.

2. Choose Format→Font from the menu bar, then make sure that the Font tab is chosen.

3. Place a checkmark in the Small Caps box in the Effects section, then click OK.

Effects
☐ Strikethrough   ☐ Shadow   ☑ Small caps
☐ Double strikethrough ☐ Outline   ☐ All caps

The lowercase letters in the name convert to uppercase style shapes. However, they are also smaller in size compared to normal uppercase letters. This format effect is often useful to give additional emphasis to names and titles.

4. Change Wednesday to **Tuesday** on the When line.
   Next, you will change the date and add a superscript after the number.

5. Click to place the insertion point just to the right of the h in 27th, then tap the (BACKSPACE) key three times.

   September 27ᵗʰ at

6. Type the numeral **6** to set a new date.

7. Choose Format→Font from the menu bar, then place a checkmark in the Superscript box and click OK.

   Effects
   ☐ Strikethrough
   ☐ Double strikethrough
   ☑ Superscript
   ☐ Subscript

8. Type **th** after the 6.
   Notice that the superscript setting not only makes these letters higher, it also makes them significantly smaller.

9. Choose Format→Font from the menu bar, then remove the checkmark in the Superscript box and click OK.

Since you are finished using this special font format, you should switch it off so that it does not affect any further typing on this line.

Apply Animated Font Formatting

To make the catered lunch item stand out, you will apply an animation effect to it.

10. Select the words *catered lunch* on the last line of the flyer.

11. Right-click (don't left-click) on the selection, then choose Font from the pop-up menu and choose the Text Effects tab.

12. Choose the Blinking Background animation effect, then click OK.

13. Click at the end of the line to dismiss the selection and view the animation effect.
    This animation effect creates a blinking black background on the selected text.

14. Select *catered lunch* again, then choose Format→Font from the menu bar.

15. Choose the Sparkle Text effect, click OK, then click at the end of the line to dismiss the selection.
    This animation will only be visible when the document is viewed in Word.

16. Compare your flyer to the one shown below. It should appear quite similar to the illustration.

Brown Bag Discussion

The Ergonomically Challenged Office

- How the setup of your office equipment can affect your productivity and health.
- Questions and answers about your computer workstation.

Where: The BAKERY CAFÉ

When: Tuesday, September 26th at 12 Noon

A catered lunch will be provided.

17. Save 🔲 the document, then close it.

Concepts Review

True/False Questions

1. Landscape indicates tall (rather than wide) page orientation.   TRUE   FALSE

2. Word is limited to a specific selection of allowable paper sizes.   TRUE   FALSE

3. You can instruct Word to align all of the contents of a page.   TRUE   FALSE

4. Most of the clip art available with Word is stored on your hard drive. TRUE   FALSE

5. Clip art includes sound and animations.   TRUE   FALSE

6. Every clip art picture is associated with one or more key words.   TRUE   FALSE

7. You can change the size of a clip art picture.   TRUE   FALSE

8. The paragraph space setting sets the distance between each line of text with in a paragraph.   TRUE   FALSE

9. Bold and italic are examples of special font format settings.   TRUE   FALSE

10. The Clip Organizer can store online images on your hard drive.   TRUE   FALSE

Multiple Choice Questions

1. Which method below will ensure that you will scale a picture proportionally so it will not appear distorted?
   a. Drag on any handle
   b. Drag on any handle while holding down the (SHIFT) key
   c. Drag on any corner handle
   d. None of the above

2. The figure at right displays a window from the

   a. Clip Organizer
   b. Clip Art task pane
   c. Both the above
   d. None of the above

3. Which of the lines below *does not* contain an example of a special font format?
   a. This is an EXAMPLE.
   b. This is an example.
   c. This is an example.
   d. This is an **example**.
   e. All of the above contain a special font format.

4. In the figure below, which letter points to an example of paragraph spacing?
   a. x
   b. y
   c. z
   d. Both y and z

   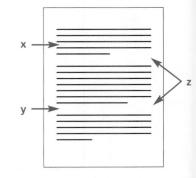

Skill Builders

Skill Builder 12.1 Insert Clip Art from the Task Pane

In this exercise, you will practice searching for and inserting clip art related to a variety of key words.

1. Start Word and create a new document. Save the document to your file storage location as **Skill Builder 12.1**.

Search in the Task Pane

2. Choose Insert→Picture→Clip Art from the menu bar. Click Later if an Add Clips to Organizer dialog box appears.

3. Follow these steps to search for clip art in the entire collection:

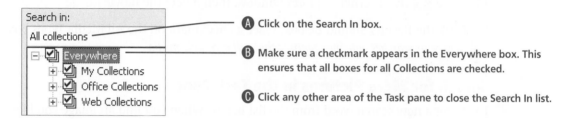

Ⓐ Click on the Search In box.

Ⓑ Make sure a checkmark appears in the Everywhere box. This ensures that all boxes for all Collections are checked.

Ⓒ Click any other area of the Task pane to close the Search In list.

4. Enter **file drawer** in the Search text box, then tap (ENTER).
The pictures on your hard drive will appear right away. After a pause, the pictures available in the Web Collection will start to appear as well.

5. Scroll down the list until you find a picture that looks attractive. Type a caption for the picture in your Word document, then click the picture in the Task pane to enter it into your document beside the caption. Your caption and picture should be similar to the figure at right.

A File Drawer

6. Click on the picture, then drag on its handles to scale it larger or smaller. (You will want to fit a total of five pictures on this page.) When you are finished scaling the picture, tap the (END) key, then tap (ENTER) to start a new line.

7. Follow these steps to change the media types setting:

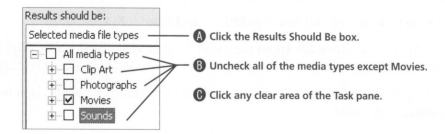

Ⓐ Click the Results Should Be box.

Ⓑ Uncheck all of the media types except Movies.

Ⓒ Click any clear area of the Task pane.

8. Click the Search button.

Now a much smaller number of pictures appear. Notice the small animation symbol at the lower-right corner of each picture.

9. Click any picture to insert it onto your document.

Although all of these pictures are "movies," this picture doesn't do anything in the Word document view. To see the animation, you must view this page as it would appear in a Web browser.

10. Choose File→Web Page Preview from the menu bar.

Word converts your brief document to Web page format and launches Internet Explorer to display it. The picture is now animated! (The picture would also be animated if it were used in a PowerPoint presentation.)

11. Close ⊠ the Internet Explorer window, then delete the movie image.

12. Click the Results Should Be box. Place a checkmark on the All Media Types box.

Now your searches will once again include all available media.

Search for More Pictures in the Task Pane

13. Enter a new search word from the list below. When you find an image you like, type a caption for it and insert it onto your document—as you did in Steps 4 to 6. Continue until you have found a picture related to the four topics listed below. Scale each picture larger or smaller so that all of the pictures fit on a single page.

- National holiday

- A group in a business meeting

- Flying to a travel destination for a travel brochure

- Washing cars for a neighborhood fundraising event

14. When you finish, Save 🖫 the document and then close it.

Skill Builder 12.2 **Use the Clip Organizer**

In this exercise, you will search for clip art using the Clip Organizer.

1. Create a new document and save it as **Skill Builder 12.2**.

2. Choose Insert→Picture→Clip Art on the menu bar then click the Organize Clips link at the bottom of the task pane. Choose Later if an Add Clips to Organizer dialog box appears.

3. Click the plus sign beside the Office Collections folder, then click the plus sign beside the Communication folder.

4. Click on the Communication folder and its subfolders to view the pictures available in this category.

   The Office Collections folder displays pictures available on the hard drive. Notice that the selection of pictures is quite limited. Notice also that one of the clip art items is actually a sound.

5. Click the minus sign beside the Office Collections folder to collapse the display of its subfolders.

6. Click the plus sign beside the Web Collections and Microsoft Office Online folders, then click on the Communications folder.

   There will be a pause as the thumbnail images for this folder download to your computer over your Internet connection. As you can see, a much larger selection of pictures is included in the Web Collection.

Insert a Picture from the Clip Organizer

7. Select any picture in the Communications folder, then click the Copy 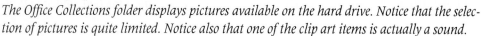 button on the Clip Organizer toolbar. Pause until the hourglass icon disappears before you proceed to the next step.

   Depending on the size of the picture and the speed of your Internet connection, several seconds or more may pass before the picture is downloaded to your computer.

8. At the end of your Word document, type a caption for the picture on a new line.

9. Click the Paste button on the Word (not the Clip Organizer) toolbar.

10. Click on the newly pasted image, then drag on its handles to scale it larger or smaller.

11. Search in the Web Collections for at least two more clip art pictures. You can choose from any category you find interesting. Enter a new line and a caption for each picture you insert. Scale the pictures so that they all fit on a single page.

Save a Picture to Favorites

12. Select any picture in the Clip Organizer, then click on its drop-down list button and choose Make Available Offline from the drop-down menu. Choose Favorites as the folder into which the picture is copied and click OK.

    The picture is copied from the collection into the Favorites folder on your hard drive.

13. Scroll to the very top of the folder list on the left side of the Clip Organizer window, then click the Favorites folder.

    The newly copied picture should be visible in this folder. Additional pictures, added to this folder by other students, may also be included.

14. Close ☒ the Clip Organizer window and close the Clip Art task pane.

15. Save 🖫 the document and close it.

Skill Builder 12.3 Use Special Character Formatting

In this exercise, you will use special character formatting to create a fraction, and to indicate an edit in text.

Create a Fraction

1. Create a new Word document and save it as **Skill Builder 12.3**.

2. Set the Zoom level to 200%, then type the line below:

   The doorway measures 19 and 15/16 inches.

3. Select the 15 in the line you just typed, then choose Format→Font from the menu bar.

4. Make sure that the Font tab is chosen, then place a checkmark in the Superscript box and click OK.

5. Select 16 in the line you just typed and set the font formatting to Subscript.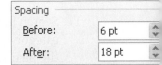
   The fraction should now match the example at right.

Indicate a Trademark

6. Choose Format→Paragraph from the menu bar.

7. Set the Paragraph Space After to 18 pts. You can use the spinner bar to make this setting, or manually type it in the After box.
   You won't see any change yet. This setting will create plenty of space after this line when you tap (ENTER) *in the next step.*

8. Tap the (END) key, tap (ENTER), then type the line below:

   Microsoft Office 2003 is a software suite.

9. Place the insertion point just to the right of the 3 in 2003, then choose Format→Font from the menu bar, set the font format to Superscript, and click OK.

10. Type **TM** in uppercase letters.
    These should appear small and elevated, to indicate a trademark.

Use Strikethrough and Animation

11. Tap the (END) key, tap (ENTER), then type the line below.

    The meeting will take place on Tuesday at 10:00 A.M.

    Notice that your previous paragraph space setting continues to function on each new paragraph you create.

12. Select the word *Tuesday* in the line you just typed, then set the font format for this word to Strikethrough.

13. Type **Wednesday** after the word Tuesday. You will have to turn off the Strikethrough setting if it appears as you type the new word.

14. Select *10:00 A.M.* at the end of the line, then choose Format→Font from the menu bar. Choose the Text Effects tab, then select any animation effect to apply to the time and click OK. Click outside the selection to deselect the text.

15. Select the time again and apply another animation effect to it.

16. Save 🖫 the document and close it.

Skill Builder 12.4 **Create a Flyer**

In this exercise, you will create a new flyer on a topic of your choice, with clip art, a page border, and other refinements.

1. Decide on a topic for your flyer, such as one of the suggestions below:

   ▪ An announcement of a job or school activity

   ▪ Publicity for a community group you in which you participate

   ▪ The opening of a new movie, or an upcoming concert

   ▪ Make up a fictional event

Set Up the Page

2. Create a new Word document, then save it as **Skill Builder 12.4**.

3. Choose File→Page Setup from the menu bar, then make the settings indicated below and click OK.

   ▪ Set the Page Orientation to Landscape.

   ▪ Set the Page Margins to 1 inch on all sides.

   ▪ Choose a Vertical Alignment for the page, such as Centered, Top, or Bottom.

4. Choose Format→Borders and Shading, then choose the Page Border tab. Add a page border in any color and line type you wish.

⚠️ **TIP!** *You might want to try using an art border. Review the options in the Art drop-down list in the Page Border dialog box.*

⚠️ **NOTE!** *If you attempt to choose Art for the page border, Word may tell you that this feature is not installed. Choose No if you receive this prompt and choose a line border instead.*

5. Save 🖫 the document.
   It's always a good habit to save your document when you complete a stage of work.

Design the Flyer

6. Choose a clip art picture to appear on the flyer. Scale the picture as you see fit.

7. Type the text for the flyer. Include information items such as the ones below:

   - A title for the flyer

   - The date and time of the event

   - Where the event will take place

   - What the event is about

   - Other details as appropriate

8. Click on the Title line and apply paragraph space after it to separate the body of the flyer from its title.

9. Select the paragraphs below the flyer title and add paragraph space above and/or below to make each paragraph easy to read. Experiment with different space settings until you like the appearance of the body paragraphs.
   Giving more space between paragraphs can give the flyer a more "open" appearance that will be more attractive to readers. Cramped information is often difficult to read.

10. Save 🖫 the document, then print it.
    Just prior to printing is another excellent stage to save your document.

11. Proofread the flyer: make corrections as appropriate and then print the final version.

Assessments

Assessment 12.1 **Find Clip Art**

In this assessment, you will find clip art related to a specific topic. You will search both on the hard drive and online.

NOTE!

You may search both the Office Collection and Web Collection clip art.

1. Create a new document named **Assessment 12.1**.

2. Using either the Task pane, Clip Organizer, or both, locate clip art pictures related to the following topics. Place each picture on a line, preceded by a caption describing the picture.

   - A picture for use in a document describing emergency first aid procedures.
   - A picture for use with a contest with an ocean voyage as the grand prize.
   - A picture for use on a flyer promoting an election.

3. Searching only the Office (and excluding the Web) Collection, locate a picture of a telephone. Place the picture and caption as you did for the items in Step 2.

4. Expand your search to include all collections (including the Web Collection), then find a photograph (not a clip art image) of a house. Place a caption and the image on a new line of your document.

5. Save 🖫 the document and close it and close the Clip Art task pane.

Assessment 12.2 **Use Special Character Formatting**

In this exercise, you will use special character formatting on text.

1. Create a new document named **Assessment 12.2**.

2. Type the line below:

   Use 1 2/3 cups of flour.

3. Convert 2/3 to a properly formatted fraction.

4. Tap the (END) key, then tap (ENTER) once and type the lines below:

   This monument is one of the most beautiful in the country, and is a short bus ride from the capital.

5. Add 21 pts of space between these lines and the previous line. (Do not tap (ENTER) again.)

6. After the period, add text that appears like the example at right:

capital. See Note 1

7. Add an animated text effect to the word *monument*.

8. Save 🖫 the document, and then close it.

Assessment 12.3 **Create a Flyer**

In this exercise, you will design a flyer to match the example below.

Take Note
Staff Meeting: 9:00^{AM} to 10:30^{AM} Thursday Morning

1. Create a new document named **Assessment 12.3**.

2. Set up the page according to the following specifications:

   ■ Page orientation = landscape.

   ■ Page Margins = 1 inch on all sides.

   ■ Page vertical alignment = bottom.

3. Add a shadow-style page border.

> **!TIP!**
>
> *Search with keywords that reflect the features of or the intended use of the picture.*

4. Search for and insert a clip art picture similar (but not necessarily identical) to the one shown in the example.

5. Add the lines of text shown below the clip art picture using the guidelines given below.

   ■ Use Comic Sans MS as the font.

   ■ Be sure to match the font setting for AM used in the meeting times.
     For example: 9:00^{AM}.

6. Scale the picture so that it fills up about 75% of the height of the page, but is not so large that the text below it is pushed down to the next page.

7. Apply a font animation effect to the Take Note flyer title.

8. Save and print the flyer.

9. Proofread your flyer and, if necessary, perform a final printout.

Critical Thinking 12.1 On Your Own—Create a Flyer Announcing a Class

Create a flyer that announces the next offering of any class you are attending now. It should indicate the subject matter of the class and use visual imagery to get the reader's attention.

Flyer Title: [The Class Name]

Main Message: The skills that enrollees in the class can expect to learn.

Create a new Word document and save it as **Critical Thinking 12.1**, then begin creating a flyer based on the title and main message notes above.

Your flyer should:

- have a title indicating the class name and number.
- use landscape orientation and 1 inch page margins.
- contain one or more relevant pictures from the clip art collections.
- have a page border with any line style and/or color you prefer.
- indicate the date, time, and location of the next offering of your class (this could be for a section later this term, or one taking place the following term).
- indicate where to enroll in the course.
- use font formatting to help the main message of the flyer stand out.

Critical Thinking 12.2 On Your Own—Create a Flyer on a Topic of Your Choice

Come up with an idea for a flyer about an event or an idea. It could be an advertisement promoting a service, a performance event (music, dance, drama, or film), or convey some other distinct message. This flyer should be about a real event, organization, or service—not a made up one. Use the space below to record the title and a brief (2 lines maximum) description of the flyer's main message.

Flyer Title: _____

Main Message: _____

_____

Create a new Word document and save it as **Critical Thinking 12.2**, then begin creating a flyer based on the title and main message notes above.

Your flyer should:

- have a title.
- use either portrait or landscape orientation, as you prefer.
- contain one or more relevant pictures from the clip art collections.
- have a page border with any line style and/or color you prefer.
- indicate the date, time, and location of the event.

Some additional tips:

- Use font formatting as appropriate to make various parts of the message stand out. However, avoid the use of too much bold type. When everything's bold, nothing's bold.
- Be selective and discriminating about the clip art you use for this flyer. Make sure each picture relates to and helps to communicate the main message.
- While big, bold images get attention, sometimes less is more. Don't allow any image to totally dominate the flyer, unless this serves a distinct purpose.
- Some clip art pictures are small, and will become jagged if you scale them too large. If this proves to be the case, look for another image or scale the picture smaller.
- Don't forget to allow some white space. Give your message room to "breathe" and give the reader's eyes a place to settle and focus. If every part of the flyer is shouting for attention, readers may feel distracted and miss your main message.

Critical Thinking 12.3 On Your Own—Quick Flash Flyer Exercise

After you create a flyer according to Critical Thinking Exercise 12.2, test its effectiveness with the steps below.

- Flash your flyer for exactly one second in front of a friend and ask the main message of it.

- Score your friend's impression according to the scale below:

    - **Strong (3 points)**—the friend's impression matches the flyer's main message exactly.

    - **Moderate (2 points)**—the friend's impression partially matches the flyer's main message.

    - **Weak (1 point)**—the friend's impression hardly relates to the flyer's main message.

    - **Missed (0 points)**—the friend's impression misses the flyer's main message completely.

Critical Thinking 12.4 On Your Own—Revise and Compare Flyers

- Revise your flyer according to the score you received in the previous exercise.

- Compare your original and revised flyers according to the points below:

    - What is the most significant visual difference between the two flyers?

    - What is the most effective change made between the original and revised versions?

    - What is the least effective change (if any) made between the original and revised versions?

    - Is this flyer ready for prime time?

Critical Thinking 12.5 Web Research—Find Other Clip Art Resources

The Web features numerous sites devoted to clip art. Some of these are free, while others charge a monthly or annual subscription fee. Use your favorite search engine to locate several clip art resources and compare the samples they display for quality and variety.

Create a Word document named **Critical Thinking 12.5**.

Complete the following:

- Give the names and URL's of at least three different clip art Web sites.

- Describe any difference you observe between "free" sites and those that charge a subscription fee.

- Describe how the variety of images available from the Web sites compare to the clip art available on Word?

- Describe how the image quality of the Web sites compares to the clip art available with Word. Do you consider it to be poorer, equal, or better? If possible, include one or two examples from a Web site to justify your description.

Critical Thinking 12.6 Web Research—Considering Copyright

Many computer users believe that if they can copy or download an image, then it is theirs to use as they please. However, this attitude ignores the reality of copyright and copyright law. The advent of the Internet has added a great deal of complexity to copyright issues. For the first time in history, an individual can steal a work of art without the artist being aware of it. Not only that, but the piece of art (if it's digital art) is exactly like the original.

Create a Word document named **Critical Thinking 12.6**.

Answer the following question for the three Web sites you wrote about in Critical Thinking exercise 12.5:

- What is the copyright (or usage) policy for clip art available from each Web site?

  You should see a prominent link on the home page or search pages that direct you to the copyright policy for artwork downloaded from that Web site. These links will have labels such as copyright or usage guidelines.

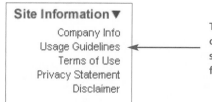

The ArtToday.com Web site has a Usage Guidelines link on its Home page. This page explains the uses to which subscribers can and cannot apply to art downloaded from the Web site.

TIP! *Navigate to the Web page, then give the command Edit→Find (on this page) from the browser's menu bar. Search for a word such as use, usage, terms, copyright, etc. This search will work best if you just search for one word at a time.*

After you have described the copyright/usage policies of the three Web sites, compare them.

- Are some policies more liberal than others? For example, do some Web sites prohibit commercial use of images and others allow such use?

- Do the three Web sites have any common restrictions?

Internet Integration: Emailing a Word Document

A Word document sent with an email message is called an attachment. This is done many of thousands of times each day in a variety of business and personal settings. Word 2003 features specific commands to help you send documents as attachments to email messages or to embed a document within the body of a message. The process of saving a file linked to a Web page onto your computer is called downloading. Some organizations link important documents to one or more Web pages so others can download and view the files from their computers. This lesson will teach you how to download a file such as a Word document and to send documents with email messages.

IN THIS LESSON

Case Study

Milena has developed the agenda for an upcoming committee meeting. She wants to distribute it to the various committee members ahead of time. Rather than print ten copies of the agenda and send them by regular mail, Milena decides to send the agenda via email as an attachment.

When Milena clicks the Email button...

Word displays a form with which she can send her document in the body of an email message.

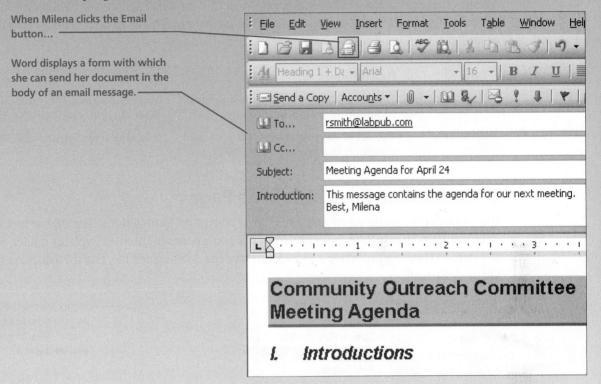

Milena can also send an email message with a Word document attached to it. When the message arrives at each committee member's email Inbox, the attachment file is visible below the subject line. Committee members can double-click to open the file in Word directly, or save it to a folder on a disk drive.

The recipient of a message with an attachment can double-click to open or save the attachment file from the message window.

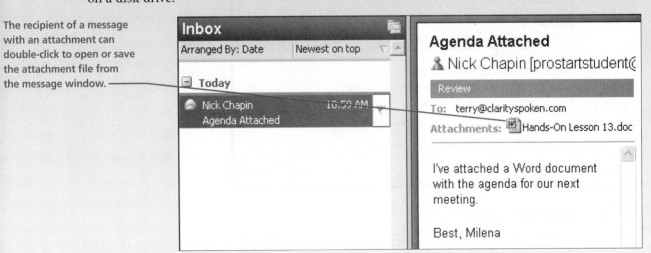

Downloading Documents

The process of exchanging files between computer systems is called uploading and downloading. When you send and receive email, your computer performs both of these tasks—uploading your outgoing messages and downloading your incoming messages. An email program such as Outlook handles these tasks for you automatically. Most of your data exchange activities will involve downloading files to your computer. For example, you may need to download a Word document or an Excel workbook from a Web page.

Task	Description	Example
Downloading	The act of copying a file from a remote computer to your own computer.	You need a tax form. You find it on a Web site and copy it to your computer.
Uploading	The act of copying a file from your own computer to a remote computer.	You send a tax form to the IRS for filing.

Downloading Files from Web Pages

You can usually download any file linked to a Web page. Simply right-click on the link in Internet Explorer, then choose Save Target As from the pop-up menu. Internet Explorer guides you through the steps to choose a disk drive and folder to save the downloaded file, and then displays the progress of the download.

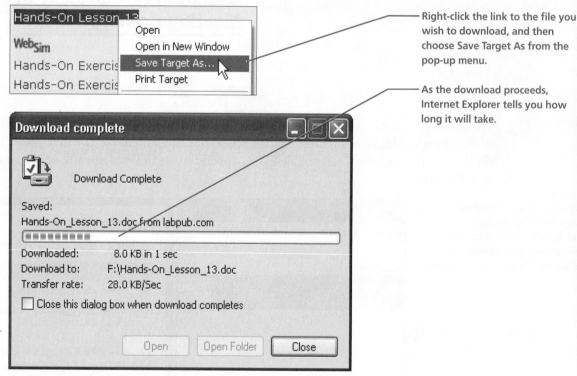

Right-click the link to the file you wish to download, and then choose Save Target As from the pop-up menu.

As the download proceeds, Internet Explorer tells you how long it will take.

!TIP!

Make sure that you can trust the source of any program or document files you download. For more information about viruses, see page 31 in Lesson 1.

Caution, Viruses!

You should be aware that certain types of attachments could contain viruses. Program files, Word documents, Excel workbooks—any of these can carry a virus. Although most viruses are harmless, some can cause damage to your system or even erase files.

Hands-On 13.1 Download a File

In this exercise, you will navigate to a Web page, then download a file from that page to your exercise diskette.

1. Launch Internet Explorer, and navigate to the Lesson 13 Web page:

   labpub.com/learn/oe3/lesson13.html

2. Follow these steps to download the Word document:

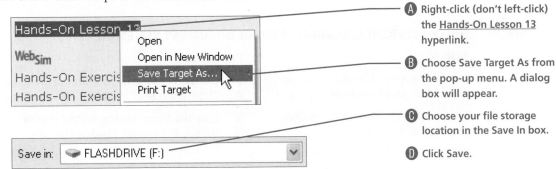

A Right-click (don't left-click) the Hands-On Lesson 13 hyperlink.

B Choose Save Target As from the pop-up menu. A dialog box will appear.

C Choose your file storage location in the Save In box.

D Click Save.

The file will download over the Internet to your exercise diskette.

3. Click the Close button after the download is complete if you see a Download Complete dialog box, otherwise continue to the next step.

4. Minimize ▄ the Internet Explorer window. You may need it again in a moment.

Emailing Word Documents

Word allows you to send documents to other email users from within the program window. You can use one of two basic methods from within Word to send a document.

- File→Send To
- Email Button

The File→Send To Method

The Send To method gives you several options for sending a Word document. The three most frequently used options are described in the table below.

Transmission Option	Description
Mail Recipient	Sends the currently displayed document in the body of an email message. (All pagination is lost.)
Mail Recipient (For Review)	Sends the entire document as an attachment to an email message and switches on Word's Track Changes feature.
Mail Recipient (As Attachment)	Sends the entire document as an attachment to an email message but does not switch on the Track Changes feature.

TIP!

If you click the E-mail button by mistake, just click it again to dismiss the command.

The Email Button

 The Word toolbar contains a button that allows you to send any document as an email message. When you click the E-mail button on the toolbar, Word immediately displays boxes for you to fill in the To: and Cc: addresses, the subject, an introduction, and a Send A Copy button to send the message. The entire document is placed into the body of the message. If you send a multipage document, all page breaks disappear—the document will appear as one long page in the message body.

QUICK REFERENCE: SENDING A WORD DOCUMENT VIA EMAIL	
Task	**Procedure**
Send a Word document as an attachment to an email message option.	▪ Choose File→Send To from the menu bar. ▪ Choose the Mail Recipient (As Attachment)
Send a Word document in the body of an email message	▪ Click the Email button on the toolbar, or choose File→Send To→Mail Recipient from the menu bar.

 ## Hands-On 13.2 Send a Word Document

WebSim

In this exercise, you will practice sending a Word document via email using the Email button and Send To (As Attachment) methods.

WebSim Users Only—If your computer cannot access an email account, restore the Internet Explorer window, then click the Hands-On Exercise 13.2 simulation link, and start working from Step 2 of this exercise.

Send a Document in the Body of a Message

1. Start Word and open the Hands-On_Lesson_13 document on your exercise diskette.
   The underscores in the filename were used to create an "Internet friendly" filename. Many computers on the Internet run an operating system called UNIX. Unlike Windows, UNIX does not allow space characters in filenames. Underscores are often substituted for the space characters.

2. Click the Email button on the toolbar.
   A new toolbar appears, allowing you to address and send the message.

3. Follow these steps to prepare and send the message:

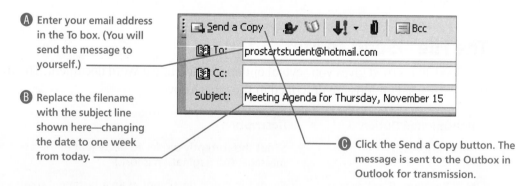

Ⓐ Enter your email address in the To box. (You will send the message to yourself.)

Ⓑ Replace the filename with the subject line shown here—changing the date to one week from today.

Ⓒ Click the Send a Copy button. The message is sent to the Outbox in Outlook for transmission.

Word sends the message to Outlook for transmission. Outlook will normally send the message immediately.

4. Choose File→Send To→Mail Recipient (As Attachment) from the menu bar. Click OK if you are asked to choose a profile. Click Cancel if the Internet Connection Wizard appears and follow the instructions for the WebSim on the previous page.
A new mail message window will appear. Notice that the document is shown as an attachment immediately below the Subject line.

5. Fill out the rest of the message according to the table below.

■ To: **[Enter Your Email Address]**
           Ask your instructor if you do not know your email address.

■ Subject: **Agenda Attached**
           Replace the existing subject.

■ Body: **I've attached a Word document with the agenda for our next meeting.**

           Best, Milena

6. Click the ⌐ Send to send the message.
The message is placed in Outlook's Outbox. Outlook will send the message the next time you start the program.

7. Close ☒ the Word window. Click No if you are asked to save any changes.

Opening Attachments

When you receive a message that includes an attachment, Outlook indicates this with a small paper clip in its row in the Inbox view. If you double-click to open an email message in a message window, Outlook displays its attachments immediately below the subject line. Outlook also displays attachments in the bar above the preview window.

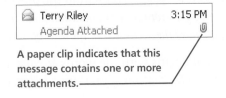

A paper clip indicates that this message contains one or more attachments.

An icon and filename for the attachment appear in the Preview Pane.

The Location of Attachments

In Outlook, attachment files are stored with your messages in the special Outlook data file on your computer's hard drive. Thus, unless you save the attachment, you will be unable to open it outside of the Outlook program.

⚠**TIP!** *Other email programs may store attachments in a special folder rather than in the program's data file.*

Methods to Open Attachments

You can use two methods to open attachments to email messages.

- **Open the attachment from within Outlook**—With this method, Outlook opens the copy of the attachment stored inside the message. If you make changes to the attachment, you can only view the changes later by opening the attachment from within the message.

- **Save the attachment first**—With this method, you give a command to save the attachment to a folder on a disk drive (explained in the next topic). Once the attachment file is saved, you can use the Open command in Word to open the file from its new location outside of Outlook.

 TIP! *Always use the Save The Attachment First Method if you intend to edit the message and open it from time to time.*

Attachments and Computer Viruses

Remember that nearly any attachment (including a Word document) might contain a computer virus. You should always be cautious when handling attachments from users you do not know well. Even trusted co-workers can unknowingly transmit a virus via an attachment.

 TIP! *Never open attachments from sources you do not know, unless you have scanned the attachments for viruses first.*

 ## Hands-On 13.3 Open an Attachment

In this exercise, you will practice opening an attachment.

WebSim ### Open the Message with the Document in the Message Body

WebSim Users Only—If necessary, restore the Internet Explorer window, then click the Hands-On Exercise 13.3 link to run the simulation for this exercise.

1. Start Outlook and display the Inbox or a Hotmail Inbox view as appropriate. Enter a password if you are prompted to do so, then click OK.

2. Click the button until you receive both messages you sent in the previous exercise. *Notice that only one of the messages has a paper clip beside the From column, indicating that it contains an attachment. That's because the first message you sent included the document in the body of the message.*

3. Double-click the message with the subject line that begins with the words *Meeting Agenda for. A line separates the text you typed in the introduction with the contents of your Word document.*

4. Scroll to the bottom of the message body.

5. Close ☒ the message window.

View an Attachment

6. Double-click the message with the subject line *Agenda Attached.*

7. Double-click the attachment name immediately below the To: line.

A dialog box appears, asking you what to do with the attachment. You can save it or open it. Since you know this attachment is safe (it does not contain a virus), you will open it. If this document came from a stranger, you would probably want to save it to a disk drive first.

8. Choose the Open option, then click OK. Choose No if you are asked to merge the changes in this document with another version of the document.
   Word may display the agenda in Reading Layout. This view makes it easier to read a document on the screen. Reading Layout view also displays two pages at a time rather than just a single page.

9. Click OK if a dialog box describing Reading Layout view appears.

10. Choose View→Print Layout to exit Reading Layout view.
    Word reverts to a normal, single page display.

11. Close ⊠ the Word window.

12. Close ⊠ the message window, and then close ⊠ the Outlook window.

UNIT 5

Excel 2003

Excel is Microsoft's powerful spreadsheet program. With it, you create worksheets that contain three types of data: text, numbers, and formulas. Excel can handle extremely complex formulas and much more. In this unit, you will be introduced to the essential Excel features. When you finish, you will be able to create worksheets by entering and editing data in them, create formulas to perform calculations on the data, produce charts to visually represent the data, and learn the basics of opening, saving, printing and closing workbooks. You'll also learn how to format data, restructure worksheets, and use several of Excel's impressive automated tools, including AutoFill, AutoComplete, AutoCorrect, and AutoFormat.

LESSON 14

Creating and Editing a Simple Worksheet

In this lesson, you will develop fundamental Excel 2003 skills. This lesson will provide you with a solid foundation of skills so that you are prepared to master the advanced features introduced in later lessons. For example, you will learn basic skills, including selecting cells, entering and editing text and numbers, and aligning cell entries. In addition, you will use Excel's powerful yet easy-to-use AutoSum tool to sum rows and columns of numbers.

IN THIS LESSON

Case Study

Susan Lee is a student intern at Computer Depot, a discount retailer of computers and computer accessories. Joel Williams, the buyer for Computer Depot, has asked Susan to report the number of PCs, laptop computers, printers, and monitors sold during a five-day period. Joel has instructed Susan to report the data on a daily basis and to include the number of units sold by each manufacturer. After analyzing Joel's request, Susan decides that Excel 2003 is the right tool for the job. She organizes the data in an Excel worksheet, a portion of which is shown below, and uses Excel's AutoSum feature to compute the necessary totals.

	A	B	C	D	E	F	G	H
1	Computer Depot Weekly Sales Data							
2								
3			Wednesday	Thursday	Friday	Saturday	Sunday	Totals
4	PCs							
5		Compaq	3	10	12	15	16	56
6		IBM	4	8	10	13	14	49
7		Acer	6	13	15	18	19	71
8		Total	13	31	37	46	49	176
9								
10	Laptops							
11		IBM	2	5	4	10	8	29
12		Apple PowerBook	3	7	5	12	10	37
13		Compaq	4	8	11	14	14	51
14		Toshiba	2	3	5	5	3	18
15		Total	11	23	25	41	35	135
16								
17	Printers							
18		IBM	3	5	5	6	8	27
19		HP	6	1	2	3	7	19
20		Canon	8	2	3	4	5	22
21		Total						

What is Microsoft Excel 2003?

Microsoft Excel is an electronic spreadsheet (also known as a worksheet) program that makes working with numbers a pleasure instead of a chore. Excel provides tools to assist you in virtually every aspect of worksheet creation and analysis. Whether you are creating dynamic charts for a presentation or interactive worksheets for group collaboration, Excel has the right tool for the job. For these and many other reasons, Excel is the most widely used worksheet program in both homes and businesses.

Why Use Excel?

Excel provides a number of important features and benefits that make it a smart choice.

1. **GUI**—Excel's Graphical User Interface is so easy to use that even beginning computer users find it simple. The interface reduces the need to memorize commands, and it will make you more productive.

2. **Charting**—Have you heard the expression, "One picture is worth a thousand words?" This is especially true with financial or numeric data. Excel's powerful charting and formatting features let you display your data in a powerful and convincing graphic format.

3. **Widely used**—Excel is the most widely used worksheet software. Excel is the right choice if you are trying to develop marketable skills and find employment.

4. **Integration with other Office programs**—Excel 2003 is part of the Microsoft Office 2003 suite of programs, which also includes Word, Access, PowerPoint, Outlook, and others. The ability to exchange data with these programs is one of the most powerful and attractive features of Excel.

5. **Web integration**—Excel 2003 lets you easily publish your worksheets to Web sites on the World Wide Web or to your company Intranet.

It's Time to Learn Excel!

It's time to put your fears behind and learn this wonderful program. You will be amazed at the power and simplicity of Excel and how easy it is to learn. The knowledge you are about to gain will give you a marketable skill and make you an Excel master.

Hands-On 14.1 **Start Excel**

In this exercise, you will start the Excel program.

1. Click the ⟨ *start* ⟩ button and choose (All) Programs, then choose Microsoft Office Excel.

⚠TIP! *You can open an existing document by navigating to the desired document in Windows Explorer or My Computer. You can also choose the desired workbook from the My Recent Documents list by clicking the Start menu.*

The Excel program will load, and the Excel window will appear. Don't be concerned if your window appears different from the example shown in the following illustration.

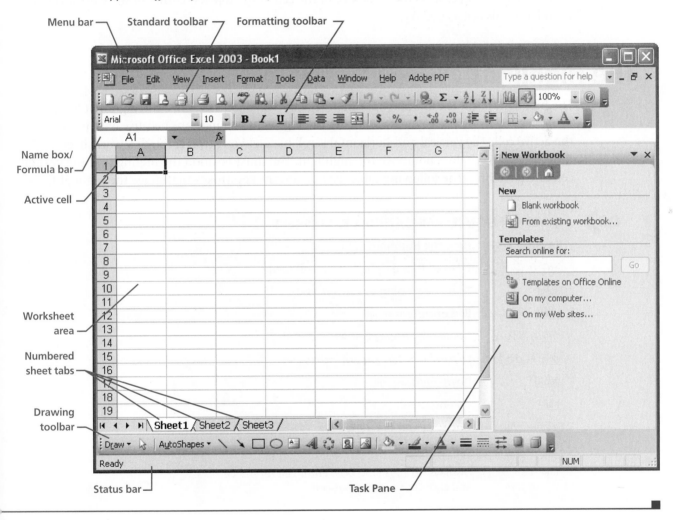

Worksheets and Workbooks

Excel displays a blank workbook the moment you start the program. A workbook is composed of worksheets. This is similar to a paper notebook with many sheets of paper. You enter text, numbers, formulas, charts, and other objects in worksheets. Excel displays three worksheets in a new workbook. The maximum number of sheets you can insert is limited to the amount of available memory.

A worksheet has a grid structure with horizontal rows and vertical columns. A new worksheet has 256 columns and 65,536 rows. However, at any given time, only a small number of the rows and columns are visible in the worksheet window. The intersection of each row and column is a cell. Each cell is identified by a reference. The reference is the column letter followed by the row number. For example, A1 is the reference of the cell in the top–left corner of the worksheet. So, we refer to this cell as Cell A1.

The Highlight

The highlight is a thick line surrounding the active cell. You can move the highlight by clicking in a cell or by using the keyboard. Moving the highlight is important because data is entered into the active cell. The vertical and horizontal scroll bars let you scroll through a worksheet. However, scrolling does not move the highlight. You must position the highlight in the desired cell after scrolling. The following table lists important keystrokes that move the highlight.

QUICK REFERENCE: NAVIGATING A WORKSHEET

Keystroke(s)	How the Highlight Is Moved
→ ← ↑ ↓	One cell to the right, left, up, or down
HOME	To the beginning of current row
CTRL + →	End of current row
CTRL + HOME	Home cell, usually Cell A1
CTRL + END	Last cell in active part of worksheet
PGDN	Down one screen
PGUP	Up one screen
ALT + PGDN	One screen to the right
ALT + PGUP	One screen to the left
CTRL + G	Displays Go To dialog box. Enter cell reference and click OK to go to that cell.

The Task Pane

The Task Pane appears on the right side of the worksheet area. You can use the Task Pane to open worksheets, create new worksheets, and perform other common activities. The Task Pane is context sensitive, displaying different options depending on the state of your worksheet. You can display or hide the Task Pane with the View→Task Pane command. You can also close the Task Pane by clicking the Close button at the top, right corner of the Task Pane window.

Close the Task Pane and Move the Highlight

In the first part of this exercise, you will close the Task Pane. You will be instructed to redisplay the Task Pane at a later time.

1. If the Task Pane is displayed on the right side of the worksheet area, choose View→Task Pane to hide it.

2. Slide the mouse, and the pointer will have a thick cross ✛ shape when it is in the worksheet area.

3. Click the pointer on any cell, and the highlight will move to that cell.

4. Move the highlight five times by clicking in various cells.

Use the Keyboard to Move the Highlight

In the next few steps, you will move the highlight with the keyboard. You can use the keys on the main part of your keyboard or on the Numeric keypad at the bottom right corner of your keyboard. Keep in mind, however, that you must have the (NUM LOCK) *key turned off if you want to move the highlight with the Numeric keypad. The word NUM will disappear from the Status bar when Num Lock is turned off.*

5. Use the arrow ⊙⊙⊙⊙ keys to position the highlight in Cell F10.

6. Tap the (HOME) key, and the highlight will move to Cell A10.
   The (HOME) *key always moves the highlight to Column A in the active row.*

7. Press (CTRL)+(HOME) to move the highlight to Cell A1.

8. Tap the (PGDN) key two or three times.
   Notice that Excel displays the next 30 or so rows each time you tap (PGDN).

9. Press and hold the ⊙ key until the highlight is in Cell A1.

Use the Scroll Bars

10. Click the Scroll Right ▶ button on the horizontal scroll bar until Columns AA and AB are visible.
    Excel labels the first 26 columns A–Z and the next 26 columns AA–AZ. A similar labeling scheme is used for the remaining columns.

11. Take a few minutes to practice scrolling and moving the highlight.

Use the Go To Command

As discussed at the bottom of the Quick Reference table on the preceding page, you can use the (CTRL)+(G) *keystroke combination to display the Go To box. You can go to a specific cell by entering the desired cell reference in the Reference box and clicking OK.*

12. Press (CTRL)+(G) to display the Go To box.

13. Type **G10** in the Reference box and click OK.
    The highlight should move to cell G10.

14. Use the Go To command to go to two or three different cells.

Explore the Excel Window

15. Follow these steps to explore the Excel window:

Ⓐ Notice the Name box on the Formula bar. Don't worry if your Formula bar is not displayed. You will learn to display and hide the Formula bar soon. The Name box displays the name or reference of the active cell. ⟶

Ⓑ Click the Sheet2 tab, and another blank worksheet will be displayed. ⟶

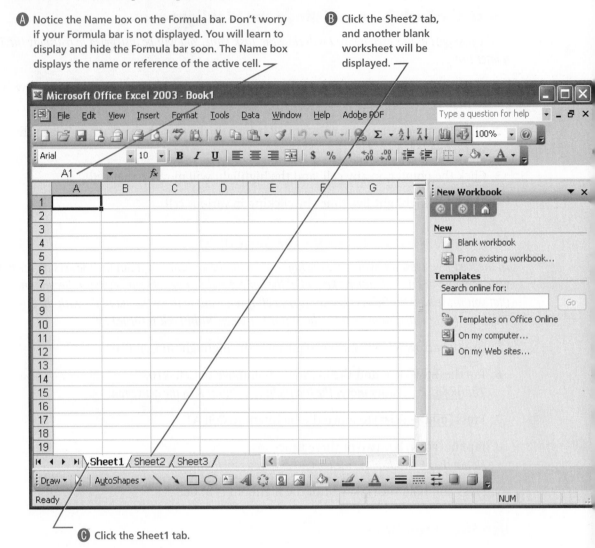

Ⓒ Click the Sheet1 tab.

16. Press ⟨CTRL⟩+⟨HOME⟩ to move the highlight to Cell A1.

Entering Data

You can begin entering data the moment Excel is started. Data is entered into the active cell (the cell with the highlight). You can enter text, numbers, or formulas into cells. Text and numbers are used for different purposes in a worksheet. Text is used for descriptive headings and entries that require alphabetic characters or a combination of alphabetic and numeric characters. Numbers can be calculated using formulas. Excel recognizes the data you enter and decides whether the entry is text, a number, or a formula.

Completing Cell Entries

Text or numbers are entered by positioning the highlight in the desired cell, typing the desired text or number, and completing the entry. You can use (ENTER) and any of the arrow (←)(→)(↑)(↓) keys to complete an entry. When you complete an entry with (ENTER), the text or number is entered in the cell, and the highlight moves down to the next cell. When you complete an entry with an arrow key, the text or number is entered in the cell, and the highlight moves to the next cell in the direction of the arrow key. If you are entering text or numbers and change your mind prior to completing the entry, you can press (ESC) to cancel the entry.

The Enter and Cancel Buttons

The Enter ☑ button and Cancel ☒ button appear on the Formula bar whenever you are entering or editing an entry. The Enter button completes the entry, and the highlight remains in the current cell. The Cancel button cancels the entry, as does the (ESC) key.

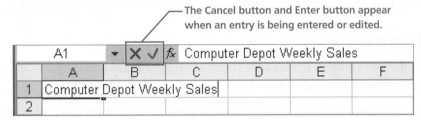

The Cancel button and Enter button appear when an entry is being entered or edited.

Deleting and Replacing Entries

You can delete an entry after it has been completed by clicking in the cell and tapping (DELETE). Likewise, you can replace an entry by clicking in the cell and typing a new entry. The new entry will replace the original entry.

Undo and Redo

Excel's Undo ↺ button lets you reverse your last 16 action(s). You can reverse simple actions such as accidentally deleting a cell's content, or you can reverse more complex actions such as deleting an entire row. Most actions can be undone. Actions that can't be undone include commands such as printing workbooks and saving workbooks.

FROM THE KEYBOARD
(CTRL)+(Z) for undo
(CTRL)+(Y) for redo

The Redo ↻ button reverses Undo. Use Redo when you Undo an action but decide to go through with that action after all.

Undoing and Redoing Multiple Actions

The arrows ▾ on the Undo and Redo buttons display lists of actions that can be undone or redone. You can undo or redo multiple actions by dragging the mouse over the desired actions. You can undo or redo up to 16 actions using this method. However, you must undo or redo actions in the order in which they appear on the drop-down list.

Repeat

The Edit→Repeat command lets you repeat your last action. For example, imagine you want to change the font size for several cells in a worksheet. To accomplish this, you could change the font size in one cell, reposition the highlight, and then issue the Repeat command. The Repeat command will set the font size for the new cell to the same size you set in the previous cell. You can repeat an action as many times as desired. However, the Repeat command is only available when the Redo button is unavailable. The Edit→Repeat command changes to Edit→Redo as soon as you undo an action.

FROM THE KEYBOARD
CTRL+Y for repeat

Text Entries

Text entries contain only text or a combination of text and numbers. They are used in headings and other areas in which descriptive text is required. Text entries cannot be used in calculations.

Long Text Entries

Text entries are often too long to fit in a cell. These entries are known as long entries. Excel uses the following rules when deciding how to display long entries.

- If the cell to the right of the long entry is empty, then the long entry displays over the adjacent cell.

- If the cell to the right of the long entry contains an entry, then Excel shortens, or truncates, the display of the long entry.

Keep in mind that Excel does not actually change the long entry, it simply truncates the display of the entry. You can always widen a column to accommodate a long entry.

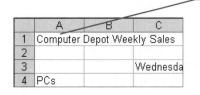

The entry, Computer Depot Weekly Sales, is a long entry. The entire phrase is entered in Cell A1 although it displays over Cells B1 and C1.

 ## Hands-On 14.3 Entering Text

Type a Long Entry

1. Make Cell A1 active by clicking the mouse pointer ✛ in it.

2. Type **Computer Depot Weekly Sales**, and tap (ENTER).
   The text should be entered in the cell, and the highlight should move down to Cell A2. Excel moves the highlight down when you tap (ENTER) because most people enter data column by column. Notice that the entry displays over Cells B1 and C1. The long entry would not display over these cells if they contained data.

Deleting Characters

Use the (DELETE) and (BACKSPACE) keys to edit entries in the Formula bar or within a cell. The (DELETE) key removes the character to the right of the insertion point, while the (BACKSPACE) key removes the character to the left of the insertion point.

FROM THE KEYBOARD

(CTRL)+(DELETE) to delete text to end of line

Hands-On 14.6 Edit Entries

The Hands-On Lesson 14 workbook should be open from the previous exercise.

Edit in the Formula Bar

1. Click Cell A1.

2. Follow these steps to edit Cell A1 using the Formula bar:

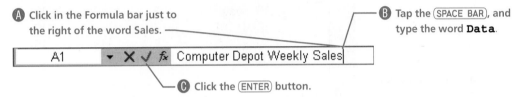

Ⓐ Click in the Formula bar just to the right of the word Sales.

Ⓑ Tap the (SPACE BAR), and type the word **Data**.

Ⓒ Click the (ENTER) button.

Replace an Entry

3. Click Cell B13.

4. Type **Compaq**, and tap (ENTER).
   The entry Compaq will replace Empower.

Use In-Cell Editing

5. Double-click Cell B12 (the cell with the word Apple).

6. Use the mouse or the (→) key to position the flashing insertion point to the right of the word Apple.

7. Tap the (SPACE BAR) once, and type **PowerBook**.

8. Tap (ENTER) or click Enter ☑ to complete the change.
   The entry should now read Apple PowerBook (although the entry will be slightly truncated). You will fix the truncation by widening the column later in this lesson.

9. Click the Save 🖫 button to update the changes.
   The Save button automatically saves changes to a workbook that has previously been saved.

Selecting Cells

In Excel, you can select cells using both the mouse and the keyboard. You can perform a variety of actions on selected cells, including moving, copying, deleting, and formatting.

A range is a rectangular group of cells. Earlier in this lesson, you learned that each cell has a reference. For example, A1 refers to the first cell in a worksheet. Likewise, a range reference specifies the cells that are included within a range. The range reference includes the first and last cells in the range separated by a colon (:). For example, the Range C3:G3 includes all cells between C3 and G3. The following illustration highlights several ranges and their corresponding range references.

The Range C3:G3 ———

The Range B5:B8 ———

The Range B11:C15 ———

	A	B	C	D	E	F	G
1	Computer Depot Weekly Sales Data						
2							
3			Wednesda	Thursday	Friday	Saturday	Sunday
4	PCs						
5		Compaq	3	10	12	15	16
6		IBM	4	8	10	13	14
7		Acer	6	13	15	18	19
8		Total					
9							
10	Laptops						
11		IBM	2	5	4	10	8
12		Apple Pow	3	7	5	12	10
13		Compaq	4	8	11	14	14
14		Toshiba	2	3	5	5	3
15		Total					

The following Quick Reference table describes selection techniques in Excel.

QUICK REFERENCE: SELECTION TECHNIQUES

Technique	How to Do It
Select a range.	Drag the mouse pointer over the desired cells.
Select several ranges.	Select a range; then press (CTRL) while selecting additional range(s).
Select an entire column.	Click a column heading, or press (CTRL)+(SPACE BAR).
Select an entire row.	Click a row heading, or press (SHIFT)+(SPACE BAR).
Select multiple columns or rows.	Drag the mouse pointer over the desired column or row headings.
Select an entire worksheet.	Click the Select All button at the top–left corner of the worksheet, or press (CTRL)+(A)
Select a range using the (SHIFT) key.	Position the highlight in the first cell you wish to select, press (SHIFT), and click the last cell in the range.
Extend a selection with the (SHIFT) key.	Press (SHIFT) while tapping any arrow key.

Hands-On 14.7 Practice Selecting

1. Position the mouse pointer ⊕ over Cell C3.

2. Press and hold the left mouse button while dragging the mouse to the right until the range C3:G3 is selected.

3. Deselect the cells by clicking anywhere in the worksheet.

Select Multiple Ranges

4. Select the range C3:G3 as you did in steps 1 and 2.

5. Press and hold (CTRL) while you select the range B5:B8, as shown to the right.
   Both the C3:G3 and B5:B8 ranges should be selected. The (CTRL) key lets you select more than one range at the same time.

5		Compaq
6		IBM
7		Acer
8		Total

6. Press and hold (CTRL) while you select another range.
   There should now be three ranges selected.

7. Deselect the ranges by releasing (CTRL) and clicking anywhere in the worksheet.

Select Entire Rows and Columns

8. Follow these steps to select various rows and columns:

Ⓐ Click on the Column A heading to select the entire column.

Ⓑ Position the mouse pointer on the Column C heading, then drag to the right until Columns C, D, and E are selected. Column A will be deselected.

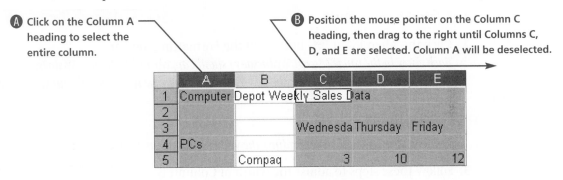

Ⓐ Click the Select All button to select the entire worksheet.

Ⓑ Click the Row 1 heading to select Row 1.

Ⓒ Drag the mouse pointer down over the headings to Rows 5–8 to select them.

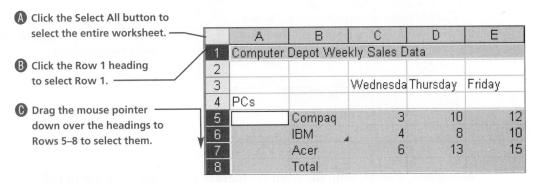

Use Keyboard Techniques

9. Click Cell B5.

10. Press and hold (SHIFT); then click Cell G8 to select the range B5:G8.

11. Click Cell B11.

12. Press and hold (SHIFT) then tap ⊕ five times, and ⊕ four times.
    The range B11:G15 should be selected. Notice that the (SHIFT) key techniques give you precise control when selecting. You should use the (SHIFT) key techniques if you find it difficult to select with the mouse.

13. Take a moment to practice selection techniques.

Aligning Cell Entries

The Align Left ▤, Center ▤, and Align Right ▤ buttons on the Formatting toolbar let you align entries within cells. By default, text entries are left-aligned and numbers are right-aligned. To change alignment, select the cell(s) and click the desired alignment button.

Hands-On 14.8 Align Text Entries and Widen Columns

In this exercise, you will align the entries in Row 3. You will also widen Columns B and C.

1. Select the range C3:G3.

   | Wednesda | Thursday | Friday | Saturday | Sunday |

2. Click the Align Right ▤ button on the Formatting toolbar.
   Each entry in the range (except Wednesday) should appear right-aligned. Wednesday does not appear right aligned because it is too wide for the cell. You will change the width of Column C in a moment.

Adjust Column Widths

In the next few steps, you will adjust the width of Columns B and C.

3. Follow these steps to adjust the width of Column B:

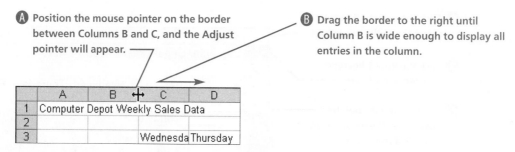

Ⓐ Position the mouse pointer on the border between Columns B and C, and the Adjust pointer will appear.

Ⓑ Drag the border to the right until Column B is wide enough to display all entries in the column.

4. Widen Column C until the word Wednesday is completely visible in Cell C3.
   You will need to drag the border between the column headings C and D.

5. Click the Save ▤ button to save the changes.

AutoSum

The power of Excel becomes apparent when you begin using formulas and functions. The most common type of calculation is when a column or row of numbers is summed. In fact, this type of calculation is so common that Excel provides the AutoSum function specifically for this purpose.

The AutoSum Σ button on the Standard toolbar automatically sums a column or row of numbers. When you click AutoSum, Excel proposes a range of numbers. You can accept the proposed range or drag in the worksheet to select a different range. When you complete the entry, Excel inserts a SUM function in the worksheet, which adds the numbers in the range.

FROM THE KEYBOARD

ALT + = for AutoSum

Other Functions Available through the AutoSum Button

The AutoSum Σ button contains a drop down button that displays a function list. Some of the functions on the list include the Sum, Average, Min, and Max functions. Functions are predefined formulas that perform calculations. You will learn how to use these and other functions in Lesson 16.

Hands-On 14.9 Use AutoSum

In this exercise, you will use AutoSum to calculate several totals. Keep in mind that this section provides an introduction to formulas. You will learn more about formulas as you progress through this course.

Calculate One Column Total

1. Click Cell C8.

2. Click the AutoSum Σ button.

3. Follow these steps to review the formula and complete the entry:

MIN	▼ X ✓ ƒx	=SUM(C5:C7)	
	A	B	C	D

	A	B	C	D
1	Computer Depot Weekly Sales Data			
2				
3			Wednesday	Thursday
4	PCs			
5		Compaq	3	10
6		IBM	4	8
7		Acer	6	13
8		Total	=SUM(C5:C7	
9			SUM(**number1**, [number2	

Ⓐ Notice that Excel proposes the formula =SUM(C5:C7) in Cell 8 and in the Formula bar. All formulas begin with an equal (=) sign. SUM is a built-in function that adds the numbers in a range (in this example the range is C5:C7).

Ⓑ Notice the flashing marquee surrounding the range C5:C7. AutoSum assumes you want to add together all cells above C8 until the first empty cell is reached. The marquee identifies this range of cells.

Ⓒ Click the Enter ✓ button on the Formula bar to complete the entry. The total should be 13.

4. Click Cell D8.

5. Click AutoSum $\boxed{\Sigma}$ and complete $\boxed{\checkmark}$ the entry.

6. Use the preceding technique to calculate the column totals in Cells E8, F8, and G8.

Calculate Several Totals With One Command

7. Select the Range C15:G15 (the cells requiring totals in Row 15).

8. Click the AutoSum $\boxed{\Sigma}$ button.
   The column totals for Cells C15, D15, E15, F15, and G15 should automatically be calculated. AutoSum displays the marquee and requires confirmation only when you are calculating a single total.

9. Use the preceding steps to calculate the totals in Rows 21 and 27.

Make Column H a Totals Column

10. Click Cell H3, type the word **Totals**, and complete the entry.

11. Use the Align Right $\boxed{\equiv}$ button to right-align the entry in Cell H3.

12. Click Cell H5.

13. Click AutoSum $\boxed{\Sigma}$ and Excel will propose the Range C5:G5, which includes all numbers in Row 5.

14. Complete $\boxed{\checkmark}$ the entry and the row sum should total 56.

15. Use the preceding steps to calculate the row total in Cell H6.

Override the Range AutoSum Proposes

16. Click Cell H7, and then click AutoSum $\boxed{\Sigma}$.
    Notice that Excel assumes you want to sum the Cells H5 and H6, above H7. This assumption is incorrect. Excel made this assumption because there were two cells above H7, which is enough to make a range. Excel will always propose a column summation if it has a choice between a column and row summation.

17. Follow these steps to override the proposed range:

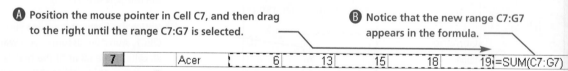

Ⓐ Position the mouse pointer in Cell C7, and then drag to the right until the range C7:G7 is selected.

Ⓑ Notice that the new range C7:G7 appears in the formula.

18. Complete the entry, and the row sum should total 71.

19. Use the preceding technique to calculate the row total in Cell H8 (the total should equal 176).
    Actually, you could have accepted the formula that AutoSum proposed for Cell H8. In this case, the column and row summations would have been the same.

Calculate Several Totals with One Command

You can eliminate the problem of AutoSum proposing the wrong formula by summing a range of row totals with one command. This is the same technique you used to sum the column totals.

20. Select the range H11:H15 as shown in the following illustration:

	A	B	C	D	E	F	G	H
9								
10	Laptops							
11		IBM	2	5	4	10	8	
12		Apple PowerBook	3	7	5	12	10	
13		Compaq	4	8	11	14	14	
14		Toshiba	2	3	5	5	3	
15		Total	11	23	25	41	35	

21. Click the AutoSum Σ button.
    The five row totals should be summed.

22. Use the preceding steps to calculate the row totals for the ranges H18:H21 and H24:H27.
    Your completed worksheet should match the worksheet shown in the Case Study at the start of this lesson.

AutoCalculate

The AutoCalculate box on the Status bar lets you view the sum of a range of numbers without actually inserting a SUM function in the worksheet. You can also right-click on the AutoCalculate box to see the average, minimum, or maximum of the selected range. The following illustration highlights these concepts.

To use AutoCalculate, first select a range. Excel displays the sum in the AutoCalculate box on the Status bar.

If desired, you can right-click the AutoCalculate box and choose another function from the pop-up menu.

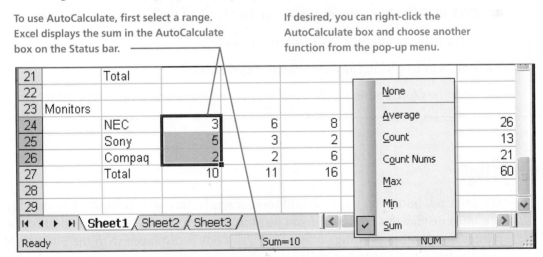

Hands-On 14.10 Use AutoCalculate

1. Select any range of numbers in your worksheet.

2. Locate the AutoCalculate box on the Status bar. The sum of the selected numbers should be displayed.

3. Right-click the AutoCalculate box, and the pop-up menu will appear.

4. Choose Average from the pop-up menu to display the average of the numbers in the AutoCalculate box.

5. Select another range to display the average in the AutoCalculate box.

6. Right-click the AutoCalculate box, and choose Sum from the pop-up menu.

Print Preview

The Print Preview button on the Standard toolbar displays the Print Preview window. Print Preview lets you see exactly how a worksheet will look when it is printed. Print Preview can save time, paper, and wear-and-tear on your printer. Print Preview is especially useful when printing large worksheets, or with worksheets containing charts and intricate formatting. It is always wise to preview a large or complex worksheet before sending it to the printer. When you display the Print Preview window, the standard toolbars are replaced by the Print Preview toolbar.

 Hands-On 14.11 Use Print Preview

1. Click the Print Preview button on the Standard toolbar.

2. Zoom in by clicking anywhere on the worksheet.

3. Zoom out by clicking anywhere on the worksheet.

4. Click the Close button on the Print Preview toolbar to exit without printing.

Printing

The Print button on the Standard toolbar sends the entire worksheet to the current printer. You must display the Print box if you want to change printers, adjust the number of copies to be printed, or set other printing options. The Print box is displayed with the File→Print command. The illustration on the following page explains the most important options available in the Print box.

FROM THE KEYBOARD

CTRL + P to display Print box

Choose a printer from this drop-down list. ────

Specify the number of copies here. The Collate option is useful when you are printing more than one copy of a multiple page worksheet. If the Collate box is checked, the first copy is printed before the second copy begins printing, etc. ────

Choose to print all pages or a range of pages. ────

Choose to print only selected cells, the active sheet(s), or the entire workbook here. ────

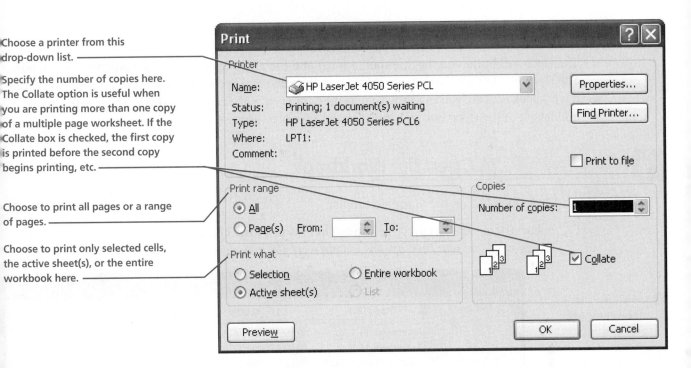

Hands-On 14.12 **Print the Worksheet**

1. Choose File→Print to display the Print box.

2. Take a few moments to review the box options.

3. When you are ready to print, make sure the options are set as shown in the preceding illustration, then click the OK button.
   Keep in mind that your printer will probably be different than the printer shown in the illustration.

4. Retrieve your worksheet from the printer.

Closing Workbooks

The File→Close command is used to close an open workbook. When you close a workbook, Excel prompts you to save the changes. If you choose Yes at the prompt and the workbook has previously been saved, then Excel saves the changes. If the workbook is new, Excel displays the Save As box, allowing you to assign a name and storage location to the workbook.

Hands-On 14.13 **Close the Workbook**

1. Choose File→Close from the menu bar.

2. Click the Yes button if Excel asks you to save the changes.
   Notice that there is no workbook in the Excel window. The Excel window always has this appearance when all workbooks have been closed.

Opening Workbooks

The Open button on the Standard toolbar and the File→Open command display the Open box. The Open box lets you navigate to any storage location and open previously saved workbooks. Once a workbook is open, you can browse it, print it, or even make editing changes. The organization and layout of the Open box are similar to the Save box discussed earlier in this lesson.

FROM THE KEYBOARD

(CTRL)+(O) to Open

Hands-On 14.14 Open the Workbook

1. Click Open on the Standard toolbar.

2. Follow these steps to open the Hands-On Lesson 14 workbook:
   Keep in mind that your Open box will contain more files than shown here.

Ⓐ Choose the disk drive containing your exercise diskette. It is most likely in 3½ Floppy (A:).

Ⓑ Choose the Hands-On Lesson 14 file.

Ⓒ Click the Open button.

TIP!

You can also double-click a document on the list.

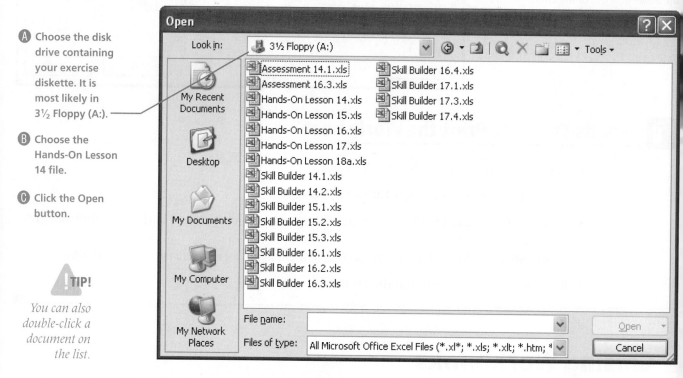

Notice that the worksheet is exactly as it was before it was closed.

Exiting from Excel

The File→Exit command is used to close the Excel program. You should close Excel and other programs if you are certain you won't be using them for some time. This will free up memory for other programs. When you exit Excel, you will be prompted to save any workbooks that have unsaved edits.

 Hands-On 14.15 **Exit from Excel**

1. Choose File→Exit from the menu bar.
   Excel will close without prompting you to save the workbook because you have not changed the workbook since it was opened last.

Concepts Review

True/False Questions

1. Each workbook can have a maximum of one worksheet. TRUE FALSE

2. A worksheet is composed of horizontal rows and vertical columns. TRUE FALSE

3. Text entries can contain spaces. TRUE FALSE

4. Numbers can only contain the digits 0–9. No other characters are permitted. TRUE FALSE

5. The Undo button lets you reverse up to the last 16 actions. TRUE FALSE

6. A colon (:) is used to separate the beginning and ending cells in a range reference. TRUE FALSE

7. You can select an entire row by clicking the row header. TRUE FALSE

8. You can use the AutoSum button to average a range of cells. TRUE FALSE

9. The Task Pane can be used to create new worksheets. TRUE FALSE

10. AutoCalculate lets you view the sum of a selected range of numbers. TRUE FALSE

Multiple Choice Questions

1. Which of the following keystrokes moves the highlight to Cell A1?
   a. HOME
   b. CTRL + PGUP
   c. CTRL + HOME
   d. CTRL + INS

2. What happens when you enter text in a cell that already contains an entry?
   a. The text replaces the original entry.
   b. Excel rejects the new entry, keeping the original entry intact.
   c. The cell contains both the original entry and the new entry.
   d. None of the above

3. What happens when you insert an entry in the cell to the right of a long text entry?
   a. The display of the long entry is truncated.
   b. The long entry is replaced by the entry in the cell to the right.
   c. It has no effect on the long entry.
   d. None of the above

4. What happens when you insert an entry in the cell to the left of a long text entry?
   a. The display of the long entry is truncated.
   b. The long entry is permanently truncated.
   c. It has no effect on the long entry.
   d. None of the above

Skill Builders

Skill Builder 14.1 Edit a Worksheet

In this exercise, you will edit a worksheet. This exercise demonstrates that sometimes it is easier to replace entries, and at other times it is easier to edit them.

Replace Several Entries

1. Start Excel and click the Open 📁 button on the Standard toolbar.

2. Navigate to your exercise diskette, and double-click the workbook named Skill Builder 14.1.

3. Click Cell A4.

4. Type **Ralph**, and tap (ENTER).
   Notice that it was easy to replace the entry because the name Ralph is easy to retype.

5. Replace the name Calvin in Cell A6 with the name **Steven**.

Edit Using the Formula Bar

6. Click Cell C4.

7. Click in the Formula bar just in front of the telephone prefix 222.

8. Tap (DELETE) three times to remove the prefix.

9. Type **333** and complete ✔ the entry.

10. Change the area code in Cell C8 from 714 to **814**.

Use In-Cell Editing

11. Double-click Cell D4.
    The flashing insertion point should appear in the cell.

12. Use ➡ or ⬅ to position the insertion point in front of the word Lane.

13. Use (DELETE) to remove the word Lane.

14. Type **Reservoir**, and complete the entry.

15. Edit the next five addresses using either the Formula bar or in-cell editing. The required changes appear bold in the following table.

Cell	Make These Changes
D5	2900 **Carlton** Drive, San Mateo, CA 94401
D6	**2300** Palm Drive, Miami, FL 33147
D7	888 Wilson Street, **Concord, CA 94518**
D8	320 Main Street, **Pittsburgh,** PA 17951
D9	132nd Street, Los Angeles, CA **90045**

16. When you have finished, choose File→Close from the menu bar, and click the Yes button when Excel asks if you wish to save the changes.

Skill Builder 14.2 Use AutoSum and Align Entries

In this exercise, you will edit a worksheet. You will use AutoSum to compute totals, and the alignment buttons to align entries.

Compute Totals

1. Click the Open ⬛ button on the Standard toolbar.

2. Navigate to your exercise diskette, and double-click the workbook named Skill Builder 14.2.

3. Click Cell C10, and then click AutoSum ⬛.
   Notice that Excel proposes the formula =SUM(C8:C9). Excel proposes this incorrect formula because there are empty cells in the range you are to sum.

4. Drag the mouse pointer over the range C5:C9. The flashing marquee will surround the range C5:C9, as shown to the right.

5. Complete the entry; the total should equal 650.

6. Use the preceding steps to compute the totals in Cells E10, G10, and I10.
   You may need to scroll to the right to see Column I.

Align the Entries

7. Follow these steps to align the cell entries for Q1:

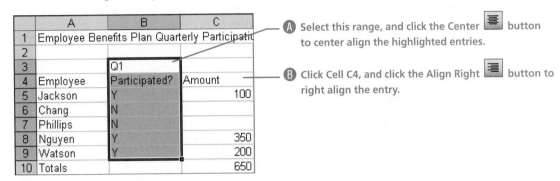

	A	B	C
1	Employee Benefits Plan Quarterly Participatio		
2			
3		Q1	
4	Employee	Participated?	Amount
5	Jackson	Y	100
6	Chang	N	
7	Phillips	N	
8	Nguyen	Y	350
9	Watson	Y	200
10	Totals		650

Ⓐ Select this range, and click the Center ▤ button to center align the highlighted entries.

Ⓑ Click Cell C4, and click the Align Right ▤ button to right align the entry.

8. Align the entries for Q2, Q3, and Q4 as you just did for Q1. You can do this quickly by using the CTRL key to select all three ranges and aligning them with a single click of the Center button.

9. Right-align the word Amount in Cells E4, G4, and I4. Once again, you can use CTRL to select all three cells and then issue the command.

10. Save the changes to your workbook, and then close the workbook.

Skill Builder 14.3 Create a Worksheet with Decimal Numbers

In this exercise, you will create the worksheet shown on the following page. You will enter numbers containing two decimal places. You will also use the alignment buttons to align the text and numbers.

Enter Text and Widen Columns

1. Click the New ▤ button on the Standard toolbar.
   You can always use the New button to display a new workbook.

2. Enter text in Rows 1–3 as shown in the following illustration.
   Make sure you enter the entire phrase Order Tracking Sheet into Cell D1. Also, the entries in Cells A3, B3, and E3 will be truncated. You will correct this by widening the columns in the following steps.

	A	B	C	D	E	F	G
1				Order Tracking Sheet			
2							
3	Customer ID	Order Status	Item #	In Stock?	Order Total	Shipping Address	

3. Position the mouse pointer on the border between the column headings A and B, and the Adjust pointer will appear.

4. Drag the border to the right until Column A is wide enough for the Customer ID entry.

5. Widen Columns B and E until the entries in those columns are completely visible.

Enter Numbers with Decimals

6. Click Cell E4.

7. Type **100.91**, and tap (ENTER).
   You should always type a decimal point if the number requires one.

8. Type **45.87**, and tap (ENTER).

9. Enter the numbers shown below in Cells E6, E7, and E8 (don't type the total 292.38 in Cell E9).

Use AutoSum

10. Click Cell E9.

11. Click AutoSum Σ, and then complete the entry.
    The total should be 292.38 as shown below.

12. Complete the worksheet as shown below. You will need to enter the numbers and text shown. Make sure you enter each shipping address into a single cell. For example, the address 1603 Catalina . . . should be entered in Cell F4. Also, you will need to select the range A3:D8 and use the Center button to center the entries. Align all other entries as shown below.

13. When you have finished, click the Save 🖫 button, and save the workbook as **Skill Builder 14.3**. Close the workbook after it has been saved.

	A	B	C	D	E	F	G	H	I	J
1				Order Tracking Sheet						
2										
3	Customer ID	Order Status	Item #	In Stock?	Order Total	Shipping Address				
4	341	S	A423	Y	100.91	1603 Catalina Avenue, Redondo Beach, CA 90277				
5	234	S	A321	Y	45.87	Will Pickup				
6	567	I	S345	N	43.23	450 Terrace Drive, Santa Clara, CA 95050				
7	879	H	D567	N	78.92	No address at this point				
8	233	I		Y	23.45	23 Maple Lane, Crawfordsville, IN 47933				
9	Total Orders				292.38					

Assessments

Assessment 14.1

1. Open the workbook named Assessment 14.1 on your exercise diskette.

2. Edit the title in Cell A1 to read **Computer Depot Sales Bonuses**.

3. Widen Column A until all names in the column are visible.

4. Right-align the headings in Row 3.

5. Use AutoSum to compute the totals in Row 9.

6. Change the name Mary Johnson in Cell A5 to **Sally Adams**.

7. Print the completed worksheet, save the changes, and then close the workbook.

Assessment 14.2

1. Click the New ⬜ button to open a new workbook.

2. Use the following guidelines to create the following worksheet:

   ▪ Widen the columns as necessary to prevent long entries from being truncated.

   ▪ Align the text entries in Row 3 as shown.

3. Use AutoSum to compute the totals. Be careful, as certain rows and columns contain blank cells. You will need to manually override the ranges proposed by AutoSum.

4. When you have finished, click the Print 🖨 button on the Standard toolbar to print the worksheet.

5. Save the workbook as **Assessment 14.2**, and then close the workbook.

	A	B	C	D	E	F	G
1	Computer Depot Employee Time Log						
2							
3	Employee	Wednesday	Thursday	Friday	Saturday	Sunday	Totals
4	Mary Johnson	6.5		5	6.5	4	22
5	Cliff Packard	4	6	6.5	6.5	4	27
6	Helen Martinez	4	6	6.5	6.5		23
7	Sarah Stonestown		4	4	4		12
8	Totals						

Assessment 14.3

1. Open a New 🗋 workbook.

2. Create the worksheet shown in the following illustration. Make sure the numbers match the worksheet. Widen columns and align entries as shown.

3. Use AutoSum to calculate the totals in Row 8, 13, 19, and 25 and in Column F.

4. Print the workbook when you have finished.

5. Save the workbook as **Assessment 14.3**, and then close the workbook.

	A	B	C	D	E	F
1	Big City Diner Q1 Expenses					
2						
3	Item		January	February	March	Q1 Totals
4	Rent and Utilities	Rent	800	800	800	
5		Utilities	340	400	250	
6		Phone	250	200	300	
7		Insurance	350	0	0	
8		Total				
9						
10	Cost of goods sold	Produce	2500	2320	1700	
11		Meat	4000	3400	3700	
12		Grains	1000	1200	890	
13		Total				
14						
15	Salaries	Simmons	800	780	800	
16		Swanson	750	650	870	
17		Martinez	900	780	680	
18		Richardson	1200	1000	990	
19		Total				
20						
21	Other	Advertising	500	300	0	
22		Uniforms	0	340	0	
23		Janitorial	200	200	200	
24		Miscellaneous	100	2000	0	
25		Total				

Critical Thinking

Critical Thinking 14.1 On Your Own

Mary Kelley is a math teacher at Washington High School. Mary wants an Excel workbook that tracks student test scores for her Trigonometry class. Students receive a final letter grade for the course that is determined by the total number of points they accumulate throughout the course. They are given four 1-hour tests, a mid term, a final, and four extra-credit homework assignments. They can receive a maximum of 100 points for each of the four tests, 200 points for the mid term, 300 points for the final exam, and 25 points for each extra-credit homework assignment. Thus, the total number of possible points for the course is 1,000. Letter grades are assigned as follows:

A 900 or more points

B 800-899 points

C 700-799 points

D 600-699 points

E less than 600 points

You have been assigned the task of setting up a worksheet for Mary. The worksheet should list the points received by each student for the four-hour tests, the mid term, final, and four homework assignments. Use AutoSum to calculate the total points for each student. In addition, assign a letter grade to each student using the scale shown above. Include scores for the following four students: Jack Simmons, Samantha Torres, Elaine Wilkins, and Tonya Robertson. Assign points to the students as you deem appropriate. Save your workbook as **Critical Thinking 14.1**.

Critical Thinking 14.2 On Your Own

Tanisha Jones is running for President of the Westmont Community College Student Association. Westmont College regulates student campaigns in various ways. In particular, the college imposes a maximum fund raising limit of $1,500 on each candidate who is running for office. In addition, there are strict reporting requirements for campaign contributions. Each contribution must be reported and must include the date of the contribution, the individual or organization making the contribution, and the amount of the contribution. The reports are made available to the public in print and on the college's Web site. You have been assigned the task of setting up a worksheet to track Tanisha's campaign contributions. List five contributions in your worksheet from the following individuals and organizations: Cindy Thomas; Richardson Vending Services; Campus Computer Equipment; Elaine Wilson; and Party Time Music and Video. You determine the contribution amounts and the dates. Include a total cell that calculates the total contributions. Make sure the total contributions do not exceed $1,500. Save your workbook as **Critical Thinking 14.2**.

Critical Thinking 14.3 On Your Own

Big Slice Pizza is a rapidly growing pizza chain that serves the best deep-dish pizza in town. An important part of Big Slice's growth strategy is the development of a franchise network using independent franchise owners. Recently, Big Slice launched a West Coast advertising campaign to attract new franchise owners. You have been assigned the task of collecting the franchise applications and creating a worksheet that summarizes the application information. Your worksheet should include each prospective franchise owner's name, city and state, investment amount, telephone number, and whether or not the prospect has previous franchise experience. Include information for the following prospects: Ben Barksdale; Sylvia Ramirez; Bill Chin; Wanda Stone; and Terry Collins. You determine the remaining information for each prospective owner. Save your workbook as **Critical Thinking 14.3**.

Critical Thinking 14.4 Web Research

Alexia Williams is the Information Systems Manager of Bellmont Health Care. Bellmont is a rapidly growing health care concern with over one billion dollars in FY 2003 revenues. Alexia has mandated that, beginning in FY 2004, at least 50% of Bellmont's technology purchases will be made using online purchasing systems. Alexia believes this strategy will reduce costs and increase the efficiency of the procurement process. As a student intern working under the direction of Alexia, you have been assigned the task of locating five vendors that allow personal computers and accessories to be purchased online. Alexia has asked you to construct a worksheet that includes the vendor's name, Web site URL, and their customer service telephone number. Use Internet Explorer and a search engine of your choice to conduct your research. Record your results in a worksheet as **Critical Thinking 14.4**.

Critical Thinking 14.5 Web Research

George Miller is the Operations Manager of Speedy Package Delivery Service. Speedy is in the business of same-day package delivery. Speedy is located in the heart of Silicon Valley. George has been instructed to purchase six new mini vans to be used for package delivery. George has assigned you the task of locating three Web sites where vehicle information can be located and where vehicles can be purchased. Use Internet Explorer and a search engine of your choice to locate three Web sites that specialize in vehicle sales. Set up a worksheet that lists the Web site name and URL of three such Web sites. For each Web site, include the posted retail price range and the dealer invoice price for Ford Windstar, Chevrolet Astro, and Dodge Caravan mini vans. Use a consistent vehicle configuration from each Web site so that the pricing comparisons are valid. Include any additional vehicle information that you think would be useful to George. Save your workbook as **Critical Thinking 14.5**.

Critical Thinking 14.6 On Your Own

Set up a worksheet to record whether or not an individual has used Windows, Outlook, Word, Excel, Access, PowerPoint, and Internet Explorer. Survey five people and record the results of your survey in the worksheet. Use a 1 to indicate that a person has experience with a particular program and a 0 to indicate no experience. Use AutoSum to calculate the totals for each program. The totals should give you some idea of how much each program is used. Save your workbook as `Critical Thinking 14.6`.

LESSON 15

Expanding on the Basics

In this lesson, you will expand upon the basic skills you learned in the previous lesson. You will use several types of formulas to create totals, calculate profits, and determine financial ratios. You will also learn powerful tools and techniques such as the fill handle and the Format Painter. When you have finished this lesson, you will have developed the skills necessary to produce more sophisticated worksheets.

Case Study

Donna Prusko is an entrepreneur and the founder of Donna's Deli. Donna recently resigned from her corporate position to pursue her dream and passion—a deli that serves delicious, healthy food at reasonable prices. Donna also realizes that the health of her business is just as important as the health of her customers. For this reason, she wants to develop a worksheet to track her income and expenses. The worksheet will use formulas to determine gross profits, net profits, and important financial ratios. Microsoft Excel is an important tool for any entrepreneur in today's highly competitive business world.

	A	B	C	D	E
1	Donna's Deli - Income and Expense Worksheet				
2					
3			Quarterly Income		
4	Food Sales	Q1	Q2	Q3	Q4
5	Dine-in Sales	21,000	23,000	28,000	42,000
6	Takeout Sales	12,000	16,000	25,000	56,000
7	Subtotal	$33,000	$39,000	$53,000	$98,000
8	Other Income				
9	Tips	2,500	2,700	3,000	4,500
10	Sublease	500	500	500	500
11	Subtotal	$3,000	$3,200	$3,500	$5,000
12	Total Income				
13					
14			Quarterly Expenses		
15	Expenses	Q1	Q2	Q3	Q4
16	Rent	3,000	3,000	3,000	3,000
17	Utilities	400	310	290	380
18	Marketing	800	800	800	800
19	Salaries	12,000	12,000	14,000	14,000
20	Supplies	15,000	15,500	18,000	24,000
21	Equipment	6,000	2,000	1,000	-
22	Total Expenses				
23					
24	Gross Profit				
25	Net Profit				
26	Gross Profit vs. Income				

The Fill Handle

The fill handle is a small black square visible at the bottom right corner of the active cell. A black cross appears when you position the mouse pointer on the fill handle. You can drag the fill handle to fill adjacent cells as described below:

- **Copying an entry**—If the entry in the active cell is a number, a formula, or a typical text entry, the fill handle copies the entry to adjacent cells.

- **Expanding a repeating series of numbers**—If you select two or more cells containing numbers, Excel assumes you want to expand a repeating series. For example, if you select two cells containing the numbers 5 and 10 and drag the fill handle, Excel will fill the adjacent cells with the numbers 15, 20, 25, etc.

- **AutoFill of date entries**—If the active cell contains a date entry, then Excel will increment the date value filling in the adjacent cells. For example, if the current cell contains the entry Q1 and you drag the fill handle, AutoFill will insert the entries Q2, Q3, and Q4 in the adjacent cells.

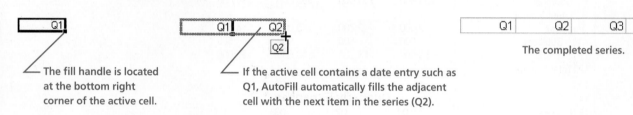

The completed series.

The fill handle is located at the bottom right corner of the active cell.

If the active cell contains a date entry such as Q1, AutoFill automatically fills the adjacent cell with the next item in the series (Q2).

AutoFill Options Button

The AutoFill Options button appears below your filled selection after you fill cells in a worksheet. A menu of fill options appears when you click the button.

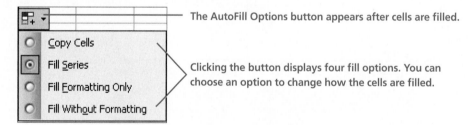

The AutoFill Options button appears after cells are filled.

Clicking the button displays four fill options. You can choose an option to change how the cells are filled.

Hands-On 15.1 Use the Fill Handle

In step 1 of this exercise, you will display the Standard and Formatting toolbars on separate rows. From this point forward, the instructions in this text will assume that the Standard and Formatting toolbars are displayed on separate rows. This will make it easier for you to locate buttons when instructed to do so.

1. Start Excel and follow these steps to display the Standard and Formatting toolbars on separate rows:

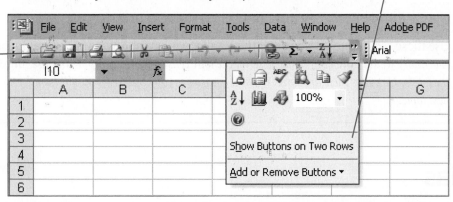

Ⓐ Click the Toolbar Options button on the right edge of the Standard toolbar.

Ⓑ If the Show Buttons on Two Rows option is available, choose it to display the Standard and Formatting toolbars on separate rows. If the Show Buttons on One Row option is available then your toolbars are already on separate rows.

2. Open the workbook named Hands-On Lesson 15 from your exercise diskette.

Use AutoFill to Expand the Q1 Series

3. Click Cell B4.
   Notice that Cell B4 contains the heading Q1. Excel recognizes Q1 as the beginning of the series Q1, Q2, Q3, and Q4.

4. Follow these steps to fill the adjacent cells:

Ⓐ Position the mouse pointer on the bottom right corner of the active cell, and a black cross will appear.

Ⓑ Drag to the right over the next three cells, and a shaded rectangle will appear.

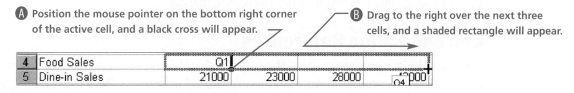

Ⓒ Release the mouse button to fill the adjacent cells.

Excel recognizes Q1, days of the week (Sunday), months (January), and other date values as the beginning of a series. You can expand any of these series with the fill handle.

5. Click the AutoFill Options 🔡 button and note the various fill options.
   If desired, you can choose an option to change how the cells are filled.

6. For now, just tap (ESC) to dismiss the menu.

7. Click Cell B15, and use the fill handle to expand Q1 to Q1–Q4, as you did in Step 4.

Use the Fill Handle to Copy Cells

8. Click Cell B7.

9. Click AutoSum $\boxed{\Sigma}$, and complete the entry.
   The subtotal should equal 33000.

10. Make sure Cell B7 is active; then drag the fill handle to the right until the shaded rectangle is over Cells C7, D7, and E7.

11. Release the mouse button. The formula should be copied to those cells.
    Excel determines whether it should copy the cell or expand a series.

12. Click Cell B11, and use AutoSum to compute the subtotal.

13. Use the fill handle to copy the formula in Cell B11 to Cells C11, D11, and E11.

14. Use these techniques to compute the total expenses in Row 22 (not total income in Row 12).
    It actually would have been easier to select the four cells in these examples and use AutoSum to compute the totals. However, there are times when it is easier to copy cells with the fill handle, as you will see in the next topic.

Formulas

FROM THE KEYBOARD

(CTRL)+(~) to display formulas

You have already learned how to compute totals with AutoSum. AutoSum provides a convenient method for summing a range of numbers. However, you will need to use many other types of formulas in Excel. In fact, many worksheets, such as financial models, require hundreds or even thousands of complex formulas.

Beginning Character in Formulas

If you are typing a formula in a cell, it is recommended that you always begin the formula with an equal (=) sign. You can also begin formulas with a plus (+) or minus (–) sign; however, it is better to adopt one method in order to create consistency.

Cell and Range References

Formulas derive their power from the use of cell and range references. For example, in the previous exercise, you used AutoSum to insert the formula =SUM(B16:B21) in Cell B22. Because the range reference (B16:B21) was used in the formula, you were able to copy the formula across the row using the fill handle. There are two important benefits to using references in formulas.

■ When references are used, formulas can be copied to other cells.

■ Since a reference refers to a cell or a range of cells, the formula results are automatically recalculated when the data is changed in the referenced cell(s).

Arithmetic Operators and Spaces

Formulas can include the standard arithmetic operators shown in the following table. You can also use spaces within formulas to improve their appearance and readability. Notice that each formula in the table begins with an equal (=) sign. Also, keep in mind that each formula is entered into the same cell that displays the resulting calculation.

QUICK REFERENCE: ARITHMETIC OPERATORS IN FORMULAS

Operator	Example	Comments
+ (addition)	=B7+B11	Adds the values in B7 and B11.
– (subtraction)	=B7–B11	Subtracts the value in B11 from B7.
* (multiplication)	=B7*B11	Multiplies the values in B7 and B11.
/ (division)	=B7/B11	Divides the value in B7 by the value in B11.
^ (exponentiation)	=B7^3	Raises the value in B7 to the third power (B7*B7*B7).
% (percent)	=B7*10%	Multiplies the value in B7 by 10% (.10).
( ) (calculations)	=B7/(C4–C2)	Parentheses change the order of calculations. In this example, C2 would be subtracted from C4, and then B7 would be divided by the result.

Hands-On 15.2 Use the Keyboard to Enter Formulas

1. Click Cell B12.

2. Type **=B7+B11**, and complete the entry.
   The result should be 36000. This is the summation of the two subtotals in Cells B7 and B11.

3. Click Cell C12.

4. Type **=C7+C11**, and complete the entry.
   The result should be 42200.

Relative Cell References

All formulas use relative cell references unless you specifically instruct Excel to use an absolute reference. Relative references make it easy to copy formulas to other cells. For example, in the Hands-On Lesson 15 worksheet, Cell C12 contains the formula =C7+C11. If this formula is copied to Cell D12, then the formula in D12 will become =D7+D11. The references to Cells C7 and C11 are updated to reflect the new location of the formula.

Point Mode

One potential danger that can occur when typing formulas is that you will accidentally type the wrong cell reference. This is easy to do, especially if the worksheet is complex and contains large numbers of cells. Point mode can help you avoid this problem. With point mode, you can insert a cell reference in a formula by clicking the desired cell as you are typing the formula. Likewise, you can insert a range reference in a formula by dragging over the desired cells. You will use point mode in the following exercise.

 ### Hands-On 15.3 Use Point Mode

1. Click Cell D12.

2. Type an equal = sign.
   Notice that Excel begins building the formula by entering the equal = sign in the Formula bar.

3. Click Cell D7.
   Notice that Excel adds the reference D7 to the formula in the Formula bar.

4. Type a plus + sign (try tapping the plus + key on the numeric keypad).

5. Click Cell D11.
   The Formula bar should contain the formula =D7+D11.

6. Complete the entry. The total should be 56500.

7. Make sure the highlight is in Cell D12, and then drag the fill handle one cell to the right.
   The formula should be copied to Cell E12, and the result should be 103000.

8. Click Cell E12, and notice the formula in the Formula bar.
   The formula should be =E7+E11. The references were updated to reflect the new formula location.

Calculate the Gross Profit

9. If necessary, scroll down until Rows 12–26 are visible.

10. Click Cell B24.
    Cell B24 will contain the gross profit. The gross profit is calculated as the total income in Cell B12 minus the total expenses in Cell B22.

11. Type an equal = sign and click Cell B12.

12. Type a minus – sign, click Cell B22, and complete the entry.
    The gross profit should equal –1200. As you can see, Donna's Deli is not profitable in the first quarter.

13. Copy the formula to the next three cells by dragging the fill handle to the right.

Calculate the Net Profit

*You will calculate the net profit in the next few steps. You will use a simplified net profit calculation: that is, the gross profit minus income taxes. We will make the assumption that Donna will pay no taxes in Q1 and Q2. This is because she lost money in Q1, and her gross profit was only $8,590 in Q2. Furthermore, we will assume that Donna's tax rate will be 15% for Q3 and 25% for Q4. The formula is, Net Profit = Gross Profit * (1–Taxrate). For example, if the tax rate is 15%, then Donna will keep 85% of her gross profit. So the Net Profit = Gross Profit * 0.85.*

14. Click Cell B24.
    Look at the Formula bar and notice the gross profit is calculated as B12–B22. In the next few steps, you will attempt to copy the gross profit formula from Cell B24 to Cell B25.

15. Follow this step to copy the formula from Cell B24 to B25:

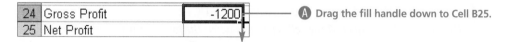
Ⓐ Drag the fill handle down to Cell B25.

16. Click Cell B24, and notice that the gross profit formula in the Formula bar is =B12–B22.

17. Click Cell B25, and notice that the net profit formula is =B13–B23.

18. Look at Cells B13 and B23 in the worksheet, and you will see they are empty.
    The formula result is 0 because Cells B13 and B23 are empty. This example demonstrates that you must be careful when copying formulas. Excel updated the cell references when you copied the formula. This produced an incorrect result because the formula is referencing incorrect cells.

19. Click Undo ↺ to reverse the copy procedure.

20. Click Cell B25, type the formula **=B24**, and complete the entry.
    This simple formula makes Cell B25 equal to Cell B24.

21. Click Cell C25, type the formula **=C24**, and complete the entry.
    Once again, the net profit and gross profit should be equal in Q2 because Donna has no tax liability in the second quarter.

22. Click Cell D25, and enter the formula **=D24*85%**.
    The result should be 16498.5. We are assuming a tax rate of 15% in Q3, so Donna gets to keep 85% of her gross profit.

23. Click Cell E25, and enter the formula **=E24*75%**.
    The result should be 45615. Keep in mind that you can either type the formulas or use point mode and the Formula bar. From this point forward, you will simply be instructed to enter a formula. You should use whichever method works best for you.

Calculate the Ratios

Donna wants to determine the ratio of gross profit to total income, or GP/TI. This ratio is important in determining the health of a business. This ratio is one indicator that will show Donna how fast she can grow her business by reinvesting the money she earns. This ratio will show Donna the amount of profit she will earn from each dollar of product she sells.

24. Click Cell B26, and enter the formula **=B24/B12**.
    The result should be –0.03333. You will convert this number to a percentage later in this lesson.

25. Use the fill handle to copy the formula to Cells C26, D26, and E26.
    The results should match the following example.

26	Gross Profit vs. Income	-0.03333	0.203555	0.34354	0.590485

26. Click Cell C26, and notice the formula =C24/C12.
    Once again, Excel updated the cell references when the formula was copied. In this case, it is good that the references were updated because the formula now refers to the correct gross profit and total income in cells C24 and C12.

27. Click the Save button to save the changes.

Number Formats

Excel lets you format numbers in a variety of ways. Number formats change the way numbers are displayed; however, they do not change the actual numbers. The following Quick Reference table describes the most common number formats.

QUICK REFERENCE: NUMBER FORMATS

Number Format	Description
General	Numbers have a General format when they are first entered. The General format does not apply any special formats to the numbers.
Comma	The Comma format inserts a comma between every third digit in the number. An optional decimal point with decimal places can also be displayed.
Currency	The Currency format is the same as the Comma format, except a dollar $ sign is placed in front of the number.
Percent	A percent % sign is inserted to the right of the number. The number is multiplied by 100, and the resulting percentage is displayed in the cell.

The following table provides several examples of formatted numbers:

Number Entered	Format	How the Number Is Displayed
1000.984	General	1000.984
1000.984	Comma with 0 decimal places	1,001
	Comma with 2 decimal places	1,000.98
1000.984	Currency with 0 decimal places	$1,001
	Currency with 2 decimal places	$1,000.98
.5366	Percent with 0 decimal places	54%
	Percent with 2 decimal places	53.66%

Applying Number Styles with the Formatting Toolbar

The Formatting toolbar contains buttons that allow you to apply the Currency, Comma, and Percent number styles. These are the most common types of number styles. The Formatting toolbar also includes buttons that allow you to increase or decrease the number of displayed decimals. The following illustration shows the number formatting buttons on the Formatting toolbar.

FROM THE KEYBOARD

(CTRL)+(SHIFT)+($)
for Currency style
(CTRL)+(SHIFT)+(%)
for Percent style
(CTRL)+(SHIFT)+(!)
for Comma style
(CTRL)+(SHIFT)+(~)
for General style

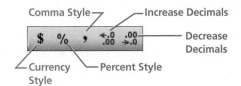

Changing the Number of Displayed Decimals

The Increase Decimal ⬚ and Decrease Decimal ⬚ buttons change the number of displayed decimal places. For example, you could enter the number 100.37 and then decrease the decimals to 0. The number would then be displayed as 100. However, the actual number would remain 100.37. The number 100.37 would be used in any calculations referencing the cell.

Hands-On 15.4 Format Numbers

In this exercise, you will format numbers using buttons on the Formatting toolbar.

Apply the Currency Style

1. Scroll up until the top row of the worksheet is visible.

2. Select the four subtotals in Row 7 (be careful not to drag the fill handle).
   The fill handle is not used to select cells. It is only used to copy cells or to expand a series. Make sure your pointer has the thick white cross shape whenever you wish to select cells.

3. Click the Currency Style $ button, and the cells should be formatted as shown below.
   Notice that the Currency style adds a dollar sign in front of the number and a comma between every third digit. It also adds a decimal point with two decimal places. Excel should also have widened the columns to accommodate the additional characters and numbers.

7	Subtotal	$33,000.00	$39,000.00	$53,000.00	$98,000.00

Decrease the Decimals

4. Make sure the four cells you just formatted are selected.

5. Click the Decrease Decimal button twice to remove the displayed decimals.
   Notice that the dollar signs $ are positioned on the left side of the cells. You will adjust this alignment later in the lesson.

6. Select the subtotal and total income cells in Rows 11 and 12, as shown below.

11	Subtotal	3000	3200	3500	5000
12	Total Income	36000	42200	56500	103000

7. Click the Currency Style $ button; then decrease the decimals to 0.

8. Format the numbers in Rows 22, 24, and 25 as Currency style with 0 decimals.

Apply the Comma Style

9. Select the numbers in Rows 5 and 6.

10. Click the Comma Style [,] button, and then decrease the decimals [.00→.0] to 0.
    Notice that the Comma style is similar to the Currency style, except a dollar sign is not displayed. Also notice that the numbers now line up with the currency formatted numbers in the subtotal row.

11. Format the numbers in the ranges B9:E10 and B16:E21 as Comma style with 0 decimals.

Apply the Percent Style

12. Select the numbers in the last row of the worksheet.

13. Click the Percent Style [%] button.
    The numbers should be formatted as Percent style with 0 decimal places. The Percent style does not display decimals; however, you can always use the Increase Decimal button to display decimals.

Setting Number Styles with the Format Cells Dialog Box

The Format→Cells command displays the Format Cells dialog box. This dialog box provides additional built-in number styles that are not available on the Formatting toolbar. You can format numbers with one of the built-in styles by displaying the dialog box and choosing the desired style. You can even create your own customized number styles to suit your needs.

FROM THE KEYBOARD

(CTRL)+(1) to display Format Cells dialog box

Accounting and Currency Styles

The dollar signs $ in the Hands-On Lesson 15 worksheet currently have a fixed format. In other words, they are fixed on the left side of the cells. You can use the Format Cells dialog box to choose a number style that floats the dollar signs next to the numbers. There are two number styles that apply currency symbols (such as dollar signs) to numbers, as discussed below.

- **Accounting style**—The Currency Style [$] button on the Formatting toolbar actually applies an Accounting style to numbers. The Accounting style lines up dollar signs and decimal points in columns. The dollar signs appear fixed at the left edges of the cells.

- **Currency style**—The Currency style floats dollar signs next to the numbers. Like the Accounting style, the Currency style displays a comma between every third digit, and it displays decimals and a decimal point.

Displaying Negative Numbers

Negative numbers can be displayed either preceded by a minus sign or surrounded by parentheses. You can also display negative numbers in red. The Currency option and Number option in the Format Cells dialog box let you choose the format for negative numbers.

The negative numbers format you choose affects the alignment of numbers in cells. If the format displays negative numbers in parentheses, then a small space equal to the width of a closing parenthesis appears on the right edge of cells containing positive numbers. Excel does this so that decimal points are aligned in columns containing both positive and negative numbers. These concepts are described in the following illustration.

15	Expenses	Q1
16	Rent	3,000
17	Utilities	400
18	Marketing	800
19	Salaries	12,000
20	Supplies	15,000
21	Equipment	6,000
22	Total Expenses	$ 37,200
23		
24	Gross Profit	$ (1,200)
25	Net Profit	$ (1,200)

Notice the slight space between positive numbers and the right edge of the cells.

Notice that the closing parenthesis of negative numbers is flush with the right edge of the cell.

15	Expenses	Q1
16	Rent	3,000.00
17	Utilities	400.00
18	Marketing	800.00
19	Salaries	12,000.00
20	Supplies	15,000.00
21	Equipment	6,000.00
22	Total Expenses	37,200.00
23		
24	Gross Profit	(1,200.00)
25	Net Profit	(1,200.00)

When the numbers are displayed with decimals, this slight shift of the positive numbers lines up the decimal points of both the positive and negative numbers.

Hands-On 15.5 Use the Format Cells Dialog Box

1. Select the numbers with the Currency style in Row 7.

2. Choose Format→Cells from the menu bar.

3. Make sure the Number tab is active at the top of the dialog box.

4. Notice that the Custom option is chosen at the bottom of the Category list.
   The Custom option is chosen because you modified the number style when you decreased the decimal places in the previous exercises, creating a custom number format.

5. Follow these steps to format the numbers with floating dollar ($) signs:

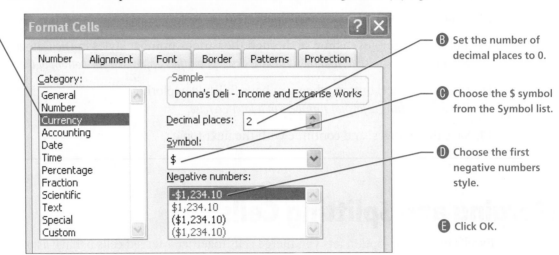

A Choose Currency.

B Set the number of decimal places to 0.

C Choose the $ symbol from the Symbol list.

D Choose the first negative numbers style.

E Click OK.

Notice that the dollar signs are now floating just in front of the numbers. Also, notice that the numbers are now shifted slightly to the right, and that they no longer line up with the numbers above them. This is because of the Negative Numbers option you set. You will adjust the Negative Numbers option in the next step.

Adjust the Negative Numbers Option

6. Make sure Cells B7:E7 are still selected, and choose Format→Cells from the menu bar.

7. Notice the various negative numbers formats.
   Formats that are red display negative numbers in red. Also notice that some of the formats are surrounded with parentheses. Formats with parentheses cause positive numbers to shift slightly to the left as discussed earlier.

8. Choose the third Negative Numbers format ($1,234), and click OK.
   The numbers should now be right-aligned with the numbers in Rows 5 and 6. The numbers in Rows 5 and 6 are formatted with the Comma style. The Comma style displays negative numbers in parentheses. This is why the positive numbers in Rows 5 and 6 are shifted slightly to the left.

Check Out the Accounting Style

9. Make sure Cells B7:E7 are still selected, and choose Format→Cells from the menu bar.

10. Choose the Accounting category.

11. Make sure the symbol type is set to $ and the decimal places are set to 0.

12. Click OK, and the dollar ($) signs will once again have a fixed placement on the left side of the cells.
   Notice that this was how the numbers were formatted when you first clicked the Currency Style button in an earlier exercise. The Currency Style button actually applies the Accounting style to numbers.

13. Click Undo ⟲ to restore the Currency style.

14. Choose Format→Cells from the menu bar.

15. Take a few minutes to browse through the various number styles in the Category list.
Feel free to choose a style, and then read the description that appears at the bottom of the dialog box.

16. Click the Cancel button when you have finished exploring.
You will continue to format numbers in a later exercise.

17. Save the changes, and continue with the next topic.

Merging and Splitting Cells

Excel's merge cells option lets you merge cells together. Merged cells behave as one large cell. You can merge cells vertically or horizontally. The merge cells option is useful if you want to place a large block of text (such as a paragraph) in the worksheet. You merge cells by selecting the desired cells, issuing the Format→Cells command, and checking the Merge Cells box on the Alignment tab. Likewise, you can split a merged cell into the original cell configuration by removing the check from the Merge Cells box.

The Merge and Center Button

The Merge and Center 🔳 button merges selected cells and changes the alignment of the merged cell to center. This technique is often used to center a heading across columns. Keep in mind that the Merge and Center button has the same effect as merging cells, and then changing the alignment of the merged cell to center. You can split a merged and centered cell the same way you would split any other merged cell. The following example shows a heading centered across Columns B through E.

The Quarterly Income heading is centered above Columns B–E.

	A	B	C	D	E
2					
3			Quarterly Income		
4	Food Sales	Q1	Q2	Q3	Q4

Hands-On 15.6 Use Merge and Center

1. Select the range B3:E3, as shown below.
   Notice that this range includes the heading you wish to center (Quarterly Income) and the range of cells you wish to center this heading across (B3:E3).

	A	B	C	D	E
1	Donna's Deli - Income and Expense Worksheet				
2					
3		Quarterly Income			

2. Click the Merge and Center ⊞ button (near the middle of the Formatting toolbar).
   Notice that the cells have been merged together and the Center button on the Formatting toolbar is highlighted.

3. Click the Align Left ≡ button and the entry will move to the left side of the merged cell.

4. Click the Center ≡ button to center the entry in the merged cell.

Split Cells

5. Choose Format→Cells from the menu bar.

6. Click the Alignment tab on the Format Cells dialog box.
   Notice that the Merge Cells box is checked. This box is checked whenever cells are merged.

7. Remove the check from the Merge Cells box and click OK.

8. Click anywhere to deselect the cells, and notice that they are no longer merged.
   You use this technique to split merged cells.

9. Click Undo ↺ to restore the merged cell.

10. Select the range B14:E14.

11. Click the Merge and Center ⊞ button to center the Quarterly Expenses heading.

Indenting Entries

The Increase Indent ⊞ button and Decrease Indent ⊞ button on the Formatting toolbar let you offset entries from the left edges of cells. Indenting is useful in conveying the hierarchy of entries. The following illustration shows indented cells.

These cells are indented to show their subordination to the Food Sales heading. ⎯

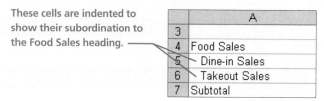

 ## Hands-On 15.7 Indent Entries

1. Click Cell A5.

2. Click the Increase Indent ⊞ button twice.
   Notice that the entry is indented slightly each time you click the button.

3. Click the Decrease Indent ⊞ button once.

4. Click Cell A6, and increase the indent ⊞ once.

5. Select Cells A9 and A10.

6. Press and hold the (CTRL) key while you select the range A16:A21.
   The range A16:A21 contains the Rent, Utilities, etc. subheadings below the Expenses heading in Column A.

7. Increase the indent ⊞ once.

Formatting Entries

FROM THE KEYBOARD
(CTRL)+(B) for Bold
(CTRL)+(U) for Underline
(CTRL)+(I) for Italics

In Excel and other Office programs, you can format text by changing the font, font size, and color. You can also apply various font formats, including bold, italics, and underline. To format cells, select the desired cells and apply formats using buttons on the Formatting toolbar. You can also choose formats from the Font tab of the Format Cells dialog box.

You can choose a font from the font list. You can also click the drop-down button and type the desired font name to rapidly scroll the list.

The Font Color button is on the right end of the Formatting toolbar. The color palette appears when you click the drop-down button. Once you choose a color, the color is displayed on the button. From that point forward, you can rapidly apply the color by clicking the button. ⎯

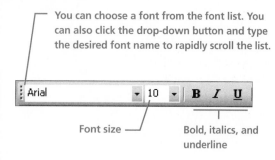

Font size ⎯

Bold, italics, and underline

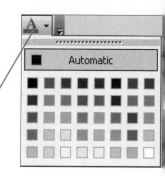

Hands-On 15.8 Format Entries

1. Click Cell A1.

2. Click the Font Size button on the Formatting toolbar, and choose 14.

3. Click the Bold **B** button on the Formatting toolbar.
   Notice that the entire title is formatted. Once again, the entire title belongs to Cell A1, even though it is displayed over the adjacent cells.

4. Click the drop-down ▾ button on the Font Color **A ▾** button located at the right end of the Formatting toolbar.

5. Choose one of the dark blue shades from the color palette.
   Notice that the color you chose is now displayed on the Font Color button. You can now apply the same color to other cells by selecting the cells and then clicking the button.

6. Click Cell B3.
   Cell B3 is now part of the large merged cell in the range B3:E3.

7. Click the Font Color **A** button, and the same color will be applied to the Quarterly Income cell.

8. Increase the size of the Quarterly Income cell to 12, and apply bold formatting.

9. Select the Q1–Q4 headings in Row 4.

10. Apply bold formatting, and then choose a different color from the Font Color **A ▾** button's color palette.
    In the next exercise, you will use the Format Painter to copy font and number formats to other cells.

The Format Painter

The Format Painter lets you copy text and number formats from one cell to another. The Format Painter copies all text and number formats from the source cell to the target cell(s). The Format Painter saves time and helps create consistent formatting throughout a workbook.

QR ⟩ **QUICK REFERENCE: USING THE FORMAT PAINTER**

- ■ Click on the cell with the format(s) you wish to copy.

- ■ Click the Format Painter once if you want to copy formats to one other cell or range. Double-click if you want to copy to multiple cell(s) or range(s).

- ■ Select the cells to which you want to copy the format(s). If you double-clicked in the previous step, the Format Painter will remain active, allowing you to select cells at multiple locations. You can even scroll through the workbook to reach the desired location(s).

- ■ If you double-clicked in the first step, then click the Format Painter when you have finished. This will turn off the Format Painter.

Hands-On 15.9 Use the Format Painter

Copy Text Formats

1. Click Cell B3 (the merged cell with the Quarterly Income heading).

2. Click the Format Painter on the Standard toolbar, and an animated paintbrush icon will be attached to the mouse pointer.

3. Click Cell B14 (the merged cell with the Quarterly Expenses heading).
   The text formats should be copied to that heading. The animated paintbrush icon also vanished because you clicked the Format Painter button just once in the previous step. If you want to copy formats to multiple locations, you must double-click the Format Painter.

4. Click Cell B4.
   This cell should contain the heading Q1.

5. Click the Format Painter .

6. Select the range B15:E15 to copy the formats to those cells, as shown below.

15	Expenses	Q1	Q2	Q3	Q4

Copy Number Formats

7. Select the cells containing numbers in Row 7, and apply bold formatting to the numbers.
   Notice that the numbers in Row 7 have a Currency style with a floating dollar sign. In the next few steps, you will use the Format Painter to copy both the number and text formats to the numbers in Rows 11, 12, and 22–25. Notice that these rows currently have fixed dollar signs on the left edges of the cells.

8. Click Cell B7.

9. Double-click the Format Painter .

10. Select the range B11:E12 to copy the formats to those cells, as shown below.

11	Subtotal	$3,000	$3,200	$3,500	$5,000
12	Total Income	$36,000	$42,200	$56,500	$103,000

11. Select the range B22:E26 to copy the formats to those cells, as shown below.

22	Total Expenses	$37,200	$33,610	$37,090	$42,180
23					
24	Gross Profit	($1,200)	$8,590	$19,410	$60,820
25	Net Profit	($1,200)	$8,590	$16,499	$45,615
26	Gross Profit vs. Income	($0)	$0	$0	$1

12. Click the Format Painter to turn it off.

Notice that you had to turn the Format Painter off this time because you double-clicked it initially. Also, notice the Percent number style in Row 26 has been removed. Be careful when you are trying to copy text formats but not number formats. In this example, you wanted to copy the bold text style to Row 26 but not the Currency style. Keep in mind that the Format Painter copies both text formats and number formats.

13. Select the numbers in Row 26 and use the Percent Style ▓ button to reapply the Percent style.

14. Save the changes, and continue with the next topic.

Clearing Cell Contents and Formats

The Edit→Clear command displays a submenu that lets you clear the content, formats, or comments from cells. The submenu also contains an All option that clears all of these items from the selected cells. Each of these items is described below.

- **Content**—Clearing the content has the same effect as tapping the (DELETE) key. This deletes a cell's contents, but any format applied to the cell will still be in effect if new data is entered in the cell.

- **Formats**—The Formats option removes all text and number formats, leaving unformatted entries in the cell(s).

- **Comments**—You can insert comments in cells to document your worksheet. The Comments option removes comments from the selected cells.

Hands-On 15.10 Clear Formats

1. Notice the formatting applied to the Q1–Q4 headings in Rows 4 and 15.
These headings will probably look better if they have simple bold formatting like the numbers in the sub-total and total rows.

2. Select the Q1–Q4 headings in Row 4 and choose Edit→Clear→Formats.
Excel will remove all formats, including the right alignment.

3. Click the Align Right ▓ button, and then apply bold formatting to the cells.

4. Clear the formats from the Q1–Q4 headings in Row 15.

5. Right-align the Q1–Q4 headings in Row 15, and apply bold formatting to the headings.
Your completed worksheet should match the worksheet shown in the case study at the start of this lesson.

6. Save the changes to your workbook.

7. Feel free to experiment with the Edit→Clear command.

8. When you have finished experimenting, close the workbook without saving the changes.
Continue with the end-of-lesson questions and exercises.

Concepts Review

True/False Questions

1. The fill handle cannot be used to copy formulas.   TRUE   FALSE

2. The Merge and Center button can only be used with numbers.   TRUE   FALSE

3. Formulas must always begin with an open parenthesis (.   TRUE   FALSE

4. Formulas can include both cell and range references.   TRUE   FALSE

5. The asterisk * is used to represent multiplication in formulas.   TRUE   FALSE

6. Point mode can be used to insert cell references in formulas.   TRUE   FALSE

7. The Comma number style inserts a dollar sign in front of the number.   TRUE   FALSE

8. The Format Painter copies text formats, but not number formats.   TRUE   FALSE

9. Tapping the Delete key on selected cells deletes the contents and any formatting.   TRUE   FALSE

10. You can drag the fill handle to copy data or expand a recognized series into adjacent cells.   TRUE   FALSE

Multiple Choice Questions

1. What should you do before clicking the Merge and Center button?
   a. Click the cell that contains the entry you wish to center.
   b. Select the cells you wish to center the entry across, while making sure the entry is included in the selection.
   c. Select the entire row that contains the entry you wish to center.
   d. None of the above

2. Which of the following symbols can be used to begin a formula?
   a. +
   b. –
   c. =
   d. All of the above

3. How would the number 10000.367 be displayed if you format it as comma with 2 decimals?
   a. 10,000.38
   b. $10,000.38
   c. 10,000
   d. None of the above

4. How is the dollar sign positioned with the Accounting number style?
   a. Floats to the immediate left of the number
   b. Fixed on the left edge of the cell
   c. The Accounting style does not place a dollar sign in front of the number.
   d. The answer depends on whether the number has a decimal point.

Skill Builders

Skill Builder 15.1 **Formatting and Formulas**

In this exercise, you will open a home budget worksheet on your exercise diskette. You will format the worksheet using the skills you have learned in this lesson.

1. Open the workbook named Skill Builder 15.1 on your exercise diskette.

2. Widen Column A until the text entries in that column are visible.

3. Select the range A1:G1, as shown below.

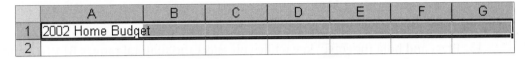

4. Click the Merge and Center [icon] button to center 2002 Home Budget above the worksheet.

Use AutoFill

5. Follow these steps to AutoFill the headings in Row 3:

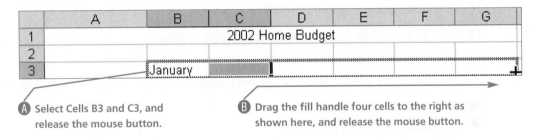

Ⓐ Select Cells B3 and C3, and release the mouse button.

Ⓑ Drag the fill handle four cells to the right as shown here, and release the mouse button.

Excel assumes you want the series January–March with an empty cell between each month. This is a correct assumption, and the resulting cells are shown below.

6. Select Cells B4 and C4 (the Budget and Spent cells).

7. Drag the fill handle over the next four cells to the right, and Excel will copy Cells B4 and C4 to those cells.
   You should now have three sets of Budget and Spent cells. As you can see, the fill handle is used for a variety of purposes.

Use Merge and Center

8. Select Cells B3 and C3 (the January cell and the blank cell to the right of it).

9. Click Merge and Center [icon] to center the January heading over the Budget and Spent columns.

10. Merge and center the February and March headings over their Budget and Spent columns.

11. Select Row 4, and right-align [icon] the Budget and Spent headings.

Calculate the Subtotals

12. Select the range B9:G9 (the subtotal cells in Row 9).

13. Press and hold the (CTRL) key while you select the subtotal ranges B14:G14 and B19:G19.
All three of the subtotal ranges should be selected.

14. Click AutoSum [Σ] to calculate all subtotals with a single command.

Calculate the Totals and Differences

15. Click Cell B21.

16. Enter the formula **=B9+B14+B19.**

17. Use the fill handle to copy the formula across the row.

18. Click Cell B22.
This cell will contain the difference between the January budget and January spent in Row 21.

19. Enter the formula **=B21−C21**.
The result should equal 158.

20. Calculate the differences in Cells D22 and F22. You may want to use some shortcut to enter these formulas. For example, you could use the fill handle to copy the formula in Cell B22 across and then delete the formulas in Cells C22, E22 and G22.
The results should equal 118 and −739.

Copy Number Formats

21. Select the subtotal numbers in Row 9.

22. Click the Currency Style [$] button.

23. Click the Decrease Decimal [icon] button twice to reduce the decimals to 0.
If you want the dollar ($) signs to float next to the numbers, make sure the cells are selected, and use the Format→Cells command. Choose the Currency style and set the number of decimal places and other options as desired.

24. Click Cell B9.

25. Double-click the Format Painter .

26. Drag the animated paintbrush over the subtotal numbers in Rows 14 and 19, and then drag over the totals and differences in Rows 21 and 22.
The Currency format will be copied to the numbers in those rows.

27. Click the Format Painter to turn it off.

Format Text Entries

28. Click Cell A1 (the large merged cell).

29. Set the font size to 16, apply bold formatting, and choose a color .

30. Apply bold formatting to the headings in Row 3, and apply the same color you used for the title in Cell A1.

31. Format the headings in Row 4 with the same color you used in Row 3.

32. Apply bold formatting to the subtotals in Rows 9, 14, and 19.

33. Format the totals and differences rows with the same color you used in Rows 3 and 4.

Recalculate Formulas

34. Click Cell G5.
Imagine you have an adjustable rate mortgage, and the monthly payment just went up. In the next step, you will change the number in Cell G5. Keep an eye on the totals and differences formulas at the bottom of the worksheet when you change the number. The formulas will automatically recalculate the numbers.

35. Type **1075**, and complete the entry.
The new total in Cell G21 should equal 2879, and the new difference in Cell F22 should equal –814.

36. Save the changes to the workbook, and then close the workbook.

Skill Builder 15.2 Formatting Practice

In this exercise, you will open a workbook on your exercise diskette. You will format the worksheet until it closely matches the completed worksheet shown below.

1. Open the workbook named Skill Builder 15.2.

2. Merge and Center ⊞ the title, Corporate Budget, across Columns A–E.

3. Use the fill handle to expand the series Q1 to Q1–Q4.

4. Right-align the headings Q1–Q4.

5. Calculate the subtotals and totals.

6. Widen Column A until the entries in the column are visible.

7. Format the numbers as shown below.

8. Format the title and headings with text formats of your choice.

9. Format the subtotal rows with italics as shown.

10. Format the total row with bold and italics as shown.

11. When you have finished, save the changes, and then close the workbook.

	A	B	C	D	E
1		Corporate Budget			
2					
3		Q1	Q2	Q3	Q4
4	Marketing	1,234,890	2,346,890	2,156,580	1,900,890
5	Sales	2,316,780	2,145,670	2,134,670	2,145,760
6	*Subtotal*	*$ 3,551,670*	*$ 4,492,560*	*$ 4,291,250*	*$ 4,046,650*
7					
8	Manufacturing	8,909,800	8,769,870	7,869,870	9,878,760
9	Distribution	3,456,570	3,245,670	2,314,560	3,897,860
10	*Subtotal*	*$ 12,366,370*	*$ 12,015,540*	*$ 10,184,430*	*$ 13,776,620*
11					
12	Customer Support	93,450	72,150	63,670	93,670
13	Human Resources	65,640	87,890	65,670	86,780
14	*Subtotal*	*$ 159,090*	*$ 160,040*	*$ 129,340*	*$ 180,450*
15					
16	***Total***	***$ 16,077,130***	***$ 16,668,140***	***$ 14,605,020***	***$ 18,003,720***

Skill Builder 15.3 Formatting and Formulas

In this exercise, you will open a workbook on your exercise diskette. You will format the worksheet until it closely matches the completed worksheet shown below.

1. Open the workbook named Skill Builder 15.3.

2. Merge and Center ⊞ the title Q2 Sales Volume Comparison across Columns A–E.

3. Use the fill handle to expand the series Store 1 to Store 1–Store 4 in Rows 3, 8, and 13.

4. Right-align the headings Store 1–Store 4.

5. Left-align all dates in Column A.

6. Widen Column A until the Percentage Increase entries fit within the column.

7. Format the numbers in Rows 4, 5, 9, 10, 14, and 15 as Comma style with 0 decimals.

8. Click Cell B6.

   In the next step, you will enter a formula that calculates the percentage increase. This formula uses parenthesis to change the order of calculations. The percentage increase is calculated as the April 03 sales minus April 02 sales. This difference is then divided by the April 02 sales. The formula is (B5–B4)/B4.

9. Enter the formula **=(B5–B4)/B4**.

10. Use the fill handle to copy the formula across the row.

11. Enter similar formulas in Cells B11 and B16, and then copy the formulas across the rows.

12. Format the numbers in the Percentage Increase rows with the Percent style ⬚% with 2 decimals.

13. In Row 1, increase the font size of the title to 12. Apply bold formatting.

14. Apply the color of your choice to the title in Row 1, and then apply the same color to the percentage increases in Rows 6, 11, and 16.

    The completed worksheet should closely match the worksheet shown below.

15. Press CTRL+~.

    The actual formulas now display in the cells—instead of the formula result.

16. When you have finished, save the changes, print the worksheet, and close the workbook.

	A	B	C	D	E
1		Q2 Sales Volume Comparison			
2					
3		Store 1	Store 2	Store 3	Store 4
4	April-02	13,234,657	34,789,564	23,000,908	65,908,456
5	April-03	14,456,900	40,987,560	28,546,905	70,987,235
6	Percentage Increase	9.24%	17.82%	24.11%	7.71%
7					
8		Store 1	Store 2	Store 3	Store 4
9	May-02	18,985,342	40,234,908	24,234,908	45,003,345
10	May-03	19,234,987	41,210,908	24,400,098	46,989,456
11	Percentage Increase	1.31%	2.43%	0.68%	4.41%
12					
13		Store 1	Store 2	Store 3	Store 4
14	Jun-02	24,234,980	65,230,980	18,230,350	51,006,983
15	Jun-03	25,235,908	66,234,908	27,908,990	58,231,900
16	Percentage Increase	4.13%	1.54%	53.09%	14.16%

Assessments

Assessment 15.1

In this assessment, you will create the completed worksheet shown below. Excel has a feature called AutoComplete that can assist you in entering data. As you are entering data in Column A, AutoComplete may propose entries in the current cell. These entries will be derived from cells that you have already typed in Column A. Just ignore this and continue typing your entries.

1. Click the New button to start a new workbook.

2. Follow these guidelines to create the worksheet shown below:

   - Enter the data as shown in the completed worksheet. You must create formulas in Columns D and F and in Rows 10, 12, and 13. You will need to use formulas in all cells containing the word Formula as shown below. The following table lists the formulas you will need to begin.

Cell	Use this Formula
D4	=C4/B4
F4	=D4*E4
Row 10	Column summations (use AutoSum)
B12	=E10/B10
B13	=F10/C10

   - Merge and center the entry in Cell A1 across the Range A1:F1 and apply Bold formatting to the entry.
   - Apply a Currency with 2 decimals format to the numbers in Columns D and F.
   - Apply a Comma with 0 decimals format to Cell B10.
   - Apply a Percent with 2 decimals format to Cells B12 and B13.
   - Adjust the column widths as necessary to display the labels.

3. Use Print Preview when you have finished, and then print the worksheet.

4. Save your workbook as **Assessment 15.1**, and then close the workbook.

	A	B	C	D	E	F
1		Donna's Deli - Produce Wastage Tracking sheet (October)				
2						
3	Item	Pounds Purchased	Total Purchased $	Cost per Lb.	Pounds Wasted	Total Wastage $
4	Sweet Potatoes	350	$101.50	Formula	52	Formula
5	Corn	220	$85.80	Formula	34	Formula
6	Greens	180	$124.20	Formula	23	Formula
7	Bean Sprouts	120	$22.80	Formula	34	Formula
8	Tomatoes	290	$258.10	Formula	80	Formula
9	Zucchini	90	$38.70	Formula	23	Formula
10	Totals	Formula	Formula	Formula	Formula	Formula
11						
12	Waste $ (Lbs.)	Formula				
13	Wast % ($)	Formula				

Assessment 15.2

In this assessment, you will develop the worksheet shown below.

1. Click the New ⬜ button to start a new workbook.

2. Follow these guidelines to create the worksheet shown below:

   ▪ Enter all text and number entries, indenting the text entries in Column A as shown below.

   ▪ Use formulas in Columns D and F to calculate the Subtotals and New Balances. Calculate each Subtotal as the Previous Balance plus the New Charges. Calculate each New Balance as the Subtotal minus the Payment Amount.

   ▪ Use AutoSum to calculate totals for the range B11:F11.

   ▪ Apply Bold formatting to Cell A1 and all cells in Row 11.

   ▪ Apply Currency formatting with 0 decimals to the totals in Row 11.

3. Use print preview when you have finished, and then print the worksheet.

	A	B	C	D	E	F
1	**Donna's Deli - Customer Credit Lines**					
2						
3	Customer	Previous Balance	New Charges	Subtotal	Payment Amount	New Balance
4	George Lopke	100	50		150	
5	Wanda Watson	230	85		315	
6	Alicia Thomas	58	100		100	
7	Bill Barton	60	35		0	
8	Latisha Robertson	140	80		0	
9	Amy Chang	200	150		350	
10	Dan Long	90	65		100	
11	**Total Credit**					

4. Save your workbook as **Assessment 15.2**, and then close the workbook.

Assessment 15.3

1. Follow these guidelines to create the worksheet shown below:

   ■ Enter all text and number entries, indenting the text entries in Column A as shown below.

   ■ Use AutoSum to calculate totals in Row 10.

   ■ Set the font size of Cell A1 to 12, and apply Bold formatting and a font color of your choice.

   ■ Apply Bold formatting to all cells in Row 10.

	A	B	C	D
1	**Donna's Deli - Customer Survey Results**			
2				
3	Category	January	February	March
4	Flavor	4.80	4.75	4.80
5	Service	4.60	4.50	4.70
6	Nutritional Value	4.95	4.95	4.83
7	Presentation	4.20	4.35	4.30
8	Price	4.20	4.20	4.45
9	Convenience	4.30	4.40	4.20
10	**Total**			

2. Press (CTRL)+(~) to display the formula results in the cells.

3. Print the worksheet, save the workbook as **Assessment 15.3**, and then close the workbook.

Critical Thinking

Critical Thinking 15.1 On Your Own

Fred Watson is the owner of Fred's Quality Lawn Care service. Fred has provided high-quality lawn care and landscaping services for over 25 years. Recently, Fred purchased a personal computer with Office 2003 preinstalled. He intends to use his new computer and Office 2003 to improve his customer service, conduct mailings, computerize his billing processes, and increase his profits. He recently took an Excel class at a local community college. Fred wants to use Excel to track his activities and help maximize his profits. You have been assigned the task of setting up a job log for Fred. The worksheet should assign a job number to each job. It should include the customer name, day of the week, type of work performed, the number of hours required to complete the activity, and the total dollar amount billed for the job. Use a formula to calculate the effective hourly rate for each job. This calculation will allow Fred to determine the types of work that yield the highest hourly rates. Include enough jobs to account for an entire week of activity with perhaps one or two jobs per day. Use the following categories of work performed:

Mowing	Irrigation system installation
Tree trimming	General maintenance

Save your workbook as **Critical Thinking 15.1**.

Critical Thinking 15.2 On Your Own

Cathy Adams works for George Miller at Speedy Package Delivery Service. Cathy has assigned you the task of setting up a worksheet to record mileage, gasoline usage, and other expenses for Speedy drivers. Cathy provides you with the following information for the month of March.

Driver	Miles Driven	Gasoline Used (gallons)	Gasoline Expense	Tolls
Harold Robinson	4,850	202	$267	$152
Jane Allen	5,232	194	$256	$165
Bill Peterson	4,100	158	$208	$ 90
Janine Rockwell	5,050	240	$317	$158

Use formulas to calculate the miles/gallon for each driver. Also, calculate the total expenses for each driver as the gasoline expense plus tolls. Format the entries as shown in the table above. Use the Format Painter to apply the same format to the Total Expense cells that is used in the Tolls cells. Use the Merge and Center tool to center a descriptive title above the worksheet data. Apply indents and any types of formats that you think are appropriate. Save your workbook as **Critical Thinking 15.2**.

Critical Thinking 15.3 On Your Own

Cindy Johnson conducts tests of PC hard drives at Data Storage Incorporated. Cindy has asked you to construct an Excel workbook to help her quantify her test results. Cindy provides you with the following data to get you started.

Unit Type	Total Produced	Passed Test	Failed but Repaired	Destroyed
CX64-64 Gigabyte	9,500	9,200	240	60
CX128-128 Gigabyte	8,000	7,450	350	200
CX256-256 Gigabyte	7,000	6,910	25	65

Use formulas to calculate the percentage of each drive type that passed the test, failed but were prepared, and were destroyed. Now use formulas to calculate totals for the columns shown in the preceding table, then calculate percentages for that total row as you did for the other rows. Format the entries as shown in the table above. Format the cells containing the percentage calculations as Percent style with two decimals. Use the Merge and Center tool to center a descriptive title above the worksheet data. Apply any types of formats that you think are appropriate. Save your workbook as **Critical Thinking 15.3**.

Critical Thinking 15.4 Web Research

Dominique Aguyo is a senior at West Side high school. Dominique is quite certain that she wants to major in Chemical Engineering when she attends college in the fall. Your task is to help Dominique identify schools that offer Chemical Engineering as a major. Use Internet Explorer and a search engine of your choice to locate at least five universities that offer Chemical Engineering majors. Record your results in an Excel spreadsheet. Include the school, city and state, size of the student population, and other information that you think would help Dominique make her decision. Save your workbook as **Critical Thinking 15.4**.

Critical Thinking 15.5 Web Research

Vivian Chu is a history major at San Francisco State University. Vivian is taking a demographics class in order to fulfill the requirements of her major. Part of the course requirements is a research paper on the effects of population growth in the 21st century. Use Internet Explorer and a search engine of your choice to help Vivian find the following population statistics for the United States, China, India, Brazil, and Germany.

Current population	Overall population growth rate
Birth rate	Estimated population in 2050
Death rate	

Use Excel to enter and organize the data. Format all cells containing rate information in Percent style with two decimals. Format cells with population numbers in Comma style with zero decimals. Center a descriptive title over the worksheet cells. Save your workbook as **Critical Thinking 15.5**.

Critical Thinking 15.6 **On Your Own**

Develop a revenue and expense worksheet for a new business venture. You can base your worksheet on the worksheet developed in the Hands-On exercises in this lesson. Decide what type of business you would like to model, what the potential revenue sources might be, and what the potential expenses might be. Include as many potential revenue sources and expense details as possible. Use formulas to determine whether or not the business can be profitable based on the model you set up. Format your worksheet and save it as **Critical Thinking 15.6**.

Powerful Features and Automated Tools

In this lesson, you will be introduced to Excel functions. Excel has hundreds of built-in functions including the AVERAGE, MIN, MAX, and COUNT functions which are introduced in this lesson. This lesson will also give you the skills necessary to move and copy cells. You will learn the Cut, Copy, and Paste techniques as well as Drag and Drop. Finally, you will learn how to apply borders and fill colors to cells and use Excel's powerful Auto-Format command.

Additional learning resources are available at labpub.com/learn/oe3/

Case Study

Lisa Wilkins is the National Sales Manager for Centron Cellular—a nationwide distributor of cellular telephone equipment. Lisa has instructed her assistant, Carl Jenkins, to provide her with a commission report for her sales force. Lisa wants the report separated into two regions. She wants to know the monthly sales and commissions for each sales rep. She also wants the total, average, minimum, and maximum sales of the reps in each region on a monthly basis. This would be a formidable task for most people, but Carl Jenkins is not concerned. Carl has expert knowledge of Excel 2003. With a little planning and the power of Excel 2003, Carl will use many tools and features to complete this worksheet with ease.

	A	B	C	D	E	F	G
1							
2							
3	Region 1						
4	Sales Rep	Jan Sales	Jan Comm	Feb Sales	Feb Comm	Mar Sales	Mar Comm
5		20000	3000	32000		23000	
6		15000	2250	32000		23890	
7		45000	6750	8900		43000	
8		23000	3450	19000		10900	
9		34000	5100	34000		32000	
10	Total						
11	Average						
12	Maximum						
13	Minimum						
14							
15							
16							
17							
18		18000		54000		36790	
19		12000		35900		45678	
20		56000		34900		72490	
21		39000		54000		21000	
22		23000		89000		38900	
23							
24							
25							

Online Help

Excel's online Help puts a complete reference book at your fingertips. Help is available for just about any topic you can imagine. Online Help is important because Microsoft does not provide reference manuals with Office 2003. The reference manuals are now integrated into online Help.

Locating Help Topics

Your goal when using online Help is to locate Help topics. There are several different search methods you can use to locate topics. All Help topics have key words that identify them. For example, a Help topic that discusses printing workbooks can probably be located by including the key word *printing* in your search method. Regardless of which search method you use, the goal is to locate a topic. Once you locate the desired topic, you can display it and follow the instructions in the topic. The Help window can be displayed using any of the following methods:

- Click the Help button on the Standard toolbar.
- Press F1.
- Choose Help→Microsoft Office Excel Help from the menu bar.

The following Quick Reference table describes the various methods for locating Help topics.

QR▶ QUICK REFERENCE: LOCATING HELP TOPICS

Search Method	Procedure
Table of Contents	The Table of Contents method is useful if you are trying to locate a topic but you aren't really sure how to describe it. The Contents method lets you navigate through a series of categories until the desired topic is located.
Type a question box	You type a phrase into a search box and execute a search.
Search For box	The Search For method lets you locate a topic by typing keywords. A list of topics is displayed from which you can choose the desired topic. This method is most useful if you know the name of the topic or feature for which you need assistance.

The Help Window Toolbar

The Help window contains a toolbar to assist you with online Help. The following illustration describes the buttons on the Help toolbar.

The AutoTile button is used to show or hide the tabbed area of the Help window. The tabbed area is used to locate Help topics.

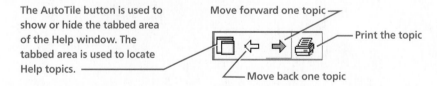

Move forward one topic

Print the topic

Move back one topic

Hands-On 16.1 Use Online Help

Use the Search For Box

1. Choose Help→Microsoft Office Excel Help from the menu bar.
   The Help window will appear.

2. Click the Start Searching ➡ button after typing the word function in the Search For box.
   The About the Syntax of Functions topic should be on the bottom of the list.

3. Click the About the Syntax of Functions topic to display the topic.
   A new pane opens and displays the topic.

4. Take a moment to read the help information. Notice the blue phrases, such as Cell References, that are scattered throughout the topic.

5. Click the Cell References phrase, and a definition will appear.

6. If the Help window is no longer displayed click the AutoTile ⊞ button on the Help toolbar.

Experiment with Help

7. Try using the Search For method to locate additional Help topics. You can type keywords in the Search For box, click the Start Searching button, and click the desired topic. Try locating Help topics for Excel features you have already learned or for new features to be covered in this lesson.

8. Try locating help topics by clicking the Table of Contents link then clicking one of the closed books in the list.

9. When you have finished, click the Close ⊠ button on the Help window.

AutoCorrect

Excel's AutoCorrect feature can improve the speed and accuracy of entering text. AutoCorrect is most useful for replacing abbreviations with a full phrase. For example, you could set up AutoCorrect to substitute *as soon as possible* whenever you type *asap*. AutoCorrect also automatically corrects common spelling errors. For example, the word *the* is often misspelled as *teh* and the word *and* is often misspelled as *adn*. These and other common spelling mistakes are built into AutoCorrect, so they are fixed automatically. AutoCorrect also automatically capitalizes the first letter of a day if you type the day in lowercase. For example, if you type *sunday* and complete the entry, AutoCorrect will enter *Sunday* in the cell. Finally, AutoCorrect fixes words that have two initial capital letters by switching the second letter to lowercase.

Expanding AutoCorrect Entries

AutoCorrect goes into action when you type a word in a text entry and tap (SPACE BAR) or when you complete a text entry. The word or entry is compared to all entries in the AutoCorrect table. The AutoCorrect table contains a list of words and their replacement phrases. If the word you type matches an entry in the AutoCorrect table, then a phrase from the table is substituted for the word. This is known as expanding the AutoCorrect entry.

Creating and Editing AutoCorrect Entries

The Tools→AutoCorrect Options command displays the AutoCorrect dialog box. You use the AutoCorrect dialog box to add entries to the AutoCorrect table, to delete entries from the table, and to set other AutoCorrect options. To add an entry, you type the desired abbreviation in the Replace box and the desired expansion for the abbreviation in the With box.

AutoComplete

The AutoComplete feature is useful if you want the same entry repeated more than once in a column. If the first few characters you type match another entry in the column, then AutoComplete will offer to complete the entry for you. You can accept the offer by completing the entry or you can reject the offer by typing the remainder of the entry yourself.

Hands-On 16.2 Use AutoCorrect and AutoComplete

In this exercise, you will open a workbook from your exercise diskette. You will experiment with AutoCorrect and AutoComplete, and create a new AutoCorrect entry.

Use AutoCorrect

1. Open the workbook named Hands-On Lesson 16.

2. Type **adn** (that's adn, not and) in Cell A1, and tap (ENTER).
   Excel should correct the misspelling and enter the word and *in the cell.*

3. Click Cell A1, and type **This adn that**, but don't complete the entry.
   Notice that AutoCorrect fixed the typo immediately after you tapped (SPACE BAR).

4. Tap (ESC) to cancel the entry.

Create a New AutoCorrect Entry

5. Choose Tools→AutoCorrect Options from the menu bar.

6. Follow these steps to create a new AutoCorrect entry:

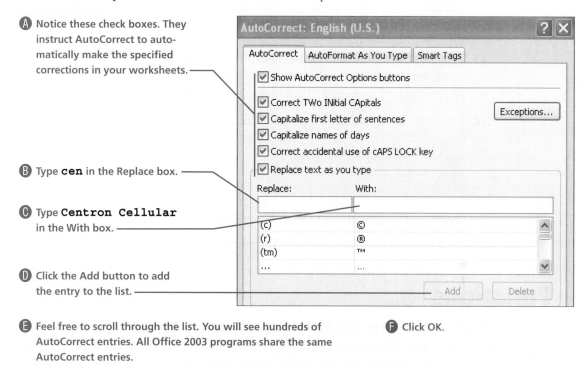

Ⓐ Notice these check boxes. They instruct AutoCorrect to automatically make the specified corrections in your worksheets.

Ⓑ Type **cen** in the Replace box.

Ⓒ Type **Centron Cellular** in the With box.

Ⓓ Click the Add button to add the entry to the list.

Ⓔ Feel free to scroll through the list. You will see hundreds of AutoCorrect entries. All Office 2003 programs share the same AutoCorrect entries.

Ⓕ Click OK.

7. Click Cell A1, type **cen**, and tap (ENTER).
   AutoCorrect should replace cen with Centron Cellular. Notice that you can use AutoCorrect as a type of shorthand. AutoCorrect can replace abbreviations with phrases you use often such as your company name or address.

Delete the AutoCorrect Entry

8. Choose Tools→AutoCorrect Options from the menu bar.

9. Scroll through the list of AutoCorrect entries and choose the cen, Centron Cellular entry. You can also type cen in the Replace box to rapidly locate the entry.

10. Click the Delete button below the AutoCorrect table, and then click OK.
   The entry is deleted from the AutoCorrect table, but the phrase Centron Cellular will remain in Cell A1.

Use AutoComplete

11. Click Cell A5, type **Branston**, and then tap (ENTER).

12. Type the letter **B** in Cell A6 and AutoComplete will display the word Branston in the cell.
You could accept this proposal by completing the entry; however, you will continue to type in the next step thus typing over the proposed entry.

13. Type **arton** (to make the entry Barton), and tap (ENTER).
AutoComplete will constantly try to assist you in completing entries. You can either ignore AutoComplete and continue typing your entries or complete the entries that AutoComplete proposes.

14. Enter the following sales rep names into the next three cells:

7	Alexander
8	Alioto
9	Chin

You will continue to enhance the worksheet throughout this lesson.

Functions

Excel has over 400 built-in functions. Functions are predefined formulas that perform calculations. Functions must be constructed using a set of basic rules known as syntax. Fortunately, most functions use the same or similar syntax. The following illustration defines the syntax of the SUM function. This syntax also applies to the MIN, MAX, AVERAGE, and COUNT functions, which are discussed in the Quick Reference table following the illustration.

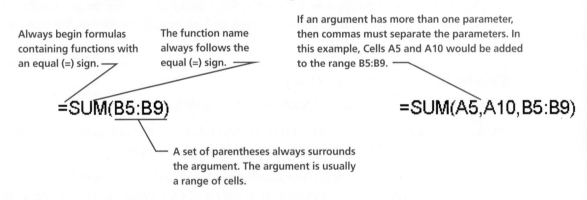

QUICK REFERENCE: COMMON FUNCTIONS

Function	What It Does	Syntax Example
MIN	Returns the minimum value of a range	=MIN(B5:B9)
MAX	Returns the maximum value of a range	=MAX(B5:B9)
AVERAGE	Returns the average of values in a range	=AVERAGE(B5:B9)
COUNT	Determines how many cells in a range contain numbers, dates, or formulas	=COUNT(B5:B9)

Entering Functions with the Keyboard

You can type a function and its argument(s) directly in the desired cell. You can also click in the desired cell and type the function in the Formula bar. If you choose to type a function, you can use point mode to assist you in entering the function arguments.

 ## Hands-On 16.3 Enter Functions with the Keyboard

Do a Little Detective Work and Use AutoSum

1. Notice that the worksheet has a January Commissions column (Jan Comm).
   The commissions in Column C are calculated with a simple formula.

2. What commission rate is being used to calculate the sales rep's commissions?
   You can find this out by clicking a commission cell in Column C and reviewing the formula in the Formula bar.

3. Click Cell C10, click AutoSum ⬛Σ, and complete the entry.
   The total commissions for January should equal 20550.

4. Look at the Formula bar and notice the function =SUM(C5:C9) that AutoSum has placed in the cell.
   The SUM function uses the standard function syntax discussed at the beginning of this topic.

Type the AVERAGE Function

5. Click Cell C11, type the function **=AVERAGE(C5:C9)**, and complete the entry.
   The result should equal 4110. This is the average of the values in the range C5:C9. Notice that the syntax is the same as the SUM function syntax, except you used the function name AVERAGE instead of SUM.

Inserting Functions

The Insert Function ⨍ button on the Formula bar displays the Insert Function box. The Insert Function box provides access to all built-in functions of Excel. The Insert Function box lets you locate a function by typing a description or searching by category. When you locate the desired function and click OK, Excel displays the Function Arguments box. The Function Arguments box assists you in constructing the function by helping you enter the arguments. The Insert Function box and the Function Arguments box are shown in the following illustrations.

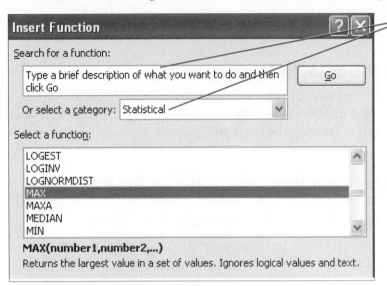

You can search for a function by typing a description or choosing a category. This example shows functions in the Statistical category.

If Most Recently Used is chosen from the Category list, then the ten most recently used functions appear in the Select a Function list.

The Function Arguments box appears when you choose a function and click OK.

You can type the argument (typically a range) in this box or select the desired range in the worksheet.

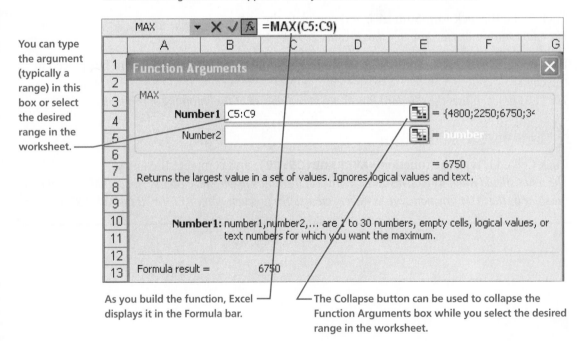

As you build the function, Excel displays it in the Formula bar.

The Collapse button can be used to collapse the Function Arguments box while you select the desired range in the worksheet.

Hands-On 16.4 Insert a Function and Use Point Mode

In this exercise, you will insert the MAX and MIN functions in your worksheet.

Insert the MAX Function

1. Click Cell C12, and then click the Insert Function ⨍ button on the Formula bar.

2. Follow these steps to choose the MAX function:

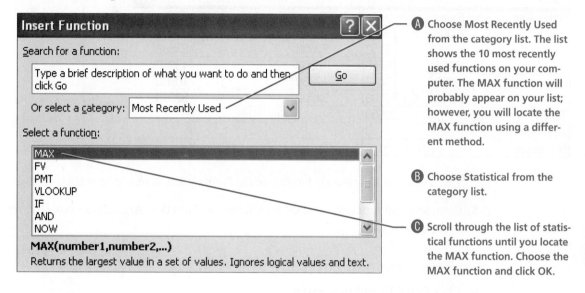

Ⓐ Choose Most Recently Used from the category list. The list shows the 10 most recently used functions on your computer. The MAX function will probably appear on your list; however, you will locate the MAX function using a different method.

Ⓑ Choose Statistical from the category list.

Ⓒ Scroll through the list of statistical functions until you locate the MAX function. Choose the MAX function and click OK.

Notice that the MAX(C11) function appears in the Formula bar. This is the correct function; however, the range C11 is incorrect. You could type the correct range, C5:C9, in the Formula bar or the Function Arguments box. However, you will insert the range by dragging in the worksheet in the following steps.

3. Follow this step to collapse the Function Arguments box:

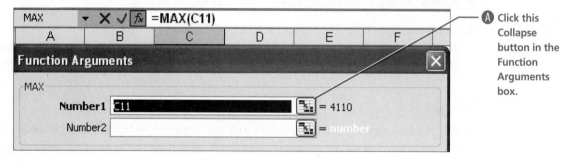

Ⓐ Click this Collapse button in the Function Arguments box.

4. Follow these steps to select the appropriate range of cells and restore the Function Arguments Box:

Ⓐ Drag the mouse over the range C5:C9, as shown here.

Ⓑ Click the Restore button to restore the Function Arguments box.

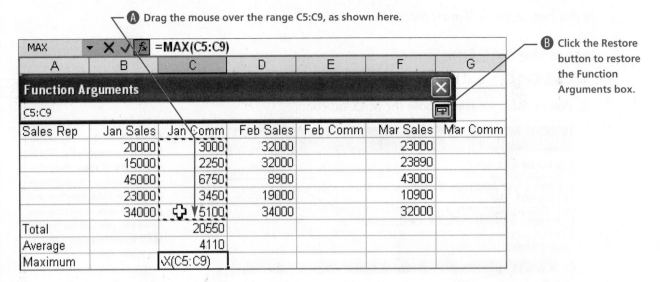

Sales Rep	Jan Sales	Jan Comm	Feb Sales	Feb Comm	Mar Sales	Mar Comm
	20000	3000	32000		23000	
	15000	2250	32000		23890	
	45000	6750	8900		43000	
	23000	3450	19000		10900	
	34000	5100	34000		32000	
Total		20550				
Average		4110				
Maximum		X(C5:C9)				

Take a moment to review the formula in the Formula bar. It should be =MAX(C5:C9).

5. Complete the function by clicking OK on the Function Arguments box (the result should equal 6750).

Use Point Mode to Enter the MIN Function

6. Click Cell C13 and type **=min(**.
   If you type a function in lowercase, Excel will convert it to uppercase when you complete the entry. Remember, you must always type the opening parenthesis when entering a function in point mode.

7. Drag the mouse down the range C5:C9.

8. Type a closing parenthesis **)**, and your formula should be =min(C5:C9).

9. Complete the entry. The result should equal 2250.
   In this exercise, you used two different methods to create functions. You can also insert functions by typing them directly into the cell or Formula bar. In the future, use whichever method you prefer.

Change the Values

You may be wondering why you used the MIN and MAX functions in this worksheet when it is relatively easy to see which sales reps had the minimum and maximum commissions. The benefit of using the functions becomes apparent when the values change or when there are a large number of rows. The functions automatically recalculate the SUM, AVERAGE, MAX, and MIN when values in the worksheet change.

10. Click Cell B5, change the sales number from 20000 to **32000**, and complete the entry.
    Notice how the functions in Cells C10 and C11 recalculate the sum and average.

11. Click Undo 🔄 to change the number back to 20000.

Cut, Copy, and Paste

Cut, Copy, and Paste are available in all Office 2003 applications. With Cut, Copy, and Paste you can move or copy cells within a worksheet, between worksheets, or between different Office applications. For example, you could use the Copy command to copy a range from one worksheet and the Paste command to paste the range into another worksheet. Cut, Copy, and Paste are most efficient for moving or copying cells a long distance within a worksheet or between worksheets. Cut, Copy, and Paste are easy to use if you remember the following concepts.

■ You must select cells before issuing a Cut or Copy command.

■ You must position the highlight at the desired location before issuing the Paste command. This is important because the range you paste will overwrite any cells in the paste area.

QUICK REFERENCE: CUT, COPY, AND PASTE

Command	Discussion	Procedure
Cut	The Cut command removes entries from selected cells and places them on the Office clipboard.	Click the Cut button, or press CTRL+X.
Copy	The Copy command also places entries on the Office clipboard, but it leaves a copy of the entries in the original cells.	Click the Copy button, or press CTRL+C.
Paste	The Paste command pastes entries from the Office clipboard to worksheet cells beginning at the highlight location.	Click the Paste button, or press CTRL+V.

The Office Clipboard

The Office Clipboard lets you collect items from any Office document or program and paste them into any other Office document. For example, you can collect a paragraph from a Word document, data from an Excel worksheet, and a graphic from a PowerPoint slide and then paste them all into a Word document. The Office Clipboard can also be used within an application like Excel to collect several items and then paste them as desired. The Office Clipboard can hold up to 24 items.

How it Works

You can place items on the Office Clipboard using the standard Cut and Copy commands; however, the Office Clipboard must first be displayed in the Task Pane. The Office Clipboard is displayed with the Edit→Office Clipboard command. Once the Office Clipboard is displayed, you can choose an item and paste it into your worksheet.

Hands-On 16.5 Use Copy and Paste

Copy the Commission Formula to Cell E5

1. Click Cell C5, and take a moment to review the formula in the Formula bar.
   Your objective is to copy this formula to the February and March commission columns. This cannot be done with the fill handle because those cells are not adjacent to Cell C5.

2. Click the Copy 🖻 button on the Standard toolbar.
   Notice the flashing marquee in Cell C5. This indicates that the sales commission formula has been copied and is ready to be pasted.

3. Click Cell E5, and then click the Paste 🖺 button.
   The formula will be pasted, and it will calculate the commission as 4800. The flashing marquee in Cell C5 indicates the formula is still available for pasting into other cells.

4. Notice that a Paste Options 🖺 button appears next to the pasted cell in the worksheet.
   The Paste Options button provides several options that allow you to control how the data is pasted.

Paste to a Range

5. Select the range E6:E9.

6. Click the Paste 🖺 button on the Standard toolbar to paste the formula.
   You can always copy a single cell and paste it into a range of cells.

7. Select the range G5:G9 and paste the formula into those cells.
   You can continue to paste as long as the marquee is flashing.

8. Tap (ESC) on the keyboard to dismiss the marquee and the Paste Options button.
   You can always turn off the flashing marquee with the (ESC) key.

9. Click any cell that you just pasted into, and review the formula in the Formula bar.
   Excel updates the references in the formulas to reflect the new formula locations.

Paste to Multiple Ranges

10. Click Cell C10, and click the Copy 🖻 button.

11. Click Cell E10.

12. Press and hold the (CTRL) key, and click Cell G10.
    Both Cells E10 and G10 should be selected.

13. Click the Paste 🖺 button to paste the formula into both cells.

14. Use the preceding techniques to copy the AVERAGE, MAX, and MIN functions from Column C to Columns E and G. You can copy the functions one at a time, or you can select all three functions, and copy and paste them simultaneously.

Copy the Heading Rows

15. Select all entries in Rows 3 and 4 by dragging over the cells.

16. Click the Copy [icon] button, and then click Cell A16.
    In the next step, you will paste the range to Cell A16. You should always paste a large range like this to one cell (A16 in this case). Excel will use Cell A16 as the starting location of the pasted range. However, you must be careful when using this technique because Excel will overwrite any cells in the pasted range.

17. Click the Paste [icon] button.
    In the next exercise, you will continue to copy cells with the drag-and-drop technique. For now, continue with the data entry task in the next step.

18. Enter the following names into the range A18:A22:

18	Richardson
19	Thomas
20	Carter
21	Williams
22	Jones

19. Change the heading in Cell A16 from Region 1 to **Region 2**.

Drag and Drop

Drag and Drop produces the same results as Cut, Copy, and Paste. However, Drag and Drop is usually more efficient if you are moving or copying entries a short distance within the same worksheet. If the original location and destination are both visible in the current window, then it is usually easier to use Drag and Drop. With Drag and Drop, you select the cells you wish to move or copy and release the mouse button. Then you point to the edge of the selected range and drag the range to the desired destination. If you press the (CTRL) key while releasing the mouse button, the cells are copied to the destination.

Right Dragging

Right dragging is a variation of the Drag and Drop technique. Many beginners find Drag and Drop difficult to use because they have difficulty controlling the mouse. This difficulty is compounded if they are trying to copy entries using Drag and Drop. This is because copying requires the (CTRL) key to be held while the selected range is dragged. With the Right-Drag method, the right mouse button is used when dragging. When the right mouse button is released at the destination, a pop-up menu appears. The pop-up menu gives you several options including Move, Copy, and Cancel. This provides more control because there is no need to use the (CTRL) key when copying, and you have the option of canceling the move or copy.

In this exercise, you will use Drag and Drop to move and copy text and formulas in the worksheet.

Move Entries

1. Follow these steps to drag and drop text entries:

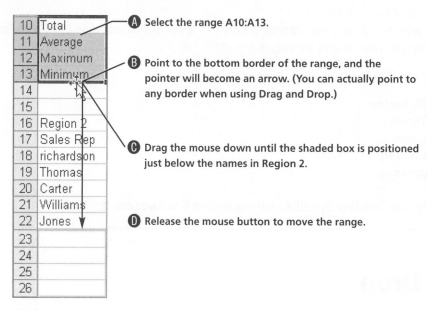

Ⓐ Select the range A10:A13.

Ⓑ Point to the bottom border of the range, and the pointer will become an arrow. (You can actually point to any border when using Drag and Drop.)

Ⓒ Drag the mouse down until the shaded box is positioned just below the names in Region 2.

Ⓓ Release the mouse button to move the range.

Notice how easy it was to move the cells using Drag and Drop. You should focus on using Drag and Drop if the move is a short distance within the same worksheet. Unfortunately, you should have copied the cells instead of moving them. You will correct this in the next few steps.

2. Click Undo ↺ to reverse the move.

Use Right Drag

3. Make sure the range A10:A13 is still selected.

4. Position the mouse pointer on the bottom edge of the selected range and press and hold the *right* mouse button.

5. Drag the mouse down until the range A23:A26 is highlighted as in the previous steps, and release the right mouse button.
A pop-up menu will appear with several choices.

6. Choose Copy Here from the pop-up menu.
The selected range will be copied.

Use Right Drag to Copy Formulas

7. Follow these steps to copy the January commission formulas to Region 2:

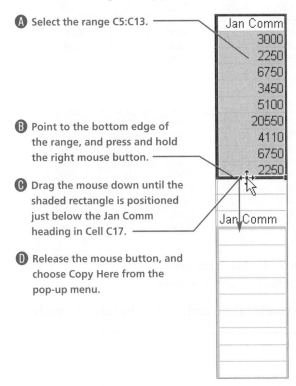

Ⓐ Select the range C5:C13.

Ⓑ Point to the bottom edge of the range, and press and hold the right mouse button.

Ⓒ Drag the mouse down until the shaded rectangle is positioned just below the Jan Comm heading in Cell C17.

Ⓓ Release the mouse button, and choose Copy Here from the pop-up menu.

Jan Comm
3000
2250
6750
3450
5100
20550
4110
6750
2250

Jan Comm

8. Use the right-drag method to copy the February and March commission formulas to Region 2.

9. Save the changes to your workbook.

At this point, your worksheet should match the following worksheet:

	A	B	C	D	E	F	G
1	Centron Cellular						
2							
3	Region 1						
4	Sales Rep	Jan Sales	Jan Comm	Feb Sales	Feb Comm	Mar Sales	Mar Comm
5	Branston	20000	3000	32000	4800	23000	3450
6	Barton	15000	2250	32000	4800	23890	3583.5
7	Alexander	45000	6750	8900	1335	43000	6450
8	Alioto	23000	3450	19000	2850	10900	1635
9	Chin	34000	5100	34000	5100	32000	4800
10	Total		20550		18885		19918.5
11	Average		4110		3777		3983.7
12	Maximum		6750		5100		6450
13	Minimum		2250		1335		1635
14							
15							
16	Region 2						
17	Sales Rep	Jan Sales	Jan Comm	Feb Sales	Feb Comm	Mar Sales	Mar Comm
18	Richardson	18000	2700	54000	8100	36790	5518.5
19	Thomas	12000	1800	35900	5385	45678	6851.7
20	Carter	56000	8400	34900	5235	72490	10873.5
21	Williams	39000	5850	54000	8100	21000	3150
22	Jones	23000	3450	89000	13350	38900	5835
23	Total		22200		40170		32228.7
24	Average		4440		8034		6445.74
25	Maximum		8400		13350		10873.5
26	Minimum		1800		5235		3150

10. Press (**CTRL**)+(~) to display the formulas in the cells.

Take a moment to examine the formulas in your worksheet.

11. Press (**CTRL**)+(~) to hide the formulas again and display the formula results in the cells.

Cell Borders

The Borders ⬚▾ button on the Formatting toolbar lets you add borders to cell edges. When you click the Borders drop-down button, a tear-off palette of popular border styles appears. You can apply a style to all selected cells by choosing it from the palette. You can also use the Format→ Cells command to display the Format Cells dialog box. The Borders tab on the dialog box lets you apply additional border combinations. You can also choose a color from the dialog box to apply colored borders.

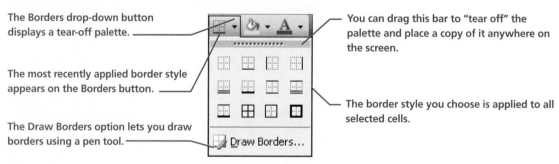

The Borders drop-down button displays a tear-off palette.

The most recently applied border style appears on the Borders button.

The Draw Borders option lets you draw borders using a pen tool.

You can drag this bar to "tear off" the palette and place a copy of it anywhere on the screen.

The border style you choose is applied to all selected cells.

Fill Colors and Patterns

The Fill Color button on the Formatting toolbar lets you fill selected cells with color. When you click the Fill Color drop-down button, a tear-off palette of colors appears. You can apply a color to all selected cells by choosing it from the palette. The fill color is independent of the font color used to format text and numbers. You can also use the Format→Cells command to display the Format Cells dialog box. The Patterns tab on the dialog box lets you apply fill colors and a variety of patterns.

Hands-On 16.7 Add Borders and Fill Colors

Format the Title Cells

1. Select the range A1:G1 in Row 1, and click the Merge and Center 🔳 button.

2. Make sure the range is selected, and click the Borders drop-down 🔳 button.

3. Follow these steps to put a thick border around the range:

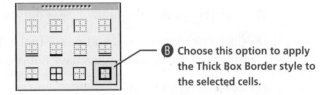

Ⓐ Take a moment to review the various border styles. The first style removes all borders from the selected cells. Notice the other styles place thin, thick, or double lines on various borders.

Ⓑ Choose this option to apply the Thick Box Border style to the selected cells.

4. Make sure the range is selected, click the Fill Color drop-down 🔳 button, and choose any color.

5. Make sure the range is selected, and click the Font Color drop-down 🔳 button.

6. Choose a color that will provide adequate contrast to the fill color you chose.

7. Click outside the range, and you will be able to see the formats.
   The lines on the top and left sides of the range may not be visible because the column and row headings are blocking them. Notice the fill color fills the range, while the font color only affects the text. Also notice that the colors and line style you chose now appear on the buttons. If desired, you could apply these same colors and line style to other selected cells by clicking the buttons.

8. Click the Print Preview 🔳 button.

9. If necessary, click anywhere on the worksheet to zoom in.
   The lines on the top and left sides of the range should now be visible.

Add Additional Borders

10. Click the Close button to exit from Print Preview.

11. Select the range A2:G26.
This range includes all cells in the active worksheet area except for the title row.

12. Click the Borders drop-down 田▾ button.

13. Choose the All Borders 田 style (second style on the bottom row).

14. Click the Print Preview 🔍 button.
Notice that the lines on every border of every cell appear too busy. You will change the borders in the next few steps.

Remove Borders and Reapply Borders

15. Close the Print Preview window.

16. Make sure the range A2:G26 is still selected.

17. Click the Borders drop-down 田▾ button, and choose Thick Box Border ◘ style.

18. Click Print Preview 🔍 and notice that a thick border has been applied to the outside of the range but the inside borders have not been removed.

19. Close the Print Preview window.

20. Click the Borders drop-down 田▾ button, and choose No Borders ⊞ style (first button).
This will remove the borders from the selected range.

21. Click the Borders drop-down 田▾ button, and choose Thick Box Border ◘ style.

22. Click Print Preview 🔍, review the results, and then close Print Preview.

Apply Fill Color and Font Color

23. Select the range A10:G13.
This range includes all cells containing entries in Rows 10, 11, 12, and 13.

24. Click the Fill Color 🖌▾ button (not the drop-down button) to apply the same fill color that was applied to the large merged cell at the top of the worksheet.

25. Click the Font Color **A**▾ button (not the drop-down button) to apply the same font color that was applied to the merged cell.

26. Apply the same fill color and font color to the range A23:G26.

27. Save the changes to your workbook.

28. Take a few moments to experiment with borders and fill colors. Use Undo to reverse any changes you make.

AutoFormat

The Format→AutoFormat command lets you choose from a variety of predefined formats. The predefined formats automatically apply number formats, borders, fill colors, font colors, font sizes, and other formats to a selected range. You may be pleasantly surprised when you see the professional formatting that AutoFormat can apply.

!NOTE!

You must select a range before applying an AutoFormat.

The AutoFormat box shows previews of the available formats.

You can scroll through the list to view additional formats. The last format on the list is the None format, which removes all formats.

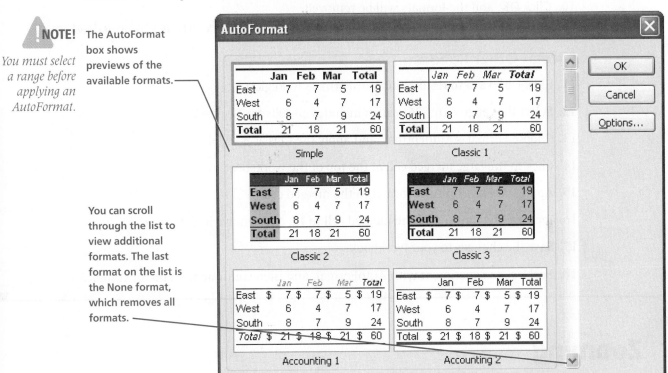

Hands-On 16.8 Use AutoFormat

Use AutoFormat on Region 1

1. Select the range A3:G13, which includes all cells for Region 1.

2. Choose Format→AutoFormat from the menu bar.

3. Click the Options button just below the Cancel button on the right side of the box.
   Check boxes will appear at the bottom of the dialog box. These boxes determine the formats that AutoFormat will apply. Make sure all of the boxes are checked.

4. Scroll through the list and notice the various formats.

5. Scroll to the top of the list and choose Classic 3 style.

6. Click OK, and then click anywhere in the worksheet to view the formats.
   Notice that AutoFormat detected rows containing formulas and formatted those rows in a different manner than the body and header rows. AutoFormat makes its formatting decisions by determining which rows and columns have text, numbers, and formulas.

Remove the AutoFormats

7. Select the range A3:G13 (the range you just formatted).

8. Choose Format→AutoFormat from the menu bar.

9. Scroll to the bottom of the list and choose the None format.

10. Click OK, and the formats will be removed.
    You can use this technique to remove all formats, whether or not they were applied with AutoFormat.

Format Other Ranges

11. Click Undo ⤴ to restore the AutoFormats to Region 1.

12. Select the range A16:G26, which includes all cells for Region 2.

13. Choose Format→AutoFormat, and apply the Classic 3 style.

14. Click in the large merged cell at the top of the worksheet.

15. Apply the Classic 3 AutoFormat to the merged cell.

16. Increase the font size of the merged cell to 12, and remove italics.

17. Save the changes to your workbook.

18. Feel free to experiment with AutoFormat, and then continue with the next topic.

Zooming

The Zoom Control lets you "zoom in" to get a close-up view of a worksheet or "zoom out" to see the full view. Zooming changes the size of the onscreen worksheet but has no effect on the printed worksheet. You can zoom from 10% to 400%.

Notice how large the onscreen worksheet appears. However, it will print in the normal size.

You can type a zoom percentage in the Zoom box and tap (ENTER) or . . .

. . . you can click the drop-down button and choose an option from the list.

	200%
	100%
	75%
	50%
	25%
	Selection

Arial   ▾ 10 ▾   **B** *I* U | ≡ ≡ ≡ ⊞ | $ % , ⁺.0 .00 | ⇥ ⇤ | ⊞ ▾

H12   ▾   *fx*

	A	B	C	D	E
1			Centron Cellular		
2					
3				Region 1	
4	**Sales Rep**	*Jan Sales*	*Jan Comm*	*Feb Sales*	*Feb Comm*
5	**Branston**	32000	4800	32000	4800
6	**Barton**	15000	2250	32000	4800
7	**Alexander**	45000	6750	8900	1335
8	**Alioto**	23000	3450	19000	2850
9	**Chin**	34000	5100	34000	5100
10	**Total**		22350		18885

Hands-On 16.9 Use the Zoom Control

1. Follow these steps to adjust the zoom percentage:

Ⓐ Click in the Zoom box, type **150**, and tap (ENTER).

Ⓑ Click the Zoom drop-down button, and choose 200%.

Ⓒ Zoom to 100%.

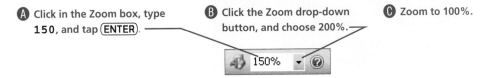

2. Select the range A4:C13.
   Imagine that you want to analyze just the January sales numbers. You can zoom in to get a close-up view of just this range.

3. Click the Zoom drop-down ⏷ button, and choose Selection.
   Excel will zoom to the maximum percentage possible for that selection.

4. Zoom to 100%, and continue with the next topic.

Hiding Rows and Columns

You can hide selected rows and columns with the Format→Row→Hide command and the Format→Column→Hide command. Hidden rows and columns are not visible in the worksheet, and they are not printed when the worksheet is printed. However, hidden rows and columns are still part of the worksheet. Their values and formulas can be referenced by other formulas in the visible rows and columns. Hiding rows and columns can be useful if you are trying to focus attention on other parts of the worksheet.

Notice that Columns B, D, and F have been hidden. These columns are hidden to draw attention to the commission columns.

	A	C	E	G
1	Centron Cellular			
2				
3	Region 1			
4	Sales Rep	Jan Comm	Feb Comm	Mar Comm
5	Branston	4800	4800	3450
6	Barton	2250	4800	3583.5
7	Alexander	6750	1335	6450

Unhiding Rows and Columns

You can unhide rows and columns with the Format→Row→Unhide command and the Format→Column→Unhide command. Before unhiding rows, you must select row(s) above and below the hidden rows. Likewise, you must select column(s) on the left and right of hidden columns before issuing the Unhide command.

To unhide Column D, you must first select Columns C and E.

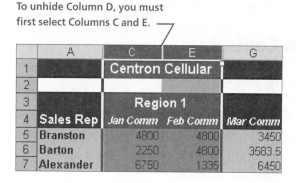

You could unhide Columns B, D, and F with a single command by selecting Columns A–G and then issuing the Unhide command.

Hands-On 16.10 Hide and Unhide Rows and Columns

1. Follow these steps to hide Columns B, D, and F:

Ⓐ Click the Column B heading to select that column. ⎯

Ⓑ Press and hold (CTRL) while clicking the Column D and F headings. ⎯

Ⓒ Choose Format→ Column→Hide from the menu bar.

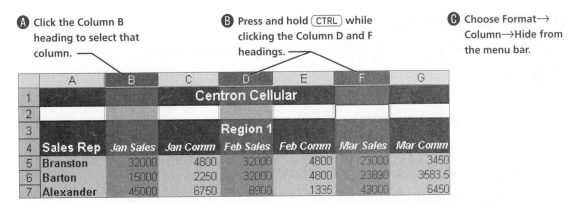

2. Follow these steps to unhide Columns B, D, and F:

Ⓐ Position the mouse pointer on the Column A heading and drag to the right until Columns A–G are selected, as shown here. ⎯

Ⓑ Choose Format→Column→ Unhide from the menu bar.

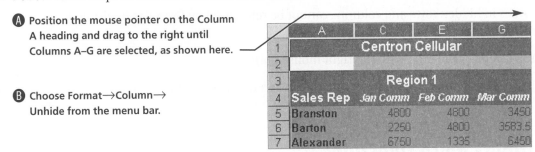

3. Click Undo ↺ to hide the columns again.

   Imagine that you are only interested in the overall results of the Centron Cellular sales force—not the performance of the individual sales reps.

4. Select Rows 5–9 by dragging the mouse down over the row headings.

5. Choose Format→Row→Hide to hide the rows.

6. Hide the rows for the individual sales reps in Region 2.

7. Feel free to experiment with any of the topics you have learned in this lesson.

8. Save the workbook when you have finished experimenting, and then close the workbook.

Concepts Review

True/False Questions

1. You cannot change the fill color of cells that contain numeric values.   TRUE   FALSE

2. AutoCorrect entries are expanded when (SPACE BAR) is tapped or when the entry is completed.   TRUE   FALSE

3. You must accept an AutoComplete entry that Excel proposes.   TRUE   FALSE

4. MIN and MAX are examples of functions.   TRUE   FALSE

5. A function's arguments are always surrounded by quotation marks " ".   TRUE   FALSE

6. You can paste a copied formula into multiple cells with one Paste command.   TRUE   FALSE

7. The maximum zoom percentage is 200%.   TRUE   FALSE

8. Values in hidden rows and columns cannot be referenced by formulas in visible rows and columns.   TRUE   FALSE

9. You can drag and drop with the right mouse button.   TRUE   FALSE

10. The only way to calculate an average is by using the Insert Function box.   TRUE   FALSE

Multiple Choice Questions

1. Which command displays the AutoCorrect dialog box?
   a. Format→AutoCorrect Options
   b. Tools→AutoCorrect Options
   c. Edit→AutoCorrect Options
   d. None of the above

2. Which command is used to display the AutoFormat dialog box?
   a. Tools→AutoFormat
   b. Format→AutoFormat
   c. Format→Cells
   d. None of the above

3. What is the maximum number of cut or copied items that can be placed on the Office Clipboard?
   a. 6
   b. 12
   c. 18
   d. 24

4. Which of the following methods of moving entries displays a pop-up menu when the mouse button is released?
   a. Cut and Paste
   b. Drag and Drop
   c. Right Drag and Drop
   d. All of the above

Skill Builders

Skill Builder 16.1 Use Copy and Paste

1. Open the workbook named Skill Builder 16.1.

2. Select the range A1:E2.

3. Click the Copy 📋 button.

4. Click Cell A10, and click the Paste 📋 button.

5. Change the year 2003 in the pasted heading to 2002.

6. Select the city names and the Total and Average headings in the range A3:A8.

7. Click Copy 📋, click Cell A12, and then click Paste 📋.

8. Use AutoSum **Σ** to compute the totals in Rows 7 and 16.

9. Click Cell B8, and enter the function =AVERAGE(B3:B6).

10. Use Copy 📋 and Paste 📋 to copy the formula with the AVERAGE function across Rows 8 and 17.
    You can safely copy this formula to both Rows 8 and 17 because the range in the function includes four cells (B3:B6). The formulas in Rows 8 and 17 both require AVERAGE functions that average four cells.

11. Click Cell B20, and enter the formula =B7−B16.

12. Copy this formula across Row 20.

13. Enter a formula in Cell B21 that computes the difference between the averages for 2003 and 2002, and then copy the formula across Row 21.
    Your completed worksheet should match the following example.

14. Save the changes to the workbook, press (CTRL)+(~), and then close the workbook.

	A	B	C	D	E
1	Quality Greeting Cards - 2003 Customer Complaints				
2		Christmas	Easter	Valentines	Thanksgiving
3	Boston	27	43	14	34
4	Los Angeles	31	47	19	39
5	New York	35	51	24	44
6	St. Louis	39	55	29	49
7	Total	132	196	86	166
8	Average	33	49	21.5	41.5
9					
10	Quality Greeting Cards - 2002 Customer Complaints				
11		Christmas	Easter	Valentines	Thanksgiving
12	Boston	19	31	16	24
13	Los Angeles	22	34	18	26
14	New York	25	37	20	28
15	St. Louis	28	40	22	30
16	Total	94	142	76	108
17	Average	23.5	35.5	19	27
18					
19	Differences Between 2003 and 2002				
20	Totals	38	54	10	58
21	Averages	9.5	13.5	2.5	14.5

Skill Builder 16.2 **Use AutoFormat**

In this exercise, you will open a workbook on your exercise diskette. You will use AutoFormat to apply an attractive format to the worksheet.

1. Open the workbook named Skill Builder 16.2.

2. Select the range A1:E16, which includes all active cells in the worksheet.

3. Choose Format→AutoFormat from the menu bar.

4. Scroll through the list, choose the List 2 style, and click OK.

5. Click outside the worksheet, and you will be able to see the format.
   The format looks good, although it may be nice to have a slightly larger title.

6. Click Cell A1, and increase the size to 12.
   You can always add your own formatting enhancements to a worksheet after AutoFormat has been used.

7. Save the changes to the workbook, and then close the workbook.

Skill Builder 16.3 **Use Copy and Paste**

1. Open the workbook named Skill Builder 16.3.

2. Select the range A3:E4, which includes all the text entries in Rows 3 and 4.

3. Click the Copy 🔳 button.

4. Click Cell A10, and Paste 🔳 the entries above the second set of numbers.
   Notice that the text formats (including the coloring) were copied with the text.

5. Click Cell A17 and Paste 🔳 the entries above the third set of numbers.

6. Change the headings to **February** and **March** for the second and third sets of numbers.

7. Select the range A5:A8, which includes the names and Totals heading in Column A.

8. Copy 🔳 the selection, and then Paste 🔳 it to Cells A12 and A19.

9. Copy 🔳 the formulas from the totals row below the first set of numbers, and Paste 🔳 them below the second and third sets of numbers.

10. Save the changes to the workbook, and then close the workbook.

Skill Builder 16.4 **Use the AVERAGE Function**

In this exercise, you will open a workbook on your exercise diskette and calculate averages using three methods. First, you will use a formula with parentheses that change the order of calculations. Then, you will enter AVERAGE functions using the keyboard and point mode.

Use a Formula with Parentheses

1. Open the workbook named Skill Builder 16.4.

2. Click Cell B18.

3. Type the formula **=(B4+B9+B14)/3**, and complete the entry.
   The result should equal 193.333 . . . Notice that the formula you entered includes parentheses ( ). The parentheses change the order of calculations. They instruct Excel to add Cells B4, B9, and B14 and then divide the result of that summation by 3. Without the parentheses, Excel would first divide Cell B14 by 3 and then add the result to B4 + B9. This would produce a very different result, and you would not receive the average you are trying to achieve. Keep in mind that the AVERAGE function does this work for you. This formula was used to demonstrate the way an average is calculated and to show how parentheses are used to change the order of calculations.

4. Use the fill handle to copy the formula across Row 18.

Type the AVERAGE Function

5. Click Cell B19.

6. Type the function **=average(b5,b10,b15)**, and complete the entry.
   The result should equal 23.3333. Once again, you can type the function name and arguments in lowercase and Excel will convert them to uppercase. Notice that the function you entered has three parameters within the argument. In this function, the parameters are cell references separated by commas. Most functions let you have multiple arguments within the parentheses. Commas always separate the arguments. In this example, the function calculates the average of Cells B5, B10, and B15.

7. Use the fill handle to copy the formula across Row 19.

Use Point Mode

8. Click Cell B20.

9. Type **=average(**.

10. Click Cell B6.
    The reference B6 will be added to the function in the Formula bar.

11. Type a comma **,** and click Cell B11.

12. Type a comma **,** and click Cell B16.

13. Type a closing parenthesis **)**, and complete the entry.
    The result should equal 8.3333. Once again, point mode is helpful in preventing typing errors.

14. Use the fill handle to copy the formula across Row 20.

15. Select the cells in Rows 18, 19, and 20, and decrease the decimals ⬛ to 2.

16. Save the changes to the workbook, and then close the workbook.

Assessments

Assessment 16.1

1. Follow these guidelines to create the worksheet shown below:

■ Enter the text and numbers shown below. You will be instructed to format the entries in a moment.

■ Use formulas to calculate the interest charge in Column E and the new balance in Column F. The formulas are as follows:

Interest Charge = 1.5% * (Beginning Balance – Payments)

New Balance = Beginning Balance + Purchases – Payments + Interest Charge

Notice that you must use parentheses in the Interest Charge formula to change the order of calculations. You want Excel to subtract the payments from the beginning balance and then multiply the result by 1.5%. Also, don't type the words Beginning Balance, etc. in the formulas. You should use the appropriate cell references in the formulas.

■ Use AutoSum to calculate the totals in row 10.

■ Use the MAX and MIN functions to calculate the highest and lowest numbers in Rows 11 and 12.

■ Format Rows 5, 10, 11, and 12 as Currency with 0 decimals.

■ Format Rows 6–9 as Comma with 0 decimals.

■ Format the title row and header rows as shown.

■ Apply bold formatting to the entries in rows 10–12.

■ Print the worksheet when you have finished.

■ Save the workbook as **Assessment 16.1**, and then close the workbook.

	A	B	C	D	E	F
1	Bill's Hot Tubs - Accounts Receivable Report					
2						
3		Beginning			Interest	
4	Customer	Balance	Purchases	Payments	Charge	New Balance
5	Zelton	$2,000	$2,300	$1,000		
6	Ranier	2,450	1,000	2,450		
7	Worthington	5,400	2,190	3,000		
8	Alonzo	3,400	500	3,400		
9	Barton	100	3,400	100		
10	Totals					
11	Highest					
12	Lowest					

Assessment 16.2

1. Follow these guidelines to create the worksheet shown on the following page:

- Enter all the numbers and text as shown. Use the Copy and Paste or Drag and Drop techniques to copy the text or numbers whenever possible. For example, all three of the Wilson family children were given the same allowances in all four years. Therefore, you can enter the data in Row 5 and then copy Row 5 to Rows 10 and 15.

- Use Increase Indent ▦ to indent the allowance, saved, and interest earned entries in Column A, as shown.

- Calculate the interest earned with the formula Interest Earned = Saved * Interest Rate. Use the interest rates shown in the following rate table. You will notice that the interest rates change from year to year.

2001	2002	2003	2004
3.5%	4.5%	6.5%	6.5%

- Use AutoSum to calculate the Total Interest in Cells F7, F12, and F17.

- Calculate the Total Family Interest in Cell F19 as the sum of Cells F7, F12, and F17.

- Apply a Currency with 2 decimals format to all cells containing formulas in Rows 7, 12, 17, and 19.

- Apply Bold formatting to all entries in rows 7, 12, 17, and 19.

- Widen all columns as necessary.

2. Your completed worksheet should match the example shown below; however, yours will contain the results to the formulas.

	A	B	C	D	E	F
1	Wilson Family Allowances					
2						
3		2001	2002	2003	2004	Total Interest
4	Jason					
5	Allowance	260	300	300	340	
6	Saved	120	110	200	220	
7	**Interest Earned**					
8						
9	Cindy					
10	Allowance	260	300	300	340	
11	Saved	120	110	200	220	
12	**Interest Earned**					
13						
14	Betty					
15	Allowance	260	300	300	340	
16	Saved	130	290	280	310	
17	**Interest Earned**					
18						
19	**Total Family Interest 2001-2004**					

3. Print the workbook, save it as **Assessment 16.2**, and then close it.

Assessment 16.3

1. Open the workbook named **Assessment 16.3**.

2. Use the Classic 3 AutoFormat style to format the worksheet as shown below.

3. Print the workbook, save the changes, and then close the workbook.

	A	B	C	D	E	F	G
1	Diane's Café - Employee Hourly Time Log						
2							
3	Employee	Wednesday	Thursday	Friday	Saturday	Sunday	Totals
4	Mary Johnson	6.5		5	6.5	4	22
5	Cliff Packard	4	6	6.5	6.5	4	27
6	Helen Martinez	4	6	6.5	6.5		23
7	Sarah Stonestown		4	4	4		12
8	Totals	14.5	16	22	23.5	8	84

Critical Thinking

Critical Thinking 16.1 On Your Own

Stacy Sanchez is a freelance graphic designer and Web site developer. Stacy specializes in helping small businesses establish corporate identities. Stacy's mastery of the computer allows her to transform creative ideas into stunning visual designs that win over customers and provide her with lucrative contracts. She wants to focus her energies on the types of customers that produce the highest rates of return. Stacy has asked you to set up a worksheet to help her analyze her customer base. She provides you with the following initial data.

Company Type	Number of Projects	Total Billings	Total Hours
Consulting	14	$25,900	235
Technology	23	$81,420	679
Manufacturing	6	$16,200	171
Food Service	8	$15,200	179
Retail Sales	12	$30,480	311

Calculate the average billings per project for each company type. Calculate the average hourly billing rate for each company type. Use the AVERAGE function to calculate the average total billings and the average hourly rate for all company types combined. Use AutoFormat to apply attractive formats to the worksheet. Save the workbook as **Critical Thinking 16.1**.

Critical Thinking 16.2 On Your Own

Marina Berkman is a manager in the research department of CTA, Inc. CTA prepares studies on consumer buying habits for companies and organizations throughout the United States. Marina has asked you to prepare a worksheet that will record the food-buying habits of consumers. The worksheet must record on a daily basis the amount of money spent on groceries, breakfast out, lunch out, dinner out, and snacks out. The worksheet should record the information for one person for an entire week. Enter the data you desire and include totals of all expenditures for each day of the week and for each expenditure type. Use the AVERAGE function to calculate the average daily expenditures for each expenditure type. Format all numbers in the worksheet as Currency style with two decimals, and apply formats of your choice using the Formatting toolbar. Save your workbook as **Critical Thinking 16.2**.

Critical Thinking 16.3 On Your Own

Mary Perkins is the Customer Service Manager at a large retail store that sells everything from potato chips to televisions sets. Mary has instructed you to set up a worksheet to track customer returns. The worksheet should include the customer name, item name, SKU code, purchase price, purchase date, return date, and reason for return. Enter five items into your worksheet using your imagination to determine the product names, SKU codes, price, dates, etc. Organize the worksheet rows by customer name in alphabetical order. Save your workbook as **Critical Thinking 16.3**.

Critical Thinking 16.4 Web Research

You have been assigned the task of setting up a worksheet that tracks and analyzes an investment portfolio of publicly traded stocks. You are given the following information as a starting point.

Symbol	Purchase Price	Shares Purchased
CORL	6	500
ORCL	25	100
LU	54	200
MSFT	70	300
GLC	45	60
HAL	25	250

Use Internet Explorer and a search engine of your choice to locate a Web site that offers free stock quotes. Use the site you locate and the symbols shown in the preceding table to determine the current price at which the stocks are trading and the company names associated with the symbols. Set up a worksheet that contains the information shown in the preceding table. Also, include the company name and current price of each stock in the worksheet. Use formulas to calculate the initial value of each investment and the current value based upon the quotes you receive. Calculate the gain or loss of each stock in dollars. Calculate the percentage gain or loss of each stock. Use the SUM function to calculate the total value of the initial portfolio and the total current portfolio value. Calculate the total gain or loss for the portfolio. Use the AVERAGE function to calculate the average gain or loss percentage of the entire portfolio. Rearrange the worksheet rows until they are sorted in alphabetical order based upon the symbols. Format the worksheet using the Autoformat of your choice. Save your workbook as **Critical Thinking 16.4**.

Critical Thinking 16.5 Web Research

Use Internet Explorer and a search engine of your choice to locate five Web sites that sell music CDs. Choose five of your favorite CDs, and set up a worksheet to categorize and analyze the information you find. In particular, include the name of the company Web site, the URL, the CD title, the artist, the price of the CD, and the freight costs. Gather this information for all five CDs from all five Web sites. Use formulas to calculate the total cost of each CD from each Web site. Use the MIN and MAX functions to determine the least expensive site and the most expensive site for each CD. Format your worksheet. Save your workbook as **Critical Thinking 16.5**.

LESSON 17

Creating an Impact with Charts

In this lesson, you will use Excel's Chart Wizard to create various types of charts. Charting is an important skill to have when using worksheets because comparisons, trends, and other relationships are often conveyed more effectively with charts. You will use the Chart Wizard to create bar charts, column charts, line charts, and pie charts. In addition, you will learn how to edit and format chart objects.

IN THIS LESSON

Additional learning resources are available at labpub.com/learn/oe3/

Case Study

Cynthia Robbins is the founder and CEO of AutoSoft—a rapidly growing software development company. Cynthia has asked her sales manager, Gary Roberts, to prepare several charts depicting revenue for the 2003 fiscal year. Cynthia wants charts that compare sales in the various quarters, the growth trend throughout the year, and the contributions of each sales rep to the total company sales. Gary uses Excel's Chart Wizard to produce impressive charts that meet Cynthia's high standards.

A column chart

A line chart

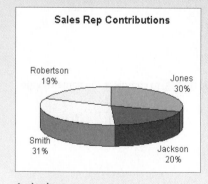

A pie chart

Managing Worksheets

!WARNING!

You cannot undo a deleted worksheet.

Excel displays three worksheets in a new workbook. You can insert new worksheets up to a maximum of 255 sheets per workbook. Each worksheet is identified by a tab located at the bottom of the sheet. You can rename, insert, delete, move, and copy worksheets.

QR > **QUICK REFERENCE: MANAGING WORKSHEETS**

Task	Procedure
Activate worksheet.	Click the desired worksheet tab.
Rename worksheet.	Double-click the worksheet tab, type a new name, and tap (ENTER).
Change Worksheet Tab Color.	Click anywhere in the desired worksheet and choose Format→Sheet→Tab Color, or right click the desired sheet tab and choose Tab Color. Choose the desired color and click OK.
Insert worksheet.	Click anywhere in the desired worksheet and choose Insert→Worksheet. The new worksheet is inserted to the left of the current sheet.
Delete worksheet.	Click anywhere in the desired worksheet, choose Edit→Delete Sheet, and click OK.
Move worksheet.	Drag the worksheet tab to the desired position in the worksheet order.
Copy worksheet.	Choose Edit→Move or Copy Sheet, choose the desired position in the Before Sheet box, click the Create a Copy box, and click OK.

Hands-On 17.1 Experiment with Worksheets

!TIP!

You can click anywhere in the worksheet to complete the name change.

1. Open the workbook named Hands-On Lesson 17.

2. Follow these steps to rename Sheet1:

A Double-click the Sheet1 tab at the bottom of the worksheet. The name Sheet1 will become selected.

```
 32
|◄ ◄ ► ►| \ Sales / Sheet2 / Sheet3 /
```

B Type the name **Sales** as shown here. ——

C Tap (ENTER) to complete the name change.

3. Choose Format→Sheet→Tab Color to display the Format Tab Color box.

4. Choose any color and click OK.
   The color you chose will appear as a thin line at the bottom of the sheet tab.

5. Click any other sheet tab and the colored sheet tab will be fully visible.

6. Follow these steps to move the sheet:

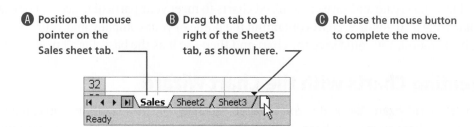

7. Now drag the Sales sheet back to the first position in the sheet order.

8. Click the Sheet3 tab and choose Edit→Delete Sheet from the menu bar.

9. Try clicking Undo, and notice that the sheet cannot be restored.
   Worksheets are permanently deleted when you issue the Edit→Delete Sheet command. The only way to recover a deleted sheet is to close the workbook without saving, and then reopen the workbook.

10. Click the Redo button.
    You had to click Redo because when you clicked Undo in Step 9 you removed the sheet tab color you assigned in Step 4.

11. Choose Insert→Worksheet from the menu bar.
    A new sheet will be inserted to the left of the current sheet.

12. Drag the new sheet to the right of Sheet2, and rename it Sheet3.

13. Click the Sales sheet tab, and continue with the next topic.

Chart Concepts

It is often easier to interpret numerical data if it is presented in a chart. Excel lets you create and modify a variety of charts. Excel provides 14 major chart types. Each chart type also has several subtypes from which you can choose. Excel literally has a chart for every occasion.

Chart Placement

You can embed a chart in a worksheet so that it appears alongside the worksheet data. You can also place a chart on a separate worksheet. This prevents the chart from cluttering the worksheet containing the data. Regardless of their placement, charts are always linked to the data from which they were created. Charts are automatically updated when worksheet data changes.

Chart Types

Each chart type represents data in a different manner. You can present the same data in completely different ways by changing the chart type. For this reason, you should always use the chart type that most effectively represents your data.

User-Defined Charts

Excel lets you create and save customized charts to meet your particular needs. For example, you could create a customized chart containing the name of your company and your company color(s) in the background. You could save the chart and then use it as the basis for all new charts of that type.

Creating Charts with the Chart Wizard

Excel's Chart Wizard 📊 guides you through each step of chart creation. You can also edit and enhance a chart after it has been created. The first, and arguably the most important step in creating a chart, is to select the data you want included in the chart. Many beginners find this step to be the most difficult because they are unsure how Excel will interpret the selected data. You will receive plenty of practice selecting data in this lesson.

Column Charts and Bar Charts

Column charts compare values (numbers) using vertical bars. Bar charts compare values using horizontal bars. Each column or bar represents a value from the worksheet. Column charts and bar charts are most useful for comparing sets of values.

Category Axis and Value Axis

The horizontal line that forms the base of a column chart or bar chart is called the *category axis*. The category axis typically measures units of time such as days, months, or quarters. The vertical line on the left side of a column chart or bar chart is known as the *value axis*. The value axis typically measures values such as dollars. Most chart types (including column charts and bar charts) have a category and value axis. The following illustrations show the column chart you will create in the next few exercises. The illustrations show the objects that are present on most column charts and the corresponding data that was used to create the chart. Take a few minutes to study these illustrations carefully.

The chart on the following page was created using the selected data shown here. Notice the Total row was not included in the selection. The column chart compares the sales numbers for the individual quarters, but it does not include the total sales from Row 9.

	A	B	C	D	E
1	Autosoft 2003 Quarterly Sales				
2					
3		Q1	Q2	Q3	Q4
4	Jones				
5	Jackson	100,000	230,000	280,000	230,000
6	Smith	50,000	130,000	170,000	200,000
7	Robertson	120,000	120,000	320,000	340,000
8		90,000	50,000	120,000	270,000
9	total	$ 360,000	$ 530,000	$ 890,000	$ 1,040,000

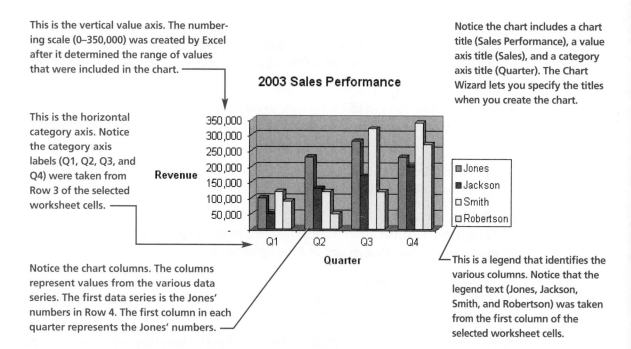

This is the vertical value axis. The numbering scale (0–350,000) was created by Excel after it determined the range of values that were included in the chart.

This is the horizontal category axis. Notice the category axis labels (Q1, Q2, Q3, and Q4) were taken from Row 3 of the selected worksheet cells.

Notice the chart includes a chart title (Sales Performance), a value axis title (Sales), and a category axis title (Quarter). The Chart Wizard lets you specify the titles when you create the chart.

Notice the chart columns. The columns represent values from the various data series. The first data series is the Jones' numbers in Row 4. The first column in each quarter represents the Jones' numbers.

This is a legend that identifies the various columns. Notice that the legend text (Jones, Jackson, Smith, and Robertson) was taken from the first column of the selected worksheet cells.

 ## Hands-On 17.2 **Create Two Charts**

The Hands-On Lesson 17 workbook should still be open from the previous exercise.

Create a Column Chart on a Separate Chart Sheet

1. Select the range A3:E7 as shown on the previous page.

2. Click the Chart Wizard 🔳 button on the Standard toolbar.
   The Chart Wizard dialog box will appear.

3. Follow these steps to explore the dialog box:

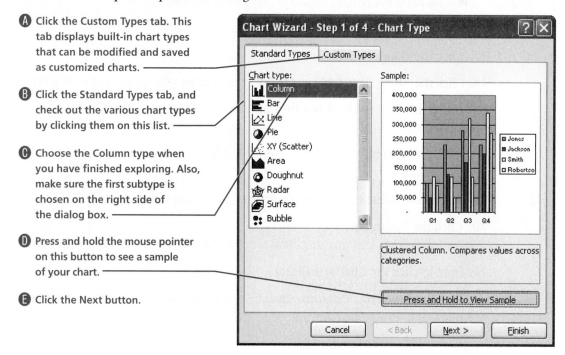

Ⓐ Click the Custom Types tab. This tab displays built-in chart types that can be modified and saved as customized charts.

Ⓑ Click the Standard Types tab, and check out the various chart types by clicking them on this list.

Ⓒ Choose the Column type when you have finished exploring. Also, make sure the first subtype is chosen on the right side of the dialog box.

Ⓓ Press and hold the mouse pointer on this button to see a sample of your chart.

Ⓔ Click the Next button.

The Chart Wizard—Step 2 of 4 box will appear. This box lets you choose a different range of cells. Notice that the range in the dialog box is =Sales!$A$3:$E$7. Sales is the worksheet name, and the dollar signs indicate that these are absolute cell references. For now, just ignore the dollar signs, and think of the range as A3:E7.

4. The range Sales!$A$3:$E$7 is correct, so click the Next button.
   The Step 3 box contains 6 tabs that let you set various chart options. You will explore these options in the next few steps.

5. Click the Titles tab and note the three available titles.
   You will add titles to a chart in the next exercise.

6. Click the Axes tab.
   The options on the Axes tab let you hide the labels on the category axis and value axis. You will almost always want to leave these options set to the default settings.

7. Click the Gridlines tab.
   Gridlines help identify the values in the chart. Your chart should have major gridlines for the value axis displayed. The gridlines are the horizontal lines across the chart.

8. Feel free to click the various gridlines boxes and notice how they appear in the Preview window.

9. Click the Legend tab.
   Notice the legend on the right side of the Preview window. The legend identifies the various columns. For example, the columns for Jones are identified by a color that also appears in the legend.

10. Remove the check from the Show Legend box, and the legend will vanish.

11. Click the Show Legend box to redisplay the legend.

12. Click the Data Labels tab.
    Data labels display the values from the worksheet on top of the columns.

13. Click the Value option to display values at the top of each column.
    The numbers will be very crowded in the Preview window.

14. Remove the check from the Value box to remove the data labels.

15. Click the Data Table tab.

16. Click the Show Data Table check box, and a table will appear below the Preview chart.

17. Take a moment to check out the data table, then remove the check from the Show Data Table box.

18. Click the Next button, and the Step 4 of 4 box will appear.

19. Click the As New Sheet option.
    This option instructs Excel to create the chart on a separate chart sheet.

20. Click the Finish button.
    Look at the sheet tabs, and notice that the chart has been created on a new sheet named Chart1.

21. Double-click the Chart1 sheet tab.

22. Type the new name **Column Chart**, and tap (ENTER) to complete the name change.

Create an Embedded 3-D Column Chart

23. Click the Sales sheet tab. The range A3:E7 should still be selected.

24. Click the Chart Wizard button.

25. Choose the fourth column chart subtype, as shown to the right.
    This subtype is known as a Clustered Column with a 3-D Visual Effect.

26. Click the Next button, then click Next again on the Step 2 of 4 box.

27. Click the Titles tab, and follow these steps in the Step 3 of 4 box:

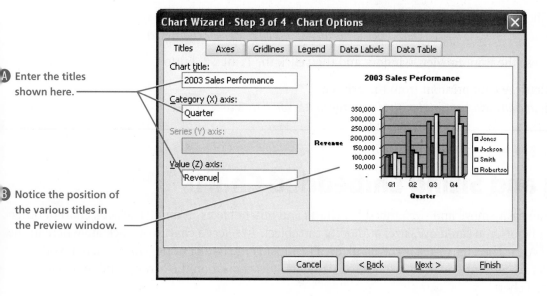

A Enter the titles shown here.

B Notice the position of the various titles in the Preview window.

28. Click the Next button.

29. Leave the chart location set to As Object In on the Step 4 of 4 box and click Finish.
    Excel will embed the chart in your worksheet. The Chart toolbar will most likely appear as well.

Previewing and Printing Charts

You can use the Print Preview and Print buttons to preview or print charts. If a chart is on a separate chart sheet, you must first activate it by clicking the sheet tab. If a chart is embedded, you must first select the chart before clicking the Print Preview or Print buttons.

Hands-On 17.3 Use Print Preview and Print a Chart

1. Click anywhere in the worksheet to deselect the chart.

2. Click the Print Preview button.
   Notice that both the worksheet and part or all of the embedded chart are displayed.

3. Click the Close button on the Print Preview toolbar.

4. Click in the blank area near one of the corners of the chart.
   Black squares known as sizing handles should appear on the corners and edges of the chart. Sizing handles indicate that the chart or one of the chart objects is selected.

5. Click the Print Preview button, and only the chart should be displayed.
   At this point, you could print the chart by using the Print button on the Print Preview toolbar. However, you will close the chart and then print it on the separate chart sheet.

6. Click the Close button on the Print Preview toolbar.

7. Click the Column Chart worksheet tab to activate that worksheet.

8. Click the Print Preview button, and notice that the chart is displayed.
   You don't need to select a chart prior to printing if it is on a separate chart sheet.

9. Close the Print Preview window, and then click the Print button.

10. Retrieve your printout from the printer.
    Your chart will be printed in shades of gray unless you have a color printer.

Moving and Sizing Embedded Charts

You can easily move and size embedded charts and other objects. You must select a chart or other object before you can move, size, or modify the object. To select a chart, you click anywhere in the Chart Area. The Chart Area is the blank area just inside the border of the chart where no other objects are present. Small squares called sizing handles appear on the corners and four sides of a selected chart.

QR▶ **QUICK REFERENCE: MOVING AND SIZING EMBEDDED CHARTS**

Task	Procedure
Move an embedded chart.	Drag the selected chart to a new location.
Change the chart size.	Drag any sizing handle.
Change the size while maintaining original proportions.	Press (SHIFT) while dragging a corner-sizing handle.

Hands-On 17.4 Move and Size the Embedded Chart

1. Click the Sales worksheet tab to activate that worksheet.

2. Click anywhere outside of the chart to deselect the chart.
   The sizing handles will vanish.

3. Use the Zoom Control to zoom to 50% of normal.
   This will give you plenty of room to move and size the chart.

4. Follow these steps to move and size the chart:

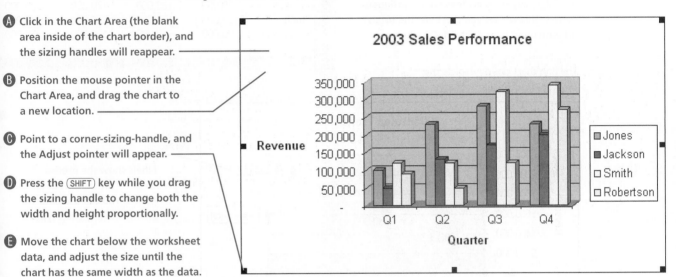

A Click in the Chart Area (the blank area inside of the chart border), and the sizing handles will reappear.

B Position the mouse pointer in the Chart Area, and drag the chart to a new location.

C Point to a corner-sizing-handle, and the Adjust pointer will appear.

D Press the (SHIFT) key while you drag the sizing handle to change both the width and height proportionally.

E Move the chart below the worksheet data, and adjust the size until the chart has the same width as the data.

5. Click anywhere outside of the chart to deselect it, then zoom to 100%.

6. Take a moment to study your chart and the worksheet data that was used to create it.
   Make sure you understand the relationship between the columns and the worksheet data.

7. Click Cell B4.

8. Enter the number **300,000** and watch the first column in the chart rise.
   Charts are linked to the worksheet data. They always reflect changes in the data even if they are placed in a separate chart sheet.

9. Click Cell B4 again, and enter the number **1,000,000**.
   Notice that 1000000 is much larger than the other numbers in the worksheet. Notice how the other columns are very small, and it is difficult to determine their values in the chart. The large number changes the scale of the value axis so much that it makes the chart difficult to interpret.

10. Click Cell B4 again, and enter the number **100,000**.

11. Save the changes, and continue with the next topic.

Line Charts

Line charts are most useful for comparing trends over a period of time. For example, line charts are often used to show stock market activity where the upward or downward trend is important. Like column charts, line charts also have a category axis and value axis. Line charts also use the same or similar objects as column charts. The illustration below shows a line chart depicting the trend in quarterly sales throughout the year. Study the illustration and the accompanying worksheet.

The chart below was created using the selected data shown here. Notice that the data is in two separate ranges. You will use the (CTRL) key to select these non-contiguous ranges. This will let you chart just the totals for each quarter, and the Q1–Q4 labels.

The line chart clearly depicts the upward trend in sales volume.

2					
3		Q1	Q2	Q3	Q4
4	Jones	100,000	230,000	280,000	230,000
5	Jackson	50,000	130,000	170,000	200,000
6	Smith	120,000	120,000	320,000	340,000
7	Robertson	90,000	50,000	120,000	270,000
8					
9	Total	$ 360,000	$ 530,000	$ 890,000	$ 1,040,000
10					

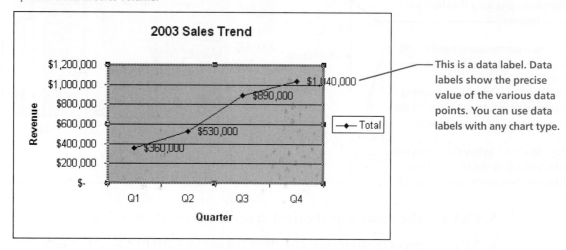

This is a data label. Data labels show the precise value of the various data points. You can use data labels with any chart type.

Hands-On 17.5 Create a Line Chart

In this exercise, you will create a line chart in the Sales sheet. When you are finished, the Sales sheet will contain the data and both the column and line charts.

Shrink and Move the Column Chart

1. Click in the chart area of the column chart, and sizing handles will appear on the chart border.

2. Press the (SHIFT) key while dragging a corner-sizing handle until the chart is very small (approximately 1" high).
   Pressing (SHIFT) while sizing the chart maintains the proportions. You will increase the size of the chart later in this exercise.

3. Position the mouse pointer in the chart area, and drag the chart to the top-right corner of the screen (just to the right of the worksheet data).

4. Click outside the chart to deselect it.

Create the Line Chart

5. Follow these steps to select the data for the line chart:

		Q1	Q2	Q3	Q4
2					
3		Q1	Q2	Q3	Q4
4	Jones	100,000	230,000	280,000	230,000
5	Jackson	50,000	130,000	170,000	200,000
6	Smith	120,000	120,000	320,000	340,000
7	Robertson	90,000	50,000	120,000	270,000
8					
9	Total	$ 360,000	$ 530,000	$ 890,000	$ 1,040,000
10					

A Select the range A3:E3.

B Press the (CTRL) key while you select the range A9:E9. Both ranges should be selected.

6. Click the Chart Wizard [image] button.

7. Choose Line from the Chart type list, and choose the fourth subtype, as shown to the right.

8. Click Next twice to display the Step 3 of 4 box.

9. If necessary, click the Titles tab on the Step 3 of 4 box.

10. Enter the titles in the Step 3 of 4 box as shown below.
    When you have completed entering the titles, your sample chart should match the chart shown in the following illustration.

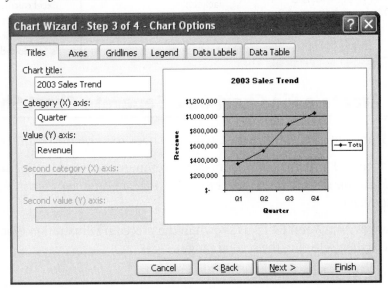

11. Click the Finish button.
    There was no need to click Next on the Step 4 of 4 box because we want the chart embedded in the current worksheet. You can click Finish at any step in the Chart Wizard.

12. Take a few moments to examine your chart. In particular, notice the relationship between the data and the points on the line.

Pie Charts

Pie charts are useful for comparing parts of a whole. For example, pie charts are often used in budgets to show how the budget is allocated. You typically select two sets of data when creating a pie chart. You select the values to be represented by the pie slices and labels to identify the slices. The following illustration shows a worksheet and accompanying 3-D pie chart. Notice that the worksheet has a total column. You will create the total column in the next exercise.

3		Q1	Q2	Q3	Q4	Total
4	Jones	100,000	230,000	280,000	230,000	840,000
5	Jackson	50,000	130,000	170,000	200,000	550,000
6	Smith	120,000	120,000	320,000	340,000	900,000
7	Robertson	90,000	50,000	120,000	270,000	530,000

The names in Column A will become labels on the pie slices. The numbers in Column F will determine the size of the slices.

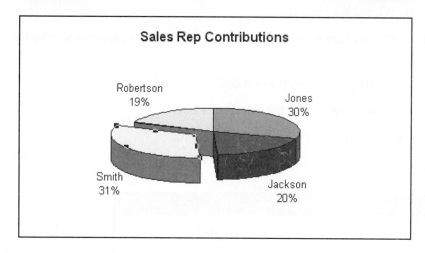

Excel calculates the percentages based upon the numbers you select. Notice that the Smith slice is "exploded" out from the pie.

 ## Hands-On 17.6 **Create a Pie Chart on a Separate Chart Sheet**

1. Click Cell F3, and enter the word **Total** (you may need to move the column or line chart).

2. Select the range F4:F7, and use AutoSum $\boxed{\Sigma}$ to compute the totals for Column F.
   The totals calculate the total annual sales for each sales rep. Your totals should match those shown in the preceding illustration.

3. Select the ranges A4:A7 and F4:F7 as shown in the preceding illustration (you will need to use the (CTRL) key when selecting the second range).

4. Click the Chart Wizard 📊 button.

5. Choose Pie from the Chart type list, and choose the second subtype as shown to the right.

6. Click Next twice to display the Step 3 of 4 box.

7. If necessary, click the Titles tab on the Step 3 of 4 box.

8. Type **Sales Rep Contributions** as the Chart title.

9. Click the Legend tab, and remove the check from the Show legend box.
   The legend won't be needed because you will add data labels in the next step.

10. Click the Data Labels tab, and check the Category Name and Percentage boxes.
    Each pie slice should have the sales rep name and percentage of the total sales displayed.

11. Click Next to display the Step 4 of 4 box.

12. Choose the As New Sheet option, and type the name **Pie Chart** in the As New Sheet box.

13. Click the Finish button.
    Notice that the chart has been created on a separate sheet, and that the name Pie Chart has been assigned to the new sheet. The sheet was named Pie Chart because you typed this name in the As New Sheet box in Step 12.

14. Save the changes to your workbook, and continue with the next topic.

Modifying Charts

You can modify any chart object after the chart has been created. For example, you can add or remove objects, such as legends or data labels. You can change the size, font, and color of titles. You can even move an embedded chart to a separate chart sheet and vice versa.

Using the Chart Wizard to Modify Charts

You can change the setup of a chart using the Chart Wizard. Simply click the desired embedded chart, or click a separate chart sheet, and then click the Chart Wizard button. You can move through all four screens in the Chart Wizard, choosing options as you do when a chart is first created.

The Chart Menu

When you activate a separate chart sheet or click an embedded chart, a Chart option appears on the menu bar. The first four options on the Chart menu display the same screens that appear in the Chart Wizard. You can add, remove, or modify chart objects using the desired screen(s) and change the chart location from embedded to separate sheet and vice versa. The 3-D View option on the Chart menu is useful for changing the elevation and rotation of pie charts.

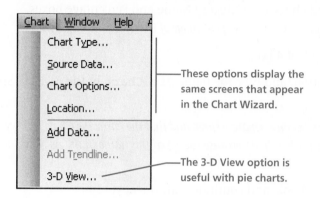

These options display the same screens that appear in the Chart Wizard.

The 3-D View option is useful with pie charts.

Hands-On 17.7 Use the Chart Wizard and the Chart Menu

Move the Line Chart to a Separate Sheet

1. Click the Sales sheet tab.

2. Click in the chart area of the line chart, and sizing handles should appear on the chart borders.
   Notice that the Chart option now appears on the menu bar because a chart is selected.

3. Choose Chart→Location from the menu bar.
   Notice that the dialog box that appears is the same one that appears in the fourth step of the Chart Wizard.

4. Choose the As New Sheet option, and type **Line Chart** in the As New Sheet box.

5. Click OK to move the chart to a separate chart sheet.
   Notice that the Chart option is available on the menu bar even though the chart is not selected. The Chart option is always available in chart sheets.

6. Choose Chart→Location from the menu bar.

7. Choose the As Object In option and choose Sales from the drop-down list of sheet names.

8. Click OK to move the chart back into the Sales sheet as an embedded chart.

9. Now move the chart back to a separate chart sheet named Line Chart as you did in steps 2 through 5.

Add Data Labels to the Column Chart

10. Click the Sales sheet tab.

11. Click in the chart area of the column chart to select the chart.

12. Now drag the chart below the worksheet data.

13. Drag a corner-sizing handle until the chart is as wide as the worksheet data. If necessary, adjust the chart position until it is just below the data.

14. Click the Chart Wizard button.

15. Click Next twice, and then click the Data Labels tab.
    Notice that the same screens appear as when you created a new chart.

16. Choose the Value option, and click the Finish button.
    Excel displays data labels at the top of each column. The data labels display the actual values from the worksheet. Notice, however, that the data labels are too crowded. Data labels aren't really appropriate in this column chart because they crowd the chart.

17. Make sure the chart is still selected, and choose Chart→Chart Options from the menu bar.
    Notice that this is the same screen that appears in Step 3 of the Chart Wizard.

18. Remove the check from the Value box, and click OK to remove the data labels.

19. Feel free to experiment with the Chart menu and the Chart Wizard, and then continue with the next topic.

Chart Objects

Charts are composed of various objects. For example, the legends, titles, and columns are all types of objects. You must select an object before you can perform an action on that object. You can select an object by clicking it with the mouse. Once an object is selected, you can delete, move, size, and format the object. You delete a selected object by tapping the (DELETE) key. You move a selected object by dragging it with the mouse. You change the size of a selected object by dragging a sizing handle.

Formatting Chart Objects

You can use buttons on the Formatting toolbar to format titles and other objects containing text. You can also use the Fill Color button on the Formatting toolbar to apply fill colors and fill effects to selected objects.

These buttons on the Formatting toolbar can be used to format text objects and add fill colors to objects.

Hands-On 17.8 Format Titles, and Fill the Chart Area

Change Text in the Titles

1. Click the chart title in the column chart, and it will become selected.

2. Click the mouse pointer I just in front of the word Performance in the title.
   The flashing insertion point should be just in front of the word Performance.

3. Type the word **Rep** and tap the (SPACE BAR) to make the title 2003 Sales Rep Performance.

4. Click the Revenue title (the title on the left side of the chart), and it will become selected.

5. Now select the word Revenue within the title box by double-clicking the word.

6. Type the replacement word **Sales**.

Format the Titles

7. Click the Chart title 2003 Sales Rep Performance.

8. Click the Font Color 🅰 drop-down button on the Formatting toolbar, and choose a blue color.

9. Format the Sales and Quarter titles with the same blue color.

Apply a Fill Color to the Chart Area

10. Click the chart area to select the entire chart.

11. Click the Fill Color 🎨 drop-down button on the Formatting toolbar, and choose a light fill color.
    The entire chart area should be filled.

12. Feel free to experiment with the formatting techniques discussed in this exercise.

The Chart Toolbar

The Chart toolbar appears when a chart sheet is active, or when an embedded chart is selected. The Chart toolbar is used primarily for formatting chart objects. You can use the View→Toolbars→Chart command to display the Chart toolbar if it does not automatically appear.

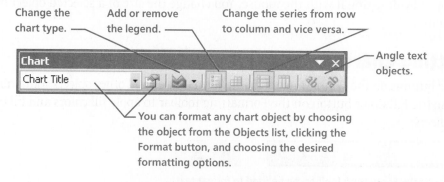

Change the chart type. Add or remove the legend. Change the series from row to column and vice versa. Angle text objects.

You can format any chart object by choosing the object from the Objects list, clicking the Format button, and choosing the desired formatting options.

 ## Hands-On 17.9 **Use the Chart Toolbar**

Change the Orientation of the Sales Title

1. Choose View→Toolbars from the menu bar.

2. If the Chart option is already checked, close the menu by clicking in the worksheet. Otherwise, choose Chart and the Chart toolbar will appear.
   The Chart toolbar may be anchored above the worksheet, or it may float in the worksheet area.

3. Click the Sales title on the left side of the chart.
   All of the buttons on the Chart toolbar should now be available.

4. Follow these steps to display a formatting box for the title:

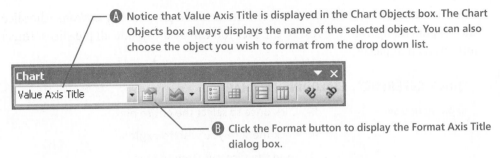

A Notice that Value Axis Title is displayed in the Chart Objects box. The Chart Objects box always displays the name of the selected object. You can also choose the object you wish to format from the drop down list.

B Click the Format button to display the Format Axis Title dialog box.

5. Click the various dialog box tabs, and notice that you can format the title text, apply a font color, and set other formatting options.

6. Click the Alignment tab.

7. Follow these steps to change the orientation to vertical:

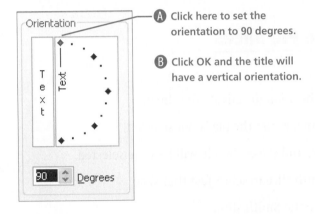

A Click here to set the orientation to 90 degrees.

B Click OK and the title will have a vertical orientation.

Experiment with the Chart Toolbar

8. Click in the chart area to select the entire chart.

9. Follow these steps to explore the Chart toolbar:

A Click the Chart Type drop down button and choose a chart type such as 3-D Cylinder from the bottom row of the list.

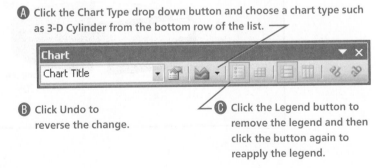

B Click Undo to reverse the change.

C Click the Legend button to remove the legend and then click the button again to reapply the legend.

10. Feel free to experiment with the options on the Chart toolbar.

Exploding Pie Slices

You can make a pie slice stand out from the rest of a pie chart by *exploding* the slice. An exploded slice is pulled out from the rest of the pie. You can also explode all pie slices, thus breaking the pie into individual pieces.

QUICK REFERENCE: EXPLODING PIE CHARTS

Explode one slice.	■ Click once to select the entire pie.
	■ Click the slice you wish to explode.
	■ Drag the slice out from the pie.
Explode all slices.	■ Click once to select the pie.
	■ Drag any slice (without clicking first), and all slices will separate.
Restore an exploded slice or an exploded pie.	■ Select the entire pie, and drag any exploded slice back into the pie.

Hands-On 17.10 Explode Pie Slices

Explode the Smith Slice

1. Click the Pie Chart worksheet tab to activate the sheet.

2. Click in the chart area to make sure the pie is not selected.

3. Click anywhere on the pie, and the entire pie will become selected.

4. Now click once on the Smith slice to select just that slice.

5. Follow this step to explode the Smith slice:

Ⓐ Position the mouse pointer on the Smith slice and drag it out of the pie, as shown here.

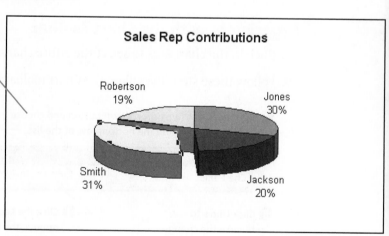

6. Drag the Smith slice back until the pie is whole again.

7. Click outside of the pie to deselect it.

8. Click anywhere on the pie, and the entire pie will become selected.

9. Drag any slice out of the pie, and all of the slices will explode.

10. Reverse the explosion by dragging any slice back to the center of the pie.

11. Now explode just the Smith slice again.

Changing the Rotation and Elevation of Pie Charts

You can rotate a pie chart to bring an important slice into view. Likewise, you can change the elevation to make an important slice more noticeable. You change the rotation and elevation using options on the 3-D View dialog box. The 3-D View dialog box is displayed with the Chart→3-D View command.

Hands-On 17.11 Change the Rotation and Elevation

1. Click outside of the pie, and then click the pie to make sure the entire pie is selected.

2. Choose Chart→3-D View from the menu bar.

3. Follow these steps to adjust the rotation and elevation:

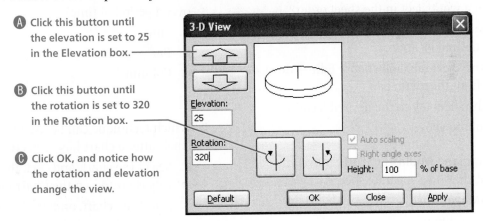

Ⓐ Click this button until the elevation is set to 25 in the Elevation box.

Ⓑ Click this button until the rotation is set to 320 in the Rotation box.

Ⓒ Click OK, and notice how the rotation and elevation change the view.

4. Feel free to experiment with any of the topics you have learned in this lesson.

5. Save your workbook when you have finished, close the workbook, and continue with the end-of-lesson questions and exercises.

Concepts Review

True/False Questions

1. You can rename a worksheet by double-clicking the sheet tab and typing the new name.   TRUE   FALSE

2. Embedded charts are updated when the worksheet data changes.   TRUE   FALSE

3. Charts on separate chart sheets are not updated when the worksheet data changes.   TRUE   FALSE

4. Column charts are most useful for comparing the parts of a whole.   TRUE   FALSE

5. Column charts have a category and value axis.   TRUE   FALSE

6. The Chart Wizard can only be used to create embedded charts.   TRUE   FALSE

7. The Chart Wizard is used to explode pie slices.   TRUE   FALSE

8. You must select a chart before you can move or resize it.   TRUE   FALSE

9. A chart cannot be moved once it is placed on a separate sheet.   TRUE   FALSE

10. Buttons on the Formatting toolbar can be used on chart text objects.   TRUE   FALSE

Multiple Choice Questions

1. Which procedure would you use to change the position of a worksheet in the sheet order?
   a. Double-click the sheet tab, and drag the tab to the desired location.
   b. Click the sheet tab, and choose Edit→Move Sheet from the menu bar.
   c. Drag the sheet tab to the desired location.
   d. None of the above

2. Which command would you use to move an embedded chart to a separate sheet?
   a. Edit→Move Chart
   b. Chart→Location
   c. Chart→Move
   d. This cannot be done.

3. Which chart would be best for showing a trend over a period of time?
   a. Line
   b. Bar
   c. Column
   d. Pie

4. Which technique can be used to insert data labels after a chart has been created?
   a. Select the chart, and click the Data Labels button on the Chart toolbar.
   b. Select the chart, and choose the Insert→Data Labels command.
   c. Select the chart, choose Chart→Chart Options, click the Data Labels tab, and choose the desired data labels format.
   d. Data labels cannot be inserted after a chart has been created.

Skill Builders

Skill Builder 17.1 Create a Column Chart

In this exercise, you will create a column chart to display student enrollments at a university.

Expand a Series

1. Open the workbook named Skill Builder 17.1.
   Notice that the enrollment data has been completed in Column B, but the years have not been completed in Column A. Notice the first two years (1988 and 1989) form the beginning of the series 1988–2004. The best way to expand this series is with the fill handle.

2. Select Cells A4 and A5.

3. Drag the fill handle down to Row 20 to expand the series.

4. Left align ▤ the years in Column A.

Create the Chart

5. Select the range A3:B20.
   This range includes the enrollment data, and the Year and Total Enrollment headings.

6. Click the Chart Wizard ▥ button.

7. Choose the Column chart type and the first subtype.

8. Click Next to display the Step 2 of 4 box.
   Take a moment to study the Step 2 dialog box, and you will notice a problem. Excel is interpreting the years 1988–2004 as numbers. The numbers are appearing as a data series in the chart. The years are the short columns to the left of the tall, thin enrollment data columns. The years should actually be displayed as labels on the horizontal category axis. You will correct this in the next few steps.

9. Click the Series tab on the dialog box.
   The Series tab lets you modify the data series that are plotted in the chart.

10. Follow these steps to remove the years from the series and to add the years as Category (X) axis labels:

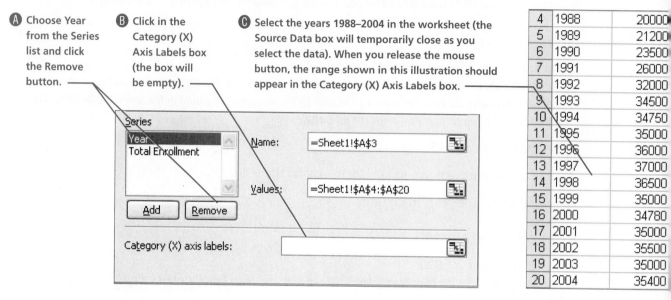

Ⓐ Choose Year from the Series list and click the Remove button. ⎯

Ⓑ Click in the Category (X) Axis Labels box (the box will be empty). ⎯

Ⓒ Select the years 1988–2004 in the worksheet (the Source Data box will temporarily close as you select the data). When you release the mouse button, the range shown in this illustration should appear in the Category (X) Axis Labels box. ⎯

4	1988	20000
5	1989	21200
6	1990	23500
7	1991	26000
8	1992	32000
9	1993	34500
10	1994	34750
11	1995	35000
12	1996	36000
13	1997	37000
14	1998	36500
15	1999	35000
16	2000	34780
17	2001	35000
18	2002	35500
19	2003	35000
20	2004	35400

Notice that the dates are now displayed in an angled fashion on the Category axis.

11. Click Next to continue with Step 3 of 4.

12. Click the Titles tab, and type the title **Student Enrollments** in the Chart Title box.

13. Click the Legend tab, and remove the legend.

14. Click Finish to complete the chart.
    Take a few moments to study your worksheet and chart. Make sure you understand the relationship between the worksheet data and the chart.

Convert the Chart to a Line Chart

Suppose you are interested in seeing only the trend in enrollments as opposed to the enrollments in individual years. You can easily convert this chart to a line chart.

15. Make sure the chart is selected.

16. Choose Chart→Chart Type from the menu bar.

17. Choose Line as the Chart type, and choose the fourth subtype.

18. Click OK to convert the chart to a line chart with data markers.

Format the Chart Title

19. Click the Student Enrollments chart title.

20. Use the Font Color **A** button to format the title with a color.

21. Feel free to format the chart and title in any other way you desire.

22. Save the changes, and then close the workbook.

Skill Builder 17.2 Create a Doughnut Chart

In this exercise, you will create a chart for Holy Doughnuts. The chart will show the contributions of various types of doughnuts to the total sales volume for two different years. What type of chart will you use? Why, a doughnut chart, what else! Like pie charts, doughnut charts are useful for comparing parts of a whole. However, doughnut charts can contain more than one data series. Each ring in a doughnut chart represents a data series.

Set Up the Worksheet

1. If necessary, start a New Workbook, and create the worksheet shown below. Format the numbers in Column C as Comma style with 0 decimals. Also, merge and center the Units Sold heading over Cells B3 and C3 and AutoFit Columns B and C.

	A	B	C	D	E
1	Holy Doughnuts Volume Comparison				
2					
3		Units Sold			
4	Type of Doughnut	2002	2003		
5	Crème Filled	12,000	14,500		
6	Frosted	10,500	9,000		
7	Nut Covered	2,300	2,500		
8	Glazed	7,000	8,200		
9	Old Fashioned	4,500	4,300		

Create the Chart

Doughnut charts function much like pie charts because they are used to compare parts of a whole. Therefore, the data is selected in a manner similar to pie charts.

2. Select the data in the range A4:C9.

3. Click the Chart Wizard button.

4. Choose Doughnut as the Chart type, and choose the first subtype.

5. Click Next twice to display the Step 3 of 4 box.

6. Click the Titles tab, and enter the Chart title **Doughnut Sales: 2002 vs. 2003**.

7. Click the Data Labels tab, and check the Percentage box.

8. Click the Finish button to create an embedded chart.

Format the Percent Labels

9. Click any of the percent labels in the outer ring of the doughnut, and all percentages for the series will be selected.

10. Use the Font Color ![A] button on the Formatting toolbar to choose a high-contrast color such as red or white.

    This will differentiate the numbers in the outer ring from those in the inner ring. Notice that the doughnut chart does not provide a title or label to identify the rings as 2002 or 2003. This is a deficiency that can only be overcome by using a textbox and arrows or lines to label the rings.

11. Save the workbook with the name **Skill Builder 17.2**, and then close the workbook.

Skill Builder 17.3 **Create Pie Charts**

In this exercise, you will create four pie charts to illustrate employee expenses for Hollywood Productions—a motion-picture production company. The pie charts will show how employee costs are divided between departments, and how each department's employee costs are allocated. You will create each chart on a separate chart sheet.

Create the Company Chart

1. Open the workbook named Skill Builder 17.3.

2. Follow these steps to select the required data:

3		Marketing	Production	Finance
4	Salaries	3,400,000	4,500,000	1,200,000
5	Benefits	1,292,000	1,980,000	336,000
6	Travel	1,700,000	1,500,000	120,000
7	**Total**	**$ 6,392,000**	**$ 7,980,000**	**$ 1,656,000**

A Use the mouse to select the range B3:D3, as shown here.

B Press the (CTRL) key while you select the range B7:D7.

3. Click the Chart Wizard ![icon] button, and create the pie chart shown to the right on a separate chart sheet.

   Make sure the chart type, title, and labels match the chart shown here. Also, notice that the chart does not include a legend.

4. Double-click the Chart1 sheet tab, and change the sheet name to **Hollywood Chart**.

   Notice that you can use long names when naming sheets.

5. Rename Sheet1 as **Employee Expense Data**.

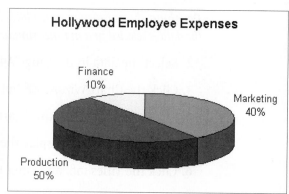

Hollywood Employee Expenses

Finance 10%
Marketing 40%
Production 50%

Create a Pie Chart for the Marketing Department

6. Select the range shown below.

3		Marketing	Production	Finance
4	Salaries	3,400,000	4,500,000	1,200,000
5	Benefits	1,292,000	1,980,000	336,000
6	Travel	1,700,000	1,500,000	120,000
7	Total	$ 6,392,000	$ 7,980,000	$ 1,656,000

7. Click the Chart Wizard button, and create a pie chart on a separate chart sheet. Use the same chart type and labels as in the previous chart, but use the title **Marketing Employee Costs**.

8. Rename the sheet as **Marketing Chart**.

9. Click the Employee Expense Data sheet tab to return to that sheet.

Create Pie Charts for the Production and Finance Departments

10. Use the techniques in this exercise to create the same style pie charts for the Production and Finance departments. Create each chart on a separate chart sheet. Use the chart titles and sheet names shown in the table below. Select data for the Production department chart as shown to the right. You will need to decide how to select the data for the Finance department (although that should be an easy decision to make).

3		Marketing	Production	Finance
4	Salaries	3,400,000	4,500,000	1,200,000
5	Benefits	1,292,000	1,980,000	336,000
6	Travel	1,700,000	1,500,000	120,000
7	Total	$ 6,392,000	$ 7,980,000	$ 1,656,000

Chart	Use This Title	Use This Sheet Name
Production	Production Employee Costs	Production Chart
Finance	Finance Employee Costs	Finance Chart

11. Follow these steps to move the Employee Expense Data sheet tab:

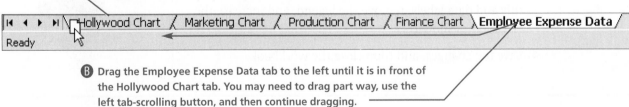

Ⓐ If necessary, scroll to the right using the tab scrolling buttons until the Employee Expense Data tab is visible.

Ⓑ Drag the Employee Expense Data tab to the left until it is in front of the Hollywood Chart tab. You may need to drag part way, use the left tab-scrolling button, and then continue dragging.

Explode Pie Slices and Increase Elevation

12. Click the Hollywood Chart tab to activate it.

13. Click once on the pie, pause, and then click the Production slice (the largest slice).

14. Drag the slice out slightly to explode it.

15. Choose Chart→3-D View from the menu bar.

16. Increase the Elevation ⬆ to 25, and click OK.

17. Click the Marketing Chart sheet tab.

18. Explode the Salaries slice (the largest slice), and increase the Elevation to 25.

19. Explode the largest slice, and increase the Elevation to 25 for the Production and Finance charts.
    Take a few moments to click the various sheet tabs and check out your charts. Feel free to format and enhance your charts in any way.

20. Save the changes, and then close the workbook.

Skill Builder 17.4 **Create a Pie Chart**

In this exercise, you will create a pie chart that shows the budget allocation for a school district.

1. Open the workbook named Skill Builder 17.4.

2. Select the data shown below.

4	Facilities	3,500,000
5	Employee Costs	4,500,000
6	Transportation	540,000
7	Students	2,300,000
8	Equipment	1,200,000

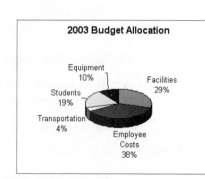

3. Use the Chart Wizard 📊 to create the embedded pie chart shown to the right. Make sure to include the chart title and data labels, remove the legend, and increase the elevation as shown.

4. Save the changes, and then close the workbook.

Skill Builder 17.5 **Create a Line Chart**

In this exercise, you will create a worksheet and line chart to track the trends in a stock portfolio.

1. Start a New Workbook 🗋 .

2. Follow these guidelines to create the worksheet shown to the right:

	A	B	C	D
1	Stock Portfolio Trends			
2				
3		Silicon Technology	Dakota Mining	Anderson Diesel
4	09/06/2003	58 1/2	32	45
5	09/13/2003	59	31	43
6	09/20/2003	56	28	45
7	09/27/2003	59	30 1/8	48
8	10/04/2003	63	33	49
9	10/11/2003	68	34	47
10	10/18/2003	70	34	42
11	10/25/2003	69	36 1/2	38

   - Notice that the dates in Cells A4 and A5 form the beginning of a series. You can enter these dates, select them, and then drag the fill handle down to Cell A11 to complete the series.
   - Columns B–D contain mixed numbers (whole numbers and fractions). Just type the numbers exactly as shown with a space between the whole numbers and the fractions.
   - AutoFit Columns B–D.

3. Select the range A3:D11 (all active cells except for the title).

4. Use the Chart Wizard 📊 to create the line chart shown below. Use the first line chart subtype, and place the chart on a separate chart sheet named Line Chart. Make sure you use the same titles and legend as shown.

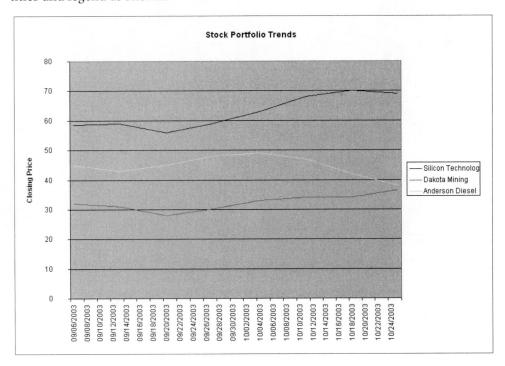

5. Save the workbook with the name **Skill Builder 17.5**, then close the workbook.

Assessments

Assessment 17.1 Create a Line Chart

1. Start a New Workbook 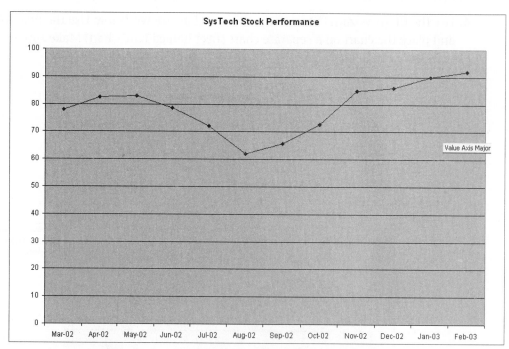, and create the following worksheet:

	A	B	C	D
1	SysTech Stock Performance			
2	March 2002 Through February 2003			
3				
4	Date	Stock Price		
5	03/01/2002	78		
6	04/01/2002	82.6		
7	05/01/2002	83		
8	06/01/2002	78.6		
9	07/01/2002	72		
10	08/01/2002	62		
11	09/01/2002	65.8		
12	10/01/2002	72.6		
13	11/01/2002	85		
14	12/01/2002	86		
15	01/01/2003	90		
16	02/01/2003	92		

2. Use the worksheet data to create the following chart on a separate chart sheet. Make sure you set up the data labels and title as shown.

3. Rename the Chart1 sheet as **Stock Performance**.

4. Rename the Sheet1 sheet as **Supporting Data**.

5. Print both the worksheet and chart.

6. Save the workbook with the name **Assessment 17.1**, then close the workbook.

Assessment 17.2 **Create an Embedded Column Chart**

1. Create the worksheet and embedded column chart shown below. Notice the column chart is two-dimensional. The differences in Row 6 are simply the budget numbers minus the spent numbers. Notice that the negative differences dip below the X-axis in the chart. Adjust the position and size of the embedded chart as shown.

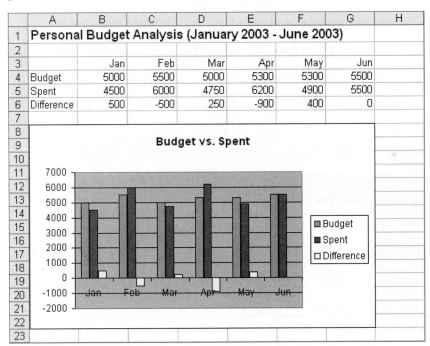

2. Print the worksheet and embedded chart on a single page.

3. Save the workbook with the name **Assessment 17.2**, then close the workbook.

Assessment 17.3 **Create a Worksheet and Pie Chart**

1. Follow these guidelines to create the worksheet and chart shown on the following page:

   ▪ Type all of the numbers and text entries as shown, but use formulas to calculate the New Balance in Column E and the Totals, Highest, and Lowest in Rows 9–11. The formula for New Balance is New Balance = Beginning Balance + Purchases – Payments. The Totals in Row 9 can be calculated with AutoSum. The Highest and Lowest calculations in Rows 10 and 11 can be accomplished with the MIN and MAX functions.

   ▪ Format the worksheet with the AutoFormat Classic 2 style.

   ▪ Create the embedded 3-D pie chart shown in the illustration. The pie chart slices represent the new balance percentages of each customer. The pie chart does not represent any of the data in Rows 9–11.

   ▪ Adjust the position and size of the embedded chart as shown in the illustration.

   ▪ Explode the Bishop slice, and adjust the chart rotation and elevation.

   ▪ Bold all of the pie slice labels, and format the chart title with bold and italics.

2. Print the worksheet and embedded chart on a single page.

3. Save the workbook as **Assessment 17.3**, then close the workbook.

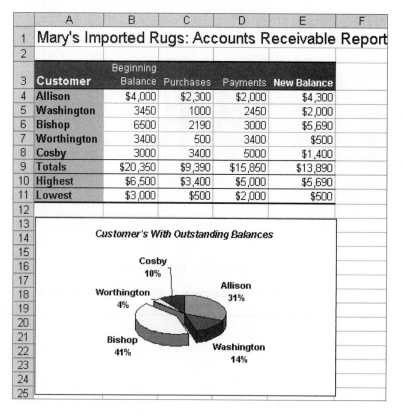

	A	B	C	D	E	F
1	Mary's Imported Rugs: Accounts Receivable Report					
2						
3	**Customer**	Beginning Balance	Purchases	Payments	**New Balance**	
4	**Allison**	$4,000	$2,300	$2,000	$4,300	
5	**Washington**	3450	1000	2450	$2,000	
6	**Bishop**	6500	2190	3000	$5,690	
7	**Worthington**	3400	500	3400	$500	
8	**Cosby**	3000	3400	5000	$1,400	
9	**Totals**	$20,350	$9,390	$15,850	$13,890	
10	**Highest**	$6,500	$3,400	$5,000	$5,690	
11	**Lowest**	$3,000	$500	$2,000	$500	

Critical Thinking

Critical Thinking 17.1 **On Your Own**

Open the workbook named Critical Thinking 15.2. You will need to complete Critical Thinking 15.2 if this workbook is not on your diskette. Create an embedded column chart that displays the miles driven by each driver. Use the chart title: Miles Driven. The name of each driver should be displayed at the base of the columns. Use data labels to display the precise number of miles driven at the top of each column.

Create another embedded column chart that displays the total expenses of each driver. Use the chart title: Total Expenses. The name of each driver should be displayed at the base of the columns. Use data labels to display the total expenses at the top of each column.

Adjust the size and position of the column charts so that they are side by side and positioned below the worksheet data. Format the worksheet to print on a single page in landscape orientation. Save the completed workbook as **Critical Thinking 17.1**.

Critical Thinking 17.2 **On Your Own**

Open the workbook named Critical Thinking 15.3. You will need to complete Critical Thinking 15.3 if this workbook is not on your diskette. Change the worksheet name to Test Results. Create a 3-D pie chart on a separate chart sheet that shows the percentage each Unit Type contributes to the total units produced. Include data labels that show the percentage and unit type label of each unit type. Do not display a legend. Use the chart title Percent of Unit Types Produced. Rotate the chart so that the largest slice is in the front of the chart. Increase the elevation of the chart and explode the largest slice. Change the sheet name to Pie Chart.

Insert a new column to the right of the Passed Test column. Use a formula in the new column to calculate the number of units that did not pass the test. Create a stacked column chart on a separate chart sheet that compares the units produced to the units that did not pass the test. Display a chart legend but no data labels. Use the title: Total Produced vs. Did Not Pass. Change the sheet name to Stacked Column Chart. Reorganize the sheets so that Test Results is first in the sheet order, Pie Chart second, and Stacked Column Chart third. Save the workbook as **Critical Thinking 17.2**.

Critical Thinking 17.3 **On Your Own**

Open the workbook named Critical Thinking 16.1. You will need to complete Critical Thinking 16.1 if this workbook is not on your diskette. Create an embedded pie chart that shows the contribution of each company type to the total billings. Include data labels that show only the company types. Do not display a legend. Use the chart title: Billing Breakdown. Position the chart below the data. Save the workbook as **Critical Thinking 17.3**.

Critical Thinking 17.4 **Web Research**

Use Internet Explorer and a search engine of your choice to locate a Web site that offers free stock quotations and charts. Search for the symbols CSCO, IBM, and ORCL, and display charts for each of the stocks. Set up an Excel workbook that includes a row for each stock and columns for each of the past 12 months. View the chart for one of the stocks and enter the approximate value of the stock into your worksheet for each of the past 12 months. Create a line chart on a separate chart sheet that includes all three stocks on the same chart. The chart should show the stock trends over the past 12 months. Use the chart title: 12 Month Stock Trends. Change the name of the chart sheet to 12-Month Trends Chart. Save the workbook as **Critical Thinking 17.4**.

Critical Thinking 17.5 **Web Research**

Use Internet Explorer and a search engine of your choice to find the Gross Domestic Product of the G7 industrial nations in any given year. The G7 nations include the United States, Germany, Japan, Great Britain, France, Italy, and Canada. Set up a worksheet that lists the nations in order by largest GDP. The GDP numbers will be measured in trillions of dollars. You can eliminate the 12 zeros from the numbers and just include the multiples. For example, if a nation has a GDP of 1.4 trillion dollars then use the number 1.4 in the worksheet. Create an embedded column chart to compare the various GDPs. Include data labels in the chart and a descriptive title. Save the workbook as **Critical Thinking 17.5**.

Critical Thinking 17.6 **On Your Own**

Open the workbook named Critical Thinking 17.6. Create a column chart on a separate chart sheet. The column chart should include columns for the purchase price and current price of each stock. Make sure that each pair of columns is identified by the appropriate stock symbol. Use the chart title: Gains and Losses. Include a legend that identifies the columns as either Purchase Price or Current Price. Name the chart sheet Gains and Losses Chart. Save the changes to your workbook.

Internet Integration: Creating Web Pages

All Office 2003 applications allow you to save your work in Web page format. For example, you can save an Excel workbook or Word document as Web pages. You can even save your Outlook calendar as a Web page. Excel and Word also offer a Web Page Preview command that allows you to preview your work in an Internet Explorer browser window. The task of making your Web pages available for viewing over the Internet is called publishing. An FTP (file transfer protocol) program is a utility that allows you to transfer Web pages from your computer to a Web server so others can browse them over the Internet.

IN THIS LESSON

Case Study

William is a grant manager at a community college. At end of the year, he is required to submit a budget report and a project narrative report covering grant-related activities over the past year. After he completes the reports, William decides to publish them to the Web site he maintains for the project. Excel and Word both have the capability to save workbooks and documents as Web pages. He can even add a title to the pages that appears when they are displayed in a Web browser.

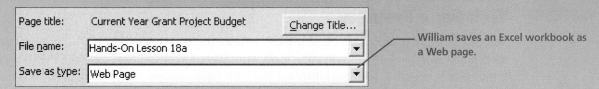

William saves an Excel workbook as a Web page.

To add some color to the Word document, William applies a theme to it. Themes are colorful formatting options that you can apply to an entire Word document with a single command.

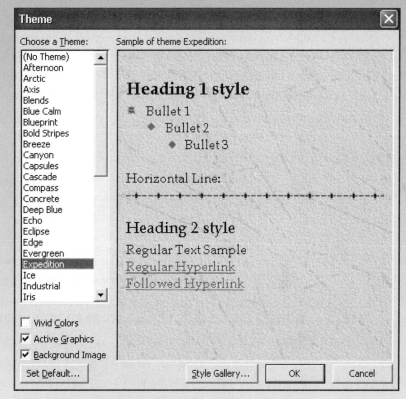

With a theme, William can apply special formatting to his entire Word document with a single command.

To publish the Web pages to the Internet, William uses an FTP (File Transfer Protocol) program. An FTP program transfers files from William's computer to a Web server, from which others can view them over the Internet.

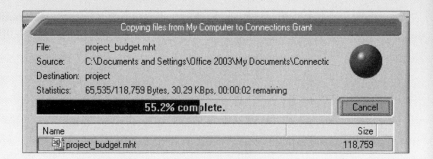

Saving an Excel Workbook as a Web Page

You can save any Excel workbook as a Web page. The workbook even retains the tabs for its individual worksheets, allowing others to navigate in the worksheets with a Web browser just as they would in Excel. Excel also allows you to convert individual worksheets in a workbook to Web page format. Workbooks and worksheets saved as Web pages can be viewed with Internet Explorer 4.0 or above and Netscape Navigator 6.0 or above.

Web Page Preview

You can preview your workbook in a Web browser prior to publishing it. This allows you to see the workbook exactly as others will view it over the Web. Excel's File→Web Page Preview command launches Internet Explorer and displays the Web page version of the workbook.

Web Page Files

When you save a workbook as a Web page, Excel converts it to HTML format. HTML is the programming language used to design most Web pages. Excel also creates a folder with the same name as the new Web page (HTML) file. This folder contains additional data required to display the Web page properly. Both the Web page file and its associated folder must always be stored together.

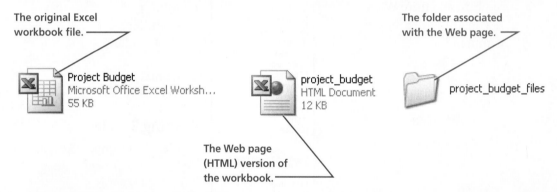

The original Excel workbook file.

Project Budget
Microsoft Office Excel Worksh...
55 KB

The Web page (HTML) version of the workbook.

project_budget
HTML Document
12 KB

The folder associated with the Web page.

project_budget_files

QUICK REFERENCE: SAVING A WORKBOOK OR DOCUMENT AS A WEB PAGE

Task	Procedure
Save an Excel workbook or Word document as a Web Page	■ Open the workbook or document file you wish to save as a Web page.
	■ Choose File→Save as Web Page from the menu bar.
	■ Click the Change Title button and enter a title to appear when the page is displayed in a Web browser.
	■ Choose a destination for the Web page. This can be a folder on a disk drive or a Web folder.

Hands-On 18.1 Save a Workbook as a Web Page

In this exercise, you will preview a workbook in Internet Explorer, then save it as a Web page.

Preview the Workbook Web Page

1. Start Excel, then open the Hands-On Lesson 18a workbook on your exercise diskette.

2. Choose File→Web Page Preview from the menu bar.
   The Internet Explorer browser will launch, displaying the workbook as it would appear as a Web page. Notice the workbook tabs at the bottom of the browser window.

3. Click the tabs at the bottom of the Web page to view each worksheet of the workbook.
   The tabs work just as they do when you view the workbook in Excel.

4. Close ⊠ the Internet Explorer window.

Save the Workbook as a Web Page

5. Choose File→Save as Web Page from the menu bar.

6. Follow these steps to save the workbook as a Web page:

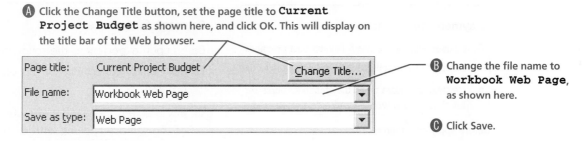

Ⓐ Click the Change Title button, set the page title to **Current Project Budget** as shown here, and click OK. This will display on the title bar of the Web browser.

Ⓑ Change the file name to **Workbook Web Page**, as shown here.

Ⓒ Click Save.

Excel converts the workbook to Web page format.

7. Close ⊠ the Excel window.

View the Web Page

8. Open a My Computer window, then display the 3½ Floppy (A:) drive.

9. Choose View→Large Icons from the menu bar, or View→Tiles if you are running Windows XP.
   Notice the Workbook Web Page folder. This folder contains additional data required to display the Web page version of your workbook. The file and its associated folder must always be stored together.

10. Scroll down the file list, then double-click to open the Workbook Web Page file.

11. Use the tabs at the bottom of the workbook to view the various worksheets.

12. Close ⊠ the Internet Explorer window.

Saving a Word Document as a Web Page

Word also allows you to save documents as Web pages. Word's File→Save as Web Page command converts most of a document's formatting into HTML format. If you save a long document as a Web page, all page breaks are deleted. For example, a 10-page document is displayed as a single Web page. You can preview your Word documents in Web page format before you save them just as you did in Excel.

Applying Themes

Word's Theme feature allows you to quickly apply colorful formatting to documents, making your Web pages more attractive. Themes also help you to format Web pages consistently. For example, if you apply the same theme to several documents, they will all have the same appearance when you save them as Web pages. You use the Format→Theme command to display the available themes and apply them to documents.

Example

The figures below display a passage in a document before and after applying a theme.

BEST PRACTICES

Payment for Services

Based upon experience, the following best practices

- Pay faculty generously for the time it takes to dev
- Pay teachers extra when they teach a course for list of things that worked and didn't work, and a

Before applying a theme

BEST PRACTICES

Payment for Services

Based upon experience, the following best practices

☐ Pay faculty generously for the time it takes to de program.

☐ Pay teachers extra when they teach a course for of the semester, along with a list of things that v

After applying the theme

Hands-On 18.2 Save a Document as a Web Page

In this exercise, you will apply a theme to a Word document, then save it as a Web page.

Review the Document

1. Start Word, then open the Hands-On Lesson 18b document on your exercise diskette.

2. Choose View→Print Layout from the menu bar, then set the Zoom Level to Whole Page.

3. Scroll through the document.
   Notice that this is a four-page document that contains several page breaks.

4. Choose View→Web Layout from the menu bar, then scroll down to the bottom of the document.
   Now the document appears as it would in a Web browser. Notice that there are no longer any page breaks. Saving a document as a Web page removes all page breaks.

5. Choose File→Web Page Preview.
   Internet Explorer launches to display your document.

6. Briefly scroll down the document, and then close ⊠ the Internet Explorer window.

Apply a Theme

7. Choose Format→Theme from the menu bar.
   A dialog box appears, listing the various themes you can apply to the document. Not all of the themes listed here are installed with Word, but many are.

8. Choose the Blends theme from the list on the left side of the dialog box.
   A preview of the theme and its formatting appears on the right. A theme affects the font formatting of the document. Most themes also apply a colorful background.

   Note: In the following step, if you choose a theme that is not installed, Word will display an Install button. Do not click Install because you would need the installation CD to install the missing theme.

9. Scroll down the list and preview several other themes. Skip any themes that do not have a preview (are not installed). Below is a list of several of the installed themes.

   - Cascade
   - Concrete
   - Expedition
   - Network
   - Profile
   - Sumi Painting

10. Choose the Water theme from the list and click OK.
    Word applies the theme formatting to the entire document.

11. Choose Format→Theme from the menu bar, then choose the Papyrus theme and click OK.

Save the Document as a Web Page

12. Choose File→Save As Web Page from the menu bar.

13. Click the Change Title button near the bottom-center of the dialog box, then set the page title to **End of Year Report** and click OK.
    This will display on the title bar of the Web browser.

14. Click Save.
    Word converts the document to Web page format.

15. Minimize ▬ the Word window, then scroll to the bottom of the My Computer window.
    Notice the Hands-On Lesson 18b_files folder and Web page file at the bottom of the file list.

16. Double-click the Hands-On Lesson 18b Web page (not the Word document) file.
    Notice that the title you just assigned in the Save dialog box appears at the top-left corner of the Internet Explorer window.

Hands-On Lesson 18b
MHTML Document
129 KB

17. Close ⊠ the Internet Explorer and My Computer windows.

Publishing with FTP

The act of placing a Web page or other type of file on the Internet so others can access it is called publishing. This requires that you upload your Web page and other files to a Web server from your computer's hard drive. There are various utilities and programs to help you do this.

FTP Utility Programs

FTP (File Transfer Protocol) utility programs help you transfer files back and forth between your local computer and a remote computer over the Internet. For example, you can transfer Web pages between your hard drive and your free ISP-provided Web space. There are several FTP programs available to download and purchase online.

An FTP program such as Doozler can transfer files to your Web server.

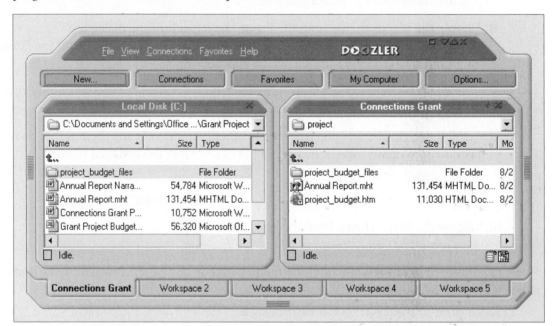

Naming Web Pages

When you create your own Web pages, you should pay careful attention to their names. Many Web servers run on an operating system called UNIX that has rules for naming files that differ from Windows. The following points will help you name the workbook files that you publish to the Web so they are compatible with most Web server systems:

QUICK REFERENCE: NAMING WEB PAGES

- Never use spaces in the filenames of Web pages and graphics—UNIX systems do not allow spaces in filenames. Use underscores instead of spaces. For example: long_file_name.

- Give the primary page on your Web site the name index.htm—This is the default page to display when browsers navigate to a folder on the Web.

- Try not to use uppercase letters in filenames—Web page filenames are case-sensitive. On UNIX server for example, MyHomePage.htm and myhomepage.htm represent different filenames.

Hands-On 18.3 Publish a Web Page

In this exercise, you will simulate copying a Web page and its associated folder to a Web server using the Doozler FTP utility from Ipswitch.com. Doozler is a user-friendly FTP program designed to make FTP tasks as easy as possible. In this simulation, you will enter the information necessary to connect to the grant project's Web server.

1. Launch Internet Explorer and navigate to the following URL:
   labpub.com/learn/oe3/

2. Click the Lesson 18 - Creating Web Pages link.

3. Click the Hands-On Exercise 18.3 link.
   A simulation of launching and running the Doozler ftp program begins.

4. Choose Start→Doozler to launch the Doozler FTP program.

5. Click the My Computer button then choose My Documents.

6. Click the New button to create a new connection to your project's Web space.

7. Type **Connections Grant Project** in the Name box and click the Next button.

8. Follow these steps to fill in the FTP server information:

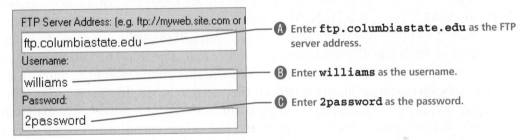

9. Click the Next button, read the information near the top of the dialog box, then click the Finished button.
   After a pause, the Web space panel appears to display its contents.

10. Double-click the Grant Project folder in the left panel.

11. While holding down the (CTRL) key, click to select the project_budget_files folder and project_budget Web page files.

12. Click the drag and drop pointer in the right panel to simulate dragging and dropping your Web page files to your project's Web space.

13. Close ⊠ the Doozler program window.
    An Internet Explorer browser window is already open for you to enter the URL of your newly transferred Web page.

14. Enter the URL **columbiastate.edu/connections_grant** in the address bar of the simulation and tap the (ENTER) key.
    The Web page you just transferred appears. Notice the URL of the Web page, indicating that it is being viewed over the Internet (not your computer).

15. Close ⊠ the Internet Explorer window.

UNIT 6

Access 2003

Keeping, storing, and retrieving information is important in our personal lives. Businesses, too, must manage information effectively. We keep information, or data, about our friends and family in an address book. If we have to look up a phone number we reach for a phone book. These are examples of physical databases. If you had to look in the phone book for everyone who lived on Main Street, it would take you quite a long time. If we had the phone book in electronic form, which is possible in Access, we could find that information in a matter of seconds. For businesses, keeping track of data is critical. They need to be able to quickly access information about payroll, accounts receivable, inventory, client, and order information. Database software like Access allows you to create a database and add, delete, change, and look up data efficiently and quickly.

LESSON 19

Creating Tables and Entering Data

In this lesson, you will begin developing a database for the Pinnacle Pet Care clinic. You will set up two Access tables and enter data in them. All data in an Access database is stored in tables. You will learn how to change the structure of tables and edit records within a database. You will also learn how to widen table columns, change the margins and page orientation, and print the contents of tables. The Pinnacle Pet Care database will continue to be developed in later lessons.

Additional learning resources are available at labpub.com/learn/oe3/

Case Study

Al Smith is a veterinarian and owner of the Pinnacle Pet Care clinic. Al recently contracted with Penny Johnson—a freelance programmer and Microsoft Access database developer—to develop an order entry system using Access 2003. Al wants to improve customer service by giving the office staff instant access to customer account information. Al chose Access as the database tool because of the customization capabilities of Access and its integration with other Office applications. Al hopes Access and the other Office applications will make Pinnacle Pet Care's customer service as excellent as the care provided to pets.

You can use forms to enter data into tables and to display records.

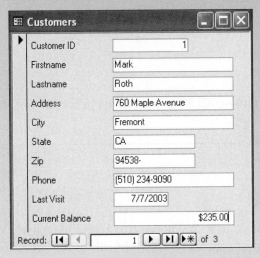

In Access, all data is stored in tables.

Firstname	Lastname	Address	City	State	Zip	Phone	Last Visit	Current Balance
Mark	Roth	760 Maple Avenue	Fremont	CA	94538-	(510) 234-9090	7/7/2003	$235.00
Tony	Simpson	312 York Lane	Richmond	CA	94804-	(510) 238-2233	9/7/2003	$185.00
Jason	Jones	2233 Crystal Street	San Mateo	CA	94403-	(415) 312-2312	7/15/2003	$48.00

You can create reports using data from your tables.

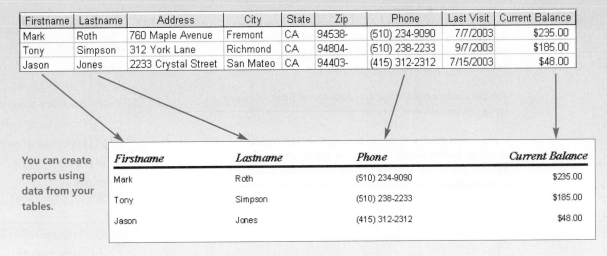

Firstname	Lastname	Phone	Current Balance
Mark	Roth	(510) 234-9090	$235.00
Tony	Simpson	(510) 238-2233	$185.00
Jason	Jones	(415) 312-2312	$48.00

What is Microsoft Access 2003?

Microsoft Access is a relational database management system that lets you store, organize, and manage information. Access is a powerful and flexible program that can handle virtually any data management task. For example, you can use Access to keep a simple contact list, or you can develop a full-featured order entry and database management system. Access gives anyone with a personal computer the ability to organize and manage data in a sophisticated manner.

Access is an integral part of the Office 2003 suite of software tools. Access plays a pivotal role in Office 2003 because it is the data storage and management tool. You can share Access data with Word, Excel, PowerPoint, and Outlook. For example, you can merge a Word form letter with an Access database to produce a mass mailing. You can also export Access data to Excel, and then use the calculating and charting capabilities of Excel to analyze the data.

 Hands-On 19.1 Start Access

1. Click the Start ⟨*start*⟩ button and choose All Programs, then choose Microsoft Access from the All Programs menu.

Creating a New Database

You can create a new Access database from scratch, or you can use Access's Database Wizard to help you build a database. The Task Pane that appears on the right side of the Access window gives you several choices.

Access 2003's Task Pane lets you open an existing database or create new databases using several methods. The Task Pane can be displayed or hidden using the View→Task Pane command.

You can create a blank database, data Access page, or Project using this section.

If you choose the On my computer... option then choose one of Access' built-in database templates, the Database Wizard is initiated and guides you step-by-step through the creation of a new database.

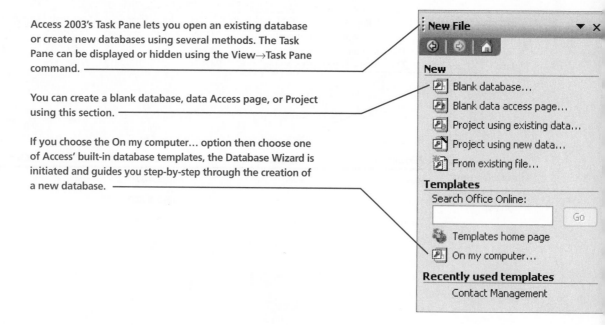

The Database Wizard

The Database Wizard lets you choose one of Access's built-in database templates as the basis for your new database. The Database Wizard takes you step-by-step through a series of screens that let you customize a built-in template to suit your needs. The resulting database is often sufficient to meet the needs of individuals and some small businesses and organizations. A database created with the wizard can also be used as a foundation from which a more sophisticated database can be developed.

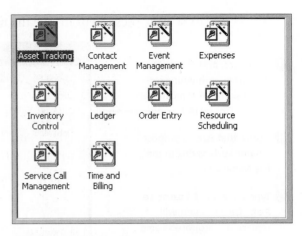

Built-in database templates.

Design View

You can also start with a blank database and add objects to your database as needed. An Access database is composed of various objects, including tables, queries, forms, and reports. Each object type can be created from scratch using a Design view for the particular type of object. Access also provides Wizards to help you set up individual objects. You will use both of these techniques as you develop the Pinnacle Pet Care database throughout this course.

Determining Data Inputs and Outputs

The first step in designing any database system is to determine the necessary data inputs and data outputs. Examples of data inputs include the name, address, telephone number, and email address of customers or contacts. Once the required data inputs are determined, the database can be designed to accommodate the inputs and store the required data. Likewise, the required data outputs must be determined before reports and other objects can be designed.

 ## Hands-On 19.2 Create a Blank Database

1. Make sure the Task Pane is displayed on the right side of the Access window. If it isn't displayed, use the View→Toolbars→Task Pane command to display it.

2. Choose Create a New File... in the Task Pane then choose the Blank Database option and the File New Database box will appear.

3. Follow these steps to save the new database to your exercise diskette:

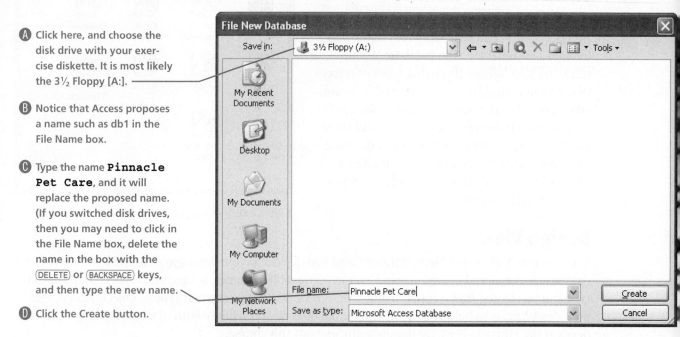

Ⓐ Click here, and choose the disk drive with your exercise diskette. It is most likely the 3½ Floppy [A:].

Ⓑ Notice that Access proposes a name such as db1 in the File Name box.

Ⓒ Type the name **Pinnacle Pet Care**, and it will replace the proposed name. (If you switched disk drives, then you may need to click in the File Name box, delete the name in the box with the (DELETE) or (BACKSPACE) keys, and then type the new name.

Ⓓ Click the Create button.

You may choose to save your database to an alternative file storage location.

4. Follow these steps to explore the Access database window:

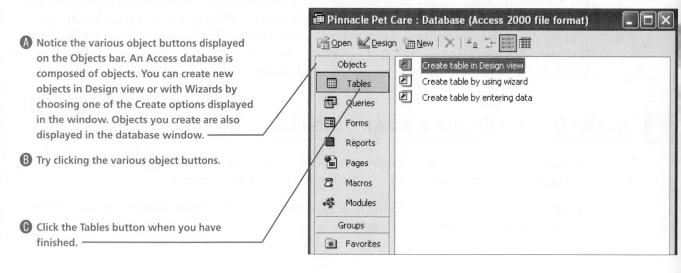

Ⓐ Notice the various object buttons displayed on the Objects bar. An Access database is composed of objects. You can create new objects in Design view or with Wizards by choosing one of the Create options displayed in the window. Objects you create are also displayed in the database window.

Ⓑ Try clicking the various object buttons.

Ⓒ Click the Tables button when you have finished.

Access Tables

In Access, data is stored in tables. Tables organize data so that it can easily be output at a later time. A simple database may have one or two tables, while a sophisticated database may have dozens or even hundreds of tables. A separate table is used for each type of related data. For example, your Pinnacle Pet Care database will initially have a table for customers and a table for pets.

Records

Tables are composed of rows, and each row is known as a record. For example, your Pinnacle Pet Care database will have a Customer table that stores all of the customer information. Each row of the Customer table will contain data for one customer.

Fields

Each record is divided into fields. A record can have many fields. For example, the Customers table will have fields for the Customer ID, name, address, telephone number, etc. In Access, each column in a table is a field. Take a few moments to study the following illustration which shows the first two tables that you will create in the Pinnacle Pet Care database.

The Customers table contains one record for each customer. All data for a customer is stored in one row of the Customers table.

The records are composed of fields.

Customer ID	Firstname	Lastname	Address	City	State	Zip	Phone	Last Visit	Current Balance
1	Mark	Roth	760 Maple Avenue	Fremont	CA	94538-	(510) 234-9090	7/7/2003	$235.00
2	Tony	Simpson	312 York Lane	Richmond	CA	94804-	(510) 238-2233	9/7/2003	$185.00
3	Jason	Jones	2233 Crystal Street	San Mateo	CA	94403-	(415) 312-2312	7/15/2003	$48.00

Pet ID	Pet Name	Pet Type	Breed	Gender	Color	Date of Birth	Last Visit	Expenditures	Number of Visits	Customer ID
CT02	Max	Cat	Unknown	Male	White	1/7/1986	9/7/2003	$1,450.55	20	2
CT16	Stripes	Cat	Tortoise shell	Male	Black and brown	10/8/1990	7/15/2003	$450.00	9	3
CT89	Puffy	Cat	Siamese	Female	White with patches	12/12/1996	7/7/2003	$30.00	1	1
DG12	Wolfy	Dog	German Shepherd	Male	Brown	6/6/1991	7/15/2003	$450.00	7	3
DG13	Dillon	Dog	Mutt	Male	Black	10/5/1994	7/7/2003	$150.55	3	1
RB23	Bugs	Rabbit	Jack	Unknown	Brown	6/7/1995	9/7/2003	$600.50	4	2

Notice that the Customer ID field appears in both the Customers and Pets tables. Eventually, this field will be used to establish a relationship between the two tables. Establishing relationships between tables is what gives Access and other relational database systems their power and flexibility.

Table Structure

In Access, you can set up tables in Design view or with the Table Wizard. In Design view, you specify the field names, the data type of each field, and any other parameters as needed. Design view lets you precisely determine the characteristics of each field. The Table Wizard automates the process of creating a table by letting you choose from a set of predefined fields. The Table Wizard lacks the flexibility of Design view; however, it is often useful for beginning Access users. Besides, you can always switch to Design view to modify a table that has been set up with the Table Wizard. Access gives you complete control in setting up and modifying tables and other Access objects.

Field Names

Each field in an Access table is identified by a unique name. The name can be up to 64 characters in length and can contain letters, numbers, spaces, and most punctuation marks. Field names cannot contain periods, exclamation marks, or square brackets [ ]. Some examples of field names from the Pinnacle Pet Care Customers table are Firstname, Lastname, Address, City, State, and Zip.

Data Types

Each field is assigned a data type that determines the type of data the field may contain. Common data types are text, number, currency, and date.

- **Text**—Text fields can contain any type of characters. The default size of text fields is 50 characters; however, you can increase or decrease the size as desired.

- **Number**—Number fields can only contain numbers. Number fields can be used in calculations. Use the Text data type if a field will contain a combination of text and numbers.

- **Currency**—Currency fields can be used in calculations. Access formats currency field numbers with dollar signs, commas, decimal points, and digits following the decimal point.

- **Date**—Date fields contain dates. Dates can also be used in calculations. For example, you could subtract two dates to determine the number of days between the dates.

Field Properties

Each data type has several field properties that can be used to customize the field. For example, you can change the Field Size property for text fields to increase or decrease the maximum number of characters allowed in the field. The field properties can be modified for each field in a table when the table is displayed in Design view.

QUICK REFERENCE: SETTING UP TABLES IN DESIGN VIEW

- Click the Tables button on the Objects bar in the Access Database window.
- Double-click the Create Table in Design View option.
- Type a field name in the Field Name column of the table that appears.
- Choose a Data Type for the new field and type a description if desired.
- If necessary, modify the field properties at the bottom of the dialog box.
- Repeat the previous three steps for all desired fields.
- Close the table and give it a name when you have finished.

Hands-On 19.3 Set up a Table in Design View

In this exercise, you will begin setting up the Pets table for the Pinnacle Pet Care database.

Define Text Fields

1. Follow these steps to display a new table in Design view:

Ⓐ Make sure the Tables button is chosen on the Objects bar.

Ⓑ Double-click the Create Table in Design View option.

2. If necessary, maximize 🔲 both the Access program window and the table design window within the Access window.

3. Follow these steps to define a text field:

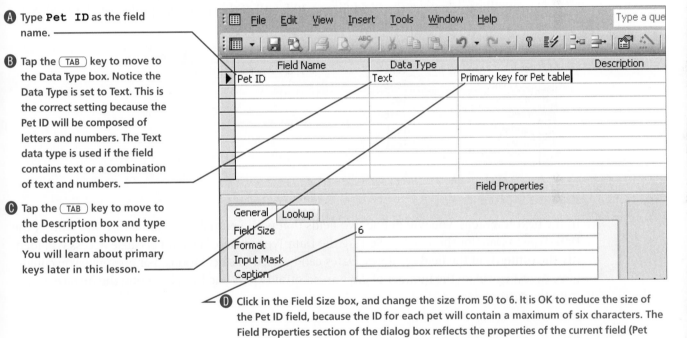

Ⓐ Type **Pet ID** as the field name.

Ⓑ Tap the (TAB) key to move to the Data Type box. Notice the Data Type is set to Text. This is the correct setting because the Pet ID will be composed of letters and numbers. The Text data type is used if the field contains text or a combination of text and numbers.

Ⓒ Tap the (TAB) key to move to the Description box and type the description shown here. You will learn about primary keys later in this lesson.

Ⓓ Click in the Field Size box, and change the size from 50 to 6. It is OK to reduce the size of the Pet ID field, because the ID for each pet will contain a maximum of six characters. The Field Properties section of the dialog box reflects the properties of the current field (Pet ID). You will learn more about these properties as you progress through this course.

You have just defined a field in your database. You will enter data into this field and other fields later in this lesson. You will use a data entry mode known as Datasheet view to enter the data. Currently, you are working in Design view, which allows you to define a table. The Text field type that you chose for the Pet ID field will allow you to enter any type of data in the field. However, the Pet ID for each pet will be restricted to six characters.

4. Follow these steps to define another text field:

Ⓐ Click in the next Field Name box, and type **Pet Name**. The Pet Name field will contain the names of the pets.

Ⓑ Tap the (TAB) key, and Text will appear as the default Data Type. Leave the Data Type set to Text, and do not enter a description for this field. Descriptions are optional and are only used when necessary.

Ⓒ Click in the Field Size box, and change the size to 30 as shown here.

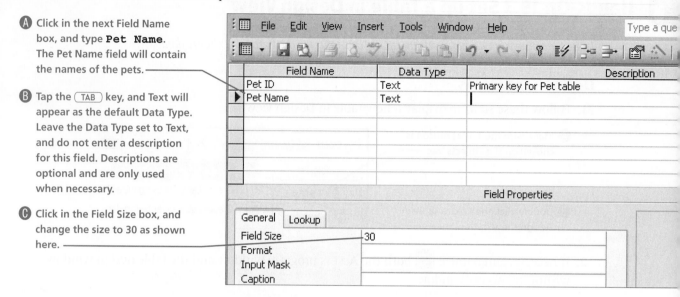

5. Follow the steps in the preceding illustration to create the next four fields, as shown in the following illustration. Set the Field Size to 30 for all of the fields except the Gender field. Set the size of the Gender field to 10.

Field Name	Data Type	Description
Pet ID	Text	Primary key for Pet table
Pet Name	Text	
Pet Type	Text	
Breed	Text	
Gender	Text	
Color	Text	

Define Date Fields

In the next few steps, you will define two fields that will eventually contain dates. You will set the Data Type to Date for these fields. Setting the Data Type to Date is useful because Access will identify the contents of the fields as dates. Dates can be used in calculations. For example, you could have Access calculate the number of days an account is past due by subtracting the invoice date from the current date.

6. Follow these steps to define a date field:

A Click in the next Field Name box, and type **Date of Birth.**

B Tap the (TAB) key, and click the drop-down button in the Data Type box. A list of data types will appear, as shown here.

C Choose Date/Time from the drop-down list.

D Notice the Field Properties section does not contain a Field Size box. You cannot set the field size for date fields. The options on the Field Properties list change for each data type.

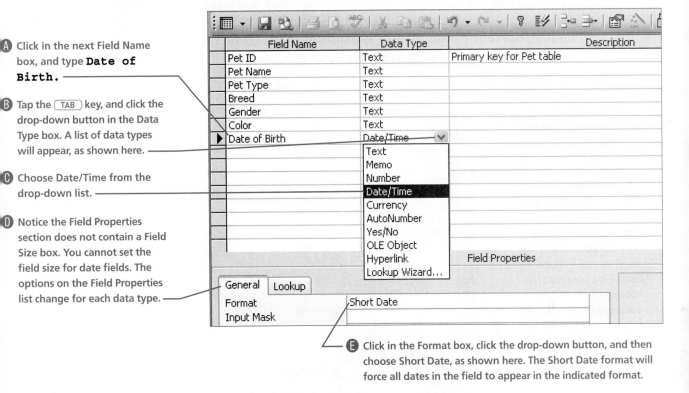

E Click in the Format box, click the drop-down button, and then choose Short Date, as shown here. The Short Date format will force all dates in the field to appear in the indicated format.

7. Now define another date field named **Last Visit**, as shown in the following illustration. Set the Format to Short Date, as shown at the bottom of the illustration.

Field Name	Data Type	Descri
Pet ID	Text	Primary key for Pet table
Pet Name	Text	
Pet Type	Text	
Breed	Text	
Gender	Text	
Color	Text	
Date of Birth	Date/Time	
Last Visit	Date/Time	

Field Properties

General | Lookup

Format   Short Date
Input Mask

Define Currency and Number Fields

In the next few steps, you will define two more fields. You will set the Data Type to Currency for one of the fields and Number for the other. Currency and number fields can be used in calculations. Furthermore, fields that are formatted with the Currency data type will display a dollar sign, a decimal point, and decimals whenever you enter data into the fields.

8. Follow this step to define the Expenditures and Number of Visits fields:

A Define the Expenditures and Number of Visits fields as shown here. Set the Data Types as shown, and enter the descriptions as shown. Leave the Field Properties at the bottom of the dialog box set to the default settings. Number fields normally have a Field Size of Long Integer as shown here. Keep in mind that choosing Field Properties can be an involved process that often requires extensive knowledge of Access.

Field Name	Data Type	Description
Pet ID	Text	Primary key for Pet table
Pet Name	Text	
Pet Type	Text	
Breed	Text	
Gender	Text	
Color	Text	
Date of Birth	Date/Time	
Last Visit	Date/Time	
Expenditures	Currency	Total expentitures on this pet from time of first visit
Number of Visits	Number	Total number of visits for this pet

Field Properties

General | Lookup

| Field Size | Long Integer |
| Format | |

9. Now continue with the next topic where you will define a primary key for the table.

Primary Keys

Every Access table should have one field defined as the primary key. The primary key field uniquely identifies each record in the table. For this reason, each record must have a unique entry in the primary key field. Most tables use numbers or codes in the primary key field. For example, the Pet ID field will be the primary key in the Pets table. A unique Pet ID will identify each pet. In table Design view, you specify a primary key by clicking in the desired field and clicking the Primary Key button on the Access toolbar. Access will also prompt you to choose a primary key field if you close a table that has not been assigned a primary key.

Hands-On 19.4 **Choose a Primary Key**

1. Follow these steps to choose a primary key:

Ⓐ **Click in the Pet ID Field Name box.** ⟶

Ⓑ **Click the Primary Key button on the Access toolbar.** ⟶

Ⓒ **Notice that a key icon appears on the Pet ID field. This icon identifies Pet ID as the primary key field.** ⟶

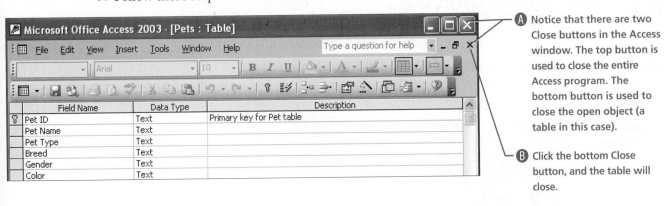

Field Name	Data Type	
Pet ID	Text	Primary key for Primary Key
Pet Name	Text	
Pet Type	Text	
Breed	Text	

Saving Database Objects

FROM THE KEYBOARD

CTRL + S to save an open object

An Access database is a "container" that holds tables and other types of objects. The entire database is saved as a single file onto a hard disk or diskette. However, you must also save the objects within the database. Database objects are assigned names when they are saved. This allows you to identify the objects at a later time. A database object name can be up to 64 characters in length and may contain letters, numbers, spaces, and other types of characters.

You save an open object by clicking the Save 🖫 button on the Access toolbar. Access will also prompt you to save an object if you attempt to close the object without saving the changes.

 ## Hands-On 19.5 **Save the Table**

1. Click the Save 🖫 button on the Access toolbar.

2. Type the name **Pets** in the Save As box, and click OK.

3. Follow these steps to close the table:

Ⓐ **Notice that there are two Close buttons in the Access window. The top button is used to close the entire Access program. The bottom button is used to close the open object (a table in this case).**

Ⓑ **Click the bottom Close button, and the table will close.**

A "Pets icon" will appear in the Tables section of the Access window. You have completed the process of setting up a table. At this point, you could set up additional tables or other types of objects. However, you will enter data into the Pets table in the next exercise. To accomplish this, you will use Datasheet view.

Opening Objects

FROM THE KEYBOARD

(ENTER) to open a
selected object

(CTRL)+(ENTER)
to open a selected
object in Design view

The Access Database window provides access to all database objects. You can select any object by clicking the appropriate objects button and then clicking the desired object. Once you select an object, you can open the object or display it in Design view.

You can open a selected object by double-clicking it or clicking the Open button.

You use this button to display a selected object in Design view.

You select an object by clicking an object button and then choosing the desired object.

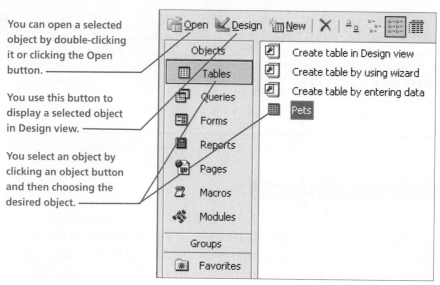

Datasheet View

In the previous exercises, you used Design view to set up the Pets table. Design view lets you set up or modify the structure of tables. However, to enter data into a table, you must display the table in Datasheet view. You can open a table in Datasheet view from the Access Database window as discussed in the previous topic. Once a table is opened in Datasheet view, you can enter data the same way it is entered into an Excel worksheet. The (TAB) key can be used to move forward one table cell and the (SHFT)+(TAB) keystroke can be used to move back one cell. You can also click in any cell and enter new data or edit existing data.

Hands-On 19.6 Enter Data

1. Follow these steps to open the Pets table in Datasheet view:

Ⓐ Make sure the Tables button is chosen, and click the Pets table icon.

Ⓑ Click the Open button. You could also have opened the Pets table by double-clicking the Pets icon.

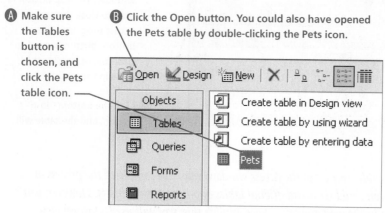

2. Follow these steps to explore the Datasheet view window:
Keep in mind that your window may have different dimensions than shown here.

Ⓐ Notice that many of the toolbar buttons are different from those in the Design view window.

Ⓑ Notice that the field names are displayed as column headings.

Ⓒ Data is entered into the rows (although you will only see one row at this point). Each row is a record. For example, each row will contain all of the data for one pet. You use the TAB key to move from one field to the next within a row (or you can click in the desired row or field).

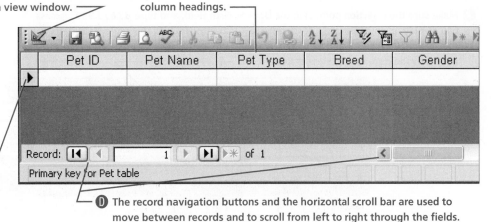

Ⓓ The record navigation buttons and the horizontal scroll bar are used to move between records and to scroll from left to right through the fields.

3. Follow these steps to begin entering a record:

Ⓐ Type **DG12** as the Pet ID, and Access will add a new row in preparation for the next record.

Ⓑ Tap the TAB key to move to the next field and type the pet name **Wolfy**.

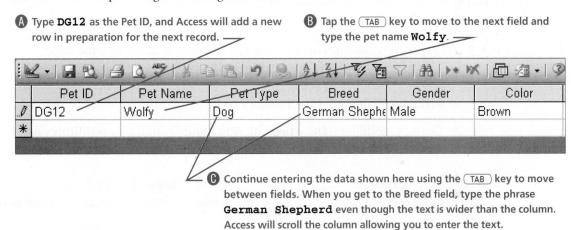

Ⓒ Continue entering the data shown here using the TAB key to move between fields. When you get to the Breed field, type the phrase **German Shepherd** even though the text is wider than the column. Access will scroll the column allowing you to enter the text.

4. Follow this step to display the remaining fields:

Ⓐ If necessary, use the horizontal scroll bar to scroll to the right until the fields shown here are visible.

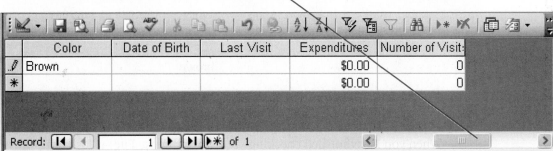

5. Follow these steps to enter data in the remaining fields:

Also notice that Access right-aligns the dates and numbers in the last four fields. Access always right-aligns entries that can be used in calculations.

Ⓐ Make sure the insertion point is in the Date of Birth field, and type **6/6/1991**. Access will display an error message if you enter a number (or text) that is not a valid date. For this reason, you must use the forward slashes / while entering dates, or enter dates using another valid date format such as 6-Jun-1991.

Ⓑ Tap the ⟨ TAB ⟩ key, and enter **7/15/2003** in the Last Visit field.

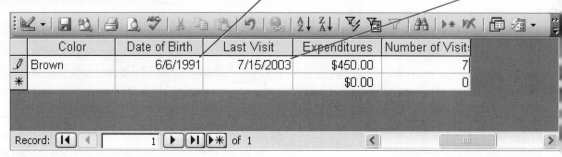

Ⓒ Tap the ⟨ TAB ⟩ key, and type **450** in the Expenditures field. Tap ⟨ TAB ⟩ again, and Access will format the number with a dollar sign ($), a decimal place, and two zeros to the right of the decimal. Access formats the number this way because you chose the Currency format for this field when you set up the table.

Ⓓ Type **7** in the Number of Visits field, and then tap ⟨ TAB ⟩ to move to the Pet ID field in the next record.

6. Follow these guidelines to enter the records shown below into the table:

- Use the ⟨ TAB ⟩ key to move between fields.

- Make sure you use forward slashes / when entering the dates.

- Do not type dollar signs when entering numbers in the Expenditures field. However, do type a decimal point followed by the indicated decimals.

Pet ID	Pet Name	Pet Type	Breed	Gender	Color	Date of Birth	Last Visit	Expenditures	Number of Visits
DG13	Dillon	Dog	Mutt	Male	Black	10/5/1994	7/7/2003	150.55	3
CT89	Puffy	Cat	Siamese	Female	White with patches	12/12/1996	7/7/2003	30.00	1
RB23	Bugs	Rabbit	Jack	Unknown	Brown	6/7/1995	9/7/2003	600.50	4
CT02	Max	Cat	Unknown	Male	White	1/7/1986	9/7/2003	1450.55	20
CT16	Stripes	Cat	Tortoise shell	Male	Black and brown	10/8/1990	7/15/2003	450.00	9

7. Check your data carefully to make sure it is error-free. Accuracy is extremely important when entering data.

8. When you have finished checking your work, choose File→Close from the menu bar.
Access will close the table, and the Database window will be displayed. You can close objects with either the File→Close command or by clicking the Close button (as you did in an earlier exercise). Notice that Access did not prompt you to save the table. Access automatically saves data entered into a table. In fact, it saves the data one record at a time as you enter it.

Changing the Structure of a Table

You can change the structure of a table after it has been set up. For example, you may need to change the size or name of a field or add a new field. Structural changes are made to a table in Design view.

Impact on Data

You must be careful when changing the structure of a table, especially if data has already been entered. For example, imagine that a field has a length of 30 and you have already entered records into the table. If you reduce the field length to 20, you may delete up to 10 characters from some records. Access will usually provide a warning message if you attempt to make a change that has the potential of destroying data in a field.

Switching Between Object Views

The Datasheet View button appears on the left end of the Access toolbar whenever you are in Design view. You can switch from Design view to Datasheet view by clicking the Datasheet View button.

Likewise, the Design View button appears on the left end of the Access toolbar when you are in Datasheet view. You can switch to Design view by clicking the Design View button.

⚠TIP! Setting the Default Value of Fields

Only set a default value if the field will have that value the majority of the time. Access lets you set default values for fields. The default value is automatically entered in new records when you enter data in Datasheet view. This can be convenient if a field is typically set to a certain value. For example, you will set the default value of the Number of Visits field to 1. Pets will be entered into the database when they make their first visit to the clinic. By setting the Number of Visits field to 1, you will be able to skip over the Number of Visits field when entering data for a new pet. In Design view, default values are set in the Field Properties area at the bottom of the dialog box.

 ## Hands-On 19.7 Change Table Structure

Change a Field's Properties

1. Click the ▦ Pets icon in the Access window, and then click the ✎ Design button on the Database toolbar. The Database toolbar is located just above the Objects bar.
   The Pets table will open in Design view.

2. Follow these steps to change the default value for the Number of Visits field:

Ⓐ Click anywhere in the Number of Visits row (you may need to scroll down).

Ⓑ Change the default value to **1**.

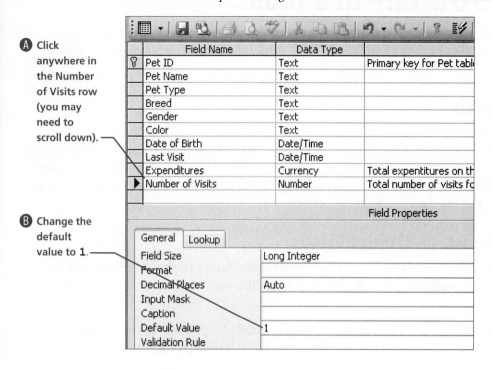

Add a Field

In the next few steps, you will add a Customer ID field to the table. The Customer ID field will eventually link the Pets table to a Customers table.

3. Follow these steps to add the Customer ID field:

Ⓐ Click in the box below Number of Visits, and type the name **Customer ID**. Make sure you include a space between Customer and ID.

Ⓑ Set the Data Type to Number.

Ⓒ Take a moment to check the spelling of every field name. Make sure the spelling is correct and matches the spelling of the field names in this illustration. It is important that the field names be spelled correctly because they will be used in other objects throughout this course.

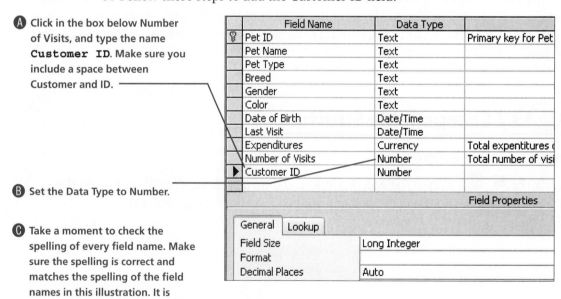

4. Click the Datasheet View button on the left end of the Access toolbar, and then click the Yes button when Access asks if you want to save the table.

   Notice that the order of the records has changed in the table. The records should now be sorted in alphabetical order based upon the primary key field. The records were sorted when you closed the table and then reopened it. One of the benefits of choosing a primary key field (such as Pet ID) is that Access will sort the records based upon the primary key field.

5. Now add the Customer IDs shown below into the table. Make sure you enter the correct Customer ID in each record. You may need to scroll to the left and right in the table to ensure that the correct Customer ID has been entered for each Pet ID. As you can see from this example, it can be difficult to add data to records after changing the structure of a table. For this reason, you should spend as much time as necessary designing and planning a database to minimize the number of changes that are required.

Pet ID	Pet Name	Pet Type	Breed	Gender	Color	Date of Birth	Last Visit	Expenditures	Number of Visits	Customer ID
CT02	Max	Cat	Unknown	Male	White	1/7/1986	9/7/2003	$1,450.55	20	2
CT16	Stripes	Cat	Tortoise shell	Male	Black and brown	10/8/1990	7/15/2003	$450.00	9	3
CT89	Puffy	Cat	Siamese	Female	White with patches	12/12/1996	7/7/2003	$30.00	1	1
DG12	Wolfy	Dog	German Shepherd	Male	Brown	6/6/1991	7/15/2003	$450.00	7	3
DG13	Dillon	Dog	Mutt	Male	Black	10/5/1994	7/7/2003	$150.55	3	1
RB23	Bugs	Rabbit	Jack	Unknown	Brown	6/7/1995	9/7/2003	$600.50	4	2

Make sure each Pet ID has the correct Customer ID.

6. Leave the table in Datasheet view, and continue with the next topic.

   You will add a record and make other changes in the next exercise.

Record Management

In Datasheet view, the Access toolbar has several buttons that let you manage records. The following quick reference table defines three of these buttons.

QR

QUICK REFERENCE: RECORD MANAGEMENT BUTTONS

Button	Function
Find	Lets you locate a record by searching for a word or phrase. The Replace option lets you replace a word or phrase with another word or phrase.
New Record	Adds a new record at the end of the table.
Delete Record	Deletes the current record.

Navigating within a Table

In Datasheet view, a record navigation bar appears at the bottom of the Access program window. The following illustration defines the buttons on the navigation bar.

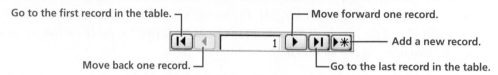

Go to the first record in the table. ⌐

Move back one record. ⌐

Move forward one record.

Add a new record.

Go to the last record in the table.

Notice the Back One Record button is "ghosted out" in this illustration. This is because the insertion point is in the first record as shown in the center of the navigation bar. In other words, there is no record to move back to.

Hands-On 19.8 **Manage Records**

The Pets table should be in Datasheet view from the previous exercise.

Add a Record

1. Click the New Record ![button] button on the Access toolbar.
   The insertion point will move to a new record at the bottom of the table.

2. Enter the following data into the new record:

Pet ID	Pet Name	Pet Type	Breed	Gender	Color	Date of Birth	Last Visit	Expenditures	Number of Visits	Customer ID
CT92	Tony	Cat	Unknown	Male	Brown with black stripes	4/3/97	7/7/2003	145	6	1

Navigate to Records

3. Follow these steps to navigate to various records:

Ⓐ Notice the Pencil icon shown in this illustration. The Pencil icon indicates that the current record is being edited.

Ⓑ If necessary, scroll to the left until the Pet ID field is visible.

Ⓒ Click the various navigation buttons to browse through the records. The navigation buttons are useful when you have a large database with many records.

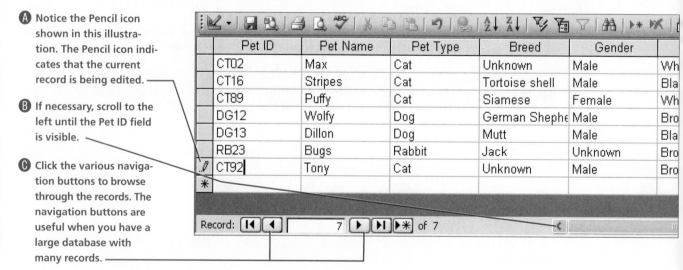

Pet ID	Pet Name	Pet Type	Breed	Gender	
CT02	Max	Cat	Unknown	Male	Wh
CT16	Stripes	Cat	Tortoise shell	Male	Bla
CT89	Puffy	Cat	Siamese	Female	Wh
DG12	Wolfy	Dog	German Shephe	Male	Bro
DG13	Dillon	Dog	Mutt	Male	Bla
RB23	Bugs	Rabbit	Jack	Unknown	Bro
CT92	Tony	Cat	Unknown	Male	Bro

Record: 7 of 7

Delete a Record

4. Follow these steps to delete a record:

Ⓐ Click the record selector (square box) to the left of the CT89 record to select the entire record. The vertical column of boxes to the left of the records is called the Selection bar. ——

Ⓑ Click the Delete Record button on the Access toolbar. ——

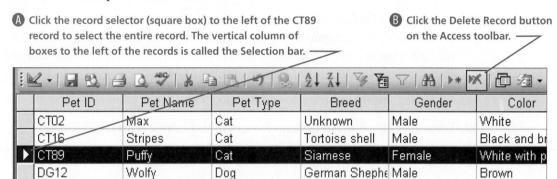

Ⓒ Click the Yes button on the warning box that appears to confirm the deletion.

In the preceding steps, you selected the CT89 record prior to deleting it. You could actually have deleted the record by clicking anywhere in the CT89 row and then clicking the Delete Record button. The Selection bar is most useful when you want to delete several records. You can select several records by dragging the mouse down the Selection bar.

Find Records

5. Click on any Pet ID in the Pet ID column.
   In the following steps, you will search for Pet IDs. You must position the insertion point somewhere in the column that you wish to search through prior to initiating the search.

6. Click the Find 🔍 button on the Access toolbar.

7. Follow these steps to conduct the search:

Ⓐ Type **ct92** in the Find What box. ——

Ⓑ Notice that the Look In field indicates that you are searching for a Pet ID. In a large database, narrowing the search to a particular field can speed up the search. ——

Ⓒ Notice the Match Case box. It should be unchecked for the current search as shown here. This is because you typed the search string in lowercase (ct92) but the actual Pet ID in the database is in uppercase (CT92). Access will still find the Pet ID because the Match Case box is unchecked. ——

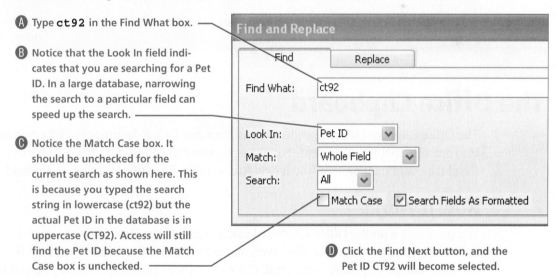

Ⓓ Click the Find Next button, and the Pet ID CT92 will become selected.

8. Use the preceding steps to find Pet ID DG12.
   Keep in mind that the Find feature is most useful when you have a large database and the item you are searching for is not visible on the screen.

Check Out the Replace Option

9. Click the Replace tab at the top of the dialog box.

10. Notice that a Replace With box and several replace buttons appear.
You can use the Replace options to replace data in a table. For example, you could enter a word or phrase in the Find What box, type a replacement word or phrase in the Replace With box, and click the Replace All button to make the replacement in all records of the table.

11. Click the Cancel button to close the dialog box.

12. Leave the table open in Datasheet view, and continue with the next topic.

Cut, Copy, and Paste

Cut, Copy, and Paste are available in all Office 2003 applications. With Cut, Copy, and Paste you can move or copy data from one table cell to another. Copying data can be useful especially when a cell's contents are lengthy. You can even use Cut, Copy, and Paste to move or copy entire rows and columns. In addition, Copy and Paste can be used to copy objects in the Database window.

QUICK REFERENCE: CUT, COPY, AND PASTE

Command	Discussion	Procedure
Cut	The Cut command removes entries from table cells and places them on the Office clipboard.	Click the Cut ✂ button or press CTRL+X.
Copy	The Copy command also places entries on the Office clipboard, but it leaves a copy of the entries in the original table cells.	Click the Copy 📄 button or press CTRL+C.
Paste	The Paste command pastes entries from the Office clipboard to table cells.	Click the Paste 📋 button or press CTRL+V.

The Office Clipboard

The Office Clipboard lets you collect items from any Office document or program and paste them into any other Office document. For example, you can collect data from an Access table and an Excel table and then paste it into a new Access table. The Office Clipboard can hold up to 24 items.

How it Works

You place items on the Office Clipboard using standard Cut and Copy commands; however, the Office Clipboard must first be displayed in the Task Pane. The Office Clipboard is displayed with the Edit→Office Clipboard command. Once the Office Clipboard is displayed, you can choose an item and paste it into a table.

Hands-On 19.9 Use Copy and Paste

In this exercise, you will use Copy and Paste to assist you in entering a new record.

1. Click the New Record ▶ button on the Access toolbar to add a new record to the table.

2. Follow these steps to enter data and to copy and paste data:

Ⓐ Type **DG14** in the Pet ID field, type **Fetch** in the Pet Name field, and type **Dog** as the Pet Type, as shown here. ⟶

Ⓑ Position the mouse pointer on the left edge of the Breed cell for Wolfy the dog, and the pointer will have a thick cross shape as shown here. ⟶

Ⓒ Click the mouse button to select the text in the Breed cell. You could also have selected the text by dragging over the cell's contents.

Ⓓ Click the Copy button on the Access toolbar.

Pet ID	Pet Name	Pet Type	Breed
CT02	Max	Cat	Unknown
CT16	Stripes	Cat	Tortoise shell
CT92	Tony	Cat	Unknown
DG12	Wolfy	Dog	German Shephe
DG13	Dillon	Dog	Mutt
▶ DG14	Fetch	Dog	

Ⓕ Click the Paste button on the Access toolbar. The phrase German Shepherd will be pasted into the cell.

Ⓔ Position the mouse pointer on the left edge of the Breed cell for the new record, and click when the thick cross appears. The entire blank cell will be selected.

3. Complete the new record by entering the data shown below.

Gender	Color	Date of Birth	Last Visit	Expenditures	Number of Visits	Customer ID
Male	Black and brown	6/12/1996	9/10/2003	345.00	3	3

Printing Tables

It is very important that you enter data accurately. There are few things more upsetting to customers and other business contacts than misspelling their names and careless data entry errors. For this reason, it is important to check your data for accuracy after it has been entered. Perhaps the best way to check data accuracy is to print out the contents of your tables. Proofreading hard copy (paper printout) is usually the best way to spot errors.

FROM THE KEYBOARD
(CTRL)+(P) to display the Print dialog box

The Print 🖨 button on the Access toolbar sends the entire contents of a table open in Datasheet view to the current printer. You must display the Print dialog box if you want to change printers, adjust the number of copies to be printed, or to set other printing options. You display the Print dialog box with the File→Print command. The illustration on the following page highlights the most frequently used options available in the Print dialog box.

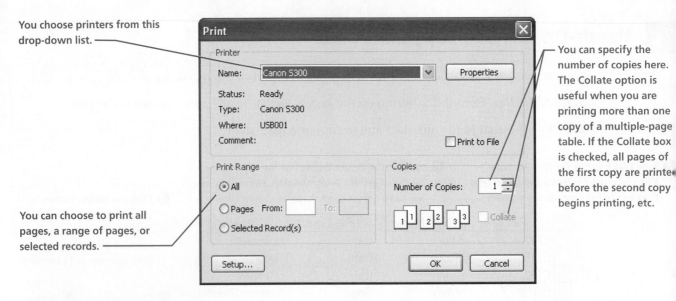

You choose printers from this drop-down list.

You can specify the number of copies here. The Collate option is useful when you are printing more than one copy of a multiple-page table. If the Collate box is checked, all pages of the first copy are printed before the second copy begins printing, etc.

You can choose to print all pages, a range of pages, or selected records.

Print Preview

The Print Preview button on the Access toolbar displays the Print Preview window. Print Preview lets you see exactly how a table will look when it is printed. Print Preview can save time, paper, and wear-and-tear on your printer. Print Preview is especially useful when printing a table with a large number of records. It is always wise to preview a large table before sending it to the printer. When you display the Print Preview window, the Access toolbar is replaced by the Print Preview toolbar.

Hands-On 19.10 Use Print Preview

1. Click the Print Preview button on the Access toolbar.

2. Zoom in by clicking anywhere on the table.

3. Zoom out by clicking anywhere on the table.
   Notice that only six of the table's columns are visible in the Print Preview window. It is a good thing that you used Print Preview before printing the table. You will hold off on printing the table until you change the page orientation and margins.

4. Click the Close button on the Print Preview toolbar to exit without printing.

Adjusting Column Widths

You may need to adjust table column widths in order to see the entire contents of table cells on a printout. In Datasheet view, you can use several techniques to adjust column widths, as described in the following table.

QUICK REFERENCE: ADJUSTING COLUMN WIDTHS

Adjustment Technique	Procedure
Manually adjust column widths.	Drag the border between two column headings.
AutoFit a column to fit the widest entry in the column.	Double-click the border between two column headings, or choose Format→Column Width, and click the Best Fit button.
Set a precise column width.	Choose Format→Column Width, and enter the desired width.
Set column widths to the default standard width.	Choose Format→Column Width, check the Standard Width box, and click OK.

Hands-On 19.11 Adjust Column Widths

1. Follow these steps to manually adjust the width of the Pet ID column:

Ⓐ Position the mouse pointer on the border between the Pet ID and Pet Name column headings, and the Adjust pointer will appear.

Pet ID	Pet Name	Pet Type
CT02	Max	Cat
CT16	Stripes	Cat
DG12	Wolfy	Dog

Ⓑ Drag the border to the left until the Pet ID column is just wide enough to display the column heading (Pet ID).

2. Follow this step to AutoFit a column to the width of the column heading:

Ⓐ Position the mouse pointer on the border between the Pet Name and Pet Type columns, and double-click when the adjust pointer appears. This technique can be tricky, so keep trying until the Pet Name column shrinks to the width of the heading. If the column has entries wider than the heading, then the width will adjust to fit the widest entry in the column.

Pet ID	Pet Name	Pet Type
CT02	Max	Cat
CT16	Stripes	Cat
DG12	Wolfy	Dog

3. Follow these steps to AutoFit the width of all columns:

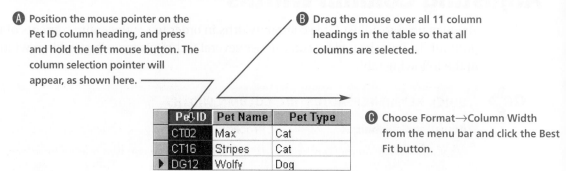

A Position the mouse pointer on the Pet ID column heading, and press and hold the left mouse button. The column selection pointer will appear, as shown here.

B Drag the mouse over all 11 column headings in the table so that all columns are selected.

C Choose Format→Column Width from the menu bar and click the Best Fit button.

Pet ID	Pet Name	Pet Type
CT02	Max	Cat
CT16	Stripes	Cat
▶ DG12	Wolfy	Dog

4. Click anywhere in the table to deselect the columns.

5. Scroll to the left, and notice that all column widths fit the widest entry (or heading) in the columns.

Margins and Page Orientation

Many tables are quite wide and may not fit on a single printed page. Fortunately, most printers can print text vertically in portrait orientation or horizontally in landscape orientation. Landscape orientation may allow a wide table (such as the Pets table) to print on a single page. You set the orientation of a page by issuing the File→Page Setup command, clicking the Page tab, and choosing the desired orientation. The margins can also be adjusted in the Page Setup dialog box.

Hands-On 19.12 Set Page Orientation and Margins, and Print

1. Choose File→Page Setup from the Access menu bar.

2. Make sure the Margins tab is active, and set all four margins to **0.25"** (that's 0.25 not 25).

3. Click the Page tab, and choose the Landscape option.

4. Click OK to complete the changes.

5. Click the Print Preview 🔍 button on the Access toolbar.

6. If necessary, zoom in by clicking anywhere on the table. Scroll left or right to view all columns in the table.
   Notice that the page orientation is now horizontal (landscape). All columns should be visible on the page.

7. Print the table by clicking the Print 🖨 button on the Print Preview toolbar.

8. Click the Close button on the Print Preview toolbar when you have finished.

9. Now close the table by choosing File→Close from the Access menu bar.

10. Click the Yes button when Access asks if you want to save the changes.
    In the next topic, you will set up another table using the Table Wizard.

The Table Wizard

Access provides a Table Wizard to help you set up common tables. The Table Wizard provides a variety of sample tables and sample fields for each table. You can choose the sample fields to include in a table and the Wizard will then build the table for you. In the next exercise, you will use the Table Wizard to set up a Customers table. Thus, you will have experience setting up tables in Design view and with the Table Wizard. In the future, you can use whichever method you prefer.

To start the Table Wizard, you click the New button on the Access Database toolbar, and choose Table Wizard from the New Table box. You can also double-click the Create Table By Using Wizard option that appears in the Tables section of the Access Database window.

Hands-On 19.13 Use the Table Wizard

Use the Table Wizard to Create a New Table

1. Click the New ▣ New button on the Access Database toolbar (located just above the Objects bar).

2. Choose Table Wizard, and click OK.

3. Follow these steps to begin setting up a table:

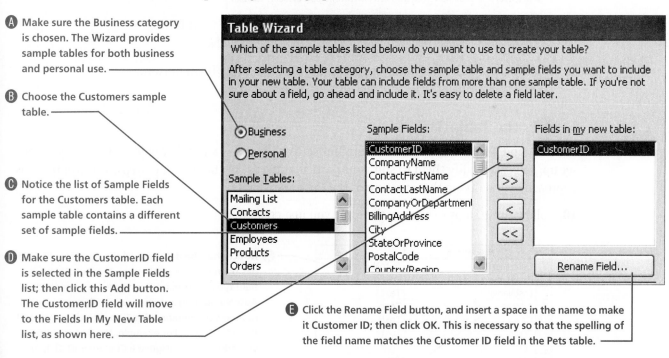

Ⓐ Make sure the Business category is chosen. The Wizard provides sample tables for both business and personal use.

Ⓑ Choose the Customers sample table.

Ⓒ Notice the list of Sample Fields for the Customers table. Each sample table contains a different set of sample fields.

Ⓓ Make sure the CustomerID field is selected in the Sample Fields list; then click this Add button. The CustomerID field will move to the Fields In My New Table list, as shown here.

Ⓔ Click the Rename Field button, and insert a space in the name to make it Customer ID; then click OK. This is necessary so that the spelling of the field name matches the Customer ID field in the Pets table.

!TIP!

You can add a field by double-clicking it.

4. Now add the ContactFirstName, ContactLastname, BillingAddress, City, StateOrProvince, PostalCode, and PhoneNumber fields by choosing them one at a time and clicking the Add button. Change the names of the fields as you add them, as shown in the following table.

Change this Field Name . . .	to This Name
ContactFirstName	Firstname
ContactLastName	Lastname
BillingAddress	Address
City	Leave as is
StateOrProvince	State
PostalCode	Zip
PhoneNumber	Phone

5. Use the Remove Field ⟨<⟩ button if you mistakenly added a field and wish to remove it. Your completed Fields In My New Table list should match the example shown to the right (although your Phone field should be completely visible).

Fields in my new table:

Customer ID
Firstname
Lastname
Address
City
State
Zip
Phone

6. Click the Next button at the bottom of the dialog box.
The next screen will propose the table name Customers and offer to set the primary key for you.

7. Leave the options set as they are by clicking the Next button.
The next screen will ask you about relationships between tables.

8. Leave the option set to Not Related To Pets by clicking the Next button.
The next screen will ask how you wish to display the completed table.

9. Choose the Modify the Table Design option and click the Finish button.
Access will create the table for you, and display it in Design view.

Modify the Table Structure

You may find Access wizards most useful for setting up tables and other objects. Once objects are set up, you can modify them to suit your particular needs. In the next few steps, you will use this approach by modifying the structure of the Customers table.

10. Follow these steps to explore the table you just created:

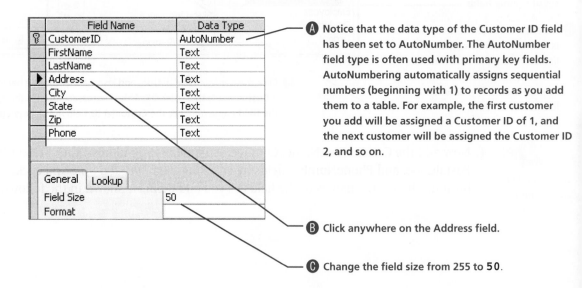

Ⓐ Notice that the data type of the Customer ID field has been set to AutoNumber. The AutoNumber field type is often used with primary key fields. AutoNumbering automatically assigns sequential numbers (beginning with 1) to records as you add them to a table. For example, the first customer you add will be assigned a Customer ID of 1, and the next customer will be assigned the Customer ID 2, and so on.

Ⓑ Click anywhere on the Address field.

Ⓒ Change the field size from 255 to **50**.

11. Follow these steps to change the default value of the State field:

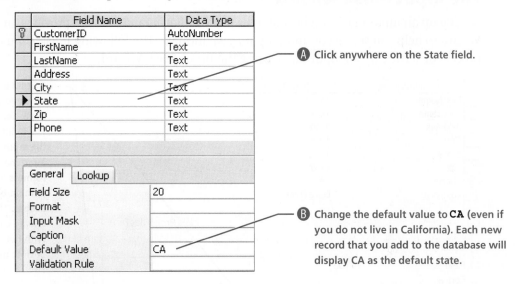

Ⓐ Click anywhere on the State field.

Ⓑ Change the default value to **CA** (even if you do not live in California). Each new record that you add to the database will display CA as the default state.

Add new Fields

12. Follow these steps to insert a new date field:

Ⓐ Click below the Phone field, and type **Last Visit**.

Ⓑ Click in the Data Type box, and choose Date/Time from the drop down list.

Ⓒ Choose Short Date as the format.

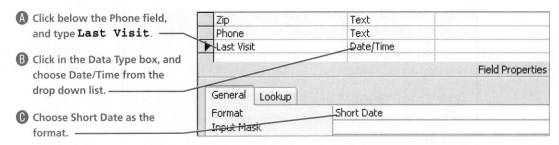

13. Now add a field named **Current Balance**, and set the Data Type to Currency. Continue with the next topic where you will create an input mask for the phone field.

Input Masks

Access lets you define input masks to help you enter formatted data. An input mask consists of a series of characters that define how the data is to be formatted. Input masks can be used for a variety of formatting tasks. For example, you can use an input mask to force all characters entered to be uppercase or to automatically insert parenthesis and dashes in phone numbers. The input masks character string is entered in the Input Mask field property in table design view. Once an input mask is set up in a table, the mask formats display data in queries, forms, and reports.

The Input Mask Wizard

Setting up an input mask can be a tedious process. Fortunately, Access provides an Input Mask Wizard to help you set up common input mask formats. The following illustration discusses the process of setting up an input mask using the Input Mask Wizard.

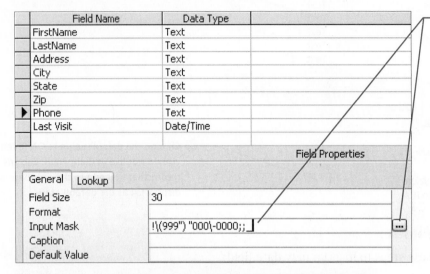

A Build button appears when you click in the Input Mask field property box. The Build button initiates the Input Mask Wizard. This input mask character string formats telephone numbers with parenthesis and dashes. The Input Mask Wizard can only be used with fields that have a Text or Date data type.

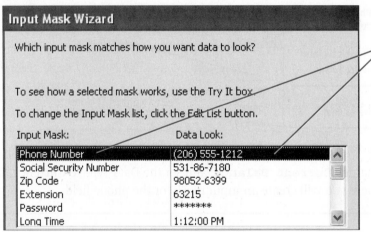

The Input Mask Wizard lets you choose common mask formats.

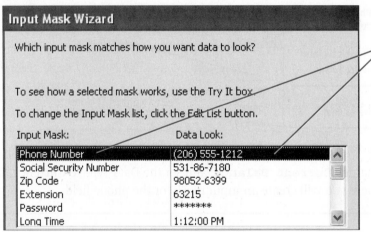 ## Hands-On 19.14 Use the Input Mask Wizard and Complete the Table

In this exercise, you will set up two input masks and complete the table.

Set Up an Input Mask for the Phone Field

1. Click in the Phone field and then click in the Input Mask box in the Field Properties section of the window.

2. Click the Build ⬛ button on the right side of the Input Mask box and choose Yes to save the table.

3. Make sure the Phone Number mask is chosen in the first Wizard screen and click Next.

4. Click Next on the second Wizard screen to accept the proposed mask format.

5. Make sure the Without the Symbols option is chosen in the third screen and then click Next.

6. Click the Finish button to complete the input mask.
   Access will display the input mask characters !(999) 000-0000;;_ in the Input Mask box.

Set Up an Input Mask for the Zip Field

7. Click in the Zip field and then click in the Input Mask box.

8. Click the Build ⊞ button and choose Yes to save the table.

9. Choose the Zip Code mask and click the Finish button to accept the default options.
   You can click the Finish button at any time while using a Wizard to accept the remaining default settings. Access will display the input mask characters 00000-9999;;_ in the Input Mask box.

Add Data to the Table

10. Click the Datasheet View ⊞ button on the Access toolbar.

11. Click Yes when Access asks if you wish to save the table.
    Notice the word (AutoNumber) is selected in the first empty record. This field is formatted with the AutoNumber data type so you will bypass it in the next step. Access will automatically assign the number 1 to the record when you begin entering data in the Firstname field.

12. Tap the ⌈TAB⌉ key to bypass the Customer ID field.

13. Type the name **Mark** in the Firstname field. The number 1 will appear in the Customer ID field.

14. Tap ⌈TAB⌉, and type **Roth** in the Lastname field.

15. Tap ⌈TAB⌉, and type **760 Maple Avenue** in the Address field.

16. Tap ⌈TAB⌉, and type **Fremont** in the City field.

17. Tap ⌈TAB⌉, and notice that the State field is set to CA.
    This is because you set CA as the default value for this field.

18. Tap ⌈TAB⌉ to bypass the State field (CA is correct) and type **94538** in the Zip field.
    You will notice that a hyphen appears to the right of the digits. This is because the Zip field has also been formatted with an input mask. The input mask inserts a hyphen between the first five and last four digits (if you use nine digits).

19. Tap ⌈TAB⌉ to bypass the last four digits of the zip code.

20. Type the area code **510** in the Phone field, and the input mask will surround the number with parenthesis.

21. Complete the phone number by typing **2349090**.
    Access will format the number by inserting a hyphen between the 4 and the 9.

22. Tap ⌈TAB⌉, and type **7/7/03** in the Last Visit field.

23. Tap TAB, and type **235** in the Current Balance field.

24. Now add the following two records to the table.
    The AutoNumber feature will insert numbers in the Customer ID field, so just tap TAB when you reach that field. Also, do not type parenthesis in the phone numbers because the input mask will automatically apply parenthesis for you.

Customer ID	Firstname	Lastname	Address	City	State	Zip	Phone	Last Visit	Current Balance
2	Tony	Simpson	312 York Lane	Richmond	CA	94804	(510) 238-2233	9/7/03	185
3	Jason	Jones	2233 Crystal Street	San Mateo	CA	94403	(415) 312-2312	7/15/03	48

Print the Table

25. Adjust the width of all columns to fit the widest entry/heading in the columns. You can accomplish this by double-clicking the borders between the column headings. You can also select all of the columns by dragging the mouse pointer across the column headings and then double-clicking the border between the column headings of any two selected columns. Finally, you can select all columns and use the Format→Column Width command, then click the Best Fit button.

26. Use the File→Page Setup command to set all four margins to **0.5"**.

27. Notice that the Print Headings box is checked on the Margins tab.
    In a moment when you preview the table printout, you will notice a header and footer appear at the top and bottom of the page. The Print Headings box displays the header and footer. The Table Wizard turned on this option.

28. Set the orientation to Landscape using the Page tab in the Page Setup dialog box, and click OK.

29. Use Print Preview to preview the table, and then print the table if desired.

30. Close Print Preview, and feel free to experiment with any of the topics that you have learned in this lesson.

31. Close the table when you have finished experimenting, and save any changes.

32. Close Access by choosing File→Exit from the Access menu bar.

33. Now continue with the end-of-lesson questions and exercises on the following pages.

Concepts Review

True/False Questions

1.	An Access database can have a maximum of 1 table.	TRUE	FALSE
2.	Datasheet view is used to set up the structure of tables.	TRUE	FALSE
3.	If you are in Design view and you want to switch to Datasheet view, you must close the table and reopen it in Datasheet view.	TRUE	FALSE
4.	A database is like a container because it can hold several types of objects, including tables.	TRUE	FALSE
5.	Changing the structure of a table will never result in lost data.	TRUE	FALSE
6.	The page orientation can be changed with the File→Print command.	TRUE	FALSE
7.	Portrait orientation causes a table to print horizontally on a page.	TRUE	FALSE
8.	The Table Wizard is used to automate data entry in a table.	TRUE	FALSE
9.	Text, Numbers, and Currency are examples of data types.	TRUE	FALSE
10.	A pencil icon in the row selector indicates a new record in which you can type.	TRUE	FALSE

Multiple Choice Questions

1. What is the maximum number of characters that a field name may contain?
   a. 8
   b. 32
   c. 64
   d. 255

2. What is the first step that you should take if you want to delete a record?
   a. Click in the desired record, or select the record.
   b. Click the Delete Record button on the toolbar.
   c. Narrow the column width.
   d. Delete all text from the cells.

3. Which of the following commands is used to change the page orientation?
   a. File→Print
   b. File→Page Setup
   c. Format→Page Orientation
   d. Format→Print Preview

4. What happens when you double-click the border between two column headings in Datasheet view?
   a. The table is closed.
   b. The column width is set to the default column width.
   c. A new column is inserted.
   d. The column width is AutoFit to the widest entry.

Skill Builders

Skill Builder 19.1 Set Up a Table in Design View

In this exercise, you will set up a new database for the Tropical Getaways travel company. Tropical Getaways is an exciting new travel company that specializes in inexpensive vacations to tropical locations worldwide. You have been asked to set up a database to track clients and trips. In this exercise, you will create the first table for the database.

1. Start Access, choose Create a New File, choose the Blank Database option from the Task Pane, and click OK.

2. Assign the name **Tropical Getaways** to your new database, and save it on your your file storage location.
   The Tables object list should be displayed in the Access Database window.

3. Double-click the Create Table in Design View option to begin setting up a new table in Design view.

4. Type **Customer ID** as the first field name, and tap the (TAB) key.

5. Click the drop-down 🔽 button in the Data Type box, and choose AutoNumber.
   Access will automatically assign sequential Customer IDs when you enter data in this table.

6. Click the Primary Key 🔑 button on the toolbar to make Customer ID the primary key.

7. Set up the remainder of this table using the field names, data types, and options shown in the following table. Keep in mind that you have already set up the Customer ID field.

Field Name	Data Type	Field Size	Primary Key	Description
Customer ID	AutoNumber		Yes	
Firstname	Text	30		
Lastname	Text	30		
Address	Text	50		
City	Text	30		
State	Text	2		
Zip	Text	9		
Profile	Text	20		The profile indicates the category of trips the customer prefers

8. When you have finished, click the Datasheet View 🖩 button on the Access toolbar.

9. Click Yes when Access asks if you wish to save the table.

10. Type the name **Customers**, click OK, and then enter the following four records. The Customer ID numbers are entered automatically because Customer ID has an AutoNumber data type.

Customer ID	Firstname	Lastname	Address	City	State	Zip	Profile
1	Debbie	Thomas	450 Crestwood Lane	Austin	TX	78752	Adventure
2	Wilma	Boyd	855 State Street	Richmond	NY	12954	Leisure
3	Ted	Wilkins	900 C Street	Fort Worth	TX	76104	Adventure
4	Alice	Simpson	2450 Ridge Road	Fort Worth	TX	76105	Family

11. When you have finished, choose File→Close from the Access menu bar to close the table. *Access automatically saves the data. You will set up another table in the next Skill Builder exercise.*

Skill Builder 19.2 Set Up a Table in Design View

In this exercise, you will set up another table for the Tropical Getaways database.

1. Double-click the Create Table in Design View option to begin setting up a new table in Design view.

2. Set up the table using the following structure:

Field Name	Data Type	Field Size/Format	Primary Key	Description
Trip ID	Text	8	Yes	Four- to eight-character unique identifier for each trip
Customer ID	Number	Long Integer		ID number from Customers table
Destination	Text	50		
Category	Text	30		All trips have a category such as Adventure, Leisure, etc.
Departure Date	Date/Time	Short Date		
Return Date	Date/Time	Short Date		
Cost	Currency			

3. Switch to Datasheet view and save the table as **Trips**.

4. Enter the following data into the Trips table. Do not type the dollar signs and commas when entering the Cost numbers. Access will add the dollar signs and commas for you because you chose the Currency data type when setting up the Cost field.

Trip ID	Customer ID	Destination	Category	Departure Date	Return Date	Cost
Adv01	1	Kenyan Safari	Adventure	8/5/04	9/4/04	$6,600
Lei01	2	Caribbean Cruise	Leisure	9/19/04	9/28/04	$2,390
Adv02	1	Amazon Jungle Trek	Adventure	8/7/04	9/14/04	$7,765
Fam01	4	Orlando	Family	3/4/04	3/10/04	$3,400

5. Close the Trips table when you have finished.
   The Tables objects list should now display both the Customers and Trips table icons. In the next exercise, you will print the Customers table.

Skill Builder 19.3 Print the Table

The Tropical Getaways database should be open, and the Customers and Trips tables should be visible in the Access Database window.

1. Double-click the Customers table to open it in Datasheet view.
   You can always open a table in Datasheet view by double-clicking it.

2. Adjust the widths of all columns to display the widest entries in the columns.

3. Use the Print Preview 🔍 button to preview the table.

4. Zoom in on the table by clicking anywhere on it.

5. Feel free to print the table and check your data for accuracy.

6. Close Print Preview when you have finished.

7. Close the table and choose Yes when Access asks if you want to save the changes.

8. Open the Trips table, and adjust the column widths to fit the widest entries in the columns.

9. Print the table, and check your data for accuracy.

10. Close the table, and save the changes when you have finished.

11. Exit from Access by choosing File→Exit from the menu bar.

Skill Builder 19.4 Use the Database Wizard

In this Skill Builder, you will use the Database Wizard to set up a database.

1. If necessary, start Access and the Task Pane will appear. If the Task Pane is not displayed, use the View→Toolbars→Task Pane command to display it.

2. Choose Create a New File in the Task Pane. In the next view of the Task Pane, choose On My Computer…

3. Click the Databases tab in the Templates box to view the available predefined databases.
   The Database Wizard is initiated when you choose any of these predefined databases.

4. Double-click the Contact Management database and save it to your exercise diskette as **Contact Management Database**.

5. Click Next to bypass the first Wizard screen.
   The second Wizard screen displays the predefined tables in the Contact Management database and the fields in each table. You can choose to remove fields by unchecking them or add additional fields by scrolling through the field list and checking the desired additional fields (shown in italics).

6. Click Next to bypass the screen accepting the default fields.

7. Continue to click the Next button on the next few screens. You will be offered various form and report formats; feel free to choose any options you desire.

8. Click the Finish button when you have finished choosing options, and the Wizard will create the database.

9. Feel free to use your new database. You will be exposed to features that you have not learned about yet and will certainly be impressed with the database the Wizard has created.
   At this point, you could add tables, fields, and other objects to your database or modify the objects already in the database.

10. When you have finished examining your database, close it and exit from Access.

Assessments

Assessment 19.1 Create a Table

In this assessment, you will begin creating a database for Classic Cars. Classic Cars is an organization devoted to tracking, categorizing, and preserving classic automobiles. You will begin by creating tables to track collectors and cars.

1. Start Access, and create a new database named **Classic Cars**.

2. Create a new table with the following structure:

Field Name	Data Type	Field Size	Primary Key	Description
Collector ID	AutoNumber	Long Integer	Yes	
Firstname	Text	30		
Lastname	Text	30		
Address	Text	50		
City	Text	30		
State	Text	2		
Zip	Text	9		
Era of Interest	Text	20		This field identifies the time period that the collector is most interested in
Collection Size	Number	Long Integer		Number of cars in collection

3. Enter the following records into the table, and name the table **Collectors**.

Collector ID	Firstname	Lastname	Address	City	State	Zip	Era of Interest	Collection size
1	Cindy	Johnson	4220 Edward Street	Northlake	IL	60164	1950s	42
2	Tammy	Olson	1200 Big Pine Drive	Moses Lake	WA	98837	1960s	6
3	Ed	Larkson	2300 Watson Street	Cainesville	OH	43701	Early 1900s	34
4	Bob	Barker	6340 Palm Drive	Rockridge	FL	32955	1950s	7

4. AutoFit the width of all columns to fit the largest entry/heading in the columns.

5. Use Print Preview to preview the table. If necessary, switch the orientation to landscape and reduce the margins until the table fits on one page.

6. Print the table.

7. Close the table when you have finished, and save any changes that you have made.

8. Create another new table with the following structure:

Field Name	Data Type	Field Size/ Format	Primary Key	Description
Car ID	Text	15	Yes	Up to 15 characters to uniquely identify each car
Collector ID	Number	Long Integer		ID number from Collectors table
Year	Text	20		
Make	Text	30		
Model	Text	50		
Color	Text	30		
Condition	Text	30		
Value	Currency			Estimated value

9. Enter the following records into the table and name the table **Cars**.

Car ID	Collector ID	Year	Make	Model	Color	Condition	Value
CJ01	1	58	Chevrolet	Corvette	Red and white	Mint	$65,000
TO05	2	62	Chevrolet	Corvette	Blue	Excellent	$30,000
CJ22	1	59	Ford	Thunderbird	Tan	Good	$20,000
BB03	4	58	Chevrolet	Corvette	Black	Excellent	$35,000

10. AutoFit the width of all columns to fit the largest entry/heading in the columns.

11. Use Print Preview to preview the table.

12. Print the table.

13. Close the table when you have finished, and save any changes that you have made.

14. Exit from Access when you have finished.

Critical Thinking

Critical Thinking 19.1 Create Tables

Linda Holmes is a real estate agent specializing in investment properties. She needs database software to help her manage her business. She has reviewed commercially available software but has found it inadequate for her needs. Instead, Linda has hired you to create a customized Access database.

Create a new, blank database for Linda named **Holmestead Realty**. The first two categories of information Linda wants to track are contact information for sellers and listing information for the properties they wish to sell. Follow these guidelines to set up two tables in your new database:

- Name the first table **Contacts** and the second table **Listings**.
- Use the field names, data types, and field properties described below.
- Leave all other field properties set to their default values.

Contacts Table

Field Name	Data Type	Field Properties
Seller ID	Auto Number	Primary key
FirstName	Text	
LastName	Text	
SpouseName	Text	Field size 30
Address	Text	
City	Text	
State	Text	Set default value to NC
Zip	Text	Apply Zip Code input mask, if necessary
Phone	Text	Apply Phone Number input mask, if necessary
Contact Type	Text	

Listings Table

Field Name	Data Type	Field Properties
MLS #	Number	Primary key No Default Value (remove 0 from Default Value property box)
Street #	Number	
Address	Text	
Price	Currency	
Listing Date	Date	Short Date format
Expiration Date	Date	Short Date format
Commission Rate	Number	Field Size: Decimal, Format: Percent, Scale: 3, Decimal Places: 1, Default Value: 0.06
Seller ID	Number	

Enter the following data into your completed tables. Be sure to check the data carefully when finished. Adjust all column widths to fit the widest entry in each column. Print copies of both tables when you have finished.

Contacts

Seller ID	FirstName	LastName	SpouseName	Address	City	ST	Zip	Phone	Contact Type
1	John	Desmond	Lydia	1020 Brevard Road	Asheville	NC	28801	(828) 298-5698	Investor
2	David	Armstrong		15 Dover Street	Swannanoa	NC	28778	(828) 669-8579	Investor
3	Sharon	Carter		9 Forest Pine Circle	Asheville	NC	28803	(828) 277-3658	Investor
4	Jeff	Jones	Susan	107 Glen Meadows Place	Arden	NC	28704	(828) 687-5786	Investor
5	Jamie	Stevens		10 Knollwood Drive	Asheville	NC	28804	(828) 274-6643	Investor
6	Phil	Wallace	Jennifer	1571 Brannon Road	Asheville	NC	28801	(828) 252-2365	Investor

Listings

MLS #	Street #	Address	Price	Listing Date	Expiration Date	Commission Rate	Seller ID
52236	1132	Richwood Road	$55,000	1/14/03	1/14/04	6.0%	4
52358	14	Dover Street	$70,000	5/30/03	11/30/03	7.0%	2
52369	6	Thoroughbred Lane	$125,000	9/25/03	3/25/04	6.0%	1
52425	218	Wildflower Road	$329,500	6/2/03	12/2/03	4.5%	2
52511	403	Hawks Landing	$150,000	9/23/03	3/23/04	6.0%	3
52524	64	Hastings Street	$112,000	4/6/03	10/6/03	4.5%	6
52526	137	Woodbridge Lane	$80,000	3/21/03	9/21/03	4.5%	6
52649	23	Edwards Avenue	$70,000	7/15/03	1/15/04	6.0%	5
52650	24	Edwards Avenue	$75,000	7/15/03	1/15/04	6.0%	5

Critical Thinking 19.2 Update Tables

Linda received the printed copies of the database tables and was quite satisfied; however, she has requested some changes. Update the database with the following changes:

- Sharon Carter was recently married to Greg Collins. On the Contacts table, locate Sharon, change her last name, and add Greg to the spouse field.

- David Armstrong's mother is moving into the house on 14 Dover Street. Delete that listing from the Listings table.

- The Wallace's bought a new investment property at 17 Keyway Avenue. Add the property to the Listings table using the following information:

  MLS #: 52912
  Price: $175,000
  Commission Rate: 6%
  Listing Date: Today's date
  Expiration Date: 6 months from today

- Linda also wants to track the style of each home. Add a field named Style to the Listings table, and then enter the data in the Style column on the next page to the listings currently in the Listings table:

MLS #	Street #	Address	Style
52236	1132	Richwood Road	Bungalow
52369	6	Thoroughbred Lane	Ranch
52425	218	Wildflower Road	Contemporary
52511	403	Hawks Landing	Ranch
52524	64	Hastings Street	2 Story
52526	137	Woodbridge Lane	1 Story w/basement
52649	23	Edwards Avenue	Duplex
52650	24	Edwards Avenue	Duplex
52912	17	Keyway Avenue	2 Story

LESSON 20

Forms and Reports

I n this lesson, you will enhance the Pinnacle Pet Care database with forms and reports. You will create forms that will make it easy to view, enter, and edit data in the Customers and Pets tables. You will also create reports to present your data in a variety of ways.

Case Study

Most of the employees at Pinnacle Pet Care have little computer experience and even less experience using Microsoft Access. For this reason, Penny Johnson must make it easy for employees to enter and extract data from the database. Penny decides to set up data entry forms that let employees enter customer information and pet information. Penny also works closely with her employees to determine the types of reports they require. Penny realizes that her employees require an outstanding customer balance report that includes the customer names and telephone numbers. Another report will list the expenditures and number of visits for each pet. This report will be sorted by expenditures so that the customers spending the most on their pets will appear at the top of the report.

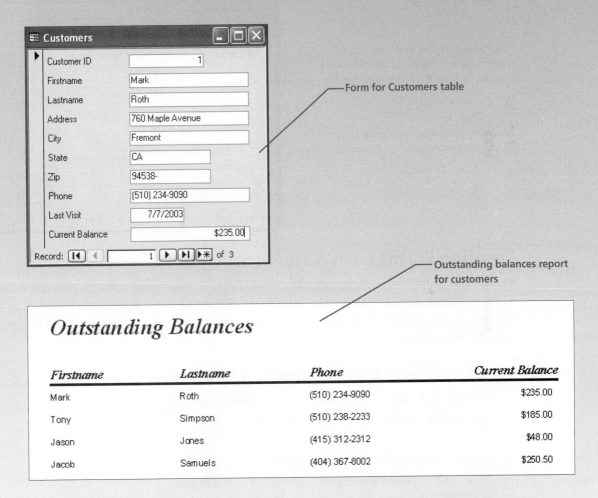

Form for Customers table

Outstanding balances report for customers

Forms

In the previous lesson, you learned that an Access database is composed of various objects. A form is a type of object that lets you view, edit, and enter data. The benefit of a form is that it allows you to focus on a single record in the database. This is in contrast to Datasheet view where you are able to view many records at the same time. The following illustration shows a form for the Customers table in the Pinnacle Pet Care database.

Notice that the form displays one complete record from the database. Forms let you focus on a single customer, pet, etc.

Fields such as Phone, Last Visit, and Current Balance are automatically formatted with symbols (as they are in Datasheet view).

The form also contains navigation buttons to let you browse through the database.

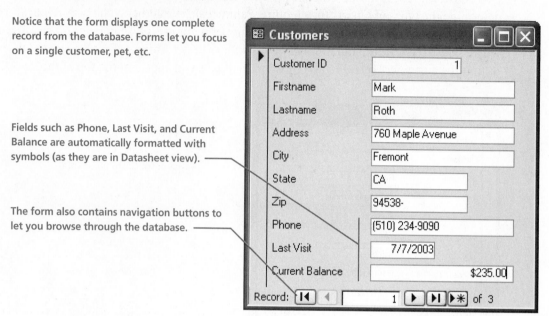

Creating Forms with AutoForm

You can use AutoForm to automatically create simple forms. AutoForm creates a form that displays all fields from a particular table. The form in the preceding illustration was created from the Customers table using AutoForm. More complex forms can be created using form Design view or with the Form Wizard.

QUICK REFERENCE: CREATING FORMS WITH AUTOFORM

- Choose the desired table in the Access Database window.
- Click the New Object [icon] drop-down button near the right end of the Access toolbar.
- Choose AutoForm from the drop-down list.
- Close the form when you have finished using it, and assign it a name.

Hands-On 20.1 Use AutoForm

In this exercise, you will open the Pinnacle Pet Care database you created in Lesson 19. You will continue to enhance the Pinnacle Pet Care database throughout this course.

1. Start Access, and follow these steps to open the Pinnacle Pet Care database:

A If the Pinnacle Pet Care database is listed in the Task Pane, then choose it and the database will open. If it is not listed, then choose More, navigate to your exercise diskette, and open the Pinnacle Pet Care file. ⎯⎯

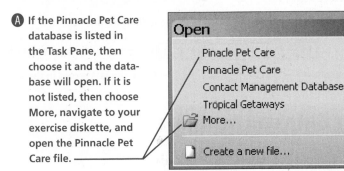

2. Follow these steps to create a form for the Customers table:

   Access will create the form, and the Mark Roth record will be displayed. This is because the Mark Roth record is the first record in the table.

A Choose the Customers table from the list of tables. You must choose the desired table before creating a form. ↗

B Click the drop-down button on the New Object button, and choose AutoForm, as shown here. ↗

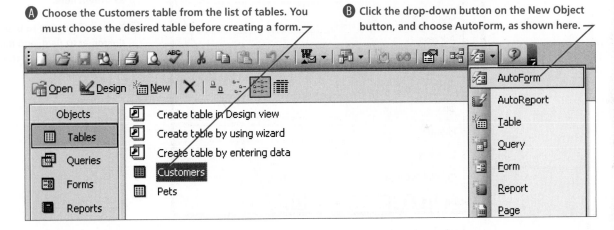

Entering Data and Navigating Records in Forms

Forms are used for viewing and entering data one record at a time. When you enter data using a form, the data is stored in the underlying table that the form is based upon. Forms also make it easy to navigate to various records. The navigation bar at the bottom of a form lets you navigate to records in the underlying table. The form navigation bar has the same buttons that appear on the navigation bar in Datasheet view.

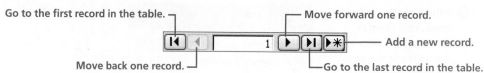

Go to the first record in the table.

Move back one record.

Move forward one record.

Add a new record.

Go to the last record in the table.

Hands-On 20.2 Enter Data and Navigate

1. Follow these steps to prepare to enter a new record:

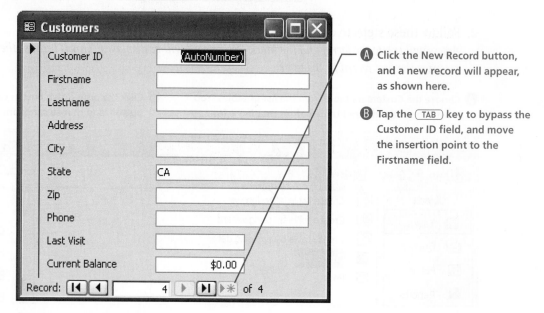

A Click the New Record button, and a new record will appear, as shown here.

B Tap the (TAB) key to bypass the Customer ID field, and move the insertion point to the Firstname field.

2. Follow this step to enter the data:

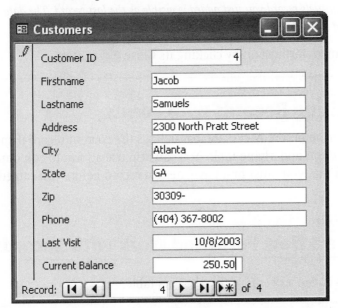

Ⓐ Enter the data shown here using the ⌈TAB⌋ key to move from one field to the next. Notice that you must change the entry in the State field from CA to GA. You can always change the default value for a record by typing a new value. You set the default value to CA when you created the table in the previous lesson. Also, the dollar sign will not appear in the Current Balance field until you go to another field or record after typing the entry in the Current Balance field.

In the next few steps, you will close the form and assign a name to it. You name forms as you name tables and all other database objects.

3. Follow this step to close the form:

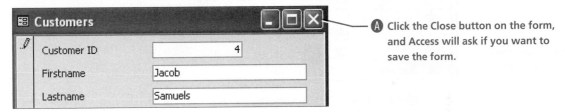

Ⓐ Click the Close button on the form, and Access will ask if you want to save the form.

4. Click the Yes button, and Access will propose the name Customers.

5. Click OK to accept the proposed name.

6. Follow these steps to confirm that the form has been created and to reopen the form:

Ⓐ Click the Forms button on the Objects bar, and the Customers icon will be visible.

Ⓑ Double-click the Customers icon to open it. (You also could have clicked the form and then clicked the Open button on the Database toolbar just above the Objects bar).

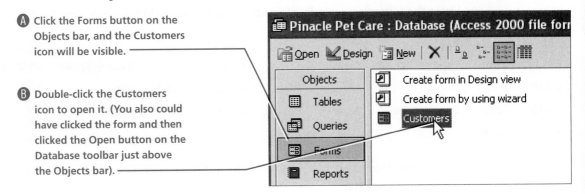

7. Use the navigation bar at the bottom of the form to browse through the records.
   Notice that the Jacob Samuels record you just added is visible as the last record. The data you entered for Jacob Samuels has been entered into the Customers table.

8. Now close the Customers form again by clicking its Close ⊠ button.

Deleting and Editing Records with Forms

The Delete Record ⊠ button on the Access toolbar deletes the current record displayed in a form. The record is deleted from the underlying table. You can also use a form to edit data in an underlying table. Keep in mind that you must first navigate to a record before you can edit the data or delete the record.

 ## Hands-On 20.3 Create a New Form and Work with Records

1. Follow these steps to create a new form for the Pets table:

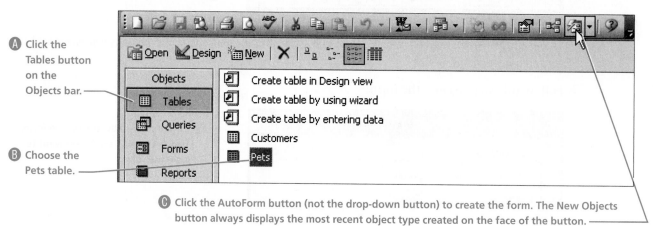

Ⓐ Click the Tables button on the Objects bar.

Ⓑ Choose the Pets table.

Ⓒ Click the AutoForm button (not the drop-down button) to create the form. The New Objects button always displays the most recent object type created on the face of the button.

Notice that the new form is based upon the fields in the Pets table.

2. Click the New Record ⊞ button on the navigation bar at the bottom of the form.

3. Enter the following records, stopping at the Breed field for Slinky the Snake:

Pet ID	Pet Name	Pet Type	Breed	Gender	Color	Date of Birth	Last Visit	Expenditures	Number of Visits	Customer ID
DG24	Ben	Dog	Terrier	Male	Black	6/1/92	10/8/03	480	3	4
DG25	Spike	Dog	Chow	Male	Brown	4/3/84	10/8/03	890	12	4
SN01	Slinky	Snake								

4. It turns out that snakes are not welcome at Pinnacle Pets, so click the Delete Record ⊠ button on the Access toolbar.

5. Click Yes to confirm the deletion of Slinky the Snake.

6. Use the navigation bar to navigate backwards through the records, and notice that the Ben the dog record and the Spike the dog record are still there.

7. Click the Close ⊠ button on the form.

8. Click Yes when Access asks if you want to save the form.

9. Click OK on the Save As box to accept the name Pets.
   Click the Forms button on the Objects bar to see both the Customer and Pets form icons.

Printing Forms

You can print the records in a table by clicking the Print 🖨 button from an open form. Access will print a copy of the form with displayed data for each record in the database. This technique can be useful if there are a large number of fields in a table. Printing a datasheet with a large number of fields is often difficult because the fields can't be displayed on a single page. A form, however, will often fit on a single page. On the other hand, printing forms may not be wise if the table has a large number of records. Forms typically take a large amount of space on the printed page, and you will use a lot of paper if you print a table with many records.

 ## Hands-On 20.4 **Preview the Pets Form**

1. Click the Forms button on the Objects bar.

2. Double-click the Pets icon in the Forms section of the database window.

3. Click the Print Preview 🔍 button on the Access toolbar.

4. If necessary, maximize ◻ the Print Preview window.

5. Click anywhere on the page in the Print Preview window to zoom in.
   Notice that a copy of the form is displayed for each record in the Pets table.

6. Use the navigation bar at the bottom of the Print Preview window to browse through the pages.
   As you can see, printing data via a form may require a lot of paper.

7. Close the Print Preview window without printing.

8. Click the Restore ⧉ button near the top right corner of the window to restore the Pets form (not the Access program window).

9. Click the Close ⊠ button on the Pets form.

Reports

You can create reports to present data in a printed format. You can specify the fields to include in reports and you can format reports using built-in report styles. In the next exercise, you will create the report shown below. Notice that the report lists just four fields from the Customers table.

Outstanding Balances

Firstname	Lastname	Phone	Current Balance
Mark	Roth	(510) 234-9090	$235.00
Tony	Simpson	(510) 238-2233	$185.00
Jason	Jones	(415) 312-2312	$48.00
Jacob	Samuels	(404) 367-8002	$250.50

Complexity of Reports

In this lesson, you will use the Report Wizard to create simple reports. However, Access reports can be quite complex. For example, reports can include calculated fields that sum up columns of numbers and grouping levels to organize records in logical groups.

AutoReport and the Report Wizard

In the previous exercises, you used AutoForm to create forms. AutoForm creates a form using all fields from a table. This is acceptable, because you will normally want all fields from a table on a form. Reports, on the other hand, usually require a subset of a table's fields. For example, the report shown in the previous illustration uses just four fields from the Customers table. Auto-Report has limited use because it inserts all fields from a table into a report. Fortunately, Access provides a Report Wizard that gives you flexibility when setting up reports. The Report Wizard lets you choose the fields to include in the report. The Report Wizard also lets you specify various formatting options.

QUICK REFERENCE: USING THE REPORT WIZARD

- Click the Reports button on the Objects bar in the Database window.

- Double-click the Create Report by Using Wizard option. You can also click the New button on the Access Database toolbar and choose Report Wizard from the dialog box.

- Choose the desired table or query that you wish to base the report on from the Tables/Queries list, and click OK.

- Follow the Report Wizard steps to create the desired report.

Previewing and Printing Reports

The Preview [🔍 Preview] button appears on the Access Database toolbar whenever the Reports button is pressed on the Objects bar and a report is chosen. You can open the report in Print Preview mode by clicking the Preview button. The Print Preview window functions the same way with reports as it does with other objects.

The Print button can be used to print reports directly from the Database window. The Print button also appears on the Print Preview toolbar when a report is chosen. You can print all pages of a report by clicking the Print button. You must use the File→Print command to display the Print dialog box if you want to print a range of pages or set other print options.

FROM THE KEYBOARD
(CTRL)+(P) to display
Print dialog box

Hands-On 20.5 Use the Report Wizard

Create an Outstanding Balances Report

1. Follow these steps to launch the Report Wizard:

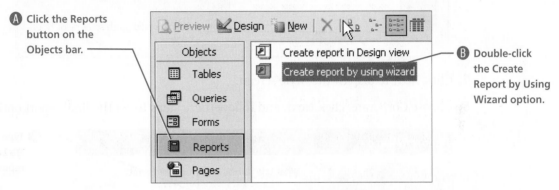

Ⓐ Click the Reports button on the Objects bar.

Ⓑ Double-click the Create Report by Using Wizard option.

2. Follow these steps to choose the Customers table as the basis for the report and to add the Firstname field to the Selected Fields list:

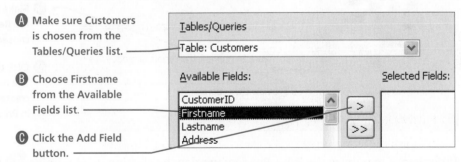

Ⓐ Make sure Customers is chosen from the Tables/Queries list.

Ⓑ Choose Firstname from the Available Fields list.

Ⓒ Click the Add Field button.

3. Now add the Lastname, Phone, and Current Balance fields. The completed Selected Fields list is shown to the right.

4. Click Next to display the Grouping Levels screen.

5. Click Next to bypass the Grouping Levels screen and display the Sort Order screen.

6. Click Next to bypass the Sort Order screen and display the Layout screen. Make sure the layout options are set as shown on the next page.

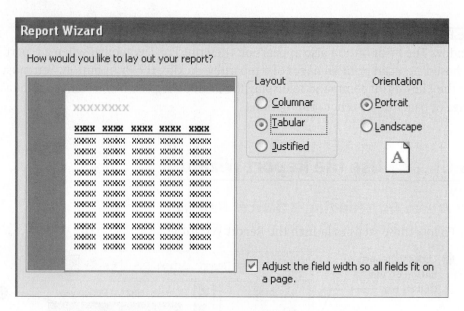

7. Click Next to display the Style screen.

8. Choose Corporate, click Next, and follow these steps to set the final report options:

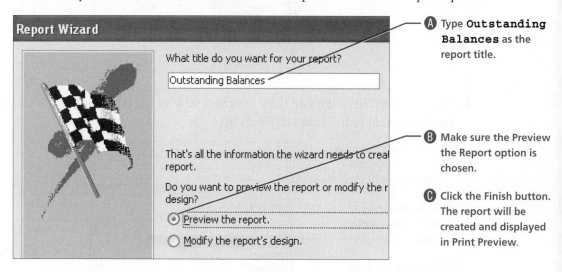

A Type **Outstanding Balances** as the report title.

B Make sure the Preview the Report option is chosen.

C Click the Finish button. The report will be created and displayed in Print Preview.

9. If necessary, maximize the Print Preview window by clicking its Maximize ▣ button.

10. Zoom in or out on the report by clicking the mouse pointer anywhere on it.
The top section of your report should match the following example (although the sort order may be different). You will sort reports in the Skill Builder exercises.

Outstanding Balances

Firstname	Lastname	Phone	Current Balance
Mark	Roth	(510) 234-9090	$235.00
Tony	Simpson	(510) 238-2233	$185.00
Jason	Jones	(415) 312-2312	$48.00
Jacob	Samuels	(404) 367-8002	$250.50

11. Click the Design View ![icon] button on the left end of the Print Preview toolbar.

    The report will display in Design view with a report header, page header, detail section, etc. In Design view, you can change the position of objects, add and remove objects, and change the properties of objects. However, you won't work in Design view at this time.

12. Click the Print Preview ![icon] button on the left end of the toolbar to return to Print Preview.

13. Feel free to print the report by clicking the Print ![icon] button on the Print Preview toolbar.

14. Choose File→Close from the menu bar to close the report.

    The Report will automatically be assigned the name Outstanding Balances, and an Outstanding Balances icon will appear in the Reports section of the database window. As you can see from this example, creating simple reports is quite easy if you use the Report Wizard. Now continue with the remainder of this exercise, where you will create a report to accompany the Pets table.

Create a Pets Report

15. Make sure the Reports button is pressed on the Objects bar, and double-click the Create Report by Using Wizard option.

16. Choose the Pets table from the Tables/Queries list.

17. Add the Pet Name, Pet Type, Expenditures, and Number of Visits fields to the Selected Fields list as shown to the right.

Selected Fields:
Pet Name
Pet Type
Expenditures
Number of Visits

18. Click the Finish button to accept all of the remaining default settings, and the completed report shown below will appear.

Pets

Pet Name	Pet Type	Expenditures	Number of Visits
Wolfy	Dog	$450.00	7
Dillon	Dog	$150.55	3
Bugs	Rabbit	$600.50	4
Max	Cat	$1,450.55	20
Stripes	Cat	$450.00	9
Tony	Cat	$145.00	6
Fetch	Dog	$345.00	3
Ben	Dog	$480.00	3
Spike	Dog	$890.00	12

19. Notice the alignment of the fields within the columns.

    Fields have the same left or right alignment in a report as they do in the table the report is based on.

20. Close the report with the File→Close command.

    The Reports section should now have an Outstanding Balance report and a Pets report.

Copying Objects

FROM THE KEYBOARD

CTRL+C to copy

CTRL+V to paste

You can copy tables, forms, reports, and other types of objects. Objects can be copied and then pasted into the same database, to a different database, or to other applications. Copying an object to the same database can be useful if you intend to modify the object. By making a copy, you will have a backup of the object in case you damage the original. You copy objects with the Copy and Paste buttons on the Access toolbar.

Deleting Objects

FROM THE KEYBOARD

DELETE to delete selected object

Objects can also be deleted from an Access database. However, you must be careful when deleting objects because they are permanently deleted from the database. Deleting objects can be useful, especially when using Wizards and tools like AutoForm. If you make a mistake or are unhappy with the results that one of these automated tools produces, you can delete the object and start over. You delete an object by choosing the desired object in the database window and issuing the Edit→Delete command or by clicking the Delete button on the Access Database toolbar.

Hands-On 20.6 Copy a Report, Then Delete the Copy

Copy the Report

1. Choose the Pets icon in the Reports section of the database window.

2. Click the Copy [icon] button on the Access toolbar.

3. Click the Paste [icon] button on the toolbar, and the Paste As box will appear.

4. Type the name **Copy of Pets** in the Paste As box, and click OK.
   The Copy of Pets report will appear in the Reports section.

5. Double-click the Copy of Pets report, and it will open.
   Notice that this report is identical to the Pets report.

6. Close the report with the File→Close command.

Delete the Report

7. Make sure the Copy of Pets report is chosen.

8. Click the Delete [X] button on the database toolbar.

9. Click Yes to confirm the deletion.
   Keep in mind that you can delete a report (or other object) whenever you want to "get a fresh start." This technique is useful when using wizards and other automated tools. You may need to use this technique in the Skill Builder and Assessment exercises on the following pages. You will create several reports in these exercises that are more complex than the reports you just created. If you make a mistake, remember to delete the report and recreate it with the Report Wizard.

10. Close the Pinnacle Pet Care database with the File→Close command.

Concepts Review

True/False Questions

1.	Forms can be used to enter data in tables.	TRUE	FALSE
2.	The main benefit of forms is that they allow you to view several records simultaneously.	TRUE	FALSE
3.	The navigation buttons at the bottom of a form can be used to move between records.	TRUE	FALSE
4.	Forms do not display currency symbols $ and other formatting characters.	TRUE	FALSE
5.	AutoForm creates a form for the table that is selected in the Tables section of the Access window.	TRUE	FALSE
6.	The Report Wizard lets you choose the fields that you wish to include in a report.	TRUE	FALSE
7.	Reports can be printed.	TRUE	FALSE
8.	The Report Wizard lets you choose portrait or landscape orientations.	TRUE	FALSE
9.	Reports can be used to enter data.	TRUE	FALSE
10.	An object can be copied and pasted to a different database.	TRUE	FALSE

Multiple Choice Questions

1. Which of the following statements is accurate?
   a. Forms can be used to enter records into a table.
   b. Forms can be used to browse through the records in a table.
   c. Forms let you focus on one record at a time.
   d. All of the above

2. Which of the following commands can you issue through the navigation buttons on a form?
   a. Add a new record.
   b. Delete a record.
   c. Change the size of a field.
   d. All of the above

3. Which of the following statements is true?
   a. The Report Wizard lets you choose portrait or landscape orientations.
   b. The Report Wizard lets you choose the fields to include in a report.
   c. The Report Wizard lets you choose a title for the report.
   d. All of the above

4. The Report Wizard is initiated from which section of the database window?
   a. The Tables section
   b. The Reports section
   c. The Forms section
   d. Any of the above

Skill Builder 20.1 **Create Forms**

The Access window should be open from the previous exercise, and all databases should be closed. In this exercise, you will open the Tropical Getaways database you created in Lesson 19. You will continue to enhance this database as you progress through the Skill Builder exercises in this course.

Create a Form for the Customers Table

1. Click the Open ⬜ button on the Access toolbar, navigate to your diskette, and open the Tropical Getaways database.

2. Make sure the Tables button is pressed on the Objects bar.

3. Choose the Customers table, click the New Object ⬜ ▾ drop-down button, and choose AutoForm.
   Access will create the form shown below. The form uses all of the fields in the Customers table.

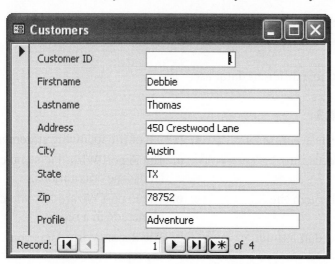

4. Click the New Record ⬜ button on the form's navigation bar, and add the following records:

Customer ID	Firstname	Lastname	Address	City	State	Zip	Profile
5	Victor	Thomas	2311 Wilmont Street	Danvers	MA	01923	Adventure
6	Lisa	Simms	100 Westside Drive	Batavia	NY	14020	Leisure
7	Ted	Carter	250 Smith Street	Charlton	MA	01507	Family

5. Click the Close ⬜ button on the form, and choose Yes when Access asks you to save the form.

6. Click OK to accept the proposed name **Customers**.

Create a Form for the Trips Table

7. Use AutoForm to create a form for the Trips table.

8. Use the form to add the following records to the Trips table:

TripID	Customer ID	Destination	Category	Departure Date	Return Date	Cost
Adv03	1	Swiss Alps	Adventure	10/10/03	11/5/03	$3,500
Adv04	5	Rocky Mountains	Adventure	5/6/04	5/22/04	$2,190
Adv05	5	Baja California	Adventure	8/8/04	8/18/04	$2,900
Lei02	6	Hawaii	Leisure	2/5/04	2/15/04	$4,500
Fam02	7	Hawaii	Family	3/7/04	3/15/04	$5,300

9. Close the form, and save it with the proposed name **Trips**.
   Leave the Tropical Getaways database open. You will continue to use it in the next exercise.

Skill Builder 20.2 **Create Reports**

In this Skill Builder exercise, you will create reports for the Tropical Getaways database. You will use the sort option in the Report Wizard to sort the records in the reports.

Create a Customer Profiles Report

1. Click the Reports button on the Objects bar.

2. Double-click the Create Report by Using Wizard option.

3. Choose Customers from the Tables/Queries list.

4. Add the Firstname, Lastname, State, and Profile fields to the Selected Fields list.

5. Click the Next button twice to display the Sorting screen.

6. Click the drop-down button on the first sorting box, and choose State as shown to the right.
   This will group all records with the same state

1	State	⌄	Ascending

   together in the report. Notice that you could set additional sort options. For example, imagine that you had a large database and you wanted the records sorted first by state and then by zip code within the states. In that situation, you would set the second sort key to zip code.

7. Click the Next button twice to display the Report Style screen.

8. Choose the Soft Gray style and click Next.

9. Type the name **Customer Profiles by State** in the title box of the last screen.

10. Click the Finish button to complete the report.

    The completed report is shown below. Notice that the State field appears first in the report, and the records for each state are grouped together. The State field appears first because you sorted on that field.

Customer Profiles by State

State	Firstname	Lastname	Profile
MA	Ted	Carter	Family
MA	Victor	Thomas	Adventure
NY	Lisa	Simms	Leisure
NY	Wilma	Boyd	Leisure
TX	Alice	Simpson	Family
TX	Ted	Wilkins	Adventure
TX	Debbie	Thomas	Adventure

11. Close the report when you have finished viewing it.

    Access will automatically name the report Customer Profiles by State.

Create a Report for the Trips Table

12. Now create the report shown below for the Trips table. You will need to start the Report Wizard and choose the appropriate fields from the Trips table. Also, sort the report on the Category field, choose the Soft Gray style, and use the report title Trips by Category.

Trips by Category

Category	Destination	Cost
Adventure	Baja California	$2,900.00
Adventure	Rocky Mountains	$2,190.00
Adventure	Swiss Alps	$3,500.00
Adventure	Amazon Jungle Trek	$7,765.00
Adventure	Kenyan Safari	$6,600.00
Family	Hawaii	$5,300.00
Family	Orlando	$3,400.00
Leisure	Hawaii	$4,500.00
Leisure	Caribbean Cruise	$2,390.00

13. Close the report when you have finished viewing it.
Your Tropical Getaways database should now have two reports: Customer Profiles by State and Trips by Category.

14. Use the File→Close command to close the database. The Access program window should remain open.

Assessments

Assessment 20.1 **Create Forms and Reports**

1. Open the Classic Cars database.
   You began setting up this database in the assessments in the previous lesson.

2. Use AutoForm to create the form shown below for the Collectors table.

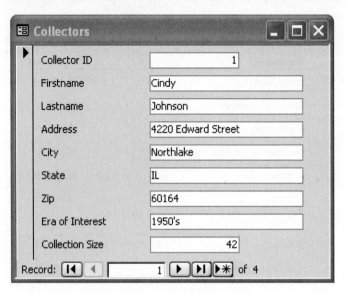

3. Use the form to enter the following new record into the Collectors table:

Collector ID	Firstname	Lastname	Address	City	State	Zip	Era of Interest	Collection Size
5	Jake	Johnson	840 Edgewood Drive	Arcadia	FL	33821	1920s	3

4. Close the form, and save it with the proposed name **Collectors**.

5. Use AutoForm to create the form shown below for the Cars table.

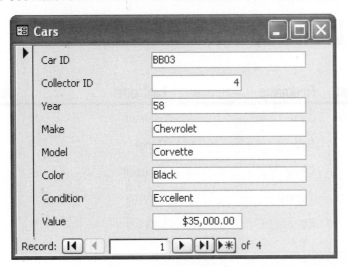

6. Use the form to enter the following new records into the table:

Car ID	Collector ID	Year	Make	Model	Color	Condition	Value
CJ04	1	48	Packard	Custom Eight Sedan	White	Fair	$15,000
JJ01	5	27	Ford	Model A	Black	Mint	$75,000
BB04	4	57	Chevrolet	Corvette	Red	Excellent	$42,000

7. Close the form, and save it with the proposed name **Cars**.

8. Create the report shown below for the Collectors table. The report sorts the records by the Era of Interest field, and it uses the Compact style. Also notice the title is Era of Interest.

9. Print the report, and then close it.

Era of Interest

Era of Interest	Firstname	Lastname	Collection Size
1920's	Jake	Johnson	3
1950's	Bob	Barker	7
1950's	Cindy	Johnson	42
1960's	Tammy	Olson	6
Early 1900's	Ed	Larkson	34

10. Create the report shown below for the Cars table. When adding the fields in the first Report Wizard screen, you will need to add them in the order shown on the report. For example, add the Model field first, the Year field second, the Condition field third, etc. This report is sorted on the Model field, and it uses the Compact style.

Models Report

Model	Year	Condition	Color	Value
Corvette	57	Excellent	Red	$42,000.00
Corvette	58	Excellent	Black	$35,000.00
Corvette	62	Excellent	Blue	$30,000.00
Corvette	58	Mint	Red and white	$65,000.00
Custom Eight Sedan	48	Fair	White	$15,000.00
Model A	27	Mint	Black	$75,000.00
Thunderbird	59	Good	Tan	$20,000.00

11. Print the report, and then close it.

12. Close the Classic Cars database when you have finished.

Critical Thinking

Critical Thinking 20.1 Create Forms

Open the Holmestead Realty database that you developed in the Critical Thinking exercises in the previous lesson. You will continue to develop this database as you progress through the Critical Thinking exercises in this course.

Linda Holmes has been working with her new database for some time and she has come to realize that working in Datasheet view can be awkward. Linda has asked you to set up a form that can be used for entering data and browsing records. Follow these guidelines to set up the form:

■ Use the AutoForm tool to create a form for the Contacts table.

■ Name the form **Contacts Data Entry**.

■ Use the new form to add the contacts in the table below to the database. If a field is empty in the table, then leave it empty on the form as well:

Seller ID	FirstName	LastName	SpouseName	Address	City	ST	Zip	Phone	Contact Type
7	Mark	Thames		76 Haywood Road	Asheville	NC	28801	(828) 252-5676	Primary Residence
8	Cindy	Johnson		24 Maple Drive	Black Mountain	NC	28711	(828) 686-3511	Trustee

It turns out that Susan Jones' name was spelled incorrectly in the Contacts table. She spells her first name Suzanne. She is the spouse of Jeff Jones. In your new form, use the Find feature to locate Jeff Jones' record in the Contacts table and make the correction.

Linda Holmes was so pleased with the form you created that she has asked you to create a form for the Listings table. Follow these guidelines to set up the form:

■ Use the AutoForm tool and name the form **Listings Data Entry**.

■ Use the form to add the following listings to the Listings table:

MLS #	Street #	Address	Price	Listing Date	Expiration Date	Commission Range	Seller ID	Style
52125	76	Haywood Road	$325,000	7/14/03	2/14/04	5%	7	3 Story
52345	625	Brevard Road	$135,000	8/5/03	12/5/03	6%	8	Ranch

You have just been informed that the Woodbridge Lane listing has expired. Use the Listings Data Entry form to remove this listing from the Listings table.

Critical Thinking 20.2 **Create Reports**

Linda Holmes has promised all of her sellers that she will call them at least once a week. She realizes that to do this she will need a report that displays contact information for her sellers. Follow these guidelines to create the necessary report:

- Use the Report Wizard to set up the report. It should extract data from the Contacts table.

- Display the FirstName, LastName, SpouseName, Contact Type, and Phone fields on the report in the same order listed here.

- Accept all of the default Report Wizard settings except for the report style: choose the Casual report style instead.

- Name the report **Contact Phone List** and print it when finished.

Linda was caught off guard by the expiration of the Woodbridge listing and she doesn't want this situation to happen again. Follow these guidelines to create a report that tracks listing expiration dates:

- Use the Report Wizard to set up the report. It should extract data from the Listings table.

- Display the MLS #, Street #, Address, Price, and Expiration Date fields on the report in the same order listed here.

- Accept all of the default Report Wizard settings except for the sort order and report style. Sort the report in Ascending order on the Expiration Date field and choose the Casual report style.

- Name the report **Expiration Date List** and print it when finished.

LESSON 21

Getting Answers with Queries

In this lesson, you will learn how to set up and use queries. Queries are an essential part of any Access database. They allow you to extract and combine data from tables. You will learn how to specify criteria in queries to extract only the records you desire. You will create calculated fields, work with statistical functions, and sort and group query results.

Additional learning resources are available at labpub.com/learn/oe3/

Case Study

The staff at Pinnacle Pet Care has used their new database for some time, and now they want answers to a variety of questions. For example,

- What is the current balance of each customer in California?

- Which customers have a current balance that is greater than $200?

- Which customers in California have a current balance that is greater than $200?

- What is the average amount of money that customers spend on cats and dogs?

Penny Johnson sets up queries in the Pinnacle Pet Care database to answer these questions. The following illustration shows a query, the Customers table, and the resulting recordset.

Field:	Firstname	Lastname	Phone	Current Balance
Table:	Customers	Customers	Customers	Customers
Sort:		Ascending		
Show:	✓	✓	✓	✓
Criteria:				>200
or:				

A query contains fields and criteria that are used to select records from a table.

Customer ID	Firstname	Lastname	Address	City	State	Zip	Phone	Last Visit	Current Balance
1	Mark	Roth	760 Maple Avenue	Fremont	CA	94538-	(510) 234-9090	7/7/2003	$235.00
2	Tony	Simpson	312 York Lane	Richmond	CA	94804-	(510) 238-2233	9/7/2003	$185.00
3	Jason	Jones	2233 Crystal Street	San Mateo	CA	94403-	(415) 312-2312	7/15/2003	$48.00
4	Jacob	Samuels	2300 North Pratt Str	Atlanta	GA	30309-	(404) 367-8002	10/8/2003	$250.50

Firstname	Lastname	Phone	Current Balance
Jacob	Samuels	(404) 367-8002	$250.50
Mark	Roth	(510) 234-9090	$235.00

Access produces a recordset when the query is run.

What are Queries?

Queries are an essential part of any Access database. Most people use queries to get answers to questions and to extract data from one or more tables. When you run a query, Access creates a temporary table using the fields and criteria you specify in the query. The temporary table is known as a recordset. The recordset is composed of data from one or more tables in your database. A query's recordset can even be used as the basis for forms and reports. Thus, queries give you the ability to produce forms and reports using data from multiple tables.

Select Queries

Select queries are the most common type of query. Select queries let you selectively extract data from one or more tables in a database. When designing select queries, you specify the fields that you wish to include in the recordset. You can also specify criteria that are used to select records from the table(s) in your database. The following illustration shows the Customers table from the Pinnacle Pet Care database and the resulting recordset. Take a few moments to study the illustration.

Customer ID	Firstname	Lastname	Address	City	State	Zip	Phone	Last Visit	Current Balance
1	Mark	Roth	760 Maple Avenue	Fremont	CA	94538-	(510) 234-9090	7/7/2003	$235.00
2	Tony	Simpson	312 York Lane	Richmond	CA	94804-	(510) 238-2233	9/7/2003	$185.00
3	Jason	Jones	2233 Crystal Street	San Mateo	CA	94403-	(415) 312-2312	7/15/2003	$48.00
4	Jacob	Samuels	2300 North Pratt Stre	Atlanta	GA	30309-	(404) 367-8002	10/8/2003	$250.50

Firstname	Lastname	Phone	Current Balance
Jacob	Samuels	(404) 367-8002	$250.50
Mark	Roth	(510) 234-9090	$235.00

A query is run that instructs Access to only choose the Firstname, Lastname, Phone, and Current Balance fields from the Customers table for those customers with a Current Balance > $200.

The query produces the recordset shown here. Notice that the recordset only includes the specified fields for customers with a Current Balance > $200.

Setting Up Queries

You can use the Query Wizard to assist you in setting up queries, or you can set them up yourself using the query design grid. The design grid gives you complete flexibility in determining the fields, criteria, and other options that you wish to use in the query. The following Quick Reference table describes how to display the Query window and how to add tables to the query. You must add table(s) to the Query window so that you can use the desired fields from the table(s) in the query.

QUICK REFERENCE: ADDING TABLES TO THE QUERY WINDOW

■ Open the desired database, and make sure the Queries button is pressed on the Objects bar.

■ Double-click the Create Query in Design View option.

■ Choose a table that you want the query to extract data from in the Show Table box, and click Add.

■ Add any other tables from which you wish to extract data.

■ Click the Close button on the Show Table box.

 ## Hands-On 21.1 **Set Up a Query**

In this exercise, you will begin setting up a query. You will display the Query window, and you will add the Customers table in the Pinnacle Pet Care database to the Query window.

Display the Query window

1. Start Access, and open the Pinnacle Pet Care database.

2. Click the Queries button on the Objects bar.

3. Double-click the Create Query in Design View option.
   The Query window will appear, and the Show Table dialog box will be displayed. The Show Table dialog box lets you choose the table(s) that you wish to use in the query. In this exercise, you will add just the Customers table to the Query window.

TIP!

You can also double-click the table name.

4. Choose Customers, and click the Add button.
   A Customers field list will appear above the design grid. The field names in the list are taken from the Customers table. In a moment, you will use the Customers field list to add fields to the query.

5. Click the Close button on the Show Table dialog box.
   You won't be using the Pets table in this exercise.

Set Up the Window

6. Make sure that the Access window is maximized ▣ and that the Query window is maximized within the Access window.

7. Follow these steps to adjust the size of the design grid and the Customers field list:

A Position the mouse pointer on the top border of the design grid and a double-headed arrow will appear.

B Drag the border down to allocate more space to the top-half of the window.

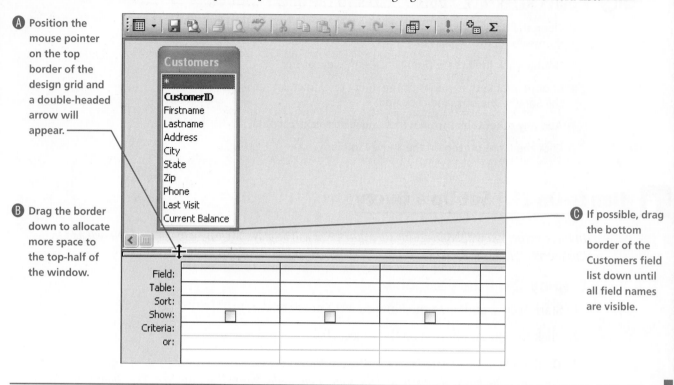

C If possible, drag the bottom border of the Customers field list down until all field names are visible.

The Query Design Grid

The design grid appears when you begin setting up a new query. The design grid lets you specify the fields to include in the query. You can also use the design grid to specify criteria and other parameters that affect the query recordset. The following illustration shows the design grid and the recordset for the sample query shown. You will develop the query shown in the illustration as you progress through the next few exercises.

The Table row indicates the table from which each field is taken. In this example, all fields are taken from the Customers table.

Fields such as Firstname, Lastname, Phone, and Current Balance are added to the columns of the design grid. These fields will be displayed in the recordset.

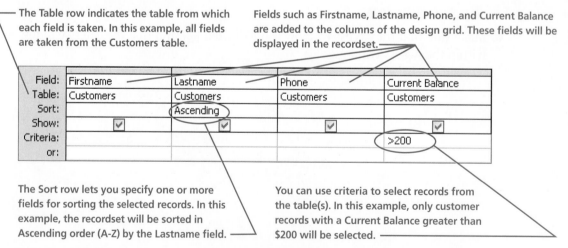

The Sort row lets you specify one or more fields for sorting the selected records. In this example, the recordset will be sorted in Ascending order (A-Z) by the Lastname field.

You can use criteria to select records from the table(s). In this example, only customer records with a Current Balance greater than $200 will be selected.

The recordset includes customer records with a Current Balance greater than $200. Only the fields specified in the query appear in the recordset.

Firstname	Lastname	Phone	Current Balance
Mark	Roth	(510) 234-9090	$235.00
Jacob	Samuels	(404) 367-8002	$250.50

Adding Fields to the Design Grid

The first step in defining a query is to add fields to the design grid. The fields you add to the design grid will appear in the recordset. Once you have added fields to the design grid, you can specify sorting options, criteria, and other options that affect the recordset. The following Quick Reference table describes the techniques you can use to add fields to the design grid.

QUICK REFERENCE: ADDING FIELDS TO THE QUERY DESIGN GRID

Technique	Description
Double-click	You can add a single field to the design grid by double-clicking the desired field in the field list.
Drop-down list	You can add a single field by clicking in a field cell, clicking the drop-down button that appears, and then choosing the desired field from the drop-down menu.
Drag	You can add a single field or multiple fields to the design grid by dragging them from a field list to the desired cell in the design grid. You can select multiple fields prior to dragging by pressing and holding the (CTRL) key while clicking the desired field names in the field list.
All fields	You can add all fields to the design grid by double-clicking the asterisk * symbol at the top of the desired field list.

Hands-On 21.2 Add Fields to the Design Grid

1. Follow these steps to add the Firstname field to the design grid:

Ⓐ Double-click the Firstname field in the field list and it will appear in the first cell of the design grid.

Ⓑ Notice the Table row specifies that the field is taken from the Customers table. Knowing which table the field is taken from can be important especially when the same field name is used in more than one table.

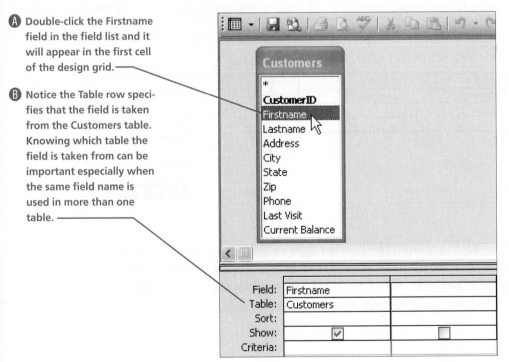

2. Now add the Lastname, Phone, and Current Balance fields to the design grid by double-clicking them on the field name list. The design grid should match the following illustration when you have finished adding the fields.

Field:	Firstname	Lastname	Phone	Current Balance
Table:	Customers	Customers	Customers	Customers
Sort:				
Show:	☑	☑	☑	☑
Criteria:				
or:				

Removing Fields from the Design Grid

You can remove fields from the design grid by clicking in the desired column and choosing Edit→Delete Columns from the menu bar. You may need to remove fields from time to time as you develop queries. Remember to use this technique if you make a mistake and add an incorrect field to the design grid.

 Hands-On 21.3 Delete a Field

1. Click anywhere in the Current Balance column in the design grid.

2. Choose Edit→Delete Columns from the menu bar, and the field will be removed.

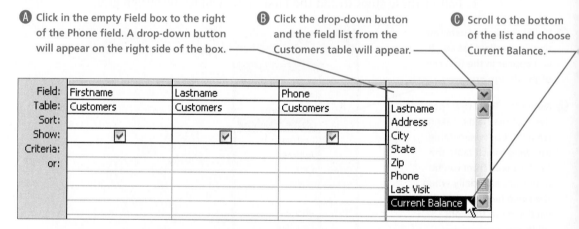

Ⓐ Click in the empty Field box to the right of the Phone field. A drop-down button will appear on the right side of the box.

Ⓑ Click the drop-down button and the field list from the Customers table will appear.

Ⓒ Scroll to the bottom of the list and choose Current Balance.

3. Follow these steps to reinsert the Current Balance field using the drop-down list technique:
The Current Balance field should be returned to the grid. As you can see, there are several ways to add fields to the design grid. Once again, feel free to remove fields from the design grid whenever you make a mistake or wish to change the order of the fields in the grid.

Running Queries

You can run a query by clicking the Run button on the Access toolbar. When you run a select query, Access selects records and fields from tables in your database and displays the recordset. You can navigate through the recordset or print it if desired. The recordset will always reflect the current data stored in the database.

Editing Data In a Recordset

When you run a select query, the recordset is connected to the underlying table(s) that the query is based upon. If you edit data in the recordset, then the data in the underlying tables is changed as well. However, most select queries are only used for viewing selective data.

Hands-On 21.4 Run the Query

1. Click the Run button on the Access toolbar.
   The query will run, and the recordset shown below will appear. Keep in mind that your query is quite basic. This query simply displays four fields from each record in the Customers table.

Firstname	Lastname	Phone	Current Balance
Mark	Roth	(510) 234-9090	$235.00
Tony	Simpson	(510) 238-2233	$185.00
Jason	Jones	(415) 312-2312	$48.00
Jacob	Samuels	(404) 367-8002	$250.50

2. Now continue with the next topic, where you will learn how to sort the query results.

Sorting the Query Results

You can instruct Access to sort the rows in a recordset using one or more fields as sort keys. For example, you may want to view the recordset with the largest current balances displayed first. You sort recordsets by setting the sort box to Ascending or Descending for one or more fields in the design grid. If you set the sort box for more than one field, then the first field is used as the primary sort key, followed by the next field, and so on.

Hands-On 21.5 Sort the Results

The recordset should be displayed from the previous exercise.

1. Notice that the records in the recordset do not appear to be sorted in any particular order.
   However, the records are actually sorted on the Customer ID field, which is the primary key for the Customers table. In the next few steps, you will set the sort key for the Lastname field in the design grid. You will run the query again, and the recordset will be sorted by last name with the Jones record first, followed by the Roth record, and so on.

2. Click the Design View button on the left end of the Access toolbar.

The design grid will reappear. You can always use the view button to switch back and forth between the recordset and the design grid.

3. Follow these steps to set a sort key:

Field:	Firstname	Lastname	Phone	Current Balance
Table:	Customers	Customers	Customers	Customers
Sort:		⌄		
Show:	✓	Ascending	✓	✓
Criteria:		Descending		
or:		(not sorted)		

A Click in the Sort box for the Lastname field. ⎯

B Click the drop-down button and choose Ascending from the list. The word Ascending will appear in the Sort box.

4. Click the Run button, and the recordset shown below will appear.

Notice that the records are sorted by the Lastname field.

Firstname	Lastname	Phone	Current Balance
Jason	Jones	(415) 312-2312	$48.00
Mark	Roth	(510) 234-9090	$235.00
Jacob	Samuels	(404) 367-8002	$250.50
Tony	Simpson	(510) 238-2233	$185.00

5. Click the Design View button to display the design grid.

6. Follow these steps to remove the Lastname sort key and to set the sort order to descending based upon the Outstanding Balance field:

A Click in the Sort box for the Lastname field. ⎯

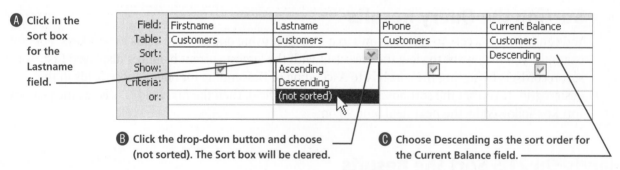

Field:	Firstname	Lastname	Phone	Current Balance
Table:	Customers	Customers	Customers	Customers
Sort:		⌄		Descending
Show:	✓	Ascending	✓	✓
Criteria:		Descending		
or:		(not sorted)		

B Click the drop-down button and choose (not sorted). The Sort box will be cleared.

C Choose Descending as the sort order for the Current Balance field. ⎯

7. Click the Run [!] button, and the recordset shown below will appear. *Notice that the records with the largest Current Balance are displayed first.*

Firstname	Lastname	Phone	Current Balance
Jacob	Samuels	(404) 367-8002	$250.50
Mark	Roth	(510) 234-9090	$235.00
Tony	Simpson	(510) 238-2233	$185.00
Jason	Jones	(415) 312-2312	$48.00

8. Click the Design View button to display the design grid.

Using Criteria to Select Records

One of the most important benefits of queries is that you can select specific records by specifying criteria. This gives you the ability to select the precise data you desire from a database. For example, you may want to know how many customers have an outstanding balance that is greater than $200. Or, perhaps you are interested in viewing only those records where the state is equal to CA (California). These and other questions are easily answered by specifying criteria in the query design grid.

Equality Criteria

You can use equality criteria to choose only those records where a field has a specific value. For example, you may want to display only those records where the state field is equal to CA. You accomplish this by entering the value that you want the field to equal in the Criteria row of the design grid. The following illustration shows how this is accomplished.

Field:	Firstname	Lastname	Phone	Current Balance	State
Table:	Customers	Customers	Customers	Customers	Customers
Sort:				Descending	
Show:	☑	☑	☑	☑	☑
Criteria:					CA
or:					

This is a Criteria row.

Entering CA in the State Criteria box instructs Access to select only those records where the state is CA.

As expected, only records where the state is CA appear in the recordset.

Firstname	Lastname	Phone	Current Balance	State
Mark	Roth	(510) 234-9090	$235.00	CA
Tony	Simpson	(510) 238-2233	$185.00	CA
Jason	Jones	(415) 312-2312	$48.00	CA

Comparison Criteria

You can use the comparison operators > (greater than), < (less than), >= (greater than or equal), <= (less than or equal), and NOT (not equal) when specifying criteria. Access will select only those records matching the criteria. For example, placing the criterion >200 in the Current Balance field instructs Access to select only records where the Current Balance is greater than 200.

The Show Check Box

The Show row in the design grid contains a check box ☑ for each field. You can prevent a field from displaying in the recordset by removing the check from the Show box. This can be useful in many situations. For example, in the preceding illustration, the State field is used to select only records where the state is equal to CA. The State field must be present in the design grid in order to specify this criteria. However, you may not want the State field to be displayed in the recordset. You could prevent the State field from being displayed in the recordset by removing the check from the State field in the design grid.

 Hands-On 21.6 Use Criteria

The design grid should be displayed from the previous exercise.

Use an Equality Criterion

1. Double-click the State field on the Customers field list to add the field to the design grid.
   The State field should be in the fifth column of the design grid.

2. Follow these steps to set an equality criterion for the State field:

Ⓐ Click in the Criteria box for the State field. ————

Ⓑ Type **CA** as shown here. You can type it in uppercase (CA) or lowercase (ca). ————

Field:	Firstname	Lastname	Phone	Current Balance	State
Table:	Customers	Customers	Customers	Customers	Customers
Sort:				Descending	
Show:	☑	☑	☑	☑	☑
Criteria:					CA
or:					

Ⓒ Click in the box below CA and Access will surround CA with quotation marks ("CA"). The quotation marks indicate that this is a text criterion (as opposed to a number or date). ————

3. Click the Run [!] button.
   The three records with the State field equal to CA should appear in the recordset.

4. Click the Design View button to display the design grid.

Use Comparison Criteria

5. Follow these steps to create a "greater than" comparison criterion for the Current Balance field:

Field:	Firstname	Lastname	Phone	Current Balance	State
Table:	Customers	Customers	Customers	Customers	Customers
Sort:				Descending	
Show:	☑	☑	☑	☑	☑
Criteria:				>200	

Ⓐ Click in the Criteria box for the Current Balance field and type **>200**. ⎯

Ⓑ Click in the Criteria box for the State field and delete the "CA" criterion. ⎯

6. Click the Run 🔳 button, to produce the recordset shown below.
Notice that the current balance is greater than $200 for each record.

Firstname	Lastname	Phone	Current Balance	State
Jacob	Samuels	(404) 367-8002	$250.50	GA
Mark	Roth	(510) 234-9090	$235.00	CA

7. Click the Design View 🔳 button again to display the design grid.

8. Change the >200 criterion to **<200** and run the query again.
Only records with current balances less than $200 will appear in the recordset.

Uncheck the Show box

In the next few steps, you will prevent the State field from appearing in the recordset by removing the check from the Show box.

9. Click the Design View 🔳 button to display the design grid.

10. Follow these steps to set up the query:

Field:	Firstname	Lastname	Phone	Current Balance	State
Table:	Customers	Customers	Customers	Customers	Customers
Sort:				Descending	
Show:	☑	☑	☑	☑	☐
Criteria:				<200	

Ⓐ Make sure the Current Balance criterion is set to <200. ⎯

Ⓑ Click the Show check box for the State field to remove the check. ⎯

11. Click the Run 🔳 button and the State field will be removed from the recordset.

12. Take 10 minutes to experiment with the query you have been using. Try entering various criteria and perhaps adding and removing fields from the design grid. Continue with the next topic when you have finished experimenting.

Clearing the Design Grid

You can clear all entries from the design grid with the Edit→Clear Grid command. This command can be used to give you a "fresh start" when working in the design grid.

 ## Hands-On 21.7 Clear the Grid and Add All Fields

1. If necessary, click the Design View button to display the design grid.

2. Choose Edit→Clear Grid to remove all fields from the grid.

3. Follow these steps to add all fields from the Customers table to the design grid:

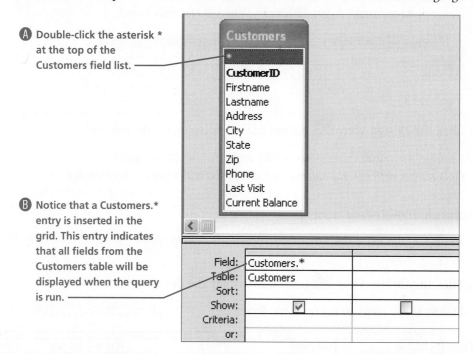

Ⓐ Double-click the asterisk * at the top of the Customers field list.

Ⓑ Notice that a Customers.* entry is inserted in the grid. This entry indicates that all fields from the Customers table will be displayed when the query is run.

4. Click the Run button. All records from the Customers table should appear in the recordset.

Use a Criterion to Select the Records

In the next few steps, you will add the Current Balance field to the design grid and specify a criterion for that field.

5. Click the Design View button to display the design grid.

6. Follow these steps to add the Current Balance field to the grid and to specify a criterion:

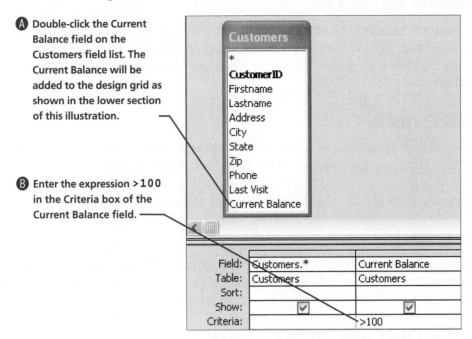

A Double-click the Current Balance field on the Customers field list. The Current Balance will be added to the design grid as shown in the lower section of this illustration.

B Enter the expression **>100** in the Criteria box of the Current Balance field.

Field:	Customers.*	Current Balance
Table:	Customers	Customers
Sort:		
Show:	☑	☑
Criteria:		>100

7. Run 🔲 the query to produce the recordset shown in the following illustration.

Notice that the last two columns of the recordset contain a Customers.Current Balance field and a Field0 field. This unusual nomenclature was used because the Current Balance field was included twice in the query design grid. It was included once as part of the Customers. entry and again as a separate field in the second column. Access cannot display the same field name twice in a table or recordset, therefore, Access changed the names of the column headings in the recordset. You will correct this by removing the check from the Show box in the next few steps.*

Customer ID	Firstname	Lastname	Address	City	State	Zip	Phone	Last Visit	Customers.Currer	Field0
1	Mark	Roth	760 Maple Avenue	Fremont	CA	94538-	(510) 234-9090	7/7/2003	$235.00	$235.00
2	Tony	Simpson	312 York Lane	Richmond	CA	94804-	(510) 238-2233	9/7/2003	$185.00	$185.00
4	Jacob	Samuels	2300 North Pratt Str	Atlanta	GA	30309-	(404) 367-8002	10/8/2003	$250.50	$250.50

8. Switch to Design View 🔲, and remove the check from the Show box of the Current Balance field. The design grid should match the example to the right.

Field:	Customers.*	Current Balance
Table:	Customers	Customers
Sort:		
Show:	☑	☐
Criteria:		>100

9. Run the query; only one Current Balance field will be visible.

The >100 criterion in the Current Balance field selects the appropriate records. However, the field is not displayed in the recordset because the Show box is unchecked.

10. Choose File→Close from the menu bar, and click the Yes button to save the query.

11. Type the name **Current Balance** in the Save As box, and click OK.

Compound Criteria

Thus far, you have worked with relatively simple queries containing one criterion. However, you will sometimes need to use more than one criterion. Criteria that are composed of two or more criteria are known as compound criteria. There are two types of compound criteria: AND criteria and OR criteria.

AND Criteria

AND criteria let you select records based on logical AND expressions. In the next exercise, you will use AND criteria to select records in the Pets table. For example, you will use an AND expression to select all records where the pet type is dog and the number of visits is greater than 5. With AND criteria, Access will only select records when all of the criteria are true.

OR Criteria

OR criteria allow you to select records based on logical OR expressions. For example, you will use an OR expression to select all records where the pet type is dog or the pet type is cat. With OR criteria, Access will select records if any of the criteria are true.

Setting up Compound Criteria

You set up compound criteria in the design grid. AND criteria are set up by placing two or more criterion in different fields within the same Criteria row. OR criteria are set up by placing two or more criteria on different rows within the design grid. The following illustration shows the compound criteria you will set up in the next exercise.

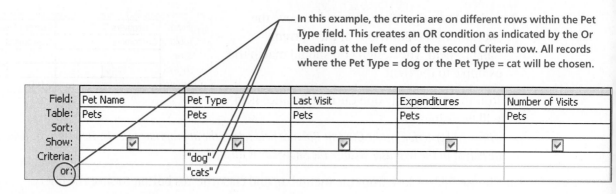

Field:	Pet Name	Pet Type	Last Visit	Expenditures	Number of Visits
Table:	Pets	Pets	Pets	Pets	Pets
Sort:					
Show:	☑	☑	☑	☑	☑
Criteria:		"dog"			>5

In this example, the criterion "dog" and >5 are on the same Criteria row. This creates an AND condition. Only records where the Pet Type is dog and the Number of Visits > 5 will be chosen.

In this example, the criteria are on different rows within the Pet Type field. This creates an OR condition as indicated by the Or heading at the left end of the second Criteria row. All records where the Pet Type = dog or the Pet Type = cat will be chosen.

Field:	Pet Name	Pet Type	Last Visit	Expenditures	Number of Visits
Table:	Pets	Pets	Pets	Pets	Pets
Sort:					
Show:	☑	☑	☑	☑	☑
Criteria:		"dog"			
or:		"cats"			

Hands-On 21.8 Use Compound Criteria

In this exercise, you will set up a new query using the Pets table from the Pinnacle Pet Care database. You will use compound criteria to query the database in various ways.

Set Up the Query Window

1. Make sure the queries are displayed in the Database window.

2. Double-click the Create Query in Design View option.

3. Choose Pets from the Show Table box, and click the Add button.

4. Click the Close button on the Show Table dialog box.

5. If necessary, maximize 🔲 the query window. Also, you may want to adjust the size of the design grid and the Pets field list to allow you to see the entire content of the Pets field list. You used this technique in the first exercise in this lesson with the Customers field list.

Create an AND Criterion

6. Double-click the Pet Name, Pet Type, Last Visit, Expenditures, and Number of Visits fields on the Pets field list to add those fields to the design grid.

7. Enter the criteria shown below into the Pet Type and Number of Visits boxes in the Criteria row.

Field:	Pet Name	Pet Type	Last Visit	Expenditures	Number of Visits
Table:	Pets	Pets	Pets	Pets	Pets
Sort:					
Show:	☑	☑	☑	☑	☑
Criteria:		"dog"			>5

8. Click the Run [!] button to produce the following recordset.
   Notice that each record has Dog as the Pet Type and that the Number of Visits is greater than 5.

Pet Name	Pet Type	Last Visit	Expenditures	Number of Visits
Wolfy	Dog	7/15/2003	$450.00	7
Spike	Dog	10/8/2003	$890.00	12

Create an OR Criterion

9. Switch to Design View , and remove the >5 criterion from the Number of Visits criteria box.

When using OR criteria, you can use as many rows as necessary. Each row that you add creates one more condition in the OR expression.

10. Add the **cat** criterion to the row below the dog criterion as shown below. It isn't necessary to type the quotation marks shown in the illustration. Access will add the quotation marks as soon as you click outside of the field after typing the criterion.

Field:	Pet Name	Pet Type	Last Visit	Expenditures	Number of Visits
Table:	Pets	Pets	Pets	Pets	Pets
Sort:					
Show:	☑	☑	☑	☑	☑
Criteria:		"dog"			
or:		"cats"			

11. Click the Run 🔘 button to produce the following recordset.
Notice that all records have a Pet Type of Dog or Cat.

Pet Name	Pet Type	Last Visit	Expenditures	Number of Visits
Wolfy	Dog	7/15/2003	$450.00	7
Dillon	Dog	7/7/2003	$150.55	3
Max	Cat	9/7/2003	$1,450.55	20
Stripes	Cat	7/15/2003	$450.00	9
Tony	Cat	7/7/2003	$0.00	1
Fetch	Dog	9/10/2003	$345.00	3
Ben	Dog	10/8/2003	$480.00	3
Spike	Dog	10/8/2003	$890.00	12

Use a Combination of AND and OR Compound Criteria

12. Switch to Design View 🔘, but do not change the "dog" and "cat" criteria.

13. Add the **>5** criteria to the Number of Visits field as shown below.
This compound criteria will choose all records where the Pet Type is dog and the Number of Visits is greater than 5 or the Pet Type is cat and the Number of Visits is greater than 5.

Field:	Pet Name	Pet Type	Last Visit	Expenditures	Number of Visits
Table:	Pets	Pets	Pets	Pets	Pets
Sort:					
Show:	☑	☑	☑	☑	☑
Criteria:		"dog"			>5
or:		"cat"			>5

14. Click the Run 🔘 button to produce the following recordset.

Pet Name	Pet Type	Last Visit	Expenditures	Number of Visits
Wolfy	Dog	7/15/2003	$450.00	7
Max	Cat	9/7/2003	$1,450.55	20
Stripes	Cat	7/15/2003	$450.00	9
Tony	Cat	7/7/2003	$145.00	6
Spike	Dog	10/8/2003	$890.00	12

632 UNIT **6** ACCESS 2003   Lesson 21: Getting Answers with Queries

15. Switch to Design view and take 10 minutes to experiment with compound criteria. *Be creative; query the Pets table for answers to any questions that may come to mind.*

16. When you have finished experimenting, choose File→Close from the menu bar, and click the Yes button when Access asks if you want to save the query.

17. Type the name **Compound Criteria** in the Save As box, and click OK.

Calculated Fields

Access lets you create calculated fields within queries. Calculated fields perform calculations using values from other fields within the query or from fields in the underlying table(s). For example, in the next exercise, you will set up a new query that will be based upon the Pets table. The Pets table contains an Expenditures field that represents the total expenditures for a particular pet. The Pets table also contains a Number of Visits field that represents the total number of visits by the pet. You will create a calculated field within the query named Expenditures Per Visit. The Expenditures Per Visit will be calculated as the Expenditures divided by the Number of Visits. The following illustration shows the design grid with the Pet Name and Pet Type fields and the Expenditures Per Visit calculated field.

Expenditures Per Visit is a calculated field, and it is too wide to be completely visible in the cell. The complete content of the cell is Expenditures Per Visit: [Expenditures]/[Number of Visits].

Field:	Pet Name	Pet Type	Expenditures Per Vis
Table:	Pets	Pets	
Sort:			
Show:	✓	✓	✓
Criteria:		dog	

The following illustration discusses the syntax that must be used with calculated fields.

A descriptive name for the calculated field is entered into an empty field cell. You can use spaces in the name. — A colon : must follow the name. The colon identifies the field as a calculated field. — An expression follows the colon. The expression can include field names, numbers, and operators such as +, -, *, and /. The various parts of the expression are surrounded with square brackets.

Expenditures Per Visit: [Expenditures]/[Number of Visits]

The Zoom Box

Calculated field expressions can be quite long and complex. For this reason, you may not be able to see the entire expression as you enter it in a cell. Fortunately, Access provides a Zoom command that displays a Zoom box. When you enter the desired expression into the Zoom box, you can see the entire expression as it is entered. In the following exercise, you will use the Zoom box to enter an expression. You display the Zoom box by right-clicking the cell where the expression will be entered and choosing Zoom from the pop-up menu.

Hands-On 21.9 **Create a Calculated Field**

The Queries section of the Database window should be displayed from the previous exercise.

1. Create a new query in Design view, and add the Pets table to the query.

2. Close the Show Tables dialog box.

3. Add the Pet Name and Pet Type fields to the design grid.

4. Follow these steps to display the Zoom box:

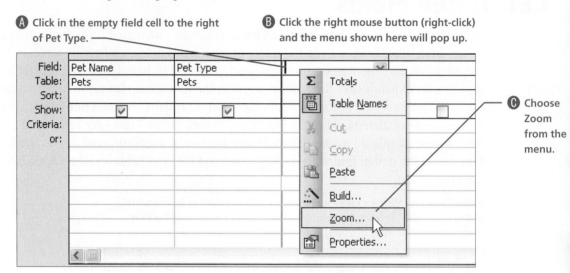

Ⓐ Click in the empty field cell to the right of Pet Type.

Ⓑ Click the right mouse button (right-click) and the menu shown here will pop up.

Ⓒ Choose Zoom from the menu.

5. Enter the calculated field expression shown in the following illustration into the Zoom box. Make sure you enter the expression exactly as shown. In particular, make sure you use a colon : (not a semicolon ;), correctly spell the field names, use the correct open and closed brackets [ ], and use the forward slash / symbol to represent division. Access is lenient when it comes to spaces, so you can omit the spaces that come after the colon and before and after the forward slash / if you desire.

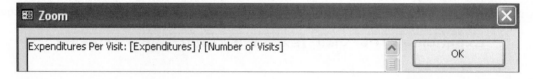

6. Click OK to insert the expression in the field.

7. Make sure the syntax is correct as shown above. If necessary, you can edit the expression within the cell or redisplay the Zoom dialog box and make any necessary changes.

8. Click the Run button to produce the recordset on the right.

The numbers shown in the Expenditures Per Visit field represent the average expenditure for each pet on each visit. Notice the excessive number of decimal places that are displayed in the calculated field. In the next exercise, you will reduce the number of displayed decimal places by changing one of the properties of the Expenditures Per Visit field.

Pet Name	Pet Type	Expenditures
Max	Cat	72.5275
Stripes	Cat	50
Tony	Cat	24.1666666667
Wolfy	Dog	64.2857142857
Dillon	Dog	50.1833333333
Fetch	Dog	115
Ben	Dog	160
Spike	Dog	74.1666666667
Bugs	Rabbit	150.125

9. Switch to Design View , and continue with the next topic.

Modifying Query Properties

The Properties button on the Access toolbar displays the Properties dialog box. You can use the Properties dialog box to change the properties of any Access object, including fields within queries. Properties can affect the appearance and format of objects. For example, in the following exercise, you will set the Format property of the Expenditures Per Visit calculated field to Currency. The Currency format will reduce the number of displayed decimal places in the recordset.

Hands-On 21.10 **Set the Format Property**

The query design grid should be displayed from the previous exercise.

1. Click the Expenditures Per Visit box, then click the Properties button on the toolbar.
   The Field Properties dialog box will appear.

2. Follow these steps to set the format of this field to Currency:
   When the query is run, the Currency format will display a dollar sign and two decimal places in the Expenditures Per Visit field.

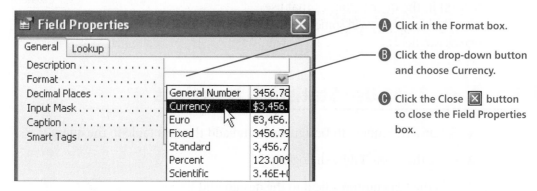

3. Click the Run button.
   The numbers in the Expenditures Per Visit field should now be formatted with the Currency format, which includes a dollar sign and two decimal places.

4. Switch to Design View .

5. Click in the Criteria box for the Pet Type field, and type **dog** as shown below.

Field:	Pet Name	Pet Type	Expenditures Per Vis
Table:	Pets	Pets	
Sort:			
Show:	☑	☑	☑
Criteria:		dog	

6. Click the Run button.

The Pet Name, Pet Type, and Expenditures Per Visit will be displayed for records where the Pet Type is Dog. As you can see, Access allows you to combine criteria, calculated fields, and other parameters within a query.

7. Choose File→Close to close the query, and save it as **Expenditures Per Visit**.

Statistical Functions

Access provides built-in statistical functions for calculating statistical information within a query. The built-in statistical functions include SUM (summation), AVG (average), MIN (minimum), MAX (maximum), COUNT, VAR (variance), FIRST, and LAST. For example, you could use the AVG function to compute the average expenditures on pets, or you may want to use the COUNT function to count the number of dogs that attend the Pinnacle Pet Care clinic.

The Total Row

To use the statistical functions, you must first click the Totals button to display a Total row in the query design grid. Once the Total row is displayed, you can choose statistical function(s) for the desired field(s) in the query. Queries that use statistical functions will sometimes have just one or two fields.

Statistical functions are entered in the Total row of the query design grid.

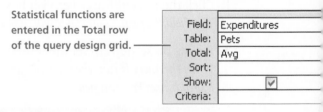

Hands-On 21.11 Use Statistical Functions

1. Set up a new query in Design view, and add the Pets table to the query.

2. Close the Show Tables dialog box.

3. Add the Expenditures field to the design grid.

4. Click the Totals Σ button on the toolbar, and a Total row will appear below the Table row.
The Total row lets you choose statistical functions and set grouping for fields. You will learn about grouping later in this lesson.

5. Follow these steps to choose the Average function for the Expenditures field:
   When you run the query, Access will determine the average expenditure for all pets. Access will display a single cell in the recordset containing the result of the average calculation.

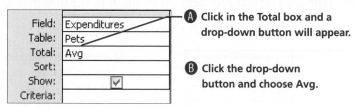

Ⓐ **Click in the Total box and a drop-down button will appear.**

Ⓑ **Click the drop-down button and choose Avg.**

6. Click the Run 🔲 button.
   The result should be $551.29. Each pet has been responsible for an average of $551.29 in revenue.

7. Switch to Design View 🔲, and click in the Total box that currently contains the Avg function.

8. Click the drop-down button, scroll to the top of the list, and choose Sum.

9. Run 🔲 the query again. This time the result should be $4,961.60.
   This number represents the summation of the expenditures for all pets.

10. Switch to Design View 🔲, and continue with the next topic.

Using Criteria with Statistical Functions

You can combine criteria with statistical functions to refine your statistical calculations. For example, imagine you are interested in determining the total expenditures for dogs at Pinnacle Pet Care. The answer can be found by summing the Expenditures of all records where the Pet Type is dog. The following illustration shows how this is expressed in the design grid.

The Pet Type field is added to the design grid and the Where function is chosen in the Total cell.

The word dog is entered in the criteria cell for the Pet Type field.

The Expenditures field uses the Sum function.

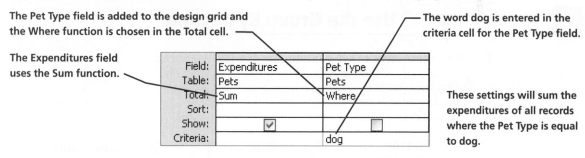

These settings will sum the expenditures of all records where the Pet Type is equal to dog.

Hands-On 21.12 Use Criteria with Statistical Functions

1. Double-click the Pet Type field on the Pets field list to add it to the design grid.

2. Follow these steps to specify criteria for the Pet Type field:

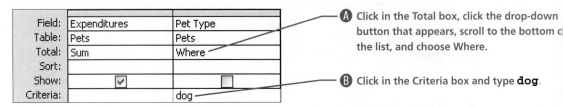

Field:	Expenditures	Pet Type
Table:	Pets	Pets
Total:	Sum	Where
Sort:		
Show:	☑	☐
Criteria:		dog

Ⓐ Click in the Total box, click the drop-down button that appears, scroll to the bottom of the list, and choose Where.

Ⓑ Click in the Criteria box and type **dog**.

3. Run the query. The result should be $2,315.55.
   This number represents the total expenditures on dogs.

4. Switch back to Design view, and continue with the next topic.

Using Grouping with Statistical Functions

The Total row in the design grid has a Group By option that can be used in conjunction with statistical functions. If you choose Group By for a field and run the query, then Access will group all records together that have the same value in the Group By field. For example, if the Pet Type field is set to Group By, then all records that have cat as the pet type will be in one group. Likewise, all records with a pet type of dog will be in another group. If you are performing a statistical calculation as well, then the statistical calculation will be performed on each group. For example, if you use the Sum function to calculate the expenditures for the groups mentioned above, then the total expenditures for cats will be calculated, as will the total expenditures for dogs.

Hands-On 21.13 Use the Group By Setting

1. Follow these steps to set grouping for the Pet Type field:

Ⓐ Click in the Total box, click the drop-down button, scroll up, and choose Group By.

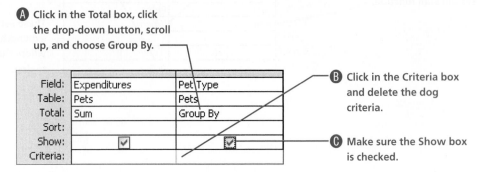

Field:	Expenditures	Pet Type
Table:	Pets	Pets
Total:	Sum	Group By
Sort:		
Show:	☑	☑
Criteria:		

Ⓑ Click in the Criteria box and delete the dog criteria.

Ⓒ Make sure the Show box is checked.

2. Run the query to produce the following recordset.
   The recordset displays the total expenditures for each pet type.

	SumOfExpend	Pet Type
	$2,045.55	Cat
	$2,315.55	Dog
▶	$600.50	Rabbit

3. Save the query as **Expenditures by Pet Type** and then close it.

Query Wizards

The button on the
Access Database toolbar
displays the New Query box as
shown to the right. The New
Query box provides access to
four different query wizards.
The query wizards can be used

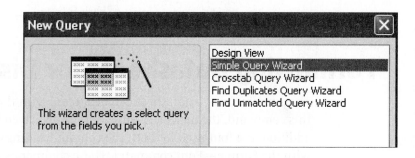

as an alternative to query design view to set up new queries. The following Quick Reference table
describes the various query wizards.

QR

QUICK REFERENCE: QUERY WIZARDS	
Wizard Type	**Description**
Simple Query Wizard	Used to set up simple, select queries. It is usually easiest to use query design view to set up select queries.
Crosstab Query Wizard	Creates a crosstab query used to display data in a spreadsheet-like format.
Find Duplicates Query Wizard	Used to locate records with duplicate field values in a table or query.
Find Unmatched Query Wizard	Locates records in one table that have no related records in another table.

 Hands-On 21.14 Use the Simple Query Wizard

In this exercise, you will set up a simple query using the Simple Query wizard.

1. Make sure the Queries button is chosen on the Objects bar and then click the button
   on the Access Database toolbar.

2. Choose Simple Query Wizard and click OK.
   The select query you will create will list customer names, telephone numbers, and last visit dates.

3. Choose the Customers table from the Tables/Queries list.

4. Choose the Firstname field and click the Add Field button to add Firstname to the Selected Fields list.

5. Now add the Lastname, Phone, and Last Visit fields to the Selected Fields list.

6. Click the Next button to display the second and final Wizard screen.

7. Type **Last Visit Date** as the query name and then click the Finish button.
   The recordset will be displayed. As you can see, it would be just as easy to set up simple queries in query design view. However, you may want to use the Wizard to help set up queries and then modify them in design view.

8. Leave the recordset open, as you will use it in the next exercise.

Formatting Datasheets for Display

The appearance of a datasheet can be altered with the Format→Datasheet command. To use this command, the datasheet must first be displayed by opening a table or running a query. In addition, the font used for both the column headings and cell text in a datasheet can be changed with the Format→Font command. These commands affect the entire datasheet and all text within the datasheet. You cannot format one part of a datasheet or change the font for a portion of a datasheet. The new datasheet appearance is visible on screen and when the datasheet is printed.

⚠ **WARNING!** *Always save a table or query before formatting because the formatting changes cannot be undone.*

 Hands-On 21.15 **Format the Datasheet**

The Last Visit Date datasheet should still be displayed from the previous exercise.

1. Choose Format→Datasheet to display the Datasheet Formatting box.

2. Choose the Raised cell effect and click OK to view the new datasheet appearance.

3. Click the Save 🖫 button to save the new appearance.

4. Choose Format→Datasheet again and experiment with the various settings. Feel free to also choose a different font or font size by using the Format→Font command.

5. When you have finished experimenting, close the query and decide whether you want to save the new appearance.

6. Close the Pinnacle Pet Care database and continue with the end-of-lesson exercises.

Concepts Review

True/False Questions

1. Criteria determine the records that are selected by a query.   TRUE   FALSE

2. The query design grid is where you define a query.   TRUE   FALSE

3. You can add fields to the design grid by double-clicking the desired fields on the field list(s) above the design grid.   TRUE   FALSE

4. You can add all fields to the design grid by double-clicking any field in the field list.   TRUE   FALSE

5. Changing data in the recordset has no impact on the underlying data in the table(s) that the query is based upon.   TRUE   FALSE

6. You must type criteria in the same case (uppercase or lowercase) as the data in the tables you are querying or Access will not select the desired records.   TRUE   FALSE

7. If a field has been entered into the design grid, then there is no way to prevent the field from appearing in the recordset.   TRUE   FALSE

8. The two types of compound criteria are Sum and Avg.   TRUE   FALSE

9. The AVG function will count the number of records in a dataset.   TRUE   FALSE

10. Queries give you the ability to use data from multiple tables.   TRUE   FALSE

Multiple Choice Questions

1. Which of the following commands can be used to remove fields from the design grid?
   a. Field→Remove
   b. Edit→Delete Columns
   c. Edit→Delete Rows
   d. File→Delete Columns

2. Which of the following symbols is used to represent greater than in query criteria?
   a. <
   b. >
   c. <=
   d. >=

3. Which of the following commands is used to clear the design grid?
   a. File→Clear All
   b. File→Clear Grid
   c. Edit→Clear Grid
   d. The grid cannot be cleared.

4. Which symbol(s) must be placed after the field name when creating a calculated field?
   a. A colon :
   b. A semicolon ;
   c. Parenthesis ( )
   d. Brackets [ ]

Skill Builders

Skill Builder 21.1 Use Comparison Criteria and Compound Criteria

In this exercise, you will use comparison criteria and compound criteria to query the Customers table in the Tropical Getaways database.

1. Open the Tropical Getaways database and click the Queries button on the Objects bar.

2. Double-click the Create Query in Design View option.

3. Choose Customers in the Show Table box, and click the Add button.

4. Click the Close button to close the Show Table dialog box.

5. If necessary, maximize the Query window, and adjust the height of the design grid and the Customers field list box.

6. Add the Firstname, Lastname, and Profile fields to the design grid by double-clicking them on the Customers field list.

7. Type the word **adventure** in the Criteria box of the Profile field as shown below.

Field:	Firstname	Lastname	Profile
Table:	Customers	Customers	Customers
Sort:			
Show:	✓	✓	✓
Criteria:			adventure

8. Run ⚡ the query. Only records with the Adventure profile will be displayed, as shown below.

Firstname	Lastname	Profile
Debbie	Thomas	Adventure
Ted	Wilkins	Adventure
Victor	Thomas	Adventure

9. Switch back to Design ⬛ view.

10. Add the State field to the design grid.

11. Set the criteria for the State field to **TX** and the sort order of the Lastname field to Ascending as shown below.

Field:	Firstname	Lastname	Profile	State
Table:	Customers	Customers	Customers	Customers
Sort:		Ascending		
Show:	✓	✓	✓	✓
Criteria:			"adventure"	TX

12. Run the query. Only records where the profile is Adventure and the state is TX will be displayed, as shown below.

Firstname	Lastname	Profile	State
Debbie	Thomas	Adventure	TX
Ted	Wilkins	Adventure	TX

13. Close the query, and save it as **Adventure Profiles**.

Skill Builder 21.2 Nest Calculated Fields

In this exercise, you will use calculated fields in the Tropical Getaways database.

1. Set up a new query in Design view, and add the Trips table to the query.

2. Close the Show Tables dialog box.

3. Add the Destination, Category, and Cost fields to the design grid.

4. Set the Sort box for the Category field to Ascending.

5. Follow these steps to display the Zoom box for a new calculated field:

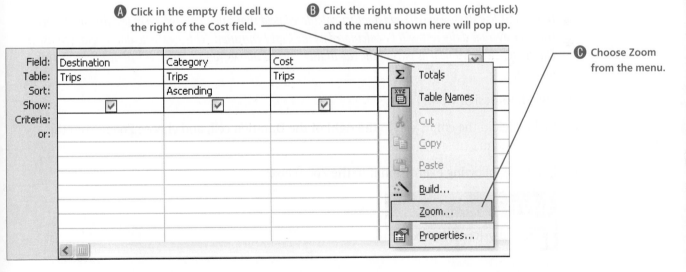

Ⓐ Click in the empty field cell to the right of the Cost field.

Ⓑ Click the right mouse button (right-click) and the menu shown here will pop up.

Ⓒ Choose Zoom from the menu.

6. Enter the expression shown below into the Zoom box. Make sure you type the expression exactly as shown, including the colon after the word Duration.
When you run the query, this expression will calculate the duration of each trip. You can perform calculations using dates in Access and Excel.

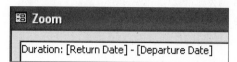

7. Click OK. Check your new calculated field for errors. Correct any errors that you find.

8. Run the query to produce the following recordset.

Destination	Category	Cost	Duration
Baja California	Adventure	$2,900.00	10
Rocky Mountains	Adventure	$2,190.00	16
Swiss Alps	Adventure	$3,500.00	26
Amazon Jungle Trek	Adventure	$7,765.00	38
Kenyan Safari	Adventure	$6,600.00	30
Hawaii	Family	$5,300.00	8
Orlando	Family	$3,400.00	6
Hawaii	Leisure	$4,500.00	10
Caribbean Cruise	Leisure	$2,390.00	9

In the next few steps, you will add another calculated field that calculates the average daily cost of each trip. The average daily cost will be calculated as the Cost / Duration. This new calculated field will use the Duration calculated field as part of the calculation. Access allows you to "nest" calculated fields in this manner.

9. Switch to Design view.

10. Right-click in the empty cell to the right of the Duration cell, and choose Zoom from the pop-up menu.

11. Enter the following expression into the Zoom box:

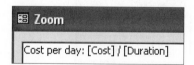

12. Click OK to insert the Cost Per Day calculated field into the cell.

13. Run the query to produce the following recordset.
Notice that the Cost Per Day numbers are not formatted with the Currency format. You will correct this in the next few steps.

Destination	Category	Cost	Duration	Cost per day
Baja California	Adventure	$2,900.00	10	290
Rocky Mountains	Adventure	$2,190.00	16	136.875
Swiss Alps	Adventure	$3,500.00	26	134.615384615
Amazon Jungle Trek	Adventure	$7,765.00	38	204.342105263
Kenyan Safari	Adventure	$6,600.00	30	220
Hawaii	Family	$5,300.00	8	662.5
Orlando	Family	$3,400.00	6	566.666666667
Hawaii	Leisure	$4,500.00	10	450
Caribbean Cruise	Leisure	$2,390.00	9	265.555555556

14. Switch to Design view.

15. Right-click on the Cost Per Day field, and choose Properties from the pop-up menu.

16. Click in the Format box, click the drop-down button, and choose Currency.

17. Close ☒ the Properties box.

18. Run the query. Format the Cost Per Day numbers as Currency with two decimal places.

19. Close the query, and save it as **Cost Per Day**.

Skill Builder 21.3 Use Statistical Functions

In this exercise, you will create a query to perform statistical calculations in the Tropical Getaways database.

1. Create a new query that uses the Trips table.

2. Add the Cost field to the design grid.

3. Display the Total row by clicking the Totals Σ button on the toolbar.

4. Choose the Avg function in the Total box, as shown below.

Field:	Cost
Table:	Trips
Total:	Avg
Sort:	
Show:	✓
Criteria:	

5. Run the query. The average cost of a trip should be calculated as $4,282.78.

6. Switch to Design view.

7. Add the Category field to the design grid.

   The Total box will automatically be set to Group By as shown below. When you run the query, the Avg function in the Cost field will calculate the average cost for each category of trip.

Field:	Cost	Category
Table:	Trips	Trips
Total:	Avg	Group By
Sort:		
Show:	✓	✓
Criteria:		

8. Run the query to produce the following recordset.

AvgOfCost	Category
$4,591.00	Adventure
$4,350.00	Family
$3,445.00	Leisure

9. Close the query, and save it as **Cost by Category**.

10. Close the Tropical Getaways database.

Assessments

Assessment 21.1 Create Queries

1. Open the Classic Cars database.

2. Create a new query, and add the Collectors table to the query.

3. Set up the query to produce the recordset shown below. Notice that this query simply chooses the indicated fields and sorts the records in descending order by Collection Size.

Firstname	Lastname	Era of Interest	Collection Size
Cindy	Johnson	1950's	42
Ed	Larkson	Early 1900's	34
Bob	Barker	1950's	7
Tammy	Olson	1960's	6
Jake	Johnson	1920's	3

4. Run the query, print the recordset, close the query, and save it as **Collection Sizes**.

5. Create a new query, and add the Cars table to the query.

6. Set up the query to produce the recordset shown below. Notice that this query only selects records where the model is Corvette and the condition is Excellent. The query also sorts the records by Value, with the largest values appearing first.

Make	Model	Year	Color	Condition	Value
Chevrolet	Corvette	57	Red	Excellent	$42,000.00
Chevrolet	Corvette	58	Black	Excellent	$35,000.00
Chevrolet	Corvette	62	Blue	Excellent	$30,000.00

7. Run the query, print the recordset, close the query, and save it as **Excellent Corvettes**.

8. Create a new query, and add the Cars table to the query.

9. Set up the query to produce the recordset shown below. Notice that this query calculates the average value of each group of models. In other words, the query groups the records on the Model field and then calculates the average value of each group. The query also sorts the records by Value, with the largest values appearing first.

Model	AvgOfValue
Model A	$75,000.00
Corvette	$43,000.00
Thunderbird	$20,000.00
Custom Eight Sedan	$15,000.00

10. Run the query, and then adjust the width of the Model column as shown in the preceding illustration to fit the widest entry in the column. You can accomplish this by double-clicking the border between the Model and AvgOfValue column headings.

11. Print the recordset, close the query, and save it as **Average Value of Model Groups**.

12. Close the Classic Cars database when you have finished, and exit from Access.

Critical Thinking

Critical Thinking 21.1 Create Select Queries

Linda Holmes has created an add-on service for investor contacts only. She has asked you to create a select query that chooses only the records from the Contacts table in which the contact type is Investor. Open the Holmestead Realty database and follow these guidelines to set up a select query:

- The recordset should display only the FirstName, LastName, SpouseName, Phone, and Contact Type fields from the Contacts table.
- Only contacts with a contact type of Investor should appear in the recordset.
- Save the query as **Investors**.

Linda has published a brochure that she sends only to contacts that have a contact type of Primary Resident or Trustee. Follow these guidelines to set up a select query:

- The recordset should display only the FirstName, LastName, Address, City, State, Zip, and Contact Type fields from the Contacts table.
- Only contacts with a contact type of Primary Resident or Trustee should appear in the recordset.
- Save the query as **Non-Investors**.

Critical Thinking 21.2 Use Calculated Fields in Queries

It is important to Linda to know how much commission she can earn for each of her listings. Follow these guidelines to set up a query that calculates the commission for each listing:

- Use the Listings table as the basis for the query.
- Include the Seller ID, MLS #, Street #, Address, Price, and Commission Rate fields in the query. All of these fields should appear in the recordset in the same order shown here except for the Commission Rate field. Do not include the Commission Rate field in the recordset (but do include it in the query).
- Create a calculated field named Commission. The commission is calculated by multiplying the Price by the Commission Rate.
- Format the Commission calculated field with the Currency format.
- Sort the recordset in Ascending order based on the Seller ID field.
- Save the completed query as **Commission**.

Critical Thinking 21.3 Use Functions in Queries

The broker in charge at Holmestead Realty wants to know the average price of all of Linda's listings. Follow these guidelines to set up the query:

■ Create a select query that calculates the average price of Linda's listings.

■ Add a criterion that calculates the average price for Ranch style houses only.

■ Save the query as **Average Price - Ranch**.

Linda's broker would also like to see the total dollar value of listings grouped by commission rate. Follow these guidelines to set up the query:

■ The recordset should display a sum of the Price field.

■ The commission rates should be grouped and displayed in the recordset next to the sums.

■ Save your completed query as **Sum by Commission Rate**.

LESSON 22

Analyzing Access Data with Excel

A ccess provides sophisticated data-storage
capabilities in Office 2003.
Excel gives you powerful tools
for analyzing data. When you
combine the two tools, you
have both a powerful database
system and a powerful tool to
analyze data in limitless ways.
In this lesson, you will use
Access 2003's OfficeLinks
feature to extract data from the
Pinnacle Pet Care database and
analyze it with Excel.

Case Study

It's the end of the year, and Al Smith wants to make important business decisions to steer Pinnacle Pet Care in the right direction. Al wants to expand the services at Pinnacle Pet Care for the types of pets that are most profitable to his fledgling enterprise. He decides to query his Access database to find the average expenditures per visit for each pet type. He uses Access to generate the query results and then sends the data to Excel. Once the data is in Excel, Al effortlessly creates a pie chart that clearly displays the results of the Access query.

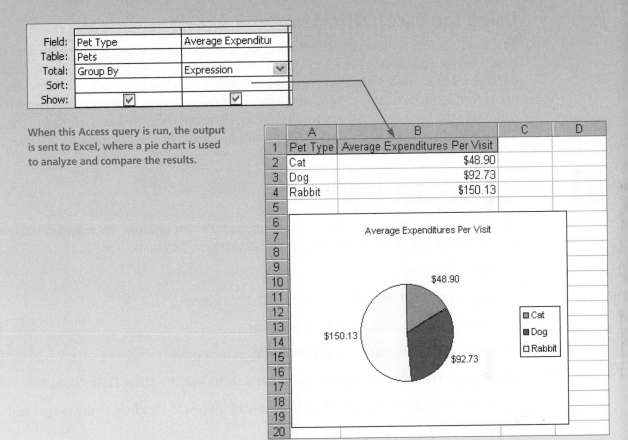

When this Access query is run, the output is sent to Excel, where a pie chart is used to analyze and compare the results.

Outputting from Access to Excel

The true power of Office 2003 lies in the integration of its various programs. Access provides the database and storage capabilities in Office 2003. Access also provides excellent tools for querying a database and generating reports. However, there are times when more sophisticated analysis of data is required. For example, you may need to perform complex calculations on Access data or create charts from Access data. The best approach in these situations is to output the data to Excel and use the analyzing and charting capabilities of Excel.

Using the Excel OfficeLink with Access

The Access toolbar contains an OfficeLinks button that lets you easily output data from Access to Word and Excel. The Excel OfficeLink button is available whenever a table or query is highlighted in the Access database window. When you click the Excel OfficeLink button, Access opens the highlighted table or runs the highlighted query. Access then opens the Excel program and copies the table data or query results to Excel. You can then use Excel to analyze the data. Changes that are made to the data in Excel have no impact on the original Access data.

Hands-On 22.1 Set Up a Query

In this exercise, you will set up a new query in the Pinnacle Pet Care database. The new query will contain a calculated field that computes the average expenditures per visit for each pet type.

Display the Query Window

1. Start Access, and open the Pinnacle Pet Care database.
2. Click the Queries button on the Objects bar.
3. Double-click the Create Query in Design View option.
4. Add the Pets table to the query window and then close the Show Table dialog box.
5. Double-click the Pet Type field in the Pets field list to add that field to the design grid.

Create a Calculated Field

6. Follow these steps to display the Zoom dialog box:

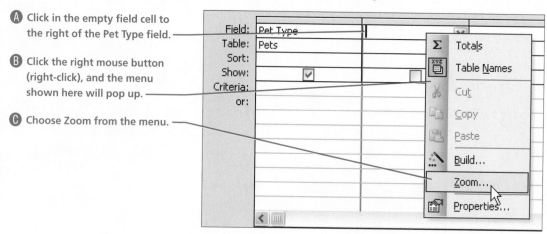

Ⓐ Click in the empty field cell to the right of the Pet Type field.

Ⓑ Click the right mouse button (right-click), and the menu shown here will pop up.

Ⓒ Choose Zoom from the menu.

7. Enter the calculated field expression shown below into the Zoom box. Make sure you enter the expression exactly as shown. In particular, make sure you use a colon : (not a semicolon ;), correctly spell the field names, use the correct open and closed parentheses ( ) and brackets [ ], and use the forward slash / symbol to represent division. This expression will eventually calculate the average expenditures per visit for each pet type.

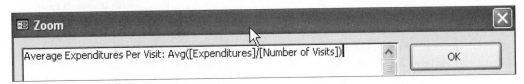

8. Click OK to insert the expression in the field.

9. Make sure the syntax is correct as shown above. If necessary, you can edit the expression within the cell or redisplay the Zoom dialog box and make any necessary changes.

Add Grouping to the Pet Type Field

10. Click the Totals **Σ** button on the toolbar, and a Total row will appear below the Table row. *The Total boxes will be set to Group By for both the Pet Type field and the calculated field.*

11. Follow these steps to set the Total box to Expression for the calculated field:

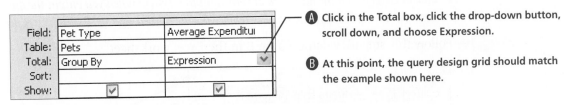

Ⓐ Click in the Total box, click the drop-down button, scroll down, and choose Expression.

Ⓑ At this point, the query design grid should match the example shown here.

These settings will group the records by Pet Type and calculate the average expenditures per visit for each group. In other words, the average expenditures per visit will be calculated for dogs, cats, and other pet types.

12. If necessary, click the Properties button on the Access toolbar to display the Field Properties dialog box.

13. Click in the Format box, click the drop-down button, scroll down, and choose Currency. *When the query is run, the resulting numbers will be formatted with dollar signs and two decimals.*

14. Click the Run button to run the query. The recordset shown to the right should appear.

Pet Type	Average Expendi
▶ Cat	$48.90
Dog	$92.73
Rabbit	$150.13

15. Close the query by clicking the Close button at the top-right corner of the query window.

16. Click the Yes button when Access asks if you want to save the query.

17. Type the name **Average Expenditures per Visit by Pet Type** in the Save As box, and click OK.

Output the Query Results to Excel

18. Follow these steps to output the query results to Excel:

Ⓐ Choose the Average Expenditures Per Visit by Pet Type query in the database window.

Ⓑ Click the OfficeLinks drop-down button and choose Analyze It with Microsoft Excel.

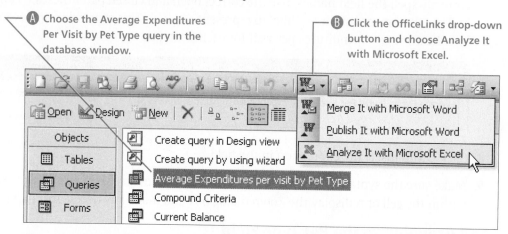

Ⓒ If Access indicates that the file named Average Expenditures Per Visit by Pet Type already exists, then click Yes to replace the file.

Excel will start, and the query results will appear in the Excel window as shown below. Access actually creates an Excel file on the hard disk of your computer system when you output the query. This is why Access may have asked if you wanted to replace the file named Average Expenditures per Visit by Pet Type.

19. Follow this step to widen Column B in the Excel worksheet:

	A	B	C
1	Pet Type	Average Expenditures Per Visit	
2	Cat	$89.18	
3	Dog	$92.73	
4	Rabbit	$150.13	

Ⓐ Double-click the border between the columns headed B and C to widen Column B, as shown here.

Create a Pie Chart

20. Select the range A1:B4.
This range includes the two heading cells and the data in Rows 2, 3, and 4.

21. Click the Chart Wizard button.

22. Choose the Pie chart type and the first subtype.

23. Click the Next button twice, and the Step 3 of 4 box will appear.

24. Click the Data Labels tab, and choose Value.
When the chart is created, the average expenditures per visit will appear next to each slice.

25. Click the Finish button, and the chart will appear in the worksheet as shown to the right.

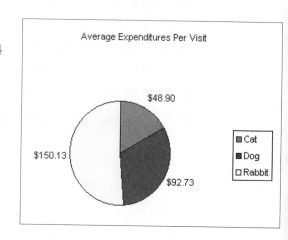

26. Save the worksheet as **Hands-On Lesson 22**.

27. Choose File→Exit from the Excel menu bar to close the Excel program. However, leave Access open, as you will continue to use Access.

Output an Entire Table to Excel

28. Click the Tables button on the Access Objects bar.

29. Notice that the OfficeLinks ▣ ▾ button now has the Excel icon on the face of the button. *This is because Excel was the last OfficeLink that you used.*

30. Choose the Pets table in the database window, and click the OfficeLinks ▣ ▾ button. *Excel will start, and Access will output the entire Pets table to Excel. If Access asks you to save the file, then click Yes to replace the existing pets.xls file.*

31. Enter **Total Expenditures** in Cell A11, which should be the first empty cell in Column A.

32. If the text wraps within Cell A11, then use the Format→Cells command to display the Format Cells dialog box. Click the Alignment tab, and uncheck the Wrap Text box.

33. Click Cell I11, which should be the first empty cell in the Expenditures column.

34. Click the AutoSum ▣ Σ button, and tap (ENTER) to calculate the total expenditures.

35. Feel free to create other totals or to chart any of the data.

36. Save the workbook as **Hands-On Lesson 22, Pets Data**.

37. Close the workbook when you have finished.

38. Use the File→Exit command to close both Excel and Access.

UNIT 7

PowerPoint 2003

PowerPoint 2003 is an intense graphics presentation application that is deceptively simple to use despite the power behind its features. You will begin by building a solid foundation by learning how to create, edit, format, print, and deliver presentations. Each step of the way, illustrations help to bring the concepts into focus. Helpful tips for design and delivery are included to guide you as the presentation evolves. Next you will see a basic presentation comes to life as you add animation schemes and transitions, clip art to color and enhance the presentation. Finally, you will practice delivery techniques for transforming a presentation into a slide show. This unit is not only informative, it's fun!

LESSON 23

Creating and Delivering a Presentation

In this lesson, you will begin developing a PowerPoint presentation for the Pinnacle Pet Care pet clinic. As you develop your presentation, you will learn basic techniques, such as adding slides to a presentation using layouts. You will format slides using bulleted lists, text formats, and paragraph formats. You will learn how to navigate through a presentation and deliver a presentation using transparencies and an electronic slide show.

Additional learning resources are available at labpub.com/learn/oe3/

Case Study

Al Smith, owner of Pinnacle Pet Care, needs to make a presentation to a large group at the annual Pet World trade show. Al wants to introduce Pinnacle to the trade show attendees and entice them with a promotional offer. Al decides to use PowerPoint to develop and deliver his presentation. The presentation will be delivered using a laptop PC attached to a video projection system. Al chose PowerPoint because it is easy to learn and seamlessly integrates with his other Microsoft Office applications. Al's dynamic speaking abilities together with PowerPoint's presentation capabilities are a powerful combination certain to win over the trade show attendees.

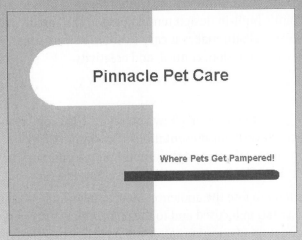

Slides from the Pinnacle Pet Care Presentation

Presenting PowerPoint 2003

PowerPoint 2003 is a presentation graphics program that allows you to easily develop dynamic presentations. Whether you are developing a one-on-one presentation for your supervisor or a sophisticated presentation for a large group, PowerPoint provides the tools to make your presentation a success. PowerPoint lets you output your presentation on transparencies for use with an overhead projector, on 35mm slides for more formal presentations, and using a projection device directly from your PC. With PowerPoint 2003, you can even create virtual presentations for delivery on the Internet or an Intranet (a network within an organization).

PowerPoint provides powerful tools that let you concentrate on the content of your presentation instead of the design details. With PowerPoint's built-in design templates, you can rapidly create highly effective professional presentations. PowerPoint makes it easy to organize your ideas, create, edit, and deliver your presentations with precision, control, and creativity.

Presentation Design Tips

Have you ever heard the expression, "It isn't what you say, it's how you say it"? This old adage remains true even when designing high-tech PowerPoint presentations. The design of your presentation will effect your audience's perception of you and the amount of information they retain. Use the following helpful hints to design effective PowerPoint presentations.

- **Keep it short**—Long presentations tend to lose the audience. Most audiences are lost after just 20 to 30 minutes. Keep your presentation focused and to the point. You can always lengthen your presentation by opening it up to questions after you have finished speaking.

- **Amount of information**—Avoid placing too much information on one slide. Too many words or pictures can distract your audience. If a slide has too much information, then try turning it into two or three slides.

- **Use bullets**—Many PowerPoint slides are set up with bullets. A typical slide should have between three and six bullets. Keep your bulleted phrases as short as possible. If you have too many bullets on a slide, break them into two columns or create a second slide.

- **Animation and special effects**—PowerPoint lets you use animation and special effects in presentations. Keep in mind that animation and special effects should draw attention to your important points. Don't get carried away with these tools and use them as entertainment. This may be enjoyable, but your audience may miss your point.

Presentation Tips

The manner in which you deliver your presentation is also important. You want the audience to focus on the presentation instead of focusing on you. Use the following helpful hints to deliver effective presentations.

- **Maintain a moderate pace**—Speaking too fast will exhaust your audience, and speaking too slow may put them to sleep. Therefore, you should try to maintain a moderate pace.

- **Pauses are important**—Try pausing for five to ten seconds after making important points. This will let your audience rest and give them time to absorb what you have said.

- **Speak to your audience**—Always face your audience while speaking. Many presenters speak while facing a white board or projection screen. Your points will definitely be missed if you turn your back to your audience while speaking.

- **Stay still**—Avoid excessive movement while presenting. Movement can be distracting because your audience's attention is drawn to your movements instead of your presentation. Excessive movement may be OK for high-energy, motivational presentations but it is a bad approach for most business presentations. The best way to avoid this is to face your audience or maintain a slight angle towards your audience. Avoid moving your feet or rocking on your feet. Move freely from the waist up, including your arms and hands. Using your body language to make points is good technique, provided you are not "running around the room" while presenting.

Hands-On 23.1 Start PowerPoint

1. Click the ⟨*start*⟩ button and choose All Programs→Microsoft Office→Microsoft Office PowerPoint from the All Programs menu.
   PowerPoint will load and the PowerPoint program window will be visible.

PowerPoint's Program Window

PowerPoint 2003's program window has not significantly changed from prior versions of the program. PowerPoint 2003 continues to include the all-important task pane on the right side of the program window. The following illustration gives an overview of the new program window.

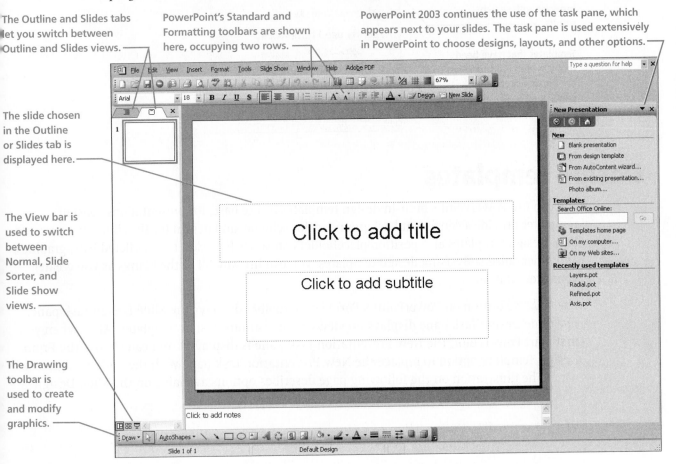

The Outline and Slides tabs let you switch between Outline and Slides views.

PowerPoint's Standard and Formatting toolbars are shown here, occupying two rows.

PowerPoint 2003 continues the use of the task pane, which appears next to your slides. The task pane is used extensively in PowerPoint to choose designs, layouts, and other options.

The slide chosen in the Outline or Slides tab is displayed here.

The View bar is used to switch between Normal, Slide Sorter, and Slide Show views.

The Drawing toolbar is used to create and modify graphics.

Task Panes

Task panes, which appear on the right side of the program window, are enhanced in PowerPoint 2003 to incorporate the Help file, Research queries, and Shared Workspace capabilities. Any of several task panes may appear, depending on the actions you perform. In addition, you can display or hide the task pane at any time with the View→Task pane command. The following illustration describes the options on the New Presentation task pane.

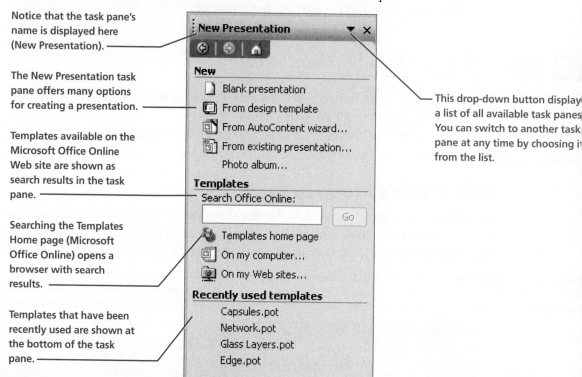

Notice that the task pane's name is displayed here (New Presentation).

The New Presentation task pane offers many options for creating a presentation.

Templates available on the Microsoft Office Online Web site are shown as search results in the task pane.

Searching the Templates Home page (Microsoft Office Online) opens a browser with search results.

Templates that have been recently used are shown at the bottom of the task pane.

This drop-down button displays a list of all available task panes. You can switch to another task pane at any time by choosing it from the list.

Design Templates

You can use PowerPoint's built-in design templates as the basis for presentations. Design templates provide a consistent background, color scheme, and design for the slides in a presentation. Design templates also position placeholders on slides for titles, text, bulleted lists, graphics, and other objects. By using design templates, you can literally fill in the blanks as you create your presentation.

The **Design** button on PowerPoint's Formatting toolbar displays the Slide Design task pane. The Slide Design task pane displays previews of the various design templates. Also, when you first start PowerPoint, the New Presentation task pane is displayed. You can choose the From Design Template option to replace the New Presentation task pane with the Slide Design task pane. The illustration on the following page describes options available on the Slide Design task pane.

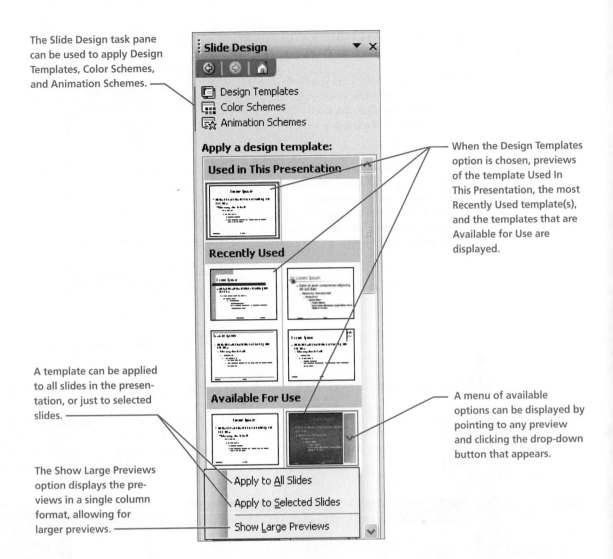

The Slide Design task pane can be used to apply Design Templates, Color Schemes, and Animation Schemes.

When the Design Templates option is chosen, previews of the template Used In This Presentation, the most Recently Used template(s), and the templates that are Available for Use are displayed.

A template can be applied to all slides in the presentation, or just to selected slides.

A menu of available options can be displayed by pointing to any preview and clicking the drop-down button that appears.

The Show Large Previews option displays the previews in a single column format, allowing for larger previews.

Hands-On 23.2 Apply a Design Template

1. Click the From Design Template option on the task pane.
   The Slide Design task pane will replace the New Presentation task pane. Currently, no design template is applied to the presentation.

2. Point to any of the design template previews on the task pane and a drop-down button will appear.

3. Click the drop-down button and choose Show Large Previews if that option is not currently checked.
   This will make viewing the previews in the following steps easier.

4. Follow these steps to choose the Capsules design template:

Ⓐ Scroll through the list until you find the Capsules template. When you point to the template, the word Capsules will be displayed. ⎯⎯⎯

Ⓑ Click the drop-down button and choose Apply to All Slides. The title slide in your presentation will be formatted with the Capsules design. The title slide has placeholders for a title and subtitle. ⎯⎯⎯

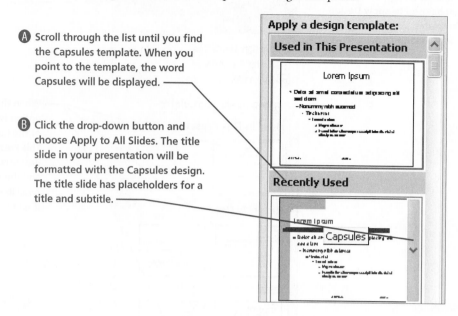

5. Follow these steps to explore the window and enter a title and subtitle in the slide:

Ⓐ Thumbnails of all slides in a presentation are displayed on the Slides tab. You can display a slide by choosing the thumbnail. ⎯⎯⎯

Ⓑ Click in the title box and type **Pinnacle Pet Care**. ⎯⎯⎯

Ⓒ Click in the subtitle box and type **Where Pets Get Pampered!** ⎯⎯⎯

Ⓓ Notice that the Capsules design template now appears at the top of the template list because it is currently in use. ⎯⎯⎯

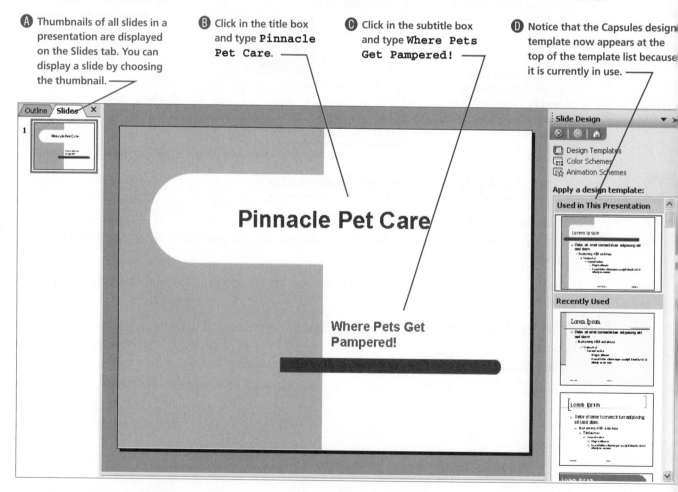

Adding Slides and Changing Layouts

PowerPoint presentations are composed of slides. Slides are composed of various objects such as titles, bulleted lists, charts, and pictures. If your presentation is based on a design template, then the slides you use will be preformatted to give your presentation a consistent background, color scheme, and design.

Adding New Slides

The button on PowerPoint's Formatting toolbar inserts a new slide after the current slide. In addition, the New Slide button displays the Slide Layout task pane. New slides can also be inserted directly from the Slide Layout task pane, as described below.

Changing Slide Layouts

The Slide Layout task pane lets you change the layout of selected slides and insert slides with a desired layout. You can apply a layout to a single slide by first choosing the slide from the Slides tab. Or, you can apply a layout to multiple slides by selecting the desired slides on the Slides tab. The following Quick Reference table describes the process of selecting multiple slides. The illustration that follows the table describes the process of inserting slides and applying layouts to selected slides.

QR ▶ **QUICK REFERENCE: SELECTING MULTIPLE SLIDES**

Selecting Miscellaneous Slides   Press the (CTRL) key while clicking the desired slides.

Selecting a Block of Slides   Click the first slide in the block, press the (SHIFT) key, and then click the last slide in the block.

Slide layouts are applied to the slide(s) selected on the Slides tab.

The New Slide button inserts a new slide and displays the Slide Layout task pane.

The Slide Layout task pane displays layouts that can be applied to slides.

Layouts can be applied to selected slides, or a new slide can be inserted with a desired layout.

Pinnacle Pet Care

Apply to Selected Slides

Reapply Layout

Insert New Slide

Hands-On 23.3 Add a Slide

In step 1 of this exercise, you will display the Standard and Formatting toolbars on separate rows. From this point forward, the instructions in this text will assume that the Standard and Formatting toolbars are displayed on separate rows. This will make it easier for you to locate buttons when instructed to do so.

1. Follow these steps to display the Standard and Formatting toolbars on separate rows:

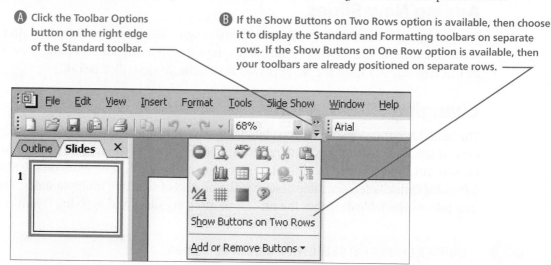

A Click the Toolbar Options button on the right edge of the Standard toolbar.

B If the Show Buttons on Two Rows option is available, then choose it to display the Standard and Formatting toolbars on separate rows. If the Show Buttons on One Row option is available, then your toolbars are already positioned on separate rows.

2. Click the ⬚ New Slide button on the Formatting toolbar.
   A new slide will be inserted below the title slide. The Slide Layout task pane will also appear.

3. Take a moment to scroll through the various layouts in the Slide Layout task pane. Remember, clicking a layout will apply it to your new slide.
   Notice that the layouts are organized in categories of Text Layouts, Content Layouts, Text and Content Layouts, and Other Layouts. Your new slide features a Title and Text layout, which allows you to easily create a slide with a title and a bulleted list.

4. Now continue with the next topic, during which you will learn about text layouts.

Text Layouts

The first category of layouts on the Slide Layout task pane is the Text Layout category. The four text layouts include two title slide layouts and two layouts, which contain both titles and bulleted lists. You can add text to any text placeholder on a slide by simply clicking in the placeholder and typing the desired text. You can edit the text using standard text editing techniques.

Bulleted List Layouts

PowerPoint makes it effortless to create bulleted lists. In fact, many of the layouts (such as the slide you just added to your presentation) already have placeholders for bulleted lists. In PowerPoint, these bulleted lists can have up to five levels. The following illustration shows the Monthly Events slide you will create in the next exercise.

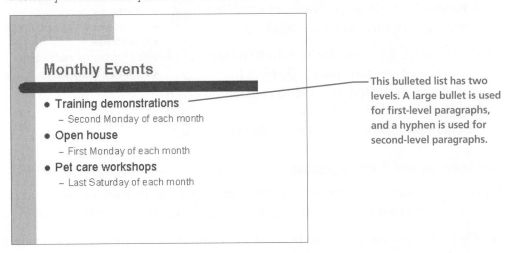

This bulleted list has two levels. A large bullet is used for first-level paragraphs, and a hyphen is used for second-level paragraphs.

Working with Bulleted Lists

If your presentation is based upon a design template, then the template automatically formats each paragraph in a bulleted list. The format impacts the bullet style, indentation level, font type, and font size for each bulleted paragraph. The following Quick Reference table describes the various techniques that can be used with bulleted lists.

QUICK REFERENCE: BULLETED LISTS

Task	Procedure
Turn bullets on and off.	Select the desired paragraph(s), and click the Bullets button on the Formatting toolbar.
Promote paragraphs.	Select the desired paragraph(s), and click the Decrease Indent button on the Formatting toolbar. Promoting reduces a paragraph's indentation level and changes the bullet character.
Demote paragraphs.	Select the desired paragraph(s), and click the Increase Indent button on the Formatting toolbar. Demoting increases a paragraph's indentation level and changes the bullet character.

Hands-On 23.4 Bulleted Lists

Enter the Title

1. Make sure the Title and Text layout is chosen in the task pane. This layout should have automatically been applied when you clicked the New Slide button in the previous exercise.

2. Click in the title box and type **Monthly Events**.

3. Click in the bulleted list box.

4. Type **Training demonstrations**, and tap (ENTER).
   PowerPoint formats the new paragraph with the same large bullet. Paragraph formats are carried to new paragraphs when you tap the (ENTER) key.

5. Complete the list shown to the right by typing the indicated text and tapping (ENTER) at the end of each paragraph. However, do not tap (ENTER) after the last paragraph.
   You will demote several items in the next few steps.

> **Monthly Events**
>
> - Training demonstrations
> - Second Monday of each month
> - Open house
> - First Monday of each month
> - Pet care workshops
> - Last Saturday of each month

Demote Several Paragraphs

The most efficient way to create multilevel bulleted lists is to first type the entire list (as you did in the previous step). Once all of the text has been typed, you can promote and demote paragraphs as desired.

6. Click anywhere on the second bulleted paragraph (Second Monday of each month).
   The flashing insertion point should be positioned on the paragraph text.

7. Click the Bullets [≡] button on the Formatting toolbar.
   The Bullets button will no longer be highlighted and the bullet will be removed from the paragraph. You can always use this technique to remove bullets from paragraphs.

8. Click the Bullets [≡] button again to reapply the bullet.

9. Click the Increase Indent [⇥] button on the Formatting toolbar.
   The paragraph will be indented, and the bullet style will change to a hyphen. Demoting a paragraph makes the paragraph subordinate to the preceding paragraph.

10. Click the Increase Indent [⇥] button several more times.
    The bullet style will change, and the indent will increase each time you click the button. Also, the font size and font style will change with each demotion. These formats are determined by the Capsule design template, which the presentation is based upon.

11. Promote the paragraph until it is at the second indentation level with the hyphen bullet style.

12. Click anywhere on the fourth paragraph (First Monday of each month).

13. Demote ⬛ the paragraph once.

14. Demote ⬛ the last paragraph (Last Saturday of each month).

15. Click outside the bulleted list box to view the completed slide.

Choosing Slides

You can choose a slide by clicking the desired slide on the Slides tab. However, if a presentation has a large number of slides, the slide you wish to choose may not be visible on the tab. The vertical scroll bar to the right of the slide lets you navigate to the desired slide. The scroll box can be dragged up and down, or the Previous Slide ⬛ and Next Slide ⬛ buttons can be used to move from one slide to the next.

Hands-On 23.5 Add Another Bulleted Slide, and Choose Slides

Add a Slide

1. Click the ⬛ New Slide button and PowerPoint will insert another bulleted list slide after the Monthly Events slide.
   The New Slide button always inserts bulleted list slides.

2. Click the Title box, and type the phrase **Services Provided**.

3. Click the bulleted list box, and type the four bulleted paragraphs shown to the right.

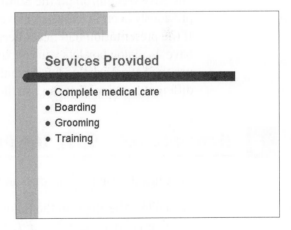

4. Follow these steps to choose slides:

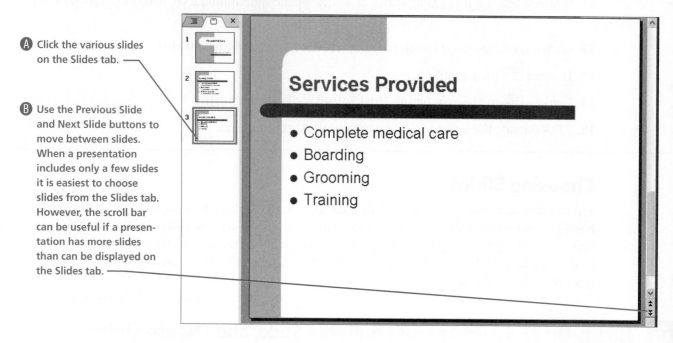

A Click the various slides on the Slides tab.

B Use the Previous Slide and Next Slide buttons to move between slides. When a presentation includes only a few slides it is easiest to choose slides from the Slides tab. However, the scroll bar can be useful if a presentation has more slides than can be displayed on the Slides tab.

Services Provided

- Complete medical care
- Boarding
- Grooming
- Training

5. Feel free to browse through your slides and make any editing changes you wish.

Saving a Presentation

The Save 🖫 button on the Standard toolbar initiates the Save command. If the presentation had previously been saved, then PowerPoint replaces the previous version with the new edited version. If the presentation had never been saved, then PowerPoint displays the Save As dialog box. The Save As dialog box lets you specify a name and storage location for the presentation. You can also use the Save As dialog box to make a copy of a presentation by saving it under a new name or to a different location. You can use filenames containing as many as 255 characters.

FROM THE KEYBOARD
CTRL + S for Save

Hands-On 23.6 Save the Presentation

1. Click the Save 🖫 button on the Standard toolbar.

2. Follow the steps on the following page to save the presentation to your exercise diskette.
   If necessary, obtain a 3½" diskette, and insert it in the diskette drive.

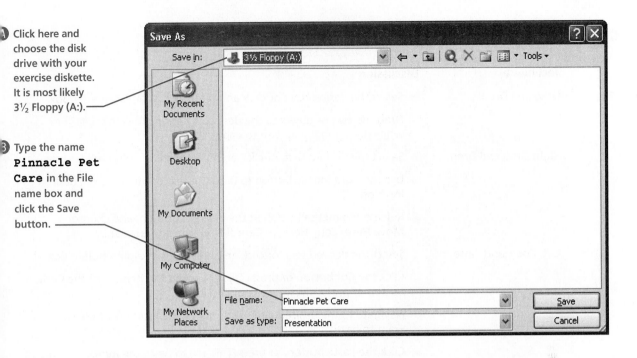

Click here and choose the disk drive with your exercise diskette. It is most likely 3½ Floppy (A:).

Type the name **Pinnacle Pet Care** in the File name box and click the Save button.

Moving and Copying Text and Objects

You can move and copy text and objects using Drag and Drop or Cut, Copy, and Paste. It is usually most efficient to use Drag and Drop if you are moving or copying within a slide or to another slide that is visible on the screen. Drag and Drop is also effective for rearranging slides. Cut, Copy, and Paste are most efficient when moving or copying to a location not visible on the current screen.

The Office Clipboard

The Office Clipboard lets you collect items from any Office document or program and paste them into any other Office document. For example, you can collect data from an Excel table and text from a Word document and paste them into PowerPoint slides. The Office Clipboard can hold up to 24 items.

How it Works

You place items on the Office Clipboard using the standard Cut and Copy commands; however, to see the pasted items the Clipboard task pane must be displayed. The Clipboard task pane is displayed using the Edit→Office Clipboard command. Once the Clipboard task pane is displayed, you can choose an item and paste it into your PowerPoint presentation.

QUICK REFERENCE: MOVING AND COPYING

Technique	Discussion
Drag and Drop	■ Select the desired text or click an object such as a placeholder box.
	■ Drag the text or object to the desired location. Press the (CTRL) key while dragging if you wish to copy.
Right Drag and Drop	■ Select the desired text, or click an object such as a placeholder box.
	■ Use the right mouse button to drag the text or object to the desired location.
	■ Release the mouse button at the desired location, and choose, Move Here, Copy Here, or Cancel from the pop-up menu.
Cut, Copy, and Paste	■ Select the desired text, or click an object such as a placeholder box.
	■ Click the Cut button or press (CTRL)+(X) to cut the item. Click the Copy button or press (CTRL)+(C) to copy the item.
	■ Navigate to the desired slide, and click at the location where you want to paste.
	■ Click the Paste button, or press (CTRL)+(V) to paste the item.

Hands-On 23.7 Add a Slide, Change the Slide Layout, and Move Paragraphs

In this exercise, you will add a new slide to the presentation. You will enter a bulleted list into the new slide. Then you will change the layout for the new slide and rearrange the paragraphs in the bulleted list. You can always change the layout for a slide after the slide has been created.

Add the Slide

1. Make sure the Services Provided slide is chosen in the presentation.
   New slides are always added after the slide that is chosen.

2. Click the New Slide button.

3. Click in the Title box, and type **Products Sold**.

4. Click in the bulleted list box, and type the bulleted paragraphs shown to the right.
   When you begin typing the last bullet, PowerPoint will reformat all of the paragraphs with a smaller font size. PowerPoint does this to allow the bullets to fit in the box. A long list of bulleted paragraphs may appear cluttered and overwhelming to an audience. For this reason, it is usually best to limit the number

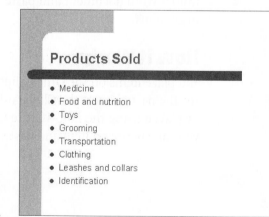

of bullets in a column to four or five. Another strategy that can be employed is to break the list into two columns. In the next two steps, you will use this technique by choosing a different layout for the slide. You can change the layout of a slide after the slide has been created.

Change the Slide Layout and Move Text

5. Follow this step to change the slide layout:

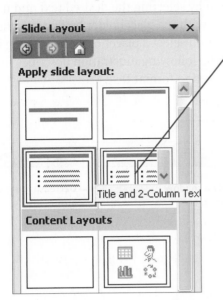

A Click the Title and 2-Column Text layout on the task pane. The new layout will be applied to the slide. Notice that you can apply a layout to selected slides by simply clicking the layout on the task pane.

6. Follow these steps to move the last four bulleted paragraphs to the second box:
The last four bulleted paragraphs should now be in the second box.

A Select the last four paragraphs by dragging the mouse over them and then release the mouse button.

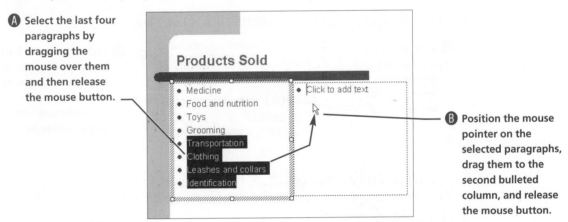

B Position the mouse pointer on the selected paragraphs, drag them to the second bulleted column, and release the mouse button.

7. Click the Save button to save the changes to your presentation.

Formatting Text and Paragraphs

FROM THE KEYBOARD

CTRL + B for Bold

CTRL + U for Underline

CTRL + I for Italics

Text within a placeholder box can be formatted by selecting the desired text and using buttons on the Formatting toolbar. You can format all text within a placeholder by first selecting the placeholder and then applying the desired formats. You select a placeholder by clicking it once and then clicking any border on the placeholder. The following illustration describes the buttons on PowerPoint's Formatting toolbar that can be used to format text.

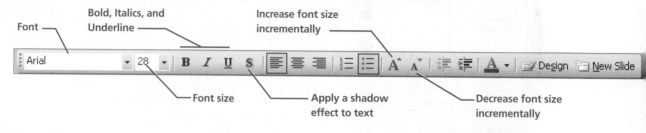

 ## Hands-On 23.8 Format Text

Use the Font Size Buttons

1. Choose the title slide (the first slide) by clicking it on the Slides tab.
   Notice that the subtitle wraps within the box. The slide will look better if the subtitle does not wrap. Also, it may look good to have the title just a little larger.

2. Follow these steps to select the subtitle placeholder box:

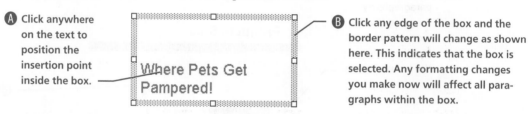

A Click anywhere on the text to position the insertion point inside the box.

B Click any edge of the box and the border pattern will change as shown here. This indicates that the box is selected. Any formatting changes you make now will affect all paragraphs within the box.

3. Notice that the Font Size box `28` is currently set to 28.
   The Capsules design template applied this font size to the subtitle.

4. Click the Decrease Font Size `A` button to reduce the size to 24.

5. Click the Bold `B` button.
   Now the text is easily visible, but the bold format has caused it to wrap within the box again.

6. Click the Decrease Font Size `A` button again.
   The subtitle should fit within the box, but now it is a little too small. The font size buttons let you easily increase or decrease the font size; however, they increment the size by four points. Fortunately, you can use the font size box to set the font size with precision.

Continue to Format the Subtitle

7. Click in the Font Size box `20`, type **22**, and tap ENTER.
   Now the text is a little larger, and it fits within the box again. You can also prevent text from wrapping by changing the box width. You will experiment with this in the next step.

8. Follow these steps to change the box width:

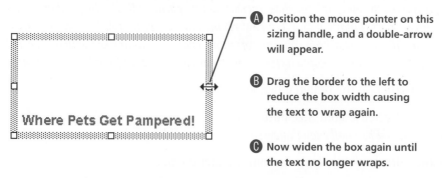

Ⓐ Position the mouse pointer on this sizing handle, and a double-arrow will appear.

Ⓑ Drag the border to the left to reduce the box width causing the text to wrap again.

Ⓒ Now widen the box again until the text no longer wraps.

You can always change the size of a placeholder box using this technique.

Format the Title

9. Click in the title box (not the subtitle), and then click a border of the box.

10. Click the Increase Font Size **A˄** button once to increase the size to 40.

Line Spacing and Paragraph Spacing

The Format→Line Spacing command displays the Line Spacing dialog box. Line spacing determines the amount of space within paragraphs and between paragraphs. The Line Spacing dialog box also lets you set the paragraph spacing before and after. The paragraph spacing settings let you increase the space before and after paragraphs, but they do not change the line spacing within paragraphs. These settings are useful if text is wrapping within a placeholder box and you want to change the spacing between paragraphs but not within the wrapped lines.

 ## Hands-On 23.9 Work with Line Spacing and Paragraph Spacing

In this exercise, you will insert a new slide. Also, you will adjust the paragraph spacing to increase the amount of space between the bullets.

1. Choose the last slide in the presentation (Products Sold).

2. Click the New Slide button to add a new bulleted list slide.

3. Click the Title box, and type the title **Our Staff**.

4. Click in the bulleted list box, and type the three bulleted paragraphs shown to the right. *Notice that the second bullet paragraph wraps to a second line. PowerPoint automatically wraps lines as you type. In this slide, the lines are long, which gives the slide a cluttered appearance. Try to avoid wrapped lines when creating slides. In the next few*

Our Staff

- Dr. Mary Boyd – Chief Veterinarian
- Alex Larkson – Boarding and Grooming Manager
- Cindy Marshall – Training Manager

steps, you will eliminate the wrapping by reducing the font size of the text. You will also increase the para-graph spacing to "open up" the slide. Increasing the spacing will also help balance the slide, since it has just three bullets. Finally, notice that PowerPoint's Check Spelling As You Type feature has put a wavy red line under the name Larkson. You can correct or ignore a word marked with a wavy red underline by right clicking the word and choosing a replacement word or Ignore All from the pop-up menu.

5. Click a border on the bulleted list box.

6. Click the Decrease Font Size button ⟨A⟩.
   The text should be small enough now so that the second line no longer wraps in the box.

7. Choose Format→Line Spacing from the menu bar.

8. Follow these steps to set the Before Paragraph spacing:
   Notice how the change has "opened up" the slide by creating more spacing between the paragraphs.

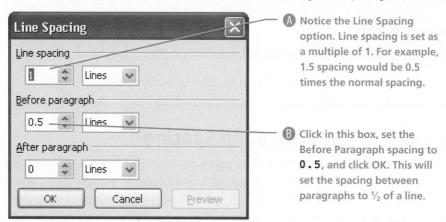

Ⓐ Notice the Line Spacing option. Line spacing is set as a multiple of 1. For example, 1.5 spacing would be 0.5 times the normal spacing.

Ⓑ Click in this box, set the Before Paragraph spacing to **0.5**, and click OK. This will set the spacing between paragraphs to ½ of a line.

9. Click the Save ⟨💾⟩ button to save the changes to your presentation.

PowerPoint Views

Thus far, you have worked in Normal view. Normal view lets you work with individual slides or with an outline. In addition to Normal view, PowerPoint has several other views that are useful for developing and delivering presentations. You can switch views by clicking buttons on the View bar, which is located on the left end of the horizontal scroll bar. You can also switch views by choosing the desired view from the View menu. The various PowerPoint views are described in the following Quick Reference table.

QUICK REFERENCE: POWERPOINT VIEWS

View	Purpose
Normal	Normal view displays thumbnails of all slides in the presentation when the Slides tab is chosen and an outline of the presentation when the Outline tab is chosen. The current slide in the outline or thumbnails is displayed in the center of the screen. Normal view is designed to let you focus on the current slide. If desired, the Outline and Slides tabs can be dismissed by clicking the Close ⊠ button next to the Slides tab. This allocates more space to the current slide. The Outline and Slides tabs can be restored using the View→Normal (Restore Panes) command.
Notes Page	Notes Page view lets you develop speaker notes to accompany the presentation. You can switch to Notes Page view with the View→Notes Page command.
Slide Sorter	Slide Sorter view displays all slides in the presentation. In Slide Sorter view, you can rearrange slides by dragging the desired slide(s) to different positions within the presentation.
Slide Show	The Slide Show button lets you run the presentation.

Hands-On 23.10 **Explore the Various Views**

1. Follow these steps to explore the various views and the PowerPoint window:

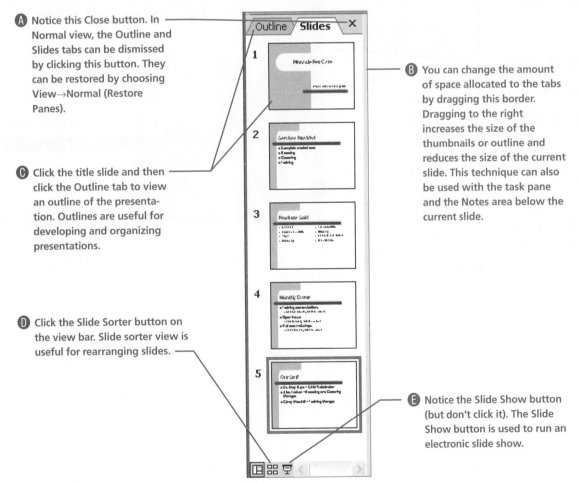

A Notice this Close button. In Normal view, the Outline and Slides tabs can be dismissed by clicking this button. They can be restored by choosing View→Normal (Restore Panes).

B You can change the amount of space allocated to the tabs by dragging this border. Dragging to the right increases the size of the thumbnails or outline and reduces the size of the current slide. This technique can also be used with the task pane and the Notes area below the current slide.

C Click the title slide and then click the Outline tab to view an outline of the presentation. Outlines are useful for developing and organizing presentations.

D Click the Slide Sorter button on the view bar. Slide sorter view is useful for rearranging slides.

E Notice the Slide Show button (but don't click it). The Slide Show button is used to run an electronic slide show.

2. Choose View from the menu bar.

3. Choose Normal to switch back to Normal view.

Working with Outlines

Outlines can be quite useful for developing your ideas and the overall structure of your presentation. Outlines are also useful for reorganizing presentations. You can add, and delete slides, move slides, and edit text within the outline.

The Outlining Toolbar

The Outlining toolbar displays buttons that are useful when working with Outlines. The Outlining toolbar is normally positioned to the left of the outline. If the Outlining tab is chosen in Normal view and the Outlining toolbar is not visible, you can display it using the View→Toolbars→ Outlining command.

You can choose a slide in an outline by clicking the slide icon or by clicking on any text within the slide.

The slide you choose is displayed in the main portion of the window.

The Outlining toolbar can be displayed on the left side of the outline using the View→Toolbars →Outlining command.

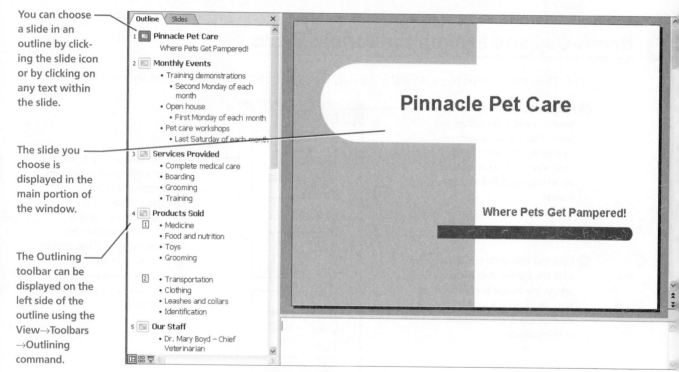

The Promote and Demote buttons let you promote or demote titles and bullets. For example, promoting a first-level bullet would create a new slide. The promoted bullet text would become the title of the new slide.

The Move Up and Move Down buttons let you rearrange bullets and entire slides.

The Summary Slide button lets you create summary slides.

This button is used to display or hide text formatting.

The Expand and Collapse buttons let you display (expand) additional levels and hide (collapse) levels. For example, you may want to collapse (hide) all bullets so that only the slide titles are displayed.

The Collapse All button displays only the slide titles. The Expand All button displays all levels.

QUICK REFERENCE: WORKING WITH OUTLINES

Task	Procedure
Select text in an outline.	Drag over the desired text.
Select an entire slide.	Click the slide icon.
Select a bulleted item and all of its subitems.	Click the bullet.
Add a new slide.	Press (CTRL)+(ENTER) when the insertion point is in slide title or a bulleted paragraph.

1. Follow these steps to add a new slide while in Outline view:

A Use this scroll bar to scroll down until the Our Staff slide is visible.

B In the outline, click on any bulleted paragraph in the Our Staff slide.

C Press (CTRL)+(ENTER) to add a new slide.

D In the Outline, type **Respected Clients** as the title of the new slide, and press (CTRL)+(ENTER).

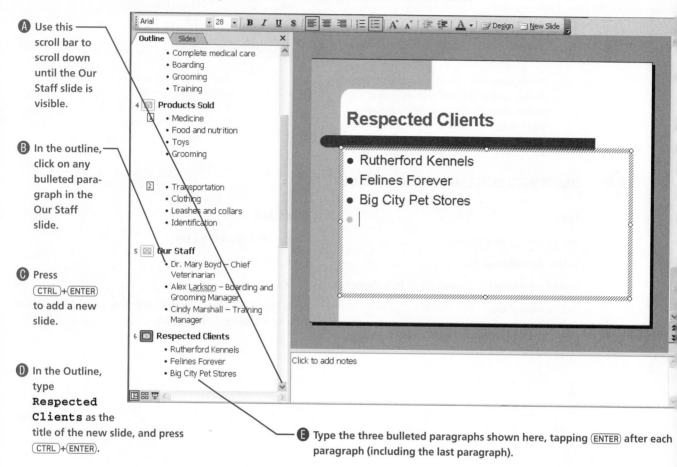

E Type the three bulleted paragraphs shown here, tapping (ENTER) after each paragraph (including the last paragraph).

As you can see, the (CTRL)+(ENTER) keystroke combination adds a bullet to the current slide if the insertion point is on the title when you press the keystrokes. This keystroke combination adds a new slide if you are on a bullet when you issue the keystrokes.

2. At this point, you should have a new bulleted paragraph visible in the outline below the Big City Pet Stores paragraph. If you don't, then tap (ENTER) to add the paragraph.

Add Two New Slides

3. Make sure the insertion point is on the blank bulleted paragraph in the outline.

4. Click the Promote 🔼 button on the Outlining toolbar. If the Outlining toolbar is not visible, then choose View→Toolbars→Outlining to display it.
   The bulleted paragraph will be promoted to a new slide.

5. Type **Welcome Aboard Special**, and tap (ENTER).
   Notice that tapping (ENTER) created a new slide. You must use the (CTRL)+(ENTER) keystroke combination to add a bulleted paragraph after a title slide. However, you will fix this by demoting the new slide in the next step.

6. Click the Demote button on the Outlining toolbar.
   The new slide should now be a bullet under the Welcome Aboard Special title.

7. Complete the new slide in the outline as shown to the right, tapping (ENTER) after each paragraph (including the last paragraph).

   ```
   7 [icon] Welcome Aboard Special
              • 25% discount on boarding
              • Free grooming (dog or cat)
              • 10% discount on products
              • Valid until July 30
   ```

8. Promote the new paragraph that follows the Valid until July 30 paragraph.

9. Type **Pinnacle Pet Care** and press (CTRL)+(ENTER) to create a bullet below the title you just typed.

10. Complete the new slide as shown to the right. Do not tap (ENTER) after the last bullet in this slide, since it is the closing slide.
    You will format this closing slide in a later exercise.

    ```
    8 [icon] Pinnacle Pet Care
               • Call
               • (510) 235-7788
               • Or
               • Visit our Web site at
               • www.pinnaclepets.com
    ```

Use Buttons On the Outlining Toolbar

11. Follow these steps to explore the outline:

    Ⓐ Scroll up until Slides 4 and 5 are visible.

    Ⓑ Notice that each slide is represented by an icon. If a slide has more than one bulleted list, numbers are used to identify the lists.

    Ⓒ Click any bullet to select the bullet text.

    Ⓓ Click this slide icon to select all text on the slide.

    Ⓔ Click on the Our Staff title to deselect the slide and prepare for the next step.

    ```
    4 [icon] Products Sold
       [1]    • Medicine
              • Food and nutrition
              • Toys
              • Grooming
       [2]    • Transportation
              • Clothing
              • Leashes and collars
              • Identification
    5 [icon] Our Staff
              • Dr. Mary Boyd – Chief
                Veterinarian
              • Alex Larkson – Boarding and
                Grooming Manager
              • Cindy Marshall – Training
                Manager
    ```

12. Click the Collapse button on the Outlining toolbar.
    The Collapse button collapses the bulleted paragraphs beneath the title.

13. Click the Expand button to redisplay the bulleted paragraphs.

14. Click the Collapse All button to display only the slide icons and titles of each slide.

15. Click the Expand All button to expand all of the slides.

Move a Slide

The easiest way to move a slide in an outline is to first collapse all slides. Then you can click on the desired slide title and use the Move Up and/or Move Down buttons on the Outlining toolbar.

16. Click the Collapse All ⬛ button.

17. If necessary, scroll up until all slide icons and titles are visible in the outline.

18. Click on the Respected Clients title, and then click the Move Down ⬇ button.
The Respected Clients title should now appear below the Welcome Aboard special title.

19. Click the Expand All ⬛ button.

20. If necessary, scroll down, and notice that the subordinate paragraphs (the bullets) below the Respected Clients title were moved along with the title. That is, the entire slide was moved.

Deleting Slides

You can delete a slide in an outline by clicking the slide icon to select the entire slide and then tapping the (DELETE) key. Likewise, slides can be deleted in Normal and Slide Sorter views by choosing the desired slide(s) and tapping (DELETE). If you inadvertently delete a slide, you can use Undo to restore the deleted slide.

Hands-On 23.12 Delete a Slide from the Outline

1. If necessary, click the Respected Clients slide icon ⬜ to select the entire slide.

2. Tap the (DELETE) key on the keyboard to delete the slide.

3. Now hide the Outlining toolbar by choosing View→Toolbars→Outlining.

Changing Paragraph Alignment

You use the Align Left ▤, Center ▤ and Align Right ▤ buttons on the Formatting toolbar to change the alignment of paragraphs. The desired paragraphs or the text box containing the paragraphs must be selected before issuing the command.

 Hands-On 23.13 Format the Closing Slide, and Use Slide Sorter View

Format the Closing Slide

1. Click the Slides tab to switch to a thumbnail view of the presentation.

2. If necessary, scroll down and double-click the closing slide at the end of the presentation.

3. Click in the bulleted list placeholder, and then click a border of the box.

4. Click the Bullets ▤ button on the Formatting toolbar to remove bullets from the paragraphs.

5. Click the Center ▤ button on the Formatting toolbar to center the paragraphs within the placeholder.

6. Choose Format→Line Spacing from the menu bar.

7. Set the Line Spacing to **1.2**, and click OK.
   This will increase the space between the paragraphs.

8. Select the entire telephone number by dragging the mouse pointer over the text.

9. Click the Increase Font Size ▤ button to increase the size to 32.

10. Now increase the size of the last line (the Web site URL) to 32.

Rearranging Slides

In a previous exercise, you rearranged slides using the Move Down button on the Outlining toolbar. PowerPoint's Slide Sorter View can also be used to rearrange slides. In Slide Sorter view, you can simply drag-and-drop slides to create the slide arrangement you desire. You can also drag-and-drop slides in Normal view. However, Normal view can only display a handful of slide thumbnails at a given time, so rearranging in this manner can be difficult.

 Hands-On 23.14 Rearrange Slides in Slide Sorter View

1. Click the Slide Sorter View ⊞ button on the View bar just below the slide thumbnails.

2. Follow these steps to move a slide:

Ⓐ If necessary, click this drop-down button, and change the zoom percentage until all seven slides are visible. Don't be concerned if your slides have a different arrangement than shown in this illustration. ————

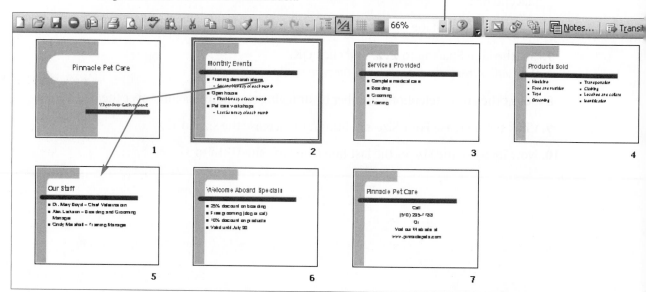

Ⓑ Drag the Monthly Events slide to the left of the Our Staff slide, and a large vertical bar will indicate the eventual position of the slide. Don't be concerned if the Our Staff slide is in a different row or column than shown here.

Ⓒ Release the mouse button, and the Monthly Events slide will become the fourth slide.

3. Click the Normal View 🖥 button on the View bar to return to Normal view.

Speaker Notes

For most people, presenting to groups can be an intimidating experience. In fact, studies have shown that speaking in front of a group is the greatest fear of most people. Adequate preparation is an important step that you can take to overcome your anxieties. PowerPoint helps you prepare for presentations by developing speaker notes. You can create speaker notes for any slide in your presentation. You can print speaker notes along with the accompanying slides. Speaker notes can help you deliver effective, anxiety-free presentations. Speaker notes are entered below the slide in Normal view, or you can use the View→Notes Page command to switch to Notes view.

 ## Hands-On 23.15 Add Speaker Notes

1. Choose View→Notes Page from the menu bar.
   PowerPoint will display a full screen view that includes the current slide and the notes area. However, notice that the phrase Click to Add Text in the notes area is difficult to read.

2. Adjust the zoom control percentage on the Formatting toolbar to 100%.

3. Use the scroll bar to navigate to the title slide at the top of the presentation.

4. If necessary, scroll down until the phrase Click to Add Text is visible in the Notes section on the title slide.

5. Click on the phrase Click to Add Text, and type **Don't forget to thank the following people:** as the replacement phrase.

6. Tap (ENTER) to move the insertion point to the next line.

7. Click the Bullets [icon] button on the Formatting toolbar.

8. Type the names and titles shown to the right, tapping (ENTER) after each line.

> Don't forget to thank the following people:
> •Pet World Trade Show Organizing Committee
> •Donald Johnson – Pet World Vendor Committee
> •Tanisha Smith – Vendor Support

9. Scroll down through the presentation until you reach the Services Provided slide.

10. Click the phrase Click to Add Text, and type the speaker note shown to the right.

> Mention the 1999 Pet World magazine article ranking us as the most comprehensive pet care facility.

11. Scroll down to the Products Sold slide, and add the speaker note shown to the right.

> Once again, mention the Pet World magazine article.

12. Scroll down to the Our Staff slide, and add the speaker notes shown to the right.
    All four slides in your presentation should contain speaker notes. Later in this lesson, you will print the speaker notes.

> •Seven other staff members
> •Combined experience is 63 years

13. Choose View→Normal to switch to Normal view.

14. Notice that the speaker note is visible in the notes area below the slide.

Print Preview

The Print Preview button on the Standard toolbar displays the Print Preview window. The Print Preview window lets you view your print job and set various options prior to printing. The following illustration describes the options available in the Print Preview window.

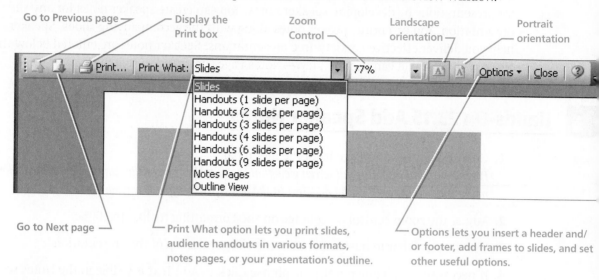

Go to Previous page

Display the Print box

Zoom Control

Landscape orientation

Portrait orientation

Go to Next page

Print What option lets you print slides, audience handouts in various formats, notes pages, or your presentation's outline.

Options lets you insert a header and/ or footer, add frames to slides, and set other useful options.

Hands-On 23.16 Use Print Preview

1. Click the Print Preview button on the Standard toolbar.

2. Follow these steps to examine the Print Preview options:

Ⓐ Click the Print What button and choose Notes Pages. Only slides with speaker notes will be displayed.

Ⓑ Feel free to choose the other Print What options and notice the effect they have on the preview of your print job.

Ⓒ Feel free to experiment with the other toolbar options.

Ⓓ When you have finished, click the Close button. This will close Print Preview without initiating the Print Command.

Printing

The Print button on the Standard toolbar sends the entire presentation to the current printer. You must display the Print box if you want to change printers, specify the number of copies to be printed, print selected slides, and to choose other print options. The Print box is displayed with the File→Print command. The Print box can also be displayed by clicking the Print button on the Print Preview toolbar. The following illustration describes options available through the Print box.

FROM THE KEYBOARD

CTRL+P to display Print box

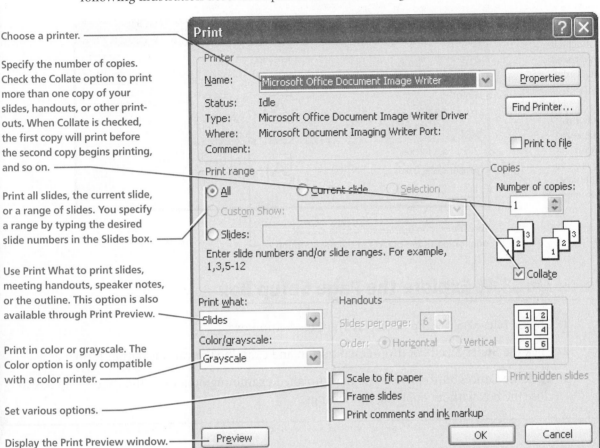

Choose a printer.

Specify the number of copies. Check the Collate option to print more than one copy of your slides, handouts, or other print-outs. When Collate is checked, the first copy will print before the second copy begins printing, and so on.

Print all slides, the current slide, or a range of slides. You specify a range by typing the desired slide numbers in the Slides box.

Use Print What to print slides, meeting handouts, speaker notes, or the outline. This option is also available through Print Preview.

Print in color or grayscale. The Color option is only compatible with a color printer.

Set various options.

Display the Print Preview window.

Hands-On 23.17 Explore the Print Box

1. Choose File→Print to display the Print Box.

2. Change one or more settings, such as the Print What setting.

3. Click the Preview button and the change should be reflected in the Print Preview window. Keep in mind that certain settings, such as the number of copies, do not affect the display in the Print Preview window.

4. When you have finished, close the Print box or the Print Preview window and make sure your presentation is displayed in Normal view.

Output Formats

In most cases, you will prepare presentations for delivery via electronic slide shows. However, you may need to deliver a presentation using transparencies, 35mm slides, or on paper. The Page Setup box lets you choose various output formats depending on how you intend to deliver the presentation. The output formats change the overall size and dimensions of the slides in your presentation. The Page Setup box is displayed with the File→Page Setup command. The following illustration describes the options available in the Page Setup box.

You choose an output format from the Slides Sized For list. Available sizes include overhead transparencies, 35mm, and various paper sizes.

PowerPoint sets the size options depending on the output format. However, you can always manually adjust the size.

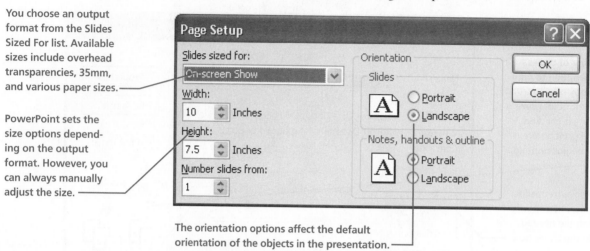

The orientation options affect the default orientation of the objects in the presentation.

 ### Hands-On 23.18 Explore the Page Setup Box

1. Choose File→Page Setup to display the Page Setup Box.

2. Click the Slides Sized For drop-down button and examine the various output formats.

3. Click the Cancel button when you have finished examining options in the Page Setup box to close the box without applying the settings.

Delivering an Electronic Slide Show

The Slide Show button on the View bar lets you initiate an electronic slide show. You can deliver a slide show using just a personal computer, or you can attach a projection device to your PC for presentations to large groups. The following table describes the options available for starting, delivering, and ending a slide show.

QUICK REFERENCE: DELIVERING A SLIDE SHOW

Task	Procedure
Start a slide show from any slide.	From Slide Sorter view, click the desired slide, and then click the Slide Show button. From Normal view, navigate to the desired slide, and then click the Slide Show button.
Advance to next slide.	Click anywhere on the current slide, or tap (PGDN), (N) (for Next), (ENTER), or (SPACE BAR).
Return to previous slide.	Tap (PGUP), (P) (for Previous), or (BACKSPACE).
End a slide show.	Tap the (ESC) key.

Using the Slide Show Toolbar

The Slide Show Toolbar Button appears at the bottom-left corner of the screen during a slide show. You can click the Slide Show Toolbar to display a menu of commands. The Slide Show Toolbar includes commands for navigating among slides, ending the slide show, and other useful functions.

FROM THE KEYBOARD

(SHIFT)+(F10) to display pop-up menu

 Hands-On 23.19 Run the Slide Show

1. Click the Slide Sorter ⊞ view button on the View bar.

2. Click the title slide in the Slide Sorter window.
   You will start your presentation by displaying the Title slide.

3. Click the Slide Show 🖳 button on the View bar.
   PowerPoint will display your title slide in a full-screen view. All toolbars and other screen objects will be hidden from view.

4. Click the mouse pointer anywhere on the screen to move to the next slide.

5. Continue to click anywhere on the screen until the closing slide appears (the slide with the phone number and Web site URL).

6. Click the closing slide, click again when the End of Show screen appears, and the slide show will end.

7. Click the fourth slide in Slide Sorter View, and then click the Slide Show 🖳 button.
   You can start a presentation on any slide.

8. Tap the (PGDN) key several times, and then tap (PGUP) several times. Use the keys near the main keyboard (not the keys on the numeric keypad).
   PowerPoint displays the next or previous slide each time you tap these keys.

9. Position the mouse pointer at the bottom-left corner of the screen and click the Slide Show Toolbar that appears.

   Notice that the pop-up menu has options to go to the Next and Previous slides and to end the slide show. The pop-up menu also lets you use a Pen tool to draw on the slide and make other enhancements. In the next step, you will use the Go to Slide option on the pop-up menu to go to a specific slide.

10. Choose Navigation→Go to Slide→Welcome Aboard Special from the pop-up menu.

    PowerPoint will display the Welcome Aboard Special slide. You can always use this technique to rapidly navigate to a specific slide.

11. Right-click (click with the right mouse button) anywhere on the current slide to display the Slide Show Toolbar.

12. Choose the Navigation button (third button) on the Slide Show Toolbar and choose Go to Slide→Products Sold.

13. Notice the many ways to navigate slides in an electronic slide show.

14. Click the Slide Show Toolbar and choose End Show from the menu.

15. Feel free to practice running your electronic slide show.

16. When you have finished, click the Save button to save the changes to your presentation.

17. We will be using this presentation as the basis of our exercises in Lesson 24. Be sure to save the changes to your presentation.

18. Choose File→Close from the menu bar to close the presentation. Click Yes when PowerPoint asks if you want to save the changes to the presentation.

Concepts Review

True/False Questions

1.	Design templates give presentations a consistent format and appearance.	TRUE	FALSE
2.	The Slide Layout task pane appears when the [New Slide] button is clicked.	TRUE	FALSE
3.	Multiple slides can be selected by pressing (ALT) and clicking the desired slides.	TRUE	FALSE
4.	A slide's layout cannot be changed once the slide has been created.	TRUE	FALSE
5.	Each slide in a PowerPoint presentation is saved as a separate file.	TRUE	FALSE
6.	The horizontal alignment of paragraphs cannot be changed.	TRUE	FALSE
7.	The number of copies to print is chosen in the Print Preview window.	TRUE	FALSE
8.	Slide Sorter view is most useful for focusing on the development of a single slide.	TRUE	FALSE
9.	You start a slide show by clicking the Slide Show button.	TRUE	FALSE
10.	While delivering a slide show, you can display the Slide Show Toolbar by clicking the left mouse button anywhere on a slide.	TRUE	FALSE

Multiple Choice Questions

1. Where are output formats such as 35mm and overhead transparency chosen?
   a. Page Setup box
   b. Print Preview window
   c. Print box
   d. None of the above

2. Which technique can be used to turn off bullets for a single paragraph?
   a. Click on the desired paragraph and click the Bullets button.
   b. Click on the desired paragraph and tap the (DELETE) key.
   c. Click the placeholder box that contains the bulleted paragraph and click the Bullets button.
   d. None of the above

3. Which of the following buttons is used to promote a bulleted paragraph?
   a.
   b.
   c.
   d.

4. Which of the following techniques can be used to move to the next slide in a slide show?
   a. Click anywhere on the current slide.
   b. Tap the (PGDN) key on the keyboard.
   c. Right-click the current slide, and choose Next from the Slide Show Toolbar.
   d. All of the above

Skill Builders

Skill Builder 23.1 Set Up a Presentation

In this exercise, you will set up a presentation for the Tropical Getaways travel service. The managers at Tropical Getaways need to deliver a presentation to audiences of up to 40 people. The presentation will be used for marketing purposes to sell potential customers a tropical getaway to paradise.

Apply a Design Template

1. If PowerPoint is still open from the previous exercise, click the New button to begin a new presentation. If PowerPoint is not currently running, then start PowerPoint and a new presentation will appear.

2. Click the Design button on the Formatting toolbar to display the Slide Design task pane.

3. Scroll through the list of designs and locate the Globe design, as shown to the right.

4. Choose the Globe design by clicking it.
   The design will be applied to the title slide in your presentation.

5. Click in the title box, and type the title **Tropical Getaways**.

6. Click in the subtitle box, and type the subtitle **Adventures in Paradise**.

Set Up Another Slide

7. Click the New Slide button on PowerPoint's Formatting toolbar.
   A single-column, bulleted list slide will be added to the presentation and the Slide Layout task pane will appear. Notice that the Globe design template is applied to the new slide.

8. Apply the Title and 2-Column Text layout (as shown to the right) to the new slide by clicking it on the Slide Layout task pane.

9. Click in the Title box, and type the title **Most Popular Destinations**.

10. Add the paragraphs shown to the right in the bulleted list boxes.

Most Popular Destinations

- Tahiti
- Maui
- Oahu
- Cancun

- Caribbean
- Fiji
- Singapore
- Australia

Set Up the Remaining Slides

11. Add another slide using the Title and 2-Column text Layout.

12. Enter the phrase **Complete Packages** in the title box.

13. Enter the phrase **Packages Include** in the first bulleted list box and tap (ENTER).

14. Click the Increase Indent [icon] button.

15. Type the word **Airfare**, and tap (ENTER).

16. Complete the slide as shown to the right.

17. Add a new slide to your presentation. Leave the layout set to Title and Text.

18. Enter the title and bulleted lists into your new slide as shown to the right. Demote the bulleted paragraphs under the headings Package 1 and Package 2. Also, notice that there is a large space above the Package 2 heading. You can create this space by tapping (ENTER) twice after typing the bulleted paragraph with the text $429 per person.

Complete Packages

- Packages Include
  - Airfare
  - Lodging
  - Rental car
  - Activities
- Low Prices
  - 3 days from $599
  - 5 days from $799
  - 7 days from $999

Travel Now and Save!

- Package 1
  - 5 days in Oahu
  - $429 per person

- Package 2
  - 7 days in Tahiti
  - $1,299 per person

---

19. Add the following slides to your presentation using the default Title and Text layout for both slides. You will need to remove the bullets from the bulleted list box in the second slide and center the paragraphs. Also, you will need to push the paragraph with the text Donna Givens down by tapping (ENTER) twice.

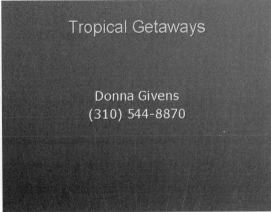

Add Speaker Notes

20. Choose View→Notes Page from the menu bar.

21. Navigate to the title slide at the top of the presentation.

22. Adjust the zoom control percentage on the Standard toolbar to 100%.

23. If necessary, scroll down until the phrase Click to Add Text is visible on the title slide.

24. Click on the phrase Click to Add Text, and type **Welcome the employees to their new travel service** as the replacement phrase.

25. Tap (ENTER), and type **Thank Glenda Johnson—Director of Human Resources**.

26. Navigate to the Most Popular Destinations slide, and type the note **Employees get a 35% discount on all destinations on the Popular Destinations list**.

27. Navigate to the Travel Now and Save slide.

28. Click on the phrase Click to Add Text in the speaker notes box.

29. Click the Bullets [::] button and enter the speaker notes shown to the right.

    - •12 preferred discount packages available to employees.
    - •No time limit on preferred discount packages.
    - •Limit of two packages per employee per year.

30. Click the Save [🖫] button, and save the presentation with the name **Tropical Getaways**.

Skill Builder 23.2 **Rearrange Slides**

In this exercise, you will reposition one of the slides in the Tropical Getaways presentation.

1. Click the Slide Sorter ⊞ button on the View bar to switch to Slide Sorter view.

2. Drag the Travel Categories slide from Position 5, and drop it in Position 2 as shown below.

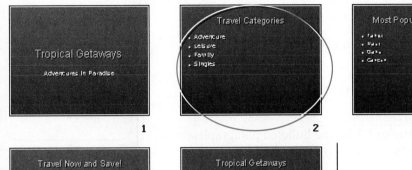

1   2   3   4

5   6

3. Save 🖫 the change, and continue with the next exercise.

Skill Builder 23.3 **Deliver an Electronic Presentation**

1. Click the first slide in the presentation, and then click the Slide Show 🖳 button.

2. Click each slide in the presentation until the presentation is complete.

3. Start the presentation again.

4. Position the mouse pointer at the bottom-left corner of the screen and click the Slide Show Toolbar that appears.

5. On the Slide Show Toolbar, click the Navigation button (third button) and choose, Go to Slide→Travel Now and Save.

6. Use the Slide Show Toolbar ⇦ ⇩ ▪ ▭ ▪ ⇨ to end the slide show.

7. Choose File→Close from the menu bar to close the presentation. Click the Yes button if PowerPoint asks you to save the changes.

Assessment 23.1 **Set Up a Presentation**

In this assessment, you will set up a presentation for Classic Cars. Classic Cars is an organization devoted to tracking, categorizing, and preserving classic automobiles. The presentation will be given to members of the Classic Cars organization at the annual Classic Cars convention.

1. Click the New button to set up a new presentation.

2. Click the Design button to display the Slide Design task pane.

3. Scroll through the design previews and choose the Radial design, as shown to the right.

4. Add the five slides shown below to your presentation, and make the following adjustments:

▨ Increase the line spacing to 1.3 for the bulleted paragraphs on the Seminar Topics and Collections on Display slides.

▨ Use the Title Slide layout for both the first and last slides.

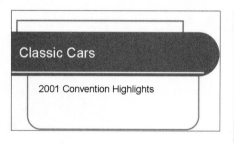

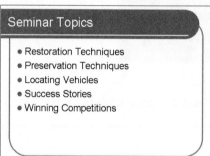

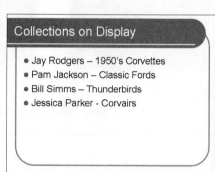

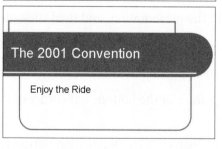

5. Add the following speaker notes to the presentation. Use the Bullets ▤ button to place bullets in front of each note.

Slide	Speaker Notes
Classic Cars (title slide)	■ Thank the organizing committee.
	■ Welcome new members.
Collections on Display	■ Thank collectors.
	■ Most valuable collection of classic cars in one location
	■ 110 cars in mint condition
Door Prizes	■ No individual limits on winning
	■ Mention the secret grand prize.

6. Use Print Preview to preview your presentation.

7. Print the Notes Pages in your presentation.
   This will print each slide and its accompanying notes on a single page.

8. Save your presentation with the name **Classic Cars**.

9. Use the File→Exit command to exit from PowerPoint.

Critical Thinking

Critical Thinking 23.1 Create a Presentation

In this exercise, you will set up a presentation for real estate agent Linda Holmes of Holmestead Realty. Linda needs to deliver a presentation to prospective sellers using her laptop computer. The purpose of the presentation is to entice sellers to list their homes with Holmestead Realty. Create a new presentation in PowerPoint using the design template of your choice. Follow these guidelines to set up the initial slides in the presentation:

Title Slide—Use **Holmestead Realty** as the title and the tagline **Stake Your Claim** as the subtitle.

Bulleted List Slides—Using the Title and Text layout, set up five bulleted list slides using the titles and bulleted list text shown below. Notice that some of the slides have two bullet levels. The bullet characters in your presentation may be different than those shown here, depending on the design template you choose.

Slide Title	Bulleted List Text

Follow Up	• Monthly reports
	  - Showing activity
	  - Feedback from other agents
	  - Market activity
	• Bimonthly calls
	  - Review advertising
	  - Review action plan
	  - Discuss concerns

Experienced Staff	• Linda Holmes—Broker and Primary Listing Agent • Joan Barnes—Personal Assistant • Chris Bell—Data Entry • Karen Rollins—Hearthfire Enterprises contact responsible for the "Feels Like Home" service

Satisfied Customers	• Zebidiah Johanson
	  - "Linda was wonderful! She really cared about my home."
	• Maria Mills
	  - "I was very pleased. When Linda said she would call, she called. I always felt like I was her most important client."
	• Jack Wilson
	  - "The Feels Like Home service increased the appeal of my house. It sold in much less time than I was expecting!"

Office Hours	• Monday through Friday • 9–5 • Saturday • 11–3 • Closed Sunday

Slide Title	Bulleted List Text
Targeted Marketing	• MLS
	• Web Page
	• Yard Signs
	• Flyers
	• IWANNA
	• Citizen Times
	• Real Estate Weekly
	• Homes and Land

Critical Thinking 23.2 Formatting Presentations

Follow these guidelines to format the slides in your new presentation:

■ Remove the bullets from all paragraphs in the Office Hours slide. Center align all paragraphs. Set the line spacing to **1.75** for all paragraphs. The line spacing setting will distribute the paragraphs vertically.

■ Change the slide layout of the Targeted Marketing slide to Title and 2-Column Text. Move the last four bullets to the second column.

■ Use the Increase Font Size button to increase the font size of the tag line (subtitle) on the title slide. Click the button twice to increase the size by two increments.

■ Rearrange the slides into the following order:

Slide Title
Targeted Marketing
Follow Up
Experienced Staff
Satisfied Customers
Office Hours

■ Add the following speaker notes:

Slide	Speaker Notes
Targeted Marketing	MLS has over 1,000 agents Web site updated weekly Color yard signs for easy viewing Professionally designed flyers IWANNA (for smaller homes) Citizen Times (color photo ads) Real Estate Weekly (published every Thursday) Homes and Land (national publication)
Follow Up	Joan makes most of the follow-up calls Clients can call me at any time on my cell phone
Experienced Staff	Over 30 years of combined experience
Satisfied Customers	Additional testimonials on file

■ Save your completed presentation as **Holmestead Realty**. Feel free to run the slide show.

Clip Art, Transitions, and Animation

In this lesson, you will enhance the Pinnacle Pet Care presentation that you created in the previous lesson. You will use clip art to add interest to the presentation. You will also create transitions between slides and use animation to "bring the presentation to life."

Additional learning resources are available at labpub.com/learn/oe3/

Case Study

After watching several of his competitors present at the Pet World trade show, Al Smith realizes that his slide show is not very exciting. Al is a talented speaker, and he needs a slide show that reflects the enthusiasm and energy level of his presentation style. Al decides to "liven up" his presentation with clip art and the powerful animation tools available in PowerPoint 2003. Al injects just the right amount of special effects to make his presentation interesting while allowing his audience to focus on the content of his presentation.

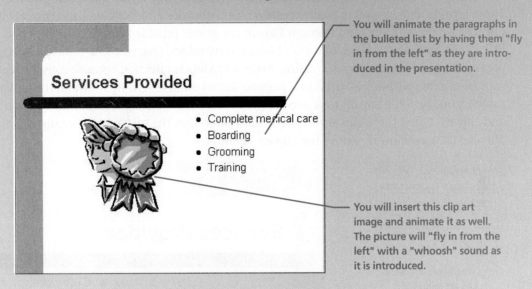

You will animate the paragraphs in the bulleted list by having them "fly in from the left" as they are introduced in the presentation.

You will insert this clip art image and animate it as well. The picture will "fly in from the left" with a "whoosh" sound as it is introduced.

Adding Clip Art to Slides

Clip art can be used to add images to presentations. Microsoft Office features an extensive clip art collection with images for just about any occasion. In addition to clip art, you can use other media types with PowerPoint slides, including photographs (pictures), movies, and sound files.

Content and Clip Art Layouts

In the previous lesson, you worked exclusively with title slide layouts and title and text layouts. These layouts allowed you to easily create slides with titles and bulleted lists. PowerPoint's Content Layout and Text and Content Layout categories provide layouts with placeholders for titles, text, and various types of content—including tables, charts, clip art, pictures, diagrams, organization charts, and movies. Using content layouts is effective because content is automatically positioned within and sized to a placeholder when inserted. In addition, the Other Layouts category on the Slide Layout task pane contains two layouts designed specifically for titles, text, and clip art. Using these clip art layouts greatly simplifies the task of positioning clip art on slides. The illustration below describes the clip art layouts.

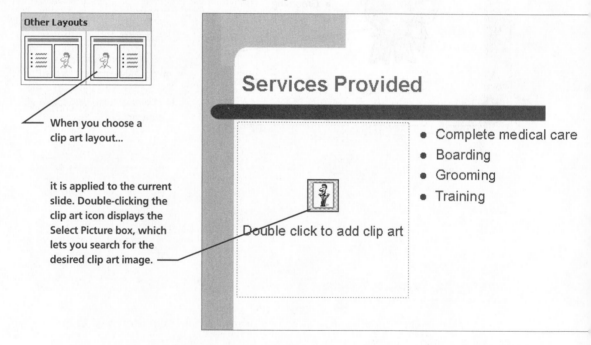

When you choose a clip art layout...

it is applied to the current slide. Double-clicking the clip art icon displays the Select Picture box, which lets you search for the desired clip art image.

Searching for Clip Art

Every clip art image provided with Microsoft Office is associated with a number of keywords that describe its characteristics. For example, the image shown to the right can be located using keywords such as awards, prizes, and ribbons. As you work with clip art in PowerPoint and other Microsoft Office programs, you will encounter several search boxes. Regardless of the search box you use, you can always locate a desired image using keywords. The following illustration describes the Select Picture box, which appears when the clip art icon is double-clicked in a clip art layout.

An image can be located by typing a keyword and clicking the Go button.

The scroll bar is used to browse through the images associated with the keyword.

The desired image can be inserted by double-clicking.

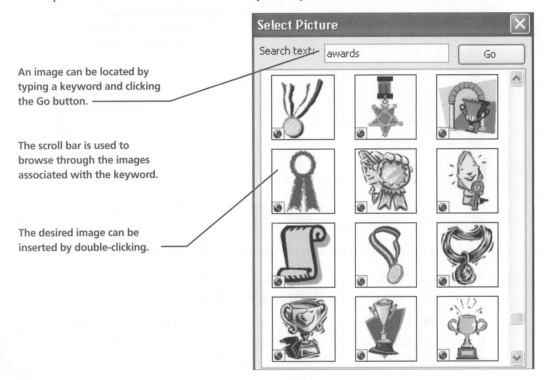

Hands-On 24.1 Insert Clip Art

In this exercise, you will open the Pinnacle Pet Care presentation you created in Lesson 23. You will enhance the presentation throughout this lesson.

Open the Presentation and Choose a Slide

1. Start PowerPoint, and the Getting Started task pane should appear.

2. If your Pinnacle Pet Care presentation is listed in the Open section of the task pane, then choose it. To ensure you are opening the correct presentation, use the More option or the Open button on the Standard toolbar to navigate to and open your presentation.

3. If necessary, click the Normal View 🖽 button to display the presentation in Normal view.

4. Scroll down to the Services Provided slide or choose it on the Slides tab.

Choose a Clip Art Layout

5. Follow these steps to display the Slide Layout task pane. For the remainder of this course, you will simply be instructed to display a particular task pane.

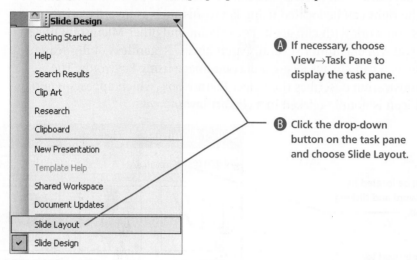

Ⓐ If necessary, choose View→Task Pane to display the task pane.

Ⓑ Click the drop-down button on the task pane and choose Slide Layout.

6. Scroll through the slide layouts until you reach the Other Layouts section.

7. Choose the Title, Clip Art, and Text layout shown to the right and it will be applied to the Services Provided slide.

8. Double-click the clip art icon on the slide to display the Select Picture box.

9. Type **awards** in the Search Text box and click the Go button.
   Clip art images associated with the keyword "awards" will appear.

10. Scroll through the list of images and locate the image shown to the right. It should appear in the middle of the list. If the image is not available on your computer, then choose any image you like.

11. Double-click on the image.
    The image will be inserted in the slide.

Moving, Sizing, and Rotating Objects

When you click an object (such as a clip art image), sizing handles and a rotate handle appear. You can easily move, size, and rotate selected objects as described in the following illustration.

Drag the yellow rotate handle to rotate an object.

Sizing handles appear on the sides and corners of a selected object. You can adjust the width or height of an object by dragging the side, top, or bottom sizing handles. Or, you can adjust both the width and height proportionately by dragging a corner handle.

The move pointer appears when you point to an object. You can move an object by dragging it while the move pointer is visible.

The Format Picture Dialog Box

You can set the size and position of a picture with precision using options on the Format Picture dialog box. The Format Picture dialog box can be displayed by right-clicking a picture and choosing Format Picture from the menu. You can also choose Format→Picture from the menu bar to display the Format Picture box for a selected object. These techniques work with all PowerPoint objects, including placeholders for titles and bulleted lists. The following illustrations describe the size and position options on the Format Picture dialog box.

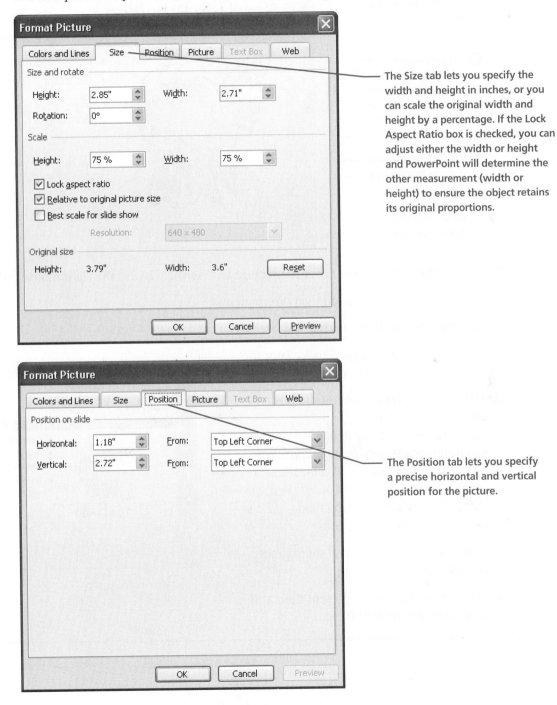

The Size tab lets you specify the width and height in inches, or you can scale the original width and height by a percentage. If the Lock Aspect Ratio box is checked, you can adjust either the width or height and PowerPoint will determine the other measurement (width or height) to ensure the object retains its original proportions.

The Position tab lets you specify a precise horizontal and vertical position for the picture.

1. Follow these steps to move and size the clip art image:

A Make sure sizing handles are visible on the image. If they aren't visible, click on the image to make them appear.

B Drag this corner sizing handle up and right slightly to reduce the height and width proportionately.

C Release the mouse button, position the mouse pointer near the center of the picture, and drag the picture to a different location on the slide.

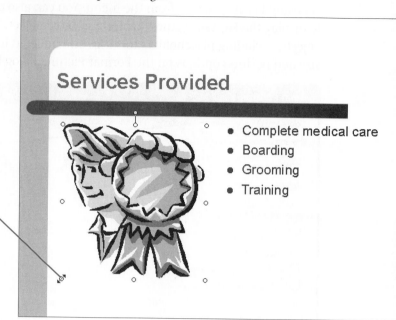

2. Position the mouse pointer over the picture and right-click (use the right mouse button).

3. Choose Format Picture from the pop-up menu.

4. Click the Size tab in the Format Picture box.

5. Set the Height scaling percentage (not the Height Size and Rotate setting) to **75%**.

6. Make sure the Lock Aspect Ratio box is checked and click OK.
   The image will be 75% of its original size. The scaling percentage overrides any adjustments previously made to the size. Because the Lock Aspect Ratio box was checked, it sets the size to 75% of the original size, maintaining both the height and width proportions.

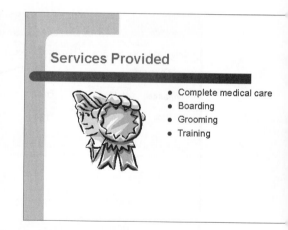

7. Now drag the picture to the approximate position shown to the right.

8. Save the changes to the presentation and continue with the next topic.

The Clip Art Task Pane

The Clip Art button on the Drawing toolbar displays the Clip Art task pane. This task pane can be used to insert clip art images on slides that do not have placeholders for clip art or other content. You search for clip art in the Clip Art task pane using keywords as you have done thus far in this lesson. The following illustration describes the Clip Art task pane.

Search for clip art using keywords.

The Search In and Results Should Be lists let you narrow your search to include only the clip art categories or media types you specify. The Clip Art task pane lets you search for media types other than clip art, including movies, sound files, and pictures.

This option displays the Microsoft Clip Organizer. The Clip Organizer lets you search clip art by browsing categorized folders on your computer.

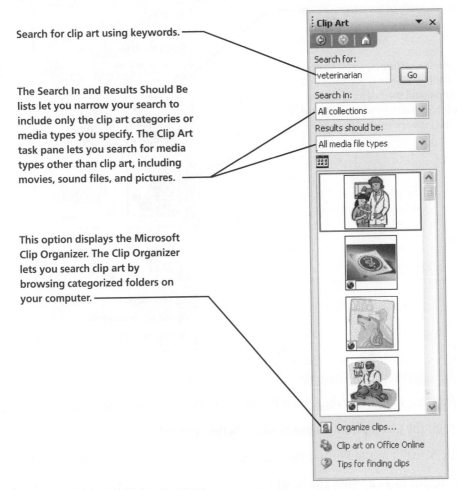

Hands-On 24.3 Use the Clip Art Task Pane

Insert the Image

1. Scroll up to the title slide, or click the title slide thumbnail on the Slides tab.

2. Click the Clip Art button on the Drawing toolbar (located at the bottom of the PowerPoint window) or choose Clip Art from the drop-down list at the top of the task pane. Either of these actions will display the Clip Art task pane.

3. Type **veterinarian** (make sure to spell it correctly) in the Search For box and click the Go button on the task pane.

4. Follow these steps to insert an image:

A Click this Expand button to temporarily widen the image display making it easier to locate an image. Clicking the button a second time restores the original width of the image display.

B Locate this picture by scrolling down (or another picture if you can't find this one) and then clicking on the picture. The picture will be inserted on the slide.

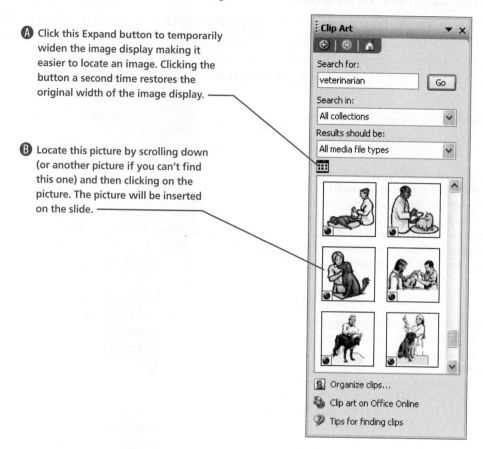

Size and Position the Image

In the next few steps, you will use the Format Picture box to specify a precise size and location for the picture.

5. Right-click the picture and choose Format Picture from the menu.

6. Click the Size tab in the Format Picture box.

7. Set the height to **2.2"** (not the height scaling), and make sure the Lock Aspect Ratio box is checked.

8. Click the Position tab.

9. Set the Horizontal position to **1"** from the Top Left Corner and the Vertical position to **4.3"** from the Top Left Corner.

10. Click OK, and your slide should have the appearance shown to the right.

11. Save the changes to your presentation and continue with the next topic.

Transitions

PowerPoint lets you create transitions between slides in electronic slide shows. Transitions can make your slide show interesting, and help create distinct break points between slides. Over 40 transition effects are available in PowerPoint.

Slide Sorter View and the Slide Transition Task Pane

Slide Sorter view is often the best view to use when setting up transitions because transitions are often applied to multiple slides. Transitions can be applied to a single slide, multiple slides, or to all slides in a presentation. Transitions are always applied to entire slides—not to individual objects on the slide.

A Slide Sorter toolbar appears whenever you are in Slide Sorter view. The Transition button is displayed on the Slide Sorter toolbar. Clicking the Transition button displays the Slide Transition task pane, which lets you choose transition effects and other transition settings. The following illustration describes the options available on the Slide Transition task pane.

The transition effect you choose from this list is applied to all selected slides. An effect is previewed on the selected slides when you choose it if the AutoPreview box at the bottom of the task pane is checked.

Set the speed at which the transition occurs and include a sound as part of the transition here.

Determine whether the presentation advances to the next slide when the mouse is clicked or automatically after a specified number of seconds using the Automatically After box.

Apply the settings to all slides in the presentation with this button.

Play the selected slides, demonstrating the transition effects here.

Start the slide show, beginning with the first selected slide.

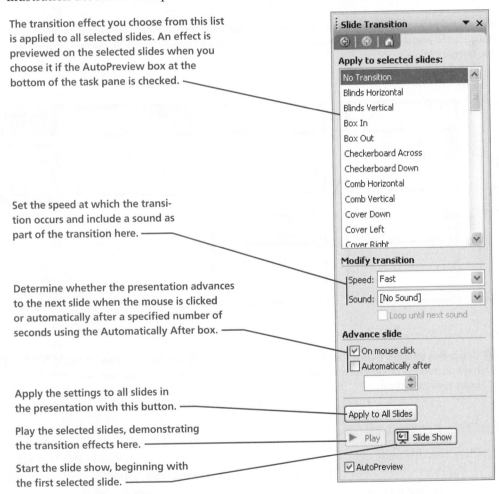

Hands-On 24.4 Apply Transition Effects

In this exercise, you will apply the Dissolve transition to all slides except the title slide. Later in this lesson, you will create a more dramatic effect for the title slide.

Choose Transition Effects

1. Click the Slide Sorter View 🔲 button on the View bar.
   The Slide Sorter toolbar will appear, although it may be positioned to the right of the Standard toolbar.

2. Click the Transition 📑 button on the Slide Sorter toolbar to display the Slide Transition task pane. If this button is not visible, click the drop-down button at the top of the task pane and choose Slide Transition.

3. Follow these steps to select multiple slides and choose a transition effect:
   You learned in the previous lesson to use the (CTRL) key while randomly selecting multiple slides or the (SHIFT) key to select a contiguous group of slides.

A Click the Services Provided slide, press and hold the (SHIFT) key, and click the last slide in the presentation. This selects all slides except the title (opening) slide. —

B Scroll through the list of transition effects and choose Dissolve. The effect will briefly be previewed on all selected slides. —

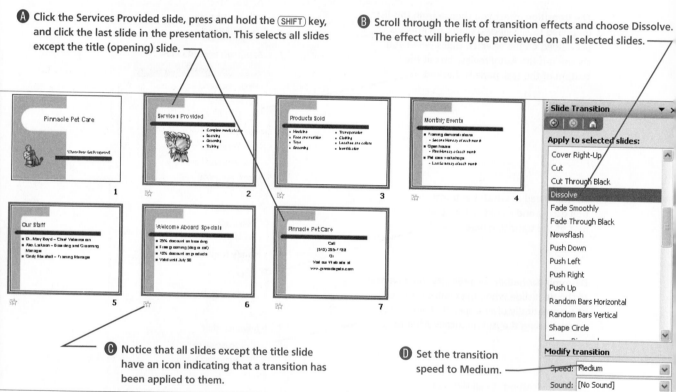

C Notice that all slides except the title slide have an icon indicating that a transition has been applied to them.

D Set the transition speed to Medium. —

Run the Presentation

4. Click the title slide.
   At this point, only the title slide should be selected. In the next step, you will run the presentation as a slide show. Selecting the title slide will force the presentation to begin with that slide.

5. Click the Slide Show 🖳 button on the View bar.
   The title slide will appear without a transition. The title slide would have opened with the Dissolve transition if you had applied the transition to it.

6. Click the mouse button, and the title slide will dissolve into the Services Provided slide.

7. Continue to click the mouse button until the presentation is complete, and the Slide Sorter window reappears.

8. Feel free to experiment with the transition effects.

9. Save the changes, and continue with the next topic.

Animation

Animation can be used to liven up presentations with exciting visual effects. PowerPoint's powerful animation tools give you control over animation effects, timing, and sequencing.

Animation Schemes

⚠TIP!

Animation schemes override transition effects.

Animation schemes are preset visual effects applied to text elements on slides. PowerPoint provides a large number of animation schemes that can easily be applied to a single slide, a group of slides, or an entire presentation. An animation scheme usually includes effects for slide titles and additional effects for the bullets or paragraphs on a slide. Animation schemes are usually applied in Slide Sorter view using the Animation Scheme option on the Slide Design task pane. The following illustration describes the animation scheme options on the Slide Design task pane.

The built-in animation schemes can be displayed by choosing the Animation Schemes option on the Slide Design task pane.

The animation schemes are organized into Subtle, Moderate, and Exciting categories depending on the level of effects in the scheme.

A chosen scheme is applied to the selected slides or to all slides in the presentation if the Apply to All Slides button is clicked.

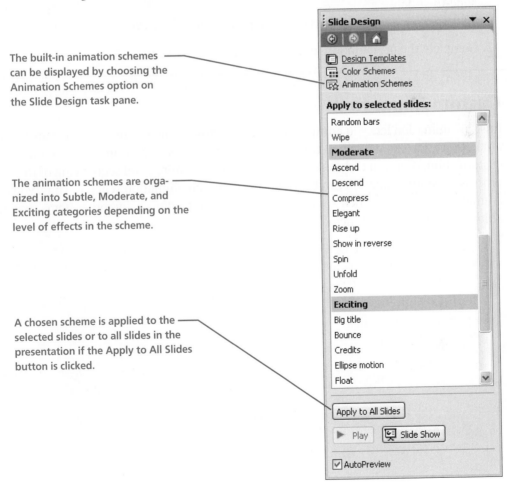

Hands-On 24.5 Apply an Animation Scheme

1. Click the ⌐ Design button on the Slide Sorter toolbar to display the Slide Design task bar.

2. Choose the Animation Schemes option at the top of the task bar to display the animation schemes.

3. Choose the Services Provided slide (second slide in the presentation) to select it.
   You will test the various animation effects on this slide. Once you choose an effect, you will apply it to all of the slides in the presentation.

4. Click any animation effect and it will be previewed on the selected slide.

5. Scroll through the list of animation effects, clicking any effects that interest you.

6. Now scroll through the list of effects until the Exciting effects category is visible.

7. Try some of the exciting effects—such as Big Title, Ellipse Motion, and Neutron.

8. Choose the Float effect when you have finished experimenting.

9. Click the Apply to All Slides button to apply the effect to all slides in the presentation.

10. Click the title slide, and then click the Slide Show button at the bottom of the task pane.

11. Work through the presentation by clicking the mouse to introduce objects and advance from slide-to-slide.
    Notice that the animation effects have replaced the transition effects.

12. Complete the presentation and return to slide sorter view.

Custom Animation

Custom animation lets you animate individual items on slides. For example, you can apply animation effects to individual titles, bulleted paragraphs, clip art images, and other objects. With custom animation, you can control the visual effects, timing, and sequencing of the animation process. Custom animation can be used to enhance an animation scheme. Thus, you can apply an animation scheme and then apply custom animation to clip art and other items that are not animated as part of the scheme.

Applying Custom Animation Effects

Custom animation effects are applied in Normal view. This is because you must first select the object(s) to which the effects will be applied. Once the desired object(s) are selected in Normal view, custom animation effects are applied using options on the Custom Animation task pane. Applying custom animation effects can be a time-consuming process because they are applied to individual objects slide-by-slide. Thus, it is usually best to use animation schemes to animate text objects and use custom animation effects for clip art and other non-text objects. The following illustration describes the options on the Custom Animation task pane.

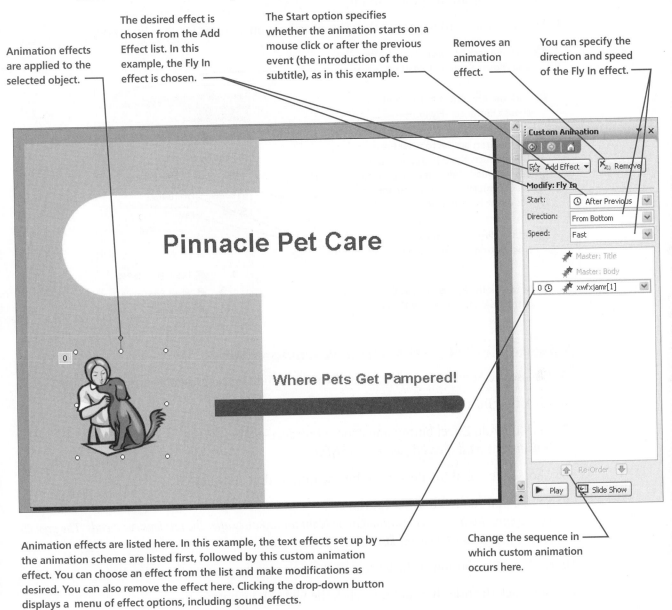

The desired effect is chosen from the Add Effect list. In this example, the Fly In effect is chosen.

The Start option specifies whether the animation starts on a mouse click or after the previous event (the introduction of the subtitle), as in this example.

Removes an animation effect.

You can specify the direction and speed of the Fly In effect.

Animation effects are applied to the selected object.

Animation effects are listed here. In this example, the text effects set up by the animation scheme are listed first, followed by this custom animation effect. You can choose an effect from the list and make modifications as desired. You can also remove the effect here. Clicking the drop-down button displays a menu of effect options, including sound effects.

Change the sequence in which custom animation occurs here.

Animate Clip Art On the Title Slide

1. Click the Normal view [image] button on the View bar.
   Custom animation is applied to individual objects on slides, so you will work in Normal view.

2. Choose the title slide to display it in the main part of the window.

3. Click the clip art image to select it.

4. Follow these steps to specify the custom animation settings for the clip art object:

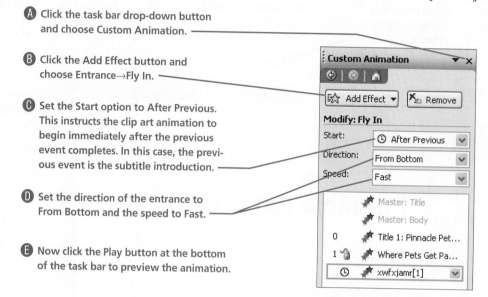

A Click the task bar drop-down button and choose Custom Animation.

B Click the Add Effect button and choose Entrance→Fly In.

C Set the Start option to After Previous. This instructs the clip art animation to begin immediately after the previous event completes. In this case, the previous event is the subtitle introduction.

D Set the direction of the entrance to From Bottom and the speed to Fast.

E Now click the Play button at the bottom of the task bar to preview the animation.

Animate Clip Art on the Services Provided Slide

5. Choose the Services Provided slide (the second slide in the presentation).

6. Click the clip art object to select it.

7. Click the Add Effect button and choose Entrance→More Effects.
   This displays a list of additional entrance effects.

8. Choose the Spiral In effect from the Exciting section and click OK.

9. Set the Start option to After Previous.
   Once again, this instructs the animation to begin immediately after the previous event ends. The previous event is the introduction of the last bullet.

10. Click the Play button at the bottom of the task pane to preview the animation.

11. Now click the title slide and then click the Slide Show button.

12. Click the mouse repeatedly to initiate the various animation events. You can end the presentation by tapping the (ESC) key after the clip art is animated on the Services Provided slide.

Sound Effects

PowerPoint provides a number of sound effects that can accompany animation effects. For example, in the next exercise you will attach the "whoosh" sound effect to the clip art objects. As the objects are introduced in a presentation, the "whoosh" sound effect will play. The following illustration describes the steps used to apply sound effects.

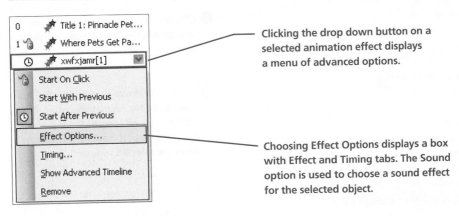

Clicking the drop down button on a selected animation effect displays a menu of advanced options.

Choosing Effect Options displays a box with Effect and Timing tabs. The Sound option is used to choose a sound effect for the selected object.

Hands-On 24.7 Apply Sound Effects and Modify Animation

Apply Sound Effects

1. Choose the title slide and then choose the clip art object.

2. Click the drop-down button for the clip art animation in the task pane and choose Effect Options.

3. Click the Sound drop-down button in the Effect tab, scroll through the list, and choose the Whoosh sound effect.

4. Click OK to preview the animation and sound.

5. Choose the Services Provided slide and apply the Whoosh sound effect to the clip art object.

Test the Slides

6. Click the title slide and then click the Slide Show button at the bottom of the task bar.

7. Click the mouse repeatedly to work through the first two slides in the presentation.

8. Tap the (ESC) key to end the presentation.

9. Now choose the last slide in the presentation and click the Slide Show button.

10. Click the mouse to work through the slide. Notice that the introduction of the name, telephone, and email information is cumbersome.
    This information should be introduced as a block. In the remainder of this exercise, you will remove the animation scheme on this slide and replace it with custom animation that introduces the text as you desire.

Remove the Animation Scheme from the Closing Slide

11. End the presentation and make sure the closing slide is visible.

12. Follow these steps to remove the animation scheme from the slide:

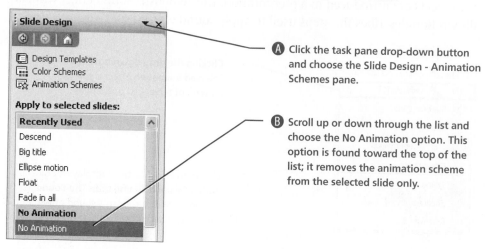

A Click the task pane drop-down button and choose the Slide Design - Animation Schemes pane.

B Scroll up or down through the list and choose the No Animation option. This option is found toward the top of the list; it removes the animation scheme from the selected slide only.

13. Notice that the Play button at the bottom of the task pane is not available. *This is because the animation scheme has been removed from the slide.*

Apply a Transition Effect

Animation schemes apply transition effects and animation to slides. In the next few steps, you will do a little detective work to identify the transition effect that was applied to slides by the Float animation scheme in an earlier exercise. Then, you will apply the same transition effect to the closing slide to create consistent transitions between all slides.

14. Choose the sixth slide in the presentation (Welcome Aboard Specials).

15. Click the Play button at the bottom of the task pane and notice the transition effect that introduces the slide. Click the button several times, if necessary, until you recognize the effect.

16. Now click the Slide Show button to begin the slide show on the sixth slide. Work through the slide by clicking the mouse and notice that when the closing slide is introduced, no transition effect occurs (nor animation for that matter).

17. End the slide show and make sure the closing slide is visible.

18. Follow these steps to apply a transition:

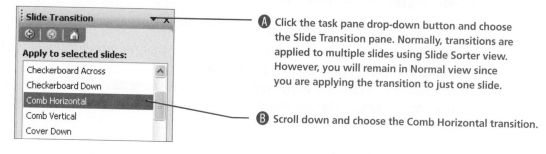

A Click the task pane drop-down button and choose the Slide Transition pane. Normally, transitions are applied to multiple slides using Slide Sorter view. However, you will remain in Normal view since you are applying the transition to just one slide.

B Scroll down and choose the Comb Horizontal transition.

19. Feel free to use the Play button one or more times to preview the transition. This is the transition that was applied to all slides by the Float animation scheme earlier in the lesson.

Animate the Title

In the next few steps, you will apply custom animation to the title and information block.

20. Make sure the closing slide is chosen and display the Custom Animation task pane.

21. Follow these steps to animate the title:

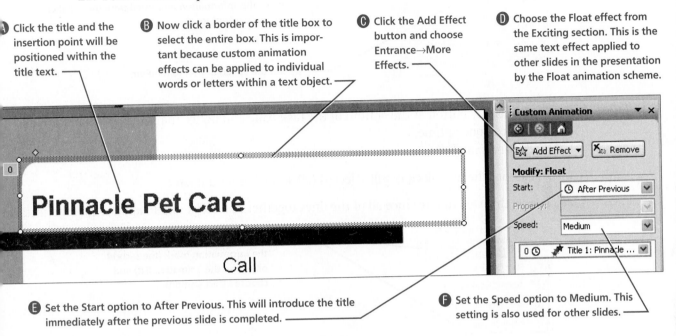

Ⓐ Click the title and the insertion point will be positioned within the title text.

Ⓑ Now click a border of the title box to select the entire box. This is important because custom animation effects can be applied to individual words or letters within a text object.

Ⓒ Click the Add Effect button and choose Entrance→More Effects.

Ⓓ Choose the Float effect from the Exciting section. This is the same text effect applied to other slides in the presentation by the Float animation scheme.

Ⓔ Set the Start option to After Previous. This will introduce the title immediately after the previous slide is completed.

Ⓕ Set the Speed option to Medium. This setting is also used for other slides.

22. Click the Play button at the bottom of the task pane to preview the slide.
   Notice that the information block is not animated. You will animate it in the next few steps, and apply the Whoosh sound effect.

Animate the Information Block

23. Click on the telephone number or some other part of the information block.

24. Now click a border of the information block to select the entire block.

25. Follow these steps to apply animation to the object:

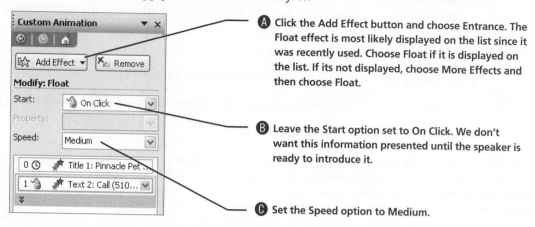

Ⓐ Click the Add Effect button and choose Entrance. The Float effect is most likely displayed on the list since it was recently used. Choose Float if it is displayed on the list. If its not displayed, choose More Effects and then choose Float.

Ⓑ Leave the Start option set to On Click. We don't want this information presented until the speaker is ready to introduce it.

Ⓒ Set the Speed option to Medium.

26. Click the Play button at the bottom of the task pane and notice that the individual lines are introduced one at time.
In this case, introducing the entire block at once with a sound effect will be more dynamic.

27. Make sure the text block is still selected (click the border if it isn't).

28. Follow this step to introduce all of the lines together as a block and to apply a sound effect:

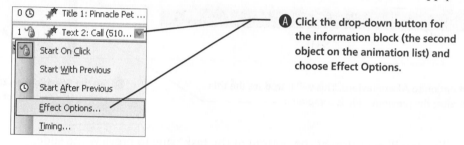

Ⓐ Click the drop-down button for the information block (the second object on the animation list) and choose Effect Options.

29. Click the Effects tab and choose the Whoosh effect from the Sounds list.

30. Click the Text Animation tab and choose the As One Object option from the Group Text list.

31. Click OK and the animation will be previewed.

32. Now click the Title slide and then click the Slide Show button.

33. Work through the slide show until it is complete.

Slide Timings

Thus far, you have advanced from slide to slide in your presentations by clicking the mouse. You can also specify timings for slides that cause them to advance after a specified number of seconds. In a traditional presentation during which an individual is presenting to a group, manually advancing from one slide to the next is the preferred method. However, PowerPoint also lets you deliver kiosk-style presentations that run automatically without user intervention. For these types of presentations, automatically advancing from slide to slide is essential.

Setting Timings Manually

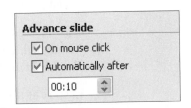

The Slide Transitions task pane includes an Advance Slide option that lets you specify the number of seconds a slide should remain displayed before advancing to the next slide. The example to the right shows the Advance Slide option with the On Mouse Click option turned on and the Automatically After option set to 10 seconds. This means the slide will advance after 10 seconds or when the mouse is clicked—whichever comes first. Timings can be set individually for each slide in a presentation.

 Hands-On 24.8 **Set Timings Manually**

1. Switch to Slide Sorter ⊞ view.

2. Display the Slide Transition task pane.

3. Set the Automatically After option to 10 seconds, as shown in the preceding illustration.

4. Click the Apply to All Slides button.
   Notice that each slide now has a 00:10 indicator below it, indicating that the automatic timing is set to 10 seconds.

5. Click the title slide and then click the Slide Show button at the bottom of the task pane. Now just sit back and watch your presentation.
   Keep in mind that you set the same timing for all slides. You can also set different timings for each slide.

Recording Timings While You Rehearse

The Slide Show→Rehearse Timings command runs a slide show in rehearsal mode. While running in Rehearsal mode, you advance through the presentation manually by clicking the mouse. As you work through the presentation, PowerPoint records the timing between each mouse click. These timings can be saved and applied to the slides, allowing you to optimize the timing of each bullet, animation, and slide transition. By using Rehearsal mode to record timings, you can allocate as much or as little time as desired to each point in your presentation. The following illustration describes the Rehearsal toolbar.

Advance to the next action. This has the same effect as clicking the mouse.

Time used on the current slide.

Time used for the presentation.

Pause the rehearsal.

Repeat the rehearsal for the current slide.

Hands-On 24.9 Record Timings in Rehearsal Mode

1. Choose Slide Show→Rehearse Timings and click the Pause ▐▐ button on the Rehearsal toolbar.

   While the rehearsal is paused, take a moment to examine the Rehearsal toolbar. In the next step, you will resume the rehearsal and work through the entire presentation by clicking the mouse. Try to imagine yourself presenting to a group and introduce actions on the various slides as you would in that situation. When you finish the presentation, a message will appear asking if you want to save the timings. You will choose Yes at that point to save the timings.

2. Now, click the Pause ▐▐ button and work through the presentation. When the presentation i finished, choose Yes when PowerPoint asks if you want to save the timings.

   Clicking the Pause button again resumes the slide show.

3. Look at the various timing indicators under the slides in Slide Sorter 🖽 view and notice that they differ for each slide.

   PowerPoint replaced the 10 second timings you set earlier with the recorded timings.

4. Click the title slide then click the Slide Show button. Sit back and watch the presentation play with your new recorded timings.

5. Save your changes and continue with the next topic.

Preparing Slide Shows for Delivery

The Slide Show→Set Up Show command displays the Set Up Show box. You can choose options in the Set Up Show box in preparation for delivering a slide show. The following illustration describes the most important options on the Set Up Show dialog box.

The Presented By a Speaker show type is the slide show format you have used thus far.

The Browsed By An Individual option runs the slide show in a standard window with menus and commands. This makes browsing and editing the presentation seamless and is useful if you want someone to review and critique your presentation.

The Browsed at a Kiosk option runs the slide show automatically.

The Loop Continuously option causes the show to continuously repeat. This option is set automatically when the Browsed At a Kiosk option is chosen.

Turn narration and animation on or off with these options.

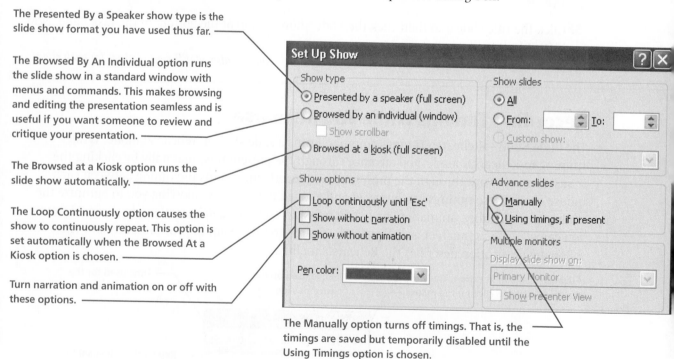

The Manually option turns off timings. That is, the timings are saved but temporarily disabled until the Using Timings option is chosen.

Hands-On 24.10 Use Set Up Show Options

Run a Kiosk Style Presentation

1. Choose Slide Show→Set Up Show from the menu bar.

2. Choose the Browsed at a Kiosk option.
   Notice that the Loop Continuously option is checked and disabled. Kiosk slide shows always loop continuously.

3. Make sure the Using Timings, If Present option is chosen and click OK.

4. Run the slide show. As the slide show runs, move the mouse and try to make the Slide Show Toolbar appear at the bottom left corner of the slide.
   Notice that the Slide Show Toolbar is not available. Users can use ⎡ESC⎤ to end a kiosk style slide show, but that is the only command they can execute.

5. Wait for the slide show to end and watch it restart.

6. Now tap ⎡ESC⎤ to end the slide show.

7. Feel free to experiment with the Set Up Show options.

8. When you have finished, choose Slide Show→Set Up Show from the menu bar.

9. Choose the Presented By a Speaker option.

10. Choose the Manually option to disable the timings and click OK.

11. Save the changes to your presentation, then close the presentation and continue with the end of lesson questions and exercises.

Concepts Review

True/False Questions

1. Clip art can be inserted while working in Normal view.   TRUE   FALSE

2. Clip art images are associated with keywords that can be used to search for clip art.   TRUE   FALSE

3. Transitions are applied to individual objects on slides.   TRUE   FALSE

4. Slide Sorter view is the best view to use when setting up transitions.   TRUE   FALSE

5. You can apply a transition to multiple slides while using Slide Sorter view.   TRUE   FALSE

6. Animation schemes override transition effects.   TRUE   FALSE

7. Text objects cannot be animated.   TRUE   FALSE

8. Clicking the mouse can initiate animation steps and transitions.   TRUE   FALSE

9. Customized animations are applied to entire slides.   TRUE   FALSE

10. Animation schemes are used to add clip art to slides.   TRUE   FALSE

Multiple Choice Questions

1. Which of the following actions can be performed on clip art while working in Normal view?
   a. Rotation
   b. Sizing
   c. Moving
   d. All of the above

2. Which item(s) are affected by animation schemes?
   a. Titles
   b. Bulleted lists
   c. Clip art
   d. Both A and B
   e. All of the above

3. Which of the following effects can be controlled through custom animation?
   a. Timing
   b. Sound
   c. Entry effects
   d. All of the above

4. To which items can custom animation be applied?
   a. Titles
   b. Bulleted lists
   c. Clip art
   d. Both A and B
   e. All of the above

Skill Builders

Skill Builder 24.1 Insert Clip Art

In this exercise, you will add clip art to the Tropical Getaways presentation that was developed in the previous lesson.

1. Open the Tropical Getaways presentation.

2. If necessary, click the Normal View 🖳 button to switch to Normal view.

3. Choose the Travel Categories slide (the second slide).

4. Display the Slide Layout task pane.

5. Scroll down toward the bottom of the layout list and choose the Title, Text and Clip Art layout as shown to the right.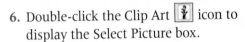

6. Double-click the Clip Art 👤 icon to display the Select Picture box.

7. Enter the keyword **safari** and click the Go button.

8. Choose a clip art image that appeals to you and click OK.

9. If necessary, size and position your clip art image. The example to the right uses the antelope image with the size reduced slightly and the position adjusted slightly.

10. Now choose the Travel Now and Save slide (the fifth slide).

11. Change the slide layout to Title, Text and Clip Art.

12. Double-click the Clip Art 👤 icon and search for clip art using the keyword **tropics**.

13. Choose an image that appeals to you, insert the image, and then size and position it if necessary.

14. Save the changes to your presentation and continue with the next exercise.

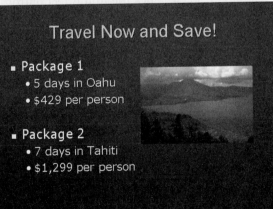

Skill Builder 24.2 Apply an Animation Scheme

1. Display the Slide Design task pane and choose Animation Schemes.

2. Scroll through the list of animation schemes and, from the Exciting section, choose Ellipse Motion.

3. Click the Apply to All Slides button to apply the scheme to all slides in the presentation.

4. Choose the title slide (first slide) and click the Slide Show button at the bottom of the task pane.

5. Work through the presentation and notice the effects introduced by the animation scheme. Feel free to choose a different scheme if you don't care for Ellipse Motion. However, if you choose a different scheme, be sure to apply it to all slides.

6. Save your changes and continue with the next exercise.

Skill Builder 24.3 Apply Custom Animation

In this exercise, you will animate the clip art images with entry effects and sound.

Animate the Safari Image

1. Make sure you are in Normal view and choose the Travel Categories slide (the second slide).

2. Display the Custom Animation task pane.

3. Click the safari clip art image to select it.

4. Click the Add Effect button and choose Entrance→More Effects.

5. Choose the Grow and Turn effect from the Moderate section and click OK.

6. Set the Start option to After Previous to make the animation begin immediately after the last slide bullet is introduced.

7. Follow these steps to add a sound effect to the animation:

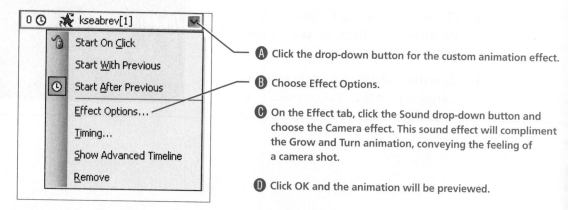

Ⓐ Click the drop-down button for the custom animation effect.

Ⓑ Choose Effect Options.

Ⓒ On the Effect tab, click the Sound drop-down button and choose the Camera effect. This sound effect will compliment the Grow and Turn animation, conveying the feeling of a camera shot.

Ⓓ Click OK and the animation will be previewed.

Animate the Tropics Image

8. Choose the Travel Now and Save slide (the fifth slide).

9. Click the island image to select it.

10. Click the Add Effect button and choose Entrance→More Effects.

11. Choose the Wedge effect from the Basic category and click OK.

12. Make the animation of the island start after the previous event has finished.

13. Apply a sound effect that you think works well with this animation, for example the Breeze effect or the Chime.

14. Play the slide to make sure the animation functions correctly.

15. Choose the title slide and run the slide show.

16. Work through the presentation, ensuring that the animation functions properly.

17. Feel free to add or modify animation in your presentation.

18. When you have finished, save your changes, and close the presentation.

Assessments

Assessment 24.1 Add Animation Effects

In this assessment, you will add animation effects to the Classic Cars presentation that was developed in the previous lesson.

1. Open the Classic Cars presentation on your exercise diskette.

Add Clip Art

2. Add clip art to the second slide as shown to the right. You can locate the picture by doing a search for the keyword phrase **classic cars**. You will need to change the slide layout for the slide and insert the picture in the placeholder box of the new layout. Reduce the size of the picture after inserting it, and adjust the position as shown. If necessary, reduce the font size of the bulleted paragraphs so that they no longer wrap.

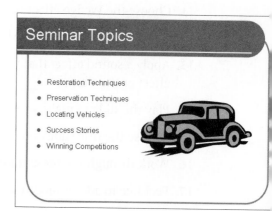

3. Choose the closing slide, and change the subtitle from Enjoy the Ride to **Enjoy the Road Ahead**.

4. Add clip art to the last slide as shown to the right. If you cannot find this clip art, choose a different one. There is no need to change the slide layout. However, you will need to use the Clip Art task pane to search for and insert the clip. Use the keyword **road** and size and position the clip art as shown.

Apply Animation

5. Apply the Big Title animation scheme to all slides in the presentation.

6. Use the following settings to apply custom animation to the car clip on the Seminar Topics slide:

   ■ Use the Fly In entrance effect.

   ■ Set the animation to begin after the previous event has finished.

   ■ Set the direction of the Fly In to From Right and the speed to Fast.

   ■ Apply a Whoosh sound effect or some other effect that you prefer.

7. Use the following settings to apply custom animation to the road clip on the closing slide:

   ■ Use the Fly In entrance effect.

   ■ Set the animation to begin after the previous event has finished.

   ■ Set the direction of the Fly In to From Top Left and the speed to Very Fast.

   ■ Apply a Whoosh sound effect or an other effect that you prefer.

8. Run the presentation when you have finished. If you used the clip art shown in this example, notice that when it is introduced in the slide show it contains built-in animation that makes the road appear to move! The road clip is introduced on the closing slide.

9. Save your changes and then close the presentation.

Critical Thinking

Critical Thinking 24.1 Add Clip Art and Animation

Open the Holmestead Realty presentation that you developed in the Critical Thinking exercises in the previous lesson.

Linda Holmes has been working with her presentation for some time and she now realizes that she needs to liven up the presentation. She asks you to add clip art and animation to the presentation. Follow these guidelines to add clip art:

- Insert a picture of a house on the title slide without changing the slide layout. If necessary, adjust the size of the picture and position it at the bottom right corner of the slide.

- Apply the Title, Text and Clip Art layout to the Follow Up slide.

- Insert a picture of a "key" in the clip art box. Choose any picture of a key you desire. Resize and reposition the picture on the slide as desired.

Follow these guidelines to animate the presentation:

- Add the Descend animation scheme to all slides in the presentation.

- Group the paragraphs on the Office Hours slide so that they descend as one object.

- Apply custom animation to the "house" picture on the title slide as follows:

Entrance Effect	Spiral In
Start	After Previous
Speed	Medium
Sound	Whoosh

- Apply custom animation to the "key" picture on the Follow Up slide as follows:

Entrance Effect	Fly In
Start	After Previous
Direction	From Top
Speed	Very Fast
Sound	Chime

ritical Thinking 24.2 **Apply Timings**

Linda decides to rent a kiosk in the local shopping mall. She wants to set up her PowerPoint presentation to run continuously at the kiosk. Follow these guidelines to prepare the presentation:

- Record timings for the entire slide show and save the timings. Use a moderate pace while recording the timings so that individuals viewing the slide show have enough time to read all bullets as they are introduced.

- Set up the show to be browsed at a kiosk. The show should run continuously once it has been started. The timings you recorded should be used while the show is running.

- Now, change the Set Up Show setting to allow the presentation to be Presented by a Speaker (Full Screen).

- Save the changes to your presentation when you have finished.

UNIT 8

Comprehensive Integration

There was a time when the holy grail of software development was to create a single program that could do everything. Today, the emphasis is on creating programs that work so well together you can use the optimal program for every computer task then bring the results of your work together in a variety of ways.

In this unit you get to experience the power of Microsoft Office 2003 programs working together in concert. You will plan and prepare for a meeting by creating Word documents, an Excel spreadsheet, a PowerPoint presentation. You will place charts created in Excel in both a Word document and a PowerPoint presentation. You will use a query in Access to generate data for another Excel chart. Finally, you will convert some of your files to Web page format for publishing to the Internet.

Integration Project: Multitasking with Office 2003

The Office 2003 applications are designed to work together seamlessly, allowing you to use the most suitable program for each part of a complex task. For example, you can place Excel charts into Word documents and PowerPoint presentations, or use Word to draft the outline of a PowerPoint presentation. This integration project gives you the opportunity to leverage the capability of Office 2003's application programs to share data and work together.

IN THIS LESSON

Additional learning resources are available at labpub.com/learn/oe3/

Case Study

Debra serves as an administrative assistant at the Help for the Homeless shelter in her community. The shelter provides year-round support and lodging for homeless persons. In addition to aiding the homeless, the shelter also helps families find permanent housing and coordinates donations of automobiles and furniture to help them get established. On a Monday morning, Debra finds the memo below in her inbox.

Help for the Homeless

Memo

To: Debra Dine

From: Allen Litton

Date: May 20, 2002

Re: Preparations for our upcoming Community Advisor Meeting

Please make preparations for our semi-annual community advisor meeting to take place four weeks from today. We need to accomplish the following tasks:

- Create an agenda for the meeting and email it to our board members for comment.
- Create a fact sheet with current data on the shelter, including:
    - Our Current year's budget
    - Data on occupancy at the shelter
- Create a PowerPoint presentation to guide the meeting.
- Prepare the meeting room and arrange for catering of a continental breakfast.

Twice a year, the shelter organizes a meeting of its community advisory committee. Committee members review the shelter's operations and make recommendations to enhance its role. They are also an important facet of community outreach—helping to recruit support in local government and corporate donations.

Debra is charged with a key role in bringing this meeting together. In order to accomplish this complex task, Debra will use the Office XP suite and all of its programs. In this Lesson, you will take on the role of Debra. The efficiency with which the Office XP applications work together will be a significant aid to putting this meeting together.

Project Task Summary

In order to make preparations for the meeting, you will use several programs. The table below list the tasks you will undertake.

Task	Brief Description	Programs
1. Plan Meeting Activities	Schedule meeting activities; ensure that the contact information for board members is current.	Outlook
2. Type and Email a Meeting Agenda	Create a new folder to hold all of the files for this project. Type up an agenda, and then email it to the board members for review and comment.	Word, Outlook
3. Check Board Member Replies	Review the board member replies and revise the agenda as advised.	Outlook, Word
4. Create a Budget Workbook	Create a worksheet with the current shelter budget and create a pie chart to display the budget.	Excel
5. Query a Database	Find out how many beds were occupied in the shelter during the past three years; find out the average number of beds occupied each week.	Access, Excel
6. Create a Column Chart	Chart the occupancy data discovered in Task 5.	Excel
7. Create a Fact Sheet Document	Create a summary of facts about the shelter, its operating budget, and its occupancy rates.	Word, Excel
8. Create a Presentation	Create a presentation to guide the meeting.	PowerPoint, Word
9. Review and Print Handouts	Review all handouts for accuracy and errors, then print originals for copying.	Word, PowerPoint
10. Publish Web Pages (Optional)	Convert the agenda, workbook, and presentation to Web page format. Optionally, publish the meeting information to the Web for current and future reference.	Word, PowerPoint, Excel, FTP Program

Multitasking

Notice that some programs are used several times. This use mirrors how most people work with programs on a project such as this. You don't necessarily foresee every need you will have for a particular program; instead, you start programs and open files as your needs dictate. You may leave a program open, then switch back and forth between it and other programs. Or you may exit a program and then launch it again later.

Task 1: Outlook—Plan Meeting Activities

In this task, you will verify the contact information for the board members to whom a copy of the meeting agenda will be sent for confirmation. You will also set appointment dates for various meeting-related activities.

 ## Hands-On 25.1 Plan Activities in Outlook

Enter Email Addresses of Board Members

1. Start Outlook and display the Contacts view.

2. Verify that the following contacts exist in the Contacts list and make sure that each email address is entered correctly.

- Jacqueline Chan   jchan@labpub.com
- Robert Smith   rsmith@labpub.com
- Terry Sanchez   terry@labpub.com

Schedule Dates for the Meeting

3. Display the Calendar view and enter the appointment below:

Item	Information
■ Subject	Community Advisory Committee Meeting
■ Location	Shelter Dining Room
■ Start Time	[4 Weeks from today] 9:00 AM
■ End Time	11:30 AM
■ Reminder	1 Week before the appointment date
■ Label	Needs Preparation
■ Notes	Will require catered continental breakfast.
■ Contacts	Jacqueline Chan Robert Smith Terry Sanchez
■ Categories	Goals/Objectives

4. Enter another appointment for a planning meeting using the following information:

Item	Information
■ Subject	Planning for Advisory Committee Meeting
■ Location	Office
■ Start Time	[1 Week from today] 2:00 PM
■ End Time	4:00 PM
■ Reminder	1 Hour before the appointment time
■ Notes Box	Finalize agenda. Flesh out topics for discussion at meeting.
■ Categories	Goals/Objectives

5. Minimize ▬ Outlook and proceed to the next task.

Task 2: Word/Outlook—
Type and Email a Meeting Agenda

In this task, you will type up a draft meeting agenda and email it to the three board members. Before you create the new document, you will create a folder on your exercise diskette to organize all of the files you use on this project. It is a common practice to make new folders for specific projects. Otherwise, the list of files in your My Documents folder (or in this case, on your exercise diskette) may become quite long.

 Hands-On 25.2 Type and Email a Meeting Agenda

Create a Project Folder

First, you will create a folder to hold all of the files that will be created and used in the course of planning for the meeting.

1. Open a My Computer window, then open the 3½ Floppy (A:) drive.

2. Choose File→New→Folder from the menu bar.
   The new folder appears with the name selected—ready for you to type the new name.

3. Name the new folder **Advisory Committee Meeting** and tap (ENTER).

4. Close ⊠ the My Computer window.

5. Start Word and type the agenda below. Use font and paragraph formatting as desired to make this document appear readable and professional.

   ▪ 12 pt. Times New Roman is recommended for the body of the agenda.

   ▪ Choose other font sizes for the title and subtitle at the top of the page.

   ▪ Place the insertion point anywhere on the Meeting Agenda (subtitle) line, then use the Format→Borders and Shading command to add a line below the subtitle.

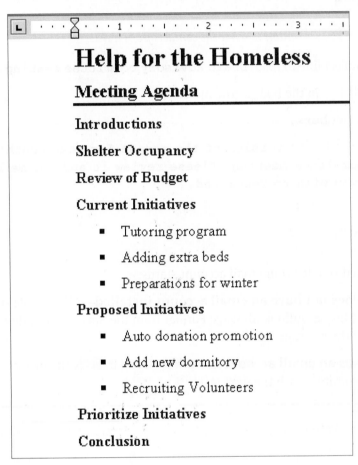

6. Save 🖫 the document to the Advisory Committee Meeting folder as **Lesson 25 Meeting Agenda**.

Email the Agenda to Board Members

7. Use File→Send To→Mail Recipient (As Attachment) to start an email message with this document attached.

8. Address the message to the three recipients listed below:

   - Jacqueline Chan

   - Robert Smith

   - Terry Sanchez

   !**TIP!** *Click the* ⬛ To... *button to select the contacts from a list.*

9. Change the subject line to read: **Draft advisory committee meeting agenda**.

10. Type the text below in the body of the message:

    Dear Board Members,

    Attached is a draft version of the agenda for next month's Community Advisory Committee meeting. Please review it and let me know of any revisions you wish to recommend.

    Regards,

    [Your Name]

11. Use the bulleted step for your email account status:

    - **Outlook does not have an email account installed**—Choose File→Save As from the menu bar. Choose Outlook Message Format from the Save As drop-down list then click Save. Close the message window.

    - **Outlook has an email account installed**—Send ⬛Send the message then minimize Word and continue with the next task.

Task 3: Outlook/Word— Check Board Member Replies

After the board members review the draft agenda, they may have some comments and recommend revisions. In this task you will check for replies and any necessary revisions.

 ## Hands-On 25.3 Check Replies and Edit the Agenda

 Before You Begin: Follow the bulleted steps below if your installation of Outlook does not have an email account installed:

- *Launch Internet Explorer and navigate to the URL* **labpub.com/learn/oe3/**.
- *Click the Lesson 25 link then click the Hands-On Exercise 25.3 link.*
- *Perform this exercise using the WebSim beginning with Step 1 below.*

Receive Replies from Board Members

1. Click its button on the Windows Taskbar to restore the Outlook window to the Desktop.

2. Display the Inbox, then use the Send/Receive command to check for replies from the board members. Continue to use the Send/Receive command until you receive replies from all three board members.

3. Review the comments from each board member on the draft agenda.

4. Open the message from Terry Sanchez. Select and copy the text with the revision he recommends.

WebSim Users Only: Minimize 🔲 *the Internet Explorer window and continue with Step 5 below.*

Edit the Agenda

5. Restore Word to the screen and open the Lesson 25 Meeting Agenda document from the Advisory Committee Meeting folder on your exercise diskette.

6. Follow these steps to edit the agenda:

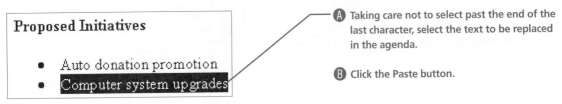

The text you saved from the email message is pasted into the document to replace the selection. Notice that the formatting from the email message in the pasted text does not match the rest of the document. You will use a SmartTag to correct this.

7. Click the Paste SmartTag at the end of the pasted text and choose Match Destination Formatting from the menu, as shown below.

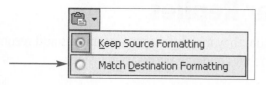

8. Save 🖫 the document, then close ⊠ the Word and Outlook windows.

Task 4: Excel—Create a Budget Workbook

In this task, you will use Excel to produce a summary of the shelter's operating expenses. You will use this budget data later for a fact sheet about the shelter. You will also use it to create charts for the fact sheet and a PowerPoint presentation.

 Hands-On 25.4 Create a Budget Workbook

Create the Budget Workbook

1. Start Excel.

2. Double-click the Sheet 1 tab, then rename the tab **Budget Summary Data**.

3. Follow these steps to delete the two extra worksheets on the workbook:

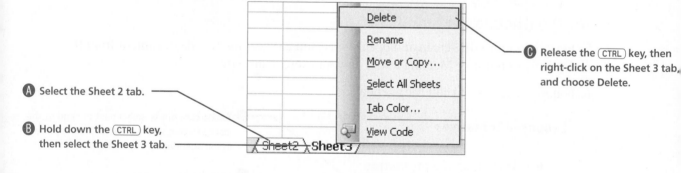

Ⓐ Select the Sheet 2 tab.

Ⓑ Hold down the (CTRL) key, then select the Sheet 3 tab.

Ⓒ Release the (CTRL) key, then right-click on the Sheet 3 tab, and choose Delete.

Menu items:
Delete
Rename
Move or Copy...
Select All Sheets
Tab Color...
View Code

4. Use the notes and data below to enter budget information for the previous year.

   ▨ Format the title, subtitle, and headings to appear similar to first two rows of this example.

   ▨ Format number cells to display commas and no decimals, as shown below.

   ▨ Create and copy formulas to calculate totals for the rows and columns.

	A	B	C	D	E	F
1	**Help for the Homeless**					
2	2004 Budget Summary					
3		Q1	Q2	Q3	Q4	Totals
4	Mortgage & Insurance	11,337	11,337	11,337	11,337	
5	Utilities	2,021	1,464	1,504	1,809	
6	Food	5,480	4,512	3,452	5,437	
7	Staff Salaries	17,685	17,685	17,685	17,685	
8	Maintenance and Repairs	2,188	3,113	3,928	3,392	
9	Outreach & Fundraising	820	2,006	576	712	
10	Grand Totals				Create Formulas	

5. Save 🖫 the workbook in the Advisory Committee Meeting folder on your exercise diskette as **Lesson 25 Advisory Committee Budget Data**.

Create a Chart

6. Follow these steps to select the data for a pie chart that will summarize the year's budget allocation:

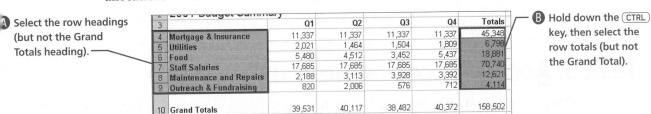

A Select the row headings (but not the Grand Totals heading).

B Hold down the CTRL key, then select the row totals (but not the Grand Total).

This technique allows you to select noncontiguous cells for the chart.

7. Click the Chart Wizard 📊 button on the toolbar, then follow these steps to select the chart type:

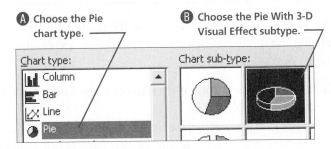

A Choose the Pie chart type.

B Choose the Pie With 3-D Visual Effect subtype.

8. Click Next. Leave the Data Range set to Columns.

9. Click Next. Do not enter a chart title.
   This chart will be pasted into a Word document and PowerPoint presentation later in this lesson. You will type titles for these charts in Word and PowerPoint rather than entering the title now in Excel.

10. Click the Legend tab, and then uncheck the Show Legend option box.
    Since you will add labels for each piece of data in the next step, you do not need a legend.

11. Click the Data Labels tab, then follow these steps to set the data labels:

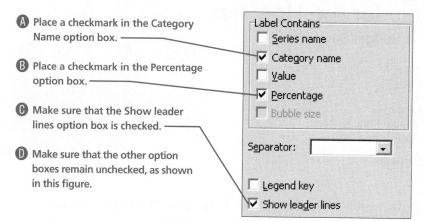

   Ⓐ Place a checkmark in the Category Name option box.

   Ⓑ Place a checkmark in the Percentage option box.

   Ⓒ Make sure that the Show leader lines option box is checked.

   Ⓓ Make sure that the other option boxes remain unchecked, as shown in this figure.

12. Click Next. Choose the As New Sheet option. Name the new sheet **Budget Summary Chart** and then click Finish.
    The new worksheet with the chart appears in front of the Budget Summary worksheet.

13. Save 🖫 the workbook, then minimize 🗕 the Excel window.

Task 5: Access/Excel—Query a Database

One piece of information required for the meeting is data on occupancy at the shelter over the past three years. The shelter maintains a database with records of each week's occupancy. You will query the database to obtain the needed information.

 ## Hands-On 25.5 Query a Database for Occupancy History

1. Start Access and open the Hands-On Lesson 25 Database file from your file storage location. Choose Yes if you are warned the database file may contain unsafe expressions, then choose Open to open the data file.

2. Choose Tables on the Objects panel, then double-click to open the Shelter Occupancy Data table. Take a moment to review the table data.
   The table contains week-to-week data on occupants of the shelter. It's always a good idea to familiarize yourself with the data before you run a query. This way, you are more likely to spot a mistake if the query does not work as you intended. In this table, you can see that about 300–500 shelter beds were occupied each week.

3. Close ☒ the table window.

4. Choose Queries on the Objects panel, then double-click the Create Query By Using Wizard item.

5. Select the Week and Occupants fields for the query as shown below, then click Next.

6. Choose the Summary option, then click the Summary Options button.

7. Place a checkmark in the Sum and Avg boxes as shown below, then click OK.

8. Click Next, then choose the Year option.

9. Click Next, then click Finish.
   The result of the query appears in a new window.

Copy the Query Results

10. Choose Edit→Select All Records from the menu bar.
    All the cells in the query are selected.

11. Click the Copy 🗐 button on the toolbar.

12. Close ☒ the Access window.

Paste the Query Results into Excel

13. Restore the Excel window to the Desktop.

14. Choose Insert→Worksheet from the menu bar.

15. Select Cell A2, then click the Paste 🖺 button.
    The results of the query are pasted onto the new worksheet.

16. Select Cell A1, then type **Annual Occupancy Data** as a heading for the worksheet.

17. Double-click the Sheet 4 tab, then rename it **Occupancy Data**.

18. Save 🖫 the workbook.

Task 6: Excel—Create a Column Chart

Now that you have the data from the Access database, you can use Excel to create a new chart of this data.

 ## Hands-On 25.6 **Create a Column Chart**

Before You Begin: The Lesson 25 Advisory Committee Budget Data workbook should be open in Excel and the Occupancy Data worksheet should be displayed.

Format the Data

1. Select Cells A2 to C5, then choose Format→Column→Autofit Selection from the menu bar.
   Notice the small green triangles at the top-left corner of each year cell. This alerts you to a possible problem with the data.

2. Select Cells A3 to A5, then click the Trace Error ⊗ SmartTag button.
   Excel displays Number Stored As Text as the error. This is not a problem in this case, since you will not be performing calculations on the years.

3. Choose Ignore Error from the Trace Error menu.
   The green triangles disappear.

Create the Column Chart

4. Select Cells A3 to B5 (the Week By Year and Sum Of Occupants data).

5. Click the Chart Wizard 📊 button on the toolbar.

6. Leave the Chart Type set to Column, then choose the Clustered Column with 3-D Visual Effect as the subtype.

7. Click Next. Leave the data range in Columns and click Next again.

8. Choose the Legend tab, and then uncheck the Show Legend box.
   You won't need a legend because your data is just a single statistic for each year.

9. Choose the Data Labels tab. Make sure all of the options are unchecked.
   This simple data does not require a label in this case.

10. Click Next. Choose the As New Sheet option, then name the sheet **Occupancy Chart** and click Finish.

11. Save 💾 the workbook, then minimize ➖ the Excel window.

Task 7: Word/Excel—Create a Fact Sheet Document

Now that the Excel data is complete, you will create a fact sheet in Word and bring some of the Excel data into the fact sheet.

Hands-On 25.7 Import Excel Data into a Document

Start Typing the Fact Sheet

1. Start Word and begin typing the fact sheet displayed below.

   ▪ Use font and paragraph formatting as desired to make this document appear readable and professional.

   ▪ Use tab settings to neatly align the fact sheet data items.

   ▪ Use the Format→Borders and Shading command to place a 2½ point line below the Fact Sheet and Current Budget subheadings.

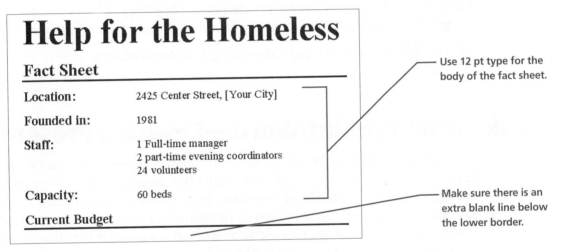

2. Save 🖫 the document in the Advisory Committee Meeting folder on your exercise diskette as **Lesson 25 Fact Sheet**.

Import the Excel Budget Data

Now you are going to copy and paste budget data from the Excel workbook into the fact sheet.

3. Activate the Excel window, then display the Budget Summary Data worksheet.

4. Select Cells A3 to F10 (all of the data and column headings, but not the worksheet title and subtitle).

5. Click the Copy 🖻 button.

6. Activate the Word window, then place the insertion point on the line below the Current Budget subheading.

7. Click the Paste 📋 button.
   Word pastes the table, keeping the Excel font formatting.

8. Click the Paste Options 📋 SmartTag button for the Excel data you just pasted, and then choose Match Destination Table Style from the SmartTag menu.
   Now the table fonts match the fonts used in the Fact Sheet.

Import the Occupancy Column Chart

Now you will copy and paste a chart from the Excel workbook into the fact sheet.

9. Activate the Excel window, then display the Occupancy Chart worksheet.

10. Click the Copy 📋 button, then restore the Word window.

11. Use (CTRL)+(END) to jump to the bottom of the Word document, then use (CTRL)+(ENTER) to create a new page.

12. Type a new subheading of **Shelter Occupancy**, and then tap (ENTER).

13. Paste 📋 the Column chart below the new subheading.
    The chart appears at the insertion point. Notice that it is scaled to fit the page margins.

14. Save 💾 the document, then minimize ➖ the Word window.

Task 8: PowerPoint/Word—Create a Presentation

Now that you have created the handouts for the meeting (Agenda and Fact Sheet), you are ready to create a PowerPoint presentation to help guide the meeting. If a computer projection display is available, the slides can be shown from a computer during the meeting. If a projection display is not available, the slides can be printed on transparencies for use with an overhead projector. You will use some of the content from the Agenda document to create the presentation. You will also place the two Excel charts on presentation slides.

Importing Slides from a Word Outline

PowerPoint can use a Word outline to create new slides in a presentation: you simply insert the Word document with your outline into the PowerPoint presentation. PowerPoint lays out the information into slides with titles and bullets according to the organization of the outline. You import slides from an outline with the Insert→Slides From Outline command.

Styles

In order for PowerPoint to interpret the outline properly, the slides must be formatted with specific heading styles. A style is a method used to apply formatting to paragraphs and text characters. An advanced topic, styles are not covered in this book. However, you will use styles to prepare your Meeting Agenda document to create slides in the presentation.

In-Place Editing of Other Office Program Objects

When you paste an object such as an Excel chart into PowerPoint, you can edit it using standard Excel commands. For example, you can edit the fonts used for the chart or change the chart type after the chart has been pasted. To activate in-place editing, simply double-click on the chart on the PowerPoint slide, and then use normal editing commands to revise the chart.

Hands-On 25.8 Create a Presentation

1. Start PowerPoint and create a new presentation by choosing From Design Template in the Task Pane. Choose any template you think will be appropriate for the advisory committee meeting.

2. On the title slide, enter the following:

   ▪ **Title:** `Community Advisory Committee Meeting`

   ▪ **Subtitle:** `Help for the Homeless`
     Now you will find a piece of clip art to place on the title slide.

3. Choose Insert→Picture→Clip Art from the menu bar.

4. Search in All Collections and in All Media File Types on the word **house**.
   Your search may produce several dozen results if you have an Internet connection.

5. Browse the search results and choose any picture of a house that seems appropriate. (It need not match the one shown below.)

6. Save the presentation in the Advisory Committee Meeting folder as **Lesson 25 Presentation**.

Prepare the Agenda Outline

Now you will use the Agenda document to fill in details on the PowerPoint presentation. In order for this to import smoothly, you must modify the Agenda document.

7. Activate the Word program. Click File on the menu bar and choose the Lesson 25 Meeting Agenda document from the file list near the bottom of the menu.
   This technique is a handy way to open a file with which you have recently worked.

8. Choose File→Save As from the menu bar, then follow these steps to save the document:

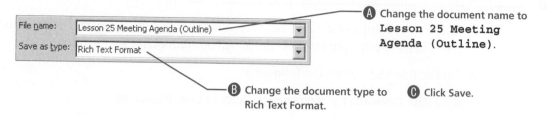

Ⓐ Change the document name to **Lesson 25 Meeting Agenda (Outline)**.

Ⓑ Change the document type to Rich Text Format.

Ⓒ Click Save.

By saving the agenda with a new name, you can freely modify it without changing the original Meeting Agenda document to be handed out at the meeting.

9. Choose View→Outline from the menu bar.
   Outline view is a special view that displays your outline with indents for each heading level. You can switch back and forth between outline view and normal or print layout views at any time.

10. Follow these steps to begin cleaning up the outline:

Ⓐ On the top row of the outline, position the pointer arrow along the left margin so that it points to the right, then drag down to select the rows above Introductions.

Ⓑ Tap the (DELETE) key to delete the selection.

11. Select and delete all blank lines in the outline, as shown in the example below.

Blank lines in the outline can cause PowerPoint to create extra slides when you import the document into your presentation later in this exercise.

12. Follow these steps to revise the Agenda document into outline form:

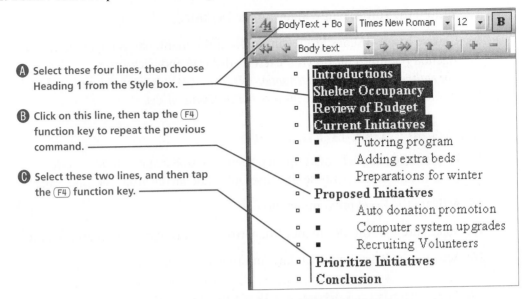

Ⓐ Select these four lines, then choose Heading 1 from the Style box.

Ⓑ Click on this line, then tap the F4 function key to repeat the previous command.

Ⓒ Select these two lines, and then tap the F4 function key.

You have promoted these lines to Heading 1 in the outline. Notice that the font formatting and paragraph spacing changed as well. These format settings are part of the Heading 1 style.

Next, you will promote the bulleted items to Heading 2.

13. Follow these steps to assign Heading 2 to the subheadings:

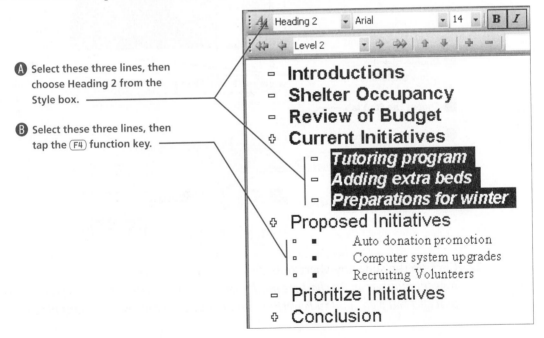

Ⓐ Select these three lines, then choose Heading 2 from the Style box.

Ⓑ Select these three lines, then tap the F4 function key.

These paragraphs also change their appearance to reflect the font and paragraph formatting of the Heading 2 style. Don't worry about the lack of bullets on these paragraphs. PowerPoint will insert them when you use the outline to add slides.

14. Save 💾 the document.

Import the Outline into the Presentation

15. Restore the PowerPoint window to the Desktop.

16. Choose Insert→Slides From Outline from the menu bar. Navigate to the Lesson 25 Meeting Agenda (Outline) file on your exercise diskette and click Insert.
The outline flows into your presentation. Notice that each Heading 1 item has created a new slide automatically. The Heading 2 lines are now bulleted items on slides.

Import an Excel Chart to a Slide

17. Display Slide 3, Shelter Occupancy, then choose Format→Slide Layout from the menu bar. Choose the Title Only slide layout from the Task Pane.

18. Activate the Excel program window.

19. Make sure that the Occupancy Chart worksheet is displayed, then click the Copy button.

20. Activate the PowerPoint window, and then click the Paste button.

Perform In-place Editing on the Excel Chart

Notice that the numbers along the axes of the chart (left and bottom sides) are too small to read. You will now edit the font setting to make these numbers readable.

21. Double-click on the column chart, then follow these steps to adjust the font size:

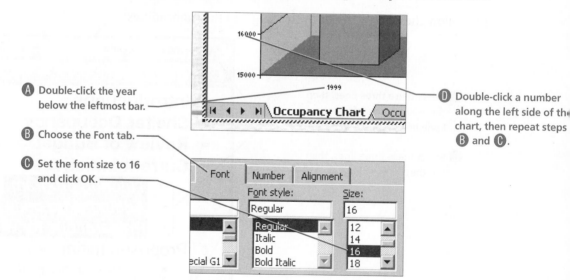

Ⓐ Double-click the year below the leftmost bar.

Ⓑ Choose the Font tab.

Ⓒ Set the font size to 16 and click OK.

Ⓓ Double-click a number along the left side of the chart, then repeat steps Ⓑ and Ⓒ.

22. Click on the slide anywhere outside the chart boundary.
Now the numbers on the chart are much more readable. As you can see, it is possible to edit an Excel chart even after you place it into a PowerPoint presentation. You can also edit charts placed in Word documents.

Import and Edit another Excel Chart

23. Activate the Excel window, then display the Budget Summary Chart worksheet and click the Copy button.

24. Activate the PowerPoint window, then select Slide 4, Review of Budget, and click the Paste button.
    The chart is centered on the slide. However, notice that the text labels are too small to read. In the next step, you will repeat the procedure you used on the column chart to change the font size of these labels.

25. Double-click on the chart, then double-click on any of the labels around the chart. Change the Font Size to 16, and then click OK. Click anywhere outside the chart boundary to view the change.

Finish the Presentation

26. Display Slide 1, click to select the picture on the slide, then click the Copy button.

27. Display Slide 2, then add the following bulleted items to the slide:

    - Shelter Staff

    - Shelter Board of Directors

    - Civic and Business Leaders

28. Display Slide 8, Conclusion, and click the Paste button.

29. Select and delete any slides remaining after Slide 8.

30. Save the presentation.

31. Display Slide 1, then tap the (F5) function key to display the slide show. Navigate through all of the slides and verify that they display properly.

32. Close PowerPoint and any other open program windows.

Task 9: Word/PowerPoint—Review and Print Handouts

Now that the files you will use as handouts in the meeting are complete, you are ready to review and print them. You will want to scan the files both before and after you print them: sometimes a mistake you overlook on the computer screen can be spotted on a printout.

 ## Hands-On 25.9 Review and Print

1. Start Word, and open the two documents listed below on your exercise diskette.

   ■ Lesson 25 Meeting Agenda

   ■ Lesson 25 Fact Sheet

2. Review each document for spelling and other types of errors. Is the formatting consistent within each document?

3. Save each document if you make any revisions, then print them.

4. Review each printout for neatness and typographical errors. Revise and reprint the documents if necessary, then close the documents and Word.

Print PowerPoint Handouts

5. Start PowerPoint and open the Lesson 25 Presentation file.

6. Review the presentation one last time, make any needed revisions, then save it.

7. Choose File→Print from the menu bar, then follow these steps to print handouts of your PowerPoint presentation:

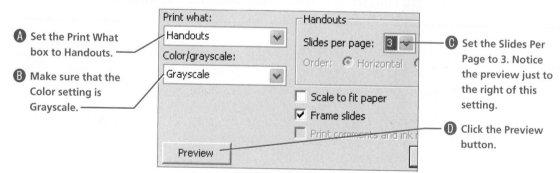

A Set the Print What box to Handouts.

B Make sure that the Color setting is Grayscale.

C Set the Slides Per Page to 3. Notice the preview just to the right of this setting.

D Click the Preview button.

8. Review the print preview. Use the Next Page ⬛ button to move from one page to the next.

9. Click Print, then click OK.

10. Retrieve the printout and review it for accuracy. If necessary, make revisions, save the presentation, and reprint the handouts.

11. Close the PowerPoint window.

Task 10: Excel/Word/PowerPoint/Web Folders— Creating and Publishing Web Pages

Help for the Homeless has its own Web site. For more and more non-profit organizations, this is the case. Given the limitations on staffing, the shelter does not have its own Webmaster, however, and Debra must maintain the site herself. Fortunately, the Office XP suite makes posting new Web pages easy to do. Combined with the utility of Web folders, Office XP allows most anyone to independently publish Web pages.

 ## Hands-On 25.10 Convert Files to Web Page Format

Save A Word Document as a Web Page

1. Open the Lesson 25 Meeting Agenda document in the Advisory Committee Meeting folder on your exercise diskette.

2. Choose Format→Theme from the menu bar. Choose and apply a theme for this page.

3. Choose File→Save as Web Page from the menu bar.

4. Click the Change Title button, then enter a title of **Advisory Committee Meeting** and click OK.
   In the next step you will give the page a Web-friendly filename. Most Web servers do not allow spaces in filenames.

5. Change the file name to **agenda**, then click Save.
   Word converts the document to Web page format.

6. Close ☒ the Word Window.

Save an Excel Workbook as a Web Page

7. Open the Lesson 25 Advisory Committee Budget Data workbook in the Advisory Committee Meeting folder.

8. Choose File→Save as Web Page from the menu bar.

9. Click the Change Title button, then enter a title of **Shelter Budget Summary** and click OK.
   In the next step, you will type an underscore between the two words in the filename. This is often done in place of using a space character.

10. Change the filename to **budget_summary**, then click Save.

11. Close ☒ the Excel window.

Save the PowerPoint Presentation as a Web Page

You can also save PowerPoint presentations in Web page format.

12. Open the Lesson 25 Presentation file in the Advisory Committee Meeting folder.

13. Choose File→Save as Web Page from the menu bar.

14. Click the Change Title button, make sure that the title reads **Community Advisory Committee Meeting**, and click OK.

15. Change the filename to **presentation**, then click Save.
   The pictures and charts in this presentation will cause it to take longer to save than the Word and Excel files—as long as two or three minutes. Wait for the save command to finish before moving on to the next step.

16. Close ⊠ the PowerPoint window.

View the Web Pages

17. Open a My Computer window, then open the 3½ Floppy (A:) drive and open the Advisory Committee Meeting folder.

 agenda
HTML Document
14 KB

 budget_summary
HTML Document
12 KB

 presentation
HTML Document
3 KB

Look for the files you just saved as Web pages. Their icons will differ from those used for normal Word, Excel, and PowerPoint files. A small globe appears on the icons to indicate that these are Web page files.

18. Double-click to open one of the Web page files.
   Internet Explorer will launch to display the Web page.

19. Activate the My Computer window, and then double-click to display one of the other two Web pages. Repeat this step for the third Web page.

20. Close ⊠ the Internet Explorer windows (but not the My Computer window) when you have viewed all three Web pages.

Publishing the Web Pages

For others to view your Web pages over the Internet, you must place them on a *server*. The act of placing a Web page or other type of file on the Internet where others can access it is called *publishing*. This requires that you *upload* (transfer from your local computer to a remote computer) your Web pages and supporting files to a Web server from your computer's hard drive.

FTP Programs

FTP (File Transfer Protocol) programs help you transfer files back and forth between your local computer and a remote computer over the Internet. For example, you can transfer Web pages between your hard drive and free ISP-provided Web space. There are several FTP programs available to download and purchase online.

In this exercise, you will simulate using the CuteFTP program to publish your Web pages by uploading them to a Web server. After the pages finish uploading, you will simulate viewing one of them over the Internet.

1. If necessary, launch Internet Explorer and navigate to the URL
   labpub.com/learn/oe3/lesson25.html.

2. Click the Hands-On Exercise 25.11 link.
   The WebSim begins with a display of the Windows Desktop.

3. Double-click the CuteFTP icon.
   CuteFTP is a program optimized to help you transfer files from your computer to a remote Internet server (upload) or to download files from a server to your computer.

4. Click the Reconnect [icon] button on the CuteFTP toolbar.
   This button reconnects you with the Help for the Homeless Web site. This connection was created previously. Now a single click reconnects you with the Web site.

5. While holding down the (CTRL) key, select files and folders for uploading in the left panel of the

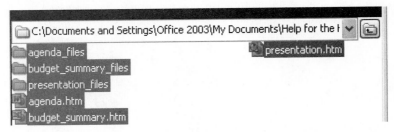

   CuteFTP window as shown below.

   Now that you have selected the files and folders to be transferred to the Internet server, you are ready to give the Upload command.

6. Click the Upload [icon] button on the CuteFTP toolbar.
   CuteFTP begins transmitting the selected files and folders. After a pause, the upload command is completed and copies of the selected files appear in the homeless folder on the remote Internet server.

7. Close [X] the CuteFTP window.
   An Internet Explorer window appears to display an example of the PowerPoint presentation over the Internet. Notice the URL in the address bar. Once an FTP program is set up it's quite easy to upload new files to a Web site.

8. Close [X] the Internet Explorer window.
   Congratulations! You've completed the final exercise of the final lesson in this book!

UNIT 9

Appendices

Appendix A

Using File Storage Media

A standard 3½ inch floppy disk comes bundled with this book. However, you may wish to use storage media besides the floppy disk referred to in most of the lessons. This appendix contains instructions for downloading and unzipping the exercise files used with this book, and an overview for using this book with various file storage media.

In This Appendix

The following topics are addressed in this appendix:

Topic	Description	See Page
Downloading the Student Exercise Files	Retrieving the exercise files and copying them to your file storage location	761
Working with File Storage Locations	Using alternative media	762
Using a Floppy Disk	Storing your work on a floppy disk	763
Using a USB Flash Drive	Storing your work on a USB flash memory drive	765
Using the My Documents Folder	Storing your work in the My Documents folder	767
Using a Network Drive Folder	Storing your work in a custom folder on a network	767

Downloading the Student Exercise Files

The files on the enclosed floppy disk and needed to complete certain Hands-On, Skill Builder, Assessment, and Critical Thinking exercises are also available for download at the Labyrinth Website. Use the following instructions to copy the files to your computer and prepare them for use with this book.

⚠️ **NOTE!** *The files needed for use with this book are already on the floppy disk enclosed on the inside back cover. Only follow this procedure if your disk is lost or the files must be replaced.*

 ## Hands-On A.1 Download and Unzip Files

Follow these steps to download a copy of the student files necessary for this book:

1. Launch Internet Explorer.

2. Enter `labpub.com/students/fdmso2003.asp` in the browser's address bar and tap ENTER.
A list of books in the applicable series appears. If you don't see the title of your book in the list, use the links on the left side of the Web page to display the list of books for your series.

3. Click the link for your book title.
A prompt to open or save a file containing the student exercise files appears.

4. Click the Save button.

5. Choose your file storage location and click Save.
After a pause, the exercise files will begin downloading to your computer. Continue with the next step after the download is complete.

6. Click the Open button on the Download Complete dialog box. Or, open your file storage location and double-click the newly downloaded file if the dialog box closed automatically.

7. Click OK, and then follow the step for your file storage location:

   ■ **Floppy Disk:** Click the Browse button, choose the 3½ Floppy A: drive, click OK, and then click the Unzip button.

   ■ **USB Flash Drive:** Click the Browse button, navigate to your USB flash drive, click OK, and then click the Unzip button.

   ■ **My Documents Folder:** Click the Browse button, navigate to the My Documents folder, click OK, and then click the Unzip button.

   ■ **Network Drive Folder:** Click the Browse button, navigate to your assigned folder on the network drive, click OK, and then click the Unzip button.

8. Click the Close button after the files have unzipped.

Working with File Storage Locations

New technologies continue to expand the variety of available computer storage media. The $3\frac{1}{2}$ inch floppy disk—such as the one bundled with this book— has been around since about 1983. That's incredibly ancient in the fast-moving field of computers. It's easy to use other storage media with this book. Potential alternative storage locations include:

- The My Documents folder

- A USB flash drive

- A folder on your local hard drive

- A folder on a network drive

Using Alternative File Storage Locations

Depending on the file storage media you select, some steps you perform in the exercises will differ from what you see illustrated. However, with a little practice you should find it easy to interpret the instructions for use with your file storage media.

Example: Using a USB Flash Drive

You are performing an exercise in which you create and save a new file. If you are using a USB flash drive, simply substitute the drive letter for your flash drive for the $3\frac{1}{2}$ Floppy (A:) drive shown in the figure instruction.

The storage location as it appears in the book

The storage location as you perform it on the screen

Using a Floppy Disk

This book assumes you will use a floppy disk to store your exercise files. However, you should be aware of space limitations. This section explains how to keep track of the available space on a floppy diskette, and how to delete unnecessary files to conserve space.

Storage Limitations of Floppy Disks

As you work through the exercises in this book, you will create numerous files that are to be saved to a storage location. A floppy diskette may not have enough storage capacity to hold all files created during the course (particularly if you perform all of the Skill Builder and Critical Thinking exercises). Thus, you may want to use an alternate storage location for all files accessed and created during the course.

Checking Available Space on a Floppy Disk

If you choose to use the floppy disk bundled with this book as your storage location, you may reach a point at which the disk fills up and no additional files can be stored on it. However, if you regularly check the available space on your floppy disk, this problem should not arise.

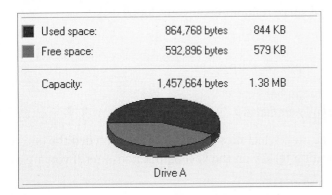

■ Used space:	864,768 bytes	844 KB
■ Free space:	592,896 bytes	579 KB
Capacity:	1,457,664 bytes	1.38 MB

Drive A

Windows can display a pie chart of the available space on your floppy disk.

Freeing Up Space on the Floppy Disk

If your floppy disk runs short of space, you will need to selectively delete files from it. You should delete files from lessons already completed, freeing up space for exercises in the current lesson.

TIP! *Using the following procedure to check your available floppy disk space before you begin work on a new lesson. If you have less than 100 KB remaining on the disk, delete some files to free up space.*

Hands-On A.2 **Check Free Space on Your Floppy Disk**

1. Open a My Computer window.

2. Right-click the 3½ Floppy (A:) drive and choose Properties from the context menu.
   Windows displays a pie chart with details on the used and available space on your floppy disk.

3. Examine the Free Space information and click OK.

4. Follow the step for the amount of disk space remaining:

   ■ Close ⊠ the Properties window. Close the My Computer window if there is more than 100 KB of space remaining on the disk. Skip the remaining steps in this procedure. You are finished and ready to proceed with the next lesson.

   ■ Close ⊠ the Properties window. Continue with the remaining steps in this exercise if there is less than 100 KB of space remaining on your floppy disk.

Delete Unnecessary Files

5. Double-click to open the 3½ Floppy (A:) drive.

6. Choose View→List from the menu bar.
   The My Computer window displays your files as a compact list.

7. While holding down the (CTRL) key, select files for lessons that preceded the one you are working on now and tap the (DELETE) key on the keyboard. Choose Yes if you are asked to confirm the deletion of these files.
   Windows deletes the selected files.

8. Close ⊠ the My Computer window.
   You now have plenty of space for your work in the next exercise.

⚠**TIP!** *If you accidentally delete an exercise file needed for a later lesson, don't worry. You can use the procedure outlined in Hands-On A.1 to download and unzip the student exercise files as many times as necessary.*

Using a USB Flash Drive

A USB flash drive stores your data on a flash memory chip. You simply plug it into a USB port on any computer and Windows immediately recognizes it as an additional disk drive. USB flash drives typically are able store 32 megabytes (MB) or more of your data files. Large capacity USB flash drives can store 512 MB or more.

Most USB flash drives are about the size of your thumb and plug into any available USB port on your computer.

USB Flash Drive Letter

When you plug in a USB flash drive to a Windows computer, Windows automatically assigns it the next available drive letter. Windows uses drive letters to identify each drive connected to the computer. For example, the primary part of the hard drive is always identified as the C: drive. The CD/DVD drive is typically the D: or E: drive.

Devices with Removable Storage

This USB flash drive is the F: drive.

 3½ Floppy (A:)   DVD/CD-RW Drive (E:)    Removable Disk (F:)

 TIP! *Your USB flash drive may receive a different drive letter on different computers. This does not affect any files stored on the drive.*

Hands-On A.3 Rename Your USB Flash Drive

You may find it convenient to rename your USB flash drive to make it easier to recognize when you save or open files.

TIP! *Some Windows systems may not give you renaming privileges for drives.*

1. Plug the USB flash drive into an available USB port.

2. Open a My Computer window.

3. Right-click your USB flash drive and choose Rename from the context menu.

NOTE! *In the next step, Windows may display a prompt that you cannot rename this flash drive. You have not done anything wrong! You can use the drive with its current name. You may also want to try renaming it later using a different login.*

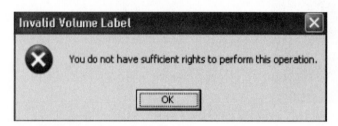

4. Type **FlashDrive** as the new drive name and tap (ENTER). Click OK if you receive a prompt that you do not have sufficient rights to perform this operation.
If you were unable to rename the flash drive, don't worry. Renaming the flash drive is a convenience for recognition and has no other effect.

Using the My Documents Folder

Windows creates a unique My Documents folder for each login. This folder resides on the main system drive (usually the C: drive). The Office 2003 application programs provide a My Documents button in their Open and Save As dialog boxes to make navigation to this folder convenient.

The My Documents button in the Word 2003 Save As dialog box

Using a Network Drive Folder

You may use a system connected to a network. There may be a folder on a network server computer in another location that is dedicated to storing your work. Usually, you will find this folder within the My Network Places folder of your computer. The Office 2003 application programs provide a My Network Places button in their Open and Save As dialog boxes to make navigation to this folder convenient. You may have to navigate deeper into the folder to locate your personal network drive folder.

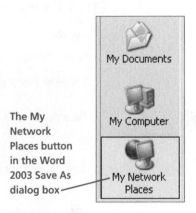

The My Network Places button in the Word 2003 Save As dialog box

Appendix B

Using Outlook with Hotmail and Other Email Services

Introduction

This appendix contains details about the use of Outlook with HTTP-type email accounts such as Hotmail. Students who use their own HTTP email accounts with Outlook must follow the special procedures contained in this appendix. These necessary procedures are also referenced in the text of each lesson.

In This Appendix

The following topics are addressed in this appendix:

Using Outlook with Hotmail

Outlook 2003 supports sending and receiving email with HTTP (Webmail) accounts. The steps used to set up Outlook for use with an HTTP account are quite similar to those used to set up a POP (Internet) email account.

> ⚠️ **NOTE!** *Depending on Microsoft policies, it is possible that only premium Hotmail accounts requiring payment of an annual fee will work with Outlook.*

 ## Hands-On B.1 Set Up a Hotmail Account

Before You Begin—The following steps assume that you have already created a Hotmail account.

1. Choose Tools→E-mail Accounts from the menu bar.

2. Choose the Add A New E-mail Account option, then click Next.

3. Choose the HTTP option, then click Next.

4. Follow these steps to begin setting up your Hotmail account:

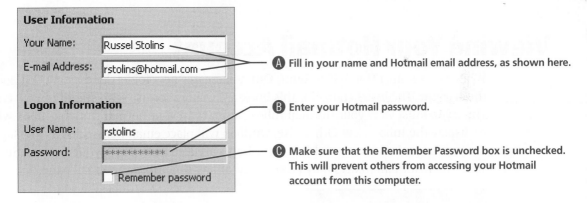

Ⓐ Fill in your name and Hotmail email address, as shown here.

Ⓑ Enter your Hotmail password.

Ⓒ Make sure that the Remember Password box is unchecked. This will prevent others from accessing your Hotmail account from this computer.

You will only need to enter your password once for each Outlook session.

5. Click the More Settings button.

6. Change the Mail Account box to indicate your name for the account, as shown below.

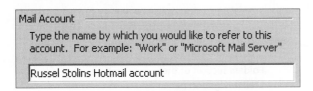

7. Click OK, click Next, then click Finish.
   Outlook displays your new Hotmail account in the Folder List panel. Also, note the new shortcut to the account's Inbox on the Outlook bar.

Set Your Account as the Default

When more than one email account is set up in Outlook, one of them is normally used to create new messages. This is the default account. You will now set your Hotmail account as the default.

8. Choose Tools→E-mail Accounts from the menu bar, then click Next. Skip to Step 10 if your account is the only one listed, otherwise continue with Step 9.

9. Choose your new Hotmail account in the email account list, then click the Set as Default button on the right side of the dialog box.
   This prompts Outlook to assume that new email messages you create should use your Hotmail account by default. Notice that your account name has jumped to the top of the account list (if more than one account is set up). The word Default should appear in parenthesis beside your account type, as shown in the example here.

Name	Type
Russel Stolins Hotmail account	HTTP (Defaul
Nick Chapin Hotmail Account	HTTP

10. Click Finish.
    Your Hotmail account name appears in the All Mail Folders section of the Navigation pane.

Read the next topic for information about how you will work with your Hotmail account in Hands-On exercises in Lessons 6, 18, and 25.

Viewing Your Hotmail Account

When you set up a Hotmail account, Outlook creates new folders and a new Outlook bar icon for the account. The instructions for this book are written for use with standard POP email accounts. Thus, you must view your Hotmail Inbox rather than your normal Outlook Inbox when instructed to display the Inbox view. Otherwise, Outlook will place email items such as message drafts and sent messages into its own folders. Sent Items are also placed into your Hotmail Sent Items folder. Your other Hotmail folders may be accessed at any time from the Email pane.

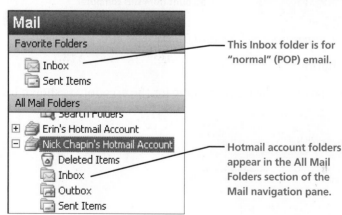

This Inbox folder is for "normal" (POP) email.

Hotmail account folders appear in the All Mail Folders section of the Mail navigation pane.

Deactivating Your Hotmail Account

At the end of a class session, you will usually want to prompt Outlook not to perform send/receive commands with your Hotmail account. This saves other students using your computer the inconvenience of clicking Cancel when asked for your account password. You should perform the exercise below whenever you finish a class session.

Hands-On B.2 Make Your Hotmail Account Inactive

In this exercise, you will instruct Outlook to exclude your account from send/receive commands.

NOTE!

If you use an HTTP email account service other than Hotmail, simply substitute the name of your account for the references to Hotmail in this exercise.

1. Choose Tools→Options from the menu bar.

2. Click the Mail Setup tab, then click the Send/Receive button.
   Outlook displays a list of send/receive groups. Most likely, just one All Accounts group will appear. Groups are a convenient way of switching on and off email accounts.

3. Make sure that the All Accounts group is selected, then click the Edit button.

4. Choose your Hotmail account in the Accounts list, then uncheck the Include the Selected Account in This Group option, as shown here.

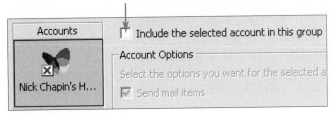

A small "X" will appear by the account icon, indicating that the account is no longer included.

5. Click OK, click Close, then click OK to close all of the dialog boxes.
   When you return to the computer lab for your next class session, you will perform a similar task to switch on your account.

Activating Your Hotmail Account

When you begin a new class session, you will want to switch on your Hotmail account. You will also want to make sure that the Hotmail account is the default email account.

 ## Hands-On B.3 Make Your Hotmail Account Active

In this exercise, you will instruct Outlook to include your account in send/receive commands.

 Activate Your Hotmail Account

If you use an HTTP email account service other than Hotmail, simply substitute the name of your account for the references to Hotmail in this exercise.

1. Choose Tools→Options from the menu bar.

2. Click the Mail Setup tab, then click the Send/Receive button.
   Outlook displays a list of send/receive groups. Most likely, just one All Accounts group will appear. Groups are a convenient way of switching on and off email accounts.

3. Make sure that the All Accounts group is selected, then click the Edit button.

4. Choose your Hotmail account in the Accounts list, then place a checkmark in the Include the Selected Account in This Group option, as shown here.

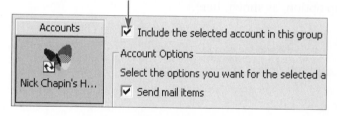

A new icon with two arrows appears, indicating that your account is now included in send/receive commands.

5. Click OK, then click Close to return to the Options dialog box.

Make Sure Your Hotmail Account is the Default Email Account

By setting your Hotmail account as the default, Outlook will assume that all new email messages are to be sent by this account.

6. Click the E-mail Accounts button, or choose Tools→E-mail Accounts from the menu bar if you have already exited the Tools dialog box.

7. Make sure that the View or Change Existing E-mail Accounts option is chosen, then click Next.

8. Choose your Hotmail account in the account list, then click the Set as Default button if your account is not already the default.

9. Click Finish, then click OK.
   Your Hotmail account is now active.

Using Outlook with Other HTTP Email Services

Besides Hotmail, Outlook 2003 can work with other HTTP (Webmail) accounts, such as YahooMail or EudoraMail accounts. Outlook 2003 can also work with MSN accounts.

 NOTE! *Outlook 2003 compatibility with other HTTP email services depends on their configuration and other details beyond the scope of this textbook. The following steps should work if the HTTP email service is compatible with Outlook.*

 NOTE! *Some HTTP email accounts require that you pay an annual fee in order to access the account with an email client such as Outlook.*

Hands-On B.4 Setting Up Other Email Accounts

The following generic instructions will get you started setting up other types of accounts, but do not provide complete information. See the email account provider's Help information for details on setting up the account to work with Outlook and other email client programs.

 NOTE!

In Step D below, you may need to enter different email servers, depending on the email service you use. Your instructor can give you this information.

1. Choose Tools→E-mail Accounts from the menu bar.

2. Choose Add a New E-mail account from the dialog box, then click Next.

3. Choose POP or HTTP as appropriate from the dialog box, then click Next.

4. Follow these steps to begin setting up your new account:

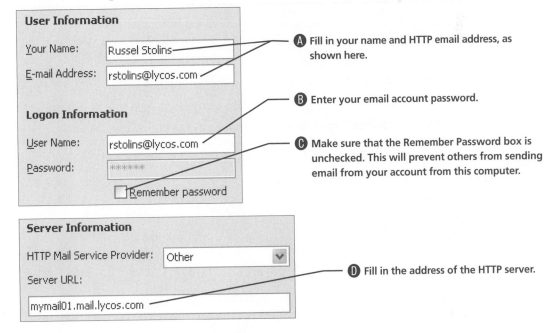

5. Click the More Settings button, then change the Mail Account box to indicate your name for the account.

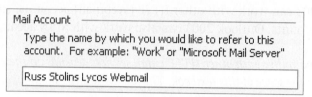

6. Click OK, then click Next.
   Outlook displays your new account in the account list.

7. Choose your new email account in the email account list, then click the Set as Default button on the right side of the dialog box.
   This prompts Outlook to assume that new email messages you create should use your Hotmail account by default. Notice that your account name has jumped to the top of the account list (if more than one account is set up). The word Default should appear in parenthesis beside your account type.

Name	Type
Russ Stolins Lycos Webmail	HTTP (Default)
Russ at Labpub	POP/SMTP

8. Click Finish.
   Your new account is ready for you to send and receive email.

Appendix C

Using Web-Based Email Simulations

Introduction

This appendix contains details about the use of Web-based simulations for institutions that cannot support the use of POP or HTTP email accounts for use with this textbook.

In This Appendix

The following topics are addressed in this appendix:

Topic	Description	See Page
Introducing Web-Based Simulations	How the Web-based email simulations work	776
Importing Outlook Data	How to import data files with email messages so that Hands-On exercises will work correctly	778

Introducing Web-Based Simulations

Some institutions cannot support the use of email accounts for use with this textbook. There may be several reasons for this:

- The institution does not have a mail server to create POP email accounts

- The institution has a firewall to provide security from unauthorized hacking, and this firewall does not permit HTTP email accounts to function

- The institution may have a policy of not supporting email accounts in its computer labs

Regardless of the reason, this book was designed to provide for situations in which email is unavailable.

How the Simulations Work

Running a Web-based simulation is just like performing the task in Outlook. The only difference is that you perform the exercise steps in a Web browser window rather than the Outlook program window. Unless indicated on the screen, you should follow all Hands-On exercise steps exactly as they are written. Each simulation uses a screen capture of the Outlook program screen and sophisticated Web programming to make the Web page appear and function exactly like the Outlook program.

When to Run a Simulation

If a Web-based simulation is available for an exercise, you will see the WebSim icon and label immediately below the Hands-On exercise heading.

 ## Hands-On C.1 Starting a Web-Based Simulation

 This procedure gets you started running the Web-based simulations for any lesson.

1. Minimize ▬ the Outlook window, then launch Internet Explorer.

2. In the Internet Explorer Address bar, enter **labpub.com/learn/oe3/** then tap ⒺⓃⓉⒺⓇ.
   The Microsoft Office 2003 Web page appears.

3. Click the link for the lesson containing WebSims you are studying.
   Links to the WebSims available for the lesson appear on this page.

4. Perform the first step number indicated in the special instructions to WebSim users. If the WebSim requires any other special instructions, they will appear on the Web page.

   ⚠**TIP!** *If you must perform any step in the simulation differently from what is written in the book, special instructions will appear at the top and bottom of the page.*

5. Continue performing the steps of the exercise until you complete it.

6. When you finish a simulation, click the Outlook 🔲 Inbox - Microsoft Offi... button on the Windows taskbar to return to Outlook.

   ⚠**TIP!** *Always leave the Internet Explorer window open until you complete the lesson.*

7. To return to a simulation, click the Internet Explorer 🔲 Microsoft Office 2003... button on the Windows taskbar.

Importing Outlook Data

If you perform the Web-based simulations for email exercises, Outlook won't have messages in the Inbox and Sent Items views that you may need in later exercises. Thus, before you begin a lesson, yo must bring these messages into Outlook. This process is called importing. Any lesson that requires additional message files will prompt you to import these files per the instructions in this appendix.

 ## Hands-On C.2 Import Data Into Outlook

Download the Data File from the Web

In this section of the exercise, you will get a copy of the Outlook data from the Web page for the lesson you are working on. You will save this file to your exercise diskette or the My Documents folder for use in the next section of this exercise.

1. Launch Internet Explorer and navigate to the Web page for the lesson you are working on. Th Web address (URL) should be listed on the opener page for the lesson or near the first Hands-On exercise for that lesson.

2. Click Download the Outlook Data File link near the top of the Web page.
   Internet Explorer will begin to download the data file.

3. Click the Save button.

4. Choose the 3½ Floppy [A:] drive or My Documents in the Save In box, then click Save.
   There will be a brief pause as the file is saved to your computer. Windows may offer to open the file when the download is complete, but this is unnecessary.

5. Click Close if you see a Download Complete dialog box.
   Now you will bring the data into Outlook with the Import command.

Delete Existing Messages

In order to follow the steps in some of the exercises, you will delete existing messages in the Inbox.

6. Launch Outlook if you have not done so already.

7. Display the Mail navigation pane and choose the Inbox.

8. Choose Edit→Select All from the menu bar.
   This selects all of the existing messages in the Inbox. If any other student needs these messages, they should already have been saved into that student's email folder.

9. Click the Delete ⊠ button on the Outlook toolbar.
   The messages are sent to the Deleted Items folder. You will learn more about deleting and undeleting messages later in Lesson 6.

Import the Outlook Data

Now you are ready to import the new data into Outlook.

10. Choose File→Import and Export from the menu bar.
    The Import/Export Wizard will guide you through the Import process.

11. Choose the Import from Another Program or File option and click Next.

12. Scroll down the file type list, choose Personal Folder File (.pst) as shown below, then click Next.

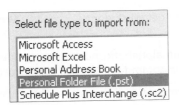

Select file type to import from:

Microsoft Access
Microsoft Excel
Personal Address Book
Personal Folder File (.pst)
Schedule Plus Interchange (.sc2)

13. Click the Browse button near the top of the dialog box, then choose the 3½ Floppy [A:] drive or My Documents in the Look In box, select the pst file for your current lesson and click Open.

14. Make sure that the Replace Duplicates with Items Imported option is chosen, then click Next.

15. Follow these steps to continue the Import command:

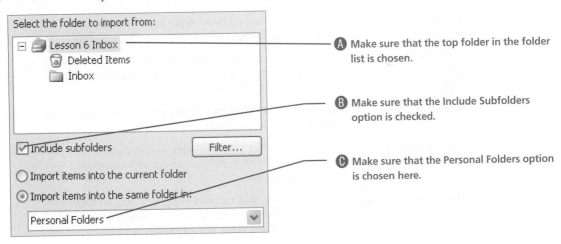

Select the folder to import from:

Lesson 6 Inbox
Deleted Items
Inbox

☑ Include subfolders   Filter...

○ Import items into the current folder
◉ Import items into the same folder in:

Personal Folders

A Make sure that the top folder in the folder list is chosen.

B Make sure that the Include Subfolders option is checked.

C Make sure that the Personal Folders option is chosen here.

16. Click Finish to execute the Import command.
    There will be a brief pause as the files are imported into the primary Outlook data file. These files have been copied into the appropriate folders for viewing later in this lesson.

Glossary of Terms

Term	Description	Example
24-bit color	Level of color resolution that allows the display of millions of colors on the monitor	See *Color Depth* (page 17)
AGP port	Short for **A**ccelerated **G**raphics **P**ort; a special slot designed for the display of high-speed 3-D graphics	
Antivirus program	Software designed to stop computer viruses from infecting files on the computer	Norton Antivirus
Application program	Software designed to help you get work done	Microsoft Word, Lot 1-2-3
ASCII	Standard code for representing alphabetic, numeric, and symbolic characters on the computer	See *Units of Measur* (page 8)
Benchmark	Program that tests the performance of a computer system	Winbench, Winston
Bit	Single on-off switch in a computer circuit	0, 1.
Byte	Single character of data; it is composed of 8 bits in a specific order	A, B, C, etc
Cable modem	Device designed to send and receive digital data over television cable system wiring	
Cache	Form of high-speed RAM designed to temporarily store the most recently processed software code	512K L2 cache
Cathode ray tube (CRT)	Technology used by large, television-style monitors; CRT monitors are gradually being replaced by thinner, more efficient LCD panels	
Data bus	Channel by which data is transmitted from expansion cards and RAM to the microprocessor	PCI, ISA, AGP
Digital camera	Still camera that stores images as computer files rather than on film; most connect to a computer via a USB cable	Nikon Coolpix 5000
Digital video camera	Video camera that records images to digital tape or disk; specially designed to transfer video directly to a computer's hard drive via a firewire port	Sony Handycam
Dots per inch (DPI)	Measure of the sharpness of a printer's output; the higher the dots per inch, the sharper the print will appear on the page	600 DPI (laser printer
Ergonomics	Science of creating work environments and furnishings well-tuned to the shape and function of the human body	Natural (split) keyboards
Expansion card	Electronic component that adds new capabilities to the computer	Internal modem, video capture
File	Group of computer data with a common purpose	A letter you have typed, a program

Term	Description	Example
Firewire port	Also called the IEEE 1394 port; popular for connecting digital video cameras and other high-speed peripherals	A connector on a digital video camera
Gigabyte	Approximately one billion bytes of data	About 3,000 books
Gigahertz (GHz)	One billion pulses of electricity in an electrical circuit in a single second; the speed of most microprocessors sold today is measured in gigahertz	3.0 GHz
Hardware	Physical components of a computer system	Disk drive, monitor, microprocessor
Hertz (Hz)	Single pulse of electricity in an electrical circuit	See *Refresh Rate* (page 17)
IDE	Type of controller for disk drives	IDE hard drive
IEEE 1394	See Firewire port	
Kilobyte (KB)	Approximately one thousand bytes of data	One single-spaced page of text
Kilohertz (kHz)	One thousand electrical pulses per second; the speed of older microprocessors is measured in kilohertz	800-kHz Pentium III microprocessor
LCD Panel	Monitor that uses liquid crystal display technology to create the screen image rather than a cathode ray tube (CRT) as in earlier monitors	
Macro virus	Computer virus transmitted in infected word processor documents and spreadsheet files	Form virus
Megabyte (MB)	Approximately one million bytes of data	3 average-length novels
Megahertz (MHz)	One million pulses of electricity in an electrical circuit in a single second	800 MHz (microprocessor clock speed rating)
Microprocessor	One single silicon chip containing the complete circuitry of a computer	Intel Pentium II, AMD K6, Intel Celleron
Modem	Device that lets a computer communicate digital data to other computers over analog telephone lines	56K modem
Monitor	The computer screen	19" monitor
MP3	Acronym for **M**oving **P**icture Experts Group Layer-**3** Audio; first popular format for highly compressed music files	A music file
Parallel port (also called LPT1)	Connection at the back of the system unit; printers are commonly connected to the parallel port	See *Ports* (page 22)
Peripherals	Hardware components outside the system unit	Monitor, keyboard
Pixel	A single dot of light on a computer monitor	See illustration on page 16
Port	A place at the back of the computer to plug in a cable	Parallel port, serial port

Term	Description	Example
RAM	Short for random access memory; computer chip designed to temporarily store data to be processed	512MB RAM
Refresh rate	How often the computer's display is redrawn each second; a refresh rate of 70 Hertz or more gives a flicker-free display that is easy on the eyes	70Hz
Resolution	Measure of the sharpness of a computer monitor display or a printout	1024x768 (monitor) 600 DPI (printer)
Scanner	Device that turns photographs and other images into computer files	HP Scanjet 5p
SCSI port	Pronounced "scuzzy"; short for Small Computer Systems Interface; commonly used to connect disk drives and scanners to the computer	
Serial port (also called COM1 and COM2)	Most computers have two serial connections at the back of the system unit; modems and mice are commonly connected to serial ports	
Software	Logical component of a computer system; composed of digital code stored in the form of files; some software exists as programs to help you get work done; also stores work	Windows XP, Internet Explorer, a document file
System unit	Main box that contains the primary components of the computer	See Computer System (page 6)
Terabyte (TB)	Approximately one trillion bytes of data	About 30,000 books.
USB port	Short for Universal Serial Bus port; a single USB port can connect several devices simultaneously, including keyboards, scanners, modems, cameras, and more; USB 2.0 standard transfers data about 40 times faster than the original USB 1.0 port	See page 23
VGA, SVGA	Short for Video Graphics Array; VGA compatible monitors display the computer screen in a variety of color and resolution settings	SVGA monitor
Virus	Program that invisibly "infects" files and disrupts operation of a computer in some way	Michelangelo, Good News
WMA	Acronym for Windows Media Audio; a recent audio format for compressing music files with better performance than available from the MP3 format	A music file

Index

Notes